BUSINESS COMMUNICATION TODAY

BUSINESS COMMUNICATION TODAY

Fifth Edition

Courtland L. Bovée

Professor of Business Communication
C. Allen Paul Distinguished Chair
Grossmont College

John V. Thill

Chief Executive Officer
Communication Specialists of America

Prentice Hall
Upper Saddle River, NJ 07458

Acquisitions Editor: Don Hull
Assistant Editor: John Larkin
Editorial Assistant: Paula D'Introno
Vice-President/Editorial Director: James Boyd
Editor-in-Chief: Natalie Anderson
Marketing Manager: Debbie Clare
Associate Managing Editor: Linda DeLorenzo
Production Coordinator: Carol Samet
Managing Editor: Dee Josephson
Manufacturing Supervisor: Arnold Vila
Manufacturing Manager: Vincent Scelta
Production/Composition: Carlisle Communications, Ltd.
Formatter/Electronic Artists: John Nestor, Christina Mahon, Annie Bartell, Erik Trinidad, Warren Fischbach, Steven Frim
Senior Production Manager: Lorraine Patsco
Permissions: Monotype Composition Company, Inc.
Design Manager: Patricia Smythe
Interior Design: Jill Yutkowitz
Cover Design: Jill Yutkowitz
Cover Art: Salem Krieger

Acknowledgements appear on pages AC-1 to AC-3, and on this page by reference.

Copyright © 1998, 1997 by Prentice-Hall Inc.
A Simon & Schuster Company
Upper Saddle River, New Jersey 07458
(Previous editions published by McGraw-Hill, Inc.)

Library of Congress Cataloging-in-Publication Data
Bovée, Courtland L.
    Business communication today / Courtland L. Bovée, John V. Thill.
  —5th ed.
        p.   cm.
    Includes bibliographical references and index.
    ISBN 0-13-783002-5
    1. Business communication—United States—Case studies.
 2. Communication in organizations—United States—Case studies.
 3. Business writing—United States—Case studies.   I. Thill, John
V. II. Title
HF5718.B66 1997
658.4'5—dc21   97–45879
                                                              CIP

Prentice-Hall International (UK) Limited, *London*
Prentice-Hall of Australia Pty. Limited, *Sydney*
Prentice-Hall Canada, Inc., *Toronto*
Prentice-Hall Hispanoamericana, S.A., *Mexico*
Prentice-Hall of India Private Limited, *New Delhi*
Prentice-Hall of Japan, Inc., *Tokyo*
Simon & Schuster Asia Pte. Ltd., *Singapore*
Editora Prentice-Hall do Brasil, Ltda., *Rio de Janeiro*

Printed in the United States of America

10 9 8 7 6 5 4 3

CONTENTS IN BRIEF

CONTENTS

PREFACE

This fifth edition marks a milestone for *Business Communication Today* and is especially exciting because it has a new publisher, Prentice Hall. Instructors and students will be well served by Prentice Hall's commitment to excellence.

This textbook serves the students who use it by giving them what they need to succeed. Demographic trends suggest that the current generation of college students will face ever tougher competition obtaining jobs and vying for top corporate positions. Simply put, today's students will have to wait longer to get ahead. Those with outstanding communication skills will have an advantage, and *Business Communication Today* gives them that crucial edge.

By presenting vivid insights into real-life business situations and employing a lively, conversational writing style, *Business Communication Today* captures the dynamics of business communication like no other textbook. It also captures the interest of students and teachers alike: In the 12 years since the first edition was published, more than 1.2 million students have learned about business communication from *Business Communication Today.*

This fifth edition covers all the basic principles in traditional sequence, as recommended by the Association of Collegiate Business Schools and Programs. Moreover, it fully integrates issues critical to successful business communication. Among the many important topics discussed in *Business Communication Today,* Fifth Edition, the following are given extensive coverage: ethics, law, cultural diversity, technology, audience-centered messages, and the writing process. Moreover, this edition strengthens the real-world examples and applications that relate to actual companies. The writing style is as involving as ever, and the eye-opening graphics crystallize chapter concepts. This text is the centerpiece of a comprehensive teaching and learning package. We believe that no other textbook in the field is as successful as *Business Communication Today* at drawing students into the subject matter, helping them understand the importance of excellent communication skills, and preparing them to obtain and pursue satisfying business careers.

A Real-World Focus

Business Communication Today, Fifth Edition, paints a realistic picture of the world of business communication—which appeals to instructors and to students. It is profoundly interesting to students and is designed to hold their attention. In every chapter, students hear from actual women and men in real companies, people with experience who cope daily with communication problems and opportunities. These role models capture students' imagination because they symbolize success; they aren't newcomers in entry-level positions but people who have proved their abilities and who hold positions that students find inspiring.

Because it encourages students to view themselves as part of an actual organization when completing assignments, this text is the next best thing to on-the-job training. It shows how standard approaches to routine assignments can help students complete work quickly and efficiently. At the same time, it stresses that every situation is different and advises students to think for themselves.

Real-Company Examples

This text offers students the opportunity to learn from other people's successes and failures. To understand our commitment to that concept, glance at the table of contents. You will see that this text was written with the cooperation of many businesses, among them such well-respected giants as Disney, Mobil, Microsoft, and General Mills as well as successful smaller organizations such as Metamorphosis Studios, Gosh Enterprises, and Rocky Mountain Institute.

Each chapter begins with an instructive Communication Close-Up featuring a communication expert who, in his or her own words, applies the chapter's concepts to common business situations. That expert reappears from time to time throughout the chapter to dramatize the connection between the chapter's contents and life on the job. This on-the-scene, internal company information was gathered through personal interviews with our business associates, friends, and contacts, and it gives *Business Communication Today* the ring of truth that students are so eager for.

Projects called Communication Challenges conclude each chapter and are related to the situations described in the Communication Close-Ups. Each chapter has one *individual challenge* (to give students "on-the-job" practice applying principles they have just learned) and one *team challenge* (to give students experience with the collaborative approach so prevalent in business today). These challenges are exclusive to *Business Communication Today,* providing a dimension of reality unmatched by any other textbook in the field.

Real-Company Documents

Throughout *Business Communication Today,* Fifth Edition, you will find up-to-date sample documents, many collected in our consulting work. These documents are superb business examples providing students with benchmarks for achievement.

The chapters on letters and memos contain outstanding examples from many types of organizations and from people working in a variety of functional areas. Many of these documents are fully formatted and presented on the letterhead of such well-known companies as Host Marriott, Blockbuster Entertainment Group, Duracell International, Office Depot, and Mattel Toys. Other documents are presented as fully formatted e-mail messages on screen. All these In-Depth Critiques are accompanied by a caption explaining the particular business situation and by a sentence-by-sentence analysis that helps students see precisely how to apply the principles discussed in the text. Additional documents are displayed in text, some including poor and improved examples to illustrate common errors and effective techniques for correcting them.

The chapters on report writing also contain numerous examples. For instance, Chapter 14 presents six case histories of reports (one a business plan), from inception through completion. And the last chapter of the unit illustrates the step-by-step development of a long report, which appears in its entirety to show how all the parts fit together.

Real-World Features

Boxed and strategically placed throughout the text, 39 special features extend the chapter material. Ever since the first edition of *Business Communication Today* was published, we have been searching publications and interviewing respected authorities to provide insights into the business world that are not found in other textbooks. These special features center on four well-integrated themes.

Sharpening Your Skills

Practical pointers and confidence-building guidelines help students improve writing and speaking skills in features such as

- How to Proofread Like a Pro: Tips for Creating the Perfect Document
- Eight Keys to Achieving Total Quality and Customer Satisfaction
- How to Take the Sting Out of Criticism and Foster Goodwill
- Sixteen Tough Interview Questions: What to Say When You're Stopped in Your Tracks

Focusing on Ethics

By examining critical ethical issues that face business communicators in today's workplace, students gain instruction on how to identify areas of ethical vulnerability, how to steer clear of ethical perils, and when to seek ethical advice. Features cover a wide range of topics, including

- The Tangled Web of Internet Copyrights
- Warning: Deceptive Résumés Can Backfire
- Visual Aids That Lie: The Use and Abuse of Charts and Graphs
- Handwriting Analysis: Should It Be Used to Determine Your Employment Potential?

Communicating Across Cultures

Tested techniques help students communicate successfully both in the global arena and across the growing cultural diversity at home. Cultural issues are well explored in features such as

- Crossing Cultures Without Crossing Signals: Your Listening Skills Can Bridge the Gap
- More than Word for Word—The Importance of Accurate Translation
- Good Ways to Send Bad News Around the World
- Understand Intercultural Audiences, and You'll Be Understood

Keeping Pace with Technology

Specific techniques offer students guidance for using technological applications to improve business communication. Features present a well-balanced selection of technological topics, including

- E-mail Etiquette: Minding Your Manners Online
- High-Tech Job Hunting: The Secrets of Finding Employment on the World Wide Web

- Writing for the Web: Sales Messages in Cyberspace
- Your Audience Will Get the Picture: Presentation Software Can Create Lively Business Speeches

Each special feature includes two questions, ranging from discussion topics to application exercises.

Real-Company Cases

Business Communication Today was the first business communication textbook to include a majority of cases featuring real companies, and we continue this tradition. Examples include

- Japanese wake-up call: E-mail at Starbucks
- Internet appliances: Persuasive letter requesting phone companies to test Oracle's software
- We won't go: Memo at Domino's Pizza requesting information
- Please don't scream: Letter from Haagen-Dazs explaining a flavor switch
- Olestra's slipping: Bad-news memo at Procter & Gamble

Real-World Issues

The boundaries of business communication are always expanding. So in addition to covering all the traditional subjects, *Business Communication Today,* Fifth Edition, examines many current issues. For example, because both the communication product and the process to achieve it are so important in today's business world, we balance our presentation of the process approach with a strong product orientation. This book also contains an unparalleled discussion of employment-related topics, including indispensable techniques for getting a job in our service-oriented economy. In addition, the text provides material to help students manage a myriad of current issues in business communication.

Ethics

Every message, whether verbal or nonverbal, communicates something about our values and ethics. Thus students must be given the means to anticipate and analyze the ethical dilemmas they will face on the job. Moreover, adhering to high ethical standards takes on a new importance in this age of wavering business behavior. Ethical questions addressed in this book include

- How much to emphasize the positive in business messages (Chapter 6)
- How to handle negative information in recommendations (Chapter 9)

- Where to draw the line between persuasion and manipulation in sales letters (Chapter 11)
- How to construct visual aids in a form that will convey a company's point of view without misleading the audience (Chapter 16)

Taking an ethical position in the face of pressures and temptations requires more than courage—it requires strong communication skills.

Crisis Communication

Whether it's the bombing of the Federal Building in Oklahoma City or the deaths from contaminated hamburger served at Jack in the Box fast-food outlets, recent catastrophes emphasize the value of planning for crisis communication (Chapter 1).

Communication Barriers

The shift toward a service economy means that more and more careers will depend on interpersonal skills. Instead of working on an assembly line, people will be interacting with other people, making it vital for people to overcome communication barriers (Chapter 2).

Cultural Diversity

The changing nature of the domestic work force requires strong communication skills to relate to older workers, women, members of various socioeconomic groups, immigrants, and others. Moreover, with such developments as European common currency and the North American Free Trade Agreement (NAFTA), and with the growth of worldwide access via the Internet, the continuing globalization of business necessitates strong skills to communicate effectively with people from other countries (Chapter 3).

Business Technology

Advances in communication technology are altering the way people communicate in organizations. More and more, students will be interacting with and through computers. To survive in the business world of today and tomorrow, students need to master ever more powerful machines and software to become comfortable with communication channels such as the Internet, e-mail, and companywide intranets (Chapter 4). Even the job of referencing documents from electronic media must be mastered (Component Chapter B).

Law

The increasing tendency of people to sue makes it important to understand the legal implications of written and oral communication. For example, students need to understand the pitfalls of writing recommendation letters (discussed in Chapter 9). Other issues include the laws that govern sales letters and collection messages (discussed in Chapter 11) and the legality of employment interview questions (discussed in Chapter 13).

Employment Search

More and more people are making radical mid-career job changes, whether by choice or because their companies are downsizing and flattening hierarchies. These people need to master new communication skills and the new electronic sources for job openings, as well as information pertaining to their new jobs (Chapter 12).

Communication Versatility

Small businesses create most of the new jobs and employ more people than large corporations do. Since these small businesses are unable to support communication specialists for specific jobs, people working for them need to be versatile in their communication skills—writing letters and reports, talking on the phone, giving speeches, making sales presentations, creating presentation slides, and producing professional-looking documents.

Real-World Internet Resources

The World Wide Web, a component of the Internet, contains a wealth of valuable resources. To acquaint students with Web sites that relate to the content of *Business Communication Today,* a Best of the Web feature describing an especially useful site is included in each chapter.

Students can access the site by using the URL provided or by going to the Web site for this text <http://www.phlip.marist.edu> where live links will take students straight to the site of their choice.

Examples of the Best of the Web feature include

* Create Your Own Web Site
* Connect Now with a Virtual Library
* Search Thousands of Full-Text Articles Instantly
* Link Your Way to a Better Résumé

Real-Company Photographs

Yet another distinctive feature of this book is its use of photographs (most of them from real companies). Each picture is accompanied by a caption that describes how it relates to business communication. The photos cover a rich assortment of people, organizations, and events, and all of them give students an intimate glimpse into the real-life application of the topic being studied.

Real-World Competencies—SCANS (Secretary's Commission on Achieving Necessary Skills)

Like no other business communication text, this edition emphasizes the skills and competencies necessary for students to make the transition from academia to the workplace. As described in the SCANS report from the Department of Labor, it is essential that students meet national standards of academic and occupational skill. To help accomplish the SCANS goal, this text offers interactive pedagogy (much of which is grounded in real-world situations): Learning Objectives, Communication Close-Ups, Communication Challenges, questions in special feature boxes, In-Depth Critiques, Documents for Analysis, Checklists, Critical Thinking Questions, boldfaced in-text key terms, a photo and illustration program, Summaries, Exercises, Cases, and Web exercises.

A RELIABLE PEDAGOGY

Having an accurate picture of how businesspeople communicate is important, but students need more if they are to develop usable skills. In *Business Communication Today,* Fifth Edition, we have included well-tested learning tools to instill good skills and enhance comprehension.

Checklists

To help students organize their thinking when they begin a communication project, make decisions as they write, and check their own work, we have included 29 checklists throughout the book and located them as close as possible to the related discussions. These checklists are reminders, however—not "recipes." They provide useful guidelines for writing, without limiting creativity. Students will find them handy when they are on the job and need to refresh their memory about effective communication techniques.

Documents for Analysis

Students can critique and revise 29 documents in 10 chapters. Documents include letters, memos and e-mail messages, a letter of application, a résumé, and visual aids. This hands-on experience in analyzing and improving documents will help students revise their own.

Exercises and Cases

A wealth of exercises (180) and cases (154), many of them e-mail and memo-writing tasks, provide assignments like those that students will most often face at work. The exercises and cases deal with all types and sizes of organizations, domestic and international. Each chapter also includes an exercise or a case that requires access to the World Wide Web, giving students practice with this fast-growing communication technology. We have written every case for a variety of majors and have categorized them for each selection. With such an array to choose from, students will have ample opportunities to test their problem-solving skills.

Component Chapters and Appendixes

For maximum flexibility in designing a course tailored to students' needs, this textbook contains two Component Chapters (placed near the end of the book): (A) Format and Layout of Business Documents and (B) Documentation of Report Sources. Also at the end of the book are two Appendixes: (I) Fundamentals of Grammar and Usage and (II) Correction Symbols (for help in proofreading, revising assignments, and interpreting an instructor's corrections; these symbols and marks also make it easier for instructors to grade assignments). Even when not assigned, students will find these component chapters and appendixes useful for reference.

Lively, Conversational Writing Style

Read a few pages of this textbook and then read a few pages of another textbook. We think you will immediately notice the difference. The lucid writing style in *Business Communication Today,* Fifth Edition, makes the material pleasing to read and easy to comprehend. It stimulates interest, promotes learning, and exemplifies the principles presented in this book. We have also carefully monitored the reading level of *Business Communication Today* to make sure it is neither too simple nor too difficult.

Learning Objectives

Each chapter begins with a concise list of goals that students are expected to achieve by reading the chapter and completing the exercises and cases. These objectives are meant to guide the learning process, motivate students to master the material, and aid them in measuring their success.

Margin Notes

Short summary statements that highlight key points and reinforce learning appear in the margins of *Business Communication Today,* Fifth Edition. They are no substitute for reading the chapters but are useful for quickly getting the gist of a section, rapidly reviewing a chapter, and locating areas of greatest concern.

Chapter Summaries

Each chapter ends with a concise overview. We have included these summaries to help students understand and remember the relationships among key concepts.

End-of-Chapter Critical Thinking Questions

The Critical Thinking Questions (120) are designed to get students thinking about the concepts introduced in each chapter. They may also prompt students to stretch their learning beyond the chapter content. Not only will students find them useful when studying for examinations, but the instructor may also draw on them to promote classroom discussion of issues that have no easy answers.

Indexes

To assist students and instructors in locating information as conveniently as possible, two types of indexes are included in the book: Organization/Company/Brand Index and a Subject Index.

Color Art and Strong Visual Program

This text has been attractively printed, and the dramatic use of full color throughout the book gives it exceptional visual appeal. In addition, students will learn from carefully crafted illustrations of important concepts in each chapter: graphs, charts, tables, and photographs.

Book Design

The state-of-the-art design is based on extensive research and invites students to delve into the content. It also makes reading easier, reinforces learning, and increases comprehension. The boxed special features and other elements do not interfere with the flow of textual material, a vital factor in maintaining attention and concentration. The design of this book, like much communication, has the simple objective of gaining interest and making a point.

A THOROUGH REVISION

When preparing the fifth edition of *Business Communication Today,* we dedicated ourselves to a thorough revision. For example, we have once again entirely rewritten the technology chapter. Moreover, we emphasize the growing influence of the Internet throughout the text. With an eye to emphasizing and integrating important topics, we have critically evaluated virtually every sentence in the text, making literally hundreds of refinements. Members of the academic and business communities have carefully reviewed it, and we have tested it in the classroom. Instructors, businesspeople, and students have all praised its competent coverage of subject matter, its up-to-date examples, its flexible organization, and its authentic portrayal of business. Here is an overview of the major content changes in the fifth edition:

Chapter 1: Communicating Successfully in an Organization

Now includes two "In-Depth Critique" sample documents to expose students as early as possible to business letters and memos; maintains emphasis on the six vital themes that recur throughout the book: open communication climate, ethics, intercultural messages, technological tools, audience-centered thinking, and efficient message flow.

Chapter 2: Understanding Business Communication

Presents a new transactional model of the communication process to help students clearly envision this basic tenet of business communication; maintains its emphasis on overcoming communication barriers.

Chapter 3: Communicating Interculturally

Now clarifies the relationship between growing technology and increasing global opportunities; shows e-mail on screen (as do many chapters throughout the text); maintains its emphasis on how intercultural differences can block successful communication, both in the U.S. work force and across national boundaries; increases the emphasis on cultural diversity in the U.S. work force and across national boundaries.

Chapter 4: Communicating Through Technology

Updates discussion emphasizing how technology affects communication; offers guidance about when it is appro-

priate to use various tools; introduces ways that the Internet is changing business communication; guides students in selecting the most appropriate messages for e-mail.

Chapter 5: Planning Business Messages

Expands the coverage of collaborative writing while emphasizing the composition process: planning (defining your purpose, analyzing your audience, establishing your main idea, and selecting the appropriate channel and medium), composing (organizing and outlining your message, and formulating your message), revising (editing, rewriting, producing, and proofing your message); strengthens discussion of electronic channels in relation to oral and written channels.

Chapter 6: Composing Business Messages

Now offers guidelines on shaping an e-mail message and advice on e-mail etiquette; also clarifies the three levels of style: informal, conversational, formal—with most business writing being conversational.

Chapter 7: Revising Business Messages

Now includes coverage of critiquing the writing of others so that students can collaborate more smoothly; expands material on active and passive voice, giving more examples; also expands coverage of parallelism and gives more examples.

Chapter 8: Writing Direct Requests

Updates discussion of salutations; increases the number of fully formatted sample documents, using the "In-Depth Critique" format; now includes new section on requesting information via the Internet and e-mail; updates all in-text sample messages; replaces nearly half of the end-of-chapter cases.

Chapter 9: Writing Routine, Good-News, and Goodwill Messages

Now includes a section on the reading and writing processes involved in summarizing; increases the number of fully formatted sample documents, using the "In-Depth Critique" format; updates all in-text sample messages; replaces nearly half of the end-of-chapter cases; updates chapter material by deemphasizing less used topics such as writing order acknowledgments, providing credit references, and sending out goodwill greetings.

Chapter 10: Writing Bad-News Messages

Expands section on rejecting job applicants; updates chapter material by deemphasizing less used topics such as negative messages about orders; increases the number of fully formatted documents, using the "In-Depth Critique" format; updates all in-text sample messages;

strengthens transitions between sections; balances discussion of the direct and indirect approaches to negative messages; replaces nearly half of the end-of-chapter cases.

Chapter 11: Writing Persuasive Messages

Completely reorganizes chapter structure to include a more thorough discussion of persuasion, including avoiding faulty logic and using the Toulmin model to test arguments; expands material on fund-raising letters and selling an idea on the job; shifts emphasis from sales letters to other persuasive messages on the job; increases the number of fully formatted sample documents, using the "In-Depth Critique" format; updates all in-text sample messages; replaces most of the end-of-chapter cases; introduces coverage of sales letters on the Web; deemphasizes collections material.

Chapter 12: Writing Résumés and Application Letters

Updates and replaces all sample résumés to be more readable, to represent computer-generated documents, to provide a résumé and application letter written by the same applicant, and to include a two-year graduate; now includes information on e-mail mailing lists, job-oriented Usenet newsgroups, and job banks on the Web; includes a new section on scannable résumés; strengthens all transitions between major sections; adds a brief section on employment portfolios; adds a discussion of how to build job experience through internships, temporary job assignments, and so forth; integrates material on intercultural differences with regard to the employment search; expands the uses for résumés; emphasizes the importance of continuously updating a résumé.

Chapter 13: Interviewing for Employment and Following Up

Strengthens transitions between major sections throughout (especially preview and review statements); expands discussion of the open-ended interview; adds a new section on video résumés/interviews; suggests advantages of videotaping mock interviews for evaluation; improves discussion of thank-you messages; expands the section on letters of resignation.

Chapter 14: Using Reports and Proposals as Business Tools

Now incorporates more material on electronic reports; updates and replaces all sample reports and extracts; expands the discussion of business plans while maintaining the clear definition and differentiation of the types of reports used in business applications.

Chapter 15: Planning and Researching Reports and Proposals

Now includes a discussion of two problem-solving methods: relative merit and hypothesis; strengthens transitions between all major sections (especially preview statements); expands discussion of problem statements; clarifies the section on factoring by simplifying the language; emphasizes the reasoning process behind selecting an appropriate organizational plan; expands the discussion of conclusions.

Chapter 16: Developing Visual Aids

Now explains where and how to cite the source of information in a visual aid; explains the concept of chartjunk; updates all computer graphics material; incorporates information on the importance of intercultural differences with regard to visual aids.

Chapter 17: Writing Reports and Proposals

Strengthens the link to concepts presented in earlier chapters (such as style, tone, "you" attitude, positive language, and concise wording); assembles all material on structural clues under the heading "Helping Readers Find Their Way"; distinguishes between transitions that link ideas within paragraphs and those that link ideas between paragraphs and sections; expands discussion of bullets and numbering; adds section on preview and review statements.

Chapter 18: Completing Formal Reports and Proposals

Now discusses how to introduce sources; uses examples from the sample business report; updates report production material with information on computerized report design; expands coverage of executive summaries; completely revises documentation and citation procedures; updates entire sample report, including citation references.

Chapter 19: Listening, Interviewing, and Conducting Meetings

Reorganizes some material for easier reading; expands coverage of telephone skills; updates and clarifies entire section on listening; adds examples of each type of listening; strengthens transitions between all major sections; strengthens link to intercultural barriers mentioned in Chapters 2 and 3.

Chapter 20: Giving Speeches and Oral Presentations

Now includes discussion to help students understand the importance of preview and review statements during a presentation or speech; discusses the benefits of using an outliner from software packages such as PowerPoint; revises writing style to raise the reading level and to delineate the discussions of preparing for and delivering a speech; expands discussion of the question-and-answer period after a speech or presentation.

Component Chapter A: Format and Layout of Business Documents

Adds e-mail formatting to the discussion; completely updates specific details of format and layout; retains the convenience of presenting all formatting material in one well-organized component chapter.

Component Chapter B: Documentation of Report Sources

Simplifies and strengthens discussion by gathering bibliographic entries and source notes into two separate figures; now includes citations for Web sites, e-mail, and newsgroups; emphasizes the reference list (or bibliography) over source notes; emphasizes the author-date method of reference citation (as do most style manuals) while deemphasizing the superscript method that requires separate source notes; maintains and greatly simplifies the discussion of source notes.

Appendix I: Fundamentals of Grammar and Usage

Clarifies the description and discussion of grammatical rules and usage problems.

Appendix II: Correction Symbols

Clarifies the use of correction symbols and abbreviations so that students can easily understand teacher evaluations and can readily use proofreading marks when evaluating their own work.

AN UNSURPASSED TEACHING PACKAGE

The instructional package for this textbook is specially designed to simplify the task of teaching and learning. The instructor may choose to use the following supplements.

Instructor's Resource Manual

This comprehensive paperback book is an instructor's tool kit. Among the many things it provides are a section on collaborative writing, suggested solutions to exercises, suggested solutions and fully formatted letters for *every* case in the letter-writing chapters, and a grammar pretest and posttest.

Test Bank

This manual is organized by text chapters and includes a mix of multiple-choice, true-false, and fill-in questions for each chapter, approximately 1,500 objective items in all, carefully written and reviewed to provide a fair, structured program of evaluation.

You can also get the complete test bank on computer disk, or you can get even more flexibility with the phone-in customized test service.

Prentice Hall Custom Test, Windows Version

Based on a state-of-the-art test generation software program developed by Engineering Software Associates (ESA), *Prentice Hall Custom Test* is suitable for your course and can be customized to your class needs. You can originate tests quickly, easily, and error-free. You can Create an exam, administer it traditionally or online, evaluate and track students' results, and analyze the success of the examination—all with a simple click of the mouse.

Color Acetate Transparency Program

A set of 100 large-type color transparency acetates, available to instructors on request, help bring concepts alive in the classroom and provide a starting point for discussion of communication techniques. All are keyed to the *Instructor's Resource Manual*. Many contrast poor and improved solutions to featured cases from the textbook.

PowerPoint Presentation Software

The overhead transparency program is also available on PowerPoint 4.0. The software is designed to allow you to present the overhead transparencies to your class electronically.

Communication Briefings Video Series and Video Guide

Accompanying the text is a series of videos from Communication Briefings, a firm known for its monthly newsletter and its video series. The video set is available without charge to adopters of *Business Communication Today.* Included in the series are the following videos:

Everyone's Teamwork Role—**NEW!**
Communicating for Results: How to Be Clear, Concise, and Credible—**NEW!**

Better Business Grammar
Make the Phone Work for You
Listen and Win: How to Keep Customers Coming Back
How to See Opportunity in a Changing Workplace
Resolving Conflicts: Strategies for a Winning Team
Make Presentations Work for You

In addition, a separate video guide is available. Features include synopses of each video and discussion questions. To order the set, please call 1-800-388-8433.

College NewsLink

Specific course-related articles from *The New York Times* and other major daily newspapers are available to professors and students by e-mail subscription and through campus intranets. Internet links within the articles will also provide access to thousands of corporate, educational, and government World Wide Web sites related to the course.

Web Site

Visit our Web site at <http://www.phlip.marist.edu>. Live links to all of the URLs in the book will take professors and students straight to the site of their choice. A wealth of other useful information is also provided.

Business Communication Update Newsletter

Delivered exclusively by e-mail every month, the newsletter provides interesting materials that can be used in class, and it offers practical ideas about teaching methods. To receive a complimentary subscription, simply send a blank message by e-mail to <BCU_ Newsletter-subscribe@lists.kz>.

PERSONAL ACKNOWLEDGMENTS

Business Communication Today, Fifth Edition, is the product of the concerted efforts of a number of people. A heartfelt thanks to our many friends, acquaintances, and business associates who agreed to be interviewed so that this business communication textbook could feature real people at actual companies: Michael Eisner, Disney; Clarence Wooten Jr. and Andre Forde, Metamorphosis Studios; Mike Stevens, Hewlett-Packard; Michael Copeland, Procter & Gamble; Jeff Hagen, General Mills; Julian Santoyo, Community Health Group; Adrianne Proeller, Turner Broadcasting System; Silva Raker, The Nature Company; Peter

Goodrich, Steinway & Sons; Yia Eason, Olmec Toys; Jeanne Anderson, AT&T Language Line; Henry Halaiko, Mobil; Jodi DeLeon, Microsoft; Wesley Van Linda, Narada Records; Charley Shin, Gosh Enterprises; Michael Fernandez, Eastman Kodak; Dierdre Ballou, Wild Animal Park; Amory and Hunter Lovins, Rocky Mountain Institute; Virginia Johnson, Minnesota Mining & Manufacturing; and Shirley Crouch and Jo Waldron, Phoenix Management.

Our thanks also to Terry Anderson, whose outstanding communication skills, breadth of knowledge, and organizational ability assured this project of clarity and completeness.

We are grateful to Bonnie Blake, Purdue University, for her remarkable talents and valuable contributions; to Lianne Downey for her unique insights and perspectives; to George Dovel for his brilliance and wise counsel; and to Jackie Estrada for her noteworthy talents and dedication.

We appreciate the remarkable talents and valuable contributions of Deborah Valentine, Emory University; Anne Bliss, University of Colorado, Boulder; Carolyn A. Embree, University of Akron; Carla L. Sloan, Liberty University; Doris A. Van Horn Christopher, California State University, Los Angeles; and Susan S. Rehwaldt, Southern Illinois University.

Recognition and thanks to Don Fitzgerald, Mary Leslie, Donald Anderson, and Quentin Decker.

We also feel it is important to acknowledge and thank the Association for Business Communication, an organization whose meetings and publications provide a valuable forum for the exchange of ideas and for professional growth.

Thanks to the many individuals whose valuable suggestions and constructive comments contributed to the success of this book. The authors are deeply grateful for the efforts of Robert Allen, Northwest Connecticut Community College; Lois J. Bachman, Community College of Philadelphia; Jane Bennett, Dekalb College; Mary Bresnahan, Michigan State University; Julian Caplan, Borough of Manhattan Community College; Donald Crawford, West Georgia College; Susan Currier, California Polytechnic State University; David P. Dauwalder, California State University, Los Angeles; Carol David, Iowa State University; Rod Davis, Ball State University; Earl A. Dvorak, Indiana University–Bloomington; Norma J. Gross, Houston Community College; Florence Grunkemeyer, Ball State University; Maxine Hart, Baylor University; Susan Hilligross, Clemson University; Louise C. Holcomb,

Gainesville Junior College; J. Kenneth Horn, Southwestern Missouri State University; Randolph H. Hudson, Northeastern Illinois University; Edna Jellesed, Lane Community College; Betty Johnson, Stephen F. Austin State University; Paul J. Killorin, Portland Community College; Lorraine Krajewski, Louisiana State University; Patricia Kuriscak, Niagara County Community College; Reva Leeman, Portland Community College; Ethel A. Martin, Glendale Community College; Kenneth R. Mayer, Cleveland State University; Gertrude M. McGuire, University of Montevallo; Willie Minor, Phoenix College; Evelyn P. Morris, Mesa Community College; Linda Munilla, Georgia Southern College; Tom Musial, Saint Mary's University; Alexa North, Georgia State University; Devern Perry, Brigham Young University; Paul Preston, University of Texas, San Antonio; Thomas P. Proietti, Monroe Community College; Nelda Pugh, Jefferson State College; Richard David Ramsey, Southeastern Louisiana University; Lillian E. Rollins, Dekalb College; W. J. Salem, Central Michigan University; Grant T. Savage, Texas Tech University; Dorothy Sibley, Brevard Community College; Roberta M. Supnick, Western Michigan University; Sumner B. Tapper, Northeastern University; Vincent Trofi, Providence College; Linda N. Ulman, University of Miami; Dona Vasa, University of Nebraska; Ruth A. Walsh, University of South Florida; John L. Waltman, Eastern Michigan University; Kathryn Jensen White, University of Oklahoma; and Mimi Will, Foothill College.

A special debt is owed to the following individuals who reviewed the fourth edition and ancillary package in preparation for the fifth edition: J. Douglas Andrews, University of Southern California; Jane Beamish, North Country Community College; Pauline Ann Buss, William R. Harper College; James L. Godell, North Michigan University; Kenneth Gorman, Winona State University; Francis N. Hamlet, Longwood College; William Hendricks, Temple University; Elizabeth Jenkins, Pennsylvania State University; Barbara Jewell, Pierce College; Eliane Krajewski, Louisiana State University; Reeva Leeman, Portland Community College; Virgil R. Pufahl, University of Wisconsin–Platteville; Jim Rucker, Fort Hays State University; Carla L. Sloan, Liberty University; Jeremiah J. Sullivan, University of Washington; Rose Ann Swartz, Ferris State University; Janet Adams, Mankato State University; Sauny Dills, California Polytechnic State University; Claudia Rawlins, California State University–Chico; Janet Adams, Mankato State University; Bill Hendricks, California University, Pennsylvania; Carol Lutz, University of Texas at Austin; Glynna Morse, Georgia College, Georgia; and David Victor, East Michigan University.

We want to extend our warmest appreciation to the devoted professionals at Prentice Hall. They include Sandra Steiner, President; James Boyd, Vice President/Editorial Director; Donald Hull, Senior Editor; all of the Prentice Hall Business Publishing group, and the outstanding Prentice Hall sales representatives. Finally, we thank Linda DeLorenzo, Associate Managing Editor, for her dedication, and we are grateful to copy editor Nancy Marcello and designer Jill Yutkowitz for their superb work.

Courtland L. Bovée
John V. Thill

FOUNDATIONS OF BUSINESS COMMUNICATION

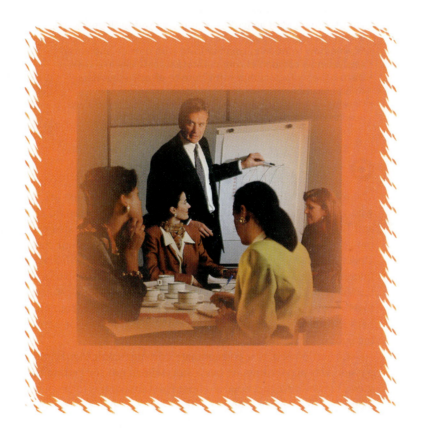

CHAPTER 1

COMMUNICATING SUCCESSFULLY IN AN ORGANIZATION

AFTER STUDYING THIS CHAPTER, YOU WILL BE ABLE TO

- Describe how managers use communication
- Contrast the formal and informal communication channels within the organization
- Explain how companies communicate with outside audiences
- Analyze how companies communicate successfully in a crisis
- Discuss the six factors that contribute to effective business communication
- Develop goals for acquiring the communication skills you will need in your career

OMMUNICATION CLOSE-UP AT DISNEY

The magic is still working at Walt Disney Company. Just ask the millions of people who visit Disneyland in California, DisneyWorld in Florida, Disney Paris in France, and Tokyo Disneyland in Japan. Of course, the company also works its spell on hotels, movies, television, records, books, a hockey team, retail merchandise, and more. Under the leadership of chief executive officer (CEO) Michael Eisner, these diverse interests compose Disney's three main divisions—theme parks and resorts, filmed entertainment, and consumer products. You may well ask what keeps this huge company together. According to insiders, the magic ingredient is communication—whether it's between managers, between managers and employees, or between the company and the public.

Eisner himself is a consummate communicator. An English major whose early passion was playwriting, he has a storyteller's gift for getting his message across. He views himself as a cheerleader whose chief function is to encourage creativity. "This is a business that succeeds on good ideas," says Eisner, and he does all he can to encourage their flow. "I use meetings, company anniversaries, anything to create some kind of catalyst to get us all going."

To keep everyone revved up, Eisner frequently holds pep talks with the rank and file. He also wanders around to get a sense of what's happening. He encourages people to call him Michael, and he solicits their opinions. He lunches on frozen yogurt in the company cafeteria and grills hamburgers at company parties.

Eisner's personality sets the tone at Disney, but he doesn't rely exclusively on his charisma. His personal presence is backed by a systematic communication program that transmits management's message to every member of the organization. An important element of this program is employee orientation, which consists of training sessions that emphasize Disney's traditions and values. The corporate message is also reinforced

Michael Eisner

When families travel to Tokyo Disneyland, or to any of Disney's theme parks, they are met by employees who exhibit strong communication skills. In fact, communication is the key to success for the Walt Disney Company, whether dealing with the public or operating within the organization.

by bulletin boards, audiovisual presentations, employee briefing sessions, and division and companywide newsletters. Disney hammers home its message by rewarding those who uphold the firm's standards. There are service awards, peer recognition programs, attendance awards, and employment banquets, as well as a variety of social events.

Getting the message down the line is one thing. Drawing information up the chain of command is another, and Disney excels at that as well. Employees are given plenty of opportunities to express themselves. One division ensures 360-degree feedback by making sure that leaders are evaluated not only by their supervisors but also by their colleagues and by the people who work for them. At Disney, even employee briefings encourage feedback. Moreover, to gather a wide range of opinions, Disney conducts regular employee opinion polls. It also runs employee focus groups so that people can comment in more detail on various issues. And employees have the incentive of cold, hard cash—being able to win up to $10,000 for submitting suggestions through the "I Have an Idea" program.

Communication between the company and the public is another important part of the Disney magic. Employees are called "cast members" and taught that their main job is to make dreams come true for Disney's guests and audiences. Cast members view themselves as entertainers, even if their role is to sweep the streets at Disneyland. They see themselves as being an important part of the show, and that perception helps them meet the public's expectations—and more.

The Disney corporation receives a lot of press, even though the corporate public relations (PR) department consists of only three people. A PR staff of 50 would be more typical for a company of Disney's size and type, but given the nature of its business, the company is inherently appealing. Moreover, Eisner has a knack for media relations. He's also fiercely protective of the company's image. Nothing annoys him more than hearing someone use the term *Mickey Mouse* to mean "small-time or trivial."[1]

COMMUNICATION, BUSINESS, AND YOU

Communication enables organizations to function.

Organizations like Disney bend over backward to see that communication both inside and outside the company is open, honest, and clear. They understand that their success depends on the ability to communicate not only with employees and customers but also with investors and with the surrounding community.[2] The demands of downsizing, materials handling, diversity, and technology are forcing today's companies to communicate more effectively with employees and outsiders. Companies are asking fewer people to do the same amount of work. They're depending on inventory and delivery systems that require perfect timing, and they're dealing with employees whose backgrounds and cultures are more and more diverse.[3] In addition, companies are embracing technological developments such as the information superhighway, videoconferencing, and interactive multimedia, so they need people to be current—to be aware of all the communication possibilities for any given situation.[4] Such coordination demands strong communication skills.

SHARPENING YOUR SKILLS

COMMUNICATION SKILLS—EIGHT GREAT WAYS THEY HELP ADVANCE YOUR CAREER

What's the main career handicap of young people today? Poor communication skills, according to a recent survey of company personnel directors and business school deans. Does this weakness stand in *your* way? Here are some reasons you should sharpen your communication skills.

- *Getting the job you want.* Employers form lasting impressions on the basis of what they see and know about a job candidate. The first items that a prospective employer is likely to see are your résumé and application letter. If they are well written, they'll make a good first impression and help you get the job. If not, you may fail to get an interview, even though you may be well qualified for the job.
- *Boosting your chances for promotion.* Many new employees soon have a chance to write a memo or report that will be read by management. These documents often stay in company files for a long time as a permanent record of employees' abilities. Good writing skills can draw attention to you and increase your chances for promotion. So can other well-honed communication skills. They make you a more effective member of the team; if your boss knows you can communicate well and deliver under pressure, you are likely to get more chances to prove your worth.

- *Helping others get ahead.* Once you are established in your career, communication skills can help you conduct impressive performance appraisals or compose letters of recommendation for employees. The ability to do a good job may show you to be a developer of people, a quality prized in any company.
- *Helping you get things done.* Good communication is important even in your daily routine. The right choice of words, even of a single word, may make the difference between settling an important issue at hand or igniting a companywide dispute.
- *Benefiting your own business.* Perhaps your goal is to start your own business. Today nearly half of the approximately 500,000 new businesses launched each year fail within 36 months. The reasons? Lack of management skills, inadequate financing, and poor communication ability—often reflected in a fear of writing. Nobody likes to do what he or she does poorly, and in a small business, there's seldom a secretary to handle what the owner doesn't do well. One aspiring entrepreneur lost credibility with his stockholders and his banker because he couldn't write a report that would sell them on giving him further support. A decade after he went bankrupt, another group, better able to communicate, made a nationwide success

Your ability to communicate increases productivity, both yours and your organization's. It shapes the impressions you make on your colleagues, employees, supervisors, investors, and customers. It allows you to perceive the needs of these **stakeholders** (the various groups you interact with), and it helps you respond to those needs. Whether you run your own business, work for an employer, invest in a company, buy or sell products, design computer chips, run for public office, or raise money for charities, your communication skills determine your success (see "Communication Skills—Eight Great Ways They Help Advance Your Career").[5]

Regardless of the field you're in or the career you choose, your chances of being hired by an organization are better if you possess strong communication skills. Out of 120 job descriptions appearing in one issue of the *National Business Employment Weekly* (published by the *Wall Street Journal*), almost every listing included this requirement: "The persons we seek must have strong oral and written communication skills." From chief financial officer to product manager, from senior economist to personnel analyst, from senior sales representative to petroleum buyer—these positions will be filled by people who can communicate well.[6]

That's because every member of an organization is a link in the information chain. The flow of information along that chain is a steady stream of messages, whether from inside the organization (staff meetings, progress reports, project proposals, research

Employers want people who can communicate.

Ask yourself what information your co-workers and supervisors need from you, and then figure out how you can supply it. Also ask yourself what information you need to do your job, and then find ways to get it.

out of his idea: a television network devoted to covering amateur and professional sporting events.

- *Advancing you socially.* The ability to communicate well can help you get along with others. It can inspire others to like and follow you. In addition, if you adopt the habit of making cordial comments to those you work with and of sending short notes to people you know, you will soon have an extensive network of contacts who wish you well.
- *Ensuring your future.* Whatever may happen with new communication technologies, the basic communication skills will always be essential. For example, letters and memos will continue to be the main carriers of business communication for years to come, whether transmitted by computer printout, electronic display, or other devices. In fact, the volume of written communication will increase with the growing use of word-processing systems, so the ability to write clearly and concisely will become ever more important.
- *Enhancing your other skills.* As you apply your improved communication skills to more and more business functions, you'll learn how to use them to motivate prospects to buy, to speed collections, to improve customer relations and claims adjustments, and to recruit and hire personnel. You'll also learn how to save time and effort. For example, you'll find you can write one letter to seal a business transaction that otherwise would have required two or three. With improved communication skills

will come new self-confidence. You'll be able to plan and send messages faster and more freely. You'll also discover that every act of communication is a potential public relations tool, and you'll try to make each one work for you.

Start your study of business communication by adopting a positive attitude. If you can't perform a task, you have a skill problem. If you won't perform a task, you have a motivation problem. With real motivation, you can learn to communicate well and advance your career.

1. As a personnel officer, you receive a brief application letter from a man who states that he really needs a job because he has been out of work for six months. He writes, "I have completed only one year of college, and my grades are just average, but I am willing to work hard." What is your reaction to this letter?
2. For the next five days, write one letter a day to a friend or relative, a business associate, someone at a newspaper, a government official, or someone in a customer relations department. Make your letters as conversational as possible. Pretend you are talking to the other person. As the week progresses, do you notice any changes in your attitude toward writing or in the ease with which you think of things to say? What responses do you receive to your letters?

results, employee surveys, and persuasive interviews) or from outside the organization (loan applications, purchasing agreements, help-wanted ads, distribution contracts, product advertisements, and sales calls). Your ability to receive, evaluate, use, and pass on information affects your company's effectiveness, as well as your own.

> You are a contact point in both the external and internal communication networks.

Within the company, you and your co-workers use the information you obtain from one another and from outsiders to guide your activities. The work of the organization is divided into tasks and assigned to various organizational units, each reporting to a manager who directs and coordinates the effort. This division of labor and delegation of responsibility depend on the constant flow of information up, down, and across the organization. So by feeding information to your boss and peers, you help them do their jobs, and vice versa.

> The manager's role is to make and carry out decisions by collecting facts, analyzing them, and transmitting directions to lower-level employees.

By analyzing how managers actually spend their time, you find that their basic function is to amass, process, and disseminate information. If you are a manager, your day consists of a never-ending series of meetings, casual conversations, speaking engagements, and phone calls, interspersed with occasional periods set aside for reading or writing. From these sources, you cull important points and then pass them on to the right people. In turn, you rely on your employees to provide you with useful data and to interpret, transmit, and act on the messages you send them.

> Employees serve as the eyes and ears of an organization, providing direct impressions from the front line.

If you are a relatively junior employee, you are likely to find yourself on the perimeter of the communication network. Oddly enough, this puts you in an important position in the information chain. Although your span of influence may be limited, you are in a position to observe firsthand things that your supervisors and co-workers cannot see: a customer's immediate reaction to a product display, a supplier's momentary hesitation before agreeing to a delivery date, a funny whirring noise in a piece of equipment, or a slowdown in the flow of customers. These are the little gems of information that managers and co-workers need to do their jobs. If you don't pass that information along, nobody will—because nobody else knows. Such an exchange of information within an organization is called **internal communication.**

THE INTERNAL COMMUNICATION NETWORK

> Each organization has its own approach to transmitting information throughout the organization.

Communication among the members of an organization is essential for effective functioning, so each organization approaches internal communication differently, depending on its particular requirements. In a small business with only five or six employees, much information can be exchanged casually and directly. In a giant organization like Disney, with hundreds of thousands of employees scattered around the world, transmitting the right information to the right people at the right time is a real challenge, whether communicating by phone, e-mail, fax, or interoffice memo (see Figure 1.1).

Some companies are better at communicating than others. At top-performing companies, communication is a way of life. For example, AT&T's audio news service delivers information to managers and employees by offering callers a choice of reports on specific subjects. AT&T also distributes a daily newsletter to employees and mails a monthly magazine to employees' homes. IBM encourages all U.S. employees to communicate any concerns electronically, using confidential and secure online systems. Because managers and employees at such companies communicate freely, employees develop a clear sense of the organization's mission, and managers are able to identify and react more quickly to potential problems. In these firms, management *is* communication.[7] To maintain a healthy flow of information, effective managers use both formal and informal channels.

As a supplier to theme parks and vacation spots such as Disney, Personalized Products, Inc. (PPI) produces souvenirs and toys printed with a wide variety of common names. In this memo, sales manager Tom Beatty reports first-quarter sales to Jacqueline Rogeine, vice president of finance.

Figure 1.1
In-Depth Critique:
Internal Communication
by Memo

INTERNAL MEMORANDUM

TO: Jacqueline Rogeine
FROM: Tom Beatty
DATE: April 10, 1997
SUBJECT: First-Quarter Sales to Disney

Our first-quarter sales to Disney theme parks show a continuing trend toward growth, although margins remain thin. We supplied thirty-eight retail outlets with fifty-two licensed or personalized items. Gross profits rose 18% from the first quarter last year, so the severe winter evidently had less impact than we originally expected.

Although you can look over the attached raw data, the items below enjoyed continued popularity:

Product & Number	1996 First Quarter	1997 First Quarter	Percent Increase
Minnie's Tea Set (M30)	$ 102,477	$ 122,460	19.5%
Mickey's Mighty Ball (B44)	204,112	249,425	22.2%
"My-Name" Note Cards (P26)	98,934	121,689	23.0%
"Needs-a-Name" Doll (D88)	407,332	5,534,827	31.3%
Character T-shirt (P102)	804,231	1,147,638	42.7%
TOTAL	**$1,617,086**	**$2,176,039**	**34.6%**

I'm recommending to Ted in marketing that we supply our field reps with character T-shirts (P102) to present to buyers. We can break a million with this product if we keep promoting it.

Our Asian suppliers assure us that they can keep the products moving our way; however, we need to carefully monitor the spelling of all names. I recommend we request a fax to proof before signing off on imprinting any item produced overseas.

Generally, the figures suggest continued strong growth with no appreciable change in our investment ratio other than adjusting for inflation. After you look over the numbers, let me know whether you have any questions or concerns before the board meets next month. If the trend continues, 1997 may prove to be a record-setting year for PPI.

The first paragraph gives the reader specific information relating to the subject.

The second paragraph presents an easy-to-read chart of data selected from the overall report.

The third and fourth paragraphs provide pertinent information relating to other areas in the company.

The final paragraph summarizes the information, asks for follow-up by a certain time, and ends on a positive note.

Formal Communication Channels

The formal flow of information follows the official chain of command.

The **formal communication network** is the official structure of an organization, which is typically shown as an organization chart like the one in Figure 1.2. Such charts summarize the lines of authority, each box representing a link in the chain of command, and each line representing a formal channel for the transmission of official messages. Information may travel down, up, and across an organization's formal hierarchy.

When managers depend on formal channels for communicating, they risk encountering **distortion,** or misunderstanding. Every link in the communication chain opens up a chance for error. So by the time a message makes its way all the way up or down the chain, it may bear little resemblance to the original idea. As a consequence, people at lower levels may have only a vague idea of what top management expects of them, and executives may get an imperfect picture of what's happening lower down the chain.

The communication climate suffers when management distorts or ignores information from below or when management limits the flow of information to employees.

One way to reduce distortion is to reduce the number of levels in the organizational structure. The fewer the links in the communication chain, the less likely it is that misunderstandings will occur.[8] Generally speaking, bigger corporations have more levels. But as Figure 1.3 illustrates, size doesn't necessarily force a company to have a hierarchy with many levels. By increasing the number of people who report to each supervisor, the company can reduce the number of levels in the organization and simplify the communication chain. In other words, a flat structure (having fewer levels) and a wide span of control (having more people reporting to each supervisor) are less likely to introduce distortion than are a tall structure and a narrow span of control. Although flat is not necessarily better in every situation, more and more companies are moving in this direction in an effort to cut costs, boost productivity, and get closer to customers.

Apart from being vulnerable to distortion, the formal communication chain has another potential disadvantage: Information may become fragmented. Unless manage-

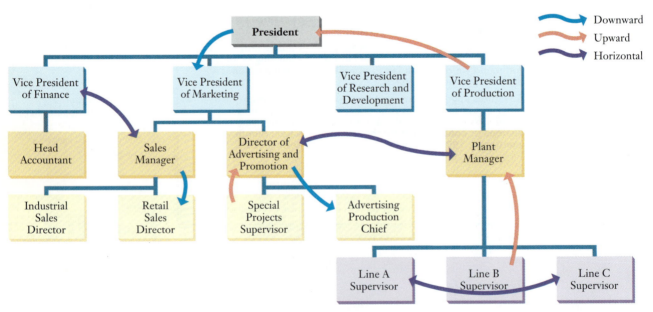

Figure 1.2
Formal Communication Network

ment encourages communication across the organization and diligently communicates down the hierarchy, only the person at the very top can see the "big picture." People lower down in the organization obtain only enough information to perform their own isolated tasks. They don't learn much about other areas, so their flexibility is limited, and they're unable to suggest ideas that cut across organizational boundaries. The solution is to make sure communication flows freely down, up, and across the organization chart.

Downward Information Flow

In most organizations, decisions are made at the top and then flow down to the people who will carry them out.[9] Downward messages might take the form of a casual conversation or a formal interview between a supervisor and an individual employee, or they might be communicated orally in a meeting, in a workshop, on videotape, or even on voice mail. Messages might also be written for e-mail or for a memo, training manual, newsletter, bulletin board announcement, or policy directive. From top to bottom, each person in the organization must be careful to understand the message, apply it, and pass it along. As pointed out by Phil Stein, vice president of H&E Do-It-Yourself Centers (in Victorville, California): "The general manager has to be able to communicate just as well as I do . . . has to be able to communicate our thoughts, our policies, and our regulations to the store managers. A store manager has to be able to communicate with the people on the floor. The 'good morning smile' has to filter all the way down."[10]

Managers direct and control the activities of lower-level employees by sending messages down through formal channels.

Tall Structure
Narrow Span of Control

Flat Structure
Wide Span of Control

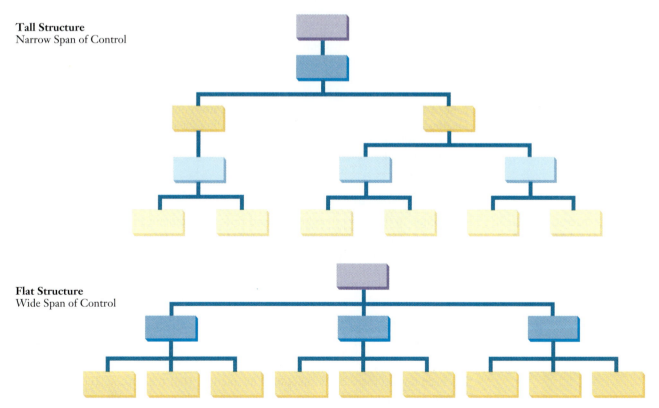

Figure 1.3
Organizational Structure and Span of Control

Most of what filters downward is geared toward helping employees do their jobs. Typical messages include briefings on the organization's mission and strategies, instructions on how to perform various jobs, explanations of policies and procedures, feedback on the employees' performance, and motivational pep talks. In hard times, downward communication is especially important, letting employees know how the organization is doing, what problems it faces, and what's expected to happen in the future.

Upward Information Flow

Messages directed upward provide managers with the information they need in order to make intelligent decisions.

Upward communication is just as vital as downward communication. To solve problems and make intelligent decisions, managers must learn what's going on in the organization. Since they can't be everywhere at once, executives depend on lower-level employees to furnish them with accurate, timely reports on problems, emerging trends, opportunities for improvement, grievances, and performance.

The danger, of course, is that employees will report only the good news. People are often afraid to admit their own mistakes or to report data that suggest their boss was wrong. Companies try to guard against the "rose-colored glasses" syndrome by creating reporting systems that require employees to furnish vital information on a routine basis. Many of these reports have a "red flag" feature that calls attention to deviations from planned results.

Other formal methods for channeling information upward include e-mail, group meetings, interviews with employees who are leaving the company, and formal procedures for resolving grievances. At Disney, two favorite methods are employee surveys (which give people a chance to comment anonymously on a wide range of issues) and focus groups (which allow employees to share their insights on specific subjects).

In recent years, many companies have also set up suggestion systems that encourage employees to submit ideas for improving the business. One of the most successful programs is run by Herman Miller, a Michigan manufacturer of office furniture. The company gets 2,000 suggestions a year from its 5,300 employees and accepts 53 percent of them. People who submit suggestions are publicly honored at departmental meetings; those who submit the most outstanding ideas qualify for the "Idea Club," whose members are invited to a special annual dinner with the CEO. The savings or profits created by the suggestions are set aside and spent for something that benefits all the employees.[11]

Horizontal Information Flow

Official channels also permit messages to flow from department to department.

In addition to the upward and downward flow of communication in the formal communication network, horizontal communication flows from one department to another, either laterally or diagonally. It helps employees coordinate tasks, and it's especially useful for solving complex and difficult problems.[12] For example, in Figure 1.2, the sales manager might write a memo or send e-mail to the vice president of finance, outlining sales forecasts for the coming period; or the plant manager might phone the director of advertising and promotion to discuss changes in the production schedule.

The amount of horizontal communication that occurs through formal channels depends on the degree of interdependence among departments. The most recent trend has been toward more cross-functional interaction. Half the Fortune 1000 companies responding to one survey report that they plan to rely more heavily on special cross-functional teams in coming years. Companies that have already moved in that direction report dramatic increases in productivity, largely because cooperation between employees from various departments breaks down the bureaucratic barriers that inhibit innovation and camouflage problems.

In many companies, advanced technology provides the physical foundation for interdepartmental communication. Sun Microsystems uses a worldwide computer network to link its 13,000 employees in the United States, England, Scotland, Brazil, Japan, Germany, the Netherlands, France, and Hong Kong. Whether implemented through technology or not, horizontal communication is crucial. Without it, co-workers aren't able to share information, and the results are missed deadlines, duplicated efforts, increased costs (due to rework), decreased product quality, and deteriorating employee relationships.[13]

Informal Communication Channels

Formal organization charts illustrate how information is supposed to flow. In actual practice, however, lines and boxes on a piece of paper cannot prevent people from talking with one another. Every organization has an **informal communication network**— a grapevine—that supplements official channels. As people go about their work, they have casual conversations with their friends in the office. They joke and kid around and discuss many things: their apartments, their families, restaurants, movies, sports, and other people in the company.

Although many of these conversations deal with personal matters, business is often discussed as well. In fact, about 80 percent of the information that travels along the grapevine pertains to business, and 75 to 95 percent of it is accurate.[14] Figure 1.4 illustrates a typical informal communication network, which is often the company's real power structure.

Some top executives are wary of the informal communication network, possibly because it threatens their power to control the flow of information. However, attempts to quash the grapevine generally have the opposite effect. Informal communication increases

> The grapevine is an important source of information in most organizations.

> The informal communication network carries information along the organization's unofficial lines of activity and power.

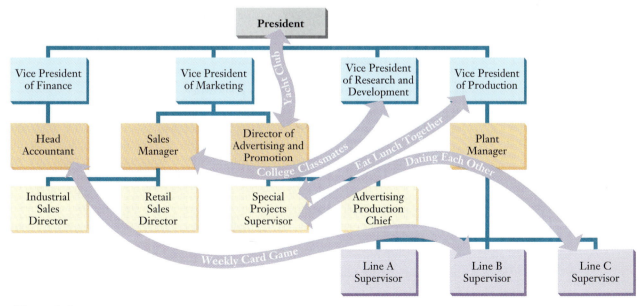

Figure 1.4
Informal Communication Network

when official channels are closed or when the organization faces periods of change, excitement, or anxiety. Instead of trying to eliminate the grapevine, sophisticated companies minimize its importance by making certain that the official word gets out.

Some companies try to tap into the grapevine.[15] One service, called In Touch, helps executives keep up with grapevine news by providing an 800 number that employees can call anonymously with any problems or worries. The recorded messages are either summarized or transcribed verbatim for top management.[16] Better yet, successful managers access the grapevine themselves to avoid being isolated from what's really happening. Hewlett-Packard trains its managers in **Management by Walking Around (MBWA),** encouraging them to be interested in employees' personal lives as well as their work lives. Disney's Michael Eisner practices MBWA, getting out of his office and making contact with other Disney employees. He often turns up in such "unexecutive" places as the carpentry shop at Disney World, where he chats with the workers.[17] Some managers actually use the grapevine to do their jobs. As chief information officer at GM Hughes Electronics in El Segundo, California, Gary Osborn can "maneuver through the business, ignoring all the official procedures and policies, and get the job done in a very informal fashion."[18]

THE EXTERNAL COMMUNICATION NETWORK

The external communication network links the organization with the outside world of customers, suppliers, competitors, and investors.

Just as internal communication carries information up, down, and across the organization, **external communication** carries it in and out of the organization. Companies constantly exchange messages with customers, vendors, distributors, competitors, investors, journalists, and government and community representatives. Whether by phone, fax, videotape, or letter (see Figure 1.5 on pages 14–15), much of this communication is carefully orchestrated, and some occurs informally.

Formal Contacts with Outsiders

Even though much of the communication that occurs with outsiders is casual and relatively unplanned, most organizations attempt to control the information they convey to customers, investors, and the general public. Two functional units are particularly important in managing the flow of external messages: the marketing department and the public relations department.

The Role of Marketing and Public Relations

The marketing and public relations departments are responsible for managing much of the organization's formal communication with outsiders.

As a consumer, you are often on the receiving end of marketing messages: face-to-face or telephone conversations with salespeople, direct-mail solicitations, TV and radio commercials, newspaper and magazine ads, blurbs advertising companies on the Internet, product brochures, and mail-order catalogs. Although these messages are highly visible, they represent just the tip of the iceberg when it comes to marketing communication. In addition to advertising and selling products, the typical marketing department is also responsible for product development, physical distribution, market research, and customer service, all of which involve both the transmission and reception of information.

Marketing focuses on selling goods and services, whereas public relations is more concerned with developing the organization's overall reputation.

Public relations is closely related to marketing and is often confused with it, but the focus of the two functions differs. Marketing has three basic responsibilities: to find out who customers are and what they want, to develop products that satisfy those needs, and to get the products into the customers' hands. The public relations department (also called the corporate communication department) manages the organization's reputation with various groups, including employees, customers, investors, government agencies, and the general public. Professional PR people may have a background in journalism, as opposed to marketing. They view their role as disseminating news about the business to the organization's various audiences.

Whereas marketing messages are usually openly sponsored and paid for by the company, public relations messages are carried by the media if they are considered newsworthy. The communication tools used by PR departments include news releases, lobbying programs, special events, booklets and brochures about the organization, letters, annual reports, audiovisual materials, speeches and position papers, tours, and internal publications for employees.

Crisis Communication

One of the most visible functions of the PR department is to help management plan for and respond to crises. A good PR professional constantly scans the business environment looking for potential problems and then alerts management to the implications and suggests the best course of action. Disneyland, for example, has anticipated the possibility of an earthquake and is prepared to provide food, water, and medical care for 10,000 people for five days. The park also has specially trained employees who would coordinate rescue efforts using walkie-talkies, cellular phones, and a public-address system. In an emergency, visitors would be assembled in "safe havens" away from major structures.[19]

Disasters of earthquake proportions fall into the category of public relations nightmares created by sudden, violent accidents. Plane crashes, oil spills, chemical leaks, and product defects all belong to this group. The other type of crisis is the sort that builds slowly and occurs because of a company's conscious, but ill-founded, decisions. One example is R. J. Reynolds's attempt to introduce a cigarette aimed at African Americans (who have historically suffered higher rates of smoking-related illness than other groups). RJR badly miscalculated the public's probable reaction to the new product. Antismoking activists accused the company of sleazy and cynical business practices, and the Department of Health and Human Services blasted the firm for promoting a "culture of cancer." The barrage of bad press prompted RJR to cancel the introduction of Uptown cigarettes.[20]

One sudden and violent event that public relations professionals had to deal with was the bombing of the Federal Building in Oklahoma City.

Figure 1.5
In-Depth Critique:
External Communication
by Letter

Montana's Save the Wolves Foundation seeks to raise funds for successfully reintroducing captured wolves from other states into the less populated habitat of Montana. The foundation communicates externally with representatives of mass media to try to educate the public and garner support.

Save the Wolves Foundation
4542 Audobon Highway • Viper, MT 32400
(406) 266-6223 • Fax (406) 723-3229
<http://www.wolves.org>

March 13, 1997

Mr. Sam Davis, Managing Editor
Montana Times Magazine
468 West Times Drive
Helena, Montana 72645

Dear Mr. Davis:

Thank you for your recent editorial supporting the Montana wolf relocation program. We are as dedicated to preserving domestic livestock herds as the ranchers who own them. However, killing the wolf predators is both a short-term and a short-sighted solution. In addition to the excellent points you made, we'd like your readers to have some additional information.

Every one of the 32 wolves we've captured and relocated this year has been examined by a veterinarian. The wolves receive inoculations to prevent rabies, among other diseases. Therefore, the relocated wolves are a safer population both to wildlife, their pack, and the occasional domestic animal or human who might encounter them.

In the wilderness areas where they will be relocated, wolves help keep the population of caribou, moose, and deer under control, and they cull injured or sick animals from the herd. However, wolves fear human beings and will avoid people whenever possible. Our North American wolves do not attack humans.

In addition, your readers will be interested to know a little more about wolves in general. Wolves have strong family ties and often mate for life with female wolves giving birth to about four to six pups. Both parents supply food and help train the pups. In fact, the wolf pack is usually a family group. And just as families

The first paragraph references what prompted the communication and ends by clearly stating the purpose of the letter to the editor. The paragraph identifies the two audiences receiving information: the editor of the magazine and magazine readers.

The second and third paragraphs provide specific information on the relocation program and reassure readers of their personal safety.

The fourth paragraph seeks to establish a special connection or link (sometimes called rapport in oral communication) with the readers.

The way a company handles a crisis can have a profound impact on the organization's subsequent performance.

An inept response to either type of crisis can destroy a company's reputation, drain its financial strength, erode morale, and invite protracted investigations, heavy fines, and negative publicity. Jack in the Box's worst nightmare began when officials linked the death of at least two children and the illness of more than 400 people to contaminated hamburger meat from its fast-food restaurants. One of the largest fast-food

Figure 1.5
(Continued)

Mr. Sam Davis, March 13, 1997, Page 2

call to their children, wolves sometimes howl to keep their pack together.

We invite those of your readers who would like to join our efforts to call 1-800-544-8333 to receive more information.

Sincerely,

Carroll Paulding

**Carroll Paulding
President**

Finally, the letter ends with a clearly stated invitation placed where readers will notice it.

chains in the United States, Jack in the Box (and parent company Foodmaker) had to fight hard to save the company's image and name.[21]

Some public relations professionals praised Jack in the Box for the steps it took to stem the crisis: (1) It established a toll-free hot line to answer questions. (2) It replaced regular product ads with special commercials to explain its response to the outbreak. (3) It paid the hospital bills of those customers affected. (4) It contributed $100,000 to fight the disease that killed the children. (5) It improved cooking procedures to exceed state and federal standards. And (6) it changed meat suppliers.[22]

Other professionals criticized the company, saying it could have reacted better: (1) It failed to include outsiders on its crisis team. (As one critic stated, ". . . in-house people can't be completely objective.") (2) It wasted precious time pointing the finger at meat suppliers. (3) It allowed too much time to pass before holding its first press conference. (After six full days of silence, too many questions were unanswered.) (4) It switched spokesmen—from Jack in the Box president Bob Nugent at the press conference to Foodmaker chairman Jack Goodall in television commercials—signaling the public that there was some confusion or lack of confidence in the company.[23]

In the first two weeks after the link was made between Jack in the Box hamburgers and the outbreak of food poisoning, business at the restaurant chain fell off 30 to 35 percent. Within a month, eight lawsuits were filed against the company, and Foodmaker in turn filed suit against its meat supplier. Within two months, sales began to rebound (with the help of regular product advertising and discounted menu items), but the company reported a second-quarter loss of $29.3 million and had to delay its expansion plans to open 85 new Jack in the Box restaurants.[24]

According to public relations professionals, when disaster strikes, a defensive posture is generally counterproductive. The best course is to be proactive, admit your mistakes, and apologize (see Table 1.1 on page 16). That's what AT&T did when its long-distance service was out of commission for nine hours in January 1990, hanging up 80 million callers. That's also what Johnson & Johnson did in its now classic handling of the Tylenol poisoning scare in 1982. More recently, however, Food Lion opted for fiercer tactics and for taking the offensive. A report was broadcast on ABC's *PrimeTime Live* accusing the fast-growing supermarket chain of dipping old meat in

Most experts recommend handling a crisis with candor and honesty.

TABLE 1.1

DO'S AND DON'TS OF CRISIS COMMUNICATION

WHEN A CRISIS HITS:

DO'S

Do be prepared for trouble. Identify potential problems in advance. Appoint and train a predesignated response team. Prepare and test a crisis management plan.

Do get top management involved as soon as the crisis hits.

Do set up a news center for company representatives and the media, equipped with phones, computers, and other electronic tools for preparing news releases.

- Issue at least two news updates a day and have trained personnel on call to respond to questions around the clock.
- Provide complete information packets to the media as soon as possible.
- To prevent conflicting statements and provide continuity, appoint a single person, trained in advance, to speak for the company.
- Tell receptionists to direct all calls to the information center.

Do tell the whole story—openly, completely, and honestly. If you are at fault, apologize.

Do demonstrate the company's concern by your statements and your actions.

DON'TS

Don't blame anyone for anything.

Don't speculate in public about unknown facts.

Don't decline to answer questions.

Don't release information that will violate anyone's right to privacy.

Don't use the crisis to pitch products or services.

Don't play favorites with media representatives.

---

bleach and disguising tainted chicken with barbecue sauce. Within hours of the blistering program, CEO Tom E. Smith made a statement to the media, often repeating the phrase, "These lies have got to stop." The next morning he contacted stock analysts in a 50-minute conference call, explaining why he believed the sources for the report lacked credibility. Smith appeared in commercials to publicize the company's position, which was also presented on 60,000 videotapes that were sent to employees with the request to show them to family, friends, and local groups.[25]

Don't ignore the impact of a crisis on employees.

When disaster hits, most companies respond, to some degree, through their public relations department, but they often ignore the audience that is likely to be hit hardest—employees. When the *New York Daily News* faced a violent 21-week union strike, morale sank. "Everyone was on edge, and even minor work-related problems were blown out of proportion," said Dawna Fields, manager of public affairs. To minimize the impact of any crisis on employees, be sure to communicate honestly, openly, and often; actively encourage employees to share their concerns; and use caution when sharing personal opinions.[26]

Informal Contacts with Outsiders

As a member of an organization, you are automatically an informal conduit for communicating with the outside world. In the course of your daily activities, you unconsciously absorb bits and pieces of information that add to the collective knowledge pool of your company. During a trip to the shopping mall, you notice how a competitor's products are selling; as you read the paper, you pick up economic and business news that relates to your work; when you have a problem at the office, you ask your family or friends for advice.

What's more, every time you speak for or about your company, you send a message. In fact, if you have a public-contact job, you don't even have to say anything. All you have to do is smile. Many outsiders may form their impression of your organization on the basis of the subtle, unconscious clues you transmit through your tone of voice, facial expression, and general appearance—which is one reason Disney enforces a strict grooming code for all employees who interact with the public.

Top managers rely heavily on informal contacts with outsiders to exchange information that might be useful to their companies. Although much of the networking involves interaction with fellow executives, plenty of high-level managers recognize the value of keeping in touch with "the real world." For example, when Stanley Gault was chairman of Rubbermaid, he cornered travelers in airports to ask for ideas on new products. Xerox executives spend one day each month handling customer complaints. Senior executives at Hyatt Hotels serve as bellhops, and Disney managers all take their turns in 80- to 100-pound character costumes at one of the theme parks. As Wal-Mart founder Sam Walton used to say when someone asked why he visited Kmart stores: "It's all part of the educational process. I'm just learning."[27]

Every employee informally accumulates facts and impressions that contribute to the organization's collective understanding of the outside world.

CHARACTERISTICS OF EFFECTIVE ORGANIZATIONAL COMMUNICATION

If good management depends on effective communication, it follows that the outstanding companies are those that have built the best internal and external communication networks. What makes these networks better? What characteristics contribute to effective communication? Six factors are involved:

- Fostering an open communication climate
- Committing to ethical communication
- Understanding the difficulties involved in intercultural communication
- Becoming proficient in communication technology
- Using an audience-centered approach to communication
- Creating and processing messages efficiently

An Open Communication Climate

An organization's communication climate is a reflection of its **corporate culture**—the mixture of values, traditions, and habits that give a place its atmosphere or personality. Some companies tend to choke off the upward flow of communication, believing that debate is time consuming and unproductive. Other companies, like Disney, foster candor and honesty. Their employees feel free to confess their mistakes, to disagree with the boss, and to express their opinions. Michael Eisner encourages an open exchange of ideas by asking plenty of questions. As he says: "I find that the best ideas always

The organization's communication climate affects the quantity and quality of the information that passes through the pipeline.

come during the final five minutes of a meeting, when people drop their guard and I ask them what they really think."[28]

The management style of the top executives influences the organization's communication climate.

Many factors influence an organization's communication climate, including the nature of the industry, the company's physical setup, the history of the company, and passing events. However, as Disney's Eisner confirms, one of the most important factors is the style of the top-management group.[29] Of all the many ways to categorize management styles, one of the most widely used is Douglas McGregor's Theory X and Theory Y.[30] Theory X managers consider workers to be lazy and irresponsible, motivated to work only by fear of losing their jobs. So these managers adopt a directive style. Theory Y managers, on the other hand, assume that people like to work and to take responsibility when they believe in what they are doing. So these managers adopt a more supportive management style.

To keep in touch with employees and encourage an open climate, effective managers
- Get out of their offices
- Talk with and listen to management and nonmanagement groups
- Travel at home and abroad to visit the troops
- Learn other languages
- Use technology

Yet another management approach, called Theory Z, was developed by William Ouchi.[31] Like athletic coaches, Theory Z managers encourage employees to work together as a team. Although the company still looks after employees, it also gives them the opportunity to take responsibility and to participate in decision making.

While many organizations are striving for the supportive style of Theory Y management or the participative style of Theory Z management, others are working toward total quality management, integrating product quality across all functions and levels in the organization. The trend today is toward any style that encourages open communication climates. Only in such a climate do managers spend more time listening than issuing orders, and only there do workers not only offer suggestions but also help set goals and collaborate on solving problems.[32]

A Commitment to Ethical Communication

The second factor contributing to effective communication is the organization's commitment to **ethics,** the principles of conduct that govern a person or a group. Unethical people are essentially selfish and unscrupulous, saying or doing whatever it takes to achieve an end. Ethical people are generally trustworthy, fair, and impartial, respecting the rights of others and concerned about the impact of their actions on society. Former Supreme Court Justice Potter Stewart defined ethics as "knowing the difference between what you have a right to do and what is the right thing to do."[33]

Ethics are the principles of conduct that govern a person or group.

Ethics plays a crucial role in communication. Language itself is made up of words that carry values. So merely by saying things a certain way, you influence how others perceive your message, and you shape expectations and behaviors.[34] Likewise, when an organization expresses itself internally, it influences the values of its employees; when it communicates externally, it shapes the way outsiders perceive it. **Ethical communication** includes all relevant information, is true in every sense, and is not deceptive in any way.

When sending an ethical message, you are accurate and sincere. You avoid language that manipulates, discriminates, or exaggerates. You do not hide negative information behind an optimistic attitude, you don't state opinions as facts, and you portray graphic data fairly. You are honest with employers, co-workers, and clients, never seeking personal gain by making others look better or worse than they are. You don't allow personal preferences to influence your perception or the perception of others, and you act in good faith. On the surface, such ethical practices appear fairly easy to recognize. But deciding what is ethical can be quite complex (see "Ethical Boundaries: Where Would You Draw the Line?").

ETHICAL BOUNDARIES: WHERE WOULD YOU DRAW THE LINE?

At the very least, you owe your employer an honest day's work for an honest day's pay, your best efforts, obedience to the rules, a good attitude, respect for your employer's property, and a professional appearance. Such duties and considerations seem clear-cut, but where does your obligation to your employer end? Some situations seem perfectly ethical . . . until you think about them. For instance, where would you draw the line in communication situations like the following?

- Writing your résumé so that an embarrassing two-year lapse won't be obvious
- Telling your best friend about your company's upcoming merger right after mailing the formal announcement to your shareholders
- Hinting to a co-worker (who's a close friend) that it's time to look around for something new, when you've already been told confidentially that she's scheduled to be fired at the end of the month
- Saying nothing when you witness one employee taking credit for another's successful idea
- Preserving your position by presenting yourself to supervisors as the only means of achieving an objective
- Buying one software package for use by three computer operators
- Making up an excuse when (for the fourth time this month) you have to pick up your child from school early and miss an important business meeting
- Calling in sick because you're taking a few days off and have already accumulated so much sick leave

At times, circumstances may seem to demand that you act in the best interests of your employer. For example, where would you draw the line in the following situation? You're returning from a bidder's conference, and you spot a competitor's product design in an airport wastebasket. Is it unethical to take advantage of your luck? Once on the plane, you're seated behind two of your competitor's engineers, who are loudly discussing their product's new design. Is it unethical if you can't help overhearing? Then you discover you're seated next to another competitor's chief engineer. He's openly studying detailed drawings of an exciting new product, which he carelessly leaves in his seat when he gets up to use the restroom. How unethical could it be to take a quick glance? When the plane finally lands, the same engineer accidentally leaves his drawings behind as he makes a mad dash for a connecting flight. Again, would it be unethical to take a look?

Is it really unethical to take advantage of a competitor's carelessness in order to benefit your employer? Is it really unethical to betray an employer's confidence or to tell your employer a lie? Wherever you are, whatever the circumstances, you owe your employer your best efforts. Nonetheless, time and again, it will be up to you to decide whether those efforts are ethical.

1. As an employer, what would you expect from your employees that isn't mentioned here?
2. As the supervisor of the office typing pool, you must deal with several typists who have a tendency to gossip about their co-workers. List five things you might do to resolve the situation.

Recognizing Ethical Choices

Every company has responsibilities to various groups: customers, employees, shareholders, suppliers, neighbors, the community, and the nation. Unfortunately, what's right for one group may be wrong for another.[35] Moreover, as you attempt to satisfy the needs of one group, you may be presented with an option that seems right on the surface but somehow feels wrong. When people must choose between conflicting loyalties and weigh difficult trade-offs, they are facing a dilemma.

An **ethical dilemma** involves choosing among alternatives that aren't clear-cut (perhaps two conflicting alternatives are both ethical and valid, or perhaps your alternatives lie somewhere in the vast gray area between right and wrong). Suppose you are president of a company that's losing money. You have a duty to your shareholders to try to cut your losses and to your employees to be fair and honest. After looking at various options, you conclude that you'll have to lay off 500 people immediately. You suspect you may have to lay off another 100 people later on, but right now you need those 100

Conflicting priorities and the vast gray areas between right and wrong pose ethical problems for an organization's communicators.

workers to finish a project. What do you tell them? If you confess that their jobs are shaky, many of them may quit just when you need them most. However, if you tell them that the future is rosy, you'll be stretching the truth.

Unlike a dilemma, an **ethical lapse** is making a clearly unethical or illegal choice. Suppose you have decided to change jobs and have discretely landed an interview with your boss's largest competitor. You get along great with the interviewer, who is impressed enough with you to offer you a position on the spot. Not only is the new position a step up from your present job, but the pay is double what you're getting now. You accept the job and agree to start next month. Then as you're shaking hands with the interviewer, she asks that when you begin your new job, you bring along profiles of your present company's ten largest customers. Do you comply with her request? How do you decide between what's ethical and what is not?

Making Ethical Choices

Laws provide ethical guide-lines for certain types of messages.

One place to look for guidance is the law. If saying or writing something is clearly illegal, you have no dilemma: You obey the law. However, even though legal considerations will resolve some ethical questions, you'll often have to rely on your own judgment and principles. You might apply the Golden Rule: Do unto others as you would have them do unto you. You might examine your motives: If your intent is honest, the statement is ethical, even though it may be factually incorrect; if your intent is to mislead or manipulate the audience, the message is unethical, regardless of whether it is true. You might look at the consequences of your decision and opt for the solution that provides the greatest good to the greatest number of people. You might also ask yourself a set of questions:[36]

Ask yourself how you would feel if you were on the receiving end of the message.

- Is this decision legal? (Does it violate civil law or company policy?)
- Is it balanced? (Does it do the most good and the least harm? Is it fair to all concerned in the short term as well as the long term? Does it promote positive win-win relationships?)
- Is it a decision you can live with? (Does it make you feel good about yourself? Does it make you proud? Would you feel good about your decision if a newspaper published it? If your family knew about it?)
- Is it feasible? (Can it work in the real world? Have you considered your position in the company, your company's competition, its financial and political strength, the likely costs or risks of your decision, and the time available?)

In addition, you might look at communication ethics in terms of stakeholders:

- ***People outside the company—customers, suppliers, investors, public officials, representatives of the media, and members of the community.*** Your goal in communicating with these outside stakeholders is to achieve mutual understanding. The best policy is to tell the truth. Lying to outsiders can lead to serious legal problems because any written communication from an organization is acceptable as legal evidence in a court of law.
- ***Supervisors.*** Management relies on lower-level employees to provide honest and accurate information about their activities. If you mislead your supervisors, you compromise the company's ability to function. Although it's sometimes tempting to cover up mistakes or exaggerate accomplishments, it's not only unethical but also counterproductive to do so.
- ***Employees.*** You have an obligation to be honest with those who report to you. Although sharing information with employees sometimes creates short-term

BEST OF THE WEB

Use the Power of the Internet to Help You Learn About Business Communication

One of the best links to information on the Internet—about business communication or any other topic—is Navigation Tools in Stockholm, Sweden. The site includes Starting Points, featuring directories and indexes for a stunning array of Internet resources. It guides you to e-mail discussion groups, news groups, search engines, and electronic newsletters. This handy site will add focus to your Web surfing and should be added to your bookmark list.

http://www.it-kompetens.com/navigate.html

Note: To reach the Web sites you find throughout this book, you don't have to type every single URL into your browser. Just type one—<http://www.phlip.marist.edu/>—which is the Web site for this book. There, you'll find live links that take you straight to the site of your choice.

problems, people have a right to know about matters that affect them. They also have a right to expect that personal information about them will be handled discreetly.

- *Co-workers.* When communicating with fellow employees, be honorable. Making a co-worker look bad, taking credit for someone else's work, spreading false rumors, and other such tactics generally backfire. Being anything but forthright with co-workers threatens your credibility and betrays people's trust. So even when such tactics advance your career, is victory worth the price?

Motivating Ethical Choices

Ethical communication promotes long-term business success and profit. However, improving profits isn't reason enough to be ethical. So how can an organization motivate employees to be ethical? First and foremost, the personal influence of chief executives and managers plays an important role. Top managers can begin encouraging ethical behavior and decision making by being more receptive communicators themselves (which requires mastering many of the skills presented in this text). They can also send the right message to employees by rewarding ethical behavior. Managers can lay out an explicit ethical policy, and in fact, more and more companies are using a written **code of ethics** to help employees determine what is acceptable. In addition, managers can use ethics audits to monitor ethical progress and to point up any weaknesses that need to be addressed.[37]

Beyond leading to success in business, being ethical is simply the right thing to do. Moreover, it's contagious. Others will follow your example when they observe you being ethical and see the success you experience both in your interpersonal relationships and in your career.[38]

Organizations can foster ethical behavior
- By helping top managers become more sensitive communicators
- By rewarding ethical actions
- By using ethics audits

An Understanding of Intercultural Communication

The third factor contributing to a positive communication climate is understanding intercultural communication. Not only are more and more businesses crossing national boundaries to compete on a global scale, but the makeup of the global and domestic work force is changing rapidly. European, Asian, and U.S. firms are establishing offices around the world and creating international ties through global partnerships, cooperatives, and affiliations.[39] These companies must understand the laws, customs, and business practices of their host countries, and they must deal with business associates and employees who are native to those countries (perhaps speaking another language and certainly more familiar with another culture). Domestically, firms are also working with more and more employees whose cultural backgrounds differ. In the United States, women and ethnic minorities are entering the work force in record numbers. By 2005, 47.7 percent of the U.S. work force will be women, 11.6 percent will be African American, 11 percent will be Hispanic, and 5.5 percent will be Asian and other minorities.[40] So whether you work abroad or at home, you will be encountering more and more cultural diversity in the workplace. To compete successfully in today's multicultural environment, most businesspeople overcome the communication barriers not only of language but of culture as well.

Chapter 3 discusses intercultural communication in detail. You'll see how the need for intercultural understanding has grown, whether your company operates within national boundaries or does business around the world. You'll learn about specific cultural differences and see how they affect communication. Chapter 3 also gives you important tips for communicating with people from other cultures.

Intercultural communication plays an important role both abroad and at home.

Culture determines how we perceive and thus how we communicate.

Intercultural communication is discussed in detail in Chapter 3.

A Proficiency in Communication Technology

Technology has such an impact on business communication that you have no choice but to master it.

The fourth factor contributing to effective organizational communication is the ability to use and adapt to technology. The increasing speed of communication and the growing amount of information to be communicated are only two results of the ever-changing technology you will encounter on the job. To succeed, businesspeople today make sure they can understand, use, and adapt to the technological tools of communication.

Technology's effects on communication are discussed in detail in Chapter 4.

Chapter 4 tells you about the impact of technology on communication, the specific tools you'll use to develop and distribute messages, and the systems that businesses use to communicate both internally and externally. Although many of you may have grown up using computers and feel comfortable with the ever-changing face of technological developments, many of you may feel apprehensive about computers or anything technical. Chapter 4 is an overview of the types of technological tools you'll encounter on the job. If you wish to learn more about communication technology, or if you would like more specific information, consult the reference notes at the end of the book for this section and for Chapter 4, and consult your instructor and your school librarian.

Technology can be an invisible ally, helping you perform the tasks necessary to succeed in business. As long as you consider it a means to an end, rather than an end in itself, technology can improve the effectiveness of your business communication.[41]

An Audience-Centered Approach to Communication

Using an audience-centered approach means keeping your audience in mind at all times when communicating.

The fifth factor contributing to effective organizational communication is an **audience-centered approach,** keeping your audience in mind at all times during the process of communication. Your ability to empathize with, be sensitive to, and generally consider your audience's feelings is the best way to be effective in your communication. Focusing on the audience is the impetus for everything else you do in the communication process. For example, being clear and correct in your communication is important not only because it's ethical but also because it ensures that your audience has an opportunity to react to your message, without having to sort out cluttered or incorrect language.

Communicate from your audience's point of view.

Because you care about your audience, you take every step possible to get your message across in a way that is meaningful to your audience. You might actually create lively individual portraits of readers and listeners to predict how they will react. You might simply try to put yourself in your audience's position. You might try adhering strictly to guidelines about courtesy, or you might be able to gather research about the needs and wants of your audience. Whatever your tactic, the point is to write and speak from your audience's point of view.

The audience-centered approach is more than an approach to business communication; it's actually the modern approach to business in general (behind such concepts as total quality management and total customer satisfaction). The advantages of using this approach include making your communication successful by making it mean something to your audience, enhancing your own credibility (because your audience perceives your sincerity), and staving off uncountable ethical questions (because when you concentrate on the benefits to your audience, your concern for others reduces the chance of an ethical lapse).

Your audience-centered approach will help you incorporate into your messages the other five factors of effective communication: an open climate, an ethical commitment, an intercultural understanding, a technological expertise, and an efficient flow.

Centering your attention on your audience helps you accomplish the other five factors that contribute to effective communication. Because you want to know what your audience's needs are and what they think of your message, you work for an open communication climate inside and outside your organization. Because you sincerely wish to satisfy the needs of your audience, you approach communication situations with good intentions and high ethical standards. Because you need to understand your audience, you do whatever it takes to understand intercultural differences and barriers. Because you make a practice of anticipating your audience's expectations, you choose the appropriate technological tools for your message and make the best use of them. Finally, because you value your audience's time, you prepare and communicate oral and written messages as efficiently as possible.

An Efficient Flow of Communication Messages

The sixth factor contributing to effective organizational communication is an efficient flow of communication messages. Think for a minute about the number of messages people send and receive, both within their organizations and throughout the world. The amount of information people must deal with is staggering. A few statistics may help put the problem in perspective:[42]

Although organizations need to document their activities, they also need to manage the flow of messages as efficiently as possible.

- Despite computer manufacturers promising the paperless office, shipments of office paper have risen 51 percent since 1983.
- People in the United States added 130 million information receivers—e-mail addresses, cellular phones, pagers, fax machines, voice mailboxes, answering machines—up 365 percent from 40.7 million in 1987 to 148.6 million in 1995 (not including their 170 million telephones, up from 143 million from 1987 to 1995).
- In one year, 11,900,000,000 messages were left on voice mailboxes.
- Even though people are clamoring to get on the Internet, they are sending even more messages through the U.S. Postal Service, and they're talking on their telephones more than ever.

How many meetings are a waste of time? How much effort is wasted handling messages during a crisis? The volume of messages is greater in large organizations than in small ones, but all companies can hold down the costs and maximize the benefits of their communication activities:

Routine communication is essential to business, but it represents a major expense.

- ***Reduce the number of messages.*** One useful way to reduce the number of messages is to think twice before sending one. It takes time and resources to produce letters and memos, so organizations have to be concerned with how many messages they create. The average cost of dictating, transcribing, and mailing a business letter is between $13.02 and $19.87.[43] If a message must be put in writing, a letter or memo is a good investment. If the message merely adds to the information overload, it's probably better left unsent or handled in some other way— say, by a quick telephone call or a face-to-face chat.

Organizations save time and money by sending only necessary messages.

- ***Speed up the preparation of messages.*** Because the value of so much information depends on its timeliness, people in business try to transmit messages as quickly as possible. One thing that helps speed up the process is to make sure that written messages are prepared correctly the first time around. Another way to increase efficiency in the preparation of messages is through standardization. Most organizations use form letters for handling repetitive correspondence, and most use a standard format for memos, reports, and e-mail messages that are prepared on a recurring basis. In the case of memos and reports (whether paper or electronic), standardization also saves the readers' time because the familiar format enables people to absorb the information more quickly.

By streamlining the preparation of messages, companies make sure that information is transmitted in a timely manner.

In-house training benefits even experienced communicators.

- ***Train the writers and speakers.*** Recognizing the importance of efficient communication, many companies train employees in communication skills. The American Society for Training and Development surveyed major employers and found that 41 percent provide writing-skills programs for their employees.[44] Many others, including Disney, offer seminars and workshops on handling common oral communication situations (such as dealing with customers, managing subordinates, and getting along with co-workers), as well as training in computers and other electronic means of communication.

Focus on building skills in the areas where you've been weak.

Even though you may ultimately receive training on the job, you can start mastering business communication skills right now, in this course. Perhaps the best place to begin is with an honest assessment of where you stand. In the next few days, watch how you handle the communication situations that arise. Try to figure out what you're doing right and what you're doing wrong. Then in the months ahead, try to focus on building your competence in areas where you need the most work.

Practice using all communication skills so that you can learn from your mistakes.

One way to improve your ability is to practice. People aren't "born" writers or speakers. Their skills improve the more they speak and write. Someone who has written ten reports is usually better at it than someone who has written only two reports. You learn from experience, and some of the most important lessons are learned through failure. Learning what *not* to do is just as important as learning what *to* do. One of the great advantages of taking a course in business communication is that you get to practice in an environment that provides honest and constructive criticism. A course of this kind also gives you an understanding of acceptable techniques, so you can avoid making costly mistakes on the job.

This book has been designed to provide the kind of communication practice that will prepare you for whatever comes along later in your career. The next chapter introduces some concepts of communication in general so that you will be better able to analyze and predict the outcome of various situations. Chapters 3 and 4 discuss the importance of intercultural and technological communication. Chapters 5, 6, and 7 explain how to plan and organize business messages and how to perfect their style and tone. The following chapters deal with specific forms of communication: letters and memos, résumés and application letters, reports, interviews and meetings, and speeches and presentations. As you progress through this book, you will also meet many business communicators like Michael Eisner of Disney. Their experiences will give you an insight into what it takes to communicate effectively on the job.

SUMMARY

Communication plays an essential part in the managerial process. When you understand how an organization communicates, you are equipped to become a productive member of the group.

Communication occurs through both formal and informal channels, and it flows up and down the hierarchy, as well as across the lines of authority. Communication also occurs with outside audiences both formally and informally.

The most successful organizations are those that communicate openly, use ethical communication, understand cultural differences, are proficient in communication technology, use an audience-centered approach, and handle messages efficiently. In such organizations, all employees have access to the information required to do their jobs.

COMMUNICATION CHALLENGES AT DISNEY

After a grueling sophomore year, you decided to take a fun summer job at Disneyland in Anaheim. The hourly jobs there are a natural fit for your excellent people skills. Besides, you enjoy the outdoors; you just can't see yourself in an office working at a computer for eight hours a day. One of the things that attracted you to Disney was the fact that it rotates jobs within the park. No employee gets "stuck" in a job that isn't fun or that doesn't suit his or her personality.

Although you began by directing cars into the parking lot, you were soon "promoted" to a job at Thunder Mountain. And that's the problem. You've been running the roller coaster inside the "mountain" for three long weeks. In a way, it's a compliment. Your supervisor, Nell Ryan, can only assign workers who are at least 20 years old, are very responsible, and have had the training course to run an action ride. She's told you you're one of the best ride operators in the park. The only trouble is that you're stuck in a dark console room within the mountain. For three weeks you haven't seen the sun or interacted with people in the park.

INDIVIDUAL CHALLENGE: Approach your supervisor in such a way that you achieve two goals: (1) get assigned to a job that involves sunshine and people, and (2) maintain your status as an exceptional employee.

After all, you're counting on a good letter of recommendation. You've asked to meet with Nell during your lunch break. What will you say?

TEAM CHALLENGE: Everyone at Disney gets along so well that you usually meet to share a pizza and talk about the crazy events and amusing people of the day. One night, everyone begins brainstorming about the new rides they would propose to CEO Michael Eisner. After all, employees who submit suggestions can win up to $10,000 through the "I Have an Idea" program. But as the hour grows late, everyone leaves but you and Lindsay Brock, another student. Together, you start formulating an idea that has tremendous possibilities: an interactive coaster ride.

Instead of being run totally by an operator, passengers on your ride would choose which of three tracks to follow, adjust the speed of the ride, and even "hang" at the top of a hill for up to ten seconds before starting the descent. You know the technology exists to design such a ride. Feverishly, you sketch out ideas on the back of a pizza box. You know the secret will be in how you pitch your idea to Eisner. Working together with a classmate, assume the roles of these two students working for Disney, and write down your ideas to be presented to Michael Eisner.

CRITICAL THINKING QUESTIONS

1. Why do you think good communication in an organization improves employees' attitudes and performance? Explain briefly.
2. Whenever you report negative information to your boss, she never passes it along to her colleagues or supervisors. You believe the information is important, but whom do you talk to? Your boss? Your boss's supervisor? A co-worker who also reports to your boss? A co-worker who reports to a different boss? Briefly explain your answer.
3. You've just been promoted to manager and you've developed a good rapport with most of your employees, but Richardson and Blake are always going to your supervisor with matters that should go through you. Both employees have been at the company for at least ten years longer than you have, and both know your supervisor very well. Should you speak with them about this? Should you speak with your supervisor? Explain briefly.
4. Because of your excellent communication skills, your boss always asks you to write his reports for him. When you overhear the CEO complimenting him on his logical organization and clear writing style, he responds as if he'd written all those reports himself. You're angry, but he's your boss. What can you do? Briefly explain your answer.
5. To save time and money, your company is considering limiting all memos to one page or less. The CEO asks your opinion. Is it a good idea? Explain briefly.
6. As long as you make sure that everyone involved receives some benefit and that no one gets hurt, is it okay to make a decision that's just a little unethical? Briefly explain your answer.

EXERCISES

1. For the following tasks, identify the necessary direction of communication (downward, upward, horizontal), suggest an appropriate type of communication (casual conversation, formal interview, meeting, workshop, videotape, newsletter, memo, bulletin board notice, etc.), and briefly explain your suggestion:
   a. As personnel manager, you want to announce details about this year's company picnic.
   b. As director of internal communication, you want to convince top management of the need for a company newsletter.
   c. As production manager, you want to make sure that both the sales manager and the finance manager receive your scheduling estimates.
   d. As marketing manager, you want to help employees understand the company's goals and its attitudes toward workers.

2. Name three ways you might encourage your employees to give you feedback on daily operations. Explain briefly.

3. In your small publishing firm, you have three top-notch editors, and as the firm grows, you need them to work more and more often as a team. One of the editors, Wilson, is rigid and unforgiving, constantly reminding others of his 20 years' experience and unwilling to compromise. Pick an option and briefly explain why it's the best course of action. Should your first step be to
   a. Fire Wilson and look for a replacement?
   b. Talk privately with Wilson about his need to cooperate?
   c. Meet with all three of your editors to forge team spirit?

4. An old college chum phoned you out of the blue to say: "Truth is, I had to call you. You'd better keep this under your hat, Chris, but when I heard my company was buying you guys out, I was dumbfounded. I had no idea that a company as large as yours could sink so fast. Your group must be in pretty bad shape over there!" Your stomach turned suddenly queasy, and you felt a chill go up your spine. You'd heard nothing about any buyout, and before you could even get your college friend off the phone, you were wondering what you should do. Of the following, choose one course of action and briefly explain it:
   a. Contact your CEO directly and relate what you've heard.
   b. Ask co-workers whether they've heard anything about a buyout.
   c. Discuss the phone call confidentially with your immediate supervisor.
   d. Keep quiet about the whole thing (there's nothing you can do about the situation anyway).

5. Your boss often uses you as a sounding board for her ideas. Now she seems to want you to act as an unofficial messenger, passing her ideas along to the staff and informing her of their responses. Are you comfortable with this arrangement? Write a short paragraph explaining your feelings.[45]

6. When Solid State Circuits accidentally released chlorine and endangered the surrounding neighborhoods, local neighbors were up in arms. Two years later, thanks to a companywide community relations campaign, the neighborhood is filled with goodwill and friendship for the company. Solid State's open door policy ranges from quarterly meetings with the neighborhood's Environmental Concerns Committee to tours of the plant to regularly held softball games between company employees and neighborhood residents—with picnics afterward. Solid State even lends facilities for neighborhood use during holiday socials and rummage sales. One residential neighbor has said, "As years go by, Solid State will be associated with community interests and involvement." In less than a page, explain why becoming involved in the surrounding community and openly sharing information with local residents should result in such support and goodwill for the company.[46]

7. In less than a page, explain why you think each of the following is or is not ethical:
   a. Deemphasizing negative test results in a report on your product idea
   b. Taking a computer home to finish a work-related assignment
   c. Telling an associate and close friend that she'd better pay more attention to her work responsibilities before management fires her
   d. Recommending the purchase of excess equipment to use up your allocated funds before the end of the fiscal year so that your budget won't be cut next year

8. Which of the following is the most effective way to encourage ethical behavior in your organization? (Briefly explain your choice.)
   a. Clearly laying out expected behavior in a written policy or code of ethics
   b. Setting up hot lines for employees to call when they have ethical questions

c. Making sure top managers set clear examples of ethical behavior

d. Punishing those who act unethically

9. For weeks, you've noticed one of your colleagues taking office supplies home at night. She's been taking pens, markers, file folders, and paper clips, and last night she took an inexpensive calculator. This morning, you asked her whether she thought taking all these supplies was okay with the company. She said: "Oh, it's nothing. Everybody does it; the management expects it. I put in a lot of overtime I don't charge for, and I work hard for this company. It just keeps everything a little more balanced." What do you do next? Explain briefly.

10. Your boss wants to send a message welcoming employees recently transferred to your department from your Hong Kong branch. They all speak English, but your boss asks you to review his message for clarity. What would you suggest your boss change in the following paragraph? (Briefly explain your decisions.)

I wanted to welcome you ASAP to our little family here in the states. It's high time we shook hands in person and not just across the sea. I'm pleased as punch about getting to know you all, and I for one will do my level best to sell you on America.

11. Technological devices such as faxes, cellular phones, electronic mail, and voice mail are making businesspeople more easily accessible at any time of day or night. Because businesspeople can be reached so easily both at work and at home, what kind of impact might frequent intrusions have on a businessperson's professional and personal life? Please explain your answer in less than a page.

12. As a manufacturer of aerospace, energy, and environmental equipment, Lockheed Martin has developed a code of ethics that it expects employees to abide by. Visit Lockheed Martin's Web site at <http://lockheed.com/ethics>, and review the 15 major ethical provisions listed there (such as "Avoid conflicts of

interest"). In a brief paragraph, describe three specific examples of things you could do that would violate these provisions. Now study those Web pages giving the "Warning Signs" of ethics violations and the "Quick Quiz." In another brief paragraph, describe how you could use these pages to avoid ethical problems as you write business letters, memos, and reports. Submit both paragraphs to your instructor.

Note: When referring to Web sites and e-mail addresses (as in exercise 12), angle brackets are used around the material to indicate that no spaces occur between the address parts. Thus the angle brackets separate the characters of the address from the rest of the text. When you type the address into your Web browser or e-mail software, be sure to leave off the angle brackets.

13. Top management has asked you to speak at an upcoming executive meeting to present your arguments for a more open communication climate. Which of the following would be most important for you to know about your audience before giving your presentation? (Briefly explain your choice.)

a. How many top managers will be attending

b. What management style members of your audience prefer

c. How firmly these managers are set in their ways

14. What would be the most efficient way (phone call, interview, memo, or newsletter) of handling the following communication situations? (Briefly explain your answer.)

a. Informing everyone in the company of your department's new procedure for purchasing equipment

b. Leaving final instructions for your secretary to follow while you're out of town

c. Disciplining an employee for chronic tardiness

d. Announcing the installation of ramps for employees using wheelchairs

15. Write a memo introducing yourself to your instructor. Keep it under one page, and use Figure 1.1 as a model for format.

CHAPTER 2

UNDERSTANDING BUSINESS COMMUNICATION

AFTER STUDYING THIS CHAPTER, YOU WILL BE ABLE TO

- List the general categories of nonverbal communication
- Explain the four channels of verbal communication
- Identify the steps in the communication process
- Describe what can go wrong when you're formulating messages
- Discuss communication barriers and how to overcome them
- Summarize what you can do to improve communication

COMMUNICATION CLOSE-UP AT METAMORPHOSIS STUDIOS

Clarence Wooten Jr.

Andre Forde

Clarence Wooten Jr. and Andre Forde were barely in their twenties when they opened their own multimedia design firm in 1993. At the time, Wooten was producing animated presentations for architects, and Forde was designing educational software. However, they shared a dream of having their own company—a company that could challenge industry giants like Sega and Microsoft, a company that would be an energizing oasis for creative people. They wanted their company to be open and nurturing, unlike the stifling corporate environments they had both experienced firsthand.

Today, their dream is a reality. Metamorphosis Studios is considered an up-and-coming competitor, thanks to its cutting-edge designs of interactive software, multimedia presentations, corporate Web pages, and edutainment products. Moreover, the company's unique working environment is attracting the industry's most talented professionals.

As CEO, Wooten is responsible for marketing, finance, project coordination, client relations, and staff management. However, these traditional corporate roles are anything but traditional at Metamorphosis. That's because the company is a "virtual corporation," for all practical purposes, located in cyberspace. The partners created this virtual corporation by default, when they decided to hire freelancers because they couldn't afford the enormous expense required for an in-house staff.

A core group of eight creative specialists work regularly for Metamorphosis, along with dozens of others who come aboard for specific projects. Based all over the country, these staffers are linked by phone, fax, and the Internet. In fact, many potential staffers contact Metamorphosis after seeing its Web page (at <http://www.mstudios.com>), which showcases products, services, creative talent, and clients. "We design our Web page with great care," says Wooten, "because we want to show that we understand the medium and that our creative designs can compete with anyone."

At Metamorphosis Studios, open communication is the key. Whether it's through the company's Web page, face-to-face meetings, weekly bulletins, or e-mail, the communication flows freely. Wooten and Forde are committed to overcoming communication barriers both inside and outside the company by planning ahead for communication opportunities, keeping the environment responsive and nonthreatening, and encouraging everyone to share their ideas.

Wooten also finds creative talent by seeking out people who display their work on the Internet and sending them e-mail that describes Metamorphosis and its special environment for contributors. "We left corporate America because we were locked in and couldn't be motivated," says Wooten. "Creative people need to explore new ways and play with new tools and ideas. They create when they want to create." To get a feeling for the creative skills of first timers, and to gauge their level of self-motivation, Wooten uses newcomers on a test project before hiring them as regular contributors. "There has to be trust," says Wooten, "because I can't be a micromanager."

A typical project takes three to six months or more to complete and requires frequent communication and coordination with each far-flung member of the creative team. Indeed, the company's open and two-way communication enables Metamorphosis to produce its trademark creative products on time and within budget.

This communication begins when Wooten and Forde assemble the entire team for a kickoff meeting. Such face-to-face communication enables team members to establish a rapport while exchanging ideas on creative strategies. During these meetings, the partners encourage feedback with informal, give-and-take discussions. "We hang out, crash on the floor, and coordinate our efforts," say Wooten. "Participation in exchanging ideas is more than encouraged—it's expected," he continues. "It's a democracy, and we listen." Wooten believes that when they have an opportunity to share ideas and give feedback, creative specialists tend to be more productive, more enthusiastic, and best of all, more creative. So he works hard to make sure that this climate of open communication and feedback continues among team members throughout the project.

Some project staffers, particularly the technical specialists, are reluctant communicators who are much less likely than the creative specialists to offer feedback. But Wooten maintains two-way communication by sending out a biweekly bulletin to everyone via electronic mail, updating them on all aspects of the project and asking for comments and reactions.

Although many people are stimulated by knowing how an entire project is progressing (even beyond their own individual roles), others feel so overloaded by unnecessary information that it actually blocks effective communication. So in addition to his update bulletins, Wooten sends individualized messages to staffers. He takes care to make these communications clear and concise. He's specific both when asking for what he needs and when providing information. At the same time, he communicates a feeling of enthusiasm and trust in the staffer, strengthening the staffer's commitment and team spirit.

Of course, Wooten's audience of freelancers are liable to be immersed in their work, no matter what time of the day or night he might try to contact them. This kind of competition for attention can be another formidable barrier to communication. But Wooten overcomes this problem by using e-mail, since it's read only when the receiver chooses to access it.

Wooten and Forde understand the importance of effective communication. They encourage two-way communication, build a solid foundation of trust, elicit feedback at every turn, and send messages that are clear and specific. Metamorphosis Studios is proving that cyberspace can be a productive environment when both staff and managers operate with trust and communicate effectively.[1]

THE BASIC FORMS OF COMMUNICATION

Actions speak louder than words.

Whether you work for a "virtual" corporation like Metamorphosis Studios or a more conventional organization, you'll discover that when all is said and done, what's done is more important than what's said. Why do Wooten and Forde begin Metamorphosis projects with a face-to-face meeting? Because action is the ultimate form of communication. What you do speaks with an unmistakable voice.

Perhaps a certain amount of inconsistency between words and actions is unavoidable. Life is full of ambiguities, and most of us have mixed feelings about things from time to time. We don't always say what we really mean; in fact, we don't always *know* what we really mean. Under the circumstances, no wonder we sometimes have trouble figuring out all the surface and underlying messages that we send and receive. Unraveling the mysteries of communication requires perception, concentration, and an appreciation of the communication process.

Nonverbal Communication

Nonverbal communication is the process of communicating without words.

The most basic form of communication is **nonverbal communication,** all the cues, gestures, vocal qualities, spatial relationships, and attitudes toward time that allow us to communicate without words. Anthropologists theorize that long before human beings used words to talk things over, our ancestors communicated with one another by using their bodies. They gritted their teeth to show anger; they smiled and touched one another to indicate affection. Although we have come a long way since those primitive times, we still use nonverbal cues to express superiority, dependence, dislike, respect, love, and other feelings.[2]

Nonverbal communication differs from verbal communication in fundamental ways. For one thing, it's less structured, which makes it more difficult to study. You can't pick up a book on nonverbal language and master the vocabulary of gestures, expressions, and inflections that are common in our culture. We don't really know how people learn nonverbal behavior. No one teaches a baby to cry or smile, yet these forms of self-expression are almost universal. Other types of nonverbal communication, such as the meaning of colors and certain gestures, vary from culture to culture.

Nonverbal communication has few rules and often occurs unconsciously.

Nonverbal communication also differs from verbal communication in terms of intent and spontaneity. We generally plan our words. When we say, "Please get back to me on that order by Friday," we have a conscious purpose. We think about the message, if only for a moment. However, when we communicate nonverbally, we sometimes do so unconsciously. We don't mean to raise an eyebrow or blush. Those actions come naturally. Without our consent, our emotions are written all over our faces.

The Importance of Nonverbal Communication

Although nonverbal communication is often unplanned, it has more impact than verbal communication alone. Nonverbal cues are especially important in conveying feelings; some researchers maintain they account for 93 percent of the emotional meaning that is exchanged in any interaction.[3] The total impact of any message is probably most affected by the blending of nonverbal and verbal communication.[4]

One reason for the power of nonverbal communication is its reliability. Most people can deceive us much more easily with words than they can with their bodies. Words are relatively easy to control; body language, facial expressions, and vocal characteristics are not. By paying attention to these nonverbal cues, we can detect deception or affirm a speaker's honesty. Not surprisingly, we have more faith in nonverbal cues than we do in verbal messages. If a person says one thing but transmits a conflicting message nonverbally, we almost invariably believe the nonverbal signal.[5] To a great degree, then, an individual's credibility as a communicator depends on nonverbal messages. If you can read other people's nonverbal messages correctly, you can interpret their underlying attitudes and intentions and respond appropriately. Successful people generally share this ability.

Nonverbal communication is more reliable and more efficient than verbal communication.

Nonverbal communication is important for another reason: It can be efficient from both the sender's and the receiver's standpoint. You can transmit a nonverbal message without even thinking about it, and your audience can register the meaning unconsciously. At the same time, when you have a conscious purpose, you can often achieve it more economically with a gesture than you can with words. A wave of the hand, a pat on the back, a wink—all are streamlined expressions of thought. Although nonverbal communication can stand alone, it usually blends with speech, carrying part of the message. Together, the two modes of expression are a powerful combination, augmenting, reinforcing, and clarifying each other.

People use nonverbal signals to support and clarify verbal communication.

The Types of Nonverbal Communication

According to one estimate, there are over 700,000 forms of nonverbal communication.[6] For discussion purposes, however, these forms can be grouped into general categories: facial expressions and eye behavior, gestures and postures, vocal characteristics, personal appearance, touching behavior, and use of time and space. Researchers have drawn some interesting conclusions about the meaning of certain nonverbal signals. But remember, the meaning of nonverbal communication lies with the observer, who both reads specific signals and interprets them in the context of a particular situation and a particular culture.

- *Facial expressions and eye behavior.* Your face is the primary site for expressing your emotions; it reveals both the type and the intensity of your feelings.[7] Your eyes are especially effective for indicating attention and interest, influencing others, regulating interaction, and establishing dominance. In fact, eye contact is so important in the United States that even when you send a positive message, averting your gaze can lead your audience to perceive a negative one.[8] Although the eyes and the face are usually a reliable source of meaning, people sometimes manipulate their expressions to simulate an emotion they do not feel or to mask their true feelings.

The face and eyes command particular attention as a source of nonverbal messages.

- *Gestures and postures.* By moving your body, you can express both specific and general messages, some voluntary and some involuntary. Many gestures—a wave of the hand, for example—have a specific and intentional meaning, such as "hello" or "good-bye." Other types of body movement are unintentional and

As director of Hong Kong Economic and Trade Office, David Tsui addresses many groups (such as this chamber of commerce). Tsui understands how body gestures and facial expressions help him emphasize important points, reveal his attitude toward topics, and even appear more natural and relaxed.

express a more general message. Slouching, leaning forward, fidgeting, and walking briskly are all unconscious signals that reveal whether you feel confident or nervous, friendly or hostile, assertive or passive, powerful or powerless.

Body language and tone of voice reveal a lot about a person's emotions and attitudes.

- **Vocal characteristics.** Like body language, your voice carries both intentional and unintentional messages. On a conscious level, we can use our voices to create various impressions. Consider the sentence "What have you been up to?" If you repeat that question four or five times, changing your tone of voice and stressing various words, you can convey quite different messages. However, your vocal characteristics also reveal many things that you are unaware of. The tone and volume of your voice, your accent and speaking pace, and all the little *um*'s and *ah*'s that creep into your speech say a lot about who you are, your relationship with the audience, and the emotions underlying your words.

Physical appearance and personal style contribute to our identity.

- **Personal appearance.** Your appearance helps establish your social identity. People respond to us on the basis of our physical attractiveness. Because we see ourselves as others see us, these expectations are often a self-fulfilling prophecy. When people think we're capable and attractive, we feel good about ourselves, and this affects our behavior, which in turn affects other people's perceptions of us. Although an individual's body type and facial features impose limitations, most of us are able to control our attractiveness to some degree. Our grooming, our clothing, our accessories, our "style"—all modify our appearance. If your goal is to make a good impression, adopt the style of the people you want to impress. In most businesses, a professional image is appropriate, but some companies, such as Metamorphosis Studios, and even some industries are more casual.

- **Touching behavior.** Touch is an important vehicle for conveying warmth, comfort, and reassurance. Even the most casual contact can create positive feelings. This fact was revealed by an experiment in which librarians alternately touched and avoided the hands of students while returning their library cards. Although the contact lasted only half a second, the students who had been touched reported far more positive feelings about themselves and the library, even though many of them didn't even remember being touched.[9] Perhaps because it implies intimacy, touching behavior is governed in various circumstances by relatively strict customs that establish who can touch whom and how. The accepted norms vary, depending on the gender, age, relative status, and cultural background of the persons involved. In business situations, touching suggests dominance, so a higher-status person is more likely to touch a lower-status person than the other way around. Touching has become controversial, however, because it can sometimes be interpreted as sexual harassment.

- ***Use of time and space.*** Like touch, time and space can be used to assert authority. In many cultures, people demonstrate their importance by making other people wait; they show respect by being on time. People can also assert their status by occupying the best space. In U.S. companies, the chief executive usually has the corner office and the prettiest view. Apart from serving as a symbol of status, space can determine how comfortable people feel talking with each other. When people stand too close or too far away, we feel ill at ease. However, attitudes toward punctuality and comfort zones and all other nonverbal communication vary from culture to culture (see "Actions Speak Louder than Words All Around the World" on page 34).

Your use of touch, your attitude toward time, and your use of space (all of which are affected by culture) help establish your social relationships.

Gender has an impact on nonverbal communication. For example, studies show that women are generally better than men at decoding nonverbal cues. Other studies reveal that in social settings with peers and in meetings with colleagues, women have less personal space and are touched more often than men (both observations indicating less power for women). Moreover, although sitting at the head of a conference table symbolizes power for a man, if a woman is at the head and at least one man is sitting elsewhere, observers assume that the man is in charge.[10]

Nonverbal communication can be different for men and women.

To improve nonverbal skills in the United States, pay more attention to nonverbal cues (especially facial expressions), engage in more eye contact, and probe for more information when verbal and nonverbal cues conflict. Most employees are frustrated and distrustful when their supervisors give them conflicting signals. So try to be as honest as possible in communicating your emotions.[11]

Improve nonverbal skills by paying more attention to cues, both yours and those of others.

Verbal Communication

Although you can express many things nonverbally, there are limits to what you can communicate without the help of language. If you want to discuss past events, ideas, or abstractions, you need symbols that stand for your thoughts. **Verbal communication** consists of words arranged in meaningful patterns. In the English language, the pool of words is growing, currently about 750,000, although most people in the United States recognize only about 20,000 of them.[12] To create a thought with these words, we arrange them according to the rules of grammar, putting the various parts of speech in the proper sequence. We then transmit the message in spoken or written form, anticipating that someone will hear or read what we have to say.

Verbal communication is the process of communicating with words.

Language is composed of words and grammar.

Speaking and Writing

As Figure 2.1 (see page 35) illustrates, businesspeople tend to prefer oral communication channels to written ones. The trade-offs between speaking and writing are discussed in more depth in Chapter 5, but basically, the preference reflects the relative ease and efficiency of oral communication. It's generally quicker and more convenient to talk to somebody than to write a memo or letter. Furthermore, when you're speaking or listening, you can pick up added meaning from nonverbal cues and benefit from immediate feedback.

Businesspeople rely more heavily on oral than on written communication channels for sharing information on a day-to-day basis, but they often put important messages in writing.

On the other hand, relying too heavily on oral communication can cause problems in a company. At Ben & Jerry's Homemade (successful seller of superpremium ice cream), this reliance has been one of the main sources of the company's growing pains.

COMMUNICATING ACROSS CULTURES

ACTIONS SPEAK LOUDER THAN WORDS ALL AROUND THE WORLD

"He wouldn't look me in the eye. I found it disconcerting that he kept looking all over the room but rarely at me," said Barbara Walters after her interview with Libya's Colonel Muammar al-Qaddafi. Like many people in the United States, Walters was associating eye contact with trustworthiness, so when Qaddafi withheld eye contact, she felt uncomfortable. In fact, Qaddafi was paying Walters a compliment. In Libya, *not* looking conveys respect, and looking straight at a woman is considered nearly as serious as physical assault.

In Australia, President George Bush waved the back of his hand from a limousine—a vulgar connotation to Australians. In an Arab country, Great Britain's Diana, Princess of Wales, sat in a posture that revealed the soles of her shoes—a grave insult to Arabs. At home in the United States, President Jimmy Carter was photographed in athletic attire while participating in a summer foot race—evoking the remark from Middle Eastern observers, "How can it be that on the front page of our newspapers, we see the leader of the free world in his underwear?"

Nonverbal communication varies widely between cultures and even between subcultures—which strongly affects communication in the workplace. Whether you're trying to communicate with your new assistant who is Asian American, the Swedish managers who recently bought out your company, the young African American college student who won a summer internship with your firm, or the French company you hope will buy your firm's new designs, your efforts will depend as much on physical cues as on verbal ones. Since most of us aren't usually even aware of our own nonverbal behavior, we have trouble understanding the body language of other cultures. The lists of differences are endless.

- In Thailand it's rude to place your arm over the back of a chair in which another person is sitting.
- Finnish female students are horrified by Arab girls who want to walk hand in hand with them.

- Canadian listeners nod to signal agreement.
- Japanese listeners nod to indicate only that they have understood.
- British listeners stare at the speaker, blinking their eyes to indicate understanding.
- People in the United States are taught that it's impolite to stare.
- Saudis accept foreigners in Western business attire but are offended by tight-fitting clothing and by short sleeves.
- Spaniards indicate a receptive friendly handshake by clasping the other person's forearm to form a double handshake.
- Canadians consider touching any part of the arm above the hand intrusive, except in intimate relationships.

It may take years to adjust your nonverbal communication to other cultures, but many options can help you prepare. Books and seminars on cultural differences are readily available, as are motion pictures from a wide range of cultures—you can even import films and TV shows from many countries. Examining the illustrations in news and business magazines can give you an idea of expected business dress and personal space. Finally, remaining flexible and interacting with people from other cultures who are visiting or living in your country will go a long way toward lowering the barriers presented by nonverbal communication.

1. Explain how watching a foreign movie might help you prepare to correctly interpret nonverbal behavior from another culture.
2. One of your co-workers is originally from Saudi Arabia. You like him, and the two of you work well together. However, he stands so close when you speak with him that it makes you very uncomfortable. Do you tell him of your discomfort, or do you try to cover it up?

Both founders are by nature face-to-face communicators. They want their organization to function like a big, happy family where people share ideas openly and informally, and for a while, it did. However, as Ben & Jerry's grew and the number of employees increased, keeping everyone adequately informed by word of mouth became difficult. As one employee pointed out, "It's hard to feel you're part of a big family if you don't know the brothers and sisters."[13]

For maximum impact, use both written and spoken channels. As a recent study suggests, the human brain may have separate systems for processing written and spoken language. If we do assign speech and writing tasks to separate compartments, then

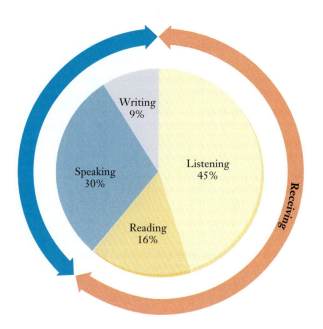

using both channels can only reinforce your message.[14] Citicorp used multiple channels when it chose the multimedia approach to explain its new employee benefits plan. Employees received a printout of their benefits, a computer disk, an extensive workbook, brochures, special face-to-face training meetings, a take-home video, and access to a hot line. With so many choices available, employees were able to use the media they felt most comfortable with. Such multimedia approaches are expected to become even more popular as work forces grow more and more culturally diverse.[15]

Listening and Reading

Take another look at Figure 2.1. Apart from underscoring the importance of oral communication, it illustrates another interesting fact: People spend more time *receiving* information than transmitting it. Listening and reading are every bit as important as speaking and writing.

Unfortunately, most of us aren't very good listeners. Immediately after hearing a ten-minute speech, we typically remember only half of what was said. A few days later, we've forgotten three-quarters of the message.[16] Worse, we often miss the subtle, underlying meaning entirely. To some extent, our listening problems stem from our education, or lack of it. We spend years learning to express our ideas, but few of us ever take a course in listening. Nevertheless, developing better listening abilities is crucial if we want to foster the understanding and cooperation so necessary for an increasingly diverse work force.[17]

At the same time, our reading skills often leave a good deal to be desired. Studies indicate that approximately 20 percent of the adults in the United States are functionally illiterate; 14 percent cannot fill out a check properly; 38 percent have trouble reading the help-wanted ads in the newspaper; and 26 percent can't figure out the deductions listed on their paychecks.[18] Even those who read adequately don't often know how to read effectively. They have trouble extracting the important points from a document, so they can't make the most of the information contained in it.

Effective business communication depends on skill in receiving messages as well as skill in sending them.

To absorb information, you must concentrate, evaluate, and retain what you read or hear.

Employees who don't listen and can't read pose obvious problems for companies. To deal with their workers' limitations, many corporations are becoming educators of last resort. General Motors spends over $200 million a year on basic-skills programs.[19] Some of the most sophisticated training in communication occurs in the airline industry, where failure to process information correctly can be fatal. To learn from others' mistakes, new pilots at most major airlines analyze cockpit tapes recorded on flights that have crashed. After hearing the tape from a plane that went down near Portland, Oregon, trainees at one airline identified the following communication problems: The captain ignored the second officer's warning that fuel was running short. The first officer never spoke up. No one corrected the captain when he made the wrong assumption about the amount of fuel remaining in each tank. By studying these and other communication problems, the trainees learn to listen for what should have been said, but wasn't.[20]

If you're listening as opposed to reading, you have the advantage of being able to ask questions and interact with the speaker. Instead of just gathering information, you can cooperate in solving problems. This interactive process requires additional listening skills, which Chapter 19 discusses.

THE PROCESS OF COMMUNICATION

The communication process consists of six phases linking sender and receiver.

Whether you are speaking or writing, listening or reading, communication is more than a single act. Instead, it is a transactional (two-way) process that can be broken into six phases, as Figure 2.2 illustrates:[21]

1. *The sender has an idea.* You conceive an idea and want to share it.
2. *The sender transforms the idea into a message.* When you put your idea into a message that your receiver will understand, you are **encoding,** deciding on the message's form (word, facial expression, gesture), length, organization, tone, and style—all of which depend on your idea, your audience, and your personal style or mood.
3. *The sender transmits the message.* To physically transmit your message to your receiver, you select a **communication channel** (verbal, nonverbal, spoken, or written) and **medium** (telephone, computer, letter, memo, report, face-to-face exchange, etc.). The channel and medium you choose depend on your message, the location of your audience, your need for speed, and the formality of the situation.
4. *The receiver gets the message.* For communication to occur, your receiver must first get the message. If you send a letter, your receiver has to read it before understanding it. If you're giving a speech, the people in your audience have to be able to hear you, and they have to be paying attention.
5. *The receiver interprets the message.* Your receiver must cooperate by **decoding** your message, absorbing and understanding it. Then the decoded message has to be stored in the receiver's mind. If all goes well, the message is interpreted correctly; that is, the receiver assigns the same basic meaning to the words as the sender intended and responds in the desired way.

Feedback is your audience's response; it permits you to evaluate your message's effectiveness.

6. *The receiver reacts and sends feedback to the sender.* **Feedback** is your receiver's response, the final link in the communication chain. After getting the message, your receiver responds in some way and signals that response to you. Feedback is the key element in the communication process because it enables you to evaluate the effectiveness of your message. If your audience doesn't understand what you mean, you can tell by the response and refine your message.

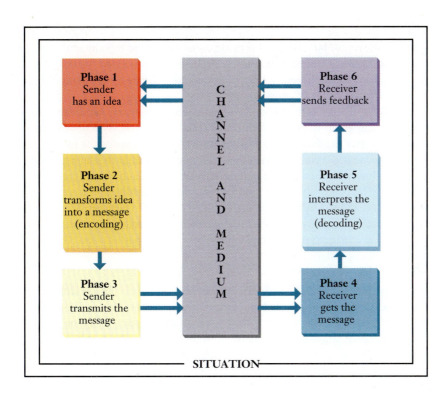

Figure 2.2
The Communication Process

The process is repeated until both parties have finished expressing themselves, but communication is effective only when each step is successful.

Formulating a Message

Communication is a dynamic process. Your idea cannot be communicated if you ignore, fail, or skip any step in that process. Unfortunately, the process can be interrupted before it really begins—while you're trying to put your idea into words. Several things can go wrong when you're formulating a message, including indecision about the content of your message, lack of familiarity with the situation or the receiver, and difficulty in expressing ideas.

Indecision About Content

Deciding what to say is the first hurdle in the communication process. Many people make the mistake of trying to convey everything they know about a subject. Unfortunately, when a message contains too much information, it's difficult to absorb. If you want to get your point across, decide what to include and what to leave out, how much detail to provide, and what order to follow. If you try to explain something without first giving the receiver adequate background, you'll create confusion. Likewise, if you recommend actions without first explaining why they are justified, your message may provoke an emotional response that inhibits understanding.

Include only the information that is useful to your audience, and organize it in a way that encourages its acceptance.

Lack of Familiarity with the Situation or the Receiver

Creating an effective message is difficult if you don't know how it will be used. If you're writing a report on the consumer market for sports equipment and you don't know the purpose of the report, it's hard to know what to say. What sort of sports equipment should you cover? Should you include team sports as well as individual sports?

Ask why you are preparing the message and for whom you are preparing it.

Should you subdivide the market geographically or according to price ranges? How long should the report be? Should it provide conclusions and recommendations or simply facts and figures? Unless you know why the report is needed, you can't really answer these questions intelligently, so you are forced to create a very general document, one that covers a little bit of everything.

Lack of familiarity with your audience is an equally serious handicap. You need to know something about the biases, education, age, status, and style of your receiver in order to create an effective message. If you're writing for a specialist in your field, for example, you can use technical terms that might be unfamiliar to a layperson. If you're addressing a lower-level employee, you might approach a subject differently if talking to your boss. Decisions about the content, organization, style, and tone of your message all depend, at least to some extent, on the relationship between you and your audience. If you don't know your audience, you will be forced to make these decisions in the dark, and at least part of your message may miss the mark.

Difficulty Expressing Ideas

Lack of experience in writing or speaking can also prevent a person from developing effective messages. Some people have limited education or a lack of aptitude when it comes to expressing ideas. Perhaps they have a limited vocabulary or are uncertain about questions of grammar, punctuation, and style. Perhaps they're simply frightened by the idea of writing something or of appearing before a group. In any case, they're unable to develop an effective message because they lack expertise in using language.

An inability to put thoughts into words can be overcome through study and practice.

Problems of this sort can be overcome, but only with some effort. The important thing is to recognize the problem and take action. Taking courses in communication at a college is a good first step. Many companies offer their own in-house training programs in communication; others have tuition reimbursement programs to help cover the cost of outside courses. Self-help books are another good, inexpensive alternative. You might even join a professional organization or other group (such as Toastmasters or the League of Women Voters) to practice your communication skills in an informal setting.

The fact is that innumerable barriers to communication can block any phase of the communication process. Effective communicators do all they can to reduce such barriers. By thinking about some of these barriers, you increase your chances of overcoming them.

Overcoming Communication Barriers

Communication barriers exist between people and within organizations.

"Good" communication is not synonymous with talking other people into accepting your point of view. Regardless of how well you express yourself, other people will not always agree with you. However, if you communicate well, they *will* understand you. **Noise** is any interference in the communication process that distorts or obscures the sender's meaning, and such communication barriers can exist between people and within organizations.[22]

Communication Barriers Between People

When you send a message, you intend to communicate meaning, but the message itself doesn't contain meaning. The meaning exists in your mind and in the mind of your receiver. To understand one another, you and your receiver must share similar meanings for words, gestures, tone of voice, and other symbols.

Differences in Perception

The world constantly bombards us with information: sights, sounds, scents, and so on. Our minds organize this stream of sensation into a mental map that represents our **perception** of reality. In no case is the map in a person's mind the same as the world itself, and no two maps are exactly alike. As you view the world, your mind absorbs your experiences in a unique and personal way. For example, if you go out for pizza with a friend, each of you will notice different things. As you enter the restaurant, one of you may notice the coolness of the air-conditioning; the other may notice the aroma of pizza.

Because your perceptions are unique, the ideas you want to express differ from other people's. Even when two people have experienced the same event, their mental images of that event will not be identical. As senders, we choose the details that seem important and focus our attention on the most relevant and general, a process known as **selective perception** (see Figure 2.3). As receivers, we try to fit new details into our existing pattern. If a detail doesn't quite fit, we are inclined to distort the information rather than rearrange the pattern.

Overcoming perceptual barriers can be difficult. Try to predict how your message will be received, anticipate your receiver's reactions, and shape the message accordingly—constantly adjusting to correct any misunderstanding. Try not to apply the same solution to every problem, but look for solutions to fit specific problems. Frame your messages in terms that have meaning for your audience, and try to find something useful in every message you receive.[23]

> Perception is our individual interpretation of the world around us.

Incorrect Filtering

Filtering is screening out or abbreviating information before a message is passed on to someone else. In business, the filters between you and your receiver are many: secretaries, assistants, receptionists, and answering machines, to name a few. Just getting

> Filtering is screening out or abbreviating information before passing the message on to someone else.

Figure 2.3
How Expectations Shape Perception

Expectations have a significant effect on perception. We see not so much what is there as what we believe ought to be there. Study the design in this illustration, and write down what you see. At first glance, most people see a maze or a group of lines. Their perception shifts, however, when they are told to look for letters of the alphabet.

BEST OF THE WEB

**Develop Your Internet
Language Skills**

Your success in Internet communication depends on how well you understand the language. That's where Netlingo can help. Keep the site's "pocket dictionary" floating toolbar on your desktop while you surf, and you'll have instant access to definitions of common Net terms, which aren't always what they appear to be. For instance, you know from this chapter that "cookie" means different things in different cultures—but do you know what a cookie means to a Netizen? Better look it up.

http://www.netlingo.com

through by telephone can take a week if you're calling someone who's protected by layers of gatekeepers (operators, secretaries, assistants). Worse yet, your message may be digested, distilled, and probably distorted before it's passed on to your intended receiver. Those same gatekeepers may also translate, embellish, and augment your receiver's ideas and responses before passing them on to you. To overcome filtering barriers, try to establish more than one communication channel (so that information can be verified through multiple sources), eliminate as many intermediaries as possible, and decrease distortion by condensing message information to the bare essentials.

Language Problems

When you choose the words for your message, you signal that you are a member of a particular culture or subculture and that you know the code. The nature of your code—your language and vocabulary—imposes its own barriers on your message. For example, the language of a lawyer differs from that of an accountant or a doctor, and the difference in their vocabularies affects their ability to recognize and express ideas.

Barriers also exist because words can be interpreted in more than one way. Language uses words as symbols to represent reality: Nothing in the word *cookie* automatically ties it to the physical thing that is a cookie. We might just as well call a cookie a zebra. Language is an arbitrary code that depends on shared definitions, but there's a limit to how completely any of us can share the same meaning for a given word.

Even on the literal (denotative) level, words are imprecise. People in the United States generally agree on what a cookie is. However, your idea of a cookie is a composite of all the cookies you have ever tasted or seen: oatmeal cookies, chocolate chip cookies, sugar cookies, and vanilla wafers. Someone from another culture may have a different range of cookie experiences: meringues, florentines, and spritz. You both agree on the general concept of cookie, but the precise image in your minds differs.

On the subjective (connotative) level, the differences are even greater. Your interpretation of the word *cookie* depends partly on how you feel about cookies. You may have very pleasant feelings about them: You may remember baking them with your mother or coming home from school on winter afternoons to cookies and milk. Or you may be on a diet, in which case cookies will be an unpleasant reminder that you think you're too fat and must say no to all your favorite foods.

Your denotative (literal) and connotative (subjective) definitions of words may differ dramatically from those of other people.

To overcome language barriers, use the most specific and accurate words possible. Always try to use words your audience will understand. Increase the accuracy of your messages by using language that describes rather than evaluates and by presenting observable facts, events, and circumstances.

Poor Listening

Listening ability decreases when information is difficult to understand and when it has little meaning for your audience.

Perhaps the most common barrier to reception is simply a lack of attention on the receiver's part. We all let our minds wander now and then, regardless of how hard we try to concentrate. People are especially likely to drift off when they are forced to listen to information that is difficult to understand or that has little direct bearing on their own lives. If they are tired or concerned about other matters, they are even more likely to lose interest. As already mentioned, too few of us listen well.

To overcome listening barriers, verify your interpretation of what's been said (by paraphrasing what you've understood). Empathize with speakers (by trying to view the situation through their eyes), and resist jumping to conclusions. Clarify meaning by asking nonthreatening questions, and listen without interrupting.

Differing Emotional States

Your audience may react either to the content of a message or to the relationship between sender and receiver that it implies.

Every message contains both a content meaning, which deals with the subject of the message, and a relationship meaning, which suggests the nature of the interaction

At Home Depot, Carolyn Fushima needs to communicate with the employees she supervises, regardless of differences in their age, their gender, or their cultural or ethnic backgrounds.

between sender and receiver. Communication can break down when the receiver reacts negatively to either of these meanings.

You may have to deal with people when they are upset—or when you are. An upset person tends to ignore or distort what the other person is saying and is often unable to present feelings and ideas effectively. This is not to say that you should avoid all communication when you are emotionally involved, but you should be alert to the greater potential for misunderstanding that accompanies aroused emotions.

You may also have conflicting emotions about the subject of your message or the audience for it. Say you've been asked to recommend ways to improve the organization of your department. You conclude that the best approach is to combine two positions, but this solution will mean eliminating the job of one of your close associates. As you prepare your report, you find yourself apologizing for your recommendation. Even though you believe your position is justified, you cannot make a convincing case.

To overcome emotional barriers, be aware of the feelings that arise in yourself and in others as you communicate, and attempt to control them. For example, choose neutral words to avoid arousing strong feelings unduly. Avoid attitudes, blame, and other subjective concepts. Most important, be alert to the greater potential for misunderstanding that accompanies emotional messages.

In business communication, try to maintain your objectivity.

Differing Backgrounds

Differences in background can be one of the hardest communication barriers to overcome. When your receiver's life experience differs substantially from yours, communication becomes more difficult. Age, education, gender, social status, economic position, cultural background, temperament, health, beauty, popularity, religion, political belief, even a passing mood can all separate one person from another and make understanding difficult. Figure 2.4 (see page 42) shows how shared experience contributes to shared meaning and understanding; the portion of each diagram where the circles overlap represents the level of understanding between sender and receiver. Communicating with someone from another country is probably the most extreme example of how background may impede communication, and culture clashes frequently arise in

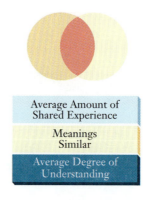

Little Shared Experience	Average Amount of Shared Experience	Large Amount of Shared Experience
Meanings Dissimilar	Meanings Similar	Meanings Very Similar
Misunderstanding	Average Degree of Understanding	High Degree of Understanding

Figure 2.4
How Shared Experience Affects Understanding

the workplace (see Chapter 3). But you don't have to seek out a person from an exotic locale to run into cultural gaps. You can misunderstand even your best friends and closest relatives, as you no doubt know from personal experience.

Try to understand the other person's point of view, and respect the inevitable differences in background and culture.

To overcome the barriers associated with differing backgrounds, avoid projecting your own background or culture onto others. Clarify your own and understand others' backgrounds, spheres of knowledge, personalities, and perceptions. And don't assume that certain behaviors mean the same thing to everyone.

Communication Barriers Within Organizations

Although all communication is subject to misunderstandings, business communication is particularly difficult. The material is often complex and controversial. Moreover, both the sender and the receiver may face distractions that divert their attention. Further, the opportunities for feedback are often limited, making it difficult to correct misunderstandings.

Information Overload

Some information isn't necessary.

Too much information is as bad as too little because it reduces the audience's ability to concentrate effectively on the most important messages. People facing information overload sometimes try to cope by ignoring some of the messages, by delaying responses to messages they deem unimportant, by answering only parts of some messages, by responding inaccurately to certain messages, by taking less time with each message, or by reacting only superficially to all messages.

To overcome information overload, realize that some information is not necessary, and make necessary information easily available. Give information meaning, rather than just passing it on, and set priorities for dealing with the information flow.

Message Complexity

When formulating business messages, you communicate both as an individual and as a representative of an organization. Thus you must adjust your own ideas and style so that they are acceptable to your employer. In fact, you may be asked occasionally to write or say something that you disagree with personally. Suppose you work as a recruiter for your firm. You've interviewed a job candidate you believe would make an excellent employee, but others in the firm have rejected this applicant. Now you have to write a letter turning down the candidate: You must communicate your firm's message, regardless of your personal feelings, a task some communicators find difficult.

Business messages may also deal with subject matter that can be technical or difficult to express. Imagine trying to write an interesting insurance policy, a set of instructions on how to operate a scraped-surface heat exchanger, the guidelines for checking credit references, an explanation of why profits have dropped by 12 percent in the last six months, or a description of your solid-waste-management program. These topics are dry, and making them clear and interesting is a real challenge.

To overcome the barriers of complex messages, keep them clear and easy to understand. Use strong organization, guide readers by telling them what to expect, use concrete and specific language, and stick to the point. Be sure to ask for feedback so that you can clarify and improve your message.

The complexity of messages relates to
- Your conflicts about the content
- The dry or difficult nature of the subject

Message Competition

Communicators are often faced with messages that compete for attention. If you're talking on the phone while scanning a report, both messages are apt to get short shrift. Even your own messages may have to compete with a variety of interruptions: The phone rings every five minutes, people intrude, meetings are called, and crises arise. In short, your messages rarely have the benefit of the receiver's undivided attention.

To overcome competition barriers, avoid making demands on a receiver who doesn't have the time to pay careful attention to your message. Make written messages visually appealing and easy to understand, and try to deliver them when your receiver has time to read them. Oral messages are most effective when you can speak directly to your receiver (rather than to intermediaries or answering machines). Also, be sure to set aside enough time for important messages that you receive.

Business messages rarely have the benefit of the audience's full and undivided attention.

Differing Status

Employees of low status may be overly cautious when sending messages to managers and may talk only about subjects they think the manager is interested in. Similarly, higher-status people may distort messages by refusing to discuss anything that would tend to undermine their authority in the organization. Moreover, belonging to a particular department or being responsible for a particular task can narrow your point of view so that it differs from the attitudes, values, and expectations of people who belong to other departments or who are responsible for other tasks.

To overcome status barriers, keep managers and colleagues well informed. Encourage lower-status employees to keep you informed by being fair-minded and respectful of their opinions. When you have information that you're afraid your boss might not like, be brave and convey it anyway.

Status barriers can be overcome by a willingness to give and receive bad news.

Lack of Trust

Building trust is a difficult problem. Other organization members don't know whether you'll respond in a supportive or responsible way, so trusting can be risky. As Metamorphosis Studios' Wooten knows well, without trust, free and open communication is effectively blocked, threatening the organization's stability. However, just being clear in your communication isn't enough.

To overcome trust barriers, be visible and accessible. Don't insulate yourself behind assistants or secretaries. Share key information with colleagues and employees, communicate honestly, and include employees in decision making.

For communication to be successful, organizations must create an atmosphere of fairness and trust.

Inadequate Communication Structures

Organizational communication is affected by formal restrictions on who may communicate with whom and who is authorized to make decisions. Designing too few formal channels blocks effective communication. Strongly centralized organizations, especially those with a high degree of formalization, reduce communication capacity, and

Structural barriers block upward, downward, and horizontal communication.

they decrease the tendency to communicate horizontally—thus limiting the ability to coordinate activities and decisions. Tall organizations tend to provide too many vertical communication links, so messages become distorted as they move through the organization's levels. To overcome structural barriers, offer opportunities for communicating upward, downward, and horizontally (using such techniques as employee surveys, open-door policies, newsletters, memos, e-mail, and task groups). Try to reduce hierarchical levels, increase coordination between departments, and encourage two-way communication.

Incorrect Choice of Medium

Your choice of a communication channel and medium depends on the
- Message
- Audience
- Need for speed
- Situation

If you choose an inappropriate communication medium, your message can be distorted so that the intended meaning is blocked. You can select the most appropriate medium by matching your choice with the nature of the message and of the group or the individual who will receive it. **Media richness** is the value of a medium in a given communication situation. It's determined by a medium's ability (1) to convey a message using more than one informational cue (visual, verbal, vocal), (2) to facilitate feedback, and (3) to establish personal focus (see Figure 2.5).

Face-to-face communication is the richest medium because it is personal, it provides immediate feedback, it transmits information from both verbal and nonverbal cues, and it conveys the emotion behind the message. Telephones and some other interactive electronic media aren't as rich; although they allow immediate feedback, they don't provide visual nonverbal cues such as facial expressions, eye contact, and body movements.[24] Written media can be personalized through addressed memos, letters,

Figure 2.5
A Continuum of Media Richness

To ensure effective communication, be sure to use richer media for messages that are complex, ambiguous, and nonroutine.

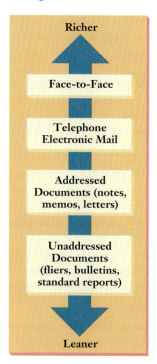

and reports, but they lack the immediate feedback and the visual and vocal nonverbal cues that contribute to the meaning of the message. The leanest media are generally impersonal written messages such as bulletins, fliers, and standard reports. Not only do they lack the ability to transmit nonverbal cues and to give feedback, they also eliminate any personal focus.

To overcome media barriers, choose the richest media for nonroutine, complex messages. Use rich media to extend and to humanize your presence throughout the organization, to communicate caring and personal interest to employees, and to gain employee commitment to organizational goals. Use leaner media to communicate simple, routine messages. You can send information such as statistics, facts, figures, and conclusions through a note, memo, or written report.[25]

Closed Communication Climate

As discussed in Chapter 1, communication climate is influenced by management style, and a directive, authoritarian style blocks the free and open exchange of information that characterizes good communication. At Metamorphosis Studios, Clarence Wooten works hard to maintain an open communication climate. To overcome climate barriers, spend more time listening than issuing orders. Make sure you respond constructively to employees, and of course, encourage employees and colleagues to offer suggestions, help set goals, participate in solving problems, and help make decisions.

Unethical Communication

An organization cannot create illegal or unethical messages and still be credible or successful in the long run. Relationships within and outside the organization depend on trust and fairness. To overcome ethics barriers, make sure your messages contain all information that ought to be there. Make sure that information applies to the situation. And make sure your message is completely truthful.

Ethical messages are crucial to any organization's credibility and success.

Inefficient Communication

Producing worthless messages wastes time and resources, and it contributes to the information overload already mentioned. Reduce the number of messages by thinking twice before sending one. Then speed up the process, first, by preparing messages correctly the first time around and, second, by standardizing format and material when appropriate. Be clear about the writing assignments you accept as well as the ones you assign.

Communication is blocked by inefficiency.

Physical Distractions

Communication barriers are often physical: bad connections, poor acoustics, illegible copy. Although noise of this sort seems trivial, it can completely block an otherwise effective message. Your receiver might also be distracted by an uncomfortable chair, poor lighting, or some other irritating condition. In some cases, the barrier may be related to the receiver's health. Hearing or visual impairment or even a headache can interfere with reception of a message. These annoyances don't generally block communication entirely, but they may reduce the receiver's concentration.

Your audience is more likely to receive your message accurately if nothing physical interrupts or distorts the message.

To overcome physical barriers, exercise as much control as possible over the physical transmission link: If you're preparing a written document, make sure its appearance doesn't detract from your message. If you're delivering an oral presentation, choose a setting that permits the audience to see and hear you without straining. When you are the audience, learn to concentrate on the message rather than the distractions.

HOW TO IMPROVE COMMUNICATION

As you learn how to overcome more and more communication barriers, you become more and more successful as a business communicator. Think about the people you know. Which of them would you call successful communicators? What do these people have in common? Chances are, the individuals on your list share five traits:

Effective communication requires perception, precision, credibility, control, and congeniality.

- *Perception.* They are able to predict how you will receive their message. They anticipate your reaction and shape the message accordingly. They read your response correctly and constantly adjust to correct any misunderstanding.
- *Precision.* They create a "meeting of the minds." When they finish expressing themselves, you share the same mental picture.
- *Credibility.* They are believable. You have faith in the substance of their message. You trust their information and their intentions.
- *Control.* They shape your response. Depending on their purpose, they can make you laugh or cry, calm down, change your mind, or take action.
- *Congeniality.* They maintain friendly, pleasant relations with you. Regardless of whether you agree with them, good communicators command your respect and goodwill. You are willing to work with them again, despite your differences.

Organizations can also use these traits to improve communication (see "Eight Keys to Achieving Total Quality and Customer Satisfaction"). Effective communicators overcome the main barriers to communication by creating their messages carefully, minimizing noise in the transmission process, and facilitating feedback.

SHARPENING YOUR SKILLS

EIGHT KEYS TO ACHIEVING TOTAL QUALITY AND CUSTOMER SATISFACTION

Quality and customer satisfaction are two of the hottest topics in communication today. Little wonder, since both focus the organization's attention squarely on the customer. It's difficult to deliver quality products or satisfy customer needs when your organization doesn't listen to customers or employees. In fact, few business activities require more of an audience-centered attitude than working toward total quality management or ensuring customer satisfaction.

Total quality management (TQM) is a comprehensive approach that involves building quality into every organizational process. When a company, nonprofit group, or government agency adopts TQM, every person in the organization—regardless of level or function—becomes responsible for improving quality. However, better quality is not, by itself, the final objective of a TQM program.

The main reason any organization uses TQM is to satisfy its customers. After all, if a customer doesn't think your product is top quality, then it isn't—all the fancy advertising and pretty packaging in the world won't change that perception. By

using TQM, the organization can hone a set of consistent, reliable internal processes to build a quality product that will more effectively satisfy customer expectations.

Improving communication improves any quality or customer-satisfaction program, and experts suggest following these eight steps:

1. *Communicate a clear vision.* A vision of quality and customer satisfaction starts at the top. Be sure that employees at every level understand exactly what they're expected to do.
2. *Focus attention on the customer.* The goal is to gear all activities toward understanding customer expectations and improving quality to meet those expectations. By clearly and consistently communicating this audience-centered viewpoint, your organization can help move employees closer to this goal.
3. *Reinforce the vision by taking action.* Talk isn't enough. Your actions lend credibility to your mes-

Create the Message Carefully

The best way to create messages carefully is to focus on your audience so that you can help them understand and accept your message. You want to create a bridge of words that leads audience members from their current position to your point, so you have to know something about your audience's current position. If you're addressing strangers, try to find out more about them; if that's impossible, try to project yourself into their position by using your common sense and imagination. Then you'll be ready to create your message:

In general terms, your purpose is to bring your audience closer to your views.

- Tell your audience at the outset what to expect from your message. Let them know the purpose of your message, and tell them what main points they will encounter. Even if you don't want to reveal controversial ideas at the beginning of a message, you can still give your audience a preview of the topics you plan to cover.

Give your audience a framework for understanding the ideas you communicate.

- Balance general concepts with specific illustrations. Once you've stated your overall idea at the beginning of your message, develop that idea by using vivid, concrete examples. The most memorable words are the ones that create a picture in your audience's mind by describing colors, objects, scents, sounds, and tastes. Specific details such as numbers, figures, and percentages can also be vivid.

To make your message memorable
- *Use words that evoke a physical, sensory impression*
- *Use telling statistics*

- Keep your messages as brief and as clean as possible. With few exceptions, one page is easier to absorb than two, especially in a business environment where so many messages compete for attention. However, you have to be careful to develop each main idea adequately. You're better off covering three points thoroughly rather than eight points superficially.

The key to brevity is to limit the number of ideas, not to shortchange their development.

sage and invite others to commit themselves to the vision.

4. ***Bring in competent, skilled people.*** Improving quality means being able to communicate up, down, and across the organization to share whatever information is needed to get the job done. You need top-notch people to accomplish this.

5. ***Move information quickly.*** By streamlining both internal and external communication, you can adapt more quickly to customer needs. With speedier communication, higher-quality products can be designed and produced more quickly.

6. ***Focus on the right things.*** If your organization emphasizes activities that don't contribute to quality or customer satisfaction, it can send the wrong signal. On the other hand, if it stresses activities that contribute to quality and customer satisfaction—and goes on to clearly communicate the results—employees will have the feedback they need to adjust their actions.

7. ***Check all organizational systems.*** You can use internal communications to explain the goal of total quality

or customer satisfaction and to provide a forum for dialogue on all levels, but make sure other systems also support the goal. If there's little or no training on a new procedure—or if people are promoted on the basis of tenure rather than improved quality or customer satisfaction—credibility will suffer.

8. ***Invite involvement.*** Organizations need to use both formal and informal communication to encourage employee commitment. When you feel that your contributions are valued, you're willing to go the extra mile, which often makes the difference between average and top quality, between customer disappointment and customer satisfaction.

1. What kind of communication goals might be set as part of a TQM or customer-satisfaction program?
2. What barriers to effective communication should a company pay special attention to when designing a customer-satisfaction program?

Tie the message to your audience's frame of reference.

- Show how new ideas are related to ideas that already exist in the minds of your audience. The meaning of the new concept is clarified by its relationship to the old. Such connections also help make the new concepts acceptable.
- When you come to an important idea, say so. By explicitly stating that an idea is especially significant, you wake people up; you also make it easier for them to file the thought in the proper place. You can call attention to an idea visually, using headlines, bold type, and indented lists and by using charts, graphs, maps, diagrams, and illustrations. If you're delivering your message orally, use your body and voice to highlight the important concepts.

By highlighting and summarizing key points, you help your audience understand and remember the message.

- Before concluding your message or even a major section of a long message, take a moment or two to review the points you've just covered. Restate the purpose, and show how the main ideas relate to it. This simple step will help your audience remember your message and help simplify the overall meaning of complex material.

Minimize Noise

Even the most carefully constructed message will fail to achieve results if it does not reach your audience. As far as possible, try to eliminate potential sources of interference. Then make sure your choice of communication channel and medium doesn't interfere with your message. Choose the method that will be most likely to attract your audience's attention and enable them to concentrate on the message. If a written document seems the best choice, try to make it physically appealing and easy to comprehend. Use an attractive, convenient format, and pay attention to such details as the choice of paper and the quality of type. If possible, deliver the document when you know the reader will have time to study it.

The careful choice of channel and medium helps focus your audience's attention on your message.

If the message calls for an oral delivery channel, try to eliminate physical barriers. The location should be comfortable and quiet, with adequate lighting, good acoustics, and few visual distractions. In addition, think about how your own appearance will affect the audience. An outfit that screams for attention creates as much noise as a squeaky air-conditioning system. Another way to reduce interference, particularly in oral communication, is to deliver your message directly to the intended audience. The more people who filter your message, the greater the potential for message distortion.

Facilitate Feedback

In addition to minimizing noise, giving your audience a chance to provide feedback is crucial. But one thing that makes business communication difficult is the complexity of the feedback loop. If you're talking face-to-face with another person, feedback is immediate and clear. However, if you're writing a letter, memo, or report that will be read by several people, feedback will be delayed and mixed. Some of the readers will be enthusiastic or respond promptly; others will be critical or reluctant to respond, and revising your message to take into account their feedback will be difficult.

When you plan a message, think about the amount of feedback you want to encourage. Although feedback is generally useful, it reduces your control over the communication situation. You need to know whether your message is being understood and accepted, but you may not want to respond to comments until you have completed your argument. If you are communicating with a group, you may not have the time to react to every impression or question.

Make feedback more useful by
- Planning how and when to accept it
- Being receptive to your audience's responses
- Encouraging frankness
- Using it to improve communication

So think about how you want to obtain feedback, and choose a form of communication that suits your needs. Some channels and media are more compatible with feedback than others. If you want to adjust your message quickly, talk to the receiver face-

Meetings can be particularly difficult to orchestrate so that you get all the feedback you want without losing the control you need to accomplish your goals. The people at Digital Review *magazine are careful to think about how much feedback they want during meetings.*

to-face or by phone. If feedback is less important to you, use a written document or give a prepared speech.

As Clarence Wooten knows from his experience at Metamorphosis Studios, feedback isn't always easy to get, even when you encourage it. In some cases, you may have to draw out the other person by asking questions. If you want to know specific things, ask specific questions, but also encourage your audience to express general reactions; you can often learn something very interesting that way.

Regardless of whether the response to your message is written or oral, encourage people to be open and to tell you what they really think and feel. Of course, you have to listen to their comments, and you must do so objectively. You can't say "Please tell me what you think" and then get mad at the first critical comment. So try not to react defensively. Your goal is to find out whether the people in your audience have understood and accepted your message. If you find that they haven't, don't lose your temper. After all, the fault is at least partially yours. Instead of saying the same thing all over again, only louder this time, try to find the source of the misunderstanding. Then revise your message. Sooner or later, if you keep trying, you'll succeed. You may not win the audience to your point of view, but at least you'll make your meaning clear, and you'll part with a feeling of mutual respect.

SUMMARY

Effective communicators use both nonverbal and verbal signals to get their messages across. They also pay as much attention to receiving information as they do to transmitting it.

Communication is a six-phase process: The sender has an idea, the idea becomes a message, the message is transmitted, the receiver gets the message, the receiver interprets the message, and the receiver reacts and sends feedback. Misunderstandings arise when any part of this process breaks down. Communication barriers exist between people and within organizations. Your ability to overcome these barriers determines your communication success and effectiveness.

To improve communication, think about your audience, let them know what to expect, use vivid language, stick to the point, connect new ideas to familiar ones, emphasize and review key points, minimize noise, and provide opportunities for feedback.

COMMUNICATION CHALLENGES AT METAMORPHOSIS STUDIOS

Although you've been with Metamorphosis Studios from the beginning as a graphics animator, you've never felt as disconnected as you do now. Every day you find 30 new e-mail messages waiting, a stack of mail several days old sits unopened in a pile on your desk, and several unread company bulletins fill your in-basket. All you can think about is the end-of-the-month deadline for the MSNBC launch. "Microsoft used to be a competitor and now they're ordering graphics from us," you think, but it brings you no pleasure. It seems that all the fun is gone.

You go back a long way with your good friend, CEO Clarence Wooten. He took a chance on hiring you, and you've always given him 150 percent. In fact, he stuck his head in the door last week to ask how the graphics were shaping up. Although you said everything was "great," you later kicked yourself for not mentioning something about the information overload. The stress of not keeping up with the flow of communication is beginning to take its toll on you in lost productivity. You vow that next time Clarence gives you the opportunity, you'll speak up.

INDIVIDUAL CHALLENGE: "How's it going, Tom?" Startled, you raise your head to see that Clarence has dropped in. He drapes himself across a chair. You take a deep breath. What will you tell him?

TEAM CHALLENGE: Clarence Wooten took Tom Webster's information about communication overload as a serious threat to both the harmony and the future profitability of Metamorphosis. He tells his partner, Andre Forde, about the problem, and together they decide to hold a series of meetings to brainstorm ideas—ways to pare down the enormous amounts of information and yet make sure key people have everything they need to work well together. They contact a professor of management communication at a nearby university. Dr. Sharon Bienvenu has a reputation for excellent work as a corporate consultant. She has suggested that Clarence and Andre not attend the first meeting to encourage employees to speak freely.

The brainstorming group includes elements from every facet of Metamorphosis. The team will consist of two freelancers, Barbara McCall and Louis Corrigan, flown in from Dallas and Chicago; two technical support people, Raji Raasad and Alice Smollen from the main office; and the two animation specialists, Tom Webster and Sandra Wooten. Assume one of these key roles and discuss the problem and possible solutions with Dr. Bienvenu. Prepare a list of key issues and suggestions considering that your first audience will be the owners of Metamorphosis.[26]

CRITICAL THINKING QUESTIONS

1. How can nonverbal communication help you run a meeting? How can it help you call the meeting to order, emphasize important topics, show approval, express reservations, regulate the flow of conversation, and invite a colleague to continue with a comment?
2. Which communication channels are more susceptible to noise, written or spoken? Why?
3. How can you as the receiver help a sender successfully communicate a message? Briefly explain.

4. Do you believe it is easier to communicate with members of your own sex? Why or why not?
5. How can you impress on your employees the importance of including negative information in messages?
6. Under what circumstances might you want to limit the feedback you receive from an audience of readers or listeners? Briefly explain.

DOCUMENT FOR ANALYSIS

Read the following document; then (1) analyze the strengths and weaknesses of each sentence, and (2) revise the document so that it follows this chapter's guidelines.

It has come to my attention that many of you are lying on your time cards. If you come in late, you should not put 8:00 on your card. If you take a long lunch, you should not put

1:00 on your time card. I will not stand for this type of cheating. I simply have no choice but to institute a time-clock system. Beginning next Monday, all employees will have to punch in and punch out whenever they come and go from the work area.

The time clock will be right by the entrance to each work area, so you have no excuse for not punching in. Anyone who is late for work or late coming back from lunch more than three times will have to answer to me. I don't care if you had to take a nap or if you girls had to shop. This is a place of business, and we do not want to be taken advantage of by slackers who are cheaters to boot.

It is too bad that a few bad apples always have to spoil things for everyone.

EXERCISES

1. Write a short description of your classroom's communication potential. What furniture is in the room? How is the room arranged? Are students seated in rows? In a circle? Where is the instructor's space? At the front of the room? In the middle? What are the acoustics like? Are there any windows in the room? Do they offer pleasing views? Could they be distracting? Are there any chalkboards or other visual aids that might affect communication? Is the temperature comfortable? Are heaters or air conditioners noisy? Explain how these and other factors influence the communication that goes on in your classroom. Conclude your description with a statement about the kind of communication your classroom encourages (An inflexible atmosphere for one-way lectures? An open forum of give and take? An intimate setting for private conversations between members of small groups?).

2. Without intruding, observe and analyze three face-to-face interactions (perhaps between a customer and a cashier at a supermarket check stand, between students in your college cafeteria, between your roommates or family members, etc.). Describe how the nonverbal behaviors you observe give the participants clues about what's being said.

3. On the World Wide Web, visit the home pages for United Airlines at <http://www.UAL.com> and Singapore Airlines at <http://www.singaporair.com>. Identify the verbal and nonverbal cues that help you understand each company as well as the products and services that each company offers. Examine the presentation of both text and visual elements, including photographs and graphics. Consider the layout of the page, background "noise," and repetition. Think about the needs of the audience. Is each page informative and easy to use? Do the links take the user to appropriate and clearly presented data? In 500 words, explain which site is more effective and why.

4. Your boss has asked you to research and report on corporate child-care facilities. Of course, you'll want to know who (besides your boss) will be reading your report. List four or five other things you'll want to know about the situation and about your audience before starting your research. Briefly explain why the items on your list are important.

5. Medical Care America's senior vice president says that when company executives stated their plans to reduce prices on selected equipment at varying rates, some analysts misinterpreted those comments during interviews with news services. So when the news media reported that Medical Care was planning to slash prices by 40 to 60 percent, investors rushed to sell their stock, fearing the company would slash prices beyond any possibility of making a profit (which of course was never Medical Care's intention). This type of message distortion could have been caused by communication barriers such as incorrect filtering or poor listening. What could Medical Care have done to reinforce its message and avoid such misunderstandings? Please explain.[27]

6. Briefly describe a miscommunication you've had with a co-worker, fellow college student, friend, or family member. Can you identify what barrier(s) prevented your successful communication? Please explain.

7. Basing your decisions on the varying richness of communication media, such as face-to-face interviews, telephone conversations, written messages (such as memos, letters, and reports), and bulletins or newsletters, advise your employees how best to send the following messages, and explain your rationale:
   a. A technical report on the durability of your production equipment
   b. A reminder to employees about safety rules
   c. A performance evaluation of an employee who has been consistently missing deadlines
   d. A confirmation of tomorrow's luncheon meeting with an important client
   e. The quarterly statistics on inventory control
   f. Your resignation before joining another company
      Briefly explain each decision

8. Selecting the site for your company's new plant was presented to you as an opportunity to prove yourself; there was even the hint of promotion. You've been in charge of everything, from soil specifications to reviewing architectural proposals. Finally, after all your research, all your negotiations with local landowners, all the cost calculations, and all the money you've already spent on ecological, social, and community impact studies, you are about to recommend the Lansing River site as the best location for the new plant. Then, right before your big presentation, you discover a tiny mistake in your cost calculations that appears to push site acquisition costs up by $50,000, nearly 10 percent over budget. You see yourself during the presentation, revealing this last-minute screwup: You feel like a fool, and you see your career sliding downhill fast. Then you think you should deemphasize the mistake for now, just until after the presentation and things get rolling. You're not sure there really is a mistake, and with the presentation scheduled in less than 15 minutes, you don't have time to recheck all your figures. By letting it go for now, you'd be acting for the good of the company.

   You believe fervently that the Lansing River site is the best location for your company's new plant—even with the possible extra expense. However, if you can't present a clean, unqualified solution, they'll never go for it. You've been around long enough to know that once a project starts, its budget often runs over original estimates anyway, so you could work the extra cost into the budget later. On your way to the meeting room, you make your final decision. In a few paragraphs, explain the decision you made.

9. You've accepted an invitation from the chamber of commerce to speak about controlled growth in the community. You know your audience will consist mostly of local businesspeople, but how can you find out more? Is it possible to determine where they stand on the issue of growth, how much they know about the topic, and what information they need to have before they'll accept your message? You have one month before the speech. List any methods you can think of that will help you learn as much as you can about the audience you'll be addressing.

10. You've agreed to help a colleague by reviewing his report. His language needs to be more specific and more memorable, so you've compiled a list of words and phrases that should be replaced. Please suggest one or two appropriate alternatives for the underlined sections in the following:
    a. A <u>pale, grayish yellow</u> cover
    b. <u>Soft</u> leather
    c. The <u>people buying this product</u>
    d. During this <u>period of business prosperity</u>
    e. Concern for <u>seriously declining</u> profits

11. You are writing a report on the U.S. sales of your newest product. Of the following topics, identify those that should and should not be included in your report (please explain your choices):
    a. Regional breakdowns of sales across the country
    b. Sales figures from competitors selling similar products worldwide
    c. Predictions of how the struggling U.S. economy will affect sales over the next six months
    d. The impact of Japanese competitors selling similar products in the United States
    e. An evaluation of your company's selling this product internationally

12. Describe the kinds of vocal signals and body movements you can use to highlight the key points of your speech.

13. You're stuck. Your boss has asked you to make your presentation to the board over lunch—a prospect you dread. It's bad enough that you have to convince such a stuffy group to spend more money on employee training and education, but to do it over lunch at one of those white-clothed tables for nine in the middle of a busy restaurant is asking a lot. What can you do to get the board members' attention, keep it, and overcome the inevitable interruptions and noise of the restaurant's waiters and lunch crowd?

14. In order to obtain just the right amount of feedback, choose the appropriate form of communication for the following (briefly explain your choices):
    a. Disclosing your idea for a new product to your five-member team
    b. Obtaining comments from your boss on your approach to completing the annual stockholders' report
    c. Convincing top management and co-workers that your plan for improving companywide communication is the best plan
    d. Getting opinions from your co-workers about remodeling the local office

15. Whenever your boss asks for feedback on an idea, she blasts anyone offering criticism—no matter how gently the news is broken to her. This defensive reaction has caused people to start agreeing with everything she says. You believe the situation is unhealthy for the company and for your boss. So despite the likelihood of her reacting defensively, you want to talk to her about it. List some of the things you'll say when you meet with her tomorrow.

CHAPTER 3

COMMUNICATING INTERCULTURALLY

AFTER STUDYING THIS CHAPTER, YOU WILL BE ABLE TO

- Outline the two trends that have made intercultural business communication so important
- Define *culture* and *intercultural communication*
- Discuss nine ways people can differ culturally
- Summarize how to learn about a particular culture
- Discuss some general skills to help communicate in any culture
- Identify some of the common sources of misunderstanding that occur in written and oral intercultural communication
- Explain the importance of speaking and listening more effectively when communicating face-to-face with people from other cultures

COMMUNICATION CLOSE-UP AT PROCTER & GAMBLE

Michael Copeland is Procter & Gamble's specialist in international training. Procter & Gamble (P&G) gets more than half its sales from outside the United States, and it is Copeland's job to help the company teach nearly 100,000 people from 140 countries how to make and sell soap, toothpaste, cake mix, coffee, deodorant, cooking oil, diapers, cough medicine, makeup, and a host of other items sold in drugstores and supermarkets. Many of these people speak English poorly, if at all, and many have work habits and job expectations that differ from those of the typical U.S. employee.

Based at headquarters in Cincinnati, Copeland guides P&G's far-flung managers as they teach their employees the skills required to do things "the P&G way." Copeland's mission is to see that the company's employees are consistently first-rate, from Argentina to Zaire. He does so by helping managers in each country plan and execute training programs, using both in-house resources and outside specialists. He tries to blend the best of both worlds so that employees not only understand P&G's traditions but also translate those traditions into behavior that makes sense on a local level. As the company fights to stay ahead of the competition, communication among employees at all levels is more important than ever.

One of Copeland's projects was to help a recently acquired Brazilian subsidiary (a manufacturer of bar soap, perfume, and personal-care products) make the transition into the P&G fold. When the company was acquired, its top managers were all Brazilians who conducted business in Portuguese. Hoping to align the company with its other Latin American operations, P&G brought in a new team of managers, most of whom were Spanish-speaking. But the change resulted in both language and cultural problems. As Copeland recalls, "After a year, it was clear that we were not succeeding

Michael Copeland

Multinational companies like Procter & Gamble believe in the importance of training domestic and foreign employees in the subtleties of intercultural communication. Training sessions, such as this one in Paris, may stress differences in social as well as in business customs.

as well as we had hoped to." Finally the human resources manager, who was Mexican, came to Copeland for help.

After listening carefully to the human resources manager, Copeland suggested a training program to reduce the linguistic and cultural barriers that separated the Brazilians from the other Latin Americans and to bring them all closer to the P&G culture. A major goal of the proposed program was to improve the English-language capabilities of all the managers of the Brazilian subsidiary—an accomplishment that would facilitate their communication with one another and with P&G's headquarters. The human resources manager liked the suggestion and asked Copeland to prepare a written document that would flesh out the details and help him sell his general manager on the program.

Copeland wrote a proposal explaining the objectives, methods, and costs associated with the effort. Because English is the second language of both the human resources manager and the general manager, Copeland kept the proposal clear and brief. "The language had to be simple, idiom-free, coldly factual, and without any embellishment," he explains. "In response to your request, this is the proposal. This is what it includes. This is the amount of time it will take. This is what it will cost." Indeed, the proposal was direct and straightforward.

The human resources manager presented Copeland's proposal and persuaded the general manager to undertake the training program, which has three elements. The first covers the grammar and vocabulary of business English and the basics of written and oral communication—letters, memos, reports, and presentations. The second deals with the subtleties of intercultural communication—maintaining appropriate eye contact, gesturing, providing verbal feedback during conversations, reaching conclusions, summarizing, and the like. The third element explores the P&G corporate culture, helping participants understand the broad values that transcend geographic boundaries. Program participants begin with a preparatory course in Brazil, followed by a three- to five-month intensive program conducted by outside consultants at a facility in Colorado.

P&G has a tradition of promoting from within. The company believes in building a corps of international managers who can maintain P&G's standards throughout the world. It's expensive, but as Michael Copeland points out, "If you want to develop organizations, this is how you do it."[1]

THE IMPORTANCE OF INTERCULTURAL BUSINESS COMMUNICATION

Procter & Gamble is by no means alone in its multinational focus. More and more companies around the world are hopping national borders to conduct business. Regardless of the organization you join, you are likely to be dealing with people who come from various national, religious, and ethnic backgrounds. Like P&G's Latin American managers, you may find yourself trying to bridge differences in both language and culture as you exchange business messages with customers, suppliers, investors, and competitors from other lands.

Of course, communicating across national borders is only one way your communication skills will be challenged. Communicating across language and cultural barriers at home will also challenge your skills. Without leaving your own country, you're likely to come into contact with people from a variety of backgrounds who work in your company, industry, and community.

Communicating with Cultures Abroad

The globalization of business is accelerating as more companies cross national borders to find customers, materials, and money.

In many ways, the world is becoming smaller and smaller for businesspeople. Thanks to technological advances in communication and transportation, companies can quickly and easily span the globe in search of new customers, new sources of materials, and new sources of money. Even firms that once thought they were too tiny to expand into a neighboring city have discovered that they can tap the sales potential of overseas markets with the help of fax machines, the Internet, overnight delivery services, and e-mail (see Figure 3.1). This rise of international business has increased international business communication by increasing exports, relaxing trade barriers, and increasing foreign competition in domestic markets.

More and more businesses report that a large part of their overall sales now come from *exports* (products sold to customers in other countries). Barco, a Belgium-based maker of electronic equipment, sells 85 percent of its products to customers in other countries; Nestlé, which is based in Switzerland, sells over 95 percent of its products in other countries. Likewise, some U.S. companies are seeing export sales dwarf sales at home: Boston-based Gillette makes 70 percent of its sales through exports, and Seattle-based Boeing exports 80 percent of its products.[2] U.S. firms sell more than $90 billion worth of goods and services every year to Canada alone (by far the largest U.S. trading partner, followed by Japan and Mexico).[3]

Relaxing trade barriers has also quickened the pace of international trade. Mexico, Canada, and the United States have agreed to lower trade barriers throughout the continent, creating a single market of 360 million people. Moreover, discussions are under way to extend that agreement throughout the Americas.[4] The goal is to increase *imports* (products purchased from businesses in other countries) by reducing the hassles of bringing goods across the borders. Similarly, the nations of the European Community have been eliminating trade barriers. Since 1993, capital, products, and employees have been flowing more freely across European borders, creating a unified market of 320 million people.[5]

Figure 3.1
In-Depth Critique: E-Mail
Is One of the Technologies
Shrinking the World

Wickman Hospital Products, Inc., a large American company, is interested in developing a client base in Mexico. Wickman's marketing department suggested a direct-mail campaign supplemented with personalized e-mail communications. Each Mexican hospital was initially sent a letter of introduction, detailed product information, and a carton of sample products. A week later, the following e-mail message was sent.

E-Mail

```
Comments: Authenticated sender is <jacksont@wickman.com>
From: "Timothy A. Jackson" <jacksont@wickman.com>
To: jHerrera@stlukeshosp.org
Date: Thurs, 19 June 1997, 10:30:23, CDT
Subject: Wickman Hospital Products, Inc.
Return-Receipt-To: jacksont@wickman.com
Priority: normal
```

The header containing routing information, subject, and so forth is a common feature of most e-mail programs.

```
Dear Sr. Herrera:

Wickman Hospital Products is eager to serve you. Did you
have time to look over the materials we sent you
recently? You may be especially interested in our fine
line of disposable pads and bedding.
```

The message begins politely and with a reminder of previous communication.

```
For your convenience, Charles Garrison can give you
detailed information about any of our products. You can
contact him by e-mail, phone, or post:

        E-mail garrison@wickman.com
        Phone (800) 773-4558
        Post   Charles Garrison
               Customer Representative
               Wickman Hospital Products
               P.O. Box 511
               Columbus, Ohio, 43216-0508
               USA
```

This paragraph gives helpful information, suggests actions, and provides an e-mail address for each action.

```
You can also place an order right away, browse through
our entire line of products, and review product
specifications. Just visit our Internet home page:
<http://www.wickman.com>. You can count on delivery
within 48 hours of the time we receive your e-mail,
Internet order form, or phone call.

Please let us help you supply St. Luke's Hospital with
the finest products available.

Timothy A. Jackson, International Sales

Wickman Hospital Products
```

The letter closes by urging use of the Internet. When this message is sent, the angle brackets placed around the Uniform Resource Locator, or URL, convert the Web address to a live link (also called a hot link). The URL appears in a distinctive color, and the angle brackets are no longer visible. To visit the linked Web page, the recipient merely clicks on the URL.

As companies move into the global marketplace, they increase the competition in domestic markets for employees, customers, and materials. They build factories abroad and buy overseas companies. In a single year, U.S. companies invested approximately $30 billion in non-U.S. facilities and equipment, employing more than 20 million people outside the United States.[6] At the same time, 30 percent of U.S. manufacturers recently reported that three of their top five competitors *in the U.S. market* are non-U.S. firms. Overall, non-U.S. corporations control nearly 15 percent of all U.S. manufacturing assets, and they employ almost 4 million people in the United States.[7] In this fast-paced global marketplace, companies are finding that good communication skills are essential for meeting customers, making sales, and working more effectively with colleagues in other countries.

Communicating with a Culturally Diverse Work Force

In addition to communicating with people in other countries, you'll be communicating with people in your own country whose culture and language differ from yours. First, if you work in the local branch of a foreign firm or if your company does business with local branches of foreign firms, you may find that differences in language and culture interfere with your message exchange. In almost any business situation—whether giving or receiving job training, discussing a customer order, or answering a question from headquarters—sending and receiving messages can be more complicated between native and nonnative businesspeople.

In many countries, the domestic work force is becoming more culturally diverse.

Second, no matter where you work, you'll face language and cultural barriers as you communicate with members of an increasingly diverse domestic work force. Few countries have an entirely homogeneous population. A country's work force reflects its **cultural diversity,** the degree to which the population is made up of people from various national, ethnic, racial, and religious backgrounds.

Cultural diversity is the degree to which the population is made up of people from varied national, ethnic, racial, and religious backgrounds.

In the United States, for example, the high degree of cultural diversity in the domestic work force has been partially shaped by immigration trends, with new arrivals from Europe, Canada, Latin America, and Asia.[8] As these immigrants join the domestic work force, they bring their own language and culture. Out of every seven people in the United States, one person speaks a language other than English when at home. After English, Spanish is by far the most commonly spoken language, followed by French, German, Italian, and Chinese. Also, because of immigration patterns, some areas of the United States have a higher concentration of non-English speakers than others. New Mexico has more Spanish-speaking residents than any other U.S. state; Maine has more French-speaking residents; and Michigan has more Arabic-speaking residents.[9]

Members of the U.S. work force also come from differing ethnic backgrounds. African Americans represent 12 percent of the U.S. population, and by the year 2000, they will represent nearly 14 percent. Hispanic Americans (including people with backgrounds from Mexico, Cuba, Puerto Rico, and Central and South America) currently account for 9 percent of the population; Asian Americans (including people with backgrounds from Vietnam, Cambodia, and other Asian nations) account for nearly 3 percent.[10] As companies hire and transfer people, their employee mix becomes more diverse.

Of course, people also differ in terms of their gender, age, physical abilities, family status, and educational background. Like language and culture, these elements contribute to the diversity of the work force. They shape how people view the world. And they also affect how business messages are conceived, planned, sent, received, and interpreted.

Solectron is a U.S. company that's making it big as an electronics contract manufacturer. It assembles printed circuit boards and complete computers for companies like IBM, Hewlett-Packard, and Compaq. Because the U.S. work force is increasing in cultural diversity, companies such as Solectron benefit from learning about intercultural communication.

THE BASICS OF INTERCULTURAL BUSINESS COMMUNICATION

As discussed in Chapter 2, differences in background can be a difficult communication barrier to overcome. When differences are extreme—when the sender and the receiver come from separate cultures—the potential for misunderstanding is even higher. So when you plan to communicate with people of another culture—whether in another country or in your own country—it's important to be aware of cultural differences.

Consider the communication challenge that Mazda's managers faced when the Japanese auto manufacturer opened a plant in the United States. Mazda officials passed out company baseball caps and told their U.S. employees that they could wear the caps at work, along with their mandatory company uniform (blue pants and khaki shirts). The employees assumed that the caps were a *voluntary* accessory, and many decided not to wear them. This upset the Japanese managers, who regarded failure to wear the caps as a sign of disrespect. Managers acknowledged that the caps were voluntary but believed that employees who really cared about the company would *want* to wear the caps. However, the U.S. employees had a different view: They resented being told what they should want to do, and they began cynically referring to all Mazda's directives as "mandatory-voluntary."[11]

As you can see, communicating with people from other cultures can be challenging. To overcome cultural barriers to effective communication, you must first learn what *culture* actually means.

Understanding Culture

You belong to several cultures. The most obvious is the culture you share with all the people who live in your own country. You also belong to other cultural groups, including an ethnic group, a religious group, and perhaps a profession that has its own special language and customs. **Culture** is a shared system of symbols, beliefs, attitudes, values, expectations, and norms for behavior. All members of a culture have similar assumptions about how people should think, behave, and communicate, and they all tend to act on those assumptions in much the same way.

BEST OF THE WEB

Master the Art of Intercultural Communication

"Building bridges between people" is the motto of the International/Intercultural Development Education Connection. On the home page, click "Communication" and then click "General Communication" to visit dozens of interesting electronic sources that will help you communicate more effectively with intercultural audiences.

http://www.escotet.com/index1.html

Culture is a shared system of symbols, beliefs, attitudes, values, expectations, and norms for behavior.

Subcultures are distinct groups that exist within a major culture.

Distinct groups that exist within a major culture are more properly referred to as **subcultures.** Groups that might be considered subcultures in the United States are Mexican Americans, Mormons, wrestling fans, Russian immigrants, and Harvard graduates.

Cultures differ in several ways that affect communication:

- *Stability.* Conditions in the culture may be stable or may be changing either slowly or rapidly. For instance, elements of Japan's culture have been changing rapidly over the past 50 years, which can interfere with receiving and decoding messages.[12]
- *Complexity.* Cultures vary in the accessibility of information. In Germany and the United States, information is contained in explicit codes, including words. However, in Japan, a great deal of information is conveyed implicitly, through body language, tone of voice, and the like.
- *Composition.* Some cultures are made up of many diverse and disparate subcultures; others tend to be more homogeneous. Indonesia, for example, is home to a wide variety of ethnic and religious subcultures; by comparison, Japan is much more homogeneous because it has only a few subcultures.[13] Generally, the fewer the subcultures in a person's background, the easier it is to communicate, because you have fewer potential differences to consider.
- *Acceptance.* Cultures vary in their attitudes toward outsiders. Some are openly hostile, some maintain a detached aloofness, and others are friendly and cooperative toward strangers. These attitudes can affect the level of trust and open communication you can achieve with people of other cultures.

Intercultural communication is the process of sending and receiving messages between people of different cultures.

By bridging these differences, you can successfully achieve **intercultural communication,** the process of sending and receiving messages between people of different cultures. You will be most effective when you learn to identify the differences between sender and receiver and to accommodate those differences without expecting either culture to give up its own identity.[14]

Recognizing Cultural Differences

A society's culture affects its members' view of the world and thus their responses to people and events.

Y. A. Cho, chief operating officer of Korean Airlines, says, "In dealing with American business people, I'm amazed at how naive most are about other cultures and the way that others do business."[15] When you write to or speak with someone in another culture, you encode your message using the assumptions of your own culture. However, the receiver decodes it according to the assumptions of the other culture, so your meaning may be misunderstood. The greater the difference between the sender's culture and the receiver's culture, the greater the chance for misunderstanding.[16]

Consider the U.S. computer sales representative who called on a client in China. Hoping to make a good impression, the salesperson brought an expensive grandfather clock as a gift. Unfortunately, the differences between the sender's culture and the receiver's culture interfered with the communication process. Instead of being pleased, the Chinese client was deeply offended, because in China receiving a clock as a gift is considered bad luck.[17]

Effective intercultural communication depends on recognizing ways in which people differ.

Such problems arise when we assume, wrongly, that other people's attitudes and lives are like ours. As a graduate of one training program said: "I used to think it was enough to treat people the way I wanted to be treated. But [after taking the course] . . . I realized you have to treat people the way *they* want to be treated."[18] Acknowledging and exploring these differences is an important step toward understanding how culture affects the communication process (see "Test Your Intercultural Knowledge"). As you'll see in the following sections, cultural differences show up in social values, ideas

COMMUNICATING ACROSS CULTURES

TEST YOUR INTERCULTURAL KNOWLEDGE

Never take anything for granted when you're doing business in a foreign country. All sorts of assumptions that are valid in one place can trip you up elsewhere if you fail to consider that customs may vary. Here are several true stories about businesspeople who blundered by overlooking some simple but important cultural differences. Can you spot the erroneous assumptions that led these people astray?

1. A Taiwanese manufacturer of drinking glasses received an order from the Middle East. The shipping clerk packed the glasses in hay, crated them in wooden boxes, and then sent them off, confident that they would arrive in one piece. He was wrong. When the glasses reached their destination, nothing remained but bits and pieces. What did the shipping clerk fail to realize?
2. When a U.S. fragrance manufacturer decided to sell its line of men's cologne in North Africa, it used its tried-and-true North American ad, which pictured a man and his dog in a rural setting. The fragrance bombed in North Africa. What did the fragrance manufacturer not realize?
3. A French firm set up an automated timber mill in East Africa, but the mill turned out to be inoperative and the company eventually tore it down. What did the French overlook?
4. A Hungarian company recently decided to export bed sheets to the United States. Company officials were dismayed when the sheets did not sell. What did the Hungarians fail to realize?

5. A U.S. manufacturer of equipment for the textile industry sent a shipment of motors to a British client. As specified, these were right-handed motors. The British returned the entire lot. What did the U.S. manufacturer fail to realize?

In each case the businesspeople acted on the basis of inaccurate assumptions. Here are the explanations of what went wrong:

1. Taiwan is a humid country, but the Middle East is arid. The hay that was moist and plump in Taiwan dried out when the shipment reached the Middle East. So the glasses rattled around and broke.
2. The fragrance manufacturer didn't know that Muslim people consider a dog to be either a sign of bad luck or a symbol of uncleanliness.
3. The French overlooked the fact that the supply of electrical power in rural East Africa was often inadequate to run the plant.
4. The Hungarians neglected to compare the size of Hungarian and U.S. mattresses. The Hungarian sheets didn't fit the U.S. beds.
5. Whether something is right-handed or left-handed depends on where you're standing. The British were standing at the front of the production line and looking at the motors from that angle when they specified right-handed motors. The U.S. manufacturer assumed the British were looking at the production line from the back end, which is the typical U.S. perspective.

of status, decision-making habits, attitudes toward time, use of space, cultural context, body language, manners, and legal and ethical behavior. Without an understanding of these differences, U.S. businesspeople can unknowingly act improperly and unacceptably when abroad, hurting their own reputations and that of their organization.[19]

Social Values

Although the United States is home to millions of people having different religions and values, the major influence is the Puritan work ethic. The predominant U.S. view is that money solves many problems, that material comfort (earned by individual effort) is a sign of superiority, and that people who work hard are better than those who don't. By and large, people in the United States assume that people from other cultures also dislike poverty and value hard work. In fact, many societies condemn materialism, and some prize a more carefree lifestyle.

As a culture, people in the United States are goal-oriented. They want to get their work done efficiently, and they assume that everyone else does too. They think they're improving things if they can figure out a way for two people using modern methods to

People from the United States emphasize hard work, material success, and efficiency more than many other people do.

do the same work as four people using the "old way." In countries such as India and Pakistan, where unemployment is high, creating jobs is more important than working efficiently. Executives in these countries would rather employ four workers than two, and their values influence their actions as well as the way they encode and decode messages.

Roles and Status

People from other cultures demonstrate their status differently than do people in the United States.

Culture dictates the roles people play, including who communicates with whom, what they communicate, and in what way. For example, in many countries women still don't play a prominent role in business, so female executives who visit these countries may find that they're not taken seriously as businesspeople. When they're in modern western Europe, women can usually behave as they would in the United States, but they should be more cautious in Latin American and eastern European countries, and they should be extremely cautious in the Middle East and the Far East.[20]

Culture can define roles by the way people refer to each other. In the United States people show respect for superiors and top managers by addressing them as "Mr. Roberts" or "Mrs. Gutierrez." However, in China, it's customary to show respect for organizational rank by addressing businesspeople according to their official titles, such as "President" or "Manager."[21]

Concepts of status also differ. Most U.S. executives send status signals that reflect materialistic values. The big boss has a large corner office, deep carpets, an expensive desk, and handsome accessories. In other cultures status is communicated in other ways. The highest-ranking executives in France sit in the middle of an open area, surrounded by lower-level employees. In the Middle East fine possessions are reserved for the home, and business is conducted in cramped and modest quarters. An executive from another culture who assumes that such office arrangements indicate a lack of status would be making a big mistake.

Decision-Making Customs

Many cultural groups take longer than U.S. and Canadian businesspeople to reach decisions, and many rely more heavily on group consensus.

In the United States and Canada, businesspeople try to reach decisions as quickly and efficiently as possible. The top people are concerned with reaching an agreement on the main points, and they leave the details to be worked out later by others. In Greece this approach would backfire. A Greek executive assumes that anyone who ignores the details is being evasive and untrustworthy. Spending time on each little point is considered a mark of good faith. Similarly, Latin Americans prefer to make their deals slowly, after much discussion.

Cultures also differ in terms of who makes the decisions. In the United States many organizations are dominated by a single figure who says yes or no to the major deals. It is the same in Pakistan, where you can get a decision quickly if you reach the highest-ranking executive.[22] In other cultures, decision making is shared. In Japan the negotiating team arrives at a consensus through an elaborate, time-consuming process. Agreement must be complete—there is no majority rule. And like businesses everywhere, Japanese firms expect their managers to follow the same decision-making process regardless of whether they're in Tokyo or in Toledo, Ohio.

Concepts of Time

Differing perceptions of time are another factor that can lead to misunderstandings. German and U.S. executives see time as a way to plan the business day efficiently, focusing on only one task during each scheduled period. Because time is so limited, German and U.S. executives try to get to the point quickly when communicating.

However, executives from Latin America and Asia see time as more flexible. In these cultures, building a foundation for the business relationship is more important than meeting a deadline for completing a task. Seen in this light, it's not surprising that people in such cultures do not observe strict schedules. Instead, they take whatever time is needed to get to know each other and explore the background issues.[23]

If a salesperson from Chicago called on a client in Mexico City and was kept waiting 30 minutes in the outer office, that salesperson would feel angry and insulted, assuming the client attaches a low priority to the visit. In fact, the Mexican client doesn't mean to imply anything at all by this delay. In Mexico, a wait of 30 minutes is a matter of course; the workday isn't expected to follow a rigid, preset schedule.[24]

Although businesspeople in the United States, Germany, and some other nations see time as a way to organize the business day efficiently, other cultures see time as more flexible.

As pictured here outside Amtex Enterprises, U.S. executives commonly maintain a five-foot comfort zone during business discussions. However, senior businessmen in Jerusalem are more comfortable conducting business up close.

Concepts of Personal Space

Like time, space means different things in different cultures. The classic story of a conversation between a U.S. executive and a Latin American executive is that the interaction may begin at one end of a hallway and end up at the other, with neither party aware of having moved. During the conversation the Latin American executive instinctively moves closer to the U.S. executive, who unconsciously steps back, resulting in an intercultural dance across the floor.

People from various cultures have different "comfort zones."

People in Canada and the United States usually stand about five feet apart during a business conversation. This distance is uncomfortably close for people from Germany or Japan. But to Arabs or Latin Americans, this distance is uncomfortably far. Because of these differing concepts of personal space, a Canadian manager may react negatively (without knowing exactly why) when a Latin American colleague moves closer during their conversation. And the Latin American colleague may react negatively (again, without knowing why) when the Canadian manager backs away.

Cultural Context

Although U.S. business-people rely more on words to convey meaning, people in other cultures rely more on situational cues and implicit understanding.

One of the ways we assign meaning to a message is according to its **cultural context,** the pattern of physical cues and implicit understanding that convey meaning between two members of the same culture. However, people convey contextual meaning differently from culture to culture. In the **high-context culture** of South Korea or Taiwan, people rely less on verbal communication and more on the context of nonverbal actions and environmental setting to convey meaning. The rules of everyday life are rarely explicit in high-context cultures; as they grow up, people learn how to recognize situational cues (such as gestures and tone of voice) and how to respond as expected.[25]

In the **low-context culture** of the United States or Germany, people rely more on verbal communication and less on circumstances and implied meaning to convey meaning. Expectations are usually spelled out in a low-context culture through explicit statements, such as "Please wait until I'm finished" or "You're welcome to browse." In this way, a businessperson in a low-context culture not only explains his or her own actions but also cues the other person about what to do or what to expect next.[26]

Imagine the confusion and frustration of someone from a low-context culture trying to sell products to a client from a high-context culture. If the client says nothing after the salesperson names a price, the salesperson may assume that the silence means rejection and may try to save the sale by naming a lower figure. However, in the high-context culture, silence means only that the client is considering the first offer. By misinterpreting this silence and lowering the price, the salesperson loses needed profits.

Body Language

Variations in the meaning of body language can cause problems because people are unaware of the messages they are transmitting.

Gestures help members of a culture clarify confusing messages, but differences in body language are a major source of misunderstanding during intercultural communication. Furthermore, don't make the mistake of assuming that someone from another country who speaks your language has mastered the body language of your culture. Instead, learn some of the basic differences in the way people supplement their words with body movement. Take the signal for *no.* People in the United States and Canada shake their heads back and forth; people in Bulgaria nod up and down; people in Japan move their right hands; people in Sicily raise their chins. Or take eye contact. Businesspeople in the United States assume that a person who won't meet their gaze is evasive and dishonest. However, in many parts of Latin America and Asia, keeping your eyes lowered is a sign of respect, and among many Native American groups, children maintaining eye contact with adults is a sign of disrespect.[27]

Sometimes people from different cultures misread an intentional signal sent by body language; sometimes they overlook the signal entirely or assume that a meaningless gesture is significant. An Arab man indicates a romantic interest in a woman by running a hand backward across his hair; most Westerners would not understand the significance of this gesture.[28] On the other hand, an Egyptian might mistakenly assume that a Westerner who exposes the sole of his or her shoe is offering a grave insult. The more open you are to nonverbal messages, the better you will communicate in your own and other cultures.[29]

Social Behavior and Manners

What is polite in one culture may be considered rude in another. In Arab countries it's impolite to take gifts to a man's wife but acceptable to take gifts to his children. In Germany giving a woman a red rose is considered a romantic invitation, inappropriate if you are trying to establish a business relationship with her. In India you might be invited to visit someone's home "any time." If you're not familiar with the culture, you may be reluctant to make an unexpected visit, and you might therefore wait for a definite invitation. But your failure to take the invitation literally is an insult, a sign that you do not care to develop the friendship.

The rules of polite behavior vary from country to country.

In any culture, rules of etiquette may be formal or informal. Formal rules are the specifically taught "rights" and "wrongs" of how to behave in common social situations, such as table manners at meals. When formal rules are violated, members of a culture can explain why they feel upset. In contrast, informal social rules are more difficult to identify and are usually learned by watching how people behave and then imitating that behavior. Informal rules govern how males and females are supposed to behave, when it is appropriate to use a person's first name, and so on. When informal rules are violated, members of a culture are likely to feel uncomfortable, although they may not be able to say exactly why.[30]

Legal and Ethical Behavior

From culture to culture, what is considered legal and ethical behavior varies widely. In some countries companies are expected to pay government officials extra fees for approving government contracts. These payments aren't illegal or unethical, merely routine. However, the same payments are seen as bribes in the United States, Sweden, and many other countries, where they are both illegal and unethical. In fact, U.S.-based companies are generally not allowed to bribe officials anywhere in the world. (The U.S. Foreign Corrupt Practices Act, which governs company payments to foreign officials, allows a few exceptions, such as small payments that speed but don't actually influence government actions.)[31]

People often encounter differing standards of legal and ethical behavior in the course of doing business in other countries.

When you conduct business around the world, you may also find that other legal systems differ from what you're accustomed to. In the United Kingdom and the United States, someone is innocent until proven guilty, a principle that is rooted in English common law. In Mexico and Turkey, someone is presumed guilty until proven innocent, a principle that is rooted in the Napoleonic code.[32] These distinctions can be particularly important if your firm must communicate about a legal dispute in another country.

Dealing with Language Barriers

Language shapes our world view, dictating our perception of the universe, so the potential for misunderstanding cross-cultural interaction is great.[33] Even the way information is approached and processed can differ greatly between various cultures. For example, an English speaker feels responsible for transmitting the meaning of a message, but a Chinese speaker is more likely to expect the receiver to discover the

English is the most prevalent language in international business, but it's a mistake to assume that everyone understands it.

meaning in a message that uses indirectness and metaphor. Further, an English speaker often places sentences in a chronological sequence to establish a cause-and-effect pattern. However, a Chinese speaker often begins by creating a context with generalizations that form a web (or frame) to receive and support a given topic.[34]

Language differences can trip you up even if you're a U.S. executive doing business in an English-speaking country. A U.S. paper products manufacturer learned this the hard way while trying to crack the English market for paper napkins by using its usual advertising slogan: "There is no finer paper napkin for the dinner table." Unfortunately for the U.S. company, *napkin* is the British term for *diaper*.[35]

Also likely are misunderstandings involving vocabulary, pronunciation, or usage when U.S. businesspeople deal with people who use English as a second language (and some 650 million people fall into this category). Some of these millions are extremely fluent; others have only an elementary command of English. Although you may miss a few subtleties when dealing with those less fluent in your own language, you'll still be able to communicate. However, don't assume that the other person understands everything you say. Your message can be mangled by slang, idioms, and local accents. One group of English-speaking Japanese employees who transferred to Toyota's U.S. office had to enroll in a special course to learn that "Jeat yet?" means "Did you eat yet?" and that "Cannahepya?" means "Can I help you?"

When you deal with people who don't speak your language at all, you have three options: You can learn their language, use an intermediary or a translator, or teach them your language. Becoming fluent in a new language requires a major commitment. At the U.S. State Department, foreign service officers take six months of language training and then continue their studies at their foreign posts. Even the Berlitz method, famous for the speed of its results, requires a month of intensive effort. Language courses can be quite expensive as well. So unless you're planning to spend several years abroad or to make frequent trips over an extended period, learning another language may take more time and more money than you can afford.

A more practical approach is to use an intermediary or a translator. An experienced translator can analyze a message, understand its meaning in the cultural context, consider how to convey the meaning in another language, and then use verbal and nonverbal signals to encode or decode the message for someone from another culture. If your company has an overseas subsidiary, you may want to seek help from local employees who are bilingual. You can also hire bilingual professionals such as advertising consultants and lawyers.

The option of teaching other people to speak your language doesn't appear to be very practical at first glance. However, many multinational companies do, in fact, offer language-training programs for employees. The program Michael Copeland devised for the managers of P&G's Brazilian subsidiary is a case in point. Learning English represented a good compromise for the Portuguese- and Spanish-speaking employees, and it reinforced their relationship with P&G headquarters.

Tenneco is another U.S.-based company that instituted an English-language training program—in this case, for its Spanish-speaking employees in a New Jersey plant. The training concentrated on practical English for use on the job, and thanks to the classes, both accidents and grievances declined, and productivity improved.[36] Nevertheless, requiring employees to use a specific language when they're on the job can create communication problems (see "Does an 'English-Only' Policy Violate Employees' Rights?" on pages 68–69). In general, the magnitude of the language barrier depends on whether you are writing or speaking. Written communication is generally easier to handle.

Watch for clues to be sure that your message is getting through to people who don't speak your language.

If you have a long-term business relationship with people of another culture, it is helpful to learn their language.

Barriers to Written Communication

Because so many international business letters are written in English, U.S. firms don't always worry about translating their correspondence. Moreover, regardless of where they're located, some multinational companies ask all their employees to use English when writing to employees in other lands. For example, Nissan employees use English for internal memos to colleagues in other countries, even though the corporation is based in Japan. Similarly, English is the official business language of Philips, the global electronics giant based in the Netherlands.[37]

However, many other forms of written communication must be translated. Advertisements are almost always translated into the language of the culture in which the products are being sold. Warranties, repair and maintenance manuals, and product labels require translation, as well. In addition, many multinational companies translate policy and procedure manuals for use in overseas offices. Reports from foreign branches to the home office may be written in one language and then translated into another. One multinational company, E. I. Du Pont de Nemours & Company, translates roughly 70,000 pages of documents per year.[38]

Most routine business correspondence is written in English, but marketing messages are generally translated into the language of the country where the product is to be sold.

When documents are translated literally, communication can break down. For example, the advertising slogan "Come alive with Pepsi" was once mistranslated for German audiences as "Come out of the grave" and for Thai audiences as "Bring your ancestors back from the dead."[39] Part of the message is almost inevitably lost during any translation process. So it's critical for you to consider the meaning of the message and the way it will appear to the receiver when translating from one language into another. To overcome barriers to written communication, follow these recommendations:[40]

Use the skills of bilingual employees or professional translators.
Write short messages.
Keep your wording clear and simple.
Avoid slang.
Use your fax to transmit the information (with speed and clarity).

Barriers to Oral Communication

Oral communication usually presents more problems than written communication. If you've ever studied another language, you know it's easier to write in that language than to conduct a conversation. Even if the other person speaks your language, you may have a hard time understanding the pronunciation if the person isn't proficient. For example, many nonnative English speakers can't distinguish between the English sounds *v* and *w,* so they say "wery" for "very." At the same time, many people from the United States cannot pronounce the French *r* or the German *ch.*

Differences in pronunciation, vocal inflections, and vocabulary can pose problems when you're speaking to people from other cultures.

Also, people use their voices in different ways, which can lead listeners to misunderstand their intentions. Russian speakers, for instance, speak in flat, level tones in their native tongue. When they speak English, they maintain this pattern, and non-Russian listeners may assume that the speakers are bored or rude. Middle Easterners tend to speak more loudly than Westerners and may therefore mistakenly be considered more emotional. On the other hand, the Japanese are soft-spoken, a characteristic that implies politeness or humility to Western listeners.

Idiomatic expressions are another source of confusion. If a U.S. executive tells an Egyptian executive that a certain product "doesn't cut the mustard," chances are communication will fail. Even when the words make sense, their meanings may differ according

DOES AN "ENGLISH-ONLY" POLICY VIOLATE EMPLOYEES' RIGHTS?

No one can disagree with striving for better communication and better safety in the workplace, but what happens when U.S. employers tell their employees to use only English on the job? When U.S. firms establish English-only rules, they raise two sticky questions: (1) Can a company legally require its employees to use *only* one language at work? (2) Is a company discriminating if it *forbids* employees to use their native language on the job?

Do English-Only Rules Ease Communication?

In a country where people predominantly speak English, many businesses believe that English-only rules smooth both internal and external communication. Atlantic Richfield (based in Los Angeles) requires its refinery employees to be able to read and write English for safety reasons. Other businesses, such as stores and banks, insist that employees be conversant in English so that they can deal with the public. Moreover, a handful of states (including Alabama, Arizona, California, Colorado, and Florida) have designated English as the *official* language. So even though the Equal Employment Opportunity Commission (EEOC) maintains that English-only rules violate laws against discrimination, U.S. firms can legally restrict employees to English if they can prove that such action has a legitimate business necessity (such as serving English-speaking customers).

Do English-Only Rules Discriminate Unfairly?

At the same time, many people condemn English-only rules. They say U.S. firms that prevent employees from using languages other than English may be violating government rules against discriminating on the basis of national origin. "English-only laws threaten the civil rights and liberties of individuals who are not proficient in English," says Edward M. Chen, a staff attorney for the American Civil Liberties Union of northern California. In fact, as more immigrants join the U.S. work force, English-only rules are being challenged in courts across the country.

English-Only Rules on Trial

Many of the nurses at Pomona Valley Hospital Medical Center in Pomona, California, are Filipino, and they often talk to each other in Tagalog, their native language. When a supervisor asked everyone to speak only English on the ward, some of the nurses were upset. They agreed that speaking English in front

to the situation. For example, suppose you are dining with a German woman who speaks English quite well. You inquire, "More bread?" She says, "Thank you," so you pass the bread. She looks confused; then she takes the breadbasket and sets it down without taking any. In German, *thank you* (*danke*) can also be used as a polite refusal. If the woman had wanted more bread, she would have used the word *please* (*bitte* in German).

When speaking in English to people who speak English as a second language, you may find these guidelines helpful:

- *Try to eliminate noise.* Pronounce words clearly, stop at distinct punctuation points, and make one point at a time.
- *Look for feedback.* Be alert to signs of confusion in your listener. Realize that nods and smiles don't necessarily mean understanding.
- *Rephrase your sentence when necessary.* If someone doesn't seem to understand you, choose simpler words; don't just repeat the sentence in a louder voice.
- *Don't talk down to the other person.* Try not to overenunciate, and don't "blame" the listener for not understanding. Use phrases such as "Am I going too fast?" rather than "Is this too difficult for you?"
- *Use objective, accurate language.* Avoid throwing around adjectives such as *fantastic* and *fabulous,* which people from other cultures might consider unreal and overly dramatic.
- *Let other people finish what they have to say.* If you interrupt, you may miss something important. You'll also show a lack of respect.

of patients was appropriate, but they saw no harm in speaking Tagalog among themselves. At times, the assistant head nurse would slip into her native language when chatting with other Filipino nurses at lunchtime and when telephoning her own family. After repeated warnings, she protested and was demoted and then transferred to another department.

At this point, the nurse filed a lawsuit, charging that the hospital had violated the Civil Rights Act of 1964, which bans discrimination on the basis of race or national origin. Hospital officials responded that they had merely urged nurses to be sensitive about speaking Tagalog around patients, who couldn't understand the language. Denying that the nurse was disciplined because she continued to speak Tagalog, the officials said that she was demoted because of her poor work performance and attitude. Following a lengthy trial, the judge decided that the nurse's rights had not been violated by the supervisor's English-only order. However, he also ruled that the hospital had illegally disciplined the nurse because she filed the suit to protest the ban on Tagalog. According to the judge, the nurse should not have been penalized for exercising her legal right to challenge the rule. He ordered the hospital to reinstate the nurse to her former position and to eliminate the unfavorable performance evaluations from her personnel records.

The courts have upheld English-only policies in other cases in which each policy was narrowly defined: Each policy (1) applied only to employees who could comply (who could speak English), (2) specified definite times when English was required, (3) was based on valid business necessity, and (4) was clearly explained to employees, along with the consequences of violating it.

However, as the U.S. population becomes more diverse, firms may find themselves looking at bilingual employees not as a problem but as a competitive advantage. Pacific Bell, for example, knows that its California customers hail from many lands. So the company invites customers to discuss service problems in English, Spanish, Chinese, Korean, or Vietnamese. Now that's intercultural communication.

1. How might a company with headquarters in Italy and a facility in Tucson, Arizona, respond to Arizona's designation of English as the official language?
2. If your multinational company insisted that English be used in all internal memos, regardless of the sender's or receiver's native language, what communication problems could you foresee?

Dealing with Ethnocentric Reactions

Although language and cultural differences are significant barriers to communication, these problems can be overcome by maintaining an open mind. Unfortunately, many of us lapse into **ethnocentrism,** the tendency to judge all other groups according to our own group's standards, behaviors, and customs. When we make such comparisons, we too often decide that our group is superior.[41]

By reacting ethnocentrically, you ignore the distinctions between your own culture and another person's culture. You assume that others will act the same way you do, that they will operate from the same assumptions, and that they will use language and symbols the same way you do. If they do not, you may mistakenly believe that they are in error, that their way is invalid, or that it's inferior to your own. An ethnocentric reaction makes you lose sight of the possibility that your words and actions will be misunderstood. It also makes you more likely to misinterpret or belittle the behavior of others.

Ethnocentric people are often prone to **stereotyping,** attempting to predict individuals' behavior or character on the basis of their membership in a particular group or class. When someone first starts to investigate the culture of another group, he or she may stereotype characteristics as a way of understanding the common tendencies of that group's members, but the next step is to move beyond the stereotypes to relationships with real people. Unfortunately, when ethnocentric people stereotype an entire group of people, they do so on the basis of limited, general, or inaccurate evidence, and

Ethnocentrism is the tendency to judge all other groups according to your own group's standards, behaviors, and customs and to see other groups as inferior by comparison.

Stereotyping is the attempt to categorize individuals by trying to predict their behavior or character on the basis of their membership in a particular group.

they frequently develop biased attitudes toward the group.[42] They fail to communicate with individuals as they really are. Instead of talking with Abdul Karhum, unique human being, ethnocentric people think only about talking to an Arab. Although they've never met an Arab, they may already believe that all Arabs are, say, hagglers. Abdul Karhum's personal qualities become insignificant in the face of such preconceptions. Everything he says and does will be forced to fit the preconceived image, even if it's wrong.

Often both parties in an intercultural exchange are guilty of ethnocentrism, stereotyping, and prejudice. Little wonder, then, that misunderstandings arise. Fortunately, a healthy dose of open-mindedness can prevent a lot of problems.

TIPS FOR COMMUNICATING WITH PEOPLE FROM OTHER CULTURES

You may never completely overcome linguistic and cultural barriers or ethnocentric tendencies, but you can communicate more effectively with people from other cultures if you work at it. Once you've acknowledged that cultural differences exist, the next step is to learn as much as possible about those cultures in which you plan to do business. You can also develop general skills for dealing with cultural diversity in your own and in other countries. If you'll be negotiating across cultures, it's important to learn how to conduct yourself and what to expect. Finally, you'll want to consider how to handle both written and oral communication with people from other cultures.

Learning About a Culture

Learning as much as possible about another culture will enhance your ability to communicate with its members.

When you're preparing to do business with people from a particular culture, you'll find that you can communicate more effectively if you study that culture in advance. Before Procter & Gamble advertises a new product in another culture, company researchers thoroughly investigate what people want and need. That way, P&G marketers can shape the advertising message to the language and customs of the particular culture.

If you're planning to live in another country or to do business there repeatedly, you might want to learn the language. The same holds true if you'll be working closely with a subculture that has its own language, such as Vietnamese Americans. Even if you're doing business in your own language, you show respect by making the effort to learn the subculture's language. In addition, you'll learn something about the culture and the customs of its people. If you don't have the time or the opportunity to learn a new language, at least learn a few words.

Read books and articles about the culture and talk to people who have done business with that culture's members. Concentrate on learning something about the culture's history, religion, politics, values, and customs. Find out about a country's subcultures, especially its business subculture, and any special rules or protocol. Here is a brief sampling of intercultural communication tips from seasoned business travelers:

- In Spain let a handshake last five to seven strokes; pulling away too soon may be interpreted as rejection. In France, however, the preferred handshake is a single stroke.
- Don't give a gift of liquor in Arab countries.
- In Pakistan don't be surprised when businesspeople excuse themselves in the middle of a meeting to conduct prayers. Muslims pray five times a day.
- Allow plenty of time to get to know the people you're dealing with in Africa; they're suspicious of people in a hurry.

- You'll insult your hosts if you turn down food, drink, or hospitality of any kind in Arab countries. But don't accept too quickly, either. A polite refusal (such as "I don't want to put you to any trouble") is expected before you finally accept.
- Stress the longevity of your company when dealing with German, Dutch, and Swiss firms.

These are just a few examples of the variations in customs that make intercultural business so interesting. This chapter's Checklist for Doing Business Abroad (see pages 72–73) can help you start your investigation of another culture by examining its social customs, concepts of time, clothing and food, political patterns, work-force diversity, religion and folk beliefs, economic and business institutions, ethics, values, and laws.

Developing Intercultural Communication Skills

Learning all you can about a particular culture is a good way to figure out how to send and receive intercultural messages more effectively. However, remember two important points: First, don't expect ever to understand another culture completely. No matter how much you study German culture, for example, you'll never be a German or share the experiences of having grown up in Germany. Second, don't fall into the overgeneralization trap; don't look at people as stereotypical "Italians" or "African Americans" and then never move beyond that view. The trick is to learn useful general information and, at the same time, to be aware of and open to variations and individual differences.

This is especially important if you interact with people from a variety of cultures or subcultures. You may not have the time or interest to learn a lot about every culture, but you can communicate more effectively if you develop general skills that help you adapt in any culture:[43]

> Learning general intercultural communication skills will help you adapt in any culture, which is important if you interact with people from a variety of cultures or subcultures.

- ***Take responsibility for communication.*** Don't assume it's the other person's job to communicate with you.
- ***Withhold judgment.*** Learn to listen to the whole story and accept differences in others without judging them.
- ***Show respect.*** Learn how respect is communicated—through gestures, eye contact, and so on—in various cultures.
- ***Empathize.*** Imagine the other person's feelings and point of view; consider what he or she is trying to communicate and why.
- ***Tolerate ambiguity.*** Learn to control your frustration when placed in an unfamiliar or confusing situation.
- ***Look beyond the superficial.*** Don't be distracted by such things as dress, appearance, or environmental discomforts.
- ***Be patient and persistent.*** If you want to communicate with someone from another culture, don't give up easily.
- ***Recognize your own cultural biases.*** Learn to identify when your assumptions are different from the other person's.
- ***Be flexible.*** Be prepared to change your habits and attitudes when communicating with someone from another culture.
- ***Emphasize common ground.*** Look for similarities to work from.
- ***Send clear messages.*** Make both your verbal and nonverbal signals clear and consistent.
- ***Increase your cultural sensitivity.*** Learn about variations in customs and practices so that you'll be more aware of potential areas for miscommunication.

CHECKLIST FOR DOING BUSINESS ABROAD

A. SOCIAL CUSTOMS

1. How do people react to strangers? Are they friendly? Hostile? Reserved?
2. What words and gestures do people use to greet each other?
3. What are the appropriate manners when you enter and leave a room? Should you bow? Nod? Shake hands?
4. How are names used for introductions? How are introductions handled (by age, gender, authority)?
5. What are the attitudes toward touching people?
6. How do you express appreciation for an invitation to lunch or dinner or to someone's home? Should you bring a gift? Send flowers? Write a thank-you note?
7. Does custom dictate how, when, or where people are expected to sit in social or business situations?
8. Are any phrases, facial expressions, or hand gestures considered rude?
9. How close do people stand when talking?
10. How do you attract the attention of a waiter in a restaurant? Do you tip the waiter?
11. When is it rude to refuse an invitation? How do you politely refuse?
12. What are the acceptable eye contact patterns?
13. What gestures indicate agreement? Disagreement? Respect?
14. What topics may be discussed in a social setting? In a business setting? What topics are unacceptable?

B. CONCEPTS OF TIME

1. How is time expressed?
2. What are the generally accepted working hours?
3. How do businesspeople view scheduled appointments?
4. How do people react to time in social situations?

C. CLOTHING AND FOOD

1. What occasions require special clothing? What colors are associated with mourning? Love? Joy?
2. Are some types of clothing considered taboo for one sex or the other?
   a. What is appropriate business attire for men?
   b. What is appropriate business attire for women?
3. What are the attitudes toward human body odors? Are deodorants/perfumes used?
4. How many times a day do people eat? How are hands or utensils used when eating?
5. What types of places, food, and drink are appropriate for business entertainment? Where is the seat of honor at a table?

D. POLITICAL PATTERNS

1. How stable is the political situation? How does this affect business inside and outside the country?
2. How is political power manifested? Military power? Economic strength?
3. What are the traditional institutions of government?
4. What channels are used for expressing political opinion?
   a. What channels are used to express official governmental positions?
   b. What channels are used to express unofficial governmental positions?
5. What media of information are important? Who controls them?

- ***Deal with the individual.*** Communicate with each person as an individual, not as a stereotypical representative of another group.
- ***Learn when to be direct.*** Investigate each culture so that you know when to send your message in a straightforward manner and when to be indirect.

These skills will help you communicate with anybody, regardless of culture. For more ideas on how to improve communication in the workplace, see this chapter's Checklist for Communicating with a Culturally Diverse Work Force (see pages 74–75).

Negotiating Across Cultures

Whether you're trying to make a sale, buy a business, or rent an office, negotiating with people from other cultures can test your communication skills. More U.S. companies than

6. In social or business situations, is it appropriate to talk politics?

E. **WORK-FORCE DIVERSITY**
1. Is the society homogeneous?
2. What minority groups are represented?
3. What languages are spoken?
4. How diverse is the work force?
5. What are the current and projected immigration patterns? How do these trends influence the composition of the work force?

F. **RELIGION AND FOLK BELIEFS**
1. To which religious groups do people belong? Is one predominant?
2. How do religious beliefs influence daily activities?
3. Which places have sacred value? Which objects? Which events?
4. Is there a tolerance for minority religions?
5. How do religious holidays affect business and government activities?
6. Does religion affect attitudes toward smoking? Drinking? Gambling?
7. Does religion require or prohibit eating specific foods? At specific times?
8. Which objects or actions portend good luck? Bad luck?

G. **ECONOMIC AND BUSINESS INSTITUTIONS**
1. What are the primary resources and principal products?
2. What kinds of vocational and technological training are offered?
3. What are the attitudes toward education?
   a. Do most businesspersons have a college degree?
   b. Are women educated as well as men?

4. Are businesses generally of one type?
   a. Are they large public corporations?
   b. Are they government owned or controlled?
   c. Are they family businesses?
5. Is it appropriate to do business by telephone?
6. Do managers make business decisions unilaterally or do they involve employees?
7. Are there any customs related to exchanging business cards?
8. How are status and seniority shown in an organization? In a business meeting?
9. Are businesspeople expected to socialize before conducting business?

H. **ETHICS, VALUES, AND LAWS**
1. Is money or a gift expected in exchange for arranging business transactions? What are the legal, ethical, and business consequences of giving what's expected? Of not giving?
2. What ethical issues might affect business transactions?
3. What legal issues might affect business transactions?
4. Is competitiveness or cooperation of greater importance?
5. What are the attitudes toward work? Toward money?
6. Is politeness more important than factual honesty?
7. How is a *friend* defined? What are the responsibilities of a friend?
8. What virtues are admired in a business associate? In a friend?

- -

ever are trying to form alliances with foreign companies, and more than half of these partnerships fail.[44] First, you may find that your approach to negotiation differs from the approach of the people you're negotiating with. For example, negotiators from the United States tend to take a relatively impersonal view of negotiations. They see their goals in economic terms and usually presume trust of the other party, at least at the outset.

In contrast, Chinese and Japanese negotiators prefer a more sociable negotiating atmosphere. They try to forge personal ties as the basis for building trust throughout the negotiating process. In their view, any immediate economic gains are less important than establishing and maintaining a long-term relationship. Unlike U.S., Chinese, and Japanese negotiators, French negotiators are likely to be somewhat less personal. They may favor an atmosphere of formal hospitality and start by distrusting the other party.[45]

People from other cultures often have different approaches to negotiation and may vary in their tolerance for open disagreement.

CHECKLIST FOR COMMUNICATING WITH A CULTURALLY DIVERSE WORK FORCE

A. ACCEPTING CULTURAL DIFFERENCES

1. Adjust the level of communication to the education level of your employees.
2. Encourage employees to openly discuss their culture's customs so that differences won't seem strange or inexplicable.
3. Create a formal forum for all employees to become familiar with the specific beliefs and practices of the cultures represented in the company work force.
4. Provide training to help employees recognize and overcome ethnocentric reactions and stereotyping.
5. Make available books, articles, and videotapes about various cultures so that interested employees can learn more.
6. Help stamp out negative or stereotyped labels by paying attention to how people identify their own groups.

B. HANDLING ORAL AND WRITTEN COMMUNICATIONS

1. Define and explain key terms that people will need to know on the job.
2. Repeat and recap information frequently to emphasize important points.
3. Use familiar words wherever possible.
4. Don't cover too much information at one time.
5. Be specific and explicit, using descriptive words, exact measurements, and examples where possible.
6. Give the reason for asking employees to follow a certain procedure and explain what happens if the procedure is not followed.
7. Use written summaries and visual aids (when appropriate) to clarify your points.
   a. Give employees written information they can take away to go over later.
   b. Use pictures that show actions (especially when explaining safety procedures).
   c. Use international symbols (such as Ø), which are understood cross-culturally.
   d. Augment written material with video presentations to make the material come alive.
8. Demonstrate and encourage the right way to complete a task, use a tool, and so on.
9. Reduce barriers caused by language differences.

Second, cultures differ in their tolerance for open disagreement. Although U.S. negotiators typically enjoy confrontational, debate-oriented negotiation, Japanese negotiators shun such tactics. To avoid the unpleasant feelings that might result from open conflict, Japanese companies use a go-between or a third person to assist in the negotiation. Chinese negotiators also try to prevent public conflict. They make concessions slowly and stay away from proposal-counterproposal methods. If you try to get a Chinese negotiating team to back down from a position they have taken, you will cause them to lose face—and you will very likely lose the deal.

In addition, negotiators from other cultures may use different problem-solving techniques, protocol, schedules, and decision-making methods. If you learn about your counterparts' culture before you start to negotiate, you'll be better equipped to understand their viewpoints. Moreover, showing flexibility, courtesy, patience, and a friendly attitude will go a long way toward finding a solution that works for both sides.

Handling Written Communication

Unless you are personally fluent in the language of your intended audience, you will ordinarily write in your own language and, if needed, have your letters or other written materials translated by a professional translator. Be especially concerned with clarity:

a. Offer managers training in the language of the employees they supervise.

b. Offer employees training in the language that most people in the company (and customers) use.

c. Ask bilingual employees and managers to serve as translators when needed, but rotate this assignment to avoid resentment.

d. Recruit bilingual employees and managers or have trained translators available to give the organization more flexibility in dealing with linguistic differences.

e. Print important health and safety instructions in as many languages as needed to enable all employees to understand.

C. **ASSESSING HOW WELL YOU'VE BEEN UNDERSTOOD**

1. Be alert to facial expressions and other nonverbal signs that indicate confusion or embarrassment.

2. Encourage employees to ask questions in private and in writing.

3. Observe how employees use the information you've provided to do their jobs, and review any points that may have been misunderstood.

4. Research the nonverbal reactions of other cultures so that you're prepared to spot the more subtle signs of misunderstanding.

D. **OFFERING FEEDBACK TO IMPROVE COMMUNICATION**

1. Focus on the positive by explaining what *should* be done rather than on the negative by discussing what *shouldn't* be done.

2. Offer feedback in terms of the person's behaviors and the situation, rather than a judgment about the person.

3. Be supportive as you offer feedback, and reassure individuals that their skills and contributions are important.

- Use short, precise words that say exactly what you mean.
- Rely on specific terms and concrete examples to explain your points.
- Stay away from slang, idioms, jargon, and buzz words. Abbreviations, acronyms (such as CAD/CAM), and unfamiliar product names may also lead to confusion.
- Construct sentences that are shorter and simpler than those you might use when writing to someone fluent in your own language.
- Use short paragraphs. Each paragraph should stick to one topic and be no more than eight to ten lines.
- Help readers follow your train of thought by using transitional phrases. Precede related points with expressions like *in addition* and *first, second, third*.

Your word choice should also reflect the relationship between you and your audience. In general, U.S. businesspeople will want to be somewhat more formal than they would be when writing to people in their own country. In many cultures, people use a more elaborate style, so your audience will expect more formal language in your letter. Consider the letter in Figure 3.2 (see pages 76–77). This letter might sound stilted to a U.S. reader, but it is typical of business letters in many other countries. In Germany, business letters usually open with a reference to the business relationship and close with a compliment to the recipient. Of course, be careful not to carry formality to extremes, or you'll sound unnatural.

International business letters generally have a formal tone and a relatively elaborate style.

Figure 3.2
In-Depth Critique:
German Business Letter,
with Translation

This letter was written by a supplier in Germany to a nearby retailer. The tone is more formal than would be used in the United States, but the writer clearly focuses on his audience.

Furtwangen Handcrafts
Kussenhofstrasse 150
Furtwangen, Germany

**Herrn
Karl Wieland
Geschäftsführer
Schwarzwald-Geschenke
Friedrichstraße 98**

**70174 Stuttgart
GERMANY**

15. Mai 1997

Sehr geehrter Herr Wieland,

Da die Touristensaison bald beginnt, möchten wir die Gelegenheit ergreifen, Ihnen unsere neue Reihe handgeschnitzter Kuckucksuhren vorzustellen. Im letzten Jahr waren Sie so freundlich, zwei Dutzend unserer Uhren zu kaufen. In Anerkennung unserer guten Geschäftsbeziehugen bieten wir Ihnen nunmehr die Möglichkeit, die neuen Modelle auszuwählen, bevor wir diese Reihe anderen Geschäften zum Kauf anbieten.

Wie Sie wissen, verwenden unsere Kunsthandwerker nur das beste Holz. Nach altbewährten Mustern, die von Generation zu Generation weitergereicht werden, schnitzen sie sorgfältig jedes Detail von Hand. Unsere Uhrwerke sind von hervorragender Qualität, und wir testen jede Uhr, bevor sie bemalt und versandt wird. Auf alle Furtwangener Kunsthandwerk-Uhren geben wir eine Garantie von 5 Jahren.

Beiliegend erhalten Sie eine Ausgabe unserer neuesten Broschüre und ein Bestellformular. Um unserer Wertschätzung Ausdruck zu verleihen, übernehmen wir die Versandkosten, wenn Sie vor dem 15, Juni bestellen.

Wir wünschen Ihnen weiterhin viel Erfolg in Ihrer neuen Stuttgarter Niederlassung. Wir sind davon überzeugt, daß Sie mit Ihrer größeren Ausstellungsfläche und erweitertem Angebot Ihre Stammkunden zufriedenstellen werden und viele neue Besucher gewinnen werden.

Mit freundlichen Grüßen

Frederick Semper

Frederick Semper

Figure 3.2
(Continued)

**Mister
Karl Wieland
Business Leader
Black Forest Gifts
Friedrichstrasse 98**

**70174 Stuttgart
GERMANY**

May 15, 1997

Very honorable Mister Wieland,

As the tourist season will begin soon, we would like to seize the opportunity to introduce our new line of hand-carved cuckoo clocks to you. Last year you were so friendly as to buy two dozen of our clocks. In recognition of our good business relationship, we now offer you the opportunity to select the new models before we offer this line to other businesses for purchase.

As you know, our artisans only use the best wood. According to time-honored patterns which are passed on from generation to generation, they carefully carve every detail by hand. Our clock-works are of superior quality, and we test every clock before it is painted and shipped. We give you a guarantee of five years on all Furtwangen Handcrafts clocks.

Enclosed you receive a copy of our newest brochure and an order form. To express our appreciation, we take over the shipping costs if you order before June 15.

We continue to wish you a lot of success in your new Stuttgart location. We are convinced that you will satisfy your regular clientele with your larger exhibition area and expanded stock and will gain many new visitors.

With friendly greetings

Frederick Semper

**Frederick Semper
Sales Leader**

The addressee's title, *Geschäftsführer,* literally means "business leader": A common English translation would be "managing director."

By offering the retailer an early selection of products, a five-year guarantee, and free shipping costs for an early order, Herr Semper shows his concern for his audience.

The closing compliment is typical of German business letters.

Also note that in German business letters, the sender's title is not included under the typed name on the closing block.

Letter writers in other countries also use various techniques to organize their thoughts. If you are aware of some of these practices, you'll be able to concentrate on the message without passing judgment on the writers. Letters from Japanese businesspeople, for example, are slow to come to the point. They typically begin with a remark about the season or weather. This is followed by an inquiry about your health or congratulations on your success. A note of thanks for your patronage might come next. After these preliminaries, the main idea is introduced (see Figure 3.3 on pages 78–79).

Figure 3.3
In-Depth Critique:
Japanese Business Letter,
with Translation

This is a letter written by a Japanese banker to a large business customer. Traditional Japanese is written vertically. Since this is a business letter, the words are written horizontally.

Sakura International Trade Bank Company, Ltd.
Marunouchi 1-5-32
Chiyoda-ku, Tokyo, Japan

Tel: (0565) 28-2121
Telex: 4537854 Sakura I
Cable: Sakura Tokyo

東京都千代田区丸の内1-5-32
さくら国際商業銀行

電話 (03) 5628-2121 大代表
テレックス 4537854 Sakura I
外電略号 Sakura Tokyo

拝啓

　秋もますます深まってきましたが、御社にはますますご繁栄のこととお喜び申し上げます。平素は格別のお引き立てにあずかり厚く御礼申し上げます。
　さて、貴社の信用限度額を5億円に設定することに決定致しましたので、お知らせ申し上げます。今回の新信用限度額設定により、貴社がさらなるご発展を遂げられるよう心よりお祈り申し上げます。さらに信用限度額の増額が必要とされます場合には、後日改めて検討させていただく所存でございますので、ご連絡下さい。
　以上、取り急ぎ、信用限度額設定の旨、お知らせ申し上げます。当行では貴社のあらゆる銀行業務に対応すべく努力する所存でございますので、今後とも倍旧のご厚配を賜わりたくお願い申し上げます。　　敬具

　1997年10月10日

　　　　　　　　　　　　副頭取　　篭田知明

王子リース株式会社経理課課長
　　　山本実様

Figure 3.3
(Continued)

Dear Sir:

With the season of fall upon us, let us congratulate your company on its growing prosperity. We are very grateful for your continued patronage.

It is a great pleasure to notify you that we decided to set your line of credit at five hundred million yen. We wish that this new line of credit will contribute to the further development of your business. If you find that you require additional credit, we would be willing to consider the details at a later date.

With this brief letter, I have quickly notified you of the arrangement of the new line of credit. We most humbly assure you of our every effort to satisfy all your banking needs, so we solicit your further patronage.

Sincerely,

October 10, 1997

Vice President
Tomoaki Kagota

The addressee's name and address do not appear above the salutation. This information appears on the envelope only.

Before getting to the point of the letter, the first paragraph mentions the season, congratulates the reader, and thanks the reader for his patronage.

The tone is not only more formal than U.S. businesspeople are accustomed to, but it is also exceedingly polite.

The date is part of the closing block, instead of coming at the top of the letter.

Handling Oral Communication

In many respects, speaking with people from other cultures is more complicated than writing to them, but it can also be more rewarding, from both a business and a personal standpoint. Some transactions simply cannot be handled without face-to-face contact. In many countries, business relationships are based on personal relationships, and until you establish rapport, nothing happens. In addition, personal contact gives you the benefit of immediate feedback so that you can clarify your own message as well as the other person's. As a consequence, executives in charge of international operations often have a hectic travel schedule. When Procter & Gamble's CEO was head of the international division, he spent nearly 70 percent of his time meeting with managers and high-level contacts in other countries.[46]

When using oral communication, be alert to the possibilities for misunderstanding. Recognize that you may inadvertently be sending conflicting signals or that you may be misreading the other person's cues. To help overcome language and cultural barriers, follow these suggestions:

Face-to-face communication lets you establish a personal relationship with people from other cultures and gives you the benefit of immediate feedback.

- Try to be aware of unintentional meanings that may be read into your message. Clarify your true intent with repetition and examples.
- Listen carefully and patiently. If you do not understand a comment, ask the person to repeat it.

- Recognize that gestures and expressions mean different things in different cultures. If the other person's body language seems at odds with the message, take time to clarify the meaning.
- Adapt your conversation style to the other person's. If the other person appears to be direct and straightforward, follow suit. If not, adjust your style to match.
- At the end of a conversation, be sure that you and the other person agree on what has been said and decided. Clarify what will happen next.
- If appropriate, follow up by writing a letter or memo summarizing the conversation and thanking the person for meeting with you.

In short, take advantage of the other person's presence to make sure that your message is getting across and that you understand his or her message too.

SUMMARY

In your capacity as a business communicator, you will have opportunities for dealing with people from other cultures. You may need to travel to another country, or you may do business with people from other cultures who are traveling or living in yours. Moreover, you may work for a foreign-owned firm or you may work with colleagues who have cultural backgrounds distinctly different from your own. In short, the growing importance of international business and the increasing diversity of the domestic work force in many countries make it essential for businesspeople to develop intercultural communication skills.

The barriers to intercultural communication include cultural differences, language problems, and ethnocentric reactions. Cultural differences and ethnocentric reactions pose the biggest problems because they frequently occur on a subconscious level and evoke an emotional response.

Learning as much as possible about the culture and language of another group will help you improve your intercultural communication. You can also overcome cultural barriers by developing general communication skills and avoiding negative value judgments. In addition, you will want to adjust the style of your written and spoken messages to accommodate the other person's customs and expectations.

COMMUNICATION CHALLENGES AT PROCTER & GAMBLE

As P&G's international operations have contributed a growing share of corporate sales and profits, Michael Copeland's job has become increasingly demanding. These days, more than 50 percent of P&G's sales revenues comes from its international businesses. What's more, 59 percent of P&G's worldwide roster of employees work outside the United States.

INDIVIDUAL CHALLENGE: Copeland has hired you to assist with the Brazilian project. Because his proposal to the Brazilian subsidiary was direct and impersonal, he wants to add a letter, addressed to the human resources manager, to express his personal enthusiasm for the training program. He has delegated the job to you.

"You have a real knack for making things sound warm and sincere," says Copeland. "Can you take a crack at drafting a letter to Carlos for me? Tell him how much I enjoyed seeing him again. Compliment him on the job he's doing in Brazil. Summarize the benefits of the program. Keep the letter short—just a couple of paragraphs."

TEAM CHALLENGE: You and several outside training consultants have been sent to Brazil to conduct the first phase of the training program. During an early session, when the participants begin discussing their cultural differences, you can see that people are becoming polarized in a "my culture is better than your culture" debate.

How can you and your fellow trainers reduce the tension and transform the discussion into a positive exchange that will help resolve rather than intensify the cultural differences dividing the members of the Brazilian management team?[47]

CRITICAL THINKING QUESTIONS

1. Your office in Turkey desperately needs the supplies that have been sitting in Turkish customs for a month. Should you bribe a customs official to speed up delivery? Explain.

2. What actions might you take to minimize the potential problems of differing concepts of time between your office in New York and your office in Venezuela?

3. A Canadian retail chain is opening a new store in Tijuana, Mexico (a border city south of San Diego, California). What cultural differences might this retailer's managers encounter when they start to hire and train local employees?

4. Your company has relocated to a U.S. city where a Vietnamese subculture is strongly established. Many of your employees will be from this subculture. What can you do to improve communication between your management and the Vietnamese Americans you are currently hiring?

5. What are some of the intercultural communication issues to consider when deciding whether to accept an overseas job with a firm that's based in your own country? A job in your own country with a local branch of a foreign-owned firm? Explain.

6. How do you think company managers from a country that has a relatively homogeneous culture might react when they have to do business with the culturally diverse staff of a company in a less homogeneous country? Explain your answer.

EXERCISES

1. You represent a Canadian toy company that's negotiating to buy miniature truck wheels from a manufacturer in Osaka, Japan. In your first meeting, you explain that your company expects to control the design of the wheels as well as the materials that are used to make the wheels. The manufacturer's representative looks down and says softly, "Perhaps that will be difficult." You press for agreement, and to emphasize your willingness to buy, you show the prepared contract you've brought with you. However, the manufacturer seems increasingly vague and uninterested. What cultural differences may be interfering with effective communication in this situation? Explain.

2. A U.S. manager wants to export T-shirts to a West African country, but a West African official expects a special payment before allowing the shipment into his country. How can the two sides resolve their different approaches without violating U.S. rules against bribing foreign officials? Team up with a classmate to role-play a meeting in which the U.S. manager tries to convince the West African official to authorize the shipment. Then discuss how the two parties handled their cultural differences.

3. Some executives believe the Foreign Corrupt Practices Act puts U.S. firms at a disadvantage. They point out that non-U.S. firms are allowed to make payments that are often part of the normal process of winning lucrative government contracts in other countries. Does this law hurt U.S. competitiveness overseas? Write a paragraph arguing for or against imposing this standard on U.S. firms, regardless of where in the world they do business.

4. You've been assigned to host a group of Swedish college students who are visiting your college for the next two weeks. They've all studied English and speak the language well. What can you tell them that will help them fit into the culture on your campus? Make a brief list of the important formal and informal behavioral rules they should understand to communicate effectively with students on your campus. Next to each item, note one problem that might occur if the Swedish visitors don't consider that rule when communicating.

5. Choose a specific country, such as India, Portugal, Bolivia, Thailand, or Nigeria—the less familiar you are with it, the better. Research the culture and write a brief summary of what a U.S. manager would need

to know about concepts of personal space and rules of social behavior to conduct business successfully in that country.

6. As the director of marketing for a telecommunications firm based in Germany, you're negotiating with an official in Guangzhou, China, who's in charge of selecting a new telephone system for the city. You insist that the specifications be spelled out in detail in the contract. However, your Chinese counterpart argues that in developing a long-term business relationship, such minor details are unimportant. What can you do or say to break this intercultural deadlock and obtain the contract without causing the official to lose face?

7. Although English is the international language of business, the English spoken in the United States differs from that spoken in Great Britain. By going to the library or interviewing someone who's lived in Great Britain, research five specific phrases that have different meanings in these two cultures. What problems would you have if you were unaware of the different meanings and misinterpreted these phrases during a business conversation?

8. Germany is a low-context culture; by comparison, France and England are more high-context. These three translations of the same message were posted on a lawn in Switzerland: The German sign read, "Walking on the grass is forbidden"; the English sign read, "Please do not walk on the grass"; and the French sign read, "Those who respect their environment will avoid walking on the grass."[48] How does the language of each sign reflect the way information is conveyed in the cultural context of each nation? Write a brief (two- to three-paragraph) explanation.

9. When a company knows that a scheduled delivery time given by an overseas firm is likely to be flexible, managers may buy in larger quantities or may order more often to avoid running out before the next delivery. Identify three other management decisions that may be influenced by differing cultural concepts of time, and make notes for a short (two-minute) presentation to your class.

10. Team up with two other students and list ten examples of slang (in your own language) that would probably be misinterpreted or misunderstood during a business conversation with someone from another culture. Next to each example, suggest other words you might use to convey the same message.

Do the alternatives mean *exactly* the same as the original slang or idiom?

11. Differences in gender, age, and physical abilities also contribute to the diversity of today's work force. Working with a classmate, role-play a conversation in which
    a. A woman is being interviewed for a job by a male human resources manager.
    b. An older person is being interviewed for a job by a younger human resources manager.
    c. A person using a wheelchair is being interviewed for a job by a person who can walk.
    How did differences between the applicant and the interviewer shape the communication? What can you do to improve communication in such situations?

12. Imagine that you're the lead negotiator for a company that's trying to buy a factory in Prague. Your parents grew up near Prague, so you understand and speak the language fairly well. However, you wonder about the advantages and disadvantages of using a translator anyway. For example, you may have more time to think if you wait for an intermediary to translate the other side's position. Decide whether or not to hire a translator, and then write a brief (two- or three-paragraph) explanation of your decision.

13. What communication problems would you face if you had to defend yourself in court in another country but didn't understand the language or the legal traditions? If you were assigned a translator, how might this additional person affect the communication process? Explain.

14. Suppose you transferred to a college in another country. How would you learn appropriate classroom behavior? Make a list of what you would need to know. For example, you might want to find out how to approach your instructors when you have questions. To get the answers to these questions, draft a letter to a college student in another nation.

15. Choose two countries from the following list: Argentina, Belgium, Canada, Egypt, Japan, Korea, Indonesia, Malaysia, Vietnam, Zaire. On the World Wide Web, read about three cultural or business aspects of each country, and then (in not more than 500 words) explain (1) why it's important to understand those aspects when communicating in your chosen country, (2) how computers and other electronic technology can help such intercultural com-

munication, and (3) how computers and other electronic technology can hinder such intercultural communication. To locate information on the World Wide Web, use Insane Search, a Web site that enables you to use 16 search engines simultaneously to locate Web sites that relate to your selections. You can find Insane Search at the following address: <http://www.cosmix.com/motherload/insane/>.

CHAPTER 4

COMMUNICATING THROUGH TECHNOLOGY

AFTER STUDYING THIS CHAPTER, YOU WILL BE ABLE TO

- Describe the technological tools now available for creating and distributing printed documents
- Discuss the internal and external databases used in business research
- Judge the benefits and limitations of spell checkers and grammar checkers
- Explore the communication role of electronic mail and Internet technologies in today's business organizations
- Describe the technologies available for group communication
- Assess the ways technology is changing business communication

COMMUNICATION CLOSE-UP AT HEWLETT-PACKARD

As a systems technology specialist at Hewlett-Packard in Colorado Springs, Mike Stevens spends a lot of his time looking at business processes to decide how they can be redesigned (or reengineered) for greater efficiency and effectiveness. That often means helping the company "reinvent the way it does business," explains Stevens. It also means using good communication skills to coordinate interaction with co-workers. The newest state-of-the-art technology helps Stevens do both.

For example, Stevens recently reengineered an aspect of his own job. Although Hewlett-Packard provides its employees with Netscape software to help them navigate the Internet, Stevens says he didn't spend much time "surfing the Net" until the day he needed to find out what kind of printer driver was available for a particular computer. "Our printer division is in Boise," he explains, and it might have taken hours on the phone just to find the person with the right information. Instead, he used his Netscape browser to access the Boise division's home page on the World Wide Web. This new technology helped Stevens quickly find the information he needed—and more. He was also able to download the actual printer driver software onto his computer in Colorado Springs. Many companies are already using the Internet in a similar fashion, to store and retrieve internal corporate information. Stevens believes that before long, businesses will be using the Internet much like mainframe computers were once used—as the software "brain" that processes and stores most of the company's computing.

Even though it's relatively easy for Stevens to find technological applications in his own job, he also helps others adapt to changes in the processes and technology they use, and that takes a team effort. It's a delicate situation: Some people enjoy change (particularly at a fast-moving company like Hewlett-Packard); others are reluctant to let go of methods that have been successful in the past, explains Stevens. So in order

Mike Stevens

Technology helps Hewlett-Packard employees communicate with speed and convenience. At the Colorado Springs division, HP employees understand that they need to adapt to evolving electronics and also that good writing and speaking skills are now more important than ever.

to communicate clearly and effectively with co-workers, it's important for Stevens and his team members to communicate well with each other. To do this, the team uses several high-tech tools.

Before re-engineering an HP process, the team's first task is to define it. How do you do that? "You write a document describing it," says Stevens. "Then once you've got your document, you want the rest of the team to review it, to add to it, to change it, to modify it, to get it right. So you mail it—you e-mail it." Using the latest e-mail and groupware programs, team members can work together on a document before it ever leaves their computers.

For instance, if two people are working together, one might insert new comments on the other's original document as they e-mail it back and forth until they agree on how something should be worded and print out the final copy. Or if the whole team is going to give feedback, the document can be sent to them via general-distribution e-mail. Each member can use a different color for comments, so when the team reaches a consensus, one key stroke eliminates the colors and incorporates everything into the finished product, which is then printed out. Another alternative is a state-of-the-art groupware program that allows individual team members to access the document directly, making any changes they wish. No matter which tool is chosen, team members can coordinate and work together seamlessly. Moreover, the document they're working on can be written, distributed, reviewed, revised, and completed without using so much as a scrap of paper.

Stevens says that technology of this type is having a major impact in the workplace. Many of the processes he re-engineers require a new way of thinking about work: Jobs that were once regarded as solitary endeavors are being "reinvented" as team efforts. Stevens and his team work together closely, and the technology they use makes such teamwork possible.

However, Stevens cautions that these rapid exchanges of information carry their own risks. Today's technology can foster a carelessness that business communicators can't afford. "The impression that you make on people is extremely important," he explains, and you can't depend on technology to supply what impresses them most:

your courtesy, intelligence, and common sense. Stevens says that good writing and speaking skills are in demand more than ever as new technology continues to help us do our jobs and communicate with each other.[1]

TECHNOLOGY IN CONTEMPORARY BUSINESS COMMUNICATION

As Hewlett-Packard and other companies try to compete in the global economy, they are always looking for better ways to communicate. Businesspeople such as HP's Mike Stevens must choose from an ever-expanding list of communication tools to remain competitive. You'll probably use most or all of the technologies discussed in this chapter, as well as some future innovations that we can only dream about right now. The better you understand the technological issues involved, the more effective you'll be as a communicator.

If a typewriter and a postage stamp were your only communication tools, you wouldn't have to spend much time thinking about how to create documents or send messages. However, when you have word processors, laser printers, satellite video links, electronic mail, notebook computers, personal communication devices, voice recognition systems, and dozens of other options, the choices you have to make as a communicator are more complicated. In business communication today, you not only have to think about what you're going to say and how you're going to say it—you also have to decide which technological tools you'll use to do so. No hard rules dictate which tool to use in each case (partly because the technology keeps changing), but here are some factors to consider:

- *Audience expectations.* What would you think if your college tried to deliver your diploma by fax? It would seem a little strange, wouldn't it? You expect the college to use a certain set of technologies (such as mail delivery or a phone-in system). Business audiences have similar expectations for various kinds of messages. Knowing what people expect is part of getting to know your audience.
- *Time and cost.* Time is often the biggest factor in your technology choice. You'd probably choose the phone to send an urgent message, for instance. Many of the technologies discussed in this chapter were designed specifically to help people communicate faster, but cost can be an issue as well, both how much you have to spend and how much is appropriate for the situation. Spending $500 to create a presentation for customers might be appropriate; however, spending that much to tell your colleagues when you'll be on vacation would be wasteful.
- *Nature of the message.* What you need to say in a document also affects your choice of technologies. For instance, business messages often require some sort of visual support (diagrams, photographs, or tables). A telephone call wouldn't be a good choice in such cases, but a printed report would be. If you need to convey emotion and excitement, delivering your message in person might be best. However, if you can't visit every member of your audience, sending your message on videotape might be a good substitute.
- *Presentation needs.* Sometimes the way you need to present your document will dictate which tools you use. If you're sending a report to an important client, you might want to stretch your budget to use typeset printing, color graphics, and professional binding. However, for short internal messages, you probably wouldn't want to spend the time or the money to present things so nicely.

Technology gives business communicators more options, but it also requires more decisions and more skills.

General guidelines for choosing communication technology include considering
- *Audience expectations*
- *Time and cost*
- *Nature of the message*
- *Presentation needs*
- *Work environment*

- *Work environment.* One of the most significant communication advances in recent years is the dramatically improved quality and availability of portable tools for creating, sending, and receiving messages. Millions of businesspeople spend some or all of their time outside traditional office settings, working from their cars, their homes, hotel rooms, and other locations. Well-equipped "road warriors" can now communicate with as much convenience and impact as their deskbound colleagues.

As you'll see throughout the rest of this chapter, some tools can create more than one type of message or document. Likewise, you may have two or three technological options when it comes to one particular message or document. The trick is to pick the tool that does the best overall job in each situation.

TECHNOLOGY IN WRITTEN COMMUNICATION

When preparing written documents, you can take advantage of technological developments at every step. You're probably familiar with some of these, but others are just now starting to appear. In business communication, a variety of tools can help you create both printed and electronic documents.

Creating Printed Documents

Whether you're writing a one-paragraph memo or a 500-page report, technology can help you create a more effective document with less time and effort. Some of these tools apply only to printed documents, but others can help you with electronic documents as well. **Word-processing software** is the dominant tool for creating printed documents, and it can do far more than you could ever attempt on a typewriter. For a text entry that involves two or more people developing a single document, you can use a category of software known as *groupware*. These systems keep track of revisions, let people attach electronic notes to each other's sections, enforce a common format for all sections, and take care of other issues that come up in any collaborative writing project (see Figure 4.1 on page 88). Groupware can include a variety of computing and communication tools to help people work together.[2]

> The most common means for creating printed documents is word-processing software.

In the same way that word-processing software was created to computerize typewriters, **desktop publishing (DTP)** software was created to computerize the process of assembling finished pages. If you wanted a first-class report with photos and drawings, the old way of doing things involved cutting strips of printed text and pasting them on a blank page along with the photos and drawings. DTP software does the same thing, only it all happens on your computer screen. Word processing and DTP are the core technologies for creating printed documents, and you can take advantage of a growing selection of specialized tools as well. The following sections present a brief overview of document creation to give you a better idea of how the various pieces of hardware and software can help you with planning, composing, revising, producing, distributing, and storing documents.

> Generally, the tool most appropriate for assembling finished pages with graphics elements is desktop publishing (DTP) software, although word-processing software can handle graphics to a limited extent.

Planning Documents

Some of the writing you'll do on the job requires very little planning. For a memo to your staff regarding the company picnic or a letter requesting information from a supplier, you can often collect a few facts and get right down to writing. In other cases, however, you won't be able to start writing until you've done extensive research. This

Figure 4.1
Groupware Helps
Businesspeople
Communicate

Netscape Composer helps the staff at *Byte* communicate about their stories. This conferencing groupware highlights hyperlinks both with underlining and color, making it easy for users to move around.

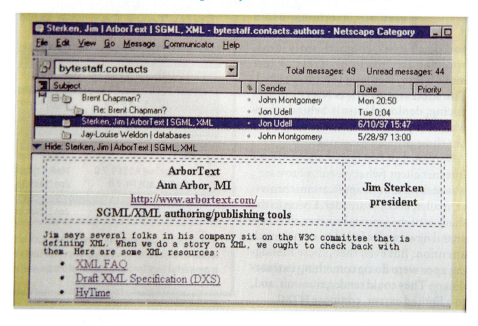

research often covers both the audience you'll be writing to and the subject matter you'll be writing about. Technology can help you with planning tasks, with research tasks, and with outlining your thoughts once you've done your research.

Managing Communication Projects

Some computer software can actually help you plan and manage communication projects. These tools fall into three general (sometimes overlapping) categories. First, *contact managers* help you maintain communication with a large number of people. They store information about the people you need to contact (names, addresses, product preferences, and so on) and help automate many tasks, such as generating follow-up letters after you've spoken with someone on the phone. Second, *personal information managers (PIMs)* help you manage all kinds of information, from to-do lists to document outlines to e-mail messages. PIMs are similar in some ways to contact managers, but they are generally much more powerful when it comes to managing, sorting, and storing information. Third, *project management software* helps you plan and coordinate the activities needed to complete projects, and it helps you communicate with others regarding project status (see Figure 4.2).

Researching Audience and Content

Sometimes the information you need for a document can be found inside your company, in its sales records, existing research reports, and other *internal sources.* Other times the information you need will be found outside the company by searching through books, magazines, and other *external sources.* Technology can help in both cases.

Much of your company's internal information may be stored in one or more **databases,** which are collections of facts ranging from financial figures to the text of reports. For information on sales trends, you might use a computer to search through your

---

Technology helps you manage communication with

- Contact managers
- Personal information managers
- Project management software

Research is often one of the most important steps in business communication, and technology provides several helpful tools, including

- Online databases, both private and public
- Statistical analysis software
- Text retrieval software
- CD-ROM information sources
- Web sites

Figure 4.2
Planning Tools

Act! organizes all the information you need about your contacts at other businesses. You can easily keep track of how to get in touch with a particular contact. You can even keep track of the names of assistants who might help you, the subject of upcoming meetings, and the tasks you need to do to prepare for those meetings.

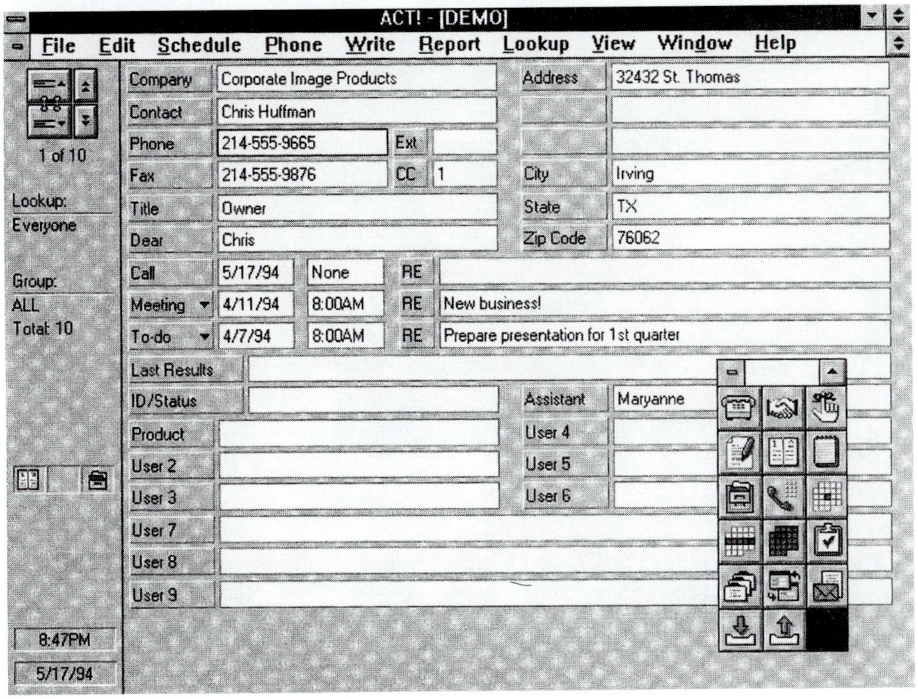

company's sales records. You can use *spreadsheets* or *statistical analysis* software to sort through numerical data and *text retrieval* software to sort through reports and other textual material (see Figure 4.3 on page 90).

The list of external sources of business information is long and getting longer all the time. If you need some recent forecasts on household income, you can tap into Econbase, a database of economic forecasts and projects. If you need to see whether Congress passed any tax laws in the last week that might affect your company, you can try accessing Tax Notes Today, which explains all recent government actions regarding federal and state taxes.[3] These and thousands of other databases, on topics ranging from accounting to zoology, are available to anyone with a properly equipped computer—although usually for a fee. (For more on data searches, see "Techniques for Finding Articles Online" on pages 92–93.) By using commercial online services or the Internet, you can access a huge number of databases and even the catalogs in many academic libraries around the world.

Another useful research tool is the **CD-ROM,** a type of compact disk that can be read by special computer equipment. An individual CD-ROM can contain either a single volume of information or collections of documents ranging from back files of newspapers to sets of books on a particular subject. For example, Microsoft Encarta is a multimedia encyclopedia that contains not only textual information but also animated drawings, short video clips, and audio tracks.[4]

Figure 4.3
Communicating with Numbers

Spreadsheets like Microsoft's Excel help you manage cumbersome information by keeping track of all the numbers, allowing you to select which particular numbers you want to look at or deal with, and converting those numbers to graphical representations.

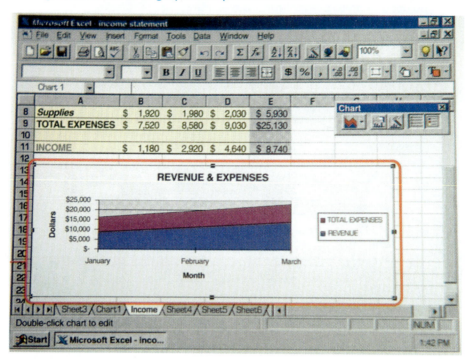

Outlining Content

Once you've collected the necessary information for your report, the next step is to outline how you want to present your ideas. You've probably outlined reports, possibly using note cards to arrange and sort the various sections. Computer-based outliners perform the same function, only without the need to fill out all those cards. Once you type in the titles of your sections, you can quickly move sections around, experimenting with order and organization. Computer outliners further boost your productivity by saving you from retyping the section titles once you've finished outlining. Most word-processing packages contain built-in outliners, although you might want to consider specialized outlining tools such as Inspiration. This tool lets you outline and organize ideas visually by moving and connecting blocks and arrows that represent a flow of ideas.[5]

Composing Documents

When you're ready to start writing, the computer once again demonstrates how it can enhance the communication process. Composing a document on your computer involves keyboarding, of course, but that's just the beginning. Technology offers a number of ways to get text into your document, and you're no longer limited to just text, either. The right software makes it relatively easy to add a wide variety of graphic elements to your document, and even audio notes if you have the right equipment.

Entering Text

Composing means sitting at the keyboard and typing. Word processors help make this as painless as possible, giving you the ability to erase and move text easily. The fact that you're on a computer, however, opens up some interesting possibilities for text entry.

To start with, if you don't know how to keyboard or don't like to, your worries may be over sooner than you think. *Pen-based computers* let you write with an electronic stylus on a special pad that converts your handwriting to text the computer can recognize. The most common uses of pen-based computers involve portable applications such as recording information in various parts of a large factory.

With some computers, you don't have to write or type at all. *Voice recognition systems* convert your voice to text, freeing you from keyboard or pen input. Such breakthroughs are particularly important for people with physical impairments, giving them the means to become more active communicators.

Some of the text that business communicators use in their documents is "prewritten," already appearing in other documents. Say that you want to announce to the media that you've developed a new product or hired an executive. Such announcements are called press releases, and they usually end with a standard paragraph about the company and its line of business. Any standard block of text used in various documents without changing it is called a *boilerplate*. With a good word processor, you don't have to retype the boilerplate each time you write a press release. You simply store the paragraph the first time you write it and then pop it into a document whenever you need it. Not only does this save time, it also reduces mistakes, since you're not retyping the paragraph every time you use it. A related concept applies to manipulating existing text. If you're a national sales manager compiling a report that includes summaries from your four regional managers, you can use your word processor's *file merge* capability to combine the four documents into one, saving yourself the trouble of retyping all four.

Using a boilerplate or file merge capability assumes that the text you want to include is in electronic format, saved on a computer disk. But sometimes you have only printed versions of the document. In such cases you can use a *scanner*, a device that essentially takes a picture of a printed document and converts it to an electronic format that your computer can handle. Scanners produce just a visual image of the document, though, and the process requires an additional step if you want to use the words from the document as normal input to your word processor. A technology called *optical character recognition (OCR)* lets your computer "read" the scanned image, picking out the letters and words that make up the text.

Scanning and OCR technologies raise the legal and ethical issues of plagiarism and image manipulation. Of course, people have had the ability to copy words and images for quite some time, but the new computer tools make it even easier. Now you can scan a photo you have on file, retouch it as you see fit, and then include it in your own document. It's also possible to make products and people look better than they really are and to depict situations or events that never actually happened. As technology continues to expand these options, business communicators will continue to face new and challenging ethical issues.

Adding Graphics and Sound to Documents

Computers can do some amazing things with text entry, but that's only part of the story. With the right equipment, you can add full-color pictures and even sound recordings to your documents. The software for creating business visuals falls into two basic groups: presentation software and graphics software. *Presentation software* helps you create overhead transparencies and other visuals for meetings, discussed later in the chapter.

Technology provides a number of options for entering text into a document:
- Keyboarding (typing)
- Pen-based computers
- Voice recognition systems
- Scanning and OCR

A boilerplate is any standard block of text used in various documents without changing it.

TECHNIQUES FOR FINDING ARTICLES ONLINE

Research tools have come a long way in the past several years, from indexes printed in books to powerful database gateways (such as Dialog) to Internet search engines that anyone with access can use. Both students and professionals have a wonderful resource in librarians who have the access and knowledge needed to use systems such as Dialog. However, you can perform a great deal of online research by yourself.

You might be familiar with popular Web tools such as Yahoo! and InfoSeek, which help you find information in Web sites and Usenet newsgroups on the Internet. You can reach a wide range of information sources with these tools, but you're likely to miss some of the most important research sources available, which are the thousands of articles published every year in newspapers, magazines, and academic journals. To find these sources, you need to use systems that can access the wide variety of databases that contain or index articles. Two such systems designed for students and other nonprofessional researchers are the Electric Library (a Web site) and Knowledge Index (a traditional database system that is actually a small part of the giant Dialog system used by librarians and other professionals).

The Electric Library has two key advantages: First, it searches through multiple types of sources, including not only articles but also book reviews, map collections, and other sources. Second, it sorts the items it finds and tries to present the most relevant items at the top of the list.

Knowledge Index, on the other hand, lets you set up very specific searches to quickly find the information you're looking for. Here's an example of a Knowledge Index search command on the subject of using computers in business training:

FIND comput? AND (train? OR learn?) AND py=1995:1997 NOT school?

Here's a breakdown of what this command does:

- The *?* attached to *comput* tells the system to find any word that starts with *comput*, including *computer, computers,* and *computing.* This way you don't have to worry about guessing the exact form of the word that may be used in an article. The same idea applies to *train?, learn?, school?,* and other such root words.

- The parentheses around *(train? OR learn?)* tell the system to do this part of the search first and to find any variation of *training* or *learning.* You use OR whenever more than one term might apply but you don't want to specify both terms.

- The two *AND* terms tell the system to find only those articles that contain all three terms connected by the *AND*s: (1) any variation of *computer,* AND (2) any variation of either *training* or *learning,* AND (3) articles published between 1995 and 1997 (*py* stands for *publication year*). An article has to match all three criteria before Knowledge Index will include it in your list.

- Finally, the *NOT school?* term tells the system to skip articles that contain any variation of the word *school,* since you're interested in business training. Using NOT can be risky, since it could, for example, exclude articles that are really about business training but that simply use the word "school" once or twice. On the other hand, NOT is a quick way to narrow down long lists of articles (it isn't unusual to locate several thousand articles on your first pass through a major database).

Graphics software can add a visual element to your message.

Graphics software ranges from products that can create simple diagrams and flowcharts to comprehensive tools designed for artists and graphic designers. You can create your pictures from scratch, use *clip art* (collections of simple images), or scan in drawings or photos. Much of the graphic design and artwork that you see in business publications was created with software packages such as CorelDRAW! and Freehand.

Inserting your visuals into a document used to be a chore, but increasing standardization of computer file formats has made the task somewhat easier. Say you want to distribute some ideas you have for a new corporate logo, and you want to include your sketches in a memo. You've already created several logos in CorelDRAW!, but your memo is in Microsoft Word. No problem—you simply save the CorelDRAW! file in a special transfer format, then switch to your memo in Microsoft Word, and activate a command to insert the picture. The logos pop into your memo, and you can shrink or enlarge them to fit.

The Electric Library allows visitors to search for information by posing questions in plain English.

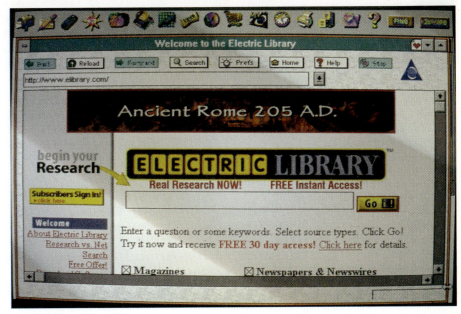

The ability to narrow down a search in this manner not only saves time (since you have fewer irrelevant articles to sort through) but also saves a significant amount of money, since these systems tend to charge by the hour or by the article.

With changes happening so fast on the Internet, it's likely that Web-based systems such as the Electric Library will continue to get more powerful and that traditional database systems such as Knowledge Index may move to some kind of Web ac-

cess. The good news is that students and business professionals can look forward to even better research tools.

1. Investigate the online research services offered at your college. Devise a question you would like researched, and use the service to conduct the information search.
2. What are the advantages and disadvantages of letting someone else do a database search for you?

Adding sound bites to your documents is an exciting new way to get your message across. Several systems now allow you to record a brief message or other sound and attach it to particular places in a document. Of course, to actually hear the sound, the person receiving the memo has to load the memo into his or her computer.

Revising Documents

When it's time to revise and polish your message, your word processor can help in a variety of ways, starting with the basics of adding, deleting, and moving text. *Cut and paste* is a term used in both word processing and desktop publishing to indicate cutting a block of text out of one section of a document and pasting it in somewhere else. The *search and replace function* helps you track down words or phrases and change them if you need to. This can be a great time saver in long documents if you need to change a word or phrase that appears in a number of places.

Spell checkers, grammar checkers, and computerized thesauruses can all help with the revision process, but they can't take the place of good writing and editing skills.

Beyond the basic revision tools, three advanced software functions can help bring out the best in your documents. A *spell checker* compares your document with an electronic dictionary stored on your disk drive, highlights words that it doesn't recognize, and suggests correct spelling. Spell checkers are a wonderful way to weed major typos out of your documents, but it's best not to use them as replacements for good spelling skills. If you use *their* when you mean to use *there,* your spell checker will fly right past the error, since *their* is in fact spelled correctly. If you're in a hurry and accidentally omit the *p* at the end of *top,* your spell checker will read *to* as correct. Or if you mistakenly type the semicolon instead of the *p,* your spell checker will read *to;* as a correctly spelled word.

A computer *thesaurus* gives you alternative words, just as your printed thesaurus does. Not only can a computer thesaurus give you answers faster and more easily than a printed thesaurus, but it may also be able to do things that your printed thesaurus could never do. The electronic version of the American Heritage dictionary provides a thesaurus and a special WordHunter function that gives you the term when all you know is part of the definition. If you're racking your brain to remember the word that means a certain quantity of paper, you simply type *quantity AND paper* and then WordHunter searches for every definition in the dictionary that includes those two terms. In a few seconds, the word *ream* pops into view, and you say, "Aha! That's the word I was looking for."

The third major revision tool is the *grammar checker,* which tries to do for your grammar what a spell checker does for your spelling. The catch here is that checking your spelling is much easier than checking your grammar. A spell checker simply compares each word in your document with a list of correctly spelled words. A grammar checker has to determine whether you're using words correctly and constructing sentences according to the complex rules of composition. Since the computer doesn't have a clue about what you're trying to say, determining whether you've said it correctly is monstrously difficult. Moreover, even if you've used all the rules correctly, a grammar checker still can't tell whether your document communicates clearly. However, grammar checkers can perform some helpful review tasks and point out things you should consider changing, such as passive voice, long sentences, and words that tend to be misused or overused.[6]

Producing Finished Documents

Consider the memo shown in Figure 4.4 on page 96. Many simple hardware and software packages are capable of producing documents like this one, combining text and graphics so that the appearance is both professional and inviting. It's important that you balance both graphics and text. The bar chart in this memo is centered to give a formal impression, and the color used in the graphic is balanced by the letterhead logo. The manner in which you package your ideas has a lot to do with how successful your communication will be. A document that looks tired and out of date will give that impression to your readers—even if your ideas are innovative. Today's computer software makes it easy for anyone to produce great looking documents in a hurry. Both word processors and desktop publishing software can help you in three ways:

Computer software can help you add a first-class look to your most important business documents.

- *Adding a first-class finish.* From selecting attractive typefaces to adding color graphics, you can use your computer tools to turn a plain piece of text into a dazzling and persuasive document. Used improperly, however, these same tools can turn your text into garish, high-tech rubbish. Knowing how to use the tools of technology is a key issue for today's business communicators.
- *Managing document style.* With so many design and formatting choices at your fingertips, it's important to maintain consistency throughout your document. *Style sheets* are collections of formatting rules available in high-end word processors

and DTP packages that can save a lot of formatting effort. Every time you need to add a section to your report, for instance, your style sheet can ensure that every section is formatted consistently (with the same typeface, margins, word spacing, etc.). You can also use style sheets to make sure that all the documents created by everyone in a department or even an entire company have a consistent look.

- ***Generating supporting elements.*** If you've ever written a report with footnotes or endnotes, an index, and a table of contents, you know how much work these supporting elements can be. Fortunately, computers can help keep track of your footnotes, renumbering them all every time you add or delete references. For indexes and tables of contents, you simply flag the terms you want to include, and the software assembles the lists for you. (For examples, see "Five Powerful Tools to Help You Create Quality Documents Quickly and Easily" on pages 98–99.)

High-end word-processing software can handle most aspects of final document production, but many communicators prefer to finish off their documents with desktop publishing instead. In addition to giving you more control over spacing, graphics, color, and other elements, DTP makes many layout and design tasks easier. When moving a column of text, for instance, with DTP you can grab it, move it wherever you want, and resize it along the way if you like.

Printing and Distributing Documents

With a thoroughly revised document, you're ready to print and distribute copies to your audience. *Printers* come in a variety of shapes, sizes, and capabilities, from low-cost portables that fit in your briefcase to high-resolution color units that can print photographs with startling accuracy. Many offices today are equipped with laser printers, which produce a printed image by drawing with a low-power laser beam. For results that look the very best, pages can be printed using a *typesetter* or an *imagesetter,* both of which are similar in concept to laser printers but which produce sharper images.

Laser and inkjet printers are popular ways of producing documents in business today.

Technology does some of its most amazing feats when it's time to distribute your documents. For multiple copies of your document, you can print as many as you like on your office printer or print a single copy and reproduce it with a *photocopier.* For high-volume and complex reproduction (involving colors or photographs, for instance), you'll want to take your document to a *print shop,* a company that has the special equipment needed for such jobs.

When you need to send the same document (sales letter, invoice, or other customer communication) to a large number of people, *mail merge* automatically combines a standard version of the document with a list of names and addresses. It will produce one copy for each person on your mailing list, saving you the trouble of inserting the name and address each time. The names and addresses can come from your own customer databases or from mailing lists you can rent from firms that specialize in collecting names and addresses.

Fax machines have had a major impact on the distribution of printed documents. Using regular telephone lines, you can transmit (fax) an exact reproduction (a facsimile) of a document from one machine to another. Fax machines are indispensable for international business, particularly since they overcome the delay problems of regular mail and the time-zone problems of trying to contact someone by telephone.[7] PCs can be equipped with *fax modems,* which combine data transmission with fax capabilities.

Fax machines (and computers equipped with fax modems) are an integral part of the business communication process, providing fast transmission of printed documents all over the world.

Many companies now distribute information on CD-ROM rather than on paper. For instance, several of HP's product catalogs are available either on CD-ROM or

Figure 4.4
In-Depth Critique: The
Importance of Appearance

An attractive, contemporary appearance can help you get your message across more effectively.

A colorful letterhead can add to a professional appearance.

Using a contemporary typeface can help your document appear lively, not tired.

Colorful graphics are great for drawing attention to important points.

Balancing graphics, text, and color creates a polished appearance that lends credibility to your message.

CaPlus

9408 Sepulveda Way • Los Angeles, California 97402 • (805) 555-4103

MEMO

DATE: April 14, 1997
TO: Alden Maxwell, Vice President, Marketing
FROM: Louise Ellison, Manager, Promotions
SUBJECT: Using sports as a selling tool for promoting our new calcium-plus soft drink

After doing a little research, I'm more convinced than ever that sponsoring a sporting event would be an excellent way to build awareness of our new calcium-plus soft drink.

The experiences of other companies show that sports sponsorship is an extremely cost-effective approach to promotion. For example, Volvo found that it can reach as many people by spending $3 million on tennis tournaments as it can by spending $25 million on media advertising.

If we decide to go forward with a sponsorship, our first priority should be to identify a sport that is popular with our target customers. As the chart below indicates, auto racing is currently the number-one sport among corporate sponsors, possibly because it appeals to both men and women:

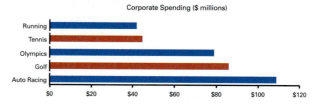

Corporate Spending ($ millions)

Over the next few days, I plan to do some more research to identify sporting events that would give us the most exposure among the health-conscious women who represent our primary market. I hope to pinpoint three or four possibilities and prepare some preliminary cost estimates for discussion at the Tuesday staff meeting.

in printed form. The cost of producing CD-ROMs is rapidly decreasing, and most personal computers now include CD-ROM drives. CD-ROMs hold a large amount of information, and their small size saves money in postage and shipping.

Creating Electronic Documents

A growing number of business documents are never put on paper; they're written on a computer and sent to other computers on the same network. A **network** is a group of computers that are connected so that they can share information. Networks vary greatly in size and nature. Small, private-office setups, sometimes called **local area networks (LANs),** connect computers in a single building or local area. **Wide area networks (WANs)** are a group of LANs, connecting computers in separate locations. Some internal networks also include software such as e-mail programs and search tools. Many LANs, WANs, or intranets also connect to larger outside networks. A **gateway** controls the passage of information between internal and external networks.

The world's largest network is the **Internet,** which is actually a network of networks.[8] Started in 1969 as a network within the U.S. Department of Defense, the Internet is now available to individuals, companies, colleges, and government agencies in countries all over the world. It is the fastest growing means of communication in the business world today. In 1985 some 1,961 computers were connected. By 1994 more than 3 million computers were connected, and in 1995 the number of connections grew about 10 percent a month.[9] Microsoft CEO Bill Gates says, "The Internet is the most important single development to come along since the IBM PC was introduced in 1981."[10]

The Internet is actually a network of networks.

You can access the Internet in one of two ways: through a commercial online service such as CompuServe, Prodigy, or America Online, or directly through a service provider. The commercial online services are actually networks in themselves. In addition to Internet connections, they provide databases, online shopping, games, and other services.[11] Service providers provide only a connection to the Internet. Some services charge a monthly fee and allow unlimited access; others charge for the amount of time you use. The best service for your company depends on how you plan to use the Internet.

Once you are connected to the Internet, you need additional software to actually do anything. The software may be provided by the online service or you may need to install it on your own computer. Here is some of the software that is available:

Some of the software available on the Internet includes
- *Electronic mail*
- *Telnet*
- *File transfer protocol*
- *Search engines*
- *World Wide Web*

- Electronic mail lets you send and receive mail via the Internet. There is more information on e-mail later in this chapter.
- **Telnet** lets you connect to a remote computer and run programs on that computer. (You must be authorized and have an account on the remote computer.)
- **File transfer protocol (FTP)** lets you copy files from a remote computer to your computer.
- Search engines (Yahoo!, Lycos, and Excite are among the most popular) help you locate information on other computers. Because the Internet is growing so fast, new search tools appear and existing ones become obsolete very quickly. You can find an annotated list of most of the currently available Internet search tools at <http://www.search.com> on the Web.
- The **World Wide Web,** or the **Web,** is a graphical approach to storing and accessing information on the Internet. There is more information on the Web later in this chapter.

SHARPENING YOUR SKILLS

FIVE POWERFUL TOOLS TO HELP YOU CREATE QUALITY DOCUMENTS QUICKLY AND EASILY

Word processors provide some handy tools for automating the layout and production of reports and other documents. These tools help ensure a consistent appearance and let you create polished documents with minimal time and effort. Here's a quick look at five useful features available in leading software packages:

Manuscript Page

26

{h1} Section 3: Employee Training

{h2} Overview
The purpose of training {XE "training:purpose of} is to make sure all employees have the skills and information they need to perform their roles successfully.
{h2}Training's Contribution
The Executive Committee {XE "Executive Committee :position on training"} has identified training as one of four factors critical to our continued success.
{h3}Improved Quality

Heading styles generate the Table of Contents

Codes generate the Index...

Table of Contents

Index

Printed Page

SECTION 3:
EMPLOYEE TRAINING

Overview
The purpose of training is to make sure all employees have the skills and information they need to perform their roles successfully.

Training's Contribution
The Executive Committee has identified training as one of four factors critical to our continued success.

Chapter 1: Factors of Success   26

... but do not print.

- *Formatting styles.* To help you maintain a consistent look for fonts, paragraphs, and other elements, most word processors use *styles,* which are formatting commands that you can save and reapply as needed. For example, a document can have a style for the main heading, another for the subheads, and a third style for paragraphs. You can apply any style to any block of text, and you can change the look of all similar elements in the document at once simply by modifying the style.
- *Table of contents.* Once you've tagged the various headings in your document with styles, most word processors can then generate a table of contents automatically. Not only does this feature save you the tiresome chore of assembling the table by hand, it can also automatically update the table of contents if you make changes to the document that change the pagination.
- *Index.* A good word processor can create an index for you, although this process tends to be more manual. By attaching a certain code to words in the text, you tag them as index entries, then the software generates the index listing.
- *Running footers/headers.* In addition to numbering pages for you automatically, most word processors let you create running headers at the top of pages and running footers at the bottom. These are sections that repeat from page to page, often with page numbers, section names, and other information.
- *Variables.* Some software packages also let you use *variables,* which are placeholders that the software fills in when you print or display the document. Microsoft Word, for instance, has more than 50 variables (which it calls *field codes*). These run from basic elements such as the author's name and the number of pages in the document to more advanced features such as equations. As a simple example, you might want to print "page X of Y" at the bottom of each page, where X is the current page number and Y is the total number of pages in the document. Variables will take care of this for you automatically.

With the word processor taking care of these chores, you can focus your attention on thinking and writing. Learn to use the tools your software provides, and you'll create first-class documents every time.

---

1. Do you see any risks in using automated tools such as these when preparing documents?
2. Can software help you become a better communicator? Explain why you agree or disagree.

Any kind of Internet service costs money, but the payback in time savings, cost savings, convenience, and visibility is well worth the investment. Here are a few of the advantages provided by the Internet.

- *Communication.* Electronic mail, or e-mail, simplifies communication within a company or with anyone in the world who is also on the Internet.
- *Research.* Most of the research information you will ever need is now available over the Internet through library catalogs, databases, and newsgroups. Yahoo!, Gopher, Archie, Veronica, and Jughead are all search tools for the Internet. A word of caution—the information on the Internet is not monitored; be cautious about quoting sources from the Internet without verifying them.
- *Discussion, collaboration, and development.* The Internet has made it easy for geographically separated people to work cohesively as a team. Besides allowing for speedy communication, the Internet also lessens the impact of time-zone differences between remote locations.
- *Cost.* Communicating over the Internet can be much cheaper than long-distance phone calls or overnight mail. You can contact anyone on the Internet anywhere in the world for just a few cents and usually within a few seconds.
- *Customer service.* Your customers can get technical advice or software upgrades electronically.[12]
- *Competitive tracking.* You can get up-to-date information on what your competition is doing and their customers' feelings about their products.

- *Globalization.* The worldwide availability of the Internet allows companies to make contacts and pursue markets all over the world.[13]
- *Employment.* The Internet is also a great place to make contacts, learn about how to find a job, learn about job opportunities, and even display your résumé on your own Web page.

As with most other things in life, there are disadvantages as well as advantages to the Internet. Downloading information onto your computer from the Internet increases the risk of introducing a "virus" into your system. A virus is a program that can destroy files on your computer. To protect your system from viruses, use an antivirus program (several are available) and back up your data frequently.

The amount of information available can be overwhelming. You can find yourself swimming in e-mail messages and files retrieved from databases and other sources. Remember, the purpose of using all these computer tools is to help you function more effectively on the job, so choose and use information wisely.

Like good news, bad news travels faster on computer networks. For example, several years ago Polaris Software released a software upgrade that had numerous problems.[14] Naturally, customers complained, and much of the complaining was done in public electronic forums read by thousands of users. The news spread quickly and widely. Even though Polaris did release an improved version of the software, it did not respond quickly enough to satisfy unhappy customers, and in one year, Polaris's market share dropped from 27 percent to 10 percent. This drop cannot be attributed solely to the Internet, but the reach and speed of this electronic forum definitely contributed to the problem.

E-mail

Electronic mail (e-mail) helps businesses communicate faster and more informally.

Electronic mail, generally called e-mail, is one of the most useful Internet features for business. **E-mail** refers to documents created, transmitted, and read entirely on computer (see Figure 4.5). The document might be a simple text message, or it might include long and complex files or programs. In fact, if you can save a file on your computer you can probably send it via e-mail. For the people who use it, e-mail has changed the style of business communication in dramatic ways. As Microsoft's Bill Gates puts it, "If we had to pick one application that would keep running no matter what, e-mail would absolutely be it." The advantages of e-mail include the following:[15]

- *Speed.* An e-mail message often arrives at its destination anywhere in the world in a matter of seconds. Regular postal mail (now often referred to as "snail mail") can take weeks or even months to reach remote areas of the world, and it takes just as long to get a reply. With e-mail, you can correspond back and forth repeatedly in the time it used to take for one message to be delivered. This speedy delivery also allows extra time to make last-minute finishing touches on a project before sending it.
- *Cost.* The cost of sending an e-mail message is usually less than the cost of a first-class stamp. It is definitely less than the cost of overnight delivery services ($6 to $20 or more). The actual cost depends on several factors: the cost of your Internet connection, the speed of your modem (if you pay an hourly access rate), and the length of the e-mail message and of any other files you send with it.[16]
- *Portability.* You can receive and send e-mail anywhere you can connect your computer to a phone line. You can read and respond to your e-mail from your personal computer at work or at home, from your laptop computer in your hotel room on a business trip, from customer sites, while waiting for your flight at the

Gretchen Plaxton, a budget analyst at Robson Brothers Manufacturing, encountered some unexpected problems in setting up her computer for an important budget briefing. Her e-mail message was waiting for Li Chau when she returned to her office, and the two women were able to solve Plaxton's problem by closing time.

Figure 4.5
In-Depth Critique:
Electronic Mail

```
╔══════════════════════ E-Mail ══════════════════════╗
║                                                      ║
╠══════════════════════════════════════════════════════╣

Date: Tues, 17 June 1997, 11:45:23, CDT
To: lichau@robson.com
From: gplaxton@robson.com (Gretchen R. Plaxton)
Subject: Help!


Li,

You're not answering your phone, so I guess you're not
back from your software demonstration. I really need
your expertise! I've spent the better part of this
morning trying to get my computer set up for tomorrow's
budget briefing, but nothing seems to help. Everything
was working fine in my office, but now that I've moved
my machine to the conference room, I keep getting
application errors in the graphics software!

I have to meet Roland from production for lunch at noon,
but I'll be back in the office by 1:00. Can you come
look at my machine after that? The budget meeting is set
for tomorrow at 9 a.m. sharp! So I can't really wait for
the consultant we started on retainer last month (she's
tied up until after 4:00). If I can't get things running
by end of business today, I'm in deep trouble. I'll be
up all night hand-drawing flip charts--and with my
artistic talent, they won't be pretty! (:<)

If you get back before I do, leave a message on my voice
mail, or e-mail me. I'm desperate, Li. Please say you'll
come rescue me.

Hope to hear from you very soon,

Gretchen
```

This computer screen shows how a timely message can be sent to anyone connected to the system—whether across the globe or in the same building.

Plaxton has the space to explain the situation so that Chau can respond without needing any more information.

At the end of the second paragraph, Plaxton has included a type of e-mail symbol known as an emoticon—in this case a sideways "sad face" that clues the reader into how the writer is feeling (see the Chapter 6 heading, "Make your E-mail Interesting").

Chau can let Plaxton know whether she will be available and what time would be convenient—again by e-mail—simply by clicking on the reply button and typing in her response.

airport, from the airplane during your flight, or from your yacht cruising the Mediterranean.

- ***Convenience.*** The person you want to contact need not be sitting at the computer or even have the computer turned on when your message arrives. This solves the problem of coordinating phone calls across time zones. For instance, HP has employees in almost every time zone around the world, and many of them need to communicate with far-flung colleagues. With e-mail, a sales representative in Germany can easily communicate with a technical specialist in California, even though the two are separated by nine time zones. E-mail also solves "phone tag" problems (when two people call back and forth leaving messages without ever connecting). Instead of leaving a brief phone message and waiting for a response, you can send and receive detailed, accurate messages. Most mail programs also include some way to alert you when new mail arrives. This is not as intrusive as a phone ringing—you have the choice of reading the message immediately or waiting until you finish your current task.

- *Record keeping.* You can save and organize e-mail messages you send and receive, which can provide a good record of the communication on a specific project.
- *News services.* Several electronic news services are available. You specify the topic or the key words of interest to you, and the service gathers articles on those topics from newspapers, magazines, and wire services, sending you the results via e-mail. Some of the services are free; others cost up to $400 a year or more.[17]
- *Egalitarianism.* E-mail has opened new channels of communication inside organizations. With most e-mail systems, anybody can send messages to just about anybody else. Lower-level employees who may otherwise have no contact with upper management can send e-mail messages to top managers as easily as to their colleagues—the electronic equivalent of an "open-door" policy.[18]
- *Open communication.* E-mail has a curious way of encouraging people to drop the inhibitions that normally govern their messages. People sometimes write things in e-mail that they wouldn't dream of saying in person or typing in a document.[19] This new openness can be beneficial, helping companies communicate better and circulating useful opinions from a wider variety of people. However, as you can imagine, such openness can also create tension and interpersonal conflict.
- *Distribution lists.* Within an e-mail program you can create distribution lists—groups of people to whom you routinely send information. Then when you want to send a message you specify the name of the list rather than typing all the names again. For example, you might have one group that includes all the people in your immediate department, another group that includes your counterparts at other company divisions, and others that include people with whom you are working on specific projects.
- *Automated mail.* Some companies use software that automatically retrieves or distributes information. For example, say you want to get information about the services and prices of Netcom On-Line Communication Services, an Internet service provider. You simply send e-mail (without an actual message) to <info@netcom.com>, and the computer automatically responds.

Some of the main benefits of e-mail also create its worst problems. Because it's so easy and cheap to send e-mail, people tend to overuse it, distributing messages more widely than necessary. Some company executives receive hundreds of messages a day—many of them the electronic equivalent of "junk mail." A vice president of a company in California estimates he spends three hours a day on e-mail, discarding 80 percent of the messages he receives.[20] Besides wasting time, overuse can also overload e-mail systems, resulting in lost messages or even system crashes. Special programs (sometimes called "Bozo filters") are available to filter out unwanted messages, but you must specify what you want to block.[21]

Privacy is another problem with e-mail. E-mail messages may seem more private than phone calls, but it is surprisingly easy for e-mail to end up in places you did not intend it to go. People do not always screen the distribution list carefully and send information to people who should not have it or do not need it. Even if your message originally goes only where you intended it to go, a recipient can easily forward it on to someone else. E-mail, like paper mail, can be used as evidence in court cases.[22] Moreover, employers have the legal right to monitor your use of e-mail on the job.[23] A good rule of thumb is don't put anything in e-mail that you would not write in any other business correspondence.[24]

Despite its growing popularity and availability, there are still times when e-mail cannot replace regular postal mail. Some situations call for a more formal message sent on official company letterhead.[25] When you need to document that a message was sent and received, it's safer to send it by registered or certified mail or via a delivery service.

Internet Discussion Groups

Two forms of discussion groups are common on the Internet: **discussion mailing lists** and **Usenet newsgroups.** A discussion mailing list (of which there are more than 100,000) consists of people with a common interest. You can subscribe by sending a message to the list's e-mail address. From then on, you will automatically receive via e-mail a copy of any message posted to that list by any other subscriber of that list. It's like subscribing to an electronic newsletter to which everyone can contribute.[26]

Usenet groups are similar to mailing lists, but they are accessed differently. Mailing lists are accessed by e-mail. Newsgroups are accessed by a newsgroup reader program in Netscape, Internet Explorer, or some other browser. Once you subscribe, you can read messages posted by other subscribers and leave messages for the other subscribers to read. You can get and submit information on more than 10,000 subjects. For example, the newsgroup <alt.business.misc> is a forum for small business owners.[27]

World Wide Web

The **World Wide Web, WWW,** or **Web,** is a powerful system of interconnections on the Internet. Being familiar with a number of terms helps you use the Web:

- *Multimedia.* When using the Web, you can access not only text files but also graphic, photograph, audio, and video files. Figure 4.6 (see page 104) shows a Web page with text and graphics.
- *Browser.* To find your way around the Web, you need a piece of software called a **browser.** As with other Internet software, it may be on your Internet service provider's computer, or you may need to install the software on your own computer. Three popular browsers are Netscape Navigator, Microsoft's Internet Explorer, and NCSA Mosaic.
- *Home page.* Every site on the Web has its own **home page,** or starting place. This site might be a very complex document containing graphics and hyperlinks (as in Figure 4.6), or it might be quite simple.
- *URL.* Each resource or site on the Web has a unique address called a Uniform Resource Locator **(URL).** For instance, the address for Hewlett-Packard's Web site is <http://www.hp.com>.
- *Hyperlinks.* Hyperlinks, or **links,** are interactive connections among these resources.

The World Wide Web is the part of the Internet that can accommodate graphics.

BEST OF THE WEB

Create Your Own Web Site

You'll learn how to create your own Web site using valuable Web development links, utilities, and online tutorials. Through this massive, user-friendly resource library, you'll learn about document and Web-page design, navigation, structure, and more. You'll even learn how to have your Web site translated into a foreign language.

http://www.stars.com

Figure 4.6
Web Pages Help
Businesses Communicate
Internally and Externally

Hewlett-Packard's site on the World Wide Web at <http://www.hp.com> shows a typical home page with graphics and hyperlinks.

- *Hypertext.* Hypertext is a method of cross-referencing between files using links. When you click on a link, hypertext uses the URL to find the file or site. This is a convenient way of finding related information.
- *Web site.* Thousands of companies and individuals now have their own Web sites. At HP's site, for instance, clicking on buttons or links provides information about new products, the company's annual report, a current press release, any job openings, or a variety of other topics. A Web site provides an interactive means of advertising. Potential customers or employees can get information directly from the Web site rather than by calling the company. This is a convenience for both the company and the customer.

Intranets

An intranet is an Internet-type network whose information and access are restricted to a single organization.

Not all Web sites are available to anyone cruising the Net. Some are reserved for the private use of a single company's employees and stakeholders. An **intranet** uses the same technologies as the Internet and the World Wide Web, but the information provided and the access allowed are restricted to the boundaries of a companywide LAN or WAN. In some cases, suppliers, distribution partners, and key customers may also have access, but intranets are protected from unauthorized access through the Internet by a *firewall,* a special type of gateway that controls access to the local network. People on an intranet can get out to the Internet, but unauthorized people on the Internet cannot get in.[28]

Hardware and software for establishing intranets are expected to be an $8 billion market within a few years, which indicates that many companies see impressive benefits in this new communication technology.[29] As a leading computer company, it's not surprising that Hewlett-Packard owns one of the largest intranets in the world.[30]

Possibly the biggest advantage of an intranet is that it eliminates the problem of employees using different types of computers within a company. On an intranet, all information is available in a format compatible with Macintosh, PC, or UNIX-based computers. This virtually eliminates the need to publish internal documents on paper because everyone can access the information electronically. Some companies have set goals of becoming "paperless." In fact, Owens-Corning Fiberglas planned no space for filing cabinets in its new headquarters (whereas filing cabinets took up 20 percent of the floor space in the old building). The leader of Owens-Corning's technology transition team says, "This is not a campaign to save the trees. This is about operating and running the business much more effectively."[31]

Besides saving paper and floor space, an intranet can save a company money in the form of employee hours. Employees can find information much faster and easier by using a well-designed database on an intranet than by digging through a filing cabinet or card catalog. Here are some of the communication uses companies have for their intranets:

- *Policy manuals.* Information is easily available to employees and always current. You don't have to reprint hundreds of copies when policies change—just make the change in one location and it is immediately available to all employees.
- *Job openings.* New positions can be posted on the intranet, and current employees can submit job applications over the intranet.
- *Presentation materials used by marketing and sales departments.* Representatives can download sales and marketing materials at customer sites all over the world. Changes made by marketing representatives at company headquarters are immediately available to field salespeople.
- *Employee benefits information.* Not only can you find out what your benefits are, but many companies have made it possible for employees to reallocate funds in their 401k plans via their intranet.
- *Record keeping.* Company records are kept in one location and are accessible from anywhere on the intranet. For instance, Federal Express tracks all its packages electronically, and the information is available to anyone on the company intranet anywhere in the world.[32]
- *Databases.* At Silicon Graphics, employees quickly find information in several databases using hyperlinks. Before their intranet was installed, finding the same information could take several days.[33]
- *Programs or bits of software that might be useful to other programmers.* Hewlett-Packard maintains a "software vending machine" of code. Before creating new code, programmers first check to see whether a program exists that they can use or modify.[34]
- *Collaboration and development.* Ford Motor's 1996 Taurus was developed by engineers at design centers in Asia, Europe, and the United States, all communicating via intranet.[35]

Other uses of intranets include scheduling meetings, setting up company phone directories, and publishing company newsletters.[36] In fact, just about any information that can help employees communicate is a good candidate for an intranet. As video and audio technologies progress, you can expect to see more multimedia applications on intranets as well.

TECHNOLOGY IN ORAL COMMUNICATION

Written documents are only part of the business communication picture. Oral communication is just as important, whether it's face-to-face or on the phone, whether it's with one other person or with a group. Here's a quick look at the technologies used to improve communication between individuals and groups.

Individual Communication

Technologies for one-on-one oral communication include the basic telephone and advanced options such as voice mail.

If you threw out fax machines, e-mail, and computers, most businesses could survive. Just don't touch the phone—that's a company's real lifeline. Phones link businesses with their customers, suppliers, news media, investors, and all the other parties that affect their success. Phones keep employees in touch with each other and give them quick access to the people and the information they need to do their jobs.

As it has in every other aspect of communication, technology has transformed the way businesspeople use their phones. Business phone systems have become less and less like the phones you use at home; many act like computers with phones attached. *Call-management systems* give companies better control over both the calls that come in and the calls that go out. For inbound calls, a *PBX (private branch exchange)* system can screen and route calls. Some are run by a human operator; others are nearly or completely computerized. To reach employees who are out of the office, a company can equip them with cellular phones or *pagers,* small radio receivers that signal employees to call the office. For outbound calls, computers can track who called whom, automatically dial numbers from a list of potential customers, and perform other time- and money-saving tasks.

The combination of phones and computers has also created an entirely new method of communication. *Voice mail* is similar to e-mail in concept, except that it doesn't require each user to have a computer (messages are stored on a central computer), and it lets you send, store, and retrieve spoken, rather than written, messages. Much more than a glorified answering machine, voice mail sends verbal messages to any number of "mailboxes" on the system. Messages can be several minutes long, and you can review your recordings before releasing them. When people need to get their messages, they enter a confidential code; then they can listen to messages, delete them, and forward messages to other people on the system. Voice mail solves time-zone difficulties when communicating across the country or internationally. It can also reduce a substantial amount of interoffice paperwork.[37]

Voice mail can make employees more productive, but it's not universally loved. The biggest complaint comes from customers who try to call a company and reach a computerized voice-mail system instead of a person. In a recent survey, 95 percent of the people questioned said they prefer reaching a person on their first call to a business.[38] Businesses that use voice mail need to balance the productivity gains with the potential effects on customer satisfaction.

Group Communication

Technologies for group presentations include teleconferencing, videoconferencing, presentation tools, and group decision-making systems.

Technology can also lend a hand when people need to communicate in groups. Group communication used to take place in person (in the same room), but technology has given people a new degree of freedom. Through *teleconferencing* (which encompasses audioconferencing and videoconferencing via phone lines and satellite), it's now possible to conduct meetings with people who are scattered across the country or around the globe.[39] New technology also allows videoconferencing over the Internet.

In more traditional gatherings, when all participants can meet in one location, technology provides an array of presentation tools to make meetings more productive and more interesting. You're no doubt familiar with *overhead transparencies.* You might also use *35 mm slides* (just like the slides you can produce with a camera), or you could make use of a *computer-based presentation* in which the computer's display is either transferred to a large-screen television or an LCD panel or LCD projector. Presentation software can help you create these visual materials. But beyond visuals, technology can even help groups make decisions and formulate plans. You can connect everyone through computers using *group decision support systems,* which range from simple vote-counting systems to advanced tools that help people consider a decision from various points of view.[40]

HOW TECHNOLOGY IS CHANGING COMMUNICATION

Communication technology is changing the way we do business. Some of the effects are unquestionably positive; others are not. New technology is increasing the flow of information. Businesspeople can now get more information on more subjects faster than ever before. At the same time, technology is producing information overload, burdening people with unwanted messages. Although much of this additional information is useful, you have to be careful not to bury yourself and your company in information you don't need. By pressing just a few keys or buttons, anyone can send e-mail, voice mail, and faxes to hundreds or even thousands of people—whether the information is actually needed or not. Of course, technology can also help you sort through all that information to find just the bits you need.

The development and evolution of technology is changing business communication, and its effects are both positive and negative.

By compressing time and distance, technology promotes teamwork and improves profits. Doing business with someone in another country is no longer the slow, complicated, even exotic adventure it once was. Electronic communication makes it easier to work with colleagues, suppliers, and customers, no matter where they are. E-mail, voice mail, and faxes facilitate communication within a company and around the world. All three technologies overcome time zones and even working hours. E-mail and faxes are even being accepted as legally binding contracts.[41] So because it costs less for people to produce and distribute messages, communication technology can directly boost profits. It can also improve profits indirectly by making a company more competitive, say, by searching databases to uncover a new market opportunity.

However, the same technology can isolate some people from business and employment opportunities. Anyone who doesn't have access to e-mail, fax machines, or other technological tools tends to be left out of the communication flow. This isolation presents a challenge to businesses who are trying to compete and to young people who lack experience with communication technology but who are applying for jobs that require some knowledge of it. By keeping up with the newest technological developments, you will be able to compete in business and for jobs.

Today's technology is also changing organizational structures, flattening the hierarchy and allowing more people to work away from the office. Although corporate structure used to define communication flow, e-mail in particular frees communication from the confines of the organizational chart. Using today's technology, anyone can send messages to anyone else with equal access, a big change from the old days when messages just moved up and down the chain of command.[42] Moreover, communication technology has loosened the strings that bind the traditional company together. In many firms, co-workers and even entire departments are no longer in a single location.

Telecommuting lets people work (linked through computers, phones, and faxes) where it is most convenient for them—whether at home, in a suburban satellite office (where people can work close to home but away from the company's main office), or on the road (traveling to sell products or to service customer accounts). Telecommuting can cover a lot more territory than the area around town, too. Technology allows many professionals to work with people across the country and around the world.

Of course, this same technology is blurring the line between work life and home life. E-mail, faxes, and other technologies that speed up and extend the reach of business communication can increase the pressure on those people who use them. From home computers to car phones to portable fax machines, technology can make it easy to feel that you're always "plugged in" and that you're expected to respond instantly to every message you receive, whether you're at home, on a business trip, or on vacation.

Mike Stevens's experience at Hewlett-Packard emphasizes some important lessons about technology: First, even though it helps him communicate with more people more efficiently, it doesn't solve *all* his problems. Second, it adds to the complexity of his job. Third, technology doesn't come cheap; Hewlett-Packard spends millions of dollars on all the communication equipment and software that Stevens and his co-workers use. Fourth, and most important, whether in the form of handwritten notes, electronic newsletters, or global videoconferences, communication efforts are only as good as the people involved. Technology cannot do the thinking, planning, or communicating. Humans must do that. Only those who learn to balance the complexity and expense of technology with good communication skills will succeed in business and in the future.

SUMMARY

Technology is changing nearly every aspect of business communication, from the way you research reports to the way you conduct meetings. The tools for written communication include word-processing software, desktop publishing, databases, CD-ROM, voice recognition, spelling and grammar checkers, e-mail, and a variety of network technologies including the Internet and private intranets. New technologies for oral communication include voice mail, teleconferencing, and videoconferencing. By themselves, these technological tools can't ensure effective communication, but with skilled writers and speakers, they increase both the speed and efficiency of the communication process.

OMMUNICATION CHALLENGES AT HEWLETT-PACKARD

Hewlett-Packard has decided to make a major change in the way employees find help with their computer hardware and software problems. Computer "help desks" (once a major function of Mike Stevens's department) have always served division employees locally, but HP has decided that help-desk functions can be handled more efficiently from a central location. From now on, employees worldwide will call the main Hewlett-Packard help desk in Atlanta, the same help desk that serves the company's external customers.

INDIVIDUAL CHALLENGE: Stevens and his team will be communicating this major change to HP employees worldwide. As a team member, your assignment is to analyze and recommend the best way to communicate news of the change and instructions for using the new system. Make up a chart comparing the advantages and disadvantages of (1) printed materials produced using desktop publishing, (2) e-mail sent to a general distribution list, (3) training videotapes, (4) formal letters sent by snail mail, (5) teleconferences, (6) face-to-face meetings and training sessions, and (7) a hard-copy memo sent to a general distribution list. Measure each option against audience expectations, time and cost, and presentation needs. Write a brief recommendation to be presented in class. You don't have to limit your recommendation to one technology.

TEAM CHALLENGE: Stevens says the initial feedback he's received has been positive, but he's concerned that

if the change in procedures isn't communicated clearly, much confusion could result. He's imagining employees with computer problems, under a tight deadline, who can't find the help they're accustomed to receiving. Brainstorm and jot down your ideas for (1) making the communication crystal clear and (2) stressing the advantages of the change (for example, employees' computer software problems will now be handled by experts with considerable experience).

CRITICAL THINKING QUESTIONS

1. Is it important for everyone in a company to know how to use the latest technological tools for document preparation? Why or why not?
2. Would you choose word-processing or desktop publishing software as a tool for writing memos to your staff? Why?
3. Considering how fast and easy it is, should e-mail replace meetings and other face-to-face communication in your company? Why or why not?

4. Why are companies interested in group technologies such as teleconferencing, groupware, and intranets?
5. How could a global corporation such as Coca-Cola take advantage of Internet technology to keep its people around the world in touch with each other?
6. What are the implications for companies that are slow to adopt new communication technologies and for employment candidates who have limited experience with such technologies?

EXERCISES

1. You are responsible for recommending word-processing software to the headquarters staff at Federal Express. Using computer magazines available in the library, read reviews of leading word-processing products. On the basis of your research, select the one product you think is best, and write a brief recommendation.
2. You're a consultant hired by Chrysler to investigate how the company and its dealers can use technology to communicate with potential customers. Interview several people who've bought a car, and ask them what types of communication technology the manufacturers and car dealers used. Ask them what types of technology they expected manufacturers and dealers to use. Did one technology seem to work better than another? Write a couple of paragraphs explaining to Chrysler what you've learned.
3. For each of the following tasks, decide which communication technology, if any, would be the best to use, and be prepared to explain your choices in class:
   a. The CEO of a major corporation wants to explain the company's performance to 27,000 employees, who are located in 14 sites across North America and Europe.

   b. A small-business owner wants to convince her bank that the normal loan qualification shouldn't apply in her case and that the bank should approve her request for a $2 million business-expansion loan.
   c. A manager needs to warn three employees that their job performance is below company standards.
4. Computer viruses are software programs designed to wreak havoc in computer systems. They can cause millions of dollars of damage in lost time and destroyed data, so they are understandably an important concern for businesses. By interviewing a computer expert or researching library articles, learn the extent of the virus problem. Then draft a brief (less than one page) explanation, listing the things that companies can do to protect themselves.
5. List the technological skills you already have and could discuss in a job interview. Can you type? Have you used e-mail or online services? Have you surfed the Web? Have you used photocopiers, calculators, answering machines, and voice-mail systems? What experience do you have with video cameras, video players, and videoconferencing equipment? Which brands, models, or systems are you familiar with? Which software do you have experience using?

6. Interview several local businesspeople or college administrators to find out the following (write a one-page summary of your findings):
   a. What communication technology they use
   b. What tasks they use the technology for
   c. The advantages of using the technology
   d. The disadvantages of using the technology
   e. How technology has affected their ability to communicate on the job

7. The year 2000 presents a surprisingly difficult challenge for many business computer systems. In the early days of the computer industry, memory was so expensive and so limited that programmers assigned only two digits to record the year in customer records and other computer files. So instead of recording 1959 or 1979, these systems recorded simply 59 or 79, and the 19 part of the date was assumed. Over the years, companies amassed huge databases with these abbreviated dates. Trouble is, when the date clicks over at 12:00 A.M. on January 1, 2000, all these systems are going to assume the year is 1900. The potential database disaster is so big that a small industry of consultants and software developers started appearing around 1995 to help companies address the issue. Assume that your company is facing this challenge and write a one-page memo to the CEO explaining why you need to hire a consultant to help solve the problem. (Do any research necessary to understand the extent of the problem.)

8. You will be out of town for the next week, attending an important meeting that was called at the last minute. While you're away, you want your clients to be able to get the personal attention they deserve, so you've made arrangements with an associate to cover for you. Of course, not every client will need help before your return on May 16; most of them should be able to leave a message on your voice mail so that you can get back to them next week. Compose a message to record on your voice-mail system letting your clients know that you haven't abandoned them and that they can either leave a message or contact your associate (Bill Comden at 578-3737). Make sure the message is brief while still containing all the necessary information.

9. Your boss refuses to adopt computers for communication purposes—choosing to rely on dictation, typewriters, and simple face-to-face contact. What arguments might you use to persuade your boss to give communication technology a try? Be prepared to discuss your arguments in class.

10. Many magazines have established Web pages in addition to using print media. For example, *Backpacker Magazine*'s BaseCamp page (at <http://www.bpbasecamp.com>) aims to give the magazine a wider audience through the Web. Consider whether the information provided on the home page and linked pages effectively addresses the needs of the intended audience. Send an e-mail message to BaseCamp, *Backpacker Magazine,* or to one of the linked information pages (including the companies that designed and maintain the home page) asking for additional information. Print both your query and your response for submission.

PART 2

THE WRITING PROCESS

PLANNING BUSINESS MESSAGES

AFTER STUDYING THIS CHAPTER, YOU WILL BE ABLE TO

- Describe the basic tasks in the composition process
- Define both the general and the specific purposes of your business messages
- Test the purpose of your business messages
- Develop an audience profile
- Analyze the needs of your audience
- Establish the main idea of your messages
- Select an appropriate channel and medium for transmitting a particular message to a particular audience

OMMUNICATION CLOSE-UP AT GENERAL MILLS

Betty Crocker never had to deal with Boo*Berry monster cereal. Most of the lengthy letters Betty received in the 1920s, when General Mills first invented her, were from women who wanted to know why their bread wasn't rising or why their meringues were weeping. To respond, General Mills established a special department to write formal, polite replies. But a lot more than Betty's hairstyle has changed since then.

Jeff Hagen is now Director of Consumer Services for General Mills, and he not only deals with Boo*Berry but also with Count Chocula, Frankenberry, and 2500 other products—as well as with 800-numbers, computerized correspondence software, voice mail information lines, e-mail, and the company's Web site. He manages a staff of 65 full-time employees who respond to between 700,000 and 1,000,000 contacts from consumers every year. And that's okay because he's got every base covered—almost. "We're not out there waving signal flags," he admits, but his staff will respond in whatever medium consumers choose.

Today's consumers are as likely to be men as women, and most of them call rather than write. Of course, Betty still gets letters, but now so do the Trix Rabbit and Sonny the Cuckoo Bird (who usually get e-mail from the kids' Web site that General Mills sponsors at <www.youruleschool.com>). If a message is from a kid, Hagen's staff makes sure the reply is in "kid language." Yes, Hagen even trains people to think about how the Trix Rabbit might respond to questions. As Hagen explains, "He wouldn't sound like a lawyer. He'd be funny; he'd be weird."

This ability to respond to consumers in their own language is the key to Hagen's success. For instance, e-mail is typically brief and sometimes irreverent, so Hagen encourages his Internet team to write responses that are "professional but not stuffy." It's a tough line to walk, he admits, but "if they're writing to you in short grunts, you don't want to write back sounding like a novel."

Jeff Hagen

Over the years, in recognition of its customers' changing interests and needs, General Mills has changed the appearance of Betty Crocker, its fictitious spokesperson. The latest Betty Crocker has been digitally "morphed" from the seven previous pictures and from the pictures of 75 real women selected across the United States. Now possessing features that appear more ethnically diverse, she has become the fuzzy reflection of us all.

With every contact, Hagen's staff inputs the information into a sophisticated computer tracking program. "Let's say somebody calls and they can't find Boo*Berry cereal in their area," explains Hagen. The call is coded as "Boo*Berry, question or request, availability." The program automatically suggests a form reply, with alternative choices varying slightly in tone or content. The system then prints the selected letter and attachments, personalizes it with the consumer's name, and signs it with a digitized replica of the staff member's actual signature.

In the case of missing Boo*Berry, the staffer checks availability on a database, and if it's not in the consumer's area, the staffer offers to ship the cereal to the consumer in 4-packs or case lots. "Even if we're talking to people on the phone, we follow up with a confirmation letter saying this is what we discussed," says Hagen. That not only puts an order form in their hands, but it gives General Mills an opportunity to explain why every product can't be on every store shelf.

"Our goal is to respond to every contact we have," says Hagen, whether it's a person in Iowa who's in love with Boo*Berry or the woman in New York who wants to know if she needs to follow the directions for high-altitude cooking because she lives on the 20th floor. The response from General Mills must demonstrate understanding, knowledge, professionalism, and efficiency—and that takes careful planning.[1]

UNDERSTANDING THE COMPOSITION PROCESS

Like Jeff Hagen and his staff, you'll face a variety of communication assignments in your career—both oral and written. Some of your tasks will be routine, needing little more than jotting down a few sentences on paper or in an e-mail message; others will be more complex, requiring reflection, research, and careful document preparation. Regardless of the job you hold, the amount of time you actually spend composing messages, or the complexity of your task, effective communication is the key.[2] Even if you have trouble thinking of what you'll say (see "Overcoming Your Fear of the Blank Page"), you can gain control over your messages by separating the various composition activities into a process.

The composition process helps you gain control over your messages.

SHARPENING YOUR SKILLS

OVERCOMING YOUR FEAR OF THE BLANK PAGE

For some people, writing is a breeze. For many of us, however, putting words on paper is a struggle. We may even get stuck so often that we develop a mental block. Here are some ways to overcome this block:

- *Use positive self-talk.* Writer's block comes from worrying about being unable to write well or easily and from believing that writing is too difficult, too time consuming, or too complicated. Replace such negative ideas about writing by telling yourself that you're a resourceful, capable person who knows how to do the job. As proof that you really can write when you want to, recall past examples of your writing that were successful.

- *Know your purpose.* What do you want to accomplish with this particular piece of writing? Without a clear purpose, writing can indeed be impossible.

- *Visualize your audience.* Picture their backgrounds, interests, knowledge of the subject, and vocabulary, including the technical jargon they're familiar with. This helps you choose an appropriate slant for your writing.

- *Create a productive environment.* When you're blocked, you're easily distracted by sights, sounds, and other elements in your environment. Make sure you write in a place that is for writing only, and make that environment pleasant. Then set "appointments" with yourself, during which you do nothing but write. A writing appointment for, say, 9:30 to 12:00 seems less imposing than an indefinite writing session. Also, be sure to build in break times to keep your mind fresh.

- *Make an outline.* Even if formal outlines make you restless, jot down at least a few notes about how your ideas fit together. As you go along, you'll probably revise these notes, which is fine, as long as you end up with a plan that gives direction and coherence to your writing.

- *Just start.* Put aside all worries, fears, and distractions— everything that gives you an excuse to postpone writing.

Then start putting down any thoughts you have about the topic. Don't worry about whether these ideas can actually be used; just let your mind range freely.

- *Write the middle first.* You don't have to start at the beginning. Start wherever your enthusiasm is greatest and your ideas are most developed. If your thoughts take you in a different direction, feel free to follow them, making notes about any ideas you want to come back to later. When you've finished with this first section, pick out another; but don't worry about sequence. The idea is to get all your thoughts in writing.

- *Push obstacles aside.* You may well get stuck at some point, but you can easily get unstuck. First, don't worry about it. These things happen. Second, get rid of any distractions. Third, if you're stuck on one thought or sentence or paragraph, go on to one that's easier for you. You can always come back later. Fourth, prime the pump; that is, simply write about why you're stuck: "I'm stuck because . . ." Before you know it, you'll be writing about your topic. Also try talking aloud about your problem. Finally, try brainstorming. Make notes about things you haven't yet covered. Soon enough, you'll feel the urge to write.

When deadlines loom, you may become paralyzed with panic. But if you keep things in perspective, you'll survive. Concentrate on the major ideas first, and save the details for later, after you have something on the page.

1. Procrastination is a skill that many writers have developed into a fine art. List the ways you procrastinate, and discuss what you can do to break these habits.
2. One reason for writer's block is negative self-talk. Analyze your own writing experiences. What negative self-talk do you use? What might you do to overcome this tendency?

A Ten-Stage Process

Although some communicators reject any structured composition process as artificial, the fact is that your final message (the product) and the way you achieve it (the process) are irrevocably linked, so successful communicators concentrate on both.[3] If you're composing for yourself, for the value of exploration and expression, your composition process will differ greatly from that of business communicators seeking to reach an audience with information, a request, or a persuasive argument. The process presented here will be most valuable if you view it not as a recipe, not as a list of how-to directives, not as a fixed sequence of steps but as a way to understand the various tasks involved in composition.[4]

The composition process varies with the situation, the communicator, and the organization. Routine messages obviously require less planning and less revision than more complex messages, and if your schedule for completing a project is tight, one or two of the stages will be slighted. Moreover, various people approach composition in various ways; some compose quickly and then revise slowly; others revise as they go along. Also, the stages do not necessarily occur in 1-2-3 order. Communicators often jump back and forth from one stage to another.

The **composition process** may be viewed as ten separate stages that fall into three simple categories—planning, composing, and revising (see Figure 5.1):

- *Planning.* During the planning phase, you think about the fundamentals of your message: your reason for communicating, your audience, the main idea of your message, and the channel and medium that will best convey your thoughts. The stages of planning include (1) defining your purpose, (2) analyzing your audience, (3) establishing your main idea, and (4) selecting the appropriate channel and medium.
- *Composing.* Having collected all the information you'll need, you decide on the organization of ideas and the tone you'll adopt. Then you formulate the message, committing your thoughts to words, creating sentences and paragraphs, and selecting illustrations and details to support your main idea. The stages of composing include (5) organizing your message and (6) formulating your message.
- *Revising.* Having formulated your thoughts, you step back to see whether you have expressed them adequately. You review the content and organization of your message, its overall style and readability, and your word choice. You revise and rewrite until your message comes across as clearly and effectively as possible. Then once you have produced the message, you proof it for details such as grammar, punctuation, and format. The stages of revision include (7) editing your message, (8) rewriting your message, (9) producing your message, and (10) proofing your message.

The composition process is flexible, not a fixed prescription of sequenced steps.

Good communicators realize that the composition process often occurs out of order as they jump back and forth from one stage to another.

Figure 5.1
The Composition Process

PLANNING	1. Define purpose
	2. Analyze audience
	3. Establish main idea
	4. Select channel and medium
COMPOSING	5. Organize message
	6. Formulate message
REVISING	7. Edit message
	8. Rewrite message
	9. Produce message
	10. Proof message

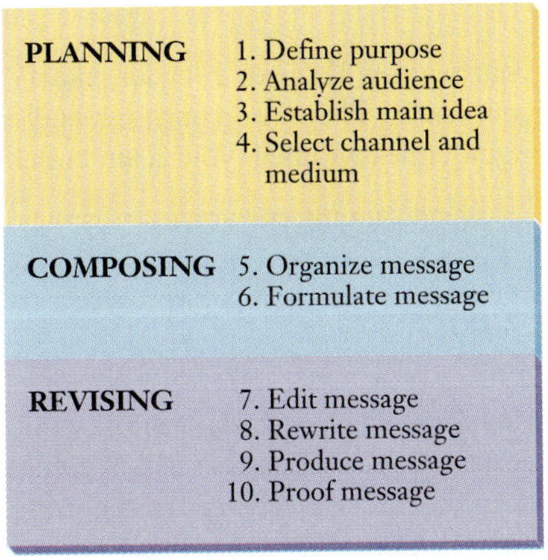

Good composition includes such important considerations as spelling and usage, but the central part of any composition process is thinking.[5] This ten-stage process helps you assess the possibilities for achieving a specific objective. It gives you control over your composition by helping you focus on the specific tasks that make up successful composition.

Collaboration

Collaboration affects the composition process.

In many organizations, the process of preparing a message is a team effort. **Collaborative writing,** in which more than one writer works on a document, can result in a better product. Collaboration brings multiple perspectives and various skills to a project. It combines the strengths of all team members to increase productivity, enrich knowledge, and enhance interpersonal relationships.[6]

Today's computers make collaborative writing more feasible. They allow you the freedom to experiment and explore various approaches to the writing process and the subject matter. Electronic tools such as groupware, e-mail, and computer conferencing help you communicate more quickly and more effectively as you maintain an ongoing dialogue with other team members.[7]

Collaborative writing isn't without problems. Of course, as a member of a collaborative team, you need writing skills such as researching, drafting, editing, and proofreading. However, team members coming from different backgrounds will have different concerns (a technical expert may focus on accuracy and meeting scientific standards; an editor may focus on organization and coherence; a manager may focus on schedules, cost, and corporate goals). So in addition to being able to write, you must also be able to attend meetings regularly, plan and organize efficiently, accept responsibility, volunteer willingly, contribute ideas freely, elicit and listen to ideas, cooperate, and resolve conflicts.[8] You must be able and willing to overcome differences in writing styles, working styles, and personality traits. You must be open to the opinions of others and focus on your team's objectives instead of your own.

Collaborative writing is used in any number of business situations, ranging from one writer asking a co-worker's opinion to many writers cooperating in an all-out team effort. You might sit down with your boss to plan a memo, work independently during the writing phase, and then ask your boss to review the message and suggest revisions. Or your message may be particularly long and important so that the process involves more people: a project manager, researchers, writers, typists, graphic artists, and editors.[9] For efforts of this type, the review and revision stages might be repeated several times to respond to input not only from various team members but also from various departments.

To get organized, your team will select a leader, clarify goals, and resolve conflict.[10] To be effective, your team will agree on purpose, audience awareness, and writing style. The following guidelines will help your team collaborate successfully:[11]

- Select members who have strong interpersonal skills, who understand group dynamics (see Chapter 19), and who care about the project.
- Clarify goals and individual expectations.
- Identify a group leader who will keep members informed and intervene when necessary.
- Create a sense of ownership and shared responsibility for the document.
- Develop members' ability to resolve conflict and negotiate.
- Assign specific roles and establish clear lines of reporting.
- Establish a time line and deadlines for every part of the project.

- Establish communication standards that are accurate and open and that create an atmosphere of trust (and agree on the technology to be used—software, e-mail, etc.).

These guidelines can help you produce a successful document that is both clear and punctual. Of course, deadline pressures must also be considered. If the message was due yesterday, you would compress the process.

Schedules

When composing a message, whether alone or in collaboration with co-workers, allotting your time properly is an important consideration. Any realistic schedule would give you the time you need for thoroughly planning, composing, and revising your message. But business messages are often composed under pressure and on a schedule that is anything but realistic. Especially when time is short, carefully schedule yourself, and stick to your schedule. Of the time you're given, try using roughly half for planning, gathering material, and immersing yourself in the subject matter. Try using less than a quarter of your time for composing, and use more than a quarter of the time for revising (so that you don't shortchange important final steps such as polishing and proofing).[12]

Scheduling affects the composition process.

EXAMINING THE COMPOSITION PROCESS

This text breaks the composition process into three chapters. Chapter 6 discusses composing business messages, and Chapter 7 covers revising business messages. The rest of Chapter 5 focuses on planning business messages. The result of planning can be as simple as a handwritten checklist of topics to cover in a phone conversation, or it can be a detailed strategy that spells out scheduling and collaborative responsibilities, objectives, audience needs, and media choices. By defining your purpose, you set clear objectives for measuring your efforts. By analyzing your audience, you focus on their needs and point of view. By establishing your main idea, you shape and control your message. And by selecting a channel and medium, you present your message in the best light possible.[13]

STAGE 1: DEFINING YOUR PURPOSE

When planning a business message, think about your purpose. Of course you want to maintain the goodwill of the audience and create a favorable impression for your organization, but you also have a particular goal you want to achieve. That purpose may be straightforward and obvious (like placing an order), or it may be more difficult to define. When the purpose is unclear, it pays to spend a few minutes thinking about what you hope to accomplish.

The purpose of the message helps you decide whether to proceed, how to respond to your audience, which information to focus on, and which channel and medium to use.

Why You Need a Clear Purpose

Suppose your boss asks you to write a memo describing the company's policy on vacation time. This is a fairly broad topic. What should you say? Knowing the purpose of your message helps you make important decisions about it. For example, you need a clear purpose to

- **Decide whether to proceed.** Frankly, many business messages serve no practical purpose and shouldn't be composed at all. Even if your message is dazzling, you can rapidly use up your credibility by writing memos that merely fill up filing cabinets. So when you're tempted to fire off a message, ask yourself: "Is this really necessary? Will it make a difference?" If you suspect that your ideas will have very little impact, hold off. Wait until you have a more practical purpose.

- ***Respond to the audience.*** If you're not certain that your purpose in composing a message is compatible with the audience's purpose in considering it, you're likely to serve fruit punch and peanut butter when they're expecting champagne and caviar. Vague assignments often give rise to this kind of mismatch. So when someone asks you to prepare a message, try to pin down the issues. What is the person's objective in requesting the information? Exactly what is expected of you? What does the audience need to know? Even when you initiate the message yourself, consider the audience's motives. Why will they pay attention to the material? What do they hope to gain? Are their expectations compatible with yours? If not, both you and the audience will fail to get what you want.

- ***Focus the content.*** It's easy to accumulate more information than you need, much of it interesting tidbits that really don't prove anything. If you include them in your message, you'll overload your audience. When you know your purpose, you include only the information necessary to accomplish your objective. Everything else is irrelevant and should be eliminated. Even though the extraneous information may be interesting, it diverts the audience from the real point and reduces the impact of your message.

- ***Establish the channel and medium.*** When you choose a channel for your message (oral, written, or electronic), and then a medium within that channel (printed memo or e-mail), your purpose influences that choice. If your purpose is to put together a company softball team, you may decide to use the written channel so that you can send the same message simultaneously to everyone in the office. Then you may decide that the appropriate medium is a casual memo or an e-mail message. The thing to remember is that if you don't know your purpose, or have only a vague definition of it, you'll make these choices haphazardly.

Common Purposes of Business Messages

Your general purpose may be to inform, persuade, or collaborate.

All business messages have a **general purpose:** to inform, to persuade, or to collaborate with your audience. These purposes determine both the amount of audience participation you need and the amount of control you have over your message (see Figure 5.2). If your message is intended strictly to inform, you require little interaction with your audience. Your readers or listeners absorb information, accept it, or reject it, but they don't contribute to message content; you control the message. If your message is persuasive, you require a moderate amount of audience participation, so you'll retain a moderate amount of message control. Finally, if you seek collaboration from your audience, you require maximum audience participation, so your control of the message is reduced. You can't adhere to a rigid plan because you need to adjust to new input and unexpected reactions.

To determine the specific purpose, think of how the audience's ideas or behavior should be affected by the message.

In addition to having a general purpose, your messages also have a **specific purpose.** Ask yourself, "What should my audience do or think after reviewing this message?" Then state your purpose as precisely as possible, identifying the members of the audience who should respond.

How to Test Your Purpose

Once you've established your purpose, pause for a moment to consider whether it's worth pursuing at this time. There's no point in creating a message that is unlikely to

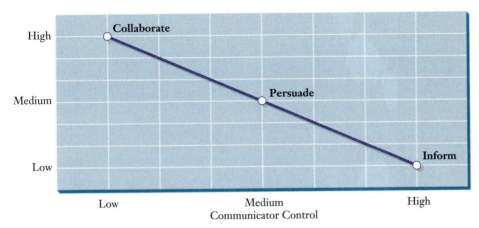

High — Collaborate

Medium — Persuade

Low — Inform

Low   Medium   High

Communicator Control

Figure 5.2
General Purposes of Business Messages

accomplish its purpose. So before you decide to pursue the message, ask yourself these
questions:

- ***Is the purpose realistic?*** Most people resist change. So if your purpose involves
  a radical shift in action or attitude, you'll do better to go slowly. Instead of suggesting your whole program at once, consider proposing the first step and viewing your message as the beginning of a learning process.
- ***Is this the right time?*** An idea that is unacceptable when profits are down, for
  example, may easily win approval when business improves. If an organization is
  undergoing changes of some sort, you may want to defer your message until
  things stabilize and people can concentrate on your ideas.
- ***Is the right person delivering the message?*** Even though you may have done all
  the work yourself, your boss may have a better chance of accomplishing results
  because of her or his higher status. Achieving your objective is more important
  than taking the credit. In the long run, people will recognize the quality of your
  work. Also bear in mind that some people are simply better writers or speakers
  than others. If the stakes are high and you lack experience or confidence, you
  might want to play a supporting role rather than take the lead.
- ***Is the purpose acceptable to the organization?*** As the representative of your
  company, you are obligated to work toward the organization's goals. Say you're a
  customer service representative who answers letters from customers (much as
  Jeff Hagen's staff does at General Mills). If you receive an abusive letter that unfairly attacks your company, your initial reaction might be to fire back an angry
  reply. Would top managers want you to counterattack, or would they want you to
  regain the customer's goodwill? Your response should reflect the organization's
  priorities.

STAGE 2: ANALYZING YOUR AUDIENCE

Once you are satisfied that you have a legitimate purpose in communicating, take a
good look at your intended audience. Who are the members, what are their attitudes,
and what do they need to know? The answers to these questions will indicate something
about the material you'll cover and the way you'll cover it.

Defer a message, or do not
send it at all

- If the purpose is not
  realistic
- If the timing is not right
- If you are not the right person to deliver the message
- If the purpose is not acceptable to the organization

Ask yourself some key questions about your audience:

- Who are they?
- What is their probable reaction to your message?
- How much do they already
  know about the subject?
- What is their relationship to
  you?

Develop Your Audience's Profile

If you're communicating with someone you know well, perhaps your boss or a co-worker, audience analysis is relatively easy. You can predict their reactions pretty well without a lot of research. On the other hand, if your audience is made up of strangers, you have to do some investigating to learn about them before you can use common sense to anticipate their reactions.

Determine Audience Size and Composition

Large audiences behave differently from small ones and require different communication techniques. If you were giving a speech to 500 people, you would limit the amount of audience participation, because fielding comments from such a large audience could be chaotic. Likewise, if you were writing a report for wide distribution, you might choose a more formal style, organization, and format than you would if the report were directed to only three or four people in your department.

Moreover, the larger your audience, the more diverse their backgrounds and interests are likely to be. People with different cultural backgrounds, education, status, and attitudes are likely to react differently to the same message, so you look for the common denominators that tie the members of the audience together.

At the same time, you want to respond to the particular concerns of individuals. The head of marketing needs different facts about a subject than the head of production or finance needs. As you compose the message, keep these differences in mind. Include a variety of evidence that touches on everyone's area of interest.

Focus on the common interests of the audience, but be alert to their individual concerns.

Identify the Primary Audience

When several people will be receiving your message, try to identify those who are most important to your purpose. If you can reach these decision makers or opinion molders, the other members of the audience will fall into place. Ordinarily, those with the most organizational status are the key people, but occasionally someone will surprise you. A person in a relatively low position may have influence in one or two particular areas.

Estimate the Audience's Probable Reaction

Your approach to organizing your message depends on your audience's probable reaction. If you expect a favorable response with very little criticism or debate, you can be straightforward about stating your conclusions and recommendations. You can also use a bit less evidence to support your points. On the other hand, when you face a skeptical audience, you may have to introduce your conclusions and recommendations more gradually and provide more proof.

In addition to considering the audience's general reaction, try to anticipate how key decision makers will respond to specific points. From past experience, you may know that the boss is especially concerned about certain issues: profits, market share, sales growth, or whatever. By anticipating this bias, you can incorporate evidence in your presentation that will address these issues.

A gradual approach and plenty of evidence are required to win over a skeptical audience.

Gauge the Audience's Level of Understanding

If you and your audience share the same general background, you can assume they will understand your material without any difficulty. If not, you'll have to decide how much you need to educate them. The trick is to provide the information they need without being stodgy or obvious. In general, you're better off explaining too much rather than too little, particularly if you're subtle about it. The audience may get a bit impatient, but at

least they'll understand your message. It may happen that most of your audience has roughly the same general level of understanding. If not, gear your coverage to the key decision makers. Of course, if your audience is from another culture, your efforts will be more involved (see "Understand Intercultural Audiences, and You'll Be Understood").

Define Your Relationship with the Audience

If you're unknown to your audience, you'll have to earn their confidence before you can win them to your point of view. The initial portion of your message will be devoted to gaining credibility. As you proceed, prove your points carefully; the audience will be judging your abilities as well as your information.

If you're communicating with a familiar group, your credibility has already been established, so you can get down to business immediately. However, you may have to overcome people's preconceptions about you. Some members of the audience may have trouble separating your arguments from your personality or your field. If they think of you as being a certain type, say, a "numbers person," they may question your competence in other areas. As you develop your message, you can overcome these prejudices by providing ample evidence for any material outside your usual area of expertise.

Your status relative to your audience also affects the style and tone of your presentation. You address your peers one way and your boss another. You use still another tone when communicating with employees of lower status, and your style with co-workers differs markedly from your style with customers and suppliers.

Satisfy Your Audience's Informational Needs

As Jeff Hagen points out, the key to effective communication is determining your reader's needs and then responding to them. You do that by telling people what they need to know in terms that are meaningful to them. A good message answers all the audience's questions.

Find Out What the Audience Wants to Know

In many cases the audience's information needs are readily apparent. When Jeff Hagen and his staff at General Mills answer messages requesting information about products or recipes, all they normally have to do is respond to the consumers' questions. In other

BEST OF THE WEB

Learn More About Analyzing an Audience

Find out more about audience analysis with a table that's based on developing information for the Web. A carefully constructed audience cluster diagram graphically illustrates the discussion and reinforces the points made in this textbook.

http//www.december.com/web/develop/wdaudience.html

Vary the tone and structure of the message to reflect your relationship with the audience.

Five questions to ask yourself that will help you satisfy the audience's information needs:
- What does the audience want to know?
- What does the audience need to know?
- Have I provided all desired and necessary information?
- Is the information accurate?
- Have I emphasized the information of greatest interest to the audience?

COMMUNICATING ACROSS CULTURES

UNDERSTAND INTERCULTURAL AUDIENCES, AND YOU'LL BE UNDERSTOOD

Perhaps you're writing a letter to a Belgian company, giving a speech to visiting Japanese business associates, or training non-English-speaking employees. Communicating successfully with an intercultural audience goes beyond avoiding idioms, jargon, long words, complicated sentences, and questionable gestures. To be clearly understood across cultures, consider how your audience thinks, how your audience learns, and what your audience expects in terms of style.

- **Does your audience think the same way you do?** If you try making a point by starting with a general statement and then elaborating on that statement without digressing, you may find your audience unimpressed. People from Slavic countries, for example, expect an intelligent expression of ideas to contain many digressions, perhaps never even stating a specific point. If you make a request by starting with the specific action desired and then explaining the benefits of such action, you may again find your audience unsatisfied. Such a request made in France would probably start by stating the problem and discussing its ramifications before requesting any specific action.
- **Does your audience learn the same way you do?** If you're writing a manual, you might require your audience first to read a brief introduction, then to look at an overview of your product, and finally to proceed through a step-by-step analysis. This approach, however, may not satisfy the way your audience prefers to learn. People in Japan, for example, tend to avoid the "big picture" until they've been exposed to each part.
- **Does your audience define good communication the same way you do?** If you focus your efforts on making your message as clear as possible, you may not satisfy your audience's aesthetic appreciation of style. In Japan, for instance, beauty, surprise, and flow are acceptable measures of good communication.
- **Does your audience perceive graphics the same way you do?** You might assume that a picture would be viewed the same by everyone, but people from differing cultures may in fact see different things. In a technical drawing, a switch labeled "MAN" (for *manual*) on the left and "AUTO" (for *automatic*) on the right would probably be called a "MAN/AUTO" switch in the United States. In Japan, engineers might call it an "AUTO/MAN" switch, perhaps because they read Japanese books from back to front. What does such a difference in perception tell you about more subtle messages?

- **Does your audience handle everyday business situations the same way you do?** You may tend to speak out clearly and directly, using forceful imperatives, when your audience expects more subtlety, delicacy, and passive grace. If you need information, you may phone an associate for the answer, but a European would probably send a memo for the same information and would consider your phone call pushy and aggressive. If you send a bright young executive to Bangkok to present a proposal, you may offend audience members who associate wisdom with age and experience and who expect an older, senior member of your firm to be entrusted with such an important task.

Clearly, analyzing an intercultural audience is more involved than analyzing one that shares your background. Thought processes, methods of learning, and expectations about style all depend on culture. Accommodating such differences may turn out to be a difficult task, but learning about these differences through audience analysis will give you the opportunity to try.

1. You researched your audience's culture, but things aren't going well during your face-to-face meeting. Your audience has also researched your culture. Is it possible you're miscommunicating because you're both too involved in accommodating the other's differences?
2. When analyzing an audience from another culture, how can you know when you have enough information?

By restating a vague request in more specific terms, you can get the requester to define his or her needs more precisely.

cases, an audience may not be particularly good at telling you what is needed. Your boss might say, "Find out everything you can about the Polaroid Corporation, and write a memo on it." That's a pretty big assignment. Ten days later, you submit your 25-page report, and instead of heaping you with praise, your boss says: "I don't need all this. All I want is Polaroid's five-year financial record."

One good way to pin down a vague request is to restate the request in more specific terms. If your boss says, "Find out everything you can about Polaroid," you might respond, "You want me to track down their market position by product line and get sales and profit figures by division for the past five years, right?" Another way to handle a vague request is to get a fix on its priority. You might ask, "Should I drop everything else and devote myself to this for the next week?" Asking a question or two forces the person to think through the request and define more precisely what is required.

Anticipate Unstated Questions

Try to think of information needs that your audience may not even be aware of. Suppose your company has just hired a new employee from out of town, and you've been assigned to coordinate this person's relocation. At a minimum, you would write a welcoming letter describing your company's procedures for relocating employees. With a little extra thought, however, you might decide to include some information about the city: perhaps a guide to residential areas, a map or two, brochures about cultural activities, or information on schools and transportation facilities.

Providing the little extras can be a big help to your audience. In some cases, you may even be a better judge of their information needs than they are. You may even tell them something they consider important but wouldn't have thought to ask. Although adding information of this sort lengthens your message, it creates goodwill.

Include any additional information that might be helpful, even though the reader didn't specifically ask for it.

Provide All the Required Information

Once you've defined your audience's needs, be certain to satisfy those needs completely. One good way to test the thoroughness of your message is to use the journalistic approach: Check to see whether your messages answer *who, what, when, where, why,* and *how.* Here's an example of a letter that fails to pass the test. It's a request for information from a large hotel:

Test the completeness of your document by making sure it answers all the important questions: who, what, when, where, why, and how.

> Dear Ms. Hill:
>
> I just got back from a great vacation in Hawaii. However, this morning I discovered that my favorite black leather shoes are missing. Since I wore them in Hawaii, I assume I left them at the Hawaii Sands Hotel. Please check the items in your "lost and found" and let me know whether you have the missing shoes.

Although the style of the letter is fine and is grammatically correct, this letter won't get the desired results because the author fails to tell Hill everything she needs to know. The *what* could be improved by a detailed description of the missing shoes (size, brand, any distinguishable marks or trim). Hill doesn't know *when* the writer stayed at the Hawaii Sands, what room the writer stayed in (*where*), or *how* to return the shoes. Hill will have to write or call the sender to get the missing details, and the inconvenience may be just enough to prevent her from complying with the request.

Whenever you request any action, take particular care to explain exactly what you are expecting. Until readers get a clear picture of what they're supposed to do, they can't possibly do it. If you want them to send you a check for $5, tell them; if you want them to turn in their time cards on Friday by 3:00 P.M., spell it out. If you want somebody to do something, be specific when stating your request, and cover all the essential points.

When you want to induce action
- *Be specific*
- *Cover all the essential points*

Be Sure the Information Is Accurate

There's no point in answering all your audience's questions if the answers are wrong. In business, you have a special duty to check things before making a written commitment, especially if you're writing to someone who is outside the company. Your organization is legally bound by any promises you make, so make sure your company is able to follow through. Whether you're promising delivery by a given date or

Be certain that the information you provide is accurate and that the commitments you make can be kept.

agreeing to purchase an item, if you have any doubt about the organization's ability or willingness to back up your promises, check with the appropriate people *before* you make the commitment. If you write the letter first and check for approval later, you may get some nasty surprises. Unreliability is embarrassing, and it damages your company's reputation.

Of course, honest mistakes are possible. You may sincerely believe that you have answered someone's questions correctly and then later realize that your information was incorrect. If that happens, the most ethical thing for you to do is to contact the person immediately and correct the error. Most people will respect you for your honesty.

You can minimize mistakes, however, by trying to be accurate and by double-checking everything you write or say. Check first to be certain that the organization can meet any commitments you make involving other people. Then check again to be certain you haven't made any errors of fact or logic. If you are using outside sources of information, ask yourself whether they are up-to-date and reliable. If your sources are international, be aware that various cultures view accuracy differently. A German bank may insist on balancing the books to the last penny, whereas an Italian bank may be more lenient. Such attitudes toward accuracy clearly influence the reliability of any information presented.[14] Be sure to review any mathematical or financial calculations. Check all dates and schedules, and examine your own assumptions and conclusions to be certain they are valid.

Emphasize Ideas of Greatest Interest to the Audience

Try to figure out what points will especially interest your audience; then give these points the most attention.

When deciding how to respond to your audience's information needs, remember that some points will be of greater interest and importance than others. Say that you're summarizing a recent conversation you had with one of your company's oldest and best customers. The emphasis you give each point of the conversation depends on the audience's concerns. The head of engineering might be interested in the customer's reaction to the design features of your product. Someone in the shipping department might be concerned about comments on delivery schedules. In other words, pick out the points that will have the most impact on your audience, and emphasize them.

If you don't know the audience, or if you're communicating with a large group of people, you'll have to use your common sense to identify points of particular interest. Such factors as age, job, location, income, or education can give you a clue. Say you're trying to sell memberships in the Book of the Month Club. How would you adjust your sales message for college students? Suburban homemakers? Retired residents of Sun City, Arizona? Traveling sales representatives? Auto mechanics? All these people would need to know the same facts about membership, but each group would be more interested in some facts than in others. Economy might be important to college students or retired people, and convenience might attract sales representatives or homemakers. Remember that your main goal as a business communicator is to tell your audience what they need to know.

Satisfy Your Audience's Motivational Needs

Rely mainly on reason to win your audience to your point of view, but don't overlook their underlying emotions.

Some types of messages, particularly persuasive messages and bad news, are intended to motivate audience members to change their beliefs or behavior. The problem is that people resist ideas that conflict with their existing beliefs and practices. If you try to sell financial planning services to someone who has always managed her own finances, she has to rethink her way of doing things. She is being asked to give up a system she's familiar with for one that's entirely new. Faced with such mutually exclusive concepts, people sometimes reject the new information without even listening.[15] They may selectively screen out threatening ideas or distort your message to fit their preconceived map of reality. To overcome resistance, arrange your message so that the information will be as acceptable as possible (see Chapter 1).

Satisfy Your Audience's Practical Needs

Many business messages are directed toward people who are themselves in business—your customers, suppliers, and co-workers. So regardless of where these people work or precisely what they do, their days are filled with distractions:

- First-level supervisors are involved in at least 200 separate activities or incidents in an 8-hour day.
- Most activities are very brief. One study of supervisors shows one activity every 48 seconds.
- A study of chief executives reports that periods of desk work average 10 to 15 minutes each.
- Responding to mail takes less than 5 percent of a manager's time, and most executives react to only about 30 percent of the mail they receive.[16]

In other words, many in your audience will review your message under difficult circumstances with many interruptions, and they are likely to give it a low priority. So make your message as convenient as possible for your audience. Try to be brief. Generally speaking, a 5-minute talk is easier to follow than a 30-minute presentation; a two-paragraph letter is more manageable than one that's two pages long, and a two-page memo is more likely to be read than a ten-page report.

If your written message has to be long, make it easy for readers to follow so that they can pick it up and put it down several times without losing the thread of what you're saying. Begin with a summary of key points, use plenty of headings, and put important points in list format so that they'll stand out. Put less important information in separate enclosures or appendixes, and use charts and graphs to dramatize important ideas.

If you're delivering a long message orally, be sure to give listeners an overview of the message's structure, and then express your thoughts clearly and logically. You might

Remember that your audience
- May have little time
- May be distracted
- May give your message low priority

Presenting the required information in a convenient format will help your audience understand and accept your message.

Devices that make your messages easier to comprehend include summaries and overviews, headings, lists, enclosures, appendixes, handouts, charts, and graphs.

For the busy executive trying to track messages from too many sources (such as voice mail, fax, pager, and e-mail), Octel Communications has come up with a system known as the Unified Messenger, which brings voice mail, e-mail, and faxes into a single mailbox that can be checked on computer screen or by telephone.

also use flip charts, slides, or handouts to help listeners understand and remember key points. You're the guide; lead audience members through your message by telling them where they've been and where they're going.

STAGE 3: ESTABLISHING THE MAIN IDEA

Every business message can be boiled down to one main idea. Regardless of the issue's complexity, one central point sums up everything. This is your theme, your main idea. Everything else in the message either supports this point or demonstrates its implications.

A topic and a main idea are different (see Table 5.1). The **topic** is the broad subject of the message. The **main idea** makes a statement about the topic—one of many possible statements—providing a rationale, explaining your purpose in terms that the audience can accept. You might give a presentation on the topic of company health clubs, with the aim of persuading management to build an on-site facility. Your main idea might be that the costs of providing a company health club would be more than offset by gains in productivity and reductions in insurance costs.

The main idea has to strike a response in the intended audience. It has to motivate people to do what you want by linking your purpose with their own. When you're preparing a brief letter, memo, or meeting, the main idea may be pretty obvious, especially if you're dealing with simple facts that have little or no emotional content for the audience. In such cases the main idea may be nothing more than "Here is what you wanted." If you're responding to a request for information about the price and availability of your company's products, your main idea would be something like "We have these items at competitive prices."

The main idea is the "hook" that sums up why a particular audience should do or think as you suggest.

Finding the "angle" or "hook" is more complicated when you're trying to persuade someone or when you have disappointing information to convey. In these situations, look for a main idea that will establish a good relationship between you and your audience. Focus on some point of agreement or common interest.

TABLE 5.1
TOPIC, PURPOSE, AND MAIN IDEA

General Purpose	Topic	Specific Purpose	Main Idea
To inform	Filing insurance claims	To teach customer service representatives how to file an insurance claim	Proper filing by employees saves the company time and money.
To persuade	Funding for research and development	To get top management's approval for increased spending on research and development	Competitors spend more than we do on research and development.
To collaborate	Incentive pay	To get the human resources and accounting departments to jointly devise an incentive system that ties wages directly to profits	Tying wages to profits will automatically reduce compensation costs in tough years while motivating employees to be more productive.

In longer documents and presentations, in which a mass of material needs to be unified, the problem of establishing a main idea becomes still more challenging. You need to identify a generalization that encompasses all the individual points you want to make. For tougher assignments like these, you may need to take special measures to come up with a main idea.

Use Prewriting Techniques

Identifying the main idea often requires creativity and experimentation. The best approach is to **brainstorm,** letting your mind wander over the possibilities, testing various alternatives against your purpose, your audience, and the facts at your disposal. How do you generate those possibilities? Successful communicators use various approaches. You have to experiment until you find a prewriting method that fits your mental style. Here are a few approaches that might work for you:

- *Storyteller's tour.* Turn on your tape recorder and pretend that you've just run into an old friend on the street. She says, "So, what are you working on these days?" Give her an overview of your message, focusing on your reasons for communicating, your major points, your rationale, and the implications for your intended audience. Listen critically to the tape; then repeat the exercise until you are able to give a smooth, two-minute summary that conveys the gist of your message. The summary should reveal your main idea.

- *Random list.* On a computer screen or a clean sheet of paper, list everything that pops into your head pertaining to your message. When you've exhausted the possibilities, study the list for relationships. Sort the items into groups, as you would sort a deck of cards into suits. Look for common denominators; the connection might be geographic, sequential, spatial, chronological, or topical. Part of the list might break down into problems, causes, and solutions; another part, into pros and cons. Regardless of what categories finally emerge, the sorting process will help you sift through your thoughts and decide what's important and what isn't.

- *FCR worksheet.* If your subject involves the solution to a problem, you might try using an FCR worksheet to help you visualize the relationships among your findings (F), your conclusions (C), and your recommendations (R). For example, you might find that you're losing sales to a competitor who offers lower prices than you do (F). From this, you might conclude that your loss of sales is due to your pricing policy (C). This conclusion would lead you to recommend a price cut (R). To make an FCR worksheet, divide a computer screen or a sheet of paper into three columns. List the major findings in the first column, then extrapolate conclusions and write them in the second column. These conclusions form the basis for the recommendations, which are listed in the third column. An analysis of the three columns should help you focus on the main idea.

- *Journalistic approach.* For informational messages, the journalistic approach may provide a good point of departure. The answers to six questions—who, what, when, where, why, and how—should clarify the main idea.

- *Question-and-answer chain.* Perhaps the best approach is to look at the subject from your audience's perspective. Ask yourself: "What is the audience's main question? What do they need to know?" Examine your answers to those questions. What additional questions emerge? Follow the chain of questions and answers until you have replied to every conceivable question that might occur to the audience. By thinking about your material from their point of view, you are more likely to pinpoint the main idea.

Some techniques for establishing the main idea:
- Storyteller's tour
- Random list
- FCR worksheet
- Journalistic approach
- Question-and-answer chain

Limit the Scope

The main idea should be geared to the length of the message.

Whether the audience expects a one-page memo or a one-hour speech, select a main idea that can be developed within that framework. So once you have a tentative statement of your main idea, test it against the length limitations that have been imposed for your message.

There's a limit to how much you can communicate in a given number of words. What can be accomplished depends on the nature of the subject, audience members' familiarity with the topic, their receptivity to your conclusions, and your existing credibility. In general, presenting routine information to a knowledgeable audience that already knows and respects you takes fewer words. Building consensus about a complex and controversial subject takes longer, especially if the audience is composed of skeptical or hostile strangers.

Although you adjust your message to fit the time or space available, don't change the number of major points. Regardless of how long the message will be, stick with three or four major points—five at the very most. According to communication researchers, that's all your audience will remember.[17]

If you're delivering a long message, say, a 60-minute presentation or a 20-page report, the major points can be developed in considerable detail. You can spend about ten minutes or ten paragraphs (or over three pages of double-spaced, typewritten text) on each of your key points and still have room for the introduction and conclusion. Instead of introducing additional points, you can deal more fully with complex issues, offer a variety of evidence, and overcome resistance. If your message is brief, four minutes or one page, you'll have only a minute or a paragraph each for the introduction, conclusion, and major points. The amount of evidence you can present is limited, which means that your main idea must be both easy to understand and easy to accept.

The scope of your message (its length and detail) also determines the amount and depth of information gathering you can do. The information you'll need for various business messages will cover a broad range. You may need only to glance at your calendar to confirm a meeting, or you may need to spend weeks conducting formal research for a complicated report. Gathering information for reports and proposals is thoroughly discussed in Chapter 15.

STAGE 4: SELECTING THE APPROPRIATE CHANNEL AND MEDIUM

Various types of messages require various communication channels.

The communication media available to businesspeople have mushroomed in the past two decades: audiotapes, videotapes, faxes, e-mail, Web sites, voice mail, teleconferences—to name a few. You can now select not only from the traditional oral and written channels but also from the newer electronic channel, which includes some features of the other two. Your selection of channel and medium can make the difference between effective and ineffective communication.[18] So when choosing a channel (whether oral, written, or electronic) and a medium (whether face-to-face conversation, telephone conversation, e-mail, voice mail, videotape, written report, etc.), do your best to match your selections to your message and your intentions.[19]

Every medium has limitations that filter out parts of the message. For example, flyers and bulletin boards are nondynamic and ineffective for communicating extremely complex messages, but they're perfect for simple ones. Moreover, every medium influences your audience's perception of your intentions. So if you want to emphasize the formality of your message, use a more formal medium, such as a written memo or letter. If you want to emphasize the confidentiality of your message, use voice mail rather than a fax, send a letter rather than a memo, or address the matter in an interview rather than during a meeting. If you want to instill an emotional commitment to corporate values, consider a visual medium, such as a videotape or videoconference.[20]

Various cultures tend to favor one channel over another. For example, the United States, Canada, and Germany emphasize written media, whereas Japan emphasizes oral media—perhaps because its high-context culture carries so much of the message in nonverbal cues and "between the lines" interpretation.[21] Within the United States, the basic choice of oral, written, or electronic channels depends on the purpose, the audience, and the characteristics of the three communication channels (see Table 5.2).

Oral Communication

The chief advantage of oral communication is the opportunity it provides for immediate feedback. This is the channel to use when you want the audience to ask questions and make comments or when you're trying to reach a group decision. Face-to-face communication is useful when you're presenting controversial information, because you can read the audience's body language and adjust your message accordingly.[22]

In general, use oral communication if your purpose is to collaborate with the audience.

TABLE 5.2

WHEN TO TALK IT OVER, WRITE IT OUT, OR APPLY TECHNOLOGY		
An Oral Message Is Best When	**A Written Message Is Best When**	**An Electronic Message Is Best When**
You want immediate feedback from the audience	You don't need immediate feedback	You don't need immediate feedback, but you do need speed
Your message is relatively simple and easy to accept	Your message is detailed, complex, and requires careful planning	Your message is emotional, you may or may not need immediate feedback, but you're physically separated (videotape, teleconference)
You don't need a permanent record	You need a permanent, verifiable record	You don't need a permanent record, but you want to overcome time-zone barriers (voice mail, fax)
You can assemble the audience conveniently and economically	You are trying to reach an audience that is large and geographically dispersed	You are trying to reach an audience that is large and geographically dispersed, and you want to reach them personally (teleconference, videotape)
You want to encourage interaction to solve a problem or reach a decision	You want to minimize the chances for distortion that occur when a message is passed orally from person to person	You want to minimize oral distortion, but you're in a hurry and in a distant location (e-mail)

Your choice between a face-to-face conversation and a telephone or conference call would depend on audience location, message importance, and your need for the sort of nonverbal feedback that only body language can reveal. In fact, oral communication takes many forms, including conversations, telephone calls, interviews, small group meetings, seminars, workshops, training programs, formal speeches, and major presentations. Chapters 19 and 20 explore these media in more detail.

In general, the smaller the audience, the more interaction among the members. If your purpose involves reaching a decision or solving a problem, select an oral medium geared toward a small audience. Be sure the program is relatively informal and unstructured so that ideas can flow freely. Gatherings of this sort can be arranged quickly and economically.

At the opposite extreme are formal presentations to large audiences, which are common at events such as sales conventions, shareholder meetings, and ceremonial functions. Often these major presentations take place in a big facility, where the audience can be seated auditorium-style. Their formality makes them unsuitable for collaborative purposes requiring audience interaction.

Written Communication

Written communication increases the sender's control but eliminates the possibility of immediate feedback.

Written messages also take many forms. At one end are the scribbled notes people use to jog their own memories; at the other are elaborate, formal reports that rival magazines in graphic quality. Regardless of the form, written messages have one big advantage: They let you plan and control the message. A written format is appropriate when the information is complex, when a permanent record is needed for future reference, when the audience is large and geographically dispersed, and when immediate interaction with the audience is either unimportant or undesirable.

For extensive coverage of letters and memos, see Chapters 8 through 11. Reports are thoroughly discussed in Chapters 14 through 18. In addition, Component Chapter A presents a detailed discussion of the accepted formats for business documents. Although many types of written communication are specialized, the most common are letters, memos, and reports.

Letters and Memos

With a few exceptions, most letters and memos are relatively brief documents, generally one or two pages. Memos are the "workhorses" of business communication, used for the routine, day-to-day exchange of information within an organization. Letters go to outsiders, and they perform an important public relations function in addition to conveying a particular message. Memos are usually brief, lacking a salutation and emphasizing the needs of readers who have time only to skim messages. They can also be sent to any number of receivers, whereas letters are sent to only one. Because of their open construction and method of delivery, memos are less private than letters. You often use memos to designate responsibility, communicate the same material to many people, communicate policy and procedure, confirm oral agreements or decisions, and place specific information on record.

Letters and memos are organized according to their purpose; the relationship between writer and reader dictates their style and tone.

Letters (see Figure 5.3), memos, and e-mail messages (see Figure 5.4 on page 132) can be classified by function into four categories: direct requests; routine, good-news, and goodwill messages; bad-news messages; and persuasive messages. Their function determines their organization, but style and tone are governed by your relationship with your audience.

Figure 5.3
In-Depth Critique: A Typical Letter

Jeff Hagen responds to a consumer who has written General Mills about his love for a company product. Hagen is careful to match the consumer's tone by keeping his approach light and cheerful.

General Mills Consumer Services

P.O. Box 1113, Minneapolis, MN 55440

March 13, 1997

Mr. Julius Croghan
231 Ruffin Avenue
Cedar Spring, South Carolina 29302

Dear Mr. Croghan:

Thank you very much for your delightful comments. It was kind of you to share your thoughts, and you've brightened our day here at General Mills.

Many of our products have long attracted loyal fans. I'm happy to see that you are among that group.

At General Mills, customer feedback is critical to our success. It's through communications like yours that we become aware of consumer concerns and preferences.

I have enclosed gift coupons and hope you will continue to use and enjoy our products.

Sincerely,

Jeffrey N. Hagen

Jeffrey N. Hagen
Director, Consumer Services

Jeff Hagen uses letterhead stationery, but doesn't let that make his message too formal or unfriendly.

The formal salutation indicates Hagen's respect for a customer he doesn't know.

The body of the letter is brief but still includes a number of friendly remarks designed to maintain goodwill.

The close is an optimistic look into the future.

Many organizations rely on form letters (and sometimes form memos) to save time and money on routine communication. Form letters are particularly handy for such one-time mass mailings as sales messages about products, explanations of policies and procedures, information about organizational activities, goodwill messages such as seasonal greetings, and acknowledgments of job applications. A variation of

Figure 5.4
In-Depth Critique: A
Typical E-mail Message

Glenda Anderson responds to a consumer who has written General Mills to inquire about a product. Anderson is careful to maintain a tone of courtesy and friendliness.

E-mail messages contain four pieces of information–to, from, date, and subject.

Glenda Anderson states her business right away.

E-mail messages are often brief and to the point.

A courteous attitude and friendly style work to keep the lines of communication open.

```
╔══════════════════════ E-Mail ══════════════════════╗

  Return-Path: <gAnderson@genmills.com>
  Date: Fri, 19 May 1997 07:11:52 (CST)
  From: Glenda Anderson <gAnderson@genmills.com>
  To: Bill B. <bbryers@aol.com>
  Subject: Love the new flavors


  Dear Bill:

  We are happy to tell you that we do make a Light Fat
  Free Yoplait yogurt in a key lime flavor. Hopefully your
  grocer will soon be carrying it. If not, let your grocer
  know that you would like to see this great new flavor on
  the shelf.

  Thank you for taking time to send us your e-mail
  message. If you should have any more questions or
  comments about our products, please contact us again.

  Sincerely,

  Glenda Anderson
  General Mills Consumer Services
  writing at 11:52 a.m.
  on Friday, May 19, 1997
```

the form letter is the **boilerplate,** a standard paragraph(s) that can be selected to suit an occasion or audience. Letters containing boilerplates are used for slightly more individualized messages, such as General Mills's replies to inquiries about its products and activities.

Reports and Proposals

Reports are generally longer and more formal than letters and memos, and they have more components.

Reports and proposals are factual, objective documents that may be distributed to either insiders or outsiders, depending on their purpose and subject. They come in many formats, including preprinted forms, letters, memos, and manuscripts. In length, they range from a few pages to several hundred. Generally, reports and proposals are longer than letters and memos, with a larger number of distinct elements.

Reports and proposals also tend to be more formal than letters and memos. As in all forms of business communication, the organization, style, and tone of reports and proposals depend on the message's purpose, on the relationship between writer and reader, and on the traditions of the organization. Thus the basic composition process is much the same for all.

Electronic Communication

Although oral messages can be in person and face-to-face, they can also be transmitted electronically using voice mail, teleconferencing, audiotape, videotape, closed-circuit television, and so on. Similarly, although written messages can be handwritten, typed, or printed, they can also be transmitted electronically using faxes, e-mail, computer conferencing, and so on. Electronic media are useful when you need speed, when you're physically separated from your audience, when you need to overcome time-zone barriers, and when you need to reach a dispersed audience personally. Chapter 4 introduces the technological features of electronic media; following are a few pointers on when to select electronic media over traditional oral or written media:[30]

In general, use electronic communication for speed, to overcome time-zone barriers, and to reach a widely dispersed audience personally.

- *Voice mail* is usually used to replace short memos and phone calls that need no response. It is most effective for short, unambiguous messages.
- *Teleconferencing* is best for informational meetings, but it's ineffective for negotiation. It's an efficient alternative to a face-to-face meeting, but it can't totally simulate it. For example, it discourages the "secondary" conversations that usually occur during a meeting of more than four or five people—which could prevent participants' sharing of valuable information or foster participants' focusing on the topic.
- *Videotape* is often effective for reaching a large number of people with a motivational message. By communicating nonverbal cues, it can strengthen your image of sincerity and trustworthiness; however, it offers no opportunity for immediate feedback.
- *Fax* messages are usually used to overcome time-zone barriers when a hard copy is required. A fax has all the characteristics of a written message, except that it may lack the privacy of a letter, and depending on the quality of your audience's machine (thermal versus plain-paper, for example), your message may appear less crisp, perhaps even less professional, than other written messages.
- *E-mail* offers advantages of speed, lower cost, and increased access to other employees. This medium is best at communicating brief, noncomplex information that's time-sensitive, but its effectiveness depends on the skills of the people using it (see Figure 5.5 on page 134).
- *Computer conferencing* offers the advantage of democracy; that is, more attention is focused on an idea than on who communicates it. However, too much emphasis on the message (to the neglect of the person communicating it) can threaten corporate culture, which needs a more dynamic medium of communication.

Message planning encompasses valuable tasks that help you gain more control over the composition process. Use this chapter's Checklist for Planning Business Messages not as a recipe for well-planned messages but as a reminder of what tasks and choices to address as you develop your business messages. Also remember that the planning stages discussed here may be useful at any time during the composition process, depending on your purpose, your audience, and your message.

Figure 5.5

*In-Depth Critique: A Brief
E-Mail Message
Conveying Time-Sensitive
Material*

The president of a chain of Texas-based pet stores, Pet Paradise, just asked his administrative assistant, Maria Hernandez, to notify all 47 store managers that their Friday meeting in San Antonio has been canceled and rescheduled for September 26. Hernandez could phone or fax the message, but either of these methods would take considerable time. By choosing e-mail, Hernandez minimized her own efforts and allowed each manager to receive the important news almost immediately.

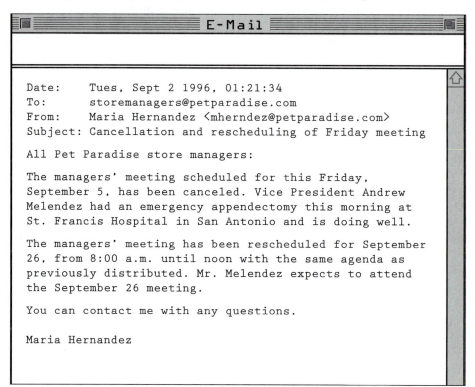

Since Hernandez has all managers' e-mail addresses in one file, she needed to key in only the name of that file to reach each manager.

Hernandez first states the critical message, followed by the reason for the cancellation.

She then gives information on the rescheduled meeting, again trying to anticipate the managers' questions.

```
Date:     Tues, Sept 2 1996, 01:21:34
To:       storemanagers@petparadise.com
From:     Maria Hernandez <mherndez@petparadise.com>
Subject:  Cancellation and rescheduling of Friday meeting

All Pet Paradise store managers:

The managers' meeting scheduled for this Friday,
September 5, has been canceled. Vice President Andrew
Melendez had an emergency appendectomy this morning at
St. Francis Hospital in San Antonio and is doing well.

The managers' meeting has been rescheduled for September
26, from 8:00 a.m. until noon with the same agenda as
previously distributed. Mr. Melendez expects to attend
the September 26 meeting.

You can contact me with any questions.

Maria Hernandez
```

SUMMARY

The composition process may be viewed as three basic categories of tasks: planning, composing, and revising. Planning stages include defining your purpose, analyzing your audience, establishing the main idea, and selecting the appropriate channel and medium. Composing stages include organizing and formulating your message. Revising stages include editing, rewriting, producing, and proofing your message.

When defining your purpose, you establish both the general and specific purposes, and you decide whether these purposes are worth pursuing. When analyzing your audience, you develop an audience profile to help you satisfy their needs, you examine their information needs to help you decide on the content of your message, you discover their motivational needs to help you organize your points in a convincing way, and you establish their practical needs to help you guide your format decisions. Your main idea summarizes what your audience should do or think as a result of your message, and it provides them with a rationale for understanding your message.

Oral communication gives you the opportunity to interact with the audience. Written communication gives you a greater opportunity to plan and control your mes-

CHECKLIST FOR PLANNING BUSINESS MESSAGES

A. PURPOSE
1. Determine whether the purpose of your message is to inform, persuade, or collaborate.
2. Identify the specific behavior you hope to induce in the audience.
3. Make sure that your purpose is worthwhile and realistic.

B. AUDIENCE
1. Identify the primary audience.
2. Determine the size and composition of the group.
3. Analyze the audience's probable reaction to your message.
4. Determine the audience's level of understanding.
5. Evaluate your relationship with the audience.
6. Analyze the audience's informational, motivational, and practical needs.

C. MAIN IDEA
1. Stimulate your creativity with brainstorming techniques.
2. Identify a "hook" that will motivate the audience to respond to your message in the way you intend.
3. Evaluate whether the main idea is realistic given the length limitations imposed on the message.
4. Collect any necessary information.

D. CHANNEL AND MEDIUM
1. If your purpose is to collaborate, give an informal, relatively unstructured oral presentation to a small group.

2. If you are celebrating an important public occasion, give a prepared speech to a large audience.
3. If you need a permanent record, if the message is complex, or if immediate feedback is unimportant, prepare a written message.
   a. Send a letter if your message is relatively simple and the audience is outside the company.
   b. Send a memo if your message is relatively simple and the audience is inside the company.
   c. Write a report if your message is objective and complex.
4. If you need to communicate quickly, overcome time-zone differences, or personally reach a widely dispersed audience, choose electronic communication.
   a. Use voice mail if your message is short and clear.
   b. Use teleconferencing for informational meetings.
   c. Use videotape for sending motivational messages to a large number of people.
   d. Use fax machines to overcome time-zone barriers.
   e. Use e-mail for speed, lower cost, and increased access to other employees.
   f. Use computer conferencing to focus attention on ideas instead of status.

sage. Electronic communication gives you greater speed and extended reach over long distances. Within these three basic channels, you can select the communication medium that best matches your intent, your message, and your audience.

COMMUNICATION CHALLENGES AT GENERAL MILLS

Although Jeff Hagen writes many of the form letters his department uses, he can't write them all. So a few senior staff members work on keeping the company's communications current and relevant as new products and new issues arise. That team is always facing bigger challenges.

INDIVIDUAL CHALLENGE: The Trix Rabbit has been getting a lot of e-mail lately. When the Web site was still

new, Internet team members would log into the tracking software, look up the suggested reply, and then cut and paste paragraphs into the e-mail program—shuffling them around to make them personal and appropriate to the medium. Now Hagen has asked you to develop a form reply for people who simply want to say, "I just love this product." Only this form reply must come via e-mail from the Trix Rabbit.

TEAM CHALLENGE: Hagen is not happy with the company's Web site at <http://www.genmills.com>, which was a first effort when the Internet was still new to General Mills. He's asking you, as his Internet team, to suggest better approaches. You'll have to analyze the audience for both the main site and the kids' site, suggest elements that should be included and some that might be avoided, and justify your reasoning before a larger committee. Use everything you've learned in this chapter to make your planning complete, and then brainstorm the list of suggestions.[31]

CRITICAL THINKING QUESTIONS

1. Some writers argue that planning messages wastes time because they inevitably change their plans as they go along. How would you respond to this argument? Briefly explain.

2. Your supervisor has asked you to prepare a message that, in your opinion, serves no worthwhile purpose. What do you do? Explain.

3. As editor of your company's newsletter, how would you go about discovering the needs of your fellow employees? Write a one-page explanation.

4. List several main ideas you might use if you were trying to persuade top management to invest in word-processing equipment and software.

5. As personnel manager, what medium would be best to use for explaining employee benefits to new employees? Explain your answer.

6. As a member of the public relations department, what medium would you recommend using to inform the local community that your toxic-waste cleanup program has been successful? Why?

EXERCISES

1. For each of the following communication tasks, state a specific purpose (if you have trouble, try beginning with "I want to . . ."):

   a. A report to your boss, the store manager, about the outdated items in the warehouse
   b. A memo to clients about your booth at the upcoming trade show
   c. A letter to a customer who hasn't made a payment for three months
   d. A memo to employees about the office's high water bills
   e. A phone call to a supplier checking on an overdue parts shipment
   f. A report to future users of the computer program you have chosen to handle the company's mailing list

2. Make a list of communication tasks you'll need to accomplish in the next week or so (a job application, a letter of complaint, a speech to a class, an order for some merchandise, etc.). For each, determine a general and a specific purpose.

3. List five messages you have received lately, such as direct-mail promotions, letters, e-mail messages, phone solicitations, and lectures. For each, determine the general and the specific purpose; then answer the following questions: Was the message well timed? Did the sender choose an appropriate channel and medium for the message? Did the appropriate person deliver the message? Was the sender's purpose realistic?

4. Barbara Marquardt is in charge of public relations for a cruise line that operates out of Miami. She is shocked to read a letter in a local newspaper from a disgruntled passenger, complaining about the service and entertainment on a recent cruise. Marquardt will have to respond to these publicized criticisms in some way. What audiences will she need to consider in her response? What channels and media should she choose? If the letter had been published in a travel publication widely read by travel agents and cruise travelers, how might her course of action differ?

5. For each communication task below, write brief answers to three questions: Who is my audience? What is my audience's general attitude toward my subject? What does my audience need to know?

   a. A final-notice collection letter from an appliance manufacturer to an appliance dealer, sent ten days before initiating legal collection procedures
   b. An unsolicited sales letter asking readers to purchase computer disks at near-wholesale prices
   c. An advertisement for peanut butter
   d. Fliers to be attached to doorknobs in the neighborhood, announcing reduced rates for chimney lining or repairs
   e. A cover letter sent along with your résumé to a potential employer

f. A request (to the seller) for a price adjustment on a piano that incurred $150 in damage during delivery to a banquet room in the hotel you manage

6. Rewrite the following message so that it includes all the information that the reader needs. (Make up any necessary details.)

> I am pleased to offer you the position of assistant buyer at Fontaine and Sons at an annual salary of $15,500. I hope to receive notice of your acceptance soon.

7. Frank Kroll has been studying a new method for testing the durability of the electric hand tools his company manufactures. Now he needs to prepare three separate reports on his findings: first, a report for the administrator who will decide whether to purchase the new equipment needed for using this method; second, a report for the company's engineers who design and develop the hand tools; and third, a report for the trainers who will be showing workers how to use the new equipment. To determine the audience's needs for each of these reports, Frank has made a list of the following questions: (1) Who are the readers? (2) Why will they read my report? (3) Do they need introductory or background material? (4) Do they need definitions of terms? (5) What level and type of language is needed? (6) What level of detail is needed? (7) What result does my report aim for? Put yourself in Frank's shoes, and answer these questions for each of the three audiences:

a. The administrator
b. The engineers
c. The trainers

8. Choose an electronic device that you know how to operate well (videocassette recorder, personal computer, telephone answering machine, etc.). Write two sets of instructions for operating the device: one set for a reader who has never used that type of machine and one set for someone familiar with that type of machine in general but who has never operated the specific model.

9. Work with a classmate to complete this task. Each partner must independently visit the site at <http://www.hrblock.com/tax>. Working together only by e-mail (not in person and not using any other electronic technology), plan, compose, and revise your joint explanation of the Web site. Summarize *what* is on the Web page and linked pages, and then critique the site. Explain why it does or does not communicate efficiently and effectively, and provide complete and accessible information for the intended audience. When you and your collaborator are satisfied with your explanation, print it out for submission to your instructor.

10. You're looking for a job as a salesperson, so you'd better be able to sell yourself first. What special qualities do you have that make you a desirable sales employee? Use the techniques described in the chapter to come up with a main idea you can use in your efforts to market yourself. In no more than a paragraph, draft a statement of your main idea that tells your audience (potential employers) what to do or think about you and why.

CHAPTER 6

COMPOSING BUSINESS MESSAGES

AFTER STUDYING THIS CHAPTER, YOU WILL BE ABLE TO

- Identify the characteristics of a well-organized message
- Explain why organization is important to both the audience and the communicator
- Break a main idea into subdivisions grouped under logical categories
- Arrange ideas in direct or indirect order, depending on the audience's probable reaction
- Compose a message using a style and tone that are appropriate to your subject, purpose, audience, and format
- Use the "you" attitude to interest the audience in your message
- Compose an appropriate e-mail message

COMMUNICATION CLOSE-UP AT COMMUNITY HEALTH GROUP

Although most people think accountants spend their days crunching numbers, Julian Santoyo says it just isn't true anymore. "Machines have taken care of a lot of that," explains the chief financial officer for Community Health Group (CHG), a nonprofit health maintenance organization (HMO) in Chula Vista, California. "Now, the more successful financial people are people who communicate and offer recommendations that support business decisions," he says. To do that, Santoyo writes memos, reports, letters, e-mail, and even news releases.

As a nonprofit organization, CHG is one of the few HMOs in the country to serve low-income recipients of government-funded medical care (known as "Medi-Cal" in California). Like commercial HMOs, CHG charges a monthly fee for each member and then contracts with doctors, hospitals, and other health-care professionals to provide the actual medical services members require. The difference is that CHG's member fees are paid by the government.

Most of CHG's 55,000 members are Hispanic or Asian, and many are non-English-speaking. Santoyo says that his co-workers reflect this diversity: Sixty percent are Hispanic, 30 percent are Anglo, and 10 percent are from a variety of cultural backgrounds. Some prefer Spanish as a primary language, others prefer English. But in addition to crossing language barriers, CHG's business spans the medical, insurance, government, and sales industries—all fields riddled with insider jargon and confusing acronyms. To be clearly understood, says Santoyo, audience awareness is essential.

"I need to take the numbers, the specific actuarial data or accounting data, and convert that information into something that's user-friendly and understandable," he says. "That means that I have to be flexible in how I structure my communication."

Julian Santoyo

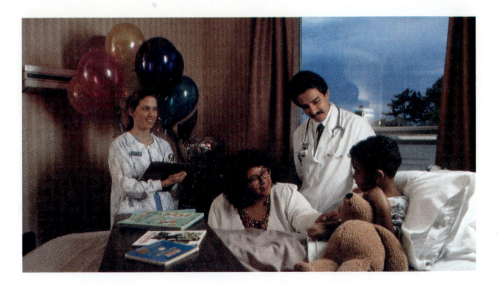

Because the majority of CHG's patients and staff members are Hispanic and Asian, employees work hard to overcome language and cultural barriers. Even when dealing with other businesses, CHG workers strive for clarity by carefully avoiding jargon and acronyms. To be as clear as possible, they strive for sound organization and a straightforward style.

He starts with an outline. If he thinks his audience will agree with him, he puts the main idea up front. If what he's writing is controversial or likely to be viewed with skepticism, he builds up to his main point. He makes these decisions before starting his first draft. The goal is to structure the message so that his readers can easily understand it, believe it, and use the information contained in it.

As Santoyo explains, it often takes two or three drafts to organize his message right. "You write it out, put it down, you come back later, and you look at it," explains Santoyo, "because when you're writing it, there's a lot of information that you're familiar with and that you assume everyone knows. A short time later or a day later, you look at it again and that 'familiar' feeling is gone and you think, 'Well, maybe I need to add this exhibit, or I need to elaborate on this point a little bit more, because I don't really think I'm getting the point across,' or 'I could write it a little bit better, rewording it a certain way.' If it's an important memo, I always recommend waiting at least half a day to distribute it."

Generally, Santoyo writes in a less formal style, in keeping with CHG's small size and casual atmosphere. He tries to avoid using technical terms. "If I'm going to use an acronym, I'll only use those that I know the audience is familiar with, or I'll define it somewhere in the text." As part of his audience-centered approach, Santoyo often uses the word 'we' to reflect CHG's team approach, as in, "We have to keep costs down because . . ."

To maintain his credibility, Santoyo never stretches his facts. "Never cry wolf," he advises. "Never exaggerate a point because you want to make sure something gets done. After a few times, they'll get wise to you and you'll end up like the kid in the story: you'll be someone's lunch." He believes in building credibility over time. "You have to have a good reputation; you see, that's all you have. You can't just say, 'Hey, I'm an honest guy,' and then go around with hidden agendas, because no matter how smart you think you are, a bright executive or co-worker is going to see through your smoke and mirrors . . . and they'll lose confidence in you." Then you'll have to work twice as hard for the same results.[1]

STAGE 5: ORGANIZING YOUR MESSAGE

Like Julian Santoyo, all business communicators face the problem of conveying a complicated web of ideas in an understandable fashion. People simply don't remember dissociated facts and figures, so successful communicators rely on organization to make their messages meaningful.[2] Before thinking about *how* to achieve good organization, however, think about *what* it means and *why* it's important.

What Good Organization Means

The definition of good organization varies from country to country. But in the United States and Canada, it is generally a linear message that proceeds point by point. If you've ever received a disorganized message, you're familiar with the frustration of trying to sort through a muddle of ideas. Consider this letter from Jill Saunders, the office manager at Boswell & Sons, mapmakers:

> Our president, Mr. Boswell, was in an accident last year, and he hasn't been able to work full-time. His absence has affected our business, so we don't have the budget we used to. His two sons are working hard, so we aren't bankrupt by any means, and soon Mr. Boswell will be coming back full-time.
>
> Boswell & Sons has been doing business with ComputerTime since I was hired six years ago. Your building was smaller then, and it was located on the corner of Federal Avenue and 2nd N.W. Mr. Boswell bought our first laser printer there. I still remember the day. It was the biggest check I'd ever written. Of course, over the years, I've gotten used to larger purchases.
>
> We have seven employees. Although all of them aren't directly involved in producing the maps we sell, they all need to have their computers working so that they can do their jobs. The 5 1/4-inch disk drive we bought for my assistant, Suzanne, has been a problem. We've taken it in for repairs three times in three months to the authorized service center, and Suzanne is very careful with the machine and hasn't abused it. She likes playing interactive adventure games on lunch breaks. It still doesn't work right, and she's tired of hauling it back and forth. We're all putting in longer hours to make up for Mr. Boswell's not being here, and none of us has a lot of spare time.
>
> This is the first time we've returned anything to your store, and I hope you'll agree that we deserve a better deal.

Most disorganized communication suffers from problems with content, grouping, or sequence.

This letter displays the sort of disorganization that U.S. and Canadian readers find frustrating. By taking a closer look at what's wrong, you can identify the four most common faults responsible for such organization problems:

- *Taking too long to get to the point.* Saunders wrote three paragraphs before introducing the topic: the faulty disk drive. Then she waited until the final paragraph to state her purpose: requesting an adjustment.
- *Including irrelevant material.* Saunders introduced information that has no bearing on her purpose or her topic. Does it matter that the computer store used to be smaller or that it was in a different location? What difference does it make whether Saunders's boss is working only part-time or whether her assistant likes playing computerized games during lunch?
- *Getting ideas mixed up.* Saunders seems to be making six points: (1) Her company has money to spend, (2) it's an old customer, (3) it pays by check, (4) it has purchased numerous items at the store, (5) the disk drive doesn't work, and (6) Saunders wants an adjustment. However, the ideas are in the wrong places. It would be more logical to begin with the fact that the machine doesn't work, and some of these ideas should be combined under the general idea that the company is a valuable customer.

- *Leaving out necessary information.* The customer service representative may want to know the make, model, and price of the disk drive; the date on which it was purchased; the specific problems the machine has had; and whether the repairs were covered by the warranty. Saunders also failed to specify what she wants the store to do. Does she want a new disk drive of the same type? A different model? Or simply her money back?

Achieving good organization can be a challenge. Nevertheless, by working with these four common faults, you can establish what good organization means. Four guidelines can help you recognize a well-organized message:

- Make the subject and purpose clear.
- Include only information that is related to the subject and purpose.
- Group the ideas and present them in a logical way.
- Include all the necessary information.

> A message is well organized when all the pieces fit together in a coherent pattern.

Each guideline not only helps you communicate clearly and logically but also helps you communicate ethically—by making sure you state all information as truthfully, honestly, and fairly as possible. Observing these four rules changes the previous letter so that the message can be effectively and ethically communicated (see Figure 6.1 on pages 142–143).

Why Good Organization Is Important

You might be asking yourself whether it matters that the message is well organized, as long as the point is eventually made. Why not just let the ideas flow naturally and trust that the audience will grasp the meaning? But when you consider the cost of misinterpreted messages (such as wasted time reading and rereading unclear messages, poor decision making, and shattered business relationships), you begin to realize the value of clear writing and good organization.[3] By arranging your ideas logically and diplomatically, you increase the chances of satisfying your audience's needs for information, motivation, and practicality. Plus you simplify your communication task.

Helping Your Audience Understand Your Message

The less work required of your audience to figure out your message, the better they understand what you're trying to say. As CHG's Julian Santoyo points out, you want your information to be "user-friendly and understandable." Read the following excerpt from a letter requesting detailed information from a hotel in order to finalize plans for a future conference. How well can the hotel manager understand the needs of the writer?

> I am chair of the planning committee for our annual conference and was considering your hotel as a possible site. I know that summer is a busy time, but we are committed to a summer conference because of scheduling problems. Can your hotel handle 350 guests for four nights? Do you have three large meeting rooms so we can have concurrent training sessions? What about dining facilities? Also, there is some concern about shuttle service to and from the airport.

From what you've read, is it possible for the hotel to send accurate helpful information to the letter writer? What are the exact dates of the conference? Is the conference this year or next? Will each guest want a single room? What does the writer want to know about the dining facilities? What is the concern about shuttle service? Now look at the revised version.

Figure 6.1
In-Depth Critique:
Letter with Improved
Organization

This letter from Boswell & Sons asking about ComputerTime's exchange policy is organized to give all needed information in a sequence that helps the reader understand the message.

Boswell & Sons

Route 7, Hancock Highway, Clear Lake, Iowa 50401
Voice: (515) 788-4343 E-mail: boswell@aol.com Fax: (515) 788-4344

September 13, 1997

Customer Service
ComputerTime
556 Seventh Avenue, N.W.
Mason City, Iowa 50401

Dear Customer Service Representative:

The first paragraph clearly states the purpose of this letter.

Boswell & Sons bought an Olympic Systems, Model PRS-2, 5-1/4-inch floppy disk drive from your store on November 15, during your pre-Christmas sale, when it was marked down to $199.95. We didn't use the unit until January, because it was bought for my assistant, who unexpectedly took six weeks' leave. You can imagine her frustration when she first tried using it and it didn't work.

The second paragraph explains the situation so that the reader will understand the problem. The writer includes no irrelevant information, and the ideas are presented logically.

We took the machine to the authorized service center and were assured that the problem was merely a loose connection. The service representative fixed the drive, but three months later it broke again—another loose connection. For the next three months, the drive worked reasonably well, although the response time was occasionally slow. Two months ago, the drive stopped working again. Once more, the service representative blamed a loose connection and made the repair. Although the drive is working now, it isn't working very well. The response time is still subject to delay, and the motor seems to drag sometimes.

The third paragraph states precisely what adjustment is being requested.

What is your policy on exchanging unsatisfactory merchandise? Although all the repairs have been relatively minor and have been covered by the one-year warranty, we are not satisfied with the drive. We would like to exchange it for a similar model from another manufacturer. If the new drive costs more than the old one, we will pay the difference, even though we generally look for equipment with heavy business discounts.

The National Association of Accountants (NAA) is considering your hotel as a site for our annual summer conference to be held on August 21, 22, 23, and 24, 1997, but we need some detailed information before coming to a final decision. Please respond to the following questions:

1. Can your hotel accommodate 350 persons for the nights of August 20, 21, 22, and 24 (with approximately three-quarters of the attendees preferring single rooms)? What is the per-room cost for a single or double room?

ComputerTime, September 13, 1997, Page 2

Boswell & Sons has done business with your store for six years and until now has always been satisfied with your merchandise. We are counting on you to live up to your reputation for standing behind your products. Please let us hear from you soon.

Sincerely,

Jill Saunders

Jill Saunders

lv

Figure 6.1
(Continued)

The letter includes all the necessary information.

2. Are three meeting rooms available on those dates (each accommodating at least 125 persons)?
3. Our preference for dining is to be able to eat together at the same time. Does your hotel have a dining room that can handle 350 persons at breakfast, lunch, and dinner? Also, please send menu suggestions and prices.
4. Does your hotel have a complimentary shuttle to and from the airport? How often does it run? If no complimentary shuttle is available, what other forms of transportation are available, and what is the cost to and from the airport?

This version contains the same topics as the initial letter, but it's organized so that the main point (the conference dates) is clear at the outset. The letter follows with the precise needs of this particular group indented and numbered. If you're interested in getting your message across, good organization is one of the handiest tools because it makes your message easier to understand. A well-organized message satisfies the audience's need for information.

The main reason for being well organized is to improve the chances that people will understand exactly what you mean.

Helping Your Audience Accept Your Message

Good organization helps motivate your audience to accept your message. Say that you're the customer with the broken disk drive referred to earlier and you get the following reply from Linda Davis, a customer service representative at the computer store:

> Your letter has been referred to me for a reply. I'm sorry, but we are unable to grant your request for a disk drive. Our store does not accept returns on sale equipment or on equipment that was purchased over six months ago. Because you bought the drive on sale ten months ago, we cannot help you. I suggest that you have it repaired before the warranty runs out. We do hope that you will understand our position and that you will continue to shop at our store. As you said yourself, this is the first problem you've ever had with our equipment.

How do you feel about the computer store now? Although Davis's letter appears at first glance to be logical enough, she's made no effort to select and organize her points in a diplomatic way. With greater care in choosing and presenting her ideas, Davis could have come up with something more acceptable, like the letter in Figure 6.2 (see page 144). Although this letter is still not likely to leave the customer totally satisfied, isn't the bad news a little easier to take?

Good organization also helps you get your ideas across without upsetting the audience.

Figure 6.2

In-Depth Critique: Letter Demonstrating a Diplomatic Organization Plan

This letter from ComputerTime responds to the inquiry from Boswell & Sons about the unsatisfactory disk drive. Although the information is effectively negative, the letter diplomatically achieves a positive feeling.

COMPUTERTIME
556 Seventh Avenue, Mason City, IA 50401
(515) 979-8870 / Comptime@netins.net

September 17, 1997

Ms. Jill Saunders
Boswell & Sons
Route 7, Hancock Highway
Clear Lake, IA 50401

Dear Ms. Saunders:

Thank you for letting us know about your experience with the Olympic disk drive that you bought last November. It's important that we learn of unusual problems with the equipment we stock.

As you know, regularly priced equipment returned to ComputerTime within 30 days is covered by the unconditional refund that has been our tradition for 22 years. Your machine, however, is still covered by the manufacturer's warranty. Your needs will receive immediate attention if you write to

Mr. George Bender
Olympic Systems
P.O. Box 7761, Terminal Annex
Los Angeles, CA 90010

From experience, I know that the people at Olympic truly care about having satisfied customers.

We, too, value your business, Ms. Saunders. Please don't miss our Tax Days sale in April, which will feature more of the low prices and high-quality equipment that you've come to rely on.

Sincerely,

Linda Davis

Linda Davis
Customer Service

hg

The letter begins with a neutral statement that the reader should not find objectionable.

The refusal is stated indirectly and is linked with a solution to the reader's problem.

The letter closes on an appreciative note and confidently assumes normal dealings in the future.

As the letter in Figure 6.2 shows, you can soften refusals, leave a better impression, and be more convincing by organizing messages diplomatically. You can also use good organization to enhance your credibility and add authority to your messages. In a recent survey of chief executives, 89 percent said that they interpret clear, well-organized writing as an indication of clear thinking.[4]

Saving Your Audience's Time

Well-organized messages are efficient. They satisfy your audience's need for convenience. They contain only relevant ideas, so your audience doesn't waste time on superfluous information. Effective organization is the foundation of brevity.

Moreover, all the information in a well-organized message is in a logical place. The audience can follow the thought pattern without a struggle. Because the organization is clear and logical, they can save even more time, if they want to, by looking for just the information they need instead of reading everything.

Well-organized messages are efficient because they contain only relevant information.

Simplifying Your Communication Task

Finally, being well organized helps you compose your message more quickly and efficiently. This is an important factor in business, where the objective is to get a job done, not to produce messages. In fact, when the chief executives in one survey were asked what they would most like to improve about their own business writing, they mentioned speed of composition more often than any other factor.[5]

By thinking about what you're going to say and how you're going to say it before you begin to write, you can proceed more confidently. As discussed in Chapter 5, the draft will go more quickly, because you won't waste time putting ideas in the wrong places or composing material you don't need. You can use your organizational plan to get some advance input from your boss to be sure you're on the right track *before* you spend hours working on a draft. If you're working on a large and complex project, you can use the plan to divide the writing job among co-workers to finish the assignment as quickly as possible.

Organizing what you're going to say before you start to write makes the job much easier.

How Good Organization Is Achieved

Understanding the *need* for good organization is half the battle. Knowing *how* to organize your messages well is the other half. Julian Santoyo of Community Health Group achieves good organization by following the two-step process: First you define and group the ideas; then you establish their sequence with a carefully selected organizational pattern.

To organize a message, first group the ideas, then put them in sequence.

Define and Group Ideas

Deciding what to say is the most basic problem that any business communicator has to solve. If the content is weak, no amount of style will camouflage that fact. Sooner or later, your audience will conclude that you really don't have anything worthwhile to say. Whether you're making a phone call, composing a three-paragraph letter, or writing a 250-page report, you begin by defining the content. The longer and more complicated the message, the more important this step is.

In business, deciding what to say is more important than deciding how to say it.

The prewriting techniques described in Chapter 5 will help generate your main idea, but they won't necessarily tell you how to develop it or how to group the supporting details in the most logical and effective way. To decide on the final structure of your message, you need to visualize how all the points fit together. One way to do this is to construct an outline. Whether you use the outlining features provided with word-processing software or simply jot down three or four points on the back of an envelope, making a plan and sticking to it will help you cover the important details.

When you're preparing a long and complex message, an outline is indispensable because it helps you visualize the relationship among the various parts. Without an outline, you may be inclined to ramble. As you're describing one point, another point may

An outline or a schematic diagram will help you visualize the relationship among parts of a message.

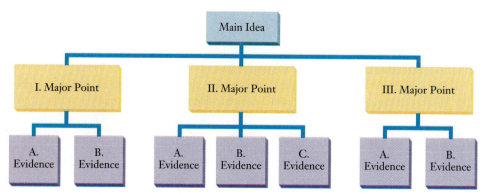

Figure 6.3
"Organization Chart" for Organizing a Message

occur to you—so you describe it. One detour leads to another, and before you know it, you've forgotten the original point. With an outline to guide you, however, you can communicate in a more systematic way, covering all the necessary ideas in an effective order and with proper emphasis. Following an outline also helps you express the transitions between points so that your message is coherent and the audience will understand the relationship among your ideas.

You're no doubt familiar with the basic alphanumeric outline, which uses numbers and letters to identify each point and indents them to show which ideas are of equal status. (Chapter 15 tells more about the various formats that can be used in this type of outlining.) A more schematic approach illustrates the structure of your message in an "organization chart" like one that depicts a company's management structure (see Figure 6.3). The main idea is shown in the highest-level box, and like a top executive, it establishes the big picture. The lower-level ideas, like lower-level employees, provide the details. All the ideas are logically organized into divisions of thought, just as a company is organized into divisions and departments.[6]

Start with the Main Idea

The main idea is the starting point for constructing an outline.

The main idea, placed at the top of an organization chart, helps you establish the goals and general strategy of the message. This main idea summarizes two things: (1) what you want your audience to do or think and (2) why they should do so. Everything in the message should either support this idea or explain its implications.

State the Major Points

The main idea should be supported by three to five major points, regardless of the message's length.

In an organization chart, the boxes directly below the top box represent the major supporting points, corresponding to the main headings in a conventional outline. These are the "vice presidential" ideas that clarify the message by expressing it in more concrete terms. To fill in these boxes, break the main idea into smaller units. Generally, try to identify three to five major points. If you come up with more than seven main divisions of thought, go back and look for opportunities to combine some of the ideas. The big question then is deciding what to put in each box. Sometimes the choices are fairly obvious. At other times you may have hundreds of ideas to sort through and group together. In either case be sure to consider both your purpose and the nature of the material.

If your purpose is to inform and the material is factual, the groupings are generally suggested by the subject itself. They are usually based on something physical that you can visualize or measure: activities to be performed, functional units, spatial or chronological relationships, or parts of a whole. When you're describing a process, the major support points are almost inevitably steps in the process. When you're describing a physical object, the vice presidential boxes correspond to the components of the object. When you're giving a historical account, each box represents an event in the chronological chain.

When your purpose is to persuade or collaborate, the major support points may be more difficult to identify. Instead of relying on a natural order imposed by the subject, develop a line of reasoning that proves your central message and motivates your audience to act. The boxes on the organization chart then correspond to the major elements in a logical argument. Basically, the supporting points are the main reasons your audience should accept your message.

Illustrate with Evidence

The third level on the organization chart shows the specific evidence you'll use to illustrate your major points. This evidence is the flesh and blood that helps your audience understand and remember the more abstract concepts. Say you're advocating that the company increase its advertising budget. To support this point, you could provide statistical evidence that your most successful competitors spend more on advertising than you do. You could also describe a specific case in which a particular competitor increased its ad budget and achieved an impressive sales gain. As a final bit of evidence, you could show that over the past five years, your firm's sales have gone up and down in unison with the amount spent on advertising.

If you're developing a long, complex message, you may need to carry the organization chart (or outline) down several levels. Remember that every level is a step along the chain from the abstract to the concrete, from the general to the specific. The lowest level contains the individual facts and figures that tie the generalizations to the observable, measurable world. The higher levels are the concepts that reveal why those facts are significant.

The more evidence you provide, the more conclusive your case will be. If your subject is complex and unfamiliar or if your audience is skeptical, you'll need a lot of facts and figures to demonstrate your points. On the other hand, if your subject is routine and the audience is positively inclined, you can be more sparing with the evidence. You want to provide enough support to be convincing, but not so much that your message becomes boring or inefficient. Of course you'll need to document your sources of information, and you may sometimes need to obtain permission to use copyrighted material. (For a closer look at the permission needed for electronic sources, see "The Tangled Web of Internet Copyrights" on page 148.)

Another way to keep the audience interested is to vary the type of detail. As you plan your message, try to incorporate the methods described in Table 6.1 (see page 149). Switch from facts and figures to narration; add a dash of description; throw in some examples or a reference to authority. Reinforce it all with visual aids. Think of your message as a stew, a mix of ingredients, seasoned with a blend of spices. Each separate flavor adds to the richness of the whole.

> Each major point should be supported with enough specific evidence to be convincing, but not so much that it's boring.

Establish Sequence with Organizational Patterns

Once you've defined and grouped your ideas, you're ready to decide on their sequence. When you're addressing a U.S. or Canadian audience with minimal cultural differences, you have two basic options:

- Direct approach *(deductive).* Putting the main idea first, followed by the evidence
- Indirect approach *(inductive).* Putting the evidence first and the main idea later

FOCUSING ON ETHICS

THE TANGLED WEB OF INTERNET COPYRIGHTS

Copyright laws restrict the copying of some kinds of materials and have existed since soon after Gutenberg invented the printing press. U.S. copyright law currently states that "original works of authorship fixed in a tangible medium of expression" created after January 1, 1978, are automatically copyrighted. It is illegal to copy such works without the author's permission. The law obviously applies to books, music, paintings, and other works that can be seen or heard. How it applies to works in electronic form on computers and networks is not clear.

Is it a copyright infringement if you download a file from the Internet to your PC? Does making a file available on the Internet automatically place it in the public domain, giving anyone the right to copy and distribute it without restriction? You can be prosecuted even if you unknowingly violate a copyright—"copyright law has no exemption for innocent infringement," according to Michael Grow, a Washington, D.C., attorney. Interest in revisions and interpretations of copyright laws concerning the Internet ranges from publishers and creators (who want strict controls on dissemination of their products) to Internet users (who do not want copyright controls to hamper the free flow of information). Many cases involving alleged copyright violations are currently being heard in courts around the world.

While the legal and ethical issues get sorted out, IBM and other companies are introducing products that make it difficult to copy things. Two of the techniques available are encryption and watermarking. Encryption involves garbling the information so that a user must have a password or decoder to make the information usable. With watermarking, the information includes a visible image that identifies the owner of the information. Microsoft, which holds electronic rights to a large number of artworks, uses watermarking to identify images.

In summary, the application of copyright laws to electronic information is not yet clearly defined. If you want to use any information from the Internet, the safest approach is to assume it is copyrighted and contact the author or owner for permission. And if you are putting information on the Internet, be aware that it is very easy for anyone to copy and reuse the information with or without your permission.

1. What if you can't find the author or owner of some online information that you'd like to use in a report? What should you do?
2. How might ethical and legal concerns slow the development of online libraries and other information resources?

These two basic approaches may be applied either to short messages (memos and letters) or to long ones (reports, proposals, presentations). To choose between the two alternatives, you must first analyze your audience's likely reaction to your purpose and message.

Use direct order if the audience's reaction is likely to be positive and indirect order if it is likely to be negative.

Your audience's reaction will fall somewhere on the continuum shown in Figure 6.4 (see page 150). As CHG's Julian Santoyo knows, the direct approach is generally fine when your audience will be receptive: eager, interested, pleased, or even neutral. If they'll be resistant to your message—displeased, uninterested, or unwilling—you'll usually have better results with the indirect approach.

Bear in mind, however, that each message is unique. You can't solve all your communication problems with a simple formula. If you're sending bad news to outsiders, for example, an indirect approach is probably best. On the other hand, you might want to get directly to the point in a memo to an associate, even if your message is unpleasant. The direct approach might also be the best choice for long messages, regardless of the audience's attitude, because delaying the main point could cause confusion and frustration. Just remember that the first priority is to make the message clear.

Short messages follow one of four organizational plans, depending on the audience's probable reaction.

Once you've analyzed your audience's probable reaction and chosen a general approach, you can choose the most appropriate organizational pattern: direct request; routine, good-news, and goodwill message; bad-news message; persuasive message. Table 6.2 (see page 150) summarizes how each type of message is structured. In each

TABLE 6.1

SIX TYPES OF DETAILS

Type of Detail	Example	Comment
Facts and figures	Sales are strong this month. We have received two new contracts worth $5 million and have a good chance of winning another with an annual value of $2.5 million.	Most common form of detail in business messages. Adds more credibility than any other form of development. May become boring if used in excess.
Example or illustration	We've spent the past four months trying to hire recent accounting graduates for our internal audit staff, and so far, only one person has agreed to join our firm. One woman told me that she would love to work for us, but she can get $5,000 more a year elsewhere.	Adds life to a message, but one example does not prove a point. Idea must be supported by other evidence as well.
Description	Upscale hamburger restaurants are designed for McDonald's graduates who still love the taste of a Big Mac but who want more than convenience and low prices. The adult hamburger establishments feature attractive waitresses, wine and beer, half-pound burgers, and substantial side dishes, such as nachos or potato skins. "Atmosphere" is a key ingredient in the formula for success.	Useful when you need to explain how something looks or functions. Helps audience visualize the subject by creating a sensory impression. Does not prove a point, but clarifies points and makes them memorable. Begins with overview of object's function; defines its purpose, lists major parts, and explains how it operates; relies on words that appeal to senses.
Narration	Under former management, the company operated in a casual style. Executives came to work in blue jeans, meetings rarely started on time, and lunch rarely ended on time. When Mr. Wilson took over as CEO, however, the company got religion—financial religion. A Harvard MBA who favors Brooks Brothers suits, Mr. Wilson has embarked on a complete overhaul of the operation. He has cut the product line from 6,000 items to 1,200 and chopped $12 million of expenses.	Good for attracting attention and explaining ideas, but lacks statistical validity.
Reference to authority	I talked with Jackie Lohman in the Cleveland plant about this idea, and she was very supportive. As you know, Jackie has been in charge of that plant for the past six years. She is confident that we can speed up the number 2 line by 150 units per hour if we add another worker.	Bolsters a case and adds variety and credibility. Works only if "authority" is recognized and respected by audience, although he or she may be ordinary person.
Visual aids	Graphs, charts, tables	Essential when presenting specific information. Used more often in memos and reports than in letters.

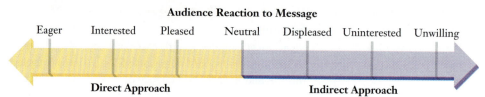

Figure 6.4
Audience Reaction and Organizational Approach

organizational plan, the opening, the body, and the close all play an important part in getting your message across. When used with good judgment, these basic types of business messages can be powerful tools of communication.[7]

Direct Requests

Direct requests get straight to the point because the audience usually wants to respond.

The most straightforward business message is the direct request. This type of message lets you get to the point in the first paragraph or, if you're talking with someone face-to-face or on the phone, allows you to get right down to business. Use this organizational pattern when your audience will be interested in complying or eager to respond. If you're inquiring about products or placing an order, your audience will usually want to comply and will welcome your request.

TABLE 6.2

FOUR ORGANIZATIONAL PLANS FOR SHORT MESSAGES

Audience Reaction	Organizational Plan	Opening	Body	Close
Eager or interested	**Direct requests**	Begin with the request or main idea.	Provide necessary details.	Close cordially and state the specific action desired.
Pleased or neutral	**Routine, good-news, and good-will messages**	Begin with the main idea or the good news.	Provide necessary details.	Close with a cordial comment, a reference to the good news, or a look toward the future.
Displeased	**Bad-news messages**	Begin with a neutral statement that acts as a transition to the reasons for the bad news.	Give reasons to justify a negative answer. State or imply the bad news, and make a positive suggestion.	Close cordially.
Uninterested or unwilling	**Persuasive messages**	Begin with a statement or question that captures attention.	Arouse the audience's interest in the subject. Build the audience's desire to comply.	Request action.

Here's a letter from Latesha Washington, the business manager for a Head Start Agency with eight centers in the St. Louis metropolitan area. She is writing to a company that manufactures children's furniture. Because she expects her agency to spend considerable money replacing furniture at all eight centers, Washington expects the company to be interested in her letter, and she looks forward to receiving a swift and favorable response.

> The St. Louis Head Start Agency intends to replace all its child-size chairs and tables in the next few months. We have eight centers that service over 700 children a day. Please send us information and detailed specifications for the chairs and tables that your company makes for small children.
>
> We currently have plastic chairs with metal legs and pressed-board tables with metal legs. Our preference is to replace our present equipment with wooden tables and chairs. We expect to purchase at least two sizes of tables and chairs to accommodate the varying ages and sizes of the children.
>
> The agency's Equipment Committee will review all the information and make a recommendation to the Head Start Board for consideration at its November meeting.
>
> If you have any questions, you may communicate with me or contact the head of the agency's Equipment Committee:
>
> Ms. Rashanda Morgan
> 6698 Hawthorne Avenue
> St. Louis, MO 63104
>
> We look forward to receiving product information from you as soon as possible.

The letter begins with the main idea and makes the request immediately.

The midsection provides essential details and describes the decision process.

In closing, the letter offers additional sources of more information and repeats the action desired.

The direct approach is appropriate in this case because it focuses attention on the main point. The reader finds out right away that the writer wants information on certain types of children's furniture. A quick scan of the remaining paragraphs yields additional details.

Aside from being easy to understand, direct requests are also easy to formulate. You can state your point directly without searching for some creative introduction. The direct approach is the most natural approach, perhaps the most useful and businesslike. This type of message is discussed in greater detail in Chapter 8.

Routine, Good-News, and Goodwill Messages

Other messages that call for the direct approach are also easy to organize. Use this organizational pattern when the audience will feel neutral about your message or will be pleased to hear from you. If you're providing routine information as part of your regular business, the audience will probably be neutral, neither pleased nor displeased. If you're announcing a price cut, granting an adjustment, accepting an invitation, or congratulating a colleague, the audience will be pleased to hear from you.

The direct approach is effective for messages that will please the reader or will cause no particular reaction.

Here's a good-news letter from Sophia Beckerman, the CEO of the Golden Oaks Retirement Community, informing the residents of the board's recent decision to construct a clubhouse on the premises. Because Beckerman knows that the residents will be delighted with this news, she comes right to the point.

> A clubhouse for the residents of Golden Oaks was approved yesterday by the board at its quarterly meeting. The architectural plans submitted by White and Scott (the firm that has designed all

The letter begins with the good news.

the buildings at this complex) were accepted, and construction is scheduled to begin in early spring. The clubhouse should be completed sometime in November.

All of the principal features sought by the residents have been incorporated into the plans: a large kitchen/dining facility, a recreation room with a large-screen television, a lap-swimming pool, and two putting greens for the golfers. Your assistance in the planning phase was most helpful. I especially want to thank the committee that surveyed the residents and collated the data.

To facilitate the building process, we need to make a small change in traffic patterns. Once the construction begins, everyone entering Golden Oaks will be asked to use the Watson Road entrance. The Valley Drive entrance will be closed to the public for the duration of the project. Construction vehicles will use Valley Drive since the clubhouse will be very near that entrance.

Thanks to all of you who have encouraged us in our planning for the clubhouse. The board and the architects were most impressed by the detailed information supplied by the residents regarding their wishes for such a facility. We will keep you informed on the progress of the construction, and we urge you to study the architect's sketches posted outside the dining room on the main bulletin board.

> All necessary details are provided in the middle part.
>
> This paragraph gives additional specifics.
>
> The letter closes with a reference to the main idea and a gracious look toward the future.

Using the direct approach for routine, good-news, and goodwill messages has many advantages. By starting off with the positive point, you put your audience in a good frame of mind and encourage them to be receptive to whatever else you have to say. This approach also emphasizes the pleasing aspect of your message by putting it right up front, where it's the first thing recipients see. This type of message is discussed in more detail in Chapter 9.

Bad-News Messages

If you have bad news, try to put it somewhere in the middle, cushioned by other, more positive ideas.

Use this organizational pattern when the audience will be displeased about what you have to say. If you're turning down a job applicant, refusing credit, or denying a request for an adjustment, the audience will be disappointed. You may be tempted to blurt out an unpleasant message in the most direct and unvarnished manner, believing that you're just being businesslike or that the audience is too far away or unimportant to matter. In many cases, however, bluntness is more expedient than practical. Astute businesspeople know that every person encountered has the potential to be a customer, a supplier, or a contributor, or to influence someone who is a customer, a supplier, or a contributor. So these people take a little extra care with their bad-news messages.

The challenge lies in being honest but kind. You don't want to sacrifice ethics and mislead the audience; at the same time, you don't want to be overly blunt. To achieve a good mix of candor and kindness, imagine you're talking face-to-face with someone you want to remain on good terms with, and focus on some aspect of the situation that makes the bad news a little easier to take (see Figure 6.5).

The first and last sections of a message make the biggest impression. If Levasseur had refused in the first sentence of the letter in Figure 6.5, the reader might never have bothered to go on to the reasons or might have been in the wrong frame of mind to consider them. By putting the explanation before the refusal, Levasseur focused attention on the reasons. Of course, you have to be sincere about your reasons. A reader can spot a phony excuse in a minute.

The following letter shows how Jamie Levasseur, advertising manager at Ballinger & Crown, responded when asked to act as industry chairperson for a dinner sponsored by the National Conference of Christians and Jews. Note how she cushions the bad news.

Figure 6.5
In-Depth Critique: Letter Delivering Bad News

BALLINGER & CROWN

676 Fifth Avenue, Ninth Floor, New York, New York 10103
Voice: (212) 397-8888 Fax: (212)397-8877

March 6, 1997

Ms. Joanne Lippman
Public Relations Officer
National Conference of Christians and Jews
2237 Welch Avenue
Houston, Texas 77219

Dear Ms. Lippman:

Your invitation to act as industry chairperson for NCCJ's upcoming Anniversary Citation Dinner is a great honor. I thoroughly enjoyed serving in the role last year. Your members are a fine group with high ideals, and working with them was a privilege.

This year I'm involved with a construction project here at B&C that is consuming all my time—and then some. Therefore, although I would enjoy repeating the experience of working with NCCJ, I believe someone else would be better able to give the assignment the attention it deserves.

Perhaps one of my colleagues would have the time to do the job the way it ought to be done. Enclosed is a brief list of colleagues (with address and phone information) who have voiced some interest in working with NCCJ. We want the advertising industry to be well represented.

I wish you and the rest of your committee the greatest success in achieving the goals set this year by NCCJ.

Sincerely,

Jamie Levasseur

Jamie Levasseur
Advertising Manager

sw

Enclosure

The letter begins with a neutral statement that provides a transition to the refusal.

The midsection explains the reason for the refusal and then states the bad news.

The writer takes care to introduce a positive thought.

The letter closes on a cordial note.

The indirect approach is neither manipulative nor unethical. As long as you can be honest and reasonably brief, you're better off opening a bad-news message with a neutral point and putting the negative information after the explanation. Then if you can close with something fairly positive, you're likely to leave the audience feeling okay—not great, but not hostile either. When you're the bearer of bad tidings, that's often about all you can hope for. This type of message is discussed further in Chapter 10.

Persuasive Messages

Using the indirect approach gives you an opportunity to get your message across to a skeptical or hostile audience.

The indirect approach is also useful when you know your audience will resist your message (will be uninterested in your request or unwilling to comply without extra coaxing). Such resistance might be the likely reaction to a sales or collection letter, an unsolicited job application, or a request for a favor of some kind. In such cases, you have a better chance of getting through to the person if you lead off with something catchy. This doesn't mean that you should go in for gimmicks, but do try to think of something that will make your audience receptive to what you have to say. Mention a possible benefit, or refer to a problem that the recipient might have. Pose a question, or mention an interesting statistic. This letter was written by Sam Guiteras to raise funds for Channel 8 public television station in Spring Valley, Ohio.

What's your favorite public television program? Children would pick *Sesame Street.* You might pick *Masterpiece Theater* or *Austin City Limits.* Would you miss these programs if they went off the air? Children would surely miss Big Bird. Would you miss the crafty Inspector Morse or the irrepressible Rumpole? Would you miss the experts who explain how to build furniture or cook or fish or paint with oils and watercolors?

> *These questions are likely to catch the reader's attention.*

With enormous cuts in the federal funding of public television, Channel 8 may have to substantially curtail its program offerings. We are working hard to avoid eliminating anyone's favorite program, but we need your help. If enough viewers offer their financial support, we may be able to continue offering you our full complement of shows.

> *The letter leads up to the main point by arousing the reader's interest.*

We believe in good educational programming for the welfare of the entire community—and so do you. Channel 8 is a source of pride for Spring Valley, and we don't want to take any steps that would diminish that sense of self-respect—and neither do you.

> *This section gives the reader a motive for complying with the request.*

So, send your contribution to Channel 8 today. In return for a gift of $100 or more, you'll receive a monthly program guide so that no one in your family misses any favorite programs. Thanks for caring about Channel 8 and about your friends and neighbors in Spring Valley.

> *The letter closes with an appeal for action and another benefit of complying.*

Although you might argue that people are likely to feel manipulated by the indirect approach, the fact remains that you have to capture people's attention before you can persuade them to do something. If you don't, you really have no way to get the message across. You also have to get your audience to consider with an open mind what you have to say; to do this, you have to make an interesting point and provide supporting facts that encourage the audience to continue paying attention. Once you have them thinking, you can introduce your real purpose. This type of message is discussed at greater length in Chapter 11.

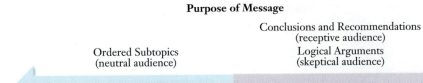

Figure 6.6
Organizational Plans for Longer Messages

Longer Messages

Most short messages can use one of the four basic organizational patterns. Longer messages (namely, reports and presentations) require a more complex pattern to handle the greater mass of information. These patterns can be broken into two general categories: informational and analytical. Figure 6.6 shows how the choice of plan for a longer message relates to the purpose.

In general, the easiest reports and presentations to organize are the informational ones that provide nothing more than facts. Operating instructions, status reports, technical descriptions, and descriptions of company procedures all fall into this category. Long informational messages have an obvious main idea, often with a descriptive or "how to" overtone. The development of subordinate ideas follows the natural breakdown of the material to be explained; subtopics can be arranged in order of importance, sequentially, chronologically, spatially, geographically, or categorically. Suppose your boss asks you to give a presentation on how to fill out time sheets. The procedure involves a series of steps, so organizing the message should be almost automatic. You simply list the steps in sequence and describe each one.

It is more difficult to organize analytical reports and presentations, which are designed to lead the audience to a specific conclusion. When your purpose is to collaborate with your audience to solve a problem or to persuade them to take a definite action, your organizational pattern must highlight logical arguments or focus the audience's attention on what needs to be done. Your audience may respond in one of two ways to your material, and your choice of organizational plan should depend on the reaction you anticipate:

- If you expect your audience to agree with you, use a structure that focuses attention on conclusions and recommendations.
- If you expect your audience to be skeptical about your conclusions and recommendations or hostile toward them, use a structure that focuses attention on the rationale that supports your point of view.

You'll learn more about organizing longer messages in Chapter 17. For now, the important thing is to master the basic steps in structuring a message.

STAGE 6: FORMULATING YOUR MESSAGE

Once you've completed the planning process, you're ready to begin composing the message. If your schedule permits, put your outline or organization chart aside for a day or two; then review it with a fresh eye, looking for opportunities to improve the flow of ideas. When you feel confident that your structure will achieve your purpose with the intended audience, you can begin to write.

The organization of a longer message should reflect both the purpose of the message and the audience's probable reaction.

When your purpose is to inform, the major points are based on a natural order implied by the subject's characteristics.

When your purpose is to persuade or collaborate, the approach is analytical, with major points corresponding to logical arguments or to conclusions and recommendations.

Some word-processing programs offer writers an outlining option to smooth the process of organization. As finance manager at Devlin Enterprises, Scott Jeffries uses Microsoft Word's outline feature to organize his reports.

Composing Your First Draft

As you compose the first draft, don't worry about getting everything perfect. Just put down your ideas as quickly as you can. You'll have time to revise and refine the material later. Composition is easier if you've already figured out what to say and in what order, although you may need to pause now and then to find the right word. You may also discover as you go along that you can improve on your outline. Feel free to rearrange, delete, and add ideas, as long as you don't lose sight of your purpose.

Composition is the process of drafting your message; polishing it is a later step.

If you're writing the draft in longhand, leave space between lines so that you'll have plenty of room for making revisions. If you're using a typewriter, leave wide margins and double-space the text. Probably the best equipment for drafting the message is a computer with word-processing software, which allows you to make changes easily. You might try dictating the message, particularly if you're practicing for an oral delivery or if you're trying to create a conversational tone.

Controlling Your Style and Tone

Style is the way you use words to achieve a certain **tone,** or overall impression. You can vary your style—your sentence structure and vocabulary—to sound forceful or passive, personal or impersonal, colorful or colorless. The right choice depends on the nature of your message and your relationship with the reader.

When composing the message, vary the style to create a tone that suits the occasion.

Your use of language is one of your credentials, a badge that identifies you as being a member of a particular group. Try to make your style clear, concise, and grammatically correct, and try also to make it conform to the norms of your group. Every organization has its own stylistic conventions, and many occupational groups share a particular vocabulary.

Although style can be refined during the revision phase (see Chapter 7), you'll save time and a lot of rewriting if you compose your message in an appropriate style. Your tone is affected by planning-stage elements such as your purpose and your audience's probable reaction to your message. Other elements affecting the tone of your message include thinking about the relationship you want to establish with your audience, using the "you" attitude, emphasizing the positive, establishing credibility, being polite, and projecting your company's image.

Think About the Relationship You Want to Establish

The first step toward getting the right tone is to think about your relationship with the audience. Who are you, and who are they? Are you friends of long standing with common interests, or are you total strangers? Are you equal in status, experience, and education, or are you clearly unequal? Your answers to these questions will help you define your relationship with the audience so that you can give the right impression in your message.

The tone of your business messages may span a continuum from informal to conversational to formal. CHG's Julian Santoyo writes in a less formal style, appropriate for his company's size and atmosphere. Most business messages fall around the conversational level of formality, using plain language that is neither stiff nor full of slang. Your conversational tone may become less or more formal, depending on the situation.

If you're addressing an old friend, your conversational tone may tend more toward an informal level. Of course, in business messages, your tone would never be as informal as it would with family members or school chums. On the other hand, if you're in the lower echelon of a large organization, your conversational tone would tend to be more formal and respectful when communicating with the people above you. Some people in high positions are extremely proud of their status and resent any gesture from a lower-level employee that is remotely presumptuous. They may not like you to offer your own opinions, and they may resent any implied criticism of their actions or decisions. If you're writing to someone of this type, your message may be ineffective unless you show a deep appreciation of rank. Also remember that businesspeople in the United States are generally less formal than their counterparts in most other cultures.[8] So to avoid embarrassment or misunderstanding when communicating across cultures, increase your level of formality.

Although various situations require various tones, most business communication sounds businesslike without being stuffy. The tone suggests that you and your audience are sensible, logical, unemotional people—objective, interested in the facts, rational, competent, and efficient. You are civilized people who share a mutual respect for each other.

To achieve this tone, avoid being too familiar. Don't mention things about anyone's personal life unless you know the individual very well. Such references are indiscreet and presumptuous. Avoid phrases that imply intimacy, such as "just between you and me," "as you and I are well aware," and "I'm sure we both agree." Also, be careful about sounding too folksy or chatty; the audience may interpret this tone as an attempt on your part to seem like an old friend when, in fact, you're not.

Humor is another type of intimacy that may backfire. It's fine to be witty in person with old friends. It's difficult, however, to hit just the right note of humor in business messages, particularly if you don't know the readers very well, because what seems humorous to you may be deadly serious to others. When communicating across cultures, the chances are slim that your audience will appreciate your humor or even realize that you're trying to be funny.[9]

Also avoid obvious flattery. Although most of us respond well to honest praise and proper respect, we're suspicious of anyone who seems too impressed. When someone

To achieve a warm but businesslike tone

- Don't be too familiar
- Use humor only with great care
- Don't flatter the other person
- Don't preach
- Don't brag
- Be yourself

says, "Only a person of your outstanding intellect and refined tastes can fully appreciate this point," little warning lights flash in our minds. We suspect that we're about to be conned.

Avoid preaching to your audience. Few things are more irritating than people who assume that they know it all and that we know nothing. People who feel compelled to give lessons in business are particularly offensive. If, for some reason, you have to tell your audience something obvious, try to make the information unobtrusive. Place it in the middle of a paragraph, where it will sound like a casual comment as opposed to a major revelation. Alternatively, you might preface an obvious remark with "as you know" or some similar phrase.

Bragging is closely related to preaching and is equally offensive. When you praise your own accomplishments or those of your organization, you imply that you're better than your audience. References to the size, profitability, or eminence of your organization may be especially annoying (unless, of course, those in your audience work for the same organization). You're likely to evoke a negative reaction with comments like "We at McMann's, which is the oldest and most respected firm in the city, have a reputation for integrity that is beyond question."

Perhaps the most important thing you can do to establish a good relationship with your audience is to be yourself. People can spot falseness very quickly, and they generally don't like it. If you don't try to be someone you're not, you'll sound sincere.

Use the "You" Attitude

Once you've thought about the kind of relationship you want to establish, remember to center your efforts on your audience. Try to project yourself into your audience's shoes. What do they want from you? What are their expectations? How will they feel about what you have to say?

By using an audience-centered approach, you try to see the subject through your audience's eyes. Then you can project this approach in your messages by adopting a **"you" attitude;** that is, by speaking and writing in terms of your audience's wishes, interests, hopes, and preferences. Talk about the other person, and you're talking about the thing that most interests him or her. Too many business messages have an "I" or "we" attitude, which causes the sender to sound selfish and uninterested in the receiver. The message tells what the sender wants; the recipient is expected to go along with it.

On the simplest level, you can adopt the "you" attitude by replacing terms that refer to yourself and your company with terms that refer to your audience. In other words, use *you* and *yours* instead of *I, me,* and *mine* or *we, us,* and *ours:*

The "you" attitude is best implemented by expressing your message in terms of the audience's interests and needs.

Instead of This	Use This
To help us process this order, we must ask for another copy of the requisition.	So that your order can be filled promptly, please send another copy of the requisition.
We are pleased to announce our new flight schedule from Atlanta to New York, which is any hour on the hour.	Now you can take a plane from Atlanta to New York any hour on the hour.
We offer the typewriter ribbons in three colors: black, blue, and green.	Take your pick of typewriter ribbons in three colors: black, blue, and green.

Avoid using *you* and *yours*
- To excess
- When assigning blame
- If your organization prefers a more formal style

Using *you* and *yours* requires finesse.[10] If you overdo it, you're likely to create some rather awkward sentences. You also run the risk of sounding like a high-pressure carnival barker at the county fair.[11] The "you" attitude is not intended to be manipulative or insincere. It is an extension of the audience-centered approach. In fact, the best way to implement the "you" attitude is to be sincere in thinking about your audience. It isn't just a matter of using one pronoun as opposed to another; it's a matter of genuine empathy. You can use *you* 25 times in a single page and still ignore your audience's true concerns. Look back at the letter in Figure 6.5. The first paragraph uses the pronoun *your* quite correctly and effectively. The third paragraph also displays effective use of the "you" attitude, even though no form of the word *you* ever appears in that paragraph. In the final analysis, it's the thought that counts, not the pronoun. If you're talking to a retailer, try to think like a retailer; if you're dealing with a production supervisor, put yourself in his or her position; if you're writing to a dissatisfied customer, imagine how you would feel at the other end of the transaction. The important thing is your attitude toward the members of your audience and your appreciation of their position.

> The word *you* does not always indicate a "you" attitude, and the "you" attitude can be displayed without using the word *you*.

On some occasions, you'll do better to avoid using *you*. For instance, when someone makes a mistake and you want to point it out impersonally to minimize the possibility of ill will, you might say, "We have a problem," instead of "You caused a problem." Using *you* in a way that might sound dictatorial is also impolite:

Instead of This	**Use This**
You should never use that kind of paper in the copy machine.	That type of paper doesn't work very well in the copy machine.
You must correct all five copies before noon.	All five copies must be corrected by noon.
You need to make sure the staff follows instructions.	The staff may need guidance in following instructions.

In addition, remember that the use of personal pronouns may not be acceptable in other cultures. In Japan, for example, people are uncomfortable with the personal touch of the "you" attitude. Japanese writers refer to their audience's company rather than to their receiver: "*Your company* [not *you*] will be pleased with the survey results."[12] You're always better off using the style and tone preferred by the culture you're dealing with.

Keep in mind the attitudes and policies of your organization as well. Some companies have a tradition of avoiding references to *you and I* in their memos and formal reports. If you work for a company that expects a formal, impersonal style, confine your use of personal pronouns to informal letters and memos.

When speaking to local service groups about the need for helping young people, Sharon Ross of San Diego's Children's Hospital and Health Center uses the "you" attitude by creating parallel situations with the audience and then building her message around that commonality. She speaks in a conversational tone to put herself on a level with her audience and to cushion the shock they may feel when she starts talking about children in trouble. She relates personal experiences (such as the first time she dealt with a child-abuse case), giving her audience a common starting point, a base on which to build. By using the "you" attitude, Ross shows an understanding of and an empathy for the people she hopes will receive her message loud and clear. She knows it's not only a highly ethical practice but a successful one as well.[13]

Emphasize the Positive

Another way of showing sensitivity to your audience is to emphasize the positive side of your message.[14] Focus on the silver lining, not the cloud. Stress what is or will be instead of what isn't or won't be. Most information, even bad news, has at least some

> Explain what you have done, what you can do, and what you will do—not what you haven't done, can't do, or won't do.

redeeming feature. If you can make your audience aware of that feature, you will make your message more acceptable.

Instead of This	**Use This**
It is impossible to repair this vacuum cleaner today.	Your vacuum cleaner will be ready by Tuesday.
We apologize for inconveniencing you during our remodeling.	The renovations now under way will help us serve you better.
We never exchange damaged goods.	We are happy to exchange merchandise that is returned to us in good condition.

When you are offering criticism or advice, focus on what the person can do to improve.

In addition, when you're criticizing or correcting, don't hammer on the other person's mistakes. Avoid referring to failures, problems, or shortcomings. Focus instead on what the person can do to improve:

Instead of This	**Use This**
The problem with this department is a failure to control costs.	The performance of this department can be improved by tightening up cost controls.
You filled out the order form wrong. We can't send you the paint until you tell us what color you want.	So that your order can be processed properly, please check your color preferences on the enclosed card.
You broke the dish by running cold water on it right after you took it from the oven.	These dishes are sensitive to temperature shock and should be allowed to cool gradually after they are removed from the oven.

Show your audience how they will benefit from complying with your message.

If you're trying to persuade the audience to buy a product, pay a bill, or perform a service for you, emphasize what's in it for them. Don't focus on why *you* want them to do something. Instead of saying, "Please buy this book so that I can make my sales quota," say, "The plot of this novel will keep you in suspense to the last page." Instead of saying, "We need your contribution to the Boys and Girls Club," say, "You can help a child make friends and build self-confidence through your donation to the Boys and Girls Club." An individual who sees the possibility for personal benefit is more likely to respond positively to your appeal.

Avoid words with negative connotations; use meaningful euphemisms instead.

In general, try to state your message without using words that might hurt or offend your audience. Substitute mild terms (euphemisms) for those that have unpleasant connotations. Instead of advertising "cheap" merchandise, announce your bargain prices. Don't talk about "pimples and zits"; refer more delicately to complexion problems. You can be honest without being harsh. Gentle terms won't change the facts, but they will make those facts more acceptable:

Instead of This	**Use This**
toilet paper	bathroom tissue
used cars	resale cars
sweaty armpits	underarm wetness
constipation	irregularity
high-calorie food	high-energy food

On the other hand, don't carry euphemisms to extremes. If you're too subtle, people won't know what you're talking about. "Derecruiting" workers to the "mobility pool" instead of telling them they have six weeks to find another job isn't really very helpful. When using euphemisms, you walk a fine line between softening the blow and hiding the facts. It would not be ethical to speak to your community about relocating refuse when you're really talking about your plans for disposing of toxic waste. Such an attempt to hide the facts would very likely backfire, damaging your business image and reputation. In the final analysis, people respond better to an honest message delivered with integrity than they do to sugar-coated double-talk.

Establish Credibility

It's to your advantage to communicate your credibility to the audience. An audience's faith in you has a profound impact on their acceptance of your message. In one experiment, three groups of U.S. college students heard the same prerecorded talk recommending leniency toward juvenile delinquents. One group was told that the speaker was a judge, another that he was an anonymous member of the audience, and the third that he was a former juvenile offender out on bail on a drug charge. As you might guess, 73 percent of the "judge's" audience said that they agreed with the speaker, but only 29 percent of the "offender's" audience agreed with the speaker.[15]

Because the success of your message may depend on the audience's perception of you, their belief in your competence and integrity is important. You want people to believe that you know what you're doing and that your word is dependable. CHG's Julian Santoyo believes in building credibility over time by carefully building one's reputation. The first step is to promise only what you can do and then to do what you promise. After that, you can enhance credibility through your writing and speaking style.

> Don't make false promises.

If you're communicating with someone you know well, your previous interactions influence your credibility. The other person knows from past experience whether you're trustworthy and capable. If the person is familiar with your company, the firm's reputation may be ample proof of your credibility.

> People are more likely to react positively to your message when they have confidence in you.

But what if you are complete strangers? Even worse, what if the other person starts off with doubts about you? First and foremost, show an understanding of the other person's situation by calling attention to the things you have in common. If you're communicating with someone who shares your professional background, you might say, "As a fellow engineer (lawyer, doctor, teacher, or whatever), I'm sure you can appreciate this situation." Another approach is to use technical or professional terms that identify you as a peer.

You can also gain the audience's confidence by explaining your credentials, but you need to be careful that you don't sound pompous. Generally, one or two aspects of your background are all you need to mention. Possibly your title or the name of your organization will be enough to impress the audience with your abilities. If not, perhaps you can mention the name of someone who carries some weight with your audience. You might begin a letter with "Professor Goldberg suggested that I contact you," or you could quote a recognized authority on a subject, even if you don't know the authority personally. The fact that your ideas are shared by a credible source adds prestige to your message.

> To enhance your credibility
> - Show that you understand the other person's situation
> - Establish your own credentials or ally yourself with a credible source
> - Back up your claims with evidence, not exaggerations
> - Use words that express confidence
> - Believe in yourself and your message

Your credibility is also enhanced by the quality of the information you provide. If you support your points with evidence that can be confirmed through observation, research, experimentation, or measurement, your audience will recognize that you have the facts, and they will respect you. Exaggerated claims, on the other hand, are unethical and do more harm than good. Here's an example from a mail-order catalog advertising rose bushes: "You'll be absolutely amazed at the remarkable blooms on this healthy plant. Gorgeous flowers with brilliant color and an intoxicating aroma will delight you week after week." Terms like *amazing, incredible, extraordinary, sensational,* and *revolutionary* exceed the limits of believability, unless they're backed up with some sort of factual proof.

You also risk losing credibility if you seem to be currying favor with insincere compliments. So support compliments with specific points:

Instead of This	**Use This**
My deepest heartfelt thanks for the excellent job you did. It's hard these days to find workers like you. You are just fantastic! I can't stress enough how happy you have made us with your outstanding performance.	Thanks for the fantastic job you did filling in for Gladys at the convention with just an hour's notice. Despite the difficult circumstances, you managed to attract several new orders with your demonstration of the new line of coffeemakers. Your dedication and sales ability are truly appreciated.

Doesn't the more restrained praise seem more credible?

The other side of the credibility coin is too much modesty and not enough confidence. Many writing authorities suggest that you avoid such words as *if, hope,* and *trust,* which express a lack of confidence on your part:

Instead of This	**Use This**
We hope this recommendation will be helpful.	We're glad to make this recommendation.
If you'd like to order, mail us the reply card.	To order, mail the reply card.
We trust that you'll extend your service contract.	By extending your service contract, you can continue to enjoy top-notch performance from your equipment.

The ultimate key to being believable is to believe in yourself. If you are convinced that your message is sound, you can state your case with authority so that the audience has no doubts. When you have confidence in your own success, you automatically suggest that your audience will respond in the desired way. If you lack faith in yourself, however, you're likely to communicate an unsteady attitude that undermines your credibility.

Be Polite

The best tone for business messages is almost always a polite one. By being courteous to your audience, you show consideration for their needs and feelings. You express yourself with kindness and tact.

Although you may be tempted now and then to be brutally frank, try to express the facts in a kind and thoughtful manner.

Undoubtedly, you'll be frustrated and exasperated by other people many times in your career. When that happens, you'll be tempted to say what you think in blunt terms. To be sure, it's your job to convey the facts, precisely and accurately. Nevertheless, venting your emotions will rarely improve the situation and may jeopardize the goodwill of your audience. Instead, be gentle when expressing yourself:

Instead of This	**Use This**
I've seen a lot of dumb ideas in my time, but this takes the cake.	This is an interesting suggestion, but I'm not sure it's practical. Have you considered the following possible problems?

Instead of This	**Use This**
You really fouled things up with that last computer run.	Let me tell you what went wrong with that last computer run so that we can make sure things run smoothly next time.
You've been sitting on my order for two weeks now. When can I expect delivery?	As I mentioned in my letter of October 12, we are eager to receive our order as soon as possible. Could you please let us know when to expect delivery.
I told you before you hired the guy that he wouldn't work out. You made your bed; now lie in it.	We all make mistakes about people from time to time, and maybe this was one of them. Why don't you give the new person a few more weeks to get adjusted?

Of course, some situations require more diplomacy than others. If you know your audience well, you can get away with being less formal. However, when corresponding with people who outrank you or with those outside your organization, you usually include an added measure of courtesy. In general, written communication requires more tact than oral communication. When you're speaking, your words are softened by your tone of voice and facial expression. You can adjust your approach depending on the feedback you get. Written communication, on the other hand, is stark and self-contained. If you hurt a person's feelings in writing, you can't soothe them right away. In fact, you may not even know that you have hurt the other person, because the lack of feedback prevents you from seeing his or her reaction.

Use extra tact when writing and when communicating with higher-ups and outsiders.

In addition to avoiding things that give offense, try to find things that might bring pleasure. Remember a co-worker's birthday, send a special note of thanks to a supplier who has done a good job, acknowledge someone's help, or send a clipping to a customer who has expressed interest in a subject. People remember the extra little things that indicate you care about them as individuals. In this impersonal age, the human touch is particularly effective.

Being courteous means taking the time to do a little extra for someone.

Another simple but effective courtesy is to be prompt in your correspondence. If possible, answer your mail within two or three days. If you need more time to prepare a reply, write a brief note or call to say that you're working on an answer. Most people are willing to wait if they know how long the wait will be. What annoys them is the suspense.

Promptness is a form of courtesy.

Project the Company's Image

Even though establishing the right tone for your audience is your main goal, give some thought to projecting the right image for your company. When you communicate with outsiders, on even the most routine matter, you serve as the spokesperson for your organization. The impression that you make can enhance or damage the reputation of the entire company. Thus your own views and personality must be subordinated, at least to some extent, to the interests and style of the company.

Subordinate your own style to that of the company.

Say you've just taken a job with a hip, young retail organization called Rappers. One of your first assignments is to write a letter canceling additional orders for clothing items that have been identified as slow sellers. Your goal is to cancel the order while maintaining the goodwill of the vendor (the business selling you the clothes).

Dear Ms. Bataglia:

I am writing to cancel our purchase order 092397AA for the amount of $12,349. Our contract with your organization specifies that we have a 30-day cancellation clause which we wish to invoke. If any shipments went out before you received this notification, they will be returned; however, we will remunerate freight charges as specified in the contract.

I am told we have ordered from you since our inception in 1993. Your previous service to us has been quite satisfactory; however, recent sales of the "Colored Denim" line have been less than previously forecast. We realize that our cancellation may have a negative impact, and we pledge to more accurately predict our needs in the future.

We maintain positive alliances with all our vendors and look forward to doing further business with you. Please keep us informed of new products as they appear.

After reading your draft, you realize the letter may be misinterpreted. Its formal tone may leave a feeling of ill will with the vendor, and it certainly doesn't reflect the corporate culture of your new employer. You try again.

Dear Ms. Bataglia:

We appreciate the relationship we've had with you since 1993. Your shipments have always arrived on time and in good order.

However, our recent store reports show a decline in sales for your "Colored Denim" line. Therefore, we're canceling our purchase order 092397AA for $12,349. If you'll let us know the amounts, we'll pay the shipping charges on anything that has already gone out.

We're making lots of changes at Rappers, but one thing remains the same—the positive relationship we have with vendors such as you. Please keep us informed of your new lines as they appear, so that we can look forward to doing business with you in the future.

This version reflects the more relaxed image of your new company. You can save yourself a great deal of time and frustration if you master the company style early in your career. In a typical corporation, 85 percent of the letters, memos, and reports are written by someone other than the higher-level managers who sign them. Most of the time, managers reject first drafts of these documents for stylistic reasons. In fact, the average draft goes through five revisions before it is finally approved.[16]

You might wonder whether all this effort to fine-tune the style of a message is worthwhile. The fact is, people in business care very much about saying precisely the right thing in precisely the right way. Their willingness to go over the same document five times demonstrates just how important style really is. For a reminder of the tasks involved in composition, see this chapter's Checklist for Composing Business Messages.

Shaping Your E-mail Message

Make your e-mail messages
- Audience-centered
- Easy to follow
- Interesting

An e-mail message is more than an electronic memo or a one-way telephone call.[17] You can send e-mail to co-workers, supervisors, and staff, but you can also send e-mail outside the company to customers, suppliers, and competitors. Moreover, you can send it across the globe as easily as across the hall.[18] Organization and style are just as important for e-mail messages as for any other type of message. So communicate your points quickly and efficiently by making your e-mail message audience-centered, easy to follow, and interesting.

Make Your E-mail Audience-Centered

Even though e-mail may have an image of speed and informality, take enough time to compose your e-mail messages carefully. Think about your audience. Consider your reader's interests, needs, and feelings.

CHECKLIST FOR COMPOSING BUSINESS MESSAGES

A. ORGANIZATION

1. Recognize good organization.
   a. Subject and purpose are clear.
   b. Information is directly related to subject and purpose.
   c. Ideas are grouped and presented logically.
   d. All necessary information is included.
2. Achieve good organization through outlining.
   a. Decide what to say.
      i. Main idea
      ii. Major points
      iii. Evidence
   b. Organize the message to respond to the audience's probable reaction.
      i. Use the direct approach when your audience will be neutral, pleased, interested, or eager.
      ii. Use the indirect approach when your audience will be displeased, uninterested, or unwilling.
3. Choose the appropriate organization plan.
   a. Short messages
      i. Direct request
      ii. Routine, good-news, and goodwill message
      iii. Bad-news message
      iv. Persuasive message
   b. Longer messages
      i. Informational pattern
      ii. Analytical pattern

B. FORMULATION

1. Compose your first draft.
   a. Get ideas down as quickly as you can.
   b. Rearrange, delete, and add ideas without losing sight of your purpose.
2. Vary the style to create a tone that suits the occasion.
   a. Establish your relationship with your audience.
      i. Use the appropriate level of formality.
      ii. Avoid being overly familiar, using inappropriate humor, including obvious flattery, sounding preachy, bragging, and trying to be something you're not.
   b. Extend your audience-centered approach by using the "you" attitude.
   c. Emphasize the positive aspects of your message.
   d. Establish your credibility to gain the audience's confidence.
   e. Use a polite tone.
   f. Use the style that your company prefers.

How formal you make your message depends on your audience, as well as your purpose. Although e-mail may at times seem transitory, it can emulate "snail mail" by having conventional business language, a respectful style, and a more formal format (including a traditional greeting, formalized headings, and a formal closing and signature).[19] Of course e-mail can be as informal and casual as a conversation between old friends—just be sure that such a style is appropriate for the situation. However, regardless of the level of formality required, do your best to use correct spelling and proper grammar. Some e-mail old-timers insist that spelling and grammar take a back seat to your readiness to communicate.[20] But in business communication, e-mail needs to be as clear and as easy to understand as possible.

> The formality of your e-mail depends on your audience.

Because e-mail is so effortlessly sent abroad, focusing on your audience also means being culturally aware. When communicating with someone in another culture, take into account cultural differences. For example, be sure to give metric measurements (followed by English-system equivalents); spell out what format or system you're using for dates, times, numbers, and money; and use more formal greetings for those parts of the world that expect it.[21]

> You need to be culturally aware when writing e-mail.

Because e-mail is read on-screen, keep your audience's terminal in mind (see Figure 6.7 on page 166). Computers and e-mail systems vary, so you want to ensure

> Consider how your message will appear on your audience's screen.

Figure 6.7
In-Depth Critique: On-Screen E-Mail Message

The following message is typical of those sent using the Eudora Pro Software package.

```
╔══════════════════════ E-Mail ══════════════════════╗


  X-Sender: joand@mail.signa.com
  Date: Mon, 06 May 1996 04:43:33 -0600
  To: signa-users@signa.com
  From: "Howard F. Jones" <Howie@signa.com>
  Subject: Now Track Your Time Online
  X-Info: SIGNA
  X-ListMember: tandy@signa.com [signa-users@signa.com]


  Dear Customer,

  An exciting change has been made at SIGNA in the past
  two weeks.

  You now have access to an online time-checking mechanism
  that allows you to track your online time usage. If you
  are on a metered service plan that is billed in an
  hourly format, this will give you the tool needed to
  maximize your connection. This tool is currently located
  on our home page.

  If you would like us to send out more reviews of our
  interesting customer sites, please drop me a line and
  let me know. I can be reached seven days a week at
  Howie@signa.com.

  Thank you,

  Howard F. Jones
  President
  SIGNA, Inc.
```

The subject line captures customer interest.

Line length is well under 80 characters.

Jones has a friendly tone in this message to his customers.

The "you" attitude is apparent in the focus of the message as well as in the request for feedback.

that your readers won't be confused by message lines that run off the screen or that wrap incorrectly. Press the *Enter* key at the end of each line, making sure your line length is less than 80 characters (or less than 60 characters if your message is likely to be forwarded, because forwarding often indents messages a tab length). And of course, don't use font features such as boldface and italics—unless you're certain your reader's computer and e-mail software can reproduce such features.[22]

Make responding easy.

Remember to make responding easy. State clearly the type of response you need. Give enough information in your e-mail message for your audience to be able to respond. Word your message so that your audience can respond as briefly as possible, perhaps with a yes or a no. Also, ask for your audience's response early in your message, perhaps even in your subject line.[23] (For more audience-centered ideas, see "E-mail Etiquette: Minding Your Manners Online" on pages 168–169.)

Make Your E-mail Easy to Follow

Some readers receive more e-mail than they can read, so your best chance of getting your message across is to make your e-mail easy to follow. Use short, focused paragraphs that are organized in a logical fashion. Consider writing like a newspaper reporter, from the top down. That way you'll be sure to get your point across as early as possible, in case your reader doesn't have the time or interest to finish reading your message.[24]

In fact, try to keep your message short and concise.[25] Many e-mail messages are less than three paragraphs long and fit into one screen.[26] Whenever possible, try to limit your message to one screen or window.[27] Of course, some e-mail messages will be longer than one screen; a few may even be longer than several screens. When it's necessary to send a long e-mail message, consider including a brief table of contents in the first screen, perhaps with a short paragraph that summarizes and highlights the key points.[28] Also, use headings to break up long passages of text. Not only do they help your reader understand you, but they can serve as shortcuts, highlighting the material your reader may want to read or skip.[29] And remember that lists are an efficient way to present information. You can use bullets (asterisks) to emphasize key points and numbered lists for sequential points. Embedding a list within text can also save you some space.[30]

Consider writing e-mail from the top down.

Make Your E-mail Interesting

When your readers are deciding which messages to spend time on, they look at who it's from, they check the subject line, and they may scan the first screen. If your message can't attract your reader's attention by that time, your e-mail will probably go unread and perhaps be deleted.[31] You can make your e-mail more interesting—from start to finish.

An interesting subject line does more than just describe or classify the content of your message.[32] By applying key words, humor, quotations, or questions, you can grab your reader's attention.[33] You have 25 to 30 characters to build interest for your message (longer lines are often truncated). Try wording your subject line so that it tells your reader what to do. For example: *Send figures for July sales* is much more informative than *July sales figures.* Of course, you don't want to use wild statements just to attract your reader's attention. Using *urgent* in your subject lines too often will soon have an effect quite different from the one intended.

E-mail's subject line offers you an opportunity to gain your reader's interest.

Your e-mail header displays who your message is to and from. Even so, adding a greeting makes your e-mail message more personal.[34] Naturally, whether you use a formal greeting *(Dear Professor Ingersoll)* or a more casual one *(Hi Marty!)* depends on your audience and your purpose.

Use a greeting to make your e-mail more personal.

Even though you can't usually use underlining, fonts, or graphics to emphasize various parts of your message, you can use keyboard characters such as asterisks, dashes, carets, hyphens, colons, slashes, pipes, and capital letters. For example, you can surround a word with asterisks to *make* it stand out. Or you can indicate underlining like _this_. You can open up your message

Create interesting typographical effects with keyboard characters.

by using white space

```
---------------------------------------------------------
|                                                       |
| and by inserting lines or boxes made of asterisks or hyphens and pipes. |
|                                                       |
---------------------------------------------------------
```

E-MAIL ETIQUETTE: MINDING YOUR MANNERS ONLINE

E-mail can be as fast as a phone call and as formal as a document. Because it's too often written hastily, it can unintentionally cause misunderstandings and hurt feelings. As you write e-mail messages, keep in mind a few rules of etiquette—be courteous, be brief, and avoid inflammatory remarks:

Be Courteous

- *Read and compose your messages offline.* Save your company money by reading, writing, and editing your messages before you connect to your service. (If you have to connect to access your mail program, try writing your message in a word-processing program and using copy-and-paste techniques to transfer it.)
- *Check your own e-mail regularly.* Try to check your mail three times a day (adapting your routine to avoid the heavy-traffic delays around 9:00, 12:00, and 5:00).
- *Don't send junk mail.* Spare your readers unnecessary broadcasting, and avoid sending trivial e-mail responses. You don't have to respond to everything.

- *Alphabetize addresses by last name.* When sending a message to more than one person, alphabetizing helps you avoid alienating anyone by listing them in the wrong place.

Be Brief

- *Don't send too much information in one message.* You don't want to burden your recipients.
- *Avoid sending big files to remote users.* When a colleague is out of town, your huge file can tie up that colleague's out-of-town connection, costing the company money and wasting your colleague's time. Instead of sending such a large file, send a short note saying where colleagues can retrieve the file or offering to send the file by request.
- *Avoid adding too many attachments to your e-mail.* Large, bulky messages tie up the network and are difficult to read.
- *Cut down your receiver lists.* Don't send copies of every memo to every colleague. You'll just clutter up everybody's mailboxes.

You can make a headline with all capital letters, but don't overdo. TOO MANY CAPITAL LETTERS LOOKS LIKE SHOUTING! You can even use extra character spaces to emphasize your most i m p o r t a n t points.[35] Of course you must guard against overusing any of these techniques, or else your message will look jumbled and confusing.

To emphasize or clarify the meaning of a comment in a less formal message, you can also use your keyboard to create little sideways pictures. For example, you can make a sideways happy face with a colon, a hyphen, and a closing parenthesis: :-) (variations might look like (:->) or d:-) or <(:->) and so on). Other emotions can also be expressed, such as boo hoo (:-<) and uh oh (:-o) and my lips are sealed (:-x) and so on. Like other enhancement techniques, emoticons can be overdone. When used sparingly, they can add power, but when overused, they can make your message look more like graffiti.[36]

Be careful not to overdo emoticons and smiley faces.

Your closing and signature also personalize your e-mail message. In most cases, use simple closings, such as *Thanks* or *Regards,* rather than more traditional business closings such as *Sincerely yours.* Of course, you may want to use a more formal closing for international e-mail.

After a simple closing, you can include a signature in several ways.

For your signature, you can simply type your name or initials on a separate line. You might put one or two hyphens before your name to set it off from the body of your e-mail.[37] Or you may want to use a signature file, a short identifier that may include your name, company name, postal address, fax number, other e-mail addresses, and sometimes even a short quotation or thought.[38] Although, some users believe you should include only the information needed to contact you.[39] Once you create a signa-

- **Cut down your reply list.** If your department manager sends a message to everyone in the department, anyone who replies without limiting the reply list will end up sending their message to everyone on the original list.
- **Change the subject line when replying.** In an ongoing communication, it isn't long before recipients can't tell whether they're getting a new message or a recycled one.

Avoid Inflammatory Remarks

- **Remember that e-mail can go where you least expect.** E-mail can go everywhere—and in the blink of an eye. Don't send anything you don't want absolutely everyone to read.
- **Be aware that companies have the right to search company mailboxes.** The 1986 Electronic Communications Privacy Act ensures that internal e-mail is the property of the company that pays for the e-mail system. So watch what you write.
- **Avoid flaming.** Sending angry or unsuitable messages is called flaming. Before sending an e-mail message, read it twice, asking yourself if you would say this to the person's face. Make sure you're calm before responding to an offensive message, and never use abusive or obscene language. Remember that in an e-mail message, you may indeed need to criticize the subject matter, but you never need to criticize another person.

The primary rule of e-mail etiquette is the golden rule: Treat others as you would like to be treated. Moreover, if a message is very important, controversial, confidential, or easily misunderstood, consider delivering it face-to-face or by phone instead of via e-mail.

---

1. Experts advise you to ask for permission before forwarding or inserting someone else's e-mail message. Explain briefly why such courteous behavior is a good idea.
2. The people in your department share a printer, which you and your colleagues sometimes use to print out e-mail messages. Since the company owns the e-mail system and the printer, and since you are part of the company, is it okay for you to read any printed e-mail messages waiting to be picked up? Or are they confidential material? Explain your answer in less than half a page.

ture file, you can save it in your mail program and add it to e-mail messages without retyping.[40] You can also use a digital copy of your handwritten signature, which is becoming acceptable as legal proof of business transactions, especially when accompanied by a date stamp that is automatically inserted by your mail program.[41]

SUMMARY

In a well-organized message, all the information is related to a clear subject and purpose, the ideas are presented in a logical order, and all necessary information is included. Good organization is important not only because it makes the message more effective but also because it simplifies the communicator's job.

Organizing a message requires grouping ideas and deciding on the order of their presentation. Direct and indirect order are the two basic organizational approaches. The direct approach presents the main idea first; the indirect approach presents the main idea later. The indirect approach is best for people who are likely to react with skepticism or hostility to the message, but the direct approach is best in most other cases.

When you communicate, you establish a relationship with the audience. The success of the relationship depends on the tone, or overall impression, that you create. Try to be both businesslike and likable; try to look at the subject through your audience's eyes. Emphasize positive ideas. Convey your credibility, and be courteous. Also remember that you represent your organization and must adjust your style to reflect its standards. Finally, be sure to shape your e-mail message according to the most appropriate style.

COMMUNICATION CHALLENGES AT COMMUNITY HEALTH GROUP

A recent newspaper article played on fears that HMOs might deny people medical care to save costs, and Julian Santoyo is concerned because CHG was mentioned along with numerous other HMOs. Since CHG's member fees are paid by taxpayers (through the state government), management must correct any damage to CHG's public reputation.

Julian Santoyo has facts at his fingertips that set CHG apart from other HMOs: CHG has been serving the indigent Hispanic and Asian communities for nearly 15 years; CHG's staff reflects this diversity (which means they understand their members and speak their language); and CHG sinks its profits back into improving services (for example, adding a telephone advice nurse for members and supplying transportation to and from appointments—important because many of CHG's members can't afford automobiles). Also, CHG encourages members and physicians to practice preventive medicine to stave off illnesses and to keep medical visits down. So CHG saves costs—not by denying services but by encouraging good health.

TEAM CHALLENGE: Santoyo will be working with management to present this information, and he's asked you as a team to help him develop the best approach. Should a letter be sent to the local news media, state government officials, or both? If both, should they receive the same letter? Why or why not? Once you've decided these factors, make an outline of the message. Will you use the direct approach or the indirect approach? Why? What is the main idea? How will you gain and hold the audience's interest? How will you conclude the message?

INDIVIDUAL CHALLENGE: Following the outline you've developed, draft a one-page version of the message in the form you've chosen, for the audience you've identified. Using the facts supplied, choose the proper style and level of formality to create a message that will counteract the article's negative publicity.[42]

DOCUMENTS FOR ANALYSIS

Document 6.A: Defining and Grouping Ideas

The writer of the following list is having trouble grouping the ideas logically for an insurance information brochure. Revise the list and develop a logical outline, paying attention to appropriate subordination of ideas. Rewrite where necessary to give phrases a more consistent sound.

Accident Protection Insurance Plan
- Coverage is only pennies a day
- Benefit is $100,000 for accidental death on common carrier
- Benefit is $100 a day for hospitalization as result of motor vehicle or common carrier accident
- Benefit is $20,000 for accidental death in motor vehicle accident
- Individual coverage is only $17.85 per quarter; family coverage is just $26.85 per quarter
- No physical exam or health questions
- Convenient payment—billed quarterly
- Guaranteed acceptance for all applicants
- No individual rate increases
- Free, no-obligation examination period
- Cash paid in addition to any other insurance carried
- Covers accidental death when riding as fare-paying passenger on public transportation, including buses, trains, jets, ships, trolleys, subways, or any other common carrier
- Covers accidental death in motor vehicle accidents occurring while driving or riding in or on automobile, truck, camper, motor home, or nonmotorized bicycle

Document 6.B: Controlling Your Style and Tone

Read the following document; then (1) analyze the strengths and weaknesses of each sentence and (2) revise the document so that it follows this chapter's guidelines.

> I am a new publisher with some really great books to sell. I saw your announcement in *Publishers Weekly* about the bookseller's show you're having this summer, and I think it's a great idea. Count me in, folks! I would like to get some space to show my books. I thought it would be a neat thing if I could do some airbrushing on T-shirts live to help promote my hot new title, *T-Shirt Art.* Before I got into publishing, I was an airbrush artist, and I

could demonstrate my techniques. I've done hundreds of advertising illustrations and have been a sign painter all my life, so I'll also be promoting my other book, hot off the presses, *How to Make Money in the Sign Painting Business.*

I will be starting my PR campaign about May 1998 with ads in *PW* and some art trade papers, so my books should be well known by the time the show comes around in August. In case you would like to use my appearance there as part of your publicity, I have enclosed a biography and photo of myself.

P.S. Please let me know what it costs for booth space as soon as possible so that I can figure out whether I can afford to attend. Being a new publisher is mighty expensive!

CRITICAL THINKING QUESTIONS

1. When organizing the ideas for your business message, how can you be sure that what seems logical to you will also seem logical to your audience?
2. Do you think that cushioning bad news is manipulative?
3. Which organizational plan would you use to ask employees to work overtime to meet an important deadline, a direct request or a persuasive message? Why?
4. Which organizational plan would you use to let your boss know that you'll be out half a day next week to attend your father's funeral, a routine message or a bad-news message? Why?
5. When composing business messages, how can you be yourself and project your company's image at the same time?
6. When writing e-mail, is it ever okay to use an indirect approach? How can you use a buffer when you have to state your purpose in the subject line? Explain.

EXERCISES

1. Suppose you are preparing to recommend to top management the installation of a new heating system (called cogeneration). The following information is in your files. Eliminate from the list topics that aren't essential; then arrange the other topics so that your report will give management a clear understanding of the heating system and a balanced, concise justification for installing it:

    History of the development of the cogeneration heating process
    Scientific credentials of the developers of the process
    Risks assumed in using this process
    Your plan for installing the equipment in your building
    Stories about its successful use in comparable facilities
    Specifications of the equipment that would be installed
    Plans for disposing of the old heating equipment
    Costs of installing and running the new equipment
    Advantages and disadvantages of using the new process
    Detailed ten-year cost projections
    Estimates of the time needed to phase in the new system
    Alternate systems that management might wish to consider

2. Indicate whether the direct or indirect approach would be best in each of the following situations; then briefly explain why. Would any of these messages be inappropriate for e-mail? Explain.
    a. A letter asking when next year's automobiles will be put on sale locally
    b. A letter from a recent college graduate requesting a letter of recommendation from a former instructor
    c. A letter turning down a job applicant
    d. An announcement that because of high air-conditioning costs, the plant temperature will be held at 78 degrees during the summer months
    e. A final request to settle a delinquent debt
3. If you were trying to persuade people to take the following actions, how would you organize your argument?

a. You want your boss to approve your plan for hiring two new people.

b. You want to be hired for a job.

c. You want to be granted a business loan.

d. You want to collect a small amount from a regular customer whose account is slightly past due.

e. You want to collect a large amount from a customer whose account is seriously past due.

4. Suppose that end-of-term frustrations have produced this e-mail message to Professor Anne Brewer from a student who feels he should have received a B in his accounting class. If this message were recast into three or four clear sentences, the teacher might be more receptive to the student's argument. Rewrite the message to show how you would improve it:

> I think that I was unfairly awarded a C in your accounting class this term, and I am asking you to change the grade to a B. It was a difficult term. I don't get any money from home, and I have to work mornings at the Pancake House (as a cook), so I had to rush to make your class, and those two times that I missed class were because they wouldn't let me off work because of special events at the Pancake House (unlike some other students who just take off when they choose). On the midterm examination, I originally got a 75 percent, but you said in class that there were two different ways to answer the third question and that you would change the grades of students who used the "optimal cost" method and had been counted off 6 points for doing this. I don't think that you took this into account, because I got 80 percent on the final, which is clearly a B. Anyway, whatever you decide, I just want to tell you that I really enjoyed this class, and I thank you for making accounting so interesting.

5. Substitute inoffensive phrases for the following:
   a. you claim that
   b. it is not our policy to
   c. you neglected to
   d. in which you assert
   e. we are sorry you are dissatisfied
   f. you failed to enclose
   g. we request that you send us
   h. apparently you overlooked our terms
   i. we have been very patient
   j. we are at a loss to understand

6. Rewrite the following letter to Mrs. Bruce Crandall (1597 Church Street, Grants Pass, Oregon 97526) so that it conveys a helpful, personal, and interested tone:

> We have your letter of recent date to our Ms. Dobson. Owing to the fact that you neglected to include the size of the dress you ordered, please be advised that no shipment of your order was made, but the aforementioned shipment will occur at such time as we are in receipt of the aforementioned information.

7. Rewrite these sentences to reflect your audience's viewpoint:
   a. We request that you use the order form supplied in the back of our catalog.
   b. We insist that you always bring your credit card to the store.
   c. We want to get rid of all our manual typewriters in order to make room in our warehouse for the new electronic models. Thus we are offering a 25 percent discount on all sales this week.
   d. I am applying for the position of bookkeeper in your office. I feel that my grades prove that I am bright and capable, and I think I can do a good job for you.
   e. As requested, we are sending the refund for $25.

8. Revise these sentences to be positive rather than negative:
   a. To avoid the loss of your credit rating, please remit payment within ten days.
   b. We don't make refunds on returned merchandise that is soiled.
   c. Because we are temporarily out of Baby Cry dolls, we won't be able to ship your order for ten days.
   d. You failed to specify the color of the blouse that you ordered.
   e. You should have realized that waterbeds will freeze in unheated houses during winter months. Therefore, our guarantee does not cover the valve damage and you must pay the $9.50 valve-replacement fee (plus postage).

9. Provide euphemisms for the following words and phrases:
   a. stubborn
   b. wrong
   c. stupid
   d. incompetent
   e. loudmouth

10. Ben Cohen and Jerry Greenfield sell millions of gallons of Ben & Jerry's Homemade ice cream each year. They are also strong advocates for global is-

sues, peace, and charity. Visit their Web site at <http://www.benjerry.com>, and consult their index. Click on various topics, and consider how Cohen and Greenfield project the company's image and their personal advocacy. Write an e-mail message to a fellow student explaining why the Web page enables Cohen and Greenfield to be themselves, advocate their causes, and advertise their business. Print your e-mail message for submission to your instructor.

CHAPTER 7

REVISING BUSINESS MESSAGES

AFTER STUDYING THIS CHAPTER, YOU WILL BE ABLE TO

- Edit your messages for content and organization, style and readability, and word choice
- Choose the most correct and most effective words to make your point
- Rewrite sentences to clarify the relationships among ideas and to make your writing interesting
- Identify elements of paragraphs
- Rewrite paragraphs using the appropriate development technique
- Choose the best design for written documents
- Proof your messages for mechanics and format

COMMUNICATION CLOSE-UP AT TURNER BROADCASTING SYSTEM

"Make sure that it's *Turner Broadcasting System* and not *'Systems,'*" coaches corporate communications manager Adrianne Proeller when asked to talk about her work at the Atlanta-based media giant (now owned by Time Warner). According to the company's corporate style manual, *TBS* or *Turner* is okay for subsequent references. "That's one of the first things you do when revising," says Proeller. "You make sure you get the name of the company right."

Not only does Proeller write speeches and statements for TBS president R. E. (Ted) Turner, she has enough other public relations duties to keep her busy during frequent ten-hour days. She enjoys her job, even when she's revising a document for the second or third time, weeding out weak verbs, complicated sentences, and unnecessary facts. She revises everything she writes, a task that she says "just comes with the territory."

The "territory" Proeller covers on a daily basis includes writing letters, memos, speeches, press releases, executive biographies, corporate fact sheets, and company histories. She also writes sample questions and answers for corporate executives before media interviews. "The Q & A prepares the executive for just about every possible question that might be asked," explains Proeller. Company founder Ted Turner is a favorite media topic, and so are the conglomerate's highly visible international divisions, which include Cable News Network (CNN), CNN Headline News, TBS Superstation, Turner Network Television (TNT), Hanna-Barbera Productions, TNT Latin America, TNT & Cartoon Asia, New Line Cinema, and Castlerock Entertainment. TBS also owns the Atlanta Braves (a major league baseball team), the Atlanta Hawks (a professional basketball team), and other sports and entertainment ventures. Reporters are al-

Adrianne Proeller

Communication is the profession of many employees of Turner Broadcasting System and its international divisions (such as CNN). Whether working with Adrianne Proeller in corporate communications at TBS, writing press releases for the Atlanta Braves, or delivering news stories on CNN, these professionals understand the importance of careful revision. The most successful communicators make sure their messages are the best they can be.

ways asking questions, and the answers executives give could turn up on tomorrow's front page or today's broadcast news. So Proeller has to be certain her memos and press releases are clear and accurate.

That doesn't mean she always has time to let her writing "cool off" before she takes a second look—which is the ideal way to approach revision. "If I have the luxury to print it out instead of just looking at it on my computer screen, then I'm doing well," laughs Proeller. Whether it's on screen or hard copy, however, she rereads the document through completely, asking herself: "What am I trying to say? Is it getting across? Is there anything that could make this better? Could anything make it stronger? Is there anything missing?"

For clarity, Proeller often narrows her communication to one primary message; then to gain her reader's attention, she makes sure that the key message is mentioned in the first paragraph. Because TBS is an international company, she also checks her copy for any cultural references that could be considered narrow-minded or biased. For instance, did she mistakenly assume a U.S. perspective? *Domestic sales* would confuse European readers, so Proeller replaces it with *U.S.-based sales* when sending memos overseas.

"Mr. Turner is very much an internationalist," Proeller explains. "A few years ago he sent around a memo to all of CNN saying that because we're an international network, he didn't want any use of the word *foreign*. In fact, I could be fined for saying that—literally fined money (about $50). Most newsrooms have a national desk and a foreign desk; Turner has a national desk and an international desk." Of course, employees have poked a little fun at the rule, joking, "Excuse me, I have an international substance in my eye." However, they don't laugh at Turner's international success.

During her revision Proeller checks the corporate style book for the proper formats and for company updates (for example, TBS Superstation used to be TBS SuperStation, and before that it was Superstation TBS). She also reconsiders her word choices. "I'm always trying to cut out unnecessary words, and I'm a big believer in strong verbs." She simplifies sentences that are too cumbersome and eliminates secondary messages if a document is too long. Overall, she makes sure the writing is positive, even when referring to TBS's competitors. That is company policy, Proeller says, because competitors of one division are often customers of another.

"Every document that passes your desk is a reflection on you," Proeller believes. "Your reputation, both internally and externally, is built one little bit at a time. I think typos are unforgivable, but beyond that—you want every document to be the best it can be. If you're not putting one hundred percent of your thought into looking at it once it has been drafted—for all of the different aspects of style and content and accuracy—you're risking your professional image."[1]

STAGE 7: EDITING YOUR MESSAGE

Once you've completed the first draft of your message, you may be tempted to breathe a sigh of relief and get on with the next project. Resist the temptation. As professional communicators like Adrianne Proeller are aware, the first draft is rarely good enough. You owe it to yourself and to your audience to review and refine your messages before sending them.

In fact, many writing authorities suggest that you plan to go over a document at least three times: once for content and organization, once for style and readability, and once for mechanics and format. The letter in Figure 7.1 has been edited using the proofreading marks shown in Appendix II. The letter in Figure 7.2 (see page 178) shows how the thoroughly revised letter looked when completed.

Although the tendency is to separate revision from composition, editing is an ongoing activity that occurs throughout the composition process. You edit and revise as you go along; then you edit and revise again after you've completed the first draft. You constantly search for the best way to say something, probing for the right words, testing alternative sentences, and arranging paragraphs in various patterns.

The basic editing principles discussed here apply to both written and oral communication. However, the steps involved in revising a speech or an oral presentation are slightly different, as Chapter 20 explains.

Evaluating Your Content and Organization

After a day or two, review your message for content and organization.

Ideally, let your draft age a day or two before you begin the editing process so that you can approach the material with a fresh eye. Then read through the document quickly to evaluate its overall effectiveness. You're mainly concerned with content, organization, and flow. Compare the draft with your original plan. Have you covered all points in the most logical order? Is there a good balance between the general and the specific? Do the most important ideas receive the most space, and are they placed in the most prominent positions? Have you provided enough support and double-checked the facts? Would the message be more convincing if it were arranged in another sequence? Do you need to add anything? Be sure to consider the effect your words will actually have on readers (not just the effect you *plan* for them to have).

Now think about what you can eliminate. In business, it's particularly important to weed out unnecessary material. Three-fourths of the executives who participated in one survey complained that most written messages are too long.[2] They are most likely to read documents that efficiently say what needs to be said.

In the first phase of editing, spend a few extra moments on the beginning and ending of the message. These are the sections that have the greatest impact on the audi-

Figure 7.1
In-Depth Critique: Sample Edited Letter

This letter responds to Louise Wilson's request for information about the Commerce Hotel's frequent-guest program.

November 12, 1997

Miss Louise Wilson
Corporate Travel Department
Brother's Electric Corporation
2300 Wacker Drive
Chicago, IL 60670

Dear Miss Wilson:

~~I enjoyed our recent conversation regarding~~ *Thank you for your interest in* the ~~FG~~ *frequent-guest* program ~~and am~~ *at the Commerce Hotel. We are* delighted to hear that the people at Brother's Electric are thinking about joining. ~~Incidentally, we are planning a special Thanksgiving weekend rate, so keep that in mind in case you happen to be in San Francisco for the Holiday.~~

The enclosed brochure explains the details of the ~~FG~~ *frequent-guest* program. *As a Corporate member, Brother's Electric will be entitled to a 20 percent discount on all rooms and services.* ~~Your FC ID card is enclosed.~~ Use ~~it~~ *the enclosed ID card* whenever you make reservations with us to obtain your corporate discount. ~~We will see to it~~ ~~that~~ your executives ~~are treated with~~ *will receive* special courtesy~~, and that they get to use the~~ health club ~~free.~~ *Of Organizations enrolled in the frequent-guest program also qualify for discounts on* ~~We also have excellent~~ convention facilities and banquet rooms~~, should you want to book a convention or meeting here.~~ We hope you and your company will take advantage of these *facilities the next time you book a convention.* ~~outstanding world-class amenities.~~ Please call me if you have any questions. I will be happy to answer them.

Sincerely,

Mary Cortez
Account Representative

Content and organization: Stick to the point (the main idea) in the first paragraph. In the middle, highlight the key advantage of the frequent-guest program, and discuss details in subsequent paragraphs. Eliminate redundancies.

Style and readability: Reword to stress the "you" viewpoint. Clarify the relationships among ideas through placement and combination of phrases. Moderate the excessive enthusiasm, and eliminate words (such as *amenities*) that may be unfamiliar.

Mechanics and format: To prevent confusion, spell out the abbreviated phrase *FG*.

---

ence. Be sure that the opening of a letter or memo is relevant, interesting, and geared to the reader's probable reaction. In longer messages, check to see that the first few paragraphs establish the subject, purpose, and organization of the material. Review the conclusion to be sure that it summarizes the main idea and leaves the audience with a positive impression.

Figure 7.2
*In-Depth Critique: Final
Revised Letter*

The revised letter gives the requested information in a more organized fashion, with a style that is more friendly and mechanics that are clearer.

333 Sansome Street ➤ San Francisco, CA 94104

(800) 323-7347 ➤ (415) 854-2447 ➤ Fax 854-7669

www.CommerceHotel.com

November 12, 1997

Miss Louise Wilson
Corporate Travel Department
Brother's Electric Corporation
2300 Wacker Drive
Chicago, Illinois 60670

Dear Miss Wilson:

Thank you for your interest in the frequent-guest program at the Commerce Hotel. We are delighted to hear that the people at Brother's Electric are thinking about joining.

The enclosed brochure explains the details of the frequent-guest program. As a corporate member, Brother's Electric will be entitled to a 20 percent discount on all rooms and services. To obtain your corporate discount, use the enclosed ID card whenever you make reservations with us. Your executives will receive special courtesy, including free use of the health club.

Organizations enrolled in the frequent-guest program also qualify for discounts on convention facilities and banquet rooms. We hope you and your company will take advantage of these facilities the next time you book a convention. Please call me if you have any questions. I will be happy to answer them.

Sincerely,

Mary Cortez

Mary Cortez
Account Representative

The first paragraph now provides a "you" attitude, spells out what was previously abbreviated, and deletes irrelevant material.

The second paragraph now clarifies the benefits of the frequent-guest program and personalizes those benefits by using the "you" attitude.

The last paragraph now combines a final benefit with more information about services available. It also concludes with a friendly tone.

Reviewing Your Style and Readability

Once you're satisfied with the content and structure of the message, look at its style and readability. Ask yourself whether you have achieved the right tone for your audience. Look for opportunities to make the material more interesting through the use of lively words and phrases.

At the same time, be particularly conscious of whether your message is clear and readable. You want the audience to understand you with a minimum of effort. Check your vocabulary and sentence structure to be sure you're relying mainly on familiar terms and simple, direct statements. You might even apply a readability formula to gauge the difficulty of your writing.

The most common readability formulas measure the length of words and sentences to give you a rough idea of how well educated your audience must be to understand your message. Figure 7.3 shows how one readability formula, the Fog Index, has been applied to an excerpt from a memo. (The "long words" in the passage have been underlined.) As the calculation shows, anyone who reads at a tenth-grade level should be able to read this passage with ease. For technical documents, you can aim for an audience that reads at a twelfth- to fourteenth-grade level; for general business messages, your writing should be geared to those who read at the eighth- to eleventh-grade level. The Fog Index of such popular business publications as the *Wall Street Journal* and *Forbes* magazine is somewhere between 10 and 11.

Of course, readability indexes can't be applied to languages other than English. Counting syllables makes no sense in other languages. For example, compare the English *forklift driver* with the German *Gabelstaplerfahrer.* Also, Chinese and Japanese characters don't lend themselves to syllable counting at all.[3]

Readability formulas are easy to apply; many are commonly done on a computer. However, they ignore some important variables that contribute to reading ease, such as sentence structure, the organization of ideas, and the appearance of the message on the page.[4] To fully evaluate the readability of your message, ask yourself whether you have effectively emphasized the important information. Are your sentences easy to decipher? Do your paragraphs have clear topic sentences? Are the transitions between ideas obvious?

Assessing Your Word Choice[5]

As a business communicator, you have two things to pay attention to when choosing and revising your words: correctness and effectiveness. Editors and grammarians occasionally have questions—and even disputes—about correct usage. The "rules" of grammar are constantly changing to reflect changes in the way people speak. For example, many experts now prefer to treat *data* as a singular noun when it refers to a body of information, even though, technically speaking, it is the plural form of *datum.* You be the judge: Which of the following sentences sounds better?

The data on our market share is consistent from region to region.
The data on our market share are consistent from region to region.

Although debating the finer points of usage may seem like nit-picking, using words correctly is important. If you make grammatical errors, you lose credibility with your audience. Poor grammar is a mark of ignorance, and—rightly or wrongly—nobody puts much faith in an ignorant source. Even if an audience is broad-minded enough to withhold judgment of the speaker, a grammatical error is distracting.

So if you have doubts about what is correct, don't be lazy. Look up the answer, and use the proper form of expression. Check the grammar and usage guide in this book (see Appendix I), or consult any number of special reference books available in libraries and bookstores. Most authorities agree on the basic conventions.

Just as important as using the correct words is choosing the best words for the job at hand. Word effectiveness is generally more difficult to achieve than correctness,

Readability depends on word choice, sentence length, sentence structure, organization, and the message's physical appearance.

The two key aspects of word choice are
- Correctness
- Effectiveness

If in doubt, check it out.

Figure 7.3
The Fog Index

> ### 1. Select writing sample.
> Keep the sample between 100 and 125 words long.
>
> I called Global Corporation to ask when we will receive copies of its <u>insur-ance policies</u> and <u>engineering</u> reports. Cindy Turner of Global said that they are putting the <u>documents together</u> and will send them by Express Mail next week. She told me that they are late because most of the <u>infor-mation</u> is in the hands of Global's <u>attorneys</u> in Boston. I asked why it was in Boston; we had <u>understood</u> that the account is serviced by the carrier's Dallas branch. Turner explained that the account <u>originally</u> was sold to Global's Boston <u>division</u>, so all paperwork stays there. She promised to <u>telephone</u> us when the package is ready to ship.
>
> ### 2. Determine average sentence length.
> Count the number of words in each sentence. Treat independent clauses (stand-alone word groups containing subject and predicate) as separate sentences. For example, "In school we studied; we learned; we improved" counts as three sentences. Then add all word counts for each sentence to get the total word count, and divide that by the num-ber of sentences. This excerpt has an average sentence length of 14:
>
> $$18 + 21 + 21 + 7 + 13 + 12 + 5 + 12 =$$
> $$109 \text{ words} \div 8 \text{ sentences} = 14$$
>
> ### 3. Determine percentage of long words.
> Count the number of long words—that is, all words that have three or more syllables (underlined in excerpt). Omit proper nouns, combina-tions of short words (such as *butterfly* and *anyway*), and verbs that gain a third syllable by adding *-es* or *-ed* (as in *trespasses* and *created*). Divide the number of long words by the total number of words in the sample. The percentage of long words in this excerpt is 10 percent:
>
> $$11 \text{ long words} \div 109 \text{ total words} = 10 \text{ percent}$$
>
> ### 4. Determine the grade level required to read the passage.
> Add the numbers for average sentence length and percentage of long words. Multiply this sum by 0.4, and drop the number following the decimal point. The number of years of schooling required to easily read this excerpt is 10:
>
> $$14 \text{ words per sentence} + 10 \text{ percent long words} =$$
> $$24 \times 0.4 = 9.6 - 0.6 = 9 \text{ (Fog Index)}$$

particularly in written communication. Professional writers like Turner Broadcasting's Adrianne Proeller have to work at their craft, using writing techniques to improve their style. The rest of this section discusses a number of these techniques.

Plain English

Plain English is close to spo-ken English and can be more easily understood.

Plain English is a way of writing and arranging language so that your audience can un-derstand your meaning. If you've ever tried to make sense of an obtusely worded legal document or credit agreement, you can understand the movement toward requiring contracts and other such documents to be written in plain English. Because it's close to the way we speak, plain English is easily understood by anyone with an eighth- or ninth-grade education.[6]

In an attempt to make government regulations more understandable, President Jimmy Carter signed an executive order requiring any regulations issued by executive agencies to be written in plain English. Since then 28 states have passed legislation regarding the readability of insurance contracts, and more than a dozen states have approved laws aimed at making consumer contracts easier to understand.[7] In Britain, the Plain English Campaign annually names British organizations that have succeeded in making themselves more easily understood.[8]

The growing focus on plain-English laws has already led to plain-English loan and credit-card application forms, insurance policies, and real estate contracts. Plain English has benefited mutual funds such as Fidelity Investments, whose documents have been rewritten, reorganized, and redesigned to emphasize important sections and to include more graphics in an attempt to make them easier to comprehend.[9] Even software programmers are trying to simplify their language to communicate with product users. Indeed, people are sometimes amazed at what their audience can't grasp—like the programmer who exclaimed, "You mean he doesn't understand what pop out to DOS means?"[10]

Of course, plain English has some limitations. It lacks the precision necessary for scientific research, intense feeling, and personal insight. Moreover, it fails to embrace every culture and dialect equally.[11] Needless to say, it's intended for areas where English is the primary language; however, the lessons of plain English can also help you simplify messages intended for audiences who may speak English only as a second or even third language. For example, you will communicate more clearly and precisely with your intercultural audience by choosing words that have only one interpretation.[12]

Functional Words and Content Words

Words can be divided into two categories. Functional words express relationships and have only one unchanging meaning in any given context. They include conjunctions, prepositions, articles, and pronouns. Your main concern with functional words is to use them correctly. Content words are multidimensional and therefore subject to various interpretations. They include nouns, verbs, adjectives, and adverbs. These words carry the meaning of a sentence. Content words are the building blocks; functional words are the mortar. In the following sentence, all the content words are in italics:

> Some *objective observers* of the *cookie market give Nabisco* the *edge* in *quality,* but *Frito-Lay is lauded* for *superior distribution.*

Both functional words and content words are necessary, but your effectiveness as a communicator depends largely on your ability to choose the right content words for your message. So let's take a closer look at two important dimensions for classifying content words.

Functional words (conjunctions, prepositions, articles, and pronouns) express relationships among content words (nouns, verbs, adjectives, and adverbs).

Connotation and Denotation

As you know from reading Chapter 2, content words have both a denotative and a connotative meaning. The **denotative meaning** is the literal, or dictionary, meaning; the **connotative meaning** includes all the associations and feelings evoked by the word. Consider *dirt,* a word that has many connotations. A disapproving parent remarks, "Just look at you; you're covered in dirt." An investigative reporter tells the editor, "I've uncovered some interesting dirt on that politician." An Iowa farmer says, "My land is good; you've never seen darker dirt." The word is the same, but the connotations are different.

Some words have more connotations than others. If you say that a student has failed to pass the test, you're making a strong statement; you suggest that the person is

Content words have both a denotative (dictionary) meaning and a connotative (associative) meaning.

inferior, incompetent, and second-rate. On the other hand, if you say that the student has achieved a score of 65 percent, you suggest something else. By replacing the word *failed,* you avoid a heavy load of negative connotations.

In business communication, generally use terms that are low in connotative meaning. Words that have relatively few possible interpretations are less likely to be misunderstood. Furthermore, because you are usually trying to deal with things in an objective, rational manner, avoid emotion-laden comments.

Abstraction and Concreteness

> The more abstract a word, the more it is removed from the tangible, objective world of things that can be perceived with the senses.

In addition to varying in connotative impact, content words also vary in their level of abstraction. An abstract word expresses a concept, quality, or characteristic instead of standing for a thing you can touch or see. Abstractions are usually broad, encompassing a category of ideas. They are often intellectual, academic, or philosophical. *Love, honor, progress, tradition,* and *beauty* are abstractions. Concrete terms are anchored in the tangible, material world. They stand for something particular: *chair, table, horse, rose, kick, kiss, red, green, two.* These words are direct and vivid, clear and exact.

You might suppose that concrete words are better than abstract words, because they are more precise. Try to rewrite this sentence without using the italicized abstract words:

> We hold these *truths* to be *self-evident,* that all men are *created equal,* that they are *endowed* by their *Creator* with certain *unalienable Rights,* that among these are *Life, Liberty,* and the *Pursuit of Happiness.*

As you can see, the Declaration of Independence needs abstractions, and so do business messages. Abstractions permit us to rise above the common and tangible. They allow us to refer to such concepts as *morale, productivity, profits, quality, motivation,* and *guarantees.*

Even though they're indispensable, abstractions can be troublesome. They tend to be fuzzy and subject to many interpretations. They also tend to be boring. It isn't always easy to get excited about ideas, especially if they're unrelated to concrete experience. The best way to minimize such problems is to blend abstract terms with concrete ones, the general with the specific. State the concept, and then pin it down with details expressed in more concrete terms. Save the abstractions for ideas that cannot be expressed any other way.

> In business communication, use concrete, specific terms whenever possible; use abstractions only when necessary.

Take a sample of your writing and circle all the nouns. How many of them point to a specific person, place, or object? The ones that do are concrete and specific. Look at the vague nouns; can you replace them with more vivid terms? Now underline all the adjectives. How many of them describe the exact color, size, texture, quantity, or quality of something? Bear in mind that words such as *small, numerous, sizable, near, soon, good,* and *fine* are imprecise. Try to replace them with more accurate terms. Instead of referring to *a sizable loss,* talk about *a loss of $32 million.*

Words That Communicate

Wordsmiths are journalists, public relations specialists, editors, letter and report writers—anyone who earns a living by crafting words. Unlike poets, novelists, or dramatists, wordsmiths don't try for dramatic effects. They are mainly concerned with being clear, concise, and accurate in their use of language. To reach this goal, they emphasize words that are strong, familiar, and short, and they avoid hiding them under unnecessary extra syllables. When you edit your message, do your best to think like a wordsmith.

Strong Words

Nouns and verbs are the most concrete words in any message, so use them as much as you can. Although adjectives and adverbs obviously have parts to play, use them sparingly. They often call for subjective judgments, and business communication strives to be objective. Verbs are especially powerful because they carry the action; they tell what's happening in the sentence. The more dynamic and specific the verb, the better. Instead of settling for *rise* or *fall*, look for something more meaningful and descriptive, like *soar* or *plummet.*

Verbs and nouns are more concrete than adverbs and adjectives.

Given a choice of words, choose the one that most clearly and specifically expresses your thought:

Avoid Weak Phrases	Use Strong Terms
wealthy businessperson	tycoon
business prosperity	boom
hard times	slump

Familiar Words

You'll communicate best with words that are familiar to your readers. At the same time, bear in mind that words familiar to one reader might be unfamiliar to another:

Familiar words are preferable to unfamiliar ones, but try to avoid overworked terms (clichés).

Avoid Unfamiliar Words	Use Familiar Words
ascertain	find out, learn
consummate	close, bring about
peruse	read, study
circumvent	avoid
increment	growth, increase
unequivocal	certain

Although familiar words are generally the best choice, beware of terms so common that they have become virtually meaningless. Readers tend to slide right by such clichés as these to whatever is coming next:

interface	time frame	strategic decisions
track record	frame of reference	dialogue
viable	prioritize	scenario

Also handle technical or professional terms with care. Used in moderation, they add precision and authority to a message. However, many people simply don't understand them, and even a technically sophisticated audience will be lulled to sleep by too many. Let your audience's vocabulary be your guide. If they share a particular jargon, you may enhance your credibility by speaking their language. When addressing a group of engineers, you might refer to *meteorological effects on microwave propagation.* When addressing an ordinary audience, you'd probably do better referring to the *effects of weather on radio waves.*

Short Words

Although certainly not true in every case, short words are generally more vivid and easier to read, whether you're writing to people at home or abroad. The thing to remember is to use short, simple words, *not* simple concepts.[13] Short words often communicate better than long words:

Short words are generally more vivid than long ones and improve the readability of a document.

Avoid Long Words	Use Short Words
During the preceding year, the company accelerated productive operations.	Last year the company sped up operations.
The action was predicated on the assumption that the company was operating at a financial deficit.	The action was based on the belief that the company was losing money.

Camouflaged Verbs

Turning verbs into nouns or adjectives weakens your writing style.

In the words you use, watch for endings such as *-ion, -tion, -ing, -ment, -ant, -ent, -ence, -ance,* and *-ency.* Most of them change verbs into nouns and adjectives. In effect, the words that result are camouflaged verbs—the heart of weak construction. Getting rid of these camouflaged verbs will strengthen your writing:

Avoid Camouflaged Verbs	Use Verbs
The manager undertook implementation of the rules.	The manager implemented the rules.
Verification of the shipments occurs weekly.	Shipments are verified weekly.

Bias-Free Language

Avoid biased language that might offend the audience.

Most of us think of ourselves as being sensitive, unbiased, ethical, and fair. But being fair and objective isn't enough; you must also *appear* to be fair.[14] **Bias-free language**

COMMUNICATING ACROSS CULTURES

MORE THAN WORD FOR WORD—THE IMPORTANCE OF ACCURATE TRANSLATION

An old Italian saying holds that *traduttori traditore* ("translators are traitors"). Of course, a translation is always slightly different from the original, but unwary translators can fall into one of two traps: (1) translating word for word and believing that this linguistic accuracy is a good translation or (2) summarizing the content of a message and believing that this general synopsis is a good translation. Because good translation involves processing ideas rather than merely processing words, neither approach achieves the equivalence of meaning necessary for effective communication. So if you need to hire a translator, how can you be sure that your intended message is actually being communicated to your intended audience? How can you proof your message when it's in a language you don't understand?

Cultural Context

Meaning equivalence can certainly be a problem, especially with culture-bound idioms. An Italian idiom, *Giovanni sta menando il cane per l'aia,* translates word for word into English as "John is leading his dog around the threshing floor." A trans-

lator might be tempted to summarize the phrase by saying, "John is avoiding the problem." The closest idiom in English turns out to be "John is beating about the bush"—which carries a meaning not present in the linguistic or the synopsis translations. A good translator understands the message in its own cultural context and chooses the best way to convey the same sense of that message in another language.

The Wrong Message

So how do you know whether you've hired a good translator? Many businesses haven't been able to tell until it was too late. Braniff airlines targeted Miami-area Hispanic residents when it created an ad campaign in Spanish to emphasize the comfort of their planes' leather seats. Unfortunately, when the airline used the headline *sentado en cuero,* it was actually inviting people to "sit naked" aboard. Even though *cuero* does mean "leather," in that context it's slang for "one's hide" or "bare skin." A food company saw its message lost in the translation when it advertised its giant burrito as *burrada,* which literally means "big

avoids unethical, embarrassing blunders in language related to culture, gender, race, ethnicity, age, and disability.

Cultural Bias

Whether working with employees from diverse cultures or dealing with businesses and customers in other countries, be careful to avoid cultural bias in your business messages. Avoid using slang ("the ball is now in your court"), acronyms ("FYI, the MIS is back on line"), or idioms ("You'll soon be moving up the organization ladder").[15] Avoid using a restrictive viewpoint, as when TBS's Adrianne Proeller made sure she changed *domestic sales* to *U.S.-based sales* in her letter to European readers. Also, if you're having your message translated into another language, the best way to avoid undetected cultural bias is to have it back-translated (see "More Than Word for Word—The Importance of Accurate Translation"). Perhaps most important of all, avoid judging international associates and intercultural workers by their use of English. Employees and associates may misuse English grammar or structure, but that fact alone indicates nothing about their creativity or talent.

> Don't use slang, idioms, or restrictive viewpoints when communicating interculturally, and don't judge associates by their grammar or language structure.

Gender Bias

Women's roles in business have changed over the years, and good communicators make every effort to change sexist language.[16] For example, the word *man* used to denote humanity, describing a human being of either gender and any age. Today, however, *man* is associated more with an adult male human being. Some of the most commonly used words contain the word *man,* but some simple solutions exist:

> Replace words that inaccurately exclude women or men.

mistake." Kentucky Fried Chicken's "finger-lickin' good" came out in Chinese as "eat your fingers off."

Back-Translation

You may want to translate safety precautions for non-English-speaking employees in your company, or you may want to translate advertising slogans to market your products globally. Either way, you need some way of proofing those translations. Your best bet is back-translation: Once a translator encodes your message into another language, a new translator retranslates (back-translates) your message into the original language. This back-translation is compared with the original message to discover any errors or discrepancies. When Heinz targeted Britain's Asian community for its vegetarian baby foods, it aired Hindi-language ads on Asian radio stations, used Hindi-language trade press ads, and made direct mailings to Asian retailers. To make sure that no meaning was misunderstood or lost, Heinz first translated every ad and mailer into Hindi and then back-translated every message into English.

No two languages can represent the same social reality. Different cultures live in different worlds, not in the same world with different labels. So a good translator knows not only the grammar and the words but also the language, and a good businessperson knows that you have to test the translation before trusting it.

1. You've hired Helene Martin to translate your big proposal to the packaging company in France. Since Martin knows both the language and the culture very well, you're tempted to ask her to help you think of what to write. Would that be a good idea? Explain.
2. You've hired George Brown to retranslate the proposal from French back into English. You compare the back-translation with the original document and find one discrepancy. When you ask Martin and Brown for the best way to say what you mean, they disagree on the proper words. Both are highly respected translators, so which one do you trust? Should you replace the English wording with something else, something that would lend itself more easily to an equivalent expression?

Unacceptable	Preferable
mankind	humanity, human beings, human race, people
if a man drove 50 miles at 60 miles per hour	if a person (or someone or a driver) drove 50 miles at 60 miles per hour
man-made	artificial, synthetic, manufactured, constructed, of human origin
manpower	human power, human energy, workers, work force

Here are some simple ways to replace occupational terms that contain the word *man* with words that can represent people of either gender:

Unacceptable	Preferable
businessman	business executive, business manager, businessperson
salesman	sales representative, salesperson, salesclerk
insurance man	insurance agent
foreman	supervisor

Avoid using female-gender words like *authoress* and *actress; author* and *actor* denote both women and men. Similarly, avoid special designations, such as *woman doctor* or *male nurse.* Use the same label for everyone in a particular group. Don't refer to a woman as a *chairperson* and then call the man a *chairman.*

The pronoun *he* has also traditionally been used to refer to both males and females. Here are some simple ways to avoid this outdated usage:

Unacceptable	Preferable
The average worker . . . he	The average worker . . . he or she
The typical business executive spends four hours of his day in meetings.	Most business executives spend four hours a day in meetings.

Avoid identifying certain roles with a specific gender:

Unacceptable	Preferable
the consumer . . . she	consumers . . . they
the nurse/teacher . . . she	nurses/teachers . . . they

If you're discussing categories of people, such as bosses and office workers, avoid referring to the boss as *he* and the office worker as *she.* Instead, reword sentences so that you can use *they,* or reword them so that you don't have to use any pronoun. In today's business world, it's also appropriate sometimes to use *she* when referring to a boss and *he* when referring to an office worker.

Another way to avoid bias is to make sure you don't always mention men first. Vary the traditional pattern with *women and men, gentlemen and ladies, she and he, her and his.*

Finally, identify women by their own names, not by their role or marital status—unless it is appropriate to the context:

Unacceptable	Preferable
Phil Donahue and Marlo	Phil Donahue and Marlo Thomas
Phil Donahue and Ms. Thomas	Mr. Donahue and Ms. Thomas

This Kentucky Fried Chicken outlet in Austin, Texas, is like any other company with a diverse work force—successful KFC executives constantly revise business messages to avoid sexism and all other biased language.

The preferred title for women in business is Ms., unless the individual asks to be addressed as Miss or Mrs. or has some other title, such as Dr.

Racial and Ethnic Bias

The guidelines for avoiding racial and ethnic bias are much the same as those for avoiding gender bias. The central principle is to avoid language suggesting that members of a racial or ethnic group have the same stereotypical characteristics:

Eliminate references that reinforce racial or ethnic stereotypes.

Unacceptable	**Preferable**
disadvantaged black children	children from lower-income families
Jim Wong is an unusually tall Asian.	Jim Wong is tall.

The best solution is to avoid identifying people by race or ethnic origin unless such a label is relevant:

Unacceptable	**Preferable**
Mario M. Cuomo, Italian American politician and ex-governor of New York	Mario M. Cuomo, politician and ex-governor of New York

Age Bias

As with gender, race, and ethnic background, mention the age of a person only when it is relevant:

Avoid references to an individual's age or physical limitations.

Unacceptable	**Preferable**
Mary Kirazy, 58, has just joined our trust department.	Mary Kirazy has just joined our trust department.

When referring to older people, avoid such stereotyped adjectives as *spry* and *frail.*

Disability Bias

There is really no painless label for people with a physical, mental, sensory, or emotional impairment. However, if you must refer to such individuals in terms of their limitations, avoid using terms such as *handicapped, crippled,* or *retarded,* and be sure to put the person first and the disability second:[17]

Always refer to people first and their disabilities second.

Unacceptable	**Preferable**
Crippled workers face many barriers on the job.	Workers who have physical disabilities face many barriers on the job.

Most of all, avoid mentioning a disability unless it is pertinent. When it is pertinent, present the whole person, not just the disability, by showing the limitation in an unobtrusive manner:

Unacceptable	**Preferable**
An epileptic, Tracy has no trouble doing her job.	Tracy's epilepsy has no effect on her job performance.

The 1990 Americans with Disabilities Act guarantees equal opportunities for people who have or have had a condition that might handicap them. The goal of bias-free communication is to abandon stereotyped assumptions about what a person can do or will do and to focus on an individual's unique characteristics. So describe people without disabilities as *typical* rather than *normal*. People having disabilities are certainly *atypical* but not necessarily *abnormal*.[18]

Critiquing the Writing of Another

In business, many documents are written for someone else's signature.[19] When you need to critique the work of another, you want to help that person communicate effectively, and to do that you must provide specific, constructive comments. To help the writer make meaningful changes, you need to say more than simply "This doesn't work" or "This isn't what I wanted" or "I don't see what you're trying to say."[20] When critiquing a document, concentrate on three elements:[21]

- ***Does the document accomplish the intended purpose?*** Is the purpose clearly stated? Does the body support the stated purpose? You might outline the key points to see whether they support the main idea. Is the conclusion supported by the data? Are the arguments presented logically? If the document fails to accomplish its purpose, it must be rewritten. Be sure to determine whether the directions given with the initial assignment were clear and complete. Making sure that directions are specific and understandable saves time both for the writer and for the person giving the critique.
- ***Is the factual material correct?*** A proposal to provide nationwide computer-training services for $15 million would be disastrous if your intention was to provide those services for $150 million. Be sure you pay strict attention to detail. All factual errors must be corrected.
- ***Does the document use ambiguous language?*** Readers must not be allowed to interpret the meaning in any way other than intended. If you interpret a message differently from what an author intended, the author is at fault, and the document must be revised to clarify problem areas.

If any one of these elements needs attention, the document must be rewritten, revised, or corrected. However, once these elements are deemed satisfactory, the question is whether to request other changes. Of course, minor changes can be made at any time in the critiquing process. But if these three elements are in fact acceptable, consider three points before requesting a major revision.[22]

- ***Can the document truly be improved?*** The answer to this question is usually yes—given enough time.
- ***Can you justify the time needed for a rewrite?*** Will deadlines be missed? Will other priorities suffer from a delay? For example, if a production line is down and the document in question is a description of what's wrong or how to fix it, then

any polishing beyond accuracy and clarity is secondary to getting the production line running again.

- ***Will your request have a negative impact on morale?*** Are the changes to be made a purely personal preference? If unexplained or inconsistent changes are regularly made to a person's writing efforts, that writer can become demoralized. (Of course, consistent style preferences can always be suggested for future use.)

STAGE 8: REWRITING YOUR MESSAGE

As you edit your business message, you'll find yourself rewriting passages, sentences, and even whole sections to improve its effectiveness. First, remember that in your search for perfection, you're probably also facing a deadline, so try to stick to the schedule you set during the planning stage of the project. Do your best to revise and rewrite thoroughly but also economically. Second, you'll probably want to keep copies of your revised versions. As TBS's Adrianne Proeller points out, someone can come back to you and say, "'Hey, I didn't approve that.' So it's very important to keep a paper trail." As you rewrite, concentrate on how each word contributes to an effective sentence and how that sentence develops a coherent paragraph.

Create Effective Sentences

In English, words don't make much sense until they're combined in a sentence to express a complete thought. Thus, *Jill, receptionist, the, smiles,* and *at* can be organized into "Jill smiles at the receptionist." Now you can begin exploring the possibilities for improvement, looking at how well each word performs its particular function. Nouns and noun equivalents are the topics (or subjects) you're communicating about, and verbs and related words (or predicates) make statements about those subjects. In a more complicated sentence, adjectives and adverbs modify the subject and the statement, and various connectors hold the words together.

> Every sentence contains a subject (noun or noun equivalent) and a predicate (verb and related word).

The Three Types of Sentences

Sentences come in three basic varieties: simple, compound, and complex. A **simple sentence** has a single subject and a single predicate, although it may be expanded by nouns and pronouns serving as objects of the action and by modifying phrases. Here's a typical example (with the subject underlined once and the predicate verb underlined twice):

> To give your writing variety, use the three types of sentences:
> - Simple
> - Compound
> - Complex

Profits have increased in the past year.

A **compound sentence** expresses two or more independent but related thoughts of equal importance, joined by *and, but,* or *or.* In effect, a compound sentence is a merger of two or more simple sentences (independent clauses) that deal with the same basic idea. For example:

Wage rates have declined by 5 percent, and employee turnover has been high.

The independent clauses in a compound sentence are always separated by a comma or by a semicolon (in which case the conjunction—*and, but, or*—is dropped).

A **complex sentence** expresses one main thought (the independent clause) and one or more subordinate thoughts (dependent clauses) related to it, often separated by a comma. The subordinate thought, which comes first in the following sentence, could not stand alone:

Although you may question Gerald's conclusions, <u>you</u> <u>must admit</u> that his research is thorough.

When constructing a sentence, use the form that best fits the thought you want to express. The structure of the sentence should match the relationship of the ideas. If you have two ideas of equal importance, express them as two simple sentences or as one compound sentence. However, if one of the ideas is less important than the other, place it in a dependent clause to form a complex sentence. This compound sentence uses a conjunction to join two ideas that aren't truly equal:

> The chemical products division is the strongest in the company, and its management techniques should be adopted by the other divisions.

In the complex sentence that follows, the first thought has been made subordinate to the second. Note how much more effective the second idea is when the cause-and-effect relationship has been established:

> Because the chemical products division is the strongest in the company, its management techniques should be adopted by the other divisions.

In complex sentences, the placement of the dependent clause should be geared to the relationship between the ideas expressed. If you want to emphasize the idea, put the dependent clause at the end of the sentence (the most emphatic position) or at the beginning (the second most emphatic position). If you want to downplay the idea, bury the dependent clause within the sentence.

Most Emphatic:	The handbags are manufactured in Mexico, *which has lower wage rates than the United States.*
Emphatic:	*Because wage rates are lower there,* the handbags are manufactured in Mexico.
Least Emphatic:	Mexico, *which has lower wage rates,* was selected as the production point for the handbags.

To make your writing as effective as possible, balance all three sentence types. If you use too many simple sentences, you can't properly express the relationship among ideas. If you use too many long, compound sentences, your writing will sound monotonous. On the other hand, an uninterrupted series of complex sentences is hard to follow.

Sentence Style

Of course, sentence style varies from culture to culture. German sentences are extremely complex with a lot of modifiers and appositives; Japanese and Chinese languages don't even have sentences in the same sense that Western languages do.[23] Basically, whether a sentence in English is simple, compound, or complex, it should be grammatically correct, efficient, readable, interesting, and appropriate for your audience. In general, strive for straightforward simplicity. For most business audiences, clarity and efficiency take precedence over literary style. The following guidelines will help you achieve these qualities in your own writing.

Keep Sentences Short

Break long sentences into shorter ones to improve readability.

Long sentences are usually harder to understand than short sentences because they are packed with information that must all be absorbed at once. Most good business writing therefore has an average sentence length of 20 words or fewer. This figure is the average, not a ceiling. To be interesting, your writing should contain both longer and shorter sentences. (Of course, for audiences abroad, varying sentence length can create translation problems for the reader, so stick to short sentences in international messages.)[24]

Long sentences are especially well suited for grouping or combining ideas, listing points, and summarizing or previewing information. Medium-length sentences (those with about 20 words) are useful for showing the relationships among ideas. Short sentences are tailor-made for emphasizing important information.

Rely on the Active Voice

Active sentences are generally preferable to passive sentences because they are easier to understand.[25] You're using **active voice** when the subject (the "actor") comes before the verb, and the object of the sentence (the "acted upon") follows the verb: "John rented the office." You're using **passive voice** when the subject follows the verb and the object precedes it: "The office was rented by John." As you can see, the passive verb combines the helping verb *to be* with a form of the verb that is usually similar to the past tense. Using passive verbs makes sentences longer and deemphasizes the subject. Active verbs produce shorter, stronger sentences:

Active sentences are stronger than passive ones.

Avoid Passive Sentences	Use Active Sentences
Sales were increased by 32 percent last month.	Sales increased by 32 percent last month.
The new procedure is thought by the president to be superior.	The president thinks the new procedure is superior.
There are problems with this contract.	This contract has problems.
It is necessary that the report be finished by next week.	The report must be finished by next week.

Of course, in some situations, using the passive voice makes sense. You may want to be diplomatic when pointing out a problem or error of some kind, so you might say, "The shipment was lost" rather than "You lost the shipment." The passive version seems less like an accusation because the emphasis is on the lost shipment rather than on the person responsible. Similarly, you may want to point out what's being done without taking or attributing either the credit or the blame, so you might say something like "The production line is being analyzed to determine the source of problems." You may want to avoid personal pronouns in order to create an objective tone, so in a formal report, you might say, "Criteria have been established for evaluating capital expenditures."

Use passive sentences to soften bad news, to put yourself in the background, or to create an impersonal tone.

Eliminate Unnecessary Words and Phrases

Some words and combinations of words have more efficient, one-word equivalents. So you would avoid saying, "This is to inform you that we have begun production" when "We have begun production" is enough.

Be on the lookout for
- *Inefficient phrases*
- *Redundancies*
- *Unneeded relative pronouns and articles*

Combinations to Avoid	Efficient Equivalents
for the sum of	for
in the event that	if
on the occasion of	on
prior to the start of	before

Other word combinations are redundant: Avoid saying "Visible to the eye" because *visible* is enough—nothing can be visible to the ear. Avoid saying "surrounded on all sides" because *surrounded* implies on all sides. Also take a close look at double modifiers. Do you really need to say "modern, up-to-date equipment," or would "modern equipment" do the job?

Relative pronouns such as *who, that,* and *which* frequently cause clutter, and sometimes even articles are excessive (mostly too many *the*'s). However, well-placed relative pronouns and articles serve an important function by preventing confusion. For example, without *that,* the following sentence is ambiguous:

Confusing: The project manager told the engineers last week the specifications were changed.

Clear: The project manager told the engineers last week *that* the specifications were changed.

Clear: The project manager told the engineers *that* last week the specifications were changed.

Here are some other ways to prune your prose:

Poor	Improved
consensus of opinion	consensus
at this point in time	at this time, now
irregardless	(no such word; use *regardless*)
each and every	(either word, but not both)
due to the fact that	because
at an early date	soon (or a specific date)
at the present time	now
in view of the fact that	since, because
until such time as	when
we are of the opinion	we believe
with reference to	about
as a result of	because
for the month of December	for December

Avoid needless repetition.

In general, be on the lookout for the needless repetition of words or ideas. Try not to string together a series of sentences that all start with the same word or words, and

Even when Los Angeles lawyer Alicia Cardeiro dictates messages and legal documents, she later examines the printed copy, closely monitoring every word to avoid confusing language. She uses active sentences and gets rid of all unnecessary words and phrases.

avoid repeating the same word too often within a given sentence. Another way to save words is to use infinitives in place of some phrases. This technique not only shortens your sentences but makes them clearer as well:

Use infinitives to replace some phrases.

Poor	Improved
In order to be a successful writer, you must work hard.	To be a successful writer, you must work hard.
He went to the library for the purpose of studying.	He went to the library to study.
The employer increased salaries so that she could improve morale.	The employer increased salaries to improve morale.

Avoid Obsolete and Pompous Language

The language of business used to be much more formal than it is today, and a few out-of-date phrases remain from the old days. Perhaps the best way to eliminate them is to ask yourself: "Would I say this if I were talking with someone face-to-face?"

Obsolete formal phrases can obscure meaning.

Obsolete	Up-to-Date
as per your letter	as in your letter (do not mix Latin and English)
hoping to hear from you soon, I remain	(omit)
yours of the 15th	your letter of June 15
awaiting your reply, we are	(omit)
in due course	today, tomorrow (or a specific time)
permit me to say that	(permission is not necessary; just say what you wish)
we are in receipt of	we have received
pursuant to	(omit)
in closing, I'd like to say	(omit)
attached herewith is	here is
the undersigned	I; me
kindly advise	please let us know
under separate cover	in another envelope; by parcel post
we wish to inform you	(just say it)
attached please find	enclosed is
it has come to my attention	I have just learned; Ms. Garza has just told me
our Mr. Lydell	Mr. Lydell, our credit manager
please be advised that	(omit)

Pompous language is similar to out-of-date phrases. It also sounds stiff, puffed up, and roundabout. People are likely to use pompous language when they are trying to impress somebody. In hopes of sounding imposing, they use big words, trite expressions, and overly complicated sentences.

The use of pompous language suggests that you are a pompous person.

Poor	Improved
Upon procurement of additional supplies, I will initiate fulfillment of your order.	I will fill your order when I receive more supplies.
Perusal of the records indicates a substantial deficit for the preceding accounting period due to the utilization of antiquated mechanisms.	The records show a company loss last year due to the use of old equipment.

Moderate Your Enthusiasm

Business writing shouldn't be gushy.

An occasional adjective or adverb intensifies and emphasizes your meaning, but too many ruin your writing:

Poor	**Improved**
We are extremely pleased to offer you a position on our staff of exceptionally skilled and highly educated employees.	We are pleased to offer you a position on our staff of skilled and well-educated employees.
The work offers extraordinary challenges and a very large salary.	The work offers challenges and an attractive salary.

Break Up Strung-Out Sentences

In many cases, the parts of a compound sentence should be separated into two sentences.

A strung-out sentence is a series of two or more sentences unwisely connected by *and*—in other words, a compound sentence taken too far. You can often improve your writing style by separating the string into individual sentences:

Poor	**Improved**
The magazine will be published January 1, and I'd better meet the deadline if I want my article included.	The magazine will be published January 1. I'd better meet the deadline if I want my article included.

Avoid Hedging Sentences

Don't be afraid to present your opinions without qualification.

Sometimes you have to write *may* or *seems* to avoid stating a judgment as a fact. Nevertheless, when you have too many such hedges, you aren't really saying anything:

Poor	**Improved**
I believe that Mr. Johnson's employment record seems to show that he may be capable of handling the position.	Mr. Johnson's employment record shows that he is capable of handling the position.

Watch for Indefinite Pronoun Starters

Avoid starting sentences with *it* and *there*.

If you start a sentence with an indefinite pronoun (an expletive) like *it* or *there*, odds are that the sentence could be shorter:

Poor	**Improved**
It would be appreciated if you would sign the lease today.	Please sign the lease today.
There are five employees in this division who were late to work today.	Five employees in this division were late to work today.

Express Parallel Ideas in Parallel Form

When you use the same grammatical pattern to express two or more ideas, you show that they are comparable thoughts.

When you have two or more similar (parallel) ideas to express, try to use a **parallel construction**; that is, use the same grammatical pattern. The repetition of the pattern tells readers that the ideas are comparable and adds a nice rhythm to your message. In the following examples, parallel construction makes the sentences more readable:

Poor	**Improved**
Miss Simms had been drenched with rain, bombarded with telephone calls, and her boss shouted at her.	Miss Simms had been drenched with rain, bombarded with telephone calls, and shouted at by her boss.
Ms. Reynolds dictated the letter, and next she signed it and left the office.	Ms. Reynolds dictated the letter, signed it, and left the office.

To waste time and missing deadlines are bad habits.	Wasting time and missing deadlines are bad habits.
Interviews are a matter of acting confident and to stay relaxed.	Interviews are a matter of acting confident and of staying relaxed.

Parallelism can be achieved through a repetition of words, phrases, clauses, or entire sentences:

Parallel Words: The letter was approved by Clausen, Whittaker, Merlin, and Carlucci.

Parallel Phrases: We have beaten the competition in supermarkets, in department stores, and in specialty stores.

Parallel Clauses: I'd like to discuss the issue after Vicki gives her presentation but before Marvin shows his slides.

Parallel Sentences: In 1994 we exported 30 percent of our production. In 1995 we exported 50 percent.

Eliminate Awkward Pointers

To save words, business writers sometimes direct their readers' attention elsewhere with such expressions as *the above-mentioned, as mentioned above, the aforementioned, the former, the latter, respectively.* These words cause the reader to jump from one point in the message to another, a process that hinders effective communication. A better approach is to be specific in your references, even if you must add a few more words:

Tell readers exactly where you want them to look.

Poor	**Improved**
Typewriter ribbons for legal secretaries and beginning clerks are distributed by the Law Office and Stenographic Office, respectively.	Typewriter ribbons for legal secretaries are distributed by the Law Office; those for beginning clerks are distributed by the Stenographic Office.

Correct Dangling Modifiers

Sometimes a modifier is not just an adjective or adverb but an entire phrase defining a noun or verb. Be careful to construct your sentences so that this type of modifier refers to something in the main part of the sentence in a way that makes sense. Consider this sentence:

Make sure that modifier phrases are really related to the subject of the sentence.

Walking to the office, a red sports car passed her.

The construction implies that the red sports car has the office and the legs to walk there. The modifier is said to be dangling because it has no real connection to the subject of the sentence—in this case, the sports car. This is what the writer is trying to say:

A red sports car passed her while she was walking to the office.

Flipping the clauses produces another correct sentence:

While she was walking to the office, a red sports car passed her.

Dangling modifiers make sentences confusing and sometimes ridiculous:

Poor	**Improved**
Working as fast as possible, the budget was soon ready.	Working as fast as possible, the committee soon had the budget ready.
After a three-week slump, we increased sales.	After a three-week slump, sales increased.

Passive construction is often the cause of dangling modifiers.

The first example shows one frequent cause of dangling modifiers: passive construction in the independent clause. When the clause is made active instead of passive, the connection with the dangling modifier becomes more obvious.

Avoid Long Sequences of Nouns

Stringing together a series of nouns may save a little space, but it causes confusion.

When nouns are strung together as modifiers, the resulting sentence is hard to read. You can clarify the sentence by putting some of the nouns in a modifying phrase. Although you add a few more words, your audience won't have to work as hard to understand the sentence.

Poor	**Improved**
The window sash installation company will give us an estimate on Friday.	The company that installs window sashes will give us an estimate on Friday.

Keep Words Together That Work Together

Subject and predicate should be placed as close together as possible, as should modifiers and the words they modify.

To avoid confusing readers, keep the subject and predicate of a sentence as close together as possible. Otherwise, readers will have to read your sentence twice to figure out who did what.

Poor	**Improved**
A 10 percent decline in market share, which resulted from quality problems and an aggressive sales campaign by Armitage, the market leader in the Northeast, was the major problem in 1994.	The major problem in 1994 was a 10 percent loss of market share, which resulted from both quality problems and an aggressive sales campaign by Armitage, the market leader in the Northeast.

The same rule applies to other parts of speech. Adjectives, adverbs, and prepositional phrases usually make the most sense when they're placed as close as possible to the words they modify:

Poor	**Improved**
We will deliver the pipe soon that you ordered last Tuesday.	We will soon deliver the pipe that you ordered last Tuesday.

Emphasize Key Thoughts

Emphasize parts of a sentence by
• Giving them more space
• Putting them at the beginning or the end of the sentence
• Making them the subject of the sentence

In every message, some ideas are more important than others. You can emphasize these key ideas through your sentence style. One obvious technique is to give important points the most space. When you want to call attention to a thought, use extra words to describe it. Consider this sentence:

The chairperson of the board called for a vote of the shareholders.

To emphasize the importance of the chairperson, you might describe her more fully:

The chairperson of the board, who has considerable experience in corporate takeover battles, called for a vote of the shareholders.

You can increase the emphasis even more by adding a separate, short sentence to augment the first:

The chairperson of the board called for a vote of the shareholders. She has considerable experience in corporate takeover battles.

Another way to emphasize an idea is to place it at either the beginning or the end of a sentence:

Less Emphatic	More Emphatic
We are cutting the *price* to stimulate demand.	To stimulate demand, we are cutting the *price*.

You can also call attention to a thought by making it the subject of the sentence. In the following example, the emphasis is on the person:

I can write letters much more quickly using a computer.

In this version, the computer takes center stage:

The *computer* enables me to write letters much more quickly.

Techniques like this one give you a great deal of control over the way your audience interprets what you have to say.

Develop Coherent Paragraphs

A paragraph is a cluster of sentences all related to the same general topic. It is a unit of thought. A series of paragraphs makes up an entire composition. Each paragraph is an important part of the whole, a key link in the train of thought. As you edit a message, think about the paragraphs and their relationship to one another.

When you're talking to someone face-to-face, you develop your paragraphs informally, using tone of voice and gestures to signal the relationship among ideas. You pause to indicate that you have completed one topic and are ready to begin another, a new "paragraph." In a written document, on the other hand, paragraphs are developed more formally. Each paragraph is separated from other units of thought by the typographical device of skipping a line or indenting the first line.

Paragraphs are functional units that revolve around a single thought.

Elements of the Paragraph

Paragraphs vary widely in length and form. You can communicate effectively in one short paragraph or in pages of lengthy paragraphs, depending on your purpose, your audience, and your message. The typical paragraph contains three basic elements: a topic sentence, related sentences that develop the topic, and transitional words and phrases.

Most paragraphs consist of a topic sentence, related sentences, and transitional elements.

Topic Sentence

Every properly constructed paragraph is **unified**; it deals with a single topic. The sentence that introduces that topic is called the **topic sentence.** In informal and creative writing, the topic sentence may be implied rather than stated. In business writing, the topic sentence is generally explicit and often the first sentence in the paragraph. The topic sentence gives readers a summary of the general idea that will be covered in the rest of the paragraph. The following examples show how a topic sentence can introduce the subject and suggest the way that subject will be developed:

The topic sentence
- *Reveals the subject of the paragraph*
- *Indicates how it will be developed*

The medical products division has been troubled for many years by public relations problems. (In the rest of the paragraph, readers will learn the details of the problems.)

Relocating the plant in New York has two main disadvantages. (The disadvantages will be explained in subsequent sentences.)

To get a refund, you must supply us with some additional information. (The details will be described.)

Related Sentences

The sentences that explain the topic sentence round out the paragraph. These related sentences must all have a bearing on the general subject, and they must provide enough specific details to make the topic clear:

> The medical products division has been troubled for many years by public relations problems. Since 1991 the local newspaper has published 15 articles that portray the division in a negative light. We have been accused of everything from mistreating laboratory animals to polluting the local groundwater. Our facility has been described as a health hazard. Our scientists are referred to as "Frankensteins," and our profits are considered "obscene."

Paragraphs are developed through a series of related sentences that provide details about the topic sentence.

The developmental sentences are all more specific than the topic sentence. Each one provides another piece of evidence to demonstrate the general truth of the main thought. Also, each sentence is clearly related to the general idea being developed, which gives the paragraph its unity. A paragraph is well developed when it contains enough information to make the topic sentence convincing and interesting.

Transitional Elements

Transitional words and phrases show readers how paragraphs and the ideas within them are related.

In addition to being unified and well developed, effective paragraphs are **coherent**; that is, they are arranged in a logical order so that the audience can understand the train of thought. Coherence is achieved through the use of transitions that show the relationship between paragraphs and among sentences within paragraphs. They show how one thought is related to another. You can establish transitions in various ways:

Some transitional devices:
- Connecting words (conjunctions)
- Repeated words or phrases
- Pronouns
- Words that are frequently paired

- Use connecting words: *and, but, or, nevertheless, however, in addition,* and so on.
- Echo a word or phrase from a previous paragraph or sentence: "A system should be established for monitoring inventory levels. This system will provide . . ."
- Use a pronoun that refers to a noun used previously: "Ms. Arthur is the leading candidate for the president's position. She has excellent qualifications."
- Use words that are frequently paired: "The machine has a minimum output of . . . Its maximum output is . . ."

These techniques help readers understand the connections you are trying to make.

Five Ways to Develop a Paragraph

Five ways to develop paragraphs:
- Illustration
- Comparison or contrast
- Cause and effect
- Classification
- Problem and solution

Paragraphs can be developed in many ways, five of the more common techniques being illustration, comparison or contrast, cause and effect, classification, and problem and solution. Your choice of technique depends on your subject, your intended audience, and your purpose. Remember also that in actual practice, you'll often combine two or more methods of development in a single paragraph. To add interest, you might begin by using illustration, shift to comparison or contrast, and then shift again to problem and solution.

Before settling for the first approach that comes to mind, think about the alternatives. Think through various methods before committing yourself. If you fall into the easy habit of repeating the same old paragraph pattern time after time, your writing will be boring.

Illustration

When you develop a paragraph by illustration, you give examples that demonstrate the general idea:

> Some of our most popular products are available through local distributors. For example, Everett & Lemmings carries our frozen soups and entrees. The J. B. Green Company carries our complete line of seasonings, as well as the frozen soups. Wilmont Foods, also a major distributor, now carries our new line of frozen desserts.

Comparison or Contrast

Similarities or differences among thoughts often provide a strong basis for paragraph development. Here's an example developed by contrast:

In previous years, when the company was small, the recruiting function could be handled informally. The need for new employees was limited, and each manager could comfortably screen and hire her or his own staff. Today, however, Gambit Products must undertake a major recruiting effort. Our successful bid on the Owens contract means that we will be doubling our labor force over the next six months. To hire that many people without disrupting our ongoing activities, we will create a separate recruiting group within the human resources department.

Cause and Effect

When you develop a paragraph using the cause-and-effect technique, you focus on the reasons for something:

The heavy-duty fabric of your Wanderer tent probably broke down for one of two reasons: (1) a sharp object punctured the fabric, and without reinforcement, the hole was enlarged by the stress of erecting the tent daily for a week; or (2) the tent was folded and stored while still wet, which gradually rotted the fibers.

Classification

Paragraphs developed by classification show how a general idea is broken into specific categories:

Successful candidates for our supervisor trainee program generally come from one of several groups. The largest group, by far, consists of recent graduates of accredited data-processing programs. The next largest group comes from within our own company, as we try to promote promising clerical workers to positions of greater responsibility. Finally, we do occasionally accept candidates with outstanding supervisory experience in related industries.

Problem and Solution

Another way to develop a paragraph is to present a problem and then discuss the solution:

Selling handmade toys by mail is a challenge because consumers are accustomed to buying heavily advertised toys from major chains. However, if we develop an appealing catalog, we can compete on the basis of product novelty and quality. In addition, we can provide craftsmanship at a competitive price: a rocking horse made from birchwood, with a hand-knit tail and mane; a music box with the child's name painted on the top; a real Indian teepee, made by Native American artisans.

Paragraph Transitions

As you edit your paragraphs, just as you check to be sure they're unified, well developed, and coherent, be sure to include appropriate transition from one paragraph to the next. When you complete a paragraph, your readers automatically assume that you've finished with a particular idea. So if you continue to discuss that idea in the next paragraph, you upset their expectations.

Each paragraph should cover a single idea.

However, some ideas are simply too big to be handled conveniently in one paragraph. Unless you break up the thoughts somehow, you'll end up with a three-page paragraph that's guaranteed to intimidate even the most dedicated reader. It's a fact that short paragraphs (of 100 words or fewer) are easier to read than long ones. Direct-mail letters almost always use very short paragraphs because the writers know their letters will be read more carefully that way. Even in memos, letters, and reports, you may want to emphasize an idea from time to time by isolating it in a short, forceful paragraph.

Short paragraphs are easier to read than long ones.

So what do you do when you want to package a big idea in a short paragraph? Break the idea into subtopics and treat each subtopic in a separate paragraph, being careful to provide plenty of transitional elements. Take a look at the following draft:

Donner Corporation had to increase the size of its facilities and staff to keep up with rapid sales growth. It had to invest more in the physical plant in 3 years ($18 million) than it had spent in the previous 17 years of its operation. It had to double its staff in three years. All this had to be accomplished in an increasingly competitive labor market, without the benefit of an experienced human resources department. The company had to transform itself from a small, single-product company into a broadly based corporation with several divisions. Much more was involved than simply adding on to the existing plant and hiring more people. The quality of the existing staff and products did not compare favorably with that of major competitors. The corporation had to develop new operations while improving and expanding its traditional activities. It also needed to add to its professional staff by recruiting high-caliber people from many fields.

By breaking the subject into three paragraphs rather than one (see Figure 7.4), the writer has done a good job of revising this draft—but many other approaches might be as effective. There is no such thing as the "right" way to develop a paragraph.

Variety is the key to making your message interesting. As you edit your message, try to mix short paragraphs with longer ones. You might even use a one-sentence paragraph occasionally for emphasis.

> To write an interesting document
> - Use different methods to develop the paragraphs
> - Vary the length and structure of sentences
> - Mix short and long paragraphs

STAGE 9: PRODUCING YOUR MESSAGE

Once you've planned, composed, edited, and rewritten your message, give some thought to its presentation. Oral presentations are discussed in Chapter 20, and visual aids are discussed in Chapter 16. In the following sections, you'll get an idea of basic decisions about the design of written documents. People have trouble comprehending long, uninterrupted pages of text. So by using design elements such as white space, headings, and boldface type (just as this textbook does), you can provide visual clues to the importance of various ideas and their relationships.[26]

> Written documents require decisions about design elements.

Design Elements

Although a few messages may traditionally be handwritten (congratulations or condolences, for example), most business messages are typeset by a professional printer, printed by computer, or typewritten. Many design elements are easiest to deal with on computers with word-processing capabilities or with page-layout software. The elements discussed here apply mostly to typeset, printed, and typed messages.

White Space

> White space is free of text and artwork.

The blank space free of text or artwork is known as **white space.** It provides contrast, and perhaps even more important, it gives readers a resting point. White space includes the open area surrounding headings, the margin space, the vertical space between columns, the space created by ragged line endings, the paragraph indents or extra space between unindented paragraphs, and the horizontal space between lines of type. You'll decide how much white space to allow for each of these areas.

Margins and Line Justification

Margins define the space around your text and between text columns. They're influenced by the way you place lines of type, which can be set (1) justified (flush on the left and flush on the right), (2) flush left with a ragged-right margin, (3) flush right with a ragged-left margin, or (4) centered.

Justified type will "darken" your message's appearance, because the uniform line lengths lack the white space created by ragged margins. It also tends to make your mes-

The following excerpt is from a report put together by Holland & Moore, a corporate research company.

```
┌─────────────────────────────────────────────────────────┐
│ ▣           E-Mail                                     ▣ │
├─────────────────────────────────────────────────────────┤
│                                                          │
│                                                          │
├─────────────────────────────────────────────────────────┤
│ Date: Thursday, 26 September 1997, 11:14:09, EST      ⇧ │
│ To: "Lee Gifford" <lgifford@research.marketpix.com>     │
│ From: "Jeffrey Coombs" <jeffc@hmr.com>                  │
│ Subject: Donner Profile                                  │
│ Cc: "Donna Holland" <Holland@hmr.com>                   │
│ Bcc:                                                     │
│ Attachments:                                             │
│                                                          │
│ Mr. Gifford, here is the information you requested on    │
│ the Donner Corporation:                                  │
│                                                          │
│ Donner Corporation faced a major transformation, growing │
│ from a small, single-product company to a large, broadly │
│ based corporation in just three years. This changeover   │
│ involved much more than simply adding on to the plant    │
│ and hiring more people, because the quality of the       │
│ existing staff and products was not good enough for a    │
│ first-rate operation. The task therefore required both   │
│ physical expansion and quality improvement.              │
│                                                          │
│ The physical expansion alone represented a major         │
│ undertaking. The investment in facilities required $18   │
│ million. Over a three-year period, the organization      │
│ spent more on the new plant and equipment than it had    │
│ spent in the past seventeen years of its operation.      │
│                                                          │
│ To raise its competitive capability, the company had to  │
│ develop new programs and organizational units and, at    │
│ the same time, expand and upgrade its existing           │
│ operations. It also needed to double the size of its     │
│ staff by recruiting high-caliber people from many        │
│ fields. This staffing had to be accomplished in an       │
│ increasingly competitive labor market and without        │
│ benefit of an experienced human resources department.    │
└─────────────────────────────────────────────────────────┘
```

Shorter paragraphs increase the message clarity and effectiveness.

Each paragraph is organized around a topic sentence.

The separate paragraphs are linked by transitional elements.

sage look more like a form letter and less like a customized message. Justified type is often considered more difficult to read because large gaps can appear between words and because more words are hyphenated. Excessive hyphenation is distracting and hard to read. Even so, many magazines and newspapers use justified type because word density is higher.

Flush-left–ragged-right type "lightens" your message's appearance. It gives a document an informal, contemporary feeling of openness. The space between each word is the same, and only long words that fall at the ends of lines are hyphenated.

Flush-left–ragged-right type gives your message an open feeling.

Centered type lends a formal tone to your message. However, centering long blocks of type causes your audience to search for the beginning of each line, which slows reading. The same problem is also true of flush-right–ragged-left type, and these two approaches are usually avoided for passages of text.

Headings and Captions

Headings and subheadings are usually set larger than the type used for text and are often set in a separate typeface. They invite readers to become involved in your message, so avoid centering heads that contain more than two lines. Like centered text, they slow your readers as they search for the beginning of each line; flush-left heads are better. Because headings and subheadings clue readers into the organization of your message's content, you want to link them as closely as possible with the text they introduce. You can do this by making sure there's more space above the heading than below it.

Next to headings, captions are the most widely read part of a message. They tie photographs and illustrations into the rest of your message. Although usually placed below the exhibits they describe, captions can also be placed beside or above their exhibits. Make sure that the width of your captions is pleasing in proportion to the width of the exhibit, the surrounding white space, and the text.

Headings help your readers quickly identify the content and organization of your message.

Typefaces

Typeface refers to the physical design of letters, numbers, and other characters. Although computers offer innumerable choices of typefaces, typewriters offer a pretty limited selection. Each typeface influences the tone of your message, making it look authoritative, friendly, expensive, classy, casual, and so on. So choose typefaces that are appropriate for your message.

Serif typefaces have small crosslines (called serifs) at the ends of each letter stroke.[27] (See Figure 7.5.) Serif faces such as Times Roman (which is built into most laser printers) are commonly used for text; they tend to look busy and cluttered when set in large sizes for headings or other display treatments. Typefaces with rounded serifs can look friendly; those with squared serifs can look official.

Serif typefaces are commonly used for text.

Sans-serif typefaces have no serifs. Faces such as Helvetica (which comes with most laser printers) are ideal for display treatments that use larger type. Sans-serif faces can be difficult to read in long blocks of text. They look best when surrounded by plenty of white space—as in headings or in widely spaced lines of text.

Sans-serif typefaces are commonly used for headings.

Limit the number of typefaces used.[28] In general, avoid using more than two typefaces on a page. Many great-looking documents are based on a single sans-serif typeface for heads and subheads with a second serif typeface for text and captions. Using too many typefaces clutters the document and your audience's comprehension.

Type Styles

Type style is any modification that lends contrast or emphasis to type. Typewriters give you the opportunity to underline text. Most computers offer you not only underlining but also boldface, italic, and other highlighting and decorative styles.

Using boldfaced type for subheads breaks up long expanses of text. Just remember that too much boldfacing will darken the appearance of your message and make it look heavy. You can set isolated words in boldface type in the middle of a text block to draw more attention to them (such as the key terms in this book). If you draw more attention than a word warrants, however, you might create a "checkerboard" appearance.

Use italic type for emphasis. Although it's sometimes used when irony or humor is intended, quotation marks are usually best for that. Italics can also indicate a quote and are often used in captions.

Figure 7.5
Common Typefaces

Although serif typefaces are considered easier to read than sans-serif, both have their place in document design.

Serif Typeface	Sans-Serif Typeface
Times Roman is often used for text.	Helvetica is often used for headings.
TIMES ROMAN IS HARDER TO READ IN ALL CAPS.	HELVETICA IS A CLEANER FACE EVEN IN ALL CAPS.

Be careful to avoid any style that slows your audience's progress through your message. Underlining can interfere with your reader's ability to recognize the shapes of words, and using all capitals slows reading.[29] Shadowed or outlined type can seriously hinder legibility, so use these styles carefully.

Make sure the size of your type is proportionate to the importance of your message and the space allotted. Small type in a sea of white space appears lost. Large type squeezed into a small area is hard to read and visually claustrophobic.

Avoid using type styles that slow your readers down.

Design Decisions

You decide on each design element according to its function. So if you're composing a half-page memo, don't confuse your audience with a boatload of design elements. Effective design guides your readers through your message, so be sure to be consistent, balanced, restrained, and detail-oriented:

For effective design, pay attention to
- *Consistency*
- *Balance*
- *Restraint*
- *Detail*

- **Consistency.** Be consistent in your design and use of certain elements within a message (and sometimes even from message to message). Throughout a message, be consistent in your use of margins, typeface, type size, and spacing (in paragraph indents, between columns, and around photographs). Also be sure you're consistent in using all recurring elements, such as vertical lines, columns, and borders.
- **Balance.** To create a pleasing design, balance the space devoted to text, artwork, and white space.
- **Restraint.** Strive for simplicity in design. Don't clutter your message with too many design elements, too much highlighting, or too many decorative touches.
- **Detail.** Track all details that affect your design and thus your message. Headings and subheads that appear at the bottom of a column or a page can offend readers when the promised information doesn't appear until the next column or page. A layout that appears off balance can be really distracting, and any typographical errors can sabotage an otherwise good-looking design.

Avoid last-minute compromises. Don't reduce type size or white space to squeeze in text. On the other hand, avoid increasing type size or white space to fill space.

If you've planned your message so that your purpose, your audience, and your message are clear, you can design your document to be effective.[30] Start by thinking about your medium: press release, magazine or newsletter article, brochure, direct mail, slide presentation, formal report, business letter, or internal memo. Once you've decided on a medium, try to make it look as interesting as you can while making it as easy as possible to read and understand.

STAGE 10: PROOFING YOUR MESSAGE

Even after you have rewritten your message from start to finish, you're not done yet. Once you're satisfied with your message's content and organization, style and readability, word choice, sentence style, and paragraph development, you'll want to produce your message in some form that allows you to check it for appearance and detail. Even if you check your message with computerized spell and grammar checkers, you'll want to proof it yourself for mechanical and formatting errors.

Proof Your Mechanics and Format

Credibility is affected by your attention to the details of mechanics and format.

When you proof your message, you ensure that it's letter-perfect (see "How to Proofread Like a Pro: Tips for Creating the Perfect Document"). Although grammar, spelling, punctuation, and typographical errors may seem trivial to some people, most readers will view your attention to detail as a sign of your professionalism. If a writer lets mechanical errors slip through, the reader automatically wonders whether the writer is unreliable in more important ways. Adrianne Proeller of TBS says, "When I get a college résumé and I see a typo on it, I instantly disregard that résumé." Companies like *The New Yorker* magazine take great pride in their editorial standards. When *The New Yorker* misspelled *Tucson* as "Tuscon," it ended up giving Arizona $66,000 worth of free advertising to set things right.[31] By spelling a word incorrectly or making an error in usage, you show a lack of pride in your work. You might want to refresh your memory of the details of grammar and usage by reviewing Appendix I.

Also, give some attention to the finer points of format. Have you followed accepted conventions and company guidelines for laying out the document on the page? Have you included all the traditional elements that belong in documents of the type you are creating? Have you been consistent in handling margins, page numbers, headings, exhibits, source notes, and other details? To resolve questions about format and layout, see Component Chapter A.

Use Grammar and Spell Checkers Wisely

Electronic grammar and spell checkers can be helpful if you don't rely too heavily on them.

If you compose your business messages on a computer, many of the mechanical and grammatical problems discussed in this chapter can be checked electronically. You can use programs of varying sophistication to help you improve your writing, but not one of them can proof your documents for content or meaning. None can replace a sharp human mind when it comes to revising business messages.

Spell checkers are discussed in Chapter 4. They're available either as part of word-processing programs like Microsoft Word, Corel WordPerfect, Word Pro, and Claris Works, or they are available as special stand-alone programs for medical, technical, and foreign language applications. Of course, some of the "errors" detected may actually be proper names, technical words, words that you misspelled on purpose for a particular reason, or simply words that weren't included in the spell checker's dictionary. It's up to you to decide whether each flagged word should be corrected or left alone.

Grammar checkers are also discussed in Chapter 4. They too can be part of a word-processing program or a self-contained program such as Grammatik, RightWriter, and

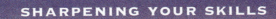

SHARPENING YOUR SKILLS

HOW TO PROOFREAD LIKE A PRO: TIPS FOR CREATING THE PERFECT DOCUMENT

You've carefully revised and polished your document, and it's been sent off to the word-processing department to be put into final form. You can breathe a sigh of relief, but only for the moment: You'll still be proofreading what comes out of the printer. To ensure that any document is error-free, always proofread the final version. Here are some hints to help make your proofreading more effective:

- **Multiple passes.** Go through the document several times, focusing on a different aspect each time. The first pass might be to look for omissions and errors in content; the second pass could be for layout, spacing, and other aesthetic features; a final pass might be to check for typographical, grammatical, and spelling errors.
- **Tricks for recognizing errors.** In normal reading, our perceptual processes have been trained to ignore transposed letters, improper capitalization, misplaced punctuation, and the like. To short-circuit these normally helpful processes, try some tricky techniques. Professional proofreaders recommend (1) reading each page from the bottom to the top, starting at the last word in each line, (2) placing your finger under each word and reading it silently, (3) making a slit in a sheet of paper that will reveal only one line of type at a time, and (4) reading the document aloud and pronouncing each word carefully.
- **Impartial reviews.** Have a friend or colleague proofread the document for you. Others are likely to catch mistakes that you continually fail to notice. (All of us have blind spots when it comes to reviewing our own work.)
- **Typos.** Look for the most common typographical errors (typos): transposed letters (such as *teh*), substitution errors

(such as *ecomonic*), and errors of omission (such as *productvity*).
- **Mechanics.** Look for errors in spelling, grammar, punctuation, and capitalization. If you're unsure about something, look it up in a dictionary, a usage book, or another reference work.
- **Accuracy.** Double-check the spelling of names and the accuracy of dates, addresses, and all figures (quantities ordered, prices, and so on). It would not do to order 500 staplers when you really want only 50.
- **Distance.** If you have time, set the document aside and proofread it the next day.
- **Vigilance.** Avoid reading large amounts of material in one sitting, and try not to proofread when you're tired.
- **Focus.** Concentrate on what you're doing. Try to block out distractions, and focus as completely as possible on your proofreading task.
- **Caution.** Take your time. Quick proofreading is not careful proofreading.

Proofreading may require patience, but it adds credibility to your document.

---

1. What qualities does a person need to be a good proofreader? Are such qualities inborn, or can they be learned?
2. Proofread the following sentence: aplication of thse methods in stores in San Deigo nd Cinncinati have resultted in a 30 drop in roberies an a 50 precent decling in violnce there, acording ot thedevelpers if the securty sytem, Hanover brothrs, Inc.

Correct Grammar. Like spell checkers, grammar checkers can flag problem areas, but they can't actually fix any of those errors for you. One thing some programs can do is run readability formulas for you (see Figure 7.6 on page 206).

By all means, use any software that you find helpful when revising your documents. Just remember that it's unwise to rely on grammar or spell checkers to do all your revision work. What such programs can do is identify "mistakes" you may overlook on your own. It's up to you to decide what, if anything, needs to be done, and it's up to you to catch the mistakes that these computer programs can't.[32] For a reminder of the tasks involved in revision, see this chapter's Checklist for Revising Business Messages.

CHECKLIST FOR REVISING BUSINESS MESSAGES

A. EDITING YOUR MESSAGE

1. Content and organization

   a. Review your draft against the message plan.

   b. Cover all necessary points in logical order.

   c. Organize the message to respond to the audience's probable reaction.

   d. Provide enough support to make the main idea convincing and interesting.

   e. Eliminate unnecessary material; add useful material.

   f. Be sure the beginning and ending are effective.

2. Style and readability

   a. Be sure you've achieved the right tone.

   b. Increase interest with lively words and phrases.

   c. Make sure your message is readable.

      i. Check vocabulary.

      ii. Check sentence structure.

      iii. Consider using a readability index.

3. Word choice

   a. Use plain English.

   b. Use concrete words that avoid negative connotations.

   c. Rely on nouns, verbs, and specific adjectives and adverbs.

   d. Select words that are strong, familiar, and short, while avoiding clichés, camouflaged verbs, and hedging words.

   e. Use bias-free language.

B. REWRITING YOUR MESSAGE

1. Sentence style

   a. Fit the sentence structure to the thought.

   b. Tailor the sentence style to the audience.

   c. Aim for an average sentence length of 20 words.

   d. Write mainly in the active voice, but use the passive voice to achieve specific effects.

   e. Eliminate unnecessary words and phrases.

   f. Avoid obsolete and pompous language.

   g. Moderate your enthusiasm.

   h. Break up strung-out sentences.

   i. Avoid hedging sentences.

   j. Watch for indefinite pronoun starters.

   k. Express parallel ideas in parallel form.

   l. Eliminate awkward pointers.

   m. Correct dangling modifiers.

   n. Avoid long sequences of nouns.

Figure 7.6
Readability Indexes Using
a Grammar Checker

Here are the readability statistics that Grammatik computed for a paragraph in one document.

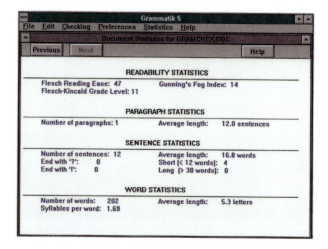

o. Keep subject and verb close together, and keep adverbs, adjectives, and prepositional phrases close to the words they modify.

p. Emphasize key points through sentence style.

2. Effective paragraphs

   a. Be sure each paragraph contains a topic sentence, related sentences, and transitional elements.

   b. Edit for unity, effective development, and coherence.

   c. Choose a method of development that suits the subject: illustration, comparison or contrast, cause and effect, classification, problem and solution.

   d. Vary the length and structure of sentences within paragraphs.

   e. Mix paragraphs of different lengths, but aim for an average of 100 words.

C. **PRODUCING YOUR MESSAGE**

   1. Design elements

      a. Use appropriate white space around headings, in margins, between columns, at line endings, in paragraph indents or between unindented paragraphs, and between lines of type.

      b. Choose margins and line justification that won't darken your document.

      c. Use headings to break up long passages of text and to guide your readers through your message.

      d. Select typefaces that complement the tone of your message.

      e. Use only as many type styles as you actually need, avoiding any style that slows the reader's progress.

   2. Design decisions

      a. Be consistent, balanced, restrained, and detail-oriented.

      b. Avoid last-minute compromises.

D. **PROOFING YOUR MESSAGE**

   1. Mechanics and format

      a. Review sentences to be sure they are grammatically correct.

      b. Correct punctuation and capitalization errors.

      c. Look for spelling and typographical errors.

      d. Review the format to be sure it follows accepted conventions.

      e. Use the format consistently throughout the message.

   2. Electronic grammar and spell checkers

      a. Use electronic checkers to point up errors you might overlook.

      b. Be aware of program limitations so that you don't rely too heavily on electronic checkers.

SUMMARY

Revision is the third category of stages in the composition process. Each message should be edited for content and organization, style and readability, and word choice. In general, rely on strong words—nouns and verbs—to convey your meaning, use familiar terms, and avoid verbs that have been turned into nouns or adjectives.

When rewriting your messages, try to balance the three types of sentences: simple, compound, and complex. Short sentences that use the active voice are more readable. Eliminate unnecessary words and phrases; avoid obsolete, pompous, or overly enthusiastic language; and try to avoid strung-out sentences, hedging sentences, pronoun starters, awkward pointers, dangling modifiers, and long sequences of nouns. Express parallel ideas in parallel form, and keep words together that work together. Emphasize your key thoughts by drawing them out and placing them in prominent positions.

Also, try to unify your paragraphs by using a topic sentence, by making sure other sentences are related, and by using transitional words and phrases. Develop paragraphs using the illustration, comparison-or-contrast, cause-and-effect, classification, and problem-and-solution techniques.

When producing your message, remember the importance of document design. Understand how to use white space, headings, typefaces, and other design elements to improve your audience's understanding. Remember that design can be established and changed at any stage of the composition process.

Be sure to leave yourself time to proof your message for mechanical and formatting errors. Make sure you don't overlook simple problems such as typographical errors or mistakes in usage, and use spell and grammar checkers only as long as they're helpful.

COMMUNICATION CHALLENGES AT TURNER BROADCASTING SYSTEM

One of Adrianne Proeller's tasks is to send out internal memos announcing new employees hired by TBS. Since you're one of the newest—hired right out of college in your field of expertise—Proeller has contacted you, asking you to provide the information she needs to write the official announcement.

INDIVIDUAL CHALLENGE: Decide which job you've been hired for (communications assistant, sales trainee, technical engineer, marketing associate, or any other you choose) and determine what qualifications you'll be bringing to the position (you may need to invent some for this exercise). For help, consult library references such as *The Dictionary of Occupational Titles,* which describes positions and qualifications. Then draft a routine memo to Proeller that supplies her with everything she needs to write her announcement. Since this is one of your first on-the-job tasks, you want your memo to look good. Scrutinize your first draft for content and organization, style and readability. Reassess word choices, sentences, and paragraphs; then produce a second draft.

TEAM CHALLENGE: In a small group, exchange copies of your memos so that everyone can mark suggestions for revision on each group member's memo. Then compare your efforts. Did everyone spot the same errors? Where did you disagree? Is it a good idea to let others review your work?[33]

CRITICAL THINKING QUESTIONS

1. You have so little time for your current project that you have to skip a few of the tasks in the composition process. You've already cut down everything you can in the planning and composing categories. Which tasks in the revision category would be best to cut: editing, rewriting, producing, or proofreading? Explain.

2. In what business situations might you want to use words of high connotative value?

3. How could cultural bias differ from racial and ethnic bias? What examples can you think of?

4. What specific techniques of style could you use to create a formal, objective tone? An informal, personal tone?

5. When designing your formal business letter, which design elements are necessary to consider, and which are not?

6. Given the choice of only one, would you prefer to use a grammar checker or a spell checker? Why?

DOCUMENTS FOR ANALYSIS

Read the following documents; then (1) analyze the strengths and weaknesses of each sentence and (2) revise each document so that it follows this chapter's guidelines.

Document 7.A: Creating Effective Sentences

The move to our new offices will take place over this coming weekend. For everything to run smooth, everyone will have to clean out their own desk and pack up the contents in boxes that will be provided. You will need to take everything off the walls too, and please pack it along with the boxes.

If you have alot of personal belongings, you should bring them home with you. Likewise with anything valuable. I do not mean to infer that items will be stolen, irregardless it is better to be safe than sorry.

On Monday, we will be unpacking, putting things away, and then get back to work. The least amount of disruption is anticipated by us, if everyone does their part. Hopefully, there will be no negative affects on production schedules, and current deadlines will be met.

Document 7.B: Assessing Your Word Choice

Dear Ms. Giraud:

Enclosed herewith please find the manuscript for your book, *Careers in Woolgathering.* After perusing the first two chapters of your 1,500-page manuscript, I was forced to conclude that the subject matter, handicrafts and artwork using wool fibers, is not coincident with the publishing program of Framingham Press, which to this date has issued only works on business endeavors, avoiding all other topics completely.

Although our firm is unable to consider your impressive work at the present time, I have taken the liberty of recording some comments on some of the pages. I am of the opinion that any feedback that a writer can obtain from those well versed in the publishing realm can only serve to improve the writer's authorial skills.

In view of the fact that your residence is in the Boston area, might I suggest that you secure an appointment with someone of high editorial stature at the Cambridge Heritage Press, which I believe might have something of an interest in works of the nature you have produced.

Wishing you the best of luck in your literary endeavors, I remain

Arthur J. Cogswell
Editor

Document 7.C: Developing Coherent Paragraphs

For delicious, air-popped popcorn, please read the following instructions: The popper is designed to pop 1/2 cup of popcorn kernels at one time. Never add more than 1/2 cup. A half cup of corn will produce three to four quarts of popcorn. More batches may be made separately after completion of the first batch. Popcorn is popped by hot air. Oil or shortening is not needed for popping corn. Add only popcorn kernels to the popping chamber. Standard grades of popcorn are recommended for use. Premium or gourmet type popping corns may be used. Ingredients such as oil, shortening, butter, margarine, or salt should never be added to the popping chamber. The popper, with popping chute in position, may be preheated for two minutes before adding the corn. Turn the popper off before adding the corn. Use electricity safely and wisely. Observe safety precautions when using the popper. Do not touch the popper when it is hot. The popper should not be left unattended when it is plugged into an outlet. Do not use the popper if it or its cord has been damaged. Do not use the popper if it is not working properly. Before using the first time, wash the chute and butter/measuring cup in hot soapy water. Use a dishcloth or sponge. Wipe the outside of the popper base. Use a damp cloth. Dry the base. Do not immerse the popper base in water or other liquid. Replace the chute and butter/measuring cup. The popper is ready to use.

EXERCISES

1. Write a concrete phrase for each of these vague phrases:
   a. sometime this spring
   b. a substantial saving
   c. a large number attended
   d. increased efficiency
   e. expanded the work area

2. List words that are stronger than the following:
   a. ran after
   b. seasonal ups and downs
   c. bright
   d. suddenly rises
   e. moves forward

3. As you rewrite these sentences, replace the clichés with fresh, personal expressions:
   a. Being a jack-of-all-trades, Dave worked well in his new selling job.
   b. Moving Leslie into the accounting department, where she was literally a fish out of water, was like putting a square peg into a round hole, if you get my drift.
   c. I knew she was at death's door, but I thought the doctor would pull her through.
   d. Movies aren't really my cup of tea; as far as I am concerned, they can't hold a candle to a good book.
   e. It's a dog-eat-dog world out there in the rat race of the asphalt jungle.

4. Suggest short, simple words to replace each of the following:
   a. inaugurate
   b. terminate
   c. utilize
   d. anticipate
   e. assistance
   f. endeavor
   g. ascertain
   h. procure
   i. consummate
   j. advise
   k. alteration
   l. forwarded
   m. fabricate
   n. nevertheless
   o. substantial

5. Revise the following sentences, using shorter, simpler words:

   a. The antiquated calculator is ineffectual for solving sophisticated problems.

   b. It is imperative that the pay increments be terminated before an inordinate deficit is accumulated.

   c. There was unanimity among the executives that Ms. Jackson's idiosyncrasies were cause for a mandatory meeting with the company's personnel director.

   d. The impending liquidation of the company's assets was cause for jubilation among the company's competitors.

   e. The expectations of the president for a stock dividend were accentuated by the preponderance of evidence that the company was in good financial condition.

6. Rewrite each sentence so that the verbs are no longer camouflaged:

   a. Adaptation to the new rules was performed easily by the employees.

   b. The assessor will make a determination of the tax due.

   c. Verification of the identity of the employees must be made daily.

   d. The board of directors made a recommendation that Mr. Ronson be assigned to a new division.

   e. The auditing procedure on the books was performed by the vice president.

7. Rewrite each of the following to eliminate bias:

   a. For an Indian, Maggie certainly is outgoing.

   b. He needs a wheelchair, but he doesn't let his handicap affect his job performance.

   c. A pilot must have the ability to stay calm under pressure, and then he must be trained to cope with any problem that arises.

   d. Candidate Renata Parsons, married and the mother of a teenager, will attend the debate.

   e. Senior citizen Sam Nugent is still an active salesman.

8. Shorten these sentences by adding more periods:

   a. The next time you write something, check your average sentence length in a 100-word passage; and if your sentences average more than 16 to 20 words, see whether you can break up some sentences.

   b. Don't do what the village blacksmith did when he instructed his apprentice as follows: "When I take the shoe out of the fire, I'll lay it on the anvil; and when I nod my head, you hit it with the hammer." The apprentice did just as he was told, and now he's the village blacksmith.

   c. Unfortunately, no gadget will produce excellent writing, but using a yardstick like the Fog Index gives us some guideposts to follow for making writing easier to read because its two factors remind us to use short sentences and simple words.

   d. Know the flexibility of the written word and its power to convey an idea, and know how to make your words behave so that your readers will understand.

   e. Words mean different things to different people, and a word like *block* may mean city block, butcher block, engine block, auction block, or several other things.

9. Rewrite each sentence so that it is active rather than passive:

   a. The raw data are submitted to the data-processing division by the sales representative each Friday.

   b. High profits are publicized by management.

   c. The policies announced in the directive were implemented by the staff.

   d. Our typewriters are serviced by the Santee Company.

   e. The employees were represented by Janet Hogan.

10. Cross out unnecessary words in the following phrases:

   a. Consensus of opinion

   b. New innovations

   c. Long period of time

   d. At a price of $50

   e. Still remains

11. Use infinitives as substitutes for the overly long phrases in these sentences:

   a. In order to live, I require money.

   b. They did not find sufficient evidence for believing in the future.

   c. Bringing about the destruction of a dream is tragic.

12. Rephrase the following in fewer words:

   a. in the near future

   b. in the event that

   c. in order that

   d. for the purpose of

   e. with regard to

   f. it may be that

   g. in very few cases

   h. with reference to

   i. at the present time

   j. there is no doubt that

13. Condense these sentences to as few words as possible:
    a. We are of the conviction that writing is important.
    b. In all probability, we're likely to have a price increase.
    c. Our goals include making a determination about that in the near future.
    d. When all is said and done at the conclusion of this experiment, I'd like to summarize the final windup.
    e. After a trial period of 3 weeks, during which time she worked for a total of 15 full working days, we found her work was sufficiently satisfactory so that we offered her full-time work.

14. Write up-to-date versions of these phrases; write *none* if you believe there is no appropriate substitute:
    a. as per your instructions
    b. attached herewith
    c. in lieu of
    d. in reply I wish to state
    e. please be advised that

15. Remove all the unnecessary modifiers from these sentences:
    a. Tremendously high pay increases were given to the extraordinarily skilled and extremely conscientious employees.
    b. The union's proposals were highly inflationary, extremely demanding, and exceptionally bold.

16. Rewrite these sentences so that they no longer contain any hedging:
    a. It would appear that someone apparently entered illegally.
    b. It may be possible that sometime in the near future the situation is likely to improve.
    c. Your report seems to suggest that we might be losing money.
    d. I believe Nancy apparently has somewhat greater influence over employees in the typing pool.
    e. It seems as if this letter of resignation means you might be leaving us.

17. Rewrite these sentences to eliminate the indefinite starters:
    a. There are several examples here to show that Elaine can't hold a position very long.
    b. It would be greatly appreciated if every employee would make a generous contribution to Mildred Cook's retirement party.
    c. It has been learned in Washington today from generally reliable sources that an important announcement will be made shortly by the White House.
    d. There is a rule that states that we cannot work overtime without permission.
    e. It would be great if you could work late for the next three Saturdays.

18. Present the ideas in these sentences in parallel form:
    a. Mr. Hill is expected to lecture three days a week, to counsel two days a week, and must write for publication in his spare time.
    b. She knows not only accounting, but she also reads Latin.
    c. Both applicants had families, college degrees, and were in their thirties, with considerable accounting experience but few social connections.
    d. This book was exciting, well written, and held my interest.
    e. Don is both a hard worker and he knows bookkeeping.

19. Revise the following sentences to delete the awkward pointers:
    a. The vice president in charge of sales and the production manager are responsible for the keys to 34A and 35A, respectively.
    b. The keys to 34A and 35A are in executive hands, with the former belonging to the vice president in charge of sales and the latter belonging to the production manager.
    c. The keys to 34A and 35A have been given to the production manager, with the aforementioned keys being gold-embossed.
    d. A laser printer and a dot-matrix printer were delivered to John and Megan, respectively.
    e. The walnut desk is more expensive than the oak desk, the former costing $300 more than the latter.

20. Rewrite these sentences to clarify the dangling modifiers:
    a. Running down the railroad tracks in a cloud of smoke, we watched the countryside glide by.
    b. Lying on the shelf, Ruby saw the seashell.
    c. Based on the information, I think we should buy the property.
    d. Being cluttered and filthy, Sandy took the whole afternoon to clean up her desk.
    e. After proofreading every word, the memo was ready to be signed.

21. Rewrite the following sentences to eliminate the long strings of nouns:
    a. The focus of the meeting was a discussion of the bank interest rate deregulation issue.

b. Following the government task force report recommendations, we are revising our job applicant evaluation procedures.

c. The production department quality assurance program components include employee training, supplier cooperation, and computerized detection equipment.

d. The supermarket warehouse inventory reduction plan will be implemented next month.

e. The State University business school graduate placement program is one of the best in the country.

22. Rearrange the following sentences to bring the subjects closer to their verbs:

a. Trudy, when she first saw the bull pawing the ground, ran.

b. It was Terri who, according to Ted, who is probably the worst gossip in the office (Tom excepted), mailed the wrong order.

c. William Oberstreet, in his book *Investment Capital Reconsidered,* writes of the mistakes that bankers through the decades have made.

d. Judy Schimmel, after passing up several sensible investment opportunities, despite the warnings of her friends and family, invested her inheritance in a jojoba plantation.

e. The president of U-Stor-It, which was on the brink of bankruptcy after the warehouse fire, the worst tragedy in the history of the company, prepared an announcement for the press.

23. In the following paragraph, identify the topic sentence and the related sentences (those that support the idea of the topic sentence):

Each year McDonald's sponsors the All-American Band, made up of two high school students from each state. The band marches in Macy's Thanksgiving Day parade in New York City and the Rose Bowl Parade in Pasadena. Franchisees are urged to join their local Chamber of Commerce, United Way, American Legion, and other bastions of All-Americana. McDonald's tries hard to project an image of almost a charitable organization. Local outlets sponsor campaigns on fire prevention, bicycle safety, and litter cleanup, with advice from Hamburger Central on how to extract the most publicity from their efforts.[34]

Now add a topic sentence to this paragraph:

Your company's image includes what a person sees, hears, and experiences in relation to your firm. Every business letter you write is therefore important. The quality of the letterhead and typing, the position of the copy on the page, the format, the kind of typeface used, and the color of the typewriter ribbon—all these factors play a part in creating an impression of you and your company in the mind of the person you are writing to.[35]

24. Explore the Web site at <http://owl.trc.purdue.edu/writing.labs.html>, and briefly explain (a) the services of each lab listed at this site and (b) the benefits each lab offers writers.

25. Write a paragraph on each of the following topics—one by illustration, one by comparison or contrast, one by discussion of cause and effect, one by classification, and one by discussion of problem and solution:

a. Types of cameras (or dogs or automobiles) available for sale

b. Advantages and disadvantages of eating at fast-food restaurants

c. Finding that first job

d. Good qualities of my car (or house, apartment, or neighborhood)

e. How to make a dessert recipe (or barbecue a steak or make coffee)

LETTERS, MEMOS, AND OTHER BRIEF MESSAGES

CHAPTER 8

WRITING DIRECT REQUESTS

AFTER STUDYING THIS CHAPTER, YOU WILL BE ABLE TO

- Clearly state the main idea of each direct request you write
- Indicate your confidence that the request will be filled
- Provide sufficient detail for the reader to be able to comply with your request
- Clarify complicated requests with lists and tables
- Close with a courteous request for specific action

COMMUNICATION CLOSE-UP AT THE NATURE COMPANY

When Silva Raker was studying zoology, she never dreamed the lizards, birds, and leopards she would spend her life with would be made of sterling silver, paper, and glass. Nevertheless, after graduation Raker landed a job in The Nature Company's warehouse. Soon she was traveling the world as a buyer for the international retail chain, and now she's been promoted to vice president of merchandise. Raker's strong communication skills help her coordinate the work of buyers and retail sales staff with that of the designers and architects who keep the atmosphere lively and interesting inside The Nature Company's stores (whether they're in the United States, Canada, France, the United Kingdom, or Japan). "I do a lot of communicating just to keep everyone informed," says Raker, and like most busy executives, she makes plenty of direct requests.

First of all, "you need to be polite and genuine," advises Raker. Her formal training as a zoologist and her travels for The Nature Company have convinced Raker that "the world's a pretty connected place . . . a web of people working together." She believes that treating people well is as important in business as it is in any other setting—and part of that treatment means considering people's needs and problems when you make a direct request.

One year Raker ordered a thousand sterling silver lizard earrings from an artist who hand-cast them in his basement, one pair at a time. Because The Nature Company's mission is "to provide fine quality products devoted to the observation, understanding, and appreciation of the natural world," its customers have come to expect true-to-life merchandise that reflects nature's fascinating diversity. They loved the realistic lizards, which dangled by their tails from the wearer's ears. Raker knew from early sales projections that she could sell ten times her original order. She decided to ask the artist to produce not 1,000, but 10,000, pairs of earrings, and she would ask him to do it in time to capture the Christmas market. It was already August, but if he could

Silva Raker

At The Nature Company, direct requests are common, both inside and outside the organization. Whether employees are dealing with customers face-to-face, composing memos to co-workers, or writing letters to suppliers, they make an effort to consider and understand their audience's needs and problems when making a request.

make the deadline, both the artist and The Nature Company would earn a nice sum from the popular lizards.

Raker understood that she would be asking the artist to expand his business substantially, to a level he probably hadn't planned to reach for many years—if ever. For such a serious request, Raker says, "You really have to establish a rapport with people, and trust." They need to know that if they expand their staff or buy new equipment, you'll still be doing business with them in the future. You want to explain how a positive response will benefit them, but at the same time, cautions Raker, "You want to make sure you don't promise more than you can deliver."

In her letter Raker got right to the request, explaining the reasons behind it and pointing out the benefits of complying with it. She also made sure to compliment the artist on his product: "You've really got something great here. Here's the response we're getting."

Raker says she tries to imagine all the ways a request might be misunderstood (something she learned from buying merchandise in other countries); then she writes her request to avoid those misunderstandings. With the lizard artist she also wanted to establish a personal rapport and a feeling of partnership. So she included questions she might ask a partner, such as, "How many earrings can you produce in a week? Tell me about your setup and your staff—what are the limiting factors? Is there a component that you can't get enough of?" She let the artist know that she cared about his business and that she would be available to offer support and advice as he increased his production. "I tried to present my request as more of a challenge rather than an impossible task," Raker recalls.

As a result of her skillful presentation, the artist accepted the challenge. He developed a method for gang-casting the earrings and met Raker's request by delivering 10,000 pairs of lizard earrings for the Christmas market—which sold even better than expected. The artist still supplies The Nature Company with some of its best-selling items.

Whether writing memos to co-workers requesting cooperation or writing letters to people outside the company requesting information or services, Raker phrases her direct requests clearly, simply, and with knowledge of her audience's point of view. She also projects a certain enthusiasm into her writing, which lets her readers know that the request involves "something that's going to matter." She's found that people sense and appreciate her concern for their needs. As a result, they're more eager to cooperate, and Raker reaps more positive replies to her direct requests.[1]

INTERCULTURAL REQUESTS

Silva Raker knows from personal experience that making requests across cultural boundaries can be frustrating, depending on the degree of red tape, the language barrier, your familiarity with the cultural differences involved, and even the mail system in a particular region or country. Just deciding whether to make your request in writing can be tricky, depending on where you're doing business. On the one hand, paper-oriented countries such as France, Germany, and England use a steady stream of correspondence to lead up to meetings and negotiations.[2] On the other hand, some Arabic, Asian, and Latin American countries consider paperwork a poor second choice for conducting business.

Whether written or oral, your request will be most effective if you follow the customs of your audience. Not all requests are organized directly. For example, an Arab letter would probably begin with a generalized blessing upon the reader and family.[3] Other cultures begin with an explanation and work up to the request at the end of the message. So whenever you can, learn about the customs of your audience and follow them to the degree possible. (See "How Direct Is Too Direct?")

ORGANIZING DIRECT REQUESTS

When you're addressing a U.S. or Canadian audience, when cultural differences are minimal, and when you can assume that your audience will be interested in what you have to say (or at least willing to cooperate with you), make a **direct request** by following the direct, or deductive, plan to organize your message. Present the request or the main idea first, follow up with necessary details, and close with a cordial statement of the action you want. This approach works well when your request requires no special tact or persuasion.

For direct requests
- State the request or main idea
- Give necessary details
- Close with a cordial request for specific action

People making direct requests (such as The Nature Company's Silva Raker) may be tempted to begin with personal introductions ("I am vice president of merchandise at a large international company, and I am looking for quality products that . . ."). However, this type of beginning is usually a mistake. The essence of the message, the specific request, is buried and may get lost. A better way to organize a direct request is to state what you want in the first sentence or two and let the explanation follow this initial request.

Even though you expect a favorable response, the tone of your initial request is important. Instead of demanding immediate action ("Send me your catalog no. 33A"), soften your request with such words as *please* and *I would appreciate*. An impatient demand for rapid service isn't necessary because you can generally assume that your audience will comply with your request once the reason for your request is understood.

Assume that your reader will comply once he or she understands your purpose.

The middle part of a direct request usually explains the original request ("Our customers appreciate nature in all its variety, so we are looking for items of exceptional

COMMUNICATING ACROSS CULTURES

HOW DIRECT IS TOO DIRECT?

Even if you're simply requesting information, is it possible to be too direct? On a visit to Mexico, the President of the United States spoke bluntly of realities, whereas the President of France spoke more abstractly—his style more grand, his words more beautiful. One man addressed the issues directly; the other was less direct. Which one had greater impact?

Neither speech changed global relationships, but the U.S. president was seen as a product of his outspoken culture, whereas the French president was seen as at least making his listeners feel better for a while. In varying degrees, Japan, Saudi Arabia, Italy, the Philippines, France, and Mexico all tend toward high-context cultures. People in these cultures depend on shared knowledge and inferred messages to communicate; that is, they gather meaning more from context and less from direct statement.

You might think you're doing your best by offering a little honest and constructive criticism to your Mexican assistant, but such a blow to pride and dignity might truly be devastating for that person. In fact, in high-context cultures, be careful to avoid saying outright, "You are wrong." People in such cultures know when they've made a mistake, but by putting it into words, you put them to shame, causing them to lose face. Although people in the United States believe that being direct is civil, considerate, and honest, people in high-context cultures view that same directness as abrupt, rude, and intrusive—even dishonest and offensive.

So when making requests outside the United States, consider what others think of your steering the straight course, meeting the problem head-on, or getting right to the point—consider whether your message is too direct. To determine whether your international audience will appreciate a direct or an implied message, consider factors such as your audience's attitudes toward destiny, time, authority, and logic.

- **Destiny.** Do people in this culture believe they can control events themselves? Or are events seen as predetermined and uncontrollable? If you're supervising employees who believe that a construction deadline is controlled by fate, then your crisp e-mail message requesting them to stay on schedule may be hard for them to understand—even insulting.

- **Time.** Do people in this culture believe that time is exact, precise, and not to be wasted? Or do they view time as relative, relaxed, and necessary for developing interpersonal relationships? If you believe that time is money and you try to get straight to business in your memo to your Mexican manager, your message may be overlooked in the confusion over your lack of relationship skills and your disregard for social propriety.

- **Authority.** Do the people in this culture conduct business more autocratically or more democratically? In Mexico, rank and status are highly valued, so when communicating downward, you may need to be even more direct than you're used to being in the United States. And when communicating upward, you may need to be much less direct in Mexico than you're used to being in the states.

- **Logic.** Do the people in this culture pursue logic in a straight line from point a to point b? Or do they communicate in circular or spiral patterns of logic? If you organize a speech or a letter in a straightforward and direct manner, your message may be considered illogical, unclear, and disorganized.

The issue of directness may be a question not only of how straightforward to be but also of whether to communicate the message at all. By finding out how much or how little a culture tends toward high-context communication, you will be able to decide whether to be direct or to rely on nuance when communicating with people in that culture.

1. Research a high-context culture such as Japan, Korea, or China, and write a one- or two-paragraph summary of how someone in that culture would go about requesting information.
2. When writing to someone in a high-context culture using American English, would it be better to (a) make the request directly in the interest of clarity or (b) try to match your audience's unfamiliar logic and make your request indirectly? Explain your answer.

quality that reflect the natural world and its wonder"). Such amplifying details help your audience fulfill your request correctly.

In the last section, clearly state the action you're requesting. You may wish to tell the audience where to send the sought-after information or product, indicate any time limits, or list details of the request that were too complex or numerous to cover in the introductory section. Then close with a brief, cordial note reminding the audience of the importance of the request ("In two months, our retail stores will be celebrating 'Nature Around the World,' a promotion that seems well suited to the African wind chimes you are known for, so please send your catalog right away").

Now let's take a closer look at the three main sections of a direct request. Although this discussion focuses on letters and memos, remember that this organizational plan may be appropriate for brief oral and electronic messages as well.

Direct Statement of the Request or Main Idea

Word the request itself carefully so that it says exactly what you want.

The general rule for the first part of a direct request is to write not only to be understood but also to avoid being misunderstood. If you request "1990 census figures" from a government agency, the person who handles your request won't know whether you want a page or two of summary figures or a detailed report running to several thousand pages. So be as specific as possible in the sentence or two that begins your message.

Also, be aware of the difference between a polite request in question form (which requires no question mark) and a question that is part of a request:

Use a period at the end of a request in question form that requires action; use a question mark at the end of a request that requires an answer in words.

Polite Request in Question Form
Would you please help us determine whether Kate Kingsley is a suitable applicant for a position as landscape designer.

Question That Is Part of a Request
Did Kate Kingsley demonstrate an ability to work smoothly with clients?

Many direct requests include both types of statements, so be sure to distinguish between the polite request that is your overall reason for writing and the specific questions that belong in the middle section of your letter or memo.

Finally, if you have more than one request, consider the following ways of writing them:

- When you have a number of requests, use headings to express categories of requests, with each category containing several requests. The reader's job is easier when you break down your needs this way.
- When you have an unusual or complex request, state the request and then provide supporting details right underneath it. This way, each request becomes a short paragraph.
- When you have a list of requests, include space beneath so that the reader can write on your letter or memo. This saves everyone's time and effort. It also controls the length of the reader's response.

Justification, Explanation, and Details

When The Nature Company's Silva Raker writes letters to potential suppliers in other countries, the middle section of her letters is of great importance. True, she's looking for product information, but she's also telling her unknown readers why she needs the information and explaining how long-term business and personal relationships might evolve.

In the middle section
- **Call attention to how the reader will benefit from granting your request**
- **Give details of your request**

To make the explanation a smooth and logical outgrowth of your opening remarks, you might make the first sentence of your message's middle section audience-centered by stating a service-to-the-reader benefit. For instance, Raker might have written, "By keeping The Nature Company informed about your products, you can help create a new distribution channel for your business. For example, if an American market exists for one of your new items, I can help you reach those customers."

Another possible approach for the middle section is to ask a series of questions, particularly if your inquiry concerns machinery or complex equipment. You might ask about technical specifications, exact dimensions, and the precise use of the product. The most important question is asked first. If cost is your main concern, you might begin with a question like "What is the price of your least expensive laser printer?" Then you may want to ask more specific but related questions about, say, the cost of toner cartridges and maintenance service.

If you're requesting several items or answers, number the items and list them in logical order or in descending order of importance. Furthermore, so that your request can be handled quickly, ask only the questions that are central to your main request. Also, avoid asking for information that you can find on your own, even if your effort takes considerable time.

If you're asking many people to reply to the same questions, consider wording them so that they can be answered yes or no or with some other easily counted response. You may even want to provide respondents with a form or with boxes they can check to indicate their answers. If you need more than a simple yes-or-no answer, pose an open-ended question. For example, a question like "How fast can you repair computer monitors?" is more likely to elicit the information you want than "Can you repair computer monitors?" Keep in mind also that phrasing questions in a way that hints at the response you want is likely to get you less than accurate information. So try to phrase your questions objectively. Finally, deal with only one topic in each question. If the questions need amplification, keep each question in a separate paragraph.

Other types of information that belong in this section include data about a product (model number, date and place of purchase, condition), your reason for being concerned about a particular matter, and other details about your request. Upon finishing this middle section, your audience should understand why the request is important and be willing to satisfy it.

> Ask the most important question first; then ask related, more specific questions.

> Use numbered lists when you're requesting several items or answers.

> When you prepare questions
> - Ask only questions that relate to your main request
> - Don't ask for information you can find yourself
> - Make your questions open-ended and objective
> - Deal with only one topic in each question

Courteous Close with Request for Specific Action

Close your letter with two important elements: (1) a request for some specific response (complete with any time limits that apply) and (2) an expression of appreciation or goodwill. Help your reader respond easily by including your phone number, office hours, and other helpful information.

However, don't thank the reader "in advance" for cooperating. If the reader's reply warrants a word of thanks, send it after you've received the reply. If you're requesting information for a research project, you might offer to forward a copy of your report in gratitude for the reader's assistance. If you plan to reprint or publish materials that you ask for, indicate that you'll get any necessary permission. When asking for information about an individual, be sure to indicate that you'll keep all responses confidential.

> Close with
> - A request for some specific response
> - An expression of appreciation
> - Information about how you can be reached

PLACING ORDERS

Because they're usually processed without objection, and because they refer to a product that the reader knows about, orders are considered one of the simplest types of direct request. When placing an order, you need not excite your reader's interest; just state your needs clearly and directly.

To see what to include in a good order letter, examine any mail-order form supplied by a large firm: It offers complete and concise directions for providing all the information needed to fill an order. After the date, the order form probably starts with

> Order letters are like good mail-order forms, although they also provide more room for explaining special needs.

"Please send the following" or "Please ship." If you complete the rest of the form and mail it, these statements constitute a legal and binding offer to purchase the goods ordered; the supplier's shipment of those goods constitutes an acceptance of the offer and thus completes a legal contract.

Order blanks are arranged to document precisely the goods you want, describing them by catalog number, quantity, name or trade name, color, size, unit price, and total amount due. This complete identification helps prevent errors in filling the order. When drafting an order letter, follow the same format, presenting information about the items you want in column form, double-spacing between the items, and totaling the price at the end.

Order blanks provide space for delivery information, such as how and where to send the shipment. In your letter be sure to specify the delivery address, especially if it is not the address from which you send your letter. (Sometimes the billing and delivery addresses are different.) Also indicate how the merchandise is to be shipped: by truck, air freight, parcel post, air express, or delivery service. Unless you specify the mode of transportation, the seller chooses.

In any letter sent with money, mention the amount of payment, explain how the amount was calculated, and if necessary, explain to what account the amount should be charged. Again, the order form provides an excellent model. Here's an example:

The general request is stated first.

Please send the following items to the above address by air freight. I am ordering from your current spring/summer catalog:

Count	Stock I.D.	Description	Price Per Item	Price Total
10	342	Navajo bracelets (turquoise and silver tubular beads)	$ 8.95	$ 89.50
10	343	Navajo necklaces (turquoise and silver tubular beads)	11.95	119.50
10	344	Navajo loop earrings (turquoise and silver)	9.95	99.50
10	574	Navajo hand-woven rugs (Windsong pattern, 20" × 38")	16.99	169.90
5	575	Navajo hand-woven rugs (Windsong pattern, 42" × 65")	49.95	249.75
3	595	Navajo hand-woven rugs (Sundance pattern, 5'5" × 8'2")	99.99	299.97
		TOTAL SALES		$1,028.12
		SHIPPING		46.00
		AMOUNT DUE		$1,074.12

All necessary details are provided (in a format similar to an order form).

Information about such additional charges as tax and shipping was provided in the catalog, so to ensure quick processing of the order, the writer calculated the amount due.

Not every item ordered through the mail, via e-mail, or by fax is neatly displayed in a catalog, Web site, or newspaper advertisement. If the goods are somewhat unusual, the problem of identifying them becomes more complex. For instance, a general contractor ordering supplies for several ongoing jobs at various sites mailed this order to Jefferson's Wood Windows:

When ordering nonstandard items, include a complete description.

Our customers have selected the following windows to replace existing construction:

♦ **3647 John Street**
   • 2 Pozzi CW2836-4 (Casement bow window, wood, true divided lite)
   • 1 Pozzi CW2836-5 (Casement bow window, wood, true divided lite)
♦ **815 Silverton Avenue**
   • 4 Kolbe FN 236 (French casement, wood, true divided lite)
   • 2 Pozzi D2830 (Double Hung, wood, true divided lite)

CHECKLIST FOR ORDERS

A. DIRECT STATEMENT OF THE REQUEST
1. Use wording that indicates an order rather than a request: "Please send me" or "please ship" instead of "I want" or "I need," which are neither polite nor legally appropriate for a business order.
2. Open with a general description of your order that encompasses all the details.

B. JUSTIFICATION, EXPLANATION, AND DETAILS
1. For complex orders, provide a general explanation of how the requested materials will be used.
2. Provide all specifications: quantity, price (including discounts), size, catalog numbers, product description, shipping instructions (date and

place), arrangements for payment (method, time, deposits), and cost totals.
3. Use a format that presents information clearly and makes it easy to total amounts.
4. Double-check the completeness of your order and the cost totals.

C. COURTEOUS CLOSE WITH REQUEST FOR SPECIFIC ACTION
1. Include a clear summary of the desired action.
2. Whenever possible, suggest a future reader benefit of complying with the order.
3. Close on a cordial note.
4. Clearly state any time limits that apply to your order, and explain why they are important.

♦ 7700 Main Street
  • 3 Andersen G436 (Gliding window, Perma-Shield, mullion fillers)

Once you have confirmed the item numbers and availability with each manufacturer, please call me at (816) 997-6040 to verify the pricing. We need these delivered by September 17, so please inform me of any possible delay.

Note the specific details included in the letter and the clarity about what is needed at each location. In any order for nonstandard items, the additional description helps the reader identify your needs accurately. In special cases, such as ordering machine parts, you may even make drawings of the parts you need and add an explanation of their particular use.

A final suggestion about placing orders: Be thorough and clear. If you supply unclear or insufficient information, your reader must make an extra effort to get the missing details. The delays and cross-communications that result will hold up delivery of your order and may lead to mistakes in filling it. To make sure your order is filled correctly, retain a copy of your letter, fax, or e-mail message. If you haven't received a response in a reasonable time (two weeks, in most cases), write or call to see whether your order has arrived and is being processed. (To remind yourself of the tasks involved in placing orders, see this chapter's Checklist for Orders.)

When placing orders, be thorough and clear.

REQUESTING ROUTINE INFORMATION AND ACTION

When you need to know about something, elicit an opinion from someone, or suggest a simple action, you usually need only ask. In essence, simple requests say, "This is what I want to know or what I want you to do, why I'm making the request, and why it may be in your interest to help me." Assuming that your reader is able and willing to do what you want, such a straightforward request gets the job done with a minimum of fuss.

Despite their simple organization, routine requests deserve a tactful touch. In many organizations, e-mail, memos, and letters like these are sent to hundreds or even thousands of employees, customers, clients, and shareholders. So the potential for creating a positive impression is second only to the risk of causing ill will through ambiguous wording or a discourteous tone. Even when writing a routine request, keep the purpose

When making a routine request, say
- *What you want to know*
- *Why you want to know*
- *Why it is in the reader's interest to help you*

of your message in mind. That is, ask yourself what you want recipients to understand or do as a result of reading the message. As you prepare the request, remember that even the briefest note can create confusion and hard feelings.

Exactly what do you want the reader to understand or do as a result of reading your request for action?

Requests to Company Insiders

Although requests to fellow employees are often oral and rather casual, some messages are better sent by e-mail or put in permanent, written form. A clear, thoughtfully written memo or e-mail message can save time and questions by helping readers understand precisely what is required.

A request in memo form
- *Provides a permanent record*
- *Saves time and questions*
- *Tells precisely what is needed*

A routine request follows the standard direct plan. Start with a clear statement of your reason for writing; then provide whatever explanation is needed to justify the request. Close with a specific account of what you expect, and include a deadline if appropriate. The memo in Figure 8.1 (see pages 224–225) was sent to all employees of a relatively small manufacturing firm.

In the following memo, the writer refers to a previous memo on the same topic and then makes the request for a response from employees:

> **Are you interested in having a day-care center on site?**
>
> Several suggestions in the cafeteria suggestion box indicate that parents at Timken want convenient, affordable child care. Therefore, your answers to the following questions will help us determine your needs.
>
> 1. How many children would you enroll in the new center?
> 2. How much do you currently pay per week for each child in day care?
> 3. Do you think the cost is too high? In your opinion, what would be a reasonable charge per week for each child?
> 4. What qualities do you look for in a day-care center?
> 5. What qualifications do you expect of the caregivers?
>
> You may respond on this form and return it to Human Resources by Friday. We appreciate your prompt response so that we may begin analyzing the possibilities.

The memo begins with the central question.

A little background information orients the reader.

The numbered questions focus responses so that they will be easier to tally.

Specific instructions for replying close the memo. The courteous tone helps ensure a prompt response.

Craft internal memos just as carefully as letters to outsiders, but adjust the writing style to take shared reference points into account.

This memo is matter-of-fact and assumes some shared background. Such a style is appropriate when you're communicating about a routine matter to someone in the same company.

When used well, memos and e-mail messages can communicate efficiently, concisely, and powerfully. When misused, these messages can waste time and effort, can swell the ocean of information that offices must deal with, and can even tarnish your business reputation. So avoid writing frequent, long, and unneeded messages. Also, don't put anything in a memo or e-mail message that you wouldn't want to share with absolutely everyone (including the press and any Senate committee you can think of).[4]

Requests to Other Businesses

Many letters and e-mail messages to other businesses are requests for information about products, like Silva Raker's letters to artists and other Nature Company suppliers. They are among the simplest of all letters to write because businesses welcome the opportunity to tell you about their goods and services. In fact, you can often fill out a coupon, a response card, or an online form and then mail or e-mail it to the correct address. In other cases you might write a brief note requesting further information about something you saw or heard in an advertisement. One or two sentences will most likely do the job. Companies commonly check on the effectiveness of their advertisements, so mention where you saw or heard about them.

Of course, many inquiries are prompted by something other than an advertisement, and they demand a more detailed letter or e-mail message. If the message will be welcome, or if the reader won't mind answering it, the direct approach is still appropriate. The following is such a letter:

When writing a letter in response to an advertisement
- *Say where you saw the ad*
- *Specify what you want*
- *Provide a clear and complete return address on the letter*

If the reader is not expecting your letter, supply more detail.

Would you please supply me with information about the lawn services you provide.	The overall request is stated at the beginning. Phrased politely in question form, it requires no question mark.
Pralle Realty owns approximately 27 pieces of rental property in College Station, and we're looking for a lawn service to handle all of them. We are making a commitment to provide quality housing in this college town, and we are looking for an outstanding firm to work with us.	The explanation for the request keeps the reader's attention by hinting at the possibility of future business.
1. **Lawn care:** What do you charge per year per location for lawn maintenance, including grass cutting and fertilizers/herbicides? 2. **Shrubbery:** What do you charge per year per location for the care of deciduous and evergreen bushes—pruning, fertilizing, and replacing as necessary? 3. **Contract:** How does Agri-Lawn Service structure such large contracts? What kind of additional information do you need from us?	To avoid burdening the reader with an impossibly broad request, the writer asks a series of specific questions, itemized in a logical sequence. To avoid receiving useless yes or no answers, the writer asks some open-ended questions.
We hope to hear from you by February 15. We want to have a lawn-care firm in place by March 15.	The courteous close specifies a time limit.

This letter should bring a prompt and enthusiastic reply because the situation is clearly described, the possibility of current and future business is suggested, and the questions are specific and easy to answer. Also, the letter implies confidence in the opinion and assistance of the reader. Because the letter will be sent to a business and pertains to a possible sale, the writer did not enclose a stamped, preaddressed envelope.

If for some reason you aren't using letterhead stationery, be sure to write your address on the letter clearly and completely. Many inquiries are not answered because the address was illegibly handwritten or was written only on the return envelope, which was discarded by the recipient.

Requests to Customers and Other Outsiders

Businesses often ask individuals outside the organization to provide information or to take some simple action: attend a meeting, return an information card, endorse a document, confirm an address, or supplement information on an order. These messages are often short and simple, but some situations require a more detailed explanation. Readers might be unwilling to respond unless they understand how the request benefits them. So more complex letters, with several paragraphs of explanation, are sometimes necessary. When the same message must be sent to many people at the same time,

Requests to customers often spell out in detail
- *What exactly is needed*
- *How filling the request will benefit them*

Figure 8.1

In-Depth Critique: Memo Requesting Routine Action from Company Insiders

Hydel Interior Alternatives (HIA) provides interior office designs for businesses. HIA recently decided to upgrade its wellness and benefits program but needs to charge employees a nominal fee to pay for use of a sports complex. The following memo seeks employee input about the new program and the possible fee.

Hydel Interior Alternatives

INTERNAL MEMORANDUM

To: All Employees
From: Mike Ortega, Human Resources
Date: October 10, 1997
Subj: New Wellness Program Opportunity

The benefits package committee has asked me to contact everyone about an opportunity to save money and stay healthier in the bargain. As you know, we've been meeting to decide on changes in our benefits package. Last week, we sent you a memo detailing the Synergy Wellness Program.

In addition to the package as described in the memo (life, major medical, dental, hospitalization), Synergy has sweetened the pot by offering HIA a 10 percent discount. To meet the requirements for the discount, we have to show proof that at least 25 percent of our employees participate in aerobic exercise at least three times a week for at least 20 minutes. (Their actuarial tables show a resulting 10 percent reduction in claims.)

During warm weather, many of us walk the nature trail on our lunch break, and this will satisfy Synergy's requirements. However, we have those nasty winters when no one can venture outside. After looking around, we discovered a gymnasium with an indoor track just a few blocks south on Haley Boulevard. Sports Midwest will give our employees unlimited daytime access to their indoor track, gym, and pool for a group fee that comes to approximately $2.50 per month per employee, if at least half of us sign up. Payroll says you can have the amount automatically deducted, if you wish.

In addition to walking, we can swim, play volleyball, jazzercise, form our own intramural basketball teams, and much more. Our spouses and children can also participate at a deeply discounted monthly fee. If you have questions, please e-mail or call me or any member of the committee. Let us know your wishes on the following form.

Because the reader is busy, it's important to state the purpose of your communication in the first paragraph.

The second and third paragraphs present the situation that makes the inquiry necessary.

The final paragraph lists reader benefits, requests action, and provides an easy-to-use response form.

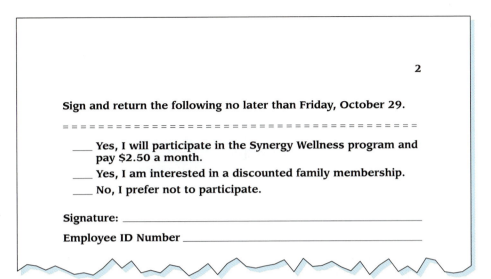

Figure 8.1
(Continued)

it can be prepared as a form letter and perhaps individualized with a word processor (see Figure 8.2 on pages 226–227).

Businesses sometimes need to reestablish a relationship with former customers. Frequently, customers who are unhappy about some purchase or about the way they were treated make no complaint: They simply stay away from the offending business. A letter of inquiry encouraging them to use idle credit accounts offers them an opportunity to register their displeasure and then move on to a good relationship. Additionally, a customer's response to an inquiry may provide the company with insights into ways to improve its products and customer service. Even if they have no complaint, customers still welcome the personal attention. Such an inquiry to the customer might begin this way:

> When a good charge customer like you has not bought anything from us in six months, we wonder why. Is there something we can do to serve you better?

Letters of inquiry sent to someone's home frequently include a stamped, preaddressed envelope to make a reply easier.

Similar inquiry letters are sent from one business to another. For example, a sales representative of a housewares distributor might send the same type of letter to a retailer. To review material discussed here, see this chapter's Checklist for Routine Requests on page 227.

The purpose of routine requests to customers is often to reestablish communication.

When sending routine requests to individuals rather than other businesses, consider enclosing a stamped, preaddressed envelope.

WRITING DIRECT REQUESTS FOR CLAIMS AND ADJUSTMENTS

Satisfied customers bring additional business to the firm, whereas angry or dissatisfied customers do not. In addition, angry customers complain to anyone who'll listen, creating poor public relations. So even though **claims** (or formal complaints) and **adjustments** (or claim settlements) may seem like unpleasant concepts, progressive organizations like The Nature Company want to know whether their customers and clients are dissatisfied with their services or merchandise. So if you have a complaint, it's in your best interests, and the company's, to bring your claim or request for an

You are entitled to request an adjustment whenever you receive a product or experience service that doesn't live up to the supplier's standards.

Figure 8.2
In-Depth Critique:
Request to Customers and
Other Outsiders

The following is an example of a well-planned, detailed form letter. The clarity of the language in this letter—the nontechnical, easily understood words and the step-by-step directions—helps ease the reader's concerns about a complex procedure.

Firestone, Inc.
2280 Kerper Boulevard, Dubuque, Iowa 52001
(319) 588-2562   •   Fax (319) 589-3951

November 24, 1997

Mr. Joseph Jakes
5101 Carlisle Place
Cedar Rapids, IA 52401

Dear Mr. Jakes:

The opening states the purpose of the letter in simple, reader-oriented terms.

For the past five years, Firestone retirees have participated in the same medical plan as active employees. Although the plan has been effective in keeping your medical costs to a minimum, you now have the opportunity to sign up for a new MetraHealth HMO. Under the improved plan, you will benefit from a simplified claim-filing process and enhanced plan offerings.

An explanation of procedures is another reader-oriented feature of the letter.

The plan works as follows: You visit any doctor in the MetraHealth network, present your membership card, and pay only the $10 co-payment. Your doctor's office will complete the claim form and send it to MetraHealth for processing. MetraHealth will then reimburse your doctor for the remainder of the fee, minus the $10 co-payment. That's it—no further costs to you and no forms to fill out.

Additional benefits in the new plan include an emergency room co-payment of only $15 and no outpatient surgery deductible.

This paragraph begins to explain the particular action being requested. Again, clear directions are provided to help ensure a response.

Providing boxes for the response helps readers comply with the request.

Please let us know your decision by December 15. If you decide to participate in the new MetraHealth medical plan, please mark the appropriate box on the enclosed form and return it to Human Resources. If you decide not to join, you don't need to reply. You will automatically be enrolled in the original plan for another year.

adjustment to the organization's attention. Communicate at once with someone in the company who can make the correction. A phone call or visit may solve the problem, but a written claim letter is better because it documents your dissatisfaction.

Your first reaction to a clumsy mistake or a defective product is likely to be anger or frustration, but the person reading your letter probably had nothing to do with the

Figure 8.2
(Continued)

Mr. Joseph Jakes, November 24, 1997, Page 2

If you have any questions or need further information about the new HMO, please refer to the enclosed brochure. You may also contact me at (319) 588-2562 during business hours.

Sincerely,

Julie Kennedy

Julie Kennedy
Human Resources/Benefits Administration

rl

> The courteous close motivates action by specifying a person to talk to and a deadline for a reply.

problem. Making a courteous, clear, concise explanation will impress the reader much more favorably than an abusive, angry letter. Asking for a fair and reasonable solution will increase your chances of receiving a satisfactory adjustment.

> Tone is of primary importance; keep your claim businesslike and unemotional.

In most cases, and especially in your first letter, assume that a fair adjustment will be made, and follow the plan for direct requests. Begin with a straightforward

CHECKLIST FOR ROUTINE REQUESTS

A. DIRECT STATEMENT OF THE REQUEST
1. Phrase the opening to reflect the assumption that the reader will respond favorably to your request.
2. Phrase the opening so clearly and simply that the main idea cannot be misunderstood.
3. Write in a polite, undemanding, personal tone.
4. Preface complex requests with a sentence or two of explanation, possibly a statement of the problem that the response will solve.

B. JUSTIFICATION, EXPLANATION, AND DETAILS
1. Justify the request, or explain its importance.
2. Explain to the reader the benefit of responding.
3. State desired actions in a positive and supportive, not negative or dictatorial, manner.
4. Itemize parts of a complex request in a numbered series.
5. List specific questions.
   a. Don't ask questions that you could answer through your own efforts.
   b. Arrange questions logically.

c. Number questions.
d. Word questions carefully to get the type of answers you need: numbers or yes's and no's if you need to tally many replies; more lengthy, detailed answers if you want to elicit more information.
e. Word questions to avoid clues about the answer you prefer so as not to bias the reader's answers.
f. Limit each question to one topic.

C. COURTEOUS CLOSE WITH REQUEST FOR SPECIFIC ACTION
1. Courteously request a specific action and make it easy to comply, perhaps by enclosing a return, postage-paid envelope or by explaining how you can be reached.
2. Indicate gratitude, possibly by promising to follow up in a way that will benefit the reader.
3. Clearly state any important deadline or time frame for the request.

statement of the problem, and give a complete, specific explanation of the details. In the middle section of your claim letter, provide any information the adjuster will need to verify your complaint about faulty merchandise or unsatisfactory service. Politely request specific action in your closing, and suggest that the business relationship will continue if the problem is solved satisfactorily.

Companies usually accept the customer's explanation of what's wrong, so ethically speaking, it's important to be entirely honest when filing claims for adjustment or refund. Also, be prepared to back up your claim with invoices, sales receipts, canceled checks, dated correspondence, catalog descriptions, and any other relevant documents. Send copies and keep the originals for your files.

If the remedy is obvious, tell your reader exactly what will return the company to your good graces—for example, an exchange of merchandise for the right item or a refund if the item is out of stock. If you're uncertain about the precise nature of the trouble, you could ask the company to make an assessment. When you're dissatisfied with an expensive item, you might request that an unbiased third person either estimate the cost of repair or suggest another solution. Be sure to supply your telephone number and the best time to call (as well as your address) so that the company can discuss the situation with you if necessary.

The following letter was written to a gas and electric company. As you read it, compare the tone with that in Figure 8.3. If you were the person receiving the complaint, which version would you respond to more favorably?

> We have been at our present location only three months, and we don't understand why our December utility bill is $115.00 and our January bill is $117.50. Businesses on both sides of us, in offices just like ours, are paying only $43.50 and $45.67 for the same months. We all have similar computer and office equipment, so something must be wrong.
>
> Small businesses are helpless against big utility companies. How can we prove that you read the meter wrong or that the November bill from before we even moved in here got added to our December bill? We want someone to check this meter right away. We can't afford to pay these big bills.

Generally, it's a good idea to suggest specific and fair compensation when asking for an adjustment. However, in some cases you wouldn't request a specific adjustment but ask the reader to resolve the problem. In a letter like this, define the problem and express your dissatisfaction in as much detail as possible, while conveying a sincere desire to find a fair solution. A courteous tone will allow the reader to save face and still make up for the mistake. (This chapter's Checklist for Claims and Requests for Adjustment, on page 230, will remind you of the tasks involved in such messages.)

MAKING ROUTINE CREDIT REQUESTS

If your credit rating is sound, your application for business credit may be as direct as any other type of simple request. Whether the application is directed to a local bank or supply company, a wholesaler or manufacturer, or a national credit-card company, the information needed is the same. You might phone the company for a credit application or write a letter as simple as this:

> We would like to open a credit account with your company. Please send an application blank, and let us know what references you will need.

Before you get a credit account, you'll have to supply such information as the name of your company, the length of time you've been in business, the name of your bank, and the addresses of businesses where you have existing accounts. Businesses trying to establish credit are also expected to furnish a financial statement and possibly a

Figure 8.3
In-Depth Critique:
Improved Letter of
Complaint

Most people will react much more favorably to this version of the complaint letter about high utility bills. As this rational and clear approach demonstrates, a courteous approach is best for any routine request. If you must write a letter that gives vent to your anger, go ahead; but then tear that one up and write a letter that will actually help solve the problem.

The European Connection
Specialist Purveyors of European Antiques
for over 30 years

P.O. Box 804 • Cayucos, California 93430
Telephone: (805) 979-7727 Fax: (805) 979-2828
EuroConnect@nemesis.net

February 24, 1997

Customer Service Representative
City of San Luis Obispo Utilities
955 Morro Street
St. Luis Obispo, CA 93401

Dear Customer Service Representative:

The utility meters may not be accurate in our office. Please send someone to check them.

We have been at our present location since December 1, almost three months. Our monthly bills are nearly triple those of neighboring businesses in this building, yet we all have similar storefronts, furnished with similar merchandise and equipment. In December we paid $115.00, and our January bill was $117.50; the highest bills that neighboring businesses have paid were $43.50 and $45.67.

If your representative could check the operation of the meters, he or she could also see how much energy we are using. We understand that you regularly provide this helpful service to customers.

We would appreciate hearing from you this week. You can reach me by calling 979-7727 during business hours.

Sincerely,

Jasper Covington

Jasper Covington
Proprietor

The problem is stated clearly and calmly in the first paragraph.

The second paragraph explains the particulars of the situation so that the person reading the letter will understand why the writer believes a problem exists.

The last paragraph requests specific action and makes responding easy by providing a phone number.

---

balance sheet. In general, the lender wants proof that your income is stable and that you can repay the loan. You might put this information in your original letter, but it will probably be requested again on the standard credit application form.

A request to buy on credit is sometimes included with a company's first-time order for goods. In such cases, the customer often sends copies of the latest financial

Order letters are often combined with a request for credit.

CHECKLIST FOR CLAIMS AND REQUESTS FOR ADJUSTMENT

A. DIRECT STATEMENT OF THE REQUEST
1. Write a claim letter as soon as possible after the problem has been identified.
2. State the need for reimbursement or correction of the problem.
3. Maintain a confident, factual, fair, unemotional tone.

B. JUSTIFICATION, EXPLANATION, AND DETAILS
1. To gain the reader's understanding, praise some aspect of the good or service, or at least explain why the product was originally purchased.
2. Present facts honestly, clearly, and politely.
3. Eliminate threats, sarcasm, exaggeration, and hostility.
4. Specify the problem: Product failed to live up to advertised standards; product failed to live up to sales representative's claims; product fell short of company policy; product was defective; customer service was deficient.
5. Make no accusation against any person or company, unless you can back it up with facts.
6. Use a nonargumentative tone to show your confidence in the reader's fairness.
7. If necessary, refer to documentation (invoices, canceled checks, confirmation letters, and the like), but mail only photocopies.

8. Ask the reader to propose fair adjustment, if appropriate.
9. If appropriate, clearly state what you expect as a fair settlement, such as credit against the next order you place, full or partial refund of the purchase price of the product, replacement of the defective merchandise, performance of services as originally contracted, or repair of the defective merchandise.
10. Do not return the defective merchandise until you have been asked to do so.
11. Avoid uncertainty or vagueness that might permit the adjusters to prolong the issue by additional correspondence or to propose a less-than-fair settlement.

C. COURTEOUS CLOSE WITH REQUEST FOR SPECIFIC ACTION
1. Summarize desired action briefly.
2. Simplify compliance with your request by including your name, address, phone number (with area code), and hours of availability.
3. Note how complying with your request will benefit the reader.

---

statement along with the order letter. If the order is made by e-mail or on the Internet, indicate that financial statements are available. If a company's credit standing is good, it may ask with confidence for the order to be accepted on a credit basis. Because the main idea in this situation is to get permission to buy on credit, the letter should open with that request. Figure 8.4 is an example of the way an order may be combined with a request for credit. Note how the request for credit is supported by documentation of financial stability. In addition, the writer has encouraged a favorable response by adopting a confident tone and mentioning the probability of future business.

A request for credit
- *Is supported by documentation*
- *Adopts a confident tone*
- *Hints at future business*

INQUIRING ABOUT PEOPLE

Some companies ask applicants to supply references before awarding credit, contracts, jobs, promotions, scholarships, memberships, and so on. Job seekers are sometimes asked to provide the names and addresses of at least three people who can vouch for their ability, skills, integrity, character, and fitness for the job.

But because some unsuccessful job and credit applicants bring suit against those who write uncomplimentary letters about them, people have become more wary about writing meaningful recommendation letters. They may simply confirm the facts of the relationship with the applicant, confine their remarks to the positive and bland, or refuse

Figure 8.4
In-Depth Critique: E-Mail Message Combining an Order with a Routine Credit Request

CrossTerrain, Inc. sells hybrid bikes (suitable on all road surfaces) to the public. This message combines an order with a request for credit.

```
┌──────────────────────────── E-Mail ────────────────────────────┐
│                                                                 │
├─────────────────────────────────────────────────────────────────┤
│ Date: Wednesday, 26 November 1997, 15:10:27, PDT                │
│ X-Sender: fapatov@CrossT.com                                    │
│ To: Willa Deerwalk <deerwalk@cai.com>                           │
│ From: "Frank Apatov" <fapataov@ctbikes.com>                     │
│ Subject: New Order                                              │
│ X-Info: Wolf.com                                                │
│                                                                 │
│ To:    Ms. Willa Deerwalk                                       │
│        Cycle Accessories, Inc.                                  │
│        468 Montmartre Road                                      │
│        Helena, Washington 45410                                 │
│                                                                 │
│ From: CrossTerrain, Inc.                                        │
│       11549 Helena Parkway                                      │
│       Helena, Washington 45442                                  │
│       (918) 367-3423 Fax (918) 323-3824                         │
│                                                                 │
│ Subj: New Order                                                 │
│                                                                 │
│ Dear Ms. Deerwalk:                                              │
│                                                                 │
│ Cycling season will soon be here, and we are planning a         │
│ spring promotion for May 1. We expect to move a large           │
│ quantity of accessories and hope you can help us by             │
│ shipping the following order by April 15:                       │
│                                                                 │
│ No.  Item   Description              Price Per  Extension        │
│ 25   RA335  Auto Rack Mount/Hybrid                              │
│             Bike                     $35.00     $ 875.00        │
│ 25   LT890  Headlight Assembly Kit    15.00       375.00        │
│ 25   MR223  Rearview Mirror Kit       10.00       250.00        │
│ 20   RF977  Reflector Set              8.00       160.00        │
│ 40   WB232  Water Bottle Kit           5.00       200.00        │
│ 32   RP447  Rain Poncho in Seat                                │
│             Pouch                     12.00       384.00        │
│             TOTAL                               $2,244.00       │
│                                                                 │
│ I've attached our standard financial statement,                │
│ including references. We ask for terms of 2/10, net 30,         │
│ FOB your dock. Please let me know if you need any               │
│ additional information.                                         │
│                                                                 │
│ Pete Weinstein at Sports West recommended you because of        │
│ the quality of your products and your record of on-time         │
│ shipping. He provided me with your catalog and price            │
│ sheet. We are trying to keep more of our orders in-state        │
│ and are looking forward to doing continued business with        │
│ Cycle Accessories.                                             │
│                                                                 │
│ Sincerely,                                                     │
│                                                                 │
│ Frank Apatov                                                    │
│ Buyer                                                           │
│                                                                 │
│ Attachment                                                      │
└─────────────────────────────────────────────────────────────────┘
```

The message starts strong with a positive statement and a possible reader benefit.

The order is clearly stated in an easy-to-read table.

Terms of 2/10 refers to a request for a 2% discount if the bill is paid within 10 days of receipt rather than the standard 30. Net 30 means the bill is due in full within 30 days of receipt. FOB your dock means "Freight on board" and indicates that shipping will be paid by the purchaser from the point of loading indicated, in this case, Cycle Accessories' dock.

Financial information necessary for granting credit accompanies the order. The message also states the terms of credit that are being requested.

The message ends on a positive note with a compliment to the receiver and an additional reader benefit.

When Julia Chartos meets with businesspeople applying for a loan or a line of credit at Bank of America, she looks for the confidence that comes from having a steady income that is sufficient to pay the loan back. She also looks for the communication skills that allow applicants to clearly describe their business situation and their reasons for applying for credit.

to recommend anyone, especially in writing. However, some states are adopting laws that make such suits more difficult, so applicants and companies may often try to solicit recommendations.[5] These recommendation letters are sent directly from the reference to the potential employer or creditor. The information is considered confidential.

Letters Requesting a Recommendation

Always ask for permission before you use someone's name as a reference.

Before volunteering someone's name as a reference, always ask that person's permission. Some people won't let you use their names, perhaps because they don't know enough about you to feel comfortable writing a letter or because they have a policy of avoiding recommendations. In any event, you are likely to receive the best recommendations from those who agree to write about you, so check first.

When asking a close personal or professional associate to serve as a reference, take the direct approach. Confidently assume that the reader will honor your request, and adopt a professional tone. In your opening paragraph, clearly state that you're applying for a position and that you want the person to write a letter of recommendation. If you haven't had contact with the person for some time, use the opening to refresh the person's memory. Recall the nature of the relationship you had, the dates of association, and any special events that might bring a clear, favorable picture of you to mind.

Refresh the memory of any potential reference you haven't been in touch with for a while.

If you're applying for a job or scholarship or the like, include a copy of your résumé to give the reader an idea of the direction your life has taken. After reading the résumé, your reader will know what favorable qualities to emphasize and will be able to write the recommendation that best supports your application. If you don't have a résumé, include in your letter any information about yourself that the reader might use to support a recommendation, such as a description of related jobs you've held.

Close your letter with an expression of appreciation and the full name and address of the person to whom the letter should be sent. When you're asking for an immediate recommendation, you should also mention the deadline. You'll make a response more likely if you enclose a stamped, preaddressed envelope. The letter in Figure 8.5 covers all these points.

Figure 8.5
In-Depth Critique: Letter Requesting a Recommendation

In Joanne Tucker's letter requesting a recommendation, she adds important information about some qualifications that might be of special interest to Global Securities.

Joanne Tucker
1181 Ashport, Tate Springs, Tennessee 38101
(901) 369-2093

April 15, 1997

Professor Lyndon Kenton
School of Business
University of Tennessee, Knoxville
Knoxville, Tennessee 37916

Dear Professor Kenton:

May I have a letter of recommendation from you? I recently interviewed with Global Securities and have been called for a second interview for their Analyst Training Program (ATP). They have requested at least one recommendation from a professor, and I immediately thought of you.

As you may recall, I took BUS 485, Financial Analysis, from you in the fall of 1996. I enjoyed the class and finished the term with an "A." Professor Kenton, your comments on assertiveness and cold-calling impressed me beyond the scope of the actual course material. In fact, taking your course helped me decide on a future as a financial analyst.

My enclosed résumé includes all my relevant work experience and volunteer activities. But I'd also like to add that I've handled the financial planning for our family since my father passed away several years ago. Although initially, I learned by trial and error, I have increasingly applied my business training in deciding what stocks or bonds to trade. This, I believe, has given me a practical edge over others who may be applying for the same job.

If possible, Ms. Blackmon in Human Resources needs to receive your letter by May 30. For your convenience, I've enclosed a stamped envelope addressed to:

Ms. Sandra Blackmon
Human Resources
Global Securities
World Financial Center, North Tower
250 Vesey Street, New York, NY 10281-1332
Voice: (212) 449-1000 • Fax: (212) 236-4384

This letter opens with the direct approach, assuming Professor Kenton will honor the request and stating the potential employer involved (Global Securities).

The next section gives enough information for Professor Kenton to recall his former student.

Tucker not only includes her résumé but also mentions experience that may set her apart from other candidates.

The close includes the name and address of the person expecting the recommendation.

Figure 8.5
(*Continued*)

In the close the writer
expresses her appreciation.

Professor Lyndon Kenton, April 15, 1997, Page 2

**I appreciate your time and effort in writing this letter of recom-
mendation for me. It will be great to put my education to work,
and I'll keep you informed of my progress.**

Sincerely,

Joanne Tucker

Joanne Tucker

Enclosure

Letters Checking on a Reference

Many companies prefer to write directly to the person named as a reference. Like letters requesting a recommendation, letters checking on a reference should be specific about the type of information needed and the use to which it will be put. If Sandra Blackmon, head of Human Resources at Global Securities, had written the letter directly to Professor Kenton, her request might have read like the one in Figure 8.6.

Guarantee confidentiality to help protect a reference from legal problems.

Promise confidentiality when you write a letter to check on a reference. The person supplying a frank recommendation could be subject to a libel suit if false or negative written information were made available. Of course, in the event of legal action, letters can be subpoenaed and made a matter of public record. Charges of discrimination are another potential problem, so avoid asking about an applicant's age, gender, race, color, religion, marital status, physical disability, or personal traits—unless it's directly related to the position you're filling and you are satisfied that you considered these factors under current laws.

Communicating about people involves more than simply adhering to the law. Ethical considerations include protecting human rights. So request facts (not opinions), request only the information needed for business purposes, and contact the source only if the applicant concerned has given you permission to make this inquiry (see "How to Check References—and Avoid Legal Traps" on page 236).

BEST OF THE WEB

**Protect Yourself When You
Check On or Write a Job
Reference**

Reduce your legal liability: Discover what employee information you can usually inquire about or provide safely. Find out how to avoid lawsuits for invasion of privacy and violation of state blacklisting laws. Learn about the types of statements that may form the basis of a lawsuit against you. Be aware of state job reference requirements (several states have laws that may require you to write a reference). Learn about when you have an absolute legal obligation to provide information about a former employee.

http://www.toolkit.cch.com/
text/pO5_8610.htm

SUMMARY

Requests made across cultural boundaries are most effective if they follow the cultural customs of your audience. The purpose of a direct request is to gain a specific response from the reader, whether the answer to a question, the delivery of goods or services, or some other sort of action. Although a favorable response is assumed, you can ensure cooperation by maintaining a cordial and you-oriented tone. Direct requests are used for placing orders, requesting routine information and action, requesting claims and adjustments, requesting credit, and inquiring about people.

When Sandra Blackmon of Global Securities writes Professor Kenton, she is careful to indicate the candidate's knowledge of the request, as well as Global Securities promise of confidentiality. When you check on a reference, you want to make it as easy and as safe as possible for your reader to respond.

Figure 8.6
In-Depth Critique: Letter
Checking on a Reference

Global $ecurities

World Financial Center, North Tower – 250 Vesey Street, New York, NY 10281-1332
Voice: (212) 449-1000 • Fax: (212) 236-4384 • http://www/globalsecurities.com

April 15, 1997

Professor Lyndon Kenton
Business Department
University of Tennessee, Knoxville
Knoxville, Tennessee 37916

Dear Professor Kenton:

We are considering Joanne Tucker for our Analyst Training Program at Global Securities. She is a promising candidate, and we need more detailed information about her education and your opinion of her ability to handle the rigors of training. Ms. Tucker submitted your name not only as her professor but also as her faculty advisor.

In addition to the long hours involved in training, candidates must have a sound, logical approach to problem solving. We are looking for people who are not afraid to express their ideas and who exude confidence in their manner and deed. The job of financial analyst requires not only technical knowledge of the market but also extensive people skills, and we appreciate any information about Joanne Tucker that will help guide our decision.

We need your letter of recommendation no later than May 30, but would appreciate it earlier, if convenient. Your evaluation will be kept strictly confidential in accordance with our governing by-laws. Thank you for your time on Ms. Tucker's behalf.

Sincerely,

Sandra Blackmon

Sandra Blackmon
Human Resources

This paragraph explains why Professor Kenton's opinions are valued.

The letter is careful to state that the applicant has authorized this request.

This section includes pertinent information about the requirements of the position and general qualities on which the applicant is being evaluated.

Because it has been written to Professor Kenton at her business address (the university) and requests information about a third party (Joanne Tucker), no stamped, preaddressed envelope has been enclosed.

SHARPENING YOUR SKILLS

HOW TO CHECK REFERENCES—AND AVOID LEGAL TRAPS

Employers who hire people without adequately checking their backgrounds not only face the possibility of expensive hiring mistakes—they could also face legal action if problems arise. Some chilling examples include the building janitor with an unchecked criminal record who murdered a tenant, the school bus driver with an unchecked record of drunk driving arrests, and the "chemist" whose difficulties on his new job were finally explained by his forged college degree. More commonly, reference checks can reveal long employment gaps, inflated accomplishments, false claims about college degrees, and potential interpersonal problems on the job.

Checking a job applicant's references has become a challenging proposition because company executives have been sued over their remarks. In fact, some companies will verify only an employee's "name, rank, and serial number," and a few companies won't verify employment at all. Even though companies realize how much they need to share relevant information on employees, many executives are uncomfortable about committing their remarks to paper. Here's some advice from the most successful reference checkers:

- *Get applicants involved.* Ask candidates to provide a list of references to check. Have them sign a waiver releasing their references from legal liability for their statements, and ask each candidate to contact references beforehand to encourage them to speak freely.
- *Take your time, and don't delegate.* Checking references is an important task and should take about two hours per candidate. Make your calls early in the morning or after five, when executives are likely to answer the phone themselves. (Be sure to check references before making a job offer so that the applicant who might be rejected won't blame his references or your procedures for not being hired.)
- *Prepare your questions carefully.* Whether writing or calling references, pose open-ended, job-related questions that elicit information about *how* a candidate performed,

not just what was accomplished. To avoid discrimination charges, ask similar questions for all applicants (don't inquire whether a female executive fears traveling alone if you wouldn't make the same inquiry of a male executive). Also, ask for additional referrals to others who can comment on the candidate's performance.

- *Know the laws in your state.* State and federal laws govern reference checks, and they're constantly being updated. In most states, it's illegal to ask direct or indirect questions about age, sex, religion, race, marital status, sexual orientation, disabilities, politics, pregnancy, drug use, medical history, or arrest records (unless the candidate will be working with minors). However, it's legal in most states to contact police departments and inquire about arrest records or to ask former employers if a person has ever been *convicted* of a crime. It's also legal (and recommended) to contact schools, or to have applicants sign requests for course transcripts to be mailed directly to the hiring company, at the applicant's expense.

You may have to rely on the telephone to check references. Prepare your questions carefully in advance, and jot down the responses for your legal and personnel records. If your phone calls are unreturned, you might write a letter of request as a last resort. If so, politely explain that you can't make a job offer until you receive a reply.

---

1. Think about who you would supply as references on an employment application. Now assume the perspective of a potential employer, and prepare the questions you'd want those references to answer about you and your work.
2. You've interviewed a job candidate who has all the right answers and seems to have the right qualifications—but your intuition tells you something isn't quite right. What checking would you do to confirm or quell your concerns?

When addressing a U.S. or Canadian audience with few cultural differences, begin with your request and then provide any justification and explanatory details that will help your reader execute the request correctly. If you request several items or pose several secondary questions, number them for clarity. The letter can then close courteously with a request for specific action and an indication of any deadline. By emphasizing a benefit to the reader, you also increase chances for a favorable and prompt response.

COMMUNICATION CHALLENGES AT THE NATURE COMPANY

The Nature Company's two Canadian stores are doing so well that the company has decided to open three more: one in Vancouver, one in Toronto, and one in Ottawa. Silva Raker is busy working with the designers and architects to create an in-store atmosphere uniquely suited to each location—The Nature Company's trademark design with a few extra touches to reflect the local region's flora and fauna.

INDIVIDUAL CHALLENGE: Getting ready for three new store openings outside the United States has created lots of extra work for Raker's staff. Nearly everyone has worked overtime, including weekends, and Raker wants to hire Jim Moody as a new staff member. She's impressed with his résumé and interview. Now she'd like to know whether Moody responds well under pressure. As public relations coordinator for Brentwell Logging in Snohomish, Washington, Moody may have dealt with pressured situations. Write the letter for Raker (making up any necessary details), and address it to Moody's su-

pervisor, Henry Watrous (at 1552 10th Avenue, Snohomish, WA 98290).[6]

TEAM CHALLENGE: Buyers in the merchandise department have already increased orders to stock the new stores, but in recent conversations with the retail staff at the established Canadian stores, Raker was clued in to a few products that are very popular among the company's northern clientele. Raker has handed your team a list of four of these extra-popular items, supplied by four separate vendors: glow-in-the-dark firefly T-shirts (which retail for $16.95 in adult sizes and $12.95 in child sizes), three-dimensional polar bear puzzles ($19.95), a digital display international-time clock ($39.95), and Greek wind chimes ($65.00). Your team is to develop a form letter explaining the circumstances and requesting a 20 percent increase in your original order from each of these vendors. Choose one of these items to use in a sample letter, making up company and individual names, wholesale prices, and quantities.

CRITICAL THINKING QUESTIONS

1. When organizing your requests, why is it important to know whether any cultural differences exist between you and your audience? Explain.
2. For U.S. and Canadian requests, why is it inappropriate to begin with a brief personal introduction? Please explain your answer.
3. What is the most important element of an order letter: the legality of the offer, the clarity of the order, or the explanation of how items will be used? Briefly explain.
4. Every time you send a direct-request memo to Ted Jackson, he delays or refuses to comply. You're be-

ginning to get impatient. Should you send Jackson a memo to ask what's wrong? Complain to your supervisor about Jackson's uncooperative attitude? Arrange a face-to-face meeting with Jackson? Bring up the problem at the next staff meeting? Explain.
5. You have a complaint against one of your suppliers, but you have no documentation to back it up. Should you request an adjustment anyway? Why or why not?
6. When checking on a reference, why should you need the applicant's permission to contact a source? Explain your answer.

DOCUMENTS FOR ANALYSIS

Read the following documents; then (1) analyze the strengths and weaknesses of each sentence, and (2) revise each document so that it follows this chapter's guidelines.

Document 8.A: Requesting Routine Information from a Business

> Our college is closing its dining hall for financial reasons, so we want to do something to help the students prepare their own food in their dorm rooms if they so choose. Your colorful ad in Collegiate Magazine caught our

eye. We need the following information before we make our decision.

> 1. Would you be able to ship the microwaves by August 15? I realize this is short notice, but our board of trustees just made the decision to close the dining hall last week and we're scrambling around trying to figure out what to do.
> 2. Do they have any kind of a warranty? College students can be pretty hard on things, as you know, so we will need a good warranty.

3. How much does it cost? Do you give a discount for a big order?
4. Do we have to provide a special plug-in?
5. Will students know how to use them, or will we need to provide instructions?

As I said before, we're on a tight time frame and need good information from you as soon as possible to help us make our decision about ordering. You never know what the board might come up with next. I'm looking at several other companies, also, so please let us know ASAP.

Document 8.B: Requesting Routine Information from a Customer

I'm writing to inquire about your recent order for a High Country backpack. You didn't tell us which backpack you wanted, and you know they make a lot of different ones. They have the canvas models with the plastic frames and vinyl trim and they have the canvas models with leather trim and they have the ones which have more pockets than the other ones. Plus they come in lots of different colors.

Also they make the ones which are large for a big-boned person and the smaller versions for little women or kids. So you can see why I didn't know which one to send you. Also, we have to have payment when you place your order and you didn't include a check or credit-card number (we need your signature if you order by credit card).

Actually, if you could drive to our store in Eureka it would help a lot because then you could see all of them and try them on. Plus we have a lot of other neat equipment you could look at. I realize you live kind of far from here, but it would be worth the trip. If you really can't come, then you just need to do the things I mentioned and we'll get it right out to you.

Document 8.C: Writing Direct Requests for Claims and Adjustments

At a local business-supply store, I recently purchased your "Negotiator Pro" for my computer. I bought the CD because I saw your ad for it in *MacWorld Magazine,* and it looked as if it might be an effective tool for use in my corporate seminar on negotiation.

Unfortunately, when I inserted it in my office computer, it wouldn't work. I returned it to the store, but since I had already opened it, they refused to exchange it for a CD that would work or give me a refund. They told me to contact you and that you might be able to send me a version that would work with my computer.

You can send the information to me at the letterhead address. If you cannot send me the correct disc, please refund my $79.95. Thanks in advance for any help you can give me in this matter.

Cases

Placing Orders

1. Paper shortage: Memo faxed to Reliable Office Supplies Your environmental consulting company, Environmental Services, is a "microbusiness"—a small business with only one or two employees. And since most of your business is conducted by phone, fax, or modem, last year you moved out of San Diego and into the surrounding foothills.

Serene as the woods may be, your company still demands lots of your time. You are everything from CEO to janitor and cafeteria chef. That's why Reliable Office Supplies, a mail-order distributor, attracted your attention.

Reliable's catalog offered you credit, free same-day shipping, 24-hour operators, and a gift of coffee mugs and cookies with your first order. How many times had you wasted half a day trekking into the city for a ream of paper? You gave Reliable a chance. You called the 800 number on Saturday and by Tuesday the paper was on your doorstep (along with the goodies, which you devoured at your desk). Then, a few weeks later, you received a promotional catalog bearing a special imprint on the cover:

PRIVATE SALE!!! On 8/02/97 you ordered Cascade Laser Paper. Only during the *Environmental Services Private Sale* will you see Cascade Laser Paper for $4.49 per ream. That's a great discount off the already low price on page 21. Call or fax us today! Use private sale item #735BC15161.

How could you resist? Moreover, the time you've been losing shopping for "bargains" at the discount store is costing you hundreds of dollars, whereas Reliable's pricing is sometimes only a few dimes higher.

Your task: You plan to fax an order to Reliable. You need six reams of the Cascade Laser Paper; one carton of PM brand standard one-ply, 2-1/4-inch calculator rolls (stock no. 02PF8677; $46.00); one AT&T brand QS2000 high-yield laser printer toner cartridge (stock no. 02QS02000; $125.99); and one dozen 8-1/2-by-11-inch Tops Prism brand perforated legal pads in orchid (stock no. Q2TP631, color code 40; $18.29).

You want to save the catalog's order blank, so type the information in memo form and fax it to Reliable at 1-800-326-3233. Your account number is BB5554432-999, and your address is 4888 Oak Road, Jamul, CA 91917. Since you don't have information on shipping charges, request that you be notified of that amount on your bill.[7]

SMALL BUSINESS
EXTERNAL COMMUNICATION

2. Wakeboard mania: Letter from Performance Ski & Surf ordering more equipment Your boss is amazed. Bill Porter, owner of Performance Ski & Surf, hasn't seen sporting equipment sell this rapidly in Orlando, Florida, since in-line skating became popular. But since May, you haven't been able to keep wakeboards in stock. It doesn't seem to matter much which brand—Wake Tech, Neptune, or Full Tilt—your customers are snapping them up and heading out to the water, locals and tourists alike. They're outselling traditional trick water skis by 20 to 1.

"Maybe it's because they don't require big, fast boats," you suggest. "I heard they're using fishing trawlers out in Seattle, and they're still catching wind because the slower boats make bigger wakes to launch from."

Porter nods thoughtfully as he gazes at a photograph of professional wakeboarder Dean Lavelle at nearby Lake Butler. He's holding the same kind of rope any water skier holds, but he's 15 feet in the air. His short, stubby, fiberglass wakeboard (which is strapped to his feet) is higher than his head, and from the grimace on his face, it looks like he's mid-flip.

"I just hope none of these kids get hurt trying to imitate the pros," Butler says.

"Nah," you say. "Extreme sports—it's the way of the 1990s. Look at what happened to snowboarding. You'll see wakeboarders at the Olympics soon."

Your task: Butler has asked you to order another 12 Wake Techs, 8 Neptunes, and 10 Full Tilts. "Don't worry about colors or models; we'll be lucky to get this order filled at all from what I hear." He suggests you draft a form letter for the three orders and he'll supply the addresses and account numbers when you're finished.[8]

BANKING
EXTERNAL COMMUNICATION

3. Vacation dreams: E-mail message ordering tourist information from Trinidad and Tobago For two years, you've been slaving away at your first management job as an assistant branch manager for Bank of America. The promotion has kept you more than busy—you never realized how much overtime salaried managers are expected to put in. You're really looking forward to that two-week paid vacation you've worked so hard to earn.

"So what's it going to be?" the branch manager asked you this morning. "Hawaii? Or DisneyWorld?"

"Huh?" you mumbled—after all, it was only 7 A.M. You caught yourself, cleared your throat, and politely answered that you hadn't decided yet. (After all, you had until December and this was still a cold day in February.)

"That may be," your manager replied, "but I need to know your plans today for a report I'm filing with the head office. Just drop your first and second choices for vacation dates on my desk by 3 P.M. I'll let you know by next week how that fits into everyone else's schedule." Then she turned on her heel and strode off toward the vault.

By 3 P.M.? First and second choices? But you don't even know where you're going! In the heart of desperation, an idea strikes. You hurry over to the customer waiting area, pick up a glossy copy of *Saveur* magazine, and begin flipping through the ads. You'd already decided you didn't want any ordinary vacation; you wanted to go somewhere exotic, somewhere tropical, like the spot where those two people are lounging in front of that plummeting waterfall. (How they got that beach umbrella to balance on the rocks, you'll never understand.) "In Tobago, Nature is in balance, as well as in abundance," reads the caption. Yes, that's it!

Your task: Striding confidently back to your computer, you spread the ad out on your desk, call up your e-mail program, and tap in the address for ordering the *Trinidad & Tobago: Come to Life* tourist information booklet: <tourism-info@tidco.co.tt>. You can almost feel that tropical heat penetrating your snow-weary bones as you type the order. Create this e-mail message and print it out for your instructor.[9]

Requesting Routine Information and Action

4. We won't go: Memo at Domino's Pizza requesting information   "They can't do this to us," fumes Tim McIntyre into his telephone. McIntyre is designated spokesman for the Domino's Pizza chain (headquartered in Ann Arbor, Michigan). The reporter at the other end of the line must have asked another question because McIntyre explodes again in a torrent of indignation. "We deliver to more inner-city areas than many other pizza chains—but we won't risk our employees' lives!" You've never heard McIntyre say an angry word before. In the PR department, courtesy, tact, and diplomacy are the order of the day for any volatile situation.

As soon as he hangs up, McIntyre turns to you with fire in his eyes. "I don't care if the law was instigated by the grandmother of the president of the United States, the San Francisco Board of Supervisors can't force Domino's, or any other business, to send delivery people into unsafe neighborhoods. We're planning to fight this.

"Get me all the information you can about Domino's restaurants in San Francisco, particularly the six stores owned by David Wilcox. The Board of Supervisors passed this ordinance after Wilcox's store refused to deliver to a supervisor's grandson. We need to convince them that this won't solve inner-city problems. Find out about the 22-year-old who was shot to death when he tried to make a delivery in 1994. I want names, dates, and locations of every incident—the robberies, the knife threats, the brick-shattered windows. So far, the California Restaurant Association supports our position that this new law violates federal worker safety legislation. In fact, every delivery business I know practices red-zoning."

You knew he was referring to the designation of unsafe areas as off-limits for deliveries. Domino's even provides outlets with a computer program that flags addresses as green (deliver), yellow (curbside only), or red (no delivery). Lives are at stake here.

Your task: Write a memo to David Wilcox, Domino's San Francisco, asking for the details that McIntyre needs.[10]

5. Maybe multimedia: E-mail message asking about computerized presentations at Rucker Fuller   As a marketing vice president for Rucker Fuller office interiors in San Francisco, you've witnessed many new developments in business presentation technology. Your office furnishings and design firm was one of the first in the industry to build a special audiovisual room for showing professionally produced slide presentations to potential clients. But that was back in the early 1980s. Now the latest developments in multimedia presentation software have caught your eye.

You've just read an article describing the features of new software packages designed to help ordinary business executives like you develop computerized presentations. According to the article, the new software not only allows you to include movies, slides, animation, audio, graphics, interactive sequences, and text, but it also lets you program a time sequence for each element.

For instance, your computerized presentation might begin by playing a recorded soundtrack while the title slides into place on the screen. Then colorful circles spin around and land behind the title (simple animation you create yourself). An electronic narrator reads the title, while the Rucker Fuller logo appears in the lower right corner. The date of the presentation fades in, then out. At any point in the presentation, you can include an interactive option: The push of a button will bring up a selection of topics that you or your client can choose on the spot.

Your task: You're no computer expert and you need some advice. Write an e-mail message asking Rucker Fuller's computer guru, Alison Blakesley at <ablakesley@RuckerFuller.com>, to research and recommend several timeline-based multimedia presentation software packages. You want to know how much these programs cost, which version has the best features, and whether they're as easy to use as the article indicates.[11]

6. Cycling and recycling: Letter from Trek USA requesting information on recycled papers Competition is hot in the bicycle business. At Trek USA in Waterloo, Wisconsin, your latest catalog is slick and sassy, demonstrating your company's focus on the latest, lightest, strongest materials and on your riders' love of biking off-road, in competition, and down a city block in style. The coated paper stock is sleek and shiny, with four-color photographs taken at action angles that show lean, mean bicycling machines poised on a rocky mountain face, in the hands of seasoned racers, and even being ferried across a rushing stream. It's a catalog any marketing director would be proud of. Then someone hands you Schwinn's latest.

Released the same month as your own, Schwinn's catalog is oversized and rough-textured. The cover shows a drawing of planet Earth with "Handle with Care—Help keep the earth a great place to ride" wrapped around it in white letters. Inside, the emphasis is on people and the environment. Short featurettes accompany the bicycle photos and describe people working to preserve the environment, to persuade cities to add more bike trails, and to teach fitness through cycling. The back cover sports the familiar triangular recycling emblem to show that Schwinn is making a serious effort at all levels, even abandoning plastic bubbles and packing its bicycles in recycled cardboard. The Schwinn catalog ends with this clincher: "Bikes and bike riding preserve our environment . . . the only energy needed is you!"

Your heart sinks for a moment. You noticed that another competitor's catalog was also printed on recycled paper. Not to be outdone or defeated, you start imagining a new campaign; maybe there's something to this recycling business. Didn't you just spot an advertisement in *The Wall Street Journal* for a recycled paper company?

Your task: As marketing director for Trek USA, write a letter to Champion International Corporation, One Champion Plaza, Stamford, CT 06921. Address your letter to Alice Bryce, as suggested in *The Wall Street Journal,* and request more information about the company's "complete line of recycled alternatives," particularly its Kromekote 2000 Recycled for your posters and its Benefit Text, Cover, and Writing papers for your catalogs and brochures. Ask for paper samples, and inquire about recycled cardboard packing materials.[12]

7. Please tell me: Request for information about a product You're a consumer, and you've probably seen hundreds of products that you'd like to buy (if not, look at the advertisements in your favorite magazine for ideas). Choose a big-ticket item that is rather complicated, such as a stereo system or a vacation in the Caribbean.

Your task: You surely have some questions about the features of your chosen product or about its price, guarantees, local availability, and so on. Write to the company or organization offering it, and ask four questions that are important to you. Be sure to include enough background information so that the reader can answer your questions satisfactorily.

If requested to do so by your instructor, mail a copy of your letter (after your instructor has had an opportunity to review it) to the company or organization. After a few weeks, you and your classmates may wish to compare responses and to answer this question: How well do companies or organizations respond to unsolicited inquiries?

8. Web site: E-mail message at Morning Star Enterprises requesting additional information In southeastern Montana they call her the "contrary warrior," a tribute to her obstinate spirit and Northern Cheyenne heritage. But Suzanne Small Trusler is the best boss you've ever had. With her husband Tom, she owns the only construction company in Lame Deer, Montana, that employs strictly Northern Cheyenne workers. As new project liaison, you've been with the company for a few months, helping develop bids for new business.

It seems reporters are always calling for interviews. They've heard of Trusler's long fight to keep Morning Star Enterprises alive. It was tougher during the 1970s. First, she's a woman, and second, she's Native American—already two strikes against her, despite her experience and education. Then she insisted on hiring workers from the local reservation, and that really stirred up trouble.

Today the controversy and politicking are behind her and Trusler's company is thriving. Annual revenues have topped $5 million. During peak season, Morning Star hires nearly a hundred workers. Now Trusler receives business awards and participates in high-profile conferences. Her success has encouraged other Native Americans to open their own businesses.

Last week one of your summer interns, Bob Beartracker, suggested that it was time to present Trusler with a new territory to conquer: the World Wide Web. He believes Morning Star Enterprises should build a Web site, not only to reach potential customers but also to spread Trusler's inspiration across a wider field.

You agree. Beartracker found an advertisement for a company that creates Web sites (Webs Are Us), but the classified ad gives little information beyond a phone number and an e-mail address.

Your task: You'll be in a strategy meeting with Trusler next week, and you need enough information to convince her of the benefits of Beartracker's idea. (You might even invite him to sit in on the meeting.) Write an e-mail message requesting more information from Webs Are Us about what the company can do for Morning Star. The e-mail address is <webs@websrus.com>.[13]

9. Scientific frontier: Memo requesting a research update at Quantum Magnetics   W. Barry Lindgren is a man of vision—as are all his colleagues at Quantum Magnetics in San Diego, California. Lindgren is president of a company that's exploring one of the scientific frontiers opened up by quantum physics. The company is using the latest developments in superconducting ceramics to develop ultrasensitive equipment that can detect extremely faint magnetic fluctuations at the molecular level.

Ultrasensitive magnetic sensors are already used in medicine as a diagnostic tool—known as Magnetic Resonance Imaging (MRI)—to create images of internal organs that can reveal serious ailments. Soon doctors will be using devices that track magnetic fields produced by heart and brain activity. Quantum Magnetics has joined a dozen new firms racing to develop additional commercial uses for these sensors.

For example, the company has developed a prototype for a sensor that will detect hidden corrosion, metal fatigue, and microscopic stress fractures in aircraft frames—a device that could one day save lives. Working with IBM and under the sponsorship of the Federal Aviation Administration (FAA), Quantum Magnetics is also developing a scanner for use in airports to distinguish the minute magnetic signals of hidden explosives (and another to scan for illegal narcotics).

In fact, Lindgren received an inquiry from the FAA yesterday, asking for a report on the company's progress on a sensor that will determine whether a bottle packed in traveling luggage is holding a common alcoholic beverage or a high-energy liquid explosive. Lindgren will write the report, but first he needs an update from the research department. The FAA wants to know what's been done on the project for the last six months and what will be done during the next six. The agency also wants an estimate of when a prototype sensor may be ready for testing.

Your task: As Lindgren's administrative assistant, draft a memo to Andrew Hibbs, director of research, requesting the information Lindgren will need to respond to the FAA's query. Lindgren needs Hibbs's information by next Tuesday.[14]

Writing Direct Requests For Claims and Adjustments

10. Spoiled in Argentina: Claim from California peach growers   When President Carlos Menem of Argentina took office, he and his economy minister Domingo Cavallo decided that competition from foreign producers would stimulate Argentine business to provide better products at competitive prices. To the delight of Argentine shoppers, the import tariffs were lowered and goods began pouring in from all over the world: calculators and copy machines, scissors and automobiles, bicycles, toothpicks—and peaches.

When Menem's new policies took effect, California peach growers responded eagerly to the opening of the new market. Individual growers banded into the California Peach Growers Association to ship their fruit to Edcadassa, the Argentine firm that oversees all imported goods while they await customs clearance at Ezeiza international airport.

As supervisor of the Argentine project for the growers' association, you were extremely pleased with the success of the first few shipments; everything had gone smoothly. Then word came back from angry Argentine buyers that the fresh, firm California peaches they had expected arrived at their stores ready for the garbage bin. They refused to pay for the rotten fruit, and your growers lost $50,000.

You made inquiries and discovered that Edcadassa was overwhelmed by the level of imported goods flowing into Argentina (an average of 150 tons a day, compared with 60 tons two years before). Your peach shipment was lost in the confusion, and by the time it was cleared through customs, three weeks late, the peaches were already rotten. Since you'd shipped the fruit when it was at the perfect stage to make the journey, await the normal customs delay, and ripen gently in the supermarkets of Buenos Aires, you believe the responsibility for the shipment's destruction rests with Edcadassa.

Your task: Write a letter to Edcadassa (Columbia 4300, 1425 Buenos Aires, Argentina) requesting full compensation for the ruined peaches.[15]

RETAILING

INTERCULTURAL COMMUNICATION

11. Bolga boo-boo: E-mail to Getrade (Ghana) Ltd. from Pier 1 Imports The way you heard it, in 1993 your employer, Pier 1 Imports, sent a buyer to Accra, Ghana, to find local handicrafts to slake your customers' insatiable thirst for African art. Free-market reforms in Ghana during the 1980s helped ease export procedures,

but so far the local entrepreneurs who sprang forward to take advantage of the change are having trouble meeting demand from large-quantity buyers like Pier 1 (and your rival, Cost Plus). The shipment that just arrived from Getrade (Ghana) Ltd., one of your best Ghanaian suppliers, is a good example of what's been going wrong.

Your customers love bowl-shaped Bolga baskets, traditionally woven by the Fra-fra people of northern Ghana. You can't keep them in stock. So this was to be a huge shipment—3,000 Bolga baskets. You requested baskets in the traditional Bolga shape but woven in solid colors (since your customers have always preferred solid to mixed colors). Getrade was to ship 1,000 green, 1,000 yellow, and 1,000 magenta. Your overseas buyer heard that the Body Shop ordered similar baskets with traditional mixed-color patterns and a flatter shape.

You sympathize with Ladi Nylander, chairman and managing director of Getrade, who is trying hard to adapt to the specific tastes of his U.S. buyers. He's hiring local artisans to carve, shape, and weave all sorts of artifacts—often from designs provided by Pier 1. You can understand how Getrade might have gotten confused, but you know Pier 1 can't sell 3,000 mixed-color, flat Bolga baskets.

Your task: As assistant buyer, it's your job to compose the e-mail message alerting Getrade to the mix-up. You decide that if you want the mistake corrected, you'd better direct your message to Nylander at <Nylander@ Getrade.co.za>. If you're lucky, it may be simply that the Body Shop's order got mixed up with yours.[16]

REAL ESTATE

ETHICS

12. Unmannered manor: Letter requesting reimbursement from Property Vision in London As executive assistant to Barry Lansdon, CEO of Lansdon Holdings, you often handle routine letter-writing tasks. But this situation is stretching your abilities.

Last May Lansdon decided to invest in some property in Great Britain. He'd heard that some of the most historically significant manor houses were on the market, and the notion of joining the landed British gentry—even part-time—fired his imagination. He contacted the people at Property Vision of London (with your help), and they replied with a dozen glowing suggestions, including Testcombe Manor in Chilbolton, Hampshire (US$2.8 million), where Edward VII once halted his private train to go fishing. You liked the seventeenth-century farmhouse in Kent (US$625,000), but it was Hunsdon House that caught your employer's fancy: The 87-acre estate (US$2.8 million) had supposedly been Henry VIII's hunting lodge.

But when Lansdon and his wife flew over to inspect this genuine Tudor mansion, they suffered quite a shock. Despite the kingly aura of wall-mounted rhinoceros trophies and wallpaper flecked with real gold, only one-quarter of the building could ever have heard Henry VIII's footsteps. It turned out that Hunsdon House had actually been demolished, then rebuilt in the 1700s—nearly two centuries after Henry's death. Moreover, the Lansdons discovered that "medieval" also applied to the plumbing system. They learned that insurers would require them to hire a full-time caretaker (at US$40,000 a year), and the sheer size of the estate demanded a butler (US$55,000), a housekeeper (US$35,000), and a gardener (US$35,000) to keep the spectacular gardens in bloom. And if the Lansdons stayed for more than 90 days a year, they'd have to pay British taxes to boot.

"We never would have made the trip if they'd told us even half of this," Mr. Lansdon sighed as he handed you a folder. "I think we have every right to ask for a reimbursement. You'll find an itemized expense list inside."

Your task: Write the claim letter to Mr. William Gething of Property Vision, 36 Brock Street, London, England W1Y 1AD, UK (Voice: 0171-493-4944, Fax: 0171-491-2548).[17]

JOURNALISM
INTERNET COMMUNICATION

13. Follow that lead: E-mail message requesting information on Patagonia   Your editor has asked you to gather information for a business profile about a unique company that would be of interest to local businesses. One such company, Patagonia, has created quite a stir in the business community, and you want to find out more about it.

Your task: Explore Patagonia's Web site <http://www.patagonia.com/menu/htm>. While you're online, get any information you can for the profile: Where is the company headquarters? What is the company best known for? What types of stores carry Patagonia's products? What products does Patagonia offer? Where are Patagonia dealers located? Finally, request product information by linking to the online guide service, sign the guest registry, order a Patagonia catalog, and send an e-mail message requesting further information.

HUMAN RESOURCES
UPWARD COMMUNICATION

14. Unfair: Memo alleging pregnancy discrimination at Midwestern Casualty   Two weeks before your honeymoon, your boss at Midwestern Casualty threatened to fire you if you came back from Tahiti pregnant. He said he'd had his share of pregnant claims adjusters this year and he wasn't going to put up with another one taking four weeks' unpaid leave. You were a little upset, but your co-workers said, "Oh, don't take it so seriously—Fred was only pulling your leg." You weren't so sure.

Two months later, you did get pregnant, as you and your husband had hoped and planned. Shortly after you informed your boss, he placed you on written probation for "poor job performance" and "neglect of duties." You know that isn't true. If you don't do something, in another two months you could be fired from your position as a claims adjuster. You're angry and upset; you and your husband are counting on your income to help support the new baby.

With a little research, you discover that your boss's behavior isn't only unfair but also illegal. The Family and Medical Leave Act of 1993 and the Civil Rights Act of 1991 guarantee protection against gender and pregnancy discrimination and require the company to grant unpaid leave time. Now if you're fired and you file a civil lawsuit, you're allowed a jury trial, and juries have been ruling in favor of other pregnant women who've alleged unfair treatment. (Jury awards have been as high as $2.7 million in compensatory and punitive damages.) All you want is to clear your reputation and keep your job.

Your task: Write a memo to Fred Johnson's superior, Randolph P. Hamilton, vice president, claiming unfair treatment and asking that your record be cleared. (If you happen to be a man, this is a good diversity exercise, giving you the opportunity to walk in the other gender's shoes, so to speak.)[18]

Making Routine Credit Requests

FINANCE
EXTERNAL COMMUNICATION

15. Footing the bill: Routine request to Bailey-Brown for retail credit   After 12 months in business, your shoe shop (named Rowdy's, after the puppy who once chewed all your shoes) seems to be succeeding. You were clever enough to locate it near a campus, and you carry a limited but appropriate variety of footwear that appeals to the college crowd. At the moment you have $5,000 worth of inventory, you just finished paying off the loan for the improvements the shop needed when you took over, and your remaining payments seem manageable, given the way business has been growing.

Today Joe Randall, the representative for Bailey-Brown Shoes, called to tell you about a new line of moderately priced, fashionable sandals that have been selling well near colleges. You're sure you could sell the sandals too, now that warm weather is approaching. Besides, Bailey-Brown's other shoes have always sold well in your shop.

The only problem is that you don't have a lot of ready cash. You mentioned the problem to Joe, but he dismissed it. "We have credit arrangements with a lot of stores like Rowdy's," he said. "All you have to do is write to us on your letterhead, asking for credit. Enclose a financial statement, but summarize your financial position in the letter. We'll also need the name of your shop's bank and the account number."

Your task: Write the letter requesting credit. Address it to Amy Provol, Manager, Credit Department, Bailey-Brown Shoes, Ltd., 602 Warden Avenue, Scarborough, Ontario M1L 3Z7 Canada. Make up any financial details that you believe are necessary; you might also provide as references the names of three people who can vouch for your creditworthiness.

SMALL BUSINESS
EXTERNAL COMMUNICATION

16. Beanie Babies: Letter requesting credit from Ty, Inc. Bubbles (the fish), Inch (the worm), Ziggy (the zebra)—if you hear another parent ask for them, you're going to walk out the door of Sandy's Gifts and never return. No, not really. You love the brightly colored, fuzzy little bean-bag toys just as much as anyone, but you hate seeing adults look as disappointed as their kids when you tell them you don't carry them.

"You mean you don't even have Bongo the monkey? Or Pinky the flamingo?"

"Sorry, not yet," you apologize. "But we've had so many requests, we're hoping to have them in stock soon. If you leave your name and phone number . . ."

Sandy Applegate, the store's owner, is sympathetic when you tell her what's been happening, but she doesn't know what to do. Her cash flow situation just doesn't allow for any new stock purchases until after Christmas.

Who would have thought the $5 bean-bag animals (called "Beanie Babies" by manufacturer Ty, Inc.) would be so popular?

"But think of the sales we're missing," you interject. "Won't they give you credit?"

"Well, we've never done business with them before," Sandy says thoughtfully, "but you might have a point. After all, Sandy's Gifts has been in business for almost ten years, at the same location. How many retail shops can say that today? And our credit with other vendors is excellent. Why don't you give it a try? You've been wanting to learn more about managing the store, haven't you?"

She's right. This is a great opportunity!

Your task: Write a letter for Sandy's signature to New Account Sales, Ty, Inc., P.O. Box 5377, Oakbrook, Illinois 60522, requesting credit to purchase two dozen Beanie Babies. Introduce the store, its reputation, and the reasons Ty might like to comply.[19]

WHOLESALE
EXTERNAL COMMUNICATION

17. Canadian braids: Credit letter from Chassman & Bem Booksellers The American Booksellers Association Convention was one of the largest trade fairs you've attended since becoming a buyer for Chassman & Bem Booksellers. Although the Vermont retailer is considered a "small independent" store (compared to the big chains), owner Randy Chudnow's business has thrived because of his good service and large inventory. He financed your scouting trip particularly to round up new books by small publishers and individual authors.

So forgoing the acres of high-tech displays in the main exhibit arena (some seven football fields' worth), you scoured the small-press exhibit hall for likely possibilities among the clutter of 3-D poster publishers, one-book authors, incense sellers, and alternative lifestyle hawkers. A corner booth caught your attention: Instead of the typical display of books on a table in front, a middle-aged woman was standing in the booth, patiently braiding the long hair of a weary convention-goer who looked grateful to be sitting down. The braid swirled down the back of her head in an attractive S-pattern you'd never seen before. The back wall of the booth sported dozens of photographs of various braided hairstyles.

The braid designer was Andrea Jeffery from Calgary, author of two self-published books on braiding.

You've seen other books on hairstyling, but nothing with such detail. Ms. Jeffery pointed out that her books include precise directions on how the braiders should hold their hands to successfully duplicate her designs.

Back in Vermont, you decide to order some books from Andrea Jeffery. You want 50 copies each of *Braids and More* by Andrea Jeffery (ISBN 0-9693543-1-2) and *Braids and Styles for Long Hair* by Andrea Jeffery and Vickie Terner (ISBN 0-9693543-0-4). You'd like the transaction to be on a credit basis (90-day payment terms, no interest, payable in U.S. funds). The U.S. retail list price is $19.95 for each book, but your wholesale discount for ordering 50 or more copies is 50 percent (or $9.98 per book).

Your task: Write the order letter, addressing it to Andrea Jeffery, P.O. Box 73054, #206, 2525 Woodview Dr. S.W., Calgary, AB, T2W 6E4 Canada.[20]

Inquiring About People

CAREER DEVELOPMENT

INTERPERSONAL COMMUNICATION

18. Remember me? Request for someone to write a letter on your behalf You are applying for a job similar to one you held before. Alonzo Montoya, your former employer, knows something of your abilities and would probably be willing to comment on your qualifications for the new job. However, it's been a while since you worked for Mr. Montoya, and he knows relatively little about your more recent accomplishments and aspirations.

Your task: Write to Mr. Montoya, Investors Plus, at 4124 Beaumont Blvd., San Antonio, TX 78200, asking him whether he would be willing to write a letter of recommendation on your behalf to a potential employer. (As an alternative, write to an actual former employer.) Describe the job, and bring Mr. Montoya up-to-date on your accomplishments since you worked for him.

HUMAN RESOURCES

INTERCULTURAL COMMUNICATION

19. And his English? Letter to Ukrainian Central Bank checking on a reference Your firm, the Canadian Bank Note Company, landed a $32 million contract to print new currency for a new country—Ukraine. Now Canadian Bank Note has agreed to deliver 1.5 billion printed bills (enough to fill 39 jumbo jets) by June, which means an ordinary year's work must be completed in just six months. To meet the delivery schedule, many of Canadian Bank Note's 350 employees have been assigned new duties, and new employees are being hired every day. On your desk is an application from Gregory Kropivnitsky, who says he once worked for Ukrainian Central Bank, your partner in the currency contract. The human resources director has advised you to contact the Kiev bank to find out whether that's true. She also wants to know whether his position there was equivalent to a Canadian bank manager's position gained in Canadian banking tradition only after a long, slow climb from the bottom to the top.

Kropivnitsky is being considered for a position with a future printing operation planned as a joint venture between Canadian Bank Note and the Ukrainian government. The new company will be located in Kiev, but it will have all the printing capabilities of your Canadian facility. From that base, Canadian Bank Note hopes to land additional currency-printing contracts from countries that were once Soviet republics. If he's qualified, Kropivnitsky could end up in a managerial position at the Kiev facility.

Your task: Write the letter to Ukrainian Central Bank, Kiev, Ukraine, asking about Kropivnitsky's qualifications. Make a special inquiry about his language skills and his managerial and supervisory background.[21]

HUMAN RESOURCES

HORIZONTAL COMMUNICATION

20. Shopping for talent: Memo inquiring about an employee at Clovine's As manager of women's apparel for Clovine's, a growing chain of moderate to upscale department stores in South Florida, you are always looking for smart, aggressive young buyers. Right now, you're particularly in need of an assistant buyer for your women's sportswear division. Because Clovine's likes to promote from within, you've been scouting store personnel for likely candidates.

Angela Ramirez, a salesclerk in the designer sportswear boutique of your main store in Miami, has caught your attention. She's quick, friendly, and good at sizing up a customer's preferences. Moreover, at recent meetings, she's made some intelligent remarks about new trends in South Florida.

Angela's supervisor is Rachel Cohen, who is on vacation this week. When Rachel returns, you'll be out of town for two weeks. Rachel could help you decide whether to interview this salesclerk, yet you need to have a list of candidates when you return.

Your task: Write a memo to Rachel Cohen, sales supervisor, asking whether she has any information that would help you evaluate Angela Ramirez's qualifications for the promotion. Mention to Rachel that you'll check with the human resources department about Angela's education and employment history; you're mainly interested in Rachel's impression of Angela's potential for advancement. Ask any specific questions you consider appropriate, and indicate when you'd like to receive Rachel's comments.

WRITING ROUTINE, GOOD-NEWS, AND GOODWILL MESSAGES

CHAPTER
9

AFTER STUDYING THIS CHAPTER, YOU WILL BE ABLE TO

- Decide when to write a routine, good-news, or goodwill message
- Adjust the basic organizational pattern to fit the type of message you are writing
- Add resale and sales promotion material when appropriate
- Encourage your reader to take any desired action
- Write credit approvals and recommendation letters
- Use the correct form for such specialized messages as instructions and news releases
- Establish the proper tone when writing goodwill letters

COMMUNICATION CLOSE-UP AT STEINWAY & SONS

Steinway & Sons is a small New York company that has been turning out the "instruments of the immortals" for nearly a century and a half. Composer Franz Liszt called the Steinway grand piano "a glorious masterpiece in power, sonority, singing quality, and perfect harmonic effects." Elton John paints his Steinways orange. Vladimir Ashkenazy believes that "Steinway is the only piano on which the pianist can do everything he wants and everything he dreams."

These performers are listed among Steinway Artists, past and present, an impressive roster of 800 pianists who personally own a Steinway piano, choose to perform only on Steinways, and are not paid a dime for this affiliation. Artists join the voluntary list for the services the company provides them, says Peter Goodrich, Steinway's vice president of worldwide concert and artist department. These special services include not only providing artists with Steinway concert grands on which to perform and practice anywhere in the world but also listening to artists' needs and complaints.

Concert performers are Steinway & Sons' best advertisers. So Goodrich spends his working hours in routine communication with a culturally and musically diverse population of musicians and their agents—by telephone, fax, letter, note, and card. He attends their concerts (always evaluating the sound of the Steinway under their capable hands), and he sends goodwill greetings (sometimes with flowers) for birthdays, anniversaries, and other special events in the performers' lives. Most of all, he solicits honest feedback about the Steinways they play.

Founded in the United States in 1853 by German immigrant Heinrich Englehard Steinweg (who later Americanized his name), Steinway & Sons developed most of the innovations in piano technology during the last 150 years. Its competitors may turn out 200,000 pianos annually, but Steinway produces only 2,500 pianos a year. From the $10,000 upright to the $60,000 concert grand, each piano is a hand-built, one-of-a-kind

Peter Goodrich

In an effort to promote its image as the small company with a big reputation, Steinway goes to great lengths to communicate positive messages to its various audiences, from the famous Steinway Artists to the local piano technicians. Such messages clearly state the company's main idea while showing a genuine understanding of the audience.

instrument that takes 400 skilled craftspeople more than a year to complete, using the finest woods and thousands of working parts. However, such a piano means nothing without the pianist.

Goodrich has adopted an easy method for routine correspondence with these luminaries of the music world, so if Steinway's pianos ever lose their "magic," the vice president will be the first to know. Every Steinway Artist receives a packet of pre-addressed, postage-paid postcards. No matter where they perform, Goodrich asks them to fill out one of these "report cards" for the Steinway they played. As you might imagine, concert pianists are not only very particular but also highly sensitive—and very busy. So a good part of Goodrich's routine letter writing serves to remind them about the piano report cards.

For instance, after visiting pianist Misha Dichter backstage and handing him one of the report cards, Goodrich wrote to him the next day, "Your program was superb and, if I may say again, the Schubert Sonata—a favorite of mine—was exquisite." After offering Steinway's assistance for a future concert, Goodrich reminded Dichter that the company was eager to learn his thoughts about the Steinway CD-385 he'd played that night. The letter closed on a friendly, appreciative note.

Goodrich also responds to artists' complaints, thanking them and explaining what action Steinway has taken. In a letter to Vladimir Ashkenazy, Goodrich mentions a new Steinway he believes the pianist will enjoy; then he relates that technicians are inspecting the pianos in Boston and Denver that hadn't met Ashkenazy's expectations. Goodrich consciously avoids clichés, writing in a warm, polite, and concerned tone. The letter to Ashkenazy opened with genuine appreciation for a recent concert and closed with additional thanks for "an evening of memorable music" and with warmest holiday wishes to the pianist's family.

When a piano receives high praise, Goodrich passes on the artist's comments to the local piano technician who keeps the instrument in good condition. Skilled Steinway concert technicians are highly trained and few, so Goodrich also uses these letters to convey his company's gratitude and respect for their fine work.

As a Steinway representative, Goodrich carefully avoids exaggeration or excess flattery. "I try to emphasize the positive," he says. "There are a lot of different ways that you can be very positive and supportive and enthusiastic without being dishonest." For instance, after a piano competition, he sends congratulations to all the participants, letting them know that Steinway stands ready to assist them in the future.

"I want to impress upon the artists that, even though Steinway has a big reputation, we're actually a small company. We take a personal interest in our artists and in their own needs and expectations," Goodrich says. Whether sending flowers or writing a recommendation to help a client obtain a temporary work visa, "It's just an effort to let them know that we are thinking about them and that we appreciate the fact that they play our pianos."[1]

ORGANIZING POSITIVE MESSAGES

Most business communication consists of messages that present neutral information, answer requests positively, and establish better relationships, so you'll probably get a lot of practice composing these **routine, good-news,** and **goodwill messages.** In addition to using letters and memos, you may send many positive messages using e-mail

KEEPING PACE WITH TECHNOLOGY

THE POSSIBILITIES AND PERILS OF E-MAIL

It's too easy: Just tap out a few irate lines on your computer keyboard, push a few more keys, and zap! Your sizzling message is on its way to a fellow worker's screen, or perhaps to the screens of several hundred workers. It's called "flaming"—sending strong, ill-considered, uncensored messages flying from electron to electron to land on someone else's computer screen. In fact, at this very moment, your boss may be reading it and wondering how you can talk about her like that or why she ever thought such an emotional person belonged in her department.

Welcome to the possibilities and perils of e-mail, the latest communication mine field in the business world. E-mail has helped us all accomplish some amazing possibilities: bypassing telephone tag, saving postage, and cutting through time-zone lags to link company employees worldwide. At the same time, e-mail has proved perilous to employer and employee alike.

People treat e-mail far more informally than other forms of business communication, primarily because they perceive it as being impermanent. In fact, e-mail can be even more permanent than traditional business documents. Backup copies can exist not only on the sender's computer but also on the receiver's computer, on your company's network, and in the archives of any number of computers used by your commercial or Internet server to route your message.

Whenever employees misuse company e-mail, the company is liable. A Chevron subsidiary recently spent $2.2 million

to settle a sex discrimination lawsuit based, in part, on an e-mail message circulated to some 30 employees describing why beer was better than women. So to avoid expensive lawsuits, companies try to ensure that employee e-mail is responsible:

- By discouraging defamatory e-mail that disparages other employees or that directly harasses other employees with unwanted or offensive messages.
- By discouraging the distribution of copyrighted materials in e-mail without the permission of the copyright owner. Copyrights cover pictures, videos, and audio materials, as well as text, and copyright owners are vigorously pursuing infringement.
- By discouraging the inclusion of trade secrets and proprietary information in e-mail messages. During litigation, attorneys have found that employee e-mail often contains revealing and sometimes quite damaging admissions.

To ensure responsible e-mail, many companies monitor their employees' messages. Of course, they must do so without violating the 1986 Electronic Communications Privacy Act (ECPA)—which prohibits unauthorized interception of or access to e-mail stored on a computer system. Some companies comply with the ECPA by requiring employees to sign an agreement acknowledging (1) that the computer and e-mail system belong to the company and are to be used for business purposes (see "The Possibilities and Perils of E-mail"). Regardless of the media, however, understanding how positive messages are organized will allow you to compose excellent examples quickly. Of course, Steinway's Peter Goodrich knows that intercultural positive messages are best when organized according to the audience's expectations, but when you're communicating with a U.S. or Canadian audience whose cultural differences are minimal, use the direct plan. Whether written or oral, positive messages begin with a clear statement of the main idea, followed by any necessary details, and they end with a courteous close.

> Organizational plan for routine, good-news, and goodwill messages:
> • Main point
> • Details
> • Close

Clear Statement of the Main Idea

Almost all business communication has two basic purposes: (1) to convey information and (2) to produce in the audience a favorable (or at least accepting) attitude or response. When you begin a message with a statement of your purpose, you're preparing your audience for the explanation that follows. Make your opening clear and concise. The following introductory statements make the same point; however, one is cluttered with unnecessary information that buries the purpose, whereas the other is brief and to the point:

only and (2) that the company has the right to monitor employee e-mail.

As an employee, you naturally want to do whatever you can to protect your company from lawsuits. You also want to avoid the personal embarrassment that can arise from irresponsible e-mail:

- *Avoid sending a message to the wrong terminal(s).* When Microsoft's Bill Gates sent a message containing his fears for his company's future and his negative views of competitors, it reached many more terminals than intended, and Microsoft's stock dropped 8-1/8 points.
- *Avoid providing legal evidence against your company or yourself.* In a lawsuit, backup tapes, individual computers, and the company's network can all be thoroughly searched for relevant e-mail. This discovery process allows lawyers to uncover nearly forgotten e-mail messages—even those you thought you had deleted.
- *Avoid assuming your e-mail is private.* The newest software "policing" programs let managers monitor workers' e-mail baskets—even while they're still typing. "In some companies, e-mail can be as private as writing on the bathroom wall," cautions an e-mail analyst at International Data.
- *Avoid inundating people with useless or irrelevant information.* People are being overwhelmed by the sheer amount of e-mail they receive. One executive in the hu-

man resource department at Sun Microsystems gets 250 e-mail messages a day—of which she needs no more than 20.

Your e-mail reflects on you as well as on your company. So plan your e-mail messages with the same care and thought you would use to plan any other business message. The best way to avoid sending an angry message to the wrong terminal is not to send it at all. If you treat e-mail the same way you treat other business correspondence, you'll avoid saying anything you wouldn't want your boss, your colleagues, or a court judge to read. Whether you're putting your words on paper or on screen, consider the consequences of what you're trying to say—before you send it off. Then once you're sure the message should be sent, cut down the overload by including only one topic per message, by providing clear headers (subject lines) that allow readers to prioritize their mail, and by sending your e-mail only to those who need it (being sure to prepare your distribution lists carefully).

1. If it's your responsibility to announce a new product to the employees at your company, which employees would you send it to? Why?
2. If you must advise a client on a sensitive matter, is it okay to send your message via e-mail as long as you run it by your supervisor? Why or why not?

Instead of This	Write This
I am pleased to inform you that after deliberating the matter carefully, our human resources committee has recommended you for appointment as a staff accountant.	You've been selected to join our firm as a staff accountant, beginning March 20.

Before you begin, have a clear idea of what you want to say.

The best way to write a clear opening is to have a clear idea of what you want to say. Before you put one word on paper, ask yourself this: What is the single most important message I have for the audience?

Necessary Details

The middle part of a positive message is typically the longest section of a routine, good-news, or goodwill message. Your reason for communicating can usually be expressed in a sentence or two, but you'll need more space or time to explain your point completely so that your audience will have no confusion or lingering doubt. The task of providing necessary details is easiest when you're responding to a series of questions. You can simply answer them in order, possibly in a numbered sequence.

Answer questions in the order they were asked.

In addition to providing details in the middle section, maintain the supportive tone established at the beginning. This tone is easy to continue when your message is purely good news, as in this example:

> Your educational background and internship have impressed us, and we believe you would be a valuable addition to Green Valley Properties. As discussed during your interview, your salary will be $3,300 per month, plus benefits. In that regard, you will meet with our benefits manager, Paula Sanchez, at 8:00 A.M. on Monday, March 20. She will assist you with all the paperwork necessary to tailor our benefit package to your family situation. She will also arrange for various orientation activities to help you acclimate to our company.

Embed negative information in a positive context.

When a routine message must convey mildly disappointing information, put the negative answer into as favorable a context as possible. Look at the following example:

Instead of This	Write This
No, we no longer carry the Sportsgirl line of sweaters.	The new Olympic line has replaced the Sportsgirl sweaters that you asked about. Olympic features a wider range of colors and sizes and more contemporary styling.

A bluntly negative explanation was replaced with a more complete description that emphasized how the audience could benefit from the change. Be careful, though: You can use negative information in this type of message only if you're reasonably sure the audience will respond positively to your message. (Otherwise, use the indirect approach, which is described more thoroughly in Chapter 10.)

Courteous Close

Make sure the audience understands what to do next and how that action will benefit them.

Your message is most likely to succeed if your audience is left with the feeling that you have their personal welfare in mind—as when Steinway's Goodrich closed his letter to Vladimir Ashkenazy with genuine appreciation and warm holiday wishes to the artist's family. In addition, if follow-up action is required, clearly state who will do what next. By highlighting a benefit to the audience, this closing statement clearly summarizes the desired procedure: "Mail us your order this week so that you can be wearing your Shetland coat by the first of October."

As sales manager at Galpin Ford in the San Fernando Valley, James Kisho gives each request for information careful consideration, taking pains to reply as promptly as possible with all the information requested.

REPLYING TO REQUESTS FOR INFORMATION AND ACTION

Whether sent by snail mail, fax, or e-mail, many memos and letters are written in response to an inquiry or a request. If the answer is yes or is straightforward information, then the direct plan is appropriate. Any request is important to the person making it, whether inside or outside the organization. That person's opinion of your company and its products, your department, and you yourself will be influenced by how promptly, graciously, and thoroughly the request is handled. Readers' perceptions are the reason Peter Goodrich of Steinway is so sensitive to the tone of his memos, letters, and other messages.

Admittedly, complying with a request isn't always easy. The information may not be immediately at hand, and decisions to take some action must often be made at a higher level. Furthermore, because a letter written on letterhead stationery is legally binding, plan your response carefully.

Fortunately, however, many requests are similar. For example, a human resources department gets a lot of inquiries about job openings. Companies usually develop form responses to handle repetitive queries like these. Although form responses are often criticized as being cold and impersonal, you can put a great deal of thought into wording them, and you can use computers to personalize and mix paragraphs. Thus a computerized form letter prepared with care may actually be more personal and sincere than a quickly dictated, hastily typed "personal" reply.

When written on letterhead stationery, a reply legally commits the company to any promised action.

When a Potential Sale Is Involved

Prospective customers often request an annual report, a catalog, a brochure, a swatch of material, or some other type of sample or information to help them make a decision about a product encountered through advertising. A polite and helpful response may prompt them to buy. When the customer has not requested the information and is not looking forward to a response, you must use persuasive techniques like those described in Chapter 11. But in a "solicited" letter that the customer is anticipating, you may use the direct plan.

When you're answering requests and a potential sale is involved, you have three main goals: (1) To respond to the inquiry and answer all questions, (2) to encourage the future sale, and (3) to leave your reader with a good impression of you and your firm. The following letter succeeds in meeting these three objectives:

Three main goals when a potential sale is involved:
- *Respond to the immediate request*
- *Encourage a sale*
- *Convey a good impression of you and your firm*

You requested a copy of our brochure "Entertainment Unlimited," and Blue Ocean Communications is pleased to send it to you. This booklet describes the vast array of entertainment options available to you with an Ocean Satellite Device (OSD).

On page 12 of "Entertainment Unlimited," you'll find a list of the 138 channels that the OSD brings into your home. You'll have access to movie, sport, and music channels; 24-hour news channels; local channels; and all the major television networks. OSD gives you a clearer picture and more precise sound than those old-fashioned dishes that took up most of your yard—and OSD uses only a small dish that mounts easily on your roof.

More music, more cartoons, more experts, more news, and more sports are available to you with OSD than with any other cable or satellite connection in this region. Yes, it's all there, right at your fingertips.

Just call us at 1-800-786-4331, and an OSD representative will come to your home to answer your questions. You'll love the programming and the low monthly cost. Call us today!

> A clear, conversational statement of the main point is all that's required to start.
>
> Key information is presented immediately, along with resale and sales promotion.
>
> A reference to superior benefits of this product should encourage the reader to take one more steps toward an actual purchase.
>
> The personal close confidently points toward the possible sale.

When No Potential Sale Is Involved

Two goals when no sale is involved:
- **Respond to the request**
- **Leave a favorable impression of your company or foster good working relationships**

Some requests from outsiders and most requests from fellow employees are not opportunities to sell a product. In replies to those requests, you have two goals: (1) to answer all the questions honestly and completely and (2) to leave a favorable impression that prepares the way for future business or smoothes working relationships. Figure 9.1 is a well-written response to a request from an outsider that does not involve an immediate sale.

When writing to a fellow employee, you can use a less formal tone.

A similar approach is appropriate for responding to requests from fellow employees, although memo format is used (see Figure 9.2 on page 257). See this chapter's Checklist for Positive Replies, on page 258, to review the primary tasks involved in this type of business message.

RESPONDING FAVORABLY TO CLAIMS AND ADJUSTMENT REQUESTS

In general, it pays to give customers the benefit of the doubt.

As anyone in business knows, customers sometimes return merchandise to a company, complain about its services, ask to be compensated, and the like. Such complaints are golden opportunities for companies to build customer loyalty.[2] The most sensible reaction is to assume that the customer's account of the transaction is an honest statement of what happened—unless the same customer repeatedly submits dubious claims, a customer is patently dishonest (returning a dress that has obviously been worn, claiming it's the wrong size), or the dollar amount in dispute is very large. Few people go to the trouble of requesting an adjustment unless they actually have a problem. Once the complaint is made, however, customers may come to view the original transaction as less important than the events that come after the complaint.[3]

Julian Zamakis wrote to McBride Department Stores for information on employment opportunities and received the following encouraging reply.

Figure 9.1
In-Depth Critique: letter
Replying to Requests (No
Potential Sale)

— McBride —
Department Stores

781 Westchester Boulevard, Hartford, Connecticut 06108
(203) 758-7733 • Fax (203) 758-7703

November 30, 1997

Mr. Julian Zamakis
40106 Glastonbury Lane
Granby, CT 06035

Dear Mr. Zamakis:

Thanks for your letter requesting information on the professional career tracks at McBride Department Stores. As a retail chain with 47 stores in the New England states, we value those recent college graduates who accept entry-level professional positions each year. Your interest is important to us, so we are pleased to provide information on two professional career paths we offer here.

McBride has created career tracks in sales management and in merchandise management. Although each track offers similar promotional opportunities, you also have the option of switching tracks and gaining important experience in both areas of retailing.

The sales management track places college graduates on the sales floor, dealing with customers and supervising all sales-clerks in a given department. The first assignment is usually in a small department, but after two or three years' experience and satisfactory performance, the sales manager has an opportunity to be assigned to a substantially larger department. Part of a sales manager's responsibilities are meeting sales quotas, setting up displays, handling customer complaints, scheduling hours, and developing basic computer skills.

The merchandising track places college graduates as assistant buyers, where they work closely with an experienced buyer, reviewing sales figures, formulating the buying plan and budget, traveling to New York and Dallas, and following up on the sales

A brief statement indicates that the requested information will be provided and comments positively on the value of new college graduates to the company.

Specific information is given in answer to the questions posed by the writer.

(continued)

Figure 9.1
(Continued)

Mr. Julian Zamakis, November 30, 1997, Page 2

of the merchandise selected. After three to five years' experience and satisfactory performance, the assistant buyer has an opportunity to be promoted to a buyer position.

A warm, personalized closing generates goodwill for McBride and encourages the letter writer to keep in touch—with the possibility that McBride may wish to hire this person in the future.

In a year or so, when you're closer to receiving your degree, come in and talk with us about opportunities with McBride Stores. Meanwhile, you will receive a packet of materials providing more information on these career tracks and detailed descriptions of our entry-level positions. By asking questions while you're still preparing for your professional career, you'll improve your chances of pursuing the career you want. Good for you. Be sure to keep the exciting field of retailing in mind.

Sincerely,

Haley Middleton

Haley Middleton
Human Resources Manager

ss

Enclosures

When the Company Is at Fault

An ungracious adjustment may increase customer dissatisfaction.

The usual human response to a bad situation is to say, "It wasn't my fault!" However, businesspeople who receive requests for claims or adjustments can't take that stance. Even when the company's terms of adjustment are generous, a grudging tone can actually increase the customer's dissatisfaction.

To protect your company's image and to regain the customer's goodwill, refer to your company's errors carefully. Don't blame an individual or a specific department, and avoid such lame excuses as "Nobody's perfect" or "Mistakes will happen." Don't promise that problems will never happen again; such guarantees are unrealistic and often beyond your control. Instead, explain your company's efforts to do a good job; in so doing, you imply that the error was an unusual incident.

Imagine that a large mail-order clothing company has decided to create a form letter to respond to the hundreds of claims it receives each year. The most common customer complaint is not receiving exactly what was ordered. The form letter can be customized through word processing and is individually signed:

Your letter concerning your recent Klondike order has arrived and has been forwarded to our director of order fulfillment. Your complete satisfaction is our goal; when you are satisfied, then we are satisfied. Our customer service representative will contact you soon to assist with the issues raised in your letter.

Whether skiing or driving a snowmobile, Klondike Gear offers you the best protection from wind, snow, and cold—and Klondike has been taking care of your outdoor needs for over 27 years! Because you're a loyal customer, enclosed is a $5 gift certificate. You may wish to consider our new line of quality snow goggles.

This message is a reply from the advertising director written to a house-wares manager whose merchandise wasn't being featured correctly in regional newspaper ads. The tone of the memo, while still respectful, is a bit less formal than the tone in the letter in Figure 9.1.

Figure 9.2
In-Depth Critique: Memo Replying to a Routine Request

```
┌──────────────────────────────────────────────────┐
│ ▦         ▦▦▦▦▦▦  E-Mail  ▦▦▦▦▦▦          ▦ │
├──────────────────────────────────────────────────┤
│                                                    │
├──────────────────────────────────────────────────┤
│                                              ⬆    │
│ Date: Tuesday, 7 January 1997, 10:15:32           │
│ X-Sender: wsimmons@west.woolworth.com             │
│ To: "Avery Mendoza, Housewares Manager"           │
│       <amendoza@lvn.woolworth.com>                │
│ From: "Wilimina Simmons" <wsimmons@west.woolworth.com> │
│ Subject: Sale ads for 12-ounce glass tumblers      │
│                                                    │
│                                                    │
│ Dear Mr. Mendoza:                                  │
│                                                    │
│ At last we've traced the problem and corrected the │
│ newspaper ads you alerted us to in your last message: │
│                                                    │
│ 1. Incorrect stock numbers have been corrected and │
│    cross-checked on all paperwork, both at the main │
│    warehouse and in advertising.                   │
│ 2. The ads that mistakenly featured 20-ounce glass │
│    tumblers have been revised to feature the 12-ounce │
│    glass tumblers you intended.                    │
│ 3. Ad layout people have been alerted to clear all │
│    future discrepancies with department managers.  │
│                                                    │
│ Apparently, the housewares vendor transposed the item │
│ numbers for these glasses on the packing slips, and the │
│ error made its way all the way through inventory at our │
│ main warehouse and onto our stock-number sheets here in │
│ the advertising department. So every time you sent us │
│ your weekly features for 12-ounce glass tumblers (stock │
│ number HW779-898), our layout people traced the number │
│ on our stock sheets and mistakenly came up with 20-ounce │
│ tumblers.                                          │
│                                                    │
│ I know you had to sell the more expensive 20-ounce │
│ tumblers for the 12-ounce sale price until we could get │
│ the ads corrected. I'm sending a message to your store │
│ manager, explaining the mix-up and taking full     │
│ responsibility for it. If there is any way I can help │
│ you with ad features in the future, please contact me. │
│                                                    │
│ Thanks,                                            │
│                                                    │
│ Wilimina Simmons                                   │
│ Regional Advertising Director                      │
└──────────────────────────────────────────────────┘
```

The good news is announced without any fanfare, and the specific actions are enumerated for easy reference.

The problem's cause and eventual solution are explained to demonstrate awareness and goodwill.

An appreciative, personal, cooperative close confirms the desire to foster good working relationships.

CHECKLIST FOR POSITIVE REPLIES

A. INITIAL STATEMENT OF THE GOOD NEWS OR MAIN IDEA

1. Respond promptly to the request.
2. Indicate in your first sentence that you are shipping the customer's order or fulfilling the reader's request.
3. Avoid such trite and obvious statements as "I am pleased to," "We have received," "This is in response to," or "Enclosed please find."
4. If you are acknowledging an order, summarize the transaction.
   a. Describe the merchandise in general terms.
   b. Express appreciation for the order and the payment, if it has arrived.
   c. Welcome a new customer aboard.
5. Convey an upbeat, courteous, you-oriented tone.

B. MIDDLE, INFORMATIONAL SECTION

1. Imply or express interest in the request.
2. If possible, answer all questions and requests, preferably in the order posed.
   a. Adapt replies to the reader's needs.
   b. Indicate what you have done and will do.
   c. Include any necessary details or interpretations that the reader may need in order to understand your answers.
3. Provide all the important details about orders.
   a. Provide any necessary educational information about the product.
   b. Provide details of the shipment, including the approximate arrival time.
   c. Clear up any questions of charges (shipping costs, insurance, credit charges, or discounts for quick payment).
4. Use sales opportunities when appropriate.
   a. Enclose a brochure that provides routine information and specifications, if possible, pointing out its main value and the specific pages of potential interest to the reader.
   b. Call the customer's attention to related products with sales promotion material.
   c. Introduce price only after mentioning benefits, but make price and the method of payment clear.
   d. Send a credit application to new customers and cash customers, if desirable.
5. If you cannot comply with part of the request, perhaps because the information is unavailable or confidential, tell the reader why this is so, and offer other assistance.
6. Embed negative statements in positive contexts, or balance them with positive alternatives.

C. WARM, COURTEOUS CLOSE

1. Avoid clichés ("Please feel free to").
2. Direct a request to the reader (such as "Please let us know if this procedure does not have the effect you're seeking") or specify the action you want the reader to take, if appropriate.
   a. Make the reader's action easy.
   b. Refer to the reader benefit of fulfilling your request.
   c. Encourage the reader to act promptly.
3. Use resale material when acknowledging orders to remind the reader of benefits to be derived from this order.
4. Offer additional service, but avoid suggestions of your answer's being inadequate, such as "I trust that," "I hope," or other doubtful statements.
5. Express goodwill or take an optimistic look into the future, if appropriate.

Thank you for taking the time to write to us. Your input helps us better serve you and all our customers.

This letter exemplifies the following points:

You may send form letters in response to claims, but word them carefully so that they are appropriate in a variety of circumstances.

- Because a form letter like this is sent to people with various types of requests or complaints, it cannot start with a clear good-news statement.
- The letter starts instead with what might be called a "good attitude" statement; it is you-oriented to put the customer at ease.

- At no time does this letter suggest that the customer was mistaken in writing to Klondike about the order in question.
- The letter includes some resale and sales promotion, made more personal by the use of *you*.
- The letter closes with a statement of the company's concern for all its customers.

A claim letter written as a personal answer to a unique situation would start with a clear statement of the good news: the settling of the claim according to the customer's request. Here is a more personal response from Klondike Gear:

> Here is your heather-blue wool-and-mohair sweater (size large) to replace the one returned to us with a defect in the knitting on the left sleeve. Thanks for giving us the opportunity to correct this situation. Customers' needs have come first at Klondike Gear for 27 years. Our sweaters are handmade by the finest knitters in this area, and Klondike inspects all our sweaters before sending them on to our customers.
>
> Our newest catalog is enclosed. Browse through it, and see what wonderful new colors and patterns we have for you. Whether you are skiing or driving a snowmobile, Klondike Gear offers you the best protection available from wind, snow, and cold. Let us know how we may continue to serve you and your sporting needs.

When the Buyer Is at Fault

Say that a customer is technically wrong (he washed a permanent-press shirt in hot water) but feels he's right ("The washing instructions were impossible to find!"). You can refuse the claim and attempt to justify this refusal to the customer, or you can simply do what the customer asks. As you try to decide which course to take, remember that refusing to make an adjustment may mean losing that customer as well as many of the customer's friends, who will hear only one side of the dispute. It makes sense, therefore, to weigh the cost of making the adjustment against the cost of losing future business from one or more customers.

If you choose not to contest the claim, start off with a statement of the good news: You're replacing the merchandise or refunding the purchase price. The explanatory section needs more attention, however. Your job is to make the customer realize that the merchandise was mistreated without falling into a tone that is condescending ("Perhaps you failed to read the instructions carefully") or preachy ("Next time, please allow the machine to warm up before using it at full power"). The dilemma is this: If the customer fails to realize what went wrong, you may commit your firm to an endless procession of returned merchandise; but if you insult the customer, your cash refund will have been wasted because the customer will make his or her next purchase elsewhere. Keep in mind that a courteous tone is especially important to the success of your message, regardless of the solution you propose (see Figure 9.3 on pages 260–261).

When complying with an unjustified claim, let the customer know that the merchandise was mistreated, but maintain a respectful and positive tone.

When a Third Party Is at Fault

At times a customer will submit a legitimate claim for a defect or damage that was not caused by either of you. If the merchandise was damaged while in transit, the carrier is responsible. If the defect was caused by the manufacturer, you have a claim for replacement from that firm.

When a third party is at fault, you have three options: (1) Honor the customer's claim with the standard good-news letter and no additional explanation; (2) honor the claim but explain that you were not really at fault; or (3) take no action on the claim and suggest that your customer file against the firm that caused the defect or damage.

Three options when a third party is at fault:
- *Honor the claim*
- *Honor the claim with an explanation of what went wrong*
- *Refer the customer to the third party for satisfaction of the claim*

Figure 9.3
In-Depth Critique: Letter Responding to a Claim When the Buyer Is at Fault

Without being offensive, the following letter educates a customer about how to treat his in-line skates.

20901 El Dorado Hills
Laguna Niguel, CA 92677
(714) 332-7474 • Fax: (714) 336-5297
skates@speed.net

February 7, 1997
Mr. Steven Cox
1172 Amber Court
Jacksonville, FL 32073

Dear Mr. Cox:

A brief statement acknowledges the problem and conveys the good news.

Thank you for letting us know about the problem with your in-line skates. Although your six-month warranty has expired, we are mailing you a complete wheel assembly replacement free of charge. The enclosed instructions make removing the damaged wheel line and replacing the new one relatively easy. If you prefer to have a technician replace the wheel assembly, please present this letter to your authorized dealer.

Here, the writer explains the problem without blaming the customer and suggests ways to avoid future problems.

The "Fastrax" (model NL 562) you purchased is our best selling and most reliable skate. However, wheel jams may occur when fine particles of sand block the smooth rotating action of the wheels. These skates perform best when used on roadways and tracks that are relatively free of sand. We suggest that you remove and clean the wheel assemblies (see enclosed directions) once a month and have them checked by your dealer about every six months.

The writer uses the opportunity to encourage the customer to "trade up," showing how to turn negative feelings about a product into future sales.

Because of your Florida location, you may want to consider our more advanced "Glisto" (model NL 988) when you decide to purchase new skates. Although more expensive than the Fastrax, the Glisto design helps shed sand and dirt quite efficiently and should provide years of trouble-free skating.

Finally, the writer adds value by enclosing a newsletter that invites future response from the customer.

Enjoy the enclosed copy of 'Rock & Roll," with our compliments. Inside, you'll read about new products, hear from other skaters, and have an opportunity to respond to our customer questionnaire.

Common business sense tells you, however, that the third option is almost always a bad choice. (The exception is when you're trying to dissociate yourself from any legal responsibility for the damaged merchandise, especially if it has caused a personal injury, in which case you would send a bad-news message.)

Of the other two options, the first is more attractive. By honoring the claim without explanation, you are maintaining your reputation for fair dealing at no cost to your-

Figure 9.3
(Continued)

Mr. Steven Cox, February 7, 1997, Page 2

We love hearing from our skaters, so keep in touch. All of us at SkatesAlive! wish you good times and miles of healthy skating.

Sincerely,

Candace Parker

Candace Parker
Customer Service Representative

Enclosure

The letter ends on a positive, "feel good" note that conveys an attitude of excellent customer service.

self; the carrier or manufacturer that caused the damage in the first place will reimburse you. Nevertheless, you may want to provide an explanation to the customer, possibly to correct any impression that the damage was caused by your negligence. In that case, you can still write the standard good-news letter, but stress the explanation. (To review the tasks involved in this type of message, see this chapter's Checklist for Favorable Responses to Claims and Adjustment Requests on page 262.)

APPROVING ROUTINE CREDIT REQUESTS

These days much of our economy runs on credit. Consumers often carry a wallet full of plastic credit cards, and businesses of all sizes operate more smoothly because they can pay for their purchases over time. Because credit is so common, most credit requests are routine.

Letters approving credit are good-news messages and the first step in what may be a decades-long business relationship. So open your letter with the main idea.

In the middle section, include a reasonably full statement of the credit arrangements: the upper limit of the account, dates that bills are sent, possible arrangements for partial monthly payments, discounts for prompt payments, interest charges for unpaid balances, and due dates. State the terms positively and objectively, not negatively or in an authoritarian manner:

State credit terms factually and in terms of the benefits of having credit.

Instead of This	**Write This**
Your credit balance cannot exceed $5,000.	With our standard credit account, you can order up to $5,000 worth of fine merchandise.
We expect your payment within 30 days of receipt of our statement.	Payment is due 30 days after you receive our statement.

Because the letter approving credit is considered a legal document, check the wording for accuracy, completeness, and clarity.

The final section of the letter provides resale information and sales promotion highlighting the benefits of buying from you. The following letter was written both to approve credit and to bring in customers:

Include resale and sales promotion information in a credit letter.

CHECKLIST FOR FAVORABLE RESPONSES TO CLAIMS AND ADJUSTMENT REQUESTS

A. INITIAL STATEMENT OF THE GOOD NEWS OR MAIN IDEA

1. State immediately your willingness to honor the reader's claim.
2. Accept your reader's account as entirely accurate unless good business reasons demand a different interpretation of some points.
3. Adopt a tone of consideration and courtesy; avoid being defensive, recriminatory, or condescending.
4. Thank the reader for taking the time to write.

B. MIDDLE, INFORMATIONAL SECTION

1. Minimize or, if possible, omit any disagreements with your reader's interpretation of events.
2. Maintain a supportive tone through such phrases as "Thank you for," "May we ask," "Please let us know," and "We are glad to work with you."
3. Apologize only under extreme circumstances; then do so crisply and without an overly apologetic tone.
4. Admit your firm's faults carefully.
   a. Avoid blaming any particular person or office.
   b. Avoid implying general company inefficiency.
   c. Avoid blaming probability ("Mistakes will happen").
   d. Avoid making unrealistic promises about the future.
   e. Remind the reader of your firm's quality controls.
5. Be careful when handling the customer's role in producing the problem.
   a. If appropriate, honor the claim in full but without negative comment.
   b. If appropriate, provide an objective, non-vindictive, impersonal explanation.

C. WARM, COURTEOUS CLOSE

1. Clarify any necessary actions that your reader must take.
2. Remind the reader of how you have honored the claim.
3. Avoid negative information.
4. Encourage the customer to look favorably on your company and/or the product in question (resale information).
5. Encourage the customer to continue buying other goods from you (sales promotion), but avoid seeming greedy.

Congratulations! Your credit application to Jake's Building Center has been approved, with $3,000 in credit available to you. Just use the enclosed card when you shop at any of our three Jake's Building Centers. With this card, you can purchase tools, appliances, paint, plumbing and electrical supplies, lawn products, and much more.

Our statements are sent out on the twentieth of each month and will list each credit purchase, the total amount due, and the monthly payment due. If you pay the total amount by the fifteenth of the following month, no interest is charged. If you elect to pay the smaller monthly amount, interest will be calculated at the rate of 1½ percent on the amount still owed and added to your next statement.

Jake's Building Centers are located in Murphysboro, Pinkneyville, and Carbondale, Illinois, with free delivery within 50 miles of each store. Come to us for everything you need to build, repair, or remodel your home or business. Count on our high quality and low prices whenever you purchase one of our top-of-the-line products. Come see us for your next building project!

The good-news opening gets right to the point.

An objective statement of the terms constitutes a legal contract. Positive, you-oriented wording avoids an authoritarian tone.

The courteous close provides resale for the store and sales promotion noting a range of customer benefits.

CHECKLIST FOR CREDIT APPROVALS

A. INITIAL STATEMENT OF THE GOOD NEWS OR MAIN IDEA

1. Cheerfully tell the reader that he or she now has approved credit with your firm.
2. Tell the reader, with brief resale, that he or she will soon be enjoying the use of any goods that were ordered with the request; specify the date and method of shipment and other purchase details.
3. Establish a tone of mutual warmth and trust.

B. MIDDLE, INFORMATIONAL SECTION

1. Explain the conditions under which credit was granted.
2. Include or attach a full explanation of your firm's credit policies and expectations of payment.
3. Stress the advantages of prompt payment in a way that assumes your reader will take advantage of them ("When you pay your account in full within ten days . . .").
4. Include legally required disclosure statements.
5. Inform or remind the reader of the general benefits of doing business with your firm (resale).
   a. Tell the consumer about free parking, mail and phone shopping, personalized shopping services, your home-decorating bureau, bridal consultants, restaurants, child care, gift wrapping, free deliveries, special discounts or purchase privileges, and other benefits, if your firm offers them.
   b. If the customer is a retailer or wholesaler, tell about nearby warehouses, factory representatives, quantity discounts, free window or counter displays, national advertising support, ads for local newspapers and other media, repair services, manuals, factory guarantees, prompt and speedy deliveries, toll-free phone number, research department, and other benefits, if your firm offers them.
6. Inform or remind the reader of a special sale, discount, or promotion (sales promotion).
7. Avoid exaggerations or flamboyant language that might make this section of your letter read like an advertisement.

C. WARM, COURTEOUS CLOSE

1. Summarize the reasons the reader will enjoy doing business with your firm.
2. Use the "you" attitude, and avoid clichés.
3. Invite the reader to a special sale or the like or provide resale information to motivate him or her to use the new account.

See this chapter's Checklist for Credit Approvals to quickly review the tasks involved in this type of message.

CONVEYING POSITIVE INFORMATION ABOUT PEOPLE

Professors, supervisors, and managers are often asked to write letters recommending students or employees for jobs, and nearly anyone may be asked to recommend acquaintances for awards, membership in organizations, and other honors. Such letters may take the direct approach when the recommendation is generally positive. Employers use the same type of organizational plan when telling job applicants the good news—that they got the job.

Recommendation Letters

Letters of recommendation have an important goal: to convince readers that the person being recommended has the characteristics required for the job or other benefit. It is important, therefore, that they contain all the relevant details:

- The full name of the candidate
- The job or benefit that the candidate is seeking
- Whether the writer is answering a request or taking the initiative
- The nature of the relationship between the writer and the candidate
- Facts relevant to the position or benefit sought
- The writer's overall evaluation of the candidate's suitability for the job or benefit sought

A recommendation letter presenting negatives may be carefully worded to satisfy both the candidate and the person or company requesting information.

Recommendation letters are usually confidential; that is, they're sent directly to the person or committee who requested them and are not shown to the candidate. However, recent litigation has made it advisable in some situations to prepare a carefully worded letter that satisfies both parties.

Oddly enough, the most difficult recommendation letters to write are those for truly outstanding candidates. Your audience will have trouble believing uninterrupted praise for someone's talents and accomplishments. So illustrate your general points with a specific example or two that point out the candidate's abilities, and discuss the candidate's abilities in relation to the "competition."

Two devices for convincing the reader when the candidate is outstanding:
- Use examples
- Use comparisons with the "competition"

Most candidates aren't perfect, however. Omitting reference to a candidate's shortcomings may be tempting, especially if the shortcomings are irrelevant to the demands of the job in question. Even so, you have an obligation to your audience, to your own conscience, and even to the better-qualified candidate who's relying on honest references to refer to any shortcoming that is serious and related to job performance. Moreover, you may be held liable for omitting negative information, especially if doing so poses a foreseeable and substantial risk of physical harm to others.[4]

A serious shortcoming cannot be ignored, but beware of being libelous:
- Include only relevant, factual information
- Avoid value judgments
- Balance criticisms with favorable points

Of course, the danger in writing a critical letter is that you might engage in libel—that is, make a false and malicious written statement that injures the candidate's reputation. On the other hand, if that negative information is truthful and relevant, it may be unethical and illegal to omit it from a recommendation. So if you must refer to a possible shortcoming, you can best protect yourself by sticking to the facts and placing your criticism in the context of a generally favorable recommendation, as in Figure 9.4.

To explore the topic further, see "Recommendation Letters: What's Right to Write?" on pages 266-267. You can also avoid trouble by asking yourself the following questions before mailing a recommendation letter:

- Does the person receiving this frank, personal information have a legitimate right to the information?
- Does all the information I have presented relate directly to the job or other benefit being sought?
- Have I put the candidate's case as strongly as I honestly can?
- Have I avoided overstating the candidate's abilities or otherwise misled the reader?
- Have I based all my statements on firsthand knowledge and provable facts?

Good News About Employment

Finding suitable job applicants and then selecting the right person is a task fraught with hard choices and considerable anxiety. In contrast, writing a letter to the successful applicant is a pleasure. Most of the time, such a letter is eagerly awaited, so the direct approach is appropriate:

> **Welcome to Lake Valley Rehabilitation Center. A number of excellent candidates were interviewed, but your educational background and recent**

Figure 9.4
*In-Depth Critique:
Recommendation Letter*

In this letter the writer supports her statements with facts and steers clear of vague, critical judgments.

S I N G H
Marketing Systems

789 E. Eisenhower Parkway, Ann Arbor, Michigan 48108-3275
Voice: (313) 930-3905 ■ Fax: (313) 930-3906
www.singh.com

March 13, 1997

Mr. Henry Paltrow
Marketing Director
Massy Young, Inc.
767 Canal Street, Suite B
Houston, TX 77061

Dear Mr. Paltrow:

I am pleased to recommend Zhe-Sheng Cheng for the marketing position at Massy Young, Inc. Zhe-Sheng has worked summers with us for the past two years, while working toward his degree in marketing and advertising.

As his supervisor, in addition to knowing his work here at SMS, I also know that Zhe-Sheng has served as secretary for the International Business Association at the University of Michigan. In addition, he tutored other international students in the university's writing center. His fluency in three languages and thorough knowledge of other cultures will make him an immediate contributor to your international operation. Although a quiet, introspective young man, Zhe-Sheng will not hesitate to contribute ideas when invited to do so. In addition, because Zhe-Sheng learns quickly, he will have no problem learning your company's routine.

I believe Zhe-Sheng will make an excellent addition to the staff of Massy Young. If you would like to further discuss Zhe-Sheng's qualifications, please call or fax me at the numbers above. I can be hard to catch at my desk, so you might want to contact me at Jenai@Singh.aol.com so that I can call you.

Sincerely,

Jenai L. Singh

Jenai L. Singh
Senior Partner

The candidate's full name and the main point are clearly stated.

The duration and nature of the relationship are specified to give weight to the evaluation.

A supportive, personal summary of the writer's evaluation provides a good close. The phone number and invitation to discuss the candidacy constitute another helpful touch.

experience at Memorial Hospital make you the best person for the position of medical records coordinator.

As we discussed, your salary is $26,200 a year. We would like you to begin on Monday, February 1. Please come to my office at 8:00 A.M. I will give you an in-depth orientation to Lake Valley and discuss the various company

FOCUSING ON ETHICS

RECOMMENDATION LETTERS: WHAT'S RIGHT TO WRITE?

You were Frank Walker's supervisor for four years. When he left the company recently, he asked you to write a letter of recommendation for him. However, your company's legal experts said, "Don't do it."

Why Not Give Recommendations?

Why? Because thousands of lawsuits have been filed (and won) by employees charging former employers with making slanderous (oral) and libelous (written) statements in job recommendations. In one seven-year period in California, employees won 72 percent of libel and related suits they brought against employers, and the average award was $582,000. One employer lost its case for saying an employee had "suddenly resigned," which implied (according to the court) that the employee had resigned under "a veil of suspicion." Another employer lost its case for saying an employee was fired "for causes." Furthermore, when employees prove that actual malice is involved, damage awards skyrocket.

In addition, a recent court ruling has held an employer liable for omitting information about a former employee. So

companies may well be confused about what sort of information should and should not be included in a recommendation. Even though some states are trying to make it easier for employers to be more open about employee performance, legal and human resources experts often advise companies to centralize all recommendations to maintain better control over what's being said. The cautious approach is to supply only dates of employment and titles of positions held—and to give that information only to people who have a legitimate right to know (or who have written authorization from former employees).

What If You Want to Give a Recommendation?

You have an ethical dilemma: Frank Walker was a terrific employee, a good friend, and someone you'd really like to help succeed. How can you refuse his request for a recommendation that you believe he really deserves? The experts suggest two alternatives. The first option is to write the letter of recommendation with Walker so that the contents satisfy both of you. Then, to be certain you're not violating company policy,

---

benefits available to you. You can also sign all the necessary employment documents.

After lunch, Vanessa Jackson will take you to the medical records department and help you settle into your new responsibilities at Lake Valley Home. I look forward to seeing you first thing on February 1.

This letter takes a friendly, welcoming tone, and it explains the necessary details: job title, starting date, salary, and benefits. The explanation of the first day's routine helps allay the bewilderment and uncertainty that might afflict the new employee.

A letter telling someone that she or he got the job is a legal document, so make sure all statements are accurate.

Although letters like these are pleasant to write, they constitute a legal job offer. You and your company may be held to any promises you make. So attorneys sometimes recommend stating salary as a monthly amount and keeping the timing of performance evaluations and raises vague; you want to avoid implying that the newly hired employee will be kept on, no matter what, for a whole year or until the next scheduled evaluation.[5]

WRITING DIRECTIVES AND INSTRUCTIONS

Directives tell employees what to do; instructions tell readers how to do something.

Directives are memos that tell employees *what* to do. Instructions tell people inside and outside the company *how* to do something and may take the form of e-mail messages, memos, letters, or even booklets. Directives and instructions are both considered routine messages because readers are assumed to be willing to comply.

The goal in writing directives and instructions is to make the point so obvious and the steps so self-explanatory that readers won't have to ask for additional help. Directives and instructions are especially important within companies: Faulty internal

discuss the letter with your human resources department before releasing it. (Walker's agreement with the contents should reassure the legal department.) If your employer is still uncomfortable, the second option is to ask Walker to list you as a *personal* reference. This removes your company from any responsibility for statements you make and gives you the freedom to say what you like. Even so, whether you're acting as a company or a personal reference, you can be held personally responsible for your comments. In fact, a common legal defense among corporations is to prove that the person who made the recommendation was acting outside company policy and should therefore be accountable for the entire amount of the lawsuit.

What If You'd Rather Not Give a Recommendation?

Of course, if it had been Sharon Brown who had asked for a recommendation, you'd be facing a different ethical dilemma. Brown wasn't the greatest employee, so do you owe her potential employer the whole story? Negative information could get you sued by Brown, and leaving out negative information could make you liable for "negligent referral" in a lawsuit filed by the hiring company. Of course, what was negative in one job situation could be irrelevant in another, so you may have no reason to convey the negative information at all. Again, consult your human resources or legal department to be sure you're supplying sufficient information and to be certain your wording is impersonal.

Regardless of the circumstances, be sure to (1) comment only on your own direct experience working with any former employee, (2) make all comments in writing, and (3) limit your remarks to provable facts (that is, don't exaggerate). Remember that honesty, integrity, and prudence are the foundations of legality and good business ethics.

1. One of your former employees was often late for work but was an excellent and fast worker and got along well with everyone. Do you think it's important to mention the tardiness to potential employers? If so, how will you handle it?
2. Step outside yourself for a moment and write a letter of recommendation about yourself from a former employer's perspective. Practice honesty, integrity, and prudence.

directives and bungled instructions are expensive and inefficient. The following directive does a good job of explaining what employees are expected to do:

> All employees will be issued new security badges between January 20 and January 24. Each employee must report in person to the human resources office (Building B, Room 106) to exchange the old (red) security badges for the new (yellow) security passes. The electronic security system will not recognize the old badges on February 1 and thereafter.
>
> If you are unable to make this exchange between January 20 and January 24, contact Theresa Gomez before January 15 either by phone at 4-6721 or by e-mail at <tgomez@biotech.com>.

This directive is brief and to the point. Drawn-out explanations are unnecessary because readers are expected simply to follow through on a well-established procedure. Yet it also covers all the bases, answering these questions: Who? What? When? Where? Why? How?

Instructions answer the same questions, but they differ from directives in the amount of explanation they provide. Peter Goodrich of Steinway might write a simple three-sentence directive to concert technicians to tell them of a change in the policies regarding employee travel expenses; however, a detailed set of instructions would be more appropriate for explaining the procedure necessary to submit such expenses for reimbursement.

When writing instructions, take nothing for granted. Assuming that readers know nothing about the process you're describing is better than risking confusion and possible damage or harm by overlooking some basic information. Figure 9.5 (see page 268) is a set of instructions for writing instructions.

Figure 9.5
Instructions for Writing Instructions

How to Write Instructions

When you need to explain in writing how to do something, a set of instructions is your best choice. By enumerating the steps, you make it easy for readers to perform the process in the correct sequence. Your goal is to provide a clear, self-sufficient explanation so that readers can perform the task independently.

Gather Equipment Needed
1. Writing materials (pen and paper, typewriter, computer)
2. Background materials (previous memos, policy manuals, manufacturer's booklets, etc.)
3. When necessary, the apparatus being explained (machine, software package, or other equipment)

Prepare to Write Useful Instructions
1. Perform the task yourself, or ask experts to demonstrate it or describe it to you in detail.
2. Analyze prospective readers' familiarity with the process so that you can write instructions at their level of understanding.

Make Your Instructions Clear
1. Include four elements as needed: an introduction, a list of equipment and materials, a description of the steps involved in the process, and a conclusion.
2. Explain in the opening why the process is important and how it relates to a larger purpose.
3. Divide the process into short, simple steps presented in order of occurrence.
4. Present the steps in a numbered list, or present them in paragraph format, making plentiful use of words indicating time or sequence, such as *first* and *then*.
5. If the process involves more than ten steps, divide them into groups or stages identified with headings.
6. Phrase each step as a command ("Do this" instead of "You should do this"); use active verbs ("Look for these signs" instead of "Be alert for these signs"); use precise, specific terms ("three weeks" instead of "several weeks").
7. When appropriate, indicate how readers may tell whether a step has been performed correctly and how one step may influence another. Supply warnings when performing a step incorrectly could result in damage or injury, but limit the number of warnings so that readers do not underestimate their importance.
8. Include diagrams of complicated devices, and refer to them in appropriate steps.
9. Summarize the importance of the process and the expected results in the conclusion.

Test Your Instructions
1. Review the instructions to be sure they are clear and complete. Also judge whether you have provided too much detail.
2. Ask someone else to read the instructions and tell you whether they make sense and are easy to follow.

WRITING BUSINESS SUMMARIES

Writing summaries involves
• Gathering information
• Organizing information
• Presenting information in your own words

Businesspeople are bombarded with masses of information, and at one time or another, everyone in business relies on someone else's summary of a situation, publication, or document. To write a summary, gather the information (whether by reading, talking with others, or observing circumstances), organize that information, and then present it in your own words. Although many people assume summarizing is a simple skill, it's actually more complex than it appears. A well-written summary has at least three characteristics.

First, as in writing any business document, be sure the content is accurate. If you're summarizing a report or a group of reports, make sure you present the information without error. Check your references, and then check for typos.

Second, make your summary comprehensive and balanced. The purpose of writing your summary is usually to help colleagues or supervisors make a decision, so include all the information necessary for your readers to understand the situation, problem, or proposal. If the issue you're summarizing has more than one side, present all sides fairly and equitably. Make sure you include all the information necessary. Even though summaries are intended to be as brief as possible, your readers need a minimum amount of information to grasp the issue being presented.

Third, make your sentence structure clear, and include good transitions.[6] The only way your summary will save anyone's time is if your sentences are uncluttered, use well-chosen words, and proceed logically. Then to help your readers move from one point to the next, your transitions must be just as clear and logical. Basically, when writing your summary, be sure to cut through the clutter. Identify those ideas that belong together, and organize them in a way that's easy to understand.[7]

Three characteristics of a well-written summary:
- Accuracy
- Comprehensiveness and balance
- Clear sentence structure and good transitions

CONVEYING GOOD NEWS ABOUT PRODUCTS AND OPERATIONS

It's good business to spread the word about such positive developments as the opening of new facilities, the appointment of a new executive, the introduction of new products or new customer services, or the sponsorship of community events. Imagine that So-Good Foods has successfully introduced a new line of vegetable chips to the stores it serves (carrot, turnip, and yam chips—not the same old potato chips). To maintain its position on supermarket shelves, So-Good decides to offer a new discount program to stores that buy large quantities of its vegetable chips. It supplements the personal visits of its sales force with a good-news message describing the new program to existing customers. The letter begins by trumpeting the news, fills in the details of the discount program in the middle, and closes with a bit of resale information and a confident prediction of a profitable business relationship.

When the audience for a good-news message is large and scattered, however, it's usually easier to communicate through the mass media. When McDonald's opened its first restaurant in Moscow, it sent announcements to newspapers, magazines, radio stations, and TV networks. The specialized documents used to convey such information to the media are called **news releases.** Written to match the style of the medium they are intended for, news releases are typed on plain 8 1/2-by-11-inch paper or on special letterhead—not on regular letterhead—and they're double-spaced for print media or triple-spaced for electronic media. Figure 9.6 (see page 270) illustrates the correct format. The content of this news release follows the customary pattern for a good-news message: good news, followed by details and a positive close. However, it avoids explicit references to any reader, displaying the "you" attitude by presenting information presumed to be of interest to all readers. To write a successful news release, keep the following points in mind:[8]

Specially formatted news releases convey good news to the media, which in turn disseminate it to the public.

- Include no marketing or sales material in your news release.
- Put your most important idea first (Don't say "Calco's president James Grall announced today that the company will move its headquarters to the Main Street

Figure 9.6
In-Depth Critique: News Release Format

The following news release demonstrates the proper format for the particular medium targeted (in this case, the medium is print).

NEWS RELEASE

FOR IMMEDIATE RELEASE
July 9, 1997

CONTACT: Wade Hyde
(214) 854 - 3196

BLOCKBUSTER.COM GIVES AWAY PATTY GRIFFIN GUITAR

DALLAS -- Blockbuster Online Services offers a rare opportunity to win a baby Taylor guitar, personally autographed by Patty Griffin. Called the "*Living With Ghosts* Sweepstakes," after the title of Griffin's debut album on A&M, anyone can enter on Blockbuster's web site, www.blockbuster.com. July 8 through July 28, 1997.

Patty Griffin was signed after an A&M rep convinced her to do a raw demo album, focusing on Patty's emotion-filled voice and acoustic guitar. That demo was so soulful it went straight to press, and now creates instant fans wherever it's played. While considered to be folk music, Patty's music reaches out and grabs the heart of a huge crossover audience.

Blockbuster's Internet site provides instant access to entertainment over the web. The site currently houses an extensive online music store, complete with online music purchasing, quick search capabilities and song sampling. Also featured is the latest scoop and interactive information on movies, music, video games and books, a web browser and web surfing suggestions. Look for future buy online options for videos and other entertainment categories to supplement the music store.

To enter the sweepstakes, visit www.blockbuster.com and complete an official online entry form anytime before July 28, 1997. A random drawing will be conducted by

The company name, address, and phone number are noted at the top, along with the names of people who can provide more information.

Most news is released immediately.

Provide your own suggestion for a title, or leave two inches so that the editor can insert a headline.

This release for a newspaper starts with a dateline and a summary (who, what, when, where, why) of the rest of the story.

office." Instead, start with the news: "Calco will move its headquarters to the Main Street office, President James Grall announced today.")
- Be brief (break up long sentences and keep paragraphs short).
- Eliminate clutter such as redundancy and extraneous facts.
- Be as specific as possible.
- Avoid adjectives and adverbs (understatement goes a long way with the media).

In addition to issuing written news releases, many large companies hold news conferences or create their own videotapes, which are sent to TV networks.

WRITING GOODWILL MESSAGES

Business isn't all business. To a great extent, it's an opportunity to forge personal relationships. You can enhance your relationships with customers and other businesspeople by sending friendly, unexpected notes with no direct business purpose. Avon's Christina A. Gold is putting heart back into the company and re-energizing its sales force by sending birthday gifts to strong performers, sending personal congratulations to high achievers, and even asking all Avon's salaried employees to handwrite 100 brief thank-you notes to sales reps.[9] Goodwill messages like these have a positive effect on business, because people prefer to deal with organizations that are warm and human and interested in more than just money.

Such goodwill messages might be considered manipulative and thus unethical unless you make every attempt to be sincere, honest, and truthful. Without sincerity, skillful writing is nothing more than clever, revealing the writer as interested only in personal gain and not in benefiting customers or fellow workers. One way to come across as sincere is to avoid exaggeration. What do you think a reader's reaction would be to these two sentences?

> We were overjoyed to learn of your promotion.

> Congratulations on your promotion.

Most likely, your audience wouldn't quite believe that anyone (except perhaps a relative or very close friend) would be "overjoyed." On the other hand, readers will accept your simple congratulations—a human, understandable intention.

To demonstrate your sincerity, back up any compliments with specific points:

Instead of This	**Write This**
Words cannot express my appreciation for the great job you did. Thanks. No one could have done it better. You're terrific! You've made the whole firm sit up and take notice, and we are ecstatic to have you working here.	Thanks for taking charge of the meeting in my absence. You did an excellent job. With just an hour's notice, you managed to pull the legal and public relations departments together so that we could present a united front in the negotiations. Your dedication and communication abilities have been noted and are truly appreciated.

Note also the difference in the words used in these two examples. Your reader would probably believe the more restrained praise to be more sincere.

Offering help in a goodwill message is fine, but promise only what you can and will provide. Avoid giving even the impression of an offer of help where none is intended. What if Peter Goodrich of Steinway ended letters to piano competition participants by saying:

> Please let us know if we can help you in any way in the future.

It's possible that in a year or two Steinway could be bombarded with requests to sponsor concerts or even entire tours.

Although goodwill messages have little to do with business transactions, they might include some sales information if you have the opportunity to be of particular service or want to remind the reader of your company's product. However, any sales message should be subdued and secondary to the helpful, thoughtful message. In the following example, the owner of a children's clothing shop succeeds in establishing a relationship with the new mother at a very special time in her life:

> Congratulations on the birth of your son at Springfield Memorial Hospital. Nothing matches the joy of a new mother welcoming her tiny baby into the world. To commemorate this joyful occasion, Bundles from Heaven is sending you this special gift—a beautifully illustrated book for you to keep track of all the important events in your son's life.
>
> Our shop serves Springfield, meeting the clothing and equipment needs of babies like yours. That's our only business. Stop in sometime and introduce us to your little son!

The mothers receiving this letter won't feel a great deal of pressure to buy but will feel that the owner took notice of this very special event in their lives. If you include a sales pitch in this type of letter, make sure that it takes a back seat to your goodwill message. Honesty and sincerity must come across above all else.

Goodwill is the positive feeling that encourages people to maintain a business relationship.

Make sure your compliments are grounded in reality.

BEST OF THE WEB

Send an Electronic Goodwill Message

Send a free electronic greeting card from the My Sentiments Fine Art Greeting Cards collection. You can choose from a variety of backgrounds and even add music. Many languages are available. The recipient will receive an e-mail notice that a greeting is waiting for him or her. Great for holidays, birthdays, or announcing a new product or service.

http://www.pathcom.com/~gfx/greetings.htm

Offer help only when you are able and willing to provide it.

If a sales pitch ever appears in a goodwill message, make it only the slightest hint.

Congratulations

One prime opportunity for sending congratulations is news of a significant business achievement—for example, being promoted or attaining an important civic position (see Figure 9.7).

Taking note of significant events in someone's personal life helps cement the business relationship.

Highlights in people's personal lives—weddings and births, graduations, success in nonbusiness competitions—are another reason for sending congratulations. You may congratulate business acquaintances on their achievements or on their spouse's or children's achievements. You may also take note of personal events, even if you don't know the reader well. Of course, if you're already friendly with the reader, you can get away with a personal tone.

Some alert companies develop a mailing list of potential customers by assigning an employee to clip newspaper announcements of births, engagements, weddings, and graduations or by obtaining information on real estate transactions in the local community. Then they introduce themselves by sending out a form letter that might read like this:

> Congratulations on your new home! Our wish is that it brings you much happiness.
>
> To help you commemorate the occasion, enclosed is a key chain with your new address engraved on the leather tab. Please accept this with our best wishes.

In this case, the company's letterhead and address is enough of a sales pitch. This simple message has a natural, friendly tone, even though the sender has never met the recipient.

Messages of Appreciation

A message of appreciation documents a person's contributions.

An important managerial quality is the ability to see employees (and other business associates) as individuals and to recognize their contributions. People often value praise more highly than monetary rewards. A message of appreciation may also become an important part of an employee's personnel file:

> Thanks for creating computerized spreadsheets to track our marketing efforts and sales by both region and product. Your personal understanding of the scope of this division's responsibilities is evident in the detail and thoroughness of the spreadsheets. I particularly appreciate the historical data you included and the fine documentation and training you provided so that the data included in the spreadsheets can be consistent over time—regardless of who is working on them.
>
> Your talents in conceptualizing the scope of the project, executing it on time, and following through with the final details are a great asset to our division.
>
> cc: Employee file, Human Resources

With its references to specific qualities and deeds, this note may provide support for future pay increases and promotions.

Anyone who does you or your organization a special favor should receive written thanks.

Suppliers also like to know that you value some exceptional product or the service you received. Long-term support deserves recognition too. Your praise doesn't just make the supplier feel good; it also encourages further excellence. The brief message that follows expresses gratitude and reveals the happy result:

> Thank you for sending the air-conditioning components via overnight delivery. You allowed us to satisfy the needs of two customers who were getting very impatient with the heat.
>
> Special thanks to Susan Brown who took our initial call and never said "it can't be done." Her initiative on our behalf is greatly appreciated.

When you write a message of appreciation to a supplier, try to mention specifically the person or people you want to praise. Your expression of goodwill might net the

Figure 9.7
In-Depth Critique: Letter Congratulating a Business Acquaintance

This sample congratulatory note moves swiftly to the subject: the good news. It gives reasons for expecting success and avoids such extravagances as "Only you can do the job!"

Office DEPOT, Inc.

2200 Old Germantown Road, Delray Beach, FL 33445   407/278-4800

March 3, 1997

Mr. Ralph Lambert, President
Lambert, Cutchen & Browt, Inc.
14355 Pasadena Parkway
Pasadena, TX 74229

Dear Mr. Lambert:

Congratulations on your firm's recent selection to design and print media advertisements for the National Association of Business Suppliers (ABS). We learned of your success at our convention in Atlanta last month.

We have long believed that the success of individual franchises is directly linked to the healthy growth of the industry at large. We can think of no better firm to help our industry achieve wide recognition than Lambert, Cutchen & Browt, Inc.

We have followed your success in promoting other associations such as soft drinks, snack foods, and recycling. Your "Dream Vision 2000" ads for the bottling industry were both inspirational and effective in raising consumer awareness, and we look for similar positive responses to your ABS campaign.

Again, accept our warm congratulations on your selection. We look forward to seeing the results of the survey you conducted during our convention. And we will follow your media campaign with great interest.

Sincerely,

Janice McCarthy

Janice McCarthy
Director, Media Relations

tw

The reason for congratulating the reader is expressed early and concisely.

The compliment becomes more effective when coupled with statements that show your knowledge of the recipient's prior work.

The letter ends with a personal note of congratulations. It expresses interest in following the future success of the individual or business.

employee some future benefit. In any case, your message honors the company that the individual represents.

Be sure to thank guest speakers at meetings, even if they've been paid an honorarium or their travel expenses—and surely if they have not. They may have spent hours gathering and organizing material for an informative and interesting presentation, so reward their hard work. Messages of appreciation are also appropriate for acknowledging money donations to campaigns or causes. They usually include a few details about the success of the campaign or how the funds are being used so that the donors will feel good about having contributed.

Condolences

In times of serious trouble and deep sadness, written condolences and expressions of sympathy leave their mark. Granted, this type of message is difficult to write, but don't let the difficulty of the task keep you from responding promptly. Those who have experienced a health problem, the death of a loved one, or a business misfortune like to know that they're not alone.

Begin condolences with a brief statement of sympathy, such as "I was deeply sorry to hear of your loss." In the middle, mention the good qualities or the positive contributions made by the deceased. State what the person or business meant to you. In closing, you can offer your condolences and your best wishes. One considerate way to end this type of message is to say something that will give the reader a little lift, such as a reference to a brighter future.

You're not obligated to offer help to the reader; a good condolence message is often help enough. However, if you want to and can offer assistance, do so. Remember, the bereaved and grieving often suffer financially as well as emotionally, and reestablishing a business or a life often takes a great deal of time and effort. A simple gesture on your part may mean much to the reader.

Here are a few general suggestions for writing condolence messages:

In condolence messages, try to find a middle path between being superficial and causing additional distress.

- *Keep reminiscences brief.* Recount a memory or an anecdote (even a humorous one), but don't dwell on the details of the loss, lest you add to the reader's anguish.
- *Write in your own words.* Write as if you were speaking privately to the person. Don't quote "poetic" passages or use stilted or formal phrases. If the loss is a death, refer to it as such rather than as "passing away" or "departing."
- *Be tactful.* Mention your shock and dismay, but keep in mind that the bereaved and distressed loved ones take little comfort in such lines as, "Richard was too young to die" or "Starting all over again will be so difficult." Try to strike a balance between superficial expressions of sympathy and heartrending references to a happier past and a possibly bleak future.
- *Take special care.* Be sure to spell names correctly and to be accurate in your review of facts.
- *Write about special qualities of the deceased.* You may have to rely on reputation to do this, but let the grieving person know the value of his or her loved one.
- *Write about special qualities of the bereaved person.* A pat on the back helps a bereaved family member feel more confident about handling things during such a traumatic time.[10]

Above all, don't let the fear of saying something wrong keep you from saying anything at all. A supervisor, George Bigalow, sent the following condolence letter to his administrative assistant, Janice Case, after learning of the death of Janice's husband:

CHECKLIST FOR GOODWILL MESSAGES

A. PLANNING GOODWILL MESSAGES

1. Choose the appropriate type of goodwill message for your purpose.
   a. Offer congratulations to make the reader feel noticed.
   b. Express praise or thanks to show your appreciation for good performance.
   c. Offer condolences to show appreciation for the deceased or the person suffering a loss.
2. Be prompt when sending out goodwill messages so that they lose none of their impact.
3. Send a written goodwill message rather than a telephone message, because a written message can be savored more than once; but keep in mind that a telephone message is better than none at all.

B. FORMAT

1. Use the format most appropriate to the occasion.
   a. Use letter format for condolences and for any other goodwill message sent to outsiders or mailed to an employee's home.
   b. Use memo format for any goodwill messages sent through interoffice mail, except for condolences.
   c. Use a preprinted greeting card for condolences (with a brief handwritten message added).

2. Handwrite condolences (and replies to handwritten invitations); otherwise, type the goodwill message.
3. Use special stationery, if available.
4. For added impact, present congratulations in a folder with a clipping or photo commemorating the special event.

C. OPENING

1. State the most important idea first to focus the reader's attention.
2. Incorporate a friendly statement that builds goodwill, right at the beginning.
3. Focus on the good qualities of the person or situation.

D. MIDDLE

1. Provide sufficient details, even in a short message, to justify the opening statement.
2. Express personalized details in sincere, not gushy, language.
3. Be warm but concise.
4. Make the reader, not the writer, the focus of all comments.

E. CLOSE

1. Use a positive or forward-looking statement.
2. Restate the important idea, when appropriate.

> My sympathy to you and your children. All your friends at Carter Electric were so very sorry to learn of John's death. Although I never had the opportunity to meet him, I do know how very special he was to you. Your tales of your family's camping trips and his rafting expeditions were always memorable.

Here's a longer condolence letter sent by a friendly competitor on the occasion of a serious business disruption:

> We just heard of the terrible fire at your furniture store, and your decision to close the store temporarily. Please accept our sympathy for your loss. However, the strength of Frankfort Furniture was not the building, but rather your family's managerial skills and team spirit. And those haven't changed.
>
> You know that Frankfort Furniture is more than just our neighbor on Main Street. Together, our stores offer this community a wide variety of furniture styles. We look forward to your store reopening in the very near future.
>
> Jack, we'd like to help. What can we do to assist? Do you need warehouse space? I have a couple of ideas. Please call me when you're ready to consider some facility options. Your many friends in Springfield wish you well and know that you and Ann have the strength and ability to rise above this setback.

Promptness is especially important in condolence messages.

These specifics reassure the reader that the store owner has friends as well as competitors.

The offer of help is not too specific, so it won't intrude on the central message of sympathy. The closing ties together a reminder of friendship and a look toward the future.

As a reminder of the tasks involved with this type of message, see the Checklist for Goodwill Messages.

SUMMARY

Positive replies, favorable responses to claims and requests for adjustment, responses to routine credit requests, positive information about people, directives and instructions, business summaries, good news about products and operations, and goodwill messages—these make up much of the daily correspondence in business. Their purpose is to convey a message that readers will either welcome or accept without question. Some of these messages also encourage readers to take a specific action.

In the United States and Canada, routine, good-news, and goodwill messages follow a straightforward pattern: first, a clear statement of the news or main point; then, the necessary explanatory details; and finally, a warm and courteous close. Some include resale information or sales promotion, which are complimentary references to the writer's company and its products. Most are rather short and depend heavily on the "you" attitude. A sincere and courteous tone highlights the positive image that such messages seek to convey and helps maintain a warm business relationship.

COMMUNICATION CHALLENGES AT STEINWAY & SONS

Peter Goodrich has been traveling more lately, and the correspondence is piling up. He's requested several temporary workers to help him catch up on routine messages so that he can devote more time to other matters, although he still plans to review his assistants' work carefully.

INDIVIDUAL CHALLENGE: You have landed a summer temporary assignment in Goodrich's office because of the business communication course you listed on your application. Now Goodrich hands you a small batch of postcards (described in the opening vignette) from well-known pianists all over the world. "I need you to come up with a brief message thanking these individuals for the time they took to fill out our evaluation cards. Give it a warm and personal feeling, but don't try to get too elaborate with compliments and flattery. I didn't attend any of these concerts, and I won't be adding personal notes, so make the form a complete letter." As you glance through the cards, you see that all the remarks in this group are complimentary.

TEAM CHALLENGE: When Billy Joel joined the roster of Steinway Artists, the Grammy-winning singer-songwriter commented, "I have long admired Steinway pianos for their qualities of tone clarity, pitch consistency, touch responsiveness, and superior craftsmanship." Now Joel is coming to New York on tour, where he'll perform on a Steinway Model B grand. It also happens that the concert takes place on his birthday. Goodrich wants to do something special for Joel, and he's asked your team to brainstorm some ideas. Goodrich suggests doing a little research on Joel's career and personal life to come up with something unique and appropriate.[11]

CRITICAL THINKING QUESTIONS

1. As a local retailer, would you take the time to reply to requests for information and action when no potential sale is involved? Why or why not?

2. Your company's error cost an important business customer a new client—you know it and your customer knows it. Do you apologize, or do you refer to the in-

cident in a positive light without admitting any responsibility? Briefly explain.

3. Your customer is clearly at fault and lying. Will you disallow her claim? Why or why not?

4. You've been asked to write a letter of recommendation for an employee who is disabled and uses a wheelchair. The disability has no effect on the employee's ability to do the job, and you feel confident about writing the best recommendation possible. Nevertheless, you know the prospective company,

and its facilities aren't well suited to wheelchair access. Do you mention the employee's disability in your letter? Explain.

5. Since press releases are published as news items, is it okay to mention the benefits of your company's products, or would that be unethical? Explain your answer.

6. Should resale and sales promotion be subdued (if included at all) in goodwill messages? Explain.

DOCUMENTS FOR ANALYSIS

Read the following documents; then (1) analyze the strengths and weaknesses of each sentence and (2) revise each document so that it follows this chapter's guidelines.

Document 9.A: Responding to Claims and Adjustment Requests When Buyer Is at Fault

We read your letter requesting your deposit refund. We couldn't figure out why you hadn't received it, so we talked to our maintenance engineer as you suggested. He said you had left one of the doors off the hinges in your apartment in order to get a large sofa through the door. He also confirmed that you had paid him $5.00 to replace the door since you had to turn in the U-Haul trailer and were in a big hurry.

This entire situation really was caused by a lack of communication between our housekeeping inspector and the maintenance engineer. All we knew was that the door was off the hinges when it was inspected by Sally Tarnley. You know that our policy states that if anything is wrong with the apartment, we keep the deposit. We had no way of knowing that George just hadn't gotten around to replacing the door.

But we have good news. We approved the deposit refund, which will be mailed to you from our home office in Teaneck, New Jersey. I'm not sure how long that will take, however. If you don't receive the check by the end of next month, give me a call.

Next time, it's really a good idea to stay with your apartment until it's inspected as stipulated in your lease agreement. That way, you'll be sure to receive your refund when you expect it. Hope you have a good summer.

Document 9.B: Responding to Claims and Adjustment Requests When Company's at Fault

Thank you for contacting us about your purchase of the "Knights of Balthazar" game for your MacIntosh. We apologize for the problem and want you to know how it happened.

We outsource our packaging to a firm called TriTech, which does the design work and prints the boxes. Unfortunately, the box that contained your CD for Balthazar was mistakenly labeled. It will work only on an IBM (or compatible) platform.

We are taking care of our customers even though this problem was caused by TriTech. If you will send the entire CD, the box, the warranty card, and your receipt, we will gladly replace it with a CD that will work in your computer. We also need to know how much memory you have and the system you are running. (Balthazar won't work on anything less than a System 7.)

Thanks for your patience. Again, we apologize for this even though it was beyond our control. We always want to do the right thing for our customers. Incidentally, I am enclosing our latest catalog of interactive CD games. We hope to do business with you in the future.

Document 9.C: Letter of Recommendation

Your letter to Tanaka Asata, President of SONY, was forwarded to me because I am the human resources director. In my job as head of HR, I have access to performance reviews for all of the SONY employees in the United States. This means, of course, that I would be the person best qualified to answer your request for information on Nick Oshinski.

In your letter of the 15th, you asked about Nick Oshinski's employment record with us because he has applied to work for your company. Mr. Oshinski was employed with us from January 5, 1992, until March 1, 1997. During that time, Mr. Oshinski received ratings ranging from 2.5 up to 9.6 with 10 being the top score. As you can see, he must have done bet-ter reporting to some managers than to others. In addition, he took all vacation days, which is a bit unusual. Although I did not know Mr. Oshinski personally, I know that our best workers seldom use all the vacation time they earn. I do not know if that applies in this case.

In summary, Nick Oshinski performed his tasks well depending on who managed him.

Cases

Replying to Requests for Information and Action

MANAGEMENT

CUSTOMER RELATIONS

1. Cooling it: Letter confirming details of a complex job　The contract has been signed. For $2,300, you have agreed to install a central air-conditioning unit in the home at 3985 Magoo Terrace, Wichita, KS 67216.

The preliminary sheet-metal work has been done, and the main unit has arrived in your shop. The main unit is guaranteed for one year (materials and labor) and an additional two years for materials only. Working with a crew of three, you believe you can install the unit and the vents in two days, starting each day at 8:30 A.M. Your customer, Mrs. Valerie Franchasia, has suggested Thursdays and Fridays as the days most convenient for her.

You want to tell Mrs. Franchasia when your crew will be working in her house, to remind her that the job will be a noisy one, and to let her know you'll need access to the house through the driveway and garage. It is also possible that you won't be able to complete the job within two days.

Your task:　You have been unable to reach Mrs. Franchasia by phone, so you must write to her. Confirm that Air-Whiz workers will install her air-conditioning system next Thursday and Friday and that they hope to have the job completed by 5:00 P.M. Friday. You usually sign letters of this type using your title, which is air-control specialist.

MARKETING

EXTERNAL COMMUNICATION

2. Blazing white: Letter to *Maclean's* magazine describing new TCF paper　Now that scientists have re-vealed the serious environmental impact of the chlorine-bleaching traditionally used to create white paper, paper companies are facing some potentially costly changes in their manufacturing techniques. Research indicates that without secondary waste-treatment facilities, the chlorine process releases highly toxic by-products (dioxins) into the environment, fouling water supplies and accumulating in both ocean and freshwater fish that humans might consume.

Most countries are considering legislation to limit or ban the use of chlorine in paper and other industries. Many paper companies have already tried producing "totally chlorine free" (TCF) paper, but industry executives complain that they just can't sell the brownish colored TCF paper. Nobody wants to read brown magazines or mail, they argue, and the TCF paper costs buyers up to 20 percent more than ordinary white paper.

Peter Sweeney, a marketing official at Cross Pointe Paper in Minnesota, isn't worried about the controversy. His company (a division of Pentair) recently developed a new line of paper made by combining TCF paper with recycled materials. Not only is it shining white, but the paper costs a mere 5 percent more than standard chlorine-bleached products. If new legislation forces a change in paper manufacturing, Cross Pointe is in a good position to lead the industry. Although the company hasn't done much advertising, requests are steadily coming in from publishers and environmental groups for more information on the new product line. Even *Maclean's*, Canada's weekly newsmagazine, has sent a request for samples.

Your task:　As a sales representative, you handle the requests for information passed on from Sweeney's department. Address a letter to Sarah Oliver, Purchasing Agent, *Maclean's* magazine (Maclean Hunter, Ltd., 777 Bay Street, Toronto, Ontario M5W 1A7, Canada), describing the new paper and providing samples and a price list for the big Canadian publisher. If the company likes your product, *Maclean's* could become one of Cross Pointe's most important accounts.[12]

PUBLIC RELATIONS
SOCIAL RESPONSIBILITY

3. Elephant fans, take note: Form letter announcing Yamaha's decision to stop using ivory for piano keys How many elephants does it take to make 350 pianos? Only five, assuming that each one has two 150-pound tusks that can be turned into ivory keys. That may not sound like many elephants, but to fans of the endangered pachyderm, it's five too many—Yamaha Corporation has the protest letters to prove it.

As the world's leading musical instrument manufacturer, Yamaha has received more than its share of complaints from elephant lovers who deplore the use of ivory in keyboards. Yamaha spokespeople have tried to defend the company by pointing out that it has substituted plastic for ivory in all but 0.2 percent of its pianos; nevertheless, the protests have increased. Finally, bowing to public pressure, Yamaha has decided to stop using ivory entirely. Realizing that this decision will be music to the ears of elephant defenders, the company is eager to spread the good news.

Your task: As a member of Yamaha's public relations department, you've been asked to develop a form letter that can be mailed to all the people who have written to the company in the past year asking management to stop using ivory in its piano keyboards. Prepare the letter announcing Yamaha's decision.[13]

MAIL-ORDER SALES
CUSTOMER RELATIONS

4. Naturally soothing: Letter describing the contents of The Body Shop by Mail's Stress Kit   Since Anita Roddick founded The Body Shop in 1976, her simple philosophy has evolved into the motto "Profits with Principles." Today, annual sales of Roddick's "naturally based hair and skin care preparations" are approaching $400 million from over 700 shops in 40 countries, and Roddick's principles are holding firm. The Body Shop has always opposed any use of animals in testing cosmetics, and employees are encouraged to spend some portion of their company time working as volunteers for community groups. The company has set up "Trade Not Aid" programs in both First and Third World countries, urged its customers to get out and vote, and worked to

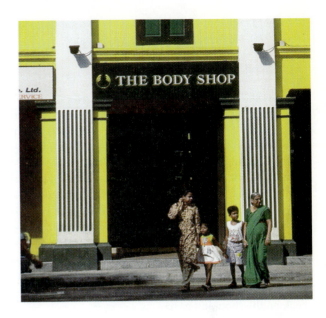

help orphans, political prisoners, and rain forest inhabitants. The Body Shop even uses price discounts to encourage customers to bring back their plastic bottles for refills.

The company has begun offering everything from Banana Shampoo to Dewberry Fruit Soap through its mail-order catalog, The Body Shop by Mail. Since customers can't sniff and dab and sample, they often send letters asking for more information. Suzanne Timmons in Warrensburg, Missouri, wants to know more about the contents of your Stress Kit and whether or not it would be suitable as a gift for her boyfriend.

The kit includes a 4.2-ounce bottle of rich pink Peppermint Foot Lotion, a 0.4-ounce jar of refreshing Elderflower Under Eye Gel (to wake up tired eyes), a 4.2-ounce bottle of unscented Body Massage Oil, and a 100 percent cotton washcloth, all tucked into a clear, plastic drawstring bag. These products are popular with both men and women. Peppermint Foot Lotion, for example, was developed for runners in the London marathon as a remedy for tired feet and is now a best seller around the world. The products are "naturally based," but they also contain synthetic ingredients to prevent contamination.

Your task: Write to Suzanne Timmons at 1255 Butcher Rd., Warrensburg, MO 64093, and answer her questions. Include copies of the appropriate pages from The Body Shop's Product Information Manual. Be sure to let her know that her purchases will also support The Body Shop's humanitarian efforts worldwide.[14]

HORIZONTAL COMMUNICATION

 5. Window shopping at Wal-Mart: Writing a positive reply via e-mail The Wal-Mart chain of discount stores is one of the most successful in the world, designing, importing, and marketing across national borders. In particular, Wal-Mart rarely fails to capitalize on a marketing scheme, and its online shopping page is no exception. To make sure the Web site remains effective and relevant, the Webmaster asks various people to peruse the site and give their feedback. As administrative assistant to Wal-Mart's director of marketing, you have just received a request from the Webmaster to visit Wal-Mart's Web site and give feedback on the shopping page.

Your task: Visit Wal-Mart at <http://www.wal-mart.com> and do some online "window shopping." As you browse through the shopping page, consider the language, layout, graphics, ease of use, and background noise. Then compose a positive reply to the Webmaster, and send your feedback to <cserve@wal-mart.com>. Print a copy of your e-mail message for submission to your instructor.

Responding Favorably to Claims and Adjustment Requests

MANAGEMENT

CUSTOMER RELATIONS

6. Good news from "Freddy Pumpkin": Letter from Teleline, granting an adjustment on a phone bill The March phone bill was a bit of a shock to Allen White (of 723 Amber Court, Cambridge, MA 02140), and April's bill was no better. The statements for both months listed $40 worth of calls that White was sure he had not made. Finally, in May, when the mystery calls totaled $100, White figured out that his four-year-old son was placing calls to "Freddy Pumpkin"—a 900 telephone line advertised on children's television shows. The irate Mr. White paid the telephone bill but fired off a letter of protest to Mr. Robert H. Lorsch, president of Teleline, a company that operates children's phone-line services.

White's letter distressed Mr. Lorsch, who feels that Teleline offers a legitimate service. Children who call

the firm's 900 numbers hear a taped message featuring cartoon or fantasy characters. At $2.45 for the first minute and 45 cents for each additional minute, the calls aren't cheap—but they aren't a big problem unless a child develops a serious habit. Teleline receives fewer than 12 complaints a month. The company is careful to state its prices in its TV ads for the phone lines, and it warns children to ask their parents for permission before calling.

Your task: Draft a letter for Mr. Lorsch's signature offering to refund $90 of Mr. White's money—half of what he paid for the calls during March, April, and May.[15]

HOTEL MANAGEMENT

CUSTOMER RELATIONS

7. The shortsighted promotion: Letter from Residence Inn to deal with objections to an ad As manager of marketing communications for Residence Inn, Joe Okon wanted his advertising to differentiate the chain from competing suite-type hotels. He thought about using a photo of the hotel chain's rooms but rejected that idea as being too similar to everybody else's ads. Instead, he decided to go with something a little bit whimsical—a picture of 12 pairs of men's undershorts: 10 to show the average stay at a Residence Inn and 2 to show the average stay at most other hotels.

In many respects, the ad was a big success. During the campaign, calls to the reservation center increased by 150 percent over the preceding year. However, there was one problem: The ad offended many female business travelers. Thirty of them took the time to complain about the "tasteless, sexist" ads. Sarah Carlston, a publicist, was typical of the women who wrote. She said: "You'd think they could have picked better symbols. I wonder what they would have used if they were trying to reach women—bras or panties?"

Your task: Write a letter to Ms. Carlston (Consumer Representative, Boyd Products, Inc., 1650 Delco Dr., Columbus, OH 43216) apologizing for the ad. Offer her a reasonable inducement to give Residence Inn another chance.[16]

MAIL-ORDER SALES

CUSTOMER RELATIONS

8. Satisfaction guaranteed: Letter from L. L. Bean granting a claim As a member of L. L. Bean's customer service department in Freeport, Maine, you've

handled plenty of claims in your day. The famous mail-order sporting goods and clothing company processes thousands of orders every month, and inevitably, some items are returned. Your job is to respond to the customer either by exchanging the merchandise or by refunding the person's money, regardless of why the item was returned. L. L. Bean guarantees satisfaction.

Today you have received a package from Arvin Bummel (212 North Star, Traverse City, MI 49684). When you open it, you find (1) one shirt, stiff as a board and two sizes smaller than it ought to be; (2) one pair of trousers, also stiff and shrunken; and (3) a nasty letter from Mr. Bummel saying that he expects better from L. L. Bean. According to him, the clothes were ruined the first time he washed them. He wants L. L. Bean to replace the shirt and pants. You are not surprised that the clothes are ruined, because the label plainly says, "Dry-clean only." Regardless, $108.50 worth of clothes are now unwearable.

Your task: In the spirit of good customer relations, write to Mr. Bummel and grant his claim. You may want to suggest gently that he look for clothing that is washable.[17]

Approving Routine Credit Requests

AGRICULTURE
CUSTOMER RELATIONS

9. Satellite farming: Letter granting credit from Deere & Company   This is the best part of your job with Deere & Co. in Moline, Illinois: saying yes to a farmer. In this case, it's Arlen Ruestman in Toluca, Illinois.

Ruestman wants to take advantage of new farming technology. Your company's new GreenStar system uses satellite technology originally developed by the defense department: the Global Positioning System (GPS). By using a series of satellites orbiting Earth, the system can pinpoint (to the meter) exactly where a farmer is positioned at any given moment as he drives his GreenStar-equipped combine over a field. For farmers like Reustman, that means a new ability to micromanage even 10,000 acres of corn or soybeans.

For instance, using the GreenStar system, farmers can map and analyze characteristics such as acidity, soil type, or crop yields from a given area. Using this information, they know exactly how much herbicide or fertilizer to spread over precisely which spot—eliminating waste and achieving better results. With cross-referencing and accumulated data, farmers can analyze why crops are performing well in some areas and not so well in others. Then they can program farm equipment to treat only the problem area—for example, spraying an insect infestation two meters wide, 300 yards down the row.

Some farms have already saved as much as $10 an acre on fertilizers alone. For 10,000 acres, that's $100,000 a year. Once Ruestman retrofits your GreenStar precision package on his old combine and learns all its applications, he should have no problem saving enough to pay off the $7,350 credit account you're about to grant him.

Your task: Write a letter to Mr. Ruestman (P.O. Box 4067, Toluca, IL 61369), informing him of the good news.[18]

ACCOUNTING
CUSTOMER RELATIONS

10. Virtual audio imager: Good news from Brown Innovations   It was just a small item in *Newsweek,* but both the Boston and Chicago offices of Brown Innovations have been swamped with orders ever since. From where you sit, it looks like every music store, arcade, and electronic equipment store in the nation wants to install the new virtual audio imagers to cut down on noise pollution. The concept is simple, really: two stereo speakers mounted beneath a clear acrylic, spherical dome.

In a store selling music CDs, multimedia computers, stereo speakers, and other consumer electronics—all with display models ready to demonstrate their sound capabilities—Saturday afternoons can be such a cacophony of noise that no one can hear anything, including the sales pitch. The virtual audio imager eliminates this problem by creating an "isolated" listening region directly beneath the speakers. In a game arcade, this means players can hear their own radical sound effects, but not everyone else's. In the stereo store, this means the rap music demo on the boombox doesn't interfere with the salesperson across the store trying to explain the benefits of a laser printer.

The applications for credit are streaming in to accounts receivable by the hundreds. As an accounts receivable supervisor, you've already reviewed 25 today, and you have just one more on your desk, a credit purchase for two virtual audio imagers from Stevens Stereo in Albuquerque, New Mexico. The financial statements have already been reviewed and approved; and the store's history is good.

Your task: Write a letter to Paul Ramirez, manager (Stevens Stereo, 87714 Malaga Road, Albuquerque, NM 87103), telling him his application has been approved and his order is being processed.[19]

Conveying Positive Information about People

11. The special courier: Reply to a request for a recommendation letter   In today's mail you get a letter from Non-Stop Messenger Service, 899 Sparks St., Ottawa, Ontario K1A 0G9, Canada. It concerns a friend of yours who has applied for a job. Here is the letter:

> Your friend has applied for the position of special courier with our firm, and she has given us your name as a reference. Our special couriers convey materials of considerable value or confidentiality to their recipients. It is not an easy job. Special couriers must sometimes remain alert for periods of up to 20 hours, and they cannot expect to follow the usual "three square meals and eight hours' sleep" routine because they often travel long distances on short notice. On occasion, a special courier must react quickly and decisively to threatening situations.
>
> For this type of work, we hire only people of unquestioned integrity, as demonstrated both by their public records and by references from people, like yourself, who have known them personally or professionally.

> We would appreciate a letter from you detailing (1) how long and in what circumstances you have known the applicant, (2) what qualities she possesses that would qualify her for the position of special courier, and (3) what qualities might be improved before she is put on permanent assignment in this job.

Your task: Write as supportive a letter as possible about your friend (choose someone you know) to Roscoe de la Penda, Human Resources Specialist, Non-Stop Messenger Service.

12. On a course for Harvard: Reply to a request for a recommendation letter   After working for several years for Zoe Coulson in Campbell Soup Company's department of consumer affairs, one of your co-workers, Angela Cavanaugh, has decided to apply for admission to the Harvard Business School's MBA program. She has asked Coulson, a Harvard graduate, to write a letter of recommendation for her. Here are the facts about Angela Cavanaugh:

1. She has an undergraduate degree in journalism from the University of Iowa, where she was an honors student.
2. She joined Campbell directly after graduating and has worked for the firm for the past five years.
3. Her primary responsibility has been to answer letters from consumers; she has done an outstanding job.
4. Her most noteworthy achievement has been to analyze a year's worth of incoming mail, categorize the letters by type and frequency, and create a series of standardized replies. The department now uses Cavanaugh's form letters to handle approximately 75 percent of its mail.
5. Although Cavanaugh has outstanding work habits and is an excellent writer, she lacks confidence as a speaker. Her reluctance to present her ideas orally has prevented her from advancing more rapidly at Campbell. This could be a problem for her at Harvard Business School, where skill in classroom discussion influences a student's chances of success.

Your task: Because you have worked closely with Cavanaugh, Zoe Coulson has asked you to draft the letter, which Coulson will sign.[20]

Writing Directives and Instructions

MANAGEMENT

DOWNWARD COMMUNICATION

13. No Kool-Aid heads: Memo to Kraft employees about hair-dyeing fad They show up glowing blue, green, or red at rock concerts and shopping malls, even college dorms: "Kool-Aid heads," a term coined by *The Wall Street Journal* for kids who insist that the flavored drink product makes a terrific (and temporary) hair dye.

You're working as assistant to Michael Polk, business director of beverages for Kraft Foods in White Plains, New York. At Kraft, the word about the fad is, "We would never, ever touch it with a 10-foot pole." So says Polk.

A few decades ago, the company endured some questionable publicity from author Tom Wolfe *(The Electric Kool-Aid Acid Test)*. Now Kraft management is determined to ignore this latest fad and its unofficial Web site, "Hey Kool-Aid!" (which apparently provides home-grown instructions for dunking your hair into a bowl of warm "Great Bluedini" without staining your forehead). When E. E. Perkins invented Kool-Aid some 70 years ago, this fad wasn't what the Nebraska home-remedy salesman intended.

"All we're about is selling a fun, fruity drink," says Polk. At three packets for $1, Kraft sold $296 million worth of Kool-Aid last year, and the hair-dyers bought only a "tiny" fraction of this amount. Kraft's target consumers are 6- to 12-year-olds, Polk believes, and the way to reach them is through smiling "Pitcher Man" TV ads or through moms who like the nutritious-sounding names like "Island Twists Man-O-Mango Berry." The wildest alternative Kraft will promote is mixing the colored powder into yogurt or cookie dough.

Your task: A few members of Kraft's marketing staff have inquired about targeting the 13- to 25-year-olds who are already mad about Kool-Aid, although not for drinking purposes. Polk wants you to write a memo for his signature, directing all employees to avoid any association with this fad.[21]

MANAGEMENT

LAW

14. Mind your own e-mail: An e-mail message about electronic privacy at *The Los Angeles Times* When you stepped into your office at *The Los Angeles Times* this morning, the place was buzzing with news of a reporter in the paper's Moscow bureau being disciplined for reading his co-workers' electronic mail. As the story goes, the newly hired correspondent was suspected of routinely snooping into his fellow reporters' e-mail. So his supervisors set up a "sting" operation, enlisting the Jerusalem bureau to send messages containing false information about shrinking travel allowances to another Moscow reporter.

The suspect took the bait, apparently using his co-worker's password to intercept the e-mail. When he later mentioned the new travel rules, he was slapped with a reassignment back to Los Angeles, to an as-yet-undesignated job (probably writing obituaries). Word of this action spread rapidly through all the paper's domestic and international bureaus.

The Los Angeles Times has always observed strict discipline with regard to journalistic ethics. But because journalists have always held confidentiality in such high regard, everyone assumed e-mail privacy needed no enforcement. Now that's changing.

As an employee of the newspaper's legal department, you're developing instructions for handling violations of e-mail privacy. Management has decided on the following penalties: reassignment, suspension without pay, or termination of employment.

Your task: Use your common sense to write an e-mail message to bureau managers (who oversee editorial offices spread around the globe) with step-by-step instructions on how to handle employees who violate e-mail privacy rules. The managers will have to use their own judgment in each case, but to avoid legal problems, they'll need some uniform guidelines. Hint: First-time offenders may be warned, but repeated problems should be dealt with more strongly.[22]

Writing Business Summaries

STRATEGIC PLANNING

EXTERNAL COMMUNICATION

15. IBM blues: E-mail message about the Olympic fiasco At the 1996 Olympic Games in Atlanta, Georgia, International Business Machines bombed big time with an $80 million information processing system that couldn't deliver scores accurately or on time. IBM spent three years developing the state-of-the-art system, but problems were evident from the first day. News organizations wound up using runners and other low-tech solutions to get the information about athletic competitions out to the world; meanwhile, fans couldn't access the information promised on IBM's highly touted Olympic Web site, and the faces of Big Blue's top executives were turning red.

As an independent public relations consultant, you've been hired by Jerry Ferguson, CEO of QualSoft, a local software company that's facing a similar situation—albeit on a far smaller scale. Both you and Ferguson are wondering whether anything can be gleaned from IBM's experience. What exactly went wrong with the high-speed information transfer network IBM had set up in Atlanta, and how did IBM respond when the system failed? Did it make the right moves to quell the negative publicity?

Your task: You've done some research and found several articles about IBM's Olympic fiasco, but the most relevant to Ferguson's situation was in *The Wall Street Journal* on July 25, 1996, "IBM Olympic Embarrassments Drag On as Computers Produce Late, Bad Data." When

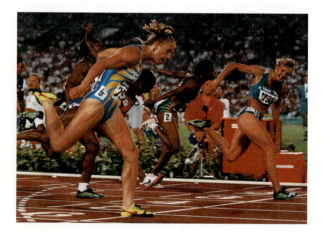

you begin explaining the article to Ferguson over the phone, he asks you to e-mail a summary of it to <jferguson@QualSoft.com>.[23]

MARKETING

UPWARD COMMUNICATION

16. Trendsetters: Memo summarizing a new marketing tactic You're working for Abbie Rose, a small clothing design company in Los Angeles—a company that was started by baby boomers in the 1980s and that has always taken pride in anticipating trends, or even starting them. But yesterday your boss, Rose Jennings, came to you with an unusual request.

"At the Kiwanis meeting last night, someone told me that Reebok, Pepsi, and other big companies have been using a kind of 'guerrilla research' to anticipate fashion trends among young people," she said. "The man said he'd read something in *The New York Times,* or somewhere, about companies sending people out to rock concerts and clubs in the city, looking for the hippest kids, the trendsetters. You know—the coolest street kids start wearing dark nail polish and six months later suburban kids are asking for it at the mall. We've always tried to know what kids want before they do—especially since it takes so long to get new styles into production and out into the marketplace. See what you can find out about this guerrilla technique. Find that article and brief me on the high points."

Your task: You looked in *The New York Times* index for the last three weeks but found nothing; then you tried an online periodicals index and found an article in *The Wall Street Journal* titled "Marketers Seek Out Cool Kids for Tomorrow's Mall Trends" (July 11, 1996). That must be it. As Jennings asked, read the article and write her a memo summarizing the facts in one or two paragraphs.[24]

Conveying Good News About Products and Operations

EDUCATION

DOWNWARD COMMUNICATION

17. Learn while you earn: Memo announcing Burger King's educational benefits Your boss, Herb Schervish, owner of a Burger King store in Detroit's downtown Renaissance Center, is worried about employee turnover. He needs to keep 50 people on his payroll to operate the outlet, but recruiting and retaining those people is tough. The average employee leaves after about seven months, which means that Schervish has to hire and train 90 people a year just to maintain a 50-person crew. At a cost of $1,500 per hire, the price tag for all that turnover is approximately $62,000 per year.

Schervish knows that a lot of his best employees quit because they think that flipping burgers is a dead-end job. But what if it weren't a dead end? What if a person could really get someplace flipping burgers? What if Schervish offered to pay his employees' way through college if they remained with the store? Would that keep them behind the counter?

He's decided to give educational incentives a try. Employees who choose to participate will continue to earn their usual salary, but in addition, they will get free books and college tuition, keyed to the number of hours they work each week. Those who work from 10 to 15 hours a week can take one free course at nearby Wayne County Community College, those who work 16 to 25 hours can take two courses, and those who work 26 to 40 hours can take three courses. The program is open to all employees, regardless of how long they have worked for Burger King, but no one is obligated to participate.

Your task: Draft a memo for Mr. Schervish to send out announcing the new educational incentives.[25]

PUBLIC RELATIONS
EXTERNAL COMMUNICATION

18. Time to grow: Press release from Wells Fargo
San Francisco–based Wells Fargo Bank has actively implemented policies that help employees develop to their full potential. Now the company has instituted a program that enables employees to take time off to pursue worthwhile personal objectives. The employees who qualify continue to receive salaries and benefits during their sabbaticals; at the end they can return to their old jobs or to positions at equivalent levels in the organization.

The program is designed to reward superior performers who have been with the bank for at least ten years. The applicants must spend their leave time on projects that will enrich both themselves and their communities. Nancy Thompson, the program's director, says: "These are not larks. We eliminate people who want to take a cruise or go to Hawaii."

Recently, the bank approved applications for two employees: Phyllis Jones, a bank operations officer who is studying Navajo rug weaving in New Mexico, and Patricia Lujan, a customer service representative who is preparing for a recital as a concert pianist.

The contact for this press release is Thomas Slattery, Director, Corporate Public Affairs, Wells Fargo Bank, 7983 Golden Gate Lane, San Francisco, CA 94101, (415) 798-0079.

Your task: Write a press release about the program that will interest newspapers and general-interest magazines.[26]

GLOBAL BUSINESS
HORIZONTAL COMMUNICATIONS

19. Japanese wake-up call: E-mail at Starbucks
You're administrative assistant to Jo Blair, project developer for Starbucks's first foray outside North America, and you're feeling pretty bad for your boss. For months, she's been working to make real a Starbucks plan to open a hundred coffee bars in major Japanese cities in the next five years. She's been tackling high rent, high labor costs, and low price requirements. It's been an uphill battle, but little by little (with your Japanese partner, Sazaby Inc.) she's overcome each obstacle. Even so, before leaving Narita Airport just hours ago for tomorrow's briefing here in Seattle, she didn't feel that Starbucks had created a market for espresso drinks. The Japanese love their coffee (they're third in consumption behind the United States and Germany), but they drink it in cans from vending machines, or as a conventional brew. You both believe that the Japanese coffee merchants are pretty secure in their market.

Blair is aboard an airplane somewhere over the Pacific, but you're at your desk in Seattle, trying to shake the blues by browsing through *The Wall Street Journal.* Suddenly you spot a headline that makes your heart jump: "Japan's Staid Coffee Bars Wake Up and Smell Starbucks"! You read the article voraciously, and then read it again to make sure you're not dreaming. One particular quote leaps out at you, from Seiji Honna, president of Pronto Corporation (which owns a chain of 94 Japanese coffee bars): "For the past few years, we've had this nightmare scenario that espresso drinks are going to swallow up Japan's coffee market, and we won't know how to make a good cup of espresso . . . If Starbucks really means business, they'll probably put some of us out of business." The article was written by a Japanese correspondent who must have had access Blair could never get. Honna even admits to making an urgent trip to the United States, where he visited 20 Starbucks stores incognito in hopes of discovering their secrets.

Another quote, this time from a Japanese industry analyst, says that all of Japan's coffee industry is "stirred up" about Starbucks's plans. According to the article, Sazaby is recognized in Japan as an expert at attracting just the kind of upscale customer Starbucks needs. Evidently, some worried merchants are already adding espresso drinks to their menus and redesigning their shops to look like Starbucks.

This should change Blair's mood! You've got to get the good news to her so that she can use it to perk up tomorrow's presentation. She'll be in Seattle in 11 hours, but you can't wait. She's got her laptop on the plane, and you know she won't go the entire flight without checking her e-mail.

Your task: Send Blair an e-mail message alerting her to the good news.[27]

Writing Goodwill Messages

MANAGEMENT
INTERPERSONAL COMMUNICATION

20. Good work: E-mail congratulating Netscape's unofficial recruiting team In spite of only 1.6 percent growth in the overall job market, so-called computer "techies" have become a hot commodity, garnering starting salaries in the high five figures. For computer "nerds" with at least three years' experience, signing bonuses of $6,000 to $10,000 are not uncommon. When you add offers of 1,500 to 2,000 company shares, you get a pretty good idea of the employment outlook for those with the necessary computer skills. "We hire the good people first, and figure out what they're going to do later," says Eric Schmidt, chief technology officer at Sun Microsystems. Competition for workers is so intense that "you have to treat your current employees as though you were recruiting them to stave off raids by rivals," he says, citing bonuses offered to employees who help recruit others.

You are Sandra Harmon, director of human resources for Netscape Communications Corp. You used to be among the 150 recruiters interviewing engineering students at the University of Illinois. This spring there were 330. You were particularly interested in 23-year-old Juan Jose Mata, a graduate student in electrical and

computer engineering. You've been in a heated battle with Hewlett-Packard, Oracle, and several others for the talents of this young man. After several trips to visit your plant, he agrees to a contract. You're not only elated but also grateful to the present cadre of computer engineers who courted Mata during his plant trips.

Your task: Now that Mata has signed with Netscape, you want to say "Congratulations, good work!" to the people who made it possible. Draft an e-mail to the following people: Ross Johnson, Tasha Blaken, Fritz Hammel, Andre Gonzalez, and Kia Vallas. Let them know that the company is awarding them $2,000 each for their time and assistance in landing this valuable recruit.[28]

MARKETING
INTERCULTURAL COMMUNICATION

21. "Got milk?" ads get in touch: E-mail message expressing thanks As executive director of California's Milk Processor Board, you are grateful to Anita Santiago. The board had already scored a national hit with its irreverent "Got milk?" ads, designed to raise state consumption. Produced in English and Spanish by Goodby, Silverstein & Partners in San Francisco, the TV ads feature zany scenarios in which people need milk but can't get it. One spot shows a detestable man who dies and believes he has gone to heaven. Spying a plate of chocolate chip cookies, he smiles and helps himself to a huge bite only to panic when he opens the refrigerator and discovers he has no milk. The spot ends with the horrified man realizing he is definitely *not* in heaven. The voice-over asks, "Got milk?"

This campaign raised the recognition level to around 90 percent for most demographic groups, but it failed miserably with Hispanic viewers—who represent one-third of the state's population. You and your staff were at a loss to understand what was wrong . . . and then you heard from Anita Santiago. As a Mexican American, she promoted her advertising agency as having roots in the Hispanic culture. You decided to hire Santiago Advertising.

The new agency pointed out two major problems with the campaign: First, the slogan "Got milk?" translates into Spanish as "Are you lactating?" Second, to the Mexican Americans in the focus groups, running out of milk was no laughing matter but indicated that you had failed your family. Santiago created an alternative ad campaign called "Generations." Now aimed at mothers, the new question put to viewers asks, "Have you given them enough milk today?" And instead of focusing on deprivation, the new ads show milk as an almost sacred ingredient in cherished recipes handed down from grandmother to mother to daughter in traditional Mexican families.

It's been four months, and you just received the figures. The product recognition factor for Hispanics just rose to 91 percent. With her knowledge of the traditional family values of the Hispanic population, Santiago helped your organization bridge the communication gap created by language and cultural differences. The new ads had saved not only your milk campaign but possibly your job.

Your task: Write an e-mail message to Anita Santiago at <anita@santiago.com> to let her know how much you appreciate her agency's contributions.[29]

22. Our sympathy: Condolence letter to an Aetna underwriter As chief administrator for the underwriting department of Aetna Health Plans in Walnut Creek, California, you're facing a difficult task. One of your best underwriters, Angela Corelli, recently lost her husband in an automobile accident (she wasn't with him at the time). Since you're the boss, everyone in the close-knit department is looking to you to communicate the group's sympathy and concern.

Someone suggested a simple greeting card that everyone could sign, but that seems so impersonal for someone you've worked with every day for nearly five years. So you've decided to write a personal note on behalf of the whole department. You didn't know Angela's husband, Jerry, but you do know that if anyone can overcome this tragedy, Angela can. She's always determined to get a job done no matter what obstacles present themselves, and she does it cheerfully. That's why everyone in the office likes her so much.

You also plan to suggest that when she returns to work, she might like to move her schedule up an hour so that she'll have more time to spend with her daughter, Kristin, after school. It's your way of helping make things a little easier for them during this period of adjustment.

Your task: Write the letter to Angela Corelli, who lives at 47 West Ave., #10, Walnut Creek, CA 94596.[30]

CHAPTER 10

WRITING BAD-NEWS MESSAGES

AFTER STUDYING THIS CHAPTER, YOU WILL BE ABLE TO

- Choose correctly between indirect and direct approaches to a bad-news message
- Establish the proper tone from the beginning of your message
- Present bad news in a reasonable and understandable way
- Write messages that motivate your audience to take constructive action
- Close messages so that your audience is willing to continue a business relationship with your firm

COMMUNICATION CLOSE-UP AT OLMEC TOYS

When her son was three years old, Yia Eason was worried about his self-image. Little Menelik, who loved all the superheroes, sadly told his mother that he couldn't be one himself because all superheroes were white. "I thought that if he couldn't see himself as a black superhero, then maybe he couldn't see himself being a black scientist or doctor," says Eason. After a fruitless search for a black superhero doll, she talked with other mothers and found that she wasn't alone in feeling left out. So she decided to start her own company, Olmec Toys, and she created SunMan, the first black superhero action figure (who gets his powers from the melanin in his skin).

Eleven years later, Olmec Toys is the largest minority-owned toy company in the United States, with annual sales approaching $10 million. The company still specializes in producing dolls created specifically for African American, Hispanic, and Asian American children, but now it also markets educational games, music videos, and even a white doll.

Eason believes that black consumers are predisposed to buy from Olmec once they know that the company is owned and operated by a black mother. "Our studies show that the black consumer doesn't believe that Mattel can make a black doll better than we can," says Eason. So Olmec puts the company's story on the back of every package and in its catalog. Of course, even though this recognition earns sales and loyalty from consumers, Eason says that people in the toy industry tend to push even harder once they know Olmec is a small company and operated by a woman. Since Olmec's sales are only a fraction of the $1.5 billion ethnic toy market and a tiny fraction of the total $17.5 billion U.S. toy industry, Olmec must fight hard to retain shelf space and maintain market share.

Surviving in the toy business hasn't been easy for Eason, who earned her MBA at Harvard and used to be a financial editor. It's a fast-paced industry, and the competi-

Yia Eason

As a small company specializing in ethnic toys, Olmec must maintain strong relationships with customers, employees, and investors. One way it builds and retains these relationships is by focusing on audience feelings. By explaining the reasons for any bad news and by focusing on the positive aspects of a negative situation, people at Olmec communicate their understanding and demonstrate their goodwill.

tion is fierce. When Eason communicates with her suppliers, customers, banks, investors, and employees, she strives to show strength and determination as well as to foster goodwill and build lasting relationships. And she's especially careful when her messages must contain bad news.

Having a single item out of stock can cost a toy company not only an immediate sale but also a long-term relationship with a retailer, especially when it's a potential first-time customer who simply turns to another toy company and is never heard from again. When Olmec receives an order or a request for a product that's no longer being produced, Eason's reply states up front that the item is not available. Then she immediately describes in-stock items that are similar. As a way of pleasing the customer and nurturing a long-term relationship, she concludes her letter by offering a discount or more attractive payment terms for any substitute items that are ordered.

Fierce competition in the consumer marketplace often leads to financial problems, especially for smaller retail stores. When a retailer places an order on credit but has numerous unpaid invoices, Eason is both firm and compassionate in the face of pleading, begging, and sometimes even threats. First she expresses her appreciation for previous business with the retailer. Then she states her reasons for adhering to Olmec's accounting department guidelines. Finally, she expresses confidence that the retailer will be able to regain solid financial footing and that their relationship will be able to continue in the future.

Key relationships for Eason are those with her investors and the members of Olmec's board of directors. She believes it's important to stay ahead of any problems, so she delivers any bad news as early as possible. She prefers to meet with the investor or board member face-to-face, because "we need to look at and address the situation eye to eye." Afterward, she puts in writing exactly what was discussed, emphasizing any positive aspects that were covered in the meeting.

She communicates with unsatisfactory employees as positively as possible. These employees require the highest level of diplomacy, says Eason. So she makes a point of focusing on what the company needs to achieve rather than on what the employee might lack.

Saying no gracefully requires tactful communication. "You always want to be able to go back someday," say Eason. When she must convey bad news, she's appreciative and cordial. But she's also careful to keep her correspondence short. Her brevity emphasizes the finality of her decision, and her warmth shows an interest in future possibilities.[1]

ORGANIZING BAD-NEWS MESSAGES

As Yia Eason realizes, some people interpret being rejected for a job or for credit as a personal failure; even rejections in less sensitive areas usually complicate people's lives. Admittedly, business decisions should not be made solely to avoid hurting someone's feelings, but mixing bad news with consideration for your reader's needs helps your audience understand that the unfavorable decision is based on a business judgment, not on any personal judgment.

As with direct requests and routine, good-news, and goodwill messages, bad-news messages are best communicated across cultures by using the tone, organization, and other cultural conventions that your audience expects. Only then can you avoid the inappropriate or even offensive approaches that could jeopardize your business relationship.[2] For example, in Latin countries, people consider it discourteous and impolite to bring negative messages to the boss, so they attempt to avoid it altogether. People in Germany tend to be more direct with bad news, but in Japan, bad news can be presented so positively that a U.S. businessperson may not detect it at all.[3]

When you need to communicate bad news to a U.S. or Canadian audience that has minimal cultural differences, consider tone and arrangement. Your tone contributes to your message's effectiveness by supporting three specific goals:

- Helping your audience understand that your bad-news message represents a firm decision
- Helping your audience understand that under the circumstances, your decision was fair and reasonable
- Helping your audience remain well disposed toward your business and possibly toward you

When establishing tone, strive for
- *Firmness*
- *Fairness*
- *Goodwill*

With the right tone, you can make an unwelcome point while preserving your audience's ego.

To accomplish the right tone, make liberal use of the "you" attitude, for example, by pointing out how your decision might actually further your audience's goals. In addition, convey concern by looking for the best in your audience; assume your audience is interested in being fair, even when they are at fault. Finally, you can ease disappointment by using positive words rather than negative ones. Just be sure that your positive tone doesn't hide the bad news behind difficult language.[4] You want to convey the bad news, not cover it up.

In a bad-news message, the "you" attitude translates into
- *Emphasizing the audience's goals instead of your own*
- *Looking for the best in your audience*
- *Using positive rather than negative phrasing*

How you arrange the main idea and supporting data can also ease your audience's disappointment. The two basic strategies described in Chapter 6 are (1) the indirect plan, which presents supporting data before the main idea, and (2) the direct plan, which presents the main idea before the supporting data.

Use the indirect plan or the direct plan, depending on the audience's needs.

Indirect Plan

The indirect plan is actually a familiar approach. You've probably used it many times to say something that might upset another person. Instead of beginning a business message with a blunt no, which could keep your audience from reading or listening to your reasons, use the indirect plan to ease your audience into the part of your message that demonstrates how you're fair-minded and eager to do business on some other terms.

The indirect plan consists of four parts: (1) a buffer; (2) reasons supporting the negative decision; (3) a clear, diplomatic statement of the negative decision; and (4) a helpful, friendly, and positive close. By presenting the reasons for your decision before the bad news itself, you gradually prepare the audience for disappointment. In most cases, this approach is more appropriate than an abrupt statement of the bad news.

Buffer

The first step in using the indirect plan is to put the audience in an accepting mood by making a neutral, noncontroversial statement closely related to the point of the message; this statement is also called a **buffer.** In a memo telling another supervisor that you can't spare anyone from your customer service staff for a temporary assignment to the order fulfillment department, you might begin with a sentence like this: "Customer service is one of our major concerns at National Investments. In addition, this department shares your goal of processing orders quickly and efficiently."

A buffer is a neutral lead-in to bad news.

If possible, base the buffer on statements made by the person you're responding to. If you use an unrelated buffer, you seem to be "beating around the bush"; that is, you appear unethical, so you lose your audience's respect. Another goal when composing your buffer is to avoid giving the impression that good news will follow. Building up the audience at the beginning only makes the subsequent letdown even more painful. Imagine your reaction to the following openings:

> Your résumé indicates that you would be well suited for a management trainee position with our company.

> Your résumé shows very clearly why you are interested in becoming a management trainee with our company.

The second opening emphasizes the applicant's favorable interpretation of her qualifications rather than the company's evaluation, so it's less misleading but still positive. Here are some other things to avoid when writing a buffer:

Use a buffer that is
- *Neutral*
- *Relevant*
- *Not misleading*
- *Assertive*
- *Succinct*

- *Avoid saying no.* An audience encountering the unpleasant news right at the beginning usually reacts negatively to the rest of the message, no matter how reasonable and well phrased it is.
- *Avoid using a know-it-all tone.* When you use phrases such as "you should be aware that," the audience expects your lecture to lead to a negative response and therefore resists the rest of your message.
- *Avoid wordy and irrelevant phrases and sentences.* Sentences such as "We have received your letter," "This letter is in reply to your request," and "We are writing in response to your request" are irrelevant. You make better use of the space by referring directly to the subject of the letter.
- *Avoid apologizing.* An apology weakens your explanation of the unfavorable decision.
- *Avoid writing a buffer that is too long.* The point is to briefly identify something that both you and your audience are interested in and agree on before proceeding in a businesslike way.

Table 10.1 (see page 292) shows types of buffers you could use to open a bad-news message tactfully.

Some critics believe that using a buffer is manipulative, dishonest, and thus unethical. In fact, buffers are unethical only if they're insincere. Breaking bad news with

TABLE 10.1
TYPES OF BUFFERS

Buffer	Strategy	Example
Agreement	Find a point on which you and the reader share similar views.	We both know how hard it is to make a profit in this industry.
Appreciation	Express sincere thanks for receiving something.	Your check for $127.17 arrived yesterday. Thank you.
Cooperation	Convey your willingness to help in any way you realistically can.	Employee Services is here to smooth the way for all of you who work to achieve company goals.
Fairness	Assure the reader that you've closely examined and carefully considered the problem, or mention an appropriate action that has already been taken.	For the past week, we have carefully monitored those using the photocopying machine to see whether we can detect any pattern of use that might explain its frequent breakdowns.
Good news	Start with the part of your message that is favorable.	A replacement knob for your range is on its way, shipped February 10 via UPS.
Praise	Find an attribute or an achievement to compliment.	Your résumé shows an admirable breadth of experience, which should serve you well as you progress in your career.
Resale	Favorably discuss the product or company related to the subject of the letter.	With their heavy-duty, full-suspension hardware and fine veneers, the desks and file cabinets in our Montclair line have become a hit with value-conscious professionals.
Understanding	Demonstrate that you understand the reader's goals and needs.	So that you can more easily find the printer with the features you need, we are enclosing a brochure that describes all the Panasonic printers currently available.

kindness and courtesy is the human way. Consideration for the feelings of others is never dishonest, and that consideration helps your audience accept your message.

After you've composed a buffer, evaluate it by asking yourself four questions: Is it pleasant? Is it relevant? Is it neutral, saying neither yes nor no? Does it provide for a smooth transition to the reasons that follow? If you can answer yes to every question, you may proceed confidently to the next section of your message.

Reasons

If you've done a good job of composing the buffer, the reasons will follow naturally. Cover the more positive points first; then move to the less positive ones. Provide enough detail for the audience to understand your reasons, but be concise; a long, roundabout explanation may make the audience impatient.

The goal is to explain *why* you have reached your decision before you explain *what* that decision is. If you present your reasons effectively, they will help convince the audience that your decision is justified, fair, and logical. However, someone who realizes

Present reasons to show that your decision is reasonable and fair.

you're saying no before he or she understands why may either quit paying attention altogether or be set to rebut the reasons when they're finally given.

When giving your reasons, be tactful by highlighting just how the decision benefits your audience, instead of focusing on why the decision is good for you or your company. For example, when saying no to a credit request, show how your decision will keep the person from becoming overextended financially. Facts and figures are often helpful in convincing members of your audience that you're acting in their best interests.

As you explain your reasons, avoid hiding behind company policy to cushion the bad news. If you say, "Company policy forbids our hiring anyone who does not have two years' management experience," you seem to imply that you haven't considered the person on her or his own merits. Although skilled and sympathetic communicators may sometimes quote company policy, they also briefly explain it so that the audience can try to meet the requirements at a later time.

Avoid apologizing when giving your reasons. Apologies are appropriate only when someone in your company has made a severe mistake or done something terribly wrong. If no one in the company is at fault, an apology gives the wrong impression.

The tone of the language you use to explain your reasons greatly influences your audience's reception of the bad news that follows. So avoid negative, counterproductive words like these:

> Focus on how the audience might benefit from your negative message.

Instead of This	**Say This**
We have received your **broken** clock.	We have received the clock you sent us.
I **cannot understand** what you mean.	Please clarify your request.
The **damage** won't be fixed for a week.	The item will be repaired next week.
There will be a **delay** in your order.	We will ship your order as soon as possible.
You are clearly **dissatisfied.**	We are doing what we can to make things right.
Your account is in **error.**	Corrections have been made to your account.
The breakage was not our **fault.**	The merchandise was broken during shipping.
Sorry for your **inconvenience.**	The enclosed coupon will save you $5 next time.
We **regret** the misunderstanding.	I'll try my best to be more clear from now on.
I was **shocked** to hear the news.	The news reached me yesterday.
Unfortunately, we haven't received it.	It hasn't arrived yet.
The enclosed statement is **wrong.**	Please recheck the enclosed statement.

Furthermore, protect the audience's pride by using language that conveys respect, and avoid an accusing tone. Use third-person, impersonal, passive language to explain your audience's mistakes in an inoffensive way. Say, "The appliance won't work after being immersed in water" instead of "You shouldn't have immersed the appliance in water." In this case, the "you" attitude is better observed by avoiding the word *you*.

When refusing the application of a management trainee, a tactfully worded letter might give these reasons for the decision not to hire:

> Sometimes the "you" attitude is best observed by avoiding the word *you*.

> Because these management trainee positions are quite challenging, our human relations department has researched the qualifications needed to succeed in them. The findings show that the two most important qualifications

are a bachelor's degree in business administration and two years' supervisory experience.

This paragraph does a good job of stating the reasons for the refusal:

Well-written reasons are
- Detailed
- Tactful
- Individualized
- Unapologetic
- Positive

- It provides enough detail to make the reason for the refusal logically acceptable.
- It implies that the applicant is better off avoiding a program in which she would probably fail, given the background of others who would be working alongside her.
- It doesn't rest solely on company policy. A relevant policy exists but is presented as logical rather than rigid.
- It offers no apology for the decision.
- It avoids negative personal expressions ("You do not meet our requirements").

Sometimes detailed reasons should not be provided.

Although specific reasons help the audience accept bad news, reasons cannot always be given. When reasons involve confidential, excessively complicated, or purely negative information, or when the reasons benefit only you or your firm (such as enhancing the company's profits), don't include them. Move directly to the next section.

The Bad News

When the bad news is a logical outcome of the reasons that come before it, the audience is psychologically prepared to receive it. However, the audience may still react emotionally if the bad news is handled carelessly. Three techniques are especially useful for saying no as clearly and as painlessly as possible. First, de-emphasize the bad news:

To make bad news less painful
- Deemphasize the bad news visually and grammatically
- Use a conditional statement
- Tell what you did do, not what you didn't do

- Minimize the space or time devoted to it.
- Subordinate it in a complex or compound sentence ("My department is already shorthanded, so I'll need all my staff for at least the next two months").
- Embed it in the middle of a paragraph.

Second, use a conditional (*if* or *when*) statement to imply that the audience could possibly have received, or might someday receive, a favorable answer: "When you have more managerial experience, you are welcome to reapply." A statement like this could motivate applicants to improve their qualifications.

Third, tell the audience what you did do, can do, or will do rather than what you did not do, cannot do, or won't do. Say "We sell exclusively through retailers, and the one nearest you that carries our merchandise is . . ." rather than "We are unable to serve you, so please call your nearest dealer." Here's the same principle applied to the letter rejecting the job applicant: "The five positions currently open have been staffed with people whose qualifications match those uncovered in our research." A statement like this need not be followed by the explicit news that you won't be hiring the reader. By focusing on the positive and only implying the bad news, you soften the blow.

Of course, when implying bad news, be sure your audience understands the entire message—including the bad news. It would not be ethical to overemphasize the positive. So if an implied message might leave doubt, state your decision in direct terms. Just be sure to avoid blunt statements that are likely to cause pain and anger. The following phrases are particularly likely to offend:

When writing a bad-news message, avoid negative wording and personal language.

Instead of This	**Use This**
I must refuse your request.	I won't be in town on the day you need me.
We must deny your application.	The position has been filled.
I am unable to grant your request.	Contact us again when you have established . . .

We cannot afford to continue the program.	The program will conclude on May 1.
Much as I would like to attend . . .	Our budget meeting ends too late for me to attend . . .
We must reject your proposal.	We've accepted the proposal from AAA Builders.
We must turn down your extension request.	Please send in your payment by June 14.

Positive Close

As Olmec's Yia Eason will attest, after giving your audience the bad news, your job is to end your message on a more upbeat note. You might propose an attainable solution to the audience's problem: "The human resources department has offered to bring in temporary workers when I need them, and they would probably consider doing the same for you." In a message to a customer or potential customer, an off-the-subject ending that includes resale information or sales promotion is also appropriate. If you've asked someone to decide between alternatives or to take some action, make sure she or he knows what to do, when to do it, and how to do it with ease. Whatever type of close you choose, follow these guidelines:

An upbeat, positive close
- Builds goodwill
- Offers a suggestion for action
- Provides a look toward the future

- Keep your close as positive as possible. Don't refer to, repeat, or apologize for the bad news, and refrain from expressing any doubt that your reasons will be accepted (avoid statements such as "I trust our decision is satisfactory").
- Encourage additional communication *only* if you're willing to discuss your decision further (avoid phrases such as "If you have further questions, please write").
- Keep a positive outlook on the future. Anticipate no problems (avoid statements such as "Should you have further problems, please let us know").
- Be sincere. Steer clear of clichés that are insincere in view of the bad news (avoid saying, "If we can be of any help, please contact us").
- Be confident about keeping the person as a customer (avoid phrases such as "We hope you will continue to do business with us").

If you are the one who has to reject the applicant for the management trainee position, you could observe these guidelines by writing a close like this:

> **Many companies seek other qualifications in management trainees, so I urge you to continue your job search. You'll certainly find an opening in which your skills and aspirations match the job requirements exactly.**

Keep in mind that the close is the last thing the audience has to remember you by. Try to make the memory a positive one.

Direct Plan

A bad-news message organized on the direct plan would start with a clear statement of the bad news, proceed to the reasons for the decision, and end with a courteous close. Stating the bad news at the beginning can have two advantages: (1) It makes a shorter message possible, and (2) the audience needs less time to reach the main idea of the message, the bad news itself.

Although the indirect approach is preferable for most bad-news messages, you may sometimes want to move right to the point. Memos are often organized so that the bad news comes before the reasons. In fact, some managers expect all internal correspondence to be brief and direct, regardless of whether the message is positive or

Use the direct plan when
- Your boss prefers that internal messages come right to the point
- The message has little personal impact
- You want to make your point emphatically

COMMUNICATING ACROSS CULTURES

GOOD WAYS TO SEND BAD NEWS AROUND THE WORLD

Bad news is unwelcome in any language—but the conventions for passing it on to business associates can vary considerably from country to country. To save yourself grief when sending and receiving bad news internationally, be familiar with the customary approach.

For instance, French business letters are very formal and writer-oriented (without reference to audience needs or benefits). That's because French businesses traditionally write for one purpose: to establish evidence for any future litigation. The preferred style is prudent, precise, and respectful, even if the writer and reader know each other very well. Letters begin with courteous titles ("Monsieur," "Madame," but not "Dear ___") and close with flowery salutations ("With our anticipated thanks, we beg you to accept, Sir, our sincere greetings," or "Awaiting your reply, we offer you, Sirs, our assiduous greetings"). Despite their respectful wording, French business letters never become personal or friendly—which is sometimes misinterpreted as coolness, nonchalance, or indifference.

When the news is bad, French writers take a direct approach. They open with a reference to the problem or previous correspondence and then state the bad news clearly. They don't try to avoid negative words, nor do they refer to the audience's needs; but they often apologize and express regret for the problem. A bad-news letter in France won't necessarily end on a positive note, but the close remains gracious: "Accept, Sirs, our distinguished greetings."

In Japan all letter writing is regarded as a troublesome task, even when the news is good. To preserve or establish the appropriate level of respect and humility for the relationship between writer and reader, Japanese letter writers select different forms of nouns, pronouns, and verbs, depending on whose actions they're referring to. Also, their letters traditionally open with remarks about the season taken from books that provide standard phrases for each month—such as, "The season for cherry blossoms is here with us and everybody is beginning to feel refreshed." This is followed by a reference to the reader's business prosperity or health.

When the message is bad news, these opening formalities serve as a buffer. Explanations and apologies follow; then comes the bad news or refusal. Also, Japanese writers protect the reader's feelings by wording the bad news ambiguously—which can sometimes be misinterpreted by Western readers as a condition of acceptance rather than as the refusal it truly is.

British bad-news letters may surprise readers who know that British culture values politeness, tact, and diplomacy. Centuries of business tradition dictate a direct approach for all business letters, even when the message is unsettling. A typical bad-news letter opens with a reference to the subject and continues with a few paragraphs explaining the bad news in an abrupt and blunt, but logical, sequence. The writer then expresses apology and regret, which further emphasizes the bad news. Some British letters end there; others close with a few words wishing the reader success or hoping for continued goodwill. Recently, however, some leading British companies have begun to see the value of considering their audiences' feelings and are using the indirect approach common in the United States.

1. Select a bad-news message and see whether you can redesign it for Japan, France, and Great Britain. How would you change the format for each country? What would you add or delete?
2. You may one day need to send bad news to a country not mentioned here. What information sources might you consult to find out how businesses convey bad news in that culture?

negative. Routine bad-news messages to other companies often follow the direct plan, especially if they relay decisions that have little or no personal impact. Using a buffer can actually cause ill will in people who see them frequently (such as people searching for employment).[5] In addition, you'll sometimes know from prior experience that your audience simply prefers reading the bad news first in any message. Of course, the direct plan is also appropriate when you want to present an image of firmness and strength; for example, the last message in a collection series, just before the matter is turned over to an attorney, usually gets right to the point.

Mony Insurance Company's best communicators go out of their way to be helpful and to keep the customer's confidence. No one does this better than Carol Trytek, working in the policyholder services area of the toll-free telephone center.

So in any number of circumstances, you may want to use the direct plan and save your positive comments for the close. Even so, remember that a tactful tone and a focus on reasons will help make any bad-news message easier to accept. (For an idea of how some other cultures handle bad news, see "Good Ways to Send Bad News Around the World").

CONVEYING BAD NEWS ABOUT ORDERS

For several reasons, businesses must sometimes convey bad news concerning orders. When Yia Eason must relate bad news to retailers about their orders, she is careful to focus her audience's attention on what she can do rather than on what she cannot. When writing to a would-be customer, you have three basic goals:

- To work toward an eventual sale along the lines of the original order
- To keep instructions or additional information as clear as possible
- To maintain an optimistic, confident tone so that your reader won't lose interest

> The basic goal of a bad-news letter about orders is to protect or make a sale.

For example, when you must back order for a customer, you have one of two types of bad news to convey: (1) You're able to send only part of the order, or (2) you're able to send none of the order. When sending only part of the order, you actually have both good news and bad news. In such situations, the indirect plan works very well. The buffer contains the good news (that part of the order is en route) along with a resale reminder of the product's attractiveness. After the buffer come the reasons for the delay of the remainder of the shipment. A strong close encourages a favorable attitude toward the entire transaction (see Figure 10.1 on page 298).

> Use the indirect plan when telling a customer that you cannot immediately ship the entire order.

Even when you're unable to send the customer any portion of an order, you still use the indirect approach. However, because you have no good news to give, your buffer only confirms the sale, and the explanation section states your reason for not filling the order promptly. For a brief outline of back-order tasks, see this chapter's Checklist for Bad News About Orders on page 299.

Figure 10.1
In-Depth Critique: Letter
Advising of a Back Order

For a customer whose order for a recliner and ottoman will be partly filled, your letter might read like this one.

1284 North Telegraph Road
Monroe, MI 48161-5138

September 9, 1997

Dr. Elizabeth Fawnworth
2524 St. Georgen Common
Boston, MA 22290-2827

Dear Dr. Fawnworth:

Thank you for your order of the special edition recliner and matching ottoman. The recliner with custom features will be shipped today. The leather trim you designated turned out beautifully, and we're sure the recliner will make a handsome addition to your study.

The roll-around ottoman has proved to be one of our most popular items. Our plant manager reports that even though he has almost doubled production this year, we are still experiencing some delays. We estimate that your ottoman will be shipped no later than November 15 to arrive by Thanksgiving.

Remember that all La-Z-Boy products carry a lifetime guarantee. We know you will enjoy your recliner and ottoman for many years. I've enclosed a catalog that includes our latest designs. Please call me at (617) 358-2899 if you'd like to talk about any of our special fabrics and custom designs. We look forward to serving you in the future.

Sincerely,

Suzanne Godfrey

Suzanne Godfrey
Manager, Custom Designs

Enclosure

Using the indirect plan, the buffer conveys the good news and confirms the wisdom of the customer's choice.

The reasons for the shipping delay are stated in such a way that indicate the ottoman is a popular choice. The bad news is cushioned by the pledge to take care of the problem by a definite time.

The bad news itself is implied by telling the reader what is being done, not what cannot be done.

The positive close also opens the door to future business.

COMMUNICATING NEGATIVE ANSWERS AND INFORMATION

The businessperson who tries to say yes to everyone probably won't win many promotions or stay in business for long. Occasionally, your response to inquiries must simply be no. It's a mark of your skill as a communicator to be able to say no clearly yet not cut yourself off from future dealings with the other person.

CHECKLIST FOR BAD NEWS ABOUT ORDERS

A. OVERALL STRATEGY
1. Use the indirect plan in most cases.
2. Use the direct plan when the situation is routine (between employees of the same company), when the reader is not emotionally involved in the message, or when you know that the reader would prefer the bad news first.

B. BUFFER
1. Express appreciation for the specific order.
2. Extend a welcome to a new customer.
3. Avoid negative words (*won't, can't, unable to*).
4. Use resale information on the ordered merchandise to build the customer's confidence in the original choice (except for unfillable orders).

C. REASONS
1. Emphasize what the firm is doing rather than what it isn't doing, what it does have rather than what it lacks.
2. Avoid apologies and expressions of sorrow or regret.
3. Handle back orders carefully.
   a. Specify shipping dates.
   b. Explain why the item is out of stock, such as high popularity or exceptional demand; that may stimulate the customer's desire for the item.
   c. Reinforce the customer's confidence with resale (for consumers, emphasize personal attention, credit, repair services, free delivery, special discounts, telephone shopping, and other services; for dealers, emphasize free counter and window displays, advertising materials, sales manuals, factory guarantees, and nearby warehousing).
   d. Refer to sales promotion material, if desirable.

D. THE BAD NEWS
1. State the bad news as positively as possible.
2. State the bad news clearly.
3. Stress the reader benefit of the decision to buy.

E. POSITIVE, FRIENDLY, HELPFUL CLOSE
1. Remind the reader of how his or her needs are being met, if appropriate.
2. Use resale information to clinch the sale, especially for back orders.
3. Adopt a tone that shows you remain in control of the situation and will continue to give customers' orders personal attention.

Depending on your relationship with the reader, you could use either the direct plan or the indirect plan when writing negative messages. If the reader is unlikely to be deeply disappointed, use the direct plan. Otherwise, use a buffer that expresses your appreciation for being thought of, assures the reader of your attention to the request, compliments the reader, or indicates your understanding of the reader's needs. Continue with the reasons for the bad news and the bad news itself, couched in terms that show how the reader's problem can be solved and what you can do to help. Then close with a statement of interest, encouragement, or goodwill. You can demonstrate your sincerity (and minimize the reader's hostility or disappointment) by promptly fulfilling any promises you make.

> Use the direct plan when your negative answer or information will have little personal impact; use the indirect plan in more sensitive situations.

Providing Bad News About Products

When you must provide bad news about a product, the situation and the reader will dictate whether to use the direct or indirect plan. If you were writing to tell your company's bookkeeping department about increasing product prices, you'd use the direct plan. The reader would have to make some arithmetical adjustments when the increases are put into effect but presumably won't be emotionally involved in the matter. However, you would probably use the indirect plan to convey the same information to customers or even to your own sales department—since a change that weakens your products' competitive edge threatens sales representatives' incomes and possibly their jobs.

> Consider the direct or indirect plan for telling the reader bad news about a product.

The e-mail message in Figure 10.2 was written to tell one company's sales managers that their request for a licensing agreement has been rejected. The middle section of this memo presents an honest statement of the bad news. The effect of the bad news is diminished by the problem-solving tone, by the avoidance of any overt statement that such a setback may affect commissions, and by the upbeat close.

Denying Cooperation with Routine Requests

Consider the direct or indirect plan to tell someone you cannot do what has been requested.

When people ask you for information or want you to do something and you can't honor the request, you may answer with either the direct plan or the indirect plan. Say that you have asked a company to participate in your research project concerning sales promotion. However, that company has a policy against disseminating any information about projected sales figures. How would you react to the following letter?

> Our company policy prohibits us from participating in research projects where disclosure of discretionary information might be necessary. Therefore, we decline your invitation to our sales staff to fill out questionnaires for your study.
> Thank you for trying to include Qualcomm Corporation in your research. If we can be of further assistance, please let us know.

This letter would offend most readers, for several reasons:

- The direct plan is used, even though the reader is outside the company and may be emotionally involved in the response.
- The tone of the first paragraph is unnecessarily negative and abrupt.
- The writer hides behind company policy, a policy that the reader may find questionable.
- The offer to help is an unpleasant irony, given the writer's unwillingness to help in this instance.

Wording, tone, and format conspire to make a letter either offensive or acceptable. The letter that follows conveys the same negative message as the previous letter without sounding offensive:

> We at Qualcomm Corporation appreciate and benefit from the research of companies such as yours. Your present study sounds interesting, and we certainly wish we could participate.
> Unfortunately, our board requires strict confidentiality of all sales information until quarterly reports are mailed to stockholders. As you know, we release press reports at the same time the quarterly reports go out and will include you in all our future mailings.
> Although we cannot release projected figures, we are more than willing to share data that is part of the public record. I've enclosed several of our past earnings reports for your inspection. We look forward to seeing the results of your study. Please let us know if there is any additional way we can help.

The buffer is supportive and appreciative.

Without falling back on references to "company policy," the reason for the policy is fully explained. The bad news is implied, not stated explicitly.

The close is friendly, positive, and helpful.

As you think about the different impact these two letters might have on you, you can see why effective business writers like Yia Eason take the time and the trouble to give negative messages the attention they deserve.

Declining Invitations and Requests for Favors

Consider the direct or indirect plan to turn down an invitation or a request for a favor.

When you must say no to an invitation or a requested favor, your use of the direct or the indirect plan depends on your relationship with the reader. For example, say the president of your community college asks you to host graduation on your

When Sybervantage pursued licensing agreements with Warner, the company expected to be entering a lucrative arrangement in which both companies would profit. But now that Warner has rejected the request, Sybervantage must adjust its strategic planning and must keep its sales force both motivated and involved.

Figure 10.2
In-Depth Critique: E-Mail Message Providing Bad News About Products

```
╔═══════════════════════ E-Mail ═══════════════════════╗
║                                                       ║
╠═══════════════════════════════════════════════════════╣

Return-Path: <leslie@Sybervant.com>
Date: Thursday, 29 Aug 1996 08:09:19
From: Frank Leslie <leslie@Sybervant.com>
To: All Sales Managers
Subject: August 29 Meeting


Thank you for your continuing efforts to make
Sybervantage a leader in video-game development. Recent
reports indicate we captured a 10 percent increase in
market share over the second quarter of last year. That
increase is directly attributable to your energy and
enthusiasm. Now, we're facing a situation that will put
us to the test.

As you know, many of us in R&D have been working to
develop concept games based on Looney Tunes characters.
Currently we have eight games in various stages of
development. However, Warner has turned down our
requests for licensing agreements. It wasn't a matter of
money; we offered them top dollar. I believe Warner saw
the tremendous potential and simply decided to develop
its own character-based games.

On August 29 we will hold day-long meetings here in
Orlando to discuss our options. We'd like all of you to
be present. Our purpose will be to decide whether we
want to pursue another licensing agreement or continue
as we started, by developing our own character-based
games. Meetings will take place at the Ramada
Renaissance by the airport with lunch provided. Call or
e-mail Shirley in my office for reservations.

We have an opportunity to reshape Sybervantage for the
twenty-first century. Our company has a great future,
and I'm looking forward to the synergy we can create.


See you there,


Frank Leslie
President
```

The memo begins on a complimentary note to buffer the bad news.

The bad news is presented along with possible explanations.

The closing paragraph indicates the action that will be taken to lessen the impact of the bad news and actively involves the readers in the possibility of a solution.

Figure 10.3
In-Depth Critique: Letter Declining a Favor

Sandra Wofford has asked Advanced Systems to host graduation ceremonies for Whittier Community College. However, Advanced Systems' facilities will be in use on the day of graduation. In the following letter, May Yee Kwan delivers the bad news in a helpful and supportive way.

2927 Dawson Valley Road • Tulsa, OK 74151

Voice: (918) 669-4428 • Fax: (918) 669-4429

http://www.adsys.com

ADVANCED SYSTEMS

March 5, 1997

Sandra Wofford, President
Whittier Community College
333 Whittier Avenue
Tulsa, Oklahoma 74150

Dear President Wofford:

The buffer recaps the request and demonstrates respect.

We appreciate Whittier Community College and the many opportunities you have provided deserving students over the years. Because of this, we at Advanced Systems have endeavored to support the college in many ways. Thank you for considering our grounds for your graduation ceremony.

The bad news is stated explicitly and in detail.

Our companywide sales meetings will be held during the weeks of May 26 and June 2. We will host over 200 sales representatives and their families with activities planned both at our corporate campus and the Ramada Renaissance. Because these activities involve many of our key staff people as well as ground maintenance and engineering, we would be unable to devote an adequate support staff for your graduation.

By suggesting an alternative, Kwan shows that she does care about the college and has given the matter some thought.

My assistant, Roberta Seagers, suggests you contact the Municipal Botanical Gardens as a possible graduation site. She recommends calling Jerry Kane who handles all their public relations. If we can help in any other way with graduation, please let us know.

The close renews the corporation's support in the future.

Even though our annual meeting will most likely prohibit us from ever hosting graduation, we remain firm in our commitment to you, President Wofford, and to the fine students you represent.

corporate grounds, but your companywide sales meetings will take place at the same time. If you don't know the president well, you'd probably use the indirect plan (see Figure 10.3).

However, if you are friends with the president and work frequently on projects for the college, you might use the direct approach.

Figure 10.3
(Continued)

Ms. Sandra Wofford, March 5, 1997, Page 2

We will continue to be a corporate partner to Whittier Community College and will support your efforts as you move into the twenty-first century.

Sincerely,

May Yee Kwan

May Yee Kwan
Public Relations Director

lc

Sandra, thanks for asking us to host your '97 graduation. You know we've always supported the college and would love to do this for you. Unfortunately, our company sales meetings will be going on during the same time. We'll have so many folks tied up with logistics, we wouldn't have the personnel to adequately take care of graduation.

Have you called Jerry Kane over at the Botanical Gardens? I can't think of a prettier site for graduation. Roberta in my office volunteers over there and knows Jerry. She can fill you in on the details, if you'd like to talk to her first.

Thanks again for considering us. Let's have lunch in mid-June to plan our involvement with the college for the next school year. You can think of all kinds of ways to make me sorry I had to say no! I'll look forward to seeing you and catching up on family news.

This letter gets right to the point but still uses some blow-softening techniques: It compliments the person and organization making the request and looks toward future opportunities for cooperation.

REFUSING ADJUSTMENT OF CLAIMS AND COMPLAINTS

In almost every instance, a customer who requests an adjustment is emotionally involved; therefore the indirect plan is generally used for a refusal. Your job as a writer is to avoid accepting responsibility for the unfortunate situation and yet avoid blaming or accusing the customer. To steer clear of these pitfalls, pay special attention to the tone of your letter. Keep in mind that a tactful and courteous letter can build goodwill while denying the claim (see Figure 10.4 on page 304).

When refusing to adjust a claim, avoid language that might have a negative impact on the reader. Instead, demonstrate that you understand and have considered the complaint. Then, even if the claim is unreasonable, rationally explain why you are refusing the request (but don't apologize or rely on company policy). End the letter on a respectful and action-oriented note. This chapter's Checklist for Refusals to Make Adjustments, on page 305, reminds you of the tasks involved in such messages.

You may be tempted to respond to something particularly outrageous by calling the person responsible a crook, a swindler, or an incompetent. Resist! If you don't,

Use the indirect plan in most cases of refusing to make an adjustment.

When refusing to make an adjustment
- Demonstrate understanding of the complaint
- Explain your refusal
- Suggest alternative action

Figure 10.4
In-Depth Critique: Letter Refusing a Claim

Brodie's Stereo/Video recently received a letter from George Pulkinen. Pulkinen purchased a portable CD player a year ago. He writes to say that the unit doesn't work correctly and to inquire about the warranty. Pulkinen believes the warranty covers one year, when it actually covers only three months.

NUMBER ONE IN ENTERTAINMENT

BRODIE'S
S/V
STEREO
VIDEO

68 Lake Itasca Boulevard • Hannover, MN 55341
Voice: (612) 878-1312 • Fax: (612) 878-1316

May 3, 1997

Mr. George Pulkinen
237 Lake Street
Hannover, MN 55341

Dear Mr. Pulkinen:

Thank you for your letter describing the problem with your portable Sony CD Walkman. We believe, as you do, that electronic equipment should be built to last. That's why we stand behind our products with a 90-day warranty.

Even though your Walkman is a year old and therefore out of warranty, we can still help. Please package your CD player carefully and ship it to our store in Hannover. Include your complete name, address, phone number, and a brief description of the problem. Include a check for $35.00 made out to Sony. After examining the unit, we will give you a written estimate of the needed parts and labor. Then just let us know whether you want us to make the repairs—either by phone or by filling out the postpaid card we will provide.

If you choose to repair the unit, the $35.00 will apply toward your bill, payable by check or major credit card. If you decide not to repair the unit, the $35.00 will pay for the technician's time in examining the unit. Sony also has service centers available in your area. If you would prefer to take the unit to one of them, please see the enclosed list.

Thanks again for inquiring about our service. It's always a pleasure to hear from our customers, and I'm glad you've enjoyed a number of our different products. I've also enclosed a catalog of

---

The buffer covers a point that reader and writer agree on.

The reason puts the company's policy in a favorable light.

The bad news, stated indirectly, tactfully leaves the repair decision to the customer.

A positive alternative action should help soothe the customer.

---

you could be sued for **defamation,** a false statement that tends to damage someone's character or reputation. (Written defamation is called *libel;* spoken defamation is called *slander.*) By this definition, someone suing for defamation would have to prove (1) that the statement is false, (2) that the language is injurious to the person's reputation, and (3) that the statement has been "published."

Figure 10.4
(Continued)

Mr. George Pulkinen, May 3, 1997, Page 2

our latest high-tech electronic gear. For the month of June, Sony is offering a "Trade-Up Special," at which time you can receive trade-in credit for your Walkman when you purchase a newer model. Your local dealers will have all the details. I hope to see you at Brodie's very soon.

Sincerely,

Walter Brodie

Walter Brodie
Proprietor

mk

Enclosure

The close blends sales promotion with acknowledgment of the customer's interests.

CHECKLIST FOR REFUSALS TO MAKE ADJUSTMENTS

A. BUFFER
1. Use a topic of mutual agreement or a neutral topic to start, but keep to the subject of the letter.
2. Indicate your full understanding of the nature of the complaint.
3. Avoid all areas of disagreement.
4. Avoid any hint of your final decision.
5. Keep the buffer brief and to the point.
6. Maintain a confident, positive, supportive tone.

B. REASONS
1. Provide an accurate, factual account of the transaction.
2. Offer enough detail to show the logic of your position.
3. Emphasize ways that the product should have been handled or the contract followed, rather than the reader's negligence.
4. Word the explanation so that the reader can anticipate the refusal.
5. Avoid relying on unexplained company policy.
6. Avoid accusing or preaching (*you should have*).
7. Do not blame or scold the reader.
8. Do not make the reader appear or feel stupid.
9. Inject a brief resale note after the explanation, if desirable.

C. THE BAD NEWS
1. Make the refusal clear using tactful wording.
2. Avoid any hint that your decision is less than final.
3. Avoid words like *reject* and *claim*.
4. Make a counterproposal for a compromise settlement or partial adjustment (if desirable) in a willing not begrudging tone, in a spirit of honest cooperation, and without making it sound like a penalty.
5. Include a resale note for the company or product.
6. Emphasize a desire for a good relationship in the future.
7. Extend an offer to replace the product or provide a replacement part at the regular price.

D. POSITIVE, FRIENDLY, HELPFUL CLOSE
1. Eliminate any reference to your refusal.
2. Avoid any apology.
3. Eliminate words suggesting uncertainty.
4. Refer to enclosed sales material.
5. Make any suggested action easy for readers to comply with.

If you can prove that your accusations are true, then you haven't defamed the person. The courts are likely to give you the benefit of the doubt because our society believes ordinary business communication should not be hampered by fear of lawsuits. However, beware the irate letter intended to let off steam: If the message has no necessary business purpose and is expressed in abusive language that hints of malice, you'll lose the case. To avoid being accused of defamation, follow these guidelines:

- Avoid using any kind of abusive language or terms that could be considered defamatory.
- If you wish to express your own personal opinions about a sensitive matter, use your own stationery (not company letterhead), and don't include your job title or position. Take responsibility for your own actions without involving your company.
- Provide accurate information and stick to the facts.
- Never let anger or malice motivate your messages.
- Consult your company's legal department or an attorney whenever you think a message might have legal consequences.
- Communicate honestly, and make sure what you're saying is what you believe to be true.

REFUSING TO EXTEND CREDIT

Use the indirect plan when turning down a credit applicant.

Credit is refused for a variety of reasons, all involving sensitive personal or legal considerations. When denying credit to the applicant with a proven record of delinquent payments and to the applicant with an unstable background, you would probably be justified in offering little hope for future credit approval. You could be more encouraging to other types of applicants. You most certainly would like their current cash business, and you may want their future credit business (see Figure 10.5).

In a letter denying credit to a business
- **Be more factual and less personal than in a letter to an individual**
- **Suggest ways to continue doing business**

Denials of business credit, as opposed to denials of individual credit, are less personally sensitive but more financially significant. Businesses have failed because major suppliers have suspended credit at inconvenient times. When refusing to extend credit to a business, explain your reasons as factually and as impersonally as possible (perhaps the firm's latest financial statements don't meet your criteria or its credit rating has fallen below an acceptable minimum). Also, explain the steps that must be taken to restore credit. Emphasize the benefits of continued dealings on a cash basis until the firm's credit worthiness has been established or restored. You might offer discounts for cash purchases or assistance in cooperative merchandising to reduce the firm's inventory and increase its cash flow. Third-party loans are another possibility you might suggest.

Be aware that credit is a legally sensitive subject.

Whether dealing with business customers or consumers, companies that deny credit exercise good judgment to avoid legal action. A faulty decision may unfairly damage a person's reputation, which in turn may provoke a lawsuit and other bad publicity for the company. Handling credit denials over the phone instead of in writing is no guarantee of avoiding trouble; companies that orally refuse credit still proceed with caution. For a reminder of the tasks involved in this type of message, see this chapter's Checklist for Credit Refusals on page 308.

CONVEYING UNFAVORABLE NEWS ABOUT PEOPLE

Use the indirect plan when giving someone bad news about his or her own job; use the direct plan when giving bad news about someone else's job.

From time to time, most managers must convey bad news about people. Letters to prospective employers may be written in direct order. On the other hand, letters to job applicants and employees are often written in indirect order, because the reader will most certainly be emotionally involved.

Figure 10.5
In-Depth Critique: Letter Refusing Credit

The following letter refuses credit for the present but points to the possibility of extending credit later. Krueger has taken pains to make the reader feel welcome and help her realize that her business is appreciated.

Best Buy Electronics

1717 Eastwood Boulevard, Atlanta, Georgia 30317
Voice: (404) 598-4747 • Fax: (404) 598-4748

September 9, 1997

Ms. Joelle Richards
818 Sandy Springs Road
Atlanta, GA 30328

Dear Ms. Richards:

Your request for a Best Buy card tells us something important: You enjoy the rewards of purchasing top-quality music and electronic equipment at bargain prices. Each year, Best Buy has grown because of a commitment to bringing you the best products at the best price.

Your excellent credit rating puts you in the top 25 percent. And although our Best Buy card requires continuous residence for 12 months, your application will remain in our database, so that it will be easier for you to reapply when you've lived a year at your present location.

In the meantime, we want you to know we value you as a customer at Best Buy. During the month of July, our Atlanta area stores are celebrating the opening of our new location in Duluth just off Interstate 85. Every store in the Metro area will be offering sales, special purchases, and additional discounts on our most popular electronic items. We'll be sending you a flyer soon. Your local paper will have all the details. We appreciate our customers and strive to give them the best at Best Buy.

Sincerely,

Evian Krueger

Evian Krueger
Customer Service Representative

The buffer expresses understanding and offers some subtle resale on the company. It establishes common ground while promoting the store.

The reason for refusal is tempered with the idea that Richards will likely be approved in the future.

The close reminds the reader that she is still a valued customer and promotes the upcoming celebration.

Refusing to Write Recommendation Letters

Even though many states have passed new laws to protect employers who provide open and honest job references for former employees, legal hazards persist.[6] That's why many former employers still refuse to write recommendation letters—especially for people whose job performance has been, on balance, unsatisfactory. Prospective employers

In letters informing prospective employers that you will not provide a recommendation, be direct, brief, and factual (to avoid legal pitfalls).

CHECKLIST FOR CREDIT REFUSALS

A. BUFFER
1. Introduce a topic that is relevant and that both you and the reader can agree on.
2. Eliminate apologies and negative-sounding words.
3. Phrase the buffer to avoid misleading the reader.
4. Limit the length of the buffer.
5. Express appreciation for the credit request.
6. Introduce resale information.

B. REASONS
1. Check the lead-in from the buffer for smoothness.
2. Make a transition from the favorable to the unfavorable message.
3. Make a transition from the general to the specific.
4. Avoid a condescending lecture about how credit is earned.
5. Avoid relying on unexplained company policy.
6. Stress the benefits of not being overextended.
7. Encourage a later credit application, if future approval is realistic.
8. Phrase reasons in terms of experience with others.
9. Carefully present reasons for the refusal.
    a. Clearly state the reasons if the reader will accept them.
    b. Explain your general credit criteria.
    c. Refer to a credit-reporting agency you have used.
    d. Use *insufficient information* as a reason only if this is the case.
    e. To avoid the risk of legal action, omit reasons entirely for extraordinarily sensitive or combative readers or when evidence is unusually negative or involves behavioral flaws.
10. Remind the reader of the benefits of cash purchases.

C. THE BAD NEWS
1. Make the refusal clear to the reader.
2. Offer only honest encouragement about considering the credit application at a later date.
3. Avoid negative words, such as *must decline*.
4. Suggest positive alternatives, such as cash and layaway purchases.
5. Handle refusals of business credit differently.
    a. Recommend cash purchases for small, frequent orders.
    b. Describe cash discounts (include figures).
    c. Suggest reducing inventory so that the business can strengthen its credit rating.
    d. Offer promotional and marketing aid.
    e. Suggest a later review of the credit application, if future approval is realistic.

D. POSITIVE, FRIENDLY, HELPFUL CLOSE
1. Avoid business clichés, apologies, and words of regret.
2. Suggest actions the reader might take.
3. Encourage the reader to look to the future, when the application may be approved.
4. Include sales promotion material only if the customer would not be offended.

---

don't usually have a personal stake in the response, so letters refusing to provide a recommendation may be brief and direct:

> We received your request for a recommendation for Yolanda Johnson. According to guidelines from our human resources department, we are authorized to confirm only that Ms. Johnson worked for Tandy, Inc., for three years from June 1995 to July 1998. Best of luck as you interview the administrative applicants.

In letters telling job applicants that you will not write a recommendation, use the utmost tact.

Letters to the applicants themselves are another matter. Any refusal to cooperate may seem a personal slight and a threat to the applicant's future. The only way to avoid ill feelings is to handle the applicant gently:

> Thank you for letting me know about your job opportunity with Coca-Cola. Your internship there and the MBA you've worked so hard to earn should place you in an excellent position to land the marketing job.

> Although we can't write formal recommendations here at PepsiCo, I can certainly send Coke a confirmation of your employment dates. For more in-depth recommendations, be sure to ask the people you worked with during your internship to write evaluations of your work performance, and don't forget to ask several of your major professors to write evaluations of your marketing skills. Best of luck to you in your career.

This letter deftly and tactfully avoids hurting the reader's feelings because it makes positive comments about the reader's recent activities, implies the refusal, suggests an alternative, and uses a polite close.

Rejecting Job Applications

It's also difficult to tell job applicants tactfully that you aren't going to offer them employment. But don't let that stop you from communicating the bad news. Rejecting an applicant with silence is unacceptable. At the same time, poorly written rejection letters do have negative consequences, ranging from the loss of qualified candidates for future openings to the loss of customers (not only the rejected applicants but also their friends and family).[7] When delivering bad news to job applicants, remember three principles:[8]

In a letter turning down a job applicant, treat the reader with respect; by applying for a job, he or she has complimented your company.

- *Open with the direct plan.* Job applicants know that good news will most probably come by phone and that bad news will most likely come by letter. So if you try to buffer the bad news that your reader is expecting, you will seem manipulative and insincere.
- *Clearly state why the applicant was not selected.* Make your rejection less personal by stating that you hired someone with more experience or whose qualifications match the position requirements more closely.
- *Close by suggesting alternatives.* If you believe the applicant is qualified, mention other openings within your company. You might suggest professional organizations that could help the applicant find employment. Or you might simply mention that the applicant's résumé will be considered for future openings. Any of these positive suggestions may help the applicant be less disappointed and view your company more positively.

A rejection letter need not be long. After all, the applicant wants to know only one thing: Did I land the job? Your brief message conveys the information clearly and with some consideration for the applicant's feelings (see Figure 10.6 on page 310).

Giving Negative Performance Reviews

A performance review is a manager's formal or informal evaluation of an employee. Few other communication tasks require such a broad range of skill and strategy as that needed for performance reviews, whether positive or negative. The main purpose of these reviews is to improve employee performance by (1) emphasizing and clarifying job requirements, (2) giving employees feedback on their efforts toward fulfilling those requirements, and (3) guiding continued efforts by developing a plan of action, along with its rewards and opportunities. In addition to improving employee performance, performance reviews help companies set organizational standards and communicate organizational values.[9]

In performance reviews, say what's right as well as what's wrong, and explain how the employee can improve performance.

Both positive and negative performance reviews share several characteristics: The tone is objective and unbiased, the language is nonjudgmental, and the focus is problem solution.[10] Also, to increase objectivity, more organizations are giving their employees feedback from multiple sources.[11]

Figure 10.6
In-Depth Critique: Letter Rejecting a Job Application

After Helen Putnam interviewed with Fiedler & McCarran, she was hopeful about receiving a job offer. Everything went well, and her résumé was in good shape. The following letter was intended to help Putnam understand that she would have been hired if she'd had more experience and that she shouldn't be discouraged.

Fiedler & McCarran

223 Brandon Street • Biloxi, Mississippi 39530 • (601) 466-9810 • Fax: (601) 466-6235

May 7, 1997

Ms. Helen Putnam
3741 Reardon Drive
Biloxi, MS 39530

Dear Ms. Putnam:

We appreciate your application for the position of customer liaison. Your academic record and community service indicate your willingness to work hard. Those of us who had the opportunity to talk with you on your visit enjoyed your obvious people skills and believe you have much to offer the right firm.

Because there were over 30 applicants for this position, the selection process was quite difficult. However, after much consideration, we have decided to hire an applicant with over 10 years' experience in mortgage lending.

Thank you for thinking of us. Your résumé and credentials show you to be a deserving candidate. And your ability to communicate will certainly help you achieve an excellent position in a recognized financial firm.

Sincerely,

Marvin R. Fichter

Marvin R. Fichter
Human Resources Director

bl

The complimentary opening should help the candidate accept the bad news better.

The explanation of choosing a candidate with ten years' experience implies the bad news about the candidate not getting the job and helps the candidate understand experience was the deciding factor, not unsatisfactory qualifications.

The positive close offers specific praise, helping the candidate finish the message with her self-confidence intact.

Be aware that employee performance reviews can play an important role in lawsuits. It's difficult to criticize employees face-to-face, and it's just as hard to include criticism in written performance evaluations. Nevertheless, if you fire an employee for incompetence and the performance evaluations are all positive, the employee can sue your company, maintaining you had no cause to terminate employment.[12] Also, your company could be sued for negligence if an injury is caused by an employee who received a negative evaluation but received no corrective action (such as retraining).[13] So as difficult as it may be, make sure your performance evaluations are well balanced and honest.

When you need to give a negative performance review, remember the following guidelines:[14]

- *Confront the problem right away.* Avoiding performance problems only makes them worse. The one acceptable reason to wait is if you need time to calm down and regain your objectivity.
- *Plan out your message.* Be clear about your concerns, and include examples of the employee's specific actions. Think about any possible biases you may have, and get feedback from others. Collect all relevant facts (both strengths and weaknesses).
- *Deliver the message in private.* Whether in writing or in person, make sure you address the performance problem privately. Don't send performance reviews by e-mail or fax. If you're reviewing an employee's performance face-to-face, conduct that review in a meeting arranged expressly for that purpose, and consider holding that meeting in a conference room, the employee's office, or some other neutral area.
- *Focus on the problem.* Discuss the problems caused by the employee's behavior (without attacking the employee). Compare the employee's performance with what's expected, with company goals, or with job requirements (not with other employees). Identify the consequences of continuing poor performance, and show you're committed to helping solve the problem.
- *Ask for a commitment from the employee.* Help the employee understand that planning for and making improvements are the employee's responsibility. However, finalize decisions jointly so that you can be sure any action to be taken is achievable. In fact, set a schedule for improvement and for following up with evaluations of that improvement.

Yia Eason would recommend that even if your employee's performance has been disappointing, you would do well to mention some good points in your performance review. Then you must clearly and tactfully state how the employee can better meet the responsibilities of the job (see "How to Take the Sting Out of Criticism and Foster Goodwill" on page 312). If the performance review is to be effective, be sure to suggest ways that the employee can improve.[15] For example, instead of telling an employee only that he damaged some expensive machinery, suggest that he take a refresher course in the correct operation of that machinery. The goal is to help the employee succeed.

Terminating Employment

When writing a termination letter, you have three goals: (1) to present the reasons for this difficult action, (2) to avoid statements that might involve the company in legal action, and (3) to leave the relationship between the terminated employee and the firm as favorable as possible. For both legal and personal reasons, present specific reasons for asking the employee to leave.[16] Make sure that all your reasons are accurate and verifiable. Avoid words that are open to interpretation, such as *untidy* and *difficult.* Make sure the employee leaves with feelings that are as positive as the circumstances allow. You can do this by telling the truth about the termination and by helping as much as you can to make the employee's transition as smooth as possible.[17] To review the tasks involved in this type of message, see this chapter's Checklist for Unfavorable News About People on page 313.

Carefully word a termination letter to avoid creating undue ill will and grounds for legal action.

SHARPENING YOUR SKILLS

HOW TO TAKE THE STING OUT OF CRITICISM AND FOSTER GOODWILL

People can't improve if they aren't evaluated, but criticism from others is often hard to take. The way you tell someone "You did it wrong" can destroy goodwill and cooperation, or it can build the relationship and improve the person's performance. The following list of suggestions will help you criticize people constructively:

- **Get all the facts first.** Don't accept hearsay or rumors. Be specific. Find out who did or said what, when, where, why, and how.
- **Don't act in haste.** Never act while you're angry, no matter how upset you or the other person may be. Take time to cool off and think things out before you start to write or speak. Remember that you're in control. Then explain your criticism calmly, rationally, and objectively.
- **Phrase your remarks impersonally.** Criticize the mistake, not the person. Focus your remarks on the action only. Analyze it thoughtfully. You'll help the person retain self-esteem and learn from the mistake.
- **Never criticize in an offhand manner.** Treat the situation seriously. Take the time to state what the problem is in detail. Explain what was wrong and why.
- **Don't ridicule, talk down, or use sarcasm.** An abusive tone will prevent the person from accepting what you have to say. To make the criticism more acceptable, respect your readers and give them the benefit of the doubt.
- **Make the offense clear.** Don't talk in generalities. Be specific. Let the person know exactly what she or he did wrong.
- **Share responsibility.** Take the sting out of your criticism by sharing some of the blame for the person's mistake. One way to do this is by saying *we*, as in "What do you think we did wrong?"
- **Preface the criticism with a kind word or compliment.** It will make the other person more receptive and put her or him at ease. Start with a few words of praise or admiration. Say how much you value the person. Put good news first; then introduce bad news.
- **Supply the answer.** When telling a person what she or he did wrong, also explain how to do it right. Don't empha-

size the mistake; emphasize how to correct it and how to avoid repeating it.

- **Ask for cooperation; don't demand it.** Asking makes the person feel like a member of your team and provides an incentive to improve.
- **Limit yourself to one criticism for each offense.** Don't drag up past mistakes or rehash any that are over and done with. Focus on the current one.
- **End on a friendly note.** Until an issue has been resolved on a positive note, it hasn't been resolved. Don't leave things up in the air, to be discussed again later. Settle them now. A friendly close works wonders. Give the other person a pat on the back. Let the last memory of the matter be a good one. The person is much more likely to accept your criticism and to feel friendly toward you.
- **Forgive and forget.** Once the criticism has been made, let the person start with a clean slate. Don't look for more mistakes. Give the person a chance to improve.
- **Take steps to prevent a recurrence.** After telling the person what to do to improve, follow up to make sure she or he is acting on your suggestions and doing things right.

If you follow these guidelines, constructive criticism can benefit you, your company, and—most important—the person you're criticizing.

1. Think back over the lessons you've learned in life. In what ways have you benefited when someone has told you the truth about something you were doing wrong?
2. With a partner, role-play a situation in which one of you is the boss and the other an employee. The boss is angry because the employee is repeatedly late for work, takes long lunches, and always leaves five to ten minutes early. However, the employee's work is always excellent. After the role-play, analyze what the boss did right and what areas could use improvement.

HANDLING BAD NEWS ABOUT COMPANY OPERATIONS OR PERFORMANCE

At least three types of situations require bad-news letters about company operations or performance: (1) a change in company policy that has a negative effect on the reader, (2) problems with company performance, and (3) controversial or unpopular

CHECKLIST FOR UNFAVORABLE NEWS ABOUT PEOPLE

A. BUFFER
1. Identify the applicant or employee clearly when writing to a third party.
2. Express the reasons for writing—clearly, completely, and objectively.
3. Avoid insincere expressions of regret.
4. Avoid impersonal business clichés.

B. REASONS
1. Include only factual information.
2. Avoid negative personal judgments.
3. Word negative job-related messages carefully to avoid legal difficulties.
   a. Avoid terms with legal definitions (*slanderous, criminal*).
   b. Avoid negative terms with imprecise definitions (*lazy, sloppy*).
   c. Whenever possible, embed negative comments in favorable or semifavorable passages.
   d. Avoid generalities, and explain the limits of your observations about the applicant's or employee's shortcomings.
   e. Eliminate secondhand information.
   f. Stress the confidentiality of your letter.
4. For letters refusing to supply a recommendation to job seekers, suggest another avenue for getting a recommendation.
5. For rejection letters, emphasize the positive qualities of the person hired rather than the shortcomings of the rejected applicant.
6. For performance reviews, describe the employee's limitations and suggest methods for improving performance.

C. THE BAD NEWS
1. Understate negative decisions.
2. Imply negative decisions whenever possible.

D. POSITIVE, FRIENDLY, HELPFUL CLOSE
1. For refusals to supply recommendations and for rejection letters, extend good wishes.
2. For performance reviews, express a willingness to help further.
3. For termination letters, make suggestions for finding another job, if appropriate.

---

company operations. In trying situations, apologies may be in order. If so, good writers usually make the apology brief and bury it somewhere in the middle of the letter. Moreover, they try to leave readers with a favorable impression by closing on a positive note.

When a change in company policy will have a negative effect on the reader, the key is to state clearly and carefully the reasons for the change. The explanation section of the letter convinces readers that the change was necessary and, if possible, that this change will benefit them.

If your company is having serious performance problems, your customers and shareholders want to learn of the difficulty from you, not from newspaper accounts or from rumors. Even if the news leaks out, counter it with your own explanation as soon as possible. Much business is based on mutual trust; if your customers and shareholders can't trust you to inform them of your problems, they may choose to work with someone they can trust. Of course, when you do inform stakeholders, use your common business sense and minimize the bad news by presenting it in as favorable a light as possible.

Companies can also find themselves caught in a political crossfire with unpopular products or controversial operations. In such cases, your general strategy might be to present the reasons the company is manufacturing the controversial item or providing the unpopular service. The goal is to show that reason and need (not villainy, carelessness, or greed) are behind the controversial decision.

When conveying bad news about the company, focus on the reasons and on possible benefits.

SUMMARY

The purpose of a bad-news message is to convey unfavorable information without alienating the audience. To accomplish both goals, first consider the audience's point of view; then if possible, explain how the bad news can work to the audience's advantage. You can be tactful and show concern by assuming that the audience is basically honest and wants to be fair.

The organizational pattern for bad-news messages can be either indirect or direct, depending on the circumstances. The indirect plan considers the audience's feelings by beginning with a buffer and moving to the reasons; it then states the bad news and closes on a courteous note that may suggest other options for the audience. The direct plan is used mainly for sending bad news that will have little emotional impact on the audience; it begins with a clear statement of the bad news, moves to the reasons, and then provides a courteous close.

COMMUNICATION CHALLENGES AT OLMEC TOYS

When Yia Eason formed Olmec Toys to produce ethnic action figures, she could not have foreseen its tremendous growth and the many challenges she would face. As each challenge has arisen, she has relied on well-trained and loyal employees and an active board of directors to provide solutions. Surrounding yourself with talented people who share the same vision can be invaluable when faced with the task of delivering bad news.

INDIVIDUAL CHALLENGE: Olmec has recently received letters from 23 consumers requesting a "family line" of dolls. The letters specifically request that dolls represent a mother, father, and children to emphasize African American family unity. As director of development and marketing, you think the motivation for the letters is commendable. However, a line of family dolls would not fit with Olmec's line of ethnic action figures.

Draft a bad-news form letter to the consumers who suggested the family line. In your letter, be careful to leave the possibility open for a future family line, and explain that the company is currently concentrating on its successful action figures. Plan carefully how you will open your communication. Will you end on a strong,

positive note? Perhaps you will want to emphasize that SunMan and the other action figures already represent family values and that Olmec as a company is committed to promoting positive role models for young people. List your objectives and major points before you begin to draft your bad-news letter.[18]

TEAM CHALLENGE: As a member of Olmec's board of directors, you have just learned that the company will not meet earnings projections for the quarter. Knowing that this news will negatively affect the price of Olmec's stock, you are meeting informally with three other board members. Your task is to suggest language to be included in a news release that will deliver the bad news and yet keep investor confidence high.

Brainstorm ideas with your group. What is the best approach, direct or indirect? What reassurances will you give investors? How will you explain the steps Olmec is taking to correct the earnings slump? You can invent numbers to help you make a convincing argument both to the media and your investors. Then write a memo to Yia Eason in which you suggest the best approach to take in the company's news releases.

CRITICAL THINKING QUESTIONS

1. You have to tell a local restaurant owner that your plans have changed and you have to cancel the 90-person banquet scheduled for next month. Do you need to use a buffer? Why or why not?

2. Why is it important to end your bad-news message on a positive note? Explain.

3. If company policy changes, should you explain those changes to employees and customers at about the

same time, or should you explain to employees first? Why?

4. If the purpose of your letter is to convey bad news, should you take the time to suggest alternatives to your reader? Why or why not?

5. The policy at your company is to refuse refunds on merchandise after 30 days. An important customer has written to request a refund on a purchase made 31 days ago, or he'll take his business elsewhere. How do you respond? Explain your answer.

6. When a company suffers a serious misfortune, should the impact be softened by letting out the bad news a little at a time? Why or why not?

DOCUMENTS FOR ANALYSIS

Read the following documents; then (1) analyze the strengths and weaknesses of each sentence and (2) revise each document so that it follows this chapter's guidelines.

Document 10.A: Conveying Bad News about Orders

We want to take this opportunity to thank you for your past orders. We have included our new catalog of books, videos, films, and slides to let you know about our great new products. We included our price list also. Please use this list rather than the old one as we've had a slight increase in price.

Per your request, we are sorry we can't send you the free examination copies of the textbooks you requested. The books, *Communication for Business* and *Winning the Presentation Game,* are two of our new titles that are enjoying brisk sales. It seems everyone is interested in communication skills these days.

We do apologize for not sending the exam copies for free. Our prices continue to rise along with everyone else's, and it's just not feasible to send everyone free copies. If you'd still like to have a look, please notice the prices in the list I've included and don't forget shipping and handling. You can also fax your order to the number shown on the sheet or e-mail your order over the Internet.

I'm sure these books would make a great addition to your collection. Again, we are sorry we couldn't grant your request, but we hope you order anyway.

Document 10.B: Communicating Negative Answers and Information

Your spring fraternity party sounds like fun. We're glad you've again chosen us as your caterer. Unfortunately, we have changed a few of our policies, and I wanted you to know about these changes in advance so that we won't have any misunderstandings on the day of the party.

We will arrange the delivery of tables and chairs as usual the evening before the party. However, if you want us to set up, there is now a $100.00 charge for that service. Of course, you might want to get some of the brothers and pledges to do it, which would save you money. We've also added a small charge for cleanup. This is only $3.00 per person (you can estimate because I know a lot of people come and go later in the evening).

Other than that, all the arrangements will be the same. We'll provide the skirt for the band stage, tablecloths, bar setup, and of course, the barbecue. Will you have the tubs of ice with soft drinks again? We can do that for you as well, but there will be a fee.

Please let me know if you have any problems with these changes and we'll try to work them out. I know it's going to be a great party.

Document 10.C: Refusing Adjustment of Claims and Complaints

I am responding to your letter of about six weeks ago asking for an adjustment on your fax/modem, model FM39Z. We test all our products before they leave the factory; therefore, it could not have been our fault that your fax/modem didn't work.

If you or someone in your office dropped the unit, it might have caused the damage. Or the damage could have been caused by the shipper if he dropped it. If so, you should file a claim with the shipper. At any rate, it wasn't our fault. The parts are already covered by warranty. However, we will provide labor for the repairs for $50.00, which is less than our cost since you are a valued customer.

We will have a booth at the upcoming trade fair there and hope to see you or someone from your office. We have many new models of office machines that we're sure you'll want to see. I've enclosed our latest catalog. Hope to see you there.

Document 10.D: Rejecting Job Applications

I regret to inform you that you were not selected for our summer intern program at Equifax. We had over a thousand résumés and cover letters to go through and simply could not get to them all. We have been asked to notify everyone that we have already selected students for the 25 positions based on those who applied early and were qualified.

We're sure you will be able to find a suitable position for summer work in your field and wish you the best of luck. We deeply regret any inconvenience associated with our reply.

CASES

Conveying Bad News About Orders

PRODUCTION

EXTERNAL COMMUNICATION

1. Seattle blend: Letter explaining delays for Cedar Grove compost Ever since word got out about your company's "gourmet compost" (with a little help from your marketing department), Pacific Northwest gardeners can't seem to get enough of Cedar Grove Composting's $20 per cubic yard blend of rotting plant materials, vegetables, and of course, coffee grounds. The fact that your company picks up its composting materials as part of a mandatory recycling program in Seattle and surrounding King County is probably part of the appeal. But some pundits think it has something to do with a nationwide mania for anything rich, aromatic, brown, and expensive coming from Seattle.

"It has a good, rich smell," Mary Heide, manager of Sky Nursery in Shoreline, Washington, told the press, while one of her employees raved about its "rich, brown coffee color—kind of a mocha color from a Seattle point of view." That was it. The orders from gardening retailers started pouring in as their customers heard of the stuff and demanded it for their gardens, despite the fact that your prices are 30 percent higher than everyone else's. It didn't help matters that your general manager, Jan Allen, publicized your $3 million, high-speed fans, cooling chambers, and other devices that "air out" the compost as it cures by telling the media that competing brands just "sit around in static piles. Ours has a higher degree of intelligence."

Your task: As manager of Cedar Grove's wholesale division, you've got a backlog of requests from retailers who are eager to fulfill their customers' demands and you've got to let them know that it's going to be about four weeks before you can fill their orders. Better write this bad-news form letter with as much care and concern as Cedar Grove puts into its compost.[19]

PRODUCTION

INTERCULTURAL COMMUNICATION

2. Please don't scream: Letter from Häagen-Dazs explaining a flavor switch Apparently, the British have never had much taste for ice cream; per capita consumption has been one-third the amount gobbled in the United States. Traditionally, Britons have been content with low-quality brands, some without so much as a spot of real cream. Now U.S.-produced Häagen-Dazs has introduced the British to the joys of superpremium ice cream—costly, but fit for a queen's palate. When it opened, the Häagen-Dazs shop in London's Leicester Square quickly broke worldwide ice cream sales records. The store scooped out $2.5 million worth of rich chocolate, vanilla, or strawberry to over a million people in the first year.

The success of the superrich ice cream in England came about when Britain's Grand Metropolitan bought Pillsbury, the producer of Häagen-Dazs. The new owners hoped to find a market hungry for superpremium ice cream both in Europe and in Asia, and they did. Despite a cost often double the price of local brands, Häagen-Dazs hit the spot with consumers. In just two years, European sales reached $30 million, and a joint venture with Suntory in Japan logged $120 million. The sales figures just keep rising.

Until a new Häagen-Dazs factory in Arras, France, can be completed, the U.S. plant has been scrambling to produce enough ice cream for the European, Asian, and U.S. markets combined. This isn't always easy—as you know; you're an overseas sales supervisor based in the Bronx, New York, where the brand originated. Right now you've got a situation on your hands that could lead to some screaming in London if you don't handle it carefully.

Europa Foods convenience stores in London have been selling so much Häagen-Dazs that the brand now accounts for over 20 percent of the chain's ice cream sales. Although that makes everyone happy, their success has put an additional strain on the shipping schedule. Europa's next shipment won't have any of the popular mocha chip they're expecting. Until production can be stepped up, coffee flavor will be substituted for all mocha chip orders.

Your task: You've been asked to communicate the substitution plans to Colleen Downey, the head of Europa Foods' purchasing department. Write to Ms. Downey at Europa Foods, Ltd., 8 Bedford Square, London WCIB 3 RA, England.[20]

3. Popular product: Letter about delayed shipping from Comfy Interamerican Sheepskins If you're paying big dollars for your automobile, you want to be sure that everything in the interior stays in the best possible condition—which is why Tom Plotkin's business is thriving. The New Zealander identified a virtually untapped U.S. market for sheepskin seat covers in 1987, so he bought Comfy Interamerican Sheepskins in Los Angeles. It was a good move; Comfy now posts $3 million in annual sales to automobile manufacturers, upscale retailers, individual car owners, and even airline pilots who like the feel, the coolness, the protection, and, of course, the status of the expensive seat covers.

Your problem, however, is handling the huge volume of special orders Comfy receives. They're complicated and they require longer production time. For instance, last week you took an order from a Corvette owner who wanted his $450, top-of-the-line, customized seat covers in pure white with sewn-on burgundy stripes to match his car's interior. Today you're looking at a letter from a Porsche owner in Baltimore, Maryland. She wants "ivory and midnight black checkerboard patterns" and she's expecting you to ship her seat covers within 24 hours (as your company promises for certain standard, in-stock merchandise). Even if you weren't backlogged, your normal shipping time for custom orders is 14 days. But right now you're running about six days behind.

Your task: Write a letter to Anamarie Haverton (4766 Elkridge Place, Baltimore, MD 21227), explaining the situation.[21]

Communicating Negative Answers and Information

4. All in the family: E-mail message resigning a position Your brother, Ruben N. Rodriguez, Jr., started the family-owned Los Amigos Tortilla Manufacturing, Inc., in 1969 with only $12,000. The job you hold as marketing director for the Latin American Division of IBM helped you support your extended family as Los Amigos

grew. Today, the Atlanta-based company enjoys annual sales of $4.5 million and its prospects look bright.

Ruben wants you to resign from IBM and work full-time for Los Amigos. Before deciding, you conducted some research into the matter. You found that Hispanic-owned businesses have exceeded overall U.S. business growth with the number of companies rising 76 percent between 1987 and 1992. The number of all U.S. companies grew 26 percent in the same period. You also found that in Georgia, Hispanic-owned businesses rose to 5,501, up 185 percent according to a U.S. census report released in 1996.

You know that many Hispanic corporate executives are leaving big companies and starting their own businesses. The estimated one million Hispanic businesses in the United States represented sales of $76.8 billion in 1992, up 134 percent from 1987. You want to be a part of this amazing trend, not only because of the profit potential but because you love your family and would like to help your brother develop the company. You hope your son will one day become a part of the organization.

You recently submitted your letter of resignation. Today, you received e-mail from the division vice president urging you to stay and offering a lucrative incentive package, including an additional week's vacation, an upgrade on your company car, and an increase of $10,000 a year in salary.

Your task: Write an e-mail message to George Packard, your division vice president <GPackard @lad.ibm.com>, thanking him for his offer. Explain the reasons behind your decision to resign and suggest that Consuela Vargas, who has worked with you for five years, would make an excellent marketing director.[22]

5. Feeling at home in Denmark: Letter to Web House critiquing its home page   Web House is an award-winning Danish company that designs home pages and other Internet materials for international clients. You have been hired as an independent consultant by Christian Broberg to critique the company's home page from a U.S. point of view. You'll need to visit the Web House home page <http://www.webhouse.dk> and study it from the perspective of a U.S. business manager. Consider all aspects of clear intercultural communication.

Your task: Write a letter to Christian Broberg, Assistant Director (Web House, Hasserisgade 30, 9000 Aalborg, Denmark), and explain why the design of the Web House home page may cause problems for English-speaking clients. Since your message is not entirely good news, take extra care in the way you explain your viewpoints to someone from another country.

6. Save the wave: Refusal to remove a large sign from Julian Surf & Sport   Ever since she bolted it to the front of her tiny sporting goods store, Marcia Hegranes has heard more than an earful of controversy over the bright blue, 14-foot, carved wooden wave cascading its message around the shop's door: "Surf's Up in Julian." Apparently, the old California mining community wasn't ready for the blond grandmother's business style. The town is buzzing with people who think that the wave clashes with Julian's rustic image as a mountain tourist stop famous for its history and its fresh apple pie. Even though Hegranes's 300-square-foot shop is tucked into the base of an old Depression-era water tower, they say the sign is too contemporary; the wave must go. Before long, Hegranes heard these demands echoed from city and county officials.

Last summer Marcia Hegranes hired you to help out because the shop had become so popular. Grandmother or not, she has a great rapport with local teenagers. Many of them are transplants from the surf-conscious coastal zone, having moved to Julian when their parents sought out the slow-paced, woodsy atmosphere that makes the town so popular with tourists; but the kids feel stuck, living a mile above sea level and an hour's drive from their beloved Pacific waves. For them, the irrever-

ent wave is a symbol—just like the half-eaten apple core on the shop's window with its defiant proclamation, "Dedicated to the Hard-Core."

Speaking for the city, Julian Architectural Review Board member Richard Zerbe says that the sign disrupts the historical character of Julian, which is modeled after area photographs dating from 1870 to 1930. He explains that the board has issued carefully developed architectural guidelines for the Julian Historical District, which encompasses the town's commercial area. As chief of zoning code enforcement for San Diego county, Sue Gray believes the wave sign is simply too big. Furthermore, Hegranes failed to go through the proper permit process for signage, so Gray has notified Hegranes that she must remove the wave within two months.

Together, you and Hegranes have decided to fight for the wave—mostly for the kids who love its spirited message. After all, the sculpted wave is more than a sign; it's a work of art. On that basis, you think you might be able to persuade officials to let it stand. You've received dozens of letters of support: "As mother and father of a teenager, we wholeheartedly support Hegrane's shop, the wave artwork, and her kindnesses to young people. The kids are watching," wrote one couple. "Why does every store have to look the same?" asked another supporter. "If all the buildings here were really historically accurate, we'd all be doing business under sheets of corrugated tin."

Your task: Write a letter stating the intention of Julian Surf & Sport to keep the wave in place as a sculptural work of art. Provide ample reasoning to back up your position. Address the letter to Sue Gray, Chief of San Diego Zoning Code Enforcement (1222 1st Ave., San Diego, CA 92101) and to the Julian Architectural Review Board (1836 Main, Julian, CA 92036).[23]

7. No time for talking: Memo about scheduling at Trident Aquaculture   Farming the ocean? You thought it was a crazy idea when you first heard of Trident Aquaculture, but you went for an interview anyway, offering your skills as an office manager. You changed your mind after winding up as administrative assistant for Michael D. Willinsky, president of the company and a skilled biologist and fish farmer who helped create the most innovative and promising sea-farming cage ever tested in the open ocean.

After trials in the blustery, icy seas off Nova Scotia and in New York's frozen St. Lawrence River, Willinsky's research team proved that their unique cage design—measuring about 41 feet in diameter and based on Buckminster Fuller's geodesic dome—could survive 80 to 110 mph winds, 6- to 12-foot waves, strong currents, and fast-moving ice floes. Thanks to regular hand-feeding and protection from predators, the Arctic charr salmon raised inside the Nova Scotia dome matured in a record 18 months (wild Arctic charr mature in 6 to 8 years).

Seaside communities are desperate for economic alternatives to the traditional fishing industry, now that overfishing, pollution, and coastal development have depleted the world's natural fish supply. About 70,000 U.S. and Canadian fishermen lost their livelihood in 1993, when several major Atlantic fishing areas were closed to commercial fishing because of severe depletion. Yet the demand for fish products has increased. Willinsky's prototype sea dome promises to provide a sustainable supply of fresh- or saltwater fish, renewing economic activity in coastal areas, and providing new jobs in the fishing industry.

One result is that Willinsky has become a popular speaker among government and industry leaders. But your boss has to divide his time between pursuing research and development, promoting aquaculture, and managing his company. Next month he travels to Hawaii to speak at an international conference on ocean farming, sponsored by the United Nations Food and Agriculture Organization. Willinsky's U.S. research partner, Michael A. Champ, wants Willinsky to appear at a joint speaking engagement for the New Bedford, Massachusetts, chamber of commerce. Unfortunately, the date falls during Willinsky's week in Hawaii.

Your task: Willinsky has asked you to fax Champ. Write the informal memo to Michael A. Champ, President, Environmental Systems Development Company (at 1-703-899-7326 in Falls Church, Virginia) and suggest an alternative date.[24]

MAIL-ORDER SALES
INTERCULTURAL COMMUNICATION

8. More to come: Letter explaining delay of Tesla videotapes Membership is expanding so rapidly at the nonprofit International Tesla Society that volunteers at the organization's headquarters and museum in Colorado Springs can hardly keep up with the daily mail. Many of the letters are orders for the rare books, diaries, patents, videotapes, audiotapes, and T-shirts advertised in the Society's Museum Bookstore Catalog.

Inventor Nikola Tesla, who emigrated from Yugoslavia to the United States in 1884, was responsible for the alternating current electrical system now used worldwide (which replaced Edison's direct current system). Called a "genius," a "mental giant," and "a man ahead of his time," Tesla also holds the patent for radio technology (although Guglielmo Marconi got the credit), and he invented a host of other devices that dazzled turn-of-the-century society: remote-controlled submarines, magnetic resonators, and lightning-generating "Tesla coils." For a time, Tesla was so well known he even appeared on the cover of *Time* magazine. Then, for reasons biographers still debate, the world forgot about Nikola Tesla.

Now people are catching up with many of Tesla's ideas—and the thousands of unexploited patents he left behind. Industrial and amateur inventors alike are developing working models from his drawings and notes for new concepts that may, like A/C power, revolutionize today's technology. That's why the International Tesla Society hosts an annual symposium at which inventors can demonstrate what they've built and attend lectures on the most esoteric aspects of Tesla research. People from many countries attend; others order videotapes of the lectures and workshops.

Last year's symposium was so popular that you've depleted your supply of videotape copies for 17 of the 29 master tapes (with an all-volunteer operation, no one rushed out to duplicate the missing tapes). Now you've received a letter from a German engineer ordering the complete set. He included $495 in U.S. funds, plus $12.50 for overseas shipping, and as a Tesla Society member, he's expecting the usual "same-day shipping." It's going to take about two weeks to get copies of the 17 missing tapes.

Your task: Write to Josef Mandelheim, Sonnenstrasse 4, 86669 Erlingshofen, Germany, explaining the back-order situation. With your letter, send the 12 lecture videotapes you have on hand.[25]

FINANCE
TECHNOLOGY

9. The check's in the mail—almost: Letter from Sun Microsystems explaining late payments You'd think that a computer company could install a new management information system without a hitch, wouldn't you? The people at Sun Microsystems thought so too, but they were wrong. When they put in their new computerized system for getting information to management, a few things fell through the cracks—like payments to vendors.

It was embarrassing, to say the least, when suppliers started clamoring for payment. Terence Lenaghan, the corporate controller, found himself in the unfortunate position of having to tell 6,000 vendors why Sun Microsystems had failed to pay its bills on time—and why it might be late with payments again. "Until we get these bugs ironed out," Lenaghan confessed, "we're going to have to finish some of the accounting work by hand. That means that some of our payments to vendors will probably be late next month too. We'd better write to our suppliers and let them know that there's nothing wrong with the company's financial performance. The last thing we want is for our vendors to think our business is going down the tubes."

Your task: Write a form letter to Sun Microsystems' 6,000 vendors explaining that bugs in the new management information system are responsible for the delays in payment.[26]

10. Everything old is new again: E-mail message reporting polyester findings   Polyester got a bad rap in the 1980s. Now it's making a comeback in both fashion and food. What? Eat and drink from polyester containers? It's an idea whose time has come according to chemical companies ranging from Dow to Amoco. The idea of sipping an ice-cold Coke from a plastic container may be tough for some Americans to swallow, but experts predict a new generation of plastic may solve many of the current problems, such as carbonation loss and heat sensitivity.

Today's drink bottles use a plastic called PET (polyethylene terephthalate). Too porous to contain the "fizz" (especially when stressed by heat), PET can now be mixed with a recently developed polyester called PEN (polyethylene naphthalate) to create a new generation of tougher plastic. Shell Chemical's director of polyester research and development, David Richardson, believes in the product. "In a few years, I'll be able to fix you a nice meal and everything in it will come out of a polyester container."

So why make the switch from aluminum or glass to plastic? "Plastic is less deadly than glass when you throw it at a soccer match," says Richard Marion, an executive at Amoco Corporation's Amoco Chemical Company. Airlines like it because it's lightweight. Their little jelly containers used in First Class will weigh less. Consumers like it because it's clear, resealable, lighter, and easily recycled. Polyester is definitely making a comeback. But one segment of the population is proving resistant to the trend: young adults.

Your task: You are Vikram Nesbet, assistant director of marketing for Coca-Cola. You were asked by your boss, Tom Ruffenach, to conduct preliminary market studies of a new PET/PEN soft drink bottle. You tested 1,000 college students and found that only 10 percent liked the idea of a plastic bottle. The students preferred aluminum cans. Write Tom an e-mail message <TomRuf@marketing.coca-cola.com> in which you report your findings and suggest ways to overcome this consumer bias.[27]

Refusing Adjustment of Claims and Complaints

11. Your monkey, your choice: Letter from Duncan's Exotic Pets refusing a damage claim   As a well-known exotic animal dealer in the Cincinnati area, your boss, Roger Duncan, has dealt with his share of customers experiencing buyer's regret. Despite his warnings, many of them still buy their exotic pets for the wrong reasons. When Melissa Carpenter bought Binky, the red-tailed guenon monkey, she begged Mr. Duncan to reduce his price to $10,000 because she had "fallen in love with Binky's soulful eyes and adorable button nose." Now she wants to return poor Binky, and you have never seen your boss so angry.

"Listen to this!" fumes Mr. Duncan as he reads Carpenter's letter:

> While I was at work, I locked your monkey in his own room—which I equipped with his own color TV (with cable) and which I spent days wallpapering with animal pictures. Then last night your monkey somehow unlocked the door, ripped out my telephone, opened the refrigerator, smashed eggs all over my kitchen and my new Persian carpet, broke 14 of the china

dishes my mother gave me when I got married, and squeezed toothpaste all over my Louis XIV settee I inherited from my grandmother!

"Not only does she demand that I take poor Binky back after she's abused him through her ignorance and neglect," snapped Mr. Duncan, "but she wants me to pay $150,000 in damages for her car, her apartment, and her state of mind."

Your boss is so upset that you decide to write Ms. Carpenter yourself.

Your task: Write to Melissa Carpenter (876 Newton Ave., Cincinnati, OH 45202) and include a copy of her contract. It clearly states Roger Duncan's policy: refunds only if animals are returned in good health, and absolutely no warranty against damages. Each pet comes with specific care instructions, including warnings about certain idiosyncrasies that could cause problems in the wrong environment.

Despite the fact that Binky is probably traumatized by his experiences, Mr. Duncan has generously agreed to accept his return, refunding Ms. Carpenter's $10,000. However, he will not accept liability for any loss of property or for any claims of mental duress on the part of Ms. Carpenter.[28]

12. Back to work: Letter from MetDisAbility refusing extended benefits   When a worker breaks an arm or leg while on the job, that's easy to diagnose, and disability insurers can easily predict approximately when that worker should be back on the job. Insurance companies have compiled mountains of data about typical illnesses and convalescent periods, and they use this actuarial data to manage the disability benefits that companies offer employees. (For example, if a disabling condition forces an insured employee out of work for more than six months, disability benefits usually replace about 60 percent of the employee's normal pay until he or she is able to return to work.)

But in recent decades, certain "self-reported" illnesses have become more common: chronic fatigue syndrome (CFS), back and muscle pain, stress, numbness, and other conditions that can't be diagnosed through conventional medical tests. (One insurer reports that claims for CFS quadrupled between 1989 and 1995.)

"Self-diagnosed" doesn't mean workers aren't really suffering or that their claims for disability leave

aren't valid. But it does mean that insurers are at a loss to determine typical healing times in these circumstances. For one thing, because of insufficient actuarial data, insurers don't know when to urge claimants back to work "in a timely fashion."

At MetDisAbility, a division of MetLife in New York, you've been following legal developments in 39 states that allow insurers to limit benefits to two years' duration for self-reported illnesses. Your company has decided to make this limit a part of all new group-disability policies, and it has notified all current customers of its intention to terminate benefits for self-diagnosed illnesses after 24 months.

Your task: Your supervisor in the claims department has handed you a letter from Alison Almonzar (338 Cumberland Avenue, Indianapolis, IN 46229), who has been out of work for 23 months with CFS. She heard about your new rule through her employer and she's asking for an extension of benefits. You must write a letter refusing her request.[29]

13. Of course they're ugly: Letter from Na-Na boutique refusing a claim over "unsightly" Doc Martens As manager of the trendy Na-Na boutique in Santa Monica, you've sold so many pairs of "Doc Martens"—the clunky, street-combat boots made by Dr. Marten—that your buyer can barely keep them in stock. Even your employees wear them because they're easy on the feet. They cater to comfort first and fashion—not at all.

Ugly as Doc Martens are, you can't remember receiving a single customer complaint about the comfy boots—until you received this unusual letter from Susan Stone of Ventura:

> Several months ago I purchased a pair of burgundy Doc Martens with black laces, after one of your salespeople convinced me that they're the most comfortable boots around. They look cool with both short and long skirts and with jeans. Then a week ago I got a job as a waitress at the Eggshell Café. After two days of eight-hour shifts, I figured I'd wear my Doc Martens and save what was left of my feet. I got fired. I argued with the manager, pointing out that she lets the girls wear whatever they want—miniskirts or leather or tank tops—but she said,

"You're out of here." Why? Customer complaints about my "unsightly footwear."

I was misled by your salesperson, who told me that Doc Martens can be worn anywhere in Los Angeles. I think I'm entitled to a full refund of the $116 that I paid for the boots, plus $1,200 compensation (a month's wages and tips) for losing my job over them.

Ms. Stone says she bought the boots "several months ago," so a full refund is out of the question. Also, because waitress dress codes in Los Angeles are liberal, you suspect that Stone's manager used the boots as an excuse to fire an employee who simply wasn't capable—particularly one who had been on the job for only two days. (It's unfortunate, but you know that some managers have difficulty telling fired employees the whole truth.) Ms. Stone makes no mention of a second chance to improve her wardrobe choice, which convinces you that she was actually fired for other reasons. In any case, the claim for job-loss compensation seems extreme for a shoe retailer, and you're not about to pay it. The boutique's owner agrees.

Your task: Write a letter to Susan Stone (235 W. Alameda, #42, Ventura, CA 93001) refusing her refund request and her claim for job-loss compensation. As a goodwill gesture, invite her to visit the store for a 20 percent discount on any of the other popular footwear the boutique sells.[30]

SMALL BUSINESS

CUSTOMER RELATIONS

14. Covering the gap: Refusal to honor a claim   You recently installed an Eazy-Air Model 77 air conditioner in the upstairs den of Mr. and Mrs. Norman E. Stocker's home (41 Citrus Place, Sumatra, FL 32691). Installation was unusually difficult, because the oak paneling in the room was old and brittle. With a lot of extra care, however, you managed to do the job with only one small problem: When you drilled a hole to bring in the 220 wiring, the paneling split a little. Fortunately, the cover plate covered all but a fraction of an inch of the gap.

When you were finished with the installation, you made sure that Mrs. Stocker was aware of the problem. She said, "Don't worry about it," and wrote out a check for $100 as the first installment on the $650 bill. Now Mr. Stocker has written to express his disappointment with the work. He gives you two alternatives: Repair the

damage, or refund $100. Mr. Stocker indicates that he will make no payments on his $550 one-year sales contract until this matter is settled.

Mr. Stocker's threat to withhold payment does not affect you directly because you have sold his sales contract (at a discount) to the Goodwin Finance Company, which now has the legal right to collect on it. You also feel justified in refusing to make any adjustment because Mrs. Stocker approved the work. Nevertheless, as a goodwill gesture, you decide that a $25 refund will more than pay for the wood putty necessary to repair the damage. Although you dislike the thought of revisiting the Stocker home to make the repairs yourself, you could stop by if that's what will make Mr. Stocker happy.

Your task: Write to Mr. Stocker, denying his request but offering an alternative. Your business address is Hatcher Air Conditioning, 2379 Coconut Lane, Sumatra, FL 32691.

ACCOUNTING

PUBLIC SECTOR

15. A taxing matter: Letter from O&Y Tax Service refusing to pay for another's mistake   During the mid-April rush at tax time last year, Hilda Black phoned to ask whether she could roll over funds from one retirement account into another without paying taxes on any gain. You answered that such a rollover was not considered a tax event, as long as the transaction was completed in 60 days. You also informed her that when she eventually draws out the funds to support her retirement income, she will pay taxes on the portion that represents interest earned on the account.

Today Ms. Black phones to say that she is being billed by the Internal Revenue Service for $1,309.72 in penalties and back interest because she failed to declare interest income earned when she cashed in "those bonds that I told you about last April." You explain that bonds are not the same thing as a retirement account. One difference, unfortunately, is that cashing in bonds requires one to pay taxes the following April on any interest income or capital gains.

Your client is not satisfied. She demands "something in writing" to show to her lawyer. Her position is that you misled her; thus you should pay the penalties and interest charges—which, by the way, are getting larger every day. She is willing to pay the actual tax on the transaction.

Your task: Write to Hilda Black (622 N. Bank Lane, Park Forest, IL 60045), explaining why you are unwilling to pay the penalties and interest charges requested by the IRS. Your position should be that you have done nothing to make yourself vulnerable in this transaction.

16. Many happy returns: Letter from Cliffs Notes refusing a claim in a complicated transaction Like most other publishers, Cliffs Notes of Lincoln, Nebraska, gives full credit to any bookstore that returns unsold copies of its publications, provided that they are received in salable condition within six months of their original shipment to the bookstore. The bookstore pays postage. Even though most large publishers have return rates of 30 to 50 percent, only about 6 percent of Cliffs Notes's 222 titles are returned.

Still, today's mail includes a large return from the University of Wyoming Bookstore, Laramie, WY 82071, containing the following:

21 copies, *Macbeth*
6 copies, *The Scarlet Letter*
12 copies, *Crime and Punishment*
5 copies, *Hamlet*

All the Cliffs Notes sell for a retail (or list) price of $6.95. Cliffs gives the bookstores a 40 percent discount off the list price.

The cover note from the University of Wyoming Bookstore indicates that 23 copies of *Macbeth* have been sent, but you count only 21. The carton has sustained some damage, but nothing appears to have spilled out. Five of the booklets are worn to the extent that they cannot be resold. One copy of *Crime and Punishment* is water-stained and cannot be resold. One copy of *The Scarlet Letter* was damaged in shipping, from a combination of careless packing and rough handling in transit.

The shipment also includes 4 copies of *A Tale of Two Cities,* published by Monarch Notes, one of Cliffs Notes's competitors. Obviously, the company does not owe the bookstore anything for these booklets.

As a customer service representative for Cliffs Notes, you have decided to return the 4 copies of *A Tale of Two Cities* to the university bookstore (and charge them $2.20 for postage); to return the unsalable copies to them with an explanation; and to tell them that they shipped you only 21 copies, not 23 copies, of *Macbeth.*

Your task: Figure out where things stand and write a letter explaining your decision.[31]

Refusing to Extend Credit

17. Grand finale: No credit for burials in space by Celestis "I know you'll understand my request," the letter began, "and I'm sure your company has enough money from its wealthy customers to cover my needs temporarily." Now, for many businesses, such a letter might well mean a new customer, but for Celestis, Inc., of Houston, Texas, those words won't start a profitable relationship.

In the first place, this company's business is space burials, or rather, "space memorials." Celestis offers "grand finale" space voyages for a symbolic portion of a person's cremated remains—about a quarter of an ounce or approximately one percent of the total.

By special arrangement with Orbital Sciences Corporation in Virginia, you are able to promise your customers a blastoff aboard a high-flying L-1011 jet, which releases a Pegasus rocket into the atmosphere. The rocket then lifts and releases a small satellite into orbit, containing 30 lipstick-sized ash capsules secured in a honeycomb arrangement. No, you won't scatter customers' ashes in space, nor do you release the 1-1/2-inch capsules (cluttering space with debris). They remain on the satellite until it reenters and burns up in Earth's atmosphere, some 18 months to 10 years later.

The cost for this service is less than $5,000 per person—a bargain, when you think of the technology involved. So far, your most famous customers have been Gene Roddenberry (creator of the *Star Trek* TV series), Timothy Leary (1960s LSD philosopher), and Gerald O'Neill (space colony advocate).

As a member of the Celestis marketing team, you think the concept is terrific and should be accessible to many people. But there's no way the company is going to offer credit for something like this. In fact, all arrangements for the Celestis space memorial must be paid for in advance.

Your task: Write a letter responding to Gerald C. Hertsbacher's request for credit, tactfully explaining why you cannot grant it. He resides at 9760 Sepulveda Blvd., Apt. R, Sherman Oaks, CA 91403).[32]

FINANCE

CUSTOMER RELATIONS

18. Pat the Painter: Letter refusing credit to a new business   Patricia Whitman (doing business as Pat the Painter, 1427 Queen St. East, Sault Sainte Marie, Ontario P6A 5P2 Canada) is a young woman of boundless ambition. She proposes to blanket the area with fliers promoting her painting and carpentry business. She tells you that she has scaffold builders, scrapers, paint mixers, and commission salespeople in place and that paint and equipment will be delivered to work sites by college students before and after their classes. She also tells you that her start-up capital is small and her start-up expenses high. She wants to purchase paint, brushes, solvents, and ladders from your firm, Hobson's Builders Supply, with payments to begin in 60 days.

You admire Pat's energy and ambition, but you are less enthusiastic about the success of her venture. You certainly want to supply her business needs but prefer to deal on a cash basis, at least for now.

Your task: Write Pat a letter, turning down her request for credit.

FINANCE

DOWNWARD COMMUNICATION

19. No more advances: Memo outlining Banc One policy against IRS refund loans   A few years ago, Banc One in Columbus, Ohio, joined a number of banking institutions in offering its customers "IRS Refund Loans." These loans allowed customers to borrow against their income tax refunds before actually receiving them. As part of the loan agreement, the Internal Revenue Service would send refunds directly to the bank to pay off the loans.

To get such a loan, customers had to file electronic tax returns, making use of newly implemented IRS technology. Once the computerized return was filed, the IRS responded with immediate confirmation of any refund due the taxpayer, and the bank made its loan based on the IRS-verified amount—which would later be repaid directly to the bank. It seemed a foolproof system—until an IRS programming error started creating problems with tax returns from all over the country.

The first year the problem emerged, the IRS was forced to apologize for errors that added up to $3 million in mistakenly confirmed refunds. Banc One lost some money on uncollected loans, but not much. The second year, IRS errors during one 17-day period, between January 10 and January 27, totaled nearly $40 million, so Banc One cashed out of the IRS Refund Loan business. Too risky, bank executives decided. If the IRS confirmed a refund that wasn't forthcoming, the bank could be left with an unsecured balance due that the customer might not be able to pay. Collection costs alone could cause the once-secure loans to become highly unprofitable for the bank.

Although news reports have quoted IRS officials stating that the computer glitch has been corrected, Banc One executives remain firm in their decision to suspend the refund loan program. The only exceptions will be made under special circumstances involving long-term customers with exemplary credit records and with whom the bank has had prior lending experience, so even if the IRS should err in confirming the refund amount, the bank could feel confident that the customer would be able to repay the loan. The bank's advertisements no longer promote the refund loans, but bank officers are expected to receive numerous requests from customers wanting to borrow against their tax refunds during the first few months of next year.

Your task: As communications director, you have been asked to issue a memo to all branch managers and credit officers, informing them of the bank's new policy.[33]

Conveying Unfavorable News About People

CAREER DEVELOPMENT

INTERPERSONAL COMMUNICATION

20. Career moves: Refusal to write a letter of recommendation Tom Terwilliger worked in the office at Opal Pools and Patios for four months, under your supervision (you're office manager). On the basis of what he told you he could do, you started him off as a word processor. His keyboard skills were inadequate for the job, however, and you transferred him to logging in accounts receivable, where he performed almost adequately. Because he assured you that his "really long suit" was customer relations, you moved him to what you aggrandize as the complaint department. After he spent three weeks making angry customers even angrier, you were convinced that no place in your office was appropriate for the talents of Mr. Terwilliger. Five weeks ago, you encouraged him to resign before being formally fired.

Today's mail brings a request from Mr. Terwilliger for you to write a letter recommending him for a sales position with a florist shop. You have no knowledge one way or the other of Mr. Terwilliger's sales abilities, but you do know him to be an incompetent word processor, a careless bookkeeper, and an insensitive customer service representative. Someone is more likely to deserve the sales job than Mr. Terwilliger is. You decide that you have done enough favors for Mr. Terwilliger for one lifetime and plan to refuse his request.

Your task: Write to Mr. Terwilliger (now living with his parents at 2344 Bob-O-Link Rd., Pineville, SC 29468), indicating that you have chosen not to write a letter recommending him for the sales job.

HUMAN RESOURCES

INTERPERSONAL COMMUNICATION

21. Bad news for 80: Form letter to unsuccessful candidates for a high-level job The Dean's Selection Committee screened 85 applications for the position of

dean of arts and sciences at your campus. After two rounds of eliminations, the top five candidates were invited to "airport interviews," where the committee managed to meet with each candidate for an hour. Then the top three candidates were invited to the campus to meet with students, faculty, and administrators.

The committee recommended to the university president that the job be given to Constance Pappas, who has a doctorate in American studies and has been chairperson of the history department at Minneapolis Metropolitan College for the past three years. The president agreed, and Dr. Pappas accepted the offer.

One final task remains before the work of the Dean's Selection Committee is finished: Letters must be sent to the 84 unsuccessful candidates. The 4 who reached the "airport interview" stage will receive personal letters from the chairperson of the committee. Your job, as secretary of the committee, is to draft the form letter that will be sent to the other 80 applicants.

Your task: Draft a letter of 100 to 200 words. All copies will be individually addressed to the recipients but will carry identical messages.

Handling Bad News About Company Operations or Performance

MARKETING

INTERNAL COMMUNICATION

22. Olestra's Slipping: Bad news memo at Procter & Gamble Ever since the Food & Drug Administration approved Procter & Gamble's new fat substitute, sucrose polyester or *olestra,* your department (consumer relations) has been fighting a product-image nightmare. Sure, the media announced your plans to use olestra in fat-free chips, but they included negative reports from medical experts and from the Center for Science in the Public Interest in Washington, D.C.

P&G spent 25 years and more than $200 million developing a calorie-free fat substitute that can be used for frying (making it ideal for chips, cheese curls, and corn chips—the junk foods U.S. consumers love, despite dire warnings about rising obesity statistics). Olestra is a combination of sugar with fatty acids, resulting in a fat molecule too large to be digested, so it passes right through the body. After 150 studies, including 48 clinical trials producing 150,000 pages of data, the FDA gave olestra its green light.

But journalists are still reporting that "hundreds of doctors and nutritionists" urged the FDA to reject olestra, citing "strong reason to suspect that the effects will include increases in cancer, heart disease, stroke, and blindness." Critics say that because olestra is a fat, it collects and carries out of the body the fat-soluble vitamins and antioxidants from other foods, even those consumed days earlier. (For this reason, P&G plans to fortify olestra with vitamin E and to add vitamins A, D, and K to foods using the fat substitute.) Other naysayers claim that the clinical tests weren't long enough, since cancer doesn't develop overnight.

Now the Center for Science in the Public Interest is focusing on the gastrointestinal side effects (cramps and diarrhea) described by 209 consumers who called its hot line. To top that, talk-show hosts are cracking olestra jokes. Your own hot line received only 85 complaints during the first 9 weeks olestra chips were on the market, and P&G has promised to include labels warning of these side effects when large quantities are consumed.

Your task: As director of consumer relations, write a memo describing the bad news for P&G's upper management.[34]

23. Kids are like that: Bad news from Crayola research   For six months, you've been working in Binney & Smith's new product development department, and in that time, you've probably smelled more Crayolas than you did throughout your entire childhood. Who can forget that distinctive waxy smell? But if all goes well, the next generation will be remembering something far different. Your Magic Scent Crayolas will make sure of that.

The idea for scented crayons isn't new; before you joined the company, Binney & Smith released the first Magic Scent crayons with much hoopla. They quickly flopped. Even though company tests proved otherwise, parents were convinced their kids would try to eat the lusciously fragrant coconut-scented white, bubble-gum pink, and chocolate brown. They refused to buy the new food-scented crayons.

But Binney & Smith didn't give up on what you all agreed was a great idea. As a researcher, you've been helping develop new "magic scents"—familiar fragrances parents won't fear and kids will still recognize and enjoy, such as Leather Jacket brown and Shampoo pink.

This morning, you have a focus group of a dozen 4- to 11-year-olds set up in the laboratory, each with a selection of unlabeled crayons laid out before them in rainbow order. Parents are hovering in the background and the videotape is rolling. Just to be sure you get everything down, you've stationed assistants with notebooks all around the table.

"Okay, kids," you announce to quiet the commotion. "Let's all sniff the first crayon, the brown one. What does it smell like to you?"

"Baloney samwich," a little redhead blurts out. "Nah—dead worms!" shouts a boy with an earring. "Smells like paint to me," a girl in plaid says softly. The two four-year-olds nod agreeably.

Well, okay, so Leather Jacket is a little off the mark. Bravely you proceed. By the end of the morning, you know that Cedar Chest smells like "dog doo," "fire," and "DNA"; Shampoo reminded them of "dead flowers"; and New Car struck their little noses as "pollution," "California," and "a vacuum cleaner." Your personal favorite, Lilac, reminded them of "mothballs," while

Eucalyptus brought shouts of "cigarettes!" The kids had great fun; your stomach is churning. Not a single child correctly identified any of the fragrances the research team has been working on for months.

Your boss has been busy out of town with another project, but he's expecting you to fax him a memo ASAP describing the results of this morning's test. Maybe after your stomach settles you can find some positive perspective to temper the dismal news.

Your task: Write the memo to Kevin Lee, manager of product research, for faxing to San Francisco.[35]

RISK MANAGEMENT

DOWNWARD COMMUNICATION

24. Watch for symptoms: Memo from GTE management announcing an outbreak of hepatitis   Dr. Frank Provato, GTE's medical director, looks grim as he addresses the group of executives assembled for the Monday morning staff meeting. "We have another confirmed case of hepatitis," he says. "That brings the total to four. The city health department has traced the problem to a cafeteria worker who's employed by ARA Services, the food-vending contractor that supplies our cafeteria. We have to assume that anyone who has eaten in the cafeteria in the last month has been exposed to the virus. That means just about all 700 employees here at corporate headquarters could come down with the disease."

"Just how serious is this?" the human resources director wants to know.

"Pretty serious. The city health department thinks the virus is hepatitis A. That's good news and bad news. People don't usually die from hepatitis A, but it's the most contagious of the strains."

"So what should we do?" someone asks.

"First," Dr. Provato says, "we have to close the cafeteria until we're sure we can operate without posing any additional health threat. Second, we need to inform the employees of the problem and tell them what symptoms to watch out for. Finally, we need to offer gamma globulin shots, which will reduce the symptoms in anyone who has contracted the disease."

"What are the symptoms?" you ask, wondering whether the scratchy feeling in your throat is the beginning of something serious.

"Basically, you feel like you've got a bad, lingering case of the flu—fever, aches and pains, loss of appetite, loss of energy. After about a week or ten days, you may notice a yellowing of the skin or the whites of the eyes.

Some people are sick for a month or more; some recover more quickly. If you get a gamma globulin shot, you're usually back on your feet in a week or two."

"When and where can the employees get these gamma globulin shots?" asks someone else.

"I'll have the serum in my office starting at noon today," says Dr. Provato. "I strongly recommend a shot for anyone who has eaten in the cafeteria in the last month."

Your task: Your boss asks you to draft a memo informing GTE's employees of the hepatitis threat.[36]

GOVERNMENT GRANT

UPWARD COMMUNICATION

25. From junk to robots: E-mail message explaining delay and requesting more money   For decades, scientists have worked to make the perfect robot: intelligent, sophisticated, and capable of multiple functions. You believe such robots would be too expensive and too complex. Working at Los Alamos National Laboratory in Los Alamos, New Mexico, you use parts from discarded tape players, worn-out toasters, and Casio watches to fabricate small one-task robots. Your goal is to make robots that are cheap and reliable.

Borrowing movement designs from nature, you built the Solar Spinner to resemble a light-seeking tarantula. Dangled by wires before a window, it wanders over the entire surface as it tries to gobble up more sunshine. Because four tiny brushes are attached to its legs, it cleans windows on its way.

Funded by a grant from the U.S. Army Research Lab at White Sands Missile Range, you are attempting to build a prototype for a robot that can unearth land mines, bombs, and other explosives. Such robots could clear the mine fields that continue to maim civilians in previously war-torn countries such as Vietnam, Afghanistan, and Bosnia.

Your task: You are robot designer Mark Tilden. Although you've been working tirelessly for six months on a prototype of a mine-sweeping robot, the desert heat of 160 degrees Fahrenheit and the sandy terrain have slowed the project. Write an e-mail message to Chuck Wullenjohn   at   White   Sands   Missile   Range <WullenjohnC@WSMR.army.mil> to let him know that the project will need additional funding of $225,000 and an extension of at least six months. Remember to use a positive approach, and inform Wullenjohn that your grant amendment will be ready for his review next week.[37]

CHAPTER 11

WRITING PERSUASIVE MESSAGES

AFTER STUDYING THIS CHAPTER, YOU WILL BE ABLE TO

- Strengthen your persuasive messages with an appropriate appeal
- Use attention, interest, desire, and action (the AIDA plan) to organize persuasive messages
- Write a message persuading your audience to take action or to grant you an adjustment
- Design a persuasive letter around selling points and benefits
- Apply the techniques of persuasion to prompt your audience to pay an overdue bill

COMMUNICATION CLOSE-UP AT AT&T'S LANGUAGE LINE SERVICES

His wife was having a baby, and he didn't know what to do, so the anxious father-to-be dialed 911. Trouble was, he spoke no English, and the operator couldn't understand what the emergency was. Neither party panicked, however; the 911 operator simply dialed an 800 number that connected her to AT&T's Language Line Services. In minutes, the AT&T operator set up a three-way call with a Spanish interpreter who helped talk the worried husband through the delivery of his first baby.

As sales director for Language Line Services, Jeanne Anderson has collected dozens of true-life stories like this, and they all illustrate the same thing: the benefits of dialing a toll-free number from any telephone and being connected at a moment's notice with an interpreter in any of 140 languages—24 hours a day. Compared to an average day rate of $500 to $700 for an on-site interpreter, AT&T's service costs from $2 to $4.50 per minute. So far, over-the-phone interpreters have closed a $12 million business deal in Taiwan, handled a marriage proposal in Russia, located a missing parent in Germany, translated an argument between a husband and wife, and helped hundreds of nurses, doctors, police officers, and business executives communicate with the diverse populations in their own local communities.

After years of experience writing persuasive messages to help sell Language Line Services, Anderson has developed a few principles she follows every time. She had to; as the anecdotes convey, the list of Language Line benefits is long. Just enumerating all the languages and dialects offered—from Asian Fukienese to African Lingala—would fill up a page. Anderson could easily mention so many applications and benefits that a potential customer would be overwhelmed—and unmoved. So she has learned to be selective and to target a persuasive message directly to an audience's needs. Her goal is not to manipulate readers, but to help them make an intelligent, in-

Jeanne Anderson

To persuade potential customers to try Language Line Services, Jeanne Anderson finds out who her audience is and what they're interested in. Then she crafts her letters to get attention, create interest, encourage desire, and motivate action. Whether working as an executive crafting letters to potential clients or as an operator serving current customers, employees of Language Line Services have strong communication skills and use them constantly.

formed decision about her message. Of course, she also makes sure she highlights specific benefits that she knows her audience will find attractive.

Anderson follows the same principles when writing persuasive memos to her staff or composing persuasive e-mail. She says the only difference is in the language and tone. "When I write an internal memo, I try to make sure that my personality comes out. I think all the same principles apply, though, because you really are competing for time with each employee. You want to make your message interesting, and you don't want to make it too long, so that people will have time to read it."

For every persuasive message, Anderson starts by answering two questions that any persuasive writer must ask: "Who is my audience, and what are they going to be interested in?" Once she knows the answers, she starts her message with what she calls a "grabber" or attention-getter, designed specifically for this particular audience. Her next paragraphs build her credibility, create interest, and encourage desire by emphasizing benefits she knows her readers care about. Depending on the nature of the message, Anderson's final paragraph will be some form of "call to action"—which may be as simple as, "Please respond to this request before Thursday." If she can tie that request to a final "grabber" or benefit, and make it easy to respond (by including her phone number, extension, or e-mail address), she knows she's written a winning message.

"You really do want to keep it simple," Anderson says, whether it's an outside client or a fellow employee. "Even if the first paragraph is interesting, your reader may think, 'Gee, there's just too much detail here. I'll just read this later when I have more time,' and unfortunately, it gets put on that pile—that 'To Do' pile that never gets done!" To keep it simple, Anderson avoids showy language, unfamiliar words, and AT&T lingo. She chooses active words and phrases that are "crisp and succinct," using the terminology of her audience's own industry when appropriate. Moreover, she always stresses the positive, for example, saying to a potential customer, "This service will save you time," instead of saying, "We know you don't have a lot of time."

Anderson's using her own skills with language to help others discover a new way to conquer language barriers—if not to save a life, then to make life simpler for everyone.[1]

PLANNING PERSUASIVE MESSAGES

Persuasion is the process of changing people's attitudes or influencing their actions.

Much more than simply asking somebody to do something, **persuasion** is the attempt to change an audience's attitudes, beliefs, or actions.[2] Persuasive messages aim to influence audiences who are inclined to resist. So they depend heavily on strategic planning—like that carried out by Jeanne Anderson of AT&T's Language Line Services. Before you begin to write a persuasive message, consider some important questions: What legal and ethical issues apply here? Who is my audience? How will my credibility affect my message? What tools can help me persuade my audience? Would emotional or logical appeals be best?

Questions to ask before you begin to write a persuasive message:
- What legal and ethical issues apply here?
- Who is my audience?
- How will my credibility affect my message?
- What tools can help me persuade my audience?
- Would emotional or logical appeals be best?

Ethical Persuasion

Positive persuasion leaves your audience free to choose.

The word *persuasion* is used negatively when associated with dishonest and unethical practices, such as coaxing, urging, and sometimes even tricking people into accepting an idea, buying a product, or taking an action they neither want nor need. However, the positive meaning of *persuasion* is influencing your audience members by informing them and by aiding their understanding, which allows them the freedom to choose.[3] Ethical businesspeople inform customers of the benefits of an idea, an organization, a product, a donation, or an action so that customers can recognize how well that idea, organization, product, donation, or action will fill a need they truly have.

To maintain the highest ethics, try to persuade without manipulating.

For anyone trying to influence people's actions, knowledge of the law is crucial. However, merely avoiding what is illegal may not always be enough. To maintain the highest standards of business ethics, make every attempt to persuade without manipulating. Choose words that won't be misinterpreted when deemphasizing negatives, and be sure you don't distort the truth. Show consideration for your audience by adopting the "you" attitude with honest concern for their needs and interests. Your consideration of audience needs is more than ethical; it's the proper use of persuasion. Moreover, it's more likely to achieve the response you intended and to satisfy your audience's needs.

Audience Needs

To motivate members of your audience, offer to satisfy their needs.

The best persuasive messages are closely connected to your audience's existing desires and interests.[4] One of the most effective ways to motivate members of your audience is offering to satisfy your audience's needs. Of course, people have many needs, but some researchers believe certain needs have priority. Figure 11.1 represents Abraham Maslow's hierarchy of needs, with the most basic needs appearing at the bottom of the figure. Only after lower-level needs have been met will a person seek to fulfill those on higher levels.[5]

For example, say that you supervise someone who consistently arrives late for work. You must either persuade him to change or fire him. First, find out why he's coming in late. Is he oversleeping because he has a second job to support his family (a safety and security need)? Is he coming in late out of a misguided desire to have people notice his arrival (an esteem and status need)? Once you've analyzed the need motivating him to arrive late, you can craft an appeal, a "hook" that will interest him in your message about changing his behavior. If the need for safety and security is behind his tardiness, you might begin by saying, "Your job is very important to you, I know."

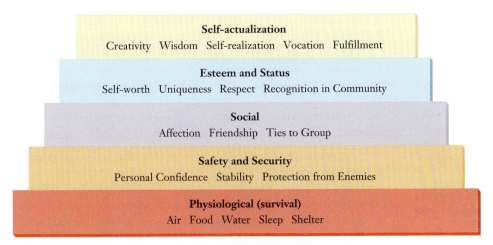

Figure 11.1
Maslow's Hierarchy of Needs

If he craves esteem and status, you could say, "You've always seemed interested in being given more responsibility, perhaps even a promotion."

Because everyone's needs differ, people respond differently to any given message. Not everyone is interested in economy, for instance, or fair play; as a matter of fact, some people's innermost needs make appeals to status and greed much more effective. To accommodate these individual differences, analyze your audience and then construct a message that appeals to their needs. A letter requesting an adjustment for defective merchandise could focus on issues of fairness or on legal issues, depending on the reader. A sales letter for sheepskin seat covers might emphasize prestige to Porsche drivers and comfort to Chevrolet drivers.

> Everybody has different needs, so appeal to the specific needs of your audience.

To assess various individual needs, you can refer to specific information such as **demographics** (the age, gender, occupation, income, education, and other quantifiable characteristics of the people you're trying to persuade) and **psychographics** (the psychological characteristics of a person, such as personality, attitudes, and lifestyle). In addition, both types of information are strongly influenced by culture.

> Demographics include characteristics such as age, gender, occupation, income, and education.

> Psychographics include characteristics such as personality, attitudes, and lifestyle.

When analyzing your audience, take into account their cultural expectations and practices so that you don't undermine your persuasive message by using an inappropriate appeal or by organizing your message in a way that seems unfamiliar or uncomfortable. Persuasion is different in different cultures. For example, in France using an aggressive, hard-sell technique is no way to win respect from your audience. In fact, such an approach would probably antagonize your audience. In Germany, where people tend to focus on technical matters, plan on verifying any figures you use for support, and make sure they are exact. In Sweden audiences tend to focus on theoretical questions and strategic implications, whereas in the United States audiences are usually concerned with more practical matters.[6] Your understanding and respect for cultural differences will not only help you satisfy the needs of audience members but also help them respect you.

> Cultural differences influence your persuasion attempts.

Writer Credibility

For you to persuade a skeptical or hostile audience, they must believe that you know what you're talking about and that you're not trying to mislead them. Your **credibility**

> Your credibility is defined by how reliable, believable, and trustworthy you are.

is your capability of being believed because you're reliable and worthy of confidence. Without such credibility, your efforts to persuade will seem manipulative.

One of the best ways to gain credibility is to support your message with facts. Testimonials, documents, guarantees, statistics, research results, and the like all provide seemingly objective evidence for what you have to say, so they add to your credibility. The more specific and relevant your proof, the better. Another good way to improve your credibility is to name your sources, especially if they're respected by your audience. Still other ways of gaining credibility include

- *Being enthusiastic.* Your excitement about the subject of your message can infect your audience.
- *Being objective.* Your understanding of and willingness to acknowledge all sides of an issue help you present fair and logical arguments in your persuasive message.
- *Being sincere.* Your honesty, genuineness, good faith, and truthfulness help you focus on your audience's needs.
- *Being an expert.* Your knowledge of your message's subject area (or even of some other area) helps you give your audience the quality information necessary to make a decision.
- *Having good intentions.* Your willingness to keep your audience's best interests at heart helps you create persuasive messages that are ethical.
- *Being trustworthy.* Your honesty and dependability help you earn your audience's respect.
- *Establishing common ground.* Those beliefs, attitudes, and background experiences that you have in common with members of your audience will help them identify with you.

Once you are committed to ethical persuasion, to satisfying the needs of your audience, and to building your credibility, you can concentrate on strengthening your message with some important persuasive tools.

Semantics and Other Persuasive Tools

When you're trying to build your credibility, how do you let your audience know that you're enthusiastic and trustworthy? Simply making an outright claim that you have these traits is sure to raise suspicion. However, **semantics** (the meaning of words and other symbols) can do much of the job for you. The words you choose to state your message say much more than their dictionary definition. For instance, *useful, beneficial,* and *advantageous* may be considered synonyms. Yet these three words are not interchangeable:

She suggested a <u>useful</u> compromise. (The compromise allowed the parties to get to work.)

She suggested a <u>beneficial</u> compromise. (The compromise not only resolved the conflict but also had a positive effect, perhaps for both parties.)

She suggested an <u>advantageous</u> compromise. (The compromise benefited her or her company more than it benefited the other party.)

Another way semantics can affect persuasive messages is in the variety of meanings that people attribute to certain words. Abstractions are subject to interpretation because they refer to things that people cannot experience with their senses. So use abstractions to enhance the emotional content of a persuasive message. For example, you may be able to sell more flags by appealing to your audience's patriotism (which may be inter-

---

Gain credibility by supporting your argument with facts such as testimonials, documents, guarantees, statistics, and research results.

Your credibility is improved if you are enthusiastic, objective, sincere, expert, and trustworthy and if your intentions are good and you establish common ground.

Semantics is the meaning of words and other symbols.

Two ways of using semantics are choosing your words carefully and using abstractions to enhance emotional content.

preted in many ways) than by describing the color and size of the flags. You may have better luck collecting an overdue bill by mentioning honesty and fair play than by repeating the sum owed and the date it was due. However, be sure to include the details along with the abstractions; the very fact that you're using abstract words leaves room for misinterpretation.

Of course, even using semantics skillfully isn't the whole story. Persuading audience members to change their attitudes or to take action can be difficult. Here are some other tools to use in persuasive messages:[7]

- *Focus on your goal.* Your message will be clearest if you shift your focus away from changing minds and emphasize the action you want your audience to take.
- *Use simple language.* In most persuasive situations, your audience will be cautious, watching for fantastic claims, insupportable descriptions, and emotional manipulation. So speak plainly and simply.
- *Anticipate opposition.* Think of every possible objection in advance. In your message, you might raise and answer some of these counterarguments, to prove you're fair-minded.
- *Be specific.* Back up your claims with evidence, and when necessary cite actual facts and figures. Let your audience know that you've done your homework.
- *Be moderate.* Asking your audience to make major changes in attitude or beliefs will most likely evoke a negative response. However, asking audience members to take one step toward that change may be a more reasonable goal.
- *Provide sufficient support.* It is up to you to prove that the change you seek is necessary.
- *Create a win-win situation.* Make it possible for both you and your audience to gain something. Audience members will find it easier to deal with change if they stand to benefit.

Other persuasive tools include focusing on your goals, using simple language, anticipating opposition, being specific, being moderate, providing sufficient support, and creating a win-win situation.

All of these tools will help your persuasive message be accepted, but none of them will actually convince your audience to take the action you want. You'll need a strong argument to persuade people, whether based on emotion or logic.

Emotion and Logic

You can diffuse negative emotions by planning carefully. For example, when people's needs are not being met, they're likely to respond emotionally. A person who lacks a feeling of self-worth is likely to be sensitive to the tone of respect in a message. So in a collection letter to such a person, you can carefully avoid any hint that the person might be considered dishonorable. Otherwise, the person might become upset and pay no attention to your message. Not even the best-crafted, most reasonable message will persuade someone who is emotionally unable to accept it.

You can diffuse negative emotions in order to help people accept your message.

But aside from simply avoiding negative emotions, how do you actually convince an audience that your position is the right one, that your plan will work best, that your company will do the most with a reader's donations? Is it better to appeal to your readers' emotions? Perhaps you're better off appealing strictly to their logic? For the best results when writing persuasive messages, appeal to both.

Both emotional and logical appeals are needed to write successful persuasive messages.

To persuade your audience, you can call on human emotion by basing your argument on the needs or sympathies of audience members, as long as your **emotional appeal** is subtle.[8] You can make use of the emotion surrounding certain words. *Freedom,* for instance, brings forth strong feelings, as do words such as *success, prestige, credit record, savings, free, value,* and *comfort.* Using words like these puts the audience in a

Emotional appeals are best if subtle.

certain frame of mind and helps them accept your message. Also, emotion works with logic in a unique way: People need to find rational support for an attitude they've already embraced emotionally.

A **logical appeal** calls on human reason. In any argument you might use to persuade an audience, you make a claim and then support your claim with reasons or evidence. When appealing to your audience's logic, you might use several types of reasoning:

Logical appeals use more than one type of reasoning:
- Analogy
- Induction
- Deduction

- *Analogy* is reasoning from specific evidence to specific evidence. To persuade employees to attend a planning session, you might use a town meeting analogy, comparing your company to a small community and your employees to valued members of that community.
- *Induction* is reasoning from specific evidence to a general conclusion. To convince potential customers that your product is best, you might report the results of test-marketing in which individuals preferred your product over others.
- *Deduction* is reasoning from a generalization to a specific conclusion. To persuade your boss to hire additional employees, you might point out industrywide projections that industry activity (and thus your company's business) will be increasing rapidly over the next three months.

Of course, regardless of the reasoning used, an argument or statement can easily appear to be true when it's actually false. Whenever you appeal to your audience's reason, do everything you can to ensure that your arguments are logically sound.

Avoiding Faulty Logic

Avoid faulty logic such as hasty generalizations, begging the question, attacking your opponent, oversimplifying, assuming a false cause, using faulty analogies, and using illogical support.

In any rational appeal, your high ethical standards dictate that you provide useful information, facts, and knowledge that can be used in decision making. To make this information persuasive, your arguments must be relevant, well-grounded, and systematic. So you make your points lucid and your arguments sound by steering clear of faulty logic:[9]

- *Avoid hasty generalizations.* Make sure you have plenty of evidence before drawing conclusions.
- *Avoid begging the question.* Make sure you can support your claim without simply restating it in different words.
- *Avoid attacking your opponent.* Be careful to address the real question. Attack the argument your opponent is making, not your opponent's character.
- *Avoid oversimplifying a complex issue.* Make sure you present all the facts rather than relying on an "either/or" statement that makes it appear as though only two choices are possible.
- *Avoid assuming a false cause.* Make sure to use cause-and-effect reasoning correctly so that you do not assume one event caused another just because it happened first.
- *Avoid faulty analogies.* Be careful that the two objects or situations being compared are similar enough for the analogy to hold. Even if *A* resembles *B* in one respect, it may not in all respects.
- *Avoid illogical support.* Make sure the connection between your claim and your support is truly logical and not based on a leap of faith, a missing premise, or irrelevant evidence.

When organizing and shaping your persuasive message, always think carefully about the argument you're using. You can test your argument to see whether it's logical. For example, the Toulmin model of logic can help you discover whether you've made hidden assumptions that your audience may not accept.

Using the Toulmin Model

As you shape your argument, you'll make it stronger (1) by finding common ground (basing your major argument on points that your audience already accepts) and (2) by stating the points in your case clearly.[10]

1. State your claim clearly.
2. Support your claim with a clear reason.
3. If your audience already accepts your reason (already holds that same belief, value, or principle presented in your reason), you may proceed to your conclusion.
4. If your audience does not already accept your reason, you must support this reason with another clearly stated claim, and support that claim with another clear reason, and so forth until you achieve common ground (find a reason based on beliefs, values, or principles that your audience already agrees with). Only then may you return to step 3.

As you can see, you are basically supporting your claim with evidence that is itself backed by a chain of reasons (all of which your audience must accept before you can move forward). This approach may remind you of the question-and-answer chain discussed briefly in Chapter 5 and at more length in Chapter 17.

ORGANIZING PERSUASIVE MESSAGES

Once you have carefully and thoroughly planned your persuasive message, you're ready to organize it. One way to organize persuasive messages is the **AIDA** plan, which has four phases: (1) attention, (2) interest, (3) desire, and (4) action. In the attention phase, you convince your audience right at the beginning that you have something useful or interesting to say. The audience wants to know, "What's in this message for me?" So try to tell them in the attention phase, without making extravagant claims or threats and without bringing up irrelevant points (see Figure 11.2 on page 336).

In the interest phase, you explain how your message relates to the audience. Continuing the theme that you started with, you paint a more detailed picture with words. Your goal is to get the audience thinking, "This is an interesting idea; could it possibly solve my problems?" In Figure 11.2, the interest section ties together a factual description and the benefits of instituting the new recycling plan. Also, the benefits relate specifically to the attention phase that precedes this section.

In the desire phase of a persuasive message, you back up claims and thereby increase your audience's willingness to take the action that you'll suggest in the next section. Whatever evidence you use to prove your claim, make sure it's directly relevant to your point.

In the action phase, you suggest the action you want your audience to take. All persuasive messages end with a section that urges specific action, but the ending is more than a statement such as "Institute this program as soon as possible" or "Send me a refund." In fact, this section offers a good opportunity for one last reminder of the main benefit the audience will realize from taking the action you want. The secret of the action phase is to make the action easy. In sales letters, AT&T's Jeanne Anderson might ask readers to call a toll-free number for more information. You might ask your audience to fill out an enclosed order form or to use a preaddressed, postpaid envelope for donations.

The Toulmin model of logic helps you uncover hidden assumptions that your audience may not accept.

Organize persuasive messages using the AIDA plan
- Attention
- Interest
- Desire
- Action

Begin every persuasive message with an attention-getting statement that is
- Personalized
- You-oriented
- Straightforward
- Relevant

In the interest section
- Continue the opening theme in greater detail
- Relate benefits specifically to the attention-getter

In the desire section
- Provide relevant evidence to prove your claim
- Draw attention to any enclosures

Close a persuasive message with an action ending that suggests a specific step the audience may take.

Figure 11.2
In-Depth Critique:
Persuasive Letter Using
the AIDA Plan

Randy Thumwolt uses the AIDA plan in this persuasive memo about a program that could solve two problems at once: (1) the high annual cost of plastics and (2) the rising number of consumer complaints about the company's failure to recycle plastics.

HOST MARRIOTT SERVICES

INTERNAL MEMORANDUM

To: Eleanor Tran, Comptroller
From: Randy Thumwolt, Purchasing Director
Date: August 22, 1997
Subject: Cost Cutting in Plastics

In the attention phase, background information and specific numbers grab the reader's attention.

As you know, we purchase five tons of plastic product containers each year. The price of the polyethylene terephthalate (PET) tends to rise and fall as petroleum costs fluctuate. You asked me earlier to find some ways to cut our annual costs for plastics. In my memo of January 5, I suggested that we bulk-purchase plastics during winter months when petroleum prices tend to be lower. Thanks for approving that suggestion. So far, I estimate we will realize a 10 percent savings this year.

In the interest phase, the writer clearly describes the problems the company is still facing.

Even so, our costs for plastic containers are still exorbitant ($2 million annually). In addition, we have received an increasing number of consumer letters complaining about our lack of a recycling program for the PET plastic containers both on the airplanes and in the airport restaurants. I've done some preliminary research and have come up with the following ideas:

In the desire phase, the writer makes suggestions in an easy-to-read list and provides detailed support in an attachment.

1. Provide recycling containers at all Host Marriott airport restaurants
2. Offer financial incentives for the airlines to collect and separate PET containers
3. Set up a specially designated dumpster at each airport for recycling plastics
4. Contract with A-Batt Waste Management for collection

I've attached a detailed report of the costs involved, but as you can see, our net savings the first year should run about $500,000. I've spoken to Ted Macy in marketing. If we adopt the recycling plan, he wants to build a PR campaign around it.

In the action phase, the writer provides another reader benefit and urges action within a specific time frame.

The PET recycling plan will help build our public image while improving our bottom line. If you agree, let's meet with Ted next week to get things started.

The Indirect Approach

The AIDA plan is tailor-made for using the indirect approach, allowing you to save your main idea for the action phase. Be sure to use the indirect approach when

- Your audience is negative (has strong resistance to your message).
- Your message is relatively short and clear (so that readers don't have to wait long for your main idea).
- You know your readers won't object to the indirect plan.

When using the indirect approach in persuasive messages, your goal is to explain your reasons and build interest before revealing your purpose. So the attention phase takes on increased importance. Getting your readers' attention is thoroughly covered during the discussion of sales letters later in this chapter.

Using AIDA with the indirect approach allows you to save your idea for the action phase.

The Direct Approach

The AIDA plan can also be adapted for the direct approach, allowing you to use your main idea as the attention-getter. You build interest with your argument, build desire with your evidence, and emphasize your main idea in the action phase with the specific action you want your audience to take. The direct approach is often shorter than the indirect approach, so it is appreciated by readers who are busy and pressed for time. Use the direct approach when

- Your audience is objective (and has no real resistance to your message).
- Your message is long and complex (so that you satisfy your reader's curiosity).
- You know your reader prefers the direct plan (for example, supervisors usually like to receive messages that will save them time and communicate the subject matter as quickly as possible).

Using AIDA with the direct approach allows you to use your main idea as your attention-getter.

However, even though you're presenting your main idea first, make sure you include a brief justification or explanation so that your reader doesn't have to accept your idea on blind faith.

Poor	Improved
I recommend building our new retail outlet on the West Main Street site.	After comparing the four possible sites for our new retail outlet, I recommend West Main Street as the only site that fulfills our criteria for visibility, proximity to mass transportation, and square footage.

Remember that your persuasive messages take careful planning and organization. Your success depends on your commitment to being ethical, analyzing your audience's needs, maintaining your own credibility, using semantics carefully, balancing emotion and logic, and choosing the most appropriate organizational plan. Following these guidelines will help you craft strong persuasive messages, no matter what the situation.

PREPARING PERSUASIVE MESSAGES ON THE JOB

Within an organization, you may write persuasive messages for any number of reasons, including to implement top management's decisions, to sell a supervisor on your idea for cutting costs, to suggest more efficient operating procedures, to elicit cooperation from competing departments, and to win employee support for a new benefits

When writing persuasive messages within an organization consider three influences:
- *Corporate culture*
- *Subcultures*
- *Position*

package. When writing a persuasive message to someone within your organization, consider three special aspects affecting your approach: corporate culture, corporate subcultures, and position or power.[11]

Every message written for a corporation adds to the corporate tradition.

An organization's culture heavily influences the types of messages that are considered effective. All the previous messages in the organization establish a tradition and practice that defines persuasive writing within that culture. If you accept and use these traditions, you are essentially establishing one type of common ground with your audience, and you will be rewarded by being accepted into the corporate culture. If you never learn these traditions or reject them, you'll have difficulty achieving that common ground, and your persuasion attempts will suffer.

Each functional area within a corporation develops its own subculture.

Organizations are made up of various functional areas such as accounting, finance, manufacturing, marketing, research, human resources, and so on. Each of these areas (or subcultures) tends to create its own approaches and traditions for helping the corporation succeed, valuing other functional areas, communicating, using language, and persuading. Moreover, each subculture tends to mistrust the language and customs of other subcultures. When writing a persuasive message within your subculture, you can use the accepted communication and language traditions with confidence. However, when writing a persuasive message outside your subculture, anticipate problems from readers whose general mind-set and specific business traditions may differ from yours.

Your position relative to your audience's position within an organization influences how you approach your persuasive message.

Holding a position in an organization affords businesspeople a commensurate amount of authority, expertise, and power. Therefore, the position you hold influences how you organize and write persuasive messages. Say you are a first-line manager. When writing a persuasive message to top management, you may try to be diplomatic and persuade using an indirect approach. But some managers may perceive your indirect persuasion as manipulative and time-wasting. On the other hand, you may consciously try to save your supervisors time by using a direct approach. But some supervisors might perceive your direct persuasion as brash and presumptuous. Similarly, when writing a persuasive message to employees, you may try to ease into a major change by persuading with an indirect approach, but your employees might perceive your indirect approach as weak or even wishy-washy. Or you may decide to persuade them with a direct approach to reinforce your image of authority, in which case your employees might perceive your direct approach as rude and unfeeling.

When writing within an organization, the way you word and organize your persuasive messages depends on organizational culture, your position, and your audience's position, not to mention the particular situation. So be sure to analyze your company's traditions, your department's practices, and your audience before deciding on an approach. In Figure 11.3, Bette McGiboney has chosen the direct plan to persuade her boss to accept her idea.

WRITING PERSUASIVE REQUESTS FOR ACTION

Many persuasive messages are written to solicit funds, favors, information, or cooperation. Within an organization, persuasive techniques are often required to get someone to change policies or procedures, to spend money on new equipment and services, to promote a person, or to protect turf.[12] Persuasive letters to outsiders might solicit donations or ask for some other type of help.

Three problems with requests for action:
- They frequently offer nothing tangible in return.
- They take time that could be used for something else.
- There are so many competing requests.

An external persuasive message is one of the most difficult persuasive tasks you could undertake. First, people are busy, so they're reluctant to do something new; it takes time and offers no guarantee of any reward in return. Second, competing requests are plentiful. In fact, the public relations departments of many large corporations

Figure 11.3
*In-Depth Critique: E-Mail
Selling an Idea to a Boss*

Bette McGiboney is administrative assistant to the athletic director of Auburn University. Each year after season tickets are mailed out, the cost of the athletic department's toll-free number skyrockets as fans call to complain about their seats or about not receiving the correct number of tickets, or to order last-minute tickets. The monthly phone bill skyrockets to over $3,000, in part because each customer is put on hold for a time while operators serve others. McGiboney has an idea that may solve the problem.

E-Mail

Date: Wednesday, 23 July 1997, 3:44:05
X-Sender: mcgibon@ath.auburn.edu
To: housel@ath.auburn.edu
From: "Bette McGiboney" <mcgibon@ath.auburn.edu>
Subject: Savings on toll-free number

Dear David:

As you know, our monthly billing for the toll-free number coming into the ticket office usually runs at least $3,000 for the month of August, compared to an average of $493 for the other eleven months. Tiger fans who call in August usually have at least a five-minute wait on hold. Here's an idea that will not only save us money but also help us manage our time and better serve our fans.

Under this plan, callers will hear the same messages and be offered the same options as before. However, if an operator isn't available when a caller presses "0" for ticket information, a new message will request a name and phone number so that we can return the call within the next two business days.

By reducing the on-hold time, I estimate we could eliminate at least $2,000 from our August bill (based on a conversation with Tandy Robertson, our AT&T representative). The good news is that the idea costs nothing and can be implemented immediately. We can use quiet times of the day to return phone calls, thus spreading our work more evenly.

I've discussed the idea informally with our operators, and they would like to try it. After football season, we can use our fall interns to call a random selection of customers to see how they liked the new message system. The plan will help us in the following ways:

•Provide better customer service
•Help us manage our time and stress levels
•Save us money on our toll-free line

I've attached a sheet with possible wording for the new message. Please let me know by the end of the month whether you'd like to give this a try.

Thanks,

Bette

This message follows the AIDA plan. The attention paragraph convinces the reader that the writer has something useful to say by presenting the main idea (a new plan for handling phone calls from fans).

The interest paragraph explains how the new plan will work, creating more interest in the idea.

The third and fourth paragraphs create desire by presenting supporting evidence such as cost savings, and the bulleted benefits draw the reader to the meat of the message.

The action paragraph is simple and direct with a specific time frame. It also takes care of a chore that might have caused the reader to delay.

receive so many requests for donations to worthy causes that they must sometimes resort to lotteries to decide which to support.

Why do people respond to requests for action on an issue that is more important to you than to them? If you're lucky, they may believe in the project or cause that you're writing about. Even so, you must convince them that your request will give them some benefit, perhaps an intangible benefit down the road or a chance to make a meaningful contribution. Also, especially in the case of requests for professional favors or information, people may believe that they are obliged to "pay their dues" by helping others.

When making a persuasive request, therefore, take special care to highlight both direct and indirect benefits. Direct benefits might include a reduced work load for the supervisor who institutes flextime or a premium for someone who responds to a survey. Indirect benefits might include better employee morale or the prestige of giving free workshops to small businesses.

The attention-getting device at the beginning of persuasive requests for action usually serves to show readers that you know something about their concerns and that you have some reason for making such requests. In this type of persuasive message, more than in most others, a flattering comment about your reader is acceptable, especially if it's sincere. The body of the letter or memo covers what you know about the problem you're trying to solve with the reader's help: the facts and figures, the benefits of helping, and your experience in attacking the problem. The goal is to give you and your request credibility, to make the reader believe that helping you will indeed help solve a significant problem. Once you've demonstrated that your message is relevant to your reader, you can request some specific action. Take a look at the request in Figure 11.4. Be aware, however, that a persuasive memo is somewhat more subdued than a letter to an outsider might be.

The most important thing to remember when preparing a persuasive request for action is to keep your request within bounds. Nothing is so distressing as a request so general, all-encompassing, or inconsiderate that it seems impossible to grant, no matter how worthy the cause. Also be careful not to doom your request to failure by asking your reader to do all your work for you: to provide information that you were too lazy to seek, to spend time saving you from embarrassment or inconvenience, or to provide total financial support for a cause that nobody else is supporting. To review the tasks involved in such messages, see this chapter's Checklist for Persuasive Requests for Action on page 342.

WRITING PERSUASIVE CLAIMS AND REQUESTS FOR ADJUSTMENT

Although persuasive claims and requests for adjustment are sometimes referred to as complaint letters, your goal is to persuade someone to make an adjustment in your favor; you're not merely getting a complaint off your chest. You reach your goal by demonstrating the difference between what you expected and what you actually got.

Persuasion is a necessity in pressing claims when you've already bought and paid for a product, for example. You can't threaten to withhold payment, so try to convey the essentially negative information in a way that will get positive results. Fortunately, most people in business are open to fair settlement of your claim. It's to their advantage to maintain your goodwill and to resolve your problem quickly so that they may continue with other business.

Highlight the direct and indirect benefits of complying with your request.

Make only reasonable requests.

The goal of a persuasive claim or request for adjustment is to satisfy your expectations for a transaction.

Figure 11.4
In-Depth Critique:
Persuasive Memo
Requesting Action

Ed Alvarez is excited about a new method of packaging bananas to decrease shipping damage and reduce costs. He needs his boss's approval to proceed and her cooperation in coordinating with another department. Following is his memo.

MEMORANDUM

To: **Kia Miamoto**
From: **Ed Alvarez**
Date: **September 3, 1997**
Subject: **Money-saving packaging**

Earlier this year you expressed concern about our damage problems in transporting our bananas from Chile using wooden crates. Recently, I came across information on plastic-lined reusable boxes that may solve our problem and save us money.

TexCrate, Inc., manufactures the corrugated boxes to any specifications. The 6 ml polyethylene lining is affixed to the walls of the boxes using a heat process. A metal U-bar inside the box provides a hanger for the bananas. The boxes feature slip-on lids that make stacking them in our containers quite easy. They can be fork-lifted using wooden pallets that we already own. We would place a desiccant pouch in each box to prevent "sweating." In addition, small heat vents can be cut into the lids and sides.

Because of the recent increase in lumber costs, the boxes cost less than the wooden crates. The boxes are also fully recyclable, which fits in with our "Earth-Friendly" campaign. Randy Farney of TexCrate says we should be able to ship repeatedly using the same boxes for several years. He would like to provide us with six sample boxes to test prior to our peak season, and he wants our specifications as soon as possible. He'll work up a dollar amount depending on the size we'll need. If we decide to use boxes, we can donate our wooden crates to Habitat for Humanity.

If you agree, I'd like to proceed with the test. Can you authorize someone from R&D to work with me on developing the specs for TexCrate? Please let me hear from you by Wednesday. If we can get the information to TexCrate within the week, we'll be able to conduct the tests and have results by early November. At that time I'll also be able to give you an estimate of our dollar savings so that we'll be ready to make a decision before mid-November—in plenty of time to make any needed changes before our peak season begins in late December.

A solution to an ongoing problem as well as an additional benefit help get the reader's attention.

By detailing the advantages and adaptability of the boxes, the writer gives the request credibility while increasing interest.

Additional cost and environmental benefits make the new method seem workable and build the reader's desire to try it.

The final paragraph tells the reader exactly what must be done and emphasizes the need to act now.

The key ingredients of a good persuasive claim are a complete and specific review of the facts and a confident and positive tone. Assume that the other person is not trying to cheat you but also that you have the right to be satisfied with the transaction. Talk only about the complaint at hand, not about other issues involving similar products or other complaints about the company. Your goal is to solve a particular problem; your

Make your persuasive claims
- Complete and specific when reviewing the facts
- Confident and positive in tone

CHECKLIST FOR PERSUASIVE REQUESTS FOR ACTION

A. ATTENTION

1. Demonstrate that you understand the audience's concerns.
2. Introduce a direct or indirect benefit that can be developed as a central selling point.
3. Construct statements so that they don't sound like high-pressure sales tactics or bribes.
4. Use an effective opening: comment or assertion the audience will agree with, compliment (if sincere), frank admission that you need the audience's help, problem that is the basis of your request, one or two rhetorical questions, statement(s) of what is being done or has been done to solve a problem.

B. INTEREST AND DESIRE

1. Early in the body of the message, introduce the reason you are writing.
   a. Mention the main audience benefit before the actual request.
   b. Thoroughly explain your reason for asking the favor.
2. Include all necessary description: physical characteristics and value of the project.
3. Include all facts and figures necessary to convince members of your audience that their contribution will be enjoyable, easy, important, and of personal benefit (as much as is true and possible).
   a. In a request for cooperation, explain the problem, facts, suggestions, other participants' roles, and the audience's part.
   b. In a request for a donation, explain the problem, past and current attempts to remedy it, future plans, your organization's involvement, and projected costs, along with suggestions about how the audience can help.
   c. Describe the possible direct benefits.
   d. Describe the possible indirect benefits.

4. Anticipate and answer possible objections.
   a. Ignore objections if they are unimportant or might not occur to the audience or if you can focus on positive facts instead.
   b. Discuss objections (usually) about half or two-thirds of the way through the body of the letter or memo.
   c. Acknowledge objections calmly; then overcome them by focusing on more important and more positive factors.
   d. Turn objections into an advantage by looking at them from another viewpoint or by explaining the facts of the situation more clearly.
   e. Overcome objections to providing restricted material by giving assurance that you will handle it in whatever limited way is specified.
5. Introduce any enclosures after you have finished the key message, with an emphasis on what to do with them or what information they offer.

C. ACTION

1. Confidently ask for the audience's cooperation.
2. Make the desired action clear and easy.
3. Stress the positive results of action.
4. Include the due date for a response (if necessary), and tie it in with audience benefits (if possible): adequate time for ordering supplies, prominent billing on the program, and so forth.
5. Replace negative or tentative statements, such as "If you can donate anything," with positive, confident statements, such as "To make your contribution, just return…"
6. Tie in the last sentence with an appeal or a statement featured in the opening paragraph (if appropriate), as a last audience-benefit plug.

audience is most likely to help when you focus on the benefits of solving the problem rather than on the horrors of neglecting your complaint.

As you read the following letter, note the improvements that could be made:

I bought an Audio-Tech sound system a few months ago to provide background music at my gift shop. Now one of the components, the compact disk (CD) player, does not work right. When we play a CD, it repeats and repeats. This is very

This opening fails to clarify for the reader the details of the purchase, the exact product involved, and the problem.

irritating to me and my customers, and Audio-Tech needs to fix this problem.

My clerks and I noticed this major mess about a month or so after I bought this fancy unit at the McNally Sound and Light Store in St. Louis, where I buy most of my video and CD stuff—although sometimes I buy through catalogs. When one of the clerks first heard the CD repeat, she tried another CD, and sure enough, it did the same thing, so it is a player-problem, not a CD problem. Then we set the CD player on digital so that we could see visually what was going on, and sure enough, the sound was repeating and even skipping.

When I finally brought the unit back to the store, Henry McNally said that the 60-day warranty had expired, and it was my gift shop's problem, but definitely not his problem. He said I probably had a "lemon."

This CD unit probably never did work right. I would think that after paying hundreds of dollars for this component, it would work for many years. Other stores here on Main Street cannot believe what a bummer it is to hear irritating background music on this Audio-Tech player. They say they will not buy the Audio-Tech brand if you don't replace my unit.

Nor does this paragraph include any acceptable reasons for Audio-Tech to consider making an adjustment.

This paragraph captures the frustration of the store owner, but it cannot persuade the reader who is still trying to grasp the dimensions of the problem.

And finally, some concluding comments touch on what the writer wants done, supported only by some additional complaining and a few vague threats.

Figure 11.5 (see pages 344–345) is a revised version of this letter, one that should yield much more favorable results. As the figure illustrates, resolving problems is more a matter of reasonable exchange than a struggle between adversaries. For a review of the tasks involved here, see this chapter's Checklist for Persuasive Claims and Requests for Adjustment on page 345.

WRITING SALES AND FUNDRAISING MESSAGES

Two distinctive types of persuasive messages are sales letters and fundraising letters. These messages often come in special direct-mail packages that can include brochures, reply forms, or other special inserts. Both types of messages are often written by specialized and highly skilled professionals like Jeanne Anderson of AT&T Language Line.

Sales and fundraising letters are distinctive types of persuasive messages that often come in special direct-mail packages.

How do sales messages differ from fundraising messages? Sales messages are usually sent by for-profit organizations seeking to solve readers' problems by persuading them to spend money on products. On the other hand, fundraising messages are usually sent by nonprofit organizations seeking to solve other people's problems by persuading readers to donate their money or time. Nevertheless, the fact is that both sales and fundraising messages are competing for business and public attention, time, and dollars.[13] Both types of messages attempt to persuade readers to spend their time or money on the value being offered—whether that value is the convenience of a more efficient vacuum cleaner or the satisfaction of helping save children's lives. Both sales and fundraising messages require a few more steps than other types of persuasive messages.

Sales and fundraising messages compete for readers' attention, time, and dollars.

Sales Letters

Whether you're selling a good, service, or company image, remember that the focus of your message is your audience. As with any message, persuasive or not, knowing the law can help you avoid serious legal problems. The laws governing sales letters are quite specific:

Know the laws governing sales letters, and avoid both legal and ethical pitfalls by being genuinely concerned about your audience's needs.

Figure 11.5
In-Depth Critique: Letter Making a Persuasive Claim

The following letter was sent to Audio-Tech Electronics to persuade the company to replace a faulty CD player.

---

ellie's special place

2201 main street, suite D • chesterfield, missouri 63071 • (314) 778-3345 • fax: (314) 778-3346

January 18, 1997

Mr. Allen Fenwick, Customer Relations
Audio-Tech Electronics
5054 Wicker Place
Chicago, IL 60622

Dear Mr. Fenwick:

As the owner of a small gift shop, I try to provide a pleasant ambiance for customers. For background music, I play "easy listening" and classical music on my Audio-Tech Pro III sound system. I play both CDs and tapes, but the CD player is not working properly. Please replace this CD unit at no charge.

I purchased the Audio-Tech Pro III system on November 1, 1996, from McNally Sound and Light at 16325 Lincoln Drive, St. Louis, Missouri 63158—about 150 miles from my store. All parts of the unit worked well for a month or so. I first noticed the problem on December 12: the CD would repeat a phrase two or three times in succession before moving on to the rest of the selection. At first I assumed it was a defective CD. On December 13, two customers asked me to turn off the CD player because it was repeating one musical phrase sporadically throughout a classical selection. The next day I checked the unit by setting it on "digital," and sure enough, every CD I played repeated phrases intermittently.

I called Mr. McNally at McNally Sound and Light, but I couldn't take the unit to St. Louis, because my shop is open extra evening and weekend hours for the Christmas holidays. There was no chance for me to take a half day away from my shop between mid-December and the end of our inventory period in early January. However, on January 10, I took the CD unit back to McNally. When I returned on January 17 to pick it up, Mr. McNally told me that he could hear the problem but was unable

---

Side annotations:

The brief opening clearly describes the problem, the product involved, how the product is used, and what adjustment is requested.

The next paragraph explains the details of purchase as well as how and when the problem was discovered.

The involvement with a third party (the dealer) is explained thoroughly.

- Sales letters are considered binding contracts in many states. So avoid even implying offers or promises that you can't deliver.
- Making a false statement in a sales letter is fraud if the recipient can prove that (1) you intended to deceive, (2) you made the statement regarding a fact rather than an opinion or a speculation, (3) the recipient was justified in relying on the statement, and (4) that the recipient was damaged by it (in a legal sense).

Figure 11.5
(Continued)

Mr. Allen Fenwick, January 18, 1997, Page 2

to fix it. He said it was a manufacturing problem, but since my warranty had expired, he could not replace the unit free of charge.

Enclosed with this letter and the CD component are copies of my original sales form and McNally's January repair order. Please replace, at no charge to me, the defective CD unit. Although the 60-day warranty theoretically expired on January 1, I discovered the problem well within the warranty period. My original decision to purchase Audio-Tech products was motivated by your reputation for both quality products and exceptional service. So I know you will stand behind your product and replace the faulty machine.

Sincerely,

Ellie Chambers

Ellie Chambers

Enclosure

> The close refers to attached receipts, restates the adjustment being requested, and provides the reader with a reason to grant the adjustment (the company's reputation for quality and customer service).

CHECKLIST FOR PERSUASIVE CLAIMS AND REQUESTS FOR ADJUSTMENT

A. ATTENTION
1. For your opening, use one of the following: sincere compliment, rhetorical question, agreeable comment or assertion, statement of the basic problem, or brief review of what has been done about the problem.
2. At the beginning, state something that you and the audience can agree on or that you wish to convince the audience about.

B. INTEREST AND DESIRE
1. State all necessary facts and details, and interweave them with audience benefits.
2. Provide a description that shows the members of your audience that their firm is responsible for the problem and that your request is factual, logical, and reasonable.
3. Appeal to the audience's sense of fair play, desire for customer goodwill, need for a good reputation, or sense of legal or moral responsibility.
4. Emphasize your goal of having the adjustment granted.
5. Present your case in a calm, logical manner.
6. Tell the audience how you feel; your disappointment with the products, policies, or services provided may well be the most important part of your argument.

C. ACTION
1. Make sure the action request is a logical conclusion based on the problem and the stated facts.
2. State the request specifically and confidently.
3. Specify a due date for action (when desirable).
4. State the main audience benefit as a reminder of benefits in earlier statements.

Misrepresenting the price, quality, or performance of a product in a sales letter is fraud. So is a testimonial by a person misrepresented to be an expert.

- Using a person's name, photograph, or other identity in a sales letter without permission constitutes invasion of privacy—with some exceptions. Using a photo of the members of a local softball team in a chamber of commerce mailer may be perfectly legal if team members are public figures in the community and if using the photo doesn't falsely imply their endorsement. On the other hand, using a photo of your governor, without consent, on a letter about the profits to be made in worm farming could be deemed an invasion of privacy.

- Publicizing a person's private life in a sales letter can also result in legal problems. Stating that the president of a local bank (mentioned by name) served six months in prison for income tax evasion is a potentially damaging fact that may be considered an invasion of privacy. You would also risk a lawsuit by publicizing another person's past-due debts or by publishing without consent another person's medical records, x-rays, or photograph.

As with other persuasive messages, following the letter of the law isn't always enough. To write sales letters of the highest ethical character, focus on solving your readers' problem rather than on selling your product. If you're genuinely concerned about your audience's needs and interests, you'll find it easier to avoid legal or ethical pitfalls. Once you're firmly committed to focusing on your audience, you can begin planning your sales letter by figuring out what features would most interest your readers.

Determining Selling Points and Benefits

Know your products' selling points, but talk about their benefits to consumers.

Selling points are the most attractive features of an idea or product; benefits are the particular advantages that readers will realize from those features. One selling point of a security system for students' dorm rooms is its portability. The benefit to students is the ability to protect their possessions from theft without investing in a full-blown permanently installed alarm system (see Figure 11.6).

Start with a thorough knowledge of the product.

Obviously, you can't write about selling points or benefits without a thorough understanding of your subject as well as of your audience. So take a good look at your product. Ask yourself (or someone else, if necessary) everything that you think a potential buyer might want to know about it. At AT&T's Language Line, Jeanne Anderson emphasizes the ease and cost-effectiveness of dialing up one of 140 languages 24 hours a day. If you were writing the sales letter in Figure 11.6, you would need to have a full description of what the portable security system looks like, what it does, and how it works. Some selling points for students receiving the SecureAbel Alarms letter would include the fact that the dormitory security system installs with a screwdriver, has an activator that hooks to your key chain or belt loop, and has a blinking red light to warn intruders to stay away. You would also investigate prices and discounts, delivery schedules, and packaging.

Form a mental picture of the product's typical buyer; then relate selling points and benefits to that picture.

Once you have a complete file on your product, collect data about your audience and try to form a mental image of the typical buyer for the product you wish to sell. This will help you formulate an idea of the central concerns of potential buyers in your audience. Then you can check the selling points you've already come up with against your audience's actual needs.

Think about how the product's features can help potential buyers; then concentrate on the most appealing benefits.

Now think about how your product can benefit your audience. The benefits for students would include ease of installation, ease of activation, and a feeling of safety and security. Be sure to focus on relatively few product benefits, and determine which benefits are most appealing to your particular audience. Ultimately, you'll single out one benefit, which will become the hallmark of your campaign. Safety seems to be the key benefit emphasized by SecureAbel Alarms.

Choosing the Format and Approach

Once you know what you need to say and who you want to say it to, decide how you're going to say it. Will you send just a letter, or will you include brochures, samples, response cards, and the like? Will the letter be printed with an additional color or special symbols or logos? How many pages will it run? You'll also need to decide whether to conduct a multistage campaign, with several mailings and some sort of telephone or in-person follow-up, or whether to rely on a single hard-hitting mailing.

All these decisions depend on the audience you're trying to reach—their characteristics, their likely acceptance of or resistance to your message—and what you're trying to get them to do. Generally speaking, expensive items and hard-to-accept propositions call for a more elaborate campaign than low-cost products and simple actions.

Getting Attention

Since sales letters are prepared according to the AIDA plan used for any persuasive message, they start with an attention-getting device. Professionals use some common techniques to attract audience attention. When you're preparing a sales letter, consider emphasizing

A number of tried-and-true attention-getting devices are used in sales letters for a wide variety of products.

- *A piece of genuine news.* "In the past 60 days, auto manufacturers' inventories have shrunk by 12 percent."
- *A personal appeal to the reader's emotions and values.* "The only thing worse than paying taxes is paying taxes when you don't have to."
- *The most attractive feature plus the associated benefit.* "New control device ends problems with employee pilferage!"
- *An intriguing number.* "Here are three great secrets of the world's most loved entertainers."
- *A sample of the product.* "Here's your free sample of the new Romalite packing sheet."
- *A concrete illustration with story appeal.* "In 1985 Earl Colbert set out to find a better way to process credit applications. After ten years of trial and error, he finally developed a procedure so simple but thorough that he was cited for service to the industry by the American Creditors Association."
- *A specific trait shared by the audience.* "Busy executives need another complicated 'time-saving' device like they need a hole in the head!"
- *A provocative question.* "Are you tired of watching inflation eat away at your hard-earned profits?"
- *A challenge.* "Don't waste another day wondering how you're going to become the success you've always wanted to be!"
- *A solution to a problem.* "Tired of arctic air rushing through the cracks around your windows? Stay warm and save energy with StormSeal Weather-stripping."

A look at your own mail will show you how many products these few techniques can be applied to. Using such attention-getting devices will give your sales letters added impact. See Figure 11.6, on pages 348–349, for a typical example.

Even so, not all attention-getting devices are equally effective. The best is the one that makes your audience read the rest of the letter. Look closely at the following three examples. Which seems most interesting to you?

Choose an attention-getter that encourages the reader to read more.

Figure 11.6
In-Depth Critique: Letter Selling a Product

The following sales letter for SecureAbel Alarms uses the AIDA plan to persuade students to buy its dorm-room alarm systems.

SecureAbel Alarms, Inc.

5654 Lakemont Drive • Altoona, PA 16602 • Voice: (814) 983-4424 • Fax: (814) 983-4422 • http://www.secure.com

October 14, 1997

Mr. Samuel Zolezzi
Penn State University, North Halls
104 Warnock Commons
State College, PA 16802

Dear Mr. Zolezzi:

Did you know that one out of four college students becomes a victim of theft? How would *you* feel if you returned to your dorm and discovered your hard-earned stereo, computer, or microwave had been stolen? Remember, locked doors won't stop a determined thief.

It happened to me when I was in college. That's why I've developed a portable security system for your dormitory room. It works like an auto alarm and installs with an ordinary screwdriver. The small activator hooks to your key chain or belt loop. Just press the "lock" key. A "beep" tells you your room is secure, and a blinking red light warns intruders to stay away.

If a thief tries to break in, a loud alarm sounds. Your possessions will be safe. And even more important, you can activate the system from your bedside, so no one can break in.

You'd expect that peace of mind to cost a fortune—something most college students don't have. But we're offering the SecureAbel Dorm Alarm System for only $75. Here's what you'll receive by return mail:

Beginning with a provocative question draws the reader into the letter and raises the awareness of a need. Benefits have both a logical appeal (protecting possessions) and an emotional appeal (personal safety).

In the second paragraph, the writer seeks to establish a common bond with the reader and explains how the product works by comparing it to something the reader is familiar with, a car alarm.

The third paragraph mentions an additional threat to safety and hence another benefit of the security system.

How would you like straight A's this semester?

Get straight A's this semester!

Now you can get straight A's this semester, with ...

If you're like most people, you'll find the first option the most enticing. The question invites your response—a positive response designed to encourage you to read on. The second option is fairly interesting too, but its commanding tone may make you wary of

Figure 11.6
(Continued)

Mr. Samuel Zolezzi, October 14, 1997, Page 2

- **The patented alarm unit**
- **Two battery-operated programmable remote units**
- **A one-year warranty on all parts**
- **Complete and easy-to-follow installation instructions**

Order additional alarm boxes to install on your window or bathroom door for only $50. Act now. Fill out the response card, and mail it along with your choice of payment in the enclosed envelope. Don't give thieves and criminals a chance. Protect yourself and your belongings. Send in your card today.

Sincerely,

Dan Abel

Dan Abel, President

Enclosures

The bulleted list creates the sense of added value to the offer.

The final paragraph urges quick action.

the claim. The third option is acceptable, but it certainly conveys no sense of excitement, and its quick introduction of the product may lead you to a snap decision against reading further.

Sales letters prepared by professionals also use a variety of formatting devices to get your attention, including personalized salutations, special sizes or styles of type, underlining, color, indentions, and so on. Whatever special techniques are used, the best attention-getter for a sales letter is a hook that gets the reader thinking about the needs your product might be able to help fill.

Emphasizing the Central Selling Point

Say that your company's alarm device is relatively inexpensive, durable, and tamper-proof. Although these are all attractive features, you want to focus on only one. Ask what the competition has to offer, what most distinguishes your product, and what most concerns potential buyers. The answers to these questions will help you select the **central selling point,** the single point around which to build your sales message. Highlight this point in your heading or first paragraph, and make it stand out through typography, design, or high-impact writing.[14]

To determine your product's central selling point, ask:
- What does the competition offer?
- What is special about my product?
- What are potential buyers really looking for?

Highlighting Benefits

Determining the central selling point will help you define the benefits to potential buyers. Perhaps your company's alarm device has been built mainly to overcome the inadequacies of the competition in resisting tampering by would-be burglars. This feature is your central selling point; the benefits of this feature are that burglars won't be able to break in so easily and therefore burglaries will be reduced. You'll want to mention this benefit repeatedly, in words and pictures (if possible), near the beginning and the end of your letter. You might get attention by using a news item to stress this benefit: "Burglaries of businesses in our county have increased 7.7 percent over the past year; police department officials cite burglars' increasing sophistication and

DOES SOME DIRECT MAIL CONTAIN DELIBERATELY DECEPTIVE COPY?

What's ethical and what's just smart selling? Some direct-mail campaigns use tokens and stickers to deter consumers from logical analysis and steer them toward a more childlike state of mind. Others set prices at $29.95 to make audiences think the product costs around $20 instead of nearer $30. One questionable practice involves the "assumptive claim": A letter states, "Here's the information you requested," when no such request was made. Some companies rationalize these methods as "affirmative puffery" and "mild misrepresentation" that do no real harm to the consumer. What do you think?

Ever since Montgomery Ward sold his first oilcloth table covers through the mail in 1872, marketers have proven that direct mail is one of the most profitable and cost-effective forms of advertising. They've also encountered some of the toughest ethical decisions in business. A few laws have been enacted to protect consumers: The federal Deceptive Mailings Preventions Act of 1990 prohibits mailings that resemble government documents, and state privacy legislation governs the nature of consumer information gathered, retained, sold, and traded as mailing lists. For the most part, however, the direct-mail seller must weigh the alternatives: How enthusiastically can I extol the benefits of my product and still maintain good ethical and legal business standards?

Skilled direct-mail copywriters try to catch their audience's attention in the first four seconds, so certain words are highly valued in the trade: *free, urgent, special, immediate, exclusive, limited supply,* and so on. "Irresistible" envelopes, personalized letters, brochures, response cards, and gimmicks such as tokens and stickers tread the narrow line between truth and exaggeration. Going overboard is easy, and professional organizations debate about how far is too far. Some researchers have even begun questioning the potential long-term negative effects of emotion-laden messages that leave a particular segment of the audience feeling depressed, anxious, hostile, or inferior.

One direct-mail expert advised businesses: "If there's a limited supply, say so." If not, you might say, "while current supply lasts" or "until inventory is sold out." This same expert suggested that even if there's no impending price increase (after the current offer expires), it might be profitable to suggest that "prices may never be this low again." Are these approaches legal? Yes. Are they ethical? You'll have to decide for yourself.

1. Plenty of honest, hard-working people use direct-mail campaigns successfully and ethically. From your own mailbox, collect some positive examples of direct-mail selling.
2. When thinking about direct-mail ethics, where would you draw the line for your own direct-mail campaign?

---

familiarity with conventional alarm devices." You might pose a provocative question: "Worried about the reliability of your current alarm system in repelling today's sophisticated burglars?"

In the rest of the letter, continue to stress this theme but also weave in references to other benefits: "You can get this worry-free protection for much less than you might think." Also, "The same technology that makes it difficult for burglars to crack your alarm system makes the device durable, even when it must be exposed to the elements." Remember, sales letters reflect the "you" attitude through references to benefits, so always phrase the selling points in terms of what such features will do for potential customers. (See "Does Some Direct Mail Contain Deliberately Deceptive Copy?")

Selling points + "you" attitude = benefits.

Using Action Terms

To give force to a message
- Use action terms
- Use colorful verbs and adjectives

Active words give force to any business message, but they are especially important in sales letters. Compare the following:

Instead of This	**Write This**
The NuForm desk chair is designed to support your lower back and relieve pressure on your legs.	The NuForm desk chair supports your lower back and relieves pressure on your legs.

The second version says the same thing in fewer words and puts more emphasis on what the chair does for the user ("supports") than on the intentions of the design team ("is designed to support").

In general, use colorful verbs and adjectives that convey a dynamic image. Be careful, however, not to overdo it: "Your factory floors will sparkle like diamonds" is hard to believe and may prevent your audience from believing the rest of your message.

Talking About Price

The price people will pay for a product depends on the prices of similar products, the general state of the economy, and the psychology of the buyer. Price is therefore a complicated issue and often a sensitive one.

Whether the price of your product is highlighted or downplayed, prepare your readers for it. Such words as *luxurious* and *economical* provide unmistakable clues about how your price compares with that of competitors, and they help your readers accept the price when you finally state it. If your price is relatively high, definitely stress features and benefits that justify it. If the price is low, you may wish to compare the features of your product with those of the competition, either directly or indirectly. In either case, if the price you eventually mention is a surprise to the reader, you've made a mistake that will be hard to overcome.

> You can prepare readers for your product's price by subtle choice and arrangement of words.

Here's an example from a sales letter offering a product at a bargain price:

All the Features of Name-Brand Pantyhose at Half the Price!

Why pay for fancy packaging or that little tag with a famous name on it when you can enjoy cotton lining, reinforced toes, and matchless durability for only $1.99?

In this excerpt the price falls right at the end of the paragraph, where it stands out. In addition, the price issue is featured in a bold headline. This technique may even be used as the opening of a letter if the price is the most important feature and the audience for the letter is value-conscious.

> If the price is an attractive feature, emphasize it by displaying it prominently.

If price is not a major selling point, you can handle it in several ways. You could leave out the price altogether or mention it only in an accompanying brochure. You could deemphasize the price by putting the actual figures in the middle of a paragraph close to the end of your sales letter, well after you've presented the benefits and selling points. The same paragraph might include a discussion of related topics, such as credit terms, special offers, and volume discounts. Mentioning favorable money matters before the actual price also reduces its impact.

> To deemphasize price
> - Bury actual figures in the middle of a paragraph near the end
> - Mention benefits and favorable money matters before the actual price
> - Break a quantity price into units
> - Compare the price with the cost of some other product or activity

Only 100 prints of this exclusive, limited-edition lithograph will be created. On June 1, they will be made available to the general public, but you can reserve one now for only $350, the special advance reservation price. Simply rush the enclosed reservation card back today so that your order is in before the June 1 publication date:

Emphasis on the rarity of the edition signals value and thus prepares the reader for the big-ticket price that follows. The actual price, buried in the middle of a sentence, is tied in with another reminder of the exclusivity of the offer.

The pros use two other techniques for minimizing price. One is to break a quantity price into units. Instead of saying that a case of wine costs $144, you might say that each bottle costs $12. The other is to compare your product's price with the cost of some other product or activity: "The cost of owning your own spa is less than you'd pay for a health-club membership." Your aim is to make the cost seem as small and affordable as possible, thereby eliminating price as a possible objection.

Tony Stone Worldwide is a stock photo agency that sends direct-mail packages to potential customers. These packages can include a sales letter, a catalog, a color brochure, a business reply form and envelope, and even a Rolodex card with important phone numbers and electronic addresses.

Supporting Your Claims

You can't assume that people will believe what you say about your product just because it's in writing. You'll have to prove your claims, especially if your product is complicated, expensive, or representative of some unusual approach.

Types of support for product claims:
- Samples
- Brochures
- Examples
- Testimonials
- Statistics
- Guarantees

Support for your claims may take several forms. Samples and brochures, often with photographs, are enclosures in the sales package and are referred to in the letter. The letter also describes or typographically highlights examples of how the product has benefited others, includes testimonials (actual quotations) from satisfied customers, or cites statistics from scientific studies of the product's performance. Guarantees of exchange or return privileges, which may also be woven into the letter or set off in a special way, indicate that you have faith in the product and are willing to back it up.

It's almost impossible to provide too much support. Try to anticipate every question your audience may want to ask. Put yourself in your audience's place so that you can ask, and answer, all the what-ifs.[15]

Motivating Action

The overriding purpose of a sales letter is to get your reader to do something. Many consumer products sold through the mail simply ask for a check—in other words, an immediate decision to buy. On the other hand, companies like AT&T's Language Line and companies selling big-ticket and more complex items frequently ask for just a small step toward the final buying decision, such as sending for more information or authorizing a call by a sales representative.

Aim to get the reader to act as soon as possible.

Try to persuade readers to take action, whatever it is, right away. Convince them that they must act now, perhaps to guarantee a specific delivery date. If there's no particular reason to act quickly, many sales letters offer discounts for orders placed by a certain date or prizes or special offers to, say, the first 500 people to respond. Others suggest that purchases be charged to a credit card or be paid off over time. Still others offer a free trial, an unconditional guarantee, or a no-strings request card for information, all in an effort to overcome readers' natural inertia. Motivating action can be a challenge in sales letters and even more of a challenge when you're trying to raise funds. (How do sales messages differ on the Internet? See "Writing for the Web: Sales Messages in Cyberspace" on pages 354–355.)

Fundraising Letters

Most of the techniques used to write sales letters can be used to write fundraising letters, as long as your techniques match your audience, your goals, and the cause or organization you're representing. Be careful to establish value in the minds of your donors. Above all, don't forget to include the "what's in it for me?" information—for example, telling your readers how good they'll feel by making a donation.[16]

Fundraising letters use many of the same techniques as used in sales letters.

Planning Fundraising Messages

To make sure that your fundraising letters outshine the competition's letters, take some time to get ready before you actually begin writing.[17] You can begin by reading the mail you receive from donors. Learn as much as you can about your audience by noting the tone of these letters, the language used, and the concerns raised. This exercise will help you write letters that donors will both understand and relate to.

By reading your mail from donors, you can learn about the tone, language, and concerns your donors prefer.

You might also keep a file of competing fundraising letters. Study these samples to find out what other fundraisers are doing and what new approaches they're taking. Most important, find out what works and what doesn't. Then you can continue with your other research efforts such as performing interviews, holding focus groups, and reading trade journals to find out what people are concerned about, what they're interested in, and what gets their attention.

By keeping a file of competing fundraising letters, you can find out what works and what doesn't.

Finally, before you start writing, know whose benefits to emphasize. Make a two-column list, and on one side, list what your organization does; then on the other side, list what your donors want. You'll discover that the two columns are quite different. Make sure that the benefits you emphasize relate to what your donors want (not what your organization does). Then you can work on stating those donor benefits in specific detail. For example: "Your donation of $100 will provide 15 people with a Christmas dinner."

Be sure to focus on the concerns of your readers, not the concerns of your organization.

Personalizing Fundraising Messages

Because fundraising letters depend so heavily on emotional appeals, keep your message personal. A natural, real-life lead-in is usually the best. People seem to respond best to slice-of-life stories. In fact, storytelling is perfect when your narrative is unforced and goes straight to the heart of the matter.[18] Professional fundraiser Conrad Squires advises you to "find and use relevant human-interest stories," to "show donors the faces of the people they are helping," and to "make the act of sending a contribution as real and memorable and personal" as you can.[19] This way your letters will make people feel the warmth of other lives.[20]

Human-interest stories are the best way to interest your readers in fundraising letters.

So that your letters remain personal, immediate, and effective, steer clear of three common mistakes:[21]

- Avoid letting your letter sound like a business communication of any kind.
- Avoid wasting space on warm-up (the things you write while you're working up to your real argument).
- Avoid assuming that the goals of your organization are more important than your readers' concerns (a deadly mistake).

This last item is crucial when writing fundraising letters. Squires suggests that "the more space you spend writing about the reader, the better response you're likely to get."[22]

Personalize fundraising letters by
- *Writing about your readers*
- *Helping your readers identify with recipients*

"You've proven you are somebody who really cares what happens to children, Mr. Jones."

KEEPING PACE WITH TECHNOLOGY

WRITING FOR THE WEB: SALES MESSAGES IN CYBERSPACE

With the World Wide Web selling everything from business consulting to gourmet foods to books, more and more business communicators are writing online sales messages. All of the principles of good persuasive writing still apply, of course, but the Web adds a few unique twists.

First, the Internet (upon which the World Wide Web operates) started as a way for government officials, scientists, and other nonbusiness users to share information. Although it has become quite commercialized in recent years, most people in this online community expect participants to follow a certain

MTV's Web site offers head-spinning amounts of information and alternative ways to receive it. The designers of this site know just who their visitors are and just how to reach them.

"Ms. Smith, your company's kindness can change the world for Meta Singh and his family."

"You are cordially invited to join..."

Also, it's up to you to help your donors identify with recipients. A busy company executive may not be able to identify with the homeless man she passes on the street every day. But every human being understands pain—we've all felt it. So do your best to portray that homeless man's pain in words the busy executive can understand.[23]

Strong fundraising letters

- Explain a specific need thoroughly
- Show how important it is for readers to help
- Spell out exactly what amount of help is being requested
- Describe in detail the benefits of helping

Strengthening Fundraising Messages

The best fundraising letters do four things: (1) explain a specific need thoroughly, (2) show how important it is for readers to help, (3) spell out exactly what amount of help is being requested, and (4) describe in detail the benefits of helping.[24] (See Figure 11.7 on pages 356–357.) To help you accomplish these four major tasks, here are some fundraising guidelines:[25]

- Do whatever you can to interest your readers at the absolute beginning of your letter. If you can't catch your readers' interest then, you never will.

approach to communication that keeps the Internet unique. This *netiquette* emphasizes content over hype, substance over style, and dialog over monologue. For sales messages, this means giving interested people information they can use to make better decisions. Avoid sensationalism, grandstanding, and competition bashing, which not only looks petty to many Internet users but can also leave you open to libel suits.

Second, many Internet users want to interact with message sources. In other words, they want to establish a dialog with you, rather than simply being on the receiving end of your monologue. They want to ask questions, explore alternatives, conduct research, download files, and compare notes with other people. Your ability to interact electronically with your audience will have a lot to do with the success of your online sales messages.

Third, in other media, people are often subjected to sales messages whether they want them or not, but on the Internet, the audience is in control. People can roam freely, moving forward and backward and following new links whenever and wherever they feel like it. They don't have to sit still for your message. Plus, search engines make it easy to find competitors' sites and jump to them within seconds. If people don't have a reason to read your sales message, they're gone in a flash.

Given that the audience is in control, how do you persuade them to visit your site and stay long enough to get your message? Most successful Web sites do some combination of the following:

- *They offer entertainment value.* The site developed by the Comedy Central cable TV channel offers humorous bits such as imaginary Web sites featuring famous people. This material is mixed in with sales messages for both the programming on Comedy Central and the T-shirts and other merchandise available for order on the site.
- *They make the shopping experience easier.* Amazon.com, the largest bookseller on the Internet, makes it easy to find and order books.
- *They provide useful information.* Hewlett-Packard, the giant computer and electronics company, offers free technical information on its Web site.

In a sense, good Web writing is all about respect for the audience. Respect your readers, and they'll have more respect for your sales messages.

---

1. Write a one-paragraph sales message for your college's Web site that doesn't rely on hype or competition bashing. (Choose either the college as a whole or any specific aspect as your subject.) Be prepared to explain how your message fits the preferred style of writing for the Internet.
2. Do you think that sending unsolicited e-mail sales messages is compatible with the preferred style of Internet writing? Why or why not?

- Tell your story with simple, warm, and personal language.
- Be sure to give readers an opportunity to accomplish something important.
- Make the need so urgent and strong that your readers find it hard to say no. "Won't you send a gift now, knowing children's lives are on the line?" Donors want to feel needed. They want the excitement of coming to your rescue.
- Make it extremely easy to respond by asking for a small gift.
- Make the amount of money you want absolutely clear and appropriate to your audience.
- Explain why the money is needed as soon as possible.
- Write no longer than you have to. For example, people expect telegram-type messages to be short. However, for fundraising letters, longer messages are usually the most effective, as long as you keep your sentences and paragraphs short, maximize content, and minimize wordiness. If you're writing a long message, just make sure it's interesting and no longer than necessary.
- Include all the basics in your reply form—your name, address, and telephone number; a restatement of your request and the gift amount; your donor's name,

Figure 11.7
In-Depth Critique: Letter Raising Funds

As president of the nonprofit Decatur High School Band Parents Association, Monty Nichols is faced with the daunting task of raising a million dollars to help send the band to Osaka, Japan, for an international band festival. Nichols and his board have decided to contact local businesses for help, and the following letter makes a compelling case for donations.

Decatur High School Band
27 Linwood Lane • Decatur, Illinois 46733
Phone: (217)-864-7788

Dear Corporate Friend:

The opening is "you" oriented, focusing on the reader's generosity and grabbing attention.

You have been a loyal supporter of our award-winning Decatur High School Band, and we appreciate what you've helped us accomplish. Because of you, we were able to participate in three festival competitions this year, and we brought home three "Grand Champion" trophies. Now we have the unprecedented opportunity to represent Decatur in the Osaka International Band Festival in 1999. Only 25 top bands from the United States have been invited, and thanks to your sponsorship, Decatur High School Band is one of them.

The next three paragraphs create interest by emphasizing benefits to the reader and providing details of the trip and costs.

Your continued support will help the Decatur High School Band accept Osaka's exciting invitation. The Decatur City Council, the Decatur School Board, and our own Parents Association Board believe the trip will be an opportunity for our 130 band members to learn about another culture. Even more important, our Decatur ambassadors will bring their experiences back to our community and their classmates in speeches, photographs, and interviews with the local media.

Let us paint your logo on our band trailer as one of our Golden Sponsors. We'll also include your name in all our programs and mailings between now and the time of the trip. You'll be helping band members

The easy-to-read list of benefits creates desire to participate in a worthwhile project.

1. Learn about other cultures
2. Share information abroad about our way of life in the United States
3. Teach others in Decatur what they learn
4. Help Decatur become recognized as a good home for international businesses

We estimate total costs at a million dollars. The city of Osaka has pledged $25,000 toward financing the trip, and we have already received pledges from Akworth Nisson and the city for $25,000 each. Our band members will be holding fundraising events such as car washes, bake sales, a spring fair, and many

Figure 11.7
(Continued)

Page 2

**other events over the next two years. But your support will make
our dream a reality.**

**Please help our young ambassadors make this trip. Mark your
pledge card and return it today. You'll receive personal letters
from the kids expressing their appreciation. And you'll be proof
of our city's motto, "Dreams come true in Decatur."**

Sincerely,

Monty Nichols

**Monty Nichols
President
Decatur High School Band Parents Association**

Enclosure

The last paragraph urges
action by naming additional
reader benefits and enclosing
a response card.

address, and code number (or space enough for a label); information on how to
make out the check; and information on tax deductibility.

- Use interesting enclosures. You will decrease returns by using enclosures that
  simply give more information about a project or the purpose of your organization.
  To increase returns, use enclosures that are fun or that give the donor something
  to do, sign, return, or keep.

These guidelines should help you reach the humanity and compassion of your readers
by focusing on specific reader benefits, detailing the unique need, emphasizing the urgency of the situation, and spelling out the exact help needed.

Like sales letters, fundraising letters are simply particular types of persuasive messages. Both categories have their unique requirements, some of which only professional writers can master. (See this chapter's Checklist for Sales and Fundraising
Letters, on pages 358–359, as a reminder of the tasks involved in these messages.)

WRITING COLLECTION MESSAGES

The purpose of the collection process is to maintain goodwill while collecting what is
owed. Collection is a sensitive issue; it's also closely governed by federal and state
laws. The Fair Debt Collection Practices Act of 1978 outlines a number of restrictions
on collection procedures. The following practices are prohibited:

- Falsely implying that a lawsuit has been filed
- Contacting the debtor's employer or relatives about the debt
- Communicating to other persons that the person is in debt
- Harassing the debtor (although definitions of harassment may vary)
- Using abusive or obscene language
- Using defamatory language (such as calling the person a *deadbeat* or a *crook*)
- Intentionally causing mental distress

CHECKLIST FOR SALES AND FUNDRAISING LETTERS

A. ATTENTION

1. Design a positive opening that awakens in the reader a favorable association with the product, need, or cause.
2. Write the opening so that it's appropriate, fresh, honest, interesting, specific, and relevant.
3. Promise a benefit to the reader.
4. Keep the first paragraph short, preferably two to five lines, sometimes only one.
5. Design an attention-getter that uses a human-interest story for fundraising letters or any of the following techniques for sales letters: significant fact about the product, solution to a problem, special offer or gift, testimonial, stimulation of the senses or emotions, reference to current events, action picture, startling fact, agreeable assertion, comparison, event or fact in the reader's life, problem the reader may face, quotation.

B. INTEREST

1. State information clearly, vividly, and persuasively, and relate it to the reader's concerns.
2. Develop the central selling point, or explain the urgency of the fundraising need.
3. Feature the product or need in two ways: physical description and reader benefits.

   a. Interweave benefits with a physical description, or place benefits first.
   b. Describe the objective details of the need or of the product (size, shape, color, scent, sound, texture, and so on).
   c. Through psychological appeals, present the sensation, satisfaction, or pleasure your reader will gain, translating the product, service, or donation into the fulfillment of needs and desires.
   d. Blend cold facts with warm feelings.

C. DESIRE

1. Enlist one or more appeals to support the central idea (selling point or fundraising goal).
   a. Provide one paragraph of desire-creating material in a one-page letter with descriptive brochure; provide several paragraphs if the letter itself is two or more pages long, with or without an enclosed brochure.
   b. Emphasize reader benefits.
   c. If the product is valued mainly because of its appearance, describe its physical details.
   d. If the product is machinery or technical equipment, describe its sturdiness of construction, fine crafting, and other technical

---

- Threatening violence
- Communicating by postcard (not confidential enough)
- Sending anonymous C.O.D. communications
- Misrepresenting the legal status of the debt
- Communicating in such a way as to make the receiver physically ill
- Giving false impressions, such as labeling the envelope "Tax Information"
- Misrepresenting the message as a government or court document

To protect people from unreasonable persecution and harassment by debt collectors, the law also delineates when you may contact a debtor, how many times you may call, and what information you must provide to the debtor (timely responses, accurate records, and understandable documents). However, that doesn't mean you can't be tough in collection letters. As long as what you state is true and lawful, it can't be construed as harassment or misrepresentation.

A debtor's response is likely to be emotional, especially when the debtor is conscientious, so use tact.

Positive appeals are usually more effective than negative ones.

    Conscientious customers are embarrassed about past-due accounts. In such an emotional state, they may consciously or unconsciously blame you for the problem, procrastinate, avoid the situation altogether, or react aggressively. Your job is to neutralize those feelings by using **positive appeals**, by accentuating the benefits of complying with your request for payment. If positive appeals fail, you may have to consider a **negative appeal**, which stresses the unpleasant consequences of not acting rather than the benefits of acting. Of course, using abusive or threatening language and ha-

details in terms that help readers visualize themselves using it.

    e. Include technical sketches and meaningful pictures, charts, and graphs, if necessary.

    f. If the main point is to elicit a donation, use strong visual details, good narrative, active verbs, and limited adjectives to strengthen the desire to help.

2. Anticipate and answer the reader's questions.

3. Use an appropriate form of proof.

    a. Include facts about users' experience with the charitable organization or product, including verifiable reports and statistics from donation recipients or product users.

    b. Provide names (with permission only) of other satisfied buyers, users, or donors.

    c. Present unexaggerated testimonials from persons or firms who have used the product or donated funds and whose judgment the reader respects.

    d. For sales letters, provide the results of performance tests by recognized experts, testing laboratories, or authoritative agencies.

    e. For fundraising letters, provide the details of how donations are spent, using recognized accounting or auditing firms.

    f. In sales letters, offer a free trial or a guarantee, and refer to samples if they are included.

4. Note any enclosures in conjunction with a selling point or reader benefit.

D. ACTION

1. Clearly state the action you desire.

2. Provide specific details on how to order the product, donate money, or reach your organization.

3. Make action easy through the use of a mail-back reply card, preaddressed envelope, phone number, or promise of a follow-up call or visit.

4. Offer a special inducement to act: time limit or situation urgency, special price for a limited time, premium for acting before a certain date, free gift for buying or donating, free trial, no obligation to buy but more information or a suggested demonstration, easy payments with no money down, credit-card payments.

5. Supply a final reader benefit.

6. Include a postscript conveying important donation information or an important sales point (if desired for emphasis).

---

rassing your customer is ineffective and illegal. Persuasion is the opposite of force, so continue to use a polite and businesslike tone as you point out some of the actions legally available to you.

    Don't forget that your real aim is to persuade the customer to make the payment. So your best approach is to try to maintain the customer's goodwill. One key to success in collecting is remembering that collection is a process, not just a single demand.[26] As the past-due period lengthens, a series of collection letters reflecting the increasing seriousness of the problem is sent to the customer at predetermined intervals: notification, reminder, inquiry, urgent notice, and ultimatum. At the later stages, the customer's past credit and buying history, the amount of money owed, and the customer's overall credit rating determine the content and style of collection messages.

If positive appeals fail, you may need to point out the actions legally available to you.

Steps in the collection series:
- *Notification*
- *Reminder*
- *Inquiry*
- *Urgent notice*
- *Ultimatum*

Notification

Most creditors send bills to customers on a regular schedule, depending on the terms of the credit agreement. Typically, this standard notification is a form letter or statement, often computerized, stating clearly the amount due, the date due, the penalties for late payment, and the total amount remaining to be paid. The standardized form, far from being an insult to the recipient, indicates the creditor's trust that all will go according to plan.

The standardized notification is a sign of trust.

Reminder

The reminder notice, which still assumes only a minor problem, may be a standardized form or an informal message.

If the payment has not been received within a few days after the due date, most creditors send out a gentle reminder. Again, the tone of the standardized letter is reassuring, conveying the company's assumption that some minor problem has delayed payment. In other words, the firm still believes that the customer has every intention of paying what is due and needs only to be reminded. Thus the tone is not too serious:

> Our records show that your September payment is more than a week overdue. If you have recently mailed your check for $154.87, we thank you. If not, please send it in quickly.

Using a different strategy, some companies send out a copy of the unpaid bill at this stage, with a handwritten note or preprinted stamp or sticker indicating that payment has not yet been received.

Inquiry

The inquiry
- Assumes that something unusual is preventing payment
- Is personalized
- Avoids any suggestion of customer dissatisfaction

As frustrating as it may be to send out a reminder and still get no response, don't assume that your customer plans to ignore the debt, especially if the customer has paid bills promptly in the past. So avoid accusations in your inquiry message. However, the time has passed for assuming that the delay is merely an oversight, so you may assume that some unusual circumstance is preventing payment:

> According to our records, we have not received your September payment of $154.87. Because this payment is four weeks overdue, we are quite concerned. You have a history of paying your bills on time, so we must conclude that there is a problem. Please contact us at (800) 536-4995 to discuss this payment, or send us your check for $154.87 right away. We want to help you correct this situation as quickly as possible.

Personalization at this stage is appropriate because you're asking your customer to work out an individualized solution. The letter also avoids any suggestion that the customer might be dissatisfied with the purchase. Instead, it emphasizes the reader's obligation to communicate about the problem and the creditor's willingness to discuss it. Including the writer's name and a phone number helps motivate a response at this stage.

Urgent Notice

An urgent notice
- Might be signed by a top company official
- Might indicate the negative consequences of noncompliance
- Should leave an opening for payment without loss of face

This stage represents a significant escalation. Convey your desire to collect the overdue payment immediately and your willingness to get serious, but avoid any overt threats. To communicate a sense of urgency, you might resort to a letter signed by a top official in the company or to a negative appeal. However, an urgent notice still leaves an opening for the debtor to make a payment without losing face:

> I was very surprised this morning when your file reached my desk with a big tag marked OVERDUE. Usually, I receive customer files only when a serious problem has cropped up.
>
> Opening your file, I found the following facts: Your order for five cases of Panza serving trays was shipped six months ago. Yet we still haven't received the $232.70 due. You're in business too, Mr. Rosen, so you must realize that this debt needs to be paid at once. If you had a customer this far behind, you'd be equally concerned.

An attention-getter focuses on the unusual circumstances leading to this letter.

The recipient is reminded of the order. Personalization and an attempt to emphasize common ground may motivate the reader to respond.

> Please see that a check for $232.70 is mailed to us at once. If you need to work out an alternate plan for payment, call me now at (712) 693-7300.
>
> Sincerely,
>
> Artis Knight
> Vice President

The preferred action is spelled out; an option is also suggested in case of serious trouble.

The name of a ranking official lends weight to the message.

Ultimatum

Some people's finances are in such disorder that you won't get their attention until this stage. However, don't send an ultimatum unless you intend to back it up and are well supported by company policy. Even then, maintain a polite, businesslike manner and avoid defaming or harassing the debtor.

By itemizing the precise consequences of not paying the bill, you can encourage debtors to reevaluate their priorities. You're no longer interested in hearing why it has taken them so long to respond; you're interested in putting your claim at the top of their list. The tone of the ultimatum need not be so personal or individualized as the inquiry or urgent notice. At this stage, you're in a position of justified authority and should no longer be willing to return to an earlier stage of communication and negotiation:

An ultimatum
- Should state the exact consequences of nonpayment
- Must avoid any hint of defamation or harassment
- Need not take a personal, helpful tone

> On December 12, 1996, you placed a catalog order with Karting Klothes for our extra-large wheeled duffel bag, and you applied for a credit account with us. We approved your application, and on December 17 mailed the duffel bag to you with an invoice for $92.87. According to our credit application, which you signed, payment is due within 20 days. As of February 1, your payment is significantly overdue.
>
> Karting Klothes sent you reminders on January 2 and again on February 2. In both these letters, we asked you to contact us to discuss your payment. We also asked you to make a partial payment as a show of your good faith. You did neither.
>
> Karting Klothes has already canceled your credit privileges, and will turn your account over to a collection agency if we do not receive your payment for $92.87 by March 10. To reinstate your account and to avoid the problems associated with a bad credit rating, mail your check immediately.

This letter outlines the steps that have already been taken, implying that the drastic action to come is the logical follow-up. Although earlier collection messages were based on persuasion, this one is essentially a bad-news letter.

If a letter like this doesn't yield results, the only remaining remedy is actually to begin legal collection procedures. As a final courtesy, you may wish to send the debtor a notice of the action you're about to take. By maintaining until the bitter end your respect for the customer, you may still salvage some goodwill.

SUMMARY

The purpose of a persuasive message is to influence attitudes and actions. Persuasive techniques are especially important for an audience that may not completely agree with you.

Planning persuasive messages includes consideration of ethics, audience needs, writer credibility, semantics, and the roles of emotion and logic. You can best motivate an audience to do as you wish by organizing your persuasive messages using the AIDA plan: attention, interest, desire, action. Stress the benefits of complying with your request. When persuading on the job, be sure to consider corporate culture, subcultures, and hierarchical position.

Persuasive messages are used in many business contexts, including requests for action and requests for adjustment. When preparing a sales letter, highlight a major feature and related benefit of the product that's being promoted; in the close, make a response easy. When preparing a fundraising letter, emphasize the specific human need and the benefit to the donor of helping. Debt-collection letters also follow the AIDA plan.

COMMUNICATION CHALLENGES AT AT&T'S LANGUAGE LINE SERVICES

The word about AT&T's Language Line Services has spread quickly among hospitals, police departments, city agencies, and businesses looking to expand into overseas markets. Jeanne Anderson's sales and marketing department is busy prospecting for new subscribers, and her staff keeps growing and growing. Anderson has her hands full, and she recently began delegating some of her responsibilities to keep up with the work load.

Individual Challenge: Every December, the sales and marketing department hosts a Holiday Open House Toy and Food Drive for all Language Line employees. Anderson sees it as a way of bringing old and new members of her department closer together and of helping local charity organizations. But she realizes it's going to take a little persuasion to get her staff to participate; the holidays are a busy time for everyone and this affair is strictly voluntary. Moreover, she's asking them, as they do every year, to bring finger food and desserts for a potluck buffet, plus a new toy or canned food to donate to the needy. The party will last from 2:00 to 4:00, with music, talk, and maybe even a little dancing.

Anderson has asked you to write the memo, which is more of a persuasive request for action than an invitation to a party. She hopes staff members will decide to attend, will bring a toy or food gift, and will contact Laura and Judy (party organizers) to let them know what potluck dish to expect. (Make up any other names or details you need to write a convincing memo.)

Team Challenge: Language Line Services became so popular so quickly among certain industries that Anderson has had little time to brainstorm ideas about new applications for new markets. She has asked your group to help out. Sooner or later, AT&T's current markets will be saturated; before that happens, Anderson wants her staff ready to target new industries. That will require special sales training and new sales literature targeted to each industry—and that means she'll need a budget increase.

First, she has asked you to brainstorm ways Language Line Services might be used by government agencies, service organizations, or any untapped industry you can identify. List applications and benefits for each industry, then decide which three sound most promising. Anderson wants you to write a persuasive memo to convince upper management that these three markets are so promising that the added expenditures for staff training and industry-specific sales literature will bring profitable returns. She's going to ask for a $50,000 total budget increase to start the three-industry campaign. "Don't worry about financial justification; I'll supply a detailed budget breakdown as an attachment to the memo," she tells you. "You just need to convince them this is an idea they can't refuse."[27]

CRITICAL THINKING QUESTIONS

1. If you must persuade your audience to take some action, aren't you being manipulative and unethical? Explain.
2. As a manager, how many of your daily tasks require persuasion? List as many as you can think of.
3. Are emotional appeals ethical? Why or why not?
4. Is it honest to use a hook before presenting your request? Explain.
5. Why is it important to maintain goodwill in your collection letter? Briefly explain.
6. For over a year, you've tried repeatedly, without success, to collect $6,000 from a client who is able to pay but simply refuses. You're writing one last letter before turning the matter over to your attorney. What sort of things can you say in your letter? What things should you avoid saying? Explain your answers.

DOCUMENTS FOR ANALYSIS

Read the following documents; then (1) analyze the strengths and weaknesses of each sentence and (2) revise each document so that it follows this chapter's guidelines.

Document 11.A: Writing Persuasive Requests for Action

At Tolson Auto Repair, we have been in business for over 25 years. We stay in business by always taking into account what the customer wants. That's why we are writing. We want to know your opinions to be able to better conduct our business.

Take a moment right now and fill out the enclosed questionnaire. We know everyone is busy, but this is just one way we have of making sure our people do their job correctly. Use the enclosed envelope to return the questionnaire.

And again, we're happy you chose Tolson Auto Repair. We want to take care of all your auto needs.

Document 11.B: Writing Persuasive Claims and Requests for Adjustment

Dear US Robotics:

I'm writing to you because of my disappointment with my new Sportster Si, 14.4 Faxmodem. The modem works all right, but the volume is set wide open and the volume knob doesn't turn it down. It's driving us crazy. The volume knob doesn't seem to be connected to anything but simply spins around. I can't believe you would put out a product like this without testing it first.

I depend on the modem to run my small business and want to know what you are going to do about it. This reminds me of every time I buy electronic equipment from what seems like any company. Something is always wrong. I thought quality was supposed to be important, but I guess not.

Anyway, I need this fixed right away. Please tell me what you want me to do.

Document 11.C: Writing Sales and Fundraising Letters

We know how awful dining hall food can be, and that's why we've developed the "Mealaweek Club." Once a week, we'll deliver food to your dormitory or apartment. Our meals taste great. We have pizza, buffalo wings, hamburgers and curly fries, veggie roll-ups, and more!

When you sign up for just six months, we will ask what day you want your delivery. We'll ask you to fill out your selection of meals. And the rest is up to us. At "Mealaweek," we deliver! And payment is easy. We accept MasterCard and VISA or a personal check. It will save money especially when compared to eating out.

Just fill out the enclosed card and indicate your method of payment. As soon as we approve your credit or check, we'll begin delivery. Tell all your friends about Mealaweek. We're the best idea since sliced bread!

Document 11.D: Writing Collection Messages

It may not seem like it to you, but your outstanding balance of $429.52 is very important to us. When we grant credit, we do it with the understanding that bills will be paid on time. Our entire operation works smoothly only when we have all our customers paying their bills in a timely fashion.

Perhaps there is some problem which you haven't called us about? We want to please our customers, but even a company with the best of intentions sometimes falls short. Take a minute from your busy day and fill out the enclosed card. We want to know if there is a problem.

Also, take a minute right now to please pay your bill. Thanks for your cooperation. We would hate to turn a valuable customer over to a collection agency.

CASES

Writing Persuasive Requests for Action

SMALL BUSINESS

EXTERNAL COMMUNICATION

1. Give me liberty: Letter persuading customers to remain loyal to Colbar Art   For many people in the United States, the Statue of Liberty is a cliché, so much a part of New York City's tourist hype that it's taken for granted. But for most immigrants, the first sight of Liberty as they enter the city brings tears along with hopes for a new life. Ovidiu Colea knows the feeling. He immigrated to the United States in the early 1980s after a difficult past that included five long years in a Romanian hard-labor camp for trying to flee the communist regime.

Colea worked two years as a cabby to save enough money to start Colbar Art, a company that produces up to 70,000 hand-crafted replicas of the Liberty statue each year. He now helps other immigrants get a start in their new country by hiring them to design and produce the Liberty models. Inspired by a letter from Lee Iacocca requesting donations to the Liberty–Ellis Island Foundation, Colea pays a royalty to the foundation for using Liberty's image. In fact, during the first year of operation, that royalty amounted to $250,000.

Recently, because much of the work is done by hand rather than by machine, Colbar Art employees have been unable to keep up with the high demand for orders. Even though Colea is arranging to lease a larger space and to hire and train more employees, the production deficits will probably continue for several months.

Your task: You work for Colbar Art as assistant manager, and Colea has asked you to write a persuasive form letter to all your customers, explaining the current delays and requesting patience. Be sure to explain the steps the company is taking to solve these delays, and describe the quality and creativity that go into the polyresin and marble-dust models. You can quote Bradford Hill (owner of the Liberty Island gift shop), who says Colbar Art's models represent 65 percent of his sales. And don't forget to mention that most of your employees are the very immigrants that the Statue of Liberty welcomes. Make a convincing argument for your customers to remain loyal to Colbar Art.[28]

MARKETING
INTERNAL COMMUNICATION

2. Cosmic catnip: Memo at Cosmic Pet suggesting a new product What do you do if your favorite cat turns up his nose at the catnip mouse you've offered him? You find a better catnip! That's what Leon Seidman of Hagerstown, Maryland, did back in the 1970s. Seidman drove as far as Shepherdstown, West Virginia, to find wild catnip—enough to fill his Volkswagen Beetle and launch a business. Today, Cosmic Pet is a $3 million company, and it uses commercially grown catnip to produce the chemical nepetalactone that triggers ecstasy in cats. Even though the company is doing well, sales have reached a plateau, and Seidman wants to add new products to boost business.

As a summer marketing intern, you've researched catnip, nepetalactone, and its historic uses. You've discovered that early European settlers used the herb in a tea to treat colic, fever, and indigestion. You believe that the herb has tremendous potential as a product to relieve gastrointestinal discomfort. You envision a marketing plan that involves touting the herb as a cure for stomach discomfort from overindulgence. Because the product is "all natural" and considered extremely safe, you believe FDA approval will not be necessary.

Your task: Write a memo to Leon Seidman. Describe your ideas for the new product, how it would be packaged and marketed, how much it would cost to produce, how much it would cost at retail, and any other pertinent details you can supply. Predict what you believe the new product would gross for the company in one to five years. Remember to focus on the concerns of your audience, and try to answer or at least address those concerns.[29]

MANAGEMENT
DOWNWARD COMMUNICATION

3. Selling sales letters: E-mail message promoting a new idea at Sears, Roebuck As marketing manager for Sears, Roebuck, you know that sales messages can make or break a business. One of your company's most difficult tasks is getting customers to read a sales letter. During a recent seminar, you heard a reference made to the "PSALM" method, and you decide to learn more about it. Explore the Web site at <http://www.socal.com/writingbiz/page1.htm> and find out what is meant by the PSALM approach. What does the author of this approach identify as the most common mistakes in sales letters? You are enthusiastic about how this new approach has changed your thinking about sales letters, and you would like everyone in your department to seriously consider it.

Your task: Write an e-mail message to everyone in your department, selling the idea of the PSALM method to your colleagues.

MARKETING
EXTERNAL COMMUNICATION

4. Internet appliances: Persuasive letter requesting phone companies to test Oracle's software "The network computer needs a network." So says Oracle CEO Lawrence Ellison. Network appliances are "stripped down" personal computers used simply to access the Internet and the data, e-mail, and other programs residing on central servers. These simple "appliances" are based on microprocessors from Intel Corporation, so they need no costly or sophisticated hardware. Of course, network appliances do need a network.

Oracle's Ellison believes that telephone companies are the best candidates to provide such services, and several phone companies are planning consumer trials of Internet appliances, with the aim of making the World Wide Web as simple to navigate as using a telephone. Instead of having to own a personal computer and periodically upgrading its software, businesses and consumers will pay one monthly fee to their phone company, which will supply the appliance and the network that links it to a central server, e-mail, the Internet, and the World Wide Web.

Oracle, a database software company based in Redwood Shores, California, is developing the standard software for hardware companies to use in the network appliances they build. Ellison's only fear is the lack of a network. Before phone companies proceed with a large-scale roll-out, they'll want to test consumer demand. Unfortunately, waiting too long could cost Oracle potential market share.

Your task: As Oracle's marketing director, your job is to encourage phone companies to test network appliances. Write a persuasive letter requesting phone companies to move quickly. You may create any data you need to support your claim. Address your e-mail to the

marketing departments of the larger long-distance providers such as AT&T, MCI, and Sprint.[30]

HUMAN RESOURCES
UPWARD COMMUNICATION

5. The downsizing dilemma: Persuasive letter at Intermed   You've heard the old saying that when your next-door neighbor loses her job, it's a recession; when you lose yours, it's a depression. After 15 years as a loyal employee of Intermed, a surgical equipment manufacturer, it's finally happening to you. In a companywide meeting this morning, your CEO informed the work force that Intermed has just been bought out by Urohealth Systems and that a substantial number of layoffs are anticipated in the near future.

As the manager of Intermed's technical support department, you're concerned both for your employees and for yourself. However, you've already learned that Urohealth is basically a holding company that has grown by acquiring smaller, regional companies like Intermed. Urohealth has few hourly or nonexempt employees, so you feel most of your staff will be kept on. You do know, however, that after Urohealth's last acquisition, dozens of middle managers like yourself disappeared.

You're determined to take a positive approach, so you begin preparing for the inevitable. You know Intermed has certain policies and procedures for terminations. However, you feel that by taking the initiative, you can negotiate a better deal for yourself. First, you look at your current compensation. You decide to ask for four weeks' severance pay for each year of service. You want to start a bit high and be prepared to settle somewhere between two and three weeks.

You have been able to purchase company stock over the years. However, you may lose some of your more recent purchases when you are terminated. You consider asking to trade some of your severance pay to be able to keep all your stock. Chances are, the value of the stock will increase after Urohealth takes over. Your 401(K) (personal retirement savings) plan may also be in jeopardy. The company matches your savings each year, provided you are employed for the entire year. You would like the company to add its matching contribution for the entire year, even though you won't be on the payroll through December 31.

Conventional wisdom says it may take up to a year for someone with your skills and experience to find another position. You intend to ask Intermed for outplacement counseling, use of an office, telephone, and office equipment, and payment of your job-hunting expenses for at least 90 days.

Your task: You know you'll get a much better deal by initiating voluntary termination and negotiating your severance package with Intermed before Urohealth takes over. Write a persuasive letter to Shirley Barnett, Intermed's director of human resources, outlining your requests. Address the letter to her at 500 Livingston Street, Northvale, NJ 07647. [31]

6. Ouch, that hurts! Persuasive memo at Technology One requesting equipment retrofit   Mike Andrews leaves your office, shutting the door behind him. The pain in his arm is reflected on his face. He's about to file a worker's compensation claim—your third this month. As human resources director for Technology One, a major software-development firm, you're worried not only about costs but also about the well-being of your employees.

Mike's complaints are much the same as those of the other two computer technicians who have already filed claims: sharp pains in the wrist, numbness, and decreased range of motion. You already know the average technician spends at least six hours a day working on the computer. Yet you've never had this many complaints in such a short time, and the severity of the symptoms seems to be increasing.

You decide to seek the advice of experts. A local sports and orthopedic medicine clinic gives you a detailed description of RSIs—repetitive strain injuries. The symptoms they describe are virtually identical to those exhibited by your technicians. You're distressed to learn that, if the cause of these injuries is not found and corrected, your technicians could require surgery or could even become permanently disabled.

The physical therapist at the clinic feels that exercises and wrist splints may help relieve symptoms and could even prevent new injuries from occurring. However, she also recommends that you consult an ergonomic analyst who can evaluate the furniture and equipment your technicians are using.

The analyst spends an entire day at your facility. After measuring desk and chair height, watching technicians at work, and conducting a detailed analysis of all your equipment, he makes two recommendations: (1) throw out all your computer keyboards and replace them with new, ergonomic keyboards, and (2) replace every mouse with a track ball. Suddenly you realize that the RSI complaints began shortly after your controller and purchasing manager bought a truckload of new computer equipment at a local merchant's going-out-of-business sale. You begin to wonder about the quality and design of your equipment and you ask the analyst what benefits the changes will provide.

The ergonomic keyboards actually split the traditional rows of keys in half and place the rows of keys at different angles. This allows the wrists to stay straight and relieves pressure on the forearm. The repetitive motions involved in using a mouse further aggravate the symptoms created by use of the traditional style keyboards. Using a track ball does not require the repetitive clicking motion of the forefinger.

Your task: You know that replacing peripheral equipment on more than 50 computers will be costly, especially when the existing equipment is nearly new. However, increasing RSIs and disability claims could be even more costly. Write a persuasive memo to Katherine Wilson, your controller, and convince her of the immediate need to retrofit the technicians' computer equipment. [32]

7. Travel turnaround: E-mail message at Travelfest convincing your boss to expand client services   As a successful travel agent with Travelfest, Inc., you have been both amazed and troubled by the recent changes in the travel industry. The upset started a year ago, when airlines stopped paying the customary 10 percent commission on airline tickets. Instead, airlines paid a flat $25 on one-way domestic flights and $50 on round-trip domestic flights. International flights were not affected.

Travelfest is located in Austin, Texas. It has four offices and more than 80 employees. Headquarters are in the center of downtown, located in the lobby of a 35-story office tower. The other three offices are located in major malls and shopping centers in upscale suburbs. The company's business is made up of about 70 percent corporate and business travel and 30 percent leisure travel. However, much of the leisure business comes from corporate customers.

Your boss, Gary Hoover, has been working night and day to make up for declining revenues brought about by the loss of airline commissions. He has tried everything, from direct-mail campaigns, to discount coupons, to drawings for cruises and weekend getaways.

Still, revenues remain flat, and there seems to be no solution in sight.

You've been doing some research and analysis of existing customer profiles. You find that many of your customers are middle- to high-income sophisticated travelers and that with the expansion of the global economy, foreign travel has increased dramatically in the past 12 months. Your research has triggered some ideas that you believe could substantially increase your revenue from existing customers.

You envision turning your suburban mall location into a travel supermarket. First, since there's such a growth in foreign travel, you'd like to sell video- and audiotape courses in Spanish, Japanese, French, and other languages. You'd like to introduce a line of travel products, including luggage, maps, travel guides, and electronics. You visualize a room with computer terminals where customers would have direct access to the Internet so that they could obtain up-to-date weather, currency-exchange rates, and other important information. You're even thinking about a special area for kids, with videos and other educational materials.

You realize your ideas don't generate a lot of direct profit. However, you believe they will get customers in the door, where you and other agents can sell them travel, particularly leisure travel to foreign destinations.

Your task: E-mail Gary Hoover at Travelfest's downtown office. Outline your ideas and volunteer to supervise the implementation as a pilot project in your store. Hoover's e-mail address is <GHoover@travelnet.com>.[33]

OPERATIONS MANAGEMENT

DOWNWARD COMMUNICATION

8. Helping out: Persuasive memo to Bread & Circus store managers Bread & Circus is a chain of organic food stores with locations in the Washington, D.C., area. The stores are big and well lit, like their more traditional grocery store counterparts. They are also teeming with a wide variety of attractively displayed foods and related products.

However, Bread & Circus is different from the average supermarket. Its products include everything from granola sold in bulk to environmentally sensitive household products. The meats sold come from animals that were never fed antibiotics, and the cheese is from cows said to be raised on small farms and treated humanely.

Along with selling these products to upscale shoppers, the company has been giving food to homeless shelters. Every third weekend, Bread & Circus donates goods and supplies to three soup kitchens downtown. Company executives believe they are in a unique position to help others.

You are the chief operating officer (COO) of Bread & Circus. You've been asked to find ways to expand the program and involve the company's eight branches, most of which are in the suburbs. Ideally, the company would be able to increase the number of people it helps and to get more of its employees involved.

You don't have a great deal of extra money for the program, so the emphasis has to be on using resources already available to the stores. One idea is to use trucks from suburban branches to make the program "mobile." Another idea is to join forces with a retailing chain to give food and clothing to individuals. The key is to be original and not exclude any ideas, no matter how absurd they might seem. The only stipulation is to keep ideas politically neutral. Bread & Circus executives want to make it clear that they do not want to be seen as supporting any party or candidate. They just want to be good corporate citizens.

Your task: Send persuasive memos to all managers at Bread & Circus, requesting ideas to expand the program. Invite employees to contribute ideas, for this or any other charitable project for the company.[34]

MANAGEMENT

EXTERNAL COMMUNICATION

9. The glass bicycle: Persuasive letter from Owens-Corning requesting bids for manufacturing rights A student design group from Brazil's University of Sao Paulo has come up with the winning bicycle design in the Global Design Challenge. Sponsored by Owens-Corning, the competition called on teams from eight top design and engineering schools in the United States, Canada, Europe, Asia, and South America to design a bicycle that would cost less than $100 and would incorporate mainly glass-fiber composites in the construction. The winning entry, called the Kangaroo, uses glass fiber reinforced polyester for its framework and has an estimated manufacturing cost of $82. Moreover, some unique features make it a product of truly worldwide potential. An adjustable wheelbase can be shortened to allow easier maneuvering in city traffic, and the seat and handlebars can be adjusted within a range to suit 95 percent of the world's population. Since more than half of the people on the globe depend on bicycles as their primary means of transportation, and since bicycles require no fossil fuel for operation, this product has tremendous potential in countries from Abu Dhabi to Zimbabwe.

As Owens-Corning's North American licensing manager, your job is to sign up companies to produce and market the Kangaroo bicycle for the U.S., Mexican, and Canadian markets. A manufacturing deal has been arranged with a Chinese producer who can deliver the bicycles to any West Coast NAFTA port for $86, including shipping, taxes and tariffs. Your problem is that you have no distribution system to handle bicycles, so you must find a marketing partner who will license the rights to distribute and market the Kangaroo in North America. Your preference is to find a single marketer to serve the entire region, and priority will be given to companies such as Schwinn, Nishiki, and Cannondale Bicycles who are currently using Owens-Corning materials in their products. You are planning to license the marketing rights for a five-year term for an initial payment of $350,000 plus 8 percent of the gross sales.

Your task: Write a persuasive letter to Mr. Gregg Bagni, Maketing Director, Schwinn Bicycle & Fitness (1690 38th Street, Boulder, CO 80301-2602), requesting a bid on the North American marketing rights and offering him first refusal. Point out the features you feel will make the Kangaroo a widespread success, and be sure to spell out the financial terms. He can then determine whether the deal makes sense from his perspective. But don't give him too much time—ask for a response within ten days.[35]

MANAGEMENT

EXTERNAL COMMUNICATION

10. The 800-pound cotton boll: E-mail at Lisle Cotton Plantations recommending genetically engineered seed   Your tour of the Delta and Pine Land Company's demonstration farm has been impressive. Mike Siegele, D&PL's chief agronomist, pointed out the increased yield of the company's NuCotn seed, which averages about 20 percent more harvestable cotton per acre. Even more impressive is the fact that this insect-resistant seed uses a gene from Bacillus thuringiensis (Bt) to kill harmful insects during the growing season. D&PL is the largest producer of cotton seed and has developed NuCotn by incorporating technology from Monsanto, which recently developed its own genetically engineered, herbicide-resistant soy-

bean and corn seeds. While genetically engineered seeds have gotten some bad publicity from unsupported claims that as part of the food supply they could endanger humans, the cotton seeds are not ingested and therefore do not pose a threat.

As chief field engineer for Lisle Cotton Plantations, you estimate that NuCotn would cost your company about $43 per acre versus $10 per acre for regular cotton seed, but it eliminates the need for pesticides and spraying, thus saving from $70 to $130 per acre. This hardy breed of seed will also make it possible for Lisle Cotton to utilize an additional 6,000 acres (previously considered substandard for cotton planting), in addition to the 40,000 acres currently in cotton production.

The problem is that NuCotn seeds are in limited supply, so you must act fast if you're going to secure enough seed for the coming season, especially since your rival, King Cotton Growers, plans to visit D&PL's demonstration farm tomorrow.

Your task: This exciting information can't wait for you to get back to the office and write a formal report. Compose an e-mail message recommending NuCotn to Lisle Cotton's general manager, Tom Costello <tcostello@lislecotton.com>. Persuade Costello to purchase the seed ASAP. Send copies to Executive Vice President Ellis Eno and CFO Gin Ellingson. Send it from your hotel as soon as you get in.[36]

MANAGEMENT

UPWARD COMMUNICATION

11. Don't take liberties with me! Persuasive memo at Taco Bell justifying an advertising stunt   "Liberty Bell Purchased by Taco Bell!" screamed the headlines. "The commercialization of America continues," read one editorial extremely critical of Taco Bell for purchasing and renaming the patriotic symbol, "The Taco Liberty Bell." "What's next?" asked many big circulation papers, "The Heinz 57 Statue of Liberty?"

You hold your head in your hands as your dream of a fast-track career in advertising suddenly dissolves into a public relations nightmare. As marketing director for Taco Bell, you approved the April Fool's joke. You were so sure that the U.S. public would "get it"—people would nod their heads and say, "Yup, those Taco Bell folks really know how to give us a chuckle." Instead, your phone hasn't stopped ringing since you came in, and now the CEO wants to hear from you.

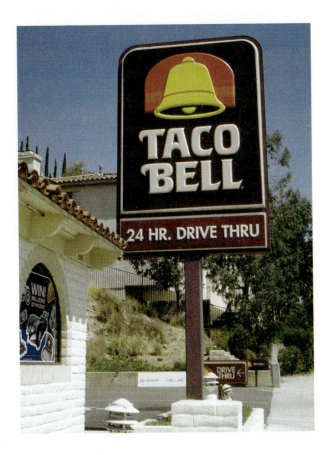

Your task: Write a memo to persuade CEO Francine Garcia that the joke accomplished some positive goals. Explain the rationale for the Taco Liberty Bell joke. Also, use bullets to list the steps you plan to take to counteract the negative publicity. For example, Taco Bell will donate $50,000 to help preserve the historic bell. Try to put what happened in the best possible light. Because of the spin-off articles in newspapers around the country, Taco Bell received millions of dollars of free advertising. Once the public is reassured that a corporation is not taking control of a national treasure, perhaps they will still remember the corporate name and the donation.[37]

Writing Persuasive Claims and Requests for Adjustment

SMALL BUSINESS

INTERPERSONAL COMMUNICATION

12. Too good to be true: E-mail to Page South requesting adjustment Page South offered its pager services for a mere $5 a month. You purchased an inexpensive pager and signed a contract for two years. You thought your pager phone number was up and running for two weeks, but your co-workers and clients say they repeatedly get a busy signal when dialing your pager number. You call Page South and get the problem resolved, but this takes an additional week. Obviously, you don't want to be charged for the time the pager wasn't in service. After discussing the situation with the local manager, she asks you to contact Judy Hinkley at the company's regional business office.

Your task: Send an e-mail message to Hinkley at <Judy@pgsouth.com> and request an adjustment to your account. Request credit or partial credit for one month of service. Remember to write a summary of events in chronological order, supplying exact dates for maximum effectiveness.

RETAIL

INTERPERSONAL COMMUNICATION

13. The great CD mystery: Persuasive letter from Digital Ear requesting adjustment As the manager of Digital Ear, a local independent music retailer, you were delighted with your sales during the recent holiday season. Although you've found it challenging to compete with the discount superstores, this year was better than usual. By making some discount deals with your key suppliers, you were able to compete on both variety and price.

Your new CD-ROM department is truly a find, especially for the last-minute shopper. You have everything from The Lion King for the youngsters to Obsidian, a new generation of the popular Myst game that keeps teenagers glued to their computer terminals. You even offer gardening CDs, challenging card games, golf, baseball, and Indy racing for sports enthusiasts. Many of your Christmas Eve shoppers purchased 15 or more CDs. You congratulated yourself on your creative solution to the last-minute shopper's dilemma—as well as on your profits.

Little did you know that your customers were in for more surprises in their Christmas stockings than just the latest in video games. The entire CD-ROM industry has been plagued with problems, centered mainly around the incompatibility of various programs with the computer hardware owned by the average consumer. Nearly 50 percent of the CD-ROM titles designed for Windows, and 30 percent of those for Apple, fail the first time the user tries to boot them up. More than 20 percent of the CD-ROMs purchased are returned to the manufacturers by retailers.

The Interactive Multimedia Association, a trade group of CD-ROM designers and manufacturers, has taken steps to help consumers through the maze of titles and compatibility issues. Free software, called "CD Match," shows users which programs are compatible with their computers. If only you had known!

The day after Christmas was your worst nightmare. Your phone rang off the hook with questions from frustrated game players. Returns were the order of the day. Reluctantly, you collected all the offending CDs and sat down at your own computer for a test run. A few worked just fine. Many more did not.

Your task: Your stock of CDs came from more than a dozen manufacturers. Write a form letter to the CD manufacturers requesting an adjustment. Explain that you would prefer to have CDs that work. Failing that, you would like all your customers' money refunded in full, and you would like the manufacturers to pay for the "CD Match" program so that you can advise future buyers *before* they purchase your products.[38]

CONSUMER

INTERPERSONAL COMMUNICATION

14. Phone frustration: Persuasive letter to Pacific Bell requesting resolution of telephone service overcharges   As a freelance business researcher, your time is valuable, especially when you're using online research facilities. These valuable resources are becoming more and more important in your work, so you can't afford to sit around waiting for your Internet searches to download files at 14,400 bits per second (14.4 Kbps) or even 28.8 Kbps. You often deal with massive files that can take forever to transfer at these rates. You determined that an ISDN (Integrated Services Digital Network) connection would be a faster alternative for your online work. You contacted Pacific Bell Telephone in November and requested residential ISDN service (since you work from home).

When the confirming work order arrived, you discovered that PacBell had your account set up as business service, so you called the service representative to change it to the lower residential rate. As a result, your business service was disconnected, and it took PacBell two weeks to reconnect you. On top of that, when the ini-

tial bill arrived, there was a $125 charge for disconnecting the business service and another $75 charge for reinstallation, but no credit for the two weeks of downtime. You have made at least 13 calls to the customer service department on this, both locally and at Midland's headquarters in Sacramento. You even left a message on the customer feedback section of PacBell's Internet home page. But none of these actions have resolved the situation.

Your task: Compose a persuasive letter to Ms. Claire Abell (PacBell's director of consumer affairs at 6640 Rosecrans Road, Sacramento, CA 99054), explaining your frustration with this billing problem and asking for immediate adjustment.[39]

Writing Sales and Fundraising Messages

MARKETING

EXTERNAL COMMUNICATION

15. The bride wore hiking boots: Persuasive letter to "We Do" bridal superstore   When Shari and Randy Almsburg of Dublin, Ohio, decided to tie the knot, they knew just what they wanted. "We always enjoyed hiking. In fact, we met each other on a hike. That's why we wanted to wrap our wedding plans around our favorite hobby." Enter "Tie the Knot," a one-owner company specializing in bizarre wedding plans.

"Actually, the bride wearing a white dress and a pair of hiking boots was NOT our most unusual wedding," explains owner and wedding consultant, Todd Dansing (whose own wedding took place a mile high just before the happy couple plunged to earth by parachute). "We recently helped plan an underwater wedding in a shark tank at the aquarium in Chicago for two marine biologists whose work involved feeding the fish. Our main problem there was this huge turtle that kept bumping into the preacher." Dansing tells you of other unusual weddings that took place in airplanes, on boats, under water, and in exotic locations such as Arizona's Painted Desert. Whatever your wedding plans, Todd believes he can find the necessary resources and save you time and money in the process.

Todd's marketing efforts to date have involved mostly word of mouth and free press coverage of his unusual weddings (although reporters kept their distance when two snake handlers from the zoo tied the knot). But his brother-in-law has invested capital in the business, so Todd hires you to help him tell the world about his services. You suggest that he consider affiliating with an established wedding service or store.

You and Todd visit "We Do," a bridal superstore located in Dublin, Ohio, and you help Todd see the potential for marketing his unusual, off-beat wedding service to this large company. We Do is a 26,000-square-foot matrimonial Mecca that sells 600 styles of bridal gowns and everything else traditional couples need for a wedding. The franchise hopes to open 40 stores eventually, so if Todd can strike a deal with We Do, his future profit potential will be high.

Your task: Write a letter for Todd's signature to Carol Feinberg, CEO of We Do. Suggest that Tie the Knot would make a great consultant for couples with offbeat wedding tastes. Emphasize Todd's past experience, and point out the ways this venture will provide additional market share for We Do. Think of possible objections, such as Todd's lack of capital and small company size, and try to assure Feinberg that Tie the Knot is the right business to help capitalize on a unique opportunity.[40]

16. Selling the Web: Sales letter from Viking Office Products Irwin Helford's company, Viking Office Products, has carved an annual $1 billion niche into the lucrative office-supply market by selling the old-fashioned way: one customer at a time. Helford created Viking Office Products in 1960 as a southern California office supply company. Challenged by the office superstores such as Staples, Office Depot, and Office Max, Helford never abandoned his belief that people want service first and then value.

Although its prices may be somewhat higher than superstore prices, Viking offers same-day delivery to the single office/home office (SOHO) market with a minimum order of just $25. Most of the mega-retailers have a higher minimum and concentrate on sales to large corporations through a network of sales representatives. Viking has also expanded into the growing European market (with locations in Germany, the United Kingdom, France, and the Netherlands) where the superstore trend lags that of the United States.

The Internet, specifically the World Wide Web, provides Helford with a golden opportunity to advertise. In fact, the company recently designed its own home page where potential customers can check on specials, request a catalog, or place their order.

Your task: As the marketing director for the SOHO division of Viking, you are planning a mailing to former customers and prospects about Viking's new Web site at <www.vikingop.com>. Because Helford is now in his sixties and looking for a successor, you know the letter has the potential to draw attention to your work. Write the sales letter so that you not only emphasize the benefits to customers but do so with creativity and style.[41]

17. You oughta be in pictures! An unusual sales letter from American Barricade about making it in the movies Judith Digon learned her business by accident, literally. Her car was totaled, and she was nearly totaled along with it. Not the best time to start a new business. But Digon's accident was caused by inadequate safety barriers at a road construction project. She decided she could do a better job, so when her broken bones healed, she began a career in the traffic safety business.

Being a woman in a male-dominated industry helped rather than hurt. Initially, Digon's presence was a surprise to a lot of customers. But she got their attention, and when they discovered she had both business savvy and competitive prices, they bought. She quickly became her employer's number 1 salesperson. After five years' working for someone else, she struck out on her own and purchased American Barricade, a company that provides safety barriers, lighted message boards, arrow boards, and traffic cones for highway construction projects. As her company grew, Digon added traffic planning and road-closure crews to her list of services.

Digon has developed her business without using loans or outside capital investment. She plows profits directly back into the company, and when funds are available for marketing, she chooses her target markets carefully. This year, she's set her sights on getting into the movies.

American Barricade is located virtually next door to one of the largest markets in the country for independent film, TV, and video production. Digon believes she can provide cost-effective traffic-control and road-closure services to independent film companies for location shooting. In order to better understand the market, she has hired out as an extra in two movies, evaluating how the process works and developing ideas for doing a better job. She and her staff have developed several prototype traffic-management and road-closure plans for various kinds of movie shoots and locations. Now Digon is ready to take American Barricade to the movies.

Your task: Write a sales letter designed to test the market by appealing to the typical independent film producer or production company manager. Convince the reader that you have the unique capabilities to manage traffic and road closures at location shoots. Address your letter to Steven Duncan, Production Manager, Fletcher Media International, 5659 Melrose Drive, Hollywood, CA, 90028.[42]

MARKETING
EXTERNAL COMMUNICATION

18. Why cellular users are hanging it up: Sales letter from Sprint Spectrum Never go anywhere without your cell phone? You may change your mind when you discover digital PCS (personal communication services). PCS has been tested in two major U.S. markets and will be available nationwide in the next few years.

Sprint Spectrum is emerging as an early leader in this dynamic market. Its marketing strategy focuses on local storefront sales outlets staffed with knowledgeable, enthusiastic people who relish the idea of head-to-head competition with cellular competitors like Nynex and Airtouch.

Here's how Sprint Spectrum's lowest-cost service plan compares with similar services offered by Nynex:

Services	Sprint Spectrum	Nynex
Cost of phone	$149 to $199	Free or deeply discounted
Monthly fee	$15	$24.95
15 minutes of air time	Free	$5.85 peak, $2.85 nonpeak
Each additional minute	31¢	39¢ peak, 19¢ nonpeak
Activation fee	None	$30 to $50
Answering service	Included	$5.95 per month

Although Sprint Spectrum's lower prices are attractive, the real excitement is in the technology. Any cell phone user who has been cut off in mid-call or who has damaged vocal cords from shouting over static interference will appreciate the sound fidelity of PCS. Why the difference? Digital versus analog technology. More than 90 percent of cellular phones use analog technology, which transmits your voice over electromagnetic waves. If the wave is broken, so is your phone call.

Before opening its doors to the public, Sprint Spectrum conducted its own research into PCS technology. First, the company purchased a dozen pocket-sized handsets at a local electronics store. Then it sent salespeople and technicians out to field-test the equipment under a variety of circumstances. They went into highrise buildings, parking garages, and subways. They tested the phones on commuter trains, in parked cars, and in moving cars. They made calls from grocery stores, restaurants, and even on the new "screamer ride" at a local amusement park. Static and cutoffs were virtually nonexistent.

For the past two years, you have been working as a corporate account salesperson for a major cellular provider. You are consistently a top producer and pride yourself on keeping up with the newest technologies. When Sprint Spectrum advertised for experienced salespeople, you jumped at the chance to join tomorrow's technology leader.

After only a month on the job at Sprint Spectrum, you've been able to provide better service at lower cost to many new PCS users and to some of your old customers as well. In addition to basic services, your customers can choose numeric paging, call waiting, call forwarding, and caller ID. Sprint Spectrum does not require a contract and imposes no cancellation fee.

Your task: You believe you have barely scratched the surface of what's possible in selling PCS. You plan to triple your customer base in the next 90 days. At the monthly sales meeting, your boss announces that Sprint Spectrum has just obtained a great mailing list—100,000 names of individuals who currently use cellular phone service in your sales territory. He is giving each salesperson a share of this list and the opportunity to sell Sprint Spectrum's PCS to these prospects. Compose a direct-mail sales letter designed to convince individual cellular phone users to switch to Sprint Spectrum.[43]

NONPROFIT
EXTERNAL COMMUNICATION

19. Finding money creatively: Fundraising letter at Long Beach Opera Long Beach Opera is a small, creative opera company, renowned for its adventuresome, sometimes offbeat, performances. Located in a major metropolitan area, it has been hampered by having to compete with larger, more affluent opera companies that have large followings and budgets to match.

But Long Beach Opera has benefited from critical acclaim, and it has built a small but loyal following since its premier performance more than 18 years ago. Now the company is at a crossroads. Most recently it mounted a production of "Elegy for Young Lovers." However, the show had to close after only a week, due to poor attendance. Bills continue to come in, and the bank account is bare. The creative director is unwilling to discuss continuing the season unless a solution can be found.

Out of the darkness comes an angel. A local university with a brand-new performing arts center would like to form an alliance with Long Beach Opera. Although the university isn't offering large sums of cash, the university's board members are willing to have the company use the performing arts center and other campus facilities at no cost. They would also consider some joint ventures in money-making educational events such as lectures and exhibitions. These events would be fairly easy and inexpensive to produce, and they could generate some immediate cash flow.

But the *pièce de résistance* for Long Beach Opera would be access to the university's key donors, alumni, and supporters of the arts. The company's management team believes that, with proper cultivation, this donor base could provide an exciting future and a sound financial base for future operations.

A recent strategy session was attended by the chair of the opera's board, the creative director, the development director, and the head of the university's fine arts department. After agreeing in principle to finalize the alliance between Long Beach Opera and the university, all agreed that the first order of business is to raise funds. It was generally agreed that business and community leaders should be informed and invited to lend their financial support to the new venture.

A symposium is planned, at which the new venture will be introduced. The symposium will include musical previews of the Long Beach's upcoming season, a presentation by the creative director, and messages from key university staff. The goal of the symposium is to raise $500,000 in pledges.

Your task: As development director of Long Beach Opera, you have been asked to draft a letter to community and business leaders. Your goals are to convince them of the opera's viability, get them to attend the symposium, and convince them to pledge their financial support.[44]

20. Buses for seniors: Fundraising letter from Morris County Senior Center The Morris County Senior Center is one of New Jersey's oldest nonprofit institutions for the elderly. Over the past 50 years, it has relied on financial support from government, businesses, and individuals.

Unfortunately, recent state and federal cutbacks have dug into the organization's budget. In addition, in the last five years, two of the county's largest companies, Hardwick Industries and McCarthy Electrical Motors, have moved offshore and shut down local operations. Both businesses were supporters of the center as were many of the workers who lost jobs.

However, the needs of the center keep growing. For many of the county's roughly 1,000 seniors who live alone, it's the only place where they can meet their peers, use a special library, avoid extreme weather, or get a well-rounded meal. The center is not a nursing home and has no overnight facilities. Most individuals get to the facility on one of the three shuttle-type buses belonging to the center. The buses are also used for various day trips to museums, plays, and similar functions. Occasionally, they are used to help people temporarily disabled get to doctors' offices or pharmacists.

Each bus is more than eight years old. Although not quite unsafe, the buses are showing their age. The constant repairs are stopgap measures at best, and most weeks at least one of the vehicles is inoperable. Monthly repairs are averaging a total of $300 for the three vehicles. In addition, when the buses aren't working, it's a major inconvenience for everyone at the center. Seniors can't get there, trips are canceled, and drivers are sometimes paid for coming to work and not being able to drive.

Conservatively, it would cost about $28,000 to replace each bus with a new one—or $84,000 total. This includes estimates on how much the center could gain from selling the old buses. It's a fair amount of money, but in the opinion of your board of directors, it would be better than continuously repairing the vehicles or risking the purchase of used buses.

Your task: As director of the center, draft a fundraising letter to send to all of the businesses in the county. Stress the good work the center does and the fact that this is a special fundraising effort. Mention that all the money collected will go directly toward the purchase of the buses.

NONPROFIT

EXTERNAL COMMUNICATION

21. Donating frequent-flier miles: A fundraising letter from Bedford Technological Institute to alumni At Bedford Technological Institute, the Office of Development has been experiencing the same difficulties encountered by all nonprofit institutions in the 1990s: donor apathy, dwindling state support, and decreased membership or participation (or student enrollment). Bedford Tech has been especially hard hit in the areas of corporate support, because dwindling profits and tightened corporate budgets have severely reduced corporate philanthropy.

As associate director, you've been asked to devise new and innovative methods of replacing or restoring these dwindling dollars. The most acute needs are for the continued support of the Technology Transfer Center (which is enabling the school to develop strategic relationships with many new corporate sponsors) and funding for equipment and supplies at the new BioMedical Center (which is establishing Bedford's reputation in new fields of science and medicine). Many of your programs have been successful in generating gifts from older alumni, but the corporate giving remains down, and recent grads have not been persuaded to begin donating at appropriate levels.

You have recently instituted a program that is squarely aimed at both these target groups—a frequent-flier mileage-redemption plan. This program begins September 1 and enables companies and individuals to donate their Delta SkyMiles to Bedford in 5,000-mile increments. Delta then converts these miles into cash donations (or exchanges them for flights for faculty and administration staff). Thus the school is able to generate cash resources and reduce development travel costs. The program has been successful for other charities, with Delta redeeming over 20 million miles in the first year. If this project is successful, Bedford will add other airlines' mileage-redemption programs.

As exciting as this program appears, the administration has approved it on a trial basis only, with results to be evaluated after the first six months. Therefore, it is imperative that mileage donations be generated rapidly and maintained at a high level so that the plan will pro-

duce acceptable results by the end of the test period. Only then can the program be expanded to include the other airlines.

Your task: As associate director of the Office of Development, create a form letter for recent alumni, urging their support for the Technology Transfer and BioMedical programs and pointing out the ease and convenience of donating their Delta SkyMiles to the school. Stress the need for their immediate attention to this matter.[45]

Writing Collection Messages

COLLECTION

CUSTOMER RELATIONS

22. Did you forget? Polite reminder from Schneider Trucking With its sophisticated use of information technology, Schneider Trucking in Green Bay, Wisconsin, has been outperforming competitors by increasing business 20 percent every year. Plenty of investors want to buy a share of Schneider Trucking, now that they've seen what can happen when you successfully pair state-of-the-art computer technology with skilled drivers (whose CB radios were long ago replaced by laptop computers linked to the company via satellite). But CEO Don Schneider isn't interested in selling the company his father built from a single truck.

However, he *is* interested in keeping up with accounts receivable. The top-drawer computer system that tracks drivers' traveling speeds, hours on the road, exact locations, and estimated arrival times, assigning them new loads based on a correlation of this computer data with customers' requirements, also keeps excellent track of the company's billing system. With a 9,000-truck fleet and some $1.25 billion in revenue to manage, there's no room for sloppy collections.

That's one reason your department (accounts receivable) is constantly striving to improve customer relations. Periodically, staff members are asked to come up with better form letters that will maintain customer goodwill and also prod sluggish accounts. Your supervisor has just asked you to take another look at the company's standard reminder letter, which is usually sent 33 days after an invoice is mailed (3 days after the payment is due).

Your task: Your supervisor is right; the letter is a little too abrasive. Write a new form letter reminding customers of their overdue bill.[46]

23. Please pay: Inquiry from Noonan Design about Sidewalk Sergeant billing   Marilyn Noonan's little boys, Conor, Ryley, Charlie, and Patrick (ages 3 through 8), loved to play in the cul-de-sac outside the family home. But their mother worried about the cars that came screeching down the La Jolla street. "Children believe that cars can stop instantly," Noonan explains, adding that traffic accidents are the number one cause of death for children her sons' ages.

Of necessity, Noonan invented a mother's helper: Sidewalk Sergeant, a bright orange traffic safety cone with the bold letters, "Children Playing," beneath a cartoon of a police officer blowing a whistle and holding his hand up in a halt signal. She put them up as a warning sign to drivers around the children's' play area. Inevitably, other parents saw the cones and before long, Noonan was taking orders and searching for a manufacturer. Now her company, Noonan Design, is selling the Sidewalk Sergeant to both large and small toy retailers. However, one of the smaller retailers is giving Noonan some trouble.

" Can you help me with this?" she greets you one Thursday morning, the day you usually spend at Noonan Design as a freelance bookkeeper. She hands you a file on "More Toys," a new account in Muncie, Indiana, for which credit was approved. More Toys bought fifty 28-inch cones (which retail for $25) and twenty-five 18-inch cones ($13 retail). The first invoice went out 120 days ago, but the small retailer hasn't sent a dime. As you peruse the paperwork, you see that, with a 40 percent wholesale discount, the company owes $945 for the cones plus $159.75 for shipping and insurance.

Your task: Since no one from Noonan Design has contacted More Toys yet, you suggest the "polite inquiry" approach—followed by stronger communications if necessary. Draft the first letter to show Noonan what you mean. Address it to her original contact: Bruce Vinchot, Manager, More Toys, 1473 Sedalia Avenue, Muncie, Indiana 47305.[47]

24. Time to pay the piper: Urgent-notice collection letter at Coast Federal Bank   You are the director of marketing at Coast Federal Bank (CFB), a consumer-oriented bank with branches mainly in southern California. Surrounded as you are by some of the top educational institutions in the country, student loans have long been an important product for you.

You've just finished reviewing this month's collection reports and you realize that, for the sixth straight month, your bad debt ratio (loans over 90 days past due) has increased. In addition, your average collection time has increased more than 20 days in the same period. This trend disturbs you, and you know your loan committee (which meets in three days) will be even more disturbed.

When CFB began an aggressive marketing campaign for student loans a little over ten years ago, tuition costs at local public and private universities were less than half what they are today. As the cost of education has skyrocketed (creating a growing demand for financing), your interest rates on these loans have remained virtually unchanged. And with your collection ratio going downhill, you can see profits eroding rapidly.

You're also concerned because many of your student loans were made to parents of college students as part of the PLUS (Parent Loans to Undergraduate Students) program. These parents are some of the bank's best customers, local executives and community leaders with whom you have other important business dealings. You are anxious to maintain your good image and relationship with these customers, so you're hesitant to implement a get-tough collection policy.

You have begun developing a strategy to improve collection of student loans. You plan to stress loyalty to your customers, commitment to supporting local educational institutions, and your desire to work with people who will demonstrate good-faith efforts. You believe refinancing and extended payment options may encourage some people to improve their payment records.

Your loan committee will meet in three days. You're aware that some committee members may want to recommend selling the entire delinquent student loan business to a collection firm. You feel this action would be extremely detrimental to your bank's reputation and long-term growth.

Your task: Develop a customer-relations collection letter designed to encourage your student loan borrowers to improve their payment records. Assume your bank's computer program will personalize each letter with the customer's name and address. Make your communication personal and directed to the individual customer.[48]

COLLECTION
EXTERNAL COMMUNICATION

25. Talk is cheap: Final-stage collection letter at Arciero Brothers   Phil Arciero was ecstatic when his concrete company, Arciero Brothers, was selected as one of the construction subcontractors for a huge entertainment complex being built by Moorfield Construction. Located near one of the country's leading vacation destinations, the complex was designed to include restaurants, theaters, a video arcade, and a kiddyland play park.

With a venture of this magnitude it wasn't surprising that over 200 subcontractors were needed to handle the variety of building and infrastructure work. Arciero Brothers specializes in building foundations, sidewalks, and parking lots. Although Arciero has been in business for more than 20 years, the entertainment complex is the largest contract he's ever been awarded.

The project took nearly 24 months to complete. Arciero Brothers was on site throughout the first 21 months of the job. Phil Arciero hired a number of new employees, including laborers and skilled tradespeople. In addition, he invested in some extra equipment, in order to handle the new work and continue to meet the needs of his existing customers.

Moorfield Construction paid Arciero 10 percent of his estimate at the beginning of the job. Interim payments have been made monthly, until the total payments reached 85 percent of the contract bid. Moorfield withheld the final 15 percent until the entire project was approved by the city building inspectors, a common practice in the construction industry.

It has been nearly five months since the entertainment complex passed final inspection and opened for business. You've already paid your workers, drawing against your credit line at the bank to do it. You have contacted Moorfield Construction on a weekly basis, repeatedly requesting payment of more than $100,000, which is still outstanding on your contract. Moorfield officials say "paperwork foul-ups" are the reason for the slow payment. You're aware that none of the other subcontractors have received their final payments and that some of them are hiring attorneys to file mechanic's liens (legal collection proceedings) directly against the owner of the complex.

Your task: As the controller of Arciero Brothers, you've talked to Phil Arciero about the dilemma. Neither of you wants to jeopardize potential future business from Moorfield Construction or from the entertainment complex owners. But to preserve your rights and to increase your chances of being paid (since liens are paid in the order filed), you and Arciero instructed your attorney to file a mechanic's lien. You recommend to Arciero that you write a polite but firm letter to Moorfield, with a copy to the owners of the entertainment center, demanding immediate payment of the full amount owed you and informing Moorfield of the lien. Address your letter to Moorfield Construction (9 Corporate Park #600, Irvine, CA 92714), and address the copy to James Penny, Vice President of Finance, Edwards Theaters Inc., 12100 Wilshire Boulevard, Los Angeles, CA 90025.[49]

PART 4

EMPLOYMENT MESSAGES

WRITING RÉSUMÉS AND APPLICATION LETTERS

AFTER STUDYING THIS CHAPTER, YOU WILL BE ABLE TO

- Analyze your work skills and qualifications
- Identify what type of job and employer you want
- List your best prospects for employment
- Develop a strategy for "selling" yourself to these prospects
- Prepare an effective résumé
- Write an application letter that gets you an interview

COMMUNICATION CLOSE-UP AT MOBIL

Looking for a career with a top-notch marketing company? How about a job that involves international business? Maybe you're more the high-tech type? Are you looking for opportunities for advancement, good pay, and excellent benefits? If so, you might want to send your résumé to Henry Halaiko, manager of recruiting operations for Mobil Corporation. Yes, Mobil. There's more to the oil business than pumping gas, and there's more to Mobil than oil, as a glance at the company's annual report will tell you. Halaiko hires as many as 800 new college graduates every year. Even though many of the recruits will be engineers, Mobil also needs people with other backgrounds to fill slots in a wide range of functions.

To find the right people, Halaiko and Mobil's recruiters conduct 11,000 interviews on 90 campuses each spring. Before visiting each campus, Mobil recruiters post job descriptions in college placement offices and then prescreen résumés from students who want to apply, using the college placement office as a conduit. The students who look the best on paper will be invited to sign up for an interview when Mobil visits the campus.

What do Mobil's recruiters look for in a résumé? Evidence of success. Take work experience, for example. "Most people simply list their job responsibilities," Halaiko points out. "They say they've worked in a toy department or a bookstore, or whatever, and they list their duties: stocking inventory, closing out a cash drawer, balancing books, and so forth. But what we're really looking for is the person who says, 'I was responsible for increasing sales by X.' We would rather see some evidence of the person's level of achievement in the job. People who mention their accomplishments convey the impression that they think in terms of results. They are people who want to do things better."

If a student hasn't had much work experience, extracurricular activities might provide evidence of accomplishment. "Instead of saying that you were on the lacrosse team or that you were active in the student council, explain what you accomplished in that role," Halaiko advises. This gives Mobil some evidence that you know how to get things done.

Henry Halaiko

Large companies like Mobil are involved in multiple industries, and even though they may actively recruit at only a small number of campuses and in only specialized fields, these firms are always interested in hiring people with good communication skills, regardless of academic field or college.

What about grade-point average? Mobil is interested in academic excellence, but according to Halaiko, you don't have to be a straight-A student. "We try to look beyond grades to how well-rounded the student is," he explains. A B student who worked full-time or took especially tough courses might be more desirable than an A student who took the easy route.

Because factors like these are difficult to show in a résumé, Halaiko recommends explaining them in the cover letter. "If you're a liberal arts student, say, but you went out of your way to take statistics because you thought it would be useful to enhance your quantitative skills, we would see that as a real plus, even if you didn't get a good grade. That would be worth explaining in the cover letter." Halaiko gives another example: If your grades are below average but you've brought them up in the last couple of years, you should mention that in the cover letter. Recruiters recognize that some really good people get off to a slow start. "What we look for is some sign of progress."

Recruiting is an art, not a science, Halaiko explains. He does not use a rigid quantitative system or checklist for ranking résumés. Instead, he reads between the lines to identify the personality traits that lead to success at Mobil: personal standards of excellence, flexibility and willingness to try new things, and strong communication skills.

Halaiko also looks for a good fit. Although it may be impractical to customize your résumé for each potential employer, it can be very helpful to indicate that you have a strong interest in a particular company or type of job. The cover letter gives you a chance to mention these points.

What if Mobil doesn't recruit on your campus? Send the company a résumé anyway. For practical reasons, most firms—even big ones like Mobil—limit their campus recruiting to a relatively small number of schools that are especially strong in certain fields. Even so, recruiters like Halaiko realize that plenty of excellent candidates attend other colleges. He and Mobil's other recruiters take unsolicited applications seriously. If something in the cover letter or résumé strikes Halaiko as being outstanding, he makes every effort to follow up. "We look at each candidate as being a potential employee," he says.[1]

THINKING ABOUT YOUR CAREER

Getting the job that's right for you takes more than sending out a few letters and signing up with the college placement office. Planning and research are important if you want to find a company that suits you. Mobil is a case in point. Unless you're an engineering major, you might say to yourself, "An oil company would never hire me." However, if you look a little deeper, you'll discover that Mobil is involved in everything from selling convenience foods to developing planned communities.

Before you limit your job search to a particular industry or functional specialty, analyze what you have to offer and what you hope to get from your work. Then you can identify employers who are likely to want you and vice versa.

Analyzing What You Have to Offer

What you have to offer:
- Functional skills
- Education and experience
- Personality traits

What are your marketable skills? One way to find out is to jot down ten achievements that you're proud of, whether they include learning to ski, taking a prizewinning photo, tutoring a child, or editing the school paper. Look carefully at each of these achievements. What specific skills did they demand? For example, leadership, speaking ability, and artistic talent may have been the skills that helped you coordinate a winning presentation to the college administration. As you analyze your achievements, you'll begin to recognize a pattern of skills. Which of them might be valuable to potential employers?

Also look at your educational preparation, work experience, and extracurricular activities. What kinds of jobs are you qualified to do based on your knowledge and experience? What have you learned from participating in volunteer work or class projects that could benefit you on the job? Have you held any offices, won any awards or scholarships, or mastered a second language?

The next step is to take stock of your personal characteristics so that you can determine the type of job you'll do best. Are you aggressive, a born leader? Or would you rather follow? Are you outgoing, articulate, great with people? Or do you prefer working alone? Make a list of what you believe are your four or five most important qualities. Ask a relative or friend to rate your traits as well.

If you're having trouble figuring out your interests and capabilities, consult your college placement office or career guidance center. Many campuses administer a variety of tests designed to help you identify your interests, aptitudes, and personality traits. Although these tests won't reveal the "perfect" job for you, they'll help you focus on the types of work that best suit your personality.

Determining What You Want

Knowing what you *can* do is one thing. Knowing what you *want* to do is another. Many students are so accustomed to doing what parents, peers, and instructors expect that they've lost sight of their own values. They need to rediscover the factors that might bring them satisfaction and happiness on the job—for example, helping others or being free to create their own ideas.

One way to get in touch with yourself is to use your imagination. Say that a rich relative offers you a one-year, fully funded opportunity to go anywhere and do anything, provided you can develop a plan in the next 15 minutes. What would you do? Say that you're given a large, prominent billboard on which you can write any message you please. What would you say?[2] Playing such "what if" games can help you understand what really matters to you. Use your self-examination as the basis for establishing some short-term career goals.

Work Content Goals

Work content goals are related to the skills you want to use in your career. Basically, you need to decide what you'd like to do every day. Of course, if you have a limited range of experience, this is tricky. One way to solve the problem is to talk to people in various occupations. That's the approach Nathan James took when he was a sophomore in college. He thought he might enjoy a career in sales, marketing research, or advertising, but he didn't know enough about the working lives of people in those fields to make an intelligent choice. So he went to his school's alumni relations office and made a list of former graduates working in the three professions. After making a few phone calls, he knew a lot more. In fact, one alumnus—an account executive with an advertising agency—invited James to spend spring break shadowing him. That experience persuaded James to focus his courses on advertising. He's now interning with a prominent advertising agency in Philadelphia.[3]

Another way to learn about various occupations is to read about them. Your college library or placement office might be a good place to start. One of the liveliest books aimed at college students is Lisa Birnbach's *Going to Work.* Among other things, Birnbach describes what it's like to test-drive cars for Ford and sell cosmetics at Bloomingdale's. Another useful source is the 13-volume *Career Information Center* encyclopedia of jobs and careers, which is arranged by industry. For each job title, there's a description of the nature of the work, entry requirements, application procedures, advancement possibilities, working conditions, earnings, and benefits.

Apart from looking at specific occupations, consider general factors, such as how much independence you want on the job, how much variety you like, and whether you prefer to work with products, machines, people, ideas, figures, or some combination thereof. Do you like physical work, mental work, or a mix? Constant change or a predictable role?

Envision the ideal "day at the office." What would you enjoy doing every day?

Personal Performance Goals

Money and opportunities for advancement are also something to think about. Establish some specific compensation targets. What do you hope to earn in your first year on the job? What kind of pay increase do you expect each year? What's your ultimate earnings goal? Would you be comfortable with a job that paid on commission, or do you prefer a steady paycheck? What occupations offer the kind of money you're looking for? Are these occupations realistic for someone with your qualifications? Are you willing to settle for less money in order to do something you really love?

Next, consider your place within the company or profession. Where would you like to start? Where do you want to go from there? What's the ultimate position you would like to attain? How soon after joining the company would you like to receive your first promotion? Your next one? Once you have established these goals, ask yourself what additional training or preparation you'll need to achieve them.

How much do you want to earn, and how high do you hope to climb?

Work Environment Preferences

Another factor to consider is the environment you want to work in. Start by thinking in broad terms about the size and type of operation that appeals to you. Do you like the idea of working for a small, entrepreneurial operation, or would you prefer to be part of a large company? How do you feel about profit-making versus not-for-profit

What type of industry and organization do you want to work for?

organizations? Are you attracted to service businesses or manufacturing operations? What types of products appeal to you? Do you want regular, predictable hours, or do you thrive on flexible, varied hours? Do you prefer to work from 9:00 A.M. to 5:00 P.M., or are you willing to work evenings and weekends, as in the entertainment and hospitality industries? Would you enjoy a seasonally varied job such as in education, which may give you summers off, or retailing, with its selling cycles?

Location can also be important. Would you like to work in a city, a suburb, or a small town? In an industrial area or an uptown setting? Do you favor a particular part of the country? Does working in another country appeal to you? Do you like working indoors or outdoors?

What about facilities? Is it important to you to work in an attractive place, or will simple, functional quarters suffice? Do you need a quiet office to work effectively, or can you concentrate in a noisy, open setting? Would you prefer to work at the company's headquarters or in a small field office? Do such amenities as an in-house gym or handball court matter to you? Is access to public transportation or freeways important?

What type of corporate culture best suits you?

Perhaps the most important environmental factor is the corporate culture. Would you be happy in a well-defined hierarchy, where roles and reporting relationships are clear, or would you prefer a less structured situation? What qualities do you want in a boss? Are you looking for a paternalistic organization or one that fosters individualism? Do you like a competitive environment or one that rewards teamwork?

Seeking Employment Opportunities

When you're looking for work, you may occasionally feel rejected. Bear in mind, however, that employers are just as eager to find good employees as you are to find a job. In fact, U.S. corporations spend roughly $11.5 billion annually to find the talent they need.[4] Somewhere an employer is looking for your skills, values, interests, and qualifications.

Sources of Employment Information

Find out where the job opportunities are.

Whether your major is business, biology, or political science, once you know what you have to offer and what you want, you can start seeking an employer to match. If you haven't already committed yourself to any particular career field, first find out where the job opportunities are. Which industries are strong? Which parts of the country are booming, and which specific job categories offer the best prospects for the future?

Begin your search for information by keeping abreast of business and financial news. If you don't already do so, subscribe to a major newspaper and scan the business pages every day. Watch some of the TV programs that focus on business, such as *Wall Street Week,* and read the business articles in popular magazines such as *Time* and *Newsweek.* You might even want to subscribe to a business magazine such as *Fortune, Business Week,* or *Forbes.*

You can obtain information about the future for specific jobs in *The Dictionary of Occupational Titles* (U.S. Employment Service), *Occupational Outlook Handbook* (U.S. Bureau of Labor Statistics), and the employment publications of Science Research Associates. For an analysis of major industries, see the annual Market Data and Directory issue of *Industrial Marketing* and Standard & Poor's industry surveys.

You might also study professional and trade journals in the career fields that interest you. Also, talk to people in these fields; for names of the most prominent, consult *Standard & Poor's Register of Corporations, Directors and Executives.* You can find recent books about the fields you're considering by checking *Books in Print* at your library. Many times, students are able to network with executives in their field of interest by joining or participating in student business organizations, especially those with ties to real-world organizations such as the American Marketing Association or the American Management Association.

Once you've identified a promising industry and a career field, compile a list of specific organizations that appeal to you. You can do this by consulting directories of employers, such as *The College Placement Annual* and *Career: The Annual Guide to Business Opportunities.* (Other directories are listed in Chapter 13.) Write to the organizations on your list and ask for their most recent annual report and any descriptive brochures or newsletters they've published. If possible, visit some of the organizations on your list, contact their human resources departments, or talk with key employees.

Of the organizations that interest you, find out which ones need your skills.

You can find ads for specific job openings by looking in local and major newspapers. (However, newspaper ads that don't list the company's name may be misleading and may not even represent a real job opening, so be careful.) In addition, check the trade and professional journals in career fields that interest you; *Ulrich's International Periodicals Directory* (available at the library) lists these publications. Job listings can also be obtained from your college placement office and from state employment bureaus. A source of growing importance to your job search is the Internet, or more specifically the World Wide Web (see "High-Tech Job Hunting: The Secrets of Finding Employment on the World Wide Web").

Employers' Sources of Information

An understanding of how employers approach the recruiting process can save you considerable time and effort when searching for the job you want (see Figure 12.1). The quickest route is to get a referral from someone you know. In a survey by the American Management Society, 70 percent of the managers interviewed said that employee referrals are a useful source of job candidates. Personal contacts appear to be the prime source of jobs for job seekers, regardless of whether they have just graduated from college or have been out of school for several years.[5]

Employers find job candidates through
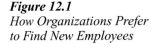
- Employee referrals
- On-campus interviews
- Unsolicited résumés
- Placement agencies
- Advertisements

Figure 12.1
How Organizations Prefer to Find New Employees

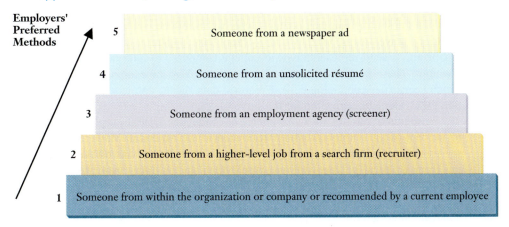

Employers prefer filling positions from within their organization or from an employee's recommendation. Placing want ads is often viewed as a last resort. In contrast, typical job-hunters begin pursuing work from the opposite direction (starting with want ads).

Employers' Preferred Methods

5 — Someone from a newspaper ad

4 — Someone from an unsolicited résumé

3 — Someone from an employment agency (screener)

2 — Someone from a higher-level job from a search firm (recruiter)

1 — Someone from within the organization or company or recommended by a current employee

HIGH-TECH JOB HUNTING:
THE SECRETS OF FINDING EMPLOYMENT ON THE WORLD WIDE WEB

The World Wide Web offers an amazing amount of employment information. Is the Web the answer to all your employment dreams? Perhaps . . . or perhaps not. But as the Web grows, the employment information it provides is constantly expanding. And you're fortunate, because you don't have to start from scratch like some intrepid adventurer. For helpful hints and useful Web addresses, you can turn to innumerable books, such as *What Color Is Your Parachute?* by Richard Nelson Bolles (which is even available in an electronic edition on the Web).

When you're dealing with the Internet, the one thing you can count on is rapid change. So exactly how using the Web will affect your job search depends on how well you prepare your job-search strategy, how many employers come to accept the Web as a source of potential employees, and how quickly the resources already available expand and adapt to the ever-changing Web environment. All major online services (such as America Online and CompuServe) already have areas for people seeking employment. The World Wide Web offers information not only from employers seeking applicants but also from people seeking work. You can use the World Wide Web for a variety of job-seeking tasks:

- *Finding career counseling.* Even when using the Web to locate particular job opportunities, you still need to analyze your skills and work expectations. For example, you can begin your self-assessment with the *Keirsey Temperament Sorter,* an online personality test. The Web offers you job-seeking pointers and counseling from online career centers, many of which are run by colleges and universities that put a lot of effort into creating interesting and helpful sites.

Other career centers are commercial and can run the gamut from award-winning to depressing. So make sure the advice you get is both useful and sensible. One good commercial site is Mary-Ellen Mort's *Job-Smart.* In addition, you can obtain online résumé assistance from sites such as Job Smart Resume Guide, The Riley Guide, Job Bank USA Resume Resources, Career Mosaic's Resume Writing Guide, and Intellimatch Power Resume Builder.

- *Making contacts.* You can use the Web to locate and communicate with potential employers. One way to locate people is through Usenet newsgroups that are dedicated to your field of interest. Newsgroup members leave messages for one another on an electronic bulletin board and retrieve messages by visiting that Web site. You might also try listservs (or Internet mailing lists). These discussion groups are similar to Usenet newsgroups, except that the group mails each message to every member's e-mail address. Commercial systems such as Prodigy, America Online, and CompuServe have their own discussion groups (called Special Interest Groups, RoundTables, Forums, Clubs, or Bulletin Boards). These commercial groups are also devoted to a particular interest, but they make a profit from the time users spend using their services. Once you've located a potential contact, you can communicate quickly and nonintrusively by using e-mail to request information or to let an employer know you're interested in working for a particular company.

- *Researching employers' companies.* When looking for information about the companies you might want to work for, don't forget the Web. Even companies that don't yet

Don't despair if you lack contacts who can introduce you to potential employers. A variety of avenues are used by both job applicants and employers. Like Mobil, many organizations send representatives to college campuses to interview students for job openings. These interviews are usually coordinated by the campus placement office, which keeps files containing college records, data sheets, and letters of recommendation for all students registered for the service.

Unsolicited résumés are a vital source of candidates for many organizations. Some 67 percent of the employers who participated in the American Management Society survey engage in this method of recruiting, and 18 percent of the job seekers graduating from a typical university found employment by sending unsolicited résumés to prospective employers. However, if you pursue this route, be prepared to buy a lot of postage stamps. For every 100 letters that you send out, you can expect to get only about six interviews.[6]

have a home page are getting one, and many of them are including job listings on their Web site. By visiting a company's Web site, you can find out about its mission, products, annual reports, employee benefits, and job openings. You can locate company web sites by knowing the URL (or Web address), by using links from other sites, or by using a search engine such as Alta Vista, Lycos, or Excite.

- *Searching for job vacancies.* In addition to visiting company home pages, you can find job vacancies at sites that list openings from multiple companies. Such online indexes include College Grad Job Hunter (offering links to organizations with entry-level jobs), Online Career Center (offering searchable information), Career Mosaic, America's Job Bank, CareerPath, Help Wanted USA, The Main Quad, Monster Board, CareerCity and many others. To easily locate any of these organizations, simply use a search engine such as Alta Vista or Excite. Of course, even the World Wide Web offers no central, unified marketplace, so plan on visiting hundreds of Web sites to learn what jobs are available. Also, remember that only a small percentage of jobs are currently listed on the World Wide Web. Employers generally prefer to fill job vacancies through the "hidden job market" (finding people without advertising, whether on the Internet or in newspapers).

- *Posting your résumé online.* You can post your résumé online either through an index service or on your own home page. To post your résumé on an index service, you would simply prepare the information to be input into the database and transmit it by mail, fax, modem, or e-mail. Then employers contact your index service, specifying all the key words to be found in qualifying résumés, and your index service sends the employer a list of names along with résumés or background profile sheets. Finally, the employer can decide whether to interview any of the people on the list. When posting your résumé on your own home page, you can retain a nicer looking format, and you can even include color photographs of yourself, links to papers you've written or recommendations you've received, and sound or video clips.

Using the World Wide Web to seek employment allows you to respond directly to job postings without going through recruiters, post résumés that have been tailored to match exactly the skills and qualifications necessary to fill a particular position, send résumés through e-mail (which is faster and less expensive than printing and mailing them), send focused cover letters directly to the executives doing the hiring, and quickly gain detailed information about your prospective employers. Moreover, most campus placement offices are retooling to help you take advantage of Web opportunities. But keep in mind just how many job openings are not listed on the Internet. The World Wide Web cannot replace other techniques for finding employment—it's just one more tool in your overall strategy.

---

1. Surfing the Web can chew up a disproportionate amount of your job-seeking time. So that you have plenty of time to spend on other sources, how can you limit the amount of time you spend on the Web and still make the Web work for you? Please explain.

2. When posting your résumé on the World Wide Web, you're revealing a lot of information about yourself that could be used by people other than employers (salespeople, people competing for similar positions, con artists). What sort of information might you leave off your Web résumé that would certainly appear on a traditional résumé?

Employers also recruit candidates through employment agencies, state employment services, and the employment bureaus operated by some trade associations, as well as through classified and display ads in newspapers, trade magazines, and campus publications.

Building Toward a Career

Employers are seeking people who are able and willing to adapt to diverse situations, who thrive in an ever-changing workplace, and who continue to learn throughout their careers. Companies like Mobil want leaders who are more versatile, and they are encouraging their managers to get more varied job experience.[7] Employers want team players with strong work records, so try to gain skills you can market in various industries.

In her efforts to find work, Marci Burkhart gets help from the Career Center at Syracuse University.

Your chances of getting a job are increased by career-building efforts:
- Developing an employment portfolio
- Gaining intercultural experience
- Participating in an internship program
- Networking with others in your field
- Taking interim jobs and classes
- Expanding your life experience

To better market yourself later on, consider keeping an employment portfolio now. Get a three-ring notebook and a package of plastic sleeves that open at the top. Collect anything that shows your ability to perform, such as classroom or work evaluations, certificates, awards, and papers you've written. A chef's apprentice may collect photographs of food presentations or ice sculptures. This employment portfolio accomplishes two things: First, employers are impressed that you're not just talking about what you've done. You have tangible evidence of your professionalism. Second, you can be more relaxed because your portfolio will let you discuss your skills and accomplishments more calmly and more enthusiastically.

Your chances of being hired are better if you've studied abroad and learned another language. At the least, employers expect graduates to have a sound understanding of international affairs. Companies are looking for employees with intercultural sensitivity and an ability to adapt in other cultures.[8]

You can gain a competitive edge by participating in an internship program. Not only will an internship help you gain valuable experience and relevant contacts, but it will provide you with important references and with items for your portfolio.[9] Remember, employers are actively seeking ways to reduce the costs of hiring permanent employees who may not work out, and these employers are using internships to try out potential workers.[10]

Whenever possible, join networks of professional colleagues and friends who can help you stay abreast of where your occupation, industry, and company are going. As you search for a permanent job that fulfills your career goals, take interim job assignments, and consider temporary work or freelance jobs. Employers will be more willing to find (or even create) a position for someone they've learned to respect, and your temporary or freelance work gives them a chance to see what you can do. You might even consider starting your own business.

If you're unable to find actual job experience, work on polishing and updating your skills. While you're waiting for responses to your résumé or to hear about your last interview, take a computer course, or use the time to gain some other educational or life experience that would be difficult to get while working full time. Become familiar with the services offered by your campus career center (or placement office). These centers offer a variety of services, including individual placement counseling, credential services, job-fair/on-campus interviews, job listings, advice on computerized résumé-writing software, workshops in job-search techniques, résumé preparation, interview techniques, and more.[11] Have a plan, but be flexible and ready to take advantage of new opportunities. That's the way you'll build your career and achieve your career goals.[12]

Once an employer hires you and you're on the job, don't think you've reached the end of the process. The best thing you can do for your long-term career is to continue learning. Listen to and learn from those around you who have experience. Be ready and willing to take on new responsibilities, and actively pursue new or better skills. Employers appreciate applicants and employees who demonstrate a willingness and enthusiasm to learn, to listen, and to gain experience.

Of course, to get hired, you usually need an interview, and to get that interview, you usually need a résumé. A good résumé can distinguish you from all the other people looking for work. So make sure your résumé is well written.

The purpose of the résumé is to get you an interview.

WRITING YOUR RÉSUMÉ

A **résumé** is a structured, written summary of a person's education, employment background, and job qualifications. Many people new to the job market have some misconceptions about résumés (see Figure 12.2 on page 388). The fact is that a résumé is a form of advertising, designed to help you get an interview. This interview may serve any number of purposes—to get a job, get a promotion, obtain membership in a professional organization, or become a member of a nonprofit board. As in all forms of advertising, your objective is to call attention to your best features and downplay your disadvantages, without distorting or misrepresenting the facts.[13] And as in any form of persuasive writing, be sure to pay particular attention to your readers. Find out what they expect from applicants. Learn about their cultural practices so that your résumé conforms to their expectations, not only in tone and format, but also in the way you arrange your information. If you're applying for work abroad, be especially careful to research the preferred form, content, and organization of résumés.

Your résumé is a structured, written summary of your educational and employment background, and it shows your qualifications for a job.

Mobil's Henry Halaiko believes that a good résumé conveys seven specific qualities that employers seek. If you're writing your résumé for employers in Canada or the United States, you might focus on these qualities. In Halaiko's view, a good résumé shows that a candidate (1) thinks in terms of results, (2) knows how to get things done, (3) is well-rounded, (4) shows signs of progress, (5) has personal standards of excellence, (6) is flexible and willing to try new things, and (7) possesses strong communication skills. As you put your résumé together, think about how the format and style, content, and organization help you convey these seven qualities.

Control the Format and Style

Quick—you've got less than 45 seconds to make a good impression. That's the amount of time a typical recruiter devotes to each résumé before tossing it into either the "maybe" or the "reject" pile.[14] If your résumé doesn't *look* sharp, chances are nobody will read it carefully enough to judge your qualifications.

It's important to use a clean typeface on high-grade, letter-size bond paper (in white, off-white, light ivory, or other light earth tone). Be sure your application letter

The key characteristics of a good résumé are
- Neatness
- Simplicity
- Accuracy
- Honesty

Figure 12.2
Fallacies and Facts About Résumés

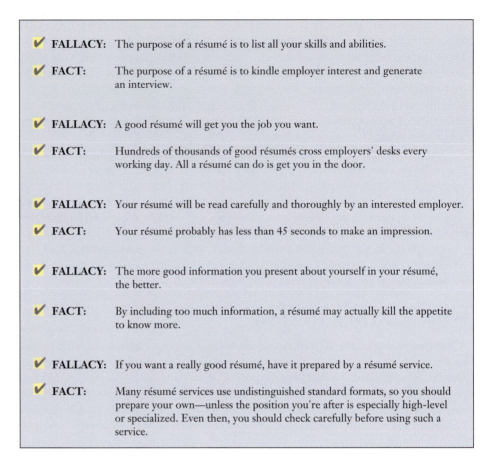

✔ **FALLACY:**   The purpose of a résumé is to list all your skills and abilities.

✔ **FACT:**   The purpose of a résumé is to kindle employer interest and generate an interview.

✔ **FALLACY:**   A good résumé will get you the job you want.

✔ **FACT:**   Hundreds of thousands of good résumés cross employers' desks every working day. All a résumé can do is get you in the door.

✔ **FALLACY:**   Your résumé will be read carefully and thoroughly by an interested employer.

✔ **FACT:**   Your résumé probably has less than 45 seconds to make an impression.

✔ **FALLACY:**   The more good information you present about yourself in your résumé, the better.

✔ **FACT:**   By including too much information, a résumé may actually kill the appetite to know more.

✔ **FALLACY:**   If you want a really good résumé, have it prepared by a résumé service.

✔ **FACT:**   Many résumé services use undistinguished standard formats, so you should prepare your own—unless the position you're after is especially high-level or specialized. Even then, you should check carefully before using such a service.

and envelope are on matching colored stationery. Leave ample margins all around, and be sure any corrections are unnoticeable. Avoid italic typefaces, which can be difficult to read. If you have reservations about the quality of your printer (dot-matrix printing is not suitable for most résumés) or typewriter, you might want to turn your résumé over to a professional service. To make duplicate copies, use offset printing or photocopying.

In terms of layout, your objective is to make the information easy to grasp.[15] Break up the text by using headings that call attention to various aspects of your background, such as your work experience and education. Underline or capitalize key points, or set them off in the left margin. Use indented lists to itemize your most important qualifications. Leave plenty of white space, even if doing so forces you to use two pages rather than one.

Pay attention to mechanics. Check the headings and itemized lists to make sure they're grammatically parallel. Be sure your grammar, spelling, and punctuation are correct. Because your résumé has only seconds to make an impression, the "you" attitude and audience focus are crucial. Think about the employer reading your résumé. Then write in a simple, direct style to save your reader time, emphasize clarity, and focus on what your reader needs to know. Absolutely avoid using the word *I*. Use short, crisp phrases instead of whole sentences, and start these phrases with action verbs such as the following:

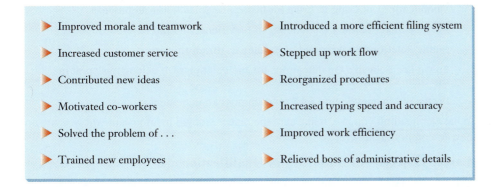

Figure 12.3
Active Accomplishment
Statements for Résumés

Administered	Implemented	Reorganized
Completed	Improved	Scheduled
Created	Influenced	Set up
Demonstrated	Initiated	Solved
Developed	Maintained	Strengthened
Directed	Performed	Succeeded
Established	Planned	Successfully systematized
Headed	Ran	Transformed

You might say, "Coached a Little League team to the regional playoffs" or "Supervised a fast-food restaurant and four employees." See Figure 12.3 for other active phrases that will improve the effectiveness of your résumé.

As a rule of thumb, try to write a one-page résumé. If you have a great deal of experience and are applying for a higher-level position, you may wish to prepare a somewhat longer résumé. The important thing is to give yourself enough space to present a persuasive but accurate portrait of your skills and accomplishments.

Tailor the Contents

Most potential employers expect to see certain items in any résumé. The bare essentials are name and address, academic credentials, and employment history. Otherwise, make sure your résumé emphasizes your strongest, most impressive qualifications. Think in terms of an image or a theme you'd like to project. Are you academically gifted? Are you a campus leader? A well-rounded person? Are you a creative genius? A technical wizard? If you know what you have to sell, you can shape the elements of your résumé accordingly. Don't exaggerate, and don't alter the past or claim skills you don't have, but don't dwell on negatives, either. By focusing on your strengths, you can convey the desired impression without distorting the facts.

Name and Address

The first thing an employer needs to know is who you are and where you can be reached: your name, address, and phone number (as well as your e-mail address or URL, if you have it). If you have an address and phone number at school and another at home, you may include both. At the same time, if you have a work phone and a home phone, list both and indicate which is which. Many résumé headings are nothing more than the name and address centered at the top of the page. You really have little need to include the word *Résumé,* but if you have a specific job in mind, you could use a heading that indicates that fact:

The opening section shows at a glance
• Who you are
• How to reach you

Qualifications of Craig R. Crisp for Insurance Sales Representative

Résumé Sheet of Mary Menendez, an Experienced Retail Fashion Buyer

Public Relations Background of Bradley R. (Brad) Howard

Susan Lee Selwyn's Qualifications for the Position of Teaching Assistant in the Dade County School District

Profile of Michael de Vito for Entertainment Management

Whatever heading you use, make sure the reader can tell in an instant who you are and how to communicate with you.

Career Objective or Summary of Qualifications

Should you state a career objective on your résumé? Opinion is divided. Some experts argue that your objective will be obvious from your qualifications. They also point out that such a statement is counterproductive (especially if you would like to be considered for a variety of openings) because it labels you as being interested in only one thing. Other experts point out that employers will undoubtedly try to categorize you anyway, so you might as well be sure they attach the right label. If you decide to state your objective, be as specific as possible about what you want to do:

Human resource management, requiring international experience

Advertising assistant, with print media emphasis

If you have two types of qualifications (such as a certificate in secretarial science and two years' experience in retail sales), prepare two separate résumés, each with a different objective. If your immediate objective differs from your ultimate one, combine the two in a single statement:

A marketing position with an opportunity for eventual managerial status

Proposal writer, with the ultimate goal of becoming a contracts administrator

As an alternative to stating your objective, you might want to summarize your qualifications in a brief statement that highlights your strongest points, particularly if you have had a good deal of varied experience. Use a short, simple phrase:

Summary of qualifications: Ten years of experience in commission selling

Hospital administrator responsible for 350-bed facility

Education

If you're still in school, education is probably your strongest selling point. So present your educational background in depth, choosing facts that support your "theme." Give this section a heading, such as "Education," "Professional College Training," or "Academic Preparation." Then starting with the school you most recently attended, list for each school the name and location, the term of your enrollment (in months and years), your major and minor fields of study, significant skills and abilities you've developed in your course work, and the degree(s) or certificate(s) you've earned. Showcase your qualifications by listing courses that have directly equipped you for the job sought, and indicate any scholarships, awards, or academic honors you've received.

The education section also includes off-campus training sponsored by business, industry, or government. Include any relevant seminars or workshops you've attended, as well as the certificates or other documents you've received. Mention high school or military training only if your achievements are pertinent to your career goals. Whether you list your grades depends on the job you want and the quality of your grades. If you choose to show grade-point averages for your total program or your major, be sure to mention the scale if a 5-point scale is used instead of a 4-point scale.

Stating your objective or summarizing your qualifications helps the recruiter categorize you.

If education is your strongest selling point, discuss it thoroughly and highlight it visually.

Education is usually given less emphasis in a résumé after you've worked in your chosen field for a year or more. If work experience is your strongest qualification, save the section on education for later in the résumé and provide less detail.

Work Experience

Like the education section, the discussion of your work experience focuses on your overall theme. Tailor your description to highlight the relationship between your previous responsibilities and your target field. Call attention to the skills you've developed and the progression from jobs of lesser to greater responsibility.

When describing your work experience, you'll usually list your jobs in chronological order, with the current or last one first. Include any part-time, summer, or intern positions even if the jobs have no relation to your present career objective. Employers will see that you have the ability to get and hold a job, which is an important qualification in itself. If you have worked your way through school, say so. Employers interpret this as a sign of character.

Each listing includes the name and location of the employer. Then, if the reader is unlikely to recognize the organization, briefly describe what it does. When you want to keep the name of your current employer confidential, identify the firm by industry only ("a large film-processing laboratory"), or use the name but request confidentiality in the application letter or in an underlined note ("Résumé submitted in confidence") at the top or bottom of the résumé. If an organization's name or location has since changed, state the current name or location and then "formerly . . ."

Before or after each job listing, state your functional title, such as "clerk typist" or "salesperson." If you were a dishwasher, say so. Don't try to make your role seem more important by glamorizing your job title, functions, or achievements. You also state how long you worked on each job, from month/year to month/year. Use the phrase "to present" to denote current employment. If a job was part-time, say so.

Be honest about the positions you've held, the companies you've worked for, and your dates of employment. You'll be courting trouble if you list jobs you never held, claim to have worked for a firm when you didn't, or change dates to cover up a gap in employment. More employers are checking candidates' backgrounds, so inaccuracies are likely to be exposed sooner or later (see "Warning: Deceptive Résumés Can Backfire").

Devote the most space to the jobs that relate to your target position. If you were personally responsible for something significant, be sure to mention it ("Devised a new collection system that accelerated payment of overdue receivables"). Facts about your accomplishments are the most important information you can give a prospective employer, so quantify your accomplishments whenever possible ("Designed a new ad that increased sales by 9 percent").

Relevant Skills

You may also want to include a section that describes other aspects of your background that pertain to your career objective. If you were applying for a position with a multinational organization, you would mention your command of another language or your travel experience. Other skills you might mention include the ability to operate a computer, word processor, or other equipment. In fact, you might title a special section "Computer Skills" or "Language Skills" and place it near your "Education" or "Work Experience" section.

If your academic transcripts, samples of your work, or letters of recommendation might increase your chances of getting the job, insert a line at the end of your résumé offering to supply these on request. If your college placement office keeps these items on file for you, you can say "References and supporting documents available from . . .";

The work experience section lists all the related jobs you've had:
- Name and location of employer
- What the organization does (if not clear from its name)
- Your functional title
- How long you worked there
- Your duties and responsibilities
- Your significant achievements or contributions

Quantify your accomplishments whenever possible.

Include miscellaneous facts that relate to your career objective:
- Command of other languages
- Computer expertise
- Date you can start working
- Availability of references

WARNING: DECEPTIVE RÉSUMÉS CAN BACKFIRE

In an effort to put your best foot forward, you may be tempted to waltz around a few points that could raise questions about your résumé. For example, given your desire for a career in sales, you'd rather not explain why you quit your summer job as a door-to-door encyclopedia sales representative, so wouldn't it be better not to mention that three-week period at all? In addition, you may be inclined to dress up a few of your accomplishments: It's true that advertising revenue increased by 25 percent shortly after you became advertising manager of the campus newspaper. Do you really have to explain that most of the credit belongs to your predecessor, who laid the groundwork for the sales campaign shortly before she graduated?

As you weigh the alternatives, you may say to yourself: "Everybody else is probably shading the facts to make their résumés look good. I'd be a fool not to do the same." Statistics on the prevalence of résumé inflation are difficult to gather, but most recruiters agree that distortion is common. The best guess is that up to 40 percent of all résumés either omit potentially damaging information or exaggerate the candidate's accomplishments. The most frequent forms of deception include:

- *Claiming nonexistent educational credits.* Candidates may state (or imply) that they earned a degree when, in fact, they never attended the school—or attended but did not complete the regular program. A typical claim might read, "Majored in business administration at Wayne State University."
- *Inflating grade-point averages.* Students who feel pressured to impress employers with their academic performance may claim a higher GPA than was actually achieved.
- *Stretching dates of employment to cover gaps.* Because periods of unemployment raise red flags for many employers, many candidates try to camouflage gaps in their work history by giving vague references to dates of employment. For example, a candidate who left a company in January 1992 and joined another in December 1993 might cover up by showing that the first job ended in 1992 and the next began in 1993.
- *Claiming to be self-employed.* Another common way people cover a period of unemployment is by saying that they were "self-employed" or a "consultant." The candi-

be sure to include the exact address of the placement office. Many potential employers prefer you to list your references on the résumé. As a convenience for the prospective employer, you may also list the month and, if you know it, the day you will be available to start work.

Activities and Achievements

Nonpaid activities may provide evidence of work-related skills.

Your résumé also describes any volunteer activities that demonstrate your abilities. List projects that require leadership, organization, teamwork, and cooperation. Emphasize career-related activities such as "member of the Student Marketing Association." List skills you learned in these activities, and explain how these skills relate to the job you're applying for. Include speaking, writing, or tutoring experience; participation in athletics or creative projects; fund-raising or community service activities; and offices held in academic or professional organizations. (However, mention of political or religious organizations may be a red flag to someone with different views, so use your judgment.) Note any awards you've received. Again, quantify your achievements with numbers wherever possible. Instead of saying that you addressed various student groups, state how many and the approximate audience sizes. If your activities have been extensive, you may want to group them into divisions like these: "College Activities," "Community Service," "Professional Associations," "Seminars and Workshops," and "Speaking Activities." An alternative is to divide them into two categories: "Service Activities" and "Achievements, Awards, and Honors."

date claims to have operated an independent business during the period in question.

- *Leaving out any reference to jobs that might cause embarrassment.* Being fired from one or two jobs is understandable when corporate mergers and downsizing are commonplace. However, when a candidate has lost several jobs in quick succession, recruiters may jump to the conclusion that the person is a poor employee. To cover up a string of such job losses, candidates often decide to drop a few positions, particularly if a reference check could prove embarrassing. To cover the gap, candidates stretch the dates of employment for the jobs held before and after.
- *Exaggerating expertise or experience.* Candidates often inflate their accomplishments by using verbs somewhat loosely. Words like *supervised, managed, increased, improved,* and *created* imply that the candidate was personally responsible for results that, in reality, were the outcome of a group effort.
- *Claiming to have worked for companies that are out of business.* Candidates who need to fill a gap in their work record sometimes say they have worked for a firm that has gone out of business. Checking such claims is difficult be-

cause the people who were involved in the disbanded business are hard to track down.

Before trying one of these ploys yourself, think twice. Experienced recruiters are familiar with the games that candidates play to make themselves look better. Many employers have a policy of firing people who have lied on their résumés. If your résumé raises suspicion, you may do yourself more harm than good by misrepresenting your background. Sure, it's fine to present your strongest, most impressive qualifications and to minimize your weaknesses. However, don't exaggerate, alter the past, or claim to have skills you don't have.

---

1. Since you'd rather not explain why you quit your summer job as a door-to-door encyclopedia sales representative, describe how you might handle that period on your résumé. Should you omit it? Can you mention it without revealing why you quit?
2. Consider one or two positions you have held (whether in a club, in a volunteer organization, or on the job). Write a realistic description that doesn't inflate them but that presents them in a positive light.

Personal Data

To differentiate your résumé, you might want to mention your hobbies, travel experiences, or personal characteristics, particularly if they suggest qualities that relate to your career goals. This section helps present you as a well-rounded person, and it can be used to spark conversation during an interview.[16] However, civil rights laws prohibit employers from discriminating on the basis of gender, marital or family status, age (although only those 40 to 70 are protected), race, color, religion, national origin, and physical or mental disability. Thus, be sure to exclude any items that could encourage discrimination.

Provide only the personal data that will help you get the job.

If military service is relevant to the position you are seeking, you may list it in this section (or under "Education" or "Work Experience"). List the date of induction, the branch of service, where you served, the highest rank you achieved, any accomplishments related to your career goals, and the date you were discharged.

Choosing the Best Organizational Plan

Although you may want to include a little information in all categories, emphasize the information that has a bearing on your career objective and minimize or exclude any that is irrelevant or counterproductive. You do this by adopting an organizational plan—chronological, functional, or targeted—that focuses attention on your strongest points. The "right" choice depends on your background and goals.

Select an organizational pattern that focuses attention on your strengths.

The Chronological Résumé

The most traditional type of résumé is the **chronological résumé,** in which a person's employment history is listed sequentially in reverse order, starting with the most recent experience. When you organize your résumé chronologically, the "Work Experience" section dominates the résumé and is placed in the most prominent slot, immediately after the name and address and the objective. You develop this section by listing your jobs in reverse order, beginning with the most recent position and working backward toward earlier jobs. Under each listing you describe your responsibilities and accomplishments, giving the most space to the most recent positions. If you are just graduating from college, you can vary the chronological plan by putting your educational qualifications before your experience, thereby focusing attention on your academic credentials.

The chronological approach is the most common way to organize a résumé, and many employers prefer it. Robert Nesbit, a vice president with Korn/Ferry International, speaks for many recruiters: "Unless you have a really compelling reason, don't use any but the standard chronological format. Your résumé should not read like a treasure map, full of minute clues to the whereabouts of your jobs and experience. I want to be able to grasp quickly where a candidate has worked, how long, and in what capacities."[17]

The chronological approach is especially appropriate if you have a strong employment history and are aiming for a job that builds on your current career path. This is the case for Roberto Cortez, whose résumé appears in Figure 12.4.

The Functional Résumé

A functional résumé focuses attention on your areas of competence.

In a **functional résumé,** you organize your résumé around a list of skills and accomplishments and then identify your employers and academic experience in subordinate sections. This pattern stresses individual areas of competence, and it's useful for people who are just entering the job market, people who want to redirect their careers, and people who have little continuous career-related experience. Figure 12.5, on page 396, illustrates how a recent graduate used the functional approach to showcase her qualifications for a career in retail.

The Targeted Résumé

A targeted résumé shows how you qualify for a specific job.

A **targeted résumé** is a résumé organized to focus attention on what you can do for a particular employer in a particular position. Immediately after stating your career objective, you list any related capabilities. This list is followed by a list of your achievements, which provide evidence of your capabilities. Employers and schools are listed in subordinate sections.

Targeted résumés are a good choice for people who have a clear idea of what they want to do and who can demonstrate their ability in the targeted area. This approach was effective for Erica Vorkamp, whose résumé appears in Figure 12.6 (see page 397).

Adapting Your Résumé to an Electronic Format

Although it was once considered unacceptable to fax a résumé to a potential employer, many executives now say they would indeed accept a résumé by fax if they've given no other specific guidelines.[18] What about sending résumés by e-mail and responding to job openings via the Internet? If employers advertise job openings online and provide an e-mail address for responses, sending your résumé by e-mail and responding via the Internet isn't only acceptable, it is preferable.

Cortez calls attention to his most recent achievements by setting them off in list form with bullets. The section titled "Intercultural Qualifications" emphasizes his international background and fluency in Spanish, which are important qualifications for his target position.

Figure 12.4
In-Depth Critique:
Chronological Résumé

Roberto Cortez
5687 Crosswoods Drive
Falls Church, Virginia 22046
Home: (703) 987-0086   Office: (703) 549-6624

OBJECTIVE

Accounting management position requiring a knowledge of international finance

EXPERIENCE

March 1993 to present — Staff Accountant/Financial Analyst, Inter-American Imports(Alexandria, VA)
- Prepare accounting reports for wholesale giftware importer with annual sales of $15 million
- Audit financial transactions with suppliers in 12 Latin American countries
- Created a computerized model to adjust accounts for fluctuations in currency exchange rates
- Negotiated joint-venture agreements with major suppliers in Mexico and Colombia

October 1989 to March 1993 — Staff Accountant, Monsanto Agricultural Chemicals (Mexico City, Mexico)
- Handled budgeting, billing, and credit-processing functions for the Mexico City branch
- Audited travel/entertainment expenses for Monsanto's 30-member Latin American sales force
- Assisted in launching an online computer system (IBM)

EDUCATION

1989 to 1993 — MBA with emphasis on international business
George Mason University (Fairfax, Virginia)

1985 to 1989 — BBA, Accounting
Universidad Naçional Autónoma de Mexico (Mexico City, Mexico)

INTERCULTURAL QUALIFICATIONS

- Born and raised in Mexico City; became U.S. citizen in 1991
- Fluent in Spanish and German
- Traveled extensively in Latin America

References available on request
Résumé Submitted in Confidence

Cortez emphasizes his achievements by using an indented list.

The chronological organization highlights Cortez's impressive career progress.

Cortez's language and cultural skills are highlighted by presenting them in a special qualifications section.

Figure 12.5
In-Depth Critique:
Functional Résumé

Although Glenda S. Johns has not held any paid, full-time positions in retail sales, she has participated in work-experience programs, and she knows a good deal about the profession from doing research and talking with people in the industry. As a result, she was able to organize her résumé in a way that demonstrates her ability to handle such a position.

Because she is a recent graduate, the applicant describes her experience first.

The use of action verbs and specific facts enhances this résumé's effectiveness.

The applicant's sketchy work history is described but not emphasized.

Glenda S. Johns

Home:	457 Mountain View Road	School:	1254 Main Street
	Clear Lake, IA 50428		Council Bluffs, IA 51505
	(515) 633-5971		(712) 438-5254

OBJECTIVE

Retailing position that utilizes my experience

RELEVANT SKILLS

- **Personal Selling/Retailing**
  - Led housewares department in fewest mistakes while cashiering and balancing register receipts
  - Created end-cap and shelf displays for special housewares promotions
  - Sold the most benefit tickets during college fund-raising drive for local community center
- **Public Interaction**
  - Commended by housewares manager for resolving customer complaints amicably
  - Performed in summer theater productions in Clear Lake, Iowa
- **Managing**
  - Trained part-time housewares employees in cash register operation and customer service
  - Reworked housewares employee schedules as assistant manager
  - Organized summer activities for children 6–12 years old for city of Clear Lake, Iowa—including reading programs, sports activities, and field trips

EDUCATION

- **AA, Retailing Mid-Management (3.81 GPA / 4.0 scale), Iowa Western Community College, June 1997**
- **In addition to required retailing, buying, marketing, and merchandising courses, completed electives in visual merchandising, business information systems, principles of management, and business math**

WORK EXPERIENCE

- **Assistant manager, housewares, at Jefferson's Department Store during off-campus work experience program, Council Bluffs, Iowa (winter 1996–spring 1997)**
- **Sales clerk, housewares, at Jefferson's Department Store during off-campus work experience program, Council Bluffs, Iowa (winter 1995–spring 1996)**
- **Assistant director, Summer Recreation Program, Clear Lake, Iowa (summer 1995)**
- **Actress, Cobblestone Players, Clear Lake, Iowa (summer 1994)**

Figure 12.6
In-Depth Critique:
Targeted Résumé

When Erica Vorkamp developed her résumé, she chose not to use a chronological pattern, which would focus attention on her lack of recent work experience. Instead, she uses a targeted approach that emphasizes her ability to organize special events.

Erica Vorkamp
Qualifications for Special Events Coordinator
in the City of Barrington
993 Church Street, Barrington, IL 60010
(312) 884-2153

CAPABILITIES

- Plan and coordinate large-scale public events
- Develop community support for concerts, festivals, and entertainment
- Manage publicity for major events
- Coordinate activities of diverse community groups
- Establish and maintain financial controls for public events
- Negotiate contracts with performers, carpenters, electricians, and suppliers

ACHIEVEMENTS

- Arranged 1997's week-long Arts and Entertainment Festival for the Barrington Public Library, involving performances by 25 musicians, dancers, actors, magicians, and artists
- Supervised the 1996 PTA Halloween Carnival, an all-day festival with game booths, live bands, contests, and food service that raised $7,600 for the PTA
- Organized the 1995 Midwestern convention for 800 members of the League of Women Voters, which extended over a three-day period and required arrangements for hotels, meals, speakers, and special tours
- Served as chairperson for the 1995 Children's Home Society Fashion Show, a luncheon for 400 that raised $5,000 for orphans and abused children

EDUCATION

- BA, Psychology, Northwestern University (Evanston, Illinois), September 1978 to June 1983, Phi Beta Kappa

WORK HISTORY

- First National Bank of Chicago, June 1983 to October 1985, personnel counselor/campus recruiter; scheduled and conducted interviews with graduating MBA students on 18 midwestern campuses; managed orientation program for recruits hired for bank's management trainee staff
- Northwestern University, November 1980 to June 1983, part-time research assistant; helped Professor Paul Harris conduct behavioral experiments using rats trained to go through mazes

The capabilities and achievements all relate to the specific job target, giving a very selective picture of the candidate's abilities.

This work history has little bearing on the candidate's job target, but she felt that recruiters would want to see evidence that she has held a paying position.

Large companies have been storing résumés in centralized databases for some time. Now, when employers look for potential employees, more and more of them are searching online databases as well as their own in-house files.[19] Depending on where you wish to apply and how you wish to be perceived, you may want to consider the unique characteristics of electronic résumés—those that are printed out but end up being scanned into a database and those that are sent to employers by e-mail or posted on the Internet.

Since many employers are lowering costs and increasing efficiency by maintaining and using database information, you may want to consider making even your paper résumé scannable; that is, able to be read by OCR scanners and digested by employers' computers. You can convert your traditional paper résumé into a scannable résumé in three steps (see Figure 12.7):[20]

An electronic résumé is helpful if your résumé will be scanned or if you post it on the Internet or submit it via e-mail.

To make your résumé scannable
- *Save it as an ASCII file*
- *Provide a list of key words*
- *Balance clear language with up-to-date jargon*

1. ***Save your résumé as a plain ASCII text file.*** ASCII is a common text language that allows your résumé to be read by any scanner and accessed by any computer. All word-processing programs allow you to save files as ASCII. However, this language does have its limitations. ASCII will not handle decorative or uncommon typefaces, underlining, italics, graphics, or shading. Stick to a popular Times Roman or Helvetica typeface, and use blank spaces to align text (rather than tabs). To help your résumé appear more readable, you might sparingly use an asterisk or a lowercase letter *o* to indicate a bullet. Be sure to use a lot of white space to allow scanners and computers to recognize when one topic ends and another begins.

2. ***Provide a list of key words.*** Emphasizing certain words will help potential employers select your résumé from the thousands they scan. Because computers scan for nouns (rather than the active verbs you've included in your traditional paper résumé), you can provide those key nouns in a separate list and place it right after your name and address. These key words may or may not actually appear in your résumé, but they accomplish two things: They give potential employers a quick picture of you, and they show that you're sensitive to the requirements of today's electronic business world. When choosing your key words, consider the following categories: job titles (staff accountant), job-related tasks (instead of "created a computerized accounting model" simply list "computerized accounting model"), skills or knowledge (Excel, fluent Spanish), degree(s) (MBA or master of business administration), major (accounting major), certifications (CPA), school (George Mason University), class ranking (top 20 percent), and interpersonal traits or skills (intercultural experience, organized, proven leader, willing to travel, written and oral communication skills).

3. ***Balance common language with current jargon.*** To maximize matches (or *hits*) between your résumé and an employer's search, use words that potential employers will understand. For example, don't call a keyboard an input device. Also, use abbreviations sparingly, except for common ones like BA or MBA. At the same time, learn the important buzz words used in your field, and use them. Places to look for the most current trends include want ads in major newspapers like *The Wall Street Journal* and the résumés in your field that are posted online. Be careful to check and re-check the spelling, capitalization, and punctuation of any jargon you include, and use only those words you see most often.

Make sure your name and address are the first lines on the résumé (with no text appearing above or alongside your name). Also, particular sections are sometimes omitted from electronic résumés—special interests and references, for example.[21] To find out what employers expect to see, check online résumés in your field. If most of them list a career objective, then perhaps you should too. If you're mailing your résumé, you may want to send both a well-designed, traditional one and a scannable one.

If Roberto Cortez knew that the employers he targeted would be scanning his résumé into a database, or if he wanted to submit his résumé via e-mail or post it on the Internet, he would change his formatting and add a key word list. However, the information he provides can remain essentially the same and appear in the same order.

Figure 12.7
In-Depth Critique:
Electronic Résumé

Roberto Cortez
5687 Crosswoods Drive
Falls Church, Virginia 22046

Home: (703) 987-0086   Office: (703) 549-6624
RCortez@silvernet.com

KEY WORDS

Financial executive, accounting management, international finance, financial analyst, accounting reports, financial audit, computerized accounting model, exchange rates, joint-venture agreements, budgets, billing, credit processing, online systems, MBA, fluent Spanish, fluent German.

OBJECTIVE

Accounting management position requiring a knowledge of international finance

EXPERIENCE

Staff Accountant/Financial Analyst, Inter-American Imports (Alexandria, VA)
March 1993 to present
    o Prepare accounting reports for wholesale importer, annual sales of
       $15 million
    o Audit financial transactions with suppliers in 12 Latin American
       countries
    o Created computerized model to adjust for fluctuations in currency
       exchange rates
    o Negotiated joint-venture agreements with suppliers in Mexico and
       Columbia

Staff Accountant, Monsanto Agricultural Chemicals (Mexico City, Mexico)
October 1989 to March 1993
    o Handled budgeting, billing, credit-processing functions for Mexico
       City branch
    o Audited travel/entertainment expenses for 30-member Latin
       American sales force
    o Assisted in launching an online computer system (IBM)

EDUCATION

MBA with emphasis on international business, George Mason University
(Fairfax, Virginia) 1989 to 1993
BBA, Accounting, Universidad Naçional Autónoma de Mexico (Mexico City,
Mexico) 1985 to 1989

Cortez has removed all boldfacing, rules, tabs, bullets, and two-column formatting.

Cortez uses a lowercase letter o in his indented lists.

Two other quick points. First, when sending your résumé to a public access area (such as a résumé database) or when posting it on your own home page, leave out Social Security numbers and other identification codes. You might also leave out the names of references and previous employers. Simply say that references are available on request, and refer to "a large accounting firm" or "a wholesale giftware importer" rather than naming companies.

Second, avoid attaching fully designed résumés to e-mail messages. Your audience will have to spend extra effort to open your résumé, and chances are that your résumé will be in a format that your audience can't read.

Writing the Perfect Résumé

Regardless of whether your résumé is electronic or paper, and regardless of what organizational plan you follow, the key to writing the "perfect" résumé is to put yourself in the reader's position. Think about what the prospective employer needs, then tailor your résumé accordingly.

People like Mobil Oil's Henry Halaiko read thousands of résumés every year and complain about the following common résumé problems:

- *Too long.* The résumé is not concise, relevant, and to the point.
- *Too short or sketchy.* The résumé does not give enough information for a proper evaluation of the applicant.
- *Hard to read.* A lack of "white space" and of such devices as indentions and boldfacing makes the reader's job more difficult.
- *Wordy.* Descriptions are verbose, with numerous words used for what could be said more simply.
- *Too slick.* The résumé appears to have been written by someone other than the applicant, which raises the question of whether the qualifications have been exaggerated.
- *Amateurish.* The applicant appears to have little understanding of the business world or of the particular industry, as revealed by including the wrong information or presenting it awkwardly.
- *Poorly reproduced.* The print is faint and difficult to read.
- *Misspelled and ungrammatical throughout.* Recruiters conclude that candidates who make these kinds of mistakes don't have good verbal skills, which are important on the job.
- *Boastful.* The overconfident tone makes the reader wonder whether the applicant's self-evaluation is realistic.
- *Dishonest.* The applicant claims to have expertise or work experience that he or she does not possess.
- *Gimmicky.* The words, structure, decoration, or material used in the résumé depart so far from the usual as to make the résumé ineffective.

Guard against making these mistakes in your own résumé, and compare your final version with the suggestions in this chapter's Checklist for Résumés on pages 402–403.

Also, update your résumé continuously. You'll need it whether you're applying for membership in a professional organization, working toward a promotion, or changing employers. People used to spend the majority of a career with one company. However, today the average person beginning a job in the United States will probably work in ten or more jobs for five or more employers before retiring.[22] So keeping your résumé updated is a good idea.

The "perfect" résumé responds to the reader's needs and preferences and avoids some common faults.

BEST OF THE WEB

Link Your Way to a Better Résumé

Learn how to stand out in a crowded job market. You'll find a helpful list of do's and don'ts, suggested résumé headings, a sample chronological résumé, a chart of action words to create an accomplishment-oriented impression, and a checklist for preparing scannable résumés.

http://www.bridgew.edu/depts/carplan/resume.htm

Whenever you submit your résumé, you accompany it with a cover or application letter. This document lets your reader know what you're sending, why you're sending it, and how your reader can benefit from reading it. Because your application letter is in your own style (rather than the choppy, shorthand style of your résumé), it gives you a chance to make a good personal impression.

WRITING APPLICATION MESSAGES

Like your résumé, your application letter is a form of advertising, so organize it like a sales letter: Use the AIDA plan, focus on the "you" attitude, and emphasize reader benefits (as discussed in Chapter 11). You need to stimulate your reader's interest before showing how you can satisfy the organization's needs. Make sure your style projects confidence; you can't hope to sell a potential employer on your merits unless you truly believe in them yourself and sound as though you do.

Of course, this approach isn't appropriate for job seekers in every culture. If you're applying for a job abroad or want to work with a subsidiary of an organization based in another country, you may need to adjust your tone. For instance, blatant self-promotion is considered bad form in some cultures. Other cultures stress group performance over individual contributions. And as for format, in some countries (including France), recruiters prefer handwritten letters to printed or typed ones. So research your company carefully before drafting your application letter.

For U.S. and Canadian companies, let your letter reflect your personal style. Be yourself, but be businesslike too; avoid sounding cute. Don't use slang or a gimmicky layout. The only time to be unusually creative in content or format is when the job you're seeking requires imagination, such as a position in advertising. In most cases you'll use a printer or typewriter to produce your application letter.

Finally, showing that you know something about the organization can pay off. Imagine yourself in the recruiter's situation: How can you demonstrate that your background and talents will solve a particular problem or fill a need? By using a "you" attitude and showing you've done some homework, you'll capture the reader's attention and convey your desire to join the organization. The more you can learn about the organization, the better you'll be able to write about how your qualifications fit its needs.[23]

Also, during your research, find out the name, title, and department of the person you're writing to. Reaching and addressing the right person is the most effective way to gain attention. So be sure to avoid phrases such as "To Whom It May Concern" and "Dear Sir."

> Follow the AIDA plan when writing your application letter: attention, interest, desire, action.

Writing the Opening Paragraph

A **solicited application letter** is one sent in response to an announced job opening. An **unsolicited letter,** also known as a *prospecting letter,* is one sent to an organization that has not announced an opening. When you send a solicited letter, you usually know in advance what qualifications the organization is seeking. However, you also have more competition because hundreds of other job seekers will have seen the listing and may be sending applications. In some respects, therefore, an unsolicited application letter stands a better chance of being read and of receiving individualized attention.

Whether your application letter is solicited or unsolicited, your qualifications are presented similarly. The main difference is in the opening paragraph. In a solicited letter, no special attention-getting effort is needed because you have been invited to apply. However, the unsolicited letter starts by capturing the reader's attention and interest.

> You write a solicited application letter in response to an announced job opening.
>
> You write an unsolicited application letter to an organization that has not announced a job opening.

CHECKLIST FOR RÉSUMÉS

A. CONTENT AND STYLE
1. Prepare the résumé before the application letter to summarize the facts the letter will be based on.
2. Present the strongest qualifications first.
3. Use short noun phrases and action verbs, not whole sentences.
4. Use facts, not opinions.
5. Avoid using too many personal pronouns.
6. Omit the date of preparation.
7. Omit mention of your desired salary, work schedule, or vacation schedule.

B. CONTACT INFORMATION
1. Use a title or your name and address as a heading.
2. List your name, address, area code, and telephone number—for both school or work and home, if appropriate.

C. CAREER OBJECTIVE AND SKILLS SUMMARY (OPTIONAL)
1. Be as specific as possible about what you want to do.
   a. State a broad and flexible goal to increase the scope of your job prospects.
   b. Prepare two different résumés if you can do two unrelated types of work.
2. Summarize your key qualifications.

3. State the month and, if you know it, the day on which you will be available to start work.

D. EDUCATION
1. List all relevant schooling and training since high school, with the most recent first.
   a. List the name and location of every post-secondary school you have attended, with the dates you entered and left, and the degrees or certificates you obtained.
   b. Indicate your major (and minor) fields in college work.
   c. State the numerical base for your grade-point average, overall or in your major, if your average is impressive enough to list. Note the numerical scale (4.0 or 5.0).
2. List relevant required or elective courses in descending order of importance.
3. List any other related educational or training experiences, such as job-related seminars or workshops attended and certificates obtained. (Give dates.)

E. WORK EXPERIENCE
1. List all relevant work experience, including paid employment, volunteer work, and internships.
2. List full-time and part-time jobs, with the most recent one first.

Getting Attention

The opening of an unsolicited application letter captures attention and raises the reader's interest.

One way to spark attention in the opening paragraph is to show how your strongest work skills could benefit the organization. A 20-year-old secretary with 1 1/2 years of college might begin like this:

> When you need a secretary in your export division who can take shorthand at 125 words a minute and transcribe notes at 70—in English, Spanish, or Portuguese—call me.

Here's another attention-getter. It describes your understanding of the job's requirements and then shows how well your qualifications fit the job:

> Your annual report states that Mobil Corporation runs training programs about work-force diversity for managers and employees. The difficulties involved in running such programs can be significant, as I learned while tutoring inner-city high school students last summer. My 12 pupils were enrolled in vocational training programs and came from an eclectic mix of ethnic and racial backgrounds. The one thing they had in common was the lack of familiarity with the typical employer's expectations. To help them learn the "rules of the game," I developed exercises that cast them in various roles: boss, customer, new recruit, and co-worker. Of the 12 students, 10 have subsequently found full-time jobs and have called or written to tell me how much they gained from the workshop.

a. State the month/year when you started and left each job.

b. Provide the name and location of the firm that employed you.

c. List your job title and briefly describe your responsibilities.

d. Note on-the-job accomplishments, such as an award or a suggestion that saved the organization time or money.

F. **ACTIVITIES, HONORS, AND ACHIEVEMENTS**

1. List all relevant unpaid activities, including offices and leadership positions; significant awards or scholarships not listed elsewhere; projects you have undertaken that show an ability to work with others; and writing or speaking activities, publications, and roles in academic or professional organizations.

2. In most circumstances, exclude mention of religious or political affiliations.

G. **OTHER RELEVANT FACTS**

1. List other information, such as your typing speed or your proficiency in languages other than English.

2. Mention your ability to operate any machines, equipment, or computer software used in the job.

H. **PERSONAL DATA**

1. Omit personal details that could be regarded negatively or be used to discriminate against you.

2. Omit or downplay references to age if it could suggest inexperience or approaching retirement.

3. Describe military service (branch of service, where you served, rank attained, and the dates of induction and discharge) here or, if relevant, under "Education" or "Work Experience."

4. List job-related interests and hobbies, especially those indicating stamina, strength, sociability, or other qualities that are desirable in the position you seek.

I. **REFERENCES**

1. Offer to supply the names of references on request.

a. Supply names of academic, employment, and professional associates—but no relatives (unless you worked for them in a family-owned/operated business).

b. Provide a name, a title, an address, and a telephone number (with area code) for each reference.

c. List no name as a reference until you have that person's permission to do so.

2. Exclude your present employer if you do not want the firm to know you are seeking another position, or add "Résumé submitted in confidence" at the top or bottom of the résumé.

Mentioning the name of a person known to and highly regarded by the reader is bound to capture some attention:

> When Janice McHugh of your franchise sales division spoke to our business communication class last week, she said you often need promising new marketing graduates at this time of year.

References to publicized company activities, achievements, changes, or new procedures can also be used to gain attention:

> Today's issue of the *Detroit News* reports that you may need the expertise of computer programmers versed in robotics when your Lansing tire plant automates this spring.

Another type of attention-getting opening uses a question to demonstrate an understanding of the organization's needs:

> Can your fast-growing market research division use an interviewer with 1 1/2 years of field survey experience, a BA in public relations, and a real desire to succeed? If so, please consider me for the position.

A catch-phrase opening can also capture attention, especially if the job sought requires ingenuity and imagination:

> Grande monde—whether said in French, Italian, or Arabic, it still means "high society." As an interior designer for your Beverly Hills showroom, not only could I serve and sell to your distinguished clientele, but I could do it in all these languages. I speak, read, and write them fluently.

Start a solicited application letter by mentioning how you found out about the open position.

In contrast, a solicited letter written in response to a job advertisement usually opens by identifying the publication in which the ad ran and then describes what the applicant has to offer:

> Your ad in the April issue of *Travel & Leisure* for a cruise-line social director caught my eye. My eight years of experience as a social director in the travel industry would allow me to serve your new Caribbean cruise division well.

Note that all these openings demonstrate the "you" attitude, and many indicate how the applicant can serve the employer.

Clarifying Your Reason for Writing

State in the opening paragraph that you are applying for a job.

The opening paragraph of your application letter also states your reason for writing: You are applying for a job, so the opening paragraph identifies the desired job or job area:

> Please consider my application for an entry-level position in technical writing.

> Your firm advertised a fleet sales position (on March 23, 1997, in the *Baltimore Sun*). With my 16 months of new-car sales experience, please consider me for that position.

Another way to state your reason for writing is to use a title at the opening of your letter:

> Subject: Application for bookkeeper position

After this clear signal, your first paragraph can focus on getting attention and indicating how hiring you may benefit the organization.

Summarizing Your Key Selling Points

The middle section of an application letter
- Summarizes your relevant qualifications
- Emphasizes your accomplishments
- Suggests desirable personal qualities
- Justifies salary requirements
- Refers to your résumé

The middle section of your application letter presents your strongest selling points in terms of their potential benefit to the organization, thereby creating interest in you and a desire to interview you. If your selling points have already been mentioned in the opening, don't repeat them. Simply give supporting evidence. Otherwise, spell out your key qualifications, together with some convincing evidence of your ability to perform.

To avoid a cluttered application letter, mention only the qualifications that indicate you can do the job. Show how your studies and your work experience have prepared you for that job, or tell the reader about how you grew up in the business. Be careful not to repeat the facts presented in your résumé; simply interpret those facts for the reader:

> Experience in customer relations and college courses in public relations have taught me how to handle the problem-solving tasks that arise in a leading retail clothing firm like yours. Such important tasks include identifying and resolving customer complaints, writing letters that build good customer relations, and above all, promoting the organization's positive image.

When writing a solicited letter responding to a help-wanted advertisement, discuss each requirement specified in the ad. If you are deficient in any of these requirements, stress other solid selling points to help strengthen your overall presentation.

Stating that you have all the necessary requirements for the job is rarely enough to convince the reader, so back up assertions of your ability by presenting evidence of it. Cite one or two of your key qualifications; then show how you have effectively put them to use.

Instead of This	**Write This**
I completed three college courses in business communication, earning an A in each course, and have worked for the past year at Imperial Construction.	Using the skills gained from three semesters of college training in business communication, I developed a collection system for Imperial Construction that reduced its 1994 bad-debt losses by 3.7 percent, or $9,902, over those of 1993. The new collection letters offered discount incentives for speedy payment rather than timeworn terminology.

This section of the letter also presents evidence of a few significant job-related qualities. The following paragraph demonstrates that the applicant is diligent and hard working:

> While attending college full-time, I trained 3 hours a day with the varsity track team. Additionally, I worked part-time during the school year and up to 60 hours a week each summer in order to be totally self-supporting while in college. I can offer your organization the same level of effort and perseverance.

Other relevant qualities worth noting include the abilities to learn quickly, to handle responsibility, and to get along with people.

Another matter to bring up in this section is your salary requirements—but only if the organization has asked you to state them. The best strategy, unless you know approximately what the job pays, is to suggest a salary range or to indicate that the salary is negotiable or open. You might also consult the latest government "Area Wage Survey" at the library; this document presents salary ranges for various job classifications and geographic areas. If you do state a target salary, tie your request to the benefits you would provide the organization, much as you would handle price in a sales letter:

> For the past two years, I have been helping a company similar to yours organize its database. I would therefore like to receive a salary in the same range (the mid-20s) for helping your company set up a more efficient customer database.

Toward the end of this section, refer the reader to your résumé. You may do so by citing a specific fact or general point covered in the résumé.

> You will find my people skills an asset. As you can see in the attached résumé, I've been working part-time with a local publisher since my sophomore year, and during that time, I have successfully resolved more than a few "client crises."

Writing the Closing Paragraph

The final paragraph of your application letter has two important functions: to ask the reader for a specific action and to make a reply easy. In almost all cases, the action you ask for is an interview. Don't demand it, however; try to sound natural and appreciative. Offer to come to the employer's office at a convenient time or, if the firm is some distance away, to meet with its nearest representative. Make the request easy to fulfill by stating your phone number and the best time to reach you. Refer again to your strongest selling point and, if desired, your date of availability:

Close by asking for an interview and making the interview easy to arrange.

> After you have reviewed my qualifications, could we discuss the possibility of putting my marketing skills to work for your company? Because I will be on spring break the week of March 8, I would like to arrange a time to talk then. You can reach me by calling (901) 235-6311 during the day or (901) 529-2873 any evening after 5:00.

An alternative approach is to ask for an interview and then offer to get in touch with the reader to arrange a time for it, rather than requesting a reply. Whichever approach you use, mail your application letter and résumé promptly, especially if they have been solicited.

Writing the Perfect Application Letter

The "perfect" application letter, like the "perfect" résumé, accomplishes one thing: It gets you an interview. It conforms to no particular model because it's a reflection of your special strengths. Nevertheless, an application letter contains the basic components. In Figure 12.8, an unsolicited letter for a retail position, the applicant gains attention by focusing on the needs of the employer. The letter in Figure 12.9 (see page 408), written in response to a help-wanted ad, highlights the applicant's chief qualifications. Compare your own letters with the tasks in this chapter's Checklist for Application Letters (see page 409).

WRITING OTHER TYPES OF EMPLOYMENT MESSAGES

In your search for a job, you may prepare three other types of written messages: job-inquiry letters, application forms, and application follow-up letters.

Writing Job-Inquiry Letters

Use a job-inquiry letter to request an application form, which is a standardized data sheet that simplifies comparison of applicants' credentials.

Some organizations will not consider you for a position until you have filled out and submitted an **application form,** a standardized data sheet that simplifies comparison of applicants' qualifications. The inquiry letter is sent to request such a form. To increase your chances of getting the form, include enough information about yourself to show that you have at least some of the requirements for the position you are seeking:

> **Please send me an application form for work as an interior designer in your home furnishings department. For my certificate in design, I took courses in retail merchandising and customer relations. I have also had part-time sales experience at Capwell's department store.**

Instead of writing a letter of this kind, you may want to drop in at the office you're applying to. You probably won't get a chance to talk to anyone other than the receptionist or a human resources assistant, but you can pick up the form, get an impression of the organization, and demonstrate your initiative and energy.

Filling Out Application Forms

Your care in filling out application forms suggests to the employer that you will be thorough and careful in your work.

Some organizations require an application form instead of a résumé, and many require both an application form and a résumé. When filling out an application form, try to be thorough and accurate, because the organization will use this as a convenient one-page source for information about your qualifications. Be sure to have your résumé with you to remind you of important information. If you can't remember something and have no record of it, provide the closest estimate possible. If the form calls for information that you cannot provide because you have no background in it—such as military experience—write "Not applicable." When filling out applications on the premises, use a pen (unless specifically requested to use a pencil). If you're allowed to take the application form with you, use a typewriter to fill it out.

Application forms rarely seem to provide the right amount of space or to ask the right kinds of questions to reflect one's skills and abilities accurately. Swallow your frustration, however, and show your cooperation by doing your best to fill out the form completely. If you get an interview, you'll have an opportunity to fill in the gaps. You might also ask the person who gives you the form if you may submit a résumé and an application letter as well.

In her application letter, Glenda Johns manages to give a snapshot of her qualifications and skills without repeating what is said in her résumé (which appears in Figure 12.5).

Figure 12.8
In-Depth Critique: Sample Unsolicited Application Letter

Glenda S. Johns

Home: 457 Mountain View Road, Clear Lake, IA 50428 (515) 633-5971
School: 1254 Main Street, Council Bluffs, IA 51505 (712) 438-5254

June 16, 1996

Ms. Patricia Downings, Store Manager
Wal-Mart
840 South Oak
Iowa Falls, Iowa 50126

Dear Ms. Downings:

You want retail clerks and managers who are accurate, enthusiastic, and experienced. You want someone who cares about customer service, who understands merchandising, and who can work with others to get the job done. When you're ready to hire a manager trainee or a clerk who is willing to work toward promotion, please consider me for the job.

Working as clerk and then as assistant department manager in a large department store has taught me how challenging a career in retailing can be. Moreover, my AA degree in retailing (including work in such courses as retailing, marketing, and business information systems) will provide your store with a well-rounded associate. Most important, I can offer Wal-Mart's Iowa Falls store more than my two years' of study and field experience: You'll find that I'm interested in every facet of retailing, eager to take on responsibility, and willing to continue learning throughout my career. Please look over my résumé to see how my skills can benefit your store.

I understand that Wal-Mart prefers to promote its managers from within the company, and I would be pleased to start out with an entry-level position until I gain the necessary experience. Do you have any associate positions opening up soon? Could we discuss my qualifications? I will phone you early next Wednesday to see whether we can arrange a meeting at your convenience.

Sincerely,

Glenda Johns

Glenda Johns

Enclosure

The applicant gains attention in the first paragraph.

The applicant points out personal qualities that aren't specifically stated in her résumé.

Knowledge of the company's policy toward promotions is sure to interest the reader.

Even though the last paragraph uses the word *I*, the concern and the focus of the letter are clearly centered on the audience with a "you" attitude.

Writing Application Follow-Ups

If your application letter and résumé fail to bring a response within a month or so, follow up with a second letter to keep your file active. This follow-up letter also gives you a chance to update your original application with any recent job-related information:

Use a follow-up letter to let the employer know you're still interested in the job.

Figure 12.9
In-Depth Critique: Sample
Solicited Application
Letter

Kenneth Sawyer grabs attention by focusing on a phrase used by the employer in a want ad: "proven skills." Sawyer elaborates on his own proven skills throughout the letter, and he even mentions the term in the closing paragraph.

Kenneth Sawyer

2893 Jack Pine Road, Chapel Hill, NC 27514

February 2, 1997

Ms. Angela Clair
Director of Administration
Cummings and Welbane, Inc.
770 Campus Point Drive
Chapel Hill, NC 27514

Dear Ms. Clair:

In the January 31 issue of the *Chapel Hill Post,* your ad mentioned "proven skills." I believe I have what you are looking for in an administrative assistant. In addition to experience in a variety of office settings, I am familiar with the computer software that you use in your office.

I recently completed a three-course sequence at Hamilton College on Microsoft Word and PowerPoint. I learned how to apply these programs to speed up letter- and report-writing tasks. A workshop on "Writing and Editing with the Unix Processor" gave me experience with other valuable applications such as composing and formatting sales letters, financial reports, and presentation slides.

These skills have been invaluable to me as assistant to the chief nutritionist at our campus cafeteria (please refer to my résumé). I'm particularly proud of the order-confirmation system I designed, which has sharply reduced the problem of late shipments and depleted inventories.

Because "proven skills" are best explained in person, I would appreciate an interview with you. Please phone me any afternoon between 3 and 5 p.m. at (919) 220-6139 to let me know the day and time most convenient for you.

Sincerely,

Kenneth Sawyer

Kenneth Sawyer

Enclosure: Résumé

The opening states the reason for writing and links the writer's experience to stated qualifications.

By discussing how his specific skills apply to the job sought, the applicant shows that he understands the job's responsibilities.

In closing, the writer asks for an interview and facilitates action.

Since applying to you on May 3 for an executive secretary position, I have completed a course in office management at South River Community College. I received straight A's in the course. My typing speed has also increased to 75 words per minute.

Please keep my application in your active file, and let me know when you need a skilled executive secretary.

CHECKLIST FOR APPLICATION LETTERS

A. ATTENTION (OPENING PARAGRAPH)

1. Open the letter by capturing the reader's attention in a businesslike way.
   a. *Summary opening.* Present your strongest, most relevant qualifications, with an explanation of how they can benefit the organization.
   b. *Name opening.* Mention the name of a person who is well known to the reader and who has suggested that you apply for the job.
   c. *Source opening.* When responding to a job ad, identify the publication in which the ad appeared, and briefly describe how you meet each requirement stated in the ad.
   d. *Question opening.* Pose an attention-getting question that shows you understand an organization's problem, need, or goal and have a genuine desire to help solve or meet it.
   e. *News opening.* Cite a publicized organizational achievement, contemplated change, or new procedure or product; then link it to your desire to work for the organization.
   f. *Personalized opening.* Present one of your relevant interests, mention previous experience with the organization, or cite your current position or status as a means of leading into a discussion of why you want to work for the organization.
   g. *Creative opening.* Demonstrate your flair and imagination with colorful phrasing, especially if the job requires these qualities.
2. State that you are applying for a job, and identify the position or the type of work you seek.

B. INTEREST AND DESIRE, OR EVIDENCE OF QUALIFICATIONS (NEXT SEVERAL PARAGRAPHS)

1. Present your key qualifications for the job, highlighting what is on your résumé: job-related education and training; relevant work experience; and related activities, interests, and qualities.

2. Adopt a mature and businesslike tone.
   a. Eliminate boasting and exaggeration.
   b. Back up your claims of ability by citing specific achievements in educational and work settings or in outside activities.
   c. Demonstrate a knowledge of the organization and a desire to join it by citing its operations or trends in the industry.
3. Link your education, experience, and personal qualities to the job requirements.
   a. Relate aspects of your training or work experience to those of the target position.
   b. Outline your educational preparation for the job.
   c. Provide proof that you learn quickly, are a hard worker, can handle responsibility, and/or get along well with others.
   d. Present ample evidence of the personal qualities and the work attitudes that are desirable for job performance.
   e. If asked to state salary requirements, provide current salary or a desired salary range, and link it to the benefits of hiring you.
4. Refer the reader to the enclosed résumé.

C. ACTION (CLOSING PARAGRAPH)

1. Request an interview at the reader's convenience.
2. Request a screening interview with the nearest regional representative, if company headquarters is some distance away.
3. State your phone number (with area code) and the best time to reach you, to make the interview request easy to comply with, or mention a time when you will be calling to set up an interview.
4. Express appreciation for an opportunity to have an interview.
5. Repeat your strongest qualification, to help reinforce the claim that you have something to offer the organization.

Even if you have received a letter acknowledging your application and saying that it will be kept on file, don't hesitate to send a follow-up letter three months later to show that you are still interested:

Three months have elapsed since I applied to you for an underwriting position, but I want to let you know that I am still very interested in joining your company.

> I recently completed a four-week temporary work assignment at a large local insurance agency. I learned several new verification techniques and gained experience in using the online computer system. This experience could increase my value to your underwriting department.
>
> Please keep my application in your active file, and let me know when a position opens for a capable underwriter.

Unless you state otherwise, the human resources office is likely to assume that you've already found a job and are no longer interested in the organization. In addition, organizations' requirements change. Sending a letter like this demonstrates that you are sincerely interested in working for the organization, that you are persistent in pursuing your goals, and that you continue upgrading your skills to make yourself a better employee—and it might just get you an interview.

SUMMARY

Before writing a résumé or an application letter, analyze what you have to offer an employer and what you want from a job or career. Then look for employment opportunities.

After you have decided what kind of work you want to do and where you might want to do it, prepare a résumé, a written summary of your qualifications, and organize it to emphasize your strong points. If you need a scannable or electronic résumé, change the format, include a list of key words, and include current language.

A résumé is always accompanied by an application letter, which is a selling piece. Therefore, follow the AIDA plan. The point of writing the letter is to win an interview.

Other types of employment messages are job-inquiry letters, written to get an application form; application forms, which are filled out as completely as possible; and application follow-up letters, written to keep your name on the active list.

COMMUNICATION CHALLENGES AT MOBIL

As a multinational corporation, Mobil receives thousands of résumés from candidates around the world. Henry Halaiko has recently revised the procedures for screening all résumés. Instead of reviewing them at Mobil's headquarters, Halaiko's staff now sorts the résumés and sends them directly to the human resources departments in the functional units that have specific openings. This enables the people who actually do the hiring to evaluate the résumés. Although this method has several advantages, Halaiko is concerned about one possible problem: inconsistency in the evaluation process.

INDIVIDUAL CHALLENGE: To ensure that all Mobil units use similar criteria to screen résumés, Halaiko wants to develop a guideline for evaluating the résumés of graduating students. The guideline will help Mobil's managers identify people who have good work habits, strong communication skills, commitment to personal accomplishment, and leadership potential. However, Halaiko wants to avoid imposing any rigid screening criteria that might arbitrarily eliminate promising candidates. He has asked you to develop the guideline and a one-page memo explaining how to use it. After you have done so, test the guideline by evaluating the résumés of three fellow students.

TEAM CHALLENGE: Henry Halaiko is planning a workshop on writing application letters for a Career Day at a nearby college. He wants to present letters that effectively portray limited work experiences in a positive light. He asks a group of you to draft letters that describe useful work skills and habits learned when (1) one applicant worked part-time as a supermarket cashier, (2) a second applicant worked as a camp counselor, and (3) a third applicant typed envelopes for a mailing service. Explain what employers may find relevant about the skills and habits described in each letter.[24]

CRITICAL THINKING QUESTIONS

1. According to experts in the job-placement field, the average job seeker places too much importance on the résumé and not enough on other elements of the job search. Which elements do you think are most important? Explain.

2. How would you locate information about overseas employment opportunities in general? About job requirements at specific overseas companies? Briefly explain.

3. As an employer, what would you do to detect résumé inflation such as misrepresented job qualifications, salaries, and academic credentials? Please explain.

4. Stating your career objective might limit your opportunities by labeling you too narrowly. Not stating your career objective, however, might lead an employer to categorize you incorrectly. Which outcome is riskier? Do summaries of qualifications overcome such drawbacks? If so, how? Briefly explain.

5. When writing a solicited application letter and describing the skills requested in the employer's ad, how can you avoid using *I* too often? Explain and give examples.

6. How can you make your letter of application unique without being cute or gimmicky? Explain and give examples.

DOCUMENTS FOR ANALYSIS

Read the following documents; then (1) analyze the strengths or weaknesses of each sentence and (2) revise each document so that it follows the guidelines presented in this chapter.

Document 12.A: Writing a Résumé

SYLVIA MANCHESTER
765 BELLE FLEUR BLVD.
NEW ORLEANS, LA 70113
(504) 312-9504

PERSONAL: Single, excellent health, 5′8″, 116 lb; hobbies include cooking, dancing, and reading.

JOB OBJECTIVE: To obtain a responsible position in marketing or sales with a good company.

Education: BA degree in biology, University of Louisiana. Graduated with a 3.0 average. Member of the varsity cheerleading squad. President of Panhellenic League. Homecoming queen.

WORK EXPERIENCE

FISHER SCIENTIFIC INSTRUMENTS, 1995 TO PRESENT, FIELD SALES REPRESENTATIVE. Responsible for calling on customers and explaining the features of Fisher's line of laboratory instruments. Also responsible for writing sales letters, attending trade shows, and preparing weekly sales reports.

FISHER SCIENTIFIC INSTRUMENTS, 1993–94, CUSTOMER SERVICE REPRESENTATIVE. Was responsible for handling incoming phone calls from customers who had questions about delivery, quality, or operation of Fisher's line of laboratory instruments. Also handled miscellaneous correspondence with customers.

MEDICAL ELECTRONICS, INC., 1991–93. ADMINISTRATIVE ASSISTANT TO THE VICE PRES-IDENT OF MARKETING. In addition to handling typical secretarial chores for the vice president of marketing, I was in charge of compiling the monthly sales reports, using figures provided by members of the field sales force. I also was given responsibility for doing various market research activities.

NEW ORLEANS CONVENTION AND VISITORS BUREAU, 1987–91, SUMMERS, TOUR GUIDE. During the summers of my college years, I led tours of New Orleans for tourists visiting the city. My duties included greeting conventioneers and their spouses at hotels, explaining the history and features of the city during an all-day sightseeing tour, and answering questions about New Orleans and its attractions. During my fourth summer with the bureau, I was asked to help train the new tour guides. I prepared a handbook that provided interesting facts about the various tourist attractions, as well as answers to the most commonly asked tourist questions. The Bureau was so impressed with the handbook they had it printed up so that it could be given as a gift to visitors.

UNIVERSITY OF LOUISIANA, 1987–91, PART-TIME CLERK IN ADMISSIONS OFFICE. While I was a student in college, I worked 15 hours a week in the admissions office. My duties included filing, processing applications, and handling correspondence with high school students and administrators.

Document 12.B: Writing an Application Message

I'm writing to let you know about my availability for the brand manager job you advertised. As you can see from my enclosed résumé, my background is perfect for the position. Even though I don't have any real job experience, my grades have been outstanding considering that I went to a top-ranked business school.

I did many things during my undergraduate years to prepare me for this job:

- Earned a 3.4 out of a 4.0 with a 3.8 in my business courses
- Elected representative to the student governing association
- Selected to receive the Lamar Franklin Award
- Worked to earn a portion of my tuition

I am sending my résumé to all the top firms, but I like yours better than any of the rest. Your reputation is tops in the industry, and I want to be associated with a business that can pridefully say it's the best.

If you wish for me to come in for an interview, I can come on a Friday afternoon or anytime on weekends when I don't have classes. Again, thanks for considering me for your brand manager position.

Document 12.C: Writing an Application Message

I saw your ad for a finance major in our paper last week. I hope the position isn't already filled because I'd like to interview for it. I've enclosed my résumé, which includes the work I've done since graduation.

Your ad said you were looking for a motivated person who wouldn't mind traveling. That would be me! I've also done the type of work you mentioned: budgeting, forecasting, and working with information systems. I know quite a bit about computers.

I know you get many résumés and mine is probably not all that special, but there's one thing that sets me apart: I'm friendly and eager to work. My present position is with a Silicon Valley company, which is in financial trouble. I'm afraid my whole division is going to be downsized, so I want to have something lined up in advance.

Could you send me some information about the financial stability of your company and its history of layoffs. I certainly wouldn't want to jump from the frying pan into the fire, so to speak. (Ha.) At any rate, thank you for considering my application and résumé. I hope you call me very soon.

Document 12.D: Writing Application Follow-Up Messages

Did you receive my résumé? I sent it to you at least two months ago and haven't heard anything. I know you keep résumés on file, but I just want to be sure that you keep me in mind. I heard you are hiring health-care managers and certainly would like to be considered for one of those positions.

Since I last wrote you, I've worked in a variety of positions that have helped prepare me for management. To wit, I've become lunch manager at the restaurant where I work, which involved a raise in pay. I now manage a wait-staff of 12 girls and take the lunch receipts to the bank every day.

Of course, I'd much rather be working at a real job, and that's why I'm writing again. Is there anything else you would like to know about me or my background? I would really like to know more about your company. Is there any literature you could send me? If so, I would really appreciate it.

I think one reason I haven't been hired yet is that I don't want to leave Atlanta. So I hope when you think of me, it's for a position that wouldn't require moving. Thanks again for considering my application.

CASES

Thinking About Your Career

CAREER DEVELOPMENT

EMPLOYMENT PREPARATION

1. Taking stock and taking aim: Application package for the right job Think about yourself. What are some things that come easily to you? What do you enjoy doing? In what part of the country would you like to live? Do you like to work indoors? Outdoors? A combination of the two? How much do you like to travel? Would you like to spend considerable time on the road? Do you like to work closely with others or more independently? What conditions make a job unpleasant? Do you delegate responsibility easily, or do you like to take charge? Are you better with words or numbers? Better at speaking or writing? Do you like to be motivated by fixed deadlines? How important is job security to you? Do you want your supervisor to state clearly what is expected of you, or do you like the freedom to make many of your own decisions?

Your task: After answering these questions, consult reference materials (from your college library or placement center) and choose a location, a company, and a job that suits the profile you have just developed. With guidance from your instructor, decide whether to apply for a job you're qualified for now or one you'll be qualified for with additional education. Then, as directed by your instructor, write one or more of the following: (a) a job-inquiry letter, (b) a résumé, (c) a letter of application, or (d) a follow-up letter to your application letter.

CAREER DEVELOPMENT

EMPLOYMENT PREPARATION

2. Scanning the possibilities: Résumé for the Internet In your search for a position, you discover that America's Job Bank is a Web site that lists hundreds of companies advertising on the Internet. Your chances of getting an interview with a leading company will be enhanced if you submit your résumé and cover letter electronically. On the Web, explore <http://www.ajb. dni.us> and <http://www.careersite.com>.

Your task: Prepare a scannable résumé that could be submitted to the site that best fits your qualifications, experience, and education. Print out the résumé for your instructor.

3. Online application: Electronic cover letter introducing a résumé   *Motley Fool* is a "Generation X" online magazine accessed via the World Wide Web. Although its founders and writers are extremely creative and motivated, they lack business experience and need a fellow "X'er" to help them manage the business. Articles in a recent edition included "The Soul of the Dead," about the influence of the Grateful Dead on more than one generation of concert-goers. Other articles deal with lifestyle issues, pop movies, music, and "trends for an old-young generation."

Your task: Write an e-mail message that will serve as your cover letter, and attach your résumé as a file to be downloaded. Address your message to Louis Corrigan, Managing Editor. Try to limit your message to one screen (about 23 lines). You'll need a creative "hook" and reassurance that you are the right person to help *Motley Fool* become financially viable.

Writing a Résumé and an Application Letter

4. "Help wanted": Application for a job listed in the classified section   Among the jobs listed in today's *New Orleans Sentinel* (500 Canal Street, New Orleans, LA 70130) are the following:

Your task: Send a résumé and an application letter to one of these potential employers.

ACCOUNTANT/MANAGER

Supervisor needed for 3-person bookkeeping department. Degree in accounting plus collection experience helpful. L. Cichy, Reynolds Clothiers, 1572 Abundance Dr., New Orleans 70119.

ACTIVIST—MAKE DEMOCRACY WORK

The state's largest consumer lobbying organization has permanent positions (full- or part-time) for energetic individuals with excellent communication skills who are interested in working for social change. Reply Sentinel Drawer 973.

ATTENDANT

For video game room, 4647 Almonaster Ave., New Orleans 70216.

CONVENIENCE FOOD STORE MANAGER

Vacancies for managers and trainees in New Orleans area. We are seeking energetic and knowledgeable individuals who will be responsible for profitable operation of convenience food stores and petroleum product sales. Applicants should possess retail sales or managerial training. Interested candidates mail résumés and salary requirements to Prestige Products, Inc., 444 Sherwood Forest Blvd., Baton Rouge, LA 70815. Equal opportunity employer M/F.

Writing Other Types of Employment Messages

5. Crashing the last frontier: Letter of inquiry about jobs in Alaska   Your friend can't understand why you would want to move to Alaska. So you explain: "What really decided it for me was that I've never seen the northern lights."

"But what about the bears? The 60-below winters? The permafrost?" asks your friend.

"No problem. Anchorage doesn't get much colder than Buffalo does. It is just windier and wetter. Anyhow, I want to live near Fairbanks, which is near the gold-mining area—and the university is there. Fairbanks has lots of small businesses, like a frontier town in the West about 50 years ago. I think it still has homesteading tracts for people who want to do their own building and are willing to stay for a certain number of years.

"Your plans seem a little hasty," your friend warns. "Maybe you should write for information before you just take off. How do you know you could get a job?"

Your task: Take your friend's advice and write to the Chamber of Commerce, Fairbanks, AK 99701. Ask what types of employment are available to someone with your education and experience, and ask who specifically is hiring year-round employees.

INTERVIEWING FOR EMPLOYMENT AND FOLLOWING UP

AFTER STUDYING THIS CHAPTER, YOU WILL BE ABLE TO

- Describe the dual purpose of the job interview
- Explain the steps in the interview process
- Identify and adapt to various types of interviews
- List the types of questions you are likely to encounter during a job interview
- Discuss how to perform well during the three phases of a typical job interview
- Write the six most common types of messages required to follow up after an interview

COMMUNICATION CLOSE-UP AT MICROSOFT

At Microsoft—the world's largest software company—focus, enthusiasm, common sense, ambition, resourcefulness, and good analytical powers could get you a job—but only if you can demonstrate to your interviewer that you actually possess these traits. To do that successfully at Microsoft, explains college recruiting manager Jodi DeLeon, you have to be able to think on your feet.

Like many other high-tech companies that conduct on-campus screening interviews, Microsoft sends employees who are trying to fill specific positions, not human resources specialists. Product managers interview potential product managers; software design engineers interview potential software design engineers. The engineers conducting those interviews may have helped design one or more of Microsoft's famous software products (MS-DOS, Windows 95, Office 97, Excel, PowerPoint, Internet Explorer), so don't try to impress them by saying, "Excel? Oh, I know everything about Excel." You could be in big trouble if your claim isn't true; Microsoft's interviewers like to dream up new questions to challenge such statements. In fact, you can expect technical questions even in the 30-minute screening interviews, where you'll be asked problem-solving questions designed to help you demonstrate whatever your résumé says you do best.

"We're not trying to intimidate or scare people at all," DeLeon explains. "We just want to find out as much as we can." If you do well in the screening interview, you're flown to Microsoft's headquarters in Redmond, Washington, for a full day of interviews. This second round of interviews is to determine whether you're a good "fit" for Microsoft—where the atmosphere may be easygoing, but the brainpower is intense.

DeLeon says Microsoft interviewers avoid the standard questions asked by many campus recruiters because they often elicit overrehearsed answers. Instead, "We just probe really deep." For example, DeLeon might ask students applying for a marketing

Jodi DeLeon

Microsoft conducts on-campus interviews and participates in job fairs. Company representatives look for enthusiasm, excitement, and an ability to think logically. Students who do well in screening interviews are flown to headquarters in Redmond, Washington, for the next round of interviews.

position how they would penetrate their school with more Microsoft products, both at the student level and at the administration level. However, she's not looking for a particular answer. "I look at how they focus their thoughts. I look at the steps they take to get from the beginning to the end. I look at all the resources they pull in, the implications that they think about. Do they ask me questions? Do they need to?"

She's been most impressed by candidates who have walked her through an idea using pen and paper or who have jumped up to sketch on a chalkboard. However, such responses can't be faked. Good interviewers know when you're being genuine or just spouting off some pat, memorized response. "For instance," says DeLeon, "it's fine if you know Excel and admit, 'I think Excel is great, but it would be a lot easier if it had X, Y, or Z.' That's the kind of thing that the Microsoft person has to think about every day. Students shouldn't be afraid to say things like that."

When evaluating candidates, DeLeon asks how they set priorities for all the various projects they're currently working on. That's where demonstrating your ability to juggle school with extracurricular activities can help. She also looks at a student's drive and ambition, resourcefulness, and analytical ability. Good grades help, of course, but she's more interested in how well a person listens to and thinks through what she says.

Although some companies differ, Microsoft doesn't consider it "cool" to dress like your interviewer, who may be in jeans and T-shirt. Dress professionally, DeLeon advises. She adds that thank-you notes help, and follow-up phone calls (made after, not before, a promised answer date) are essential to demonstrate your continued interest in the job. Most of all, avoid attention-getting gimmicks. One of the worst blunders DeLeon ever encountered was a résumé sent in a pizza—and the candidate didn't stop there. "She just went above and beyond good judgment to get her foot in the door here," DeLeon recalls. After the pizza came fortune cookies with her qualifications in them, and then balloons. DeLeon finally had to write and ask her to stop.

The best way to prepare for an interview, suggests DeLeon, is to think about the job itself. "Ask yourself, what have I done in my life that is related to some aspect of this job?" Although that question may never be asked in the interview, your understanding of the answer will shine through every statement you make. Most important, she adds, be yourself and take your chances. "If you feel like you're taking a risk by telling the truth or being honest, you're probably doing the right thing," says DeLeon.[1]

INTERVIEWING WITH POTENTIAL EMPLOYERS

As Jodi DeLeon points out, the best way to prepare for a job interview is to think carefully about the job itself. With the right job, you stand to be happy in your work. Thus it pays to approach job interviews with a sound appreciation of their dual purpose. The organization's main objective is to find the best person available for the job; the applicant's main objective is to find the job best suited to his or her goals and capabilities.

By focusing on your audience, your potential employer, you will learn about the organization you want to work for and the people who will make the hiring decision. Be sure to consider any cultural differences when preparing for interviews, and base your approach on what your audience expects. The advice in this chapter is most appropriate for companies and employers in the United States and Canada.

To be more successful in your employment interviews, you can learn what employers look for, what applicants need to find out, how to prepare for a job interview, and how to be interviewed. But first, what can you expect from the interview process? Is more than one interview required for a particular job? What types of interviews are there? Will you have to take any sort of preemployment tests?

The Interview Process

Various types of organizations approach the recruiting process in various ways, so adjust your job search accordingly. Major corporations like Microsoft hire hundreds of new employees every year, so they take a more systematic approach to recruiting than small local businesses that add only a few new people a year. Table 13.1 (see page 418) contrasts the recruiting procedures of large companies with those of smaller companies and provides tips for increasing your chances of getting an interview with either type of employer. In general, the easiest way to connect with a big company is through your campus placement office; the most efficient way to approach a smaller business is by contacting the company directly.

In either case, once you get your foot in the door, you move to the next stage and prepare to meet with a recruiter during an **employment interview,** a formal meeting during which an employer and an applicant ask questions and exchange information to see whether the applicant and the organization are a good match. Applicants often face a series of interviews.

The Typical Sequence of Interviews

Most employers conduct two or three interviews before deciding whether to offer a person a job. The first interview, generally held on campus, is the **preliminary screening interview,** which helps employers eliminate (screen out) unqualified applicants from the hiring process. Those candidates who best meet the organization's requirements are invited to visit company offices for further evaluation. Some organizations make a decision at that point, but many schedule a third interview to complete the evaluation process before extending a job offer.

Margin notes:

An interview helps both the interviewer and the applicant achieve their goals.

Companies take various approaches to recruiting, depending on their hiring needs. Successful applicants vary their job searches accordingly.

An employment interview is a formal meeting in which employers and applicants ask questions and exchange information to learn more about each other.

Most organizations interview an applicant several times before extending a job offer.

At Microsoft, line managers are responsible for conducting preliminary screening interviews on campus. However, many organizations assign the job to members of their human resources department, who may conduct hundreds of screening interviews each year. Screening interviews are fairly structured, so applicants are often asked roughly the same questions. Many companies use standardized evaluation sheets to "grade" the applicant so that each candidate is measured against the same criteria. Preliminary screening interviews enable an organization to sort through a large number of candidates efficiently, which is a practical necessity when, say, 50 people respond to a help-wanted ad or 50 students sign up for interviews through their campus placement office.

Your best approach to a screening interview is to follow the interviewer's lead. Keep your responses short and to the point. Talking too much can be a big mistake. As pointed out by Sandra Moersdorf, a recruiting manager for Procter & Gamble, "Some people are just motor mouths; they never shut up, and I'd like to be able to ask more than one question in the interview."[2] However, if an opportunity presents itself, emphasize the "theme" you used in developing your résumé. You want to give the interviewer a way to differentiate you from other candidates, and at the same time, you want to demonstrate your strengths and qualifications.

The next round of interviews is designed to help the organization narrow the field a little further. Typically, if you're invited to visit a company, you will talk with several people: a member of the human resources department, one or two potential colleagues, and your potential supervisor. You might face a **panel interview,** meeting with several interviewers who ask you questions during a single session. Your interviewers will try to determine from your answers, actions, and attitudes whether you're right for the job. By noting how you listen, think, and express yourself, they can decide how likely you are to get along with colleagues. Your best approach during this round of interviews is to show interest in the job, relate your skills and experience to the organization's needs, listen attentively, ask insightful questions, and display enthusiasm.

If the interviewers agree that you're a good candidate, you may receive a job offer, either on the spot or a few days later by phone or mail. In other cases, you may be invited back for a final evaluation by a higher-ranking executive who has the authority to make the hiring decision and to decide on your compensation. An underlying objective of the final interview is often to sell you on the advantages of joining the organization.

Because these three steps take time, start seeking interviews well in advance of the date you want to start work. According to experts, it takes an average of 10 interviews to get one job offer. If you hope to have several offers to choose from, you can expect to go through 20 or 30 interviews during your job search.[3] So some students start their job search as much as nine months before graduation. Early planning is even more crucial during downturns in the economy because many employers become more selective when times are tough. Moreover, many corporations reduce their campus visits and campus hiring programs during bad times, which puts more of the job-search burden on you.

> In a typical job search, you can expect to have 20 or 30 interviews before you accept a job offer.

Types of Interviews

Interviews take various forms, depending on what the recruiter is attempting to discover about the applicant. In the **directed interview,** generally used in screening, the employer controls the interview by preparing a series of questions to be asked in a set order. Working from a checklist, the interviewer asks you each question in order, staying within a specific time period. Your answers are noted. Although useful in gathering

> Companies use a variety of interviewing techniques to evaluate various attributes.

TABLE 13.1

RECRUITING PROCEDURES OF BIG COMPANIES VERSUS SMALL COMPANIES: THE BEST WAY TO GET YOUR FOOT IN THE DOOR

	Big Companies	**Small Companies**
Number and type of applicants sought	Consistently hire thousands of new employees each year; have relatively specific hiring criteria, depending on the position; tend to be highly selective	Hire a handful of new people each year, but requirements fluctuate widely depending on ups and downs in the business; may have specific requirements, but are often looking for flexibility, versatility; are often somewhat more open-minded than big corporations about candidate's background
Person or department in charge of recruiting	Handled by human resources or personnel department	Companies at larger end of the small-company scale may have a specialized human resources department, but many depend on line managers to staff their own functions; in really small companies, the founder/top manager makes all hiring decisions
General recruiting and interviewing style	Governed by formal policies and procedures; typically involves series of several interviews on campus and at company facility; approach is generally systematic, well planned, and well financed	Conducted informally on an as-needed basis without a standard procedure; hiring decision may be made after first interview or may drag on for several months; company generally lacks budget/motive for conducting elaborate recruiting programs
Where/how they advertise	Use national and local newspapers, trade journals, campus placement offices, word of mouth	Rely heavily on word of mouth and local newspapers; may post openings at local colleges or at a few colleges whose graduates have specific qualifications

facts, the directed interview is generally regarded as too structured to measure an applicant's personal qualities.

In contrast, the **open-ended interview** is a less formal, unstructured interview with an open, relaxed format. By posing broad, open-ended questions, the interviewer encourages you to talk freely, perhaps even to divulge more than you should. This type of interview is good for bringing out an applicant's personality. However, be careful you don't reveal more than you should. Some interviewers use an open-ended format to test your judgment in professional situations. So avoid rambling on about personal or family problems that have nothing to do with your qualifications for employment, your ability to get along with co-workers, or any personal interests that could benefit your performance on the job. You need to strike a careful balance between being friendly and remembering that you're in a business situation.

One of the latest twists in open-ended interviewing involves asking behavioral or situational questions to determine how candidates would handle real-life work problems. This approach has been used by companies such as Hershey Foods and Scott

	Big Companies	**Small Companies**
Use of employment agencies, search firms	Roughly 60 percent use employment agencies, whereas 40 percent use executive search firms; however, new college graduates are generally recruited directly without help of intermediaries	Agency use varies widely among small companies; cost may be a factor
Responsiveness to unsolicited résumés	Receive hundreds of unsolicited résumés, which typically get less attention than résumés obtained through department's own planned recruiting program; although most companies review unsolicited résumés, they hire a relatively small percentage of candidates who approach them this way; best to send résumé directly to line manager or potential co-worker in department where you want to work	Receive relatively few unsolicited résumés, so they pay close attention to them; however, given limited hiring needs, chances are slim that your résumé will arrive when company has a corresponding opening
Reliance on campus recruiting	Roughly 80 percent rely heavily on campus recruiting programs to fill entry-level professional, technical, and managerial positions; however, most limit their recruiting to a relatively small number of campuses	Companies at large end of small-company scale (500 employees) may have limited campus recruiting programs; the smaller the company, the less likely it is to recruit in this manner, and the fewer schools it is likely to visit
Best way for candidate to approach company	Use campus placement office to schedule interviews with companies that recruit on your campus; if these interviews are by invitation only, send a letter and résumé to company asking to be included on its schedule; if company does not recruit on your campus, call the person in charge of college recruiting, explain your situation, and ask for advice on best way to get an interview	Check with campus placement office; try to make direct personal contact with owner/manager or department head; get names and addresses from chamber of commerce, business directories, or local economic development agency; send résumé and application letter; follow up with phone call

Paper. To determine your managerial skills, the recruiter might ask, "What motivators and disciplinary actions would you use to improve employees' performance?" To test your ability to get along with colleagues, the question might be, "Can you tell me how you handled a particular argument or disagreement that came up among the people you worked with on your last job?"[4]

Another approach to evaluating interpersonal skills is to interview several candidates simultaneously to see how they interact. The Walt Disney Company uses this technique when hiring people for its theme parks. During a 45-minute session the Disney recruiter watches to see how three candidates relate to one another. Do they smile? Are they supportive of one another's comments? Do they try to score points at each other's expense?[5]

Yet another approach, used by such companies as General Electric, Sears, and AT&T, is to ask the candidate to participate in a series of simulated exercises, either individually or in a group. Candidates who'll be working on team projects might be asked to collaborate on a decision or to develop a group presentation. Trained observers evaluate the candidates' performance using predetermined criteria and then advise management on how well each person is likely to handle the challenges normally faced on the job.[6]

Perhaps the most unnerving type of interview is the **stress interview,** an interview designed to see how well a candidate handles stressful situations (an important qualification for certain jobs). During a stress interview you might be asked pointed questions designed to irk or unsettle you. You might be subjected to long periods of silence, criticisms of your appearance, deliberate interruptions, and abrupt or even hostile reactions by the interviewer. Although the late Admiral Hyman Rickover was famous for using such techniques to identify people who could cope with life on a nuclear submarine, many corporate managers believe that stress interviews are inappropriate and unethical.[7]

Interviewing by video is an option that has worked for some job seekers. The University of Tennessee uses a videoconferencing system that allows recruiters to interview students from the Tullahoma campus (some 3-1/2 hours away from the main campus in Knoxville).[8] Some applicants use video "résumés" on CD-ROMs that can be played on office computers. These videos are more like interviews than résumés, and they require the same strategies as interviews. Such video interviews can save you time, showcase your strong personality, and facilitate long-distance job searches. But video interviews entail a risk: Your appearance may jog a negative memory or a dislike that the recruiter is unaware of, or you may encounter discrimination that you'll never know about.[9] Whatever types of interviews you face, if you are successful, you may be asked to take one or more preemployment tests before starting your new job.

Preemployment Testing

Preemployment tests attempt to provide objective, quantitative information about candidates' skills, attitudes, and habits.

Given the high cost of hiring unsuitable employees, more and more companies are turning to preemployment testing to determine whether applicants have the necessary skills and psychological characteristics to handle a particular job. According to a survey by the American Management Association, your chances of being asked to take some form of preemployment test are roughly 1 in 6 if you're applying for a managerial position and 1 in 4 if you're applying for a nonsupervisory job.[10] Even though many of the tests are related to specific job skills such as typing ability, the real growth is occurring in tests designed to weed out dishonest candidates and substance abusers.

Companies are concerned about these issues for good reason. The Commerce Department estimates that employee crime costs U.S. businesses roughly $40 billion a year, not counting the economic loss associated with time spent loafing, taking unwarranted sick days, and handling personal business at the office.[11] Moreover, the National Institute on Drug Abuse reports that 44 percent of all work-force entrants have used illegal drugs within the past year and that 23 percent of all U.S. employees use dangerous drugs on the job.[12] Alcohol abuse alone is responsible for 47 percent of all industrial accidents and 40 percent of all industrial fatalities.[13] Statistics like these are enough to worry any businessperson, particularly given the threat of being held liable for negligent hiring practices if an employee harms an innocent party on the job.

To combat such problems, many employers now require newly hired employees to undergo drug and alcohol testing. Many also administer "honesty" tests, which ask applicants questions designed to bring out their attitudes toward stealing and work habits. As many as 2,500 U.S. companies use handwriting analysis to evaluate candidates' personalities in areas considered necessary for good job performance.[14] (See "Handwriting Analysis: Should It Be Used to Determine Your Employment Potential?") Some companies administer medical and psychological exams, and some of the larger companies

---

FOCUSING ON ETHICS

HANDWRITING ANALYSIS: SHOULD IT BE USED TO DETERMINE YOUR EMPLOYMENT POTENTIAL?

Your résumé looked great, you wore your best suit, you performed with calm and confidence during the interview—the employer has all the information needed to select you as the best candidate for the job. Not so fast. Prospective employers want to know as much as possible about you, and a growing number appear to be using handwriting analysis to find the answers.

Also known as graphology, handwriting analysis involves a search for telltale signs of a person's character and personality in a handwriting sample. According to Pace Graphology, an organization that helps employers screen job candidates, "handwriting reveals abilities, aptitudes, outer personality attributes, and deeper features of the inner character."

In the United States, handwriting analysis is often dismissed as an entertaining trick, something you explore at parties or the county fair. However, it is taken very seriously in some other countries. If you're applying for a job in France, don't be surprised if the employer requests a handwriting sample. As many as 80 percent of French companies apparently screen new hires through handwriting analysis. The figure is 90 percent in Israel. The number of companies using handwriting analysis in the United States is hard to pin down, but one researcher estimates it's about 5 percent, and growing all the time. The Central Intelligence Agency and the American Management Association are among the organizations that have hired graphology consultants to conduct seminars.

This interest in a technique dismissed by many as a gimmick or pseudoscience raises some important questions: Does it really work, and should it be part of the hiring process?

Does Handwriting Analysis Work?

Employers who use graphology/handwriting believe it is another form of communication and that it's more revealing than the things you or your acquaintances say about you. Proponents claim that exhaustive research dating back hundreds of years proves that a person's true nature is revealed in the details of his or her handwriting. A temporary placement firm, Olsten's, has been using graphology for more than 20 years and calls it "shockingly accurate." The president of a California produce distributor claims it is 85 percent accurate.

On the other hand, psychology professor and author Rod Plotnik says that handwriting analysis fails the basic scientific test of validity. It can be *reliable,* he notes—it can deliver consistent answers each time a person is tested. However, to be *valid* the analysis must actually measure what it claims to measure. According to the research Plotnik has reviewed, "graphology has poor validity because little relationship is found between handwriting characteristics and personality traits or job success." However, Pace Graphology maintains that handwriting analysis can reveal personality; it just can't predict the future.

Is Applicant Handwriting Analysis Ethical?

No matter which side you believe, using handwriting analysis in the hiring process is an important ethical issue. Writing in the *Online Journal of Ethics,* Dr. Daryl Koehn asserts that using graphology in employee screening is unethical for two reasons. First, graphology is an invasion of privacy because it reveals things that the person may not want to reveal. Assuming it works, she says, graphology reveals a lot more about a person than an employer has any right (both ethically and legally) to know.

Second, Koehn claims that graphology fails to respect the individuality that is a core value in our culture. She says that the formulaic approach of graphology pigeonholes human beings and removes their ability to communicate one-on-one with an interviewer. And she raises another key question: If a peer group or a teacher encourages a young child to write in a particular style, then is graphology measuring the personality of the peer group, the teacher, or the child?

Don't be surprised if you run into a handwriting test, but make sure you understand what the test means and how the employer plans to use the results.

---

1. Do you agree or disagree with Daryl Koehn that graphology is an invasion of privacy? Why or why not?
2. Would you submit to a handwriting test if a potential employer requested it? If not, how would you explain your choice?

---

are even using gene testing to screen out applicants who may develop expensive and debilitating diseases.[15]

Tests have their critics, of course. Some employers prefer not to go to the extra expense of administering them or feel that educated judgment works just as well. Some applicants question the validity of honesty and drug tests or consider them an invasion of privacy. However, used in conjunction with other evidence, the tests attempt to provide an objective, quantitative measure of applicants' qualifications, which may work to the advantage of both employer and applicant. To protect candidates' interests, employment tests must meet strict criteria of fairness set forth by the Equal Employment Opportunity Commission.

What Employers Look For

Interviewers try to determine what you can do and what kind of person you are.

In general, employers are looking for two things: proof that a candidate can handle a specific job and evidence that the person will fit in with the organization. Employers are most concerned with attitude, communication skill, and work experience.[16] They also care about intelligence, enthusiasm, creativity, and motivation.

Qualifications for the Job

Suitability for the specific job is judged on the basis of
- Academic preparation
- Work experience
- Job-related personality traits

Every position requires specific qualifications. To become an auditor, for example, you must know accounting; to become a sales manager, you must have several years of sales experience. When you're invited to interview for a position, the interviewer may already have some idea of whether you have the right qualifications, based on a review of your résumé. During the interview, you'll be asked to describe your education and previous jobs in more depth so that the interviewer can determine how well your skills match the requirements. In many cases, the interviewer will be seeking someone with the flexibility to apply diverse skills in several areas.[17]

Another consideration is whether a candidate has the right personality traits for the job. A personal interview is vital because a résumé can't show whether a person is lively and outgoing, subdued and low-key, able to take direction, or able to take charge. Each job requires a different mix of personality traits. The task of the interviewer is to find out whether a candidate will be effective in the job.

A Good Fit with the Organization

Compatibility with the organization is judged on the basis of
- Appearance
- Age
- Personal background
- Attitudes and style

Interviewers try to determine more than whether the applicant has the right professional qualifications and personality for a particular job. They also try to decide whether the candidate will be compatible with the other people in the organization. Every interviewer approaches this issue a little differently.

Physical appearance is often a consideration because clothing and grooming reveal something about a candidate's personality and professionalism. IBM, for example, is a conservative firm, so showing up for an interview in blue jeans would probably be a big mistake. Even in companies like Microsoft, where interviewers may dress casually, it's important to show good judgment by dressing (and acting) in a professional manner. Apart from noticing a candidate's clothes, interviewers also consider such physical factors as posture, eye contact, handshake, facial expressions, and tone of voice.

An interviewer might consider age when deciding whether an applicant will fit in with the organization. Job discrimination against middle-aged people is prohibited by law, but if you feel your youth could count against you, counteract its influence by emphasizing your experience, dependability, and mature attitudes.

Some interviewers believe personal background can also indicate how well the candidate will fit in with the organization. So you might be asked about your interests, hobbies, awareness of world events, and so forth. You can expand your potential along these lines by reading widely, making an effort to meet new people, and participating in discussion groups, seminars, and workshops.

Employers may also consider a candidate's attitudes and personal style. Openness, enthusiasm, and interest are likely to impress an interviewer. So are courtesy, sincerity, willingness to learn, and a positive, self-confident style—all of which help a new employee adapt to a new workplace and new responsibilities.

What Applicants Need to Find Out

What things should you find out about the prospective job and employer? By doing a little advance research and asking the right questions during the interview, you can probably find answers to all the following questions and more:

Candidates are responsible for deciding whether the work and the organization are compatible with their goals and values.

- *Are these my kind of people?* Arrange to talk with an employee if you can, and when you go for an interview, observe the interviewer and other employees. Would you enjoy working with them?
- *Can I do this work?* Compare your qualifications with the requirements described in the notice for the job, in the job description on file at the placement office, or by the interviewer.
- *Will I enjoy the work?* To answer this one, you must know yourself and what is important to you. Is the work challenging? Will it give you feelings of accomplishment and satisfaction? Of making a real contribution?
- *Is the job what I want?* You may never find a job that fulfills all your wants, but the position you accept should satisfy at least your primary ones. Will the job make use of your best capabilities? Does it offer a career path to the long-term goals you've set for yourself?
- *Does the job pay what I'm worth?* Is the position comparable to those held by people with qualifications like your own? Is the pay in line with that for similar jobs in the field? By comparing jobs and salaries before you're interviewed, you'll know what's reasonable for someone with your skills in your industry.
- *What kind of person would I be working for?* You can find out quite a bit by watching how others interact with your interviewer (if the interviewer is the supervisor for the position), by tactfully querying other employees, or by posing a careful question or two during the interview. If the interviewer is not your prospective boss, ask who will be and find out her or his job title and responsibilities. Try to learn all you can, because that one person will have quite a bit to do with whether you'll like the job and whether it will lead you somewhere or nowhere.
- *What sort of future can I expect with this organization?* This is a key question to ask during the interview and to research on your own. How healthy is the organization? Can you look forward to advancement? Does the organization offer exciting career opportunities or fast salary improvement? What benefits does the organization offer (insurance, pension, vacation)?

In order to find out the answers to these questions, you'll need to keep your wits about you. The best way to do that is to be prepared before the interview even begins.

How to Prepare for a Job Interview

It's perfectly normal to feel a little anxious before an interview. So much depends on it, and you don't know quite what to expect. But don't worry too much; preparation will help you perform well. Before the interview, do some basic research, think ahead about questions, bolster your confidence, polish your interview style, plan to look good, and be ready when you arrive.

Do Some Basic Research

Be prepared to relate your qualifications to the organization's needs.

Learning about the organization and the job is important because it enables you to review your résumé from the employer's point of view (see Figure 13.1). With a little research, you would discover that Microsoft is moving aggressively into international markets and now operates in 48 countries around the world. You'd also learn that the company is making its largest commitment ever to research and development, enhancing its entire range of products to encompass the Internet.[18] Knowing these facts might help you pinpoint aspects of your background (such as language capabilities and communication skills) that would appeal to Microsoft's recruiters.

The fastest way to learn about a company is by visiting its Web site. If you land an important interview and you need information on a company fast, you can use a Web search engine to find the location of information about mission statements, product descriptions, annual reports, and job listings. The largest companies also post press releases and employee news.[19]

Think Ahead About Questions

Most job interviews are essentially question-and-answer sessions: You answer the interviewer's questions about your background, and you ask questions of your own to determine whether the job and the organization are right for you. By planning for your interviews, you can handle these exchanges intelligently. (See "Sixteen Tough Interview Questions: What to Say When You're Stopped in Your Tracks".)

Practice answering interview questions.

Employers usually gear their interview questions to specific organizational needs, and many change their questions over time. In general, you can expect to be asked about your skills, achievements, and goals; your attitude toward work and school; your relationships with work supervisors, colleagues, and fellow students; and, occasionally, your hobbies and interests. For a look at the types of questions that are often asked, see Figure 13.2 (on page 428). Jot down a brief answer to each one. Then read the answers over until you feel comfortable with each one. You may want to tape-record them and then listen to make sure they sound clear and convincing. Although practicing your answers will help you feel prepared and confident, you don't want to memorize responses or sound overrehearsed. Another suggestion is to give a list of interview questions to a friend or relative and have that person ask you various questions at random. This way you'll learn to articulate answers and to look at the person as you answer.

The questions you ask in an interview are just as important as the answers you provide. By asking intelligent questions, you can demonstrate your understanding of the organization and steer the discussion into those areas that allow you to present your qualifications to peak advantage. More important, you can get the information you need in order to evaluate the organization and the job.

Types of questions to ask during an interview:
- Warm-up
- Open-ended
- Indirect

Before the interview, prepare a list of about a dozen questions, using a mix of formats to elicit various types of information. Start with a warm-up question to help break the ice. You might ask recruiter Jodi DeLeon, "What Microsoft departments usually hire new graduates?" After that, you might build rapport by asking an open-ended question that draws out her opinion—for example, "Do you think the Internet's popularity will affect Microsoft's ability to continue growing?" Indirect questions are another approach. You can get useful information and show that you've prepared for the interview with comments like "I'd really like to know more about Microsoft's plans for handwriting-recognition software" or "That recent *Business Week* article about the company was very interesting." Of course, any questions you ask should be put into your own words so that you don't sound like every other candidate. For a list of other good questions you might use as a starting point, see Figure 13.3 (page 429).

Where to Look for Information

■ *Annual report*	Summarizes year's operations; mentions products, significant events, names of key personnel
■ *In-house magazine or newspaper*	Reveals information about company operations, events, personnel
■ *Product brochures and publicity releases*	Provide insight into organization's operations and values (obtain from public relations office)
■ *Stock research reports*	Help you assess stability and prospects for growth (obtain from local stockbroker)
■ *Business and financial pages of local newspapers*	Contain news items about organizations, current performance figures
■ *Periodicals indexes*	Contain descriptive listings of magazine and newspaper articles about organizations (obtain from library)
■ *Better Business Bureau and Chamber of Commerce*	Distribute information about some local organizations
■ *Former and current employees*	Have insight into job and work environment
■ *College placement office*	Collects information on organizations that recruit and on job qualifications, and salaries

What to Find Out About the Organization

■ *Full name*	What the organization is officially known as (for example, 3M is Minnesota Mining & Manufacturing Company)
■ *Location*	Where the organization's headquarters, branch offices, and plants are
■ *Age*	How long the organization has been in business
■ *Products*	What goods and services the organization produces and sells
■ *Industry position*	What the organization's current market share, financial position, and profit picture are
■ *Earnings*	What the trends in the organization's stock prices and dividends are (if the firm is publicly held)
■ *Growth*	What changes in earnings and holdings the organization has experienced in recent years and its prospects for expansion
■ *Organization*	What subsidiaries, divisions, and departments make up the whole

What to Find Out About the Job

■ *Job title*	What you will be called
■ *Job functions*	What the main tasks of the job are
■ *Job qualifications*	What knowledge and skills the job requires
■ *Career path*	What chances for ready advancement exist
■ *Salary range*	What the organization typically offers and what pay is reasonable in this industry and geographic area
■ *Travel opportunities*	How often, long, and far you'll be allowed (or required) to travel
■ *Relocation opportunities*	Where you might be allowed (or required) to move and how often you might be moved

Figure 13.1
Finding Out About the Organization and the Job

SIXTEEN TOUGH INTERVIEW QUESTIONS: WHAT TO SAY WHEN YOU'RE STOPPED IN YOUR TRACKS

The answers to challenging interview questions can reveal a lot about a candidate. You can expect to face several such questions during every interview. If you're prepared with thoughtful answers that relate to your specific situation, you're bound to make a good impression. Here are 16 tough questions and guidelines for planning answers that put your qualities in the best light.

- *What is important to you in a job?* Mention one or two specific rewards (other than a paycheck) that you desire, such as meeting a challenge, feeling a sense of accomplishment, or knowing that you've made a contribution.
- *Why do you want to work for this organization?* Cite its reputation, the opportunities it offers, or the working conditions. Stress that you want to work for *this* organization, not just *any* organization.
- *Why should we employ you?* Depending on your strengths, point to your academic preparation, job skills, and enthusiasm about the firm. Mention your school or work performance to show that you can learn and become productive quickly. If the job involves managerial responsibilities, refer to past activities as proof of your ability to get along with others and to work as part of a team.
- *If we hire you, how long will you stay with us?* Your answer might be like this: "As long as my position here al-

lows me to learn and to advance at a pace consistent with my abilities."
- *Can we offer you a career path?* Reply that you believe so, but you need to know more about the normal progression within the organization. The answer may be revealing.
- *What are your greatest strengths?* Here's your chance to really shine. Answer sincerely with a summary of your strong points: "I can see what needs to be done, and I do it" or "I'm willing to make decisions" or "I work well with others."
- *What are your greatest weaknesses?* Describing a weakness so that it sounds like a virtue is a good way to honestly reveal something about yourself while showing how it works to an employer's advantage. If you say that you sometimes drive yourself too hard, you can also add that this has been helpful when you've had to meet deadlines.
- *What didn't you like about previous jobs you've held?* State what you didn't like; then discuss what the experience taught you about your own abilities or the workplace. Avoid making slighting references to former employers.
- *How do you spend your leisure time?* Mention a cross section of interests—active and quiet, social and solitary—rather than just one.

Take your list of questions to the interview on a notepad or clipboard. If you need to, jot down the briefest notes during the meeting, and be sure to record them in more detail afterward. Having a list of questions should impress the interviewer with your organization and thoroughness. It will also show that you're there to evaluate the organization and the job as well as to sell yourself.

Bolster Your Confidence

If you feel shy or self-conscious, remember that recruiters are human too.

By overcoming your tendencies to feel self-conscious or nervous during an interview, you can build your confidence and make a better impression. The best way to counteract apprehension is to try to remove its source. You may be shy because you think you have some flaw that will prompt other people to reject you. Bear in mind, however, that you're much more conscious of your limitations than other people are. If some aspect of your appearance or background makes you uneasy, correct it or exercise positive traits to offset it, such as warmth, wit, intelligence, or charm. Instead of dwelling on your weaknesses, focus on your strengths so that you can emphasize them to an interviewer. Make a list of your good points and compare them with what you see as your shortcomings. Remember, too, that all the other candidates for the job are probably just as nervous as you are. In fact, even the interviewer may be nervous.

- *Are there any weaknesses in your education or experience?* Take stock of your weaknesses before the interview. Practice discussing them in a positive light. You'll find that they're minor when discussed along with the positive qualities you have to offer.
- *Where do you want to be five years from now?* Saying you'd like to be president is unrealistic, yet few employers want people who are content to sit still. Your answer should reflect your long-term goals as well as the organization's advancement opportunities.
- *What are your salary expectations?* If you're asked this at the outset, it's best to say, "Why don't we discuss salary after you decide whether I'm right for the job?" If the interviewer asks this after showing real interest in you, speak up. If you need a clue about salary levels, say, "Can you discuss your salary range with me?"
- *What would you do if . . .* This question is designed to test your resourcefulness. For example: "What would you do if your computer broke down during an audit?" Your answer isn't nearly as important as your approach to the problem, and a calm approach is best. You might say, "One thing I might do is . . ." and then give several alternatives.
- *What type of position are you interested in?* Job titles and responsibilities vary from firm to firm. So state your skills instead, such as "I'm good at figure work," and the positions that require these skills, such as "accounts payable."
- *Tell me something about yourself.* Say you'll be happy to talk about yourself, and ask what the interviewer wants to know. If this point is clarified, respond. If not, say how your skills can contribute to the job and the organization. This question gives you a great opportunity to sell yourself.
- *Do you have any questions about the organization or the job?* Employers like candidates who are interested in the organization. This is the time to convey your interest and enthusiasm.

Of course, many other responses might be appropriate, depending on your own circumstances. Just be sure that your answers are sincere, truthful, and positive. Take a moment to compose your thoughts before responding so that your answers are to the point.

---

1. What makes an effective answer to an interviewer's question? Consider some of the ways answers can vary: specific versus general, assertive versus passive, informal versus formal.
2. Think of four additional questions that pertain specifically to your résumé. Practice your answers.

Polish Your Interview Style

Confidence helps you walk into an interview, but the only way you'll walk out with a job is if you also give the interviewer an impression of poise, good manners, and good judgment. One way to develop an adept style is to stage mock interviews with a friend. After each practice session, have your friend critique your performance, using the list of interview faults shown in Figure 13.4 (see page 429) to identify opportunities for improvement. You can even videotape these mock interviews and then evaluate them yourself. The taping process can be intimidating, but it helps you work out any problems before you begin actual job interviews.

Staging mock interviews with a friend is a good way to hone your style.

As you stage your mock interviews, pay particular attention to your nonverbal behavior. In the United States, you are more likely to be invited back for a second interview or offered a job if you maintain eye contact, smile frequently, sit in an attentive position, and use frequent hand gestures. These nonverbal signals convince the interviewer that you are alert, assertive, dependable, confident, responsible, and energetic.[20] Of course some companies based in the United States are owned and managed by people from other cultures. So during your basic research, find out about the company's cultural background and preferences regarding nonverbal behavior.

Nonverbal behavior has a great effect on the interviewer's opinion of you.

Questions About College

1. What courses in college did you like most? Least? Why?
2. Do you think your extracurricular activities in college were worth the time you devoted to them? Why or why not?
3. When did you choose your college major? Did you ever change your major? If so, why?
4. Do you feel you did the best scholastic work you are capable of?
5. Which of your college years was the toughest? Why?

Questions About Employers and Jobs

6. What jobs have you held? Why did you leave?
7. What percentage of your college expenses did you earn? How?
8. Why did you choose your particular field of work?
9. What are the disadvantages of your chosen field?
10. Have you served in the military? What rank did you achieve? What jobs did you perform?
11. What do you think about how this industry operates today?
12. Why do you think you would like this particular type of job?

Questions About Personal Attitudes and Preferences

13. Do you prefer to work in any specific geographic location? If so, why?
14. How much money do you hope to be earning in five years? In ten years?
15. What do you think determines a person's progress in a good organization?
16. What personal characteristics do you feel are necessary for success in your chosen field?
17. Tell me a story.
18. Do you like to travel?
19. Do you think grades should be considered by employers? Why or why not?

Questions About Work Habits

20. Do you prefer working with others or by yourself?
21. What type of boss do you prefer?
22. Have you ever had any difficulty getting along with colleagues or supervisors? With other students? With instructors?
23. Would you prefer to work in a large or a small organization? Why?
24. How do you feel about overtime work?
25. What have you done that shows initiative and willingness to work?

The way you speak is almost as important as what you say.

Like other forms of nonverbal behavior, the sound of your voice can have a major impact on your success in a job interview.[21] You can work with a tape recorder to overcome voice problems. If you tend to speak too rapidly, practice speaking more slowly. If your voice sounds too loud or too soft, practice adjusting it. Work on eliminating speech mannerisms such as *you know, like,* and *um,* which might make you sound inarticulate. Speak in your natural tone, and try to vary the pitch, rate, and volume of your voice to express enthusiasm and energy. If you speak in a flat, emotionless tone, you convey the impression that you are passive or bored.

1. What are this job's major responsibilities?
2. What qualities do you want in the person who fills this position?
3. Do you want to know more about my related training?
4. What is the first problem that needs the attention of the person you hire?
5. What are the organization's major strengths? Weaknesses?
6. Who are your organization's major competitors, and what are their strengths and weaknesses?
7. What makes your organization different from others in the industry?
8. What are your organization's major markets?
9. Does the organization have any plans for new products? Acquisitions?
10. What can you tell me about the person I would report to?
11. How would you define your organization's managerial philosophy?
12. What additional training does your organization provide?
13. Do employees have an opportunity to continue their education with help from the organization?
14. Would relocation be required, now or in the future?
15. Why is this job now vacant?

Figure 13.3
Fifteen Questions to Ask the Interviewer

1. Has a poor personal appearance
2. Is overbearing, overaggressive, conceited; has a "superiority complex"; seems to "know it all"
3. Is unable to express self clearly; has poor voice, diction, grammar
4. Lacks knowledge or experience
5. Is not prepared for interview
6. Has no real interest in job
7. Lacks planning for career; has no purpose or goals
8. Lacks enthusiasm; is passive and indifferent
9. Lacks confidence and poise; is nervous and ill at ease
10. Shows insufficient evidence of achievement
11. Has failed to participate in extracurricular activities
12. Overemphasizes money; is interested only in the best dollar offer
13. Has poor scholastic record; just got by
14. Is unwilling to start at the bottom; expects too much too soon
15. Makes excuses
16. Is evasive; hedges on unfavorable factors in record
17. Lacks tact
18. Lacks maturity
19. Lacks courtesy; is ill-mannered
20. Condemns past employers
21. Lacks social skills
22. Shows marked dislike for schoolwork
23. Lacks vitality
24. Fails to look interviewer in the eye
25. Has limp, weak handshake

Figure 13.4
Marks Against Applicants (in General Order of Importance)

When nonverbal behavior is less of a concern, you can use live chat rooms on the Internet to simulate interviews. For example, by using the chat rooms on America Online, CompuServe, or Prodigy, you can create a private room and invite other Internet users to meet you there for a one-on-one mock interview.[22] You'll be able to practice answering questions, but of course you'll have no way of evaluating gestures, voice, or appearance over the Internet.

Plan to Look Good

When your parents nagged at you to stand up straight, comb your hair, and get rid of your gum, they were right. You can impress an interviewer just by the way you look. The best policy is to dress conservatively. Wear the best-quality businesslike clothing you can, preferably in a dark, solid color. Avoid flamboyant styles, colors, and prints.

Good grooming makes any style of clothing look better. Make sure your clothes are clean and unwrinkled, your shoes unscuffed and well shined, your hair neatly styled and combed, your fingernails clean, and your breath fresh. If possible, check your appearance in a mirror before entering the room for the interview. Don't spoil the effect by smoking cigarettes during the interview. Finally, remember that one of the best ways to look good is to smile at appropriate moments.

Be Ready When You Arrive

For the interview, plan to take a small notebook, a pen, a list of the questions you want to ask, two copies of your résumé protected in a folder, an outline of what you have learned about the organization, and any past correspondence about the position. You may also want to take a small calendar, a transcript of your college grades, a list of references, and your portfolio containing samples of your work, performance reviews, and certificates of achievement. Recruiters are impressed by such tangible evidence of

To look like a winner
- *Dress conservatively*
- *Be well groomed*
- *Smile when appropriate*

Be prepared for the interview:
- *Take proof of your accomplishments*
- *Arrive on time*
- *Wait graciously*

When Natalie Minton interviews potential employees for Texas Instruments in Fort Worth, Texas, she looks for people who communicate well. Part of good communication is being prepared with résumés and work samples; another part is knowing how to look. This graphic designer is showing more than her portfolio: She is also demonstrating her ability to communicate and her concern for a professional appearance.

your job-related accomplishments. In an era when many people exaggerate their qualifications, visible proof of your abilities carries a lot of weight.[23]

Be sure you know when and where the interview will be held. The worst way to start any interview is to be late. Check the route you will take, even if it means phoning the interviewer's secretary to ask. Find out how much time it takes to get there; then plan to arrive early. Allow a little extra time just in case you run into a problem on the way.

Once you arrive, relax. You may have to wait a little while, so bring along something to read or occupy your time (the less frivolous or controversial, the better). If company literature is available, read it while you wait. In either case, be polite to the interviewer's assistant. If the opportunity presents itself, ask a few questions about the organization or express enthusiasm for the job. Refrain from smoking before the interview (since nonsmokers can smell smoke on the clothing of interviewees), and avoid chewing gum in the waiting room. Anything you do or say while you wait may well get back to the interviewer, so make sure your best qualities show from the moment you enter the premises. That way you'll be ready for the interview itself once it actually begins.

How to Be Interviewed

The way to handle the actual interview depends on where you stand in the interview process. If you are being interviewed for the first time, your main objective is often to differentiate yourself from the many other candidates who are also being screened. Say you've signed up to talk with a recruiter on campus, who may talk with 10 or 15 applicants during the course of the day. Without resorting to gimmicks, you need to call attention to one key aspect of your background so that the recruiter can say, "Oh yes, I remember Jones—the one who sold used Toyotas in Detroit." Just be sure the trait you accentuate is relevant to the job in question. In addition, you'll want to be prepared in case an employer such as Microsoft expects you to demonstrate a particular skill (such as problem solving) during the screening interview.

Present a memorable "headline" during a screening interview.

If you have progressed to the initial selection interview, you should broaden your sales pitch. Instead of telegraphing the "headline," give the interviewer the whole story. Touch at least briefly on all your strengths, but explain three or four of your best qualifications in depth. At the same time, probe for information that will help you evaluate the position objectively. As important as it is to get an offer, it's also important to learn whether the job is right for you.

Cover all your strengths during a selection interview.

If you're asked back for a final visit, your chances of being offered a position are quite good. At this point, you'll talk to a person who has the authority to make the offer and negotiate terms. This individual may already have concluded that you have the right background for the job, so she or he will be concerned with sizing up your personality. In fact, both you and the employer need to find out whether there is a good psychological fit. Be honest about your motivations and values. If the interview goes well, your objective should be to clinch the deal on the best possible terms.

Emphasize your personality during a final interview.

Regardless of where you are in the interview process, every interview will proceed through three stages: the warm-up, the question-and-answer session, and the close.

The Warm-Up

Of the three stages, the warm-up is most important, even though it may account for only a small fraction of the time you spend in the interview. Psychologists say that 50 percent of the interviewer's decision is made within the first 30 to 60 seconds, and another 25 percent is made within 15 minutes. If you get off to a bad start, it's extremely difficult to turn the interview around.[24]

The first minute of the interview is crucial.

Body language is important at this point. Because you won't have time to say much in the first minute or two, you must sell yourself nonverbally. Begin by using the interviewer's name if you're sure you can pronounce it correctly. If the interviewer extends a hand, respond with a firm but gentle handshake. Then wait until you are asked to be seated. Let the interviewer start the discussion, and listen for cues that tell you what he or she is interested in knowing about you as a potential employee.

The Question-and-Answer Stage

Questions and answers will consume the greatest part of the interview. During this phase, the interviewer will ask you about your qualifications and discuss many of the points mentioned in your résumé. You'll also be asked whether you have any questions of your own.

As questions are asked, tailor your answers to make a favorable impression. Don't limit yourself to yes or no answers. Be sure you pause to think before responding if you're asked a difficult question. Consider the direction of the discussion, and guide it where you wish with your responses.

Another way you can reach your goal is to ask the right questions. If you periodically ask a question or two from the list you've prepared, you'll not only learn something but demonstrate your interest as well. It's especially useful to probe for what the company is looking for in its new employees. Once you know that, you can show how you meet the firm's needs. Also try to zero in on any reservations the interviewer might have about you so that you can dispel them.

Paying attention when the interviewer speaks can be as important as giving good answers or asking good questions. Listening should make up about half the time you spend in an interview. For tips on becoming a better listener, read Chapter 19. Be alert to nonverbal communication. The interviewer's facial expressions, eye movements, gestures, and posture may tell you the real meaning of what is being said. If the interviewer says one thing but sends a different message nonverbally, you may want to discount the verbal message. Be especially aware of how your comments are received. Does the interviewer nod in agreement or smile to show approval? If so, you're making progress. If not, you might want to introduce another topic or modify your approach.

Bear in mind that employers cannot legally discriminate against a job candidate on the basis of race, color, gender, age (from 40 to 70), marital status, religion, national origin, or disability. Although questions that touch on these areas are not prohibited by federal law, the Equal Employment Opportunity Commission considers such questions with "extreme disfavor."[25] In the course of your interviews, you may be asked questions that are directly or indirectly related to

- Your religious affiliation or organizations and lodges you belong to
- Your marital status or former name
- The names or relationships of people you live with
- Your spouse, spouse's employment or salary, dependents, children, or child-care arrangements
- Your height, weight, gender, pregnancy, or any health conditions or disabilities that are not reasonably related to job performance
- Arrests or criminal convictions that are not related to job performance or that occurred more than seven years ago

How you respond depends on how badly you want the job, how you feel about revealing the information asked for, what you think the interviewer will do with the in-

Paying attention to both verbal and nonverbal messages can help you turn the question-and-answer stage to your advantage.

Think about how you might respond if you are asked to answer unlawful interview questions.

formation, and whether you want to work for a company that asks such questions. If you don't want the job, you can tell the interviewer that you think a particular question is unethical and mention that you plan to contact the proper government agency. You can also simply refuse to answer—which, in many cases, will leave an unfavorable impression on the interviewer.[26]

However, if you want the job (and you don't want to leave an unfavorable impression), you can choose a more tactful approach. You might (1) ask how the question relates to your qualifications for the job, (2) explain that the information is personal, (3) respond to what you think is the interviewer's real concern, or (4) answer both the question and the concern. Of course, if you answer an unethical question, you still run the risk that your answer may hurt your chances, so think carefully before answering.[27]

When a business can show that the safety of its employees or customers is at stake, it may be allowed to ask questions that would seem discriminatory in another context. Despite this exception, if you believe that an interviewer's questions are unreasonable, unrelated to the job, or designed to elicit information in an attempt to discriminate, you may complain to the Equal Employment Opportunity Commission or to the state agency that regulates fair employment practices. To report discrimination on the basis of age or physical disability, contact the employer's equal opportunity officer or the U.S. Department of Labor. Be prepared to spend a lot of time and effort if you file a complaint—and remember that you may not win.[28]

The Close

Like the opening, the end of the interview is more important than its duration would indicate. In the last few minutes, you need to evaluate how well you've done and correct any misconceptions the interviewer might have.

You can generally tell when the interviewer is trying to conclude the session by watching for verbal and nonverbal cues. The interviewer may ask whether you have any more questions, sum up the discussion, change position, or indicate with a gesture that the interview is over. When you get the signal, respond promptly, but don't rush. Be sure to thank the interviewer for the opportunity and express an interest in the organization. If you can do so comfortably, try to pin down what will happen next, but don't press for an immediate decision.

If this is your second or third visit to the organization, the interview may culminate with an offer of employment. You have two options: Accept it or request time to think it over. The best course is usually to wait. If no job offer is made, the interviewer may not have reached a decision yet, but you may tactfully ask when you can expect to know the decision.

If you do receive an offer during the interview, you'll naturally want to discuss salary. However, let the interviewer raise the subject. If asked your salary requirements, say that you would expect to receive the standard salary for the job in question. If you have added qualifications, point them out: "With my 18 months of experience in the field, I would expect to start in the middle of the normal salary range."

If you don't like the offer, you might try to negotiate, provided you're in a good bargaining position and the organization has the flexibility to accommodate you. You'll be in a fairly strong position if your skills are in short supply and you have several other offers. It also helps if you're the favorite candidate and the organization is booming. However, many organizations are relatively rigid in their salary practices, particularly at the entry level. Still, in the United States and some European countries, it is acceptable to ask, "Is there any room for negotiation?"

Conclude the interview with courtesy and enthusiasm.

Be realistic in your salary expectations and diplomatic in your negotiations.

CHECKLIST FOR INTERVIEWS

A. PREPARATION

1. Determine the requirements and general salary range of the job.
2. Research the organization's products, structure, financial standing, and prospects for growth.
3. Determine the interviewer's name, title, and status in the firm.
4. Prepare (but don't overrehearse) answers for the questions you are likely to be asked about your qualifications and achievements, your feelings about work and school, your interests and hobbies.
5. Develop relevant questions to ask, such as what training the organization might offer after employment, what type of management system the firm has, whether its executives are promoted from within, and why the position is vacant.
6. Plan your appearance.
   a. Dress in a businesslike manner, regardless of the mode of dress preferred within the organization.
   b. Select conservative, good-quality clothing to wear to the interview.
   c. Check your clothing to make sure it's clean and wrinkle-free.
   d. Choose traditional footwear, unscuffed and well shined.
   e. Wear a minimum of jewelry, but wear a wristwatch to keep track of the time.
   f. Use fragrances sparingly, and avoid excessive makeup.
   g. Choose a neat, well-groomed, conventional hairstyle.
   h. Clean and manicure your fingernails.
   i. Check your appearance just before going into the interview, if possible.
7. In a briefcase or portfolio, take a pen and paper, a list of questions, two copies of your résumé, and samples of your work (if appropriate).
8. Double-check the location and time of the interview.
   a. Map out the route beforehand, and estimate the time you'll need to get there.
   b. Plan your arrival for 10 to 15 minutes before the interview.
   c. Add 10 or 15 more minutes to cover problems that may arise en route.

B. INITIAL STAGES OF THE INTERVIEW

1. Greet the interviewer by name, with a smile and direct eye contact.

Even if you can't bargain for more money, you may be able to win some concessions on benefits and perquisites. The value of negotiating can be significant because benefits often cost the employer 25 to 45 percent of your salary. In other words, if you're offered an annual salary of $20,000, you'll ordinarily get an additional $5,000 to $9,000 in benefits: life, health, and disability insurance; pension and savings plans; vacation time; or even tuition reimbursement.[29] If you can trade one benefit for another, you may be able to enhance the value of the total package. For example, life insurance may be relatively unimportant to you if you're single, whereas extra vacation time might be very valuable indeed. Don't inquire about benefits, however, until you know you have a job offer.

Interview Notes

Keep a written record of your job interviews.

If yours is a typical job search, you'll have many interviews before you accept a final offer. For that reason, keeping a notebook or binder of interview notes can be helpful. To refresh your memory of each conversation, as soon as the interview ends, jot down the names and titles of the people you met. Next write down in capsule form the interviewer's answers to your questions. Then briefly evaluate your performance during the interview, listing what you handled well and what you didn't. Going over these notes can help you improve your performance in the future.[30] Whenever you need to review important tips, try consulting this chapter's

2. Offer a firm but not crushing handshake if the interviewer extends a hand.
3. Take a seat only after the interviewer invites you to be seated or has taken his or her own seat.
4. Sit with an erect posture, facing the interviewer.
5. Listen for cues about what the interviewer's questions are trying to reveal about you and your qualifications.
6. Assume a calm and poised attitude.
7. Avoid gum chewing, smoking, and other displays of nervousness.

C. BODY OF THE INTERVIEW
1. Display a genuine, not artificial, smile when appropriate.
2. Convey interest and enthusiasm.
3. Listen attentively so that you can give intelligent responses.
4. Take few notes, and expand on key points later.
5. Sell the interviewer on hiring you.
    a. Relate your knowledge and skills to the position you are seeking.
    b. Stress your positive qualities and characteristics.
6. Answer questions wisely.
    a. Keep responses brief, clear, and to the point.

    b. Avoid exaggeration, and convey honesty and sincerity.
    c. Avoid slighting references to former employers.
7. Avoid alcoholic drinks if you are interviewed over lunch or dinner.

D. SALARY DISCUSSIONS
1. Put off a discussion of salary until late in the interview, if possible.
2. Let the interviewer initiate the discussion of salary.
3. If asked, state that you would like to receive the standard salary for the position. (Know the standard salary for the position in your region of the country.)

E. CLOSING STAGES OF THE INTERVIEW
1. Watch for signs that the interview is about to end.
2. Tactfully ask when you will be advised of the decision on your application.
3. If you're offered the job, either accept or ask for time to consider the offer.
4. Thank the interviewer for meeting with you, with a warm smile and a handshake.

"Checklist for Interviews." In addition to improving your performance during interviews, interview notes will help you keep track of any follow-up messages you'll need to send.

FOLLOWING UP AFTER THE INTERVIEW

Touching base with the prospective employer after the interview, either by phone or in writing, shows that you really want the job and are determined to get it. It also brings your name to the interviewer's attention once again and reminds him or her that you're waiting to know the decision. As Jodi DeLeon at Microsoft points out, following up shows your continued interest in the job.

The two most common forms of follow-up are the thank-you message and the inquiry. These are generally handled by letter, but a phone call is often just as effective, particularly if the employer seems to favor a casual, personal style. The other four types of follow-up messages—request for a time extension, letter of acceptance, letter declining a job offer, and letter of resignation—are sent only in certain cases. These messages are better handled in writing, because it's important to document any official actions relating to your employment. However, regardless of your method of communicating, the principles outlined here will help you write better messages.

Six types of follow-up messages:
- Thank-you message
- Inquiry
- Request for a time extension
- Letter of acceptance
- Letter declining a job offer
- Letter of resignation

Thank-You Letter

Express your thanks within two days after the interview, even if you feel you have little chance for the job. Acknowledge the interviewer's time and courtesy, and be sure to restate the specific job you're applying for. Convey the idea that you continue to be interested. Then ask politely for a decision.

Keep your thank-you message brief (less than five minutes for a phone call or only one page for a letter), and organize it like a routine message. Like all good business messages, it demonstrates the "you" attitude, and it sounds positive without sounding overconfident. You don't want to sound doubtful about your chances of getting the job, but you don't want to sound arrogant or too sure of yourself either.

The following sample thank-you letter shows how to achieve all this in three brief paragraphs:

A note or phone call thanking the interviewer
- *Is organized like a routine message*
- *Closes with a request for a decision or future consideration*

> After talking with you yesterday, touring your sets, and watching the television commercials being filmed, I remain very enthusiastic about the possibility of joining your staff as a television/film production assistant. Thanks for taking so much time to show me around.
>
> During our meeting, I said that I would prefer not to relocate, but I've reconsidered the matter. I would be pleased to relocate wherever you need my skills in set decoration and prop design.
>
> Now that you've explained the details of your operation, I feel quite strongly that I can make a contribution to the sorts of productions you're lining up. You can also count on me to be an energetic employee and a positive addition to your crew. Please let me know your decision as soon as possible.

The opening reminds the interviewer of the reasons for meeting and graciously acknowledges the consideration shown to the applicant.

This paragraph indicates the writer's flexibility and commitment to the job if hired. It also reminds the recruiter of special qualifications.

The letter closes on a confident and you-oriented note, ending with the request for a decision.

Even if the interviewer has said that you are unqualified for the job, a thank-you message like that shown in Figure 13.5 may keep the door open. A letter of this type will probably go into the file for future openings because it demonstrates courtesy and interest.

Letter of Inquiry

If you're not advised of the interviewer's decision by the promised date or within two weeks, you might make an inquiry. An inquiry is particularly appropriate if you have received a job offer from a second firm and don't want to accept it before you have an answer from the first. The following inquiry letter follows the general plan for a direct request; the writer assumes that a simple oversight, and not outright rejection, is the reason for the delay:

An inquiry about a hiring decision follows the plan for a direct request.

> When we talked on April 7 about the fashion coordinator position in your Park Avenue showroom, you said you would let me know your decision before May 1. I would still like the position very much, so I'm eager to know what conclusion you've reached.
>
> To complicate matters, another firm has now offered me a position and has asked that I reply within the next two weeks.
>
> Because your company seems to offer a greater challenge, I would appreciate knowing about your decision by Thursday, May 12. If you need more information before then, please let me know.

The opening paragraph identifies the position and introduces the main idea.

The reason for the request comes second. The writer tactfully avoids naming the other firm.

The courteous request for a specific action comes last, in the context of a clearly stated preference for this organization.

After Michael Espinosa's interview with Gloria Reynolds, he sent the following thank-you message.

Figure 13.5
In-Depth Critique: Thank-You Note

MICHAEL ESPINOSA
585 MONTOYA ROAD
LAS CRUCES, NM 88005

January 16, 1997

Ms. Gloria Reynolds, Editor
Las Cruces News
317 N. Almendra Street
Las Cruces, NM 88001

Dear Ms. Reynolds:

Our conversation on Tuesday about your newspaper's opening for a food-feature writer was enlightening. Thank you for taking time to talk with me about it.

Your description of the profession makes me feel more certain than ever that I want to be a newspaper writer. Following your advice, I am going to enroll in an evening journalism course soon.

After I achieve the level of writing skills you suggested, I would deeply appreciate the chance to talk with you again.

Sincerely,

Michael Espinosa

Michael Espinosa

The main idea is the expression of thanks for the interviewer's time and information.

The writer specifically refers to points discussed in the interview. Enthusiasm and eagerness to improve skills are qualities that will impress the interviewer.

The letter closes with a specific and cordial request.

Request for a Time Extension

A request for a time extension follows the plan for a direct request but pays extra attention to easing the reader's disappointment.

If you receive a job offer while other interviews are still pending and you want more time to decide, write to the offering organization and ask for a time extension. Employers understand that candidates often interview with several companies. They want you to be sure you are making the right decision, and most of them are happy to accommodate you with a reasonable extension. Just be sure to preface your request with a friendly opening like the one shown in the following sample letter. Ask for more time, stressing your enthusiasm for the organization. Conclude by allowing for a quick decision if your request for additional time is denied. Ask for a prompt reply confirming the time extension if the organization grants it.

> The customer relations position in your snack foods division seems like an exciting challenge and a great opportunity. I'm very pleased that you offered it to me.
>
> Because of another commitment, I would appreciate your giving me until August 29 to make a decision. Before our interview, I scheduled a follow-up interview with another company. I'm interested in your organization because of its impressive quality-control procedures and friendly, attractive work environment. But I do feel obligated to keep my appointment.
>
> If you need my decision immediately, I'll gladly let you know. However, if you can allow me the added time to fulfill the earlier commitment, I'd be grateful. Please let me know right away.

The letter begins with a strong statement of interest in the job.

The writer stresses professional obligations, not her desire to learn what the other company may offer. Specific reasons for preferring the first job offer help reassure the reader of her sincerity.

The expression of willingness to yield or compromise conveys continued interest in the position

This type of letter is, in essence, a direct request. However, because the recipient may be disappointed, be sure to temper your request for an extension with statements indicating your continued interest.

Letter of Acceptance

A letter of acceptance follows the good-news plan.

When you receive a job offer that you want to accept, reply within five days. Begin by accepting the position and expressing thanks. Identify the job that you're accepting. In the next paragraph, cover any necessary details. Conclude by saying that you look forward to reporting for work.

> I'm delighted to accept the graphic design position in your advertising department at the salary of $1,575 a month.
>
> Enclosed are the health insurance forms you asked me to complete and sign. I've already given notice to my current employer and will be able to start work on Monday, January 18.
>
> The prospect of joining your firm is very exciting. Thank you for giving me this opportunity for what I'm sure will be a challenging future.

The good-news statement at the beginning confirms the specific terms of the offer.

Miscellaneous details are covered in the middle.

The letter closes with another reference to the good news and a look toward the future.

As always, a good-news letter should convey your enthusiasm and eagerness to cooperate.

Acceptance of a job offer is legally binding.

Be aware that a job offer and a written acceptance of that offer constitute a legally binding contract, for both you and the employer. So before you write an acceptance letter, be sure you want the job.

Letter Declining a Job Offer

After all your interviews, you may find that you need to write a letter declining a job offer. The best approach is to open warmly, state the reasons for refusing the offer, decline the offer explicitly, and close on a pleasant note, expressing gratitude. By taking the time to write a sincere, tactful letter like the one shown here, you leave the door open for future contact:

A letter declining a job offer follows the bad-news plan.

> One of the most interesting interviews I have ever had was the one last month at your Durham textile plant. I'm flattered that you would offer me the computer analyst position that we talked about.
>
> During my job search, I applied to five highly rated firms like your own, each one a leader in its field. Both your company and another offered me a position. Because my desire to work abroad can more readily be satisfied by the other company, I have accepted that job offer.
>
> I deeply appreciate the hour you spent talking with me. Thank you again for your consideration and kindness.

The opening paragraph is a buffer.

Tactfully phrased reasons for the applicant's unfavorable decision precede the bad news and leave the door open.

A sincere and cordial ending lets the reader down gently.

The bad-news plan is ideally suited to this type of letter.

Letter of Resignation

If you get a job offer and are presently employed, you can maintain good relations with your current employer by writing a letter of resignation to your immediate supervisor. Make the letter sound positive, regardless of how you feel. Say something favorable about the organization, the people you work with, or what you've learned on the job. Then state your intention to leave and give the date of your last day on the job. Be sure you give your current employer at least two weeks' notice.

A letter of resignation also follows the bad-news plan.

> My sincere thanks to you and to all the other Emblem Corporation employees for helping me learn so much about serving the public these past 11 months. You have given me untold help and encouragement.
>
> You may recall that when you first interviewed me, my goal was to become a customer relations supervisor. Because that opportunity has been offered to me by another organization, I am submitting my resignation. I regret leaving all of you, but I can't pass up this opportunity.
>
> I would like to terminate my work here two weeks from today but can arrange to work an additional week if you want me to train a replacement.
>
> My sincere thanks and best wishes to all of you.

An appreciative opening serves as a buffer.

Reasons stated before the bad news itself and tactful phrasing help keep the relationship friendly, should the writer later want letters of recommendation.

An extra paragraph discusses necessary details.

A cordial close tempers any disappointment.

This letter follows the bad-news plan. By sending one like it, you show that you are considerate and mature, and you also help ensure the good feeling that may help you get another job in the future. Compare your messages to the suggestions in this chapter's "Checklist for Follow-Up Messages" (see page 440).

CHECKLIST FOR FOLLOW-UP MESSAGES

A. THANK-YOU MESSAGES

1. Thank the interviewer in writing within two days after the interview, and keep your letter to one page.
2. If you have no alternative, thank the interviewer by phone, keeping the message under five minutes.
3. In the opening express thanks and identify the job and the time and place of the interview.
4. Use the middle section for supporting details.
    a. Express your enthusiasm about the organization and the job after the interview.
    b. Add any new facts that may help your chances.
    c. Try to undo any negative impressions you may have left during the interview.
5. Use an action ending.
    a. Offer to submit more data.
    b. Express confidence that your qualifications will meet the organization's requirements.
    c. Look forward to a favorable decision.
    d. Request an opportunity to prove that you can aid the organization's growth or success.

B. INQUIRIES

1. Phone or write an inquiry if you are not informed of the decision by the promised date, especially if another organization is awaiting your reply to a job offer.
2. Follow the plan for direct requests: main idea, necessary details, specific request.

C. REQUESTS FOR A TIME EXTENSION

1. Send this type of letter if you receive a job offer while other interviews are pending and you want more time before making your decision.

2. Open with an expression of warmth.
3. In the middle section explain why you need more time and express your continuing interest in the organization.
4. Conclude by allowing for a quick decision if your request for more time is denied and by asking the interviewer to confirm the time extension if it is granted.

D. LETTERS ACCEPTING A JOB OFFER

1. Send this message within five days of receiving the offer. State clearly that you accept the offer with pleasure, and identify the job you're accepting.
2. Fill out the letter with vital details.
3. Conclude with a statement that you look forward to reporting for work.

E. LETTERS DECLINING A JOB OFFER

1. Open a letter of rejection warmly.
2. Fill out the letter with an explanation of why you are refusing the offer and an expression of appreciation.
3. End on a sincere, positive note.

F. LETTERS OF RESIGNATION

1. Send a letter of resignation to your current employer as soon as possible.
2. Begin with an appreciative buffer.
3. Fill out the middle section with your reasons for looking for another job and the actual statement that you are leaving.
4. Close cordially.

SUMMARY

Job interviews have a dual purpose. An organization that invites you to an interview wants to find out whether you're the best person to fill a job opening. Your goal is to find out about the job and the organization so that you can make a decision should the job be offered. In the course of a job search, you'll move through a series of interviews from preliminary screening interview to job offer. Some may be directed interviews, some may be open-ended interviews, and some may even be stress interviews.

You can relieve the anxious and nervous feelings that often accompany interviews by preparing for the steps in the interview process ahead of time. First analyze the organization, the job, and your own qualifications and needs. Then plan answers to the interviewer's likely questions, and devise some questions of your own. Be sure to plan your appearance and take along appropriate material. The interview itself will go more smoothly if you adopt a relaxed style and an enthusiastic attitude.

Follow-up messages to the interviewer, such as thank-you messages and inquiries, may increase your chances of getting a job offer. Other courteous, well-planned employment letters—whether requesting a time extension, accepting an offer, declining an offer, or resigning—also demonstrate that you're a professional.

COMMUNICATION CHALLENGES AT MICROSOFT

Cooking up new questions for interviews has become a favorite pastime at Microsoft (right up there with lunchtime Frisbee games). Says Jodi DeLeon, "You'll often walk down the hall and see a group of technical people bouncing a new idea for an interview question off each other." The challenge is to attract the best and brightest from the nation's campuses, while making sure these candidates will fit in at Microsoft.

DeLeon believes it's important for every applicant to leave the screening interview with a positive feeling toward Microsoft. "They may not get a job here, but they may turn out to be a major consumer of our products." So she advises Microsoft interviewers to be fair and considerate, giving equal time to everyone and allowing candidates time to add information about their qualifications and to ask questions.

INDIVIDUAL CHALLENGE: Microsoft needs communication assistants in the busy Office Products division. If hired, the new employees will help handle public relations for Microsoft Office, Word, Excel, PowerPoint, Access, FrontPage, Project, Schedule+, Publisher, and

Team Manager. The best candidates will know how to organize and write letters, memos, press releases, and possibly advertising copy, but they'll also be innovative in their thinking. DeLeon has come up with a problem-solving question for the campus interviews that she wants to test on you: What are some of the ways you might use written or spoken communications to promote Microsoft's Office software to teachers and administrators? Write your answer just as you would explain it in an interview, drawing on everything you've learned so far in this course.

TEAM CHALLENGE: To test your answers, divide your group so that one member role-plays the job candidate being "interviewed" by the others. Start by posing the problem-solving question. Then, if time allows, ask a few follow-up questions to determine more about the "applicant's" knowledge of good communication principles. Take turns until each of you plays the role of job candidate. This will give you some practice thinking on your feet and also a chance to experience the interviewer's perspective.[31]

CRITICAL THINKING QUESTIONS

1. How can you distinguish yourself from other candidates in a screening interview and still keep your responses short and to the point? Explain.

2. What can you do to make a favorable impression when you discover that an open-ended interview has turned into a stress interview? Briefly explain your answer.

3. Should applicants ask about preemployment testing during an interview? Explain your answer.

4. Why is it important to distinguish unethical or illegal interview questions from acceptable questions? Explain.

5. If you want to switch jobs because you can't work with your supervisor, how can you explain this to a prospective employer? Give an example.

6. If you feel you've gotten off to a bad beginning during a preliminary screening, what can you do to try to save the interview? Explain your answer.

DOCUMENTS FOR ANALYSIS

Read the following documents; then (1) analyze the strengths or weaknesses of each sentence and (2) revise each document so that it follows this chapter's guidelines.

Document 13.A: Thank-You Letter

Thank you for the really marvelous opportunity to meet you and your colleagues at Starret Engine Company. I really enjoyed touring your facilities and talking with all the people there. You have quite a crew! Some of the other companies I have visited have been so rigid and uptight that I can't imagine how I would fit in. It's a relief to run into a group of people who seem to enjoy their work as much as all of you do.

I know that you must be looking at many other candidates for this job, and I know that some of them will probably be more experienced than I am. But I do want to emphasize that my two-year hitch in the Navy involved a good deal of engineering work. I don't think I mentioned all my shipboard responsibilities during the interview.

Please give me a call within the next week to let me know your decision. You can usually find me at my dormitory in the evening after dinner (phone: 877-9080).

Document 13.B: Letter of Inquiry

I have recently received a very attractive job offer from the Warrington Company. But before I let them know one way or another, I would like to consider any offer that your firm may extend. I was quite impressed with your company during my recent interview, and I am still very interested in a career there.

I don't mean to pressure you, but Warrington has asked for my decision within ten days. Could you let me know by Tuesday whether you plan to offer me a position? That would give me enough time to compare the two offers.

Document 13.C: Letter Declining a Job Offer

I'm writing to say that I must decline your job offer. Another company has made me a more generous offer, and I have decided to accept. However, if things don't work out for me there, I will let you know. I sincerely appreciate your interest in me.

CASES

Interviewing with Potential Employers

MANAGEMENT

INTERPERSONAL COMMUNICATION

1. Interviewers and interviewees: Classroom exercise in interviewing Interviewing is clearly an interactive process involving at least two people. So the best way to practice for interviews is to work with others.

Your task: You and all other members of your class are to write letters of application for an entry-level or management-trainee position requiring a pleasant personality and intelligence but a minimum of specialized education or experience. Sign your letter with a fictitious name that conceals your identity. Next polish (or prepare) a résumé that accurately identifies you and your educational and professional accomplishments.

Three members of the class, who volunteer as interviewers, divide equally among themselves all the anonymously written application letters. Then each interviewer selects a candidate who seems the most pleasant and convincing in his or her letter. At this time the selected candidates identify themselves and give the interviewers their résumés.

Each interviewer then interviews his or her chosen candidate in front of the class, seeking to understand how the items on the résumé qualify the candidate for the job. At the end of the interviews, the class may decide who gets the job and discuss why this candidate was successful. Then retrieve your letter, sign it with the right name, and submit it to the instructor for credit.

CROSS DISCIPLINE

INTERPERSONAL COMMUNICATION

2. Internet interview: Exercise in interviewing Using the Commercial Sites Index at <http://www.directory.net>, locate the Web home page of a company you would like to work for. Then within the company, identify a position you would like to apply for. Working with a partner, review each other's company home page.

Your task: Interview your partner in person for his or her chosen position. Take notes during the interview. Now revisit your company's home page, and consider the information generated during your interview. Write a follow-up letter thanking your interviewer, and print it out along with your interview notes for submission to your instructor.

Following Up After the Interview

RETAIL

INTERPERSONAL COMMUNICATION

3. "Dear Mr. Chacon": Follow-up letter to straighten out possible confusion   You have been interviewed for the position of assistant manager of a retail outlet in the In-a-Minute chain, consisting of company-owned stores that sell groceries, some medications, and petroleum products. The chain is successful, with new outlets opening regularly in Missouri, Kentucky, and Tennessee. You would appreciate a chance to join the firm.

During the interview, Roger Chacon asked you several questions about your academic record. Your answers, you feel, were somewhat scattered and left Mr. Chacon with no clear understanding of the courses you've taken, your proficiency in several key areas, or the date you expect to graduate—matters that he seemed most interested in.

Your task: Working with your own record, draft a follow-up letter to send to Mr. Chacon with a copy of your college transcript. Describe what you have accomplished in one or two academic areas. Mr. Chacon is with the human resources department at the corporation's headquarters, 99 Litzinger Lane, St. Louis, MO 63124.

MARKETING

INTERPERSONAL COMMUNICATION

4. A slight error in timing: Letter asking for delay of an employment decision   You botched up your timing and applied for your third-choice job before going after what you really wanted. What you want to do is work in retail marketing with Neiman-Marcus in Dallas; what you have been offered is a similar job with Longhorn Leather and Lumber, 55 dry and dusty miles away in Commerce, just south of the Oklahoma panhandle.

You review your notes. Your Longhorn interview was three weeks ago with the human resources manager, R. P. Bronson, a congenial person who has just written to offer you the position. The store's address is 27 Sam Rayburn Dr., Commerce, TX 75428. Mr. Bronson notes that he can hold the position open for ten days. You have an interview scheduled with Neiman-Marcus next week, but it is unlikely that you will know the store's decision within this ten-day period.

Your task: Write to R. P. Bronson, requesting a reasonable delay in your consideration of his job offer.

CAREER DEVELOPMENT

INTERPERSONAL COMMUNICATION

5. Journey to Long Island City: Letter accepting a good job offer   Today's mail brings you the following letter from Rhonda Frederick, Human Resources Director, Chesterton Ceramics, 3 Chesterton Place, Long Island City, NY 11101:

> We are pleased to offer you the position of chemical technician beginning 60 days from the date of this letter at a monthly salary of $1,650. Please let us know of your acceptance of this position within ten days.
>
> Your work will be given 6-month and 12-month reviews; we offer 4 percent salary increases at these points if the employee's work progress is satisfactory. As was indicated to you in the interview, employee participation in the company pension plan is voluntary during the first full year of employment; after that, participation is required. We will fund your moving expenses up to $850, with 50 percent of this amount sent to you in advance if you desire.
>
> We hope that you will accept this position. Your academic record and experience indicate that you should do well in our laboratories, and you will find that Long Island City provides easy access to Manhattan. We maintain a file of house and apartment listings; if you let me know your housing needs, I will send you whatever information you require.
>
> If you plan to join our pension program during your first year, please let me know so that I can start the paperwork before your arrival.
>
> Enclosed is our check for $232.76, covering your interview expenses.

Your task: Write a letter accepting the job and answering the questions that Ms. Frederick asks.

CAREER DEVELOPMENT

INTERPERSONAL COMMUNICATION

6. Job hunt: Set of employment-related letters to a single company   Where would you like to work? Pick a real or an imagined company, and assume that a month ago you sent your résumé and application letter. Not long afterward, you were invited to come for an interview, which seemed to go very well.

Your task: Use your imagination to write the following: (a) a thank-you letter for the interview, (b) a note of inquiry, (c) a request for more time to decide, (d) a letter of acceptance, and (e) a letter declining the job offer.

REPORTS AND PROPOSALS

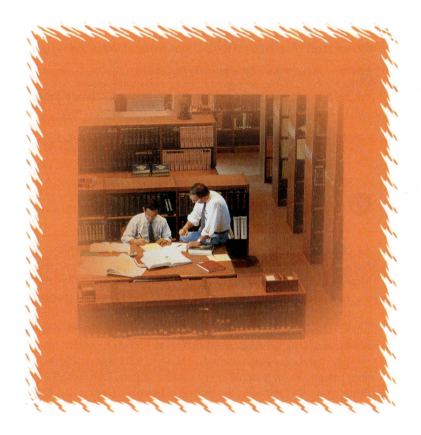

CHAPTER 14

USING REPORTS AND PROPOSALS AS BUSINESS TOOLS

AFTER STUDYING THIS CHAPTER, YOU WILL BE ABLE TO

- Define what is meant by a business report
- Identify the qualities of a good business report or proposal
- Make decisions about report format, style, and organization based on six factors: who, what, when, where, why, and how
- Discuss six general purposes of reports
- Explain how six types of reports are developed
- Weigh the advantages and disadvantages of electronic reports

COMMUNICATION CLOSE-UP AT NARADA PRODUCTIONS

"It comes down to information management," says Wesley Van Linda, president of Narada Productions. Founded in 1983 by Van Linda's partner, John Morey, the Milwaukee-based company is a "small, boutique, specialty label" among the giants of the recording industry, producing contemporary instrumental, New Age, jazz, and electronic music. With annual sales in the range of $10 million to $30 million, Van Linda relies on reports from every department (from sales to shipping) to track performance and to make managerial decisions based on current needs.

Van Linda says his system for using reports was developed by necessity as Narada grew rapidly from a small distribution company into two distinct companies: Narada Productions (which records and sells the music of David Lanz, David Arkenstone, Michael Jones, and other New Age artists) and Music Design (which distributes children's music, meditation music, environmental sounds, and unusual recordings by other record producers). These recordings don't get a lot of radio play, so Narada first sold tapes and CDs through mail-order catalogs, then in gift stores and bookstores (where in-store play helped acquaint customers with the new sounds), and later in local record stores. This market diversity saved the company during a tough economy, but it also made Van Linda's job harder—with so much sales information coming from so many directions.

The reports Van Linda receives are daily sales reports from his staff, monthly sales reports from MCA (which distributes Narada-label recordings), and weekly reports from Soundscan (a computerized cash-register-monitoring service for the music industry from which popularity charts are derived). To put all his reports into perspective, he developed a computerized spreadsheet program. Now he takes a few minutes every day to enter the facts from each of these reports into his personal computer, and at a glance, he can analyze everything from how well a particular artist's recordings are

Wesley Van Linda

At Narada Productions, reports of all kinds are used to track product performance as well as to assemble the information needed for making managerial decisions. Electronic reporting helps Narada president Wesley Van Linda quickly review the mountain of sales information he must sort through.

selling to how long customers have to wait before their phone calls are returned. If something isn't right, he can fix it immediately.

Van Linda believes that good reports and good management go hand in hand, and one key is having enough historical information available to compare with the company's current performance. "If you know where you've been, you can project where you're going, based on the current information," he says. The spreadsheet program allows him to compare current monthly figures with monthly figures dating back seven years. He can quickly determine whether his business is growing or declining and what sort of pattern is developing for the year. He uses this information to make smarter decisions about the company's needs.

"I'm a firm believer in summary reports for a manager," says Van Linda. "Managers should know what's going on in their company but should also allow people the space and flexibility to do the job that they know how to do." For example, when his in-house computer specialist suggested that their system required an upgrade, Van Linda sent her off to do extensive research and analysis so that she could write a report for him, summarizing her findings and backing up her recommendations with hard facts. She spent three months evaluating Narada's current system, meeting with vendors, and working with a financial consultant to develop a justification report for purchasing a new computer system.

Her report opened with a brief overview that Van Linda could read quickly (an executive summary). It included sections on hardware and software selections, diagrams of the new system, information and data flow diagrams and descriptions, a financial impact analysis, and her own conclusions and recommendations. The report was well researched and clearly presented, which helped Van Linda reach the determination he believed was best for the company: He decided the new system would be "overkill."

Although his decision probably wasn't what his computer specialist wanted to hear, Van Linda relied on her expertise to help him make the right choice. "Usually someone who knows how to write well," says Van Linda, "also knows how to think well and clearly and creatively." He believes good reports are essential for keeping a business on track—and good report writers are invaluable.[1]

WHAT MAKES A GOOD BUSINESS REPORT

A business report is any factual, objective document that serves a business purpose.

You may be surprised at the variety of messages that qualify as reports. The term covers everything from a fleeting image on a computer screen to preprinted forms to informal letters and memos to formal three-volume manuscripts. Many reports are delivered orally, as discussed in Chapter 20. In general, however, most businesspeople think of **reports** as written, factual accounts that objectively communicate information about some aspect of the business. Reports can be printed on paper or distributed electronically.

In large part, reports are a managerial tool. Even the most capable managers must rely on other people to observe events or collect information for them. Like Wesley Van Linda, they are often too far away to oversee everything themselves, and they don't have enough time. In addition, they often lack the specialized background required to research and evaluate certain subjects. Thus reports are usually prepared for managers or on their behalf.

When developing a report, the goal is to make the information as clear and convenient as possible. Because time is precious, you tell your readers what they need to know—no more, no less—and you present the information in a way that is geared to their needs. Wesley Van Linda likes to use a computer to compare information from the reports he receives. Some managers like to get their reports orally, face-to-face; but many managers prefer the convenience and permanence of paper reports and, increasingly, of electronic reports distributed over the Internet or corporate intranets.

Select a format, a style, and an organization that reflect the reader's needs.

Regardless of the medium you use for your message, try to keep the likes and dislikes of your readers in mind. As you make decisions about the content, format, style, and organization of the report, your readers' needs are your main concern. Before you write, decide whether to use letter, memo, or manuscript format (see Component Chapter A for details), whether to employ a formal or informal style, and how to group your ideas.

When making decisions about the format, style, and organization of a report, consider its
- *Origin*
- *Subject*
- *Timing*
- *Distribution*
- *Purpose*
- *Probable reception*

When thinking about these issues, ask yourself the following questions and tailor the report accordingly:

- ***Who initiated the report?*** **Voluntary reports,** which are prepared on your own initiative, usually require more detail and support than **authorized reports,** which are prepared at the request of someone else. When writing a voluntary report, you give more background on the subject, and you explain your purpose more carefully. An authorized report is organized to respond to the reader's request.
- ***What subject does the report cover?*** A report's vocabulary and format are dictated by its subject matter. For example, audit reports (that verify an accountant's inspection of a firm's financial records) contain a lot of numbers, often in the form of tables. Reports from the legal department (perhaps on the company's patents) contain many legal terms. When you and your reader are familiar with the subject and share the same background, you don't need to define terms or explain basic concepts. The presentation format, style, and organization are dictated by the characteristics of the subject.
- ***When is the report prepared?*** **Routine reports** are submitted on a recurring basis (daily, weekly, monthly, quarterly, annually), like the reports that Wesley Van

Linda receives at Narada Productions. They require less introductory and transitional material than do *special reports,* nonrecurring reports that deal with unique situations. Routine reports are often prepared on preprinted or computerized forms (either of which the writer simply fills in), or they're simply organized in a standard way.

- *Where is the report being sent?* **Internal reports** (used within the organization) are generally less formal than **external reports** (sent to people outside the organization). Many internal reports, especially those under ten pages, are written in memo format. On the other hand, external reports may be in letter format (if they are no longer than five pages) or in manuscript format (if they exceed five pages).

- *Why is the report being prepared?* **Informational reports** focus on facts; **analytical reports** include analysis, interpretation, conclusions, and recommendations. Informational reports are usually organized around subtopics; analytical reports are generally organized around logical arguments and conclusions. (Chapter 17 explains this difference in greater detail.)

- *How receptive is the reader?* When the reader is likely to agree with the content of the report, the material is presented in direct order, starting with the main idea (key findings, conclusions, recommendations). If the reader may have reservations about the report, the material is presented in indirect order, starting with the details and leading up to the main idea.

As you can see, the origin, subject, timing, distribution, purpose, and probable reception of a report have quite an impact on its format, style, and organization.

HOW COMPANIES USE REPORTS AND PROPOSALS

Reports are like bridges, spanning time and space. Organizations use them to provide a formal, verifiable link among people, places, and times. Some reports are used for internal communication; others are vehicles for corresponding with outsiders. Some serve as a permanent record; others solve an immediate problem or answer a passing question (see "Do You Make These Costly Mistakes When Writing Business Reports?"). Many move upward through the chain of command to help managers monitor the various units in the organization; some move downward to explain managerial decisions to lower-level employees responsible for day-to-day operations. However, any useful report follows common-sense guidelines.

Business reports may appear in many guises, but the reasons for preparing a report provide the best clues about how to organize and write it. Although business reports serve literally hundreds of purposes, most reports are used for one of the following six general purposes:

- To monitor and control operations
- To help implement policies and procedures
- To comply with legal or regulatory requirements
- To obtain new business or funding
- To document work performed for a client
- To guide decisions on particular issues

Each of these purposes imposes different requirements on the report writer (see Table 14.1 on page 452). If your readers need information to oversee an operation, you would present your message differently than if you were contributing to a decision on a complex issue. In other words, the purpose of a report affects its form.

BEST OF THE WEB

Spotlight on Sample Business Reports

So that you can better understand report organization, style, and format, it's helpful to look at a wide variety of actual business reports. To do this, enter the phrase "business reports" in the search window of Cyber411, a parallel search engine that contacts 13 other search engines to do the actual work and then collates the results from all the engines and presents them to you.

Note: In the option windows, choose "phrase" and "fast" for the most effective search.

http://www.cyber411.com

Before you start writing a report, ask yourself why it's being prepared.

DO YOU MAKE THESE COSTLY MISTAKES WHEN WRITING BUSINESS REPORTS?

When you write a report, or even a simple memo, you're creating a permanent record that may be read by an unintended audience. Once the document leaves your hands, it leaves your control. So don't expect the contents to remain confidential. Put nothing in writing that you're unwilling to say in public, and write nothing that may embarrass or jeopardize your employer. Your report or memo may end up as evidence in a courtroom or as a headline in the newspaper:

- The Ford Motor Company was ordered to pay $128 million in damages to a teenager injured in a car accident. One of the most telling pieces of evidence against Ford was an internal memo that acknowledged a design flaw in the Pinto's gas tank but argued against spending the $10 per car required to fix it.
- After TV newscaster Bryant Gumbel wrote a candid memo criticizing a popular co-worker, someone leaked the story to the press, where it was page-one news for days.
- When American Airlines refused to turn over a confidential maintenance report on a plane that crashed and killed 273 people, the company was ordered to pay over $2 million in penalties.

Does this mean you should cover up problems? No, of course not. However, when you're dealing with sensitive information, think about what you're going to write. Maybe the best course is to present the information orally. However, if a written record is required, be discreet. Focus on presenting the information in such a way that it will help the reader resolve the problem. Avoid personal gripes, criticisms, alibis, attempts to blame other people, sugar-coated data, and unsolicited opinions.

To be useful, the information must be accurate, complete, and honest. However, bear in mind that being honest is not always a simple matter. Each of us sees reality a little differently, and we describe what we see in our own way. To restrict the distortions introduced by differences in perception, follow these guidelines:

- ***Describe facts or events in concrete terms.*** It's better to say, "Sales have increased from $400,000 to $435,000 in the past two months" rather than "Sales have skyrocketed." Indicate quantities whenever you can. Be specific.
- ***Report all the relevant facts.*** Regardless of whether these facts will support your theories or please your readers, they are included. Omitting the details that undermine your position might be convenient, but it isn't accurate. Readers will be misled if you hesitate to be the bearer of bad news and leave out unpleasant information.
- ***Put the facts in perspective.*** If you tell readers, "The value of the stock has doubled in three weeks," you are giving only a partial picture. They will have a much clearer understanding if you say, "The value of the stock has doubled in three weeks, rising from $2 to $4 per share

Reports for Monitoring and Controlling Operations

Monitor/control reports help managers find out what's happening in the operations under their control.

One of the most common applications for business reports is to monitor and control the operations of the organization. Because managers cannot be everywhere at once, they rely on reports to find out what's happening to the operations under their control.

Monitor/control reports focus on data. If you're new in an organization, use previous reports of the same type as examples. Your objective is to make your report similar in appearance, style, and organization to the reports your boss is used to reviewing so that he or she can more easily absorb the information.

Pay special attention to the accuracy, thoroughness, and honesty of monitor/control reports. It is tempting to cover up the bad news and emphasize only the accomplishments, but such distortions defeat the purpose of a monitor/control report. In the final analysis, the problems will show up anyway, so you might as well get them out in the open.

Three types of reports used for monitoring and controlling operations are plans, operating reports, and personal activity reports. In general, plans are written for both internal and external audiences. However, operating reports and personal activity reports are usually written for internal audiences only.

on the rumor of a potential merger." Taken out of context, even the most concrete facts can be misleading.

- *Give plenty of evidence for your conclusions.* You can't expect readers to fully understand your conclusions unless you offer substantial supporting evidence. Statements like "We have to reorganize the sales force or we're bound to lose market share" may or may not be true. Readers have no way of knowing unless you provide enough data to support your claim.

- *Present only objective evidence and verifiable conclusions.* Of course, your facts and figures must be checked, and your sources must be reliable. In addition, try to avoid drawing conclusions from too little information. Just because one sales rep reports that customers are dissatisfied with your product doesn't mean that all customers are dissatisfied. Also, don't assume that a preceding event is the cause of what follows. The fact that sales declined right after you switched ad agencies doesn't necessarily mean that the new agency is to blame. Other factors may be responsible, such as the general state of the economy.

- *Keep your personal biases in check.* Even if you have strong feelings about the subject of your report, try to keep those feelings from influencing your choice of words. Don't say, "Locating a plant in Kraymore is a terrible idea because the people there are mostly students who would rather play than work and who don't have the ability to op-

erate our machines." Such language not only offends but also obscures the facts and provokes emotional responses.

---

1. When would you avoid concrete detail in favor of language that is more vague? Would this action be unethical or merely one form of emphasizing the positive?
2. Describe each of the following situations in a single sentence that reveals nothing about your personal feelings or prejudices but that clearly shows your position:
   a. Your competitor has been dumping toxic waste into the local river for years, and local government has ordered your company to share in the cost of cleanup—which accounts for a major part of next year's budget. You're writing a report on the financial impact for your CEO.
   b. An employee in your department has been taking supplies from company storage and selling them wholesale to unsuspecting small businesses—which has cost your department a bundle in overhead expenses. You're writing a brief report on the inventory discrepancy for upper management.
   c. Recent budget cuts have endangered the day-care program at your local branch of a national company, and the effect on employees is grave. You're writing a report for headquarters about the impact on employees.

Plans

One of the most widely used monitor/control reports is the **plan,** a written report that establishes guidelines for future action. Plans come in all shapes and sizes: annual budgets, five-year plans, strategic plans, sales plans, recruiting plans, production plans, and so on. Just about every functional area of a company develops a plan to direct its activities. These plans are generally used by internal audiences to improve organizational coordination, to guide the distribution of money and material, and to motivate employees.

    One particular type of plan, the **business plan,** documents an organization's overall goals and the operational methods it will use to reach those goals.[2] Small businesses, divisions of larger businesses, and nonprofit organizations write business plans for internal use to guide operations and to provide benchmarks for measuring progress toward goals.[3] In addition, top managers frequently send their business plans to external audiences (such as bankers or consultants) when they need financing or are contracting for managerial support services. (For a nonprofit venture, see this chapter's case study, "Bruce Rogow's Business Plan Proposal.") In most cases, business plans (and supporting documents such as marketing plans and engineering plans) are

Plans help managers
- Coordinate the various activities of a business
- Guide the distribution of resources
- Motivate employees

TABLE 14.1

THE SIX MOST COMMON USES OF REPORTS

Purpose of Report	Common Examples	Preparation and Distribution	Features
To monitor and control operations	Plans, operating reports, personal activity reports	Internal reports move upward on a recurring basis; external reports go to selected audiences	**Format:** Standard memo or preprinted form **Style:** Telegraphic **Organization:** Topical **Order:** Direct
To implement policies and procedures	Lasting guidelines, position papers	Internal reports move downward on a non-recurring basis	**Format:** Matches policies and procedures manual **Style:** Fully developed text **Organization:** Topical **Order:** Direct
To comply with regulatory requirements	Reports for IRS, SEC, EEOC, Revenue Canada, Canadian Human Rights Commission, and other industry regulators	External reports are sent on a recurring basis	**Format:** Standardized; perhaps preprinted or electronic form **Style:** Skeletal **Organization:** To follow reader's instructions **Order:** Direct
To obtain new business or funding	Sales proposals	External reports are sent on a nonrecurring basis	**Format:** Letter or manuscript **Style:** Fully developed text **Organization:** Problem-solution **Order:** Commonly direct
To document client work	Interim progress reports, final reports	External reports are sent on a nonrecurring basis	**Format:** Letter or manuscript **Style:** Fully developed text **Organization:** Around sequential steps or key findings **Order:** Usually direct
To guide decisions	Research reports, justification reports, troubleshooting reports	Internal reports move upward on a nonrecurring basis	**Format:** Memo or manuscript **Style:** Fully developed text **Organization:** Around conclusions or logical arguments **Order:** Direct or indirect

considered highly confidential and are released to outsiders very selectively. External readers are frequently asked to sign *nondisclosure agreements* to prevent them from using or sharing anything they read.

Operating Reports

Many managers get detailed information about operations from a management information system (MIS), which captures statistics about everything happening in the organization. In most companies the MIS is computerized, but operating reports can be created manually as well. In either case, someone must decide what facts to gather and in what form to report them. Either system then provides a constant stream of statistics on all operations of the company—sales, production, inventory, shipments, backlogs, costs, personnel—whatever management is interested in measuring. All this information can be given to management in its raw state through computer terminals, printouts, or pages of accounting numbers; or it can be analyzed and reported in paragraph form by staff members.

A management information system comprises many operating reports that provide managers with statistics on company performance.

Personal Activity Reports

In addition to using statistical MIS reports, companies rely on a variety of personal activity reports to keep track of what individuals are doing. Sales-call reports are one example. In a sales-call report, the salesperson summarizes the events that occurred during an appointment with a customer. The report outlines the topics that were discussed and gives the salesperson's evaluation of the prospects for a sale, together with plans for follow-up action.

Personal activity reports keep managers abreast of employees' work-related activities.

Marilyn Ounjian, the owner and chief executive officer of Careers USA, a fast-growing personnel-placement service based in Philadelphia, reads sales-call reports to track her salespeople's effectiveness and to check sales trends in 21 offices spread across 9 states. "I want to know what's happening now," she says. "Salespeople are on the front lines. If they're not growing, we're not growing."[4] Other examples are conference reports, expense reports, performance reviews, recruiting reports, and any other document intended to keep management posted on the activities of individuals.

Case Study: Juan Martinez's Annual Recruiting Report

Juan Martinez is in charge of hiring for a Seattle-based software company. As part of his job in the human resources department, he keeps statistics and writes reports on the company and its employees. Some of the reports are for internal information; others are submitted to the federal government to document the company's compliance with federal employee regulations. One of Martinez's responsibilities is organizing on-campus recruiting interviews. Every spring, company representatives visit several colleges and universities to interview and recruit new employees.

Although headquartered in Seattle, the company has divisions in Europe and Asia, and some of its software products are joint efforts of programming teams in several countries. Language differences can be a barrier to communication, so the company prefers to hire programmers who are fluent in at least one language besides English. "Our most recent product was developed collaboratively by teams in the U.S., Germany, and Japan," says Martinez. "The U.S. team included two members fluent in German and one who is fairly comfortable in Japanese. The team members in Germany and Japan all speak some English, but I believe the development cycle was shortened considerably by the U.S. team's ability to communicate with the other teams in their native languages. Hiring programmers who speak the language of one of our international divisions makes sense in a couple of ways. It conveys a message to these other divisions that they are important to the corporation. It also saves the company money in shortened product development cycles."

Each summer, after college interviewing and hiring is finished, Martinez analyzes statistics about these interviews and includes the information in his annual report to the company's human resources director. The information in the report includes how many students applied, how many were interviewed on campus, how many of those were flown to corporate headquarters for further interviews, and how many were eventually hired. Also included in the report are recruiting costs, broken down by college, company department, and new employee. Besides documenting expenses, the report helps the company determine which institutions are most appropriate for recruiting in the future. (See Figure 14.1.)

Reports for Implementing Policies and Procedures

Policy/procedure reports help managers communicate the company's standards.

Another common use for business reports is to help put company policies and procedures into effect. Like reports for monitoring and controlling operations, reports that implement policies and procedures are necessary because managers cannot be everywhere at once. They need to communicate with employees, but they aren't usually able to talk firsthand with every person in the organization. Written policies and procedures can be read and reread by anyone who needs to know about a particular issue. Some of these documents are preserved as lasting guidelines; others are one-time explanations.

In general, make statements of policies and procedures as broad and simple as possible.

Reports for implementing policies and procedures have a straightforward organization, but they can be difficult to write well. The goal is to strike the right balance between the general and the specific. You may be tempted to answer every question that every possible reader might have, but this approach often creates more confusion than illumination. Try to keep the policies broad and the procedures as simple as possible. Nordstrom, one of the country's most respected retailing chains, has carried simplification to the extreme. Its policy manual is one sentence: "Use your best judgment at all times."[5]

Lasting Guidelines

Some policies and procedures provide lasting "recipes" for how things should be done.

Each organization typically has a collection of lasting policies and procedures. The head of personnel might write a memo announcing a new reimbursement program for employees who continue their education; the head of production might develop guidelines for standardizing quality-control procedures; the office manager might issue a memo explaining how to reserve the conference room for special meetings; the assistant to the president might draft a policy on business ethics for use in international operations. Many companies distribute a written report of their ethics policy to employees on their first day of work. Such reports on policies and procedures then become part of the company's large body of lasting guidelines for doing things a certain way.

Position Papers

Other policies and procedures explain management's position on passing events.

In contrast to lasting guidelines, position papers treat less permanent issues. They explain management's views on particular issues or problems as they arise. An office manager might write a report on the need for extra security precautions following a rash of burglaries in the area. Countless other situations also call for written statements aimed at informing various groups about management's position on special, nonrecurring events.

Because this report includes so much data, Martinez has organized it mostly in tables. Also, he has wasted no time with extensive introductory material, since the human resources director is already familiar with the purpose and general content of the report.

Figure 14.1
In-Depth Critique: Juan Martinez's On-Campus Interview Report (Monitor/Control Excerpt)

MEMO

TO: **Stephanie Brogan**
FROM: **Juan Martinez**
DATE: **July 15, 1997**
SUBJECT: **1997 U.S. On-Campus Recruiting Report**

For the first time in five years, our projections for U.S. on-campus recruiting efforts have surpassed the previous year's. With our first-quarter 1997 sales nearly doubling from first-quarter 1996, we've had to scramble to fill positions in marketing, production, and product development. Programmers have been especially difficult to come by this year, but we have succeeded in filling all crucial positions. Following is a general overview of our U.S. on-campus recruiting efforts:

SUMMARY

Campuses visited	27
Applications received	810
Campus interviews	725
Corporate interviews	540
Offers tendered	216
Offers accepted	198
Total cost	$686,664
Cost per new employee	$3,468

As you can see from the following information, our ratio of hires to corporate interviews is very high, and our ratio of hires to campus interviews isn't bad either.

INFORMATION BY CAMPUS VISITED

Campus	Applications received	Campus interviews	Corporate interviews	Offers tendered	Offers accepted	New hires fluent in another language		
						French	German	Italian
Minnesota Central	57	35	15	13	12	4	2	2
Ohio Southern	43	20	9	7	5	1	0	0
Georgia A&M	23	17	14	12	11	4	3	1

TAILOR YOUR REPORT

WHO: Authorized

WHAT: Annual recruiting report

WHEN: Routine, recurring

WHERE: Internal, upward

WHY: Informational

HOW: Receptive reader

ORGANIZE REPORT
Use direct order, emphasizing the items being monitored. For readers tracking hiring by campus, organize table by campus visited. For readers' ease in tracking results and cost of the entire effort, present a summary first.

CRAFT REPORT STYLE
These reports provide a lot of information as efficiently as possible. Being routine and recurring, they need little introductory and transitional material. Headings establish topics, and major points are often made in lists or visuals.

FORMAT REPORT
Submit these reports on preprinted forms, or write to conform to a standard plan. The high degree of standardization allows readers to compare one report with another.

PREPARE AND DISTRIBUTE REPORT
These routine reports are prepared by various employees for submission to top management. Some high-level readers see similar reports from many employees.

Case Study: William Lawson's Building Access Policy

William Lawson is in charge of security for a medical research lab. Many of the scientists employed there work odd hours—late at night or on weekends—especially when a deadline approaches. During normal working hours, a company receptionist sits at the front desk, greeting everyone who enters the building. At night and on weekends, no one is at the front desk. Employees who need to work during those hours are issued a key to the outside door so that they can get into the building.

Until last year, only ten scientists and technicians worked in the lab, and the receptionist at the security desk recognized them on sight. This year the company has several new government contracts and the number of employees has tripled. Moreover, the new receptionist can't be expected to recognize everyone who works in the lab. So Lawson believed it was time to establish a more formal procedure for entering the building (see Figure 14.2).

Reports for Complying with Government Regulations

Compliance reports explain what a company is doing to conform to government regulations.

The regulation of business by government agencies requires another common type of report: the compliance report. All compliance reports are written in response to regulations of one sort or another, most of them imposed by government agencies. In a sense, compliance reports are monitor/control reports for the government. These reports play a major role in relations between private industry and government agencies. (In fact, government reporting requirements are often a major point of dissatisfaction among business owners and managers because of the time and attention those reports require.)

The regulatory agency issues instructions on how to write compliance reports, and the important thing is to be honest, thorough, and accurate. Remember that these reports are required by law, that they generally serve the public interest, and that you and your company can get into trouble if you're caught being dishonest. Depending on its size and industry, a company may also encounter more specialized reporting requirements. For example, the Food and Drug Administration regulates pharmaceutical companies operating in the United States, while the Interstate Commerce Commission watches over transportation companies that do business across state lines.

Annual Compliance Reports

Many compliance reports are prepared on an annual basis.

Perhaps the most common example of an annual compliance report is the income tax return. Also, both the U.S. Internal Revenue Service and Revenue Canada require a yearly report from every corporation with a pension plan. Another common compliance report that must be prepared every year by companies selling stock to the public is the annual report to the shareholders. This report is required in the United States by the Securities and Exchange Commission (SEC) and in Canada by the provincial securities commissions. Annual reports also serve a public relations function. The second half of annual reports must conform to information requirements laid out by the SEC, but the first half gives corporations a forum for educating and persuading readers about everything from corporate strategy to public misperceptions of company business. In fact, some companies show remarkable creativity and playfulness with their annual reports. Eskimo Pie produced a report in the shape of a popsicle, Comcast had a jigsaw puzzle for a front cover, and Oracle put its annual report on CD-ROM.[6] Many other annual and quarterly documents are required as well, all of which contain financial information related to a company's stock and bond offerings.

Companies that do business with the U.S. government are required to submit a yearly report to the Equal Employment Opportunity Commission describing the

The following excerpt is from the policy report prepared by Lawson. "In the past we got by with a loose, informal policy," explains Lawson. "There were only a few people working in the lab, and everyone knew everyone else. Anyone working in the building would recognize an unauthorized visitor and report the matter to security. Since we have expanded, we need to formalize a policy regarding building access. With so many new faces, it would be too easy for an unauthorized person to walk right in."

Figure 14.2
In-Depth Critique:
William Lawson's Building
Access Policy
(Policy/Procedure
Excerpt)

BUILDING ACCESS PROCEDURES

PURPOSE

The nature of our business demands a balance between free access to lab facilities and security for both equipment and information. One of the implications of our success in recent years is a dramatic increase in the number of employees, so much so that we can no longer rely on an informal approach to security. We've designed this new program to minimize the burden on employees while maximizing security. The program involves four elements:

- Photo ID badges for all employees
- A building access checkpoint
- A procedure for reporting unauthorized or suspicious entry
- Policies regarding personal guests and professional visitors

Employee ID Badges

To make personnel identification both easy and accurate, each employee will be issued a photo ID badge that must be worn at all times while in the building. The Human Resources Department will arrange photo sessions for all current employees. Badges for future new hires will be made during the new-employee orientation session.

Access Checkpoint

During normal working hours, 8:00 a.m. to 5:00 p.m. Monday through Friday, all employees will enter the building through the front door. Employees must show their photo ID badges to the receptionist before entering the lab.

For access after hours, all department heads will identify which employees need to enter the building outside normal working hours. A list of these employees will be kept at the receptionist's desk. After hours and on weekends the desk will be manned by a security guard. Each employee wanting to enter the building must show the guard a valid company ID card and must be included on the authorization list. If the employee is not on the list, the security guard will deny access.

Reporting Unauthorized or Suspicious Entry

We all stand to benefit from improved security, so the company considers it everyone's responsibility to watch for and report unauthorized or suspicious entry to the building.

TAILOR YOUR REPORT

WHO: Voluntary

WHAT: Security policy

WHEN: Special (periodic update)

WHERE: Internal, downward

WHY: Informational

HOW: Receptive readers

ORGANIZE REPORT
Use direct order, emphasizing either the important elements of the policy or the steps in the procedure.

CRAFT REPORT STYLE
These reports establish lasting guidelines or clarify management's position. They are comprehensive, detailed documents, written in paragraph form and containing ample introductory and background information.

FORMAT REPORT
Use the format established in the policies and procedures manual (provided in most large companies), but realize that the variety of subjects covered limits the standardization possible.

PREPARE AND DISTRIBUTE REPORT
These nonroutine reports are prepared by management and distributed to a wide audience throughout the organization. They respond to specific situations and are usually retained (sometimes in a loose-leaf binder) and periodically updated.

composition of their work force and their plans for ensuring full use of qualified women, minorities, and other protected groups. The Canadian Human Rights Commission has similar reporting requirements.

Case Study: Tai Chen's Child-Care Facility Report

Tai Chen operates a child-care facility in her home. To keep her state license current, she must submit regular reports on how her facility meets various state requirements. The report lists such things as the size of the facility, number of bathrooms, whether the outdoor play area is fenced, and the number of staff members.

"I started my daycare center when I had my first child," Chen said. "That way I can stay home with my own children while still earning an income. Before I applied for my license, I had no idea how many regulations apply to child care and how much paperwork is involved. Even though I care for only five children, I have to submit the same reports as a larger facility." Figure 14.3 provides an excerpt.

Proposals for Obtaining New Business or Funding

Proposals are reports written to get products, plans, or projects accepted by outside business or government clients.

A **proposal** is an attempt to get products, plans, or projects accepted by outside business or government clients. Thus it's often called a sales proposal. Such a proposal spells out precisely what the seller will provide under specific terms and conditions. If the proposal is accepted, it becomes the basis of a contract between the buyer and the seller.

Proposals to outsiders are similar to justification reports (which solicit approval of projects within an organization—discussed later in the chapter). However, proposals have some important differences:

- Unlike justification reports, proposals are legally binding, so they are prepared with extreme care. If you propose to sell 500 units at a price of $250 each, you are bound to deliver at that price, come what may.
- Proposals compete with proposals from other organizations; justification reports do not. In a proposal, you try to convince the buyer that your organization is the best source of the product. So you devote a considerable amount of space to explaining your experience, qualifications, facilities, and equipment. Also, to be persuasive, you try to prove that you clearly understand the buyer's problem or need.[7]

The two basic types of proposals are those solicited by a prospective client and those sent without a specific invitation from a prospective client.

Solicited Proposals

A solicited proposal demonstrates that your organization is better qualified than competitors to handle a particular contract.

Solicited proposals are prepared at the request of clients who need something done or want a certain product manufactured. The solicitation, or invitation to bid on the contract, is called a *request for proposal (RFP)*. You respond to an RFP by preparing a proposal that shows how you would meet the potential customer's needs.

Say that the National Aeronautics and Space Administration decides to develop a new satellite. Nobody makes this particular satellite yet; it hasn't been invented. Nevertheless, NASA knows what the satellite ought to do and wants to get the best design at the lowest cost. Typically, NASA first prepares an RFP that specifies exactly what the satellite should accomplish. The agency sends this RFP to several aerospace companies and invites them to bid on the job.

NASA isn't the only branch of the U.S. government that awards contracts on the basis of written proposals. Every agency from the Library of Congress to the Department of Health and Human Services issues RFPs, as do many states, provinces,

Figure 14.3
In-Depth Critique: Tai Chen's Child-Care Facility Report (Compliance Excerpt)

Chen's report is straightforward and takes little time to prepare from the records that Chen keeps.

DEPARTMENT OF HEALTH AND SOCIAL SERVICES
ANNUAL COMPLIANCE REPORT

State law requires that all day-care facilities file this form by March 31 of each year. Failure to complete this form fully and accurately may result in loss of your day-care license. All questions on the form must be answered; if you need to speak with a licensing advisor before submitting the form, call the Department of Health and Social Services at 555-1754.

FACILITY	
Type of facility:	Private home
Owner:	Tai and Hoa Chen
Type and age of building:	Brick, 14 years
Street address:	1625 Grandview
City:	Peterborough
Hours of operation:	7:00 a.m. to 6:00 p.m. Monday through Friday
Square footage of facility:	2,300 sq. ft total; 600 sq. ft used for child care
Play area provided:	600 sq. ft indoor playroom; 2,000 sq. ft fenced backyard
Number of bathrooms: Location of emergency exits:	2.5 total, 1 opening directly off playroom Door leads directly from room to fenced backyard
Number of children cared for:	Five
Age range:	2 to 9 years old
Meals provided:	Breakfast, lunch, snacks
STAFF	
Number of staff:	One
Education level:	B.A. in Elementary Education
Medical training:	Certified in first aid and CPR

TAILOR YOUR REPORT

WHO: Authorized

WHAT: Child-care compliance

WHEN: Routine, recurring

WHERE: External

WHY: Informational

HOW: Receptive reader

ORGANIZE REPORT
Use the direct order dictated by the regulatory agency's instructions.

CRAFT REPORT STYLE
These reports emphasize concise detail, not broad concepts. They need no lengthy introductions or transitions (audience sees hundreds of similar reports). Language is impersonal and legalistic.

FORMAT REPORT
These reports are highly standardized; many are essentially long forms filled out according to instructions from the regulatory agency.

PREPARE AND DISTRIBUTE REPORT
These routine reports are prepared for external readers who review many reports of the same type. They are often recurring documents prepared on an annual basis.

---

counties, and cities. The federal government publishes RFPs both on paper and in electronic format, making it easy for firms to search for contracts of interest.

In addition, private industry awards major contracts on the basis of proposals. The items procured in this fashion range from office equipment to power plants. Whenever a customer is spending a lot of money—especially for something that is unique, sophisticated, and difficult to produce—the managers involved want to know as much as possible about potential suppliers and their ability to deliver the desired solution.

When a company gets an RFP, the managers have to decide whether they are interested in the job and whether they have a reasonable chance of winning the contract. If they decide to submit a bid, the proposal effort begins in earnest. The company reviews the requirements, defines the scope of the work, determines the methods and procedures to be used, and estimates time requirements, personnel requirements, and costs. Then the proposal writers put it all on paper, responding meticulously to every point raised by the RFP—and following the exact format specified by the RFP.[8]

Most proposals are organized in the same way: They begin with an introductory section that states the purpose of the proposal, defines the scope of the work, presents background information, and explains any restrictions that might apply to the contract. The body of the proposal gives details on the proposed effort and specifies what the anticipated results will be. The discussion covers the methods, schedule, facilities, equipment, personnel, and costs that will be involved in the contract. A final section generally summarizes the key points of the proposal and asks for a decision from the client.

Unsolicited Proposals

In an unsolicited proposal, establish the need for your product.

The other major type of proposal, the unsolicited proposal, is initiated by an organization that is attempting to obtain business or funding on its own, without a specific invitation from the client. Unsolicited proposals differ from solicited proposals in one important respect: The client has to be sold on the idea of buying (or funding) something. As a consequence, unsolicited proposals generally spend more time explaining why the client should take action.

Unsolicited proposals vary widely in form, length, and purpose. A university seeking funding for a specific research project might submit an unsolicited proposal to a large local corporation. To be convincing, the proposal would show how the research could benefit the corporation, and it would demonstrate that the university has the resources and expertise to conduct the research.[9] As another example, an entrepreneur seeking funding for a new venture might modify a business plan to create a proposal showing potential investors the return they should expect in exchange for the use of their funds. Of course, such a proposal would try to convince investors of the viability of the new business.

Case Study: Bruce Rogow's Business Plan Proposal

Bruce Rogow was a junior engineering major at San Diego State University when he was first struck by the idea of leading a team of students to design, build, and race a solar car at the World Solar Challenge race across the Australian outback. The race itself would be the least of Rogow's challenges: First he had to convince students and faculty of the project's benefits; then he had to keep them motivated (and working long, hard hours) while he tackled administrative and engineering roadblocks even he couldn't predict.

Ultimately, the SDSU Solar Car Project succeeded, and it drew involvement from various academic departments, dozens of student volunteers, several corporate benefactors, and many news organizations. Rogow challenged science, engineering, and computer students to design and test *Suntrakker* (as the car was named). But he also challenged SDSU's business students to come up with a proposal that would help him raise the support *Suntrakker* required.

"We needed to raise $145,000," Rogow recalls. "And since we had no faculty support in the beginning, we had to have something that would give us credibility. The business plan gave us much more than that."

Bruce Rogow with Suntrakker *in Australia. Rogow wrote his business plan proposal to raise financial and team support for designing, building, and racing* Suntrakker. *The project involved 35 students, who raised $145,000. Their solar car finished 42nd out of 52 cars in Australia's World Solar Challenge race.*

Three students from an entrepreneurship class agreed to work with Rogow on a plan that eventually filled over 70 pages. "The business plan mapped out every detail of our project, from start to finish, and made us look at things we had not considered. It also earned us respect from the faculty and was responsible for a $5,000 donation from our local power company." Rogow now believes the business plan made the difference between "thriving and just surviving" (see Figure 14.4).

With the students' combined skills and Rogow's determined leadership, *Suntrakker* gave an impressive showing in Australia. In fact, the futuristic-looking solar car now tours schools as part of a university recruiting program, and both a book and a documentary film (*Warriors of the Sun*) have been produced about the project. Meanwhile, the Solar Car Project's business plan is still at work, helping students produce a second-generation *Suntrakker* for the next World Solar Challenge.

Reports for Documenting Client Work

Winning a contract often marks the beginning of another stage of writing, as the company must now document its work for the customer. Reports that document client work vary in importance and complexity. Some are a mere formality; others are a vital element in the relationship with the client. These reports may be difficult to write, particularly if the work is not going well or if the customer is unusually demanding. The important thing is to anticipate the reader's needs and to provide the required information clearly and tactfully.

Progress reports to clients are generally submitted on a regular basis. They may be required monthly or weekly, or they may be keyed to phases of the project. In many cases these periodic progress reports are followed by a final report at the conclusion of the contract.

Reports documenting progress on a contract provide all the information the client needs.

Interim Progress Reports

Interim progress reports naturally vary in length, depending on the period covered and the complexity of the contract. Their purpose is to give the customer an idea of the work that has been accomplished to date. These reports are often keyed to the work plan that was established at the beginning of the contract. The writer tells the customer what tasks have been accomplished, identifies problems, and outlines future steps. Important findings are summarized. Making such reports available whenever they're needed can give a company an important competitive edge.

A long or complex project is documented with periodic updates on the progress that has been made.

Figure 14.4
In-Depth Critique: Bruce Rogow's Proposal (Business Plan Excerpt)

Bruce Rogow's business plan is a type of unsolicited proposal, with the benefits up front and the financial information at the close. Detailed and thorough, it includes sections describing the vehicle, the management team, and even "Critical Risks." Appendixes include an organization chart, résumé, design schematics, letters of support, lists of volunteers and contributors, and a telemarketing script. Following is an excerpt from the executive summary (a miniversion of the report that gives busy executives a detailed overview).

TAILOR YOUR REPORT

WHO: Voluntary

WHAT: Business plan

WHEN: Special, nonrecurring

WHERE: External

WHY: Analytical

HOW: Receptive readers

ORGANIZE REPORT
For a business plan intended to raise funds, use the indirect approach to introduce your objectives, justification, and benefits. Include ample details supported by facts, figures, personnel qualifications, endorsements, and so forth.

CRAFT REPORT STYLE
Convey a confident tone by writing thoughtful, well-developed paragraphs. Provide good introductions and transitions, headings, and lists.

FORMAT REPORT
For solicited proposals, use the format outlined in the client's RFP (to ease competitor comparison). Unsolicited proposals can be more creative.

THE EXECUTIVE SUMMARY

Purpose of the Plan

This document will acquaint the reader with three principal areas by

- Showing what the San Diego State University (SDSU) SUNTRAKKER project is
- Showing that the team-oriented, interdepartmental disciplines at SDSU possess the tenacity and know-how to build and race a solar-powered vehicle in the World Solar Challenge Race in Australia in 1993
- Defining and articulating how this business team expects to promote and generate the necessary support, funds, and materials from the student body, alumni, community, and local businesses to seize and execute this opportunity

Project Profile

The SUNTRAKKER Solar Car Project was conceived in July of 1990 when a small group of San Diego State University engineering students, motivated by the successes of the General Motors Sunrayce, committed themselves to designing and building a superior solar-powered vehicle to compete in the World Solar Challenge.

From modest beginnings, the SUNTRAKKER project quickly evolved into a cross-disciplinary educational effort encompassing students from many colleges of San Diego State University. The Project has provided student participants and volunteers with valuable real-life experiences, and brought them together in an effort that benefits not only the students and the university but also the environment.

Sponsors of this project are not only contributing to the success of the overall SUNTRAKKER project but will enhance their goodwill, advertising, and name promotion by association with the project. In addition, the SUNTRAKKER offers a unique opportunity for companies that can donate parts and accessories to showcase their name and field test their products in this highly publicized international contest.

Figure 14.4
(Continued)

2

The Nature and Value of the Product

The explicit purpose of the project is to design, build, test, and race a world-class solar-powered car with the express purpose of spurring the technological development of energy efficient vehicles. While winning the World Solar Challenge is the explicit focus of the project, the implicit goal is to promote the ongoing technological research in the field of alternative energy sources, with a view toward conserving the earth's precious nonrenewable natural resources and encouraging international cooperation.

Competitions such as the World Solar Challenge are catalysts for innovation; they provide focus and expand our perspectives beyond the present technology horizon in many different disciplines. The competition stimulates development of seemingly "impractical" vehicles, yet actually promotes interest and involvement in real-life educational and practical experiences culminating in tangible benefits to the global community. Futuristic and evolutionary projects such as the SUNTRAKKER provide a stimulus to researchers and forward-thinkers to strive toward the common goal of making alternative energy sources a viable reality.

Form of Organization

The SDSU SUNTRAKKER project has been founded as a tax-exempt, nonprofit student organization. The organization's primary purpose is to build the SUNTRAKKER and to represent SDSU in the World Solar Challenge Race in 1993.

The SUNTRAKKER project is organized by function with directors of marketing, design, production, logistics, public relations, and finance. Together, the departments compose the management review committee in charge of all activities. Each department director reports to the project manager, Bruce Rogow. In turn, Mr. Rogow, who is responsible for coordinating the whole team effort, reports to a board of advisors. The advisory board, headed by Dr. William Guentzler, oversees the project and acts as a resource think tank to assist in critical problem solving. (See Appendix A for an organizational chart of the SUNTRAKKER project.)

Growth Trend of Market

Technology developed from the SUNTRAKKER project has direct

PREPARE AND DISTRIBUTE REPORT

Business plans may be prepared for external and internal readers. Not usually compared with competing plans (as are solicited proposals or bids), business plans must still motivate readers to invest or contribute. Many businesses periodically update their plans as their objectives change and as they seek funding from new sources.

(continued)

Final Reports

Final reports are generally more elaborate than interim reports and serve as a permanent record of what was accomplished. They focus on results rather than progress. They deal with what was discovered, not with how the work got done.

At the end of the project, a final report provides a wrap-up of results.

Case Study: Carlyce Johnson's Progress Report

Carlyce Johnson runs the office for her family's landscaping business. She works with a landscape architect to design landscaping for homes and businesses. The jobs vary from replanting a few beds to new installation of thousands of square feet of lawn and

Figure 14.4
(Continued)

3

applicability to the coming hybrid electric and solar-powered vehicle markets throughout the world, especially here in Southern
California. Because of massive pollution problems and rising
population growth rates, transportation needs mandate that alternative energy sources be found for the fossil-fueled emissions
vehicles now in popular use.

In many areas of California, pollution has become the driving
factor in the search for alternative vehicle power sources. The
South Coast Air Quality Management District, encompassing the
greater Southern California area, has enacted a plan to replace
40 percent of gasoline-powered vehicles now operating in metropolitan areas with nonemissions vehicles. The plan directs that
government and commercial fleets greater than 15 vehicles be
required to buy alternative powered vehicles if they want to increase their fleet size.

beds. Each customer must approve the design before installation can begin, and
Johnson is responsible for monitoring and reporting progress on every job. For an excerpt from one of Johnson's interim progress reports, see Figure 14.5.

Reports for Guiding Decisions

Reports that help managers make decisions about problems and opportunities are especially interesting to write.

In many respects, the most interesting business reports are those that help the managers
in your organization make major decisions. Before responding to problems or opportunities, most managers study the pros and cons of alternatives. For this, they rely on
reports from lower-level staff members that provide information, analyses, and recommendations. Thus decision-oriented reports require a strong foundation of facts combined with good insight and excellent communication skills on the part of the writer.
When you prepare one of these reports, you have the chance to present your skills to
top management. You naturally want to give these assignments your best effort.

Although decision-oriented reports are extremely varied, all of them tend to have
a "should we or shouldn't we" quality: Should we expand into this market? Should we
reorganize the research department? Should we invest in new equipment? Should we
close this plant? Should we make Minoru Yoshida a vice president? Because people
performing the various functions of a company make various kinds of decisions, they
require various types of decision-oriented reports. Some of the more common types are
research reports, justification reports, and troubleshooting reports.

Research Reports

Research reports provide management with background information and analysis of options.

People in management rely heavily on research reports, which analyze the pros and
cons of various actions. The question may be whether to launch a new product, expand
into a new territory, change the pricing strategy, withdraw from a business venture,
redesign a product, or acquire another company. At Narada Productions, Wesley Van
Linda used his computer specialist's research report to help reach a decision about investing in a new computer system.

When making these and similar decisions, managers need both basic information
and analysis of the various options. The research report might cover supply and

Figure 14.5
*In-Depth Critique:
Carlyce Johnson's
Progress Report (Interim
Progress Excerpt)*

Johnson explains, "Our landscaping jobs vary in length from part of a day to several months. Often the only report required is a short final report sent to the customer with the billing for the job. For longer jobs, I send the customer weekly or monthly progress reports. The reports can vary from a single page to 20 pages, depending on the complexity of the installation."

Johnson Landscaping

1500 Dakota, Seattle, WA 98105 • (206) 745–8636 / Fax: 745–6361

May 31, 1997

Steve Gamvrellis, Facilities Manager
United Food Processing
9000 235th St. SW
Everett, WA 98204

Dear Mr. Gamvrellis:

This report will bring you up to date on the landscaping done for your company by Johnson Landscaping during the month of May 1996.

Ground Preparation and Sprinkler System Installation

Initial ground preparation is complete. We cleared, tilled, leveled, and raked 25,000 square feet for lawn and beds. Installation of the sprinkler system for 15,000 square feet of lawn and beds was completed on May 20. The system includes an automatic timer. The entire area was roped off to prevent foot traffic.

Bed Planting

From May 21 to May 30, shrubs and ornamental perennials were planted in 7,000 square feet of beds. Beds were prepared for 3,000 square feet of annuals.

Problem Areas

We've resolved the flooding problem discovered last month near the south end of the shipping and receiving dock. It appears that an old plumbing repair had begun to come apart under the employee cafeteria, causing water to flow under the building and occasionally flood a small portion of the new lawn area. The problem has been fixed.

Unfortunately, we have uncovered a potential problem in several of the perennial borders we've created along the east side of the main building. A series of soil samples indicates an extremely high level of acidity, much higher than would occur under natural

---

TAILOR YOUR REPORT

WHO: Authorized

WHAT: Interim progress

WHEN: Nonrecurring series

WHERE: External

WHY: Analytical

HOW: Receptive readers

ORGANIZE REPORT

For interim progress reports, use direct order, emphasizing what has been accomplished during the reporting period. Main headings correspond to the tasks performed. In the final section, outline plans for the coming period. For final reports, focus on results rather than progress.

CRAFT REPORT STYLE

Use a formal style. Interim reports need less attention to introductions and transitions than final reports, which are lasting records covering the contract.

FORMAT REPORT

Interim reports are often in letter format and tend to be brief. Final reports are generally longer and often in manuscript form.

PREPARE AND DISTRIBUTE REPORT

These reports are written for outsiders and are submitted over the life of a contract. As many as five or six progress reports are followed by a final report.

(continued)

Figure 14.5
(Continued)

Mr. Steve Gamvrellis, May 31, 1997, Page 2

conditions. We suspect that the problem may have been caused by a small chemical spill at some point in the past. We'll try to resolve the problem next month, and I'll contact you if the solution to this problem is likely to affect your budget planning.

Plans for June
1. We'll distribute beauty bark and plant remaining annuals after the lawn is sufficiently established.
2. We'll resolve the soil quality issue in the perennial bed and make soil amendments as needed.
3. We'll monitor and adjust the automated sprinkling system to ensure adequate watering while keeping water usage to an absolute minimum, as you requested last month.

demand, growth projections, competitor profiles, and company strengths and weaknesses. If the report is prepared on a computer, it might include a financial model that allows managers to compare various scenarios by plugging in different assumptions and projections.

Justification Reports

A justification report is a proposal to upper-level management from lower- or middle-level management.

Another common type of decision-oriented report is the justification report (or internal proposal), which is used to persuade top management to approve a proposed investment or project. The writer might want to build a new plant, buy some new production equipment, or automate the warehouse system. Although many justification reports deal with the acquisition of tangible assets, others do not. The proposed project might be the reorganization of a department, the revision of recruiting procedures, a change in the company's training programs, the redesign of the information storage and retrieval system, or any one of hundreds of other ideas for improving the operations of a company that do not require the addition of physical assets. When preparing such documents, managers explain why the project is needed, what it will involve, how much it will cost, and what the benefits will be.

A capital appropriation request is a specific type of justification report that deals with a request for equipment or facilities. Most capital appropriation requests are aimed at justifying the investment from a financial standpoint. In many organizations these requests are submitted on a standardized form so that all projects can be evaluated according to the same financial criteria.

Justification reports vary widely in style and format. Some are brief informal memos; others are lengthy, formal documents in manuscript format.

Troubleshooting Reports

Troubleshooting reports analyze problems and propose solutions.

Troubleshooting reports are another common decision-oriented document prepared for submission to top management. Whenever a problem exists, somebody has to investigate it and propose a solution. The vehicle for communicating this analysis is the troubleshooting report. Regardless of the specific problem at hand, these reports deal with the same basic questions: How did this problem arise, what's the extent of the damage, and what can we do about it? These reports usually start with some background information on the problem. Then they analyze alternative solutions and recommend the best approach.

Case Study: Shandel Cohen's Justification Report

Shandel Cohen manages the customer response section of the marketing department for a Midwest personal computer manufacturer. Her section is responsible for sending out product information requested by customers and the field sales force.

Over the last two years the company has introduced a new line of computers and several upgrades to existing lines. Cohen has observed that the demand for information fluctuates significantly, with greater demand when a new product is released and diminishing demand as the product matures. This varying demand means drastic changes in her section's work load.

"It seems that in our unit, it's either feast or famine. We either have more work than we can possibly handle, or we don't have enough to keep us busy. I don't want to get into a hiring-and-firing cycle to deal with the fluctuating work load."

Cohen is also concerned about the amount of printed material that is discarded when products are upgraded or replaced. She believes she has found a viable solution to both problems (see Figure 14.6).

Because decision-oriented reports represent both a challenge and an opportunity for business report writers, they are the main focus of the remaining report-writing chapters. Consult Table 14.1 again for an overview of all the types of reports discussed in this chapter.

HOW ELECTRONIC TECHNOLOGY AFFECTS BUSINESS REPORTS

Reports aren't necessarily confined to paper in today's business environment. Virtually all of the reports discussed in this chapter can and are being adapted to computerized formats. Businesses have envisioned the *paperless office* for years, and it's finally coming true for many organizations. You can now file your taxes electronically, the SEC actually requires corporations to file reports electronically, and thousands of companies have set up electronic reporting procedures to communicate with employees, customers, and suppliers (see "Gain the Competitive Edge with Online Reporting" on page 471).[10]

Electronic reports are becoming more popular.

Electronic reports fall into two basic categories: First are those that essentially replace paper reports. You can draft a report using your word processor, but rather than printing it and making copies, you can distribute the file electronically. Most e-mail systems now have the ability to attach files to support electronic document distribution. The other category of electronic reports includes those that are unique to the electronic format. For example, an intranet site can offer text, video, and sound in a single integrated "report."

If you explore software for electronic reports, you'll discover a class of software known as *report writers* or *reporting tools*. Unfortunately, these tools don't magically write business reports for you. They are designed to extract and format data from computerized databases. For instance, you can utilize a personnel database to generate a report that ranks employees by income or a customer database to generate mailing labels for all your customers. Once the report is generated, you can print it or distribute it electronically. Also, some report writers allow you to work interactively with the database, in effect creating a "live" report that responds to your queries and inputs.[11]

Report-writing software can pull information out of computerized databases and organize it in any format you want.

Figure 14.6
In-Depth Critique: Shandel Cohen's Justification Report (Guiding Decisions Report)

Cohen's proposal is to install an automatic mail-response system. Because the company manufactures computers, she knows that her boss will have no objections to a computer solution to the problem. She also knows that company profits are always of concern, so her report emphasizes the financial benefits of the proposed system. Her report describes the problem, her proposed solution, and the benefits to the company.

TAILOR YOUR REQUEST

WHO: Authorized

WHAT: Justification

WHEN: Special, nonrecurring

WHERE: Internal, upward

WHY: Analytical

HOW: Receptive readers

ORGANIZE REPORT
Organize by readers' likely reaction. Use direct order for receptive readers (as in this example), with conclusions or recommendations first. Use indirect order for skeptical or hostile readers, emphasizing the reasons underlying the final conclusions or recommendations.

CRAFT REPORT STYLE
Include ample background information, facts, and analysis to guide both the decision and its implementation. Write in complete paragraphs. Use strong introductions and transitions. Use headings, lists, and visuals to guide readers.

FORMAT REPORT
Write in manuscript or memo format. Some companies have guidelines for formatting capital appropriation requests (because most are evaluated in a similar fashion).

MEMO

TO: Jamie Engle
FROM: Shandel Cohen
DATE: July 8, 1997
SUBJECT: Proposed automatic mail-response system

THE PROBLEM:
SLOW RESPONSE TO CUSTOMER REQUESTS FOR INFORMATION

Our new product line has been very well received, and orders have surpassed our projections. This very success, however, has created a shortage of printed catalogs and data sheets, as well as considerable overtime for people in the customer response center. As we introduce upgrades and new options, our printed materials quickly become outdated. If we continue to rely on printed materials for customer information, we have two choices: Distribute existing materials (even though they are incomplete or inaccurate) or discard existing materials and print new ones.

THE SOLUTION:
AUTOMATED MAIL-RESPONSE SYSTEM

With minor modifications to our current computer system and very little additional software, we can set up an automated mail-response system to respond to customer requests for information. This process can save us time, money, and keep our distributed information current.

Automated mail-response systems have been tested and proven effective. Many companies already use this method to respond to customer information requests, so we won't have to worry about relying on untested technology. Both customer and company responses have been positive.

Ever-Current Information

Rather than discard and print new materials, we would need to update only the electronic files. We would be able to provide customers and our field sales organization with up-to-date, correct information as soon as the upgrades or options are available.

Instantaneous Delivery

Within a very short time of requesting information, customers would have that information in hand. This is especially advanta-

---

Electronic reports offer both advantages and disadvantages, compared with their paper counterparts. Several potential advantages include the following:

Electronic reports have distinct advantages.

- **Cost savings.** Assuming you have the necessary hardware and software in place, electronic reports can save a significant amount of money in terms of paper, printing or photocopying, and distribution.

Figure 14.6
(Continued)

2

geous for our international customers. Regular mail to remote locations sometimes takes weeks to arrive, by which time the information may already be out of date. Both customers and field salespeople will appreciate the automatic mail-response system.

Minimized Waste

With our current method of sending printed information, we discard virtually tons of obsolete catalogs, data sheets, and other materials.

By maintaining and distributing the information electronically, we would eliminate this waste. We would also free up a considerable amount of floor space and shelving that is required for storing printed materials.

Of course, some of our customers may still prefer to receive printed materials, or they may not have access to electronic mail. For these customers we could simply print copies of the files when we receive requests.

Lower Overtime Costs

Besides savings in paper and space, we would also realize considerable savings in wages. Because of the increased interest in our new products, we must continue to work overtime or hire new people to meet the demand. An automatic mail-response system would eliminate this need, allowing us to deal with fluctuating interest without a fluctuating work force.

Setup and Operating Costs

The necessary equipment and software costs approximately $15,000. System maintenance and upgrades are estimated at $5,000 per year.

We expect the following annual savings from eliminating printed information:

PREPARE AND DISTRIBUTE REPORT
These nonroutine reports are prepared for managers in response to unique situations. They're directed upward, and some are written by outside consultants.

(continued)

- *Space savings.* A basic CD-ROM can hold the equivalent of hundreds of pages of text (and higher-capacity CD-ROMs and other massive storage devices are on the way), so electronic reports can be stored in far less space than paper reports. This can be a significant advantage for large businesses, businesses with heavy government reporting requirements, and businesses that must keep historical records for many years.
- *Faster distribution.* Electronic documents can reach their audiences in a few seconds, compared to the few hours or days it can take to send paper documents to other locations.

Figure 14.6
(Continued)

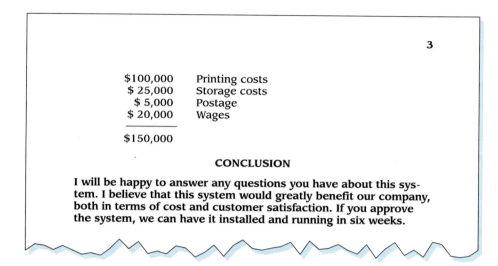

3

$100,000	Printing costs
$ 25,000	Storage costs
$ 5,000	Postage
$ 20,000	Wages

$150,000

CONCLUSION

I will be happy to answer any questions you have about this system. I believe that this system would greatly benefit our company, both in terms of cost and customer satisfaction. If you approve the system, we can have it installed and running in six weeks.

- *Multimedia communication.* You can integrate sound and video with some electronic reports, bringing text to life.
- *Easier maintenance.* Documents on intranet and Internet Web sites are great examples of how much easier it is to correct and update electronic documents. If a single figure changes in a sales report after you've distributed it, your options with a paper report are to reprint and redistribute the entire thing, send out a corrected page, or send a memo to all the recipients asking them to pencil in the correction by hand. With an electronic report, you simply make the change and let everyone know via e-mail. When you offer your readers access to an electronic report on an intranet site, you have an added bonus: Since the only existing copy of the report is always current, you don't have to worry about people hanging on to obsolete or incorrect information.

Electronic reports have some disadvantages.

For all their advantages, however, electronic reports are not a cure-all for business communication problems, nor are they without some risks and disadvantages:

- *Hardware and software costs.* Naturally, you need some kind of computer equipment to distribute electronic documents. If those systems aren't already in place, their purchase, installation, and maintenance is an extra expense.
- *System compatibility.* As discussed in Chapter 4, corporate intranets are helping businesspeople get around the computer compatibility problem, but companies that lack intranets may find themselves with incompatible computer systems that inhibit the use of electronic documents.
- *Training.* Beyond the ability to read, there is little training involved in reading most paper business reports. However, reading electronic reports can require training in using Web browsers, accessing databases, or other skills.
- *Data security and integrity.* Because information in electronic reports is not fixed on paper, it's vulnerable to tampering and inadvertent corruption. The growth of electronic commerce on the Internet will be determined to a large degree by how much confidence the public has in the security and privacy of credit-card transactions and other purchase details. And even innocent computer errors can affect electronic reports. Sending word-processor files over the Internet is still a shaky proposition: Since the files are handled by various systems that don't always work in harmony, your carefully crafted document can end up as electronic rubbish.[12]

KEEPING PACE WITH TECHNOLOGY

GAIN THE COMPETITIVE EDGE WITH ONLINE REPORTING

Mrs. Fields uses them. Mrs. Paul's uses them. However, you don't have to be in the cookie or fish business to work with electronic reports. Today more and more managers and employees are using computers to write and send reports for virtually every business purpose. Computerized cash registers in Mrs. Fields cookie outlets are the heart of a sophisticated reporting system for monitoring and controlling operations. Rather than taking the time to write reports by hand, store managers enter data into the computer system by following report formats on their screen. Then they electronically transmit these reports to corporate headquarters in Park City, Utah. The computer system also serves as a two-way communication device, allowing store and corporate personnel to send messages back and forth in seconds. So Mrs. Fields corporate managers can quickly receive the information they need to track sales and productivity trends—and to spot potential problems—in more than 500 outlets around the world.

At Mrs. Paul's, a computerized reporting system allows production managers to continuously monitor and control the yield from the company's fish processing operation. The system calculates the production yield using the weight of the fish before it's processed, the weight of any scraps, and the weight of the finished fish meals. If the reports show that the actual yield drops below the expected yield, the managers can immediately adjust the equipment to improve the yield. The production managers have instant access to electronic monitor and control reports at each stage of the operation, so they can find and fix problems more quickly than if they had to wait for printed reports.

Federal Express, the well-known package-shipping firm, uses electronic reporting to let customers know the status of their shipments at any time. One of the most popular sites on the World Wide Web belongs to Federal Express. The company uses extensive satellite and computer technologies to track the location of every package in the system, and customers can log onto the FedEx site to find out where their packages are. This not only helps the company serve its customers better but cuts down on costs as well, since FedEx doesn't need to have so many people on the phones answering questions for customers.

1. What advantages and disadvantages do you see in asking store managers at Mrs. Fields to file troubleshooting reports immediately by entering data into the computerized cash register system?
2. How would an electronic reporting system help a company track the activity of personnel who frequently travel to customer sites or other locations?

Many businesses see electronic documents as a way to cut costs while improving worker productivity and customer service, so you'll probably write and read many such reports on the job.

SUMMARY

A business report is a factual, objective document that serves a legitimate business purpose. It may be 3 pages or 300 pages long. It may be a preprinted form, a memo, a letter, a manuscript, or an electronic form submitted over the company's intranet. The style may be abbreviated and specific or fully developed and generalized; the organization may be direct or indirect. The length, format, style, and organization of a business report all depend on who originates it, what subject it covers, when it is prepared, where it is sent, why it is prepared, and how receptive the reader is.

The way a report will be used suggests how it should be developed. Companies use reports for six basic functions: to monitor and control operations, to implement policies and procedures, to comply with legal or government regulations, to obtain new business or funding, to document client work, and to guide decisions.

Another key factor when planning a report is whether you'll be using a traditional paper format or some kind of electronic format. Electronic reports can lower costs, cut storage space requirements, increase distribution speed, and open up new possibilities such as integrated sound and video.

COMMUNICATION CHALLENGES AT NARADA PRODUCTIONS

Now that his daily reporting system has helped smooth the wrinkles from Narada's operations, Wesley Van Linda has time to focus on other important issues. One of them involves a marketing test he wants to conduct to determine how cover art affects the sales of a compact disk or audiocassette. Although other companies have conducted similar research into the dynamics of consumer buying and package design, Van Linda wants to know whether the buying habits of Narada listeners differ from those of conventional listeners, since they're choosing music that is unconventional. To conduct the test, Van Linda plans to issue one recording by pianist David Lanz, with two distinct covers throughout the country.

INDIVIDUAL CHALLENGE: Van Linda has asked you to help with the project by recommending a reporting method for tracking how the cover designs affect sales. (He wanted to enlist someone who wasn't busy with other projects, and he heard you were one of the best report writers among Narada's new employees.) Van Linda explains: "Here's what we need to know: Does one cover sell better than the other? Are there regional distinctions? In other words, do this artist's fans respond positively to the same artwork no matter where they live, or do West Coast buyers differ from East Coast buyers? If so, this could affect how we issue future releases. Don't worry about the psychology behind the choices of artwork—we'll let marketing handle that. I want you to determine what kinds of reports we'll need for tracking the sales patterns, who should write them, and what information they should include. Let me have your recommendations as soon as possible."

TEAM CHALLENGE: Another possibility might be to incorporate the marketing test into reports Van Linda is already receiving from the field. He's asked your group to look into it. Refer to the vignette for descriptions of these operational reports, and discuss with your team how they might be used. Would this be more efficient? Why or why not? What would be the advantages and disadvantages of handling the marketing test through a separate set of reports?[13]

CRITICAL THINKING QUESTIONS

1. If you want to make a specific recommendation in your research report, should you include information that might support a different recommendation? Explain.
2. Could the increased speed of electronic reporting create any problems with the quality of the information people see or the decisions they make? Explain your answer.
3. What are the advantages and disadvantages of asking your employees to "fill in the blanks" on standardized reporting forms? Briefly explain.
4. If you want to use your business plan as an unsolicited proposal for obtaining funds for a new business venture, what changes would you have to make to the report? Think about the who, what, when, where, why, and how of both types of report, and explain your answer.
5. If you were writing a troubleshooting report to help management decide how to reduce quality problems at a manufacturing plant, what ethical issues might you face? How would these issues relate to your need to report all the relevant facts and to offer evidence for your conclusions? Explain briefly.
6. Discuss one internal issue and one external issue that might spark managers to draft a position paper. Identify the audience for each position paper you discuss.

EXERCISES

1. Using the information presented in this chapter, identify the type of report represented by each of the following examples. In addition, write a paragraph about each, explaining who the audience is likely to be, what type of data would be used, and whether conclusions and recommendations would be appropriate.
   a. A statistical study of the pattern of violent crime in a large city during the last five years
   b. A report prepared by a seed company demonstrating the superiority of its seed corn for farmers
   c. A report prepared by an independent testing agency evaluating various types of cold remedies sold without prescription
   d. A trip report submitted at the end of a week by a traveling salesperson
   e. A report indicating how 45 acres of undeveloped land could be converted to an industrial park

f. An annual report to be sent to the shareholders of a large corporation

g. A report from a U.S. National Park wildlife officer to Washington, D.C., headquarters showing the status of the California condor (an endangered species)

h. A written report by a police officer who has just completed an arrest

2. Go to the library and review the annual reports recently released by two corporations in the same industry. Analyze each report and be prepared to discuss the following questions in class:

a. What differences do you see in the way each corporation reports its financial data? Is the data presented clearly so that shareholders can draw conclusions about each corporation's financial results?

b. What goals, challenges, and plans do top managers emphasize in their discussion of results?

c. How do the format and organization of each report enhance or detract from the information being presented?

3. Call the public affairs department of a nearby company and ask for a copy of the policy statement concerning one of the following three topics:

a. Environmental affairs

b. Equal opportunity employment practices

c. Buy-American policies

Then write a one-page report discussing whether the policy offers sufficient guidance without being too specific to be implemented. How can you improve the way this policy statement communicates with employees?

4. Interview several people working in a career you might like to enter, and ask them about the types of written reports they receive and prepare. How do these reports tie into the decision-making process? Who reads the reports they prepare? Summarize your findings in writing, give them to your instructor, and be prepared to discuss them with the class.

5. Find a copy of *Commerce Business Daily* through your library, or check your local newspaper for advertisements placed by government agencies that are issuing RFPs on construction contracts or other projects. Call or write for a copy of the RFP guidelines. Does the RFP specify a particular format for company bids? Is any specialized language used in the RFP form? What restrictions are mentioned? What financial points must be covered in each bid?

6. Imagine you're the manager of campus recruiting for Nortel, a Canadian telecommunications firm. Each of your four recruiters interviews up to 11 college seniors every day. What kind of personal activity report can you design to track the results of these interviews? List the areas you would want each recruiter to report on, and explain how each would help you manage the recruiting process (and the recruiters) more effectively.

7. You're the vice president of operations for a Florida fast-food chain. In the aftermath of a major hurricane, you're drafting a report on the emergency procedures to be followed by personnel in each restaurant when storm warnings are in effect. Answer who, what, when, where, why, and how, and then prepare a one-page draft of such a report.

8. Visit the Narada Productions home page <http://www.narada.com>, and consider the factual information it provides: company intentions, products, services, and so forth. Based on this information, prepare a short memo to Wesley Van Linda in which you justify the cost and the effort of maintaining this Web site—its fulfillment of company goals, and its effectiveness with Web browsers and customers. (Create any details necessary to complete your memo.)

9. As the director of your college's placement office, you're always searching for employers who will hire students part-time during the school year. However, because three other colleges are located within 25 miles of your campus, most area employers are bombarded with similar requests. Now you're planning to send an unsolicited proposal to the nearby American Airlines reservations office. Your proposal must convince the airline that students from your college are better qualified to serve as reservations operators than students from other colleges. Make a list of the specific points you'll cover to be convincing; then note any restrictions you may have to mention in such a proposal.

10. You're an engineer training your assistant to write monthly progress reports. The current report is on a project in Singapore that's behind schedule. This report will go to Singapore government officials as well as to your own supervisors at corporate headquarters. Is it a voluntary report or an authorized report? What information should you ask your assistant to report? In what order should this information be presented? How formal do you want this report to be? Will the report be organized around conclusions or subtopics? Draft a brief (one- to two-page) memo, giving your assistant instructions on how to prepare this report.

PLANNING AND RESEARCHING REPORTS AND PROPOSALS

AFTER STUDYING THIS CHAPTER, YOU WILL BE ABLE TO

- Develop a statement defining the problem to be solved and a statement defining the purpose of the report
- Identify and outline the issues that have to be analyzed during your study
- Prepare a work plan for conducting the investigation
- Organize the research phase of the investigation, including the identification of secondary and primary sources of data
- Draw sound conclusions and develop practical recommendations

---

COMMUNICATION CLOSE-UP AT GOSH ENTERPRISES

Charley Shin opened his first Philly cheesesteak restaurant—Charley's Steakery—when he was a junior at Ohio State. Today he is the millionaire owner of Gosh Enterprises, franchiser of over 50 Charley's Steakery restaurants. How did he reach this pinnacle of achievement so early in life? Through hard work and vision—backed up by lots of research and planning.

Shin says that running his first Charley's Steakery (near the Ohio State campus) was "a fun time—a lot of hard work. Going to school and running a restaurant was a bit overwhelming, but I juggled my way through it okay."

Shin and his older sister had come to the United States from South Korea when he was 13. They joined their mother in Columbus, Ohio, where she'd settled two years before. "I don't know if all the immigrants are poor, but we were poor," he recalls. To make ends meet, his mother worked days as a hospital housekeeper and three nights a week at a Japanese steakhouse. In 1980, she bought a small Japanese restaurant, and Shin started washing dishes there when he was 14 or 15 (reading *Forbes* in his spare time). By 17 he was thinking big. He convinced his mother that the little restaurant wasn't going anywhere and she should sell it, bank the profits, and wait until he graduated from college so that he could support her. "She, having all the faith in her son, did just that," says Shin. Trouble was, by the time he was a junior, the banked profits were running out. It was time to make his move—and that's how the first Charley's Steakery began.

A year after it opened, Shin graduated, and a year after that he opened the second Charley's Steakery, followed by a third, and then a fourth and fifth with partners. "At that point, I had to decide on the venue for growth: whether to continue with company-owned restaurants, pursue equity-interested partnerships, or start franchising," explains Shin. Before drafting a new plan for the future, he knew he needed to do some research.

Charley Shin

Competing directly with burgers and fries, the Philly cheesesteak sandwich sold at Charley's Steakery outlets is fresh food (not frozen or microwaved). This distinction is just one of the concepts described in the original business plan written at Gosh Enterprises. To guide the company's focus and progress, the business plan spelled out specifics such as marketing strategy, franchising policy, location preference, and financial projections.

"Franchising was very interesting to me because it does not require a lot of capital but it has a venue for quick expansion. So, I read a lot of articles," says Shin. "I went to the library almost every day for over a month, and I read everything I could about franchising and the Philly cheesesteak concept." He studied newspaper articles on microfiche, read magazines and books, looked at statistics and trends, and learned what everyone else was doing in the field.

Shin also interviewed a fellow restaurant owner who had long years of experience. The man advised Shin to stick with the "fresh food" concept (instead of precooked or prepackaged sandwiches) and to concentrate on the "captive audience" in shopping-center food courts. Shin now credits this advice as some of the best he ever followed.

After weeks of this research, Shin started writing a formal plan. "I wish there had been a place that could really have given me sound advice about how to write a business plan," he says now. Using what he did know, he wrote an overview, a description of the concept, and a summary of his plans for the future. He hired professionals to help him develop a marketing strategy to include in the plan, but he prepared all the financial statements and projections himself.

Because of Shin's careful research and planning, Gosh Enterprises has done so well that Shin recently directed his senior staff in the preparation of a new three-year plan for future growth. This time, he went all out. Meeting on Saturdays to avoid distractions, Shin and his top people first developed a "work plan" for the writing project. They assigned themselves two months to complete the new business plan, and they divided the research and writing tasks according to their individual expertise.

Shin says he's fortunate that his vice president of franchise operations is an "expert" at preparing business plans; she brought up all the issues to be addressed and made sure all staff members did their part. In fact, Shin thinks business plans are so important that today all his franchise owners must prepare a written business plan during their training. They aren't certified until they complete at least a rough draft.

"The plan is just a road map to where I want to go," explains Shin. "It really disciplines one's thought process. I think it's a lot easier for me to justify in my own mind how I'm going to do certain things; I may have a happy and fuzzy idea in my head, but if I start to write it down on paper, I really have to think things through."[1]

FIVE STEPS IN PLANNING REPORTS

As Charlie Shin knows, it's too easy to let "happy and fuzzy" thinking interfere with effectiveness—especially when preparing a proposal as detailed and important as Gosh Enterprise's new three-year growth plan. Writing a report involves careful planning. Before putting a single word on the page, follow the series of steps that form the foundation of any report:

1. Define the problem and the purpose.
2. Outline the issues for investigation.
3. Prepare a work plan.
4. Conduct research.
5. Analyze and interpret data, drawing conclusions and developing recommendations.

> When planning most business reports, you define the problem and the purpose, outline the issues for investigation, prepare a work plan, conduct research, and then analyze and interpret data.

The relative importance of these five steps depends on the type of assignment. **Informational reports,** which contain facts alone, may require very little in the way of conclusions and recommendations. Monitor/control reports, statements of policies and procedures, interim progress reports, and many compliance reports are examples. On the other hand, **analytical reports** include conclusions and recommendations and require all five steps. Examples include decision-oriented reports, proposals, and final reports to clients. Charley Shin's three-year business plan is also an example of an analytical report.

STEP 1: DEFINING THE PROBLEM AND THE PURPOSE

> Narrow the focus of your investigation by defining your problem.

Before you begin writing any report, you usually have some planning to do. Even if you're preparing a strictly informational report simply to transmit facts, you must still gather those facts and arrange them in a convenient format. But even before you do that, you write a **problem statement,** a statement that defines the problem your report will cover. This problem may be negative or positive; it may deal with the problem of shrinking sales or the need for more child-care facilities. The problem you cover is merely the matter you intend to deal with, whether you're gathering information, supporting a decision, or actually solving a problem. Be careful not to confuse a simple topic (campus parking) with a problem (the lack of enough campus parking). A clear problem statement helps you decide what information you'll need in order to complete your report. Also, be sure to consider the company's perspective and the individual perspectives of the people who will read your report.[2] If you're the only person who thinks this issue is a problem, the audience won't be very interested in your solution. You may have to spend some time convincing people that a problem exists.

Linda Moreno is a cost accounting analyst for Electrovision, a high-technology company based in San Francisco. She was recently asked to find ways of reducing employee travel costs (her complete report appears in Chapter 18). Because she was supposed to suggest specific cost reductions, she phrased her problem statement carefully:

"Electrovision needs to find ways to reduce travel costs while still enabling employees to work effectively." If her assignment had been restricted to simply reporting on spending patterns, her problem statement would have been phrased differently: "We need to understand how our travel budget is being spent." You can see from these two statements how much influence the problem statement has on your investigation. If Moreno's manager expected her to suggest cost reductions but all she did was collect cost data, her report would have failed to meet expectations. Because she was assigned an analytical report rather than an informational report, Moreno had to go beyond mere data collection to draw conclusions and make recommendations. However, no matter what kind of report you're doing, defining the problem and the purpose requires asking questions to clarify the assignment.

Asking the Right Questions

As in Moreno's case, the problem is often defined for you by the person who authorizes the report. When this is the case, talk over the objectives of the report before you begin your investigation—to ensure that you understand exactly what is required. Specifically, try to answer the following questions:

- What needs to be determined?
- Why is this issue important?
- Who is involved in the situation?
- Where is the trouble located?
- When did it start?
- How did the situation originate?

Not all these questions apply in every situation, but asking them helps you clarify the boundaries of your investigation. You can then draft a written statement of the problem being investigated, which will serve as a guide to whatever problem you're trying to solve or whatever question you're trying to answer in the report.[3]

> *Your investigation takes its shape from the questions you ask and the problem you delineate.*

Developing the Statement of Purpose

Once you've asked some preliminary questions and determined the problem, you're ready to write a clear **statement of purpose,** which defines the objective of the report. In contrast to the statement of problem, which defines only what you're going to investigate, the statement of purpose defines what the report should accomplish.[4]

> *Prepare a written statement of your purpose; then review it with the person who authorized the study.*

The most useful way to phrase your purpose is to begin with an infinitive phrase. If Linda Moreno had been given an informational assignment, she might've stated her purpose this way:

> *Purpose:* To summarize Electrovision's spending on travel and entertainment

However, her analytical report had to go beyond information:

> *Purpose:* To analyze Electrovision's travel costs and suggest practical ways to reduce these costs while still enabling employees to work effectively

Using an infinitive phrase (*to* plus a verb) encourages you to take control and decide where you're going before you begin. When you choose such a phrase—*to inform, to confirm, to analyze, to persuade, to recommend*—you pin down your general goal in preparing the report. At the same time, be sure to define the benefit (the information or the recommended action) that your reader will gain from reading your report. The more specific your purpose, the more useful it will be as a guide to planning and writing the report. For example, the purpose of Charley Shin's latest business plan is *to recommend the best direction for Gosh Enterprises to take over the next three years.* So Shin's report does more than merely inform; it's expected to suggest a practical plan.

Your audience's reaction dictates all the decisions you'll make about content, structure, outline, and so forth. So it's important to anticipate that reaction. Double-check your statement of purpose with the person who authorized the report. When the authorizer sees the purpose written down in black and white, he or she may decide to direct the study in another direction.

STEP 2: OUTLINING ISSUES FOR INVESTIGATION

Outline the issues you plan to study.

Once you've defined the problem and established the purpose of your report, you're ready to begin your investigation. To organize the research effort, you can break the problem into a series of logical, connected questions that try to identify causes and effects. This process is sometimes called **problem factoring.** You probably subconsciously approach most problems this way. When your car's engine won't start, what do you do? You use the available evidence to organize your investigation, to start a search for cause-and-effect relationships. If the engine doesn't turn over at all, for instance, you might suspect a dead battery. In contrast, if the engine does turn over but won't fire, you can conclude that the battery is okay but perhaps you're out of gas. When you speculate on the cause of a problem, you're forming a **hypothesis,** a potential explanation that needs to be tested. By subdividing a problem and forming hypotheses based on available evidence, you can tackle even the most complex situations.

Linda Moreno used the factoring process to structure her investigation into cost reduction at Electrovision (see Figure 15.1). "I began with a two-part question," says Moreno. "Why have our travel costs grown so dramatically, and how can we reduce them? Then I factored that question into two subquestions: Do we have adequate procedures for tracking and controlling costs? Are these procedures being followed?

"Looking into cost-control procedures, I speculated that the right kind of information was not reaching the executives who were responsible for these costs. From there, the questioning naturally led to the systems and procedures for collecting this information. If we didn't have the right procedures in place or if people weren't following procedures, the information wouldn't reach the people in charge."

The outline of issues for analysis is often different from the outline of the final report.

Once Moreno had determined what was wrong with Electrovision's cost-control system, she could address the second part of the main question: the problem of recommending improvements. The process of outlining the issues enabled Moreno and her colleagues to solve a problem methodically, just as outlining a report enables you to write in a systematic way. It's worth noting, however, that the way you outline an investigation may be different from the way you outline the resulting report. Solving the problem is one thing; "selling" the solution is another. During your investigation, you might analyze five possible causes of a problem and discover that only two causes are relevant. In your report, you might not even introduce the three unrelated causes.

Developing a Logical Structure

Informational and analytical studies are factored differently.

Because any subject can be factored in many ways, your job is to choose the most logical method, the one that makes the most sense. Start by looking carefully at the purpose of your report. Informational assignments are structured differently from analytical ones.

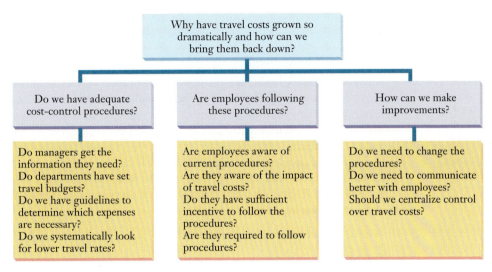

Figure 15.1
Factoring the Travel-Cost Problem at Electrovision

Many assignments require both information and analysis, so it's up to you to discern the overall purpose of the report. Is your general goal to provide background information that someone else will use or interpret? Then an informational outline is appropriate overall, even though subsections of the study may require some analysis to discover and emphasize important facts. Is the purpose of your report to scrutinize the data and generate your own conclusions and recommendations? Then use an analytical outline overall, even though your opinions will obviously be based on facts. For problem solving you may use a variety of structural schemes, as long as you take care to avoid errors in logic.

Informational Assignments

Investigations that lead to factual reports, offering little analysis or interpretation of the data, are generally organized on the basis of subtopics dealing with specific subjects. These subtopics can be arranged in various ways:

Studies that emphasize discovering and reporting facts may be factored by subtopic.

- *According to importance.* If you're reviewing five product lines, you might organize your study in order of the sales for each product line, beginning with the line that produces the most revenue and proceeding to the one that produces the least revenue.
- *According to sequence.* If you're studying a process, proceed step-by-step—1, 2, 3, and so on.
- *According to chronology.* When investigating a chain of events, organize the study according to what happened in January, what happened in February, and so on.
- *According to spatial orientation.* If you're studying a physical object, study it left to right (or right to left in some cultures), top to bottom, outside to inside.
- *According to geography.* If location is important, factor your study geographically.
- *According to category.* If you're asked to review several distinct aspects of a subject, look at one category at a time, such as sales, profit, cost, or investment.

These methods of subdivision are commonly used when preparing monitor/control reports, policies and procedures, compliance reports, and interim progress reports.

Analytical Assignments

Studies that focus on problem solving may be structured around hypotheses that the report writer plans to prove or disprove during the investigation.

Analytical studies result in decision-oriented reports, final reports for clients, and some compliance reports. Such reports usually contain analyses, conclusions, and recommendations, and they're generally categorized by a problem-solving method. The two most common structural approaches for this method are (1) relative merit and (2) hypothesis.

When the problem is to evaluate how well various alternatives meet your criteria, the natural way to subdivide your analysis is to focus on the criteria. For example, if the problem is to decide where to build a new plant, you might factor the investigation along the following lines:

Where should we build a new plant?

1. Construction costs
   a. Location A
   b. Location B
   c. Location C

2. Labor availability
   a. Location A
   b. Location B
   c. Location C

3. Transportation facilities
   a. Location A
   b. Location B
   c. Location C

Another way of using relative merits is to identify the alternatives first and then analyze how well each alternative meets your criteria.

When the report's purpose is to discover causes, predict results, or suggest a solution to a problem, one natural way to proceed is to formulate hypothetical explanations. If your problem is to determine why your company is having trouble hiring secretaries, you'd begin factoring this problem by speculating on the causes. Then you'd collect information to confirm or disprove each reason. Your outline of the major issues might look something like this:

Why are we having trouble hiring secretaries?

1. Salaries are too low.
   a. What do we pay our secretaries?
   b. What do comparable companies pay their secretaries?
   c. How important is pay in influencing secretaries' job choices?

2. Our location is poor.
   a. Are we accessible by public transportation and major roads?
   b. Is the area physically attractive?
   c. Are housing costs affordable?
   d. Is crime a problem?

3. The supply of secretaries is diminishing.
   a. How many secretaries were available five years ago as opposed to now?
   b. What was the demand for secretaries five years ago as opposed to now?

SHARPENING YOUR SKILLS

SEVEN ERRORS IN LOGIC THAT CAN UNDERMINE YOUR REPORTS

For your report to be effective, it must be logical. If you learn how to think logically, you'll also write more logically. Here are some common errors to avoid:

- **Lack of objectivity.** Seeing only the facts that support your views and ignoring any contradictory information:

  Although half the survey population expressed dissatisfaction with our current product, a sizable portion find it satisfactory. (*You may be tempted to ignore the dissatisfied half instead of investigating the reasons for their dissatisfaction.*)

- **Hasty generalizations.** Forming judgments on the basis of insufficient evidence or special cases:

  Marketing strategy Z increased sales 13 percent in Atlanta supermarkets. Let's try it in Fairbanks. (*Atlanta and Fairbanks are probably vastly different markets.*)

- **Hidden assumptions.** Hiding a questionable major premise:

  We are marketing product X in trade journals because we marketed product Y in trade journals. (*Who says product X and product Y should be marketed the same way?*)

- **Either-or.** Setting up two alternatives and not allowing for others:

  We must open a new plant by spring, or we will go bankrupt. (*Surely there are other ways to avoid bankruptcy.*)

- **False causal relationships.** Assuming that event A caused event B merely because A preceded B:

Sales increased 42 percent as soon as we hired the new sales director. (*Something besides the new sales director may be responsible for increased sales.*)

- **Begged questions.** Assuming as proven what you are seeking to prove:

  We need a standard procedure so that we will have standard results. (*But why is standardization important?*)

- **Personal attacks/appeals to popular prejudice.** Sinking people or ideas you don't like by chaining them to irrelevant but unpopular actions or ideas:

  Ellen mishandled the budget last year, so she can't be expected to motivate her staff. (*Ellen's accounting ability may have nothing to do with her ability to motivate a staff.*)

  It's un-American to impose government regulations. (*Regulations are unpopular, but they do exist in the United States.*)

---

1. Discuss some newsworthy business problem that arose from errors in logic. For example, Huffy tried to sell a combination mountain-and-racing bicycle through Kmart and other large stores that sold Huffy bicycles. Unfortunately, the reasoning that this special bike (priced higher than other Huffy models) could be sold by salespeople who weren't knowledgeable about bicycles was faulty, and Huffy lost $5 million on the product.
2. Go through the "Letters to the Editor" columns in recent newspapers or news magazines. Examine the arguments made, and point out errors in logic.

In many cases, however, identifying and clarifying problems is only part of the challenge. You'll often be called on to suggest and implement solutions. Developing solid problem-solving skills will help not only your business reports but many other aspects of your career as well. You will be able to solve problems efficiently and effectively if you follow a clear problem-solving process:[5]

1. Define and limit the problem so that you know exactly what you're trying to solve—and what you're not trying to solve.
2. Analyze the problem and gather data about it.
3. Establish criteria for possible solutions.
4. Brainstorm possible solutions.
5. Choose the best possible solution, based on the criteria you set in step 3.
6. Implement the chosen solution.

You won't cover all six of these steps in every report you write, of course, but knowing how to solve problems will help you make better decisions and recommendations in your reports. (See "Seven Errors in Logic That Can Undermine Your Reports" on page 481.)

Preparing a Preliminary Outline

Organize your study by preparing a detailed preliminary outline.

As you go through the factoring process, you may want to use an outline format to represent your ideas. Of course, if a few notes are enough to guide you through a short, informal report in memo form, perhaps an outline isn't necessary. However, a preliminary outline gives you a convenient frame of reference for your formal investigation. Furthermore, a detailed outline can definitely be worthwhile under certain circumstances:

- When you're one of several people working on an assignment
- When your investigation will be extensive and will involve many sources and types of data
- When you know from past experience that the person who requested the study will revise the assignment during the course of your investigation and you want to keep track of the changes

Two widely used systems of outlining, the alphanumeric system and the decimal system, are illustrated in Figure 15.2. Both are perfectly acceptable, but some companies favor one method over the other. Many outlining programs for personal computers give you a choice and then help you switch from outline format to report format as you write.

Use the same grammatical form for each group of items in your outline.

You usually write the headings at each level of your outline in the same grammatical form. In other words, if item I uses a verb, items II, III, and IV also use verbs. This parallel construction enables readers to see that the ideas are related, of similar importance, and on the same level of generality. It makes the outline a more useful tool for establishing the table of contents and headings in your final report, and it is considered the correct format by most of the people who might review your outline. When wording the outline, you must also choose between descriptive (topical) and informative (talking) headings. As Table 15.1 indicates, descriptive headings label the subject that will be discussed, whereas informative headings (in either question or summary form) suggest more about the meaning of the issues.

Informative outlines are generally more helpful than descriptive outlines.

Although outlines with informative headings take a little longer to write, they're generally more useful in guiding your work, especially if written in terms of the questions you plan to answer during your investigation. In addition, they're easier for others to review. If other people are going to comment on your outline, they may not have a very clear idea of what you mean by the descriptive heading "Advertising." However, they will get the main idea if you use the informative heading "Cuts in Ad Budget May Explain Sales Decline."

Remember that at this point you're only developing a preliminary outline to guide your investigation. Later on, when you've completed your research and are preparing a final outline or a table of contents for the report, you may want to switch from an outline of your questions to an outline that summarizes your findings.

Following the Rules of Division

Follow the rules of division to ensure that your study will be organized in a logical, systematic way.

Once you've prepared your outline, sit back for a minute and check it over. Ask yourself whether the structure is significant, consistent, exclusive, and complete:

ALPHANUMERIC	DECIMAL
I. ______	1.0 ______
A. ______	1.1 ______
B. ______	1.2 ______
1. ______	1.21 ______
2. ______	1.22 ______
a. ______	1.221 ______
b. ______	1.222 ______
3. ______	1.23 ______
C. ______	1.3 ______
II. ______	2.0 ______
A. ______	2.1 ______
1. ______	2.11 ______
a. ______	2.111 ______
b. ______	2.112 ______
2. ______	2.12 ______
3. ______	2.13 ______
B. ______	2.2 ______

Figure 15.2
Two Common Outline Formats

- ***Divide a topic into at least two parts.*** A topic cannot be divided into only one part. For example, if you wanted to divide a topic such as "Alternatives for Improving Division Profits," you wouldn't look only at increasing sales. You would need at least one other subtopic, such as reducing production costs or decreasing employee absenteeism. If you were interested only in increasing sales, then that would be your topic, which you would probably divide into at least two subtopics.
- ***Choose a significant, useful basis or guiding principle for the division.*** You could subdivide production problems into two groups: problems that arise when the machines are turned off and problems that occur when the machines are turned on. However, this basis for breaking down the subject would not be of much use to anyone. A better choice might be dividing the subject into problems caused by human error versus problems caused by machine failure.

TABLE 15.1

TYPES OF OUTLINE HEADINGS

Descriptive (Topical) Outline	Informative (Talking) Outline: *Question Form*	Informative (Talking) Outline: *Summary Form*
I. Industry characteristics	I. What is the nature of the industry?	I. Flour milling is a mature industry.
A. Annual sales	A. What are the annual sales?	A. Market is large.
B. Profitability	B. Is the industry profitable?	B. Profit margins are narrow.
C. Growth rate	C. What is the pattern of growth?	C. Growth is modest.
1. Sales	1. Sales growth?	1. Sales growth averages less than 3 percent a year.
2. Profit	2. Profit growth?	2. Growth in profits is flat.

- *When subdividing a whole into its parts, restrict yourself to one category at a time.* If you switch from one category to another, you get a mixed classification, which can confuse your analysis. Say you're subdividing your study of the market for toothpaste according to sales of fluoride versus nonfluoride brands. You would upset the investigation by adding another category to your analysis (such as sales broken down by geographic region). If you are dealing with a long, complex subject, you'll no doubt have to use several categories of division before you complete your work, but the shift from one category to another must be made at a logical point, after you've completed your study of a particular issue. For example, after you've looked at sales of fluoride versus nonfluoride toothpaste, you might then want to look at toothpaste sales by geographic location or socioeconomic group.
- *Make certain that each group is separate and distinct.* As you divide a topic into groups, those groups must be mutually exclusive, or you'll end up talking about the same item twice, under two separate headings. Subdividing a population into males, females, and teenagers wouldn't make any sense because the categories overlap.
- *Be thorough when listing all the components of a whole.* It would be misleading to subdivide an engine into parts without mentioning the pistons. An important part of the whole would be missing, and the resulting picture of the engine would be wrong.

Most important, of course, is whether your outline follows a logical flow when compared to your investigation and its results. For instance, if you're searching for cause-and-effect relationships, you might want to start with the observed effects and work backward to the causes in a logical manner.

Step 3: Preparing the Work Plan

Once you've defined the problem and outlined the issues for analysis, you are ready to establish a work plan based on your preliminary outline. In business, most report-writing situations involve a firm deadline with finite time and resources to get the job done. In other words, you not only have to produce quality reports, you have to do so quickly and efficiently. A carefully thought-out work plan is the best way to make sure you produce quality work on schedule.

Prepare a work plan that identifies the tasks you will perform.

If you are preparing this work plan for yourself, it can be relatively informal: a simple list of the steps you plan to take, an estimate of their sequence and timing, and a list of the sources of information you plan to use. If you're conducting a lengthy, formal study, however, you'll want to develop a detailed work plan that can guide the performance of many tasks over a span of time. Most proposals require a detailed work plan, which becomes the basis for a contract if the proposal is accepted. A formal work plan might include these elements (especially the first two):

- *Statement of the problem.* Include the problem statement so that anyone working with you is clear about the nature of the challenge you face. Including the problem statement can also help you stay focused on the core problem and avoid distractions that are likely to arise during your investigation and writing.
- *Statement of the purpose and scope of your investigation.* As you saw earlier in the chapter, your statement of purpose describes what you plan to accomplish with this report. The scope defines the boundaries of your work, explicitly stating which issues you will cover and which issues you won't cover. If you've ever misunderstood a homework assignment and delivered something that didn't meet expectations, you know how frustrating such misunderstandings can be for both the writer and the reader. Particularly with complex, lengthy investigations, make

sure that the task is clearly defined before you start. If it's possible and appropriate, verify your purpose and scope with your intended audience before starting. As with homework, you usually won't have time to rework business reports if you discover at the last minute that you're on the wrong track.

- *Discussion of the sequence of tasks to be accomplished.* Indicate sources of information, required research, and any restrictions (on time, money, personnel, or available data). For simple reports, the list of necessary tasks will be short and probably rather obvious. Longer reports and complex investigations, however, require thorough planning. You may need to reserve time with customers or executives or schedule outside services such as telephone researchers or print shops.

- *Description of the end products that will result from the investigation.* In many cases, the output of your efforts will be the report itself. In other cases, though, you'll need to produce something above and beyond a report, such as a new marketing plan, some improvements to a business process, or even a tangible product. As with the rest of your work plan, make sure these expectations are clear up front, and make sure you've scheduled enough time and resources to get the complete job done.

- *Review of project assignments, schedules, and resource requirements.* Indicate who will be responsible for what, when tasks will be completed, and how much the investigation will cost. You may also want to include a brief section on coordinating the writing and production of the report if more than one person will be involved. Collaborative writing has some important advantages over writing a report by yourself, of course, but making sure everyone works together productively can also be a challenge.

- *Plans for following up after the report is delivered.* Follow-up can range from something as simple as making sure people received the information they needed to something as complex as conducting additional research to evaluate the results of proposals contained in the report. Even if follow-up isn't required or expected, doing some informal follow-up can help you find ways to improve your future reports. Following up is also a good way to communicate to your audience that you care about the effectiveness of your work and the impact you can have on the organization.

Some work plans also include a tentative outline of the report (see Figure 15.3). With a plan in place, you're ready to get to work, which usually means starting with research.

STEP 4: CONDUCTING THE RESEARCH

The value of your report depends on the quality of the data it's based on. So when the time comes to gather facts and figures, your first concern is to get organized. If you're working alone on a project, getting organized may mean nothing more than setting up a file and checking out a few books and periodicals from the nearest library. If you're part of a team, you will work out your assignments and coordinate activities. Your work plan will be a big help during this research effort.

Work plans contain a list of the sources you'll consult. *Primary sources* of information provide, as the name implies, firsthand information that is collected for your report's specific purpose. In contrast, *secondary sources* of information have been previously collected for other purposes.[6] Most business reports call for a mix of both secondary and primary sources. However, you're likely to find that much of what you need to know has never been collected, which means you'll have to conduct your own

Consult primary and secondary sources of information.

Figure 15.3
In-Depth Critique: Sample Work Plan for a Formal Study

The following is an example of a work plan developed for a report on whether to launch a company newsletter.

Statement of the problem is clear enough for anyone to understand without background research.

Statement of purpose is specific, delineating exactly what will be covered in the report.

Tasks to be accomplished are clearly laid out.

Although no description of the end product is included here, a preliminary outline is presented for guidance.

STATEMENT OF THE PROBLEM
The rapid growth of our company over the past five years has reduced the sense of community among our staff. People no longer feel like part of an intimate organization where they matter as individuals.

PURPOSE AND SCOPE OF WORK
The purpose of this study is to determine whether a company newsletter would help rebuild employee identification with the organization. The study will evaluate the impact of newsletters in other companies and will attempt to identify features that might be desirable in our own newsletter. Such variables as length, frequency of distribution, types of articles, and graphic design will be considered. Costs will be estimated for several approaches. In addition, the study will analyze the personnel and the procedures required to produce a newsletter.

SOURCES AND METHODS OF DATA COLLECTION
Sample newsletters will be collected from 50 companies similar to ours in size, growth rate, and types of employees. The editors will be asked to comment on the impact of their publications on employee morale. Our own employees will be surveyed to determine their interest in a newsletter and their preferences for specific features. Production procedures and costs will be analyzed through conversations with newsletter editors and printers.

PRELIMINARY OUTLINE
    I. Do newsletters affect morale?
        A. Do people read them?
        B. How do employees benefit?
        C. How does the company benefit?
    II. What are the features of good newsletters?
        A. How long are they?
        B. What do they contain?
        C. How often are they published?
        D. How are they designed?
    III. How should a newsletter be produced?
        A. Should it be written, edited, and printed internally?
        B. Should it be written internally and printed outside?
        C. Should it be totally produced outside?
    IV. What would a newsletter cost?
        A. What would the personnel costs be?
        B. What would the materials costs be?
        C. What would outside services cost?

research. Reliance on primary sources is one of the main differences between business reports and school reports. Even so, business report writers begin by researching secondary sources.

Reviewing Secondary Sources

Even though you may plan to rely heavily on primary sources, it's a good idea to begin your study with a thorough review of the information that has already been collected. By searching the literature, you avoid the embarrassment of failing to report something

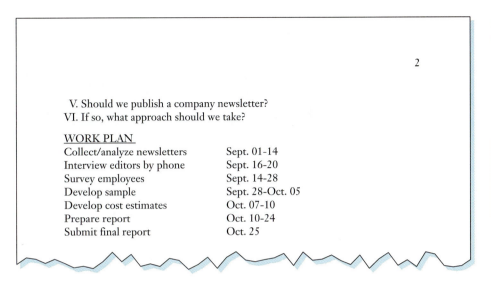

Figure 15.3
(Continued)

2

V. Should we publish a company newsletter?
VI. If so, what approach should we take?

WORK PLAN
Collect/analyze newsletters	Sept. 01-14
Interview editors by phone	Sept. 16-20
Survey employees	Sept. 14-28
Develop sample	Sept. 28-Oct. 05
Develop cost estimates	Oct. 07-10
Prepare report	Oct. 10-24
Submit final report	Oct. 25

This plan includes no plans for following up, but it clearly states the assignments and the schedules for completing them.

that's common knowledge. You also save yourself the trouble of studying something that has already been done. Once you gain a feel for the structure of the subject, you can decide what additional research will be required.

Finding Sources

Depending on your subject, you may find useful information in general reference works, popular publications, or government documents. CD-ROM products now offer a wide variety of research materials, from product databases to nationwide phone directories. You can also search online databases via the Internet or using services such as Dialog (a gateway to more than 450 databases). As you learned in Chapter 4, the Internet offers a variety of search and retrieval tools to help you find articles, research reports, Web sites, and other sources of information (see Figure 15.4).

Conduct secondary research by locating information that has already been collected, usually in the form of books, periodicals, and reports.

In addition, each field of business has a handful of specialized references that are considered indispensable. You'll quickly come to know these sources once you've joined a particular industry. In addition, don't overlook internal sources. Often the most useful references are company reports, memos, and information stored in the company's databases. Also check company brochures, newsletters, and annual reports to shareholders.

If you're working for a large organization with a company library, you may have the help of a professional librarian in identifying and obtaining other useful materials for your investigation. If not, look for the nearest public library or university library, and ask the librarians there for help. Reference librarians are trained to know where to find just about everything, and many of them are pleased to help people pursue obscure information.

Choosing and Using Sources

When it comes to choosing your references, be selective. Avoid dated or biased material. If possible, check on who collected the data, the methods they used, their qualifications, and their professional reputations.[7] Common sense will help you judge the credibility of the sources you plan to use. Ask yourself the following questions about each piece of material:

Ask questions about the reference works you use:
- Are they up to date?
- Are they objective?
- Who collected the data? How?
- What are the authors' qualifications and reputations?

- ***Does the source have a reputation for honesty and reliability?*** Naturally, you'll feel more comfortable with information from a source that has established a reputation for accuracy. But even a good reputation doesn't mean you should let your guard down completely, since even the finest reporters and editors can make mistakes.

Figure 15.4
Using Search Engines on the Internet

Chances are good you'll find information on the Internet about almost any research topic. However, finding that information can be frustrating if you don't know where or how to look. *Search engines* are Internet research tools that can help you identify and screen resources. The search engines described here are the most popular ones. Keep in mind, however, that there are literally hundreds of search engines, many of them designed for finding specialized information. To quickly locate other possibilities, enter "search engines" in the key word field of the search engines described in this figure.

A search engine travels the Web, indexes documents it finds on Web sites, and places those documents in a database. When you enter key words or phrases to be searched, the engine scans its database and returns all documents or "hits" that contain a match. Effective searches often require linking key words together. *Boolean search operators*, such as *AND, WITH, NEAR, OR,* and *NOT,* can help you limit or expand your search. For example, if you searched for "Ford AND automobiles," you would receive documents that contain both words. Entering "Ford WITH automobiles" would return hits where the two words appear beside each other. Entering "Ford NEAR automobiles" would return hits where the two words appear in close proximity to one another. Searching for "Ford OR automobiles," would return documents containing at least one, but not necessarily both words. And if you entered "Ford NOT automobiles" you would see all documents that refer to Ford but do not mention automobiles. The *NOT* operator can be especially effective for limiting unwanted hits. Most search engines recognize Boolean search operators, although some substitute symbols, such as plus and minus signs, to achieve the same results.

Each engine has qualities that distinguish it from the others. Some engines index all the pages they find. Others index only the most popular pages. Many will also search Usenet newsgroups instead of Web sites, depending on which one you specify when you enter your query. And each search engine updates its database on a different schedule. These differences create great variation in search results. It is always best, therefore, to try your search on several engines. Yahoo!, Infoseek, Alta Vista, Excite, Open Text, and Cyber411 represent a few of the more popular search engines available. There are many others, however, some of which are designed for locating specific types of information.

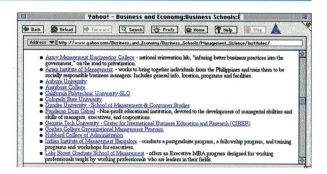

Yahoo! is actually called a *Web directory* because it files all of its documents in categories. It works best when you want to locate many similar sites under a particular subject or title. Yahoo! supports case-sensitive matching, which can be very helpful when searching for documents containing proper names. For example, by entering "China," you are assured of receiving only documents that refer to the country, and not to porcelain dishes. The documents that Yahoo! returns are given priority when key words appear either in the title or multiple times in the text. Also, more general categories are ranked higher than narrowly focused categories.

Infoseek has a reputation for consistently finding the most relevant Web sites. It ranks sites by the proximity of the search terms to each other within the document. With Infoseek, you can search for documents by their title, Internet address (URL), or text. The engine also supports case-sensitive searches and searching by phrases. In addition to its search engine capabilities, Infoseek maintains a Web directory similar to Yahoo!'s. Infoseek excels at bringing you specific information without making you wade through a lot of irrelevant documents.

Alta Vista is commonly known as having the largest search engine database on the Web. It claims to contain well over 20 million pages. This makes it the engine of choice when you want the most comprehensive results or when you are searching for obscure information. Alta Vista allows you to limit your returns by date or by instructing the engine to prioritize documents that contain particular words. However, its document relevance ranking is not the best, so you may have to sift through several pages of less pertinent documents before finding the ones you want.

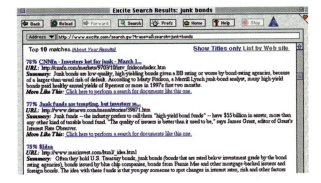

Excite is known for having the broadest search capabilities and one of the most up-to-date databases of any search engine. Excite maintains a Web directory and is capable of searching by phrases. In addition, it allows you to sort the hits by the number of pages they contain so that you may identify the documents that hold the most information. However, Excite ranks its hits by popularity, as determined by the number of links that point to each site. This means that the most relevant hits are not always retrieved first. Excite performs best with mainstream topics that are widely discussed.

(continued)

Figure 15.4
(Continued)

Open Text has received excellent reviews for its design, layout, and comprehensive search tools. You may search for up to five search terms and use any of five Boolean operators between them. You may also specify whether you want the engine to search the title, summary, first heading, URL, or anywhere in the document. You can even create a "weighted search," in which you rank different search terms. However, Open Text does not identify misspellings or plural forms of search terms. Furthermore, the engine will find hits for phrases only if the search terms appear in the document exactly as they were entered in the search. Open Text is excellent for finding specific information if you make an effort to structure your search well.

Cyber411 is a *metasearch engine*, searching 15 major search engines at once, including all of those described here. This broad approach can make your search much more efficient when you are looking for large amounts of information. However, Cyber411's

search parameters are not very complex. Consequently, you may also want to search individual engines if you are looking for a very focused topic.

Regardless of which search engine you choose, your results will be best if you spend a few minutes becoming acquainted with it before initiating your search. Each engine has a "tips" or "help" page that explains which operators it uses, whether it recognizes misspellings, whether case-sensitivity is supported, how it ranks pages for relevancy, and whether it is capable of searching phrases. You should also become acquainted with each engine's advanced search capabilities, because they will usually bring you better hits. Getting to know each engine's strengths and weaknesses at the start of your search can save you a lot of time and frustration later.

- ***Is the source potentially biased?*** Some of the information you'll find in your research will have been produced and distributed by people or organizations with a particular point of view. Bias isn't necessarily bad; in fact, getting people to believe one thing and not another is the purpose of much of the world's communication efforts. If you gather some facts from the Tobacco Institute or the American Association of Retired Persons, you have a fairly clear idea of what these organizations stand for and what biases their messages may have. However, organizations with neutral names, such as the Heritage Foundation, People for the American Way, or the U.S. Committee for Energy Awareness, aren't as easy to categorize. Without knowing what these organizations stand for, you're at their mercy when it comes to interpreting the information they produce. Also, an organization's source of funding may influence its information output. Again, there is nothing inherently unethical about this; you just need to be aware of it when you interpret the information.

- ***Where did the source get its information?*** Many secondary sources are themselves derived from other sources, making you even further removed from the original information. If a newspaper article says that pollutants in a local river dropped by 50 percent in the last year, chances are the reporter who wrote the article didn't make those measurements directly. He or she got the number from someone else.

- *Can you verify the material independently?* A good way to uncover mistakes or biases is to search for the same information from another source. This can be particularly important when the information goes beyond simple facts to include projections, interpretations, and estimates.
- *Will the source's claims stand up to thoughtful scrutiny?* Finally, step back and ask yourself whether the things you read or hear make sense. If a researcher claims that the market for a particular product will triple in the next five years, ask yourself what will have to happen for that prediction to come true. Will three times as many customers buy the product? Will existing customers buy three times as much as they currently buy? Why?

You probably won't have time to conduct a thorough background check on all your sources, so focus your efforts on the most important or most suspicious pieces of information.

The amount of library research you do depends on the subject you're studying and the purpose of your investigation. Linda Moreno conducted fairly extensive research, both to analyze Electrovision's expense problems and to find potential solutions. Since travel costs are a concern to so many companies, business newspapers and magazines publish quite a few articles on the subject.

Regardless of the amount of research you do, retain complete and accurate notes on the sources of all the material you collect, using one of the systems explained in Component Chapter B, "Documentation of Report Sources." Documenting your sources through footnotes, endnotes, or some similar system lends credibility to your report. It also helps you steer clear of plagiarism (see "How to Avoid Plagiarism").

Stop when you reach the point at which additional effort provides little new information.

Collecting Primary Data

When the information you need is not available from secondary sources, you collect and interpret the data yourself by doing primary research, going out into the real world to gather information through your own efforts. The four main ways of collecting primary data are examining documents, making observations, surveying people, and conducting experiments.

Conduct primary research by collecting basic information yourself.

Documents

In business a great deal of information is filed away for future reference. By scouring a company's files, you can often piece together an accurate, factual, historical record from the tidbits of evidence revealed in various letters, memos, and reports. Philadelphia National Bank has cataloged five generations of correspondence so that its senior managers can understand past events and operations. By researching the bank's previous positions on certain issues or by studying the roots of company trends, managers can gain valuable insight into current problems and situations.[8]

Business documents that qualify as primary data include sales reports prepared by field representatives, balance sheets and income statements, policy statements, correspondence with customers and suppliers, contracts, and log books. Many government and legal documents are also primary sources because they represent a decision made by those present at some official proceeding.

Documentary evidence and historical records are sources of primary data.

HOW TO AVOID PLAGIARISM

Is it right to kidnap someone else's ideas, words, or original research? *Plagiarism* (a word derived from the Latin for "kidnapping") occurs when one person misappropriates without permission or acknowledgment any ideas, facts, words, or structures that were reported or originated by others. In general, you're flirting with plagiarism when your business documents fail to alert your audience that you have

- Repeated someone else's information word for word
- Paraphrased another's material too closely
- Lifted a series of phrases and put them together with your own words
- Borrowed a unique term that originated elsewhere

Of course, plagiarism is completely unacceptable in the academic world, where term papers, research projects, and other materials must include the proper documentation to indicate when information is taken from other sources. Plagiarism is similarly unacceptable in the business world, although authorship is cited differently.

For example, many organizations downplay the role of individual writers. Whereas academic documents take great pains to show the name of every individual who contributed ideas, criticism, or words, some companies prefer to show the name of an entire department, division, or company as the author of a business document. When your company follows this con-

vention, it's usually not necessary to give credit to any individuals if you cite internal documents in your own report.

Another example is the memo, letter, or other document that you write but that is issued under someone else's name, such as that of your supervisor. In contrast to the college environment, where putting your name on a term paper written by another student would be considered plagiarism, putting a supervisor's name on a business report written by an employee would rarely be seen as plagiarism. After all, drafting documents on behalf of a supervisor is a legitimate part of the employee's job in most organizations.

As a business communicator, you'll often face decisions about how and when to use information from other sources as you draft reports, letters, memos, speeches, articles, manuals, brochures, and other materials. In general, using quotation marks when quoting from a source—and then citing the original source—enables you to properly credit the person whose words you're using. It also tells your audience where to look if they want more information. Similarly, even if you paraphrase from a source, it's important to indicate who originated the information you are using. Although your company may have more specific guidelines, here are a few general tips on how to handle situations that commonly arise when you plan business documents that include information from other sources:

A single document may be both a secondary source and a primary source. When citing summaries of financial and operations data from an annual report, you're using it as a secondary source. That same report, however, would be considered a primary source if you were analyzing its design features or comparing it with annual reports from other years or other companies.

Observations

Observation applies your five senses and your judgment to the investigation.

Informal observations are a rather common source of primary data in business. You simply use your five senses (especially your eyes and ears) to gather information. For instance, many reports are based on the writer's visiting a facility and observing operations. More objective information can be gathered through formal observations, which give observers a structure for noting what they see, thereby minimizing opportunities for interpretation.

In general, observation is a useful technique when you're studying objects, physical activities, processes, the environment, or human behavior. However, it can be expensive and time consuming, and the value of the observation depends on the reliability of the observer. Many people have a tendency to see what they want to see or to interpret events in light of their own experience. However, if the observer is trustworthy and has proper instructions, observation can provide valuable insights.[9]

- *Repeating information from another company document.* If you reuse information that appeared in other company documents, your audience may believe that you've independently verified the repeated material and eliminated any errors that were in the original report. To avoid such misunderstandings, it's best to mention where the material appeared earlier. That way, your readers can check the source for further details.

- *Using the same sources as a noncompany document.* Consulting someone else's sources for further information is perfectly acceptable. Plagiarism deals with the way information is reported or analyzed, not with whether you can access the sources used by someone else. When you approach cited sources to get the same information yourself, you're being absolutely ethical.

- *Repeating information protected by copyright.* When you want to repeat information from books, published articles, songs, and other copyrighted materials, be sure to avoid infringing on the originators' legal rights. Even when you document your sources, you may find that your use of outside information has inadvertently violated copyright laws. Although ideas can't be copyrighted, words, illustrations, graphs, maps, cartoons, poetry, and other creative expressions of ideas can be legally protected against unauthorized use by others. To be safe, talk to your company's attorney before you repeat information or reprint artwork that is protected by copyright.

At the very least, people often lose respect for someone who has been caught kidnapping the words of another. At worst, plagiarism in business documents can lead to more serious consequences. For example, a scientific researcher lost government funding when the National Institutes of Health found that he had published as his own the conclusions and experimental protocol from another researcher's manuscript. In another case, a *Denver Post* art critic was fired after editors found that she had falsely claimed authorship of two short stories that were written by others.

Consider how you would feel if you saw your words used without proper credit. On the other hand, you would probably feel flattered if a business report mentioned your work and cited you as the source. So to avoid even the most unintentional plagiarism, the best approach in most cases is to acknowledge the contributions of others by citing sources carefully and completely.

1. How might you indicate to listeners that a specific passage in your speech is taken word for word from a document written by someone else?
2. If you were the general manager of a marketing research firm, what rules might you establish to help your staff avoid unintentional plagiarism when writing analytical reports for clients?

Surveys

Often the best way to obtain answers to your questions is to ask people with relevant experience and opinions. Such surveys include everything from a single interview to the distribution of thousands of questionnaires.

When you need specialized information that hasn't been recorded anywhere, you may want to conduct a personal interview with an expert, which is the simplest form of survey. Many experts come from the ranks of your own organization: people from other departments who have specialized knowledge, your predecessor in the job, or long-time employees who have seen it all. On occasion you may also want to talk with outsiders who have some special expertise. Gosh Enterprises' Charley Shin may want to survey fast-food customers to keep up with their preferences in fast-food preparation.

A common way to conduct primary research is to interview well-qualified experts.

Doing an interview may seem an easy way to get information, but it requires careful preparation. You don't want to waste anyone's time, and you want your efforts to be productive. Chapter 19 presents some helpful pointers on conducting effective interviews.

Although they have the same purpose, interviews are quite different from formal, large-scale surveys in which a sample population answers a series of carefully tested questions. In Linda Moreno's work at Electrovision, she needed to know why people were traveling and whether there were suitable alternatives to frequent travel.

A formal survey is a way of finding out what a cross section of people thinks about something.

When Harris Research's Jodi Hart administers surveys in a face-to-face interview, she takes great pains not to waste anyone's time—whether conducting the survey in a formal office setting or in a more casual public place.

A formal survey requires a number of important decisions:

- Will face-to-face interviews, phone calls, printed questionnaires, or computer-based surveys be more useful?
- How many individuals will you contact to get results that are *reliable* (that is, reproducible if the same study were repeated)? Who will those people be? What sample is an accurate reflection of the population?
- What specific questions will you ask to get a *valid* picture, a true reflection of the group's feelings on the subject?[10]

Two important research criteria are:
- Reliability—when the same results would be obtained if the research were repeated
- Validity—when research measures what it is intended to measure

Your answers to these questions have a profound effect on the results of your survey.

Having seen rival preelection polls that come up with conflicting projections of who's going to win, you may wonder whether it makes sense to rely on survey results at all. The answer is yes, as long as you understand the nature of surveys. For one thing, surveys reveal only what people think about something at a specific time. For another, pollsters ask various people different questions in various ways and, not surprisingly, get differing answers. Just because surveys produce differing results doesn't mean that surveys are a poor form of research. Conducting a reliable, valid survey is not an easy matter. Generally speaking, it helps to have the advice of a specialist.

Developing an effective questionnaire requires care and skill.

One of the most critical elements of a survey is the questionnaire. To develop one, begin by making a list of the points you're trying to determine. Then break these points into specific questions, choosing an appropriate type of question for each point (Figure 15.5 shows some variations). The following guidelines will help you produce valid results:

- ***Provide clear instructions.*** Respondents need to know exactly how to fill out the questionnaire.
- ***Keep the questionnaire short and easy to answer.*** People are more likely to respond if they can complete the questionnaire within 10 or 15 minutes. So ask only questions that are relevant to your research. In addition, don't ask questions that require too much work on the respondent's part. People aren't willing to dig up the answers to questions like "What was your monthly rate of water consumption in 1996?"

Figure 15.5
Types of Survey Questions

QUESTION TYPE	EXAMPLE
Open-ended	How would you describe the flavor of this ice cream?
Either-or	Do you think this ice cream is too rich? _____ Yes _____ No
Multiple Choice	Which description best fits the taste of this ice cream? (Choose only one.) a. Delicious b. Too fruity c. Too sweet d. Too intensely flavored e. Bland f. Stale
Scale	Please make an X on the scale to indicate how you perceive the texture of this ice cream. Too light Light Creamy Too creamy
Checklist	Which flavors of ice cream have you had in the past 12 months? (Check all that apply.) _____ Vanilla _____ Chocolate _____ Strawberry _____ Chocolate chip _____ Coffee
Ranking	Rank these flavors in order of your preference, from 1 (most preferred) to 5 (least preferred): _____ Vanilla _____ Cherry _____ Maple nut _____ Chocolate ripple _____ Coconut
Short-answer Questions	In the past month how many times did you buy ice cream in the supermarket? _____ In the past month how many times did you buy ice cream in ice cream shops? _____

- *Formulate questions that provide easily tabulated or analyzed answers.*
  Numbers and facts are easier to deal with than opinions are. Nevertheless, you
  may be able to elicit countable opinions with multiple-choice questions or to
  group open-ended opinions into a limited number of categories.
- *Avoid questions that lead to a particular answer, because they bias your survey.*
  This question obviously calls for a yes answer: "Do you prefer that we stay open
  in the evenings for the convenience of our customers?" A less biased alternative
  would be: "What time of day do you normally do your shopping?"
- *Ask only one thing at a time.* When you pose a compound question like "Do you
  read books and magazines regularly?" you don't allow for the respondent who
  reads one but not the other.
- *Avoid questions with vague or abstract words.* Instead of asking "Are you frequently troubled by colds?" ask, "How many colds did you have in the past
  12 months?"

Figure 15.6
Computer-Based
Interviewing

Sawtooth Technologies offers interviewing software that helps you create questionnaires that can be specifically adapted to fit the requirements of your company.

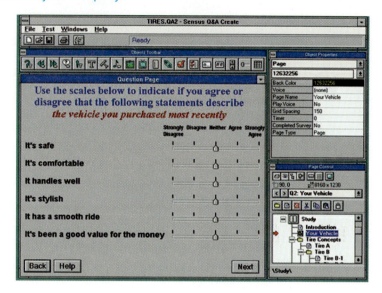

- *Include a few questions that rephrase earlier questions.* Such questions will
  help you cross-check the validity of respondents' responses.
- *Pretest the questionnaire.* Have a sample group identify questions that are subject to misinterpretation.[11]

If you're mailing your questionnaire, rather than administering it in person, include a
persuasive cover letter that explains why you're conducting the research. Try to convince the person that her or his response is important to you. If possible, offer to share
the results with the respondent. Mention that you won't disclose information that
can identify individual respondents. Include a preaddressed envelope with prepaid
postage so that the respondent won't have to find an envelope or postage to return the
questionnaire to you. Remember, however, that even under the best of circumstances
you may not get more than a 10 to 20 percent response.

Computer-based interviewing (CBI) can be an excellent way to gather and analyze
data (see Figure 15.6). Two big advantages of CBI are real-time customization (the
computer can change the flow and content of the interview based on each person's answers) and the ability to automatically sort and compile data during the interview. CBI
can be conducted in several ways, including mailing survey disks or inviting people to
respond at an Internet Web site. TK Associates International is a consulting firm in
Portland, Oregon, that helps U.S. companies market to Japanese consumers and businesses, and it has used its Web site to conduct a survey with more than 2,000 Japanese
computer users.[12] This application of CBI was particularly helpful because the company was researching Web-based marketing opportunities.

Experiments

Experiments are far more common in technical fields than in general business. That's
because an experiment requires extensive manipulation of the factors involved, which
is often very expensive (and may even be unethical when people are one of the factors).

Nevertheless, experiments do have their place. Say you want to find out whether a change in lighting levels increases the productivity of the pattern cutters in your dressmaking business. The most objective approach is to conduct an experiment using two groups of cutters: one working under existing conditions and the other working under the new lighting.

When conducting an experiment, it's important to carefully control the factors (called variables) you're not testing. Thus, in the lighting experiment, for the results to be valid, the only difference between the two groups and their environments should be the lighting. Otherwise, differences in productivity could be attributed to such factors as age differences between the two groups or experience on the job. It's even possible that introducing any change in the pattern cutters' environment, whether it be lighting or something else entirely, is enough to increase their productivity.

> The aim when conducting an experiment is to keep all variables the same except for the one you're testing.

STEP 5: ANALYZING AND INTERPRETING DATA

After you've completed your research, you're ready to analyze your data and interpret the findings. The analytical process is essentially a search for relationships among the facts and bits of evidence you've compiled. By themselves, the data you've collected won't offer much meaning or insight. It's the *analysis* of these facts and the *interpretation of the findings* that give you the information you need in order to understand or solve a problem.

> Analyze your results by calculating statistics, drawing reasonable and logical conclusions, and if appropriate, developing a set of recommendations.

Looking at the data from various angles, you attempt to detect patterns that will enable you to answer the questions outlined in your work plan. Your mind begins to fit pieces together and to form tentative conclusions. As your analysis proceeds, you either verify or reject these conclusions. Your mind constantly filters, sorts, and combines ideas, so this is where your critical thinking skills will be put to the test.

Calculating Statistics

Much of the information you compile during the research phase will be in numerical form. Assuming that it's been collected carefully, this factual data is precise, measurable, and objective—and therefore credible. However, statistical information in its raw state is of little practical value. It must be manipulated so that you and your readers can interpret its significance.

Averages

One useful way of looking at data is to find the **average,** which is a number that represents a group of numbers. Consider the data presented in Figure 15.7, for example, showing the sales booked by a group of nine salespeople over one week. To analyze this information, you could calculate the average—but which average? Depending on how you planned to use the data, you could choose the mean, the median, or the mode.

> The same set of data can be used to produce three kinds of averages: mean, median, and mode.

The most commonly used average is the *mean,* or the sum of all the items in the group divided by the number of items in the group. The mean is useful when you want to compare one item or individual with the group. In the example, the mean is $7,000. If you were the sales manager, you might well be interested in knowing that Wimper's sales were average; that Wilson, Green, and Carrick had below-average sales; and that Keeble, Kemble, O'Toole, Mannix, and Caruso were above average. One problem with using the mean, however, is that it can give you a false picture if one of the numbers is extreme. Say that Caruso's sales for the week were $27,000. The mean would then be $9,000, and eight of the nine salespeople would be performing "below average."

Figure 15.7
Three Types of Averages:
Mean, Median, and Mode

SALES-PERSON	SALES	
Wilson	$ 3,000	
Green	5,000	
Carrick	6,000	
Wimper	7,000	Mean
Keeble	7,500	Median
Kemble	8,500	
O'Toole	8,500	Mode
Mannix	8,500	
Caruso	9,000	
Total	$ 63,000	

The *median* is the "middle of the road" average: It's found in the midpoint of a series.[13] Above and below the median are an equal number of items. In a numerical ranking like the one shown in Figure 15.7, the median is the number right in the middle of the list: $7,500. The median is useful when one (or a few) of the numbers is extreme. For example, even if Caruso's sales were $27,000, the median would still be $7,500.

The *mode* is the number that occurs more often than any other in your sample.[14] It's the best average for answering a question like "What is the usual amount?" If you wanted to know what level of sales was most common, you would answer with the mode, which is $8,500. Like the median, the mode is not affected by extreme values. It's much easier to find than the median, however, when you have a large number of items or individuals.

While you're analyzing averages, you should also consider the *range,* or the spread of a series of numbers. In the example, the fact that sales per person ranged from $3,000 to $9,000 may raise the question of why there is such a wide gap between Wilson's and Caruso's performances. A range tells you the context in which the averages were calculated and demonstrates what values are possible.

Trends

If you were overseeing the work of Wilson, Caruso, and the other salespeople, you might be tempted to make some important personnel decisions on the basis of the week's sales figures. You would be a lot smarter, however, to compare them with sales figures from other weeks, looking for a **trend,** a steady upward or downward movement in a pattern of events taking place over time. By examining the pattern over a number of weeks, you could begin to see which salespeople were consistently above average and which were consistently below. You could also see whether sales for the group as a whole were increasing, declining, or remaining steady and whether there were any seasonal fluctuations in the sales pattern.

Trend analysis involves an examination of data over time so that patterns and relationships can be detected.

This type of trend analysis is very common in business. By looking at data over a period of time, you can detect patterns and relationships that will help you answer important questions.

Correlations

Once you have identified a trend, look for the cause. Say that Caruso consistently produces the most sales. You would undoubtedly be curious about the secret of her success. Does she call on her customers more often? Is she a more persuasive person? Does she have larger accounts or a bigger sales territory? Is she simply more experienced than the others?

To answer these questions, you could look for a **correlation,** a statistical relationship between two or more variables. For example, if salespeople with the largest accounts consistently produced higher sales, you might assume that these two factors were correlated, or related in a predictable way. You might conclude that Caruso's success was due, at least in part, to the average size of her accounts.

A correlation is a statistical relationship between two or more variables.

However, your conclusion might be wrong. Correlations are useful evidence, but they do not necessarily prove a cause-and-effect relationship. Caruso's success might well be the result of several other factors. To know for sure, you would have to collect more evidence.

Drawing Conclusions

Regardless of how much evidence you amass, at some point in every analysis you move beyond hard facts that can be objectively measured and verified. When you reach that point, you begin to formulate a **conclusion,** which is a logical interpretation of what the facts in your report mean. Reaching good conclusions based on the evidence at hand is one of the most important skills you can develop for your business career. A sound conclusion meets the following criteria:

Conclusions are interpretations about what the facts mean.

- *It must fulfill the original statement of purpose.* After all, this is why you took on the project in the first place.
- *It must be based strictly on the information included in the rest of the report.* In other words, the conclusion must consider all the information in the report and no information not included in the report. While drawing a conclusion, you can introduce no new information. (If it's that important, it should be in the body of the report.) Nor can you ignore any information in your report that doesn't support your conclusion.
- *It must be logical.* People sometimes toss the word *logical* into a conversation without thinking much about its true meaning. For the purposes of writing a business report, a logical conclusion is one that follows accepted patterns of reasoning.

Check the logic that underlies your conclusions.

Reasoning falls into two distinct categories. With **inductive reasoning,** you arrive at a general conclusion after analyzing many specific pieces of evidence. If every one of your stores experienced a sales decline during a recent blizzard (specific evidence), you could reasonably conclude that harsh weather can have a negative effect on sales (general conclusion).

Deductive reasoning, in contrast, works from general principles to specific conclusions. This includes the classic form of argumentation called a syllogism, in which you state a general principle (the major premise), then a specific case (the minor premise), and then draw a conclusion based on the relationship of the two premises. Say that you study employee productivity problems and discover that radios distract some employees from their work. If you were to conclude that radios are affecting productivity, you could construct a syllogism such as this:

Major premise: Things that distract employees reduce productivity (general principle).

Minor premise: Radios are distracting employees (specific case).

Conclusion: Therefore, radios reduce productivity.

To support your conclusion, you have to be able to demonstrate that both premises are true. In addition, you need to consider cause-and-effect relationships. Maybe it's not radios themselves that are distracting people but the fact that employees argue constantly about which stations to listen to. The music may in fact help relieve stress or boredom, if only you could get people to agree.

Conclusions need to be logical, but this doesn't mean they automatically flow from the evidence. Most business decisions require assumptions and judgment; relatively few are based strictly on the facts. Your personal values or the organization's values may also influence your conclusions; just be sure that you are conscious of how these biases may be affecting your judgment. Nor can you expect members of a team to examine the evidence and all arrive at the same conclusion. One of the key reasons for bringing additional people into a decision is to gain the value of their unique perspectives and experiences.

Developing Recommendations

Drawing a conclusion is one thing; deciding what to do about it and then recommending action is another. Recommendations are inappropriate in a report when you're not expected to supply them, so be sure you know the difference between conclusions and recommendations. Recall that a conclusion is an opinion or interpretation of what the facts mean; a **recommendation** suggests what ought to be done about the facts. Here's an example of the difference:

> *Recommendations are suggestions for action.*

Conclusion
I conclude that on the basis of its track record and current price, this company is an attractive buy.

Recommendation
I recommend that we write a letter to the president offering to buy the company at a 10 percent premium over the market value of its stock.

When you've been asked to take the final step and translate your conclusions into recommendations, be sure to make the relationship between them clear. Keep in mind that your assumptions and personal values may enter into your recommendations, but to be credible they must be based on logical analysis and sound conclusions.

When you develop recommendations of your own, consider whether your suggestions are practical and acceptable to your readers; they're the people who have to make the recommendations work. Be certain that you have adequately described the steps that come next. Don't leave your readers scratching their heads and saying, "This all sounds good, but what do I do on Monday morning?"

> *Good recommendations are*
> - *Practical*
> - *Acceptable to readers*
> - *Explained in enough detail for readers to take action*

SUMMARY

Effective business reports begin with a clear definition of the problem to be investigated and a statement of purpose, which outlines what the report should accomplish. Once the problem has been defined, you can determine what information will be required to solve it and develop a plan for obtaining that information.

During the research phase, review such secondary sources as books, periodicals, and reports. You may also conduct primary research to obtain information that is not available from existing sources. This research may involve reading documents, conducting surveys, designing experiments, and conducting firsthand observation.

When you've completed your research and analyzed the data, you're ready to develop conclusions, which are interpretations about what the facts mean. In some cases, you'll offer recommendations, which are suggestions for taking action based on your conclusions. Be certain that your suggestions are logical, practical, and acceptable to the report's readers.

COMMUNICATION CHALLENGES AT GOSH ENTERPRISES

Charley Shin always keeps one eye on the marketplace and one eye on his plans for expansion. Are his ideas still in line with consumer interests? He learned the importance of paying attention to the customer's perspective shortly after opening the first Charley's Steakery. The restaurant was named simply "Charley's"—until Shin realized that the name didn't communicate what kind of food customers could expect from "Charley." When he spelled it out with a sign that said "Charley's Steakery," business increased by 50 percent.

That's why, in addition to the three-year-growth plan, Shin wants to take another look at fast-food trends. Charley's Steakery made its reputation by serving fresh sandwiches with everything prepared to order—no frozen, microwaved entrees. This "fresh food" concept has been popular with customers since 1986. Is it still important to them? Some of his burger-selling competitors have returned to greasier, less healthy cuisine (boosting business tremendously, they claim), but Shin isn't so sure their figures are giving an accurate picture; a double-digit increase in sales doesn't mean much if it's preceded by a huge plummet, as in the case of one competitor.

INDIVIDUAL CHALLENGE: As part of Shin's marketing staff, you've been asked to begin setting up the study. First task: Define the problem and draft a statement of purpose. Start putting your version on paper for presentation during a brainstorming session with the rest of your team.

TEAM CHALLENGE: After the team members have presented their ideas and the problem and purpose statements have been agreed on, your team needs to write a preliminary outline for the investigation and the report you will be developing. A formal work plan will be produced from your team's outline, so be thorough. You can structure the outline either in statement form or in question form.[15]

CRITICAL THINKING QUESTIONS

1. What are the advantages and disadvantages of knowing a lot about the problem you are researching? Explain.
2. Analyze any recent school or work assignment that required you to conduct research. Was the assignment informational, analytical, or a mix? How did you approach your investigation? Did you rely mostly on primary or secondary sources? After studying this chapter, can you identify two ways to improve the research techniques you used during that assignment? Briefly explain.
3. Imagine you've detected a correlation in the trend data collected for an analytical report. What kind of research might help you determine whether a cause-and-effect relationship exists between the two variables? Why?
4. Put yourself in the position of a manager who is supervising an investigation but doing very little of the research personally. Why would a work plan be especially useful to the manager? To the researcher? Explain.
5. If you have a clear and detailed statement of purpose, why do you need a problem statement as well? Would it be a good idea to combine the two? Why or why not?
6. After an exhaustive study of an important problem, you have reached a conclusion that you know your company's management will reject. What do you do? Explain your answer.

EXERCISES

1. You're getting ready to launch a new lawn-care business offering mowing, fertilizing, weeding, and other services. The lawn surrounding a nearby shopping center looks like it could use better care, so you target that business for your first sales proposal. To help prepare this proposal, write your answers to these questions:
   a. What problem statement and statement of purpose would be most appropriate? (Think about the reader's viewpoint.)
   b. What questions will you need answered before you can write a proposal to solve the reader's problem? Be as specific as possible.
   c. Will you conduct primary or secondary research? Why? What sources will you use?
   d. What conclusions and recommendations might be practical, acceptable to the reader, and specific enough for the shopping center to take action? (Think about the purpose of the report.)

2. Now turn the situation around and assume that you're the shopping center's facilities manager. You report to the general manager, who must approve any new contracts for lawn service. Before you contract for lawn care, you want to prepare a formal study of the current state of your lawn's health. The report will include conclusions and recommendations for your boss's consideration. Draft a work plan, including the problem statement, the statement of purpose and scope, a description of what will result from your investigation, the sources and methods of data collection, and a preliminary outline.

3. Assume that your college president has received many student complaints about campus parking problems. You are appointed to chair a student committee organized to investigate the problems and recommend solutions. The president turns over to you the file labeled "Parking: Complaints from Students," and you jot down the essence of the complaints as you inspect the contents. Your notes look like this:

— Inadequate student spaces at critical hours
— Poor night lighting near the computer center
— Inadequate attempts to keep resident neighbors from occupying spaces
— Dim marking lines
— Motorcycles taking up full spaces
— Discourteous security officers
— Spaces (usually empty) reserved for college officials
— Relatively high parking fees
— Full fees charged to night students even though they use the lots only during low-demand periods
— Vandalism to cars and a sense of personal danger
— Inadequate total space
— Resident harassment of students parking on the street in front of neighboring houses

Your first job is to organize for committee discussion four or five areas that include all (or most) of these specific complaints. Choose the main headings for your outline, and group these specific complaints under them.

4. The college administration has asked you to head a student committee that will look into how the bookstore can ease the long lines during the first two weeks of every term, when students need to buy books. Select two other students to serve on your committee and help plan a feasibility study and an analytical report showing your recommendations. As a first step, your committee should prepare a brief memo to the administration in which you cover the following points:
   a. Draft the problem statement and the statement of purpose.
   b. Identify two or three likely alternatives to be investigated.
   c. Determine clear criteria for selecting among the options.
   d. Identify the primary and secondary sources of information to be used in the study.

5. Deciding how to collect primary data is an important part of planning a business report. Which one or more of the four methods of data collection (examining documents, making observations, surveying people, and conducting experiments) would you use if you were testing the following hypotheses? Explain your answers.
   a. The litter problem on campus has been reduced because the cafeteria is offering fewer take-out choices this year than in past years.
   b. Your school would attract more transfer students if it waived the formal application process and allowed students at other colleges to simply send their transcripts and a one-page letter of application.
   c. The school needs more computers, because students who compose their term papers on computers finish faster than those who use typewriters.
   d. The number of traffic accidents at the school's main entrance could be reduced if the stop signs at that intersection were placed more prominently.

6. As the new manager at The Gap clothing store, located in your local mall, you've been assigned to research and write a factual report about the day-to-day variations in store sales throughout a typical week. What's the most logical way to factor this problem and structure your informational report? Why? Indicate the subtopics you might use in your report.

7. After years of work, you've almost completed your first motion picture, the story of a group of unknown musicians finding work and making a reputation in a difficult world. Unfortunately, some of your friends leave the first complete screening saying that the 132-minute movie is simply too long. Others can't imagine any more editing cuts. You decide to test the movie on a regular audience, members of which will be asked to complete a questionnaire that may or may not lead to additional editing. You obtain permission from a local theater manager to show your film at 4:30 and 8:15, in between the regularly scheduled presentation. Design a questionnaire that can solicit valid answers.

8. Visit the Xerox Web site at <http://www.xerox.com> and carefully review the products and services discussed on the home page and linked pages. Prepare a survey instrument that Xerox could use for customer feedback on these products. Remember to avoid questions that are leading, and pretest your questionnaire on family and friends before submitting it to your instructor.

9. Some students on your campus have complained about the high cost of college textbooks. Team up with three other students to study the average cost of the textbooks purchased by students in this class. Start by designing a survey; then conduct the research, tabulate your results, and report the findings.
    a. List the survey questions you'll ask and decide whether you'll interview the students or ask them to write down their own answers.
    b. Pretest the questionnaire on several students to see whether the questions make sense.
    c. Conduct the research.
    d. Analyze the survey answers by determining the mean, the median, and the mode of the amounts spent on textbooks.
    e. Write a one- or two-page summary of your findings, including an interpretation of the data you've gathered.

10. You're conducting research for a supermarket chain, and you're trying to answer two questions: Do men or women make larger supermarket purchases? Does the age of the customer help predict the size of the purchase? Visit a local supermarket during a busy time, such as Saturday afternoon, and observe customers passing through one cash register for half an hour. You're interested in the gender and approximate age of the customers, the size and composition of the groups they're in, and the size of their purchases. Before your investigation prepare a sheet that will help you collect data systematically; afterward draft a brief narrative and statistical report of your findings.

11. Because of the success of your pizza delivery service, you're considering whether to expand. You'll need at least one additional delivery van if you expand, but you know that buying a van will lead to other expenses, such as maintenance, insurance, and so on. Before you can make a decision, you want to factor the problem and develop an outline to guide your investigation. As you do so, include a list of at least six questions to research and answer.

12. Your boss has asked for a report on sales for the first nine months of this year. Using the following data

from company invoices, calculate the mean for each quarter and all averages for the year to date. Then identify and discuss the quarterly sales trends.

January:	$24,600	June:	$26,800
February:	$25,900	July:	$29,900
March:	$23,000	August:	$30,500
April:	$21,200	September:	$26,600
May:	$24,600		

13. You're the advertising manager at a regional ice cream company. Your boss, the director of marketing, has asked you to report on how the company should use advertising to support new-product introductions, using this statement of purpose:

Statement of purpose: To analyze various methods of advertising new products when they are introduced and to recommend the most effective and cost-efficient program

    a. How should you factor this problem? Will you use descriptive or informative headings for your preliminary outline?
    b. Develop an outline, following the rules of division.
    c. Exchange outlines with a student in your class and critique each other's work. Comment on the organization, the logic, the consistency, and the completeness of the other student's outline. On the basis of the suggestions you receive, revise your own outline.

14. Now put yourself on the other side of the desk: You're the regional ice cream company's director of marketing. Your advertising manager has submitted a full report, and you're reviewing the conclusions. Identify and discuss the errors of logic underlying the following conclusions and recommendations in the report:
    a. As soon as we started advertising the new Apricot Swirl on television, sales increased, so we need to advertise every new fruit-flavored product on television.
    b. Coupons really work, and if we don't use them to promote every new product we introduce, they will all fail.
    c. Newspaper advertising didn't help Apricot Swirl, so let's not use it on any other new-product launch.
    d. Peanut Swirl isn't as good a flavor as the other new products, so it shouldn't receive the same extensive advertising support.

CHAPTER 16

DEVELOPING VISUAL AIDS

AFTER STUDYING THIS CHAPTER, YOU WILL BE ABLE TO

- Decide when using a visual aid would be appropriate
- Develop visual aids that conform to the principles of effective graphic design
- Select the right table, chart, or other illustration to simplify and dramatize your information
- Produce visual aids in an efficient manner
- Fit visual aids into the text of your report
- Analyze the effectiveness of a visual aid

COMMUNICATION CLOSE-UP AT EASTMAN KODAK COMPANY

The object is to get your message across, says Michael Fernandez, director of management communications for Eastman Kodak Company. Visuals greatly enhance a message. They increase the amount of information an audience takes home, whether the communication is oral or written. Just as you'd expect from a company like Kodak, the visual aids Fernandez uses range from the very simple (pie charts, tables, and flow charts) to the most sophisticated (images produced on digital cameras, color-corrected on computers, and stored on Photo CDs).

In 1888 George Eastman set out "to make the camera as convenient as the pencil." Today, Michael Fernandez has at his fingertips image manipulation tools that Eastman probably never dreamed of.

For instance, Kodak and four of its Japanese competitors have set standards for a new photo-imaging technology that moves photography closer to computing. The new cameras use drop-in cassettes loaded with film that features state-of-the-art emulsions and a magnetic strip. Today this magnetic strip records information used by film processors. But since it has the potential to store as much information as a 3 1/2-inch computer diskette, the strip's future applications boggle the imagination: Your snapshot of the CEO may one day include the sound of her voice, recorded when you snapped the image. And that's just one of a new generation of products that includes digital cameras (which allow images to be manipulated just like computer data) and new processing services (which supply a computer diskette with your standard prints so that you can call up your images on your PC and e-mail them anywhere in the world).

Fernandez is undaunted by this huge array of choices. Every visual tool still has its place, he believes, from bar charts in the annual report to computer-generated graphics rolled in over live video, a technique he used for a product announcement extrava-

Michael Fernandez

Whether you include a simple pie chart in your written report or emphasize your speech with state-of-the-art computer graphics, Kodak's Michael Fernandez believes that visuals greatly enhance your message by increasing the amount of information your audience comes away with.

ganza that took place simultaneously in Hollywood, Tokyo, London, and Rochester, New York.

With only 3 1/2 weeks to plan, Fernandez cooked up a visual feast of images for the event, including a 115-pound product prop that flew across the auditorium and landed at the CEO's feet, a wall-sized bank of video screens, and live satellite transmissions beamed around the world. The event was a terrific success, but Fernandez says it brings home two challenges facing today's communicators: First, he warns that "because the technology is making certain things easier to do, people begin to think that you can do just about anything; expectations are higher." Second, it's easy to become so involved with the imaging technology that you forget the importance of the words your images accompany.

"You're basically striving for something that is relatively simple, that has a great deal of clarity, and that provides people with strong images," says Fernandez. You need to know your audience, but before you begin to think about visual aids, you must be certain of your objectives. "What do you hope to achieve? Do you want an article in the newspaper? Do you want employees to think well of your benefits package?" Only after you know the primary message can you decide which visual elements to present. Pie charts, line graphs, and other visual aids are meant to enlighten. Visuals help you "hammer away at the fundamental points you're trying to make," says Fernandez.

Taking its message worldwide is common for Kodak, but it means that, in addition to clarifying information, Kodak's visual aids must work in diverse cultures. For instance, when Fernandez prepares written materials, he makes sure the visual aids will "translate" appropriately. He wants to avoid the kind of confusion Kodak ran into years ago, when it marketed a type of film called "Royal Pan." In Great Britain, recalls

Fernandez, "they didn't know whether we were referring to bedpans or passing judgment on the Royal family." Before he releases any material to a foreign audience, Fernandez tries it out on his overseas colleagues—and they've saved him from embarrassment more than once.

As a final step, Fernandez proofs the visual aids as carefully as the written text. Obvious errors are easy to spot, but everyone interprets visuals differently, so "it's important to look at an image as conveying some strategic idea," says Fernandez. Does it fulfill the objectives? Is it necessary, convenient, accurate, and honest? If not, it might be more of a visual distraction than a visual aid.[1]

PLANNING VISUAL AIDS

Conveying an important idea is the main reason businesspeople like Michael Fernandez include visual aids in their reports and proposals, but which comes first: visual aid or text? Say you've just completed the research for an important report or oral presentation. You're about to begin the composition phase. Your first impulse might be to start with the introduction and proceed page by page until you've completed the text or script. Almost as an afterthought you might throw in a few **visual aids**—tables, charts, graphs, schematic drawings, illustrations, photographs—to illustrate the words.

Although this approach makes some sense, many experienced businesspeople prefer to begin with the visual aids, which has three advantages. First, if much of the fact-finding and analytical work is already in tabular or graphic form, you already have a visual point of departure. Sorting through and refining your visuals will help you decide exactly what you're going to say. Second, many important business projects involve both a written report and an oral presentation of results. Similar visual aids, modified for different media, can be used for both communication situations. By starting with the visual aids, you develop a graphic story line that serves two purposes. Finally, the text or script explains and refers to the tables, charts, and graphs, so you save time by having them ready before you start to compose, particularly if you plan to use quite a few visuals.

> A visual aid is an illustration in tabular, graphic, schematic, or pictorial form.

Why Business Professionals Use Visual Aids

You may be wondering why visual aids are used at all. In business your audience is generally quite wide, and you may find yourself trying to communicate with people who have little or no interest in your ideas. Moreover, in the numbers-oriented world of work, people rely heavily on visual images. They think in terms of trend lines, distribution curves, and percentages. An upward curve means good news in any language, be it English or Japanese. Visual aids also attract and hold people's attention and help them understand and remember the message. In one study, 36 audiences were exposed to oral presentations with and without graphic aids, with the following results:

> Visual aids help communicators get through to an audience.

- In presentations where visual aids were used, the speaker was able to persuade the audience to accept the message two-thirds of the time. Speakers who did not use visuals won the audience to their point of view only half the time.
- The audience reached a consensus 79 percent of the time when graphics were used, but they agreed on a decision only 58 percent of the time when graphics weren't used.
- Meetings involving graphic presentations were 28 percent shorter than meetings involving no graphics.[2]

Although the study focused on oral presentations, to a considerable degree its results pertain to written reports as well.

TABLE 16.1

WHEN TO USE VISUAL AIDS

Purpose	Application
To clarify	Support text descriptions of "graphic" topics: quantitative or numerical information; explanations of trends; descriptions of procedures, relationships, locations; or composition of an item
To simplify	Break complicated descriptions into components that can be depicted with conceptual models, flow charts, organization charts, or diagrams
To emphasize	Call attention to particularly important points by illustrating them with line, bar, and pie charts
To summarize	Review major points in the narrative by providing a chart or table that sums up the data
To reinforce	Present information in visual and written form to increase readers' retention
To attract	Make material seem more interesting by decorating the cover or title page and by breaking up the text with visual aids
To impress	Build credibility by putting ideas in visual form to convey the impression of authenticity and precision
To unify	Depict the relationship among points—for example, with a flow chart

Despite their value, recommends Michael Fernandez of Kodak, use visual aids selectively, including only those elements that support your primary message. The illustrative material in a report or presentation should supplement the written or spoken word, not replace it, so restrict your use of visual aids to situations in which they do the most good. Table 16.1 helps you identify those situations.

The Process of "Visualizing" Your Text

Translating words and numbers into graphic format is generally an integral part of the process of preparing a report or presentation. As you sort through the information you've compiled during the research phase, you begin seeing relationships and drawing conclusions. An outline begins to take shape in your mind, and you select the facts you'll use to support each point. Some of these facts lend themselves to a prose presentation; others may be expressed more easily in graphic form. As you think about how to convey your message, you begin to envision the balance between verbal and graphic elements.

When planning visual aids
- *Decide what you want to say*
- *Pick out the points that can best be made visually*
- *Judge whether you have too many or too few graphics*

Decide on the Message

When you begin to compose a report or presentation, you usually have a lot of raw data that can be molded into a number of messages. Your first step then is to decide what you're trying to say. You do this by sorting through the facts you've compiled.

Suppose you've been asked to compare your company's recent sales with those of a competitor. You have the following data on market share for the past month:

Sales Region	Your Company's Share	Competitor's Share
North	10%	25%
South	40	8
East	32	32
West	20	23

Analyze raw data to identify the points supporting your main idea.

Now, what message can you derive from this set of data? Some of the possibilities are listed here:

- The two companies perform differently in different regions. Your company is strongest in the South, where your competitor is weakest.
- The two companies' performances are similar in the East and West.
- Both companies are uneven in their market share from region to region.

All these messages are true, and all of them might be useful. You decide which interpretation of the data is most useful for your purposes. As you sort through your facts, looking at various interpretations, you find that an outline of a message begins to emerge.

Identify Points That Require Visual Support

Use visual aids to simplify, clarify, and emphasize important information.

Once you have an outline in mind, you can begin to identify which points to illustrate graphically. Ask yourself how to visually dramatize the key elements of your message (which Kodak's Fernandez calls the strategic ideas). Think of each main point on your outline as a separate scene, and then try to visualize a chart or graph that would communicate the point to your audience.

Take your analysis a step further by considering other visual aids. Undoubtedly, some of the supporting items on your outline involve detailed facts and figures. This sort of information may be confusing and tedious when presented in paragraph form, but tables can conveniently organize and display such detail. If some points in your outline require a detailed description of physical relationships or procedures, you might use flow charts, drawings, or photographs to clarify the discussion.

Maintain a Balance Between Illustrations and Words

When planning the illustrations for your report or presentation, aim to achieve a reasonable balance between the verbal and the visual. The ideal blend depends on the nature of the subject. Some topics are more graphic than others and require more visual aids.

In general, use visual aids only to supplement the story you are telling in words.

Illustrating every point dilutes the effectiveness of all your visual aids. In a written report, particularly, telling your audience every paragraph or two to consult a table or chart is likely to obscure the thread of your argument. Furthermore, readers tend to assume that the amount of space allocated to a topic indicates its relative importance. So by using visual aids to illustrate a minor point, you may be sending a misleading message about its significance.

When deciding on the mix of words and visuals, give some thought to your readers' needs and thought patterns. Some people ignore the visuals and focus on the words; others do the opposite. If you know that your audience prefers one form of communication over the other—or has special communication needs—you can adjust the balance accordingly.

When General Mills redesigned its Hamburger Helper package, management decided to include both drawings and step-by-step photographs. These visual aids helped the company communicate with audiences who speak English as their second language. The illustrations also provided additional explanation for people who have limited cooking experience. "It's critically important that customers can read the directions, because if they don't have a successful experience with the food, they won't buy the product again," says Craig Shulstad, a General Mills spokesperson.[3]

Another factor to consider is your production schedule. If you're producing the report or presentation without the help of an art department or appropriate computergraphics tools, you may want to restrict the number of illustrations. Making charts and tables takes time, particularly if you're inexperienced.

DESIGNING VISUAL AIDS

Knowing what points you want to present visually and knowing exactly what format to use are separate things. The construction of visual aids requires a good deal of both imagination and attention to detail. Your main concern is always your audience. What format is most meaningful and convenient for them?

Understanding the Art of Graphic Design

You may not think of yourself as being the "artistic type," but chances are you have a better sense of design than you realize. Most people seem to subconsciously recognize good design when they see it, although they don't often know how to achieve the same effects on their own.[4]

Few of us have studied the "language" of line, mass, space, size, color, pattern, and texture. When arranged in certain ways, these elements of visual design are pleasing to the eye. More important for the business communicator, however, they have a meaning of their own. A thick line implies more power than a thin one; a bold color suggests strength; a solid mass seems substantial. To create effective visual aids, become conscious of both the aesthetic and the symbolic aspects of graphic art so that you won't send the wrong message. Here are a few principles to be aware of:

The elements of design convey meaning in subtle ways.

- **Continuity.** An audience views a series of visual aids as a whole and assumes that you'll use the elements of design in a consistent way from one page to the next. You'll confuse people if you make arbitrary changes in color, shape, size, texture, position, scale, or typeface. If your first chart shows results for division A in blue, the audience will expect division A to be shown in blue throughout the report or presentation.
- **Contrast.** The audience also expects that visual distinctions will match verbal distinctions. If you're contrasting A and B, depict them in a visually contrasting manner: red versus blue, black versus white. On the other hand, if you want to indicate similarities between two items, make the visual distinction between them would be more subtle. You might have a pie chart in which two similar items are shown in two shades of blue and a dissimilar item is shown in yellow.
- **Emphasis.** An audience assumes that the most important point will receive the most visual emphasis. Therefore, present the key item on the chart in the most prominent way—through color, position, size, or whatever. Visually downplay less important items. Avoid using strong colors for unimportant data, and de-emphasize background features such as the grid lines on a chart. Take care to avoid *chartjunk,* a term coined by information expert Edward Tufte to describe decorative elements that clutter documents (and confuse readers) without adding any relevant information.[5] Computers make it far too easy to add chartjunk, from

When designing visual aids, observe the principles of continuity, contrast, and emphasis.

clip art illustrations to three-dimensional bar charts that really display only two dimensions of data (see Figure 16.1).

- **Expectations.** Culture, education, and other experiences condition people to expect things to look certain ways, and these expectations can affect the way people respond to your visuals. Green is a color easily associated with money in the United States, but not so in countries that print currency in red, blue, yellow, and other colors. A red cross on a white background, the logo of the International Red Cross, symbolizes emergency medical care in many countries. However, since the cross is also a Christian symbol, the International Red Cross uses a red crescent in Islamic countries.[6]

The best time to think about the principles of good design is before preparing your visual aids; making changes after the fact increases the amount of time required to produce them.

Selecting the Right Visual Aid for the Job

Various types of messages call for various types of visual aids.

Once you've decided on the general design features for your report or presentation, you can begin developing the individual visual aids. Be sure to choose the specific form that best suits your message and that communicates your message most clearly to your audience.

Tables

Use tables to help your audience understand detailed information.

When you have to present detailed, specific information, choose a **table,** a systematic arrangement of data in columns and rows. Tables are ideal when the audience needs the facts, all the facts, and when the information would be either difficult or tedious to handle in the main text.

Most tables contain the standard parts illustrated in Figure 16.2 (see page 512). What makes a table a table is the grid that allows you to find the point where two factors intersect. So every table includes vertical columns and horizontal rows, with useful headings along the top and side. Tables projected onto a screen during an oral presentation should be limited to three column heads and six row heads; tables presented on paper may include from one or two heads to a dozen or more. If the table has too many columns to fit comfortably between the margins of the page, turn the paper horizontally and insert it in the report with the top toward the binding.

Although formal tables set apart from the text are necessary for complex information, you can present some data more simply within the text. You make the table, in essence, a part of the paragraph, typed in tabular format. These text tables are usually introduced with a sentence that leads directly into the tabulated information. Here's an example:

Half the people surveyed are very concerned about artificial coloring in the prepackaged foods they eat. Women and older people are most concerned:

	Percentage Who Are Very Concerned	Percentage Who Are Slightly Concerned
Men	44	40
Women	53	39
Adults 18–49	49	40
Adults 50–65	55	32

Source: "Artificial Coloring in Prepackaged Food," *Food Processing News,* January 1995, 113.

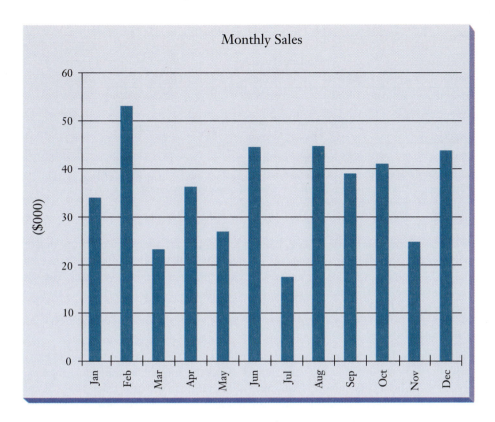

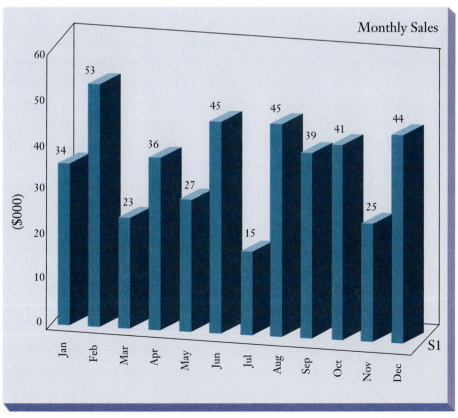

Figure 16.1
Simplify Graphics to Avoid
Clutter and Confusion

These two charts show
the same information,
but the second one is
cluttered with useless
decoration. The three-
dimensional bars don't
show anything more
than the simple two-
dimensional bars in the
first chart.

Figure 16.2
Parts of a Table

	TABLE 1 Title			
	Multicolumn Head		Single-Column Head*	Single-Column Head
Stub head	Subhead	Subhead	Head*	Head
Line head	XXX	XXX	XX	XX
Line head				
Subhead	XX	XXX	XX	XX
Subhead	XX	XXX	X	XX
Totals	XXX	XXX	XX	XX

Source: (in the same format as a text footnote; see Component Chapter B)
*Footnote (for explanation of elements in the table; a superscript number or small letter may be used instead of an asterisk or other symbol)

When preparing a numerical table, be sure to identify the units you're using: dollars, percentages, price per ton, or whatever. All items in a column are expressed in the same unit. Although many tables are numerical, word tables can be just as useful. They are particularly appropriate for presenting survey findings or for comparing various items against a specific standard.

Line and Surface Charts

Use line charts
- To indicate changes over time
- To plot the interaction of two variables

A **line chart** illustrates trends over time or plots the relationship of two variables. In line charts showing trends, the vertical axis shows the amount, and the horizontal axis shows the time or the quantity being measured. Ordinarily, both scales begin at zero and proceed in equal increments; however, in Figure 16.3, the vertical axis is broken to show that some of the increments have been left out. A broken axis is appropriate when the data are plotted far above zero, but be sure to clearly indicate the omission of data points.

A simple line chart may be arranged in many ways. One of the most common is to plot several lines on the same chart for comparative purposes, as shown in Figure 16.4. Try to use no more than three lines on any given chart, particularly if the lines cross. Another variation of the simple line chart has a vertical axis with both positive and negative numbers (see Figure 16.5). This arrangement is handy when you have to illustrate losses.

Figure 16.3
Line Chart with Broken Axis

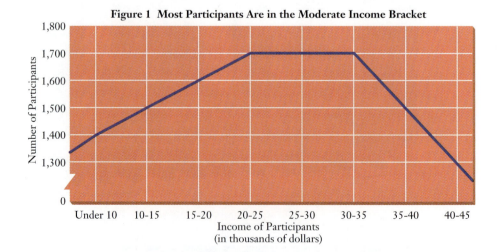

Figure 1 Most Participants Are in the Moderate Income Bracket

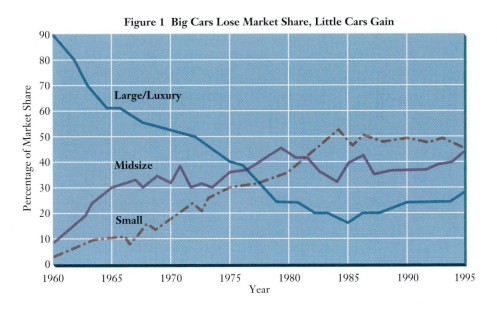

Figure 16.4
Line Chart Plotting
Three Lines

A **surface chart** is a form of line chart with a cumulative effect; all the lines add up to the top line, which represents the total (see Figure 16.6). This form of chart helps you illustrate changes in the composition of something over time. When preparing a surface chart, put the most important segment against the baseline, and restrict the number of strata to four or five.

A surface chart is a kind of line chart showing cumulative effect.

Bar Charts

A **bar chart** is a chart in which amounts are visually portrayed by the height or length of rectangular bars. Bar charts are almost as common in business reports as line charts, and in some ways they're more versatile. As Figure 16.7 illustrates, bar charts are particularly valuable when you want to

Bar charts, in which numbers are visually portrayed by rectangular bars, can take a variety of forms.

- Compare the size of several items at one time
- Show changes in one item over time

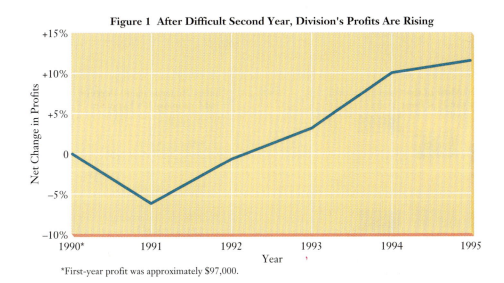

Figure 16.5
Line Chart with Positive and Negative Values on Vertical Axis

Figure 16.6
Surface Chart

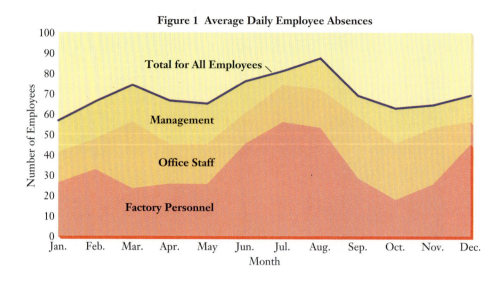

Figure 1 Average Daily Employee Absences

Total for All Employees

Management

Office Staff

Factory Personnel

Number of Employees

Jan. Feb. Mar. Apr. May Jun. Jul. Aug. Sep. Oct. Nov. Dec.

Month

Figure 16.7
The Versatile Bar Chart

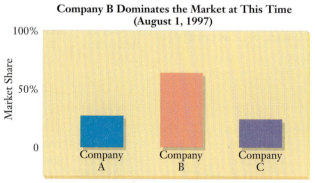

Company B Dominates the Market at This Time
(August 1, 1997)

Market Share

100%

50%

0

Company A   Company B   Company C

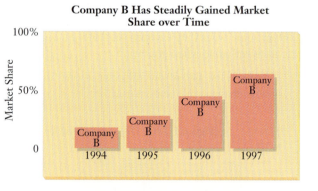

Company B Has Steadily Gained Market
Share over Time

Market Share

100%

50%

0

Company B 1994   Company B 1995   Company B 1996   Company B 1997

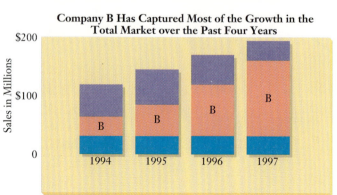

Company B Has Captured Most of the Growth in the
Total Market over the Past Four Years

Sales in Millions

$200

$100

0

B 1994   B 1995   B 1996   B 1997

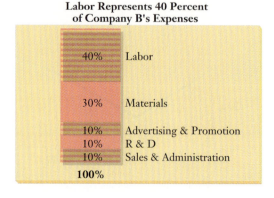

Labor Represents 40 Percent
of Company B's Expenses

40% Labor

30% Materials

10% Advertising & Promotion
10% R & D
10% Sales & Administration

100%

Figure 1 **Starting Salaries for Sales Careers (in thousands)**

Source: Adapted from David J. Rachman, Michael H. Mescon, Courtland L. Bovée, and John V. Thill, "Careers in Business," *Business Today*, 7th ed. (New York: McGraw-Hill, 1993), 657–670.

Figure 16.8
Pictogram

- Indicate the composition of several items over time
- Show the relative size of components of a whole

You can be creative with bar charts in many ways. You might align the bars either vertically or horizontally and double the bars for comparisons. You might even use bar charts to show both positive and negative quantities.

You can also convert the bars into a line of symbols, the number of symbols indicating the number of items (see Figure 16.8). A chart that uses symbols instead of words or numbers to portray data is known as a **pictogram.** The chief value of pictograms is their novelty. However, pictograms leave a lot to be desired from the standpoint of both preparation time and accuracy (the inability to show exact amounts, as in Figure 16.8 where showing part of a thousand is difficult). Although they occasionally enhance a report, they tend to be less useful than other types of bar charts.

Closely related to the bar chart is the **timeline chart,** which shows how much time is needed to complete each task in a given project. When you want to track progress toward completing a project, you can use a type of timeline chart known as a **Gantt chart** (named for management theorist Henry L. Gantt). The Gantt chart in Figure 16.9 shows

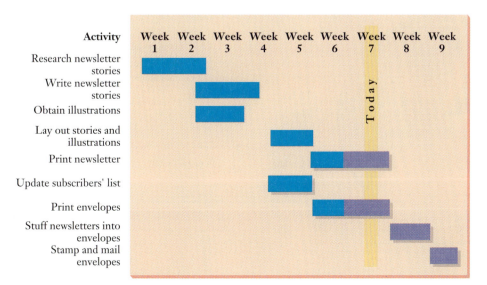

Figure 16.9
Gantt Chart

the activities involved in preparing and mailing a newsletter, which is running behind schedule. The dark bars indicate completed tasks; the lighter bars indicate activities not yet completed.

Pie Charts

Another type of chart you see frequently in business reports is the **pie chart,** in which numbers are represented as slices of a complete circle, or *pie.* As you can see from the pie chart in Figure 16.10, this type of chart helps you show exactly how each part relates to the whole. You can combine pie charts with tables to expand the usefulness of such visuals.

When composing pie charts, try to restrict the number of slices in the pie to seven. Otherwise, the chart looks cluttered and is difficult to label. If necessary, lump the smallest pieces together in a "miscellaneous" category. Ideally, the largest or most important slice of the pie, the segment you want to emphasize, is placed at the twelve o'clock position; the rest are arranged clockwise either in order of size or in some other logical progression. You might want to shade the segment that is of the greatest interest to your readers or use color to distinguish the various pieces. In any case, label all the segments and indicate their value in either percentages or units of measure so that your readers will be able to judge the value of the wedges. The segments must add up to 100 percent.

Flow Charts and Organization Charts

If you need to show physical or conceptual relationships rather than numerical ones, you might want to use a flow chart or an organization chart. A **flow chart** illustrates a sequence of events from start to finish. Flow charts are indispensable when illustrating processes, procedures, and relationships. The various elements in the process you want

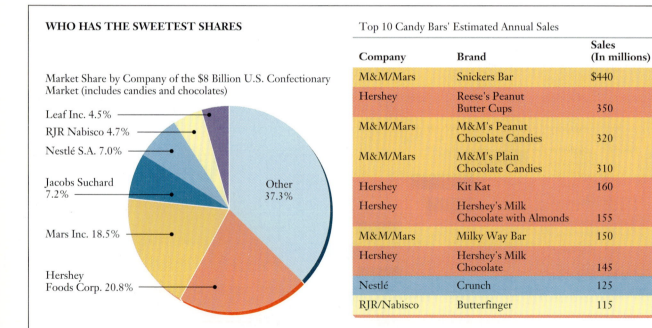

WHO HAS THE SWEETEST SHARES

Market Share by Company of the $8 Billion U.S. Confectionary Market (includes candies and chocolates)

Leaf Inc. 4.5%
RJR Nabisco 4.7%
Nestlé S.A. 7.0%
Jacobs Suchard 7.2%
Mars Inc. 18.5%
Hershey Foods Corp. 20.8%
Other 37.3%

Top 10 Candy Bars' Estimated Annual Sales

Company	Brand	Sales (In millions)
M&M/Mars	Snickers Bar	$440
Hershey	Reese's Peanut Butter Cups	350
M&M/Mars	M&M's Peanut Chocolate Candies	320
M&M/Mars	M&M's Plain Chocolate Candies	310
Hershey	Kit Kat	160
Hershey	Hershey's Milk Chocolate with Almonds	155
M&M/Mars	Milky Way Bar	150
Hershey	Hershey's Milk Chocolate	145
Nestlé	Crunch	125
RJR/Nabisco	Butterfinger	115

Figure 16.10
Pie Chart Combined with Table

to portray may be represented by pictorial symbols or geometric shapes, as shown in Figure 16.11.

An **organization chart,** as the name implies, illustrates the positions, units, or functions of an organization and the way they interrelate. An organization's normal communication channels are almost impossible to describe without the benefit of a chart like the one in Figure 16.12.

Use organization charts to depict the interrelationships among the parts of an organization.

Maps

For certain applications, maps are ideal. One of the most common uses is to show concentrations of something by geographic area. In your own reports, you might use maps to show regional differences in such variables as your company's sales of a product. You might indicate proposed plant sites and their relationship to key markets.

Most U.S. office-supply stores carry blank maps of various regions of the world, including all or part of the United States. You can illustrate these maps to suit your needs, using dots, shading, color, labels, numbers, and symbols. In addition, you can use specialized computer programs to select maps of various regions and insert just the portions you need into your business documents.

Use maps
- To represent statistics by geographic area
- To show location relationships

Figure 1 Flow of Clients Through Health Center

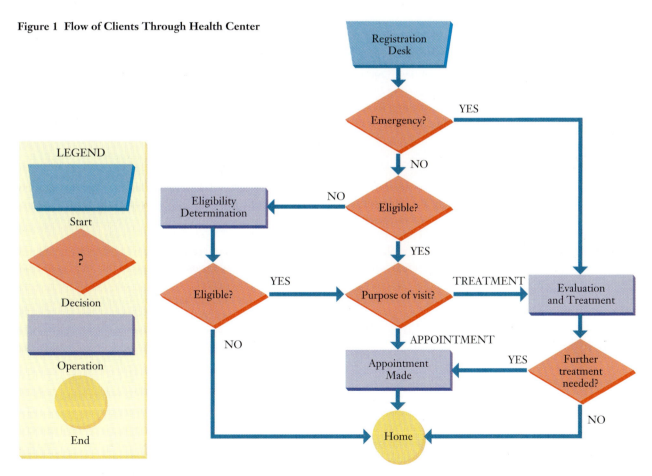

Figure 16.11
Flow Chart

Figure 1 Administration of Atlantic College

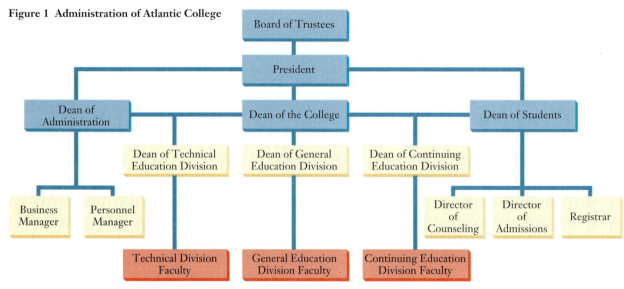

Figure 16.12
Organization Chart

Drawings, Diagrams, and Photographs

Use drawings and diagrams
to show
- How something looks
  or works
- How something is made
  or used

Although less common than other visual aids, drawings, diagrams, and photographs are also used in business reports. Drawings and diagrams are most often used to show how something looks or operates. Figure 16.13 is from an article explaining how a new satellite network will let people place calls to any point on earth from any point on earth. This diagram was professionally prepared, but even a hand-drawn sketch can be much clearer than words alone when it comes to giving your audience an idea of how an item looks or how it can be used. In industries such as engineering and architecture, computer-aided design systems produce detailed diagrams and drawings. A variety of widely available software programs for microcomputers provide a file of symbols and pictures of various types, which can be used (sparingly) to add a decorative touch to reports and presentations.

Use photographs
- For visual appeal
- To show exact appearance

Photographs have always been popular in certain types of business documents, such as annual reports, where their visual appeal is used to capture the interest of readers. As the technology for reproducing photographs improves and becomes less expensive, even analytical business reports for internal use are beginning to include more photographs. Digital cameras now make it easy to drop photographic images directly into a report or presentation. Nothing can demonstrate the exact appearance of a new facility, a piece of property or equipment, or a new product the way a photograph can. In some situations, however, a photograph shows too much detail. This is one of the reasons repair manuals, for instance, frequently use drawings instead of photos. With a drawing, you can select how much detail to show and focus the reader's attention on particular parts or places.

Technology has created new opportunities and an important new ethical concern for people who use photography in reports and other materials. Software tools such as Photoshop now make it easy for computer users to make dramatic changes to photos—without leaving a clue. Small changes to photos have been possible for a long time, of course (more than a few people have blemishes airbrushed out of their yearbook

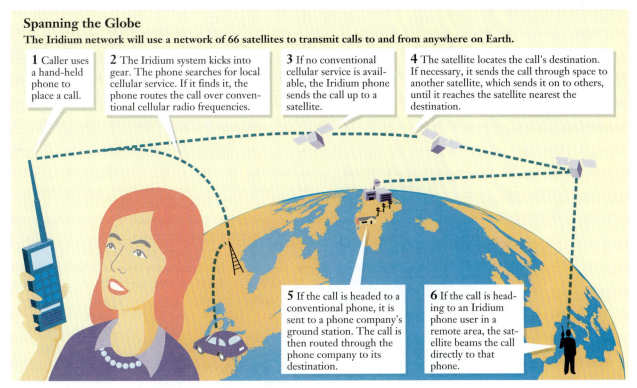

Spanning the Globe
The Iridium network will use a network of 66 satellites to transmit calls to and from anywhere on Earth.

1 Caller uses a hand-held phone to place a call.

2 The Iridium system kicks into gear. The phone searches for local cellular service. If it finds it, the phone routes the call over conventional cellular radio frequencies.

3 If no conventional cellular service is available, the Iridium phone sends the call up to a satellite.

4 The satellite locates the call's destination. If necessary, it sends the call through space to another satellite, which sends it on to others, until it reaches the satellite nearest the destination.

5 If the call is headed to a conventional phone, it is sent to a phone company's ground station. The call is then routed through the phone company to its destination.

6 If the call is heading to an Iridium phone user in a remote area, the satellite beams the call directly to that phone.

Figure 16.13
Diagram

photos), but computers make drastic changes easy and undetectable. You can remove people from photographs, put Person A's head on Person B's body, and make products look more attractive than they really are. As with other technological tools, stop and ask yourself where the truth lies before you start making changes.[7]

PRODUCING VISUAL AIDS

Professional-looking visual aids used to be extremely expensive and time consuming to produce, but personal computer technology has changed all that. Graphics that used to cost hundreds of dollars and take several days to complete can now be done in minutes for little cost. Companies are cutting the cost and time involved in preparing visual aids by turning to **computer graphics,** charts and graphs that are created and produced using a computer program.

Computer programs are having a tremendous impact on how companies create and use visual aids. Instead of relying on graphic designers, businesspeople are turning out their own professional-looking visual aids. The simplicity of the production process encourages people to present data in a graphic format. In fact, the technology is so seductive that some people can't resist going overboard and putting so much into graphic form that they diminish the effect they had hoped to achieve.

Computer-graphics systems cut the time and cost involved in producing visual aids.

Creating Graphics with Computers

Presentation-graphics programs, drawing programs, painting programs, and spreadsheet programs can all be used to develop visual aids.

With today's powerful computers, it's faster and easier than ever to produce good-looking graphics in printed form or as slides, transparencies, or screen images. Your choices include presentation-graphics programs such as Harvard Graphics, which help you prepare slides, charts, and other materials; drawing programs such as CorelDraw!, which allow you to create freehand drawings; painting programs such as Painter, which let you manipulate existing images; and spreadsheet programs such as Lotus 1-2-3, QuattroPro, and Excel, which help you calculate, sort, and then display numbers in graphic form. Some word-processing programs, such as Microsoft Word, can also be used to prepare charts.

A computer-graphics system does more than draw charts; it also enhances your analytical capabilities.

If you spend a lot of time working with numbers, you'll find a spreadsheet program particularly handy because it can serve as both an analytical tool and a communication tool. As you enter numerical data into your computer, you can use the graphics program to automatically calculate trend lines and growth curves. You can print these out for use in reports or presentations, or you can simply use them in your own analysis. You can also save the results and then enter additional data later. So if you track sales or profits by month, you can easily add the latest month's figures and create a new graph that shows the cumulative pattern.

Computer-Graphics Tools

The personal computers found in most offices can handle basic graphics tasks, from adding a simple drawing in a word processor to charting numbers in a spreadsheet. However, more advanced tasks can require special hardware and software components. In the computer itself, complicated graphics place heavy demands on processing speed and memory capacity. High-resolution images, particularly color photographs, require large files. In fact, a single brochure can consume more disk space than most computers had available just a few years ago. Computers set up for graphics work have high-capacity disk drives and usually feature special removable optical drives or other mechanisms for moving and storing large files.

A standard keyboard and mouse provide the means for getting basic information into the computer, but again, more involved graphics can require additional equipment. A scanner converts printed images to electronic format, a CD-ROM drive provides access to a growing number of image libraries, and a modem lets users download images and information from the Internet and other sources. Most new computers come equipped with modems and CD-ROM drives, and scanners are now cheap enough to be a common office tool, too.

Finally, specialized tools enable your computer to print or display the finished graphic. Most businesspeople are connected to at least a black-and-white printer, usually an inkjet or laser printer. For internal reports and many external reports, inkjet printers provide a low-cost option for producing full-color printouts. Color laser printers provide higher-quality output, but these printers cost several times more than inkjet devices. To display graphics, you can create overhead transparencies on most office printers or have a graphics company produce 35 mm slides. For live presentations, an increasing number of businesses now use LCD projectors or display panels. These products re-create the images on your computer screen and display them on the same projection screens used for viewing slides. This has the advantage of including real-time manipulation of numbers, animation, video clips, and even sound (see Chapter 20 for more information).

BEST OF THE WEB

Design Effective Computer Graphics

Mambo is a jump station to more than 65 Web sites containing the latest information about the imaginative world of computer graphics. The site provides links to company, university, and government labs displaying colorful portfolios; Usenet groups; and software companies. It also includes frequently asked questions (FAQs), bibliographies, conferences, and utilities.

http://mambo.ucsc.edu/psl/cg.html

Computer-Graphics Skills

For the power and possibilities they offer, computer-graphics tools are not without some potential drawbacks. Using this equipment efficiently and effectively requires skills that many businesspeople may not possess, including the ability to use hardware and software and to make good design decisions. Many products have become easier to use, but most continue to offer more and more options to choose from—type of graph, color and design of the background, typefaces, line weights, and so on. Most businesspeople lack the visual arts training to make informed design decisions; moreover, making all those choices takes time.

Fortunately, some graphics products, such as Harvard Graphics and Microsoft PowerPoint, can simplify the situation by making many of these decisions for you. Some products, particularly those used to create overhead transparencies and other displays, provide a set of *templates*. You simply type in the information you want to use, and the software makes all the design choices for you. (Be careful with templates, however. Even though they are designed by professional graphic artists, some are "overdesigned" and inappropriate for serious business uses, and some clutter the image with overly fancy borders and backgrounds that can distract the audience from the real message.)

Before you take advantage of any computer-graphics tools, think about the kind of image you want to project. The style of your visual aids communicates a subtle message about your relationship with the audience. A simple, hand-drawn diagram is fine for a working meeting but inappropriate for a formal presentation or report. On the other hand, elaborate, full-color visuals may be viewed as extravagant for an informal memo but may be entirely appropriate for a message to top management or influential outsiders. In other words, the image you want to project should determine your production technique (see "Creating Colorful Visual Aids with Computers for Maximum Clarity and Impact").

The sophistication of visual aids matches the communication situation.

Fitting Visual Aids into the Text

Once you've produced your visual aids, you face the problem of displaying them in an appropriate way. Fit your visuals into your text in a manner that is convenient for your audience and practical from a production standpoint. (For information on how to handle visual aids in oral presentations, see Chapter 20.)

To some extent, your approach to integrating text and visuals depends on the type of report you're preparing. If you're working on a glossy public relations document, you'll handle the visual aids as though they were illustrations in a magazine, positioning them to attract interest and tell a story of their own. However, in most business documents, where the visual aids clarify the text, you'll tie them closely to the discussion.

To tie visual aids to the text
- *Introduce them in the text*
- *Place them near the points they illustrate*
- *Choose a meaningful title and legend for each one*

Introduce Illustrations in the Text

Every visual aid you use should be clearly referred to by number in the text of your report. Some report writers refer to all visual aids as exhibits and number them consecutively throughout the report; many others number tables and figures separately (everything that isn't a table is regarded as a figure). In a very long report with numbered chapters (as in this book), visual aids may have a double number (separated by a period or a hyphen) representing the chapter number and the individual illustration number within that chapter.

Help your readers understand the significance of any visual aids by referring to them before they appear in the text. The reference helps readers understand why the

In-text references tell readers why the illustration is important.

CREATING COLORFUL VISUAL AIDS WITH COMPUTERS FOR MAXIMUM CLARITY AND IMPACT

More and more people are learning to use graphics software to create striking and attractive visual aids. No matter which type of software you use, your design is likely to look more professional than a graphic drawn by hand. Once you've designed your visual, you can also use your computer and software to plan the colors.

You know from your own experience that color helps make a point more effectively than black and white. However, there's more to using color than simply picking hues that appeal to you. To choose an effective color scheme, ask yourself these questions:

- *What colors will best convey the effect I want?* As a general rule, bright, solid colors are more pleasing to the eye and easier to distinguish than pastel or patterned colors. Yellow, blue, and green are usually good choices, but the possibilities are numerous. Just

keep in mind that too many colors may overwhelm the message. Use color as an accent, bright color for emphasis and darker or lighter colors for background information.

table or chart is important. The following examples show how you can make this connection in the text:

> Figure 1 summarizes the financial history of the motorcycle division over the past five years, with sales broken into four categories.

> Total sales were steady over this period, but the mix of sales by category changed dramatically (see Figure 2).

> The underlying reason for the remarkable growth in our sales of low-end fax machines is suggested by Table 4, which provides data on fax machine sales in the United States by region and model.

Use references similar to these to prepare your readers for all your visual aids.

When describing the data shown in your visual aids, be sure to emphasize the main point you are trying to make. Don't make the mistake of simply repeating the data to be shown. Paragraphs like this are guaranteed to put the reader to sleep:

> Among women who replied to the survey, 14.6 percent earn less than $5 per hour; 26.4 percent earn $5–$7; 25.7 percent, $8–$12; 18.0 percent, $13–$24; 9.6 percent, $25–$49; and 2.9 percent, $50 and over.

Color can also visually connect related points or set apart points that represent significant change.

- *Are these colors appropriate for my message, purpose, and audience?* Liking red is not a good reason for using it in all your graphic designs. It's too "hot" for some people and conveys the wrong message in some instances; for example, using red to show profits in an annual report might confuse readers because they're likely to associate your graphic with "red ink," or losses. Also remember that people in other cultures will make color associations that differ from yours.
- *Is my audience familiar with these colors?* Unless your aim is to shake up your audience, avoid uncommon colors or unusual combinations. In general, conventional colors are best for conventional audiences. However, young or trendy audiences probably won't be jarred by unfamiliar colors.
- *Can I improve the effect by changing any of the colors?* When you have the opportunity to use more than one color, choose those that contrast. Colors without contrast blend together and obscure the message. At the same time, be careful to use vivid or highly saturated colors sparingly.

Of course, your color choices may be limited or dictated in certain situations. Some organizations specify the exact color or combination to be used on company logos and other official symbols or illustrations. At other times you'll be free to decide on any combination of colors that works best for the visual aid you're preparing. That's when you'll find graphics software especially useful.

Depending on the capabilities of your software and your computer monitor, you can try out various colors and combinations and see the results immediately. Even the most basic program offers three colors. More sophisticated programs can give you thousands or even millions of color and shading choices.

To start, select a background color from the program's "palette" of available colors. Then choose a dominant color to set the tone for the overall color scheme. Continue adding colors as necessary, until you find the combination that works best. Because you can test many colors and combinations with a quick click of the mouse, you can come to a final decision more quickly (and with less effort) than if you had to do it without the software.

Once you've decided on colors, you can print out a hard copy or an acetate transparency using a color printer or color plotter. You can also create full-color slides using a film recorder, or you can simply project the colorful image from your computer screen through an overhead projector to a large viewing screen.

---

1. Would you use green or red to shade a visual aid showing the geographic areas where your firm does business? Would you use green or red to shade the areas where your firm does not do business? Why?
2. How can you use color in a line chart to help your audience differentiate between current and projected sales? Between expected and actual sales? Explain your answers.

The chart will provide these details; there is no need to repeat them in the text. Instead, use round numbers that sum up the message:

Over two-thirds of the women who replied earn less than $12 per hour.

Place Visual Aids Near the Points They Illustrate

Ideally, it is best to place each visual aid right beside or right after the paragraph it illustrates so that readers can consult both the explanation and the visual aid at the same time. Many word-processing programs and desktop publishing systems let you create layouts with artwork and text on the same page. If you don't have these programs, the most practical approach is to put visual aids on separate pages and mesh them with the text after the report has been typed.

This solution raises the question of where to put the pages with the visual aids. Some writers prefer to cluster them at the end of the report, either as a separate section or as an appendix. Others group them at the end of each chapter. Still others prefer to place them as close as possible to the paragraphs they refer to. Although a case can be

Put a visual aid as close as possible to its in-text reference to help readers understand the illustration's relevance.

made for each approach, the best one is generally to place the pages of visual aids right after the pages containing references to them. This arrangement encourages readers to look at the visual aids when you want them to, in the context you have prepared.

Choose Titles and Legends with a Message

Titles and legends should
- Reinforce the point you want to make
- Be specific

One of the best ways to tie your visual aids to the text is to choose titles (or captions) and descriptions (or legends) that reinforce the point you want to make. This precaution is especially necessary when the visual aids are widely separated from the text.

The title of a visual aid, when combined with labels and legends on the piece itself, should be complete enough to tell the reader what the content is. The title "Petroleum Tanks in the United States" is sufficient if it's the title of a line chart labeled "Year" along the horizontal axis and "Number (in thousands)" along the vertical axis. However, if the visual aid is a map overlaid with dots of different sizes, the title would need to explain a bit more: "Concentrations of Petroleum Tanks in the United States in 1997." A legend might then explain how many petroleum tanks each size of dot represents.

When you place a visual aid next to the text discussion that pertains to it, clear labeling and a good title are usually enough; the text can explain the visual aid's significance and details. However, when you place a visual aid elsewhere or when the illustration requires considerable explanation that would disrupt the flow of the text, you may need to add a description (or legend). Legends are generally written as one or more complete sentences, and they do more than merely repeat what's already clear from the title and figure labels. It's better to be too specific than too general when you're identifying the content of an illustration. As a check, ask yourself whether you've covered the who, what, when, where, why, and how of the illustration.

If you're using informative headings in your report, carry this style over into the titles and legends. In other words, instead of using a **descriptive title,** which identifies the topic of the illustration, call attention to the conclusion that ought to be drawn from the data by using an **informative title.** Here's the difference:

Descriptive Title:	Relationship Between Petroleum Demand and Refinery Capacity in the United States
Informative Title:	Shrinking Refinery Capacity Results from Stagnant Petroleum Demand

Regardless of whether your titles and legends are informative or descriptive, phrase them consistently throughout the report. At the same time, be consistent in your format. If the title of the first visual aid is typed entirely in capital letters, type all the remaining titles that way as well. Although an employer may specify the placement of titles, as a general rule place all table titles at the top. Figure titles may be placed at the top or the bottom. When legends are used, make them all roughly the same length.

Checking Over the Visual Aids

Before you give your visual aids a final stamp of approval, take a few extra minutes to review them. Ask yourself whether each one is necessary, convenient, accurate, and honest.

Is It Necessary?

Avoid cluttering a report with too many visual aids.

As the old saying goes, "One picture is worth a thousand words." Of course, that doesn't mean you should include one picture for every thousand words. A few well-placed visual aids clarify and dramatize your message, but an avalanche of illustrations may bury it. So avoid the temptation to overload your reports with unnecessary tables, graphs, and charts. Remember that your audience is busy. Don't give people information they don't need simply because you want to impress them or because you've fallen in love with the computer-graphics system.

Is It Convenient?

Be aware of convenience, particularly when reviewing tables. The information should be laid out so that the audience can grasp the important points easily. Be sure that columns are labeled properly and that units of measure are clearly identified. Ask yourself whether separating columns or rows with lines or extra spaces might make the table easier to follow.

Also check the placement of your visual aids. Try to position them so that your audience won't have to flip back and forth too much between the visuals and the text, and make sure each visual is clearly and correctly referred to in the text. If you have four or more visual aids, prepare a separate list of them that can be placed with the table of contents at the front of the report. Some writers list tables separately from figures. The two lists should start on separate pages unless both lists will fit on the same page.

Make sure the audience can locate your visual aids and figure out what they mean.

Is It Accurate?

Proofreading visual aids is a chore, but it has to be done, preferably several times. Before you release the final product, make sure that every number is correct, that every line is plotted accurately, that every scale is drawn to reflect reality, and that every bit of information is consistent with the text.

If you rely on others to prepare the visual aids, you may be tempted to let them catch all the errors, but resist the temptation. Even the most conscientious staff members will miss a few mistakes, particularly because they may lack the information necessary to spot a data point that doesn't make sense.

When you're proofreading, be sure to check the source notes and the content notes too. Regardless of where reference notes for the text are placed, those for illustrations should appear right below the visual material (as Component Chapter B recommends). If you are the source, you may omit the source note, identify the source as "primary" or "internal" data, or refer simply to the nature of the information (for example, "interviews with 50 soybean farmers").

Proofread visual aids carefully for errors in data and for consistency with the text.

Is It Honest?

Accuracy and honesty are two distinct qualities. You can have all the numbers right and still give your audience a false impression by presenting those numbers in a distorted way. Graphs and charts, in particular, tend to oversimplify some numerical relationships, and deliberately leaving out important data points that don't fit your needs is highly unethical.

Another possible source of distortion is omitting an outside influence on the data being portrayed. You might develop a bar or line chart that shows big improvements in your company's profits. Your audience might attribute this gain to lasting changes in the way the company does business, even though the source of the improvement might actually be a one-time change in accounting methods. If events not shown on the graph or chart are actually responsible for creating the results, let your audience know. A footnote is helpful, but the best solution is to revise the visual aid to create a more realistic picture of events.

The choice of scale on a graph or chart also introduces the possibility of distortion. As Figure 16.14 illustrates, you can transform modest results into dramatic ones

To make sure your graphs and charts don't create a false impression
- Avoid omitting key data points
- Avoid ignoring an important outside influence on the data
- Avoid shifting the scale of measurement

Figure 16.14

The Impact of Scale on the Slope of a Curve

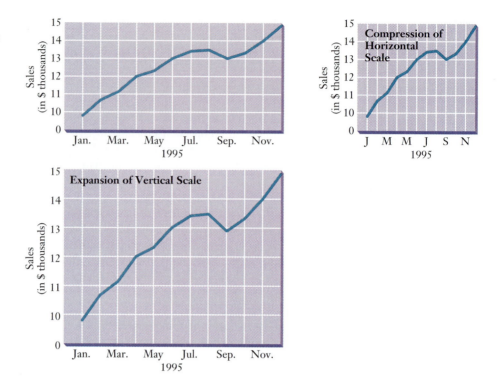

by compressing the horizontal scale or expanding the vertical scale, but you abandon good business ethics and mislead your audience in the process. So be sure that the visual impression you create is an honest representation of the facts. Choose a scale that conveys a realistic picture of what's happening. Likewise, maintain the same scale in successive charts comparing the same factors (see "Visual Aids That Lie: The Use and Abuse of Charts and Graphs").

When you are the audience interpreting the data presented in a visual format, remember to consider the possibilities for distortion. Ask yourself whether any important data might have been omitted. Look closely at the scale. Don't let a pretty curve fool you. Bear in mind that visual images tend to oversimplify reality.

Finally, be sure to cite the source of any data you use in creating a visual. You may be the creator of the actual graphic design, but if you use someone else's data, you need to give the source credit. To avoid cluttering your graphic, use either a shortened citation on the graphic itself or include a complete citation elsewhere in the report.

SUMMARY

Visual aids are illustrations in tabular, graphic, schematic, or pictorial form. They are used to reduce lengthy verbal descriptions and to emphasize key points. When presenting data graphically, observe conventions of continuity, contrast, and emphasis.

Tables are commonly used to present detailed, specific information; line, bar, and pie charts are used to clarify and dramatize trends and numerical relationships. Flow charts, organization charts, maps, drawings, and photographs are useful but somewhat less common.

FOCUSING ON ETHICS

VISUAL AIDS THAT LIE: THE USE AND ABUSE OF CHARTS AND GRAPHS

The ease with which computers help people create visual displays of numerical information can obscure some important ethical issues. Here's a quick example of how easy it is to obscure information or otherwise mislead an audience (the data are all fictional in this example). The line graph in Chart A shows the number of insecticide poisonings by age from 0 to 20. Chart B shows the same data, with one crucial difference:

The vertical axis is scaled to fit the data. By expanding the axis way beyond the data, Chart A can create the impression that accident levels are far below the "maximum"—after all, the chart has all that extra room above the data.

Chart C shows another ethical problem. By sampling the data and showing incidence levels for just four ages, the chart hides the fact that 4- and 5-year-olds suffered the most poisonings and that more 3-, 4-, and 5-year-olds died from poisoning. Six-year-olds *appear* to be the age hardest hit, but they aren't.

When it comes to presenting information, a good way to make ethical decisions is to ask what the audience needs to know in order to make an informed choice. If the audience needs the information, you need to show it.

1. How might your choice of a base unit affect your reader's perception of progress when viewing a Gantt chart?
2. Can you construct a pie chart from data that's been rounded up to equal more than 100 percent? Explain.

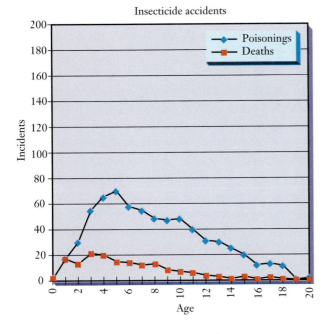

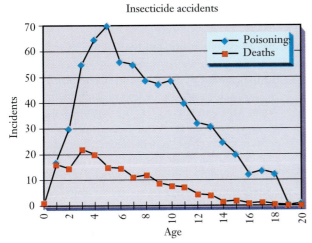

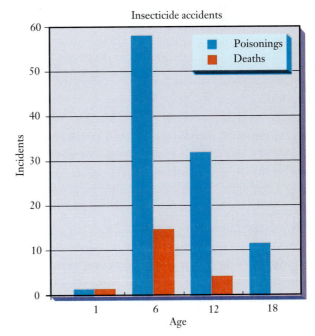

The production of visual aids is becoming increasingly automated as computers supplant graphic artists. Regardless of how you produce it, label each visual aid clearly and refer to it in the text. Also be sure that each visual passes the four-question test: Is it necessary? Is it convenient? Is it accurate? Is it honest?

COMMUNICATION CHALLENGES AT EASTMAN KODAK COMPANY

Whether putting together a report or a multimedia extravaganza, Kodak employees definitely have plenty of images and state-of-the-art technology to work with. Nevertheless, adequately illustrating complex information always presents a challenge. For a speech to be given at the annual shareholders' meeting by the chief executive officer (and a written report to be developed later), Michael Fernandez needs easy-to-comprehend visuals that will convey the following information:

- In 1989 Eastman Kodak's Health, Safety, and Environment Council began efforts to reduce the company's worldwide chlorofluorocarbon (CFC) emissions. In 1989 direct manufacturing processes were annually pumping 760 million pounds of CFCs into the atmosphere. That figure has dropped steadily: 1990, 390 million pounds; 1991, 380 million pounds; 1992, 240 million pounds; 1993, 160 million pounds; 1994, 150 million pounds; 1995, zero CFC emissions.
- The new Kodak Advantix consumer imaging products were announced in April 1996. Advantix cameras require a drop-in film cassette that uses Kodak's best-ever film emulsions and includes a magnetic strip carrying information for the developer. The cassette also stores the exposed negatives after developing. With each shutter click, consumers can indicate a different print size choice: C for classic, H for HDTV (or wide-angle), and P for panoramic.
- At the end of 1994, Kodak's stock price was $47.75 per share, and at the end of 1995, it was $67.00. In 1994 sales were $13,557 million and net earnings were $557 million; by 1995, sales were $14,980 million and net earnings were $1,252 million.

INDIVIDUAL CHALLENGE: Choose two of the three items, decide how best to illustrate them, and make sketches to submit to Fernandez. Bear in mind that the finished visual aid will be professionally polished on a computer-graphics system and then reproduced as a slide for the speech and as a printed image for Kodak's annual report.

TEAM CHALLENGE: Exchange and discuss your preliminary sketches as a group. How could they be improved, enhanced, colorized, and captioned or titled? As you evaluate the sketches, be sure to apply the four most important questions: Is it necessary? Is it convenient? Is it accurate? Is it honest? Using your discussion as a basis, work as a group to develop one enhanced sketch for each of the three items (use colored pens or pencils to indicate your color choices).[8]

CRITICAL THINKING QUESTIONS

1. In what ways might visual aids help people overcome some of the barriers to communication discussed in Chapter 2? Please explain.
2. What similarities do you see between visual aids and nonverbal communication? Explain your answer.
3. You're writing a report to the director of human resources on implementing participative management throughout your company. You want to emphasize that since the new approaches were implemented six months ago, absenteeism and turnovers have been sharply reduced in all but two departments. How do you visually present your data in the most favorable light? Explain.
4. Besides telling readers why an illustration is important, why refer to it in the text of your document?
5. When you can't use color in a printed document, what can you do to visually accentuate your major point in a line chart? In a bar chart? In a pie chart? In a table? Explain your answers.
6. When you read a graph, how can you be sure that the visual impression you are receiving is an accurate reflection of reality? Please explain.

DOCUMENTS FOR ANALYSIS

Document 16.A

Examine the pie charts in Figure 16.15, and point out
any problems or errors you notice.

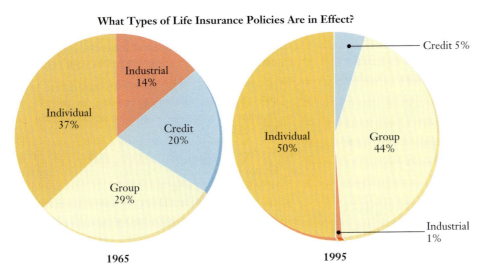

What Types of Life Insurance Policies Are in Effect?

Document 16.B

Examine the line chart in Figure 16.16, and point out any
problems or errors you notice.

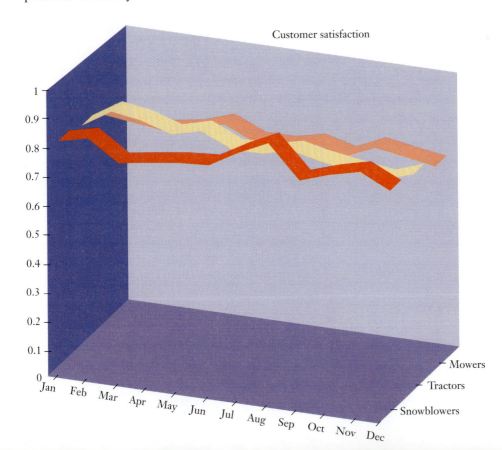

EXERCISES

1. As a market researcher for a statewide bank, you're examining home ownership and rental patterns among single-person households in various age groups. You're particularly interested in pinpointing when these households tend to switch from renting to owning a home. Using the following information, prepare a bar graph comparing the number of owners with the number of renters in each age category. Be sure to label your graph and include combined totals for owners and renters ("total households"). Then prepare a pie chart showing the proportion of owners and renters in the one age group you believe holds the most promise for mortgage loans. Write a sentence that prepares your bank's management for the information shown in the pie chart.

Age Group	Owners (in 000s)	Renters (in 000s)
18–24	1,143	1,208
25–29	1,454	1,796
30–34	1,596	1,326
35–44	1,816	1,545
45–54	1,824	1,207
55–64	1,697	1,348
65–74	2,513	1,655
75+	2,344	1,767

2. As the head of the career center at a midwestern journalism school, you want to show students that they have many options after graduation. Create a pie chart based on the following information, which shows career areas that journalism school graduates pursued during a recent year. Summarize these findings (in two or three sentences) for publication in the student newspaper.

Media jobs	11,276
Newspapers/wire services	3,162
Broadcast/radio/TV	1,653
Public relations	2,407
Advertising	2,142
Magazines	286
Other media	1,626
Graduate study	1,346
Nonmedia jobs	5,324
Unemployed	2,454
Total graduates	20,400

3. The pet-food manufacturer you work for is interested in the results of a recent poll of U.S. pet-owning households. Look at the statistics that follow and decide on the most appropriate scale for this chart; then create a line chart of the trends in cat ownership. What conclusions do you draw from the trend you've charted? Draft a paragraph or two discussing the results of this poll and the potential consequences for the pet-food business. Support your conclusions by referring readers to your chart.

In 1980, 22 million U.S. households owned a cat. In 1985, 24 million households owned a cat. In 1990, 28 million households owned a cat. In 1995, 32 million households owned a cat.

4. You're preparing the annual report for FretCo Guitar Corporation. For each of the following types of information, what form of visual aid would you choose to illustrate the text? Explain your choices.
   a. Data on annual sales for the past 20 years
   b. Comparison of FretCo sales, product by product (electric guitars, bass guitars, amplifiers, acoustic guitars), for this year and last year
   c. Explanation of how a FretCo acoustic guitar is manufactured
   d. Explanation of how the FretCo Guitar Corporation markets its guitars
   e. Data on sales of FretCo products in each of 12 countries
   f. Comparison of FretCo sales figures with sales figures for three other competing guitar makers over the past 10 years

5. Team up with a classmate to design graphics based on a comparison of the total tax burden of the U.S. taxpayer with that of people in other nations. One teammate should sketch a horizontal or vertical bar chart and the other should sketch a pictogram from the estimates that follow. Then exchange visual aids and analyze how well each conveys the situation of the U.S. taxpayer. Would the bar chart look best with vertical or horizontal bars? Why? What scale is best? How does the symbol used in the pictogram enhance or obscure the meaning or impact of the data? What suggestions can each student make for improving the other's visual aid?

Estimates show that Swedish taxpayers spend 51 percent of their incomes on taxes, British taxpayers spend 48 percent, French taxpayers spend 37 percent, Japanese taxpayers spend 28 percent, and U.S. taxpayers spend 27 percent.

TABLE 16.2

STORE SALES IN 1997, IN THOUSANDS (EXERCISE 6)

Month	Lingerie	Sporting Goods	Housewares
January	$39	$55	$83
February	37	50	81
March	37	51	78
April	25	55	77
May	26	60	79
June	30	65	85
July	30	65	79
August	27	60	77
September	27	51	77
October	27	53	78
November	31	60	82
December	40	65	85

6. Last year's sales figures are in for the department store where you work (see Table 16.2). Construct visual aids based on these figures that will help you explain seasonal sales variations among the departments to the store's general manager.

7. Look back at Figure 16.10, which compares the U.S. market shares of leading candy makers. What type of visual aid would most effectively communicate the annual candy-bar sales data shown in the table? Make a sketch and discuss your choice of visual aid as well as your choice of scale. How could you use color to visually portray which company makes each of the top ten candy bars?

8. Search through recent newspapers and magazines to find a map created to accompany an article, then find a road map or other comprehensive map of the same general area. After comparing the two maps, answer the following questions:

a. What kinds of information were left off the newspaper/magazine map?

b. Did the loss of that information hamper your ability to understand the article?

c. Was the newspaper/magazine map accurate enough for the purpose of the article? Why or why not?

d. Why wouldn't newspapers and magazines simply use road maps or other existing maps in their articles?

9. Make a copy of the organization chart in Figure 16.12 and modify it to indicate a temporary task force consisting of the personnel manager, the director of admissions, the dean of the technical education division, and the president.

10. Re-create the line chart in Figure 16.3 as a bar chart and as a pie chart. Which of these three formats does the best job of conveying the information? Are any of the formats definitely inappropriate for this information? Explain your answers.

11. With a team of three or four other students, brainstorm and then sketch at least three ways to visually compare the population of all 50 states in the United States. You can use any of the graphic ideas presented in this chapter, as well as any ideas or examples you find from other sources.

12. Because of your experience with creating and designing presentation materials, your company asks you to design its Web page. No one else in your company has the technical expertise to help you, so you begin by searching the Internet. You discover the Web sites at <http://www.pstbbs.com/tammyb/web/html> and <http://www.kudonet.com/%7Erhondamo/create.html>. Explore the following links: *Search Engines; Shareware & Freeware; Icons, graphics, color, and styles;* and *General Help.* Now try your hand at Web page design, and print a copy of your sample home page for submission.

WRITING REPORTS AND PROPOSALS

AFTER STUDYING THIS CHAPTER, YOU WILL BE ABLE TO

- Choose the proper format and length for your report
- Use direct or indirect order when appropriate
- Subdivide informational reports by using topical divisions of thought
- Subdivide analytical reports by using conclusions and recommendations or various types of logical arguments
- Establish an appropriate degree of formality in a report
- Establish a consistent time perspective
- Use openings, headings, lists, transitions, and summaries to guide readers through the report

COMMUNICATION CLOSE-UP AT THE SAN DIEGO WILD ANIMAL PARK

Whether encountering a cheetah, feeding a giraffe, or crossing a floating bridge to a "field biologist's research island," visitors to the San Diego Wild Animal Park aren't likely to be thinking about business proposals. But if it weren't for a dedicated team of five park employees and a particularly impressive proposal, the park's brand new, 30-acre "Heart of Africa" safari tour would not exist. Hardy tourists would not be trekking through the artificially created African forestland, savannah, wetlands, waterholes, and islands to enjoy raging waterfalls, African native plants, and lots of animals—grazing antelope, wattled cranes, sacred ibis, colobus monkeys, rhinos, wildebeests, gazelles, and some 250 other mammals and birds. If not for those determined park employees who put their communication skills to work to sell a concept that was initially nixed by the park's brainstorming committee, there would be no interpretive guides posing as "research scientists" and no demonstrations of radio telemetry tracking.

This is a communication success story. As education manager for the Wild Animal Park, Deirdre Ballou was part of the enthusiastic group that rescued the Heart of Africa concept from its early rejection. "We felt the idea was good, and that if we carried it out a little bit more, we could try again." In addition to Ballou, this group included the public relations manager and the curators of birds, mammals, and zoology. These five colleagues agreed among themselves to meet on their own time to develop a proposal that the rest of the committee just couldn't refuse. They would do their homework, they vowed, and then return with a comprehensive, clear, impressive, and persuasive proposal for the Heart of Africa project.

Ballou says their smartest move was to first identify the best skills of everyone in the group. One was a terrific writer, another was a sparkling presenter, and others were extremely knowledgeable about the park's animal collection. Ballou contributed her

Deirdre Ballou

Whether working on new concepts like the Heart of Africa project, raising funds, or educating sponsors and visitors, Deirdre Ballou often finds herself writing reports and proposals. Ballou pays special attention to her communication skills in order to do her best while researching, organizing, analyzing, and presenting her ideas.

knowledge of education and interpretation, as well as her proposal-writing experience. Identifying their individual strengths "was really key" to the team's success, says Ballou.

The next step was to write an evocative scenario using "very creative words" to walk committee members through an imaginary tour of the team's vision for the Heart of Africa. They put the sizzle before the steak, as the old adage goes—also known as using the indirect approach. All contributed their expertise to the scenario, but the team's "best writer" did the honors, says Ballou.

The park committee liked the scenario, challenging the team to take the next step: a slide-show presentation for the committees of the Board of Trustees of the Zoological Society of San Diego, nonprofit owner of the Wild Animal Park. Now Ballou and her colleagues really knuckled down, researching statistics published by zoo and museum professional organizations and drawing on their own experience working with the public and with the park's animal collections. They poured this information into a script that began with an overview to be presented by their best speaker, followed by detailed information from the animal curators. Ballou came next with information about the terrific educational opportunities at the research island and with justification for hiring interpretive staff to portray "field researchers." The PR manager closed the presentation, reemphasizing the "selling points" of the Heart of Africa and research island project, reminding committee members how well it would fulfill the park's stated mission and purpose. The team knew the committee members' preference for short presentations, so they kept it under 20 minutes, concluding with questions and answers.

"Committees and board members respect (and will listen to) people who have done their homework," Ballou says now, remembering the excitement of winning the committees' approval. Before long, she was out in the middle of a human-made lagoon in jeans and T-shirt, helping builders complete the final details in time for the Heart of Africa's official opening.

Ballou still routinely writes dozens of reports and proposals—funding proposals, budget and labor reports, and project status reports. And she still starts by asking: Will my audience be receptive? Have we met with them before and are they expecting a formal presentation or a more casual approach? Then she chooses the right format, length, order, and tone to meet their expectations. But she also recalls with great fondness her participation on the team that saved the Heart of Africa and unique research island project. Who would have thought an ordinary business proposal could be so much fun—and so rewarding?[1]

ORGANIZING REPORTS AND PROPOSALS

Writing reports and proposals is an important part of Deirdre Ballou's role at the San Diego Wild Animal Park. Like Ballou, when you need to translate your own research into a finished report or an oral presentation, you face the challenge of finding the most effective way to communicate your message to an audience. The division of ideas that helped you conduct your research may be quite different from the division of ideas that will help your audience understand and accept your message, particularly if your message contains controversial material or if you're communicating with someone from another culture. When writing your report, be sure to follow the customs your audience expects—these expectations differ from company to company and from culture to culture. In addition to your audience, consider your purpose in writing the report and the subject matter of your report. All three elements influence the format and length of your report, the information you include, the order you use, and the way you structure your ideas.

Before you write your report, you may have to revise the outline you used to guide your research effort.

Deciding on Format and Length

One of the first issues to decide is whether to create a written report or an oral presentation. You'll often need to prepare both: a presentation to brief management on the results of your work and a written report to provide a lasting record. You can generally use the same basic outline for both, but reports and oral presentations obviously require different preparation methods. (Chapter 20 provides details on how to handle oral presentations; however, the organizational principles discussed here apply equally to both oral and written material.)

When you're writing a report, decisions about format and length may be made for you by the person who requests the document. Such guidance is often the case with monitor/control reports, justification reports, proposals, progress reports, and compliance reports. Generally speaking, the more routine the report, the less flexibility you have in deciding format and length. Monthly status reports, for example, are usually pretty routine, so they will have the same basic appearance and structure. Within that framework, however, there is room for flexibility, depending on the nature of the information being reported.

When you do have some leeway in length and format, your decisions are based on your readers' needs. As the Wild Animal Park's Deirdre Ballou can attest, your goal is to tell your audience what they need to know in a format that is easy for them to use. When selecting a format for your report, you have four options:

You may present a report in one of four formats: preprinted form, letter, memo, or manuscript.

- **Preprinted form.** Basically for "fill in the blank" reports. Most are relatively short (five or fewer pages) and deal with routine information, often mainly numerical. Use this format when it's requested by the person authorizing the report.
- **Letter.** Common for reports of five or fewer pages that are directed to outsiders. These reports include all the normal parts of a letter, but they may also have headings, footnotes, tables, and figures.
- **Memo.** Common for short (fewer than ten pages) informal reports distributed within an organization. Memos have headings at the top: *To, From, Date,* and

Subject. In addition, like longer reports, they often have internal headings and sometimes have visual aids. Memos exceeding ten pages are sometimes referred to as memo reports to distinguish them from their shorter cousins. They also begin with the standard memo headings. The Checklist for Short Informal Reports at the end of this chapter provides guidelines for preparing memo reports and other short informal reports.

- *Manuscript.* Common for reports from a few pages to several hundred pages that require a formal approach. As their length increases, reports in manuscript format require more elements before the text of the report (prefatory parts) and after the text (supplementary parts). Chapter 18 explains these elements and includes additional instructions as well as a checklist for preparing formal reports.

Component Chapter A, "Format and Layout of Business Documents," contains more specific guidelines for physically preparing these four kinds of reports. (Also see "Be Careful—Your Computer Can Create Work!")

The length of your report obviously depends on your subject and purpose, but it's also affected by your relationship with your audience. If they are relative strangers, if they are skeptical or hostile, if the material is nonroutine or controversial, you usually have to explain your points in greater detail, resulting in a longer document. You can afford to be brief if you are on familiar terms with your readers, if they are likely to agree with you, and if the information is routine or uncomplicated. Generally speaking, short reports are more common in business than long ones, and you'll probably write many more 5-page memos than 250-page formal reports.

> Length depends on
> - Your subject
> - Your purpose
> - Your relationship with your audience

Selecting the Information to Include

Should you cover all the material obtained during your research, or should you eliminate some of the data? When deciding on the content of your report, the first step is to put yourself in the audience's position. What major questions do you think your audience has about the subject? By developing a **question-and-answer chain,** you can think ahead to the questions your readers may have and anticipate their sequence. Your objective is to answer all those questions in the order that makes the most sense.

> Reports answer the audience's key questions.

Your audience usually has one main question of greatest importance: "Why are we losing money?" "What's the progress on this project?" At the San Diego Wild Animal Park, Deirdre Ballou's audience was the brainstorming committee, and members had one major question: "Why should the Wild Animal Park pursue the Heart of Africa concept?" No matter what the main question is, be sure to define it as precisely as you can before you begin formulating your answer. Nine times out of ten the main question is simply the reason you've been asked to write the report or make the presentation. Once you've defined the main question, you can sketch a general answer, based on the results of your research. Your answer, like the question, should be broad.

Now you're ready to determine what additional questions your audience is likely to ask, based on your answer to the main question. A typical question-and-answer chain might look like the following:

Main Question: Why are we losing money?

General Answer: We're losing money because our production costs are higher than our prices.

Question 1: Why are our production costs high?

Question 2: Why are our prices low?

BE CAREFUL—YOUR COMPUTER CAN CREATE WORK!

Computers have given business communicators some wonderful tools for planning, developing, and producing reports. They can clearly make a person more efficient than a typewriter could, but only up to a point. Because they give you so much flexibility and so many design choices, computers can actually create work and waste time if you don't use them carefully.

Back in the days of typewriters, reports tended to look more or less alike. Without resorting to extraordinarily slow (and expensive) custom artwork, it was hard to add anything special to a report. So because it was impossible to turn routine reports into works of art, no one wasted time trying to do so. Now you can choose from thousands of typefaces, create full-color graphics, scan in photos (or upload them directly from digital cameras), down-

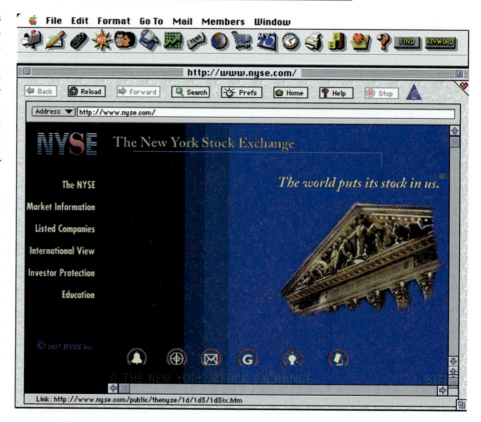

Pursue the chain of questions and answers from the general to the specific.

Your next step is to answer these questions, and your answers again raise additional questions. As you forge the chain of questions and answers, the points multiply and become increasingly specific (see Figure 17.1). When you've identified and answered all your audience's probable questions, you've defined the content of your report or presentation. The process is similar to factoring the issues in order to conduct an investigation.

The question-and-answer chain clarifies the main idea of the report (your answer to the main question) and establishes the flow of ideas from the general to the specific. Effective reports and presentations use a mix of broad concepts and specific details. When the mix is right, the message works: Members of the audience grasp both the general meaning of the ideas and the practical implications of those ideas. The general ideas sum up and give direction to the message, and the specific ideas clarify and illustrate their meaning. For every piece of information you are tempted to include, ask why the audience needs it and how it relates to the main question.

load Web pages (such as the home page for the New York Stock Exchange shown here), and produce dazzling printouts on standard office equipment. Computers have made it incredibly easy to turn a one-page memo into a one-day design project.

Clearly, many of these advancements represent tremendous increases in efficiency and quality. Others offer questionable benefits, particularly if they are misused. Yes, you can now create your own printer fonts (even to imitate your own handwriting), but do you really need to? Color printers can make reports come to life, but they also present another set of design choices. When you add color, you start worrying about which colors look good together, whether the company logo prints in the same color on every printer, whether flesh tones in photographs look right, and on and on.

Moreover, your computer tools themselves can be a source of work. No one spent time customizing their typewriters; they couldn't. With a computer, however, you could spend all day playing around with screen savers, macros, icons, sounds, and video clips—not to mention the biggest time waster of them all, computer games. You can scan in a picture of your cat and convert it to "wallpaper" for your monitor. Some experts predict that object-oriented software will soon enable you to create your own word processor. In other words, you can spend all day working on your computer, without actually getting any work done.

Managers and supervisors need to set the tone for computer usage. If a manager applauds one employee for a dazzling, full-color report with extensive graphics, guess what all the other employees will be doing the next time they write a report?

Employees need be conscious of how they're spending their computer time. Does a report really need fancy charts with clip art decorations, or will a simple table of numbers suffice? Do you need a handsomely bound printed report, or will corner-stapled photocopies get the job done? In the same way that you consider *what* should go in your report, stop and consider *how* you should package it. Don't fall into the trap of using computer tools just because you have them.

---

1. How can style sheets help people develop reports more efficiently? (If you're not familiar with style sheets, ask someone with a good word processor to give you a demonstration.)
2. What role do you think audience expectations play in the temptation to overuse computer design tools?

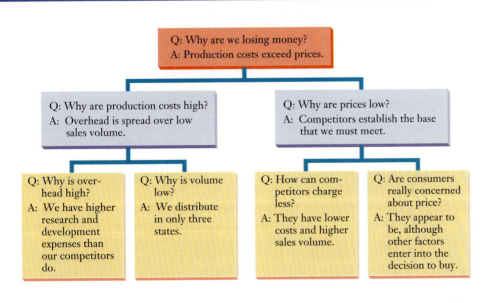

Figure 17.1
A Typical Question-and-Answer Chain

Choosing Direct or Indirect Order

What psychological approach is best for your particular readers? As Chapter 1 explains, audience attitude is the basis for decisions about organization. When the audience is considered either receptive or open-minded, use the direct approach: Lead off with a summary of your key findings, conclusions, and recommendations. This "upfront" approach is by far the most popular and convenient order for business reports. Direct order saves time and makes the rest of the report easier to follow. For those who have questions or want more information, later parts of the report provide complete findings and supporting details.

The direct approach also produces a more forceful report. You sound sure of yourself when you state your conclusions confidently at the outset. However, confidence may sometimes be misconstrued as arrogance. If you're a junior member of a status-conscious organization or if your audience is skeptical or hostile, you may want to use indirect order: Introduce the complete findings and supporting details before the conclusions and recommendations, which come last. The indirect approach gives you a chance to prove your points and gradually overcome your audience's reservations. Deirdre Ballou used this approach to pull her audience into her vision. By deferring the conclusions and recommendations, you imply that you've weighed the evidence objectively without prejudging the facts. You also imply that you're subordinating your judgment to that of the audience, whose members are capable of drawing their own conclusions when they have access to all the facts.

Although the indirect approach has its advantages, some report readers will always be in a hurry to get to "the answer" and will flip to the recommendations immediately, thus defeating your purpose. For this reason, consider length when deciding on direct or indirect order. Generally speaking, the longer the message, the less effective an indirect approach is likely to be. Furthermore, an indirect argument is harder to follow than a direct argument.

Because both the direct and indirect approaches have merit, businesspeople often combine them. They reveal their conclusions and recommendations as they go along, rather than putting them either first or last. Figure 17.2 presents the introductions from two reports with the same general outline. In the direct version, a series of statements summarize the conclusion reached in relation to each main topic on the outline. In the indirect version, the same topics are introduced (in the same order) without drawing any conclusions about them. The conclusions appear within the body of the report instead. So is this second report direct or indirect? Business reports are often difficult to classify.

Structuring Ideas

What method of subdivision will make your material both clear and convincing? Should you use a **topical organization,** based on order of importance, sequence, chronology, location, spatial relationships, or categories? Should you use **logical organization** to arrange your ideas around logical arguments that reflect the reasoning behind the report's conclusions and recommendations?

Regardless of whether you use the direct or indirect approach, you must still deal with the question of how your ideas will be subdivided and developed. Say you're writing a controversial report recommending that your company revise its policy on who reports to whom. You know that some of your readers will object to your ideas, so you decide to use indirect order. How do you develop your argument? The key is first to de-

The direct approach saves time and makes the report easier to understand by giving readers the main idea first.

The indirect approach helps overcome resistance by withholding the main idea until later in the report.

Topical organization is based on order of importance, sequence, chronology, location, spatial relationships, or categories. *Logical organization* is based on logical arguments that reflect the reasoning process behind the conclusions and recommendations.

Figure 17.2
*Direct Approach versus
Indirect Approach in an
Introduction*

THE DIRECT APPROACH	THE INDIRECT APPROACH

Since the company's founding 25 years ago, we have provided regular repair service for all our electric appliances. This service has been an important selling point as well as a source of pride for our employees. However, we are paying a high price for our image. Last year, we lost $500,000 on our repair business.
 	
    Because of your concern over these losses, you have asked me to study the pros and cons of discontinuing our repair service. With the help of John Hudson and Susan Lefkowitz, I have studied the issue for the past two weeks and have come to the conclusion that we have been embracing an expensive, impractical tradition.
 	
    By withdrawing from the electric appliance repair business, we can substantially improve our financial performance without damaging our reputation with customers. This conclusion is based on three basic points that are covered in the following pages:
• It is highly unlikely that we will ever be able to make a profit in the repair business.
• Service is no longer an important selling point with customers.
• Closing down the service operation will create few internal problems.
	Since the company's founding 25 years ago, we have provided repair service for all our electric appliances. This service has been an important selling point as well as a source of pride with our employees. However, the repair business itself has consistently lost money.
	
	    Because of your concern over these losses, you have asked me to study the pros and cons of discontinuing our repair business. With the help of John Hudson and Susan Lefkowitz, I have studied the issue for the past two weeks. The following pages present our findings for your review. Three basic questions are addressed:
	• What is the extent of our losses, and what can we do to turn the business around?
	• Would withdrawal hurt our sales of electric appliances?
	• What would be the internal repercussions of closing down the repair business?

cide whether the purpose of the report is to provide information or analysis. From there, you can choose an organizational plan that suits your topic and goals.

Informational reports differ from analytical reports in their purpose and thus in their organization. Informational reports are intended mainly to educate readers, but analytical reports are designed to persuade readers to accept certain conclusions or recommendations. In informational reports the information alone is the focus of attention. In analytical reports the information plays a supporting role. The facts are a means to an end rather than an end in themselves. Typically, the end is either a decision or an action.

Informational reports are usually written to explain something in straightforward terms. Having hundreds of uses in business, informational reports include those for monitoring and controlling operations, statements of policies and procedures, most compliance reports, most personal activity reports, some justification reports, some reports documenting client work, and some proposals.

Analytical reports are usually written to respond to special circumstances. Most of the decision-oriented reports mentioned in Chapter 14 are analytical, such as justification reports, research reports, and troubleshooting reports. So are many proposals and final reports to clients.

Subdividing Informational Reports

When writing informational reports, you don't usually have to be too concerned about reader reaction. Because readers will presumably respond unemotionally to your material, you can present it in the most direct fashion possible. What you do need to be

The purpose of informational reports is to explain, whereas analytical reports are meant to convince the audience that the conclusions and recommendations developed in the text are valid.

Make clarity your main objective in informational reports.

concerned about with informational reports is reader comprehension. The information must be presented logically and accurately so that readers will understand exactly what you mean and be able to use the information in a practical way.

When structuring an informational report, you can let the nature of whatever you're describing serve as the point of departure. If you're describing a machine, each component can correspond to a part of your report. If you're describing an event, you can approach the discussion chronologically, and if you're explaining how to do something, you can describe the steps in the process. As vice president of the plant sciences division of Monsanto Agricultural Company in St. Louis, Missouri, Milton P. Wilkins submits monthly status reports about his division's activities to Monsanto's top management. Wilkins lets the organizational structure of his division serve as the framework for these monthly reports. He summarizes results for his group as a whole and then for each of the six departments under his supervision.[2]

Some informational reports, especially compliance reports and internal reports prepared on preprinted forms, are organized according to instructions supplied by the person requesting the information. In addition, many proposals conform to an outline specified in the request for proposal issued by the client, which might include statement of the problem, background, scope of work, restrictions, sources and methods, work schedule, qualifications of personnel, facilities, anticipated costs, and expected results.

Informational reports take many forms. The two examples that follow, a brief periodic report and a personal activity report on a seminar, will give you an idea of the typical organization and tone.

A Periodic Report

Periodic reports are recurring monitor/control reports that keep managers informed about departments reporting to them.

A periodic report is a monitor/control report that describes what has happened in a department or division during a particular period. Corporate annual reports are periodic reports that are more formal and polished. Milt Wilkins's monthly status reports to Monsanto are a prime example of periodic reports. The purpose of these recurring documents is to provide a picture of how things are going so that corporate managers will be up-to-date and can take corrective action if necessary.

Periodic reports are usually written in memo format and don't need much of an introduction; a subject line on the memo is adequate. They should follow the same general format and organization from period to period. Most are organized in this sequence:

- *Overview of routine responsibilities.* Briefly describe activities related to each of the writer's normal responsibilities. In some cases the overview focuses on statistical or financial results; in other cases it's written in paragraph form.
- *Discussion of special projects.* Briefly describe any new or special projects that have been undertaken during the reporting period.
- *Plans for the coming period.* Give a schedule of activities planned for the next reporting period.
- *Analysis of problems.* Discuss the possible causes of and solutions for any problems. Although often included in the overview of routine responsibilities or in the discussion of special projects, this analysis is sometimes set off in a separate section to call attention to areas that may require high-level intervention.

Periodic reports expose any problems that exist.

The important thing to remember when writing periodic reports is to be honest about problems as well as accomplishments. In fact, the bad news is probably more important than the good news because problems require action whereas good news often does not.

The periodic report in Figure 17.3 was prepared by Roger Watson, real estate director for a San Francisco coffee retailer. According to Watson, "Real estate scouting

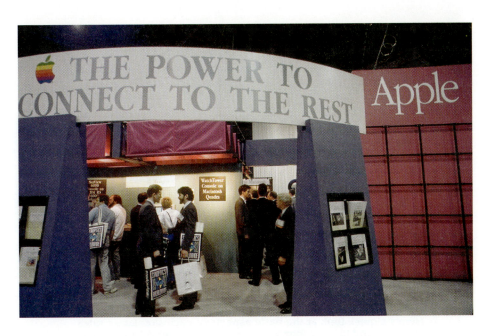

Businesspeople attending this Interop conference in Washington, D.C., might well be asked to write a personal activity report about the booths they visited, the representatives they met, and the products that most impressed them.

is a crucial activity for our company as we expand eastward from our California base. My manager needs to know that my department is making good decisions when we select new store locations."

A Personal Activity Report

A personal activity report is a form of monitor/control report that calls for a person's description of what occurred during a conference, convention, trip, or other activity. It's intended to inform management of any important information or decisions that emerged during the activity.

Personal activity reports are ordinarily written in memo format. Because they're nonrecurring documents, they require more of an introduction than periodic reports. They're often organized chronologically, but some are organized around topics that reflect the audience's interests. Figure 17.4 (see pages 544–545) is an example of a personal activity report organized by topic. This seminar attendance report was prepared by Carrie Andrews, the human resources manager of a small insurance firm based in Indianapolis.

Personal activity reports describe the facts and decisions that emerge during conventions, trips, and business meetings.

Subdividing Analytical Reports by Conclusions or Recommendations

When writing an analytical report for people from your own organization who have asked you to study something, you're writing for your most receptive readers. They may know from past experience that you'll do a thorough job, and they may trust your judgment. So they're likely to accept your conclusions, and you can usually use the direct approach by organizing your report around conclusions or recommendations.

Analytical reports may be organized around conclusions and recommendations (direct approach) when the audience is receptive.

Focusing on Conclusions: A Research and Analysis Report

The direct approach does have some drawbacks, however. If your readers have reservations about either you or your material, strong statements at the beginning may intensify their resistance. Focusing on conclusions and recommendations may also make everything seem too simple. Your readers could criticize your report as being superficial: "Why didn't you consider this option?" or "Where did you get this number?" You're generally better off taking the direct approach in a report only when your

Figure 17.3
In-Depth Critique: Sample Periodic Report

With over 500 stores in the company, Roger Watson doesn't want to burden his boss with a lot of details about every single site. His monthly reports are concise and presented in a summary format. "If Joan has questions about a specific location and needs more information," says Watson, "we usually just talk by phone after she gets my report."

The brief introduction orients the reader but doesn't waste time with unnecessary explanations.

Headings stand out to make report review easier for the reader.

The table organizes summary information in the most time-saving format.

MEMO

TO:	Joan Chen, V.P. New Business Development	**DATE:** August 1, 1997	
FROM:	Roger Watson, Real Estate Director	**SUBJECT:** July location scouting	

During the last two weeks of July, I scouted four Denver locations for our coffee outlets. George Spindle recommended these sites in his business development report (which is on the intranet under "Regional reports" if you'd like to review it). All four sites are in existing office buildings.

HOW THE DENVER SITES COMPARE

Here's a quick look at the basic aspects of each site. Lease rates are comparable at all four locations, ranging from $34 to $38 a square foot.

	Space	**Availability**	**Competition**	**Visibility**
Lakewood	260 square feet	Now	Starbucks has begun construction 4 blocks north; no other stores within a 16-block radius	None; on the second of two retail floors in this building
Glendale	525 square feet; with additional 150 square feet in one year	January	2 Starbucks (2 blocks south and 8 blocks west); Chicago Blues (across street, but poor visibility)	Superb corner location; windows on both streets
McNichols Arena	420 square feet	December	JavaLand 3 blocks east; Starbucks 4 blocks south	Good visibility but little evening/weekend traffic
University of Denver	Two options: 340 square feet, 655 square feet	Now for the smaller site; March for the larger	Five independents in the immediate area; Starbucks on campus (2 blocks west)	Good visibility, and street is a major retail location

SCOUTING PLANS FOR SEPTEMBER

Our schedule has been pretty tight for the last six months. Following are the plans for our efforts in September:

2

> **Denver:** I'll contract Shure Research to conduct foot traffic counts at all four sites (we should have those numbers in 10 days). I've asked George's team to do a permits search to study future building plans in each location. I'll be talking with Melissa Hines next week about construction restrictions. (She's the Smith, Allen broker who helped us with the Grand Junction sites last year.)
>
> **Minneapolis:** Jean-Luc Goddard wants us to review several sites he's had his eye on. I'll send Margie or visit them myself if my schedule permits.
>
> **Dallas:** We've run into some problems with the lease negotiations at the airport site. My staff will investigate and try to clear it up by September 15.

Figure 17.3
(Continued)

Details of upcoming efforts help the reader maintain a timely overview of the progress.

BEST OF THE WEB

Write an Outline with Confidence

The Purdue University Online Writing Lab (OWL) offers a variety of resources and direct assistance for any writer in need of help. Over 100 valuable handouts are available for your use. For information about outlining, start on the home page, then click on the following items in order: "Handouts & Writing Links," "Index of Handouts," "General Writing Concerns." Under this last heading, click "Developing an Outline" and "Sample Outline" for information that will reinforce the points made in this chapter.

http://owl.english.purdue.edu

credibility is high, when your readers trust you and are willing to accept your conclusions and recommendations.

Cynthia Zolonka works on the human resources staff of a bank in Houston, Texas, that decided to have an outside firm handle its employee training. A year after the outsourcing arrangement was established, Zolonka was asked to evaluate the results. She explains: "Moving our training programs to an outside supplier was a tough—and controversial—decision for the entire company. Some people were convinced outsourcing would never work, while others thought it might save money but hurt training quality. To convince them, I took special care to do a thorough analysis of the data, and I supported my conclusion with objective answers not personal opinions." Consider Zolonka's outline in Figure 17.5 (see page 545) and an excerpt from her report in Figure 17.6 (see page 546).

You can use a similar organization whenever you're asked to analyze a problem or an opportunity. Readers who are interested mainly in your conclusions can grasp them quickly, and readers who want to know more about your analysis can look at the data you provide.

When the reader is concerned with conclusions, use them as the main points.

Focusing on Recommendations: A Justification Report

A slightly different approach is useful when your readers want to know what they ought to do as opposed to what they ought to conclude. You'll often be asked to solve a problem rather than just study it. If so, the things you want your readers to do become the main subdivisions of your report.

When the reader is concerned about what action to take, use recommendations as the main points.

When organizing a report around recommendations, you usually take five steps:

1. Establish the need for action in the introduction, generally by briefly describing the problem or opportunity.
2. Introduce the benefit that can be achieved, without providing any details.
3. List the steps (recommendations) required to achieve the benefit, using action verbs for emphasis.
4. Explain each step more fully, giving details on procedures, costs, and benefits.
5. Summarize the recommendations.

Figure 17.4
In-Depth Critique: Sample
Personal Activity Report

Carrie Andrews attended a seminar on legal issues in employee recruiting and interviewing. Says Andrews, "I prepared this report for my boss, the company president, and the four people who work for me. We can't afford to send everyone in the department to seminars such as this, so it's important that I share the information I received with the people who couldn't attend."

The introduction states the reason for Andrews attending the seminar in the first place.

Organizing this report around the three areas of knowledge gained by Andrews helps readers focus on what is important.

Bullets make the new knowledge stand out for easy reader reference.

MEMO

TO:	Jeff Balou; all members of HR staff	**DATE:**	March 14, 1997
FROM:	Carrie Andrews	**SUBJECT:**	Recruiting and hiring seminar

As you all know, the process of recruiting, screening, and hiring new employees can be a legal mine field. Since we don't have an in-house lawyer to help us make every decision, it's important for all of us to be aware of what is legally acceptable and what isn't.

Last week I attended an American Management Association seminar on this subject. I got enough useful information to warrant updating our online personnel handbook and perhaps developing a quick training session for all interviewing teams. First, here's a quick idea of the things I learned.

AVOIDING LEGAL MISTAKES
- How to write recruiting ads that accurately portray job openings and that don't discriminate
- How best to comply with the Americans with Disabilities Act
- How to use an employment agency effectively and safely (without risk of legal entanglements)

SCREENING AND INTERVIEWING MORE EFFECTIVELY
- How to sort through résumés more efficiently (including looking for telltale signs of false information)
- How to avoid interview questions that could get us into legal trouble
- When and how to check criminal records

MEASURING APPLICANTS
- Which types of preemployment tests have proven most effective
- Which drug-testing issues and recommendations affect us

As you can see, the seminar addressed a lot of important information. We cover the basic guidelines for much of this already, but a number of specific recommendations and legal concepts should be emphasized.

One eye-opening part of the seminar was learning about the mistakes other companies have made. Some companies have

Figure 17.4
(Continued)

2

lost millions of dollars in employment-discrimination lawsuits. The risks are huge, so we have to protect ourselves and avoid discriminating against any applicants.

It will take me a couple of weeks to get the personnel handbook updated, but we don't have any immediate hiring plans anyway. I'll keep the seminar handouts and my notes on my desk, in case you want to peruse them. After I've updated the handbook, we can get together and decide whether we need to train the interviewing team members. Although we have a lot of new information, I think we can highlight what people need to be aware of and let them read the new sections as their schedules allow.

If you have any questions in the meantime, don't hesitate to e-mail me or drop by for a chat.

Although reporting on personal activity, this report wastes no time on unimportant activities such as how many sessions were offered during the seminar or what was served for lunch. Rather, the report is full of the information needed by department members and the plans for how to disseminate it.

Figure 17.5
In-Depth Critique: Outline of a Research Report Based on Conclusions

The audience for Zolonka's report on outsourcing employee training included some very skeptical readers. They assumed the outsourcing experiment would fail, but Zolonka's analysis showed it was a success. Zolonka decided to organize her report in four main sections, as this outline illustrates.

I. Introduction

II. Conclusion: Outsourcing employee training has reduced costs and improved quality

III. Cost reductions
   A. Cost reduction goal was 15 percent over the first year
   B. Actual reduction achieved was 22 percent
   C. Reassigned the three staffers who used to work on training full-time
   D. Reduced the management time needed to oversee training
   E. Sold the computers that used to be reserved for training and eliminated the equipment budget for next year

IV. Quality improvements
   A. Employees say they are more confident in seven out of ten key skill areas
   B. Measurable mistakes have dropped by 12 percent

V. Areas needing improvement
   A. Two trainers received approval ratings below 80 percent
   B. The outside trainers aren't always up to speed on internal company issues
   C. We've lost some flexibility for scheduling courses

VI. Summary

The conclusion is stated first: that the outsourcing was successful because it met most of the goals established for the program.

The next two sections explore the two categories of goals: cost savings and quality improvements.

The last main section discusses some areas of concern.

Figure 17.6
In-Depth Critique:
Excerpt Showing the
Development of
Conclusions in an
Analytical Report

The following is an excerpt from Cynthia Zolonka's report on outsourcing employee training. The excerpt is taken from the beginning of the section describing the quality improvements.

21

MEASURING QUALITY IMPROVEMENTS

As you know, we survey employees once a year on training issues, and two of the areas we measure are confidence levels employees have in job-related skills and error rates in each job task. The numbers this year look quite favorable when compared with last year's.

Employee Confidence

The following table demonstrates the success of our new training programs in boosting employee confidence; the numbers indicate the percentage of employees who feel "confident" or "very confident" in the skills indicated.

	1/14/96	1/12/97		1/14/96	1/12/97
Order entry	95%	98%	Shipping	91%	93%
Refunds	85%	91%	Receiving	82%	88%
Restocking	97%	99%	Reordering	85%	84%
Troubleshooting	88%	93%	Negotiating	72%	68%
Kitting	95%	98%	Discounting	64%	62%

Naturally, we'd like to make improvements in the last three areas as well. We're working with Temple & Associates to find out why the training hasn't improved the scores here.

Error Rates

We want confidence to translate into improved performance, of course, so another important quality-control measurement is error rates. The following table shows that error rates decreased in every category, as measured during first-quarter quality audits.

	Q1 96	Q1 97		Q1 96	Q1 97
Order entry	5%	3%	Shipping	4%	3%
Refunds	8%	7%	Receiving	2%	0%
Restocking	4%	1%	Reordering	5%	4%
Troubleshooting	12%	9%	Negotiating	11%	5%
Kitting	8%	5%	Discounting	8%	6%

Zolonka introduces this main section and its two subsections with statements describing the success of the program (which support her overall conclusion at the beginning of the report).

Zolonka does not gloss over the lack of improvement in employee confidence in three areas. Moreover, she emphasizes what's being done to bring those numbers up.

Tables make it easy for readers to see the change in numbers.

Alycia Jenn, the business development manager at a Chicago-based retail chain, was asked by the company's board of directors to suggest whether the company should set up a retailing site on the World Wide Web, and if so, how to implement the site. As Jenn noted, "Setting up shop on the Internet is a big decision for our company. We don't have the big computer staffs that our larger competitors have, and our business development team is stretched rather thin already. On the other hand, I know that more and more people are shopping online, and we don't want to be left out if this mode of retailing really takes off. After studying the issue for several weeks, I concluded that we should go ahead with a site, but we had to be careful about how we implement it." Her memo appears in Figure 17.7.

Subdividing Analytical Reports by Logical Argument

Focusing on conclusions or recommendations is the most forceful and efficient way to organize an analytical report, but it isn't the best solution for every situation. Sometimes you can achieve better results by encouraging readers to weigh all the facts before you present your conclusions or recommendations.

> Analytical reports may be organized around logical arguments (indirect approach) when the audience is unreceptive.

When you want your audience to concentrate on *why* your ideas make sense, your best bet is to let your logical arguments provide the structure for your report, making your organization reflect the thinking process that will lead readers to your conclusions. The main points in your outline correspond to the main points in favor of your conclusions and recommendations. Three basic organizational plans may be used to argue your case: the $2 + 2 = 4$ approach, the scientific method, and the yardstick approach. The best choice depends on the nature of the facts at your disposal. Essentially, you choose an organizational plan that matches the reasoning process you used to arrive at your conclusions.

> Three organizational plans are useful for convincing skeptical readers that your conclusions and recommendations are well-founded: the $2 + 2 = 4$ approach, the scientific method, and the yardstick approach.

The three approaches are not mutually exclusive. When analyzing a problem, you often pursue several lines of thought to arrive at a solution; you might want to lead readers along the same mental pathways in hopes they will follow you to the same conclusions. In a long report, particularly, you may find it convenient to use differing organizational plans for various sections. Generally speaking, however, simplicity of organization is a virtue. You need a clear, comprehensible argument in order to convince skeptical readers to accept your conclusions or recommendations.

The 2 + 2 = 4 Approach: A Troubleshooting Report

Reports based on the accumulation of facts and figures are developed around a list of reasons that collectively add up to the main point you're trying to prove. Essentially, to convince readers of your point of view, you demonstrate that $2 + 2 = 4$. The main points in your outline are the main reasons behind your conclusions and recommendations. You support each of these reasons with the evidence you have collected during your analysis.

> Use reasons as the main divisions in your outline to gradually build a case for your conclusions and recommendations.

Binh Phan, the national sales manager of a New Hampshire sporting goods company, was concerned about his company's ability to sell to its largest customers. His boss, the vice president of marketing, shared these concerns and asked Phan to analyze the situation and recommend the solution. As Phan says, "We sell sporting goods to retail chains across the country. Large nationwide chains with superstores modeled after Toys R Us have been revolutionizing the industry, but we haven't had as much success with these big customers as we've had with smaller companies that operate on only a local or regional basis. With more and more of the industry in the hands of the large chains, we knew we had to fix the situation." Phan's troubleshooting report is outlined in Figure 17.8 (see page 550). The main idea is that the company should establish separate sales teams for these major accounts, rather than continuing to service them through the company's four regional divisions. However, Phan knew his plan would be controversial since it required a big change in the company's organization.

Figure 17.7
In-Depth Critique: Sample Justification Report Focusing on Recommendations

In her justification report, Alycia Jenn uses her recommendations to organize her thoughts. Because the board of directors wouldn't be interested in a lot of technical detail, she keeps her discussion at a fairly high level. She also maintains a formal and respectful tone for this audience.

MEMO

TO: Board of Directors, Executive Committee members
FROM: Alycia Jenn, Business Development Manager
DATE: July 6, 1997
SUBJECT: World Wide Web retailing site

In response to your request, my staff and I investigated the potential for establishing a retailing site on the World Wide Web. After analyzing the behavior of our customers and major competitors and studying the overall development of electronic retailing, we have three recommendations:

1. Yes, we should establish an online presence within the next six months.
2. We should engage a firm that specializes in online retailing to design and develop the Web site.
3. We must take care to integrate online retailing with our store-based and mail-order operations.

WE SHOULD SET UP A WEB SITE

First, does a Web site make financial sense today? Studies suggest that our competitors are not currently generating significant revenue from their Web sites. Stallini's is the leader so far, but its sales haven't broken the $1 million mark. Moreover, at least half our competitors' online sales are from current customers who would have purchased the same items in-store or by mail order. Since the cost of setting up a retailing site is around $120,000, it isn't possible to justify a site based solely on current financial return.

Second, do we need to establish a presence now in order to remain competitive in the future? The online situation is too fluid and unpredictable to answer this question in a quantitative profit-and-loss way, but a qualitative view of strategy indicates that we should set up a site:

• As younger consumers (more comfortable with online shopping) reach their peak earning years (ages 35–54), they'll be more likely to buy online than today's peak spenders.
• The Web is erasing geographical shopping limits, presenting both a threat and an opportunity. Even though our customers can now shop Web sites anywhere in the world (so that we have thousands of competitors instead of a dozen), we can now target customers anywhere in the world.

Jenn clarifies the purpose and origin of the report in the introduction.

For clarity, her recommendations are simple and to the point.

Her reasons for recommending the firm establish a Web site are logically and clearly presented.

Figure 17.7
(Continued)

2

- If the growth in online retailing continues, this will eventually be a viable market. Establishing a site now and working out any problems will prepare us for high-volume online business in the years ahead.

WE SHOULD ENGAGE A CONSULTANT TO IMPLEMENT THE SITE

Implementing a competitive retailing site can take anywhere from 1,000 to 2,500 hours of design and programming time. We have some of the expertise needed in-house, but the marketing and information systems departments have only 300 person-hours in the next six months. I recommend that we engage a Web-design consultant to help us with the design and to do all of the programming.

WE MUST INTEGRATE THE WEB INTO EXISTING OPERATIONS

The studies we reviewed showed that the most successful Web retailers are careful to integrate their online retailing with their store- and mail-based retailing. Companies that don't integrate carefully find themselves with higher costs, confused customers, and Web sites that don't generate much business. Before we begin designing our Web site, we should develop a plan for integrating the Web into our existing marketing, accounting, and production systems. The online site could affect every department in the company, so it's vital that everyone has a chance to review the plans before we proceed.

SUMMARY

1. Yes, establish a Web site now even though it doesn't make immediate financial sense, because we might lose business if we don't have a site in the near future.
2. Use the services of a Web designer, since we don't have enough person-hours available in-house.
3. Integrate the Web site with existing operations, particularly in marketing, accounting, and production.

Her recommendations include not only establishing a Web site but also hiring a consultant to implement it and making sure to integrate it with existing systems.

Her close briefly summarizes her recommendations and the reasons behind them.

When Phan wrote the actual report, he used descriptive rather than informative headings to give his report an objective feel:

 I. Introduction

 II. Organizational Issues

III. Commission Issues

IV. Recommendation

 V. Summary

By phrasing his headings in an objective manner, he reassured his readers and prevented them from reacting negatively to ideas that had not yet been fully explained. Figure 17.9 (see page 551) is a copy of Phan's report.

Soften the force of controversial points by
- Using descriptive (not informative) headings
- Writing a "neutral" introduction
- Placing recommendations at the end

Figure 17.8
In-Depth Critique: Outline of a Troubleshooting Report Using the 2 + 2 = 4 Approach

Binh Phan's proposal would change the way his company's sales representatives are paid, and that's obviously an important personal issue for everybody. Plus, there was some risk to the company as a whole because Phan was suggesting a fairly major change to the way it does business. Consequently, Phan's analysis had to be thorough and objective, and his thinking had to be clear and easy to follow.

Phan has made his main points the very reasons for his recommendations.

Each main point is supported with concrete evidence.

His recommendation is a logical culmination of the main points he has presented so carefully.

Main Idea: We should set up a national account team to sell to customers that are located in more than one region, and our sales commissions should reflect this change.

I. Introduction

II. Reason #1: Our sales department is not organized to match our customer base.

    A. The sales force is now organized into four separate regions, but some of our biggest accounts are national companies with operations in two or more regions.

    B. Sales reps from two or more regions often end up competing with each other by pursuing the same customers from different locations.

    C. National customers are sometimes confused and frustrated; they want a single contact point with us.

III. Reason #2: Our sales commission program isn't providing the right kind of motivation and reward.

    A. Salespeople in one region can invest a lot of time in pursuing a sale, only to have the customer place the order in another region. Moreover, the sales rep in the second region ends up with a commission that was earned by someone in the first region.

    B. Sales reps occasionally don't pursue leads in their regions if they think a rep in another region will get the commission.

IV. Recommendation: Establish national account teams that cross all four regions, and change the compensation plan to encourage team selling.

V. Summary

The 2 + 2 = 4 approach works well when you have many reasons for your point of view but no single reason is overwhelming.

Organizing an analytical report around a list of reasons that collectively support your main conclusions or recommendations is a natural approach to take. Many problems are solved this way, and readers tend to accept the gradual accumulation of evidence, even though they may question one or two points. Because of its naturalness and versatility, the 2 + 2 = 4 approach is generally the most persuasive and efficient way to develop an analytical report for skeptical readers. When writing your own reports, this is the structure to try first. You'll usually find that your arguments fall naturally into this pattern. However, not every problem or reporting situation can be handled with this organizational plan.

The Scientific Method: A Proposal

When you're trying to discover whether an explanation is true, whether an option will solve your problem, or which one of several solutions will work best, you're likely to find the scientific method useful. Every day hundreds of managers ask themselves,

Binh Phan's troubleshooting report would definitely stir emotions, so he had to make sure the logic was solid. Moreover, he was careful that his introduction didn't reveal his position.

MEMO

TO: Robert Hernandez, Vice President of Marketing
FROM: Binh Phan, National Sales Manager
DATE: September 12, 1997
SUBJECT: Major accounts sales problems

INTRODUCTION

This report outlines the results of my investigation into the recent slowdown in sales to major accounts and the accompanying rise in sales- and service-related complaints from some of our largest customers.

As we discussed at last quarter's management retreat, major account sales dropped 12 percent over the last four quarters, whereas overall sales were up 7 percent. During the same time, we've all noticed an increase in both formal and informal complaints from larger customers regarding how confusing and complicated it has become to do business with us.

My investigation started with in-depth discussions with the four regional sales managers, first as a group and then individually. The tension I felt in the initial meeting eventually bubbled to the surface during my meetings with each manager. Staff members in each region are convinced that other regions are booking orders they don't deserve, with one region doing all the legwork only to see another region get credited with the sale and naturally the commission and quota credit.

I followed the sales manager discussions with informal talks and e-mail exchanges with a number of sales reps from each region. Virtually everyone who is involved with our major national accounts has a story to share. No one is happy with the situation, and I sense that a number of reps are walking away from major customers because the process is so frustrating.

ORGANIZATIONAL ISSUES

When we divided the national sales force into four geographic regions last year, the idea was to focus our sales efforts and clarify responsibilities for each prospective and current customer. The regional managers have gotten to know their market territories very well, and sales have increased beyond even our most optimistic projections.

Instead of summarizing his recommendations, Phan begins by discussing the report's purpose and scope, the background of the study, and his methods of research.

In the body, Phan presents the facts and his observations in an objective tone, without revealing his own point of view.

(continued)

"What's wrong with this operation, and what should we do about it?" They approach the problem by coming up with one or several possible solutions (hypotheses) and then conducting experiments or gathering information to find the most effective one.

Reports based on the scientific method begin with a statement of the problem and a brief description of the hypothetical solution or a list of possible solutions. The body of the report discusses each alternative in turn and offers evidence that will either

When organizing a report to reflect the scientific method, you discuss, one by one, hypothetical solutions to the problem.

Figure 17.9
(Continued)

2

Unfortunately, while solving one problem, we seem to have created another. In the past 12 to 18 months, several regional customers have grown to national status. In addition, a number of national retailers have taken on (or expressed interest in) our products. As a result, a significant portion of both our current sales and our future opportunities lie with these large national accounts.

I uncovered more than a dozen cases in which sales reps from two or more regions found themselves competing with each other by pursuing the same customer from different locations.

Moreover, the complaints from our major accounts about overlapping or nonexistent account coverage are a direct result of the regional organization. In some cases, customers aren't sure which of our reps they're supposed to call with problems and orders. In others, no one has been in contact with them for several months.

An example should help illustrate the problem. AmeriSport, with retail outlets across the lower tier of the country, was being pitched by reps from our West, South, and East regions. Since we give our regional offices a lot of negotiating freedom, all three were offering the client different prices. However, all buying decisions are made at their headquarters in Tampa, so all we did was confuse the customer.

The irony of this situation is that we're often giving our weakest selling and support efforts to the largest customers in the country.

COMMISSION ISSUES

The regional organization issues are compounded because of the way we assign commissions and quota credit. Salespeople in one region can invest a lot of time in pursuing a sale, only to have the customer place the order in another region. So some sales rep in the second region ends up with the commission on a sale that was partly or even entirely earned by someone in the first region.

Also, sales reps sometimes don't pursue leads in their regions if they think a rep in another region will get the commission. For example, Athletic Express, with outlets in 35 states spread across all four regions, finally got so frustrated with us that the

---

confirm the alternative or rule it out. Because many problems have multiple causes and complex solutions, several alternatives may be relevant. The final section of the report summarizes the findings and indicates which solution or solutions are valid. The report concludes with recommendations for solving the problem or eliminating the causes.

The scientific method, which is used in planning many studies, also provides a suitable outline for a proposal.

A variation of this pattern is often useful for the main section of a proposal. After defining the problem, you can suggest several solutions that you plan to investigate. For each alternative, you explain why it may have a bearing on the problem, and you describe how you plan to investigate it. The next section of the proposal is a work plan showing the schedule for investigating each alternative. Additional sections describe your organization's past experience, facilities, personnel, and projected costs.

Figure 17.9
(Continued)

3

company president called our headquarters. Athletic Express has been trying to place a large order for tennis and golf accessories, but none of our local reps seem interested in paying attention. I spoke with the rep responsible for Nashville, where the company is headquartered, and asked her why she wasn't working the account more actively. Her explanation was that last time she got involved with Athletic Express, the order was actually placed from their L.A. regional office, and she didn't get any commission after more than two weeks of selling time.

RECOMMENDATION

Our sales organization should reflect the nature of our customer base. To accomplish this, we need a group of reps who are free to pursue accounts across regional borders—and who are compensated fairly for their work. The most sensible answer is to establish a national accounts group. Any customer whose operations place them in more than one region would automatically be assigned to the national group.

Further, we need to modify our commission policy to reward people for team selling. I'll talk with the sales managers to work out the details, but in general, we'll need to split commissions whenever two or more reps help close a sale. This will also involve "finder's fees" for reps who pull in leads at the regional level that are passed on to the national account teams.

SUMMARY

The regional sales organization is working at the regional and local levels, but not at the national levels. We should establish a national accounts group to handle sales that cross regional boundaries.

To make sure the sales reps (at both the regional and national levels) are adequately motivated and fairly compensated, we need to devise a system of commission splitting and finder's fees. We'll then have a set of reps focused on the local and regional levels, and a set who pursue national accounts. The two groups will have incentives to work together, rather than against each other as the case is now.

He saves his recommendations for the fourth section, where he adds up the reasons (2 + 2 = 4).

An example of a proposal using the scientific method was prepared by Fredrik Swensen, an executive with a Miami restaurant management firm. (See the outline in Figure 17.10 on page 554.)

Swensen's proposal approach, analyzing each alternative, is useful when you're trying to unify a divided audience. Your chances of bringing about a consensus are much better when you show the strengths and weaknesses of all the ideas. The main drawback to the scientific method is that many of the alternatives may turn out to be irrelevant or unproductive, but you have to discuss them all. The more ideas you discuss, the more confused your readers may become and the more trouble they may have comparing pros and cons.

When readers have their own ideas about how to solve a problem, you have to discuss those notions before you can sell your own solution.

Figure 17.10
In-Depth Critique: Outline of a Proposal Using the Scientific Method

The purpose of Fredrik Swensen's proposal was to help the company decide which of four franchise operations to invest in. "We wanted to buy 45 or 50 more franchise outlets across the country, so this was a major investment decision. Our company already owns several hundred fast-food franchises, so we have a good idea of how to evaluate which ones are right for us."

This report covers two major steps: (1) establishing the decision criteria, and then (2) testing each of four alternatives against those criteria.

All four alternatives are separated into matching and comparable subdivisions: description, pros, cons, and conclusion (priority).

Main Idea: We should purchase the 45 franchises currently for sale in the Burger World chain.

I. **Statement of problem and purpose of this proposal**
II. **Scope of the investigation**
III. **Method used to compare the business opportunities**
 A. **Establish decision criteria**
 B. **Get input from consultants**
 C. **Gather secondary research**
 D. **Conduct market surveys for primary research**
 E. **Meet with franchisor management teams**
 F. **Analyze quantitative and qualitative data**
 G. **Prioritize and select the best opportunity**
IV. **Analysis of the four franchise operations**
 A. **Wacky Taco**
  1. **Description: Low-fat Mexican food; most locations in malls**
  2. **Pros: 58 units available within a year; consultants believe the concept has significant growth potential; operations easy to manage**
  3. **Cons: Company recently hit with employment discrimination lawsuit; franchise fees are 30 percent above average**
  4. **Conclusion: Priority = 3; lawsuit may be indicative of mismanagement; fees too high**
 B. **Thai in the Sky**
  1. **Description: Thai food served in New Age settings**
  2. **Pros: Healthy and interesting food; unusual theme concept; no franchised competition**
  3. **Cons: Complexity of food preparation; only 40 franchises available; franchisor's top management team replaced only six months ago**
  4. **Conclusion: Priority = 4; too risky and not enough units available**
 C. **Dog Tower**
  1. **Description: Gourmet hot dogs**
  2. **Pros: No nationwide competition; more than 60 franchises available within a year; easy to manage; fees lower than average**
  3. **Cons: Limited market appeal; many stores need updating**
  4. **Conclusion: Priority = 2; needs too much investment**
 D. **Burger World**
  1. **Description: Mainstream competitor to McDonald's and Burger King**

Figure 17.10
(Continued)

> 2. **Pros: Aggressive franchisor willing to invest in national marketing; start-up costs are low; unique demographic target (teenagers and young adults; not a little kids' place)**
> 3. **Cons: Fierce competition in burgers overall; some units in unproved locations**
> 4. **Conclusion: Priority = 1; finances look good; research shows that teenagers will support a chain that doesn't cater to small children**
>
> V. **Summary**
> VI. **Appendixes**
>   A. **Financial data**
>   B. **Research results**

The decision is never black and white, of course, but it's Swensen's job to present the alternatives objectively.

The Yardstick Approach: A Research Report

One way to reduce the confusion presented by having a lot of alternatives is to establish a yardstick for evaluating all of them. You begin by discussing the problem, as with the scientific method, but then you set up the conditions that must be met to solve the problem. These are the criteria against which you evaluate all possible solutions. The body of the report evaluates those alternatives in relation to the criteria. The main points of the outline are either the criteria themselves or the alternatives.

Yardstick reports are similar in some respects to those based on the scientific method, but in criteria-based reports, each alternative is reviewed against the same standards. Another distinction is that criteria-based reports can be used to prove the need for action: The current situation can be measured against the criteria and shown to be wanting.

The yardstick approach is useful for certain kinds of proposals because the client who requests the proposal often provides a list of criteria that the solution must meet. Say that your company has been asked to bid on a contract to install a computer for a large corporation. The client has listed the requirements (criteria) for the system, and you've developed a preliminary design to meet them. In the body of your proposal, you could use the client's list of requirements as the main headings and under each one explain how your preliminary design meets the requirement.

Figure 17.11 is an outline of a yardstick report that was provided by J. C. Hartley, a market analyst for a large Sacramento company that makes irrigation equipment for farms and ranches. "We've been so successful in the agricultural market that we're starting to run out of customers to sell to. To keep the company growing, we needed to find another market. Two obvious choices to consider were commercial buildings and residences."

Of course, if there is any disagreement on the decision criteria, you'll spin your wheels if you try to push forward to a decision. In Hartley's case, the criteria had been agreed to before she began her investigation, so her goal in including the criteria here was to remind her readers and make it easy for them to evaluate the options available.

The yardstick approach has one other drawback: It can be a little boring. You may find yourself saying the same things over and over again: "Opportunity A has high growth potential; opportunity B has high growth potential; opportunity C has high growth potential"; and so on. One way to minimize the repetition is to compare the

In the yardstick approach, the report is organized around criteria; the solution is the alternative that best meets the criteria.

Some proposals are best organized by using the client's criteria as the main points.

For the yardstick approach to work, readers must accept your criteria.

Figure 17.11
Outline of a Research Report Using the Yardstick Approach

J. C. Hartley knows that moving into a new market is not a trivial decision: "I had a responsibility to make careful recommendations. Even though I don't make the final decision, the information and professional opinion that I provide in my report both weigh heavily in the decision process."

After introducing the report and explaining the scope of her investigation, Hartley defines the criteria for evaluating and choosing the market opportunities.

The section on irrigation equipment trends gives readers valuable background information for understanding this report and its recommendations.

Communicating the decision criteria is particularly important in yardstick evaluation reports because you want readers to evaluate the options using a consistent and conscious set of factors.

Main Idea: We should move into the commercial irrigation equipment market but not into the residential market.

I. **Introduction**
II. **Criteria for entering new markets**
   A. Size and growth
   B. Profit potential
   C. Ability to compete
   D. Distribution costs and opportunities
   E. Fit with current capabilities
III. **Irrigation equipment trends**
   A. Water shortages leading to demand for more efficient irrigation
   B. Labor costs encouraging automation
   C. More homeowners attempting do-it-yourself projects
IV. **Comparison of new market opportunities**
   A. Commercial landscapers and building owners
      1. Size and growth
      2. Profit potential
      3. Ability to compete
      4. Distribution costs and opportunities
      5. Fit with current capabilities
   B. Residential landscapers and homeowners
      1. Size and growth
      2. Profit potential
      3. Ability to compete
      4. Distribution costs and opportunities
      5. Fit with current capabilities
V. **Recommendations**
   A. Enter the commercial segment
      1. Select a test market
      2. Learn from the test and refine our approach
      3. Roll out product marketing nationwide
   B. Do not attempt to enter the residential market at this point

Tables are useful in the yardstick approach
• To avoid repetition
• To make the options easier to compare

options in tables and then highlight the more unusual or important aspects of each alternative in the body so that you get the best of both worlds. This way you compare all the alternatives against the same yardstick but call attention to the most significant differences among them.

FORMULATING REPORTS AND PROPOSALS

Choosing format, length, and a basic organizational plan for your report is an important set of decisions. A number of other decisions also affect the way your report will be received and understood by readers: the degree of formality, a consistent time perspective, and appropriate structural clues.

Choosing the Proper Degree of Formality

The issue of formality is closely related to considerations of format, length, and organization. If you know your readers reasonably well and if your report is likely to meet with their approval, you can generally adopt a less formal tone. In other words, you can speak to readers in the first person, referring to yourself as *I* and to your readers as *you*. This personal approach is often used in brief memo or letter reports, although there are many exceptions.

Longer reports, especially those dealing with controversial or complex information, are traditionally handled in a more formal vein. You'll also tend to use a more formal approach when writing a report to be sent beyond your own work area to other parts of the organization, customers, and suppliers. Communicating with people in other cultures often calls for more formality, for two reasons. First, the business environment outside the United States tends to be more formal in general, and that formality must be reflected in our communication style. Second, the things you do to make a document informal, such as using humor and idiomatic language, are the hardest things to transfer from culture to culture. Less formality in these cases increases the risk of offending people and of miscommunicating.

You achieve a formal tone by using the impersonal style, eliminating all references to *I* (including *we, us,* and *our*) and *you*. The style is borrowed from journalism, which stresses the reporter's objectivity. However, be careful that avoiding personal pronouns doesn't lead to overuse of such phrases as *there is* and *it is,* which are both dull and wordy. Also, avoiding personal pronouns makes it easier to slip into passive voice, which can be dull and wordy. Instead of saying "I think we should buy TramCo" you might end up saying "It is recommended that the company buy TramCo."

When you write in a formal style, you impose a certain distance between you and your readers. You remain businesslike, unemotional, and objective. You use no jokes, no similes or metaphors, and very few colorful adjectives or adverbs. You eliminate your own subjective opinions and perceptions and retain only the objective facts.

The formal style does not guarantee objectivity of content, however. When determining the fairness of a report, the selection of facts is far more important than the way they're phrased. If you omit crucial evidence, you're not being objective, even though you're using an impersonal style. In addition, you can easily destroy objectivity by exaggerating and using overblown language: "The catastrophic collapse in sales, precipitated by cutthroat pricing on the part of predatory and unscrupulous rivals, has jeopardized the very survival of the once-soaring hot-air balloon division." This sentence has no personal references, but its objectivity is highly questionable.

Despite such drawbacks, the impersonal style is a well-entrenched tradition in many business organizations. You can often tell what tone is appropriate for your readers by looking at other reports of a similar type in your company. If all the other reports on file are impersonal, you should probably adopt the same tone yourself, unless you're confident that your readers prefer a more personal style. Most organizations, for whatever reasons, expect an unobtrusive, impersonal writing style for business reports.

> Write informal reports in a personal style, using the pronouns *I* and *you.*

> Being formal means putting your readers at a distance and establishing an objective, businesslike relationship.

> You are not being objective if you
> - Omit crucial evidence
> - Use exaggerated language

Establishing a Time Perspective

In what time frame will your report exist? Will you write in the past or present tense? The person who wrote this paragraph never decided:

> Twenty-five percent of those interviewed <u>report</u> that they <u>are</u> dissatisfied with their present brand. The wealthiest participants <u>complained</u> most frequently, but all income categories <u>are</u> interested in trying a new brand. Only 5 percent of the interviewees <u>say</u> they <u>had</u> no interest in alternative products.

> Be consistent in the verb tense you use.

By flipping from tense to tense when describing the same research results, you only confuse your readers. Is the shift significant, they wonder, or are you just being sloppy? Such confusion can be eliminated by using tense consistently.

Also be careful to observe the chronological sequence of events in your report. If you're describing the history or development of something, start at the beginning and cover each event in the order of its occurrence. If you're explaining the steps in a process, take each step in proper sequence.

Follow a proper chronological sequence in your report.

Helping Readers Find Their Way

As you begin to write, remember that readers have no concept of how the various pieces of your report relate to one another. Because you have done the work and outlined the report, you have a sense of its wholeness and can see how each page fits into the overall structure; but readers see the report one page at a time (see Figure 17.12). As you begin to write, your job is to give readers a preview or road map of the report's structure so that they can see how the parts of your argument relate to one another. These directions are particularly important for people from other cultures and countries, whose language skills and business expectations may differ from yours.

In a short report, readers are in little danger of getting lost. As the length of a report increases, however, so do readers' opportunities for becoming confused and losing track of the relationship among ideas. If you want readers to understand and accept your message, help them avoid this confusion. Five tools are particularly useful for giving readers a sense of the overall structure of your document and for keeping them on track as they read along: the opening, headings and lists, smooth transitions, previews and reviews, and the ending.

The Opening

In the opening tell readers what to expect, tell them why your subject is important, and orient them toward your organizational plan.

As the name suggests, the **opening** is the first section in any report. A good opening accomplishes at least three things:

- Introduces the subject of the report
- Indicates why the subject is important
- Previews the main ideas and the order in which they will be covered

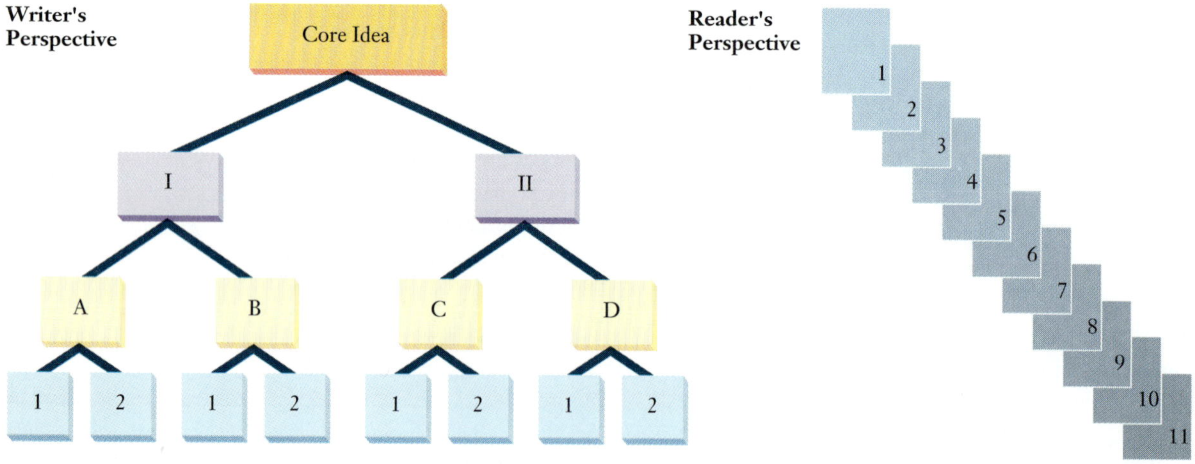

Figure 17.12
Differences in the Perspective of Writer and Reader

If you fail to provide readers with these clues to the structure of your report, they'll read aimlessly and miss important points, much like drivers trying to find their way through a strange city without a map.

If your audience is skeptical, the opening downplays the controversial aspects of your message while providing the necessary framework for understanding your report. Here's a good example of an indirect opening, taken from the introduction of a controversial memo on why a new line of luggage has failed to sell well. The writer's ultimate goal is to recommend a shift in marketing strategy.

> **The performance of the Venturer line can be improved. In the two years since its introduction, this product line has achieved a sales volume lower than we expected, resulting in a drain on the company's overall earnings. The purpose of this report is to review the luggage-buying habits of consumers in all markets where the Venturer line is sold so that we can determine where to put our marketing emphasis.**

This paragraph quickly introduces the subject (disappointing sales), tells why the problem is important (drain on earnings), and indicates the main points to be addressed in the body of the report (review of markets where the Venturer line is sold), without revealing what the conclusions and recommendations will be.

Headings and Lists

A **heading** is a brief title at the start of a subdivision within a report that cues readers about the content of the section that follows. Headings are useful markers for clarifying the framework of a report. They visually indicate shifts from one idea to the next, and when *subheadings* (lower-level headings) and headings are both used, they help readers see the relationship between subordinate and main ideas. In addition, busy readers can quickly understand the gist of a document simply by scanning the headings. (See "Writing Headings That Spark Reader Interest.")

Use headings to give readers the gist of your report.

Headings within a given section that are of the same level of importance should be phrased in parallel form. In other words, if one heading begins with a verb, all same-level headings in that section should begin with verbs. If one is a noun phrase, all should be noun phrases. Putting comparable ideas in similar terms tells readers that the ideas are related. The only exception might be such descriptive headings as "Introduction" at the beginning of a report and "Conclusions" and "Recommendations" at the end. Many companies specify a format for headings. If yours does, use that format. Otherwise, you can use the scheme shown in Figure 17.13 (see page 561).

Phrase all same-level headings within a section in parallel terms.

A **list** is a series of words, names, or items arranged in a specific order. Setting off important ideas in a list provides an additional structural clue. Lists can show the sequence of ideas or visually heighten their impact. In addition, they facilitate the skimming process for busy readers. Like headings, list items should be phrased in parallel form. You might also consider multilevel lists, with subentries below each major item (much like an outline).[3]

Use lists to set off important ideas and to show sequence.

When you're creating a list, you can separate items with numbers, letters, or bullets (a general term for any kind of graphical element that precedes each item). Numbers are the best choice when you want to indicate sequence or priority, as in this example:

1. Find out how many employees would like on-site day-care facilities
2. Determine how much space the day-care center would require
3. Estimate the cost of converting a conference room for the on-site facility

These three steps need to be taken in the order indicated, and the numbers make that clear. Letters and bullets help you indicate choices without implying order or hierarchy:

SHARPENING YOUR SKILLS

WRITING HEADINGS THAT SPARK READER INTEREST

Headings help your audience follow the main points presented in your report. Furthermore, when carefully developed, headings do much more. They capture your readers' attention and interest, inform them, and make them want to read the whole report.

Each heading offers you an opportunity to make an important point. For example, instead of "Introduction," your opening section might be called "An Insight into the Need." This title catches attention and sparks interest. The title "Chart of Proposed Organization" gains impact when reworded as "Organization for Results." So does "Cost Considerations" when retitled "A New Way to Cut Costs."

Headings fall into two categories. Descriptive (topical) headings, such as "Cost Considerations," identify a topic but do little more. However, they are fine for routine reports and in controversial reports, where they may defuse emotional reactions. Informative (talking) headings, such as "A New Way to Cut Costs," convey more information about the main theme or idea of the report. They are helpful because they guide readers to think in a certain way about the topic. For more effective reports, concentrate on developing informative headings rather than descriptive ones. However, be aware that informative headings are more difficult to create.

Try to avoid vague headings. In a chronological history of your company, headings such as "The Dawning of a New Era" and "The Times They Are a-Changin'" may sound distinguished or cute, but readers will have no idea what time period you are referring to. Preferable headings would be "The War Years: Gebco Outfits Our GIs" or "The 1990s See International Expansion."

Whatever types of headings you choose, try to keep them grammatically parallel. For example, this series of headings is parallel: "Cutting Costs," "Reducing Inventory," "Increasing Profits." This series of headings is not: "Cutting Costs," "Inventory Reduction," "How to Increase Profits."

1. Think about the headlines in a newspaper. What functions do they perform? How are they usually phrased? What can you learn from journalistic headlines that applies to report writing?
2. For practice in writing headings, collect some brochures, newsletters, or similar items and rewrite the headings to convey more information about the theme or main idea. Can you draw any conclusions about what works best?

A. Convert an existing conference room
B. Build an add-on room
C. Lease space in an existing day-care center

Bullets can add a decorative touch while helping readers distinguish the items in a list. Most word processors make it easy to add a variety of bullet styles, some more appropriate than others. The first list here is fine in this context; the second is too frivolous:

• Cut everyone's salary by 10 percent
• Close the employee cafeteria
• Reduce travel expenses

✂ Cut everyone's salary by 10 percent
✂ Close the employee cafeteria
✂ Reduce travel expenses

When you use lists, make sure to introduce them clearly so that people know what they're about to read. If necessary, add further discussion after the lists (such as this paragraph is doing). Moving your readers smoothly into and out of lists requires careful use of transitions—the subject of the next section.

Transitions

Use transitions consisting of a single word, a few words, or a whole paragraph to provide additional structural clues.

Such phrases as *to continue the analysis, on the other hand,* and *an additional concept* are another type of structural clue. These are examples of **transitions,** words or phrases that tie ideas together within a report and keep readers moving along the right track.

Figure 17.13
Heading Formats for Reports

TITLE

The title is centered at the top of the page in all capital letters, usually boldfaced (or underlined if typewritten), often in a larger font (type size), and often using a sans serif typeface. When the title runs to more than one line, the lines are usually double-spaced and arranged as an inverted pyramid (longer line on the top).

FIRST-LEVEL HEADING

A first-level heading indicates what the following section is about, perhaps by describing the subdivisions. All first-level headings are grammatically parallel, with the possible exception of such headings as "Introduction," "Conclusions," and "Recommendations." Some text appears between every two headings, regardless of their levels. Still boldfaced and sans serif, the font may be smaller than that used in the title but still larger than the typeface used in the text and still in all capital letters.

Second-Level Heading

Like first-level headings, second-level headings indicate what the following material is about. All second-level headings within a section are grammatically parallel. Still boldfaced and sans serif, the font may either remain the same or shrink to the size used in the text, and the style is now initial capitals with lowercase. Never use only one second-level heading under a first-level heading. (The same is true for every other level of heading.)

Third-Level Heading

A third-level heading is worded to reflect the content of the material that follows. All third-level headings beneath a second-level heading should be grammatically parallel.

Fourth-Level Heading. Like all the other levels of heading, fourth-level headings reflect the subject that will be developed. All fourth-level headings within a subsection are parallel.

Fifth-level headings are generally the lowest level of heading used. However, you can indicate further breakdowns in your ideas by using a list:

1. *The first item in a list.* You may indent the entire item in block format to set it off visually. Numbers are optional.
2. *The second item in a list.* All lists have at least two items. An introductory phrase or sentence may be italicized for emphasis, as shown here.

Good writers use transitions to help readers move from one section of a report to the next, from one paragraph to the next, and even from one sentence to the next. (The last sentence in the previous paragraph was a transition to help you move from the subject of lists to the subject of transitions.) Here is a list of transitions frequently used to move readers smoothly between sentences and paragraphs:

Additional Detail: moreover, furthermore, in addition, besides, first, second, third, finally

Causal Relationship: therefore, because, accordingly, thus, consequently, hence, as a result, so

Comparison: similarly, here again, likewise, in comparison, still

Contrast:	yet, conversely, whereas, nevertheless, on the other hand, however, but, nonetheless
Condition:	although, if
Illustration:	for example, in particular, in this case, for instance
Time Sequence:	formerly, after, when, meanwhile, sometimes
Intensification:	indeed, in fact, in any event
Summary:	in brief, in short, to sum up
Repetition:	that is, in other words, as I mentioned earlier

Although transitional words and phrases are useful, they're not sufficient in themselves to overcome poor organization. Your goal is first to put your ideas in a strong framework and then to use transitions to link them together even more strongly.

Consider using a transition device whenever it might help the reader understand your ideas and follow you from point to point. You can use transitions inside paragraphs to tie related points together and between paragraphs to ease the shift from one distinct thought to another. In longer reports transitions that link major sections or chapters are often complete paragraphs that serve as mini-introductions to the next section or as summaries of the ideas presented in the section just ending. Here's an example:

> Given the nature of this problem, the alternatives are limited. As the previous section indicates, we can stop making the product, improve it, or continue with the current model. Each of these alternatives has advantages and disadvantages. The following section discusses pros and cons of each of the three alternatives.

Previews and Reviews

You may have heard the old saying "tell 'em what you're going to tell 'em, tell 'em, then tell 'em what you just told 'em." The more formal way of giving this advice is to tell you to use *preview sections* before and *review sections* after important material in your report. Using a preview section to introduce a topic helps readers get ready for new information. Previews are particularly helpful when the information is complex or unexpected. You don't want the reader to get halfway into a section before figuring out what it's all about.

Review sections, obviously enough, come after a body of material and summarize the information for your readers. For example, the summary section at the end of this chapter is a review section. Long reports and reports dealing with complex subjects can often benefit from multiple review sections, and not just a single review at the very end.

Swimming is a good analogy for using preview and review sections. Before you jump into the water, you look around, get your bearings, and get an idea of what you're about to dive into. A preview section serves the same purpose for your reader. After you dive in and swim for a few moments, you come back up for air. You look around and get your bearings again. This is like a review section. Whenever you've had your readers "swimming in details" for any length of time, bring them back to the surface with a review section so they can get their bearings again.

The Ending

Reemphasize your main ideas in the ending.

Research shows that the **ending,** the final section of a report, leaves a strong and lasting impression. That's why it's important to use the ending to emphasize the main points of your message. In a report written in direct order, you may want to remind readers

CHECKLIST FOR SHORT INFORMAL REPORTS

A. FORMAT

1. For brief external reports, use letter format, including a title or a subject line after the reader's address that clearly states the subject of the document.
2. For brief internal reports, use memo or manuscript format.
3. Present all short informal reports properly.
   a. Single-space the text.
   b. Double-space between paragraphs.
   c. Use headings where helpful, but try not to use more than three levels of headings.
   d. Call attention to significant information by setting it off visually with lists or indention.
   e. Include visual aids to emphasize and clarify the text.

B. OPENING

1. For short, routine memos, use the subject line of the memo form and the first sentence or two of the text as the introduction.
2. For all other short reports, cover these topics in the introduction: purpose, scope, background, restrictions (in conducting the study), sources of information and methods of research, and organization of the report.
3. If using direct order, place conclusions and recommendations in the opening.

C. BODY (FINDINGS AND SUPPORTING DETAILS)

1. Use direct order for informational reports to receptive readers, developing ideas around subtopics (chronologically, geographically, categorically).
2. Use direct order for analytical reports to receptive readers, developing points around conclusions or recommendations.
3. Use indirect order for analytical reports to skeptical or hostile readers, developing points around logical arguments.

4. Use an appropriate writing style.
   a. Use an informal style (*I* and *you*) for letter and memo reports, unless company custom calls for the impersonal third person.
   b. Use an impersonal style for more formal short reports in manuscript format.
5. Maintain a consistent time frame by writing in either the present or the past tense, using other tenses only to indicate prior or future events.
6. Give each paragraph a topic sentence.
7. Link paragraphs by using transitional words and phrases.
8. Strive for readability by using short sentences, concrete words, and terminology that is appropriate for your readers.
9. Be accurate, thorough, and impartial in presenting the material.
10. Avoid including irrelevant and unnecessary details.
11. Include documentation for all material quoted or paraphrased from secondary sources, using a consistent format.

D. ENDING

1. In informational reports summarize major findings at the end, if you wish.
2. Summarize points in the same order in which they appear in the text.
3. In analytical reports using indirect order, list conclusions and recommendations at the end.
4. Be certain that conclusions and recommendations follow logically from facts presented in the text.
5. Consider using a list format for emphasis.
6. Avoid introducing new material in the summary, conclusions, or recommendations.

---

once again of your key points or your conclusions and recommendations. If your report is written in indirect order, end with a summary of key points (except in short memos). In analytical reports, end with conclusions and recommendations as well as key points. Be sure to summarize the benefits to the reader in any report that suggests a change of course or some other action. In general, the ending ties up all the pieces and reminds readers how those pieces fit together. It provides a final opportunity to emphasize the wholeness of your message. Furthermore, it gives you one last chance to check that the report says what you really wanted to say.[4]

SUMMARY

Preparing the final draft of a report involves decisions on format, length, and organization. Short informal reports often take the form of memos or letters; longer, more formal reports are presented in manuscript form.

When readers are receptive or open-minded, you may present your ideas in direct order, with the main point first. When readers are hostile or skeptical, use indirect order, with key findings, conclusions, and recommendations last. Informational reports such as periodic reports and personal activity reports are organized around subtopics. Analytical reports are organized around conclusions or recommendations or around a logical argument, such as the $2 + 2 = 4$ approach, the scientific method, or the yardstick approach.

The task of organizing a report is not complete until you decide on the proper degree of formality, establish a time perspective, and develop such structural clues as the opening, headings, lists, transitions, and the ending.

COMMUNICATION CHALLENGES AT THE SAN DIEGO WILD ANIMAL PARK

Deirdre Ballou often helps the Zoological Society of San Diego's development department solicit funding for the nonprofit organization from outside sources. Educational projects are a favorite among corporate sponsors, so Ballou's expertise is invaluable. For the past three years, one corporation has underwritten an annual Educators' Event at the Wild Animal Park, which allows Ballou and staff to host and inform groups of teachers about the wonderful and unique educational opportunities the park offers. For example, imagine trying to get school kids excited about keeping a detailed information log. Then picture them visiting the park's simulated "research station," learning about logs from a guide portraying a "real scientist" who is tracking and recording the behavior of colobus monkeys that inhabit a nearby island.

Although some sponsors want only the facts about a project (proposal followed by preliminary, interim, and final reports), Ballou knows that this particular company likes colorful proposals and reports, describing everything from the menu served to how well the weather cooperated. But they also want to see a proposed timeline and budget spreadsheets. For this year's event, Ballou is planning a behind-the-scenes tour led by WAP animal experts, culminating in a visit to the research island where her interpretive guides will demonstrate how they entertain and inform visitors with their

lab equipment, charts, maps, logs, microscopes, centrifuges, water purification equipment, discovery scopes, and radio telemetry tracking—not to mention their hand-reared animals. An aardvark is a permanent resident on the island, and ten other creatures—including a pygmy falcon, a lilac-breasted roller, a leopard tortoise, a spring haas, and a fennec fox—are brought to the station throughout each day for demonstrations.

INDIVIDUAL CHALLENGE: Ballou is meeting again with company representatives, and she wants to take along a preliminary proposal for this year's Educators' Event. Use what you've learned in this chapter to suggest an outline for Ballou's preliminary proposal. Make up any details you need to make your outline authentic. Suggest a length, format, organization, and level of formality.

TEAM CHALLENGE: Ballou will also need to convince park management that hiring extra interpretive guides for a new exhibit is a necessity. Trouble is, their special knowledge and training costs more per hour than other park personnel—and keeping labor costs low is a primary concern for the General Manager. Brainstorm ideas for solving Ballou's dilemma. How should she broach the subject and convince the GM that the cost is justified? Make detailed notes explaining and justifying your recommended strategy.[5]

CRITICAL THINKING QUESTIONS

1. Would you use an opening, headings, and a closing in informal reports that stay within your own department? In routine status reports to your manager? Explain your answers.
2. Should a report always explain the writer's method of gathering evidence or solving a problem? Why or why not?
3. Would you use the direct or indirect approach to document inventory shortages at your manufacturing plant? To propose an employee stock-option plan? Why?
4. Have you ever written any reports that led to a decision or action? Did your report achieve the desired results? Did you use direct or indirect order? Why? How did you subdivide the ideas, and why did you use that structure? How might you have applied some of the ideas presented in this chapter to make the report more effective?
5. Why do you think some organizations prefer a formal tone for internal reports? What are the advantages and disadvantages of such a tone? Explain briefly.
6. What tense is better for most business reports, past or present? Explain.

EXERCISES

1. Look through recent issues (print or online) of *Business Week, Fortune,* or other business publications for an article that describes how an executive's conclusions about his or her company's current situation or future opportunities led to changes in policy, plans, or products. Construct an outline of the material, using (a) direct order and (b) indirect order. Which approach do you think the executive would use when reporting these conclusions to stockholders? When reporting to other senior managers? Explain your answers.
2. You're the human resources manager for an office-products company. Your boss, the president, has decided that the company needs to lay off ten people because competition has squeezed revenue so much that the company has run at a loss for three months in a row. You'd like to propose that the company share employees with a firm across the street that is trying to hire a number of experienced employees. Outline a report that will explain your idea of having some of your people work at both companies (such as in the morning for your company and in the afternoon for the other company). Make up whatever details you need.
3. Check the business pages of your local newspaper for an article about an entrepreneur who recently started a new business. Play the role of a banker who is considering this business's loan application. Construct a question-and-answer chain that you could use to find out about the entrepreneur's plans and financial projections for a report to the bank's loan committee. Diagram your question-and-answer chain, bearing in mind that your audience for this report will be the bank officials who decide whether or not to approve the loan.
4. Of the organizational approaches introduced in the chapter, which is best suited for reporting on each of the following problem statements? Briefly explain why.
   a. In which market segment—root beer, cola, or lemon-lime—should Fizz Drinks, Inc., introduce a new soft drink to take advantage of its enlarged research-and-development budget?
   b. Major Manufacturing, Inc., should close down operations of its antiquated Bellville, Arkansas, plant in spite of the economic impact on the town that has grown up around the plant.
   c. Should you and your partner adopt a new accounting method to make your financial statements look better to potential investors?
   d. Your boss asked you to look at two black-only laser printers to replace old equipment in your office. You have decided a single color laser printer would be better.
   e. Should Grand Canyon Chemicals buy disposable test tubes to reduce labor costs associated with cleaning and sterilizing reusable test tubes?
   f. What are some reasons for the recent data loss at the college computer center, and how can we avoid similar problems in the future?
5. Team up with a classmate to research one of the following topics. Working together, plan an analytical report focusing on your conclusions. Write out the main idea, and draft an informative outline with first- and second-level headings.

a. Trends in the U.S. trade deficit with China and Japan, and the implications for business in the next century

b. The impact on small businesses of recent increases in the minimum wage

c. The impact of drug abuse in the workplace

6. Select one of the following topics and plan an analytical report focusing on your recommendations. Develop the main idea, and draft an informative outline with first- and second-level headings.

a. How to reduce the amount of electricity consumed by your college

b. How to prepare your home to endure a severe weather problem, such as a strong hurricane or a major snowstorm

c. How to reduce the cost of car insurance

7. Select one of the following conclusions and plan an analytical report using the 2 + 2 = 4 approach. Write out the main idea, and draft an informative outline with first- and second-level headings (make up whatever details you need).

a. Your overcrowded college should arrange to rent excess meeting room space from nearby businesses

b. Your company should hire a training firm to teach employees better presentation skills

c. Your company should purchase a new computer system that allows customers to check the status of their orders through touch-tone phones, rather than speaking with an employee

8. Plan an analytical report, using the scientific method, for one of the following topics. Write out the main idea, and draft an informative outline with first- and second-level headings. (Make up any details you need.)

a. We should hire more counter help or keep the store open later on weeknights; people stopping by after work are encountering long, frustrating delays in service.

b. We need to find the cheapest way to deliver packages to local customers; the alternatives are to lease a truck and hire a delivery driver, contract with a courier service, or use UPS.

c. Our work load always increases during the winter holiday season; we should consider hiring students on school break, hiring retired workers, or asking our current employees to work overtime.

9. Select one of the following topics and plan an analytical report using the yardstick approach. Establish your criteria, write out the main idea, and draft an informative outline with first- and second-level headings.

a. Which buildings should the college modernize next semester?

b. Where should the college install additional pay phones to be used by both students and instructors?

c. How should the college change the physical layout of the cafeteria to accommodate more students?

10. Team up with a classmate to practice writing informative openings. For the analytical report you outlined in any of exercises 5 through 9, draft an opening that tells what the report covers, explains why the subject is important, and previews the main ideas and the order in which ideas will be presented. Swap with your teammate and critique each other's opening section. Does each opening give sufficient clues to the structure of the report? How can these openings be improved?

11. Team up with a classmate to practice writing emphatic and informative endings. For the analytical report you outlined in any of exercises 5 through 9, draft an ending that includes conclusions, recommendations, and key points. Swap with your teammate and compare each ending with the Checklist for Short Informal Reports. How well does each ending communicate the main points and the overall message? How can these endings be improved?

12. Attend the next meeting of the college's student government and take notes on what occurs. Then write a brief (two-page) personal activity report on that meeting, using the memo format. Think about what your audience, the other students in your business communication class, will want to know about the issues discussed and conclusions reached during that meeting. What key question should you answer in this report?

13. Obtain the annual report of any public corporation. Read through the management report made by the president, chief executive officer, or chairperson. Outline this report and indicate whether it's in direct or indirect order. Why do you think the direct or indirect order was chosen? Can you easily distinguish the main idea? Does the opening explain the report's structure and indicate the importance of the information? How well does the ending pull all the details together?

14. Using the management report you obtained for exercise 13, write informative headings that clue readers about the content of the various sections. Be sure to keep all headings grammatically parallel,

and check whether the headings are interesting enough to encourage the reader to continue reading for the details.

15. American Management Systems (AMS) has, for more than a quarter century, developed and implemented management plans and placed management personnel in positions around the globe. The company's Web site <http://www.amsinc.com> provides perspective on the company as well as information about positions in management. Following suggestions in this text's Checklist for Short Informal Reports, prepare a brief internal report analyzing the clarity of presentation and the persuasive aspects of the AMS Web page.

CASES

Informal Informational Reports

CAREER DEVELOPMENT
UPWARD COMMUNICATION

1. My progress to date: Periodic report on your academic career   As you know, the bureaucratic process involved in getting a degree or certificate is nearly as challenging as any course you could take.

Your task: Prepare a periodic report detailing the steps you've taken toward completing your graduation or certification requirements. After examining the requirements listed in your college catalog, indicate a realistic schedule for completing those that remain. In addition to course requirements, include such steps as completing the residency requirement, filing necessary papers, and paying necessary fees. Use memo format for your report, and address it to anyone who is helping or encouraging you through school.

EDUCATION
HORIZONTAL COMMUNICATION

2. Here's why: Personal report on how a class influenced a life decision   Think of a class that has helped influence a life decision. For example, you may have decided to pursue finance as a career because of a particularly dynamic professor. Or you may have decided never again to use products tested on animals after learning about the issue in a presentation by a fellow student in business communication.

Your task: Prepare an e-mail memo in which you explain your decision. Think of your target audience (your family or friends) as you decide on pertinent details to include. Remember that your task is not to persuade them to follow your decision, but to inform them of the reasoning that led to your own.

EDUCATION
HORIZONTAL COMMUNICATION

3. Gavel to gavel: Personal report of a meeting Meetings, conferences, and conventions abound in the academic world, and you have probably attended your share.

Your task: Prepare a report on a meeting, convention, or conference that you have recently attended. Use memo format, and direct the report to other students in your field who were not able to attend.

Informal Analytical Reports

SMALL BUSINESS
EMPLOYMENT PREPARATION

4. A new venture: Report organized around conclusions   Read the classified ads in your local newspaper. Select a business for sale or a business opportunity.

Your task: Write a memo to yourself evaluating the item you read in the classifieds (assuming you had the money required for the venture). Call the person running the ad to get any information you need to complete this assignment.

CAREER DEVELOPMENT
EMPLOYMENT PREPARATION

5. My next career move: Report organized around recommendations   If you've ever given yourself a really good talking-to, you'll be quite comfortable with this project.

Your task: Write a memo report directed to yourself and signed with a fictitious name. Indicate a possible job that your college education will qualify you for, mention the advantages of the position in terms of your long-range goals, and then outline the actions you must take to get the job.

EDUCATION

UPWARD COMMUNICATION

6. Staying the course: Report using the 2 + 2 = 4 approach   Think of a course you would love to see added to the core curriculum at your school. Conversely, if you would like to see a course offered as an elective rather than being required, write your e-mail report accordingly.

Your task: Write a short e-mail report using the 2 + 2 = 4 approach. Prepare your report to be submitted to the academic dean by e-mail. Be sure to include all the reasons supporting your idea.

EDUCATION

UPWARD COMMUNICATION

7. Planning my program: Report using the scientific method   Assume that you will have time for only one course next term.

Your task: List the pros and cons of four or five courses that interest you, and use the scientific method to settle on the course that is best for you to take at this time. Write in memo format, addressing the memo to your academic adviser.

EDUCATION

UPWARD COMMUNICATION

8. Section A, section B: Report using the yardstick approach   Choose a course that is taught by at least two instructors at different times, either one that you actually need to take or one that interests you. Which section should you enroll in?

Your task: Write a memo to your academic adviser that explains which section you plan to enroll in and why you chose it. Use three or four important criteria as a basis for analyzing the two sections or instructors.

MARKETING

CUSTOMER RELATIONS

9. "Would you carry it?" Sales proposal recommending a product to a retail outlet   Select a product you are familiar with, and imagine that you are the manufacturer trying to get a local retail outlet to carry it.

Your task: Write a sales proposal in letter format to the owner (or manager) of the store, proposing that the item be stocked. Making up some reasonable figures, tell what the item costs, what it can be sold for, and what services your company provides (return of unsold items, free replacement of unsatisfactory items, necessary repairs, and the like).

FINANCE

UPWARD COMMUNICATION

10. The importance of a good breakfast: Justification report for longer business hours   Imagine that you work for a restaurant that is near campus that's open only for lunch and dinner. You think there is significant demand for a good place to eat breakfast, and you believe the restaurant could more than make up for the additional cost of opening at 6:00 A.M. instead of 11:30 A.M.

Your task: Develop a budget for the expanded hours of operation, including personnel costs, management time, utilities, and changes to the food inventory. Next write a report explaining your concept, describing the major budget items, and briefly predicting the future benefits that this expansion will bring. (Feel free to make up any details you need, but keep it realistic.) Write your report in memo format to the owner or manager of the business.

Short Informal Reports

PROMOTION

CUSTOMER RELATIONS

11. Selling something special: Proposal to a business   Pick a company or business that you know something about. Now think of a customized item or service that you believe the business needs. Examples might be a specially designed piece of equipment, a workshop for employees on improving their communication skills, a program for curtailing shoplifting, a catering service to a company's construction site, or a customized word-processing system, to name just a few possibilities.

Your task: Write a proposal to the owners or managers of this business. Convince them that they need the product you're selling. Include a statement of the problem, purpose (benefits), scope (areas in which your product will help the business), methods and procedures, work plan and schedule, your qualifications, projected costs, and any other pertinent information. Use letter format.

12. Who's best? Report comparing job candidates
Imagine that a family from another country (pick any country) has engaged you to help find a tutor for their two children (aged 9 and 11). You have just interviewed four people for the position.

Your task: Write a report in memo format to the parents. In it, describe the four candidates (use four friends) and recommend them, in rank order, for the position. Consider at least the following areas for comparison of the candidates: education, experience, and personal attributes.

13. Restaurant review: Report on a restaurant's food and operations Visit any restaurant, possibly your school cafeteria. The workers and fellow customers will assume that you are an ordinary customer, but you are really a spy for the owner.

Your task: After your visit write a short memo to the owner, explaining (a) what you did and what you observed, (b) any violations of policy that you observed, and (c) your recommendations for improvement. The first part of your report (what you did and what you observed) will be the longest. Include a description of the premises, inside and out. Tell how long the various steps of ordering and receiving your meal took. Describe the service and food thoroughly. You are interested in both the good and bad aspects of the establishment's decor, service, and food. For the second section

(violations of policy), use some common sense. If all the servers but one have their hair covered, you may assume that policy requires hair to be covered; a dirty window or restroom obviously violates policy. The last section (recommendations for improvement) involves professional judgment. What management actions will improve the restaurant?

14. Taste test: Report on the results of consumer research Here's your chance to check the advertising claims of soft-drink manufacturers. Blindfold four or five friends (one at a time), and ask them to taste several competing soft drinks.

Your task: After you have conducted the test, write a memo that summarizes your findings. Could your friends tell the difference between the soft drinks? If so, how did they describe the difference? Did they seem to prefer one of the brands? Did the order in which they tasted the drinks seem to have any bearing on the results? You might also address the problem of whether soft drinks without sugar or caffeine taste as good to your friends as drinks containing these ingredients.

15. Mansfield Center or Cat Spring? Report comparing potential plant locations Current plant capabilities are inadequate for manufacturing Victory Valve's new line of gate valves, globe valves, check valves, ball valves, and butterfly valves. The company is seeking a new location removed from the strains of rapid urbanization and union pressures but still close to potential markets. Two locations have been proposed: Mansfield Center, Connecticut, and Cat Spring, Texas. Fellow members of the site-selection committee (you're in charge) submitted the following raw data about these two locations:

- *Mansfield Center, Connecticut.* An attractive town of about 5,000 near the Mansfield Hollow Reservoir, with rivers and forested recreation areas. Good schools, with moderately expensive housing available. Tax rates generally low and subject to negotiation; the town might forgive taxes during a three- to five-year start-up period. Adequate rail and road transportation available. Located within

50 miles of markets in Hartford, Providence, Springfield, Worcester, and New Haven. Energy costs ranging from average to high and rising. Experienced factory workers available. Steel must be brought in by rail, probably from Pennsylvania or the Chicago-Gary area. Moderate climate. The University of Connecticut, at nearby Storrs, might provide research facilities and assistance, as well as a supply of seasonal workers. In this heavily industrialized area, valves are in constant demand, but the presence of nearby competitors would force heavy price competition.

- *Cat Spring, Texas.* A tiny, dry town about 50 miles from the Gulf of Mexico; conveniently located on the Houston–Fort Worth rail line. Real estate prices low and taxes minuscule. Adequate labor available from the Houston and Dallas–Fort Worth areas, but housing would have to be built to accommodate the influx of workers. Local schools presently inadequate for any increase from workers' families but could presumably be expanded. Steel from Europe arrives at the port of Houston and could be delivered economically by rail to Cat Spring. The climate is hot and dry nine months of the year, making air-conditioning of the plant necessary. Markets in Houston, Waco, Fort Worth, Dallas, and Austin are all about 200 miles away. The need for our type of valves appears to be growing as industrialization increases in southern Texas. Electricity and water expensive, although recent developments in solar power appear to be reducing the costs of air-conditioning.

Your task: Write a memo in which you recommend one of the two locations and justify your recommendation. The report has been requested by Ron Wasserman, chief executive officer of Victory Valves, Inc.

MANAGEMENT

UPWARD COMMUNICATION

16. In the driver's seat: Report on the best route for obtaining a new truck   City Heights News Service, a partnership that supplies periodicals to various outlets in the area, has had the same used truck since the company was founded three years ago. Business has expanded since then, and the old truck has become a little unreliable, so the owners of City Heights, Pam and Bill Oster, have decided to get a new set of wheels. They've given you the job of analyzing three options:

- Lease a truck for $640 per month for two years. At the end of that time, purchase the truck for $12,000. The lease payments are tax-deductible; thus 40 percent of the lease expense is covered through lower taxes.
- Lease the same truck for $1,400 a month for a two-year period, and then purchase it for a token payment of $1. Again, the lease payments are tax-deductible.
- Purchase a similar truck for $23,000.

Your task: Select an option and justify your choice in a brief memo.

MANAGEMENT CONSULTING

UPWARD COMMUNICATION

17. On the books: Report on improving the campus bookstore   Imagine that you are a consultant hired to improve the profits of your campus bookstore.

Your task: Visit the bookstore and look critically at its operations. Then draft a memo offering recommendations to the bookstore manager that would make the bookstore more profitable, perhaps suggesting products that the store should carry, hours that the store should remain open, or added services that the store should make available to students. Be sure to support your recommendations.

ARCHITECTURE

UPWARD COMMUNICATION

18. With an eye toward change: Report on converting a building to a new use   The company you work for, Video Vendors, Inc., has just bought an abandoned fast-food restaurant with the intention of converting it to an outlet for renting and selling videotapes and video equipment. You are a planning specialist with Video Vendors, and it's your job to outline the architectural changes that will be necessary for successful remodeling.

Your task: Visit any fast-food restaurant in your area and draw a diagram that shows its current use of indoor and outdoor space. Next determine the architectural changes that will be necessary to convert the building into a video outlet, the major fixtures that must be removed, and the major items that must be purchased. Present your findings in a memo to Angelica Smythe, vice president of planning for Video Vendors, Inc. Include a diagram showing the proposed layout of the video outlet.

19. Prospects for growth: Report on a small firm Choose a small independent business in your area, and assume that the owners have hired you to help them approach a local bank for financial help with their expansion. The bank will require a complete financial statement and a brief narrative description of the business, covering such topics as the length of time it has been operating, its chief product lines and services, the size of its market area, its usual mix of customers, and the general prospects for growth in its neighborhood.

Your task: Draft the report that you will submit to the bank for your client. Several paragraphs of objective writing will be sufficient, and no financial figures are necessary because they will appear in accompanying financial statements. Remember that your job is to describe the business, not to recommend that the bank lend money to it.

20. Pumping up gasoline sales: Report on suggested advertising approaches Gasoline advertising is heating up in Brazil, where Esso, Shell, Atlantic-Arco, Texaco, and Ipiranga compete with Petrobras, the state-owned monopoly. All are in a race to increase their share of Brazil's 5-billion-liter gasoline-products market. However, Brazilian drivers know that Petrobras actually produces and refines the gasoline that every one of its competitors sells. What differentiates one brand from another are the additives that the oil companies put into their individual formulations. Esso's advertising in Brazil is handled by the ad agency J. Walter Thompson. Knowing that rivals put a variety of ingredients into their formulations, the agency recommends that Esso use a new advertising approach: Alert drivers to the differences among brands and warn them to look closely at the quality of the gasoline they use.

Your task: As the J. Walter Thompson manager assigned to the Esso account, draft a one-page memo to Esso's managers in which you justify your agency's recommendation. Use your contact's first name, Don, and your own first name in the memo heading. Explain why you believe Esso should adopt this new advertising approach, discuss the main benefit you see in using this approach, and summarize your position.[6]

21. Chasing a good story: Report on a reporter's activities It's June 30, and the 25 reporters on the *Newtown Advocate* have to file their monthly progress reports. The editor-in-chief uses these personal activity reports to track each reporter's progress in researching and writing assigned articles. You're assigned to write about how local officials are fighting the state's attempt to build a superhighway through Newtown farmland. You spent the first week of the month talking with state legislators, agricultural experts, and Newtown's mayor. After writing the initial two-part story, you attended public hearings about the proposal and interviewed Newtown residents about their reactions. From that research you were able to write one brief article a day for the two middle weeks of the month. In the final week of the month, you telephoned environmental experts to ask about the superhighway's impact on adjacent farmland. Getting answers has been slow, however, so the articles based on these expert interviews won't appear until next month.

Your task: Plan and write a personal activity report summarizing the progress you've made this month in covering the superhighway story. Determine how to organize this informal memo, and address it to Janice Schneider, the editor-in-chief. Be sure to mention any problems you've encountered and discuss how these affected your progress.

22. Check that price tag: Report on trends in college costs Are tuition costs going up, down, or remaining the same? Your college's administration has asked you to compare your college's tuition costs with those of a nearby college and determine which has risen more quickly. Research the trend by checking your college's annual tuition costs for each of the most recent four years. Then research the four-year tuition trends for a neighboring college. For both colleges, calculate the percentage change in tuition costs from year to year and between the first and fourth year.

Your task: Prepare an informal report (using the letter format) presenting your findings and conclusions to the president of your college. Include graphics to explain and support your conclusions.

23. Preparing for the worst: Report on crisis management   When the anonymous call came in, Campbell Soup officials refused to take any chances. The caller claimed to have put poison in Campbell's tomato juice cans at a New England supermarket. The company quickly decided to yank the product from 84 area stores. Even though the call turned out to be a hoax, Campbell Soup believes it's best to be prepared for the worst. Moreover, an important part of any crisis-management plan is the way company officials tell the public about the situation.

Your task: You're a public relations consultant with special expertise in crisis management. You've been asked to recommend how and when Campbell Soup should reveal any threats and the steps that have been taken in response. In addition, you want to suggest ways of reassuring consumers that Campbell Soup products are pure and completely safe. Draft the outline for an impersonal but informal analytical report to CEO David W. Johnson that includes your recommendations and the justifications for those recommendations. Be sure the headings you choose show what your report will cover, including the need for action, the benefits to be achieved, the list of recommendations (without details), and a summary.[7]

24. Fishing for more revenue: Report for a nonprofit organization   The Historic Fishing Village of Puget Sound has asked you to determine why revenues have been lower than expected and to suggest how to improve revenues. You've found two probable causes for the low revenue: (1) unusually bad weather during prime tourism periods and (2) shoddy, inexpensive merchandise in the gift shop.

Your task: Draft a two-page troubleshooting report to present to the nonprofit's trustees. Use the 2 + 2 = 4 approach to support your conclusions, and address the report to the trustees as a group. Make up whatever details you need about the merchandise and about ways to improve revenues. Bear in mind that the trustees originally approved the purchase of merchandise for the gift shop, so you'll want to use objective language to avoid offending them.

25. Press 1 for efficiency: Report on a telephone interviewing system   How can a firm be thorough yet efficient when considering dozens of applicants for each position? One tool that just may help is IntelliView, a ten-minute question-and-answer session conducted by touch-tone telephone. The company recruiter dials up the IntelliView computer and then leaves the room. The candidate punches in answers to roughly 100 questions about work attitudes and other issues. In a few minutes, the recruiter can call Pinkerton, which offers the service, and find out the results. On the basis of what the IntelliView interview revealed, the recruiter can delve more deeply into certain areas and, ultimately, have more information on which to base the hiring decision.

Your task: As a recruiter for Curtis Box and Crate, you think that IntelliView might help your firm. Write a brief memo to Wallace Jefferson, the director of human resources, in which you suggest a test of the IntelliView system. Your memo should tell your boss why you believe your firm should test the system before making a long-term commitment.[8]

26. The check's in the mail: A report on collecting overdue tuition payments   As student representatives on your college's campus administration committee, you and three classmates are considering ways to collect from students who are late in paying their tuition bills. Decide on the criteria you'll use to evaluate alternatives; then come up with at least four ideas.

Your task: Weigh each idea against the criteria. Then draft a research report about your findings, and address it to Heather Anderson, who heads the committee.

27. Hit a home run: Report on plans for starting a local softball league   The local chamber of commerce has agreed to sponsor a local softball league for teens and young adults. As the planning starts, you've volunteered to list the items that need to be purchased (such as equipment and uniforms) and come up with several possible sources of revenue to offset those purchases (such as selling league T-shirts and snacks to fans who attend the games).

Your task: Write a brief, impersonal report to the chamber of commerce that includes your listing of both expenditures and revenue sources. Rather than including figures in this report, indicate where you think such figures can be obtained as the planning progresses.

PROMOTION
CUSTOMER RELATIONS

28. Sampling success: Report on a program to promote a new cracker   To help food manufacturers promote their new products, Sample U.S.A. offers supermarket shoppers bite-size samples of everything from cheese and ice cream to pretzels and cookies. This month Sample U.S.A. gave away a total of 12,800 samples of Cheezy sesame crackers in 11 New Orleans supermarkets. The Cheezy Company wants Sample U.S.A. to give away 14,000 sesame cracker samples in 13 Houston supermarkets during the coming month. However, one large supermarket chain hasn't yet agreed to let Sample U.S.A. set up a tasting booth.

Your task: As the southwest regional manager for Sample U.S.A., you send your clients a monthly report on results and future sampling plans. Prepare this month's report to Jacques D'Aprix, the director of marketing at the Cheezy Company. Be sure to include future plans as well as any problems that may affect next month's activities.

RETAILING
UPWARD COMMUNICATION

29. Day and night: Report on stocking a 24-hour convenience store   When a store is open all day, every day, when's the best time to restock the shelves? That's the challenge at Store 24, a retail chain that never closes. Imagine you're the assistant manager of a Store 24 branch that just opened near your campus. You want to set up a restocking schedule that won't conflict with prime shopping hours. Think about the number of customers you're likely to serve in the morning, afternoon, evening, and overnight hours. Consider, too, how many employees you might have during these four periods.

Your task: Using the scientific approach, write a report in letter form to the store manager (Isabel Chu) and the regional manager (Eric Angstrom), who must agree on a solution to this problem. Discuss the pros and cons of each of the four periods, and include your proposal for restocking the shelves.

COMPLETING FORMAL REPORTS AND PROPOSALS

AFTER STUDYING THIS CHAPTER, YOU WILL BE ABLE TO

- Describe how organizations produce formal reports and proposals
- Prepare all the necessary parts of a formal report
- Assemble all the parts of a formal report in the proper order, using an appropriate format
- Prepare and assemble all the parts of a formal proposal
- Critique formal reports prepared by someone else

COMMUNICATION CLOSE-UP AT THE ROCKY MOUNTAIN INSTITUTE

The Rocky Mountain Institute (RMI) has plans to save the world's resources by convincing governments, corporations, utilities, architects, and anyone else who will listen that "it's cheaper to save energy than to waste it." The nonprofit environmental think tank spends its own energy getting this message to the world. Its primary tool? Reports. The institute's 40 researchers produce thousands of pages of written reports each year for some 200 clients in over 32 countries. Although many of these reports are highly technical, the institute's founders, Amory and Hunter Lovins, make sure they're presented in witty, straightforward language that anyone can understand. The couple has even invented words when necessary—like "negawatt" (a measure of electricity *saved*).

A child prodigy who became a Harvard and Oxford scholar, Amory Lovins built his reputation as an energy wizard in the mid-1970s when his book *Soft Energy Paths* correctly predicted that economic growth could be accompanied by lowered energy consumption. Energy experts said he was crazy—until his prediction came true; now they flock to him for advice. Hunter Lovins is RMI's president and executive director. She's an attorney-turned-activist who rides rodeo and dirt bikes in her spare time. For years the married couple traveled the world, working as energy-efficiency consultants, but in 1982 they settled in Snowmass, Colorado, in a state-of-the-art, environmentally sound building that serves as home and office for RMI's research team (it also demonstrates that $5 monthly electric bills are possible, even in Colorado winters).

The institute's programs cover five areas: energy efficiency, water usage, economic renewal of rural areas, sustainable agriculture, and global security through more efficient resource usage and distribution. Hunter explains that they do very little testing, invention, or "fiddling around with" hardware. Instead, staffers use the telephone—contacting officials who have successfully implemented efficiency programs. The researchers ask what worked and what didn't, how much it cost, what roadblocks were overcome, and where to obtain any equipment that was used. This information

Hunter and Amory Lovins

Rocky Mountain Institute in Snowmass, Colorado, is both home and office to the Lovinses and their staff of 40. The institute's goal is to save the world's resources, and it pursues this objective by preparing written reports for such clients as governments, corporations, utility companies, and architects. Employees at RMI understand how important it is to produce reports that are easily understood, logical, attractive, persuasive, and thorough.

may be combined with hardware evaluations, supply sources, and implementation recommendations, all of which winds up in analytical reports that can run as long as 600 pages ("tomes as big as a Manhattan phone book," says Hunter). Other reports are informational; smaller and friendlier, they sometimes become popular with consumers, as happened with RMI's soft-cover *Practical Home Energy Savings,* which caught fire with the media and landed Hunter and Amory on television talk shows.

Hunter admits that organizing and producing lengthy reports can be challenging. Amory is RMI's most prolific writer, she says. "He can knock out 100 pages in a day if he really puts his mind to it." Hunter is often the one who rewrites early drafts of analytical reports to make sure readers can follow the flow of what she calls "the argument."

When the U.S. Environmental Protection Agency (EPA) commissioned a 100-page analytical report from RMI to serve as a manual for local water utilities, "The agency was interested in what water-efficiency measures existed and in how to implement them," says Hunter. RMI pulled together all the information, which a junior researcher compiled into a first draft of the report. Then Hunter went to work.

She organized the report using the indirect approach. She divided the text into three sections: (1) Basic Concepts, Benefits, and Economics; (2) Efficiency Tools; and (3) Implementation Techniques. So the benefits of water conservation were presented first, followed by detailed information on what conservation measures are available and how they can be implemented. She wrote a "Final Note" (or summary) restating RMI's recommendations and added a fourth section for appendixes. The table of contents lists headings and subheads, so it serves as a quick outline of the report, and at the beginning of each section Hunter added an overview to explain what the section covers.

A year (and several EPA reviews) later, the 114-page spiral-bound report was finally finished. It's rich with case studies, and it includes 172 footnotes, 7 appendixes, 9 figures, and 5 tables. It doesn't have a bibliography or an index, but one of the appendixes lists over a hundred names and addresses of water-efficiency contacts.

Hunter believes that the hard work of producing a lengthy report is well worth it. Many RMI reports have already influenced changes that are improving life for millions of people—now and in the future. That's ample encouragement for RMI researchers, who often spend long hours laboring over their computers, making sure a report is clearly written, well organized, professionally presented, convincing, and complete.[1]

REPORT PRODUCTION

Experienced business communicators such as Amory and Hunter Lovins realize that planning a report or proposal, conducting the necessary research, developing visual aids, organizing the ideas, and drafting the text are demanding and time-consuming tasks. They also know that the process of writing a report or proposal doesn't end with these steps. After careful editing and rewriting, you still need to produce a polished final version.

In organizations that produce many reports and proposals, the preparation process involves teamwork.

How the final version is actually produced depends on the nature of your organization. The traditional approach was usually a team effort, with secretaries or other support personnel handling the typing, formatting, and other tasks. For important, high-visibility reports, a graphics department could sometimes help with charts, drawings, covers, and other visual elements.

Personal computers can automatically handle many of the mechanical aspects of report preparation.

However, as personal computers have become commonplace in the business office, more and more employees are expected to handle most or even all of the formatting and production of their own reports. In fact, many of the advances in computer hardware and software in recent years have been designed specifically to give all businesspeople the ability to produce great-looking reports by themselves. The good news is that these computer tools are now generally easy enough for the average businessperson to use productively. A software "suite" such as Microsoft Office makes it easy to produce reports with graphics, tables, spreadsheet data, and even database records. Even advanced report features such as photography are relatively simple these days, with the advent of low-cost, color desktop scanners. And inexpensive color printers with near photo-quality output have put color reports within just about everybody's reach. Used effectively, color helps improve both the reader's interest in your material and the effectiveness of your message.

The bad news is that continually improving computer tools increase your audience's expectations. People are influenced by packaging, and a handsomely bound report with full-color graphics will influence many readers more than a plain, typewriter-style report containing the exact same information. To make matters even more challenging, paper reports are starting to compete with various multimedia electronic reports, such as Web sites and CD-ROMs. More and more computers are connected to the Internet and able to read CD-ROMs, and the cost and skill requirements for creating both options continues to drop. Instead of producing a lengthy report full of tables and other information, you can now provide the information electronically and let readers pick and choose what they want to read. And when it comes to razzle-dazzle, sending a potential client a custom-made CD-ROM with your new business proposal might be a lot more effective than a paper report.

Be sure to schedule enough time to turn out a document that looks professional.

No matter which tools you use, make sure you leave enough time for formatting and production. Murphy's law (which says that if something can go wrong, it will) applies to just about every aspect of using computers. Data communication problems, incompatible or corrupted disk files, printing problems, and other glitches can consume hours. You don't want computer trouble to sabotage all your thinking, planning, and writing, so make sure you can create and produce the report before the deadline.

Once you've completed a major report and sent it off to your audience, you'll naturally expect a positive response, and quite often you'll get one—but not always. You may get half-hearted praise or no action on your conclusions and recommendations. Even worse, you may get some serious criticism. Try to learn from these experiences. Sometimes you won't get any response at all. If you don't hear from your readers within a week or two, you might want to ask politely whether the report arrived. In hopes of stimulating a response, you might also offer to answer any questions or provide additional information.

Ask for feedback, and learn from your mistakes.

Regardless of how the final product is produced, it will be up to you to make sure that all necessary components are included. Depending on the length and formality of your report, various prefatory and supplementary parts may be necessary. The more formal your report, the more components you'll include.

COMPONENTS OF A FORMAL REPORT

A formal report's manuscript format and impersonal tone convey an impression of professionalism. A formal report can be either short (fewer than ten pages) or long (ten pages or more). It can be informational or analytical, direct or indirect. It may be directed to readers inside or outside the organization. What sets it apart from other reports is its polish.

A formal report conveys the impression that the subject is important.

The parts included in a report depend on the type of report you are writing, the requirements of your audience, the organization you're working for, and the length of your report. The components listed in Figure 18.1 fall into three categories, depending on where they are found in a report: prefatory parts, text of the report, and supplementary parts. For an illustration of how the various parts fit together, see Linda Moreno's Electrovision report in "In-Depth Critique: Analyzing a Formal Report" on page 586.

The three basic divisions of a formal report:
- Prefatory parts
- Text
- Supplementary parts

Many of the components in a formal report begin on a new page, but not always. Inserting page breaks consumes more paper and adds to the bulk of your report (which may be a significant financial concern if you plan to distribute many copies). On the other hand, starting a section on a new page helps the reader navigate through the report and recognize transitions between major sections or features of the report.

When a particular section is designed to stand apart, it generally starts on a new page, and the material after it starts on a new page as well. Most prefatory parts (such as the table of contents, for example), should be placed on their own pages. However, the various parts in the text of the report may not often need to stand alone. If your introduction is only a paragraph long, don't bother with a page break before moving into

PREFATORY PARTS	TEXT OF THE REPORT	SUPPLEMENTARY PARTS
Cover	Introduction	Appendixes
Title fly	Body	Bibliography
Title page	Summary	Index
Letter of authorization	Conclusions	
Letter of acceptance	Recommendations	
Letter of transmittal	Notes	
Table of contents		
List of illustrations		
Synopsis or executive summary		

Figure 18.1
Parts of a Formal Report

the body of your report. If the introduction runs longer than a page, however, a page break can signal the reader that a major shift is about to occur in the flow of the report.

You can use this textbook as a model for deciding where to put page breaks. Each chapter starts on new page, which provides a clear break between chapters. On the other hand, the opening vignettes at the beginning of each chapter flow right into the body of the chapter without a page break because they are designed to lead readers into the chapter.

Prefatory Parts

Prefatory parts may be written after the text has been completed.

Although the prefatory parts are placed before the text of the report, you may not want to write them until after you've written the text. Many of these parts—such as the table of contents, list of illustrations, and executive summary—are easier to prepare after the text is complete because they directly reflect the contents. Other parts can be prepared at almost any time.

Cover

Many companies have standard covers for reports, made of heavy paper and imprinted with the company's name and logo. Report titles are either printed on these covers or attached with gummed labels. If your company has no standard covers, you can usually find something suitable in a good stationery store. Look for a cover that is appropriate to the subject matter, attractive, and convenient. Also, make sure it can be labeled with the report title, the writer's name (optional), and the submission date (also optional).

Put a title on the cover that is informative but not too long.

Think carefully about the title you put on the cover. A business report is not a mystery novel, so give your readers all the information they need: the who, what, when, where, why, and how of the subject. At the same time, try to be reasonably concise. You don't want to intimidate your audience with a title that's too long, awkward, or unwieldy. One approach is to use a subtitle. You can reduce the length of your title by eliminating phrases like *A report on, A study of,* or *A survey of.*

Title Fly and Title Page

The **title fly** is a plain sheet of paper with only the title of the report on it. You don't really need one, but it adds a touch of formality to a report.

The title page usually includes four blocks of information.

The **title page** includes four blocks of information, as shown in Moreno's Electrovision report: (1) the title of the report; (2) the name, title, and address of the person, group, or organization that authorized the report (usually the intended audience); (3) the name, title, and address of the person, group, or organization that prepared the report; and (4) the date on which the report was submitted. On some title pages the second block of information is preceded by the words *Prepared for* or *Submitted to,* and the third block of information is preceded by *Prepared by* or *Submitted by.* In some cases the title page serves as the cover of the report, especially if the report is relatively short and intended solely for internal use.

Letter of Authorization and Letter of Acceptance

A letter of authorization usually follows the direct-request plan.

If you were authorized in writing to prepare the report, you may want to include in your report the letter or memo of authorization (and sometimes even the letter or memo of acceptance). The **letter of authorization** (or *memo of authorization*) is a document requesting that a report be prepared. It normally follows the direct-request plan described in Chapter 8, and it typically specifies the problem, scope, time and money restrictions, special instructions, and due date.

The **letter of acceptance** (or *memo of acceptance*) acknowledges the assignment to conduct the study and to prepare the report. Following the good-news plan, the acceptance confirms time and money restrictions and other pertinent details. This document is rarely included in reports.

Use the good-news plan for a letter of acceptance.

Letter of Transmittal

The **letter of transmittal** (or *memo of transmittal*) conveys your report to your audience. (In a book this section is called the preface.) The letter of transmittal says what you'd say if you were handing the report directly to the person who authorized it, so the style is less formal than the rest of the report. For example, the letter would use personal pronouns (*you, I, we*) and conversational language. Moreno's Electrovision report includes a one-page transmittal memo from Moreno to her boss (the person who requested the report).

Use a less formal style for the letter of transmittal than for the report itself.

Generally, the transmittal letter appears right before the table of contents. However, if your report will be widely distributed, you may decide to include the letter of transmittal only in selected copies, in order to make certain comments to a specific audience. If your report discusses layoffs or other issues that affect people in the organization, you might want to discuss your recommendations privately in a letter of transmittal to top management. If your audience is likely to be skeptical of or even hostile to something in your report, the transmittal letter is a good opportunity to acknowledge their concerns and explain how the report addresses the issues they care about.

The letter of transmittal follows the routine and good-news plans described in Chapter 9. Begin with the main idea, officially conveying the report to the readers and summarizing its purpose. Such a letter typically begins with a statement like "Here is the report you asked me to prepare on . . ." The rest includes information about the scope of the report, the methods used to complete the study, and the limitations that became apparent. In the middle section of the letter you may also highlight important points or sections of the report, make comments on side issues, give suggestions for follow-up studies, and offer any details that will help readers better understand and use the report. You may also wish to acknowledge help given by others. The concluding paragraph is a note of thanks for having been given the report assignment, an expression of willingness to discuss the report, and an offer to assist with future projects.

Use the good-news plan for a letter of transmittal.

If the report does not have a synopsis, the letter of transmittal may summarize the major findings, conclusions, and recommendations. This material would be placed after the opening of the letter.

The synopsis of short reports is often included in the letter of transmittal.

Table of Contents

The table of contents indicates in outline form the coverage, sequence, and relative importance of the information in the report. In fact, the headings used in the text of the report are the basis for the table of contents. RMI's report to the EPA on water-efficiency measures lists headings and subheadings in the table of contents to serve as a quick outline of the report. Depending on the length and complexity of the report, your contents page may show only the top two or three levels of headings, sometimes only first-level headings. Of course, excluding some levels of headings may frustrate readers who want to know where to find every subject you cover. On the other hand, a simpler table of contents helps readers focus on the major points. No matter how many levels you include, make sure readers can easily distinguish between them (see Exhibit 17.13 in the previous chapter for examples of various levels of headings).

The table of contents outlines the text and lists prefatory and supplementary parts.

The table of contents is prepared after the other parts of the report have been typed so that the beginning page numbers for each heading can be shown. The headings

Be sure the headings in the table of contents match up perfectly with the headings in the text.

should be worded exactly as they are in the text of the report. Also listed on the contents page are the prefatory parts (only those that follow the contents page) and the supplementary parts. If you have fewer than four visual aids, you may wish to list them in the table of contents, too; but if you have four or more visual aids, show them separately in a list of illustrations.

List of Illustrations

Put the list of illustrations on a separate page if it won't all fit on one page with the table of contents; start the list of figures and the list of tables on separate pages if they won't both fit on one page.

For simplicity's sake, some reports refer to all visual aids as illustrations or exhibits. In other reports, as in Moreno's Electrovision report, tables are labeled separately from other types of visual aids, which are called figures. Regardless of the system used to label visual aids, the list of illustrations gives their titles and page numbers.

If you have enough space on a single page, include the list of illustrations directly beneath the table of contents. Otherwise, include the list on a separate page following the contents page. When tables and figures are numbered separately, they should also be listed separately. Both lists can appear on the same page if they fit; otherwise, start each list on a separate page.

Synopsis or Executive Summary

Provide an overview of the report in a synopsis or an executive summary.

A **synopsis** is a brief overview (one page or less) of a report's most important points, designed to give readers a quick preview of the contents. It's often included in long informational reports dealing with technical, professional, or academic subjects, and can also be called an *abstract*. Because it's a concise representation of the whole report, it may be distributed separately to a wide audience; interested readers can then order a copy of the entire report.

An informative synopsis summarizes the main ideas; a descriptive synopsis states what the report is about.

The phrasing of a synopsis can be either informative or descriptive, depending on whether the report is in direct or indirect order. With an informative synopsis, you present the main points of the report in the order in which they appear in the text. A descriptive synopsis, on the other hand, simply tells what the report is about, in only moderately greater detail than the table of contents; the actual findings of the report are omitted. Here are examples of statements from each type:

Informative Synopsis: Sales of super-premium ice cream make up 11 percent of the total ice cream market.

Descriptive Synopsis: This report contains information about super-premium ice cream and its share of the market.

Use a descriptive synopsis for a skeptical or hostile audience, an informative synopsis for most other situations.

The way you handle a synopsis reflects the approach you use in the text. If you're using an indirect approach in your report, you're better off with a descriptive synopsis. An informative synopsis, with its focus on conclusions and key points, may be too confrontational if you have a skeptical audience. You don't want to spoil the effect by providing a controversial beginning. No matter which type of synopsis you use, however, be sure to present an accurate picture of the report's contents.[2]

Put enough information in an executive summary so that an executive can make a decision without reading the entire report.

Many business report writers prefer to include an **executive summary** instead of a synopsis or an abstract. A synopsis is essentially a prose table of contents that outlines the main points of the report; an executive summary is a fully developed "mini" version of the report itself, intended for readers who lack the time or motivation to study the complete text. So an executive summary is more comprehensive than a synopsis, often as much as 10 percent as long as the report itself.

Unlike a synopsis, an executive summary may contain headings, well-developed transitions, and even visual aids. It is often organized in the same way as the report, using a direct or an indirect approach, depending on the audience's receptivity. However, executive summaries can also deviate from the sequence of material in the remainder of the report.

After reading the summary, audience members know the essentials of the report and are in a position to make a decision. Later, when time permits, they may read certain parts of the report to obtain additional detail. However, from daily newspapers to Web sites on the Internet, businesspeople are getting swamped with more and more data and information all the time. People are looking for ways to cut through all the clutter, and reading executive summaries is a popular shortcut. Consequently, you can usually assume that many of your readers will not read the main text of your report, so make sure you cover all your important points (along with significant supporting information) in the executive summary.

Linda Moreno's Electrovision report provides one example of an executive summary. Another good example is in a report published by the National Association of Recording Manufacturers (NARM). Covering the results of NARM's annual survey of music and video retailing, this report addresses such issues as which types of music are most popular, how CDs are selling relative to cassettes and vinyl LPs, age distribution of music consumers, and so on. The "Consumer Profile" section of the report is two pages of data tables, which are summarized in one five-sentence paragraph in the executive summary. In other words, the executive summary highlights important trends, such as the fact that traditional record stores are losing market share to other retailers (such as mail order). Then readers who want more details can turn to the data tables in the body of the report.[3]

Many reports require neither a synopsis nor an executive summary. Generally speaking, length is the determining factor. Most reports of fewer than 10 pages either omit such a preview or combine it with the letter of transmittal. However, if your report is over 30 pages long, you'll probably include either a synopsis or an executive summary as a convenience for readers. Which one you'll provide depends on the traditions of your organization.

Text of the Report

Apart from deciding on the fundamental issues of content and organization, you must also make decisions about the design and layout of the report. You can use a variety of techniques to present your material effectively. Many organizations have format guidelines that make your decisions easier, but the goal is always to focus readers' attention on major points and on the flow of ideas. Headings, typographical devices (such as capital letters, italics, and boldface type), white space, and so on are useful tools, as are visual aids. Also, as discussed in Chapter 17, use preview and review statements to frame sections of your text. This strategy keeps your audience informed and reinforces the substance of your message. For example, in RMI's report to the EPA on water-efficiency measures, Hunter Lovins included an overview at the beginning of each major section to explain what the section covers.

Aids to understanding the text of a report:
- Headings
- Typographical devices
- Visual aids
- Preview and review statements

Introduction

The introduction of a report serves a number of important functions:

- Putting the report in a broader context by tying it to a problem or an assignment
- Telling readers the report's purpose
- Previewing the report's contents and organization
- Establishing the tone of the report and the writer's relationship with the audience

An introduction has a number of functions and covers a wide variety of topics.

The length of the introduction depends on the length of the report. In a relatively brief report, the introduction may be only a paragraph or two and may not be labeled with a heading of any kind. On the other hand, the introduction to a major formal report may extend to several pages and can be identified as a separate section by the first-level heading "Introduction." (See Linda Moreno's Electrovision report.)

Here's a list of topics to consider covering in an introduction, depending on your material and your audience:

- **Authorization.** When, how, and by whom the report was authorized; who wrote it; and when it was submitted. This material is especially important when no letter of transmittal is included.
- **Problem/purpose.** The reason for the report's existence and what is to be accomplished as a result of the report's being written.
- **Scope.** What is and what isn't going to be covered in the report. The scope indicates the report's size and complexity.
- **Background.** The historic conditions or factors that have led up to the report. This section enables readers to understand how the problem developed and what has been done about it so far.
- **Sources and methods.** The secondary sources of information used and the surveys, experiments, and observations carried out. This section tells readers what sources were used, how the sample was selected, how the questionnaire was constructed (a sample questionnaire and cover letter should be included in the appendix), what follow-up procedures were employed, and the like. It provides enough detail to give readers confidence in the work and to convince them that the sources and methods were satisfactory.
- **Definitions.** A brief introductory statement leading into a list of terms used in the report and their definitions. Naturally, if your audience is familiar with the terms you've used throughout the report, a list of definitions isn't necessary. Moreno's Electrovision report doesn't include a list of definitions because the topic doesn't involve any unfamiliar terminology. However, if you have any question about your readers' knowledge, be sure to include definitions of any terms that might lead to misinterpretation. In addition, if you've used familiar or general terms in a specific way, be sure to explain exactly what you mean. For example, the term *market* could be used in a number of different ways, from a physical location to a collection of potential customers. Note that terms may be defined in other places as well: in the body (as the terms are used), in explanatory footnotes, or in a glossary (an alphabetical listing of terms placed at the end of the report).
- **Limitations.** Factors affecting the quality of the report, such as a budget too small to do all the work that should have been done, an inadequate amount of time to do all the necessary research, unreliability or unavailability of data, or other conditions beyond your control. This is the place to mention doubts about any aspect of the report. Although candor may lead readers to question the results, it will also enable them to assess the results more accurately and help you maintain the integrity of your report. However, limitations are no excuse for conducting a poor study or writing a bad report.
- **Report organization.** The organization of the report (what topics are covered and in what order), along with a rationale for following this plan. This section is a road map that helps readers understand what's approaching at each turn of the report and why.

Some of these items may be combined in the introduction; some may not be included at all. Consider the items included in the 44-page introduction to *Management*

Education and Development: Drift or Thrust into the 21st Century? This report on the future of business education was sponsored by the American Assembly of Collegiate Schools of Business (AACSB). Part 1 of the introduction discusses the background and objectives of the project, the issues addressed, the project's design (including limits to the project's scope), and the report's structure. Part 2 offers some background on various views of the future (including a brief overview of what other writers see for the future); an examination of future trends in economics, demographics, and societal variables; and a commentary about anticipating and responding to future changes.[4]

You can decide what to include by figuring out what kind of information will help your readers understand and accept the report. Also give some thought to how the introduction relates to the prefatory parts of the report. In longer reports you may have a letter of transmittal, a synopsis or an executive summary, and an introduction, all of which cover essentially the same ground. To avoid redundancy, balance the various sections. If the letter of transmittal and synopsis are fairly detailed, for example, you might want the introduction to be relatively brief.

However, remember that some people may barely glance at the prefatory parts, so be sure your introduction is detailed enough to provide an adequate preview of your report. If you feel that your introduction must repeat information that has already been covered in one of the prefatory parts, simply use different wording.

Body

The body of the report follows the introduction. It consists of the major sections or chapters (with various levels of headings) that present, analyze, and interpret the findings gathered as part of your investigation. These chapters contain the "proof," the detailed information necessary to support your conclusions and recommendations. (See the body of Linda Moreno's Electrovision report.)

One of the decisions to make when writing the body of your report is how much detail to include. Your decision depends on the nature of your information, the purpose of your report, and the preferences of your audience. Some situations call for detailed coverage; others lend themselves to shorter treatment. In general, provide only enough detail in the body to support your conclusions and recommendations, and put additional detail in tables, charts, and appendixes.

> Restrict the body to those details necessary to prove your conclusions and recommendations.

You can also decide whether to put your conclusions in the body or in a separate section or both. If the conclusions seem to flow naturally from the evidence, you'll almost inevitably cover them in the body. However, if you want to give your conclusions added emphasis, you may include a separate section to summarize them. Having a separate section is particularly appropriate in longer reports; the reader may lose track of the conclusions if they're given only in the body.

Summary, Conclusions, and Recommendations

The final section of the text of a report tells readers "what you told them." In a short report this final wrap-up may be only a paragraph or two. A long report generally has separate sections labeled "Summary," "Conclusions," and "Recommendations." Here's how the three differ:

- **Summary.** The key findings of your report, paraphrased from the body and stated or listed in the order in which they appear in the body.
- **Conclusions.** The writer's analysis of what the findings mean. These are the answers to the questions that led to the report.

> Summaries, conclusions, and recommendations serve different purposes.

- ***Recommendations.*** Opinions, based on reason and logic, about the course of action that should be taken. The author of the Electrovision report lists four specific steps the company should take to reduce travel costs.

If the report is organized in direct order, the summary, conclusions, and recommendations are presented before the body and are reviewed only briefly at the end. If the report is organized in indirect order, these sections are presented for the first time at the end and are covered in detail. Many report writers combine the conclusions and recommendations under one heading because it seems like the natural thing to do. It is often difficult to present a conclusion without implying a recommendation. (See Moreno's Electrovision report.)

Whether you combine them or not, if you have several conclusions and recommendations, you may want to number and list them. An appropriate lead-in to such a list might be, "The findings of this study lead to the following conclusions." A statement that could be used for a list of recommendations might be, "Based on the conclusions of this study, the following recommendations are made." Present no new findings either in the conclusions or in the recommendations section.

In action-oriented reports, put all the recommendations in a separate section and spell out precisely what should happen next.

In reports that are intended to lead to action, the recommendations section is particularly important; it spells out exactly what should happen next. It brings all the action items together in one place and gives the details about who should do what, when, where, and how. Readers may agree with everything you say in your report but still fail to take any action if you're vague about what should happen next. Your readers must understand what's expected of them and must have some appreciation of the difficulties that are likely to arise. So providing a schedule and specific task assignments is helpful because concrete plans have a way of commanding action.

Source Documentation

Give credit where credit is due.

When writing the text of the report, you need to decide how to acknowledge your sources. You have an ethical and a legal obligation to give other people credit for their work. Acknowledging your sources also enhances the credibility of your report. By citing references in the text, you demonstrate that you have thoroughly researched the topic. Mentioning the names of well-known or important authorities on the subject also helps build credibility for your message. In fact, it's often a good idea to mention a credible source's name several times if you need to persuade the audience.

On the other hand, you don't want to make your report read like an academic treatise, dragging along from citation to citation. The source references should be handled as conveniently and inconspicuously as possible. One approach, especially for internal reports, is simply to mention a source in the text:

> According to Dr. Lewis Morgan of Northwestern Hospital, hip replacement operations account for 7 percent of all surgery performed on women ages 65 and over.

However, if your report will be distributed to outsiders, include additional information on where you obtained the data. Most college students are familiar with citation schemes suggested by the Modern Language Association (MLA) or American Psychological Association (APA). *The Chicago Manual of Style* is a reference often used by typesetters and publishers. All of these encourage the use of *in-text citations,* in which you insert the author's last name and a year of publication or a page number directly in the text. An alternative is to use numbered footnotes (bottom of the page) or endnotes (end of the report). (Linda Moreno's Electrovision report uses the author-date system, whereas this textbook uses endnotes.) For more information on citing sources, see Component Chapter B, "Documentation of Report Sources."

Supplementary Parts

Supplementary parts follow the text of the report and include the appendix(es), bibliography, and index. They are more common in long reports than in short ones.

An **appendix** contains materials related to the report but not included in the text because they're too lengthy or bulky or because they lack direct relevance. One of the appendixes in RMI's report to the EPA on water-efficiency measures includes more than 100 names and addresses of water-efficiency contacts. Frequently included in appendixes are sample questionnaires and cover letters, sample forms, computer printouts, and statistical formulas; a glossary of terms may be put in an appendix or may stand as a separate supplementary part. The best place to include visual aids is in the text body nearest the point of discussion. If any graphics are too large to fit on one page or are only indirectly relevant to your report, they too may be put in an appendix. Some organizations specify that all visual aids be placed in an appendix.

Each type of material deserves a separate appendix. Identify the appendixes by labeling them, for example, "Appendix A: Questionnaire," "Appendix B: Computer Printout of Raw Data," and the like. All appendixes should be mentioned in the text and listed in the table of contents.

A **bibliography** is a list of sources consulted when preparing the report. Linda Moreno labeled her bibliography as "Sources" in her Electrovision report. You might also call this section "Works Cited" or "References." The construction of a bibliography is shown in Component Chapter B.

An **index** is an alphabetical list of names, places, and subjects mentioned in the report and the pages on which they occur, as in the index for this book. An index is rarely included in unpublished reports.

COMPONENTS OF A FORMAL PROPOSAL

As discussed in Chapter 14, certain analytical reports are called proposals, including bids to perform work under a contract and pleas for financial support from outsiders. Such bids and pleas are nearly always formal. The goal is to impress the potential client or supporter with your professionalism, and this goal is best achieved through a structured and deliberate approach.

Formal proposals contain many of the same components as other formal reports (see Figure 18.2). The difference lies mostly in the text, although a few of the prefatory parts are also different. With the exception of an occasional appendix, most proposals have few supplementary parts (text continues on page 605).

Marginal notes:

Put into an appendix materials that are
- Bulky or lengthy
- Not directly relevant to the text

List your secondary sources in the bibliography.

PREFATORY PARTS	TEXT OF THE PROPOSAL	SUPPLEMENTARY PARTS
Cover	Introduction	Appendixes
Title fly	Body	
Title page	Summary	
Letter of transmittal		
Letter of acceptance		
Table of contents		
List of illustrations		
Synopsis or executive summary		

Figure 18.2
Parts of a Formal Proposal

IN-DEPTH CRITIQUE: ANALYZING A FORMAL REPORT

The report presented in the following pages was prepared by Linda Moreno, manager of the cost accounting department at Electrovision, a high-tech company based in Los Gatos, California. Electrovision's main product is optical character recognition equipment, which is used by the U.S. Postal Service for sorting mail. Moreno's job is to help analyze the company's costs. She has this to say about the background of his report:

"For the past three or four years, Electrovision has been on a roll. Our A-12 optical character reader was a real breakthrough, and the post office grabbed up as many as we could make. Our sales and profits kept climbing, and morale was fantastic. Everybody seemed to think that the good times would last forever. Unfortunately, everybody was wrong. When the Postal Service announced that it was postponing all new-equipment purchases because of cuts in its budget, we woke up to the fact that we are essentially a one-product company with one customer. At that point management started scrambling around looking for ways to cut costs until we could diversify our business a bit.

"The vice president of operations, Dennis McWilliams, asked me to help identify cost-cutting opportunities in the travel and entertainment area. On the basis of his personal observations, he felt that Electrovision was overly generous in its travel policies and that we might be able to save a significant amount by controlling these costs more carefully. My investigation confirmed his suspicion.

"I was reasonably confident that my report would be well received. I've worked with Dennis for several years and know what he likes: plenty of facts, clearly stated conclusions, and specific recommendations for what should be done next. I also knew that my report would be passed on to other Electrovision executives, so I wanted to create a good impression. I wanted the report to be accurate and thorough, visually appealing, readable, and appropriate in tone."

When writing the analytical report that follows, Moreno used an organization based on conclusions and recommendations, presented in direct order. The first two sections of the report correspond to Moreno's two main conclusions: that Electrovision's travel and entertainment costs are too high and that cuts are essential. The third section presents recommendations for achieving better control over travel and entertainment expenses. As you review the report, analyze both the mechanical aspects and the way Moreno presents her ideas. Be prepared to discuss the way the various components convey and reinforce the main message.

REDUCING ELECTROVISION'S TRAVEL
AND ENTERTAINMENT COSTS

Prepared for
Dennis McWilliams,
Vice President of Operations
Electrovision, Inc.

Prepared by
Linda Moreno, Manager
Cost Accounting Services
Electrovision, Inc.

February 15, 1997

Capitalize the title; use uppercase and lowercase letters for all other lines.

Follow the title with the name, title, and organization of the recipient.

Balance the white space between the items on the page.

When centering the lines horizontally on the title page, allow an extra 1/2-inch margin on the left side if it's a left-bound report.

For future reference, include the report's publication date.

The "how to" tone of Moreno's title is appropriate for an action-oriented report that emphasizes recommendations. A more neutral title, such as "An Analysis of Electrovision's Travel and Entertainment Costs," would be more suitable for an informational report.

Use memo format for transmitting internal reports, letter format for transmitting external reports.

Present the main conclusion or recommendation right away if you expect a positive response.

Use an informal, conversational style for the letter or memo of transmittal.

Acknowledge any help that you have received.

Close with thanks, an offer to discuss results, and an offer to assist with future projects, if appropriate.

MEMORANDUM

TO: Dennis McWilliams, Vice President of Operations

FROM: Linda Moreno, Manager of Cost Accounting Services

DATE: February 15, 1997

SUBJECT: Reducing Electrovision's Travel and Entertainment Costs

Here is the report you requested January 30 on Electrovision's travel and entertainment costs.

Your suspicion was right. We are spending far too much on business travel. Our unwritten policy has been "anything goes," leaving us with no real control over T&E expenses. Although this hands-off approach may have been understandable when Electrovision's profits were high, we can no longer afford the luxury of going first class.

The solutions to the problem seem rather clear. We need to have someone with centralized responsibility for travel and entertainment costs, a clear statement of policy, an effective control system, and a business-oriented travel service that can optimize our travel arrangements. We should also investigate alternatives to travel, such as videoconferencing. Perhaps more important, we need to change our attitude. Instead of viewing travel funds as a bottomless supply of money, all traveling employees need to act as though they were paying the bills themselves.

Getting people to economize is not going to be easy. In the course of researching this issue, I've found that our employees are deeply attached to their first-class travel privileges. I think they would almost prefer a cut in pay to a loss in travel status. We'll need a lot of top management involvement to sell people on the need for moderation. One thing is clear: People will be very bitter if we create a two-class system in which top executives get special privileges while the rest of the employees make the sacrifices.

I'm grateful to Mary Lehman and Connie McIllvain for their help in rounding up and sorting through five years' worth of expense reports. Their efforts were truly Herculean.

Thanks for giving me the opportunity to work on this assignment. It's been a real education. If you have any questions about the report, please give me a call.

In this report Moreno decided to write a brief memo of transmittal and include a separate executive summary. Short reports (fewer than ten pages) often combine the synopsis or executive summary with the memo or letter of transmittal.

CONTENTS

Word the headings exactly as they appear in the text.

Include no element that appears before the "Contents" page.

Include only the page numbers where sections begin.

iii

Moreno included only first- and second-level headings in her table of contents, even though the report contains third-level headings. She prefers a shorter table of contents that focuses attention on the main divisions of thought. She used informative titles, which are appropriate for a report to a receptive audience.

LIST OF ILLUSTRATIONS

Number the contents pages
with lowercase roman
numerals centered at the
bottom margin.

Because figures and tables were numbered separately in the text, Moreno listed them separately here. If
all were labeled as exhibits, a single list of illustrations would have been appropriate.

EXECUTIVE SUMMARY

This report analyzes Electrovision's travel and entertainment (T&E) costs and presents recommendations for reducing those costs.

Travel and Entertainment Costs Are Too High

Travel and entertainment is a large and growing expense category for Electrovision. The company spends over $16 million per year on business travel, and these costs have been increasing by 12 percent annually. Company employees make roughly 3,390 trips each year at an average cost per trip of $4,720. Airfares are the biggest expense, followed by hotels, meals, and rental cars.

The nature of Electrovision's business does require extensive travel, but the company's costs appear to be excessive. Every year Electrovision employees spend more than twice as much on T&E as the average business traveler. Although the location of the company's facilities may partly explain this discrepancy, the main reason for Electrovision's high costs is the firm's philosophy and managerial style. Electrovision's tradition and its hands-off style almost invite employees to go first class and pay relatively little attention to travel costs.

Cuts Are Essential

Although Electrovision has traditionally been casual about travel and entertainment expenses, management now recognizes the need to gain more control over this element of costs. The company is currently entering a period of declining profits, prompting management to look for every opportunity to reduce spending. At the same time, rising airfares and hotel rates are making travel and entertainment expenses more important to the bottom line.

Electrovision Can Save $6 Million per Year

Fortunately, Electrovision has a number of excellent opportunities for reducing its travel and entertainment costs. Savings of up to $6 million per year should be achievable, judging by the experience of other companies. American Express suggests that a sensible travel-management program can save companies as much as 35 percent a year (Gilligan 1995). Given that we purchase many more first-class tickets than the average, we should be able to achieve even greater savings. The first priority should be to hire a director of travel and entertainment to assume overall responsibility for T&E spending. This individual should establish a written travel and entertainment policy and create

v

Begin by stating the purpose of the report.

Present the points in the executive summary in the same order as they appear in the report; use subheadings that summarize the content of the main sections of the report without repeating those that appear in the text.

Type the synopsis or executive summary in the same manner as the text of the report. Use single-spacing if the report is single-spaced, and use the same format as used in the text for margins, paragraph indentions, and headings.

Moreno decided to include an executive summary because her report was aimed at a mixed audience. She knew that some readers would be interested in the details of her report and some would prefer to focus on the big picture. The executive summary was aimed at the "big picture" group. Moreno wanted to give these readers enough information to make a decision without burdening them with the task of reading the entire report.

The hard-hitting tone of this executive summary is appropriate for a receptive audience. A more neutral approach would be better for hostile or skeptical readers.

a budget and a cost-control system. The director should also retain a nation-wide travel agency to handle our reservations and should lead an investigation into electronic alternatives to travel.

At the same time, Electrovision should make employees aware of the need for moderation in travel and entertainment spending. People should be encour-aged to forgo any unnecessary travel and to economize on airline tickets, ho-tels, meals, rental cars, and other expenses.

In addition to economizing on an individual basis, Electrovision should look for ways to reduce costs by negotiating preferential rates with travel providers. Once retained, a travel agency should be able to accomplish this.

Finally, we should look into alternatives to travel. Although we may have to invest money in videoconferencing systems or other equipment. we may be able to recover these costs through decreased travel expenses. I recommend that the new travel director undertake this investigation to make sure it is well integrated with the rest of the travel program.

These changes, although necessary, are likely to hurt morale, at least in the short term. Management will need to make a determined effort to explain the rationale for reduced spending. By exercising moderation in their own travel arrangements, Electrovision executives can set a good example and help other employees accept the changes. On the plus side, cutting back on travel with videoconferencing or other alternatives will reduce the travel burden on many employees and help them balance their business and personal lives.

Number the pages of the executive summary with lowercase roman numerals centered about 1 inch from the bottom of the page.

vi

This executive summary is written in an impersonal style, which adds to the formality of the report. Some writers prefer a more personal approach. Generally speaking, you should gear your choice of style to your relationship with the readers. Moreno chose the formal approach because several members of her audience were considerably higher up in the organization. She did not want to sound too familiar. In addition, she wanted the executive summary and the text to be compatible, and her company prefers the impersonal style for formal reports.

REDUCING ELECTROVISION'S TRAVEL
AND ENTERTAINMENT COSTS

INTRODUCTION

Electrovision has always encouraged a significant amount of business travel, believing that it is an effective way of operating. To compensate employees for the inconvenience and stress of frequent trips, management has authorized generous travel and entertainment (T&E) allowances. This philosophy has been good for morale, but the company has paid a price. Last year Electrovision spent $16 million on T&E—$7 million more than it spent on research and development.

This year the cost of travel and entertainment will have a bigger impact on profits, owing to changes in airline fares and hotel rates. The timing of these changes is unfortunate because the company anticipates that profits will be relatively weak for a variety of other reasons. In light of these profit pressures, Dennis McWilliams, Vice President of Operations, has asked the accounting department to take a closer look at the T&E budget.

Purpose, Scope, and Limitations

The purpose of this report is to analyze the T&E budget, evaluate the impact of recent changes in airfares and hotel costs, and suggest ways to tighten management's control over T&E expenses. Although the report outlines a number of steps that could reduce Electrovision's expenses, the precise financial impact of these measure is difficult to project. The estimates presented in the report provide a "best guess" view of what Electrovision can expect to save. Until the company actually implements these steps, however, we won't know exactly how much the travel and entertainment budget can be reduced.

Sources and Methods

In preparing this report, the accounting department analyzed internal expense reports for the past five years to determine how much Electrovision spends on travel and entertainment. These figures were then compared with average statistics compiled by Dow Jones (publisher of *The Wall Street Journal*) and presented as the Dow Jones Travel Index. We also analyzed trends and suggestions published in a variety of business journal articles to see how other companies are coping with the high cost of business travel.

Center the title of the report on the first page of the text, 2 inches (2-1/2 inches if top-bound) from the top of the page.

Begin the introduction by establishing the need for action.

Mentioning sources and methods increases the credibility of a report and gives readers a complete picture of the study's background.

Use the arabic numeral 1 for the first page of the report; center the number about 1 inch from the bottom of the page.

In a brief introduction like this one, some writers would omit the subheadings within the introduction and rely on topic sentences and on transitional words and phrases to indicate that they are discussing such subjects as the purpose, scope, and limitations of the study. Moreno decided to use headings because they help readers scan the document. Also, to conserve space, Moreno used single spacing and 1-inch side margins.

2

Report Organization

This report reviews the size and composition of Electrovision's travel and entertainment expenses, analyzes trends in travel costs, and recommends steps for reducing the T&E budget.

THE HIGH COST OF TRAVEL AND ENTERTAINMENT

Although many companies view travel and entertainment as an "incidental" cost of doing business, the dollars add up. At Electrovision the bill for airfares, hotels, rental cars, meals, and entertainment totaled $16 million last year. Our T&E budget has increased by 12 percent per year for the past five years. Compared to the average U.S. business traveler, Electrovision's expenditures are high, largely because of management's generous policy on travel benefits.

$16 Million per Year Spent on Travel and Entertainment

Electrovision's annual budget for travel and entertainment is only 8 percent of sales. Because this is a relatively small expense category compared with such things as salaries and commissions, it is tempting to dismiss T&E costs as insignificant. However, T&E is Electrovision's third-largest controllable expense, directly behind salaries and information systems.

Last year Electrovision personnel made about 3,390 trips at an average cost per trip of $4,720. The typical trip involved a round-trip flight of 3,000 miles, meals and hotel accommodations for two or three days, and a rental car. Roughly 80 percent of the trips were made by 20 percent of the staff—top management and sales personnel traveled most, averaging 18 trips per year.

Figure 1 illustrates how the travel and entertainment budget is spent. The largest categories are airfares and lodging, which together account for $7 out

Figure 1
Airfares and Lodging Account for Over Two-Thirds of Electrovision's Travel and Entertainment Budget

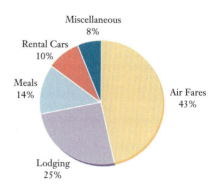

3

of every $10 that employees spend on travel and entertainment. This spending breakdown has been relatively steady for the past five years and is consistent with the distribution of expenses experienced by other companies.

Although the composition of the T&E budget has been consistent, its size has not. As mentioned earlier, these expenditures have increased by about 12 percent per year for the past five years, roughly twice the rate of the company's growth in sales (see Figure 2). This rate of growth makes T&E Electrovision's fastest-growing expense item.

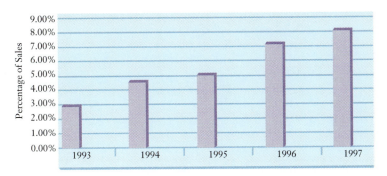

Figure 2
Travel and Entertainment Expenses Have Increased as a Percentage of Sales

Electrovision's Travel Expenses Exceed National Averages

Much of our travel budget is justified. Two major factors contribute to Electrovision's high travel and entertainment budget:

- With our headquarters on the West Coast and our major customer on the East Coast, we naturally spend a lot on cross-country flights.
- A great deal of travel takes place between our headquarters here on the West Coast and the manufacturing operations in Detroit, Boston, and Dallas. Corporate managers and division personnel make frequent trips to coordinate these disparate operations.

However, even though a good portion of Electrovision's travel budget is justifiable, the company spends considerably more on travel and entertainment than the average business traveler (see Figure 3).

Introduce visual aids before they appear, and indicate what readers should notice about the data.

Number the visual aids consecutively, and refer to them in the text by their numbers. If your report is a book-length document, you may number the visual aids by chapter: Figure 4-2, for example, would be the second figure in the fourth chapter.

Moreno originally drew the bar chart in Figure 2 as a line chart, showing both sales and T&E expenses in absolute dollars. However, the comparison was difficult to interpret because sales were so much greater than T&E expenses. Switching to a bar chart expressed in percentage terms made the main idea much easier to grasp.

4

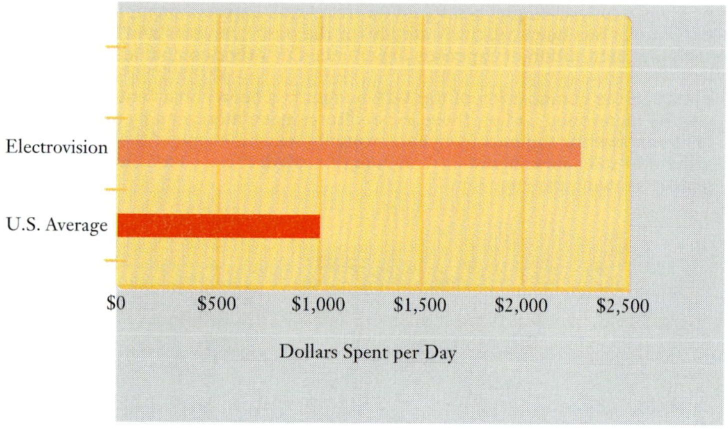

Figure 3
Electrovision People Spend Over Twice as Much as the Average Business Traveler
Source: Wall Street Journal and company records

The Dow Jones Travel Index calculates the average cost per day of business travel in the United States, based on average airfare, hotel rates, and rental car rates. The average fluctuates weekly as travel companies change their rates, but it has been running at about $1,000 per day for the last year or so. In contrast, Electrovision's average daily expense over the past year has been $2,250—125 percent higher than average. This figure is based on the average trip cost of $4,720 listed earlier and an average trip length of 2.1 days.

Spending Has Been Encouraged

Although a variety of factors may contribute to this differential, Electrovision's relatively high T&E costs are at least partially attributable to the company's philosophy and management style. Because many employees do not enjoy business travel, management has tried to make the trips more pleasant by authorizing first-class airfare, luxury hotel accommodations, and full-size rental cars. The sales staff is encouraged to entertain clients at top restaurants and to invite them to cultural and sporting events.

The cost of these privileges is easy to overlook, given the weakness of Electrovision's system for keeping track of T&E expenses:

Leaving a bit more white space above a heading than below it helps readers associate that heading with the text it describes.

Moreno was as careful about the appearance of her report as she was about its content. The chart in Figure 3 is very simple, but it creates an effective visual comparison. Moreno included just enough data to make her point.

5

- The monthly financial records provided to management do not contain a separate category for travel and entertainment; the information is buried under Cost of Goods Sold and under Selling, General, and Administrative Expenses.
- Each department head is given authority to approve any expense report, regardless of how large it may be.
- Receipts are not required for expenditures of less than $100.
- Individuals are allowed to make their own travel arrangements.
- No one is charged with the responsibility for controlling the company's total spending on travel and entertainment.

GROWING IMPACT ON THE BOTTOM LINE

During the past three years, the company's healthy profits have resulted in relatively little pressure to push for tighter controls over all aspects of the business. However, as we all know, the situation is changing. We're projecting flat to declining profits for the next two years, a situation that has prompted all of us to search for ways to cut costs. At the same time, rising airfares and hotel rates have increased the impact of T&E expenses on the company's financial results.

Lower Profits Underscore the Need for Change

The next two years promise to be difficult for Electrovision. After several years of steady increases in spending, the Postal Service is tightening procurement policies for automated mail-handling equipment. Funding for the A-12 optical character reader has been canceled. As a consequence, the marketing department expects sales to drop by 15 percent. Although Electrovision is negotiating several promising R&D contracts with nongovernment clients, the marketing department does not foresee any major procurements for the next two to three years.

At the same time, Electrovision is facing cost increases on several fronts. As we've known for several months, the new production facility now under construction in Salt Lake City, Utah, is behind schedule and over budget. Labor contracts in Boston and Dallas expire within the next six months, and plant managers there anticipate that significant salary and benefits concessions may be necessary to avoid strikes. Moreover, marketing and advertising costs are expected to increase as we attempt to strengthen these activities to better cope with competitive pressures. Given the expected decline in revenues and increase in costs, the Executive Committee's prediction that profits will fall by 12 percent in the coming fiscal year does not seem overly pessimistic.

Airfares and Hotel Rates Are Rising

Business travelers have grown accustomed to frequent fare wars and discounting in the travel industry in recent years. Excess capacity and aggressive price competition, particularly in the airline business, made travel a relative bargain.

Bulleted lists make it easy for readers to identify and distinguish related points.

Informative headings focus readers' attention on the main points of the report. Thus they are most appropriate when the report is in direct order and is aimed at a receptive audience. Descriptive headings are more effective when a report is in indirect order and the readers are less receptive.

Because airfares represent Electrovision's biggest T&E expense, Moreno included a subsection that deals with the possible impact of trends in the airline industry. Airfares are rising, so it is especially important to gain more control over employees' air travel arrangements.

6

Documenting the facts adds
weight to Moreno's argument.

However, that situation has changed, as weaker competitors have been forced
out and the remaining players have grown stronger and smarter. Airlines and
hotels are better at managing inventory and keeping occupancy rates high,
and high occupancy translates into higher prices because suppliers have less
reason to compete on price. Last year saw some of the steepest rate hikes in
years. Business airfares (tickets most likely to be purchased by business travelers) jumped over 40 percent in many markets. The trend is expected to continue, with rates increasing another 5 to 10 percent overall (Phillips 1996;
"Travel Costs Under Pressure" 1996; Dahl 1995).

Given the fact that air and hotel costs account for 70 percent of
Electrovision's T&E budget, the trend toward higher prices in these two categories will have serious consequences on the company's expenses unless
management takes action to control these costs.

METHODS FOR REDUCING TRAVEL AND ENTERTAINMENT COSTS

Pointing out both the benefits
and risks of taking action
gives recommendations an
objective flavor.

By implementing a number of reforms, management can expect to reduce
Electrovision's T&E budget by as much as 40 percent. This estimate is based
on the general assessment made by American Express (Gilligan 1995) and the
fact that we have an opportunity to significantly reduce air travel costs by reducing or eliminating first-class travel. However, these measures are likely to
be unpopular with employees. To gain acceptance for such changes, management will need to sell employees on the need for moderation in travel and entertainment allowances.

Four Ways to Trim Expenses

By researching what other companies are doing to curb travel and entertainment expenses, the accounting department has identified four prominent opportunities that should enable Electrovision to save about $6 million annually
in travel-related costs.

Institute Tighter Spending Controls

A single individual should be appointed director of travel and entertainment to
spearhead the effort to gain control of the T&E budget. More than a third of all
U.S. companies now employ travel managers in an effort to keep costs in line
("Businesses Use Savvy Managers" 1995). The director should be familiar with
the travel industry and should be well versed in both accounting and information technology. The director should also report to the vice president of operations. The director's first priorities should be to establish a written travel and
entertainment policy and to implement a system for controlling travel and entertainment costs.

Moreno created a forceful tone by using action verbs in the third-level subheadings of this section. This
approach is appropriate to the nature of the study and the attitude of the audience. However, in a status-
conscious organization, the imperative verbs might sound a bit too presumptuous coming from a junior
member of the staff.

7

Electrovision currently has no written policy on travel and entertainment, a step widely recommended by air travel experts (Smith 1995). Creating a policy would clarify management's position and serve as a vehicle for communicating the need for moderation. At a minimum, the policy should include the following provisions:

- All travel and entertainment should be strictly related to business and should be approved in advance.
- Except under special circumstances to be approved on a case by case basis, employees should travel by coach and stay in mid-range business hotels.
- The travel and entertainment policy should apply equally to employees at all levels in the organization. No special benefits should be allowed for top executives.

To implement the new policy, Electrovision will need to create a system for controlling travel and entertainment expenses. Each department should prepare an annual T&E budget as part of its operating plan. These budgets should be presented in detail so that management can evaluate how travel and entertainment dollars will be spent and recommend appropriate cuts.

To help management monitor performance relative to these budgets, the director of travel should prepare monthly financial statements showing actual travel and entertainment expenditures by department. The system for capturing this information should be computerized and should be capable of identifying individuals who consistently exceed approved spending levels. The recommended average should range between $2,000 and $2,500 per month for each professional employee, depending on the individual's role in the company. Because they make frequent trips, sales and top management personnel can be expected to have relatively high travel expenses.

The director of travel should also be responsible for retaining a business-oriented travel service that will schedule all employee business trips and look for the best travel deals, particularly in airfares. In addition to centralizing Electrovision's reservation and ticketing activities, the agency will negotiate reduced group rates with hotels and rental car agencies. The agency selected should have offices nationwide so that all Electrovision facilities can channel their reservations through the same company. By consolidating its travel planning in this way, Electrovision can increase its control over costs and achieve economies of scale. This is particularly important in light of the dizzying array of often wildly different airfares available between some cities. It's not uncommon to find dozens of fares along commonly traveled routes (Rowe 1995).

The director should also work with the agency to explore low-cost alternatives, such as buying tickets from airfare consolidators (the air travel

The bulleted list format not only calls attention to important points but adds visual interest. You can also use visual aids, headings, and direct quotations to break up large, solid blocks of print.

When including recommendations in a report, specify the steps required to implement them.

Moreno decided to single-space her report to save space; however, double-spacing can make the text of a long report somewhat easier to read, and it provides more space for readers to write comments.

8

equivalent of factory outlet malls). In addition, the director can help coordinate travel across the company to secure group discounts whenever possible (Barker, 1996; Miller 1995).

Reduce Unnecessary Travel and Entertainment

One of the easiest ways to reduce expenses is to reduce the amount of traveling and entertaining that occurs. An analysis of last year's expenditures suggests that as much as 30 percent of Electrovision's travel and entertainment is discretionary. The professional staff spent $2.8 million attending seminars and conferences last year. Although some of these gatherings are undoubtedly beneficial, the company could save money by sending fewer representatives to each function and by eliminating some of the less valuable seminars.

Similarly, Electrovision could economize on trips between headquarters and divisions by reducing the frequency of such visits and by sending fewer people on each trip. Although there is often no substitute for face-to-face meetings, management could try to resolve more internal issues through telephone, electronic, and written communication.

Electrovision can also reduce spending by urging employees to economize. Instead of flying first class, employees can fly tourist class or take advantage of discount fares. Instead of taking clients to dinner, Electrovision personnel can hold breakfast meetings, which tend to be less costly. Rather than ordering a $50 bottle of wine, employees can select a less expensive bottle or dispense with alcohol entirely. People can book rooms at moderately priced hotels and drive smaller rental cars. In general, employees should be urged to spend the company's money as though it were their own.

Obtain Lowest Rates from Travel Providers

Apart from urging individual employees to economize, Electrovision can also save money by searching for the lowest available airfares, hotel rates, and rental car fees. Currently, few Electrovision employees have the time or specialized knowledge to seek out travel bargains. When they need to travel, they make the most convenient and most comfortable arrangements. However, if Electrovision contracts with a professional travel service, the company will have access to professionals who can more efficiently obtain the lower rates from travel providers.

Judging by the experience of other companies, Electrovision may be able to trim as much as 30 to 40 percent from the travel budget by looking for bargains in airfares and negotiating group rates with hotels and rental car companies. Electrovision should be able to achieve these economies by analyzing its travel patterns, identifying frequently visited locations, and selecting a few

Pointing out possible difficulties demonstrates that you have considered all the angles and builds readers' confidence in your judgment.

9

hotels that are willing to reduce rates in exchange for guaranteed business. At the same time, the company should be able to save up to 40 percent on rental car charges by negotiating a corporate rate.

The possibilities for economizing are promising, but it's worth noting that making the best arrangements is a complicated undertaking, requiring many trade-offs such as the following:

- The best fares might not always be the lowest. Indirect flights are often less expensive than direct flights, but they take longer and may end up costing more in lost work time.
- The cheapest tickets may have to be booked 30 days in advance, often impossible for us.
- Discount tickets may be nonrefundable, which is a real drawback if the trip has to be canceled at the last minute.

Electrovision is currently ill-equipped to make these and other trade-offs. However, by employing a business-oriented travel service, the company will have access to computerized systems that can optimize its choices.

Replace Travel with Technological Alternatives

We might be able to replace a significant portion of our interdivisional travel with electronic meetings that utilize videoconferencing, real-time document sharing on PC screens, and other alternatives. Naturally, we don't want to reduce employee or team effectiveness, but many companies are using these new tools to cut costs and reduce wear and tear on employees.

Rather than make specific recommendations in this report, I suggest that the new travel director conduct an in-depth study of the company's travel patterns as part of an overall cost-containment effort. A thorough analysis of why employees travel and what they accomplish will highlight any opportunities for replacing face-to-face meetings. Part of this study should include limited-scope tests of various communication systems as a way of measuring their impact on both workplace effectiveness and overall costs.

The Impact of Reforms

By implementing tighter controls, reducing unnecessary expenses, negotiating more favorable rates, and exploring "electronic travel," Electrovision should be able to reduce its travel and entertainment budget significantly. As Table 1 illustrates, the combined savings should be in the neighborhood of $6 million, although the precise figures are somewhat difficult to project.

Note how Moreno made the transition from section to section. The first sentence under the second heading on this page refers to the subject of the previous paragraph and signals a shift in thought.

The use of informative titles for exhibits is consistent with the way headings are handled and is appropriate for a report to a receptive audience. The use of complete sentences helps readers focus immediately on the point of the illustrations.

Even though estimated savings may be difficult to project, including dollar figures helps management envision the impact of your suggestions.

10

TABLE 1

ELECTROVISION CAN TRIM TRAVEL AND ENTERTAINMENT COSTS BY AN ESTIMATED $6 MILLION PER YEAR

Source of Savings	Amount Saved
Switching from first-class to coach airfare	$2,300,000
Negotiating preferred hotel rates	940,000
Negotiating preferred rental car rates	460,000
Systematically searching for lower airfares	375,000
Reducing interdivisional travel	675,000
Reducing seminar and conference attendance	1,250,000
TOTAL POTENTIAL SAVINGS	**$6,000,000**

To achieve the economies outlined in the table, Electrovision will incur expenses for hiring a director of travel and for implementing a T&E cost-control system. These costs are projected at $95,000: $85,000 per year in salary and benefits for the new employee and a one-time expense of $10,000 for the cost-control system. The cost of retaining a full-service travel agency is negligible because agencies receive a commission from travel providers rather than a fee from clients.

The measures required to achieve these savings are likely to be unpopular with employees. Electrovision personnel are accustomed to generous travel and entertainment allowances, and they are likely to resent having these privileges curtailed. To alleviate their disappointment

- Management should make a determined effort to explain why the changes are necessary.
- The director of corporate communication should be asked to develop a multifaceted campaign that will communicate the importance of curtailing travel and entertainment costs.
- Management should set a positive example by adhering strictly to the new policies.
- The limitations should apply equally to employees at all levels in the organization.

The table on this page puts Moreno's recommendations in perspective. Note how she called attention in the text to the most important sources of savings and also spelled out the costs required to achieve these results.

11

CONCLUSIONS AND RECOMMENDATIONS

Electrovision is currently spending $16 million per year on travel and entertainment. Although much of this spending is justified, the company's costs appear to be high relative to competitors', mainly because Electrovision has been generous with its travel benefits.

Electrovision's liberal approach to travel and entertainment was understandable during years of high profitability; however, the company is facing the prospect of declining profits for the next several years. Management is therefore motivated to cut costs in all areas of the business. Reducing T&E spending is particularly important because the impact of these costs on the bottom line will increase as a result of fare increases in the airline industry.

Electrovision should be able to reduce travel and entertainment costs by as much as 40 percent by taking four important steps:

1. *Institute tighter spending controls.*   Management should hire a director of travel and entertainment who will assume overall responsibility for T&E activities. Within the next six months, this director should develop a written travel policy, institute a T&E budget and a cost-control system, and retain a professional, business-oriented travel agency that will optimize arrangements with travel providers.
2. *Reduce unnecessary travel and entertainment.*   Electrovision should encourage employees to economize on travel and entertainment spending. Management can accomplish this by authorizing fewer trips and by urging employees to be more conservative in their spending.
3. *Obtain lowest rates from travel providers.*   Electrovision should also focus on obtaining the best rates on airline tickets, hotel rooms, and rental cars. By channeling all arrangements through a professional travel agency, the company can optimize its choices and gain clout in negotiating preferred rates.
4. *Replace travel with technological alternatives.*   With the number of computers already installed in our facilities, it seems likely that we could take advantage of desktop videoconferencing and other distance-meeting tools. This won't be quite as feasible with customer sites, since these systems require compatible equipment at both ends of a connection, but it is certainly a possibility for communication with Electrovision's own sites.

Because these measures may be unpopular with employees, management should make a concerted effort to explain the importance of reducing travel costs. The director of corporate communication should be given responsibility for developing a plan to communicate the need for employee cooperation.

Use a descriptive heading for the last section of the text. In informational reports, this section is generally called "Summary"; in analytical reports, it is called "Conclusions" or "Conclusions and Recommendations."

Emphasize the recommendations by presenting them in list format, if possible.

Do not introduce new facts in this section of the text.

Because Moreno organized her report around conclusions and recommendations, readers have already been introduced to them. Thus she summarizes her conclusions in the first two paragraphs. A simple list is enough to remind readers of the four main recommendations. In a longer report she might have divided the section into subsections, labeled "Conclusions" and "Recommendations," to distinguish between the two. If the report had been organized around logical arguments, this would have been the readers' first exposure to the conclusions and recommendations, and Moreno would have needed to develop them more fully.

Moreno decided this major supplementary part should allow a 2-inch top margin.

List references alphabetically by the author's last name or, when the author is unknown, by the title of the reference. See Component Chapter B for additional details on preparing reference lists.

SOURCES

Barker, Julie. "How to Rein in Group Travel Costs." *Successful Meetings* Feb. 1996: 31.

"Businesses Use Savvy Managers to Keep Travel Costs Down." *Christian Science Monitor* 17 July 1995: 4.

Dahl, Jonathan. "1995: The Year Travel Costs Took Off." *Wall Street Journal* 29 Dec. 1995: B6.

Gilligan, Edward P. "Trimming Your T&E Is Easier than You Think." *Managing Office Technology* Nov. 1995: 39–40.

Miller, Lisa. "Attention, Airline Ticket Shoppers." *Wall Street Journal* 7 July 1995: B6.

Phillips, Edward H. "Airlines Post Record Traffic." *Aviation Week & Space Technology* 8 Jan. 1996: 331.

Rowe, Irene Vlitos. "Global Solution for Cutting Travel Costs." *European* 12 Oct. 1995: 30.

Smith, Carol. "Rising, Erratic Air Fares Make Company Policy Vital." *Los Angeles Times* 2 Nov. 1995: D4.

"Travel Costs Under Pressure." *Purchasing* 15 Feb. 1996: 30.

12

Moreno's list of references follows the style recommended in *The MLA Style Manual.*

Prefatory Parts

The cover, title fly, title page, table of contents, and list of illustrations are handled the same as in other formal reports. However, other prefatory parts are quite different:

- *Copy of the RFP.* Instead of having a letter of authorization, a formal proposal may have a copy of the **request for proposal (RFP),** which is a letter or memo soliciting a proposal or bid for a particular project. The RFP is issued by the client to whom the proposal is being submitted and outlines what the proposal should cover. If the RFP includes detailed specifications, it may be too long to bind into the proposal; in that case, you may want to include only the introductory portion of the RFP. Another option is to omit the RFP and simply refer to it in your letter of transmittal.

- *Letter of transmittal.* The way you handle the letter of transmittal depends on whether the proposal is solicited or unsolicited. If the proposal is solicited, the transmittal letter follows the pattern for good-news messages, highlighting those aspects of your proposal that may give you a competitive advantage. If the proposal is unsolicited, the transmittal letter takes on added importance; in fact, it may be all the client reads. The letter must persuade the reader that you have something worthwhile to offer, something that justifies the time required to read the entire proposal. The transmittal letter for an unsolicited proposal follows the pattern for persuasive messages (see Chapter 11).

- *Synopsis or executive summary.* Although you may include a synopsis or an executive summary for your reader's convenience if your proposal is quite long, these components are somewhat less useful in a formal proposal than they are in a formal report. If your proposal is unsolicited, your transmittal letter will already have caught the reader's interest, making a synopsis or an executive summary pointless. It may also be pointless if your proposal is solicited, because the reader is already committed to studying the text to find out how you propose to satisfy the terms of a contract. The introduction to a solicited proposal would provide an adequate preview of the contents.

> Formal proposals contain most of the same prefatory parts as other formal reports.
>
> Use a copy of the request for proposal in place of the letter of authorization.
>
> Use the good-news pattern for the letter of transmittal if the proposal is solicited; use the persuasive plan if the proposal is unsolicited.
>
> Most proposals do not require a synopsis or an executive summary.

Text of the Proposal

The text of a proposal performs two essential functions: It persuades the client to award you a contract, and it spells out the terms of that contract. The trick is to sell the client on your ideas without making promises that will haunt you later.

If the proposal is unsolicited, you have some latitude in arranging the text. However, the organization of a solicited proposal is governed by the request for proposal. Most RFPs spell out precisely what you should cover, and in what order, so that all bids will be similar in form. This uniformity enables the client to evaluate the competing proposals in a systematic way. In fact, in many organizations a team of evaluators splits up the proposals and looks at various sections. An engineer might review the technical portions of all the proposals submitted, and an accountant might review the cost estimates.

> A proposal is both a selling tool and a contractual commitment.
>
> Follow the instructions presented in the RFP.

Introduction

The introduction orients readers to the rest of the proposal. It identifies your organization and your purpose and outlines the remainder of the text. If the proposal is solicited, the introduction should refer to the RFP; if not, it should mention any factors that led you to submit the bid. You might refer to previous conversations you've had with the client, or you might mention mutual acquaintances. Subheadings often include the following:

> In the introduction, establish the need for action and summarize the key benefits of your proposal.

- ***Background or statement of the problem.*** Briefly reviews the client's situation, worded to establish the need for action. In business selling situations, the reader may not have the same perception of the problem as the writer has. With unsolicited proposals, potential clients and other readers may not even think they have a problem. You have to convince them a problem exists before you can convince them to accept your solution. You can do this by discussing the reader's current situation and explaining how things could be better—in a way that is meaningful to your reader.

- ***Overview of approach.*** Highlights your key selling points and their benefits, showing how your proposal will solve the client's problem. The heading for this section might also be "Preliminary Analysis" or some other wording that will identify this section as a summary of your solution to the problem.

- ***Scope.*** States the boundaries of the study, what you will and will not do. This brief section may also be labeled "Delimitations."

- ***Report organization.*** Orients the reader to the remainder of the proposal and calls attention to the major divisions of thought.

Body

The core of the proposal is the body, which has the same purpose as the body of other reports. In a proposal, however, the body must cover some specific information:

In the approach section, demonstrate the superiority of your ideas, products, or services.

- ***Proposed approach.*** May also be titled "Technical Proposal," "Research Design," "Issues for Analysis," or "Work Statement." Regardless of the heading, this section is a description of what you have to offer: your concept, product, or service. If you're proposing to develop a new airplane, you might describe your preliminary design by using drawings or calculations to demonstrate the soundness of your solution. To convince the client that your proposal has merit, focus on the strengths of your product in relation to the client's needs. Point out any advantages that you have over your competitors. In this example, you might describe how your plane's unique wing design provides superior fuel economy, a particularly important feature specified in the client's request for proposal.

Use the work plan to describe the tasks to be completed under the terms of the contract.

- ***Work plan.*** Describes how you will accomplish the work that must be done (necessary unless you're proposing to provide a standard, off-the-shelf item). For each phase of the work plan, describe the steps you'll take, their timing, the methods or resources you'll use, and the person or persons who will be responsible. Indicate any critical dates when portions of the work will be completed. If your proposal is accepted, the work plan will become contractually binding. Any slippage in the proposed schedule may jeopardize the contract or cost your organization a considerable amount of money. Therefore don't promise to deliver more than you can realistically achieve within a given period.

In the qualifications section, demonstrate that you have the personnel, facilities, and experience to do a competent job.

- ***Statement of qualifications.*** Describes your organization's experience, personnel, and facilities in relation to the client's needs. If you work for a large organization that frequently submits proposals, you can usually borrow much of this section intact from previous proposals. Be sure, however, to tailor any of this boilerplate material to suit the situation. The qualifications section can be an important selling point, and it deserves to be handled carefully.

The more detailed your cost proposal is, the more credibility your estimates will have.

- ***Costs.*** Typically has few words and many numbers but can make or break the proposal. If your price is out of line, the client will probably reject your bid. However, before you deliver a low bid, remember that you'll have to live with the price you quote in the proposal. It's rarely worthwhile to win a contract if you're doomed to lose money on the job. Because it's often difficult to estimate costs on experimental projects, the client will be looking for evidence that your costs are realistic. Break down the costs in detail so that the client can see how you got your numbers: so much for labor, so much for materials, so much for overhead.

In a formal proposal it pays to be as thorough and accurate as possible. Carefully selected detail enhances your credibility. So does successful completion of any task you promise to perform.

Summary or Conclusion

You may want to include a summary or conclusion section because it's your last opportunity to persuade the reader to accept your proposal. Summarize the merits of your approach, reemphasize why you and your firm are the ones to do the work, and stress the benefits. Make this section relatively brief, assertive, and confident. To review the ideas and procedures presented in this chapter, consult the Checklist for Formal Reports and Proposals.

SUMMARY

Preparing a formal report or proposal requires a team effort. Be sure to allow enough time for the various phases in the production process. Once you've sent off your report, don't expect a positive response every time.

It's up to you to make sure your report has all the necessary components. Long formal reports have a greater number of separate elements. The text of the report (introduction, body, and final summary/conclusions/recommendations) is usually prepared first. Various prefatory and supplementary parts—such as the cover, title page, table of contents, appendixes, and bibliography—are added as needed, depending on the length and formality of the document.

Formal proposals are prepared in much the same way as other formal reports, although they differ somewhat in prefatory parts, text elements, and supplementary parts.

COMMUNICATION CHALLENGES AT THE ROCKY MOUNTAIN INSTITUTE

Although they've worked as consultants for governments, utilities, and corporations around the world, Hunter and Amory Lovins have turned down consulting jobs that would prevent them from republishing the resulting reports. They want to guard against anyone's *burying* RMI research that could benefit the public, explains Hunter. Now that the EPA report is finished, RMI is preparing to republish it for wider distribution. In addition, Amory is working on a report that will probably stir international controversy.

INDIVIDUAL CHALLENGE: Hunter wants to be sure that the EPA report gets to all the water utilities, municipalities, and rural governments that could benefit from implementing efficiency measures. She plans to republish the report under a new title, *Water Efficiency—A Resource for Utility Managers, Community Planners,*

and Other Decisionmakers, and she'll be mailing it directly to a list of individuals responsible for water-usage policies throughout the United States. Hunter has asked you to write a new letter of transmittal directed to this audience. Be sure to mention that the report was produced by RMI "through cooperative agreement with the U.S. Environmental Protection Agency, Office of Water, Office of Wastewater Enforcement and Compliance."

TEAM CHALLENGE: Amory Lovins has researched and written a groundbreaking treatise proving that plutonium waste from nuclear power reactors can be used to build nuclear weapons—a finding contrary to public reassurances made by some officials in the nuclear power industry. The implication of Amory's work is that any government that helps developing nations gain energy through nuclear power programs is also,

CHECKLIST FOR FORMAL REPORTS AND PROPOSALS

A. QUALITY OF THE RESEARCH
1. Define the problem clearly.
2. State the purpose of the document.
3. Identify all relevant issues.
4. Accumulate evidence pertaining to each issue.
5. Check evidence for accuracy, currency, and reliability.
6. Justify your conclusions by the evidence.
   a. Do not omit or distort evidence in order to support your point of view.
   b. Identify and justify all assumptions.

B. PREPARATION OF REPORTS AND PROPOSALS
1. Choose a format and length that are appropriate to your audience and the subject.
2. Prepare a sturdy, attractive cover.
   a. Label the cover clearly with the title of the document.
   b. Use a title that tells the audience exactly what the document is about.
3. Provide all necessary information on the title page.
   a. Include the full title of the document.
   b. Include the name, title, and affiliation of the recipient.
   c. Give the name, title, and affiliation of the author.
   d. Provide the date of submission.
   e. Balance the information in blocks on the page.
4. Include a copy of the letter of authorization or request for proposal, if appropriate.
5. Prepare a letter or memo of transmittal.
   a. Use memo format for internal documents.
   b. Use letter format for external documents.
   c. Include the transmittal letter in only some copies if it contains sensitive or personal information suitable for some but not all readers.
   d. Place the transmittal letter right before the table of contents.
   e. Use the good-news plan for solicited proposals and other reports; use the persuasive plan for unsolicited proposals.
   f. Word the letter to "convey" the document officially to the readers; refer to the authorization; and discuss the purpose, scope, background, sources and methods, and limitations.

   g. Mention any special points that warrant readers' attention.
   h. If you use direct order, summarize conclusions and recommendations (unless they are included in a synopsis).
   i. Acknowledge all who were especially helpful in preparing the document.
   j. Close with thanks, offer to be of further assistance, and suggest future projects, if appropriate.
6. Prepare the table of contents.
   a. Include all first-level headings (and all second-level headings or perhaps all second- and third-level headings).
   b. Give the page number of each heading.
   c. Word all headings exactly as they appear in the text.
   d. Include the synopsis (if there is one) and supplementary parts in the table of contents.
   e. Number the table of contents and all prefatory pages with lowercase roman numerals centered at the bottom of the page.
7. Prepare a list of illustrations if you have four visual aids or more.
   a. Put the list in the same format as the table of contents.
   b. Identify visual aids either directly beneath the table of contents or on a separate page under the heading "List of Illustrations."
8. Develop a synopsis or an executive summary if the document is long and formal.
   a. Tailor the synopsis or executive summary to the document's length and tone.
   b. Condense the main points of the document, using either the informative approach or the descriptive approach, according to the guidelines in this chapter.
   c. Present the points in the synopsis in the same order as they appear in the document. Remember that an executive summary can deviate from the order of points made in the report.
9. Prepare the introduction to the text.
   a. Leave a 2-inch margin at the top of the page, and center the title of the document.

b. In a long document (ten pages or more), type the first-level heading "Introduction" three lines below the title.

c. In a short document (fewer than ten pages), begin typing three lines below the title of the report or proposal without the heading "Introduction."

d. Discuss the authorization (unless it's covered in the letter of transmittal), purpose, scope, background, sources and methods, definitions, limitations, and text organization.

10. Prepare the body of the document.

a. Carefully select the organizational plan (see Chapter 15).

b. Use either a personal or an impersonal tone consistently.

c. Use either a past or a present time perspective consistently.

d. Follow a consistent format in typing headings of different levels, using a company format guide, a sample proposal or report, or the format in this textbook as a model (see Component Chapter A).

e. Express comparable (same-level) headings in any given section in parallel grammatical form.

f. Group ideas into logical categories.

g. Tie sections together with transitional words, sentences, and paragraphs.

h. Give ideas of equal importance roughly equal space.

i. Avoid overly technical, pretentious, or vague language.

j. Develop each paragraph around a topic sentence.

k. Make sure all ideas in each paragraph are related.

l. Double-space if longer than ten pages.

m. For documents bound on the left, number all pages with arabic numerals in the upper right-hand corner (except for the first page, where the number is centered 1 inch from the bottom); for top-bound documents, number all pages with arabic numerals centered 1 inch from the bottom.

11. Incorporate visual aids into the text.

a. Number visual aids consecutively throughout the text, numbering tables and figures (other visual aids) separately if that style is preferred.

b. Develop explicit titles for all visual aids except in-text tables.

c. Refer to each visual aid in the text, and emphasize the significance of the data.

d. Place visual aids as soon after their textual explanations as possible, or group them at the ends of chapters or at the end of the document for easy reference.

12. Conclude the text of reports and proposals with a summary and, if appropriate, conclusions and recommendations.

a. In a summary, recap the findings and explanations already presented.

b. Place conclusions and recommendations in their order of logic or importance, preferably in list format.

c. To induce action, explain in the recommendations section who should do what, when, where, and how.

d. If appropriate, point up the benefits of action, to leave readers with the motivation to follow recommendations.

13. Document all material quoted or paraphrased from secondary sources, using a consistent format (see Component Chapter B).

14. Include appendixes at the end of the document to provide useful and detailed information that is of interest to some but not all readers.

a. Give each appendix a title, such as "Questionnaire" or "Names and Addresses of Survey Participants."

b. If there is more than one appendix, number or letter them consecutively in the order they're referred to in the text.

c. Type appendixes in a format consistent with the text of the report or proposal.

15. Include a bibliography if it seems that readers would benefit or the document would gain credibility.

a. Type the bibliography on a separate page headed "Bibliography" or "Sources."

b. Alphabetize bibliography entries.

c. Use a consistent format for the bibliography (see Component Chapter B).

inadvertently, providing that nation with the tools to build nuclear weapons. Amory believes it's crucial for government policymakers around the world to understand this implication. He's assigned your team the job of organizing and formatting his treatise in report form, to be published by RMI and distributed to government officials internationally. Discuss the organizational plan, style, length, and format appropriate for this report. What prefatory and supplementary parts will the report require? What visual aids might be included? Make a list of the points the letter of transmittal should cover. Remember that this report will be crossing cultural boundaries; talk over any additional steps you might take to ensure that Amory's message is clear.[5]

CRITICAL THINKING QUESTIONS

1. What are the advantages and disadvantages of managers and professional staffers (e.g., lawyers, accountants, engineers, and consultants) using such computer tools as page layout programs, graphic design software, and scanners? Explain your answer.

2. When businesspeople prepare unsolicited proposals, they often have to make assumptions about timing and other issues that are under the client's control. Where in the formal proposal should these assumptions be included? Why?

3. Under what circumstances would you include more than one index in a lengthy report? Explain your answer.

4. If you were submitting a solicited proposal to build an indoor pool, would you include as references the names and addresses of other clients for whom you recently built similar pools? Would you include these references in an unsolicited proposal? Where in either proposal would you include these references? Why?

5. How would you report on a confidential survey in which employees rated their managers' capabilities? Employees and managers alike expect to see the results. Would you give the same report to employees and managers? What components would you include or exclude for each audience? Explain your choices.

6. Would you include a letter of authorization with a periodic personal activity report? What about a letter of transmittal? Why or why not?

CASES

Short Formal Reports

RESEARCH

UPWARD COMMUNICATION

1. What do frequent travelers want? Report using statistical data to analyze attitudes about lodging You are a research assistant for the American Hotel & Motel Association, which recently commissioned a survey of frequent travelers and lodging satisfaction. The study's purpose was to provide member hotels and motels with up-to-date data on the demographics and lodging preferences of frequent travelers. The hotels could use this information to adapt their services to changing consumer needs.

The results presented in Tables 18.1, 18.2, and 18.3 were obtained from detailed questionnaires mailed to people identified as "frequent travelers": male or female heads of households who had stayed one or more nights at any hotel or motel five or more times in the previous 12 months.

Your task: Write a report to the president of your organization that explains the results of the survey and its implications for hotels that wish to cater specifically to frequent travelers. What trends should they be concerned about? What changes should they make? Justify your conclusions and your recommendations by referring to the data in the tables.[6]

HUMAN RESOURCES

UPWARD COMMUNICATION

2. Keeping an eye on the kids: Report that summarizes survey data for an on-site day-care facility You're the human resources manager at a 200-employee manufacturing firm. Employees at your company have expressed a strong desire for some kind of on-site child-care facility. You're in charge of investigating the situation and developing the company's response. You know that any facility will require a balance between what the company can afford to pay and what employees are willing to pay, relative to other day-care alternatives.

TABLE 18.1

FREQUENT TRAVELER DEMO- GRAPHICS: TRENDS OVER TIME

Demographic Characteristics	1992	1994	1996
Age			
Under 35 years	21%	28%	22%
35–50 years	40	42	45
Over 50 years	38	30	33
Gender			
Male	68	64	61
Female	32	36	39
Annual Household Income			
Less than $20,000	26	16	5
$20,000–$29,999	30	18	12
$30,000–$49,999	32	40	31
$50,000 or more	12	26	52
Number of Trips			
5–10 trips	70	63	64
More than 10 trips	30	37	35
Number of Nights Stayed			
5–10 nights	19	10	8
11–20 nights	35	31	30
21–30 nights	21	21	25
31 or more nights	25	38	37
Type of Travel			
Business	73	74	69
Pleasure	27	26	31

TABLE 18.2

HOTEL SELECTION FACTORS

Factor	Rank in Initial Selection	Rank in Initial Decision
Clean appearance	1	1
Convenient location	2	3
Price/reasonable rate	3	4
Good service	4	2
Name/reputation	5	7
Security/safety	6	5
Company/family discount	7	6
Reservation service	8	8
Recommendation	9	10
Recreational facilities	10	9
Chain frequency program	11	11
Business facilities	12	13
Other	13	12

TABLE 18.3

IMPORTANCE OF HOTEL SERVICES

Facilities, Services, and Amenities	Likely to Use All or Most of the Time		
	Total	*Male*	*Female*
Television	94%	95%	93%
Bar soap	89	89	86
Restaurant/coffee shop	83	81	85
More than 2 towels	81	79	84
Personal-care amenities	80	78	82
Choice of smoking/ nonsmoking room	78	76	82
Wake-up call	77	78	75
Complimentary newspaper	75	78	71
In-room refrigerator	63	59	68
In-room coffeemaker	59	57	62
Pool	49	48	52
Auto check-in	40	40	41
Hair dryer	36	32	43
Auto check-out	33	35	33
In-room safety deposit box	29	28	34
Bar/lounge	28	30	25
Room service	28	26	31
Robes	27	24	21
Pay TV	23	26	21
Exercise facilities	22	24	21
Check cashing	21	18	24
VCR	15	16	13
Executive-level rooms	14	16	10
Valet dry cleaning	10	12	8
Coin laundry	8	7	10
Video games	8	8	6
Fax machine	7	7	7
Typing services	3	3	2
Day-care facilities	2	1	4

Table 18.4 indicates trends in on-site day care among local employers. Because you have to compete with other organizations for employees, offering comparable employee benefits such as on-site day care is an important business decision. Tables 18.5, 18.6, and 18.7 show the data collected in an internal employee survey.

Your task: Write a report to your boss summarizing the survey results and suggesting the next step in the planning process.

TABLE 18.4

DAY-CARE FACILITIES OFFERED BY LOCAL EMPLOYERS

Organization Type	Percentage with On-Site Day Care	
	1990	*1995*
By Industry		
Retailing	6%	14%
Consumer services	8	11
Business services	11	25
Government and nonprofit	15	17
Manufacturing	27	30
By Size		
Fewer than 50 employees	2	2
51–100 employees	5	6
101–250 employees	12	14
251–500 employees	28	32
More than 500 employees	35	45

TABLE 18.5

AGES OF EMPLOYEE DEPENDENTS

Age Range	Number of Children
Under 1	14
2–3	32
4–5	25
6–7	22
8–9	13
10–11	28
Over 12	112

TABLE 18.6

SERVICES AND FEATURES DESIRED IN AN ON-SITE DAY-CARE FACILITY

Service or Feature	Must Have	Nice to Have	Not Important
Nurse	3%	77%	0%
Arts and crafts	54	41	5
Outdoor play area	36	52	12
Educational activities	25	59	16
Organized games and contests	12	62	26
Sleeping arrangements	34	34	32
Evening hours (after 6 P.M.)	33	52	15
Early morning hours (before 8 A.M.)	7	48	45
Snacks	74	21	5
Lunch	88	12	0

TABLE 18.7

AMOUNT EMPLOYEES ARE WILLING TO PAY

Per Child per Month	Percentage of Employees Willing to Pay
Less than $100	100%
$101–$200	95
$201–$300	89
$301–$400	64
$401–$500	50
$501–$600	28
More than $600	12

STRATEGIC PLANNING

UPWARD COMMUNICATION

3. Who's eating what: Report using statistical data to analyze industry trends   You are the assistant to Christie Thurber, the president of Restaurant Association of America, which recently commissioned a study of consumer eating habits. The association undertakes studies like these so that it can relay the results to its member restaurants. The restaurants can then adapt to suit changing consumer needs.

To get the results shown in Tables 18.8, 18.9, and 18.10, telephone interviews were conducted with a na-tionwide sample of 1,035 people over 18. The interviewers prefaced their questions with this statement:

> In recent years some people say they have changed their diets by *increasing* their consumption of fruits, vegetables, and whole grains and by *decreasing* their consumption of refined sugar, animal fats, and salts.

Your task: Write a report to your boss that explains the results of the survey and its implications for restau-

TABLE 18.8

PERCENTAGE OF CONSUMERS WHO HAVE CHANGED EATING HABITS AT HOME

Demographic Characteristics	Yes	No	Don't Know	Demographic Characteristics	Yes	No	Don't Know
Gender				**Women's Employment Status**			
Male	54%	46%	—%	Employed full-time	69	31	—
Female	67	33	—	Employed part-time	65	35	—
				Not employed	66	34	—
Age							
18–24 years	48	52	—	**Region**			
25–34 years	61	38	1	East	65	34	1
35–49 years	64	36	—	Midwest	59	41	—
50–64 years	60	40	—	South	52	48	—
65 years and older	65	35	—	West	66	34	—
Marital Status				**Frequency of Eating Out in Average Week**			
Married	62	38	—	None	56	44	—
Not married	57	43	—	One	64	35	1
				Two or three	62	38	—
Education				Four or more	54	45	1
College graduate	69	31	—				
High school graduate	62	38	—				
Not high school graduate	46	54	—				
Annual Household Income							
$30,000 and over	67	33	—				
$20,000–29,999	61	38	1				
$15,000–19,999	60	40	—				
Under $15,000	60	40	—				

TABLE 18.9

PERCENTAGE OF CONSUMERS WHO HAVE CHANGED EATING HABITS AT RESTAURANTS OR OTHER EATING PLACES

Demographic Characteristics	Yes	No	Don't Know	Demographic Characteristics	Yes	No	Don't Know
Gender				**Women's Employment Status**			
Male	35%	64%	1%	Employed full-time	51	49	—
Female	44	54	2	Employed part-time	42	58	—
				Not employed	38	59	3
Age							
18–24 years	30	70	—	**Region**			
25–34 years	42	57	1	East	41	56	3
35–49 years	41	58	1	Midwest	42	57	1
50–64 years	45	54	1	South	35	64	1
65 years and older	39	58	3	West	42	58	—
Marital Status				**Frequency of Eating Out in Average Week**			
Married	41	58	1	None	31	65	4
Not married	38	61	1	One	40	59	1
				Two or three	45	55	—
Education				Four or more	40	60	—
College graduate	47	52	1				
High school graduate	41	58	1				
Not high school graduate	27	70	3				
Annual Household Income							
$30,000 and over	48	51	1				
$20,000–$29,999	39	60	1				
$15,000–$19,999	33	67	—				
Under $15,000	42	55	3				

TABLE 18.10

PERCENTAGE OF CONSUMERS WHO HAVE MADE VARIOUS TYPES OF CHANGES WHEN DINING OUT

Demographic Characteristics	Less Salt	More Salt	Less Sugar	More Vegetables	More Salads	Fewer Fats
Age						
18–34	20%	16%	21%	24%	24%	12%
35–49	26	18	21	16	16	16
50 and older	31	25	17	16	12	20
Education						
College graduate	18	28	20	23	15	15
Not a college graduate	28	17	19	17	19	16
Annual Household Income						
$30,000 and over	25	27	21	18	13	17
$15,000–29,999	22	17	22	20	21	18
Under $15,000	31	16	19	19	21	9
Women's Employment Status						
Employed	23	24	19	14	20	11
Not employed	31	16	14	20	21	18
Region						
East	24	22	18	17	20	13
Midwest	30	19	21	15	21	23
South	17	22	18	25	13	13
West	30	17	20	18	14	14
Frequency of Eating Out in Average Week						
None	32	22	13	18	16	22
One	30	14	21	24	19	13
Two or three	22	18	23	14	16	18
Four or more	19	20	17	19	21	12
Average	25	20	20	18	18	16

rants. What trends in eating habits should they be concerned about? What changes should they make? Justify your conclusions and your recommendations by referring to the data in the tables.

ADVERTISING

DOWNWARD COMMUNICATION

4. Sailing past the sunsets: Report using statistical data to suggest a new advertising strategy As manager of Distant Dreams, a travel agency in Waco, Texas, you are interested in the information in Table 18.11. It seems dollar income is shifting toward the 35–44 age group. Tables 18.12 and 18.13 are also broken down by age group.

Traditionally, your agency has concentrated its advertising on those nearing retirement, people who are closing out successful careers and now have the time and money to vacation abroad. After examining the three sets of data, however, it occurs to you that a major shift in emphasis is desirable.

Your task: Write a report to Mary Henderson, who writes your advertisements, explaining why future ads should still be directed to people who want to explore far reaches of the world but to people besides those in their fifties and sixties. Justify your explanation by referring to the data you have examined.

MANAGEMENT CONSULTING

INTERPERSONAL COMMUNICATION

5. Picking the better path: Report assisting a client in a career choice You are employed by Open Options, a career-counseling firm, and your main function is to

TABLE 18.11
PERCENTAGE OF TOTAL U.S. HOUSEHOLD INCOME EARNED BY VARIOUS AGE GROUPS

Age Group	1985	1990	1995
25–34	23%	24%	26%
35–44	22	25	28
45–54	22	21	19
55–64	19	17	15
Over 65	14	13	12

TABLE 18.12
PREFERENCES IN TRAVEL AMONG VARIOUS AGE GROUPS

Travel Interests	Age Group 18–34	35–54	55+
I am more interested in excitement and stimulation than rest and relaxation.	67%	42%	38%
I prefer to go where I haven't been before.	62	58	48
I like adventuresome travel.	62	45	32
I love foreign and exotic things.	41	25	21
Vacation is a time for self-indulgence, regardless of the cost.	31	16	14
I don't see the need for a travel agent.	67	63	52

TABLE 18.13
BASIC DESIRE FOR TRAVEL AMONG VARIOUS AGE GROUPS

Attitude Toward Travel	Age Group 18–34	35–54	55+
Travel is one of the most rewarding and enjoyable things one can do.	71%	69%	66%
I love the idea of traveling and do so at every opportunity.	66	59	48
I often feel the need to get away from everything.	56	55	33

help clients make career choices. Today a client with the same name as yours (a truly curious coincidence!) came to your office and asked for help deciding between two careers, careers that you yourself had been interested in (an even greater coincidence!).

Your task: Do some research on the two careers and then prepare a short report that your client can study. Your report should compare at least five major areas, such as salary, working conditions, and education required. Interview the client to understand her or his personal preferences regarding each of the five areas. For example, what is the minimum salary the client will accept? By comparing the client's preferences with the research material you collect, such as salary data, you will have a basis for concluding which of the two careers is best. The report should end with a career recommendation.

MARKETING
INTERCULTURAL COMMUNICATION

6. Selling overseas: Report on the prospects for marketing a product in another country Select (a) a product and (b) a country. The product might be a novelty item that you own (an inexpensive but accurate watch or clock, a desk organizer, or a coin bank). The country should be one that you are not now familiar with. Imagine that you are with the international sales department of the company that manufactures and sells the novelty item and that you are proposing to make it available in the country you have selected.

The first step is to learn as much as possible about the country where you plan to market the product. Check almanacs and encyclopedias for the most recent information, paying particular attention to descriptions of the social life of the inhabitants and their economic conditions. If your library carries resources such as *Yearbook of International Trade Statistics, Monthly Bulletin of Statistics,* or *Trade Statistics* (all put out by the United Nations), you may want to consult them. In addition, check the card catalog and recent periodical indexes for sources of additional information; look for (among other matters) cultural traditions that would encourage or discourage use of the product. If you have online access, check both Web sites and any relevant databases you can find.

Your task: Write a short report that describes the product you plan to market abroad, briefly describes the country you have selected, indicates the types of people in this country who would find the product attractive, explains how the product would be transported into the country (or possibly manufactured there if materials and labor are available), recommends a location for a regional sales center, and suggests how the product should be sold. Your report is to be submitted to the chief operating officer of the company, whose name you can either make up or find in a corporate directory. The report should include your conclusions (how the product will do in this new environment) and your recommendations for marketing (steps the company should take immediately and those it should develop later).

MARKETING

UPWARD COMMUNICATION

7. Who uses coupons? Report summarizing important demographics   You are employed by Supermarket Coupons Incorporated. Your company is interested in distributing its manufacturing client's coupons to supermarket customers in the most cost-conscious manner. Your boss is advocating using the Internet exclusively to deliver client's coupons. She believes that a major shift from the print media to computer media would result in substantial savings for all concerned (your company, your manufacturing clients, customers, and supermarkets). Your responsibility is to determine (a) which demographic groups (by age, sex, economic class, profession) use coupons received via postal service, newspapers, magazines, and in-store displays and then (b) whether these groups would be interested in downloading coupons from the Internet.

Here are a few Internet sources to get you started on your search. (Most sites provide an e-mail link that might be beneficial in obtaining additional sources of information for your report.)

- <http://www.interstate.net/gscable/demograp.html>
- <http://www.marketingtools.com/publications/AD/95-AD/9501af02.html>
- <http://www.xenon.chem.vidaho.edu/hypermail/demograph/0011.html>
- <http://www.marketingtools.com/ad_current/AD752.html>

Your task: Write a short formal report that summarizes your findings on which demographic groups use manufacturer's coupons and which of those groups would be interested in downloading coupons.

ADVERTISING

UPWARD COMMUNICATION

8. Is anyone out there listening? Report on radio advertising   Martha McCreary is a vice president at Knowles-Mead, a small stock brokerage house in your city. In order to increase its clientele, the firm has decided to run a series of radio advertisements designed to catch the attention of potential investors.

Knowing of your interest in local radio, Martha asks your advice. Of the local stations, which one or two would be best for the low-key, factual advertisements that her firm has in mind? At what times during the day and the week might these spots be most effective?

Your task: Listen systematically to three or four radio stations in your area to determine (a) what types of products their advertisers are generally selling, (b) what their programming generally consists of, and (c) what type of listener they seem to appeal to. Listen to each station at several times during the day and during the week. Chart your findings.

Then draft a formal report for Martha that contains the results of your research and your conclusions and recommendations. If the report is successful, Knowles-Mead should be able to choose the appropriate times and stations for a series of advertisements that would win new clients.

STRATEGIC PLANNING

PUBLIC SECTOR

9. A park inspection: Report on the condition of public facilities   As an employee of the city, you have been assigned to inspect some of its parks.

Your task: Visit a city park, and report back to your supervisor (Ben Willis, Commissioner of Parks) on the use and condition of the park that you have inspected. Your report should include at least the following information: the date and time of your inspection, a general description of the park and its facilities, an indication of who (if anyone) was on duty at the time of your inspection, an estimate of the number of people using the park at the time of your inspection, a breakdown by age and

activity of these people, conclusions about the general use and condition of the park, recommendations for making the park more useful or attractive, and a statement of any problems more significant than ordinary day-to-day maintenance (such as inadequate parking or inadequate facilities).

Show in your report that you have inspected the park carefully. Check the bolts in the swings (for rust, wear, or inadequate lubrication), and make other observations necessary for a conscientious inspection. Write factually. A serious inspector would write "The swing area was littered with 12 empty soda cans," not "The swing area was filthy."

Long Formal Reports Requiring No Additional Research

SMALL BUSINESS

INTERCULTURAL COMMUNICATION

10. Breaking U.S. boundaries: A report on the international trade efforts of small businesses Small business is a significant part of the U.S. economy. The over 20 million small businesses in the United States employ 58 percent of the private work force and account for nearly half of all new jobs. As a research analyst for the U.S. Chamber of Commerce in Washington, D.C., you have been asked to prepare a report on the extent to which U.S. small businesses are involved in international trade. The report's main function will be to help those in the chamber's publishing division (which produces *Nation's Business,* among other periodicals) decide whether to produce a regular publication for small-business operators about international trade. Other researchers will be preparing reports on the financing, circulation, and production aspects of producing such a magazine; your focus is on learning whether there is really a need for the magazine and, if so, what would constitute the target audience.

Your task: Write a formal report that presents the results of your findings about the current international trade efforts of small U.S. businesses, as displayed in Figures 18.3, 18.4, 18.5, 18.6, and 18.7. Your primary source for information is National Small Business United (NSBU), a private, nonprofit association representing more than 60,000 small businesses. Along with Arthur Andersen's Enterprise Group, NSBU has contracted with the Gallup Organization to conduct an ongoing research study of small businesses, including such aspects as demographics, business growth, access to credit, health-care programs, and tax issues. For the most recent survey, 634 questionnaires were returned out of 6,000 mailed to member businesses. The demographics of these businesses are presented in Tables 18.14, 18.15, and 18.16.

Your report should indicate not only what you consider the specific target market for the proposed publication but also what sorts of topics a publication aimed at this market should address.[7]

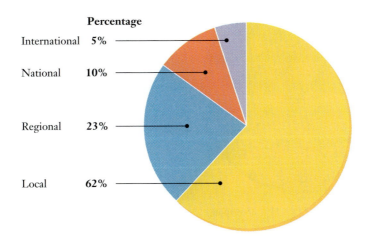

Percentage

International **5%**

National **10%**

Regional **23%**

Local **62%**

Figure 18.3
Extent of Small Business Involvement in Marketplace Levels

Figure 18.4
Marketplace Levels by Size of Company

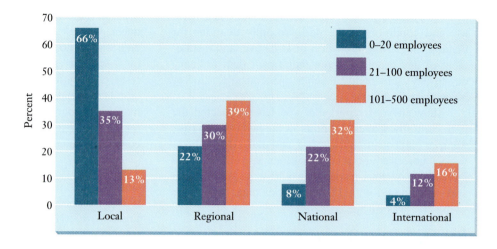

Figure 18.5
Marketplace Levels by Region of the United States

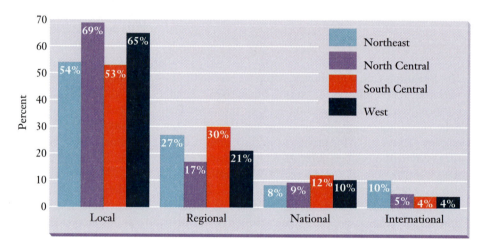

Figure 18.6
Importing and Exporting Goods and Services

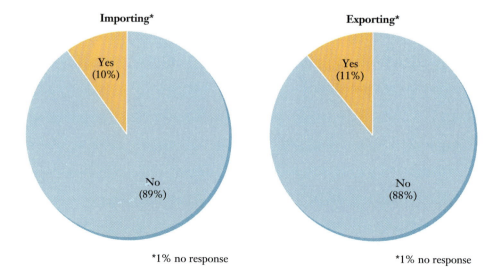

Figure 18.7
Barriers to Exporting by Region of the United States

TABLE 18.14
TYPES OF SMALL BUSINESSES RESPONDING

Type	Percentage
Retail trade	15%
Construction	12
Business services	12
Manufacturing	10
Insurance	9
Personal services	8
Social services	6
Wholesale distribution	4
Other	24

TABLE 18.16
BUSINESS SIZE BY ANNUAL SALES

Most Recent Fiscal Year Sales	Percentage of Businesses
Less than $200,000	31%
$200,000–$499,999	18
$500,000–$999,999	15
$1,000,000–$4,999,999	17
$5,000,000–$9,999,999	9
$10,000,000–$24,999,999	3
$25,000,000–$49,999,999	2
$50,000,000–$74,999,999	0
$75,000,000 or over	2

TABLE 18.15
BUSINESS SIZE BY NUMBER OF EMPLOYEES

Number of Employees	Percentage Full-Time	Percentage Part-time
0	8%	11%
1–5	56	41
6–10	14	6
11–20	5	3
21–50	9	5
51–100	2	1
101–500	1	4

CUSTOMER SERVICE

PROBLEM SOLVING

11. Customer service crisis: Report summarizing and explaining customer service problems You are the operations manager for Continental Security Systems (CSS), a mail-order supplier of home-security systems and components. Your customers are do-it-yourself homeowners who buy a wide range of motion sensors, automatic telephone dialers, glass breakage detectors, video cameras, and other devices.

The company's aggressive pricing has yielded spectacular growth in the last year, and everyone is scrambling to keep up with the orders that arrive every day. Unfortunately, customer service has often taken a back seat to filling those orders. Your boss, the company's founder and president, knows that service is slipping, and she wants you to solve the problem. You started with some internal and external surveys to assess the situation. Some of the more significant findings from the research are presented in Tables 18.17, 18.18, and 18.19.

Your task: Prepare a report that explains the data you collected in your research. Keep the report factual and objective; everyone knows that growth has strained the company's resources, so you have no need to place blame. (For the purposes of this exercise, feel free to make up any facts you need regarding the company.)

Long Formal Reports Requiring Additional Research

MANAGEMENT

UPWARD COMMUNICATION

12. Equipment purchase: Report on competitive product features   Say that your office or home needs some new equipment. Choose one of the following, and figure out which brand and model would be the best buy.

a. Cellular phone
b. Calculator
c. Telephone answering machine
d. Home security system
e. Photocopier
f. Personal computer
g. Word-processing software
h. Desktop scanner

Your task: Write a long formal report describing the features of the available alternatives, listing the benefits and drawbacks of each, and making a clear recommendation. Be sure to include a discussion of the factors on which you've based your decision (including cost, reliability, and so on).

PUBLIC RELATIONS

LAW

13. Is there any justice? Report critiquing legislation   Plenty of people complain about their state legislators, but few are specific about their complaints. Here's your chance.

Your task: Write a long formal report about a law that you believe should not have been enacted or should be

TABLE 18.17

CUSTOMER COMPLAINTS OVER THE LAST 12 MONTHS

Type of Complaint	Number of Occurrences	Percentage of total
Delays in responding	67	30%
Product malfunction	56	25
Missing parts	45	20
No answer when calling for help	32	14
Rude treatment	18	8
Overcharge	5	2

Note: Percentages don't add to 100 because of rounding

TABLE 18.18

HOW COMPLAINTS WERE RESOLVED

Resolution	Percentage
Employee receiving the phone call solved the problem	20%
Employee referred customer to his/her manager	30
Customer eventually solved the problem by himself/herself	12
Unable to solve problem	23
Resolution unknown	15

TABLE 18.19

CUSTOMER PERCEPTIONS AND OPINIONS

Statement	Percentage That Agree	Percentage That Disagree
CSS offers a competitive level of customer service	12%	88%
I recommended CSS to friends and colleagues	4	96
I plan to continue buying from CSS	15	85
I enjoy doing business with CSS	9	91

enacted. Be objective. Write the report using specific facts to support your beliefs. Reach conclusions and offer your recommendation at the end of the report. As a final step send a copy of the report to an appropriate state official or legislator.

14. Employment opportunities: Report comparing two employers   For a student, the task of getting a job looms large. Because you don't want just any job, you're going to be doing some research.

Your task: Prepare a lengthy comparative study of two organizations that you might like to work for. Using annual reports, brochures, discussions with present or past employees, and all the other types of company information described in Chapter 12, analyze the suitability of these organizations to your own career goals and preferences for work environment. At the end of the report, recommend the best company to work for.

15. Group effort: Report on a large-scale topic   The following topics may be too big for any one person, yet they need to be investigated:

a. A demographic profile (age, gender, socioeconomic status, residence, employment, educational background, and the like) of the students at your college or university
b. The best part-time employment opportunities in your community
c. The best of two or three health clubs or gyms in your community
d. Actions that can be taken in your community or state to combat alcohol (or other drug) abuse
e. Improvements that could be made in the food service at your college or university
f. Your college's or university's image in the community and ways to improve it
g. Your community's strengths and weaknesses in attracting new businesses

Your task: Because these topics require considerable research, your instructor may wish to form groups to work on each. If your group writes a report on the first topic, summarize your findings at the end of the report. For all the other topics, reach conclusions and make recommendations in the report.

16. Secondary sources: Report based on library research   Perhaps one of the following questions has been keeping you awake at night:

a. What's the best way for someone in your financial situation to invest a $5,000 inheritance?
b. What can be done about parking problems on campus?
c. Of three careers that appeal to you, which best suits you?
d. How do other consumers regard a product that you use frequently?
e. Which of three cities that you might like to live in seems most attractive?
f. What's the surest and easiest route to becoming a millionaire?

Your task: Answer one of these questions, using secondary sources for information. Be sure to document your sources in the correct form. Give conclusions and recommendations in your report.

17. Business problem: Report relating to business   In the business or profession that you are in or are studying for, there are undoubtedly some issues that have not been resolved.

Your task: Choose one of these problems and write a long formal report on it, complete with your own conclusions and recommendations.

Formal Proposals

18. Top dogs: Proposal to furnish puppies to Docktor Pet Centers   You are the business manager for Sandy's Kennels of Alma, Kansas, one of the country's largest dog-breeding operations. Every year you sell 7,500 puppies to pet shops around the country, at an average price of $130 per dog. The pet stores then sell the dogs for $225 to $300, depending on the breed.

Your business involves both breeding and reselling animals. In your own kennels you raise 52 kinds of dogs;

in addition, you buy dogs from other breeders at approximately $60 per dog and resell them to pet stores. Your dogs are all pedigreed animals with American Kennel Club (AKC) papers. In addition, they come with all the required puppy vaccinations and are guaranteed to be healthy.

For several years you've been trying to win a long-term contract to supply puppies to Docktor Pet Centers, the country's largest pet-store chain. Finally, you've been invited to submit a proposal to provide 2,000 dogs per year to Docktor Pet's 220 retail outlets. The specifications stipulate that you will ship approximately 150 dogs per month from January through October and 250 dogs in November and in December. The puppies should be eight to ten weeks old at the time of shipment and should have all the necessary shots and AKC papers. Docktor is willing to accept a variety of breeds but has requested that each shipment contain a mix of large and small dogs and males and females. The chain is willing to pay from $115 to $130 per dog, depending on the breed.

Your task: Using your imagination to supply the details, write a proposal describing your plan to provide the dogs.[8]

PROMOTION
CUSTOMER RELATIONS

19. A new kind of campus "party": Proposal to hold a promotional event at colleges   Marketers of all kinds have their eyes on college students. Besides being

consumers of a wide variety of products, students seem to have the discretionary funds to be able to purchase everything from stereo equipment to cosmetics to snack foods. The problem for marketers is reaching their targets—college students are notoriously difficult for advertisers to get to.

A new approach is meeting with some success: the product festival. College Fest, a two-day event held at a Massachusetts convention center, drew some 19,000 students from 50 Boston-area colleges, who each paid a $5 admission fee. While rock bands played, 150 companies ranging from Guess? to Revlon to Toyota pushed their products via contests, free samples, and such activities as mechanical bull rides and complimentary manicures. Most of the companies were enthusiastic, since the festival allowed target consumers to interact directly with their products and even make purchases on the spot.

Your employer, MarketSource Corporation, based in Cranbury, New Jersey, is also engaged in college "party marketing," but on a smaller scale. MarketSource's Campus Fest is held directly on college campuses, where 20 to 25 companies set up their booths under a giant tent. Exhibitors are encouraged to provide activities and displays that contribute to the festival atmosphere. So far, Campus Fest has been held at more than 60 universities all over the United States.

Your task: Write a proposal that can be sent to colleges and universities where MarketSource would like to hold Campus Fests. Use your imagination to provide details about such things as the benefits to the university, the types of companies that will participate, and the activities that the companies will sponsor.[9]

HUMAN RESOURCES
UPWARD COMMUNICATION

20. A losing proposition: Proposal to run a weight-loss program for General Electric employees   One of your duties as a marketing representative for Weight Watchers International is to encourage corporations to sponsor weight-loss programs for their employees. You are a firm believer in the value of such programs because you have seen what they can do for a company's employees. As a result of one of your recent five-week, company-sponsored programs, a group of 110 employees lost a total of 750 pounds. At the conclusion of the program you had the satisfaction of knowing that you had left a healthier, happier staff. One woman who lost 20 pounds said, "You've changed my life!"

Weight Watchers' outstanding reputation in the diet industry helps make your job relatively easy. The program involves a combination of psychological support and nutritional counseling. Groups of dieters meet once a week to discuss their eating problems, check their progress, and learn good eating habits. A group leader, usually a successful Weight Watchers "graduate," runs the meeting and provides nutritional information and moral support. Participants are encouraged to use a variety of Weight Watchers products, which include cookbooks and frozen dinners.

The approach sounds simple, but it works. Since the organization was founded in 1963, 25 million people have joined Weight Watchers. Some 15,000 meetings are held each week, and over 700,000 dieters are currently enrolled in the program.

You recently met with the director of employee health and safety at General Electric headquarters in Fairfield, Connecticut. During your meeting you proposed that Weight Watchers conduct a seven-week weight-loss program for GE employees. You suggested that the sessions be held during lunch hour and that as many employees as possible be encouraged to participate. You would subdivide the enrollees into groups of 25 to facilitate discussions. Each group would be headed by a professional Weight Watchers trainer. Participants would meet for an hour each day to share low-calorie lunches, prepared by the GE cafeteria using Weight Watchers recipes. During their meal enrollees would get a pep talk from the group leader and share their own experiences.

After lunch each group would take a brisk 15-minute walk before returning to work. In addition, employees would be encouraged to spend an hour each day working out in the GE gym before or after work. Weight Watchers trainers would be on hand at these times to run aerobics classes and advise participants on exercise programs.

The seven-week program would culminate with a ceremony honoring participants who had lost the most pounds and inches. The grand prize would be a one-week trip for two to Hawaii. General Electric would pay Weight Watchers a fee of $50 for each employee who enrolled in the program and would cover the costs of the award ceremony and the prizes.

Your task: Your contact at GE was very enthusiastic about your suggestions. He urged you to submit a formal, written proposal describing your program. Write the proposal.[10]

21. When is a program not a program? Proposal to produce a television infomercial   If you have cable television, you already know something about "infomercials." As you flip through the channels, you can't help noticing these half-hour "programs" that extol the benefits of products ranging from baldness cures to exercise equipment to car wax. Many of the ads are in a talk-show format and feature celebrities talking with people who have used the product and want to share their success stories. Other infomercials focus primarily on product demonstrations.

This form of "direct-response television" has proliferated because the ads are relatively inexpensive to produce and because cable air time often comes cheap. Whereas producing a 30-second network commercial might cost $200,000, a marketer can get by with as little as $150,000 to produce a 30-minute infomercial. In addition, placing the spots can cost in the hundreds or thousands of dollars instead of the ten-thousands or hundred-thousands.

You've recently joined the staff of American Telecast, one of the three major producers of infomercials. With annual revenues of $150 million, American Telecast's claims to fame include the highly successful Richard Simmons weight-loss-plan "long-form marketing program." Your boss has handed you a magazine ad for Audio-Forum, a company that sells audiocassettes that teach people how to speak foreign languages, how to play the piano or read music, how to improve their vocabulary or their speech, and even how to touch-type. "This looks like the kind of product we could really run with in an infomercial—especially the foreign language stuff," says your boss. She wants you to come up with an unsolicited proposal that will entice Audio-Forum into entering the infomercial game.

You look through the company's highly detailed ad, which you remember seeing in a variety of magazines. The portion of the ad devoted to language-learning tapes says, "Learn to speak a foreign language fluently on your own and at your own pace" and goes on to give the course's credentials (developed for the U.S. State Department for diplomatic personnel who need to learn a language quickly), to describe what each course consists of, and to list the languages available. Both an order form and a toll-free number are provided. You remember reading somewhere that Audio-Forum has been quite successful with its magazine direct-marketing approach.

Your task: Write a proposal to Audio-Forum, 96 Broad St., Guilford, CT 06437, indicating American Telecast's desire to produce an infomercial for Audio-Forum's language-learning tapes. Use your imagination to fill in any additional details.[11]

PROBLEM SOLVING
CUSTOMER RELATIONS

22. Customer service crisis: Proposal solving the problem Continental Security Systems (CSS) is the company whose customer service problems were the subject of Case 11. After the company president read the information in your report, she agreed that the situation needs to be addressed immediately.

Your task: Write a two-part proposal to solve CSS's customer service problems. In the first part, focus on an immediate, stop-gap measure to minimize customer defections. In the second part, outline a long-term plan to emphasize excellent customer service in CSS's culture and daily operations. Some library research will help you find examples of companies that have improved customer service dramatically. Be sure to consider all aspects of a potential solution, including reorganizing the company, training employees, and so on.

ORAL COMMUNICATION

CHAPTER 19
Listening, Interviewing, and Conducting Meetings

CHAPTER 20
Giving Speeches and Oral Presentations

LISTENING, INTERVIEWING, AND CONDUCTING MEETINGS

OMMUNICATION CLOSE-UP AT 3M

Excellent speaking and listening skills probably had a lot to do with the once-in-a-career promotion that advanced 3M's Virginia Johnson from marketing administration manager in Austin, Texas, to director of human relations at company headquarters in St. Paul, Minnesota. Johnson had plenty of opportunities to hone her communication skills. In addition to her marketing job, she served several years as head of 3M's Meeting Management Institute, traveling the nation to show executives how to make their meetings more effective. She found that effectiveness always came down to those two basic skills: speaking and listening. Most businesspeople are fairly good speakers, but they're often poor listeners.

Listening is important at all levels of business, but especially for meeting leaders and participants, says Johnson. In fact, most of what a leader does to prepare for and conduct a successful meeting (determining the purpose, creating an agenda, keeping the ball rolling, summarizing the results) is to help participants "listen" more effectively.

"If a leader speaks more than 15 or 20 percent of the time, he or she is not being effective," explains Johnson, and the participants have probably stopped listening out of sheer boredom. Instead, a meeting leader should spend most of the time listening to others, since "the role of the facilitator is to help other people get their opinions or questions out and responded to. Speeches are not meetings." Through 3M-funded research, Johnson also learned that a good meeting leader can help people listen by using a few visual aids, which enables meeting participants to visualize and retain information. Sticking to the agenda also helps, and summarizing the results reinforces or clarifies what everyone has heard.

Of course, half the responsibility for a successful meeting belongs to the participants. When Johnson attends meetings, she keeps herself actively involved. "If it's a formal meeting, I'll take notes to help me listen and for later recall," says Johnson. "At

Virginia Johnson

To be successful at 3M, employees are skilled in oral communication. Their skills are constantly put to the test, whether they're participating in one-on-one interviews, dealing with clients or customers, or participating in meetings.

creative sessions, I may have to listen intently or shout out my responses." Either way, she uses her knowledge of group dynamics to get more out of the time she spends in meetings (top executives spend about 38 percent of a 61-hour workweek in meetings).

When Johnson conducts a meeting, she first determines whether her goals can best be accomplished through an interview (two people), a meeting (three or more people), or a memo (unlimited but less personal). "You can't accomplish some things without getting your people together—when you want to provide them with direct access to an expert, for example, or show that avenues of communication in the company are open," she explains. "Meetings here at 3M serve other needs too. They allow us to share information, build teams, brainstorm solutions, reach decisions, and train people. Young companies especially, and companies in trouble, may find meetings indispensable." Johnson's favorite test of the need for a meeting is to write one 25-word sentence stating what she expects people to know, do, and believe after attending. "If I can't create that sentence, the need for a meeting isn't apparent." However, if a meeting is needed, she goes on to develop her agenda and then gathers the visual aids she'll use to help present the main points.

"For me," says Johnson, "the toughest meeting to run is the creative session—trying to bring out the child in adults. Achieving fantasy and free thinking by breaking down management roles is very demanding." To generate new ideas for sales training, Johnson used something she calls a "brain writing sheet." She asked the eight sales managers in the meeting to write down three things about sales training they'd like to see added or changed. Then the managers exchanged sheets and added three more ideas. "After a few rounds of this, they'd forgotten their jobs and titles and were busy scribbling. Each round triggered new ideas."

Johnson understands how important it is to know your audience. In meetings and interviews, she tries to identify nonverbal signals, to stay in control of the situation, and to be sensitive to listeners' needs (which must be met before they'll actually hear and absorb what's being said). She also tries to slow down nonstop talkers, stimulate quiet participants, and draw out information using various types of questions. "My personal style is to be natural and extemporaneous," says Johnson. "My agenda, visuals, and notes help me achieve that tone."

Johnson's new position puts her at the head of a department charged with smoothing human relations. Keeping everyone happy at a company with thousands of employees is no easy task. So more than ever, Johnson will be relying on her listening and speaking skills to meet that challenge.[1]

COMMUNICATING ORALLY

Virginia Johnson's job at 3M may involve more oral communication than many jobs do, but her experience is by no means unusual. Speaking and listening are the communication skills we use most. Given a choice, people would rather talk to each other than write to each other. Talking takes less time and needs no composing, keyboarding, rewriting, duplicating, or distributing.

Oral communication saves time and provides opportunities for feedback and social interaction.

More important, oral communication provides the opportunity for feedback. When people communicate orally, they can ask questions and test their understanding of the message; they can share ideas and work together to solve problems. They can also convey and absorb nonverbal information, which reveals far more than words alone. By communicating with facial expressions, eye contact, tone of voice, gestures, and postures, people can send subtle messages that add another dimension to spoken words. Oral communication satisfies our common need to be part of the human community and makes us feel good. Talking things over helps people in organizations build morale and establish a group identity.

The spontaneous quality of oral communication limits your ability to edit your thoughts.

Nonetheless, oral communication also has its dangers. Under most circumstances, oral communication occurs spontaneously. You have far less opportunity to revise your spoken words than to revise your written words. You can't cross out what you just said and start all over. Your dumbest comments will be etched in the other person's memory, regardless of how much you try to explain that you really meant something else entirely. Moreover, you can't go back and reread what was just said. If you let your attention wander while someone else is speaking, you miss the point. You either have to muddle along without knowing what the other person said or admit you were daydreaming and ask the person to repeat the comment.

People often judge the substance of a remark by the speaker's style.

Another problem is that oral communication is personal. People tend to confuse your message with you as an individual. They're likely to judge the content of what you say by your appearance and delivery style. Nobody will reject your sales letter because you're wearing white socks with a blue suit or because you say "um" a lot. However, people might very well reject your oral presentation on those grounds.

Intercultural barriers can also be as much a problem in oral communication as in written communication. Naturally, it's best to know your audience, including any cultural differences they may have. Then communicate your message in the tone, manner, and situation your audience will feel most comfortable with. (Chapter 2 has more information on intercultural barriers.)

Whether you're using the telephone, engaging in a quick conversation with a colleague, participating in a formal interview, or attending a meeting, oral communication is the vehicle you use to get your message across. When communicating orally, make it your goal to take advantage of the positive characteristics while minimizing the dangers. To achieve that goal, work on improving two key skills: speaking and listening.

Speaking

Because speaking is such an ingrained activity, we tend to do it without much thought, but that casual approach can be a problem in business. Be more aware of using speech as a tool for accomplishing your objectives in a business context. To do this, break the habit of talking spontaneously, without planning *what* you're going to say or *how* you're going to say it. Learn to manage the impression you create by consciously tailoring your remarks and delivery style to suit the situation. Become as aware of the consequences of what you say as you are of the consequences of what you write.

Learn to think before you speak.

With a little effort, you can learn to apply the composition process to oral communication. Before you speak, think about your purpose, your main idea, and your audience. Organize your thoughts in a logical way, decide on a style that suits the occasion (for example, formal/informal, lecture/conversation), and edit your remarks mentally. Try to predict how the other person will react and organize the message accordingly. Your audience may not react the way you expect, so have alternative approaches ready. As you speak, watch the other person, judging from verbal and nonverbal feedback whether your message is making the desired impression. If not, revise and try again.

Just as various writing assignments call for different writing styles, various situations call for different speaking styles. Your speaking style depends on the level of intimacy between you and the other person and on the nature of your conversation. When you're talking with a friend, you naturally speak more frankly than when you're talking with your boss or a stranger. When you're talking about a serious subject, you use a serious tone. As you think about which speaking style is appropriate, also think about the nonverbal message you want to convey. People derive less meaning from your words than they do from your facial expressions, vocal characteristics, and body language. The nonverbal message should reinforce your words. Perhaps the most important thing you can do to project yourself more effectively is to remember the "you" attitude, earning other people's attention and goodwill by focusing on them. For example, 3M's Virginia Johnson maintains that a meeting leader's job is to help other participants state opinions, ask questions, and listen to responses.

Adjust your speaking style to suit the situation.

Apply the "you" attitude to oral communication.

An important tool of oral communication, the telephone can extend your reach across town and around the world. However, if your telephone skills are lacking, you may waste valuable time and appear rude.[2] You can minimize your time on the phone while raising your phone productivity by delivering one-way information by fax or e-mail, jotting down an agenda before making a call, saving social chit-chat for the end of a call (in case your conversation is cut short), saving up all the short calls you need to make to one person during a given day, and making sure your assistant has a list of people whose calls you'll accept even if you're in a meeting.[3]

Much telephone communication now happens through voice mail rather than directly person-to-person. Organize your thoughts before you make the phone call so that your message will be concise and accurate. Be sure to take advantage of the system's review and editing features to make your message as effective as possible. And keep in mind that voice mail messages aren't necessarily private. Many systems make it easy to forward messages to other people, so be careful when recording sensitive or personal messages.

Listening

The ability to listen is a vital skill in business.

Speaking is, of course, only one side of the oral communication story. If you're typical, you spend over half your communication time listening.[4] Listening supports effective relationships within the organization, enhances the organization's delivery of products, alerts the organization to the innovation growing from both internal and external forces, and allows organizations to manage the growing diversity both in the work force and in the customers they serve.[5] An individual with good listening ability is more likely to succeed; good listening enhances performance, leading to raises, promotions, status, and power.[6] However, no one is born with the ability to listen; the skill is learned and improved through practice.[7] Someone who believes in the importance of listening is Jennifer Lawson, executive vice president of programming for PBS. Lawson was called on to unite 341 stations across the country, and she has learned a lot about listening:

> I've learned that if you want to change a bureaucracy from within, the most important thing you can do is listen. You have to give people a chance to vent their frustrations with a new system, and then build on the basis of that. My advice is to ask the right questions and be genuinely interested in the answers.[8]

Cultural barriers present a potential challenge with listening as well as with speaking. You might misinterpret what you hear if you fail to consider any cultural differences between you and the speaker. (See "Crossing Cultures Without Crossing Signals: Your Listening Skills Can Bridge the Gap," and for more on intercultural barriers, see Chapter 2.)

Most people need to improve their listening skills.

Most of us like to think of ourselves as being good listeners, but the average person remembers only about half of what's said during a 10-minute conversation and forgets half of that within 48 hours.[9] Furthermore, when questioned about material they've just heard, people are likely to get the facts mixed up. In one study people were exposed to two 30-second clips taken from TV programs and commercials. The subjects replied incorrectly to questions about these broadcasts about 30 percent of the time.[10] Understanding the process of listening will help you understand why oral messages get lost so often.

What Happens When You Listen

Listening involves five steps: sensing, interpreting, evaluating, remembering, and responding.

Listening involves five related activities, which most often occur in sequence:[11]

- *Sensing* is physically hearing the message and taking note of it. This reception can be blocked by interfering noises, impaired hearing, or inattention. Tune out distractions by focusing on the message.
- *Interpreting* is decoding and absorbing what you hear. As you listen, you assign meaning to the words according to your own values, beliefs, ideas, expectations, roles, needs, and personal history. The speaker's frame of reference may be quite different, so the listener may need to determine what the speaker really means. Pay attention to nonverbal cues—things such as gestures, body language, and facial expressions—but be careful not to assign meanings that aren't there. For example, a speaker who nervously stumbles over his or her words might be hiding something or might simply be nervous.
- *Evaluating* is forming an opinion about the message. Sorting through the speaker's remarks, separating fact from opinion, and evaluating the quality of the evidence requires a good deal of effort, particularly if the subject is complex or emotionally charged. Avoid the temptations to dismiss ideas offered by people

CROSSING CULTURES WITHOUT CROSSING SIGNALS: YOUR LISTENING SKILLS CAN BRIDGE THE GAP

Listening to other people and achieving a common understanding can be a tough job under any circumstances, but when participants come from different cultures the job can be even tougher because listening (and communication in general) involves much more than just the words spoken. Every culture views communication from a unique perspective. Western cultures value individual aggressiveness, and participants from such cultures often question authority. Other cultures downplay the importance of the individual, valuing the group as a whole and deferring to the statements of authority figures. People from such cultures may be reluctant to speak up and voice their opinions or even to discuss ideas generated by meeting leaders. Some cultures consider interruptions, corrections, and direct questions to be rude, while other cultures consider such behavior a part of normal conversation. In some cultures a meeting begins with social conversation; in other cultures this sort of "chit-chat" is considered a waste of time, and participants get down to business immediately. You must consider all these differences if you want to listen effectively.

The face-saving practices common to many cultures can prevent effective listening and create confusion. You might notice that when leaders or authority figures speak, their comments generate nods and smiles—not because their ideas are necessarily good or their listeners understand, but simply because they are the figures of authority. Those nods and smiles are offered to help these speakers save face. So if you're the leader or the authority figure in a group and you greet someone's idea by saying, "Hey, that's a great suggestion," you won't hear any argument—your opinion has already swayed other listeners.

Nuances of language are also a barrier to effective listening. Idioms, slang, and jargon cause massive confusion. Even Americans and Britons, who theoretically speak the same language, sometimes have trouble understanding one another. Phrases that seem perfectly innocent on one side of the Atlantic might be offensive to someone on the other side. For example, in Britain "on the job" is slang for sexual intercourse, and "knock you up" is a reference to a morning wake-up call.

When you are listening to someone from a different cultural background, a few guidelines can help prevent misunderstandings:

- Make no assumption that you understand the speaker; review and confirm important information.
- When a misunderstanding does occur, back up until you solve it.
- Request clarification of any idioms, slang, and jargon or of anything you don't understand.
- Educate yourself about the customs of other cultures so that you can better interpret both spoken and unspoken language.
- Above all, be patient; effective communication takes time.

1. You disagree with a point made by another meeting participant, but you know he will lose face if you correct him. What do you do?
2. The meeting is drawing to a close, but you are not sure that the participants, who come from various cultural backgrounds, all understand and agree with what has been decided. How do you ensure that everyone understands?

who are unattractive or abrasive and to embrace ideas offered by people who are charismatic speakers.
- *Remembering* is storing a message for future reference. As you listen, retain what you hear by taking notes or by making a mental outline of the speaker's key points.
- *Responding* is acknowledging the message by reacting to the speaker in some fashion. If you're communicating one-on-one or in a small group, the initial response generally takes the form of verbal feedback. If you're one of many in an audience, your initial response may take the form of applause, laughter, or silence. Later on you may act on what you have heard. Actively provide feedback to help the speaker refine the message.

Listening requires a mix of physical and mental activities and is subject to a mix of physical and mental barriers.

The Three Types of Listening

To be a good listener, vary the way you listen to suit various situations.

Various situations call for different listening skills. When you attend a briefing on the company's new medical insurance, you listen mainly for content. You want to know what the policy is. As the speaker describes the prescription drug plan, you begin to listen more critically, assessing the benefits of the new plan relative to your own needs. Later, as a friend talks to you about his medical problems, you listen empathetically, trying to understand his feelings.

The three forms of listening:
- Content listening enables you to understand and retain the message.
- Critical listening enables you to evaluate the information.
- Active listening is used to draw out the other person.

These three types of listening differ not only in purpose but also in the amount of feedback or interaction that occurs. The goal of **content listening** is to understand and retain information imparted by a speaker. You may ask questions, but basically information flows from the speaker to you. Your job is to identify the key points of the message, so be sure to listen for clues to its structure: previews, transitions, summaries, enumerated points. In your mind create an outline of the speaker's remarks; afterward silently review what you've learned. You may take notes, but you do this sparingly so that you can concentrate on the key points. It doesn't matter whether you agree or disagree, approve or disapprove—only that you understand.[12] When you listen to a regional sales manager's monthly report on how many of your products sold that month, you are listening for content.

The goal of **critical listening** is to evaluate the message at several levels: the logic of the argument, strength of the evidence, and validity of the conclusions; the implications of the message for you or your organization; the speaker's intentions and motives; the omission of any important or relevant points. Because absorbing information and evaluating it at the same time is hard, reserve judgment until the speaker has finished. Critical listening generally involves interaction as you try to uncover the speaker's point of view. You are bound to evaluate the speaker's credibility as well. Nonverbal signals are often your best clue.[13] When the regional sales manager presents sales projections for the next few months, you listen critically, evaluating whether the estimates are valid and what the implications are for your manufacturing department.

The goal of **active** or **empathic listening** is to understand the speaker's feelings, needs, and wants so that you can appreciate his or her point of view, regardless of whether you share that perspective. By listening in an active or empathic way, you help the individual vent the emotions that prevent a dispassionate approach to the subject. Avoid the temptation to give advice. Try not to judge the individual's feelings. Just let the other person talk.[14] You listen empathetically when your regional sales manager tells you about the problems he had with his recreational vehicle while vacationing with his family.

All three types of listening can be useful in work-related situations, so it pays to learn how to apply them.

How to Be a Better Listener

Regardless of whether the situation calls for content, critical, or active listening, you can improve your listening ability by becoming more aware of the habits that distinguish good listeners from bad (see Figure 19.1). Try particularly to guard against being self-centered or defensive. The minute a speaker mentions *his* or *her* problem, self-centered listeners take control of the conversation and talk about *their* problem. They trivialize the speaker's concerns by pointing out that their difficulties are twice as great. They can top the positive experiences as well. No matter what subject is being discussed, they know more than the speaker does—and they're determined to prove it.

Defensive listeners view every comment as a personal attack. If someone says, "Golly, it's warm in here," they assume that person is blaming them for mismanaging

TO LISTEN EFFECTIVELY	THE BAD LISTENER	THE GOOD LISTENER
1. Find areas of interest	Tunes out dry subjects	Opportunizes; asks "What's in it for me?"
2. Judge content, not delivery	Tunes out if delivery is poor	Judges content; skips over delivery errors
3. Hold your fire	Tends to enter into argument	Doesn't judge until comprehension is complete; interrupts only to clarify
4. Listen for ideas	Listens for facts	Listens for central themes
5. Be flexible	Takes extensive notes using only one system	Takes fewer notes; uses four to five different systems, depending on speaker
6. Work at listening	Shows no energy output; fakes attention	Works hard; exhibits active body state
7. Resist distractions	Is distracted easily	Fights or avoids distractions; tolerates bad habits; knows how to concentrate
8. Exercise your mind	Resists difficult expository material; seeks light, recreational material	Uses heavier material as exercise for the mind
9. Keep your mind open	Reacts to emotional words	Interprets emotional words; does not get hung up on them
10. Capitalize on the fact that thought is faster than speech	Tends to daydream with slow speakers	Challenges, anticipates, mentally summarizes, weighs the evidence; listens between the lines to tone of voice

Figure 19.1
Distinguishing Good Listeners from Bad Listeners

the thermostat. Their immediate reaction is to prove that the speaker is wrong and they're right. To protect their self-esteem, they may distort a message by tuning out anything that doesn't confirm their view of themselves.

We're all occasionally guilty of self-centeredness and defensiveness. The important thing is to recognize these counterproductive communication patterns in ourselves and in others so that we can take appropriate action. To improve listening skills, follow these ten steps:[15]

- Look beyond the speaker's style by asking yourself what the speaker knows that you don't.
- Depersonalize your listening so that you decrease the emotional impact of what's being said and are better able to hold your rebuttal until you've heard the total message.
- Listen for ideas as well as for facts, and know the difference between fact and principle, idea and example, and evidence and argument.
- Keep an open mind by asking questions that clarify understanding.
- Make meaningful notes that are brief and to the point.
- Fight distractions by closing doors, turning off radios or televisions, and moving closer to the speaker.
- Stay ahead of the speaker by anticipating what will be said next and by thinking about what's already been said.
- Use nonverbal skills to help you focus: maintain eye contact, react responsively with head nods or spoken signals, and pay attention to the speaker's body language.

- Evaluate and criticize the content not the speaker.
- Practice your listening skills by attending museum lectures, city council hearings, and so forth.

One way to assess your listening skills is to pay attention to how you listen. When someone else is talking, are you really hearing what is said, or are you mentally rehearsing how you will respond? Above all, try to be open to the information that will lead to higher-quality decisions, and try to accept the feelings that will build understanding and mutual respect. Becoming a good listener will help you in many business situations—especially those that are emotion-laden and difficult.

Effective listening involves being receptive to both information and feelings.

HANDLING DIFFICULT INTERPERSONAL SITUATIONS

Improving your listening habits will help you cope with some of the difficult situations that inevitably arise in business. You need a great deal of communication skill to maintain your composure and achieve your goals when the stakes are high and emotions are aroused—for example, when you're trying to resolve conflict, overcome resistance, or handle negotiations.

Resolving Conflict

Conflict is not necessarily bad, as long as it is handled in a constructive fashion.

Many business dealings involve conflict. People in organizations often compete for scarce resources or clash over differences in goals and values. Misunderstandings based on cultural differences may arise. These conflicts can be valuable, forcing important issues into the open and bringing out creative ideas about solving problems.

Although conflict itself can be healthy, some approaches to resolving conflict are destructive. If you believe that the only solution is for one party to win and the other party to lose (win-lose strategy), the outcome of the conflict will surely make someone unhappy. Unfortunately, some conflicts degenerate to the point that both parties would rather lose than see the other party win (lose-lose strategy). On the other hand, if you approach the conflict with the idea that both parties can satisfy their goals at least to some extent (win-win strategy), then no one loses.

Look for win-win solutions to conflict.

The principle behind the win-win strategy is that the parties in conflict can better solve their problems by working together than by waging war. However, for the win-win strategy to work, everybody must believe that it's possible to find a solution both parties can accept, that cooperation is better for the organization than competition, that the other party can be trusted, and that higher status doesn't entitle one party to impose a solution. Here are seven measures a manager can take to successfully resolve conflict:

- Deal with minor conflict before it becomes major conflict.
- Get those most directly involved in the conflict to participate in solving it, and make sure they know that you expect them to communicate with each other.
- Get feelings out in the open before dealing with the main issues; try to understand each party's motivations, biases, and vested interests.
- Seek reasons for the problem before seeking solutions, but don't blame either party; make sure that reasons are based on fact, not on differing perceptions.
- Don't let anyone become locked into a position before considering other solutions.
- Don't let anyone avoid a fair solution by hiding behind the rules.
- Try to get the parties to fight together against an "outside force" instead of against each other.

By applying these techniques, a manager can turn potentially disastrous conflict into an opportunity for creative change.

Overcoming Resistance

Part of dealing with conflict is learning how to persuade other people to accept your point of view. In a business situation, reason usually prevails. Sometimes, however, you encounter people who react emotionally. When you face irrational resistance, you may well become frustrated, but the best strategy is to remain calm and detached so that you can avoid destructive confrontations and present your position in a convincing manner.

When you encounter resistance or hostility, try to maintain your composure and address the other person's emotional needs.

Start by expressing understanding. Most people are ashamed when they react emotionally, especially in business situations. They're insulted when you say, "Your reaction is emotional," and they respond by rejecting you and your viewpoint. Show that you sympathize; you don't necessarily have to agree with someone who is reacting emotionally, but respond with understanding and acceptance. You might say, "I can understand that this change might be difficult, and if I were in your position, I might be reluctant to do it myself." The point is to make the other person relax and talk about his or her anxiety so that you have a chance to offer reassurance.[16]

Be aware that the person's resistance and behavior might be the result of cultural differences. What seems like irrational behavior to you might seem perfectly rational to the other person. For example, people in our culture try not to react emotionally in a business setting, while in other cultures emotional reactions at work may be quite acceptable. (See Chapter 2 for more on cultural barriers.)

Make the person aware of her or his resistance. When you encounter a noncommittal, silent reaction, you know that you aren't getting through to the other person. Although not actively resisting you, the person is tuning you out, possibly without even being aware of why. In such situations continuing to present your own point of view is futile. Deal directly with the resistance, but not in an accusing way. You might say, "You seem cool to this idea. Have I made some faulty assumptions somewhere?" This sort of question will force the person to face up to her or his resistance and define it.[17]

Evaluate others' objections fairly. Don't just continue repeating yourself. Focus instead on what the other person is saying. Listen carefully to both the words and the feelings being expressed. Get the person to open up so that you can understand the basis for his or her resistance. The person may raise some legitimate points. If your suggestions are going to create problems for people, you'll have to discuss ways of minimizing those problems.[18]

When you're trying to convince someone of your viewpoint, hold your arguments until the other person is ready for them. Your success in getting your points across depends as much on the other person's frame of mind as it does on your arguments. You can't assume that a strong argument will speak for itself. Be sure to address the other person's emotional needs first.

Handling Negotiations

Life is full of transactions. Whether you're bargaining over the terms of your employment, the conditions of a lease, the price of a car, or the evening's dishwashing responsibilities, you want to get the best deal you can, preferably without alienating the other person. However, if you're like many other people, you may have doubts about your negotiating skills. Perhaps you were taught as a child that it's impolite to haggle over money, or perhaps you lack experience negotiating.

Everyone can learn to negotiate better. First, know as much as you can about your audience. Understand that negotiating across cultures may involve differences in the

The key to being an effective negotiator is to be prepared.

way the negotiation process is viewed, in the amount of trust between negotiating parties, in the protocol accepted, in the skills needed by a good negotiator, and in how the decision-making process is viewed.[19] Moran, Stahl & Boyer International, a company specializing in cross-cultural training, proposes that culture consists of two levels: surface culture, the more obvious level, including the obvious things such as food, holidays, and styles; and deep culture, the attitudes and values on which the culture is based.[20] The differences resulting from deep culture can be hidden pitfalls for the uninformed negotiator.

Next, be sure you know what you want. Before you enter negotiations, define your goals. If you know what you hope to obtain, you can explain your position more clearly to the other side. Furthermore, you'll be less likely to make concessions on the spur of the moment. You can prepare by doing your homework. Always approach the negotiations armed with information that supports your position. Say that you're trying to persuade a potential employer to give you a more generous starting salary. If you know of comparable employers who are paying that much for similar employees, you'll have stronger support for your position.[21]

Preserve the "you" attitude by considering the other person's needs. You can always get what you want more easily if the other person benefits too. Before your meeting try to find out what might be acceptable to the other party. For example, if you're buying a new car, get the wholesale list price so that you know the dealer's break-even cost. You can extend the "you" attitude by searching for mutually satisfactory solutions. Keep your eyes and ears open; ask questions that will help you understand the other person's wants. Look for compromises that result in joint gain.[22]

Finally, know your strengths and weaknesses. In any negotiation you're bound to have some advantages and disadvantages. Try to think of ways to minimize or offset your disadvantages, and be prepared to make the most of your strong points. Increase your strengths by being aware of pressure tactics so that you can resist the pressure to cave in. Experienced negotiators sometimes win concessions by using time pressure ("This sale ends tomorrow"), fear of loss ("Another customer wants the car, but . . ."), or extreme proposals ("You must be crazy to ask for $10,000—$5,000 is my best offer").

Negotiating is a lot like acting; the more you rehearse, the better your performance will be. Stand in front of a mirror and play out the scene. Practice what you'll say, and think of how you'll respond to various proposals and tactics.[23] The important thing to remember about negotiations is that both parties can usually get what they want if both are willing to work together. In many cases, the negotiating process is chiefly an exchange of opinions and information that gradually leads to a mutually acceptable solution.

CONDUCTING INTERVIEWS ON THE JOB

An interview is any planned conversation with a specific purpose involving two or more people.

In addition to handling difficult interpersonal situations, planning what to say and developing good listening skills will also help you participate in on-the-job interviews. From the day you apply for your first job until the day you retire, you'll be involved in a wide variety of business **interviews**—planned conversations with a predetermined purpose that involve asking and answering questions. In a typical interview the action is controlled by the interviewer, the person who scheduled the session. This individual poses a series of questions designed to elicit information from the interviewee. Interviews sometimes involve several interviewers or several interviewees, but more often only two people participate. The conversation bounces back and forth from interviewer to interviewee. Although the interviewer guides the conversation, the interviewee may also seek to accomplish a purpose, perhaps to obtain or provide information, to solve a problem, to create goodwill, or to persuade the other person to take action. If the participants establish rapport and stick to the subject at hand, both parties have a chance of achieving their objectives.

When both the interviewer and the interviewee achieve their purpose, the interview is a success.

Categorizing Interviews

The interviewer establishes the style and structure of the session, depending on the purpose of the interview and the relationship between the parties, much as a writer varies the style and structure of a written message to suit the situation. Each situation calls for a slightly different approach, as you can imagine when you try to picture yourself conducting some of these common business interviews:

The various types of interviews call for different communication skills.

- *Job interviews.* The job candidate wants to learn about the position and the organization; the employer wants to learn about the applicant's abilities and experience. Both hope to make a good impression and to establish rapport. Initial job interviews are usually fairly formal and structured, but later interviews may be relatively spontaneous as the interviewer explores the candidate's responses.
- *Information interviews.* The interviewer seeks facts that bear on a decision or contribute to basic understanding. Information flows mainly in one direction: One person asks a list of questions that must be covered and listens to the answers supplied by the other person. This kind of interview is a valuable form of primary research. Of course, the person you interview must be credible and knowledgeable about the subject. It is also important to decide in advance what kind of information you want and how you will use it—this planning will save time and build goodwill.
- *Persuasive interviews.* One person tells another about a new idea, product, or service and explains why the other should act on the recommendations. Persuasive interviews are often associated with, but are certainly not limited to, selling. The persuader asks about the other person's needs and shows how the product or concept is able to meet those needs. Thus persuasive interviews require skill in drawing out and listening to others as well as the ability to impart information.
- *Exit interviews.* The interviewer tries to understand why the interviewee is leaving the organization or transferring to another department or division. A departing employee can often provide insight into whether the business is being handled efficiently or whether things could be improved. The interviewer tends to ask all the questions while the interviewee provides answers. Encouraging the employee to focus on events and processes rather than on personal gripes will elicit more useful information for the organization.
- *Evaluation interviews.* A supervisor periodically gives an employee feedback on his or her performance. The supervisor and the employee discuss progress toward predetermined standards or goals and evaluate areas that require improvement. They may also discuss goals for the coming year, as well as the employee's longer-term aspirations and general concerns.
- *Counseling interviews.* A supervisor talks with an employee about personal problems that are interfering with work performance. The interviewer is concerned with the welfare of both the employee and the organization. The goal is to establish the facts, convey the company's concern, and steer the person toward a source of help. (Only a trained professional should offer advice on such problems as substance abuse, marital tension, and financial trouble.)

When Herb Silverman holds an evaluation interview at Fluor-Daniel in Irvine, California, he focuses on giving constructive feedback, encouraging positive goals, and adopting a supportive demeanor.

- *Conflict-resolution interviews.* Two competing people or groups of people (such as Smith versus Jones, day shift versus night shift, General Motors versus the United Auto Workers) explore their problems and attitudes. The goal is to bring the two parties closer together, cause adjustments in perceptions and attitudes, and create a more productive climate.
- *Disciplinary interviews.* A supervisor tries to correct the behavior of an employee who has ignored the organization's rules and regulations. The interviewer tries to get the employee to see the reason for the rules and to agree to comply. The interviewer also reviews the facts and explores the person's attitude. Because of the emotional reaction that is likely, neutral observations are more effective than critical comments.
- *Termination interviews.* A supervisor informs an employee of the reasons for the termination. The interviewer tries to avoid involving the company in legal action and tries to maintain as positive a relationship as possible with the interviewee. To accomplish these goals, the interviewer gives reasons that are specific, accurate, and verifiable.

Planning Interviews

Planning an interview is similar to planning any other form of communication. You begin by stating your purpose, analyzing the other person, and formulating your main idea. Then you decide on the length, style, and organization of the interview.

To accomplish their objectives, interviewees develop a communication strategy.

Even as an interviewee, you have some control over the conversation by anticipating the interviewer's questions and then planning your answers so that the points you want to make will be covered. You can also introduce questions and topics of your own. In addition, by your comments and nonverbal cues, you can affect the relationship between you and the interviewer. Think about your respective roles. What does this person expect from you? Is it to your advantage to confirm those expectations? Will you be more likely to accomplish your objective by being friendly and open or by conveying an impression of professional detachment? Should you allow the interviewer to dominate the exchange, or should you try to take control?

The interviewer assumes the main responsibility for planning the interview.

If you're the interviewer, responsibility for planning the session falls on you. On the simplest level, your job is to schedule the interview and see that it's held in a comfortable and convenient location. Good interviewers are good at collecting information, listening, and probing.[24] So you'll also develop a set of interview questions and decide on their sequence. Having a plan will enable you to conduct the interview more efficiently, even if you find it advantageous to deviate from the plan during the interview. If your questions might require research or extensive thinking, or if you'd like to quote the interviewee in writing, consider providing a list of questions a day or two before the interview. This will give the person time to prepare more complete (and therefore more helpful) answers. You might also want to tape-record the interview if the topic is complex or if you plan to quote or paraphrase the interviewee in a written document.

Interview Questions

The purpose of the interview and the nature of the participants determine the types of questions that are asked. When you plan the interview, bear in mind that you ask questions (1) to get information, (2) to motivate the interviewee to respond honestly and appropriately, and (3) to create a good working relationship with the other person. While you're drafting your questions, be aware of ethical implications. For example, asking someone to divulge personal information about a co-worker may be asking that person to make an unethical decision. Always be careful about issues of confidentiality, politics, and other sensitive issues.

To obtain both factual information and underlying feelings, you'll probably use various types of questions. **Open-ended questions** invite the interviewee to offer an opinion, not just a yes, no, or one-word answer: "What do you think your company wants most from its suppliers?" This kind of question is useful when you want to learn the reasons behind a decision rather than just the facts. You can learn some interesting and unexpected things from open-ended questions, but they diminish your control of the interview. The other person's idea of what's relevant may not coincide with yours, and you may waste some time getting the interview back on track. Use open-ended questions to warm up the interviewee and to look for information when you have plenty of time to conduct the conversation.

To suggest a response, use **direct open-ended questions.** For example, asking "What have you done about . . " assumes that something has been done and calls for an explanation. With direct open-ended questions you have somewhat more control over the interview, but you still give the other person some freedom in framing a response. This form is good to use when you want to get a specific conclusion or recommendation from someone, for example, "What would you do to improve customer satisfaction in the southern region?" Take care to avoid biasing the response with the way you word the question, however. Asking "What should Roger Vanque do to improve customer satisfaction in his region?" implies that Vanque is doing something wrong, which may not be the case.

Closed-ended questions require yes or no answers or call for short responses: "Did you make a reservation for the flight?" "What is your grade-point average, 3.5 to 4.0, 3.0 to 3.5, 2.5 to 3.0, 2.0 to 2.5?" Questions like these produce specific information, save time, require less effort from the interviewee, and eliminate bias and prejudice in answers. The disadvantage is that they limit the respondent's initiative and may prevent important information from being revealed. They're better for gathering information than for prompting an exchange of feelings.

Questions that mirror a respondent's previous answer are called **restatement questions.** They invite the respondent to expand on an answer: "You said you dislike completing travel vouchers. Is that correct?" They also signal the interviewee that you're paying attention. Restatements provide opportunities to clarify points and correct misunderstandings. Use them to pursue a subject further or to encourage the other person to explain a statement. You can also use restatement questions to soothe upset

Four basic types of interview questions:
- Open-ended questions
- Direct open-ended questions
- Closed-ended questions
- Restatement questions

Figure 19.2
Choosing Questions with
the Appropriate Degree
of Openness

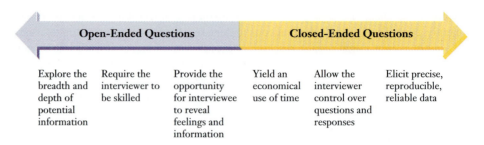

Open-Ended Questions			Closed-Ended Questions		
Explore the breadth and depth of potential information	Require the interviewer to be skilled	Provide the opportunity for interviewee to reveal feelings and information	Yield an economical use of time	Allow the interviewer control over questions and responses	Elicit precise, reproducible, reliable data

customers or co-workers. By acknowledging the other person's complaint, you gain credibility.

Figure 19.2 gives another view of question differences. As the figure implies, most questions fall along a continuum of openness. To achieve any of the purposes listed in the figure, frame a question toward the appropriate end of the spectrum.

Interview Structure

Organize an interview much as you would organize a written message.

Good interviews have an opening, a body, and a close. The opening establishes rapport and orients the interviewee to the remainder of the session. You might begin by introducing yourself, asking a few polite questions, and then explaining the purpose and ground rules of the interview.

Use the opening to set the tone and orient the interviewee.

The questions in the body of the interview reflect the nature of your relationship with the interviewee. For an informational session, such as a market research interview, you may want to structure the interview and prepare a detailed list of specific questions. This approach enables you to control the interview and use your time efficiently. It also facilitates repeating the interview with other participants. On the other hand, if the interview is designed to explore problems or to persuade the interviewee, you may prefer a less structured approach. You might simply prepare a checklist of general subjects and then let the interview evolve on the basis of the participant's responses. Figure 19.3 summarizes the effect of structure on interviews.

Use a mix of question types to give the body of the interview rhythm.

In the body of the interview, use a mix of question types. One good technique is to use closed-ended questions to pin down specific facts that emerge during an open-ended response. You might follow up an open-ended response by asking, "How many people did you contact to get this information?" or "Can we get this product in stock before May 15?"

Use the close to sum up the interview and leave the interviewee with a cordial feeling.

The close of the interview is when you summarize the outcome, preview what comes next, and underscore the rapport that has been established. To signal that the interview is coming to an end, you might lean back in your chair, smile, and use an open, palms-up gesture as you say, "Well, I guess that takes care of all my questions.

Figure 19.3
Choosing the Right
Amount of Structure for
an Interview

Unstructured Interviews			Structured Interviews		
Explore the breadth and depth of potential information	Require the interviewer to be skilled	Provide the freedom to adapt to various responses and situations	Require careful preparation	Allow the interviewer control over questions and responses	Elicit precise, reproducible, reliable data

Would you like to add anything?" If the interviewee has no comments, you might go on to say, "Thank you so much for your help. You've given me all the information I need to finish my report. I should have it completed within two weeks; I'll send you a copy." Then you might rise, shake hands, and approach the door. In parting, you could add a friendly comment to reaffirm your interest in the other person: "I hope you have a nice trip to Yellowstone. I was there when I was a kid, and I've never forgotten the experience."

From a practical standpoint, you need to be certain that your interview outline is about the right length for the time you've scheduled. People can speak at the rate of about 125 to 150 words (roughly one paragraph) per minute. Assuming that you're using a mix of various types of questions, you can probably handle about 20 questions in a half-hour (or about the same amount of information that you would cover in a 10- to 12-page single-spaced document). However, you may want to allow more or less time for each question and response, depending on the subject matter and the complexity of the questions. Bear in mind that open-ended questions take longer to answer than other types do.

Don't try to cover more questions than you have time for.

When you've concluded the interview, take a few moments to write down your thoughts. If it was an information-gathering session, go over your notes. Fill in any blanks while the interview is fresh in your mind. In addition, you might write a short letter or memo that thanks the interviewee for cooperating, confirms understandings between you, and if appropriate, outlines the next steps. (As a reminder of the tasks involved in interviews, see this chapter's Checklist for Interviews on the Job.)

CHECKLIST FOR INTERVIEWS ON THE JOB

A. PREPARATION
1. Decide on the purpose and goals of the interview.
2. Outline your interview based on your goals and the interview category.
   a. Set the level of formality.
   b. Choose a structured or unstructured approach.
3. Determine the needs of your interviewee, and gather background information.
4. Formulate questions as clearly and concisely as possible, and plot their order.
5. Project the outcome of the interview, and develop a plan for accomplishing the goal.
6. Select a time and a site.
7. Inform the interviewee of the nature of the interview and the agenda to be covered.
8. Provide a list of questions in advance if the interviewee will need time to research and formulate quality answers.

B. CONDUCT
1. Be on time for the interview appointment.
2. Remind the interviewee of the purpose and format.

3. Clear the taking of notes or the use of a tape recorder with the interviewee.
4. Use ears and eyes to pick up verbal and nonverbal cues.
5. Follow the stated agenda, but be willing to explore relevant subtopics.
6. At the end of the interview, restate the interviewee's key ideas, reviewing the actions, goals, and tasks each of you has agreed to.
7. Close the interview; restate the interviewee's key ideas, reviewing the actions, goals, and tasks each of you has agreed to.

C. FOLLOW-UP
1. Write a thank-you memo or letter that provides the interviewee with a record of the meeting.
2. Provide the assistance that you agreed to during your meeting.
3. Monitor progress by keeping in touch through discussions with your interviewee.

PARTICIPATING IN SMALL GROUPS AND MEETINGS

As in interviews, your speaking and listening skills are also put to the test during meetings. Moreover, the skills you develop to handle difficult interpersonal situations and interviews are just as helpful when operating in small groups. By being a good listener, relying on a win-win strategy, and using the appropriate types of questions for each situation, you can contribute positively to any small group or meeting.

As more and more corporations embrace the concept of **participative management** and involve employees in the company's decision making, the importance of teamwork has increased. Companies are looking for people who can interact successfully in small groups and make useful contributions during meetings. When Hewlett-Packard studied its most successful managers to identify the personality traits that contribute to their effectiveness, it found that all of them are good at team building. This finding prompted the company to emphasize team-building skills in its management development program.[25]

Meetings are called to solve problems or share information.

At their best, meetings can be an extremely useful forum for making key decisions and coordinating the activities of people and departments. Theoretically, the interaction of the participants should lead to good decisions based on the combined intelligence of the group. Whether the meeting is held to solve a problem or to share information, the participants gain a sense of involvement and importance from their attendance. Because they share in the decision, they accept it and are committed to seeing it succeed.

At their worst, meetings are unproductive and frustrating. They waste everyone's time and they're expensive. More important, poor meetings may actually be counterproductive, because they may result in bad decisions. When people are pressured to conform, they abandon their sense of personal responsibility and agree to ill-founded plans.

Understanding Group Dynamics

A meeting's success depends not only on what the goal is but also on how the group approaches the task.

A meeting is called for some purpose, and this purpose gives form to the meeting. In addition, however, the interactions and processes that take place during a meeting, the **group dynamics,** also affect the outcome. People are assembled to achieve a work-related task, but at the same time, each person has a **hidden agenda,** private motives that affect the group's interaction. Sam might want to prove that he's more powerful than Sherry; Sherry might be trying to share the risk of making a decision; Don might be looking for a chance to postpone doing "real" work; and Rachel might be looking for approval from her peers. Each person's hidden agenda either contributes to or detracts from the group's ability to perform its task. Bear in mind that it would be unethical for any group member to make decisions solely on the basis of his or her hidden agenda.

Role-Playing

We all have many-faceted personalities: Sometimes we're carefree and fun-loving; sometimes we're serious and hard working. We assume various roles to suit various occasions, playing the part that's expected of us in a particular context. The roles are all consistent with our self-concept, but we vary the image we project depending on the demands of the situation and the cues we receive from other people.

Each member of a group plays a role that affects the outcome of the group's activities.

The roles people play in meetings fall into three categories (see Figure 19.4). Members who assume **self-oriented roles** are motivated mainly to fulfill personal needs, and they tend to be less productive than the other two types. Far more likely to contribute to group goals are those who assume **group maintenance roles** to help

At Motorola in Phoenix, Arizona, this microme-chanics design team meets frequently to make sure everyone's efforts are focused toward the same goal. As in any meeting, their understanding of the dynamics of their group helps them accomplish their objectives.

members work well together and those who assume **task-facilitating roles** to help members solve the problem or make the decision.

To a great extent, the role we assume in a group depends on our status in that group. The people with more status play dominant roles; those with less status play more passive parts. Status depends on many variables, such as personal attractiveness, competence in a particular field, past successes, education, age, social background, and organizational position. It also varies from group to group: You may have a good deal of status in one group (say, a college fraternity) and less status in another (say, a Fortune 500 company).

In most groups a certain amount of "politics" occurs as people try to establish their relative status. One or two people typically emerge as the leaders, but often an undercurrent of tension remains as members of the group vie for better positions in the pecking order. These power struggles often get in the way of the real work. One

Group members' personal motives may interfere with the group's efforts to accomplish its mission.

SELF-ORIENTED ROLES	GROUP-MAINTENANCE ROLES	TASK-FACILITATING ROLES
Controlling: dominating others by exhibiting superiority or authority **Withdrawing:** retiring from the group either by becoming silent or by refusing to deal with a particular aspect of the group's work **Attention seeking:** calling attention to oneself and demanding recognition from others **Diverting:** focusing group discussion on topics of interest to the individual rather than those relevant to the task	**Encouraging:** drawing out other members by showing verbal and non-verbal support, praise, or agreement **Harmonizing:** reconciling differences among group members through mediation or by using humor to relieve tension **Compromising:** offering to yield on a point in the interest of reaching a mutually acceptable decision	**Initiating:** getting the group started on a line of inquiry **Information giving or seeking:** offering (or seeking) information relevant to questions facing the group **Coordinating:** showing relationships among ideas, clarifying issues, summarizing what the group has done Procedure setting: suggesting decision-making procedures that will move the group toward a goal

Figure 19.4
Roles People Play in Groups

person might refuse to go along with a decision simply because it was suggested by a rival. Until roles and status have stabilized, the group may have trouble accomplishing its goals.

Group Norms

A group that meets regularly develops unwritten rules governing the behavior of the members. To one degree or another, people are expected to conform to these norms. For example, there may be an unspoken agreement that it's okay to be 10 minutes late for meetings but not 15 minutes late. In the context of work, the most productive groups tend to develop norms that are conducive to business.

Some groups are more cohesive than others. When the group has a strong identity, the members all observe the norms religiously. They're upset by any deviation, and individuals feel a great deal of pressure to conform. This sense of group loyalty can be positive: Members generally have a strong commitment to one another, and they're highly motivated to see that the group succeeds. However, such group loyalty can also lead members into **groupthink,** the willingness of individual members to set aside their personal opinions and go along with everyone else, even if everyone else is wrong, simply because belonging to the group is important to them. Because decisions based on groupthink are more a result of group loyalty and conformity than of carefully considered opinion and fact-finding, groupthink can lead to poor-quality decisions and ill-advised actions. Groupthink can even induce people to act against their own sense of ethics.

> Because they feel pressured to conform, members of a group may agree to unwise decisions.

Group Decision Making

> Group decision making passes through four phases: orientation, conflict, emergence, reinforcement.

Groups usually reach their decisions in a predictable pattern. The process can be viewed as passing through four phases. In the *orientation phase,* group members socialize, establish their roles, and agree on their reason for meeting. In the *conflict phase* members begin to discuss their positions on the problem. If group members have been carefully selected to represent a variety of viewpoints and expertise, disagreements are a natural part of this phase. The point is to air all the options and all the pros and cons fully. At the end of this phase, group members begin to settle on a single solution to the problem. In the *emergence phase* members reach a decision. Those who advocated different solutions put aside their objections, either because they're convinced that the majority solution is better or because they recognize that arguing is futile. Finally, in the *reinforcement phase* group feeling is rebuilt, and the solution is summarized. Members receive their assignments for carrying out the group's decision and make arrangements for following up on these assignments.[26]

These four phases almost always occur, regardless of what type of decision is being considered. Group members naturally employ this decision process, even when they lack experience or training in group communication. However, just as a natural athlete can improve by practicing, this "natural" decision process will proceed more smoothly if the group leader prepares carefully.

Group decision-making software (also called electronic meeting systems) can save time and streamline the decision process. These systems can also make meetings more democratic by putting everyone on equal footing.

Arranging the Meeting

By being aware of how small groups of people interact, meeting leaders can take steps to ensure that their meetings are productive. The three most frequently reported problems with meetings are (1) getting off the subject, (2) not having an agenda, and

(3) meeting for too long.[27] The key to productive meetings is careful planning of purpose, participants, agenda, and location. The trick is to bring the right people together in the right place for just enough time to accomplish your goals.

Determining the Purpose

Virginia Johnson of 3M warns that the biggest mistake in holding meetings is not having a specific goal. So before you call one, satisfy yourself that a meeting is truly needed. Perhaps your purpose doesn't require the interaction of a group, or maybe you could communicate more effectively in a memo or through individual conversations.

> Before calling a meeting, ask yourself whether it is really needed.

Generally, the purpose of a meeting is either informational or decision making, although many meetings comprise both purposes. An informational meeting is called so that the participants can share information and, possibly, coordinate actions. This type of meeting may involve individual briefings by each participant or a speech by the leader followed by questions from the attendees.

Decision-making meetings are mainly concerned with persuasion, analysis, and problem solving. They often include a brainstorming session that is followed by a debate on the alternatives. These meetings tend to be somewhat less predictable than informational meetings. When planning a decision-making meeting, remember that your purpose is to develop a course of action that the group can support. Therefore each participant must be aware of the nature of the problem and the criteria for its solution.

Selecting the Participants

In many organizations, being invited to this or that meeting is a mark of status, and as the one calling the meeting, you may be reluctant to leave someone out. Despite the pressure to include everyone even remotely concerned, try to invite only those whose presence is essential. The number of participants should reflect the purpose of the meeting. If the session is purely informational and one person will be doing most of the talking, you can include a relatively large group. However, if you're trying to solve a problem, develop a plan, or reach a decision, try to limit participation to between 6 and 12 people.[28] The more people who attend, the more comments and confusion you're likely to get, and the longer the whole thing will take.

> Limit the number of participants, but include all key people.

Although you don't want to invite too many people, be sure to include those who can make an important contribution and those who are key decision makers. Holding a meeting to decide an important matter is pointless if the people with the necessary information aren't there. If your purpose is to develop the schedule for launching a new product, you'd better be sure you've invited someone from production as well as all the marketing people. Otherwise, you may end up with a great promotional campaign but nothing to sell.

Setting the Agenda

Although the nature of a meeting may sometimes prevent you from developing a fixed agenda, at least prepare a list of matters to be discussed. Distribute the agenda to the participants several days before the meeting. The more participants know ahead of time about the purpose of the meeting, the better prepared they'll be to respond to the issues at hand.

> Prepare a detailed agenda well in advance of the meeting.

Agendas include the names of the participants and the time, place, and order of business (see Component Chapter A). Some argue that the most important items should be scheduled first, but others favor an arrangement that provides warm-up time to accommodate latecomers. Regardless of the order of business, starting and ending meetings on time sends a signal of good organization and allows attendees to meet other commitments. In fact, one of Virginia Johnson's favorite solutions for improving meetings is simply telling people what time it will end (as well as what time it will start).

Preparing the Location

Give attention to the small details that help participants focus on the task at hand.

Decide where you'll hold the meeting, and reserve the location. For work sessions, morning meetings are usually more productive than afternoon sessions. If you work for an organization with technological capabilities, you may want to use teleconferencing or videoconferencing for your meeting. A number of firms now offer videoconferencing facilities that companies can rent by the hour. (See "Electronic Meetings: Work Together—Wherever You Are—to Get the Results You Want.")

Consider the seating arrangements. Are rows of chairs suitable, or do you need a conference table? Give some attention to such details as room temperature, lighting, ventilation, acoustics, and refreshments. These things may seem trivial, but they can make or break a meeting.

KEEPING PACE WITH TECHNOLOGY

ELECTRONIC MEETINGS: WORK TOGETHER— WHEREVER YOU ARE—TO GET THE RESULTS YOU WANT

Someday you may attend a virtual meeting in the morning and then head down the hall to the decision room where an electronic meeting system will help you and your colleagues brainstorm ideas. Afterward, you'll use the groupware on the PC in your office to work out the details. If you understand such jargon, then you're already part of the electronic meeting revolution. If not, don't worry. Even the techno-whizzes are having trouble keeping up with the remarkable flood of technology that's redefining the word *meeting*.

Virtual Meetings Can Save Time and Money

Attending a *virtual meeting* means joining (via computer) an ongoing dialogue between two or more individuals communicating over telephone lines through computer modem devices. The exchange is similar to e-mail, but it's interactive; that is, everyone sees everyone else's message as soon as it's sent. These meetings can occur over a private business's computer network or through a wider Internet-based setup. It's a "virtual" meeting because even though the participants may be separated by miles, they can exchange ideas as if they were in the same room. As companies all over the world have gained access to the Internet and the World Wide Web, the number of virtual meetings has increased dramatically. The speed and ease-of-use has made this type of communication even more practical for businesses.

Decision Rooms Make Meetings More Productive

A *decision room* is a dedicated meeting room filled with fax machines, telephones, and special equipment called electronic meeting systems (EMS), group decision support systems (GDS or GDSS), or electronic voting systems (the European term). The simplest of these hardware/software configurations include a large viewing screen, one personal computer (PC), and individual keypads. More sophisticated systems feature a group of individual computer workstations linked through a local area network (LAN) and using a type of *groupware*—software that allows several people to work on a document at the same time.

Whatever the level of sophistication, the function is basically the same: The computer software tallies and sorts information keyed in by meeting participants and displays the results almost instantaneously. With the simple keypad system, a vote can be taken on an idea, and the results will be immediately displayed on the large screen, either as a graph, as a simple number tally, or as a complex breakdown of categories and voting trends. Discussion follows, along with subsequent votes on every aspect of the issue at hand. At the end of the meeting, the system provides printed summaries for everyone.

Companies that rent or purchase EMS equipment are often surprised by the amount of time they save. Also, because the keypads provide anonymity, participants tend to be more hon-

Contributing to a Productive Meeting

Whether the meeting is conducted electronically or conventionally, its success depends largely on how effective the leader is. If the leader is prepared and has selected the participants carefully, the meeting will generally be productive. Moreover, according to 3M's Virginia Johnson, listening skills are especially important to meeting leaders. The leader's ability to listen well facilitates good meetings.

As meeting leader, you're responsible for keeping the ball rolling. Avoid being so domineering that you close off suggestions, but don't be so passive that you lose control of the group. If the discussion lags, call on those who haven't been heard from. Pace the presentation and discussion so that you'll have time to complete the agenda. As time begins to run out, interrupt the discussion and summarize what has been accomplished. Another leadership task is either to arrange for someone to record the proceedings or to ask a participant to take notes during the meeting. (Component Chapter A includes an example of the format for minutes of meetings.)

The meeting leader's duties:
- Pacing the meeting
- Appointing a note taker
- Following the agenda
- Stimulating participation and discussion
- Summarizing the debate
- Reviewing recommendations
- Circulating the minutes

est. This equalizes power structures, which can have a dramatic effect: In one instance, a manager resigned on the spot when he learned what his subordinates really thought about his work. "The group thinks, sees, reacts, and rethinks in quick succession," says Robert Bostrom of the University of Georgia. The quick feedback and printed reports also eliminate the need for follow-up meetings, according to Cathe Johnson, a manager at Motorola's semiconductor division, where an EMS cut the number of required meetings by 50 percent.

More expensive systems include brainstorming software, which works well when the decision room features individual computer screens. Participants type in their ideas and then view and comment on the ideas of others—anonymously and simultaneously. Again, differences of rank, gender, or personality disappear, so the decision-making process becomes truly democratic. Using a decision room rented from IBM, a group of Blue Cross/Blue Shield executives brainstormed 400 ideas in 30 minutes. In two days the group developed a written plan for future developments. The company figures the task would have taken five times as long in traditional meetings.

Videoconferencing Is the Next Best Thing to Being There

The cost of videoconferencing once limited its appeal to a handful of large companies that could afford the specialized equipment and satellite rental time. However, business communicators can now choose from more economical options as well. The first is renting time from a videoconferencing service com-

pany. These rental facilities use high-bandwidth satellite links that offer high-quality video transmission for interactive conferencing between two sites or one-way broadcasts from one site to multiple reception sites.

The second option is desktop videoconferencing, which involves low-cost systems that use personal computers and telephone lines instead of satellite transmissions. The ProShare system from Intel is a good example. With compatible hardware and software on each person's PC, a team of people can send audio, video, and data across town or around the world. These PC-based systems don't offer the same video speed as dedicated videoconferencing systems, but they are much less expensive. They also offer additional benefits, such as the ability for two or more people to work on a document or drawing at the same time.

Decreasing costs have made videoconferencing a highly economical alternative to long-distance travel. So don't be surprised if you find yourself smiling and talking over a television-type monitor to a colleague who's thousands of miles away. You'll be working together—wherever you are.

1. Do in-person, face-to-face meetings have any advantages over electronic meetings?
2. What potential risks face employees and companies that don't keep up with trends in electronic meeting technology?

As leader, you're expected to follow the agenda; participants have prepared for the meeting on the basis of the announced agenda. However, don't be rigid. Allow enough time for discussion, and give people a chance to raise related issues. If you cut off discussion too quickly or limit the subject too narrowly, no real consensus can emerge.

You can improve the productivity of a meeting by using **parliamentary procedure,** a time-tested method for planning and running effective meetings. Anyone belonging to an organization should understand the basic principles of parliamentary procedure. Used correctly, it can help groups in several important ways:[29]

- Transact business efficiently
- Protect individual rights
- Maintain order
- Preserve a spirit of harmony
- Help the organization accomplish its goals

The most common guide to parliamentary procedure is *Robert's Rules of Order,* available in various editions and revisions. Also available are less technical guides based on "Robert's Rules." You can determine how strictly you want to adhere to parliamentary procedure. For small groups you may be quite flexible, but for larger groups you'll want to use a more formal approach.

As the meeting gets under way, you'll discover that some participants are too quiet and others are too talkative. To draw out the shy types, ask for their input on issues that particularly pertain to them. You might say something like, "Roberto, you've done a lot of work in this area. What do you think?" For the overly talkative, simply say that time is limited and others need to be heard from. The best meetings are those where everyone participates, so don't let one or two people dominate your meeting while others doodle on their notepads. As you move through your agenda, stop at the end of each item, summarize what you understand to be the feelings of the group, and state the important points made during the discussion.

At the conclusion of the meeting, tie up the loose ends. Either summarize the general conclusion of the group or list the suggestions. Wrapping things up ensures that all

CHECKLIST FOR MEETINGS

A. PREPARATION
1. Determine the meeting's objectives.
2. Work out an agenda that will achieve your objectives.
3. Select participants.
4. Determine the location, and reserve a room.
5. Arrange for light refreshments, if appropriate.
6. Determine whether the lighting, ventilation, acoustics, and temperature of the room are adequate.
7. Determine seating needs: chairs only or table and chairs.

B. CONDUCT
1. Begin and end the meeting on time.

2. Control the meeting by following the announced agenda.
3. Encourage full participation, and either confront or ignore those who seem to be working at cross-purposes with the group.
4. Sum up decisions, actions, and recommendations as you move through the agenda, and restate main points at the end.

C. FOLLOW-UP
1. Distribute the meeting's notes or minutes on a timely basis.
2. Take the follow-up action agreed to.

participants agree on the outcome and gives people a chance to clear up any misunderstandings. Before the meeting breaks up, briefly review who has agreed to do what by what date.

As soon as possible after the meeting, the leader gives all participants a copy of the minutes or notes, showing recommended actions, schedules, and responsibilities. The minutes will remind everyone of what took place and will provide a reference for future actions.

Like leaders, participants have responsibilities during meetings. If you've been included in the group, try to contribute to both the subject of the meeting and the smooth interaction of the participants. Use your listening skills and powers of observation to size up the interpersonal dynamics of the people; then adapt your behavior to help the group achieve its goals. Speak up if you have something useful to say, but don't monopolize the discussion. (To review the tasks that contribute to productive meetings, see this chapter's Checklist for Meetings.)

SUMMARY

Oral communication is of primary importance in business. The two key skills are speaking and listening, both of which contribute to effective interpersonal relationships. Speaking well requires a conscious effort to plan and edit your remarks in light of your audience's needs. Listening also requires conscious effort. Both skills enhance your ability to resolve conflicts, overcome resistance, and handle negotiations.

An interview is any planned, purposeful conversation involving at least two people. Various types of interviews require different mixes of the four main types of questions: open-ended, direct open-ended, closed-ended, and restatement. Planning an interview is much like planning a written message. The interview should be tailored to the subject, purpose, and audience and should include an opening, a body, and a close.

In business a great deal of time is spent in meetings. Their effectiveness depends on careful planning and skillful leadership. The personal motives of the participants can affect the outcome of the meeting. The goal is to get all participants to share information or to contribute to a sound decision.

● OMMUNICATION CHALLENGES AT 3M

As director of 3M's human relations department, Virginia Johnson constantly faces demands for effective communication—with her own staff, with executives throughout the company, in one-on-one interviews, and in meetings. Her department (an offshoot of human resources) is charged with making sure the company meets all its legal responsibilities to employees (through equal-hiring, affirmative-action, and family-leave policies, for instance). Johnson's department is also the place employees can bring problems they would feel uncomfortable discussing with supervisors. So Johnson is sometimes supporting employees and sometimes explaining management's perspective—she's always striving to achieve a balanced and fair conclusion that meets everyone's needs. Work like this requires every person in her eight-member department to be a good listener and a good speaker.

INDIVIDUAL CHALLENGE: Several members of your department have been confused by Johnson's way of doing things, which are slightly different from her predecessor's. A fellow staffer explains to you that by the time he retired, Johnson's predecessor was "a well-loved man throughout the company. They all miss him." Johnson wants to clear the air and establish her own way of doing things. As Johnson's assistant, you have been asked to advise her whether to (1) write a memo clarifying procedures, (2) call each of the eight department members into her office for a one-on-one interview, or (3) hold a meeting of the entire department. Decide on the best approach and explain your reasoning in a brief memo to Johnson. Then develop an outline, an agenda, questions, or whatever is appropriate for the method you suggest. (Invent any details you need.)

TEAM CHALLENGE: Johnson has asked your group to conduct research on family-leave policies. She wants to know whether managers at all 3M locations around the country are following the same procedures regarding unpaid leave for new parents and whether men and women are being treated equally, as company policy prescribes. She also wants to know whether workers are be-

ing restored to jobs of equal pay and responsibility when they return.

You'll be interviewing supervisors and managers via telephone to determine their procedures, attitudes, and opinions on family-leave policies. (On the basis of recent complaints, Johnson suspects returning workers might be subject to subtle prejudices that are denying them the raises and promotions they deserve.) Follow the Checklist for Interviews on the Job in this chapter to make all necessary preparations for the interviews. Discuss your ideas as a group and record them for further class discussion.[30]

CRITICAL THINKING QUESTIONS

1. Do you believe that you're better at sending written, oral, or nonverbal messages? Why does this particular form of communication appeal to you? When receiving messages, are you better at reading, listening, or interpreting nonverbal cues? Why do you think this is true?
2. Have you ever made a comment you later regretted? Describe the circumstances of your verbal blunder, and explain the consequences.
3. When communicating across cultures, U.S. businesspeople tend to be impatient. What are the drawbacks of such impatience? How would you suggest dealing with this trait? Explain.

4. When was the last time you negotiated for something? Were you successful in achieving your aims? If you could repeat the experience, what would you do differently? Briefly explain.
5. Should meeting leaders always use a participatory style, or are there some circumstances when this might not be advisable? Explain your answer.
6. During your meeting with members of your project team, one member keeps raising objections to points of style in a rough draft of your group's report. At this rate you'll be here for hours debating whether to use the word *criteria* or the word *parameter* on page 27. What should you do? Explain your answer.

EXERCISES

1. As a middle manager, you report to your supervisor monthly in an informative interview. The only problem is, your boss keeps interrupting the interview to accept phone calls, leaving you sitting, staring at the ceiling, until she's finished. Make a list of what, if anything, you can do about her behavior. Explain the rationale for each item on your list.
2. With a partner, attend the same meeting, and each of you take notes. Compare your notes. What differences are apparent in your perceptions? What in the listening process accounts for those differences? Summarize what you learn in a memo to your instructor.
3. Visit the 3M home page on the Internet at <http://www.3m.com>. To gain more information from 3M, write an e-mail message in which you ask two open-ended and two closed-ended questions about products and markets. Print out your e-mail message for submission.

4. What kinds of questions (open-ended, direct open-ended, closed-ended, restatement) are most likely to be asked by the interviewers in these situations? Explain your answers.
   a. A management consultant evaluating a proposed personnel policy
   b. A job interviewer attempting to solicit additional information from a shy respondent
   c. A supervisor trying to settle a dispute between co-workers
   d. An accountant preparing a client's tax returns
   e. A human resources counselor probing for more information in a sensitive area
5. Read through the following situations, and think about them from the viewpoint of both participants:
   a. A high school debate coach has scheduled an appointment with the school principal in an attempt to obtain $250 to take her debate team to the state finals in Peoria, Illinois. The team is strong, and

she feels that it has a good chance of winning some type of award. However, the school activities budget is limited.

b. A counselor has scheduled an interview with a company employee who has a long, consistent record of excellent work. Recently, however, the employee has been coming to work late and often appears distracted on the job.

c. As part of the job-evaluation process and in an attempt to have her civil service position upgraded, an employee has submitted a job description of her work. An evaluator from the civil service has scheduled an interview at the job location to discuss the candidate's requested upgrading.

For each participant, what is the general purpose of the interview? What sequence of conversation might best accomplish this purpose? What type of information should be sought or presented? Explain your answers.

6. Plan to conduct an informational interview with a professional working in your chosen career area. Plan the tone and structure of the interview, and create a set of interview questions. Using the information you gather, write a summary describing for another student the tasks, pitfalls, and advantages this career entails. (Your reader is a person who plans to enter this career.)

7. Attend a campus meeting (preferably of a preprofessional organization). Evaluate the meeting with regard to (a) the leader's ability to clearly articulate the meeting's goals, (b) the leader's ability to engage members in a meaningful discussion, (c) the group's dynamics, and (d) the group's listening skills. Prepare a memo summarizing your evaluations.

8. It's up to you to decide (a) whether to have one class meeting off campus and (b) at what location. Your instructor will divide the class into groups of no more than five or six. In the time allowed, the members of each group will discuss the possibilities and reach a decision. Inform your instructor of your decision in a memo.

9. Analyze the dynamics of the group you participated in for the previous exercise. Identify the role played by each member of your group. Describe the phases your group passed through to reach the decision.

10. In a memo to your instructor, prepare a detailed agenda of the off-campus class meeting discussed in exercise 8.

11. You belong to a professional organization that meets monthly. Members are all professionals in your career area, and the organization's purpose is to provide networking and educational opportunities in the form of lectures, talks, roundtable discussions, and presentations. Your meetings are well attended (about 20 members each month), but the members are stiff with one another, few of them engage in casual conversation, and the atmosphere is generally strained. As meeting leader, what can you do to put other members more at ease and encourage them to get to know one another? Put your ideas in a memo to your instructor, and be prepared to discuss them in class.

12. Two of your employees have personal differences that are beginning to interfere with their work. Suggest some ways that you might resolve the conflict. Put your suggestions and explanations into a memo to be submitted.

13. At your department staff meetings one person tends to dominate the discussion, presenting her ideas and ignoring the contributions of others. As department manager, you can see that the more forceful this person becomes, the more others in the group withdraw and the less they contribute to the discussion. How would you encourage more equitable participation? Please explain.

14. Your company is opening a new office in Japan, and you are unfamiliar with Japanese culture and business practices. Suggest some ways you and your coworkers could learn more about the cultural differences that might affect work relationships. Briefly explain your suggestions.

15. Every month, each employee in your department is expected to give a brief oral presentation of his or her project status. However, your department has recently been joined by an employee with a severe speech impediment that prevents people from understanding most of what he has to say. As department manager, how would you resolve this dilemma? Please explain your answer.

16. You're conducting an information interview with a high-level executive in another division of your company. Partway through the interview, this person shows clear signs of impatience. How should you respond? Explain your answer.

CHAPTER 20

GIVING SPEECHES AND ORAL PRESENTATIONS

AFTER STUDYING THIS CHAPTER, YOU WILL BE ABLE TO

- Categorize speeches and presentations according to their purpose
- Identify the audience characteristics that govern decisions about the style and content of speeches and presentations
- Discuss four steps required in planning a speech or presentation
- Develop an introduction, a body, and a close for a long formal presentation
- Select, design, and use visual aids that are appropriate for various types of speeches and presentations
- Explain techniques you can use to improve your public speaking skills

COMMUNICATION CLOSE-UP AT PHOENIX MANAGEMENT

Shirley Crouch and Jo Waldron aren't just two women in business—they're two women with physical challenges who refuse to believe that "it can't be done." Together they formed Phoenix Management, a small Colorado company that has developed a revolutionary device to help people with hearing impairment. It's called HATIS.

HATIS stands for "Hearing Aid Telephone Interconnect System." The device consists of a small box that connects to a telephone receiver and diverts the sound directly to an over-the-ear coupler that interfaces with the telecoil in a person's hearing aid. Before HATIS was invented, people with hearing loss could use systems requiring relay operators, but no form of wireless (cellular) communication was accessible to them. That's changing—thanks to Crouch and Waldron.

Crouch says the two women had to start "from the ground up" to educate executives at companies such as Motorola, AT&T, Nokia, Ericsson/GE, Fujitsu, IBM, SEGA, and Audiovox about what HATIS could do. The result is that these companies are all developing newly accessible telecommunication products using the HATIS system. Some are even giving the products away to those who need them, and this makes the owners of Phoenix Management extremely happy.

Undoubtedly, their skill at giving outstanding presentations has been a major factor in Crouch and Waldron's success. Today, when they speak before a room full of people, they have everything going for them.

First, they have credibility. Their personal experiences and their credentials give meaning to everything they say. Waldron has a 97 percent hearing loss (which is classified as "totally deaf"), plus she's challenged by "post-polio syndrome," a painful condition that affects muscle tissues. In 1987 Ronald Reagan presented her with the

Shirley Crouch and Jo Waldron

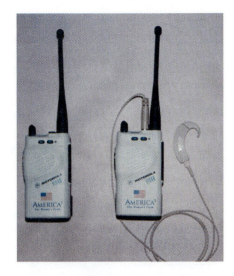

The HATIS equipment has always been the most powerful visual aid that Crouch and Waldron could use during presentations. The over-the-ear interface helps people with hearing aids use telephones and cellular equipment. Whether demonstrating the equipment by using a volunteer from an auditorium audience or by using Waldron's HATIS-equipped cellular phone in a corporate office, the impact is always exciting.

Handicapped American Award, and she still serves on the President's Committee on the Employment of People with Disabilities. Although HATIS won't work for everyone, it makes telephone communication possible even for Waldron. Furthermore, she's not a shy speaker—in fact, it was Waldron who coined the term, "physically challenged." Crouch also has nearly total hearing loss in one ear and a 46 percent loss in the other, plus she faces the challenge of rheumatoid arthritis. She, too, has spoken on behalf of a national organization for people with disabilities.

Second, Crouch and Waldron start every presentation with a sure-fire attention-getter. If they're addressing an audience that includes people with hearing loss—along with families, doctors, or teachers—they start by asking for a volunteer who has never been able to use a telephone. It's the volunteer's facial expression that wins the audience over, says Crouch—they're watching a person who's hearing someone on the other end of the phone *for the first time,* and everyone in the room understands what that means.

"If you bring your audience to you and involve them, then it flows a lot easier than having a staunch and rigid presentation," says Crouch. Waldron has a favorite way of doing this for corporate audiences. She'll stride confidently into the front office and ask to use a telephone, knowing that many companies still don't have accessible equipment available for people with hearing loss. Then, to quell everyone's flustered embarrassment, Waldron pulls out her HATIS-equipped cellular phone and starts the kind of presentation that has landed the two women so many important contracts.

They also use visual aids to create interest. HATIS itself is their best visual aid, says Crouch. Sometimes they also bring along a few of the actual devices (or visuals of them) that many HATIS users can now enjoy, such as multimedia computers, stereos, video games, televisions, cassette players, and so on.

To keep audiences emotionally involved, Crouch and Waldron use meaningful anecdotes and examples. They might describe the little boy who was suddenly willing to use school learning equipment—to the astonishment of his teachers. Or they'll tell of the elated business executive who discovered that he would be able to talk to his girlfriend over the phone—without an interpreting operator.

Finally, Crouch says they possess two important ingredients for successful presentations: sincerity and conviction. "We feel strongly that we have developed a product that will enable millions throughout the world to finally have freedom of communication and the self-confidence that brings. The world has been opened to them," Crouch explains. "If I don't believe in something, I can't promote it and I cannot actively get excited or pretend that I can get somebody else excited about it." But when it comes to HATIS and its potential for the 120 million to 150 million people in the world who are hearing impaired, Crouch and Waldron have no problem conveying genuine enthusiasm and ending every presentation on a positive note.[1]

SPEAKING AND PRESENTING IN A BUSINESS ENVIRONMENT

As Shirley Crouch will tell you, giving speeches and oral presentations can be an integral part of your business career. Chances are you'll have an opportunity to deliver a number of speeches and presentations throughout your career. You may not speak before large audiences of employees or the media, but you'll certainly be expected to present ideas to your colleagues, make sales presentations to potential customers, or engage in other kinds of spoken communication. For most speeches and formal presentations, you'll follow three general steps:

1. Prepare to speak (by defining your purpose, analyzing your audience, and planning your speech's content, length, and style)
2. Develop your speech or presentation (including the introduction, body, close, question-and-answer period, and visual aids)
3. Deliver your speech or presentation

PREPARING TO SPEAK

Preparing speeches and oral presentations is much like preparing any other message: You define your purpose, analyze your audience, and plan how to present your points. However, because speeches and presentations are delivered orally under relatively public circumstances, they require a few special communication techniques. A speech is a one-shot event—your audience cannot leaf back through pages to review something you said earlier. For this reason, you must make sure audience members will hear what you say and remember it.

Define Your Purpose

During your career you may be called on to give speeches and presentations for all sorts of reasons. If you're in the human resources department you may give orientation briefings to new employees or explain company policies, procedures, and benefits at assemblies. If you're a department supervisor, you may conduct training programs. If you're a problem solver or consultant, you may give analytical presentations on the merits of various proposals.

These speeches and presentations can be categorized according to their purpose, which helps you determine content and style. The four basic categories are to inform, to persuade, to motivate, and to entertain. Here are sample statements of purpose for business speeches:

- To inform the accounting department of the new remote data-access policy
- To explain to the executive committee the financial ramifications of OmniGroup's takeover offer
- To persuade potential customers that our bank offers the best commercial banking services for their needs
- To motivate the sales force to close 10 percent more business this quarter

The amount of audience interaction varies from presentation to presentation, depending on your purpose.

Many of your business speeches and presentations will be informative, and if you're involved in a marketing or sales position, you'll need to do persuasive presentations as well. Motivational speeches tend to be more specialized. Many companies bring in outside speakers who specialize in motivational speaking. Entertainment speeches are perhaps the rarest in the business world, and they are usually limited to after-dinner speeches and speeches at conventions or retreats. But no matter which kind of speech you plan to make, it will always start with understanding your audience.

Analyze Your Audience

Once you have your purpose firmly in mind, you should think about another basic element of your speech or presentation: your audience. As Shirley Crouch of Phoenix Management points out, analyzing your audience is a particularly important step because you'll be gearing the style and content of your speech to your audience's needs and interests. When you're preparing to speak, be sure to review the discussion of audience analysis in Chapter 5. This chapter's Checklist for Audience Analysis also provides a good summary. Of course, for even more insight into audience evaluation (including emotional and cultural issues) consult a good public speaking textbook.

The nature of the audience affects your strategy for achieving your purpose.

If you're involved in selecting the audience, you'll certainly have information about their characteristics. However, you'll often be speaking to a group of people you know very little about. You'll have a much better chance of achieving your purpose if you investigate the audience's characteristics before you show up to speak. Ask your host or some other contact person for help with audience analysis, and supplement that data with some informed estimates of your own.

Gear the content, organization, and style of your message to the audience's size, background, and attitude.

Plan Your Speech or Presentation

Planning an oral message is similar to planning a written message: You establish the main idea, organize an outline, estimate the appropriate length, and decide on the most effective style. At every step, your work is driven by what you know about your audience. For example, if you're planning a sales presentation, focus on how much your

CHECKLIST FOR AUDIENCE ANALYSIS

A. AUDIENCE SIZE AND COMPOSITION
  1. Estimate how many people will attend.
  2. Consider whether they have some political, religious, professional, or other affiliation in common.
  3. Analyze the mix of men and women, age ranges, socioeconomic and ethnic groups, occupations, and geographic regions represented.

B. PROBABLE AUDIENCE REACTION
  1. Analyze why audience members are attending the speech or presentation.
  2. Determine the audience's general attitude toward the topic.
     a. Decide whether the audience is very interested, moderately interested, or unconcerned.
     b. Review how the audience has reacted to similar issues in the past.
     c. Determine which facets of the subject are most likely to appeal to the audience.
     d. Decide whether portions of your message will create problems for any members of the audience.
  3. Analyze the mood that people will be in when you speak to them: tired from listening to other presentations like yours or fresh because your presentation comes early in the agenda, interested in hearing a unique presentation, restless from sitting too long in one position and needing a minute to stretch.
  4. Figure out which sort of backup information will most impress the audience: technical data, statistical comparisons, cost figures, historical information, generalizations, demonstrations, samples, and so on.
  5. Predict audience response.
     a. List ways that the audience will benefit from your message.
     b. Formulate an idea of the most desirable audience reaction and the best possible result (what you want the audience to believe or do afterward).
     c. Anticipate possible objections or questions.
     d. Analyze the worst thing that might happen and how you might respond.

C. LEVEL OF AUDIENCE UNDERSTANDING
  1. Determine whether the audience already knows something about the subject.
     a. Analyze whether everybody has about the same amount of knowledge.
     b. Consider whether the audience is familiar with your vocabulary.
  2. Estimate whether everybody is equally capable of understanding the message.
  3. Decide what background information the audience will need to understand the subject.
  4. Think about the mix of general concepts and specific details you will need to explain.
  5. Consider whether the subject involves routine, recurring information or an unfamiliar topic.

D. AUDIENCE RELATIONSHIP WITH THE SPEAKER
  1. Analyze how this audience usually reacts to speakers.
  2. Determine whether the audience is likely to be friendly, open-minded, or hostile toward your purpose in making the speech or presentation.
  3. Decide how the audience is likely to respond to you.
     a. Analyze what the audience expects from you.
     b. Think about your past interactions with the audience.
     c. Consider your relative status.
     d. Consider whether the audience has any biases that might work against you.
     e. Take into account the audience's probable attitude toward the organization you represent.
  4. Decide which aspects of your background are most likely to build credibility.

product will benefit the people in your audience, not on how great the product is. If you're explaining a change in medical benefits for company employees, address the concerns your audience is likely to have, such as cost and quality of care.

Establishing the Main Idea

The main idea points up how the audience can benefit from your message.

What is the main idea, or theme, that you want to convey to the audience? Look for a one-sentence generalization that links your subject and purpose to the audience's frame of reference, much as an advertising slogan points out how a product can benefit consumers:

- Demand for low-calorie, high-quality frozen foods will increase because of basic social and economic trends.
- Reorganizing the data-processing department will lead to better service at a lower cost.
- We should build a new plant in Texas to reduce operating costs and to capitalize on growing demand in the Southwest.
- The new health plan reduces our costs by 12 percent while maintaining quality coverage.

Each of these statements puts a particular slant on the subject, one that is positive and directly related to the audience's interests. This sort of "you" attitude helps keep the audience's attention and convinces people that your points are relevant. For example, a group of new employees will be much more responsive to your discussion of plant safety procedures if you focus on how the procedures can save their lives rather than on how the rules conform to Occupational Safety and Health Administration guidelines.

Organizing an Outline

With a well-crafted main idea to guide you, you can begin to outline your speech or presentation. This outline is affected by your subject, your purpose, and your audience, as well as the time allotted for your presentation. If you have ten minutes or less to deliver your message, organize your thoughts much as you would a letter or brief memo, using the direct approach if the subject involves routine information or good news and using the indirect approach if the subject involves bad news or persuasion. Plan your introduction to arouse interest and to give a preview of what's to come. For the body of the presentation, be prepared to explain the who, what, when, where, why, and how of your subject. In the final paragraph or two, review the points you've made, and close with a statement that will help your audience remember the subject of your speech (see Figure 20.1).

Structure a short speech or presentation like a letter or memo.

Longer speeches and presentations are organized like reports (see Chapter 17 for specific suggestions). If the purpose is to entertain, motivate, or inform, use direct order and a structure imposed naturally by the subject (importance, sequence, chronology, spatial orientation, geography, category—as discussed in Chapter 15). If the purpose is to analyze, persuade, or collaborate, organize your material around conclusions and recommendations or around a logical argument. Use direct order if the audience is receptive and indirect if you expect resistance (see Figure 20.2 on pages 659–660).

Organize longer speeches and presentations like formal reports.

Regardless of the length of your speech or presentation, bear in mind that simplicity of organization is especially useful in oral communication. Once listeners lose the thread of your comments, they have a hard time catching up and following the remainder of your message. They can't review a paragraph or flip pages back and forth, as they can when reading. So look for the most obvious and natural way to organize your ideas, using a direct order of presentation whenever possible. Explain at the beginning how you've organized your material, and try to limit the number of main points to three or four—even when the speech or presentation is rather long. To keep the audience's attention, be sure to include only the most useful, interesting, and relevant supporting evidence. In addition, reorient the audience at the end of each section by summarizing the point you've just made and explaining how it fits into your overall framework.

Use a clear, direct organization to accommodate your listeners' limitations.

A carefully prepared outline may be more than just the starting point for composing a speech or presentation. If you plan to deliver your presentation from notes rather than from a written text, your outline can also become your final "script." For this reason the headings on the outline should be complete sentences or lengthy phrases rather

Use an outline as your "script," but be prepared to deviate in response to audience feedback.

Figure 20.1
In-Depth Critique: Sample Outline for a Brief Speech

The following is the outline of a brief persuasive speech delivered by a human resources manager to persuade a group of executives to invest in an on-site fitness center.

PHYSICAL FITNESS IS GOOD FOR BUSINESS

> **Purpose: To convince company officers to approve an on-site fitness center.**

This introduction will arouse interest and preview what is coming in the presentation.

I. **Introduction**
Mention the words "computer programmer," and the picture that comes to mind is a person spending 12 or more hours a day in a cubicle pounding away at a keyboard. This may be the stereotype, but it is outdated. Programmers and employees in general are more and more aware that physical activity makes them more healthy, happy, and productive. Corporations have also learned the benefits of having healthy, fit employees.

Items II, III, and IV support the main idea (that an on-site fitness center would be a good investment).

II. **The most obvious improvement is in lowered health-related costs. [slides]**
A. People who are physically active are generally healthier and take fewer sick days.
B. Increased activity leads to better general health and fewer visits to the doctor, which means lower health insurance costs for the company.
C. Better physical fitness results in a reduction in work-related injuries.

III. **Improving employees' physical fitness increases company profitability.**
A. Studies show that improved physical fitness increases employee productivity. [slide]
B. Physical activity also increases creativity.

IV. **A survey of college seniors showed fringe benefits to be the second most important factor (after salary) in choosing a company.**

The conclusion summarizes all the evidence that makes the installation of the center such a good business decision.

V. **Conclusion: Installing an on-site fitness center makes good business sense.**

---

than one- or two-word topic headings. Many speakers also include notes that indicate where visual aids will be used. You might want to write out the transitional sentences you'll use to connect main points. Experienced speakers often use a two-column format, which separates the "stage directions" from the content (see Figure 20.3 on page 661).

Presentation software can help you organize your speech. Packages such as PowerPoint and Freelance Graphics include special outline tools that simplify organizing and formatting your outline. Both provide a variety of ways to print notes and hand-

Figure 20.2
In-Depth Critique: Sample Outline for a 30-Minute Presentation

The following is the outline of a 30-minute analytical presentation organized around conclusions and presented in direct order. This outline is based on Chapter 18's Electrovision report, written by Linda Moreno. This presentation follows the same basic organization as the report did.

OUR TRAVEL AND ENTERTAINMENT COSTS
ARE OUT OF CONTROL

> **Purpose: To explain why Electrovision's travel and entertainment (T&E) costs are so high and to propose a series of changes to bring them under control.**

I. **Introduction**
    Our T&E costs are way above average, and they pose a threat to the company's financial health; fortunately, we can fix the problem in four straightforward steps that could save as much as $6 million a year.

II. **How we approached the investigation**
    A. We analyzed internal expense reports.
    B. We compared our cost data with nationwide averages.
    C. We analyzed published information on trends and cost-control suggestions.

III. **Analysis of spending patterns**
    A. The amount we've been spending on T&E:
        1. Airfares, hotels, rental cars, restaurants, and entertainment totaled $16 million last year.
        2. T&E budget has increased by 12 percent per year for the past five years.
    B. Where that money goes:
        1. We took 3,390 trips last year at an average cost per trip of $4,725.
        2. Airfares and lodging represent 70 percent of T&E expenses.
    C. How our spending compares with national averages:
        1. Facilities and customers spread from coast to coast force us to spend a lot on travel.
        2. However, we spend 125 percent more than the national average for every travel day.
    D. Why do we spend so much?
        1. First-class travel has been viewed as compensation for the demands of extensive travel.
        2. The sales staff is encouraged to entertain clients.

The overall organization is logical and simple.

The Introduction highlights the problem.

Items II through IV explain why the problem exists.

(continued)

outs. For example, PowerPoint allows you to view all your overhead transparencies and slides in thumbnail to help you choose the items you want to discuss and display (see Figure 20.4 on page 662).

Of course, you may have to adjust your organization in response to feedback from your audience, especially if your purpose is to collaborate. You can plan ahead by

Figure 20.2
(Continued)

3. **T&E costs are hard for managers to view and study.**
4. **No one has central responsibility for controlling costs.**

IV. **Impact on profits**
   A. **T&E costs continue to rise, as are other company costs.**
   B. **Revenue is projected to decline in coming years.**
   C. **Bottom line: we're headed for trouble.**

V. **Solution**
   A. **We should institute tighter spending controls:**
      1. **Hire a travel manager to control costs and negotiate group discounts.**
      2. **Develop a formal, written policy to contain costs.**
      3. **Give departmental managers the data they need to make smarter decisions.**
   B. **We can reduce unnecessary travel and entertainment costs:**
      1. **Cut down on discretionary trips (seminars, etc.).**
      2. **Reduce the number of intracompany trips and employees sent on each trip.**
      3. **Encourage employees to economize.**
   C. **We can find lower travel rates:**
      1. **Negotiating corporate discounts.**
      2. **Planning trips more carefully to take advantage of lower fares.**
   D. **We can replace some travel with technological alternatives:**
      1. **Conference calls**
      2. **Videoconferences**
      3. **Other possibilities**
   E. **Potential impact of all these changes: as much as $6 million in reduced costs**

VI. **Conclusion**
   We spend more on T&E than we should, and four fairly obvious steps will yield significant cost savings.

Item V explores alternatives and makes a recommendation.

thinking of several organizational possibilities (based on "what if" assumptions about your audience's reactions). Then if someone says something that undercuts your planned approach, you can switch smoothly to another one.

Estimating Length

The average speaker can deliver about one paragraph, or 125 to 150 words, in a minute.

Time for speeches and presentations is often strictly regulated, so you'll need to tailor your material to the available time. You can use your outline to estimate how long your speech or presentation will take. The average speaker can deliver about 125 to 150 words a minute (or roughly 7,500 to 9,000 words an hour), which corresponds to 20 to 25 double-spaced, typed pages of text per hour. The average paragraph is about

The following excerpt is taken from a presentation that was made to persuade a company's marketing department to reassess its strategies.

SLIDE 1:
  Text
  Overview

SLIDE 2:
  Web site screen
  Highlight 1st point

SLIDE 3:
  Bar chart
  Internet usage,
  1975 to present

SLIDE 4:
  Bar chart
  Internet advertising,
  1985 to present

SLIDE 5:
  Table
  Current costs vs.
  Internet marketing
  estimates

SLIDE 6:
  Text
  Preview second point

INTRO: Have our marketing techniques become stale?

I. The Internet and World Wide Web open up totally new marketing possibilities.

  A. Usage of the Internet has mushroomed since its introduction.

      1. The number of business advertising outlets on the Internet has increased significantly in the last few years.

      2. Selling products via the Internet is gaining popularity.

  B. Marketing via the Internet can increase profitability.

Transition: Compared to the excitement of the Internet, our marketing techniques seem dated.

The introduction is geared to arouse interest.

Outline items are in complete sentences.

Each slide noted here highlights a point being made and can even be used by the speaker as a prompt during delivery.

The transition leads listeners to the second main point: a view of marketing techniques currently being used.

125 to 150 words in length, so most of us can speak at a rate of about one paragraph per minute.

Say you want to make three basic points. In a 10-minute speech, you could take about 2 minutes to explain each of these points, using roughly two paragraphs for each point. If you devoted a minute each to the introduction and the conclusion, you would have 2 minutes left over to interact with the audience. If you had an hour, however, you could spend the first 5 minutes introducing the presentation, establishing rapport with the audience, providing background information, and giving an overview of your topic. In the next 30 to 40 minutes, you could explain each of the three points, spending about 10 to 13 minutes per point (the equivalent of 5 or 6 typewritten pages). Your conclusion might take another 3 to 5 minutes. The remaining 10 to 20 minutes would then be available for responding to questions and comments from the audience.

Which is better, the 10-minute speech or the hour-long presentation? If your speech doesn't have to fit into a specified time slot, the answer depends on your subject, your audience's attitude and knowledge, and the relationship you have with your audience. For a simple, easily accepted message, 10 minutes may be enough. On the other hand, if your subject is complex or your audience is skeptical, you'll probably need more time. Don't squeeze a complex presentation into a period that is too brief, and don't draw out a simple talk any longer than necessary.

Be sure that your subject, purpose, and organization are compatible with the time available.

Figure 20.4
Using Presentation Software to Print Your Speaker's Notes

By allowing you to view a thumbnail layout of your slides (or overheads), PowerPoint lets you choose your most important points and visually organize your speech around them.

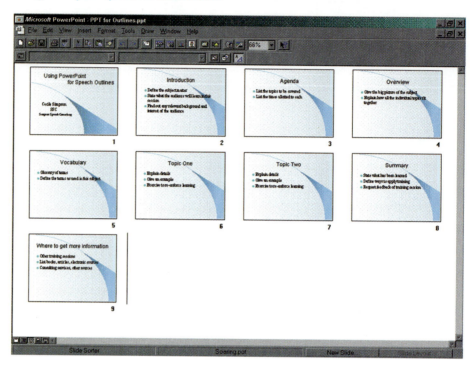

Deciding on Style

Another important element in your planning is the style you choose. Will you present a formal speech in an impressive setting, with professionally produced visual aids? Or will you lead a casual, roll-up-your-sleeves working session? Choose your style to fit the occasion. The size of the audience, the subject, your purpose, your budget, and the time available for preparation all determine the style.

Use a casual style for small groups; use a formal style for large groups and important events.

In general, if you're speaking to a relatively small group, you can use a casual style that encourages audience participation. A small conference room, with the audience seated around a table, may be appropriate. Use simple visual aids. Invite the audience to interject comments. Deliver your remarks in a conversational tone, using notes to jog your memory if necessary. This is the approach taken by Edward McQuade, a vice president of Campbell Soup. He prefers a casual style, talking from notes rather than a script and emphasizing his main points by using hand gestures naturally—just as he would in a personal conversation.[2]

On the other hand, if you're addressing a large audience and the event is an important one, you'll want to establish a more formal atmosphere. A formal style is well suited to announcements about mergers or acquisitions, new products, financial results, and other business milestones. Executives of Hewlett-Packard and other public companies regularly meet with securities analysts to discuss financial performance. Because the analysts are responsible for recommending particular stocks, companies are eager to make a good impression. During these formal presentations, the speakers generally stand on a stage or platform, positioned behind a lectern and using a microphone so that their remarks can be heard throughout the room. These speeches are often accompanied by multimedia presentations showcasing major products, technological breakthroughs, and other information that the speakers want audience members to remember.

DEVELOPING YOUR SPEECH OR PRESENTATION

Developing a major speech or presentation is much like writing a formal report, with one important difference: You need to adjust your technique to an oral communication channel. This channel presents both an opportunity and a challenge.

The opportunity lies in the interaction that is possible between you and the audience. When you speak before a group, you can receive information as well as transmit it. So you can adjust both the content and the delivery of your message as you go along, editing your speech or presentation to make it clearer and more compelling. Instead of simply expressing your ideas, you can draw out the audience's ideas and use them to reach a mutually acceptable conclusion.

To realize the benefits of oral communication, though, you need to plan carefully. The challenge of this channel is controlling what happens. As you develop each part of your speech or presentation, stop and think about how you plan to deliver the information. The more you plan to interact with your audience, the less control you'll have. Halfway through your presentation a comment from someone in the audience might force you to shift topics. If you can anticipate such shifts, you'll have a chance to prepare for them.

How formal speeches and presentations differ from formal reports:
- *More interaction with the audience*
- *Use of nonverbal cues to express meaning*
- *Less control of content*
- *Greater need to help the audience stay on track*

The Introduction

You'll have a lot to accomplish during the first few minutes of your speech or presentation, including arousing your audience's interest in your topic, establishing your credibility, and preparing the audience for what will follow. That's why preparing the introduction often requires a disproportionate amount of your attention.

The introduction captures attention, inspires confidence, and previews the contents.

Arousing Interest

Some subjects are naturally more interesting than others. If you will be discussing a matter of profound significance that will personally affect the members of your audience, chances are they'll listen regardless of how you begin. All you really have to do is announce your topic ("Today I'd like to announce the reorganization of the company").

Other subjects, however, call for more imagination. How can you get anyone to listen if you're explaining the pension program to a group of new clerical employees, none of whom will be full participants for another five years and most of whom will probably leave the company within two? The best approach to dealing with an uninterested audience is to appeal to human nature. Encourage people to take the subject personally. Show them how they'll be affected as individuals. You might plan to begin your address to new clerical employees like this:

Connect the topic to the listeners' needs and interests.

> If somebody offered to give you $200,000 in exchange for $5 per week, would you be interested? That's the amount you can expect to collect during your retirement years if you choose to contribute to the voluntary pension plan. During the next two weeks, you will have to decide whether you want to participate. Although for most of you retirement is many years away, this is an important financial decision. During the next 20 minutes, I hope to give you the information you need to make that decision intelligently.

Experienced speakers always make sure that the introduction matches the tone of the speech or presentation. If the occasion is supposed to be fun, you may begin with something light; but if you're talking business to a group of executives, don't waste their time with cute openings. Avoid jokes and personal anecdotes when you're discussing a serious problem. If you're giving a routine oral report, don't be overly dramatic. Most of all, be natural. Nothing turns off the average audience faster than a trite, staged beginning. (See "Tired of Being Ignored? Five Ways Guaranteed to Get Attention and Keep It.")

Building Credibility

One of the chief drawbacks of overblown openings is that they damage the speaker's credibility, and building credibility is probably even more important than arousing interest. A speaker with high credibility is more persuasive than a speaker with low credibility.[3] So it's important to establish your credentials—and quickly; people will decide within a few minutes whether you're worth listening to.[4] You want the audience to like you as a person and to respect your opinion, and you have to plan for this while you're developing your speech.

Establishing credibility is relatively easy if you're speaking to a familiar, open-minded audience. The difficulty comes when you try to earn the confidence of strangers, especially those predisposed to be skeptical or antagonistic.

One way to handle the problem is to let someone else introduce you. That person can present your credentials so that you won't appear boastful, but make sure the person introducing you doesn't exaggerate your qualifications. Some members of the audience are likely to bristle if you're billed as being the world's greatest authority on your subject.

Without boasting, explain why you are qualified to speak on the subject.

If you're introducing yourself, plan to keep your comments simple. At the same time, don't be afraid to mention your accomplishments. Your listeners will be curious about your qualifications, so tell them briefly who you are and why you're there. Generally speaking, one or two aspects of your background are all you need to mention: your position in an organization, your profession, and the name of your company. You might plan to say something like this:

> I'm Karen Whitney, a market research analyst with Information Resources Corporation. For the past five years, I've specialized in studying high-technology markets. Your director of engineering, John LaBarre, has asked me to brief you on recent trends in computer-aided design so that you'll have a better idea of how to direct your R&D efforts.

This speaker would establish credibility by tying her credentials to the purpose of her presentation. By mentioning her company's name, her position, and the name of the audience's boss, she will let her listeners know immediately that she's qualified to tell them something they need to know. She connects her background to their concerns.

Previewing the Presentation

Let the audience know what lies ahead.

Phoenix Management's Crouch and Waldron strongly believe that you need to "Tell them what you're going to tell them." Giving your audience a preview of what's ahead adds to your authority and, more important, helps people understand your message. A reader can get an idea of the structure of a report by looking at the table of contents and scanning the headings. In an oral presentation, however, the speaker provides the framework. Otherwise, the audience may be unable to figure out how the main points of the message fit together.

Your introduction should summarize your main idea, identify the supporting points, and indicate the order in which you'll develop those points. Tell your listeners in so many words, "This is the subject, and these are the points I will cover." Once

SHARPENING YOUR SKILLS

TIRED OF BEING IGNORED? FIVE WAYS GUARANTEED TO GET ATTENTION AND KEEP IT

In any speech or presentation (especially in a long formal one), using attention-getters throughout your speech maintains and revives the audience's interest. Here are five possibilities:

- **Use humor.** In business the subject of most presentations is serious. Nevertheless, you can still include a light comment now and then to perk up the audience. Just be sure the humor is relevant to the presentation. However, if you're not comfortable telling jokes, don't try to do it in a speech. Also, be very careful about offending your audience with inappropriate humor.
- **Tell a story.** Most audiences will pay attention to a story, and you can generally find one that illustrates an important point. A speaker who was trying to explain his company's strategy of buying old, low-priced houses and fixing them up told this story: "One of the first properties we bought was in a very poor part of town, and we had serious reservations about buying it. We were especially worried about the motorcycle tracks on the wall, but we fixed that with a coat of paint. In fact, that house taught me the value of paint in general. Most of our properties don't look like much on the surface, but they are solid underneath. All they need is a few coats of paint, some basic carpentry, new landscaping, and *voilà*! The ugly duckling emerges as a beautiful swan."
- **Pass around a sample.** Psychologists say that you can get people to remember your points by appealing to their senses. The best way to do that is to pass around a sample. If your company is in the textile business, let the audience handle some of your fabrics. If you sell chocolates, give everybody a taste.

- **Ask a question.** Asking questions will get the audience actively involved in your speech and, at the same time, give you information about them and their needs. A securities broker whose presentation was designed to arouse interest in tax-free municipal bonds used these questions at various points in her talk: "How many of you paid over $10,000 in taxes last year?" "What's the biggest risk you run when you invest in common stocks?" "How important is safety to your investment strategy?" "What kind of return do you want on your investments?" These questions made the audience think about what she was saying, and their answers helped her understand them.
- **State a startling statistic.** People love details. If you can interject an interesting statistic, you can often wake up an audience. In a presentation on opportunities in the computer field, you might say, "Experts estimate that by the turn of the century, 80 percent of the gross domestic product will depend on computers in one way or another."

Regardless of the attention-getters you use, remember to use them in moderation and with good taste. If you're giving a serious business presentation, keep the tone of your remarks on a businesslike level.

1. Which of your lecture classes do you enjoy the most? What techniques does the instructor use to keep students interested?
2. Say you're giving a presentation on white-collar crime. By using creative thinking or by conducting research, come up with three attention-getters you might use to enliven your talk.

---

you've established the framework, you can move into the body of the presentation, confident that the audience will understand how the individual facts and figures relate to your main idea.

The Body

The bulk of your speech or presentation is devoted to a discussion of the three or four main points in your outline. Use the same organizational patterns you'd use in a letter, memo, or report, but keep things simple. Your goals are (1) making sure the structure of your speech or presentation will be clear and (2) making sure your organization will keep your audience's attention.

Limit the body to three or four main points.

Emphasizing Structure

Help your audience follow
your presentation
• By summarizing as you go
along
• By emphasizing the transitions from one idea to the
next

A written report uses typographical and formatting clues—headings, paragraph indentions, white space, lists—to show how ideas are related. However, an oral presentation relies more on words.

For the small links between sentences and paragraphs, one or two transitional words
are enough: *therefore, because, in addition, in contrast, moreover, for example, consequently, nevertheless, finally.* To link major sections of the speech or presentation, you
need complete sentences or paragraphs, such as "Now that we've reviewed the problem, let's take a look at some solutions." Every time you shift topics, stress the connection between ideas. Summarize what's been said, and then preview what's to come.

The longer your presentation, the more important the transitions become. If you
will be presenting many ideas, the audience will have trouble absorbing them and seeing the relationship among them. Listeners need clear transitions to guide them to the
most important points. Furthermore, they need transitions to pick up any ideas they
may have missed. If you plan to repeat key ideas in the transitions, you can compensate for lapses in the audience's attention. When you actually deliver your speech, you
might also want to call attention to the transitions by using gestures, changing your tone
of voice, or introducing a visual aid.

Holding the Audience's Attention

Make a special effort to capture wandering attention.

To communicate your points effectively, you have to maintain the audience's attention.
Here are a few helpful tips for developing memorable speeches:

* *Relate your subject to the audience's needs.* People are interested in things that
  affect them personally. Plan to present every point in light of the audience's needs
  and values.
* *Use clear, vivid language.* People become bored quickly when they don't understand the speaker. If your presentation will involve abstract ideas, plan to show
  how those abstractions connect with everyday life. Use familiar words, short sentences, and concrete examples.
* *Explain the relationship between your subject and familiar ideas.* Plan to show
  how your subject relates to ideas the audience already understands so that you
  give people a way to categorize and remember your points.[5]

You can also hold the audience's interest by introducing variety into your presentation. One useful technique is to pause occasionally for questions or comments from
the audience. This helps you determine whether the audience understands key points
before you launch into another section; it also gives the audience a chance to switch for
a time from listening to participating. Plan your pauses, even going so far as to note
them in your outline so that you won't forget them once you're on stage. Visual aids
will also help clarify points and stimulate interest.

The Close

The close should leave a
strong and lasting impression.

The close of a speech or presentation is almost as important as the beginning because
audience attention peaks at this point. Plan to devote about 10 percent of the total time
to the ending. When developing your conclusion, begin by telling listeners that you're
about to finish so that they'll make one final effort to listen intently. Don't be afraid to
sound obvious. Consider saying something like "in conclusion" or "to sum it all up."
You want people to know that this is the home stretch.

Restating the Main Points

Once you've planned how to get everyone's attention, you'll repeat your main idea. Be sure to emphasize what you want the audience to do or think. Then state the key motivating factor. Reinforce your theme by repeating the three or four main supporting points. A few sentences are generally enough to refresh people's memories. Here's how one speaker ended a presentation on the company's executive compensation program:

> We can all be proud of the way our company has grown. If we want to continue that growth, however, we will have to adjust our executive compensation program to reflect competitive practices. If we don't, our best people will look for opportunities elsewhere.
> In summary, our survey has shown that we need to do four things to improve executive compensation:
>
> - Increase the overall level of compensation.
> - Install a cash bonus program.
> - Offer a variety of stock-based incentives.
> - Improve our health insurance and pension benefits.
>
> By making these improvements, we can help our company cross the threshold of growth into the major leagues.

The speaker repeats his recommendations and then concludes with a memorable statement that motivates the audience to take action.

Summarize the main idea, and restate the main points.

Describing the Next Steps

Some speeches and presentations require the audience to reach a decision or agree to take specific action. In such cases the close provides a clear wrap-up. If the audience agrees on an issue covered in the presentation, plan to review the consensus in a sentence or two. If not, make the lack of consensus clear by saying something like "We seem to have some fundamental disagreement on this question." Then you'll be ready to suggest a method of resolving the differences.

If you expect any action to occur, you must explain who is responsible for doing what. One effective technique is to list the action items, with an estimated completion date and the name of the person responsible. Plan to present this list in a visual aid that can be seen by the entire audience, and ask each person on the list to agree to accomplish his or her assigned task by the target date. This public commitment to action is the best insurance that something will happen.

If the required action is likely to be difficult, make sure everyone understands the problems involved. You don't want people to leave the presentation thinking their tasks will be easy, only to discover later that the jobs are quite demanding. If that happens, they may become discouraged and fail to complete their assignments. You'll want everyone to have a realistic attitude and to be prepared to handle whatever arises. So when planning your presentation, use the close to alert people to potential difficulties or pitfalls.

Be certain that everyone agrees on the outcome and understands what should happen next.

Ending on a Positive Note

Make sure your final remarks will be enthusiastic and memorable. Even if parts of your speech are downbeat, plan to close on a positive note. You might stress the benefits of action or express confidence in the listeners' ability to accomplish the work ahead. An alternative is to end with a question or a statement that will leave your audience thinking.

Remember that your final words round out the presentation. You'll want to leave the audience with a satisfied feeling, a feeling of completeness. The close is not the place to introduce new ideas or to alter the mood of the presentation. Although you want to close on a positive note, avoid using a staged finale. Keep it natural. As with everything else in your speech, plan your closing remarks carefully. You don't want to wind up on stage with nothing to say but, "Well, I guess that's it."

The Question-and-Answer Period

Along with the introduction, body, and close, include in your speech or presentation an opportunity for questions and answers. Otherwise, you might just as well write a report. If you aren't planning to interact with the audience, you're wasting the chief advantage of an oral format.

Specifics about handling questions from the audience are discussed in this chapter under the heading "Mastering the Art of Delivery." In general, the important thing to consider when you're developing your speech is the nature and timing of that audience interaction. Responding to questions and comments during the presentation can interrupt the flow of your argument and reduce your control of the situation. If you're addressing a large group, particularly a hostile or an unknown group, questions can be dangerous. Your best bet in this case is to ask people to hold their questions until after you have concluded your remarks. On the other hand, if you're working with a small group and need to draw out ideas, encourage comments from the audience throughout the presentation.

Regardless of when you respond to questions, remember that they're one of the most important parts of your presentation. Questions give you a chance to obtain important information, to emphasize your main idea and supporting points, and to build enthusiasm for your point of view. Try to anticipate as many questions as you can, and rehearse your answers. The more you know about your audience, the better you'll be at anticipating both positive and negative questions.

Encourage questions throughout your speech if you are addressing a small group, but ask a large audience to defer questions until later.

The Visual Aids

Phoenix Management's Crouch and Waldron use visual aids to create interest and clarify important points. From a purely practical standpoint, visuals are a convenience for the speaker, who can use them as a tool for remembering the details of the message (no small feat in a lengthy presentation); novice speakers also like visual aids because they draw audience attention away from the speaker. More important, visual aids dramatically increase the audience's ability to absorb and remember information. Audiences remember only 10 percent of a speaker's message when it's presented solely through words; however, they remember 50 percent when the information is supported with such visual aids as slides and overhead transparencies.[6] Although the visual aids used in speeches and presentations are similar in many respects to those used in documents (see Chapter 16), they also differ significantly. Special software packages can simplify the design and presentation of visual aids (see "Your Audience Will Get the Picture: Presentation Software Can Create Lively Business Speeches").

Visual aids help both the speaker and the audience remember the important points.

Designing and Presenting Visual Aids

Two types of visual aids are used to supplement speeches and presentations. Text visuals consist of words and help the audience follow the flow of ideas. Because text visuals are simplified outlines of your presentation, you can use them to summarize and preview the message and to signal major shifts in thought. On the other hand, graphic visual aids illustrate the main points. They help the audience grasp numerical data and other information that would be hard to follow if presented orally.

Two kinds of visual aids:
- *Text visuals help listeners follow the flow of ideas.*
- *Graphic visuals present and emphasize important facts.*

KEEPING PACE WITH TECHNOLOGY

YOUR AUDIENCE WILL GET THE PICTURE: PRESENTATION SOFTWARE CAN CREATE LIVELY BUSINESS SPEECHES

As personal computers become more and more powerful, many software products are becoming easier to use. Multimedia packages that were once only used by experts are now so user-friendly that you can quickly learn how to prepare and present your own visual materials for oral presentations.

However, when choosing a presentation software package, it's vital to consider who will be using the software and for what purpose. Programs developed for graphics designers trained in creating visual materials would not be appropriate for employees with no training in graphic arts. Some of the more popular presentation software programs now available include Harvard Graphics (from Software Publishing Corp.), PowerPoint (from Microsoft), Charisma (from Micrografx), and Freelance Graphics (from Lotus). A good presentation software package should make it easy for you to do four tasks:

1. Choose an appropriate chart or graph format to present your information. Some information is best conveyed by a bar chart. Other information is more easily understood in table or pie chart form.
2. Enhance the graphic so that it grabs the audience's attention without distracting from the information presented. You should be able to add color, shading, drawings, clip art, or even your company's logo.
3. Organize the visuals in a logical manner and provide continuity throughout. Good software packages include an outline mode that helps organize your presentation in a logical order and then create the visuals to support your message. Most packages also allow you to specify graphical elements that you want repeated

on every visual, such as a border, company logo, or background graphic.

4. Select the most appropriate output formats for your presentation. Such formats can range from paper handouts to slides or transparencies to computer-based presentations. You can even use the computer to present as well as create the visuals. The choice of output format depends largely on your audience. Slides and transparencies work well for large groups, but they require a projector. Paper handouts are simpler, but people tend to read through the handout instead of focusing on your presentation. Computer-based presentations let you avoid the trouble of printing slides or transparencies, but they require some fairly expensive equipment.

Multimedia presentations can be quite complex, including sound, graphics, video, and text information. One pitfall of this technology is the tendency to create a multimedia blitz that overwhelms and confuses the audience. Whether you use simple bar charts or complex multimedia, remember that the purpose of presentation packages is to *support* your message—visual aids are not the message itself.

1. Watch several television or in-person speeches made by political candidates, social activists, or business leaders. How do these speakers make use of computer tools for preparing and presenting their messages? How could they use these tools more effectively?
2. How might companies use a Web site to supplement or perhaps even replace some live presentations?

Simplicity is the key to effectiveness when designing both types of visual aids. Because people can't read and listen at the same time, the visual aids have to be simple enough for the audience to understand them within a moment or two. At the same time, visual aids should be just that—aids that enhance your speech by explaining and emphasizing key points. Having too many visuals or visuals that are too complicated or too flashy can detract from your message.

As a rule, text visuals are more effective when they consist of no more than six lines, with a maximum of six words per line. Produce them in large, clear type, using uppercase and lowercase letters, with extra white space between lines of text. Make sure the type is large enough to be seen from any place in the room. Phrase list items in parallel grammatical form. Use telegraphic wording ("Compensation Soars," for example) without being cryptic ("Compensation"); you are often better off including both a noun and a verb in each item.

Many speeches and presentations begin with several text visuals. The first is usually the equivalent of a title page: It announces the subject and signals the audience that the presentation is under way. The second typically lists the three or four major points you'll cover, providing a road map of what's to come. The remaining text visuals are used to emphasize the transitions between the main points. Like the headings in a written report, they signal that a new topic is about to be introduced.

You can use any of the graphic visuals you might show in a formal report, including line, pie, and bar charts, as well as flow charts, organization charts, diagrams, maps, drawings, and tables. However, graphic visuals used in oral presentations are simplified versions of those that appear in written documents. Eliminate anything that is not absolutely essential to the message. To help the audience focus immediately on the point of each graphic visual, use headings that state the message in one clear phrase or sentence: "Earnings have increased by 15 percent."

When you present visual aids, you want people to have the chance to read what's there, but you also want them to listen to your explanation:

> **Visual aids are counter-productive if the audience can't clearly see or understand them within a few moments.**

- Be sure that all members of the audience can see the visual aids.
- Allow the audience time to read a visual aid before you begin your explanation.
- Limit each visual aid to one idea.
- Illustrate only the main points, not the entire presentation.
- Avoid visual aids that conflict with your verbal message.
- Paraphrase the text of your visual aid; don't read it word for word.
- When you've finished discussing the point illustrated by the visual aid, remove it from the audience's view.[7]

Remember that you want the audience to listen to you, not to study the visual aids. The visual aids are there to supplement your words—not the other way around.

Selecting the Right Medium

> **Visual aids may be presented in a variety of media.**

Visual aids for documents are usually limited to paper. For speeches and presentations, however, you have a variety of media to choose from:

- **Handouts.** Even in a presentation, you may choose to distribute sheets of paper bearing an agenda, an outline of the program, an abstract, a written report, or supplementary material such as tables, charts, and graphs. Listeners can keep the handout to remind them of the subject and the main ideas of your presentation. In addition, they can refer to it while you're speaking. Handouts work especially well in informal situations where the audience takes an active role; they often make their own notes on the handouts. However, handouts can be distracting because people are inclined to read the material rather than listen to you, so many speakers distribute handouts after the presentation.
- **Chalkboards and whiteboards.** When you're addressing a small group of people and want to draw out their ideas, use a board to list points as they are mentioned. Because visual aids using this medium are produced on the spot, boards provide flexibility. However, they're too informal for some situations.
- **Flip charts.** Large sheets of paper attached at the top like a tablet can be propped on an easel so that you can flip the pages as you speak. Each chart illustrates or clarifies a point. You might have a few lines from your outline on one, a graph or diagram on another, and so on. By using felt-tip markers of various colors, you can highlight ideas as you go along. Keep it simple: Try to limit each flip-chart page to three or four graphed lines or to five or six points in list format.

- *Overheads.* One of the most common visual aids in business is the overhead transparency, which can be projected on a screen in full daylight. Because you don't have to dim the lights, you don't lose eye contact with your audience. Transparencies are easy to make using a typed original on regular paper, a copying machine, and a page-size sheet of plastic. Opaque projections are similar to transparencies but do not require as much preparation. You could use an opaque projector to show the audience a photograph or an excerpt from a report or manual.

- *Slides.* The content of slides may be text, graphics, or pictures. If you're trying to create a polished, professional atmosphere, you might find this approach worthwhile, particularly if you'll be addressing a crowd and don't mind speaking in a darkened room. However, remember that you may need someone to operate the projector and that you'll need to coordinate the slides with your speech. Take a few minutes before your speech to verify that the equipment works correctly.

- *Computers.* With special projection equipment, a personal computer can be turned into a large-screen "intelligent chalkboard" that allows you to create and modify your visual aids as the presentation unfolds. If you're discussing financial projections, you can show how a change in sales forecasts will affect profits by typing in a new number. When the presentation is over, you can print out hard copies of the visual aids and distribute them to interested members of the audience. Using this technology, you can prepare a multimedia presentation incorporating photos, sound, video, and animation.[8]

- *Other visual aids.* In technical or scientific presentations, a sample of a product or material allows the audience to experience your subject directly. Models built to scale are convenient representations of an object. Audiotapes are often used to supplement a slide show or to present a precisely worded and timed message. Filmstrips and movies can capture the audience's attention with color and movement. Television and videotapes are good for showing demonstrations, interviews, and other events. In addition, filmstrips, movies, television, and videotapes can be used as stand-alone vehicles (independent of a speaker) to communicate with dispersed audiences at various times. For example, PepsiCo's CEO, Wayne Calloway, videotapes many of his important presentations and sends them to all the company's operating divisions to keep employees updated on the business.[9]

Table 20.1 (see page 672) summarizes some of the factors to consider when selecting a visual medium.

With all visual aids, the crucial factor is how you use them. Properly integrated into an oral presentation, they can save time, create interest, add variety, make an impression, and illustrate points that are difficult to explain in words alone.

Use visual aids to highlight your spoken words, not as a substitute for them.

MASTERING THE ART OF DELIVERY

When you've planned all the parts of your presentation and have your visual aids in hand, you're ready to begin practicing your delivery. You have a variety of delivery methods to choose from, some of which are easier to handle than others:

- *Memorizing.* Unless you're a trained actor, avoid memorizing an entire speech, particularly a long one. You're likely to forget your lines. Furthermore, a memorized speech often sounds stiff and stilted. And in many business speaking situations, you'll need to address questions and comments from the audience during your speech, so you have to be flexible and sometimes adjust your speech as you go. On the other hand, memorizing a quotation, an opening paragraph, or a few concluding remarks can bolster your confidence and strengthen your delivery.

TABLE 20.1

GUIDELINES FOR SELECTING VISUALS

Visual	Optimum Audience Size	Degree of Formality	Design Complexity	Equipment and Room Requirements	Production Time	Cost
Handouts	Fewer than 110	Informal	Simple	Typed text and photocopying machine	Typing or drawing time; photocopying time	Inexpensive
Boards and Flip Charts	Fewer than 20	Informal	Simple	Chalkboard or whiteboard or easel and chart, with writing implements	Drawing time only	Inexpensive
Overheads	About 100	Formal or informal	Simple	Text, copy machine, plastic sheets, and projector screen	Drawing or typing time; photocopying time	Inexpensive— unless designed or typeset professionally
Slides	Several hundred	Formal	Anything that can be photo- graphed	Slides, projec- tor, and screen; dim lighting	Design and photographing time; at least 24 hours' pro- duction time	More expensive

- *Reading.* If you're delivering a technical or complex presentation, you may want to read it. Policy statements by government officials are sometimes read because the wording may be critical. If you choose to read your speech, practice enough so that you can still maintain eye contact with the audience. Triple-spaced copy, wide margins, and large type help too. You might even want to include stage cues for yourself, such as *pause, raise hands, lower voice.*

Speaking from notes is gener- ally the best way to handle delivery.

- *Speaking from notes.* Making a presentation with the help of an outline, note cards, or visual aids is probably the most effective and easiest delivery mode. It gives you something to refer to and still allows for eye contact and interaction with the audience. If your listeners look puzzled, you can expand on a point or put it another way. (Generally, note cards are preferable to sheets of paper; ner- vousness is more evident in shaking sheets of paper.)

- *Impromptu speaking.* You might give an impromptu, or unrehearsed, speech in two situations: when you've agreed to speak but have neglected to prepare your re- marks or when you're called on to speak unexpectedly. Avoid speaking unprepared unless you've spoken countless times on the same topic or are an extremely good public speaker. When you're asked to speak "off the cuff," take a moment or two to think through what you're going to say. Then avoid the temptation to ramble.

Regardless of which delivery mode you use, be sure that you're thoroughly familiar with the subject. Knowing what you're talking about is the best way to build your self-confidence. It's also helpful to know how you'll approach preparing for successful speaking, delivering the speech, and handling questions.

Getting Ready to Give Your Presentation

In addition to knowing your material, you can build self-confidence by practicing, especially if you haven't had much experience with public speaking. Even if you practice in front of a mirror, try to visualize the room filled with listeners. Put your talk on tape to check the sound of your voice and your timing, phrasing, and emphasis. If possible, rehearse on videotape to see yourself as your audience will. Go over your visual aids and coordinate them with the talk.

Whenever you can, check the location for your presentation in advance. Look at the seating arrangements, and make sure they're appropriate for your needs. If you want the audience to sit at tables, be sure tables are available. Check the room for outlets that may be needed for your projector or microphone. Locate the light switches and dimmers. If you need a flip-chart easel or a chalkboard, be sure it's on hand. Check for chalk, an eraser, extension cords, and any other small but crucial items you might need.

If you're addressing an audience that doesn't speak your language, consider using an interpreter. Working with an interpreter adds some constraints to your presentation. You must speak slowly enough that the interpreter can keep up with you, but not so slowly that the rest of the audience loses interest. Send your interpreter a copy of your speech—and any visual aids—as far in advance as possible. Of course, any time you make a speech or presentation to people from other cultures, take into account cultural differences in appearance, mannerisms, and other customs, in addition to adapting the content of your speech. If you are working with an interpreter, the interpreter will be able to suggest appropriate changes for the audience or occasion. When you're addressing a U.S. or Canadian audience with few cultural differences, follow the specific guidelines in this chapter.

Before you speak
- Practice
- Prepare the location

Delivering the Speech

When it's time to deliver the speech, you may feel a bit of stage fright. Most people do, even professional actors. A good way to overcome your fears is to rehearse until you're thoroughly familiar with your material.[10] Communication professionals have suggested other tips:

A little stage fright is normal.

- Prepare more material than necessary. Extra knowledge, combined with a genuine interest in the topic, will boost your confidence.
- Think positively about your audience, yourself, and what you have to say. See yourself as polished and professional, and your audience will too.
- Be realistic about stage fright. After all, even experienced speakers admit that they feel butterflies before they address an audience. A little nervous excitement can actually provide the extra lift that will make your presentation sparkle.
- Use the few minutes while you're arranging your materials, before you actually begin speaking, to tell yourself you're on and you're ready.
- Before you begin speaking, take a few deep breaths.
- Have your first sentence memorized and on the tip of your tongue.
- If your throat is dry, drink some water.

- If you feel that you're losing your audience during the speech, don't panic. Try to pull them back by involving them in the action.
- Use your visual aids to maintain and revive audience interest.
- Keep going. Things usually get better, and your audience will silently be wishing you success.

Perhaps the best way to overcome stage fright is to concentrate on your message and your audience, not on yourself. When you're busy thinking about your subject and observing the audience's response, you tend to forget your fears. Even so, as you deliver your presentation, try to be aware of the nonverbal signals you're transmitting. To a great degree, your effectiveness will depend on how you look and sound.

Don't rush the opening.

As you approach the speaker's lectern, breathe deeply, stand up straight, and walk slowly. Face the audience. Adjust the microphone. Count to three slowly; then survey the room. When you find a friendly face, make eye contact and smile. Count to three again; then begin your presentation.[11] Even if you feel nervous inside, this slow, controlled beginning will help you establish rapport.

Use eye contact, posture, gestures, and voice to convey an aura of mastery and to keep your audience's attention.

Once your speech is under way, be particularly careful to maintain eye contact with the audience. Pick out several people positioned around the room, and shift your gaze from one to another. Doing this will make you appear to be sincere, confident, and trustworthy; moreover, it will help you perceive the impression you're creating.

Your posture is also important in projecting the right image. Stand tall, with your weight on both feet and your shoulders back. Avoid gripping the lectern. In fact, you might step out from behind the lectern to help the audience feel more comfortable with you and to express your own comfort and confidence in what you're saying. Use your hands to emphasize your remarks with appropriate gestures. At the same time, vary your facial expressions to make the message more dynamic.

Finally, think about the sound of your voice. Studies indicate that people who speak with lower voice tones at a slightly faster than average rate are perceived as be-

When speaking before a large audience, such as this Chamber of Commerce meeting in Dubuque, Iowa, Richard Gaines tries to make his audience's experience more personal by making an eye-to-eye connection with individuals throughout the room.

ing more credible.[12] Speak in a normal, conversational tone but with enough volume so that everyone in the audience can hear you. Try to sound poised and confident, varying your pitch and speaking rate to add emphasis. Don't ramble or use meaningless filler words like *um, you know, okay,* and *like.* Speak clearly and crisply, articulating all the syllables, and sound enthusiastic about what you're saying.

Handling Questions

The question-and-answer period is a valuable section of an oral presentation. It gives you a chance to emphasize points you made earlier, work in material that didn't fit in the formal presentation, identify audience resistance, and work to overcome resistance. Many speakers do well delivering the speech or presentation, only to falter during the question-and-answer period. Phoenix Management's Shirley Crouch believes that preparation is the key to handling this segment effectively. Spend time before your speech thinking about the questions that might arise—including abrasive or difficult questions. Then be ready with answers. In fact, some experts recommend that you hold back some dramatic statistics as ammunition for the question-and-answer session.[13] However, bear in mind that circumstances may require some changes in the answers you prepare.

When someone poses a question, focus your attention on that individual. Pay attention to body language and facial expression to help determine what the person really means. Nod your head to acknowledge the question; then repeat it aloud to confirm your understanding and to ensure that the entire audience has heard it. If the question is vague or confusing, ask for clarification. Then give a simple, direct answer. Don't say more than you need to if you want to have enough time to cover all the questions. If giving an adequate answer would take too long, simply say, "I'm sorry that we don't have time to get into that issue right now, but if you'll see me after the presentation, I'll be happy to discuss it with you." If you don't know the answer, don't pretend that you do. Instead, say something like "I don't have those figures. I'll get them for you as quickly as possible." Remember that you don't always have to answer every question that is asked.

Keep your answers short and to the point.

If the message you delivered is unpopular, be prepared for hostile questions. Treat hostile questions as legitimate requests for information. Maintaining your professionalism will improve your credibility.

Don't allow one or two people to monopolize the question period. Try to give everyone a chance to participate; call on people from different parts of the room. If the same person keeps angling for attention, say something like "Several other people have questions; I'll get back to you if time permits." If audience members try to turn a question into an opportunity to mount their own soapboxes, it's up to you to maintain control. You might admit that you and the questioner have a difference of opinion and offer to get back to the questioner after you've done more research. Then call on someone else. Another approach is to respond with a brief answer, thus avoiding a lengthy debate or additional questions.[14] Finally, you might thank the person for the question and then remind the questioner that you were looking for specific questions. Don't indulge in put-downs, which may backfire and make the audience more sympathetic to the questioner.

Don't let any member of the audience monopolize your attention or turn a question into a debate.

If you're ever on the hot seat, remember to be honest, but keep your cool. Look the person in the eye, answer the question as well as you can, and try not to show your feelings. Don't get into an argument. If questioners challenge your ideas, logic, or facts,

Respond unemotionally to tough questions.

they may be trying to push you into overreacting. Defuse hostility by paraphrasing the question and asking the questioner to confirm that you've understood it correctly. Break long, complicated questions into parts that you can answer simply. State your response honestly, accurately, and factually, and move on to the next question. Avoid postures or gestures that might seem antagonistic. Maintain a businesslike tone of voice and a pleasant expression.[15]

In case your audience is too timid or hostile to ask questions, you might want to plant some of your own. If a friend or the meeting organizer gets the ball rolling, other people in the audience will probably join in. You might also ask a question yourself: "Would you like to know more about . . ." If someone in the audience answers, act as if the question came from that person in the first place. When all else fails, say something like, "I know from past experience that most questions are asked after the question period. So I'll be around afterward to talk."[16]

When the time allotted for your presentation is up, call a halt to the question-and-answer session, even if more people want to talk. Prepare the audience for the end by saying: "Our time is almost up. Let's have one more question." After you've made your reply, summarize the main idea of the presentation and thank people for their attention. Conclude the way you opened: by looking around the room and making eye contact. Then gather your notes and leave the podium, shoulders straight, head up. (The Checklist for Speeches and Oral Presentations is a reminder of the tasks involved in these types of oral communication.)

CHECKLIST FOR SPEECHES AND ORAL PRESENTATIONS

A. DEVELOPMENT OF THE SPEECH OR PRESENTATION
1. Analyze the audience.
2. Begin with an attention-getter.
3. Preview the main points.
4. Limit the discussion to no more than three or four points.
5. Explain who, what, when, where, why, and how.
6. In longer presentations include previews and summaries of major points as you go along.
7. Close by reviewing your main points and making a memorable statement.

B. VISUAL AIDS
1. Use visual aids to show how things look, work, or relate to one another.
2. Use visual aids to highlight important information and create interest.
3. Select appropriate visual aids.
   a. Use flip charts, boards, or transparencies for small, informal groups.
   b. Use slides or films for major occasions and large groups.

4. Limit each visual aid to three or four graphed lines or five or six points.
5. Use short phrases.
6. Use large, readable type.
7. Make sure equipment works.

C. DELIVERY
1. Establish eye contact.
2. Speak clearly and distinctly.
3. Do not go too fast.
4. Be sure everyone can hear.
5. Speak in your natural style.
6. Stand up straight.
7. Use gestures in a natural, appropriate way.
8. Encourage questions.
   a. Allow questions during the presentation if the group is small.
   b. Ask the audience to hold their questions until the end if the group is large or hostile.
9. Respond to questions without getting sidetracked.
10. Maintain control of your feelings in spite of criticism.

SUMMARY

At some point in your career you're likely to be called on to give a speech or presentation. Brief speeches (5 to 15 minutes) are organized like letters and short memos. Formal presentations, lasting up to an hour or more, generally involve more complex subjects and require more interaction with the audience. They're organized like formal reports, with an introduction, a body, and a close.

Many long speeches and presentations make use of visual aids such as handouts, chalkboards, flip charts, overheads, slides, computers, and audiovisual equipment. These visuals are selected to suit your purpose and the size and needs of your audience.

Practice your presentation thoroughly in advance. As you address the audience, use nonverbal communication skills to enhance your effectiveness. Be sure to make eye contact and to speak so that everyone can understand you. If you encounter difficult questions, remain unemotional. Respond as well as you can, and then move on.

COMMUNICATION CHALLENGES AT PHOENIX MANAGEMENT

Shirley Crouch and Jo Waldron have just learned of an opportunity to participate in an upcoming telecommunications convention. They'll be setting up a booth for their company that will have sufficient wiring and space to display working HATIS systems integrated with telephones, multimedia computers, and a CD-player. Other exhibitors will be displaying technological wonders, but Crouch and Waldron figure they'll be the only ones with specialized equipment for people with hearing loss.

The organizers expect attendance at the convention to top 100,000 over three days. It's open to the public, but it's scheduled during the week to attract purchasing agents from both large and small companies. The Phoenix booth might even attract executives from the few telecommunications manufacturers who are not yet incorporating HATIS into their products.

INDIVIDUAL CHALLENGE: Crouch, Waldron, and their interns (recruited to help out at the booth) will ac-

tually be making small oral presentations every time they speak with a booth visitor. They want you, one of their interns, to prepare by making notes. First define your purpose and analyze your audience. (Is there more than one?) Outline your mini-presentation, and decide on the appropriate style. Explain how you'll arouse interest, establish credibility, hold attention, and back up your claims. How can you incorporate the HATIS equipment? What questions do you anticipate? Try to imagine everything that might come up, and use what you know about HATIS to make your notes as detailed as possible.

TEAM CHALLENGE: Set up a mock "booth" with props to indicate where you'd place the HATIS equipment, printed literature, company representatives, and so on. Then using your notes, take turns role-playing Phoenix Management representatives and curious passers-by. After everyone has taken a turn as a presenter, talk over your experiences. What would you do differently next time?[17]

CRITICAL THINKING QUESTIONS

1. Would you rather (a) give a speech to an outside audience, (b) be interviewed for a news story, or (c) make a presentation to a departmental meeting? Why? How do the communication skills differ in each situation? Explain.

2. How might the audience's attitude affect the amount of audience interaction during or after a presentation? Explain your answer.

3. Have you ever attended a presentation or a speech in which the speaker's style seemed inappropriate? What effect did that style have on the audience? Briefly explain.

4. What similarities and differences would you expect to see in the introduction to a formal presentation and the introduction to a formal report? Explain.

5. What problems could result from using visual aids during your speech?

6. From the speaker's perspective, what are the advantages and disadvantages of responding to questions from the audience throughout a speech or presentation? From the listener's perspective, which approach would you prefer? Why?

EXERCISES

1. For many years, Toastmasters has been dedicated to helping its members give speeches. Instruction, good speakers as models, and practice sessions aim to teach members to convey information in lively and informative ways. Visit the Toastmasters Web site at <http://www.toastmasters.com> and carefully review the linked pages about listening, speaking, voice, and body. Evaluate the information and outline a three-minute presentation to your class telling why Toastmasters and its Web site would or would not help you and your classmates write and deliver an effective speech.

2. Attend a speech at your school or in your area, or watch a speech on television. Categorize the speech as one that motivates or entertains, one that informs or analyzes, or one that persuades or urges collaboration. Then compare the speaker's delivery and use of visual aids with the Checklist for Speeches and Oral Presentations. Write a two-page report analyzing the speaker's performance and suggesting improvements.

3. Analyze the speech given by someone introducing the main speaker at an awards ceremony, a graduation, or some other special occasion. Does the speech fit the occasion, relate to the audience's interests, and grab attention? How well does the speech motivate the audience to listen to the featured speaker? Does the speech provide the information necessary for the audience to understand, respect, and appreciate the speaker's background and viewpoint? Put yourself in the shoes of the person who made that introduction. Draft a brief (two-minute) speech that prepares the audience for the featured speaker.

4. You've been asked to give an informative ten-minute talk on vacation opportunities in your home state. Draft your introduction, which should last no more than two minutes. Then pair off with a classmate and analyze each other's introductions. How well do these two introductions arouse the audience's interest, build credibility, and preview the presentation? Suggest how these introductions might be improved.

5. Pick a speech from *Vital Speeches of the Day,* a publication of recent speeches on timely and topical subjects. Examine both the introduction and the close; then analyze how these two sections work together to emphasize the main idea. What action(s) does the speaker want the audience to take? Prepare a brief (two-minute) oral presentation summarizing your analysis for your class.

6. Look again at the speech you selected in exercise 5. What nonverbal signals do you think the speaker would have used to emphasize key points? Mark specific phrases you think would be more persuasive or better understood if accompanied by gestures or other nonverbal cues. Which nonverbal signals would you suggest to enhance the delivery of these sections? Explain the effect you would expect these cues to have on the audience.

7. In the speech you selected for exercise 5, note all the transitional sentences or phrases that clarify the speech's structure for listeners. In particular, focus on the transitions that help the speaker shift between supporting points. Using these transitions as clues, list the main message and supporting points; then indicate how each transitional phrase links the current supporting point to the succeeding one.

8. Which media would you use for the visual aids that accompany each of the following speeches? Explain your answers.
   a. An informal ten-minute speech explaining the purpose of a new training program to 300 assembly-line employees
   b. An informal ten-minute speech explaining the purpose of a new training program to five vice presidents
   c. A formal five-minute presentation explaining the purpose of a new training program to the company's 12-member board of directors
   d. A formal five-minute speech explaining the purpose of a new company training program to 35 members of the press

9. For the next meeting of the student government, you're preparing a presentation about the diversity of your college's student population. Prepare an introduction using humor, an introduction using a story, and an introduction using a question. Swap introductions with a classmate and critique how well each of your introductions gets attention. Which works best? Why?

10. With three classmates, practice audience analysis by analyzing the audience of a particular television program. Note the age, gender, race, marital status, relationships, and occupations of the characters. Also pay attention to the commercials that run during the program. On the basis of these clues, who do you think watches this program? Now choose a topic that this audience is likely to feel strongly about. How would you prepare a speech on that topic if you believed the audience would probably be hostile? What would you do differently if you believed the audience would be sympathetic? Present your group's analysis to the class, and defend your answers.

11. Select one of the following main ideas and outline a brief (three- to five-minute) persuasive speech to your business communication class:

   a. As a requirement for graduation, every college student should demonstrate proficiency in basic writing skills by passing a standardized national test.

   b. College students should be allowed access to their confidential academic records at least once a year and, if they choose, submit a written statement disputing or correcting information in the files.

   c. Rather than ask all students to pay an activities fee to support campus sports, require only those students who participate to pay a special sports fee.

   d. The campus computer laboratory should remain open 24 hours a day throughout the week to give students the opportunity to complete their assignments at their own convenience.

   e. All college students should be required to complete a period of community service during their junior or senior years.

12. Prepare a list of questions you might be asked during the question-and-answer period following one of the speeches in exercise 11. Highlight the two or three most difficult or controversial questions, and write your answers. Then team up with a classmate to evaluate how well your answers might satisfy a hostile or skeptical questioner. What can you do to improve these answers?

13. Read the jacket of a book for information about the author. Analyze the author's biography to see how his or her credentials are established. Next, use this biographical information to draft a brief introduction you might use when presenting this speaker to an audience of people who haven't read the book. How can you build the speaker's credibility without exaggerating?

14. Examine the nonverbal signals sent by a political figure who is making a live or televised speech. How do the speaker's gestures, facial expressions, eye contact, and posture contribute to the message? Do these nonverbal signals detract from your confidence in the speaker? Do you detect any signs of nervousness? Is there any aspect of his or her delivery that you think this speaker should work to improve? Explain your answer.

PART
7

SPECIAL TOPICS IN BUSINESS COMMUNICATION

COMPONENT CHAPTER A
Format and Layout of Business Documents

COMPONENT CHAPTER B
Documentation of Report Sources

FORMAT AND LAYOUT OF BUSINESS DOCUMENTS

An effective letter, memo, or report does more than store words on paper. It communicates with the right person, makes an impression, and tells the recipient who wrote it and when it was written. It may even carry responses back to the sender, if only to relate how and by whom it was received and processed.

Over the centuries certain conventions have developed for the format and layout of business documents. Of course, conventions vary from country to country, and even within the United States, few hard-and-fast rules exist. Many organizations even develop variations of standard styles to suit their own needs, adopting the style that's best for the types of messages they send and for the kinds of audiences that receive them. The conventions described here are more common than others. Whether you handle all your own communication via computer or rely on your secretary to handle it for you, knowing the proper form for your documents and knowing how to make them attractive to your readers is crucial.

FIRST IMPRESSIONS

A letter or other written document is often the first (sometimes the only) contact you have with an external audience. Memos and other documents used within an organization represent you to supervisors, colleagues, and employees. So it's important that your documents look neat and professional and that they're easy to read. Your audience's first impressions come from the paper you use, the way you customize it, and the general appearance of your document. These elements tell readers a lot about you and about your company's professionalism.

Paper

From your own experience, you know that a flimsy, see-through piece of paper gives a much less favorable impression than a richly textured piece. Paper quality is measured in two ways: The first measure of quality is weight, specifically the weight of four reams (each a 500-sheet package) of letter-size paper. The quality most commonly used by U.S. business organizations is 20-pound paper, but 16- and 24-pound versions are also used. The second measure of quality is the percentage of cotton in the paper. Cotton doesn't yellow over time the way wood pulp does, and it's both strong and soft. In general, paper with a 25 percent cotton content is an appropriate quality for letters and outside reports. For memos and other internal documents, lighter-weight paper and paper with a lower cotton content may be used. Also, airmail-weight paper may be more cost-effective for international correspondence, but make sure it isn't too flimsy.[1]

In the United States the standard size of paper for business documents is 8-1/2 by 11 inches. Standard legal documents are 8-1/2 by 14 inches. Executives sometimes have heavier 7-by-10-inch paper on hand (with matching envelopes) for such personal messages as congratulations and recommendations.[2] They may also have a box of correspondence note cards imprinted with their initials and a box of plain folded notes for condolences or for acknowledging formal invitations.

Stationery may vary in color. Of course, white is standard for business purposes, although neutral colors such as gray and ivory are sometimes used. Memos are sometimes produced on pastel-colored paper so that internal correspondence can be more easily distinguished from external, and memos are sometimes printed or typed on various colors of paper for routing to separate departments. Light-colored papers are distinctive and often appropriate, but bright or dark colors make reading difficult and may appear too frivolous.

Customization

For letters to outsiders, U.S. businesses commonly use letterhead stationery printed with the company's name and address, usually at the top of the page but sometimes along the left side or even at the bottom of the page. Other information may be included in the letterhead as well: the company's telephone number, fax number, cable address, Web site address, product lines, date of establishment, officers and directors, slogan, and symbol (logo). The idea is to give the recipient of the letter pertinent reference data and a better idea not only of what the company does but also of the company's image.[3] Nevertheless, the letterhead should be as simple as possible; too much information gives the page a cluttered look, cuts into the space needed for the letter, and may become outdated before all the letterhead has been used. If you correspond frequently with people in foreign countries, your letterhead can be misleading. If you do a lot of business abroad, be sure your letterhead is intelligible to foreigners, and make sure it includes the name of your country as well as your cable, telex, e-mail address, or fax information.

In the United States, company letterhead is always used for the first page of a letter. Successive pages are plain sheets of paper that match the letterhead in color and quality, or some companies use a specially printed second-page letterhead bearing only the company's name. Other countries have other conventions. For example, Latin American companies use a cover page with their printed seal in the center.

Many companies also design and print standardized forms for memos and for reports that are written frequently and always require the same sort of information (such as sales reports and expense reports). These forms may be printed in sets for use with carbon paper or in carbonless copy sets that produce multiple copies automatically with the original. More and more, organizations are using computers to generate their standardized forms. These electronic forms can save money and time.[4]

Appearance

Most business documents are produced using either a letter-quality (not a dot-matrix) printer or a typewriter. Some short informal memos are handwritten, and it's appropriate to handwrite a note of condolence to a close business associate. Of course, the envelope is handwritten, printed, or typed to match the document. However, even a letter on the best-quality paper with the best-designed letterhead may look unprofessional if it's poorly produced.

Companies in the United States make sure that documents (especially external ones) are centered on the page, with margins of at least an inch all around (unlike documents produced in Latin America, which use much wider margins and thus look much longer.) Using word-processing or desktop publishing software, you can achieve this balanced appearance simply by defining the format parameters. If you are using a typewriter, such balance can be achieved either by establishing a standard line length or by establishing a "picture frame."

The most common line length is about 6 inches. Lines aren't usually right-hand justified because the resulting text can be hard to read, even with proportional spacing, and because the document generally looks too much like a form letter. Varying line length looks more personal and interesting. If you're using a typewriter, the larger, pica type will give you 60 characters in a line; the smaller, elite type will give you 72 characters in a line. Sometimes a guide sheet, with the margins and the center point marked in dark ink, is used as a backing when typing a page. The number of lines between elements of the document (such as between the date line and inside address in a letter) can be adjusted to ensure that a short document fills the page vertically or that a longer document extends to at least three lines of body on the last page.

Fitting type into a picture frame with even margins all around requires more skill on a typewriter than on a computer. First, estimate the length of the document; then determine the number of characters for each line. Table A.1 gives the most commonly used guidelines for estimating line length; however, tables, set-off quotations, and exceptionally long or short opening and closing elements all affect the size of the margins.

Another important aspect of a professional-looking document is the proper spacing after punctuation. For example, U.S. conventions include (1) leaving one space after commas and semicolons and (2) leaving two spaces after periods at the ends of sentences and after colons (unless your typeface is proportional, requiring only one space). Each letter in a person's initials is followed by a period and a single space. Abbreviations for organizations, such as P.T.A., may or may not have periods, but they never have internal spaces. On computers and typewriters that have no special characters for dashes, use two hyphens with no space before, between, or after. Other details of this sort are provided in your company's style book or in most secretarial handbooks.

Finally, messy corrections are dreadfully obvious and unacceptable in business documents. Be sure that any letter, report, or memo requiring a lot of corrections is reprinted or retyped. Self-correcting typewriters and word-processing software can produce correction-free documents at the push of a button.

LETTERS

For a long time, letters have begun with some kind of phrase in greeting and have ended with some sort of polite expression before the writer's signature. In fact, books printed in the sixteenth century prescribed letter formats for writers to follow. Styles have changed

TABLE A.1

GUIDELINES FOR ESTABLISHING LINE LENGTHS USING THE "PICTURE FRAME" METHOD

Length of Letter	Number of Words	Line Lengths		
		Inches	Elite Characters	Pica Characters
Short	Under 100	4	50	40
Medium	100–200	5	60	50
Long	200–300	6	70	60
Two pages	Over 300	6	70	60

some since then, but all business letters still have certain elements in common. Several of these elements appear in every letter; others appear only when desirable or appropriate. In addition, these letter parts are usually arranged in one of three basic formats.

Standard Letter Parts

All business letters typically include seven elements, in the following order: (1) heading, (2) date, (3) inside address, (4) salutation, (5) body, (6) complimentary close, and (7) signature block. The letter in Figure A.1 shows the placement of these standard letter parts.

Heading

Letterhead (the usual heading) shows the organization's name, full address, and (almost always) telephone number. Executive letterhead also bears the name of an individual within the organization. Computers allow you to design your own letterhead (either one to use for all correspondence or a new one for every correspondence). If letterhead stationery is not available, the heading consists of a return address (but not a name) starting 13 lines from the top of the page, which leaves 2 inches between the return address and the top of the page.

Date

If you're using letterhead, place the date at least one blank line beneath the lowest part of the letterhead. Without letterhead, place the date immediately below the return address. The standard method of writing the date in the United States uses the full name of the month (no abbreviations), followed by the day (in numerals, without *st, rd,* or *th*), a comma, and then the year: July 14, 1997 (7/14/97). The U.S. government and some U.S. industries place the day (in numerals) first, followed by the month (unabbreviated), followed by the year—with no comma: 14 July 1997 (14/7/97). This convention is similar to the one used in Europe, except that European convention replaces the U.S. solidus (diagonal line) with periods when the date appears all in numerals: 14 July 1997 (14.7.1997). The international standard places the year first, followed by the month and the day, using commas in the all-numeral form: 1997 July 14 (1997,7,14). To maintain the utmost clarity, always spell out the name of the month in dates for international correspondence.[5]

When communicating internationally, you may also experience some confusion over time. Some companies in the United States refer to morning (A.M.) and afternoon (P.M.), dividing a 24-hour day into 12-hour blocks so that they refer to four o'clock in the morning (4:00 A.M.) or four o'clock in the afternoon (4:00 P.M.). The U.S. military and European companies refer to one 24-hour period so that 0400 hours (4:00 A.M.) is always in the morning and 1600 hours (4:00 P.M.) is always in the afternoon.[6] Make sure your references to time are as clear as possible, and be sure you clearly understand your audience's time references.

Inside Address

The inside address identifies the recipient of the letter. For U.S. correspondence, begin the inside address one or more lines below the date, depending on how long the letter is. Precede the addressee's name with a courtesy title, such as *Dr., Mr.,* or *Ms.* The accepted courtesy title for women in business is Ms., although a woman known to prefer the title *Miss* or *Mrs.* is always accommodated. If you don't know whether a person is a man or a woman (and you have no way of finding out), do not use a courtesy title. For example, Terry Smith could be either a man or a woman. The first line of the inside address would be just Terry Smith, and the salutation would be Dear Terry Smith. The same is true if you know only a person's initials, as in S. J. Adams.

Figure A.1
In-Depth Critique:
Standard Letter Parts

The writer of this business letter had no letterhead available but correctly included a heading.

Heading

Date

Inside Address

Salutation

Body

Complimentary Closing

Typewritten Name

6412 Belmont Drive
New Weston, OH 45348
June 22, 1997

Mr. Richard Garcia
Director of Franchises
Snack Shoppes
2344 Western Avenue
Seattle, WA 98123

Dear Mr. Garcia:

Last Monday, my wife and I were on our way home from a long weekend, and we stopped at a Snack Shoppe for a quick sandwich. A sign on the cash register gave your address in the event customers were interested in operating a franchise of their own somewhere else. We talked about the idea all evening and into the night.

Although we had talked about changing jobs—I'm an administrative analyst for a utility company and my wife sells real estate—the thought of operating a franchised business had never occurred to us. We'd always thought in terms of starting a business from scratch. However, owning a Snack Shoppe is an intriguing idea.

We would appreciate your sending us full details on owning our own outlet. Please include the names and telephone numbers of other Snack Shoppe owners so that we can talk to them before we make any decision to proceed further. We're excited about hearing from you. Please write soon.

Cordially,

Peter Simond

Peter Simond

☐ One blank space
* Variable spacing, depending on length of letter, except for the top margin which should be 2 inches

Spell out and capitalize titles that precede a person's name, such as *Professor* or *General* (see Table A.2 for the proper forms of address). The person's organizational title, such as *Director,* may be included on this first line (if it is short) or on the line below; the name of a department may follow. In addresses and signature lines, don't forget to capitalize any professional title that follows a person's name:

Mr. Ray Johnson, Dean

Ms. Patricia T. Higgins
Assistant Vice President

However, professional titles not appearing in an address or signature line are capitalized only when they directly precede the name.

President Kenneth Johanson will deliver the speech.
Maria Morales, president of ABC Enterprises, will deliver the speech.
The Honorable Helen Masters, senator from Arizona, will deliver the speech.

If the name of a specific person is unavailable, you may address the letter to the department or to a specific position within the department. Also, be sure to spell out company names in full, unless the company itself uses abbreviations in its official name.

Other address information includes the treatment of buildings, house numbers, and compass directions. Capitalize the names of buildings, and if you specify a location within a building (suite, room, etc.), capitalize it and use a comma to separate it from the building name.

Empire State Building, Suite 1073

Use figures for all house or building numbers, except the number *one*.

One Trinity Lane

637 Adams Avenue, Apt. 7

Spell out compass directions that fall within a street address, but abbreviate compass directions that follow the street address:

1074 West Connover Street

783 Main Street, N.E., Apt. 27

Also remember that apartment, suite, and room numbers always appear in figures (as in the examples already listed in this paragraph). The following example shows all the information that may be included in the inside address and its proper order for U.S. correspondence:

Ms. Linda Coolidge, Vice President
Corporate Planning Department
Midwest Airlines
Kowalski Building, Suite 21-A
7279 Bristol Avenue
Toledo, OH 43617

Canadian addresses are similar, except that the name of the province is usually spelled out:

Dr. H. C. Armstrong
Research and Development
Commonwealth Mining Consortium
The Chelton Building, Suite 301
585 Second Street SW
Calgary, Alberta T2P 2P5

When addressing correspondence for other countries, follow the format and information that appear in the company's letterhead.[7] You want to be especially careful about the format of international correspondence because you want everything to be as clear as possible.[8] The order and layout of address information varies from country to country, so follow the conventions of the country you're writing to. However, when you're sending mail from the United States, be sure the name of the destination country appears on the last line of the address in capital letters. Also, use the English version of

TABLE A.2
FORMS OF ADDRESS

Person	In Address	In Salutation
Personal Titles		
Man	Mr. [first & last name]	Dear Mr. [last name]:
Woman (marital status unknown)	Ms. [first & last name]	Dear Ms. [last name]:
Woman (single)	Ms. *or* Miss [first & last name]	Dear Ms. *or* Miss [last name]:
Woman (married)	Ms. *or* Mrs. [wife's first & last name] *or* Mrs. [husband's first & last name]	Dear Ms. *or* Mrs. [last name]:
Woman (widowed)	Ms. *or* Mrs. [wife's first & last name] *or* Mrs. [husband's first & last name]	Dear Ms. *or* Mrs. [last name]:
Woman (separated or divorced)	Ms. *or* Mrs. [first & last name]	Dear Ms. *or* Mrs. [last name]:
Two men (or more)	Mr. [first & last name] and Mr. [first & last name]	Dear Mr. [last name] and Mr. [last name]: *or* Dear Messrs. [last name] and [last name]:
Two women (or more)	Ms. [first & last name] and Ms. [first & last name] *or* Mrs. [first & last name] and Mrs. [first & last name] *or* Miss [first & last name] and Mrs. [first & last name]	Dear Ms. [last name] and Ms. [last name]: *or* Dear Mses. [last name] and [last name]: Dear Mrs. [last name] and Mrs. [last name]: *or* Dear Mesdames [last name] and [last name]: *or* Mesdames: Dear Miss [last name] and Mrs. [last name]:
One woman and one man	Ms. [first & last name] and Mr. [first & last name]	Dear Ms. [last name] and Mr. [last name]:
Couple (married)	Mr. and Mrs. [husband's first & last name]	Dear Mr. and Mrs. [last name]:
Couple (married with different last names)	[title] [first & last name of husband] [title] [first & last name of wife]	Dear [title] [husband's last name] and [title] [wife's last name]:
Couple (married professionals with same title & same last name)	[title in plural form] [husband's first name] and [wife's first name] [last name]	Dear [title in plural form] [last name]:
Couple (married professionals with different titles & same last name)	[title] [first & last name of husband] [title] [first & last name of wife]	Dear [title] and [title] [last name]:

the country name so that your mail is routed from the United States to the right country. Then, to be sure your mail is routed correctly within the destination country, use the foreign spelling of the city name (using the characters and diacritical marks that would be commonly used in the region). For example, the following address uses Köln, instead of Cologne:

Person	In Address	In Salutation
Professional Titles		
President of a college or university (doctor)	Dr. [first & last name], President	Dear Dr. [last name]:
Dean of a school or college	Dean [first & last name] *or* Dr., Mr., Ms., Mrs., *or* Miss [first & last name], Dean of (title)	Dear Dean [last name]: Dear Dr., Mr., Ms., Mrs., *or* Miss [last name]:
Professor	Professor [first & last name]	Dear Professor [last name]:
Physician	[first & last name], M.D.	Dear Dr. [last name]:
Lawyer	Mr., Ms., Mrs., *or* Miss [first & last name]	Dear Mr., Ms., Mrs., *or* Miss [last name]:
Service personnel	[full rank, first & last name, abbreviation of service designation] (add *Retired* if applicable)	Dear [rank] [last name]:
Company or corporation	[name of organization]	Ladies and Gentlemen:
Governmental Titles		
President of the United States	The President	Dear Mr. *or* Madam President:
Senator of the United States	Honorable [first & last name]	Dear Senator [last name]:
Cabinet member Postmaster General Attorney General	Honorable [first & last name]	Dear Mr. *or* Madam Secretary: Dear Mr. *or* Madam Postmaster General: Dear Mr. *or* Madam Attorney General:
Mayor	Honorable [first & last name] Mayor of [name of city]	Dear Mayor [last name]:
Judge	The Honorable [first and last name]	Dear Judge [last name]:
Religious Titles		
Priest	The Reverend [first & last name], [initials of order, if any]	Reverend Sir: (formal) *or* Dear Father [last name]: (informal)
Rabbi	Rabbi [first & last name]	Dear Rabbi [last name]:
Minister	The Reverend [first & last name] [title, if any]	Dear Reverend [last name]:

H. R. Veith
Director
Eisfieren Glaswerk
BlaubachstraBe 13
Postfach 10 80 07
D-5000 Köln I
GERMANY

Addressee

Company name
Street address
Post office box
District, city
Country

Additional addresses might look similar to the following:

Mr. Toru Hasegawa
7-35 Kitashinagawa
6 Chome—141 Shinagawa-ku
Tokyo
JAPAN

Cairo
Cleopatra
165 El Corniche Road
Mrs. Ahmed Abbas Zaki
EGYPT

Crédit Lyonnais
c/o Claude Rubinowicz
19, Boulevard des Italiens
75002 Paris
FRANCE

Sr. Ari Matos Cardoso
Superintendent of Human Resources and Personnel
Av. República do Chile, 65
Centro-Rio de Janeiro, RJ
CEP 20035
BRAZIL

Be sure to get organizational titles right when addressing international correspondence. Unfortunately, job designations vary around the world. In England, for example, a managing director is often what U.S. companies call their chief executive officer or president, and a British deputy is the equivalent of a vice president. In France responsibilities are assigned to individuals without regard to title or organizational structure, and in China the title *project manager* has meaning, but the title *sales manager* may not. To make matters worse, businesspeople in some countries sign correspondence without their names typed below. In Germany, for example, the belief is that employees represent the company, so it's inappropriate to emphasize personal names.[9]

Salutation

In the salutation of your letter, follow the first line of the inside address. That is, if the first line is a person's name, the salutation is *Dear Mr. or Ms. Name.* Base the formality of the salutation on your relationship with the addressee. If in conversation you would say "Mary," your letter's salutation should be *Dear Mary,* followed by a colon. In letters to people you don't know well enough to address personally, include the courtesy title and last name, followed by a colon. Presuming to write *Dear Lewis* instead of *Dear Professor Chang* demonstrates a disrespectful familiarity that a stranger will probably resent. If the first line is a position title such as Director of Personnel, then use *Dear Director;* if the addressee is unknown, use a polite description, such as *Dear Alumnus, Dear SPCA Supporter,* or *Dear Voter.* If the first line is plural (a department or company), then use *Ladies and Gentlemen* (look again at Table A.2). When you do not know whether you're writing to an individual or a group (for example, when writing a reference or a letter of recommendation), use *To whom it may concern.*

In the United States some letter writers use a salutopening on the salutation line. A salutopening omits *Dear* but includes the first few words of the opening paragraph along with the recipient's name. After this line the sentence continues a double space below as part of the body of the letter, as in these examples:

Thank you, Mr. Brown,	Salutopening
for your prompt payment of your bill.	Body
Congratulations, Ms. Lake!	Salutopening
Your promotion is well deserved.	Body

Don't overlook an especially important point with personalized salutations: Whether they're informal or formal, make sure names are spelled right. A misspelled name is glaring evidence of carelessness, and it belies the personal interest you're trying to express.

Body

The body of the letter is your message. Almost all letters are single-spaced, with double spacing (one blank line) before and after the salutation or salutopening, between paragraphs, and before the complimentary close. The body may include indented lists, entire paragraphs indented for emphasis, and even subheadings. If so, all similar elements should be treated in the same way. Your department or company may select a format to use for all letters.

Complimentary Close

The complimentary close begins on the second line below the body of the letter. A number of alternatives for wording are available, but currently the trend seems to be toward using one-word closes, such as *Sincerely* and *Cordially.* In any case the complimentary close reflects the relationship between you and the person(s) you're writing to. Avoid closes that are too cute, such as *Yours for bigger profits.* If your audience doesn't know you well, your sense of humor may be misunderstood.

Signature Block

Leave three blank lines for a written signature below the complimentary close, and then include the sender's name (unless it appears in the letterhead). The person's title may appear on the same line as the name or on the line below:

Cordially,

Raymond Dunnigan
Director of Personnel

Your letterhead indicates that you're representing your company. However, if your letter is on plain paper or runs to a second page, you may want to emphasize that you're speaking legally for the company. The accepted way of doing that is to place the company's name in capital letters a double space below the complimentary close and then include the sender's name and title four lines below that:

Sincerely,

WENTWORTH INDUSTRIES

(Mrs.) Helen B. Taylor
President

If your name could be taken for either a man's or a woman's, a courtesy title indicating gender should be included, with or without parentheses. Also, women who prefer a particular courtesy title should include it:

Mrs. Nancy Winters

(Miss) Juana Flores

Ms. Pat Li

(Mr.) Jamie Saunders

Additional Letter Parts

Letters vary greatly in subject matter and thus in the identifying information they need and the format they adopt. The following elements may be used in any combination, depending on the requirements of the particular letter, but generally in this order:

- Addressee notation
- Attention line
- Subject line
- Second-page heading
- Company name
- Reference initials
- Enclosure notation
- Copy notation
- Mailing notation
- Postscript

The letter in Figure A.2 shows how these additional parts should be arranged.

Addressee Notation

Letters that have a restricted readership or that must be handled in a special way should include such addressee notations as *Personal, Confidential,* or *Please Forward.* This sort of notation appears a double space above the inside address, in all capital letters.

Attention Line

Although an attention line is not commonly used today, you may find it useful if you know only the last name of the person you're writing to. An attention line can also be used to direct a letter to a position title or department. An attention line may take any of the following forms or variants of them: *Attention Dr. McHenry, Attention Director of Marketing,* or *Attention Marketing Department.* You may place the attention line on the first line and use the company name as the second line of the inside address.[10] With either approach, the address on the envelope should always match the style of the inside address shown in Figure A.2, to conform to postal specifications.

Subject Line

The subject line lets the recipient know at a glance what the letter is about; it also indicates where to file the letter for future reference. It usually appears below the salutation—against the left margin, indented as the paragraphs in the body of the letter, or centered on the line. Sometimes the subject line is placed above the salutation or at the very top of the page. The subject line may take a variety of forms, including the following:

Subject: RainMaster Sprinklers

About your February 2, 1997, order

FALL 1995 SALES MEETING

Reference Order No. 27920

Sometimes the subject line (or the last line of a long subject "line") is underscored. Some writers omit the word *Subject* and put the other information all in capitals to distinguish it from the other letter parts. Organizations such as insurance and financial institutions, attorneys, and government offices may use the words *Re:* or *In re:* (meaning "concerning" or "in the matter of") rather than using the word *SUBJECT:*.

Second-Page Heading

If the letter is long and an additional page is required, use a second-page heading. Some companies have second-page letterhead, with the company name and address on one line and in a smaller typeface than the regular letterhead. In any case, the second-page heading bears the name that appears in the first line of the inside address (the person or organization receiving the letter), the page number, and the date of the letter; you can also include a reference number. All the following are acceptable:

Ms. Melissa Baker
May 10, 1997
Page 2

Ms. Melissa Baker, May 10, 1997, Page 2

Ms. Melissa Baker   -2-   May 10, 1997

Triple-space (leave two blank lines) between the second-page heading and the body. If a paragraph must be continued on a second page, make sure at least two lines of that paragraph appear on the first page and on the second page. Also, the closing lines of a business letter must never appear alone on a continued page. At least two lines of the body must precede the complimentary close or signature lines. And finally, don't hyphenate the last word on a page.

Company Name

If you include the company's name in the signature block, put it all in capital letters a double space below the complimentary close. You usually include the company's name in the signature block only when the writer is serving as the company's official spokesperson or when letterhead has not been used.

Reference Initials

Because it can happen in business that one person may dictate or write a letter and another person may produce it, reference initials are used to show who helped prepare the letter. Reference initials appear at the left margin, a double space below the last line of the signature block. When the writer's name has been included in the signature block, only the preparer's initials are necessary. If only the department name appears in the signature block, both sets of initials should appear, usually in one of the following forms:

RSR/sm

RSR:sm

RSR:SM

The first set of initials is the writer's; the second set is the preparer's.

Sometimes the writer and the signer of a letter are different people. In that case, at least the file copy of a letter should bear both their initials as well as those of the typist: JFS/RSR/sm (signer, writer, preparer). When businesspeople keyboard their own letters, reference initials are not included, so such initials are becoming more and more rare.

Figure A.2
In-Depth Critique:
Additional Letter Parts

This excerpt from J. Elizabeth Spencer of the Worldwide Talent Agency includes many of the elements often appearing in business letters.

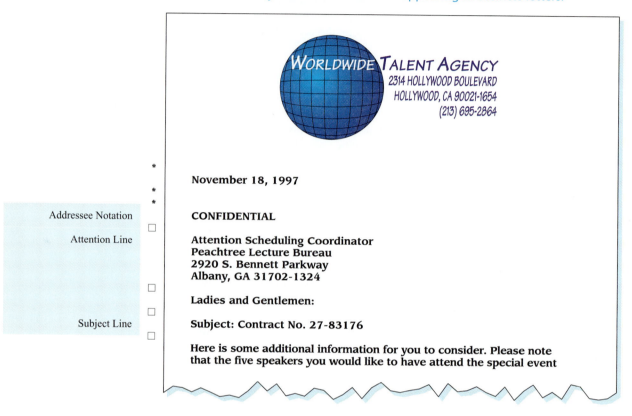

Addressee Notation

Attention Line

Subject Line

☐   One blank space
*   Variable spacing, depending on length of the letter

Enclosure Notation

Enclosure notations also appear at the bottom of a letter, one or two lines below the reference initials. Some common forms:

Enclosure

Enclosures (2)

Enclosures: Résumé

Photograph

Attachment

Copy Notation

Copy notations may follow reference initials or enclosure notations. They indicate who's receiving a *courtesy copy* (*cc*). Some companies indicate copies made on a photocopier (*pc*), or they simply use copy (*c*). Recipients are listed in order of rank or (rank being equal) in alphabetical order. Among the forms used:

cc: David Wentworth

pc: Martha Littlefield

Peachtree Lecture Bureau
November 18, 1995
Page 2

This information should clarify our commitment to you. I look forward to good news from you in the near future.

Sincerely,

Worldwide Talent Agency

J. Elizabeth Spencer

J. Elizabeth Spencer
President

nt

Enclosures: Talent Roster
Commission Schedule

Copy to Everett Cunningham, Chairperson of the Board, InterHosts, Inc.

Special Delivery

PS: The lunch you treated me to the other day was a fine display of Southern hospitality. Thanks again.

Second-Page Heading

Company Name

Reference Initials

Enclosure Notation

Copy Notation

Mailing Notation

Postscript

☐   One blank space
*   Variable spacing, depending on length of letter, except for the top margin which should be 2 inches

Copy to Hans Vogel

c: Joseph Martinez

In addition to the name of an individual, copy notations may include any combination of that person's courtesy title, position, department, company, and complete address, along with notations about any enclosures being sent with the copies.

On occasion, copies are sent to benefit readers other than the person who receives the original letter. In that case, place the notation *bc, bcc,* or *bpc* (for blind copy, blind courtesy copy, or blind photocopy) with the name, where the copy notation would normally appear—but only on the copy, not on the original.

Mailing Notation

You may place a mailing notation (such as *Special Delivery* or *Registered Mail*) at the bottom of the letter, after reference initials or enclosure notations (whichever one is last) and before copy notations. Or you may place it at the top of the letter, either above the inside address on the left-hand side or just below the date on the right-hand side. For greater visibility, mailing notations may appear in capital letters.

Postscript

Letters may also bear postscripts: afterthoughts to the letter, messages that require emphasis, or personal notes. The postscript is usually the last thing on any letter and may be preceded by *P.S., PS., PS:,* or nothing at all. A second afterthought would be designated *P.P.S.,* meaning "post postscript."

Postscripts usually indicate poor planning, so generally avoid them. However, they're commonly used in sales letters, not as an afterthought but as a punch line to remind the reader of a benefit for taking advantage of the offer.

Letter Formats

Although the basic letter parts have remained the same for centuries, ways of arranging them do change. Sometimes a company adopts a certain format as its policy; sometimes the individual letter writer or secretary is allowed to choose the format most appropriate for a given letter or to settle on a personal preference. In the United States, three major letter formats are commonly used:

- *Block format.* Each letter part begins at the left margin. The main advantage is quick and efficient preparation (see Figure A.3).
- *Modified block format.* Same as block format, except the date, complimentary close, and signature block start near the center of the page (see Figure A.4 on pages 700–701). The modified block format does permit indentions as an option. This format mixes preparation speed with traditional placement of some letter parts. It also looks more balanced on the page than the block format does.
- *Simplified format.* Instead of using a salutation, this format often works the audience's name into the first line or two of the body and often includes a subject line in capital letters (see Figure A.5 on page 702). It also omits the complimentary close—so you sign your name after the body of the letter, followed by the printed (or typewritten) name (customarily in all capital letters). The advantages include convenience when you don't know your audience's name. However, some people object to this format because it seems mechanical and impersonal (a drawback that may be overcome with a warm writing style). In this format, the elimination of certain letter parts changes some of the spacing between lines.

These formats differ in the way paragraphs are indented, in the way letter parts are placed, and in some punctuation. However, the elements are always separated by at least one blank line, and the printed (or typewritten) name is always separated from the line above by at least three blank lines to allow space for a signature. If paragraphs are indented, the indention is normally five spaces.

The most common formats for intercultural business letters are the block style and the modified block style. Use either the U.S. or the European format for dates. For the salutation, use *Dear (Title/Last name)*. Close the letter with *Sincerely* or *Cordially,* and sign it personally.

In addition to these three letter formats, letters may also be classified according to the style of punctuation they use. *Standard,* or *mixed, punctuation* uses a colon after the salutation (a comma if the letter is social or personal) and a comma after the complimentary close. *Open punctuation* uses no colon or comma after the salutation or the complimentary close. Although the most popular style in business communication is mixed punctuation, either style of punctuation may be used with block or modified block letter formats. Because the simplified letter format has no salutation or complimentary close, the style of punctuation is irrelevant.

ENVELOPES

The quality of the envelope is just as important for first impressions as the quality of the stationery. In fact, letterhead and envelopes should be of the same paper stock, have the same color ink, and be imprinted with the same address and logo. Most envelopes used by U.S. businesses are No. 10 envelopes (9 1/2 inches long), which are sized to contain an 8 1/2-by-11-inch piece of paper folded in thirds. Some occasions call for a smaller, No. 6 3/4, envelope or for envelopes proportioned to fit special stationery. Figure A.6 (see page 703) shows the two most common sizes.

Addressing the Envelope

No matter what size the envelope, the address is always single-spaced and in block form—that is, with all lines aligned on the left. The address on the envelope is in the same style as the inside address and presents the same information. The order to follow is from the smallest division to the largest:

1. Name and title of recipient
2. Name of department or subgroup
3. Name of organization
4. Name of building
5. Street address and suite number, or post office box number
6. City, state or province, and ZIP code or Postal Code
7. Name of country (if the letter is being sent abroad)

Because the U.S. Postal Service uses optical scanners to sort mail, envelopes for quantity mailings, in particular, should be addressed in the prescribed format. As in the mailing address on the No. 10 envelope in Figure A.6, everything is in capital letters, no punctuation is included, and all mailing instructions of interest to the post office are placed above the address area. Canada Post requires a similar format, except that only the city is all in capitals and the Postal Code is placed on the line below the name of the city. The post office scanners read addresses from the bottom up, so if a letter is to be sent to a post office box rather than a street address, the street address should appear on the line above the box number. Figure A.6 also shows the proper spacing for addresses and return addresses.

The U.S. Postal Service and the Canada Post Corporation have published lists of two-letter mailing abbreviations for states, provinces, and territories (see Table A.3), to be used without periods or commas. Nevertheless, some executives prefer that state

Figure A.3
In-Depth Critique:
Block Letter Format

Rogers can be sure that her company's letterhead and the block format give her letter a crisp, businesslike appearance.

September 5, 1997

Mr. Clifford Hanson
General Manager
The Toy Trunk
356 Emerald Drive
Lexington, KY 40500

Dear Mr. Hanson:

You should receive your shipment of Barbie dolls and accessories within two weeks, just in time for the holiday shopping season. The merchandise is being shipped by United Parcel Service. As the enclosed invoice indicates, the amount due is $352.32.

When preparing to ship your order, I noticed that this is your fifteenth year as a Mattel customer. During that period, you have sold over 3,750 Barbie dolls! We sincerely appreciate the part you have played in marketing our toys to the public.

Your customers should be particularly excited about the new Barbie vacation outfits that you have ordered. Our Winter advertising campaign will portray Barbie trekking through the jungle in her safari suit, climbing mountains in her down parka, and snorkeling off a coral reef in her skin diving gear.

Next month, you'll be receiving our spring catalog. Notice the new series of action figures that will tie in with a TV cartoon featuring King Arthur and the Knights of the Round Table. As a

and province names be spelled out in full and that a comma be used to separate the city and state or province names. Thus the use of a comma between the name of the city and the state or province name is an unresolved issue. Most commonly, the comma is included; sometimes, however, the comma is eliminated to conform with post office standards.

Quantity mailings follow post office requirements. For letters that aren't mailed in quantity, a reasonable compromise is to use traditional punctuation and uppercase and

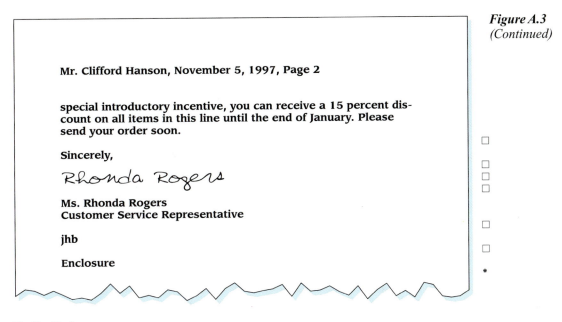

□   One blank space
*   Variable spacing, depending on length of letter

lowercase letters for names and street addresses but two-letter state or province abbreviations, as shown here:

> Mr. Kevin Kennedy
> 2107 E. Packer Drive
> Amarillo, TX 79108

For all out-of-office correspondence use ZIP codes and Postal Codes, assigned to
speed mail delivery. The U.S. Postal Service has divided the United States and its territories into ten zones, each represented by a digit from 0 to 9; this digit comes first in
the ZIP code. The second and third digits represent smaller geographic areas within a
state, and the last two digits identify a "local delivery area." Canadian Postal Codes are
alphanumeric, with a three-character "area code" and a three-character "local code"
separated by a single space (K2P 5A5). ZIP codes and Postal Codes should be separated from state and province names by one space. As an alternative, a Canadian Postal
Code may be put on the bottom line of the address all by itself.

The U.S. Postal Service has introduced ZIP + 4 codes, which add a hyphen and
four more numbers to the standard ZIP codes. The first two of the new numbers may
identify an area as small as a single large building, and the last two digits may identify
one floor in a large building or even a specific department of an organization. The ZIP
+ 4 codes are especially useful for business correspondence. The Canada Post
Corporation achieves the same result with special postal codes assigned to buildings
and organizations that receive a large volume of mail.

Folding to Fit

Trivial as it may seem, the way a letter is folded also contributes to the recipient's
overall impression of your organization's professionalism. When sending a standard-
size piece of paper in a No. 10 envelope, fold it in thirds, with the bottom folded up

Figure A.4
In-Depth Critique:
Modified Block Letter
Format

Gomez's choice of a modified block format appears no less crisp or businesslike than the previous figure, but indenting the date and the signature block can make the letter appear somewhat more balanced.

Chiquita
Brands
International

April 20, 1998

Mr. Robert Thomson
Shoeshine Productions
2378 Hector Avenue
Pittsburgh, PA 15217

Dear Mr. Thomson:

We are flattered that you've requested the use of our company logo for your "Top Banana" musical skit in your upcoming stage production. Your human-sized banana costume, as evidenced by the sketches you submitted, is very clever and, we must admit, the concept for the musical production sounds quite entertaining.

We've worked hard to build our company reputation, and as your request indicates, Chiquita has become a worldwide symbol for bananas and for quality. As you must surely realize, corporations such as ours invest heavily in creating brand recognition. The giant-sized Chiquita label you've proposed stitching onto your costume is certainly accurate, your ideas are creative, and the proposed song lyrics are not offensive. Even so, we realize that the demands of your business may require future changes in your stage presentation. We have considered your request very carefully and find that we just aren't comfortable placing our brand name in a situation over which we would have so little control in the future. We certainly appreciate your courtesy in taking the time to ask before borrowing our name.

Let us thank you by treating your cast members to a banana split "on us." We are enclosing coupons for bananas, ice cream, and fudge topping that we hope you'll all enjoy. If we can offer you

first and the top folded down over it (see Figure A.7 on page 705); the open end should be at the top of the envelope and facing out. Fit smaller stationery neatly into the appropriate envelope simply by folding it in half or in thirds. When sending a standard-size letterhead in a No. 6 3/4 envelope, fold it in half from top to bottom and then in thirds from side to side.

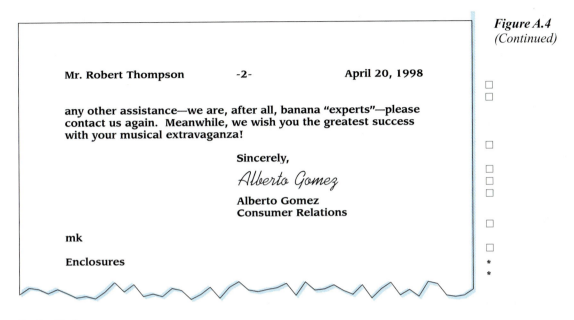

Mr. Robert Thompson   -2-   April 20, 1998

any other assistance—we are, after all, banana "experts"—please contact us again. Meanwhile, we wish you the greatest success with your musical extravaganza!

Sincerely,

Alberto Gomez

Alberto Gomez
Consumer Relations

mk

Enclosures

☐   One blank space
*   Variable spacing, depending on length of letter

INTERNATIONAL MAIL

When sending mail internationally, remember that postal service differs from country to country. For example, street addresses are uncommon in India, and the mail there is unreliable.[11] It's usually a good idea to send international correspondence by air mail and to ask that responses be sent that way as well. Also, remember to check the postage; rates for sending mail to most other countries aren't the same as the rates for sending mail within your own country.

Three main categories of international mail are the following:

- *LC mail.* An abbreviation of the French *Lettres et Cartes* ("letters and cards"), this category consists of letters, letter packages, aerograms, and postcards.
- *AO mail.* An abbreviation of the French *Autres Objets* ("other articles"), this category includes regular printed matter, books and sheet music, matter for the blind, small packets, and publishers' periodicals (second class).
- *CP mail.* An abbreviation of the French *Colis Postaux* ("parcel post"), this category resembles fourth-class mail, including packages of merchandise or any other articles not required to be mailed at letter postage rates.

The U.S. Postal Service also offers Express Mail International Service (EMS), a high-speed mail service to many countries; International Priority Airmail (IPA), an international service that's as fast as or faster than regular airmail service; International Surface Air Lift (ISAL), a service providing quicker delivery and lower cost for all kinds of printed matter; Bulk Letter Service to Canada, an economical airmail service for letters weighing 1 ounce or less; VALUEPOST/CANADA, a reduced postage rate for bulk mailings; International Electronic Post (INTELPOST), a service offering same or next-day delivery of fax documents; International Postal Money Orders, a service for transferring funds to other countries; and several optional special services.

Figure A.5
In-Depth Critique:
Simplified Letter Format

Davis's use of the simplified format seems less personal than either the block or the modified block formats.

DURACELL INTERNATIONAL INC.

Berkshire Industrial Park · Bethel, Connecticut 06801   USA
Telephone 203-796-4000

May 5, 1998

Mr. Michael Ferraro
Pacific Coast Appliances
5748 Catalina Avenue
Laguna Beach, CA 92677

NEW PRODUCT INFORMATION

Thank you, Mr. Ferraro, for your recent inquiry about Duracell's product line. We appreciate your enthusiasm for Duracell products, and we are confident that your customers will enjoy the improved performance of the new product line.

I have enclosed a package of information for your review, including product specifications, dealer prices, and an order form. The package also contains reprints of Duracell Product reviews and a comparison sheet showing how our products measure up against competing brands.

Please call with any questions you may have about shipping or payment arrangements.

Joanna Davis

JOANNA DAVIS
PRODUCT SPECIALIST

ek

Enclosures

☐ One blank space
* Variable spacing, depending on length of the letter

To prepare your mail for international delivery, follow the instructions in the U.S. Postal Service Publication 51, *International Postal Rates and Fees.* Be sure to note instructions for the address, return address, and size limits. Envelopes and wrappers must be clearly marked to show their classification (letter, small packet, printed matter, air mail). All registered letters, letter packages, and parcel post packages must be

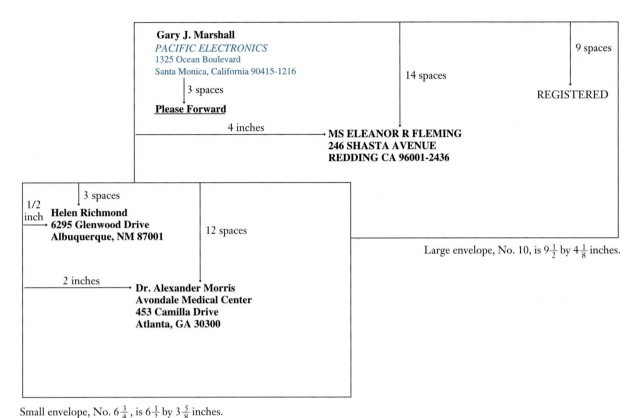

Figure A.6
Prescribed Envelope Format

securely sealed. Printed matter may be sealed only if postage is paid by permit imprint, postage meter, precanceled stamps, or second-class imprint. Otherwise, prepare contents so that they're protected but without hindering inspection. Finally, because international mail is subject to customs examination in the country of destination, the contents and value must be declared on special forms.

MEMOS

Interoffice memos aren't distributed outside the organization, so they may not need the best-quality paper. However, they still convey important information, so clarity, careful arrangement, and neatness are important. As with those for letters, the guidelines for formatting memos help recipients understand at a glance what they've received and from whom.

Many organizations have memo forms printed, with labeled spaces for the recipient's name (or sometimes a checklist of all departments in an organization or all persons in a department), the sender's name, the date, and the subject (see Figure A.8 on page 705). If such forms don't exist, you can use plain paper or sometimes letterhead.

When using plain paper or letterhead, include a title such as *Memo* or *Interoffice Correspondence* (all in capitals) centered at the top of the page or aligned with the left margin. Also include the words *To, From, Date,* and *Subject*—followed by the appropriate information—at the top with a blank line between, as shown here:

TABLE A.3

TWO-LETTER MAILING ABBREVIATIONS FOR THE UNITED STATES AND CANADA

State/Territory/Province	Abbreviation	State/Territory/Province	Abbreviation	State/Territory/Province	Abbreviation
United States		Massachusetts	MA	Texas	TX
Alabama	AL	Michigan	MI	Utah	UT
Alaska	AK	Minnesota	MN	Vermont	VT
Arizona	AZ	Mississippi	MS	Virginia	VA
Arkansas	AR	Missouri	MO	Virgin Islands	VI
American Samoa	AS	Montana	MT	Washington	WA
California	CA	Nebraska	NE	West Virginia	WV
Canal Zone	CZ	Nevada	NV	Wisconsin	WI
Colorado	CO	New Hampshire	NH	Wyoming	WY
Connecticut	CT	New Jersey	NJ		
Delaware	DE	New Mexico	NM	*Canada*	
District of Columbia	DC	New York	NY	Alberta	AB
Florida	FL	North Carolina	NC	British Columbia	BC
Georgia	GA	North Dakota	ND	Labrador	LB
Guam	GU	Northern Mariana Is.	CM	Manitoba	MB
Hawaii	HI	Ohio	OH	New Brunswick	NB
Idaho	ID	Oklahoma	OK	Newfoundland	NF
Illinois	IL	Oregon	OR	Northwest Territories	NT
Indiana	IN	Pennsylvania	PA	Nova Scotia	NS
Iowa	IA	Puerto Rico	PR	Ontario	ON
Kansas	KS	Rhode Island	RI	Prince Edward Island	PE
Kentucky	KY	South Carolina	SC	Quebec	PQ
Louisiana	LA	South Dakota	SD	Saskatchewan	SK
Maine	ME	Tennessee	TN	Yukon Territory	YT
Maryland	MD	Trust Territories	TT		

MEMO

TO:
FROM:
DATE:
SUBJECT:

Sometimes the heading is organized like this:

MEMO

TO: DATE:
FROM: SUBJECT:

You can arrange these four pieces of information in almost any order. The date sometimes appears without the heading *Date.* The subject may be presented with the letters *Re:* (in place of *SUBJECT:*) or may even be presented without any heading (but put it

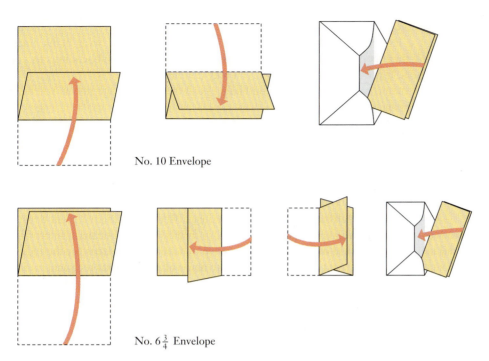

No. 10 Envelope

No. 6$\frac{3}{4}$ Envelope

Figure A.7
Letter Folds for Standard-Size Letterhead

in capital letters so that it stands out clearly). You may want to include a file or reference number, introduced by the word *File*.

If you send a memo to a long list of people, include the notation *See distribution list* or *See below* in the *To* position at the top; then list the names at the end of the memo. Arranging such a list alphabetically is usually the most diplomatic course, although high-ranking officials may deserve more prominent placement. You can also address memos to groups of people—*All Sales Representatives, Production Group, or Assistant Vice Presidents*.

You don't need to use courtesy titles anywhere in a memo; in fact, first initials and last names, first names, or even initials alone are often sufficient. As a general rule, however, use a courtesy title if you would use one in face-to-face encounters with the person.

The subject line of a memo helps busy colleagues find out quickly what your memo is about. Although the subject "line" may overflow onto a second line, it's most helpful when it's short (but still informative).

Figure A.8
Preprinted Memo Form

MEMO

Date: _____

To: _____   From: _____

Dept: _____   Telephone: _____

Subject: _____   *For your*
❏ APPROVAL ❏ INFORMATION ❏ COMMENT

Start the body of the memo on the second or third line below the heading. Like the body of a letter, it's usually single-spaced. Separate paragraphs with blank lines. Indenting them is optional. Handle lists, important passages, and subheadings as you do in letters. If the memo is very short, you may double-space it.

If the memo carries over to a second page, head the second page just as you head the second page of a letter.

Unlike a letter, a memo doesn't require a complimentary close or a signature, because your name is already prominent at the top. However, you may initial the memo—either beside the name appearing at the top of the memo or at the bottom of the memo—or you may even sign your name at the bottom, particularly if the memo deals with money or confidential matters. Treat all other elements—reference initials, enclosure notations, and copy notations—as you would in a letter.

Memos may be delivered by hand, by the post office (when the recipient doesn't work at the same location as the memo writer), or through interoffice mail. Interoffice mail may require the use of special reusable envelopes that have spaces for the recipient's name and department or room number; the name of the previous recipient is simply crossed out. If a regular envelope is used, the words *Interoffice Mail* appear where the stamp normally goes so that it won't accidentally be stamped and mailed with the rest of the office correspondence.

Informal, routine, or brief reports for distribution within a company are often presented in memo form (see Chapter 17). Don't include such report parts as a table of contents and appendixes, but write the body of the memo report just as carefully as you'd write a formal report.

E-MAIL

Since e-mail messages can act both as memos (carrying information within your company) and as letters (carrying information outside your company and around the world), their format depends on your audience and purpose. You may choose to have your e-mail resemble a formal letter or a detailed report, or you may decide to keep things as simple as an interoffice memo. In fact, a modified memo format is probably appropriate for most e-mail messages.[12] All e-mail programs include two major elements: the header and the body (see Figure A.9).

Header

The e-mail header depends on the particular program you use. Some programs even allow you to choose between a shorter and a longer version. However, most headers contain similar information.

The *To:* line contains your audience's e-mail address. The most common e-mail addresses are Internet addresses, like the following:

• NMAA.BETSY@IC.SI.EDU	Smithsonian Institute's National Museum of American Art
• webwsj@dowjones.com	*Wall Street Journal*'s home page
• mailto:cci31@iway.fr	Chamber of Commerce and Industry in Toulouse, France

On the Internet, everything on the left side of the @ symbol is the user name; everything on the right side describes the computer where that user has an account. This machine name usually ends with a country code (such as fr for France, dk for Denmark,

Figure A.9
In-Depth Critique: A Typical E-Mail Message

```
┌─────────────────────────────────────────────────┐
│ ▣                    E-Mail                    ▣ │
├─────────────────────────────────────────────────┤
│                                                 │
│                                                ▲│
│ Date: Tuesday, 17 May 1997, 9:34:27, PDT       │
│ X-Sender: KeithW@Bluecrane.com                 │
│ To: bookco@artech.demon.co.uk                  │
│ From: "Keith D. Wells" <keithw@bluecrane.com>  │
│ Subject: Please confirm shipping date          │
│                                                 │
│ To:    Jeffrey Coombs, International Sales Desk │
│        Artech House, London                    │
│                                                 │
│ From:  Keith Wells, Proprietor                 │
│        Blue Crane Books, Laguna Beach          │
│                                                 │
│ Re:    Order # 1-SD-95466                      │
│        Dated: 7 April 1997                     │
│                                                 │
│ Dear Jeffrey:                                  │
│                                                 │
│ On 7 April 1997, we ordered the following books:│
│                                                 │
│  1 copy    _Electronic Mail_                   │
│            by Jacob Palme                       │
│            (ISBN# 0-89006-802-X)               │
│                                                 │
│  2 copies  _Distance Learning Technology and   │
│            Applications_                        │
│            by Daniel Minoli                     │
│            (ISBN# 0-89006-739-2)               │
│                                                 │
│ Please confirm the date you shipped this order. My│
│ customers are eager to receive their copies and have│
│ been calling me almost daily.                  │
│                                                 │
│ You said in your last message that you would be shipping│
│ them UPS on 10 April, so I would have expected to│
│ receive them by now. Of course, I am used to ordering│
│ through your Boston office, so I may have misjudged the│
│ time it takes from London.                     │
│                                                 │
│ Anything you can tell me about when they were shipped│
│ will be most helpful.                          │
│                                                 │
│ Thank you,                                     │
│                                                 │
│ Keith                                          │
│                                                 │
└─────────────────────────────────────────────────┘
```

HEADER (May vary from program to program—see page 201 for another example)

Date: Includes the day, date, time, and time zone
To: Includes the recipient's address (perhaps addressee's proper name)
From: Includes your address (perhaps your proper name)
Subject: Describes what your message concerns (an opportunity to gain interest)
Cc: Includes the address of anyone you want to receive a copy of the message
Bcc: Includes the address of anyone you want to receive a copy of the message but don't want listed as a receiver
Attachments: Includes the name of any files you have attached to your message

BODY (Format depends on your audience and purpose)

Your own header (optional): Used only if this information isn't easily obtained from program's header
Greeting: Makes the message more personal
Message: Includes line space between paragraphs, and can include headings, lists, and other common devices used in letters and memos
Closing: Personalizes your message and resembles simple closings in letters
Signature: Can be simply your name typed or can be a signature file

hk for Hong Kong, ca for Canada). But within the United States, the country code is replaced with the type of organization that operates that particular computer.[13]

- .com   business and commercial users
- .edu   educational institutions
- .gov   nonmilitary government and related groups
- .mil   military-related groups
- .net   network providers
- .org   organizations and nonprofit groups

Most e-mail programs will also allow you to send mail to an entire group of people all at once. First, you create a distribution list. Then you type the name of the list in the *To:* line instead of typing the addresses of every person in the group.[14]

The *From:* line contains your e-mail address. The *Date:* line contains the day of the week, date (day, month, year), time, and time zone. The *Subject:* line describes the content of the message and presents an opportunity for you to build interest in your message. The *cc:* line allows you to send copies of a message to more than one person at a time. It also allows everyone on the list to see who else received the same message. The *Bcc:* line lets you send copies to people without the other recipients knowing—a practice considered unethical by some.[15] The *Attachments:* line contains the name(s) of the file(s) you attach to your e-mail message. The file can be a word-processing document, a digital image, an audio or video message, a spreadsheet, or a software program.[16]

Other lines containing more detailed information can be listed in your e-mail's header, including *Message-Id* (the exact location of this e-mail message on the sender's system), *X-mailer:* (the version of the e-mail program being used), and *Content type:* (a description of what kind of text and character set is contained in the message). Also, the *Received:* lines include information about each of the systems your e-mail passed through en route to your mailbox.[17] Most e-mail programs now allow you the choice of hiding or revealing this sort of detailed information.

Body

You might consider your mail program's header to be something like letterhead, because the rest of the space below the header is for the body of your message. In the *To:* and *From:* lines, some headers actually print out the names of the sender and the receiver (in addition to the e-mail addresses). Other headers do not. If your mail program includes only the e-mail addresses, you might consider including your own memo-type header, as was done in Figure A.9. Wells even included a subject line in his memo-type header that is more specific than the one in the mail program header. Although some may applaud the clarity such a second header provides, others may criticize the space it takes. Your decision depends on the formality you're striving for.

Do include a greeting in your e-mail. As pointed out in Chapter 6, greetings personalize your message. Leave one line space above and below your greeting to set it off from the rest of your message. Again, depending on the level of formality you want, you may choose to end your greeting with a colon (most formal), a comma (conversational), or even two hyphens (informal).

Your message begins one blank line space below your greeting. Just as in memos and letters, skip one line space between paragraphs and include headings, numbered lists, bulleted lists, and embedded lists when appropriate. Limit your line lengths to a maximum of 80 characters by inserting hard returns at the end of each line.

One blank line space below your message, include a simple closing, often just one word. A blank line space below that, include your signature. Whether you type your name or use a signature file, including your signature personalizes your message.

TIME-SAVING MESSAGES

If there's a way to speed up the communication process, the organization stands to gain. Telephones and electronic mail systems are quick, as are mailgrams, telegrams, faxes, and the like. In addition, organizations have developed special formats to reduce the amount of time spent writing and typing short messages:

- *Fax cover sheets.* When faxing messages, you may use a fax cover sheet, which includes the recipient's name, company, fax number, and city; the sender's name, complete address, fax number, and telephone number; the number of pages being sent; a phone number to call if the faxed transmission isn't successful; and enough space for any brief message.[18] The format for this information varies widely. When a document is self-explanatory, a cover sheet may not be necessary, so be sure not to waste paper or transmission time.
- *Memo-letters.* Printed with a heading somewhat like a memo's, memo-letters provide a space for an inside address so that the message may be sent outside the company (see Figure A.10). When the memo is folded properly, the address shows through a window in the envelope, thereby eliminating the need to address the envelope separately. Memo-letters often include a space for a reply message so that the recipient doesn't have to print out or type a whole new letter in response; carbonless copy sets allow sender and recipient to keep on file a copy of the entire correspondence.
- *Short-note reply technique.* Popular in many organizations, this technique can be used even without a special form. The recipient of a memo (or sometimes a letter) simply handwrites a response on the original document, makes a copy for the files, and sends the annotated original back to the person who wrote it.
- *Letterhead postcards.* Ideal for short, impersonal messages, letterhead postcards are preprinted with a list of responses so that the "writer" merely checks the appropriate response(s) and slips the postcard into the mail. Organizations such as mail-order companies and government agencies use these time-saving devices to communicate frequently with individuals by mail.

The important thing to realize about these and all other message formats is that they've developed over time to meet the need for clear communication and to speed responses to the needs of customers, suppliers, and associates.

REPORTS

You can enhance your report's effectiveness by paying careful attention to its appearance and layout. Follow whatever guidelines your organization prefers, but remember to be neat and consistent throughout. If it's up to you to decide formatting questions, the following conventions may help you decide how to handle margins, headings, spacing and indention, and page numbers.

Margins

All margins on a report page are at least 1 inch wide. Margins of 1 inch are customary for double-spaced pages, and margins of between 1-1/4 and 1-1/2 inches are customary for single-spaced pages. The top, left, and right margins are usually the same, but the bottom margins can be 1-1/2 times deeper. Some special pages also have wider top margins. Set top margins as deep as 2 inches for pages that contain major titles: prefatory parts such as the table of contents or the executive summary, supplementary parts such as the reference notes or bibliography, and textual parts such as the first page of the text or the first page of each chapter.

If you're going to bind your report at the left or at the top, add half an inch to the margin on the bound edge (see Figure A.11). Because of the space taken by the binding on left-bound reports, make the center point of the page a quarter inch to the right of the

Figure A.10
In-Depth Critique: Memo-Letter

Memo-letters such as this one are convenient for the writer, and with the space for a reply message, they can be convenient for the recipient. However, they are much less formal than a business letter for outside correspondence.

MEMO

TO: **Green Ridge Gifts**
1786 Century Road
Nashua, NH 03060
USA

FROM: **Whiteside Import/Export, Ltd.**
1601 Ronson Drive
Toronto, Ontario M9W 523
CANADA

SUBJECT: **Order for Royal Dorchester china**
completer sets

DATE: **October 11, 1997**

MESSAGE:

The six Wellington pattern completer sets that you ordered by telephone October 9 are on their way and should reach your shop by October 18.

The three Mayfield pattern completer sets are coming from the factory, however, and will not arrive here until October 26 or 27. That means you will get them around November 2 or 3.

Do you still want the Mayfield sets? Would you like us to bill you for the Wellington sets only so that you can pay for the Mayfield order separately? Please add your reply below, retain the yellow copy for your records, and send us the white and pink copies.

SIGNED: *Barbara Hutchins*

REPLY: PLEASE SEND THE MAYFIELD SETS AS SOON AS POSSIBLE. YOU MAY BILL FOR BOTH MAYFIELD AND WELLINGTON SETS.

DATE: OCT. 15, 1997

SIGNED: William L. Smith

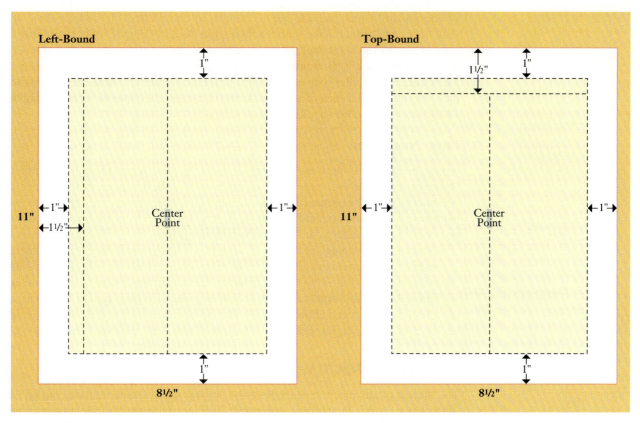

Figure A.11
Margins for Formal Reports

center of the paper. Be sure that centered headings are centered over the typed portion, not centered on the paper. Of course, computers can do this for you automatically. Other guidelines for formatting a report can be found in the sample in Chapter 18.

Headings

Headings of various levels provide visual clues to a report's organization. Figure 17.13, on page 561, illustrates one good system for showing these levels, but many variations exist. No matter which system you use, be sure to be consistent.

Spacing and Indentions

The spacing and indention of most elements of a report are relatively easy. If your report is double-spaced (perhaps to ease comprehension of technical material), indent all paragraphs five character spaces (or about 1/2 inch). In single-spaced reports, you can block the paragraphs (no indentions), leaving one blank line between them.

When using a typewriter, properly spacing the material on the title page is more complicated. For reports that will be bound on the left, start a quarter inch to the right of center. From that point, backspace once for each two letters in the line so that the line will appear centered once the report is bound.

To correctly place lines of type on the title page, first count the number of lines in each block of copy, including blank lines. Subtract the total from 66 (the total number of lines on an 11-inch page) to get the number of unused lines. To allocate these unused lines equally among the spaces between the blocks of copy, divide the number of unused lines by the number of blank areas (always one more than the number of blocks of copy). The result is the number of blank lines to devote to each section. Of course, when using a computer with a good word-processing program, these calculations are done for you with the click of a mouse. As the title page of the sample report in Chapter 18 shows, the title page should look well balanced.

Page Numbers

Remember that every page in the report is counted but that not all pages have numbers shown on them. The first page of the report, normally the title page, is not numbered. All other pages in the prefatory section are numbered with a lowercase roman numeral, beginning with ii and continuing with iii, iv, v, and so on. The unadorned (no dashes, no period) page number is centered at the bottom margin.

Number the first page of the text of the report with the unadorned arabic numeral 1, centered at the bottom margin (double- or triple-spaced below the text). In left-bound reports, number the following pages (including the supplementary parts) consecutively with unadorned arabic numerals (2, 3, and so on), placed at the top right-hand margin (double- or triple-spaced above the text). For top-bound reports and for special pages having 2-inch top margins, center these page numbers at the bottom margin.

MEETING DOCUMENTS

The success of any meeting depends on the preparation of the participants and on the follow-up measures they take to implement decisions or to seek information after the meeting. Meeting documents—agendas and minutes—aid this process by putting the meeting plan and results into permanent, written form. Although small informal meetings may not require a written agenda, any meeting involving a relatively large number of people or covering a lot of ground will run more smoothly if an agenda is distributed in advance. A written agenda helps participants prepare by telling them what will be discussed, and it helps keep them on track once the meeting begins. The typical agenda format (shown in Figure A.12) may seem stiff and formal, but it helps structure a meeting so that as little time as possible is wasted. It also provides opportunities for discussion, if that's what is called for.

The presentation, a special form of meeting that allows for relatively little group interaction, may also require an agenda or a detailed outline. Special visual aids such as flip charts help attendees grasp the message, and copies of the charts are often provided for future reference.

After a meeting the secretary who attended prepares a set of minutes for distribution to all attendees and to any other interested parties. The minutes are prepared in much the same format as a memo or letter, except for the heading, which takes this form:

MINUTES

PLANNING COMMITTEE MEETING

MONDAY, AUGUST 21, 1997

Present: [All invited attendees who were present are listed here, generally by rank, in alphabetical order, or in some combination.]

Absent: [All invited attendees who were not present are listed here, in similar order.]

AGENDA

**PLANNING COMMITTEE MEETING
TUESDAY, AUGUST 21, 1997
10:00 A.M.
EXECUTIVE CONFERENCE ROOM**

 I. Call to Order

 II. Roll Call

 III. Approval of Agenda

 IV. Approval of Minutes from Previous Meeting

 V. Chairperson's Report

 VI. Subcommittee Reports

  A. New Markets

  B. New Products

  C. Finance

 VII. Unfinished Business

 VIII. New Business

  A. Carson & Canfield Data

  B. Reassignments

 IX. Announcements

 X. Adjournment

Figure A.12
Agenda Format

The body of the minutes follows the heading, and it notes the times the meeting started and ended, all major decisions reached at the meeting, all assignments of tasks to meeting participants, and all subjects that were deferred to a later meeting. In addition, the minutes objectively summarize important discussions, noting the names of those who contributed major points. Outlines, subheadings, and lists help organize the minutes, and additional documentation (such as tables or charts submitted by meeting participants) are noted in the minutes and attached.

At the end of the minutes, the words *Submitted by* should be added, followed by a couple of blank lines for a signature and then the signer's printed (or typed) name and title (if appropriate). If the minutes have been written by one person and prepared by another, the preparer's initials should be added, as in the reference initials on a letter or memo.

An informal meeting may not require minutes. Attendees simply pencil their own notes onto their copies of the agenda. Follow-up is then their responsibility, although the meeting leader may need to remind them through a memo, phone call, or face-to-face talk.

DOCUMENTATION OF REPORT SOURCES

Documenting a report is too important a task to undertake haphazardly. By providing information about your sources, you improve your own credibility—as well as the credibility of the facts and opinions you present. By documenting your work, you give readers the means for checking your findings and pursuing the subject further. Also, documenting your report is the accepted way to give credit to the people whose work you have drawn from.

The specific style you use to document your report may vary from the styles recommended here. Experts recommend various forms, depending on your field or discipline. Moreover, your employer or client may use a form different from any the experts suggest. Don't let this discrepancy confuse you. If your employer specifies a form, use it; the standardized form is easier for colleagues to understand. However, if the choice of form is left to you, adopt a style like one of those described here. Just be consistent within any given report, using the same order, punctuation, and format from one reference citation or bibliography entry to the next. Of course, to document report sources, you have to find the information you need.

FINDING SOURCES

Chapter 15 describes the difference between primary data and secondary data and tells how to gather both kinds of research. Primary research (such as conducting studies and surveys yourself) is documented within the text of your report through descriptions of your methods and findings. However, this component chapter describes how to present the results of secondary research in your report. Secondary sources for business research can be obtained from libraries and computerized databases.

Libraries

Today the first hurdle in getting information is to figure out which library to visit or to phone with your query. The *American Library Directory* lists more than 30,000 public, college, university, and special libraries in the United States and 3,000 in Canada. In addition, many companies have their own libraries. The Internet can help you get a better idea of what a library has to offer. Many libraries can be reached online for general information, access to the computerized catalog, and even information about which books are out on loan and thus unavailable.

Basic References

Once you've decided which library to use, head for the reference section. A librarian with specialized knowledge of general sources of information can direct you to the appropriate dictionaries, encyclopedias, almanacs, atlases, biographical reference books, hand-

- *Biography Index:* Indexes biographical data from more than 2,400 periodicals as well as from English-language books.
- *Books in Print:* Lists more than 425,000 books in 62,000 subject categories currently available from over 6,000 U.S. publishers. Also indexes books by author and by title.
- *Business Periodicals Index:* Lists articles from about 280 business-related periodicals; companion is *Canadian Business Index.*
- *Current Biography:* Features biographical data about individuals who have achieved fame during the period covered.
- *Directory of Directories:* Indexes several thousand business, industrial, and professional directories.
- *Dun & Bradstreet, Inc., Million Dollar Directory:* Lists more than 120,000 U.S. companies by net worth. Includes names of officers and directors, goods and services, approximate sales, and number of employees.
- *Encyclopedia of Associations:* Indexes thousands of associations by broad subject category, by specific subject, by name of association, and by geographic location.
- *Moody's Manuals:* In a series of publications for specific industries—such as banks and financial institutions, public utilities, and international companies—lists financial data of the sort found in corporate annual reports.
- *Reader's Guide to Periodical Literature:* Indexes articles in some 190 popular periodicals by subject and author.
- *Standard & Poor's Register of Corporations:* Indexes more than 37,000 U.S., Canadian, and major international corporations. Lists officers, products, sales volume, and number of employees.
- *Standard Periodical Directory:* Describes more than 66,000 U.S. and Canadian periodicals.
- *Statistical Abstract of the United States:* Presents U.S. economic, social, political, and industrial statistics.

- *Survey of Current Business:* Features national business statistics on construction, real estate, employment and earnings, finance, foreign trade, transportation, communication, and other key topics.
- *Thomas Register of American Manufacturers:* Presents information on thousands of U.S. manufacturers, indexed by company name and product.
- *U.S. Government Publications: Monthly Catalog:* Lists titles of more than 1,000 new U.S. government publications in each issue.
- *Who's Who in America:* Summarizes the achievements of living U.S. citizens who have gained prominence in their fields; *Canadian Who's Who* and *Who's Who in Business and Finance* are similar.
- *World Almanac and Book of Facts:* Presents statistical information about many events, people, and places. Index contains both general subject headings and specific names. Similar information is available in the *Canadian Yearbook* and the *Corpus Almanac of Canada.*
- Other indexes of articles in newspapers, magazines, and journals:

  Accountants' Index
  Applied Science and Technology Index
  Art Index
  Biological and Agricultural Index
  Computer Literature Index
  Education Index
  Engineering Index
  General Science Index
  Humanities Index
  Index Medicus
  Index to Legal Periodicals
  The New York Times Index
  Predicasts (U.S. and international editions)
  Public Affairs Information Bulletin
  Social Sciences Index
  The Wall Street Journal Index

Figure B.1
Major Reference Works

books, manuals, directories of companies and associations, and perhaps even a collection of corporations' annual reports. In the absence of a knowledgeable reference librarian, consult *Reference Books: A Brief Guide* or *Business Information Sources,* or you can refer to Figure B.1, which lists the major reference books used by business researchers.

Books and Articles

Both books and articles provide in-depth coverage of specific topics. Although articles are more timely than books, books have a broader focus. A combination of the two often provides the best background for your report.

Numerous books and articles are published every year, and libraries must be selective when choosing works to put on their shelves. So when you need specialized information, a public library may not be very useful. You'll have better luck finding books and articles on technical subjects at college libraries (assuming the college offers courses in those subjects) and in company libraries.

All libraries provide bibliographies of the books and back issues of the publications they stock. The traditional card catalog contains vast numbers of index cards organized by subject, title, and author; a code on each card directs you to the shelf where the book or publication is located. However, some libraries have converted their card catalogs to microfilm or microfiche, which takes up far less space. Many other libraries have computerized the information about their holdings.

Abstracts

One way to find out a lot relatively quickly is to consult abstracts. Instead of just supplying a categorized list of article titles, as indexes do, abstracts summarize each article's contents as well. Many fields are served by abstracts that regularly review articles in the most useful periodicals. Here are the names of a few abstracts that may prove useful:

ABS Guide to Recent Publications in the Social and Behavioral Sciences
Book Review Digest
Business Publications Index and Abstracts
Computer Abstracts
Dissertation Abstracts International
Educational Research Information Center (ERIC)
Personnel Management Abstracts
Psychological Abstracts
Sociological Abstracts

Government Documents

When you want to know the exact provisions of a law, the background of a court decision, or the current population patterns and business trends, you can consult the government documents section of a library. This sort of research can be rather complicated, but a librarian will direct you to the information you need. All you have to know is the government body you're interested in (U.S. Congress, Ninth Court of Appeals, or Department of Labor) and some sort of identification for the specific information you need (such as the Safe Drinking Water Act of 1974, *Price* v. *Shell Oil,* or 1990 Census). If you have a date and the name of a publication containing the document, so much the better.

Computerized Databases

Many companies maintain their own computerized databases containing company-generated statistics on sales and expenses, product specifications, inventory status, market research data, and perhaps reports and correspondence as well. Your access to information expands greatly when you use Internet sources, online services such as CompuServe or America Online, or commercial databases such as Knowledge Index, Management Contents, National Newspaper Index, and Trade and Industry Index. A lot of this information can be downloaded directly, but some magazine articles will need to be ordered either by e-mail, phone, or regular mail.

USING SOURCE INFORMATION

Locating all this information is just the first step, of course. Once you have the necessary information, you'll want to use what you've found. You begin by recording information effectively. By taking down information that's complete and well organized, you'll capture the information you need and avoid backtracking to look up something you forgot. Moreover, to maintain your credibility and ethics, you'll want to keep current with the issues of copyright and fair use.

Recording Information

The recording system that most students use (and many instructors recommend) is taking notes on 3-by-5-inch index cards, noting only one thought, quote, or other piece of information per card. Try to summarize information in your own words, unless you think specific data or quotations may be useful. Using note cards has several advantages: Cards are easy to use, easy to carry around, and easy to sort and rearrange.

You're using these note cards to help you remember and retrieve useful information for your report, so be sure to record all bibliographic information carefully. Write the author's name, the title of the book or article, the publication information, and page numbers at the top of each card. (As an alternative when you're collecting several pieces of information from each source, you might prepare a bibliography card for each one, number the cards, and then use these numbers to cross-reference your note cards.) It's helpful to note at the top of the card the general subject of the material (either in a simple phrase or with identifying numbers from your preliminary outline) so that you can sort your notes more easily when it comes time to write your report. Also indicate whether the information is a direct quote, a paraphrase of someone else's idea, or an idea of your own.[1] Figure B.2 shows a sample note card.

The card system works, without question. You won't go wrong with it. Up until recently, people generally agreed that taking notes on computer was slower and more cumbersome than using index cards. Computers simply didn't have the tools to make this task easy, and they tended to get in the way more than they helped. However, advances in software are changing this picture. Here are several ways that computers can help you capture and organize research information:[2]

- *Organizing and outlining.* If you've used the outlining capability in a good word processor, you already know how helpful it can be. You can quickly move headings and blocks of information—about as easily as you can shuffle a deck of

---

11-B-2a

Emily Card and Adam Miller, <u>Business Capital for Women: An Essential Handbook for Entrepreneurs</u> (New York: MacMillan, 1996), 4.

One of today's fastest-growing corporate categories is composed of female-owned companies—especially in the small business sector, which is expanding rapidly.

(Great graph showing statistics!)

Figure B.2
Sample Note Card

index cards. And outliners have a major advantage over index cards in that they let you select the amount of information you want to see at any given time. Sometimes it's hard to see the big picture if you have 30 or 40 pieces of detailed information strewn across on the table. Outliners let you collapse or expand your outline, showing as many levels as you want. This can be a great help when you're trying to organize the flow of your speech.

- **Searching.** Now where was that quote about water pollution? If you have more than a few dozen cards, which is easy to do, finding a specific piece of information can be time consuming. With the notes in your computer, you simply use the "find" function to locate the information. It's faster, and you have much less chance of missing whatever information you're looking for.
- **Linking.** This is not a feature found in the typical word processor, but software packages such as Info Select make it easy to weave "threads" through your research materials. For instance, for some research on water pollution, information-management software could highlight for you all the research notes that involve government regulation. If you had organized your notes by problems and solutions, in chronological order, or from general concepts to specific details, these bits of information about regulation would probably be spread throughout your outline. By reminding you of such links, the software helps you handle all the themes and subthemes of your report clearly and consistently.

You may find that using a combination of index cards (to capture information while you're reading it) and computer software (to manage the information once you've captured it) is the best solution. Whichever method you choose, be sure to record all the facts you need to responsibly credit your sources. Being thorough not only saves you time if you need to go back and check facts or quotes, but it is also your ethical responsibility.[3]

Understanding Copyright and Fair Use

You have an important reason for carefully documenting the sources you consult during secondary research: Although ideas belong to no one person, the way they're expressed provides the livelihood for many scholars, consultants, and writers. To protect the interests of these people, most countries have established copyright laws. If you transgress those laws, you or your company could be sued, not to mention embarrassed.

In addition to covering printed materials like books and magazines, copyright law covers audiovisual materials, many forms of artistic expression, computer programs, maps, mailing lists, even answering machine messages. However, copyright law does not protect

- Titles, names, short phrases, and slogans
- Familiar symbols or designs
- Lists of ingredients or contents
- Ideas, procedures, methods, systems, processes, concepts, principles, discoveries, or devices (although it does cover their description, explanation, or illustration)

A work is considered copyrighted as soon as it's put into fixed form, even if it hasn't been registered.[4]

As discussed in Chapter 15, you can avoid plagiarism whenever you quote another person's work by telling where you found the statement. This documentation applies to books, articles, tables, charts, diagrams, song lyrics, scripted dialogue, letters, speeches, anything that you take verbatim (word for word) from someone else. Even if you paraphrase the material (change the wording somewhat), it's best to give credit to the person who has found an effective way of expressing an idea.

However, for general knowledge or for specialized knowledge that's generally known among your readers, you do not have to cite a source. For example, everyone knows that Franklin Roosevelt was elected to the presidency of the United States four times. You can say so on your own authority, even if you've read an article in which the author says the same thing.

Of course, merely crediting the source is not always enough. The fair use doctrine says that you can use other people's work only as long as you don't unfairly prevent them from benefiting as a result. For example, if you reproduce someone else's copyrighted questionnaire in a report you're writing (and identify the source thoroughly), you're preventing the author from selling a copy of that questionnaire to your readers.

Generally, you do best to avoid relying to such a great extent on someone else's work. However, when you can't avoid it, contact the copyright holder (usually the author or publisher) for permission to reprint. You'll usually be asked to pay a fee.

Fair use is decided in the courts on a case-by-case basis. So you won't find any hard-and-fast rules about when to get permission. In general, however, you would probably request permission to use

- More than 250 words quoted from a book
- Any reproduction of a piece of artwork (including fully reproduced charts and tables) or excerpt from commercially produced audiovisual material
- Any dialogue from a play or line from a poem or song
- Any portion of consumable materials, such as workbooks
- Multiple copies of copyrighted works that you intend to distribute widely or repeatedly, especially for noneducational purposes

You do not need permission to use materials published before 1907, news articles more than three months old, or materials originally published by the government. Nor do you need permission to use copies as the basis for "criticism, comment, news reporting, teaching, scholarship, or research."[5]

When deciding whether you may use someone else's work without permission, remember that the courts (if they get involved) will consider the length of your quotation in relation to the total length of the work from which it is taken, the type of work you are taking it from, your purpose, and the effect your action has on the original author's efforts to distribute the work. If you think you may be infringing on the author's rights, write for permission and provide a credit line. In any case, be sure to acknowledge the original author's work with a source note.

PREPARING REFERENCE LISTS

In every report you write, you'll need to give your readers a complete list of the sources you used. You can assign a title to this list, such as *Sources, Bibliography, Reference List, Works Cited* (if you include only those sources you actually cited in your report), or *Works Consulted* (if you include uncited sources as well). Your reference list also serves as a reading list for readers who want to pursue the subject of your report further, so you may want to annotate each entry—that is, comment on the subject matter and viewpoint of the source, as well as its usefulness to your readers. Annotations may be written in either complete or incomplete sentences:

Helgeson, Donald V. *Engineer's and Manager's Guide to Winning Proposals.* Boston: Artech House, 1994. Makes proposal writing almost as easy as filling in the blank pages; contains a step-by-step process for analyzing a request for proposal; 283 pages.

Depending on the length of your report and the complexity and number of your sources, you may either place the entire bibliography at the end of the report (after the endnotes) or place relevant sections at the end of each chapter. Another way to make a long bibliography more manageable is to subdivide it into categories (a classified bibliography), either by type of reference (such as books, articles, and unpublished material) or by subject matter (such as government regulation, market forces, and so on).

Reference List Construction

When preparing the reference list, start each entry at the left margin, with the author's last name first. Entries are alphabetized and single-spaced (with a double space between each entry). After the first line, these entries are usually indented (customarily five spaces or as few as two). See Figure B.3 and the Electrovision report that appears in Chapter 18.

Many schemes have been proposed for organizing the information in source notes, but all of them break the information into three main parts: (1) information about the author, (2) information about the work, and (3) information about the publication. The first part includes the author's name, last name first. The second part includes the title of the work, and such other identifying information as the edition and volume number. The third part includes the place of publication, the publisher, and the date of publication, followed by relevant page numbers. A few details about these elements are described in the sections that follow.

Author's Name

If the author of the work is only one person, spell out the name (last name first) and follow it with a period. For multiple authors, only the first author's name appears in reversed order. Two authors' names are separated with *and*. For three or more authors, separate the names with commas and insert *and* before the last author's name. For more than three authors, you usually list all the authors; however, it's also acceptable simply to insert *et al.* or *and others* after the first author's name, with no preceding comma.

Title of the Work

Titles commonly appear uppercase and lowercase, which means that the first and last words start with a capital letter, as do all nouns, pronouns, verbs, adverbs, and adjectives. However, prepositions, conjunctions, and articles start with a lowercase letter; exceptions include prepositions that are an inseparable part of an expression (as in "Looking Up New Words") and often prepositions and conjunctions with more than four letters. For works that have a two-part title, use a colon to separate the two parts, and capitalize the letter that comes right after the colon:

> Managerial Communications: A Strategic Approach

Titles of books, periodicals (journals and magazines published at regular intervals), and other major works are usually italicized on computer (or underlined on a typewriter). Sometimes they appear in all capitals (with no italics or underlining) to make the keyboarding task easier and to make the title stand out more. Titles of articles, pamphlets, chapters in books, and the like are most often placed in quotation marks.

"Acquired Immunodeficiency Syndrome." In Mesh vocabulary file [database online]. Bethesda, Md.: National Library of Medicine, 1990 [cited 3 October 1990] Identifier no. D000163. [49 lines]

Asakawa, Frances. "Recommendations for Replacing the Sales Fleet Based on a Comparison of Three Midsize Automobiles." Report to Daniel Standish, Director of Sales, Midwest Marketing, Inc., 17 November 1994.

Baron, Robert A. <rabaron@pipeline.com> "Copyright and Fair Use of Images." 9 February 1997. <fj.soc.copyright> (3 Mar 1997).

Choon, Tang Meng. <tanmeng@biomed.nus.sg> "Broadcasting Standards." 29 January 1997. Personal e-mail (30 January 1997).

Conrad, Charles. *Strategic Organizational Communication: An Integrated Perspective.* 2d ed. Fort Worth, Tex.: Holt, Rinehart and Winston, 1990.

Donaldson, John, ed. *Business Ethics.* San Diego: Academic Press, 1992.

Fenwick, Rose et al. *Guidelines for Teaching Persuasive Writing.* Chicago: Illinois State Department of Education, Chicago Division of Education Services, July 1990. 87, DIALOG, ERIC, ED 179423.

"Forecasters Predict Economy Won't Change Much." *Wall Street Journal,* 12 October 1993, sec. A, 16.

Gabbei, Dorothy. Interview with the author. Emporia, Kansas, 14 July 1992.

Group Productivity. Del Mar, Calif.: CRM/McGraw-Hill Films, 1995. Videotape, 22 min.

Hawkins, Katherine W. "Effects of Gender and Communication Content on Leadership Emergence in Small Task-Oriented Groups." Paper presented at the 78th annual meeting of the Speech Communication Association, Chicago, Illinois, 1992.

Ivey, Keith C. "Joining a Usenet Community," *The Editorial Eye,* n.d., <http://www.eeicom.com/eye/utw/96dec.html> (10 February 1997).

"Jericho's Walls." In History Log9008 [electronic bulletin board]. S.l. 27 August 1990–[cited 15 December 1990]. Available from <listserv@FINHUTC.BITNET>.

Lamude, Kevin G., and Joseph Scudder. "Compliance-Gaining Techniques of Type-A Managers," *Journal of Business Communication 30,* no. 1 (1993): 63–79.

Landes, Les L. "Down with Quality Programitis." *IABC Communication World.* February 1992, 31.

Lotus 1-2-3 Rel. 2. Lotus Development Corporation, Cambridge, Mass.

Presner, Lewis A. *The International Business Dictionary and Reference.* New York: Wiley, 1991.

Steele, Peter A. "Implementation of Cyber Appliances Through Cable Television." Master's thesis, San Diego State University, 1996.

"Time to Call in the Boss." *Brandweek.* 27 July 1992, 32–36, 60.

U.S. Bureau of the Census. *Statistical Abstract of the United States: 1996.* 116th ed. Washington, D.C.: GPO, 1996.

U.S. Congress. Senate Committee on Foreign Relations. *Famine in Africa: Hearing Before the Committee on Foreign Relations.* 99th Cong., 1st sess., 17 January 1985. [pp. 53–57 for footnote]

U.S. Department of Commerce. *Falling Through the Net: A Survey of the "Have Nots" in Rural and Urban America.* July 1995. <http://www.ntia.doc.gov/ntiahome/fallingthru.html>. [accessed online 5 December 1996]

Wallace, Mike. *60 Minutes.* CBS-TV, 22 August 1993.

Figure B.3
Sample Reference List

Publication Information

Bibliographic entries referring to periodicals don't usually include the publisher's name and place of business, but entries for books, pamphlets, and other hard-to-find works do include such publication information. In a book entry, the first item of publication data is the city where the publisher is located. If the city is large and well known and if there are no other well-known cities by the same name, its name can appear alone. However, if necessary for proper identification, the state, province, or country should also be indicated. Abbreviations are used for states and provinces. A colon follows the name of the place.

The publisher's name comes after the colon, often in a shortened form. For example, Prentice Hall, Inc., can easily be identified when shortened to Prentice Hall. If you begin with shortened publishers' names, be sure to carry through with the same short forms throughout. Use a publisher's full name if it's not well known or if it might be confused with some other organization. The publisher's name is followed by a comma.

The publication date is the most recent year on the copyright notice. Ignore the dates of printing.

MANUALS OF STYLE

For more specific format guidelines about capitalization, punctuation, abbreviation, and order of the elements within these three main parts, follow the style established by your employer or consult a style manual. A wide variety of style manuals provide information on constructing reference lists (and on documentation in general):

Achtert, Walter S., and Joseph Gibaldi. *The MLA Style Manual.* New York: Modern Language Association, 1985. Basis for the note and bibliography style used in much academic writing and recommended in many college textbooks on writing term papers; provides a lot of examples in the humanities.

American Psychological Association. *Publication Manual of the American Psychological Association.* 4th ed. Washington, D.C.: American Psychological Association, 1994. Details the author-date system, which is preferred in the social sciences and often in the natural sciences as well.

The Chicago Manual of Style. 14th ed. Chicago: University of Chicago Press, 1993. Known as the *Chicago Manual* and widely used in the publishing industry; detailed treatment of documentation in Chapters 15, 16, and 17.

Gibaldi, Joseph. *MLA Handbook for Writers of Research Papers.* 4th ed. New York: Modern Language Association, 1995. One of the standard style manuals for footnote and bibliography form.

Harnack, Andrew, and Eugene Kleppinger. *Online! A Reference Guide to Using Internet Sources.* New York: St. Martin's Press, 1997. A comprehensive review of style for citing online references.

Slade, Carol. *Form and Style: Research Papers, Reports, Theses.* 10th ed. Boston: Houghton Mifflin, 1997. A comprehensive review of Chicago Manual style, Modern Language Association style, and American Psychological Association style.

Turabian, Kate L. *A Manual for Writers of Term Papers, Theses, and Dissertations.* Revised and expanded by Bonnie Birtwhistle Honigsblum. 6th ed. Chicago: University of Chicago Press, 1995. Based on the *Chicago Manual*, but smaller and limited to matters of concern to report writers; many examples of documenting nonstandard references.

Warren, Thomas L. *Words into Type.* 3d ed. Englewood Cliffs, N.J.: Prentice Hall, 1992. Useful information on the classic use of scholarly notes and bibliographies.

Reference List Entries

Because you're referring your reader to a work as a whole, bibliographic entries do not usually include page numbers (unless you're citing a chapter in a book or an article). To be sure you have all the information you need when it's time to construct a reference list, use the same format during your research that you'll be using in your report. Figure B.3 contains some sample bibliographic entries, based on guidelines recommended in *The Chicago Manual of Style.*

Books

In their simplest form, references to books look like the Presner entry in Figure B.3. Sometimes, however, you'll want to include additional information:

- For the edition of a book, place the information after the title (using abbreviations such as 1st, 2d, 3d, 4th, and so on—as in the Conrad entry in Figure B.3).
- For more than one work by the same author, use three em dashes (or six hyphens) in place of the author's name. (However, repeat the name if one of the books is by a single author and another is by that author with others.)
- To cite a volume number, place *vol. 3* (or the correct number) after the title or edition number and before the publication data.
- To use the name of an editor instead of an author, simply place *ed.* after the editor's name (as in the Donaldson entry).

Periodicals

The typical periodical reference looks like the Landes entry in Figure B.3. The article author's name (if there is one) is handled as a book author's is, but the title of the article appears in quotation marks. Like the title of a book, the title of the magazine or journal appears either in italics (underlined) or in all capital letters. The page numbers are always inclusive (that is, they show the page numbers for the entire article). Entries that have no author are listed alphabetically by title.

The rest of the periodical entry can be tricky, however. For popular and business magazines, you need include only the date and page number(s) after the title (as in the "Time to Call in the Boss" entry in Figure B.3). Be sure the date is inverted (14 June 1997)—unlike the dates you use in text. For scientific or academic journals, include the volume number and treat the page number(s) as shown in the Lamude entry in Figure B.3.

As a rule of thumb, use the more scholarly style if your report is weighted heavily toward serious research in professional journals; however, if popular and trade magazines dominate your references, you may stick with the simpler style that leaves out the volume number. Another option is to employ both styles, depending on the type of periodical being referenced. Your guiding principle in choosing a style is to provide the information that your readers need to find your source easily.

Newspapers

When a newspaper article doesn't have an author, the citation begins with the name of the article (and the entry is alphabetized by the first word of that title). The name of the newspaper is treated like the title of a book or periodical. Many of the best-known newspapers—such as *The New York Times, The Wall Street Journal,* and *The Christian Science Monitor*—are not easily mistaken for other newspapers, but many smaller newspapers are less easily identified. If the name of the city (plus the state or province for obscure or small cities) doesn't appear in the title of these newspapers, put the place name in brackets after the title. Finally, a newspaper reference specifies the date of publication in the same way a magazine does, and it ends with a section name or number (if appropriate) and a page number (see the entry in Figure B.3 that begins "Forecasters Predict Economy . . .").

Public Documents

Government documents and court cases are often useful in business reports, but bibliographic entries referring to them can be difficult to construct. As you struggle with a complex set of "authors" and publication data, remember that the goal is to provide just enough information to identify the work and to distinguish it from others. In Figure B.3, the entries for the U.S. Bureau of the Census and for the U.S. Congress are examples of how to format government documents.

Unpublished Material

Theses, dissertations, and company reports—which are usually prepared for a limited audience of insiders—are handled similarly. The title, like an article title, is in quotation marks, and "publication" data is included to help the reader find the work (see Figure B.3 entries for Asakawa and for Steele). This format can be used for any written source that doesn't fall into one of the other categories, such as a sales brochure or a presentation handout. Identify the author, title, and place and date of publication as completely as you can so that your readers have a way to refer to the source.

Formal letters, speeches, interviews, and other types of unpublished references are also identified as completely as possible to give readers some means of checking your sources. Begin with the name, title, and affiliation of the "author"; then describe the nature of the communication, the date and possibly the place, and if appropriate, the location of the files containing the document (as in Figure B.3, entries for Gabbei and Hawkins). Casual letters, interviews, and telephone conversations are rarely included in bibliographies; however, in notes you can identify the communication as personal (see Figure B.3 entry for Choon).

Electronic Media

Television and radio programs, films, computer programs, Internet sources, electronic databases, and the like are also documented. It may be more difficult for a reader to refer to some of these media (especially television and radio programs), but you still want to acknowledge ideas and facts borrowed from someone else. Figure B.3 lists ten electronic entries. To more easily identify the types of sources cited, the electronic entries are listed here as well:

Source	Reference List Entry
Electronic database	"Acquired Immunodeficiency Syndrome." In Mesh vocabulary file [database online]. Bethesda, Md.: National Library of Medicine, 1990 [cited 3 October 1990] Identifier no. D000163. [49 lines]
Computer service	Fenwick, Rose et al. *Guidelines for Teaching Persuasive Writing.* Chicago: Illinois State Department of Education, Chicago Division of Education Services, July 1990. 87, DIALOG, ERIC, ED 179423.

Videotape	*Group Productivity.* Del Mar, Calif.: CRM/McGraw-Hill Films, 1995. Videotape, 22 min.
Electronic bulletin board	"Jericho's Walls." In History Log9008 [electronic bulletin board]. S.l. 27 August 1990–[cited 15 December 1990]. Available from <listserv@FINHUTC.BITNET>.
Computer software	Lotus 1-2-3 Rel. 2. Lotus Development Corporation, Cambridge, Mass.
Web site	U.S. Department of Commerce. *Falling Through the Net: A Survey of the "Have Nots" in Rural and Urban America.* July 1995. <http://www.ntia.doc.gov/ntiahome/fallingthru.html>. [accessed online 5 December 1996.]
Web site	Ivey, Keith C. "Joining a Usenet Community," *The Editorial Eye,* n.d., <http://www.eeicom.com/eye/utw/96dec.html> (10 February 1997).
E-mail	Coon, Tang Meng. <tanmeng@biomed.nus.sg> "Broadcasting Standards." 29 January 1997. Personal e-mail (30 January 1997).
Newsgroup	Baron, Robert A. <rabaron@pipeline.com> "Copyright and Fair Use of Images." 9 February 1997. <fj.soc.copyright> (3 Mar 1997).
TV program	Wallace, Mike. *60 Minutes.* CBS-TV, 22 August 1993.

The information provided in these entries is sufficient to give readers a clear idea of the works you consulted. For more details on the formatting of electronic sources, consult style manuals such as *The Chicago Manual of Style* and *The MLA Style Manual.*

CHOOSING A METHOD OF IN-TEXT CITATION

Once you have constructed a complete and well-organized reference list, you can choose from several methods of documenting report sources in text. Three popular ways of handling citations are the author-date system, the key-number system, and the superscript system. Although the author-date system is preferred by many style manuals, the classic superscript system is still often used in scholarly works. The key-number system is least preferred by most authorities.

Author-Date System

When using the author-date system to make a reference citation in text, simply insert the author's last name and the year of the publication within parentheses. You can add a page number when necessary:

> . . . a basic understanding of the problem" (Landes 1992, 31).

An alternative is to weave the name of the author into the sentence:

> According to Landes (1992), no solution is likely to come . . .

When no author is named, use a short form of the title of the work. If the "author" is an organization, then shorten the name of the organization. In either case, make sure a reader can easily find this entry in the reference list:

> . . . with an emphasis on environmental matters (U.S. Department of Commerce 1995).

If this entry were identified as "Department of Commerce," your reader would be searching the *D*'s instead of the *U*'s for the correct reference.

When listing more than one work by the same author, rely on the year of publication to distinguish between them. A lowercase letter (*a, b,* and so on) after the year differentiates two works by the same author published in the same year.

The author-date system requires a reference list containing all your sources with all the pertinent publication information. The only variable is the placement of the year of publication. If your reference list has many instances of multiple works by one author or if you want to highlight the currency of your research, place the year of publication in the spot just after the author's name:

> Presner, Lewis A. 1991. *The International Business Dictionary and Reference.* New York, Wiley.

> Landes, Les L. 1992. "Down with Quality Programitis." *IABC Communication World (*February): 31.

A modification of the author-date system uses author-page information. Like the author-date system, the author-page system lets you weave references into the text. However, instead of using the author's name with the year of publication, this system uses the author's name and a page reference:

> . . . giving retailers some additional options (Landes, 31).

Parenthetical references can often be reduced to just the page number or year:

> In his article on management cooperation, Lamude emphasizes type-A managers (63–79).

> Conrad (1990) offers specific guidelines for handling problems with organizational communication.

Key-Number System

To use the least preferred method of documenting sources, you number each reference-list entry in sequence, with an arabic numeral followed by a period. When using this approach, the reference list is sometimes arranged in order of the appearance of each source in the text (rather than in alphabetical order).

In the text, references are documented with numbers. The first is the number assigned to the source, the second is the page number:

> . . . a basic understanding of the problem (12:7).

This reference cites page 7 of item 12 in the reference list.

The goal of using the author-date, author-page, and key-number systems is to simplify the traditional method of documentation using superscripts.

Superscript System

Source information has been traditionally handled using superscripts, which are arabic numerals placed just above the line of type. Scholarly works are still documented using this method. The superscript lets the reader know to look for source information either in a **footnote** (at the bottom of report pages) or in an **endnote** (at the end of each chapter or at the end of the report). Footnotes can be handier for readers, but some readers find them distracting. Endnotes are less intrusive, but readers may become annoyed with flipping to the end of the report to find them.

For the reader's convenience, you can use footnotes for **content notes** (which may supplement your main text with asides about a particular issue or event, provide a cross-reference to another section of your report, or direct the reader to a related source). Then you can use endnotes for **source notes** (which document direct quotations, paraphrased passages, and visual aids). Consider which type of note is most common in your report, and then choose whether to present them all as endnotes or all as footnotes. If all your sources are listed as endnotes, you may find that a bibliography is unnecessary. However, the larger and more formal the report, the greater the need for a separate reference list. Regardless of the method you choose for referencing textual information in your report, both content notes and source notes pertaining to visual aids are placed on the same page as the visual aid.

Superscripts usually come at the end of the sentence containing the referenced statement; but occasionally, to avoid confusion, a superscript is placed right after the referenced statement:

> Rising interest rates put a damper on third-quarter profits in all industries,[1] and profits did not pick up again until the Federal Reserve loosened the money supply.[2]

The first superscript in this example comes after the comma. Superscripts follow all punctuation marks except the dash (which follows the superscript).

Superscripts are numbered consecutively throughout the report. (In very long reports, they may be numbered consecutively throughout each chapter instead, as in this textbook.) If a note is added or deleted, all the reference marks that follow must be changed to maintain an unbroken sequence. If you change the superscript, be sure to renumber the corresponding notes as well. (Of course, word-processing software contains a note feature that will automatically do this for you.) Content notes appearing in visual aids are marked with asterisks and other symbols (or italicized lowercase letters if the visual aids contain many numbers).

Source Note Mechanics

Source notes generally follow the same order as bibliographic entries; however, commas are often substituted for periods, and the publication information appears in parentheses. A source note often refers to a specific page number. If so, the closing parenthesis is followed by a comma, which in turn is followed by the page number(s):

> 4. Lewis A. Presner, *The International Business Dictionary and Reference* (New York: Wiley, 1991), 62–63.

Notes of all varieties are single-spaced and separated from one another by a double space. In footnotes to textual information, the identifying number is indented five spaces and followed by a period (as in the Presner note just cited). However, endnotes begin at the left margin (see the "References" section at the end of this book). Notes referring to visual aids are handled differently too: A source note, preceded by the underlined (italicized) word *Source* and a colon, is placed at the bottom of the visual aid; content notes, if any, are listed below the source note. Figure 16.2, on page 512, shows the placement of these notes on visual aids.

When using footnotes, plan carefully to leave enough space for the footnote at the bottom of the page and still maintain the standard margin. Word-processing software handles the layout and numbering of notes for you, whether footnotes or endnotes. When using a typewriter, separate the footnote(s) from the text with a line (made using the underscore key) about 1-1/2 inches long (15 spaces in pica type, 20 in elite).

Quotations

Quotations from secondary sources must always be followed by a reference mark. However, quotations may appear in one of two forms, depending on their length. A brief quotation (three lines or less) can be typed right into the main body of the text. Quotation marks at the beginning and end of the quotation separate the other person's words from your own.

Longer quotations must be set off as extracts. An extract begins on a new line, and both right and left margins are indented five to seven spaces. No quotation marks are needed. Although the main text may be single- or double-spaced, an extract is always single-spaced.

You'll often want to leave out some part of a quotation. Ellipsis points (or dots) are the three periodlike punctuation marks that show something is missing.

> Brant has demonstrated . . . a wanton disregard for the realities of the marketplace. His days at the helm are numbered. . . . Already several lower-level executives are jockeying for position.[3]

The second sentence in this example shows you how ellipsis points are handled between sentences: A period is followed by the three dots. Also, make sure ellipsis points appear with spaces before, after, and between them.

Repeated Notes

When you cite the same reference more than once in the course of your report, you can save time and effort by using a full citation for the first source note and a shortened form for later references. The information in repeated source notes can be handled in two ways: in a formal, traditional style or in an informal style. The formal style uses Latin abbreviations to indicate certain information; the informal style uses shortened versions of the source information instead. Here are some repeated source notes using the formal style:

> 4. Lewis A. Presner, *The International Business Dictionary and Reference* (New York: Wiley, 1991), 62–63.
> 5. Ibid., 130. [refers to page 130 in the Presner book]
> 6. Charles Conrad, *Strategic Organizational Communication: An Integrated Perspective,* 2d ed. (Fort Worth, Tex.: Holt, Rinehart and Winston, 1990), 107.
> 7. Les L. Landes, "Down with Quality Programitis," *IABC Communication World,* February 1992, 31.
> 8. Conrad, op. cit., 28. [refers to a new page in the book cited in note 6]
> 9. Landes, loc. cit. [refers to page 31 of Landes]

Ibid. means "in the same place"—that is, the same reference mentioned in the immediately preceding entry but perhaps a different page (indicated by giving the page number). *Op. cit.* means "in the work cited"; because it's used when at least one other reference has come between it and the original citation, you must include the last name of the author. You must also use a new page number; otherwise, you would use *loc. cit.* ("in the place cited") and omit the page number.

The informal style, which is commonly used today, avoids Latin abbreviations by adopting a shortened form for the title of a reference that is repeated. In this style, the previous list of source notes would appear as follows:

> 4. Lewis A. Presner, *The International Business Dictionary and Reference* (New York: Wiley, 1991), 62–63.
> 5. Presner, *The International Business Dictionary and Reference,* 130.
> 6. Charles Conrad, *Strategic Organizational Communication: An Integrated Perspective,* 2d ed. (Fort Worth, Tex.: Holt, Rinehart and Winston, 1990), 107.
> 7. Les L. Landes, "Down with Quality Programitis," *IABC Communication World,* February 1992, 31.
> 8. Conrad, *Strategic Organizational Communication,* 28.
> 9. Landes, "Down with Quality Programitis," 31.

Books

10. Lewis A. Presner, *The International Business Dictionary and Reference* (New York: Wiley, 1991), 62–63.

11. Charles Conrad, *Strategic Organizational Communication: An Integrated Perspective,* 2d ed. (Fort Worth, Tex.: Holt, Rinehart and Winston, 1990), 107.

12. John Donaldson, ed., *Business Ethics* (San Diego: Academic Press, 1992), 74.

Periodicals and Newspapers

13. Les L. Landes, "Down with Quality Programitis," *IABC Communication World,* February 1992, 31.

14. "Time to Call in the Boss," *Brandweek,* 27 July 1992, 32–36, 60.

15. Kevin G. Lamude and Joseph Scudder, "Compliance-Gaining Techniques of Type-A Managers," *Journal of Business Communication* 30, no. 1 (1993): 63–79.

16. "Forecasters Predict Economy Won't Change Much," *Wall Street Journal,* 12 October 1993, sec. A, 16.

Public Documents

17. U.S. Bureau of the Census, *Statistical Abstract of the United States: 1996* (Washington, D.C.: GPO, 1996), 337.

18. U.S. Congress, Senate Committee on Foreign Relations, *Famine in Africa: Hearing before the Committee on Foreign Relations,* 99th Cong., 1st sess., 17 January 1985, 53–57.

19. *Simpson v. Union Oil Co. of California,* 377 U.S. 13 (U.S. Sup. Ct. 1964).

Unpublished Materials

20. Katherine W. Hawkins, "Effects of Gender and Communication Content on Leadership Emergence in Small Task-Oriented Groups" (paper presented at the 78th annual meeting of the Speech Communication Association, Chicago, Illinois), 1992.

21. Peter A. Steele, "Implementation of Cyber Appliances Through Cable Television" (Master's thesis, San Diego State University, 1996), 56–61.

22. Frances Asakawa, "Recommendations for Replacing the Sales Fleet Based on a Comparison of Three Midsize Automobiles." Report to Daniel Standish, Director of Sales, Midwest Marketing, 17 November 1994, 12.

23. Dorothy Gabbei, interview with the author, Emporia, Kansas, 14 July 1992.

Electronic Media

24. Mike Wallace, *60 Minutes*, CBS-TV, 22 August 1993.

25. *Group Productivity* (Del Mar, Calif.: CRM/McGraw-Hill Films, 1995), videotape, 22 min.

26. Lotus 1-2-3 Rel. 2, Lotus Development Corporation, Cambridge, Mass.

27. "Acquired Immunodeficiency Syndrome," in Mesh vocabulary file [database online] (Bethesda, Md.: National Library of Medicine, 1990 [cited 3 October 1990]) identifier no. D000163 [49 lines].

28. Department of Commerce, *Falling Through the Net: A Survey of the "Have Nots" in Rural and Urban America.* July 1995. <http://www.ntia.doc.gov/ntiahome/fallingthru.html>. [accessed online 5 December 1996].

29. Rose Fenwick et al., *Guidelines for Teaching Persuasive Writing* (Chicago: Illinois State Department of Education, Chicago Division of Education Services, July 1990), 87, DIALOG, ERIC, ED 179423.

30. "Jericho's Walls," in History Log9008 [electronic bulletin board]. s.l. 27 August 1990–[cited 15 December 1990]. available from <listserv@FINHUTC.BITNET>.

31. Keith C. Ivey, "Joining a Usenet Community," *The Editorial Eye,* n.d., <http://www.eeicom.com/eye/utw/96dec.html> (10 February 1997).

32. Tang Meng Choon, <tanmeng@biomed.nus.sg> "Broadcasting Standards," 29 January 1997, personal e-mail (30 January 1997).

33. Robert A. Baron, <rabaron@pipeline.com> "Copyright and Fair Use of Images," 9 February 1997 <fj.soc.copyright> (3 March 1997).

Only the author's last name, a short form of the title, and the page number are used in this style of repeated source note. If your report has a comprehensive alphabetical bibliography, you may opt to use the short form for all your source notes, not just first citations.

Source Note Format

Source notes present the same information as bibliographic entries, in some cases with the addition of page numbers. Source note punctuation differs from bibliographic style, and parentheses are placed around the publication data. To emphasize the differences between source notes and bibliographic entries, the examples in Figure B.4 use the same sources as the references appearing in Figure B.3.

Remember, even though legal cases such as reference note 19 are often not listed in bibliographies, they may be mentioned in the text or cited in source notes. Be sure to provide the name of the case, the volume and page numbers of the law report, the name of the court that decided the case (the U.S. Supreme Court here), and the date of the decision. References to unpublished sources such as notes 20–23 may also be woven into the text of your report and thus require no source note.

The exact information you provide for electronic references such as notes 24–30 depends on your subject and audience and on the context of the reference. For example, when citing a film, it may be appropriate to note the scriptwriter or director. When constructing source notes for electronic media, consult a good style manual and use good judgment about how much information is needed.

APPENDIX 1

FUNDAMENTALS OF GRAMMAR AND USAGE

Grammar is nothing more than the way words are combined into sentences, and usage is the way words are used by a network of people—in this case, the community of businesspeople who use English. You'll find it easier to get along in this community if you know the accepted standards of grammar and usage. What follows is a review of the basics of grammar and usage, things you've probably learned but may have forgotten. Without a firm grasp of these basics, you risk not only being misunderstood but also damaging your company's image, losing money for your company, and possibly even losing your job.

1.0 GRAMMAR

The sentence below looks innocent, but is it really?

> We sell tuxedos as well as rent.

You might sell rent, but it's highly unlikely. Whatever you're selling, some people will ignore your message because of a blunder like this. The following sentence has a similar problem:

> Vice President Eldon Neale told his chief engineer that he would no longer be with Avix, Inc., as of June 30.

Is Eldon or the engineer leaving? No matter which side the facts are on, the sentence can be read the other way. You may have a hard time convincing either person that your simple mistake was not a move in a game of office politics. Now look at this sentence:

> The year before we budgeted more for advertising sales were up.

Confused? Perhaps this is what you meant:

> The year before, we budgeted more for advertising. Sales were up.

Maybe you meant this:

> The year before we budgeted more for advertising, sales were up.

The meaning of language falls into bundles called sentences. A listener or reader can take only so much meaning before filing a sentence away and getting ready for the next one. So as a writer, you have to know what a sentence is. You need to know where one ends and the next one begins.

If you want to know what a thing is, you have to find out what goes into it, what its ingredients are. Luckily, the basic ingredients of an English sentence are simple. They're called the parts of speech, and the content-bearing ones are nouns, pronouns, verbs, adjectives, and adverbs. They combine with a few functional parts of speech to convey meaning. Meaning is also transmitted by punctuation, mechanics, and vocabulary.

1.1 Nouns

A noun names a person, place, or thing. Anything you can see or detect with one of your other senses has a noun to name it. Some things you can't see or sense are also nouns—ions, for example, or space. So are things that exist as ideas, such as accuracy and height. (You can see that something is accurate or that a building is tall, but you can't see the idea of accuracy or the idea of height.) These names for ideas are known as abstract nouns. The simplest nouns are the names of things you can see or touch: car, building, cloud, brick.

1.1.1 Proper Nouns and Common Nouns

So far, all the examples of nouns have been common nouns, referring to general classes of things. The word *building* refers to a whole class of structures. Common nouns like *building* are not capitalized.

However, if you want to talk about one particular building, you might refer to the Glazier Building. The name is capitalized, indicating that *Glazier Building* is a proper noun.

Here are three sets of common and proper nouns for comparison:

Common	Proper
city	Kansas City
company	Blaisden Company
store	Books Galore

1.1.2 Plural Nouns

Nouns can be either singular or plural. The usual way to make a plural noun is to add *s* to the singular form of the word:

Singular	Plural
rock	rocks
picture	pictures
song	songs

Many nouns have other ways of forming the plural. Letters, numbers, and words used as words are sometimes made plural by adding an apostrophe and an *s*. As a rule, *'s* is used with abbreviations that have periods, lowercase letters that stand alone, and capital letters that might be confused with other words when made into plurals:

Spell out all *St.*'s and *Ave.*'s.

He divided the page with a row of *x*'s.

Sarah will register the *A*'s through the *I*'s at the convention.

In other cases, however, the apostrophe may be left out:

They'll review their *ABC*s.

The stock market climbed through most of the 1980s.

Circle all *the*s in the paragraph.

In these examples, the letters and words used as words are *italicized* (discussed later in the appendix).

Other nouns, like those below, are so-called irregular nouns; they form the plural in some way other than simply adding *s*:

Singular	Plural
tax	taxes
specialty	specialties
cargo	cargoes
shelf	shelves
child	children
woman	women
tooth	teeth
mouse	mice
parenthesis	parentheses
son-in-law	sons-in-law
editor-in-chief	editors-in-chief

Rather than memorize a lot of rules about forming plurals, use a dictionary. If the dictionary says nothing about the plural of a word, it's formed the usual way—by adding *s*. If the plural is formed in some irregular way, the dictionary shows the plural or has a note something like this: *pl* -es.

1.1.3 Possessive Nouns

A noun becomes possessive when it's used to show the ownership of something. Then you add *'s* to the word:

the man's car   the woman's apartment

However, ownership does not need to be legal:

the secretary's desk   the company's assets

Also, ownership may be nothing more than an automatic association:

a day's work   a job's prestige

An exception to the rule about adding *'s* to make a noun possessive occurs when the word is singular and already has two *s* sounds at the end. In cases like the following, an apostrophe is all that's needed:

crisis' dimensions   Mr. Moses' application

When the noun has only one *s* sound at the end, however, retain the *'s*:

Chris's book   Carolyn Nuss's office

With hyphenated nouns (compound nouns), add *'s* to the last word:

Hyphenated Noun	Possessive Noun
mother-in-law	mother-in-law's
mayor-elect	mayor-elect's

To form the possessive of plural nouns, just begin by following the same rule as with singular nouns: add *'s*. However, if the plural noun already ends in an *s* (as most do), drop the one you've added, leaving only the apostrophe:

the clients's complaints   employees's benefits

1.2 Pronouns

A pronoun is a word that stands for a noun; it saves repeating the noun:

> *Drivers* have some choice of weeks for vacation, but *they* must notify this office of *their* preference by March 1.

The pronouns *they* and *their* stand in for the noun *drivers*. The noun that a pronoun stands for is called the antecedent of the pronoun; *drivers* is the antecedent of *they* and *their*.

When the antecedent is plural, the pronoun that stands in for it has to be plural; *they* and *their* are plural pronouns because *drivers* is plural. Likewise, when the antecedent is singular, the pronoun has to be singular:

> We thought the *contract* had been signed, but we soon learned *it* had not been.

1.2.1 Multiple Antecedents

Sometimes a pronoun has a double (or even a triple) antecedent:

> Kathryn Boettcher and Luis Gutierrez went beyond *their* sales quotas for January.

Kathryn Boettcher, if taken alone, is a singular antecedent. So is *Luis Gutierrez.* However, when both are the antecedent of a pronoun, they're plural and the pronoun has to be plural. Thus the pronoun is *their* instead of *her* or *his.*

1.2.2 Unclear Antecedents

In some sentences the pronoun's antecedent is unclear:

> Sandy Wright sent Jane Brougham *her* production figures for the previous year. *She* thought they were too low.

Which person does the pronoun *her* refer to? Someone who knew Sandy and Jane and knew their business relationship might be able to figure out the antecedent for *her.* Even with such an advantage, however, a reader still might receive the wrong meaning. Also it would be nearly impossible for any reader to know which name is the antecedent of *she.*

The best way to clarify an ambiguous pronoun is usually to rewrite the sentence, repeating nouns when needed for clarity:

> Sandy Wright sent her production figures for the previous year to Jane Brougham. *Jane* thought they were too low.

Repeat the noun only when the antecedent is unclear.

1.2.3 Gender-Neutral Pronouns

The pronouns that stand for males are *he, his,* and *him.* The pronouns that stand for females are *she, hers,* and *her.* However, you'll often be faced with the problem of choosing a pronoun for a noun that refers to both females and males:

> Each manager must make up (his, her, his or her, its, their) own mind about stocking this item and about the quantity that (he, she, he or she, it, they) can sell.

This sentence calls for a pronoun that's neither masculine nor feminine. The issue of gender-neutral pronouns

responds to efforts to treat females and males evenhandedly. Here are some possible ways to deal with this issue:

Each manager must make up *his* . . .
(Not all managers are men.)

Each manager must make up *her* . . .
(Not all managers are women.)

Each manager must make up *his* or *her* . . .
(This solution is acceptable but becomes awkward when repeated more than once or twice in a document.)

Each manager must make up *her* . . . Every manager will receive *his* . . . A manager may send *her* . . .
(A manager's gender does not alternate like a windshield wiper!)

Each manager must make up *their* . . .
(The pronoun can't be plural when the antecedent is singular.)

Each manager must make up *its* . . .
(*It* never refers to people.)

The best solution is to make the noun plural or to revise the passage altogether:

Managers must make up *their* minds . . .

Each manager must decide whether . . .

Be careful not to change the original meaning.

1.2.4 Case of Pronouns

The case of a pronoun tells whether it's acting or acted upon:

> *She* sells an average of five packages each week.

In this sentence *she* is doing the selling. Because *she* is acting, *she* is said to be in the nominative case. Now consider what happens when the pronoun is acted upon:

> After six months Ms. Browning promoted *her.*

In this sentence the pronoun *her* is acted upon. The pronoun *her* is thus said to be in the objective case.

Contrast the nominative and objective pronouns in this list:

Nominative	Objective
I	me
we	us
he	him
she	her
they	them
who	whom
whoever	whomever

Objective pronouns may be used as either the object of a verb (like *promoted*) or the object of a preposition (like *with*):

Rob worked with *them* until the order was filled.

In this example *them* is the object of the preposition *with* because Rob acted upon—worked with—them.

Here's a sample sentence with three pronouns, the first one nominative, the second the object of a verb, and the third the object of a preposition:

He paid *us* as soon as the check came from *them.*

He is nominative; *us* is objective because it's the object of the verb *paid; them* is objective because it's the object of the preposition *from.*

Every writer sometimes wonders whether to use *who* or *whom:*

(Who, Whom) will you hire?

Because this sentence is a question, it's difficult to see that *whom* is the object of the verb *hire.* You can figure out which pronoun to use if you rearrange the question and temporarily try *she* and *her* in place of *who* and *whom:* "Will you hire *she*?" or "Will you hire *her*?" *Her* and *whom* are both objective, so the correct choice is "*Whom* will you hire?" Here's a different example:

(Who, Whom) logged so much travel time?

Turning the question into a statement, you get:

He logged so much travel time.

Therefore, the correct statement is:

Who logged so much travel time?

1.2.5 Possessive Pronouns

Possessive pronouns are like possessive nouns in the way they work: They show ownership or automatic association.

her job	their preferences
his account	its equipment

However, possessive pronouns are different from possessive nouns in the way they are written. That is, possessive pronouns never have an apostrophe.

Possessive Noun	**Possessive Pronoun**
the woman's estate	her estate
Roger Franklin's plans	his plans
the shareholders' feelings	their feelings
the vacuum cleaner's attachments	its attachments

The word *its* is the possessive of *it.* Like all other possessive pronouns, *its* doesn't have an apostrophe. Some people confuse *its* with *it's,* the contraction of *it is.* Contractions are discussed later.

1.3 Verbs

A verb describes an action:

They all *quit* in disgust.

It may also describe a state of being:

Working conditions *were* substandard.

The English language is full of action verbs. Here are a few you'll often run across in the business world:

verify	perform	fulfill
hire	succeed	send
leave	improve	receive
accept	develop	pay

You could undoubtedly list many more.

The most common verb describing a state of being instead of an action is *to be* and all its forms:

I *am, was,* or *will be;* you *are, were,* or *will be*

Other verbs also describe a state of being:

It *seemed* a good plan at the time.
She *sounds* impressive at a meeting.

These verbs link what comes before them in the sentence with what comes after; no action is involved. (See Section 1.7.5 for a fuller discussion of linking verbs.)

1.3.1 Verb Tenses

English has three simple verb tenses: present, past, and future.

Present: Our branches in Hawaii *stock* other items.

Past: When we *stocked* Purquil pens, we received a great many complaints.

Future: Rotex Tire Stores *will stock* your line of tires when you begin a program of effective national advertising.

With most verbs (the regular ones), the past tense ends in *ed;* the future tense always has *will* or *shall* in front of it. But the present tense is more complex:

Singular	**Plural**
I stock	we stock
you stock	you stock
he, she, it stocks	they stock

The basic form, *stock,* takes an additional *s* when *he, she,* or *it* precedes it.

In addition to the three simple tenses, there are three perfect tenses using forms of the helping verb *have.* The present perfect tense uses the past participle (regularly the past tense) of the main verb, *stocked,* and adds the present-tense *have* or *has* to the front of it:

(I, we, you, they) *have stocked.*

(He, she, it) *has stocked.*

The past perfect tense uses the past participle of the main verb, *stocked,* and adds the past-tense *had* to the front of it:

(I, you, he, she, it, we, they) *had stocked.*

The future perfect tense also uses the past participle of the main verb, *stocked,* but adds the future-tense *will have:*

(I, you, he, she, it, we, they) *will have stocked.*

Keep verbs in the same tense when the actions occur at the same time:

When the payroll checks *came* in, everyone *showed* up for work.

We *have found* that everyone *has pitched* in to help.

Of course, when the actions occur at different times, you may change tense accordingly:

A shipment *came* last Wednesday, so when another one *comes* in today, please return it.

The new employee *had been* ill at ease, but now she *has become* a full-fledged member of the team.

1.3.2 Irregular Verbs

Many verbs don't follow in every detail the patterns already described. The most irregular of these verbs is *to be:*

	Singular	**Plural**
Present:	I *am*	we *are*
	you *are*	you *are*
	he, she, it *is*	they *are*
Past:	I *was*	we *were*
	you *were*	you *were*
	he, she, it *was*	they *were*

The future tense of *to be* is formed the same way the future tense of a regular verb is formed.

The perfect tenses of *to be* are also formed as they would be for a regular verb, except that the past participle is a special form, *been,* instead of just the past tense:

Present Perfect:	you *have been*
Past Perfect:	you *had been*
Future Perfect:	you *will have been*

Here's a sampling of other irregular verbs:

Present	**Past**	**Past Participle**
begin	began	begun
shrink	shrank	shrunk
know	knew	known
rise	rose	risen
become	became	become
go	went	gone
do	did	done

Dictionaries list the various forms of other irregular verbs.

1.3.3 Transitive and Intransitive Verbs

Many people are confused by three particular sets of verbs:

lie/lay   sit/set   rise/raise

Using these verbs correctly is much easier when you learn the difference between transitive and intransitive verbs.

Transitive verbs convey their action to an object; they "transfer" their action to an object. Intransitive verbs do not. Here are some sample uses of transitive and intransitive verbs:

Intransitive	**Transitive**
We should include in our new offices a place to *lie* down for a nap.	The workers will be here on Monday to *lay* new carpeting.
Even the way an interviewee *sits* is important.	That crate is full of stemware, so *set* it down carefully.
Salaries at Compu-Link, Inc., *rise* swiftly.	They *raise* their level of production every year.

The workers *lay* carpeting, you *set* down the crate, they *raise* production—each action is transferred to something. In the intransitive sentences, one *lies* down, an interviewee *sits,* and salaries *rise* without (at least grammatically) affecting anything else. Intransitive sentences are complete with only a subject and a verb; transitive sentences are not complete unless they also include an object, or something to transfer the action to.

Tenses are a confusing element of the *lie/lay* problem:

Present	Past	Past Participle
I *lie*	I *lay*	I have *lain*
I *lay* (some-thing down)	I *laid* (some-thing down)	I have *laid* (some-thing down)

The past tense of *lie* and the present tense of *lay* look and sound alike, even though they're different verbs.

1.3.4 Voice of Verbs

Verbs have two voices, active and passive:

Active: The buyer paid a large amount.

Passive: A large amount was paid by the buyer.

The passive voice uses a form of the verb *to be.*

Also, the passive-voice sentence uses eight words, whereas the active-voice sentence uses only six words to say the same thing. The words *was* and *by* are unnecessary to convey the meaning of the sentence. In fact, extra words usually clog meaning. So be sure to opt for the active voice when you have a choice.

At times, however, you have no choice:

> Several items *have been taken,* but so far we don't know who took them.

The passive voice becomes necessary when you don't know (or don't want to say) who performed the action; the active voice is bolder and more direct.

1.3.5 Mood of Verbs

You have three moods to choose from, depending on your intentions. Most of the time you use the indicative mood to make a statement or ask a question:

The secretary *mailed* a letter to each supplier.

Did the secretary *mail* a letter to each supplier?

When you wish to command or request, use the imperative mood:

> Please *mail* a letter to each supplier.

Sometimes, especially in business, a courteous request is stated like a question; in that case, however, no question mark is required.

> Would you *mail* a letter to each supplier.

The subjunctive mood, most often used in formal writing or in presenting bad news, expresses a possibility or a recommendation. The subjunctive is usually signaled by a word such as *if* or *that.* In these examples the subjunctive mood uses special verb forms:

If the secretary *were to mail* a letter to each supplier, we might save some money.

I suggested that the secretary *mail* a letter to each supplier.

Although the subjunctive mood is not often used anymore, it's still found in such expressions as *Come what may* and *If I were you.*

1.4 Adjectives

An adjective modifies (tells something about) a noun or pronoun:

an *efficient* staff	a *heavy* price
brisk trade	*poor* you

Each of these phrases says more about the noun or pronoun than the noun or pronoun would say alone.

Adjectives always tell us something we wouldn't know without them. So you don't need to use adjectives when the noun alone, or a different noun, will give the meaning:

a *company* employee
(An employee ordinarily works for a company.)

a *crate-type* container
(*Crate* gives the entire meaning.)

At times, adjectives pile up in a series:

> It was a *long, hot,* and *active* workday.

Such strings of adjectives are acceptable as long as they all convey a different part of the phrase's meaning.

Verbs in the *ing* form can be used as adjectives:

> A *boring* job can sometimes turn into a *fascinating* career.

So can the past participle of verbs:

> A freshly *painted* house is a *sold* house.

Adjectives modify nouns more often than they modify pronouns. When adjectives do modify pronouns, however, the sentence usually has a linking verb:

They were *attentive.*	It looked *appropriate.*
He seems *interested.*	You are *skillful.*

Most adjectives can take three forms: simple, comparative, and superlative. The simple form modifies a single noun or pronoun. Use the comparative form when comparing two items. When comparing three or more items, use the superlative form.

Simple	Comparative	Superlative
hard	harder	hardest
safe	safer	safest
dry	drier	driest

The comparative form adds *er* to the simple form, and the superlative form adds *est*. (The *y* at the end of a word changes to *i* before the *er* or *est* is added.)

A small number of adjectives are irregular, including these:

Simple	Comparative	Superlative
good	better	best
bad	worse	worst
little	less	least

When the simple form of an adjective is two or more syllables, you usually add *more* to form the comparative and *most* to form the superlative:

Simple	Comparative	Superlative
useful	more useful	most useful
exhausting	more exhausting	most exhausting
expensive	more expensive	most expensive

The only exception might be a two-syllable adjective that ends in *y:*

Simple	Comparative	Superlative
happy	happier	happiest
costly	costlier	costliest

If you choose this option, change the *y* to *i,* and tack *er* or *est* onto the end.

1.5 Adverbs

An adverb modifies a verb, an adjective, or another adverb:

Modifying a Verb:	Our marketing department works *efficiently.*
Modifying an Adjective:	She was not dependable, although she was *highly* intelligent.
Modifying Another Adverb:	His territory was *too* broadly diversified, so he moved *extremely* cautiously.

Most of the adverbs mentioned are adjectives turned into adverbs by adding *ly,* which is how many adverbs are formed:

Adjective	Adverb
efficient	efficiently
high	highly
extreme	extremely
special	specially
official	officially
separate	separately

Some adverbs are made by dropping or changing the final letter of the adjective and then adding *ly:*

Adjective	Adverb
due	duly
busy	busily

Other adverbs don't end in *ly* at all. Here are a few examples of this type:

often	fast	too
soon	very	so

1.6 Other Parts of Speech

Nouns, pronouns, verbs, adjectives, and adverbs carry most of the meaning in a sentence. Four other parts of speech link them together in sentences: prepositions, conjunctions, articles, and interjections.

1.6.1 Prepositions

Prepositions are words like these:

of	to	for	with
at	by	from	about

They most often begin prepositional phrases, which function like adjectives and adverbs by telling more about a pronoun, noun, or verb:

of a type	*by* Friday
to the point	*with* characteristic flair

1.6.2 Conjunctions, Articles, and Interjections

Conjunctions are words that usually join parts of a sentence. Here are a few:

and	but	because
yet	although	if

Using conjunctions is discussed in Sections 1.7.3 and 1.7.4.

Only three articles exist in English: *the, a,* and *an.* These words are used, like adjectives, to specify which item you are talking about.

Interjections are words that express no solid information, only emotion:

Wow!   Well, well!
Oh no!   Good!

Such purely emotional language has its place in private life and advertising copy, but it only weakens the effect of most business writing.

1.7 Sentences

Sentences are constructed with the major building blocks, the parts of speech.

Money talks.

This two-word sentence consists of a noun (*money*) and a verb (*talks*). When used in this way, the noun works as the first requirement for a sentence, the subject, and the verb works as the second requirement, the predicate. Now look at this sentence:

They merged.

The subject in this case is a pronoun (*they*), and the predicate is a verb (*merged*). This is a sentence because it has a subject and a predicate. Here is yet another kind of sentence:

The plans are ready.

This sentence has a more complicated subject, the noun *plans* and the article *the;* the complete predicate is a state-of-being verb (*are*) and an adjective (*ready*).

Without these two parts, the subject (who or what does something) and the predicate (the doing of it), no collection of words is a sentence.

1.7.1 Commands

In commands the subject (always *you*) is only understood, not stated:

(You) Move your desk to the better office.

(You) Please try to finish by six o'clock.

1.7.2 Longer Sentences

More complicated sentences have more complicated subjects and predicates, but they still have a simple subject and a predicate verb. In the following examples, the simple subject is underlined once, the predicate verb twice:

<u>Marex</u> and <u>Contron</u> <u>enjoy</u> higher earnings each quarter.
(<u>Marex</u> [and] <u>Contron</u> did something; <u>enjoy</u> is what they did.)

My <u>interview</u>, coming minutes after my freeway accident, <u>did</u> not <u>impress</u> or <u>move</u> anyone.
(<u>Interview</u> is what did something. What did it do? It <u>did</u> [not] <u>impress</u> [or] <u>move</u>.)

In terms of usable space, a steel <u>warehouse</u>, with its extremely long span of roof unsupported by pillars, <u>makes</u> more sense.
(<u>Warehouse</u> is what <u>makes</u>.)

These three sentences demonstrate several things. First, in all three sentences the simple subject and predicate verb are the "bare bones" of the sentence, the parts that carry the core idea of the sentence. When trying to find the simple subject and predicate verb, disregard all prepositional phrases, modifiers, conjunctions, and articles.

Second, in the third sentence the verb is singular (*makes*) because the subject is singular (*warehouse*). Even though the plural noun *pillars* is closer to the verb, *warehouse* is the real subject. So *warehouse* determines whether the verb is singular or plural. Subject and predicate must agree.

Third, the subject in the first sentence is compound (*Marex* [and] *Contron*). A compound subject, when connected by *and,* requires a plural verb (*enjoy*). Also in the second sentence, compound predicates are possible (*did* [not] *impress* [or] *move*).

Fourth, the second sentence incorporates a group of words—*coming minutes after my freeway accident*—containing a form of a verb (*coming*) and a noun (*accident*). Yet this group of words is not a complete sentence for two reasons:

- *Accident* is not the subject of *coming.* Not all nouns are subjects.
- A verb that ends in *ing* can never be the predicate of a sentence (unless preceded by a form of *to be,* as in *was coming*). Not all verbs are predicates.

Because they don't contain a subject and a predicate, the words *coming minutes after my freeway accident* (called a phrase) can't be written as a sentence. That is, the phrase can't stand alone; it can't begin with a capital letter and end with a period. So a phrase must always be just one part of a sentence.

Sometimes a sentence incorporates two or more groups of words that do contain a subject and a predicate; these word groups are called clauses.

My <u>interview</u>, because <u>it</u> <u>came</u> minutes after my freeway accident, <u>did</u> not <u>impress</u> or <u>move</u> anyone.

The independent clause is the portion of the sentence that could stand alone without revision:

> My <u>interview</u> <u>did</u> not <u>impress</u> or <u>move</u> anyone.

The other part of the sentence could stand alone only by removing *because:*

> (because) <u>It</u> <u>came</u> minutes after my freeway accident.

This part of the sentence is known as a dependent clause; although it has a subject and a predicate (just like an independent clause), it's linked to the main part of the sentence by a word (*because*) showing its dependence.

To summarize, the two types of clauses—dependent and independent—both have a subject and a predicate. Dependent clauses, however, do not bear the main meaning of the sentence and are therefore linked to an independent clause. Neither can phrases stand alone, because they lack both a subject and a predicate. Only independent clauses can be written as sentences without revision.

1.7.3 Sentence Fragments

When an incomplete sentence (a phrase or dependent clause) is written as though it were a complete sentence, it's called a fragment. Consider the following sentence fragments:

> Marilyn Sanders, having had pilferage problems in her store for the past year. Refuses to accept the results of our investigation.

This serious error can easily be corrected by putting the two fragments together:

> Marilyn Sanders, having had pilferage problems in her store for the past year, refuses to accept the results of our investigation.

Not all fragments can be corrected so easily:

> Employees a part of it. No authority or discipline.

Only the writer knows the intended meaning of these two phrases. Perhaps the employees are taking part in the pilferage. If so, the sentence should read:

> Some employees are part of the pilferage problem.

On the other hand, it's possible that some employees are helping with the investigation. Then the sentence would read:

> Some employees are taking part in our investigation.

It's just as likely, however, that the employees are not only taking part in the pilferage but are also being analyzed:

> Those employees who are part of the pilferage problem will accept no authority or discipline.

In fact, even more meanings could be read into these fragments. Because fragments like these can mean so many things, they mean nothing. No well-written memo, letter, or report ever demands the reader to be an imaginative genius.

One more type of fragment exists, the kind represented by a dependent clause. Note what *because* does to change what was once a unified sentence:

Our stock of sprinklers is depleted.

Because our stock of sprinklers is depleted.

Although it contains a subject and a predicate, adding *because* makes the second version a fragment. Words like *because* form a special group of words called subordinating conjunctions. Here's a partial list:

since	though	whenever
although	if	unless
while	even if	after

When a word of this type begins a clause, the clause is dependent and cannot stand alone as a sentence. However, if a dependent clause is combined with an independent clause, it can convey a complete meaning. The independent clause may come before or after the dependent clause:

We are unable to fill your order because our stock of sprinklers is depleted.

Because our stock of sprinklers is depleted, we are unable to fill your order.

Another remedy for a fragment that is a dependent clause is to remove the subordinating conjunction. That solution leaves a simple but complete sentence:

> Our stock of sprinklers is depleted.

The actual details of a transaction will determine the best way to remedy a fragment problem.

The ban on fragments has one exception. Some advertising copy contains sentence fragments, written knowingly to convey a certain rhythm. However, advertising is the only area of business in which fragments are acceptable.

1.7.4 Fused Sentences and Comma Splices

Just as there can be too little in a group of words to make it a sentence, there can also be too much:

> All our mail is run through a postage meter every afternoon someone picks it up.

This example contains two sentences, not one, but the two have been blended so that it's hard to tell where one ends and the next begins. Is the mail run through a meter every afternoon? If so, the sentences should read:

> All our mail is run through a postage meter every afternoon. Someone picks it up.

Perhaps the mail is run through a meter at some other time (morning, for example) and is picked up every afternoon:

> All our mail is run through a postage meter. Every afternoon someone picks it up.

The order of words is the same in all three cases; sentence division makes all the difference. Either of the last two cases is grammatically correct. The choice depends on the facts of the situation.

Sometimes these so-called fused sentences have a more obvious point of separation:

> Several large orders arrived within a few days of one another, too many came in for us to process by the end of the month.

Here the comma has been put between two independent clauses in an attempt to link them. When a lowly comma separates two complete sentences, the result is called a comma splice. A comma splice can be remedied in one of three ways:

- Replace the comma with a period and capitalize the next word: ". . . one another. Too many . . ."
- Replace the comma with a semicolon but do not capitalize the next word: ". . . one another; too many . . ." This remedy works only when the two sentences have closely related meanings.
- Change one of the sentences so that it becomes a phrase or a dependent clause. This remedy often produces the best writing, but it takes more work.

The third alternative can be carried out in several ways. One is to begin the blended sentence with a subordinating conjunction:

> Whenever several large orders arrived within a few days of one another, too many came in for us to process by the end of the month.

Another way is to remove part of the subject or the predicate verb from one of the independent clauses, thereby creating a phrase:

> Several large orders arrived within a few days of one another, too many for us to process by the end of the month.

Finally, you can change one of the predicate verbs to its *ing* form:

> Several large orders arrived within a few days of one another, too many coming in for us to process by the end of the month.

At other times a simple coordinating conjunction (such as *or, and,* or *but*) can separate fused sentences:

You can fire them, *or* you can make better use of their abilities.

Margaret drew up the designs, *and* Matt carried them out.

We will have three strong months, *but* after that sales will taper off.

Be careful using coordinating conjunctions: Use them only to join simple sentences that express similar ideas.

Also, because they say relatively little about the relationship between the two clauses they join, avoid using coordinating conjunctions too often: *and* is merely an addition sign; *but* is just a turn signal; *or* only points to an alternative. Subordinating conjunctions such as *because* and *whenever* tell the reader a lot more.

1.7.5 Sentences with Linking Verbs

Linking verbs were discussed briefly in the section on verbs (Section 1.3). Here you can see more fully the way they function in a sentence. The following is a model of any sentence with a linking verb:

> A (verb) B.

Although words like *seems* and *feels* can also be linking verbs, let's assume that the verb is a form of *to be:*

> A *is* B.

In such a sentence, A and B are always nouns, pronouns, or adjectives. When one is a noun and the other's a pronoun, the sentence says that one is the same as the other:

> She is president.

When one is an adjective, it modifies or describes the other:

> She is forceful.

Remember that when one is an adjective, it modifies the other as any adjective modifies a noun or pronoun, except that a linking verb stands between the adjective and the word it modifies.

1.7.6 Misplaced Modifiers

The position of a modifier in a sentence is important. The movement of *only* changes the meaning in the following sentences:

Only we are obliged to supply those items specified in your contract.

We are obliged *only* to supply those items specified in your contract.

We are obliged to supply *only* those items specified in your contract.

We are obliged to supply those items specified *only* in your contract.

In any particular set of circumstances, only one of these sentences would be accurate. The others would very likely cause problems. To prevent misunderstanding, modifiers like *only* must be placed as close as possible to the noun or verb they modify.

For similar reasons, whole phrases that are modifiers must be placed near the right noun or verb. Mistakes in placement create ludicrous meanings:

> Antia Information Systems has bought new computer chairs for the programmers *with more comfortable seats.*

The anatomy of programmers is not normally a concern of business writing. Obviously, the comfort of the chairs was the issue:

> Antia Information Systems has bought new computer chairs *with more comfortable seats* for the programmers.

Here is another example:

> I asked him to file all the letters in the cabinet *that had been answered.*

In this ridiculous sentence the cabinet has been answered, even though no cabinet in history is known to have asked a question. *That had been answered* is too far from *letters* and too close to *cabinet.* Here's an improvement:

> I asked him to file in the cabinet all the letters *that had been answered.*

In some cases, instead of moving the modifying phrase closer to the word it modifies, the best solution is to move the word closer to the modifying phrase.

2.0 PUNCTUATION

On the highway, signs tell you when to slow down or stop, where to turn, and when to merge. In similar fashion, punctuation helps readers negotiate your prose. The proper use of punctuation keeps readers from losing track of your meaning.

2.1 Periods

Use a period (1) to end any sentence that is not a question, (2) with certain abbreviations, and (3) between dollars and cents in an amount of money.

2.2 Question Marks

Use a question mark after any direct question that requests an answer:

> Are you planning to enclose a check, or shall we bill you?

Don't use a question mark with commands phrased as questions for the sake of politeness:

> Will you send us a check today.

2.3 Exclamation Points

Use exclamation points after highly emotional language. Because business writing almost never calls for emotional language, you will seldom use exclamation points.

2.4 Semicolons

Semicolons have three main uses. One is to separate two closely related independent clauses:

> The outline for the report is due within a week; the report itself is due at the end of the month.

A semicolon should also be used instead of a comma when the items in a series have commas within them:

> Our previous meetings were on November 11, 1994; February 20, 1989; and April 28, 1995.

Finally, a semicolon should be used to separate independent clauses when the second one begins with a word such as *however, therefore,* or *nevertheless* or a phrase such as *for example* or *in that case:*

Our supplier has been out of part D712 for 10 weeks; however, we have found another source that can ship the part right away.

His test scores were quite low; on the other hand, he has a lot of relevant experience.

Section 4.4 has more information on using transitional words and phrases like these.

2.5 Colons

Use a colon (1) after the salutation in a business letter and (2) at the end of a sentence or phrase introducing a list, a quotation, or an idea:

Our study included the three most critical problems: insufficient capital, incompetent management, and inappropriate location.

In some introductory sentences, phrases such as *the following* or *that is* are implied by using a colon.

A colon should not be used when the list, quotation, or idea is a direct object or part of the introductory sentence:

We are able to supply

staples	wood screws
nails	toggle bolts

This shipment includes 9 videotapes, 12 CDs, and 14 cassette tapes.

2.6 Commas

Commas have many uses, the most common being to separate items in a series:

He took the job, learned it well, worked hard, and succeeded.

Put paper, pencils, and paper clips on the requisition list.

Company style often dictates omitting the final comma in a series. However, if you have a choice, use the final comma; it's often necessary to prevent misunderstanding.

The second place to use a comma is between clauses. A comma should separate independent clauses (unless one or both are very short):

She spoke to the sales staff, and he spoke to the production staff.

I was advised to proceed and I did.

A dependent clause at the beginning of a sentence is also separated from an independent clause by a comma:

Because of our lead in the market, we may be able to risk introducing a new product.

However, a dependent clause at the end of a sentence is separated from the independent clause by a comma only when the dependent clause is unnecessary to the main meaning of the sentence:

We may be able to introduce a new product, although it may involve some risk.

A third use for the comma is after an introductory phrase or word:

Starting with this amount of capital, we can survive in the red for one year.

Through more careful planning, we may be able to serve more people.

Yes, you may proceed as originally planned.

However, with short introductory prepositional phrases and some one-syllable words (such as *hence* and *thus*), the comma is often omitted:

Before January 1 we must complete the inventory.

Thus we may not need to hire anyone.

In short the move to Tulsa was a good idea.

Fourth, commas are used to surround parenthetical phrases or words, which can be removed from the sentence without changing the meaning:

The new owners, the Kowacks, are pleased with their purchase.

Fifth, commas are used between adjectives modifying the same noun:

She left Monday for a long, difficult recruiting trip.

To test the appropriateness of such a comma, try reversing the order of the adjectives: *a difficult, long recruiting trip*. If the order cannot be reversed, leave out the comma (*a good old friend* isn't the same as *an old good friend*). A comma is also not used when one of the adjectives is part of the noun. Compare these two phrases:

a distinguished, well-known figure

a distinguished public figure

The adjective-noun combination of *public* and *figure* has been used together so often that it has come to be considered a single thing: *public figure*. So no comma is required.

Sixth, commas should precede *Jr., Sr., Inc.,* and the like:

Cloverdell, Inc.	Daniel Garcia, Jr.

In a sentence, a comma also follows such abbreviations:

Belle Brown, Ph.D., is the new tenant.

Seventh, commas are used both before and after the year when writing month, day, and year:

It will be sent by December 15, 1997, from our Cincinnati plant.

Some companies write dates in another form: 15 December 1997. No commas should be used in this case. Nor is a comma needed when only the month and year are present (December 1997).

Eighth, a comma may be used after an informal salutation in a letter to a personal friend. (In business letters, however, salutations are followed by colons.)

Ninth, a comma is used to separate a quotation from the rest of the sentence:

> Your warranty reads, "These conditions remain in effect for one year from date of purchase."

However, the comma is left out when the quotation as a whole is built into the structure of the sentence:

> He hurried off with an angry "Look where you're going."

Finally, a comma should be used whenever it's needed to avoid confusion or an unintended meaning. Compare the following:

Ever since they have planned new ventures more carefully.

Ever since, they have planned new ventures more carefully.

2.7 Dashes

Use a dash to surround a parenthetical comment when the comment is a sudden turn in thought:

> Membership in the IBSA—it's expensive but worth it—may be obtained by applying to our New York office.

A dash can also be used to emphasize a parenthetical word or phrase:

> Third-quarter profits—in excess of $2 million—are up sharply.

Finally, use dashes to set off a phrase that contains commas:

> All our offices—Milwaukee, New Orleans, and Phoenix—have sent representatives.

Don't confuse a dash with a hyphen. A dash separates words, phrases, and clauses more strongly than a comma does; a hyphen ties two words so tightly that they almost become one word.

When typing a dash, type two hyphens with no spacing before, between, or after.

2.8 Hyphens

Hyphens are mainly used in three ways. The first is to separate the parts of compound words beginning with such prefixes as *self, ex, quasi,* and *all:*

self-assured	quasi-official
ex-wife	all-important

However, hyphens are usually left out and the words closed up when using such prefixes as *pro, anti, non, un, inter,* and *extra:*

prolabor	nonunion
antifascist	interdepartmental

Exceptions occur when (1) the prefix occurs before a proper noun or (2) the vowel at the end of the prefix is the same as the first letter of the root word:

pro-Republican	anti-American
anti-inflammatory	extra-atmospheric

When in doubt, consult your dictionary.

Hyphens are also used in some compound adjectives, which are adjectives made up of two or more words. Specifically, you should use hyphens in compound adjectives that come before the noun:

an interest-bearing account

well-informed executives

However, do not hyphenate when the adjective follows a linking verb:

This account is interest bearing.

Their executives are well informed.

You can shorten sentences that list similar hyphenated words by dropping the common part from all but the last word:

> Check the costs of first-, second-, and third-class postage.

Finally, hyphens may be used to divide words at the end of a typed line. Such hyphenation is best avoided, but when you have to divide words at the end of a line, do so correctly (see Section 3.4). A dictionary will show how words are divided into syllables.

2.9 Apostrophes

Use an apostrophe in the possessive form of a noun (but not in a pronoun):

On *his* desk was a reply to *Bette Ainsley's* application for the *manager's* position.

Apostrophes are also used in place of the missing letter(s) of a contraction:

Whole Words	Contraction
we will	we'll
do not	don't
they are	they're

2.10 Quotation Marks

Use quotation marks to surround words that are repeated exactly as they were said or written:

> The collection letter ended by saying, "This is your third and final notice."

Remember: (1) When the quoted material is a complete sentence, the first word is capitalized. (2) The final comma or period goes inside the closing quotation marks.

Quotation marks are also used to set off the title of a newspaper story, magazine article, or book chapter:

> You should read "Legal Aspects of the Collection Letter" in *Today's Credit*.

The book title is shown here in italics. When typewritten, the title is underlined. The same treatment is proper for newspaper and magazine titles. (Component Chapter B explains documentation style in more detail.)

Quotation marks may also be used to indicate special treatment for words or phrases, such as terms that you're using in an unusual or ironic way:

> Our management "team" spends more time squabbling than working to solve company problems.

When using quotation marks, take care to put in both sets, the closing marks as well as the opening ones.

Although periods and commas go inside any quotation marks, colons and semicolons go outside them. A question mark goes inside the quotation marks only if the quotation is a question:

> All that day we wondered, "Is he with us?"

If the quotation is not a question but the entire sentence is, the question mark goes outside:

> What did she mean by "You will hear from me"?

2.11 Parentheses

Use parentheses to surround comments that are entirely incidental:

> Our figures do not match yours, although (if my calculations are correct) they are closer than we thought.

Parentheses are also used in legal documents to surround figures in arabic numerals that follow the same amount in words:

> Remittance will be One Thousand Two Hundred Dollars ($1,200).

Be careful to put punctuation (period, comma, and so on) outside the parentheses unless it is part of the statement in parentheses.

2.12 Ellipses

Use ellipsis points, or dots, to indicate that material has been left out of a direct quotation. Use them only in direct quotations and only at the point where material was left out. In the following example, the first sentence is quoted in the second:

The Dow Jones Industrial Average, which skidded 38.17 points in the previous five sessions, gained 4.61 to end at 2213.84.

According to the Honolulu *Star Bulletin,* "The Dow Jones Industrial Average . . . gained 4.61" on June 10.

The number of dots in ellipses is not optional; always use three. Occasionally, the points of ellipsis come at the end of a sentence, where they seem to grow a fourth dot. Don't be fooled: One of the dots is a period.

2.13 Underscores and Italics

Usually a line typed underneath a word or phrase either provides emphasis or indicates the title of a book, magazine, or newspaper. If possible, use italics instead of an underscore. Italics (or underlining) should also be used for defining terms and for discussing words as words:

In this report *net sales* refers to after-tax sales dollars.

The word *building* is a common noun and should not be capitalized.

3.0 MECHANICS

The most obvious and least tolerable mistakes that a business writer makes are probably those related to grammar and punctuation. However, a number of small details, known as writing mechanics, demonstrate the writer's polish and reflect on the company's professionalism.

3.1 Capitals

You should, of course, capitalize words that begin sentences:

> *Before* hanging up, he said, "*We'll* meet here on Wednesday at noon."

A quotation that is a complete sentence should also begin with a capitalized word.

Capitalize the names of particular persons, places, and things (proper nouns):

We sent *Ms. Larson* an application form, informing her that not all *applicants* are interviewed.

Let's consider opening a branch in the *West,* perhaps at the *west* end of *Tucson, Arizona.*

As *office buildings* go, the *Kinney Building* is a pleasant setting for *TDG Office Equipment.*

Ms. Larson's name is capitalized because she is a particular applicant, whereas the general term *applicants* is left uncapitalized. Likewise, *West* is capitalized when it refers to a particular place but not when it means a direction. In the same way, *office* and *buildings* are not capitalized when they are general terms (common nouns) but are capitalized when they are part of the title of a particular office or building (proper nouns).

Titles within families, governments, or companies may also be capitalized:

My *Uncle David* offered me a job, but I wouldn't be comfortable working for one of my *uncles.*

We've never had a *president* quite like *President* Sweeney.

In addition, always capitalize the first word of the salutation and complimentary close of a letter:

Dear Mr. Andrews: *Yours* very truly,

Finally, capitalize the first word after a colon when it begins a complete sentence:

Follow this rule: When in doubt, leave it out.

Otherwise, the first word after a colon should not be capitalized.

3.2 Abbreviations

Abbreviations are used heavily in tables, charts, lists, and forms. They're used sparingly in prose paragraphs, however. Here are some abbreviations often used in business writing:

Abbreviation	Full Term
b/l	bill of lading
ca.	circa (about)
dol., dols.	dollar, dollars
etc.	et cetera (and so on)
FDIC	Federal Deposit Insurance Corporation
Inc.	Incorporated
L.f.	Ledger folio
Ltd.	Limited
mgr.	manager
NSF or N/S	not sufficient funds
P&L or P/L	profit and loss
reg.	regular
whsle.	wholesale

Because *etc.* contains a word meaning *and,* never write *and etc.*

3.3 Numbers

Numbers may correctly be handled many ways in business writing, so follow company style. In the absence of a set style, however, generally spell out all numbers from one to ten and use arabic numerals for the rest.

There are some exceptions to this general rule. First, never begin a sentence with a numeral:

Twenty of us produced *641* units per week in the first *12* weeks of the year.

Second, use numerals for the numbers one through ten if they're in the same list as larger numbers:

Our weekly quota rose from *9* to *15* to *27.*

Third, use numerals for percentages, time of day (except with *o'clock*), dates, and (in general) dollar amounts.

Our division is responsible for *7* percent of total sales.

The meeting is scheduled for *8:30* A.M. on August 2.

Add *$3* for postage and handling.

Use a comma in numbers with four digits (*1,257*) unless the company specifies another style.

When writing dollar amounts, use a decimal point only if cents are included. In lists of two or more dollar amounts, use the decimal point either for all or for none:

He sent two checks, one for *$67.92* and one for *$90.00.*

3.4 Word Division

In general, avoid dividing words at the ends of lines. When you must, follow these rules:

- Don't divide one-syllable words (such as *since, walked,* and *thought*); abbreviations (*mgr.*); contractions (*isn't*); or numbers expressed in numerals (*117,500*).
- Divide words between syllables, as specified in a dictionary or word-division manual.
- Make sure that at least three letters of the divided word are moved to the second line: *sin-cerely* instead of *sincere-ly.*
- Do not end a page or more than three consecutive lines with hyphens.
- Leave syllables consisting of a single vowel at the end of the first line (*impedi-ment* instead of *imped-*

iment), except when the single vowel is part of a suffix like *-able, -ible, -ical,* or *-ity* (*respons-ible* instead of *responsi-ble*).

- Divide between double letters (*tomor-row*), except when the root word ends in double letters (*call-ing* instead of *cal-ling*).
- Divide hyphenated words after the hyphen only: *anti-independence* instead of *anti-inde-pendence.*

4.0 Vocabulary

Using the right word in the right place is a crucial skill in business communication. However, many pitfalls await the unwary.

4.1 Frequently Confused Words

Because the following sets of words sound similar, be careful not to use one when you mean to use the other:

Word	Meaning
accede	to comply with
exceed	to go beyond
accept	to take
except	to exclude
access	admittance
excess	too much
advice	suggestion
advise	to suggest
affect	to influence
effect	the result
allot	to distribute
a lot	much or many
all ready	completely prepared
already	completed earlier
born	given birth to
borne	carried
capital	money; chief city
capitol	a government building
cite	to quote
sight	a view
site	a location
complement	complete amount; to go well with
compliment	to flatter
corespondent	party in a divorce suit
correspondent	letter writer

Word	Meaning
council	a panel of people
counsel	advice; a lawyer
defer	to put off until later
differ	to be different
device	a mechanism
devise	to plan
die	to stop living; a tool
dye	to color
discreet	careful
discrete	separate
envelop	to surround
envelope	a covering for a letter
forth	forward
fourth	number four
holey	full of holes
holy	sacred
wholly	completely
human	of people
humane	kindly
incidence	frequency
incidents	events
instance	example
instants	moments
interstate	between states
intrastate	within a state
later	afterward
latter	the second of two
lead	a metal
led	guided
lean	to rest at an angle
lien	claim
levee	embankment
levy	tax
loath	reluctant
loathe	to hate
loose	free; not tight
lose	to mislay
material	substance
materiel	equipment
miner	mineworker
minor	underage person
moral	virtuous; a lesson
morale	sense of well-being
ordinance	law
ordnance	weapons

overdo	to do in excess
overdue	past due
peace	lack of conflict
piece	a fragment
pedal	a foot lever
peddle	to sell
persecute	to torment
prosecute	to sue
personal	private
personnel	employees
precedence	priority
precedents	previous events
principal	sum of money; chief; main
principle	general rule
rap	to knock
wrap	to cover
residence	home
residents	inhabitants
right	correct
rite	ceremony
write	to form words on a surface
role	a part to play
roll	to tumble; a list
root	part of a plant
rout	to defeat
route	a traveler's way
shear	to cut
sheer	thin, steep
stationary	immovable
stationery	paper
than	as compared with
then	at that time
their	belonging to them
there	in that place
they're	they are
to	a preposition
too	excessively; also
two	the number
waive	to set aside
wave	a swell of water, a gesture
weather	atmospheric conditions
whether	if

In the above list only enough of each word's meaning is given to help you distinguish between the words in each group. Several meanings are left out entirely. For more complete definitions, consult a dictionary.

4.2 Frequently Misused Words

The following words tend to be misused for reasons other than their sound. A number of reference books (including *The Random House College Dictionary,* Revised Edition; Follett's *Modern American Usage;* and Fowler's *Modern English Usage*) can help you with similar questions of usage.

a lot: When the writer means "many," *a lot* is always two separate words, never one.

correspond with: Use this phrase when you are talking about exchanging letters; use *correspond to* when you mean "similar to." Use either *correspond with* or *correspond to* when you mean "relate to."

disinterested: This word means "fair, unbiased, having no favorites, impartial." If you mean "bored" or "not interested," use *uninterested.*

etc.: This is the abbreviated form of a Latin phrase, *et cetera.* It means "and so on" or "and so forth." The current tendency among business writers is to use English rather than Latin.

imply/infer: Both refer to hints. Their great difference lies in who is acting. The writer *implies;* the reader *infers,* sees between the lines.

lay: This is a transitive verb. Never use it for the intransitive *lie.* (See Section 1.3.3.)

less: Use *less* for uncountable quantities (such as amounts of water, air, sugar, and oil). Use *fewer* for countable quantities (such as numbers of jars, saws, words, pages, and humans). The same distinction applies to *much* and *little* (uncountable) versus *many* and *few* (countable).

like: Use *like* only when the word that follows is just a noun or pronoun. Use *as* or *as if* when a phrase or clause follows:

She looks *like* him.

She did just *as* he had expected.

It seems *as if* she had plenty of time.

many/much: See *less.*

regardless: The *less* ending is the negative part. No word needs two negative parts, so it is illiterate to add *ir* at the beginning.

to me/personally: Use these phrases only when personal reactions, apart from company policy, are being stated (not often the case in business writing).

try: Always follow with *to,* never *and.*

verbal: People in the business community who are careful with language frown on those who use *verbal* to mean "spoken" or "oral." Many others do say "verbal agreement." Strictly speaking, *verbal* means "of words" and therefore includes both spoken and written words. Be guided in this matter by company usage.

4.3 Frequently Misspelled Words

All of us, even the world's best spellers, sometimes have to check a dictionary for the spelling of some words. People who've never memorized the spelling of commonly used words must look up so many that they grow exasperated and give up on spelling words correctly.

Don't expect perfection, and don't surrender. If you can memorize the spelling of just the words listed here, you'll need the dictionary far less often and you'll write with more confidence.

absence	calendar	disbursement
absorption	campaign	discrepancy
accessible	category	dissatisfied
accommodate	ceiling	dissipate
accumulate	changeable	
achieve	clientele	eligible
advantageous	collateral	embarrassing
affiliated	committee	endorsement
aggressive	comparative	exaggerate
alignment	competitor	exceed
aluminum	concede	exhaust
ambience	congratulations	existence
analyze	connoisseur	extraordinary
apparent	consensus	
appropriate	convenient	fallacy
argument	convertible	familiar
asphalt	corroborate	flexible
assistant	criticism	fluctuation
asterisk		forty
auditor	definitely	
	description	gesture
bankruptcy	desirable	grievous
believable	dilemma	
brilliant	disappear	haphazard
bulletin	disappoint	harassment

holiday	newsstand	repetition
	noticeable	rescind
illegible		rhythmical
immigrant	occurrence	ridiculous
incidentally	omission	
indelible		salable
independent	parallel	secretary
indispensable	pastime	seize
insistent	peaceable	separate
intermediary	permanent	sincerely
irresistible	perseverance	succeed
	persistent	suddenness
jewelry	personnel	superintendent
judgment	persuade	supersede
judicial	possesses	surprise
	precede	
labeling	predictable	tangible
legitimate	preferred	tariff
leisure	privilege	technique
license	procedure	tenant
litigation	proceed	truly
	pronunciation	
maintenance	psychology	unanimous
mathematics	pursue	until
mediocre		
minimum	questionnaire	vacillate
		vacuum
necessary	receive	vicious
negligence	recommend	
negotiable		

4.4 Transitional Words and Phrases

The following two sentences don't communicate as well as they might because they lack a transitional word or phrase:

> Production delays are inevitable. Our current lag time in filling orders is one month.

A semicolon between the two sentences would signal a close relationship between their meanings, but it wouldn't even hint at what that relationship is. Here are the sentences, now linked by means of a semicolon, with a space for a transitional word or phrase:

> Production delays are inevitable; _____, our current lag time in filling orders is one month.

Now read the sentence with *nevertheless* in the blank space. Now try *therefore, incidentally, in fact,* and *at any rate* in the blank. Each substitution changes the meaning of the sentence.

Here are some transitional words (called conjunctive adverbs) that will help you write more clearly:

accordingly	furthermore	moreover
anyway	however	otherwise
besides	incidentally	still
consequently	likewise	therefore
finally	meanwhile	unfortunately

The following transitional phrases are used in the same way:

as a result	in other words
at any rate	in the second place
for example	on the other hand
in fact	to the contrary

When one of these words or phrases joins two independent clauses, it should be preceded by a semicolon and followed by a comma, as shown here:

> The consultant recommended a complete reorganization; moreover, she suggested that we drop several products.

Practicing Grammar and Usage

1. Possessive Nouns
Review Section 1.1.3. Then, beside each noun, write its possessive form.

a. women _____

b. secretaries _____

c. worker _____

d. Matthew Kitsos _____

e. editor-in-chief _____

f. children _____

g. Betsy Daniels _____

h. *Daily Times* _____

i. nobody _____

j. month _____

k. Jules _____

l. desks _____

m. today _____ .

n. the Rosses _____

2. Antecedents
Review Section 1.2.1. Then, for each sentence below, underline the correct pronoun and write its antecedent and its number (*S* for singular, *P* for plural) in the appropriate columns.

	Antecedent	Number
a. Joe, Frank, and Bob gave (their, his) opinions.	a. _____	_____
b. Any company worth (its, their) salt has one.	b. _____	_____
c. Los Angeles, as well as San Francisco, has (its, their) advantages.	c. _____	_____
d. Because office decor is important to employees, (it, they) should be planned by professionals.	d. _____	_____
e. Neither newcomers nor veterans knew (his, her, their) way around.	e. _____	_____
f. Was it Marilyn or Lupe who sent (her, their) résumé?	f. _____	_____
g. Both candidates did well in (his, their) interviews.	g. _____	_____
h. Each of the sales representatives went (his or her, their) own way.	h. _____	_____
i. This ad campaign, despite excessive costs, has had (its, their) successes.	i. _____	_____

j. Nancy is one of
those people who
know (her, their)
business.   j. _____ _____

3. Case of Pronouns
Review Section 1.2.4. Then underline the correct pronoun in each sentence.

a. (We, Us) sales representatives are overworked.
b. (Who, Whom) do you trust to do a good job?
c. Just between you and (I, me), the pay is poor.
d. The programmer (who, whom) gets this job will
have to work overtime.
e. Give Terry and (I, me) that office.
f. The best positions went to Randolph and (she, her).
g. It's (he, him) who should get the raise.
h. I'll give the assignment to (whoever, whomever) is-
n't busy with another one.
i. He turned as large a profit as (I, me) did.
j. (Who, Whom) will you talk to?

4. Possessive Pronouns
Review Section 1.2.5. Then underline the correct word
choice in each sentence.

a. (Its, It's) imperative that we close escrow today.
b. In (its, it's) final clause, the contract states that we
are accountable for defects.
c. BGT and Ramp Industries have changed the design
of (there, their, they're) brakes recently.
d. It is (are, our) conviction that we can complete this
job before the deadline.
e. Always be sure that (your, you're) employees understand what is expected of them.
f. Give each secretary a copy of (her or his, their) new
schedule.
g. Do you know what (there, their, they're) planning
for the sales meeting?
h. Take note of (your, you're) mistakes.
i. If (its, it's) warranty has not expired, we will not
charge you for fixing it.
j. (Your, you're) mistaken if you think she will budge
on that issue.

5. Verb Tenses
Review Section 1.3.1. Then write the correct form of
each verb in the space provided.

To Provide
a. present: I   _____

b. past: you   _____

c. future: we   _____

d. present perfect: they   _____

e. past perfect: she   _____

To Allow
f. present: he   _____

g. past: it   _____

h. future: you   _____

i. present perfect: they   _____

j. past perfect: I   _____

To Shrink
k. present: they   _____

l. past: she   _____

m. future: it   _____

n. present perfect: you   _____

o. past perfect: we   _____

To Become
p. present: we   _____

q. past: I   _____

r. future: you   _____

s. present perfect: he   _____

t. past perfect: it   _____

To Be
u. present: you   _____

v. past: she   _____

w. future: we _____

x. present perfect: they _____

y. past perfect: I _____

6. Transitive and Intransitive Verbs
Review Section 1.3.3. Then underline the correct verb in each sentence.

a. After the walls are poured, there must be a way to (rise, raise) them into position.
b. (Sit, Set) up your display against that wall.
c. The contract has (laid, lain) forgotten in our safe for months.
d. I could see when I (lay, laid) it on Mary's desk that she was surprised.
e. It's important to know why production costs have (raised, risen).

7. Voice of Verbs
Review Section 1.3.4. Then rewrite these sentences so that their verbs are in the active voice.

a. The delivery was made by Mercury Message

Service._____

_____

_____

b. Your report has been read by three of us.

_____

_____

_____

c. A choice of color must be made by the buyer.

_____

_____

_____

d. Complaints are handled by Jane Harper.

_____

_____

_____

e. New ideas were picked up at the trade fair by our

representatives._____

_____

_____

8. Adjectives
Review Section 1.4. Then, for each simple adjective in parentheses, give the comparative or superlative (whichever is more appropriate) in the space provided.

a. Of the three, Paul's sales record is (good)

_____.

b. Which check is the (large) _____ of the two?
c. Inspect our five branches before choosing the

(promising) _____ one.

d. Send the (practical) _____ frame you have from the group.
e. Having lifted both, I can pick out the (heavy)

_____ one.

9. Adverbs
Review Section 1.5. Then turn the following adjectives into adverbs.

a. intense _____

b. poor _____

c. real _____

d. full _____

e. complete   _____

f. good   _____

g. whole   _____

h. busy   _____

i. secondary   _____

j. due   _____

10. Prepositions
Review Section 1.6.1. Then underline all the prepositions in these sentences.

a. Providing a few samples of cheese created better sales in many areas.
b. Lead into the letter without a break.
c. He brought with him the habit of using quick-freeze equipment.
d. If the right people are informed of your offer, word of mouth will take care of the rest.
e. The committee will meet behind closed doors for several reasons, none of which are secret.

11. Conjunctions, Articles, and Interjections
Review Section 1.6.2. Then, beside each word below, write *C, A,* or *I* to indicate whether the word is a conjunction, an article, or an interjection.

a. the   _____   f. an   _____

b. although   _____   g. Good!   _____

c. Oh no!   _____   h. if   _____

d. but   _____   i. unless   _____

e. because   _____   j. and   _____

12. Longer Sentences
Review Section 1.7.2. Then underline the word that makes each sentence correct.

a. His presentation, coming after two of the most boring speeches I have ever heard, (was, were) refreshing.
b. When the full slate of officers (is, are) present, she doesn't write out their names.
c. (Although, However,) it was over by the time we got there.
d. The (secretary, secretaries) working in corporate headquarters the longest are going to be recognized.
e. All who are in the group (meet, meets) the selection criteria.

13. Sentence Fragments
Review Section 1.7.3. Some of the following are sentence fragments; others are correct as they stand. Rewrite the sentence fragments to make them complete sentences; write *correct* in the space following sentences that are complete.

a. In just 14 days, with lots of promotion, the new outlet will open._____

_____

_____

b. Nearly ten one-week sessions, beginning the first week in June, with no breaks.

_____

_____

_____

c. Drop the economy model. _____

_____

_____

d. Who of all our employees?_____

_____

_____

e. Although Joan is well grounded in office

procedure._____

_____

_____

f. Charging our office with the task of counting

supplies. _____

_____

_____

g. Having ordered a large quantity of wheat from the

United States. _____

_____

_____

h. Our coats, water-repellent, sleek, and undeniably

tough. _____

_____

_____

i. Because the action would absorb the available supplies of short-term government securities.

_____

_____

_____

a. You like the idea of owning your own business, particularly because you have the capital to begin one.

_____

_____

_____

b. Having met at a previous sales convention, we often
had lunch with him you never know where you stand.

_____

_____

_____

c. The big question is financing, will you have enough

money?_____

_____

_____

d. If satisfaction is not forthcoming, we will be forced
to cancel our order, find another supplier, and take

legal action. _____

_____

_____

e. Over half of them are badly damaged, it looks like

water damage. _____

_____

_____

14. Fused Sentences and Comma Splices
Review Section 1.7.4. Some of the following are fused
sentences; others are correct as they stand. Rewrite the
fused sentences to make them correct; write *correct* in
the space following correct sentences.

15. Misplaced Modifiers
Review Section 1.7.6. Then rewrite each of the following
sentences so that modifiers are placed correctly.

a. Deliver the fastback to the customer with the

leather upholstery. _____

_____

_____

b. An unauthorized caller can't get through this
    "smart" telephone, no matter how clever.

_____

_____

_____

c. We interviewed several applicants with great speed.

_____

_____

_____

d. The letters should be filed in the green cabinet
    from clients who have complaints.

_____

_____

_____

e. I passed the new business center driving through

Emerson City._____

_____

_____

16. Punctuation A
Review Section 2.0. Then, in the space provided, write
C if the sentence is punctuated correctly, *I* if punctua-
tion is incorrect.

a. "Johnson and Kane, Inc., is gone,
    comments one Wall Street merger
    expert.   _____

b. OPEC's uncertain outlook—its
    production has fallen drastically
    since 1978—makes attempts to
    defend the cartel's official price
    appear futile.   _____

c. Over half the combined debt loads of
    Argentina; Brazil; and Mexico
    fluctuates with the movement of the
    U.S. prime rate.   _____

d. About 100 products bore the Can-Man
    trademark last May; there are nearly
    300 today.   _____

e. Stephen Raken says Oak Tree Realty
    now: "realizes that it can't keep up if
    it does it all in-house."   _____

f. Seasoned, well-managed companies
    should explore this alternative. As
    they search for capital.   _____

g. Several insurers (Gaston, Regis, DMA)
    maintain offices in Tennessee.   _____

h. Is the private placement extinct? Yes.
    And no.   _____

i. "Bricks and mortar," Johnson says,
    are history."   _____

j. At Simtex, however, the union
    recently gave up a three-year-old
    profit-sharing plan—which has
    produced no bonuses—because the
    workers wanted an immediate wage
    increase; they had not had a raise in
    nearly two years.   _____

17. Punctuation B
Review Section 2.0. Then correct the punctuation in
the following sentences.

a. Will you please send us a check today so that we
    can settle your account?

b. I find it hard to believe that we could miss such a
    promising opportunity!

c. His writing skills are excellent, however he still
    needs to polish his management style.

d. We'd like to address the issues of: efficiency, prof-
    itability, and market penetration.

e. During the highest level trials we will resume
    operations.

f. The letter should be dated no later than April 14, 1997
    if it is to prove the point.

g. All along the production designers have insisted on using robots.

h. My boss the most senior executive in the company is well known for her concern for employees.

i. Mark is a bright competent young man.

j. What is your career goal the interviewer asked.

18. Punctuation C
Review Section 2.0. Then insert correct punctuation in the following business letter:

Hardball Bearing Company
2206 Wheeler Boulevard
Newark New Jersey 07127

November 13 1997

Mr James R Capp Accounts Payable Manager
The Rollem Company
8321 Clearspring Way
Boston Massachusetts 02109

Dear Mr Capp

We are happy after five years of pleasant dealings with you to announce a change in our billing procedure one that will prove helpful to both of us

Until recently we have billed all our customers on the first of each month beginning January 1996 we will mail billings in alphabetical order you will enjoy the following benefits of this change

> **For the month of January the balance of your account with us will be in effect an interest-free loan**

> **Because most other suppliers continue to bill on the first our bill will not arrive during your peak accounting period**

> **Our company newsletter Bearing Up will continue to be enclosed with our billing**

We know that an accountants life is never simple but we are doing our best to make it so

Yours very truly

Now count the number of items of punctuation you inserted and enter the total in this space: _____. Your instructor will tell you if you have missed some.

19. Capitals
Review Section 3.1. Then capitalize the appropriate words below by putting three short parallel lines under each letter that should be capitalized. (The first item in the first sentence is done for you.)

a. He was questioned about lifting the post-afghanistan embargo on grain sales to russia.

b. what did the senate foreign relations committee say about her as a human rights official?

c. at northern natural gas company, for one, president samuel f. segnar holds monthly luncheons with employees who have hit the five-year service mark.

d. margaret d. steele, head of faribault college's business department, recently conducted a semester-long program involving monthly lunches with professors.

e. "book me a flight to atlanta on airtrans airlines," he said, "so that i can visit our southern wholesalers."

20. Word Division
Review Section 3.4. Then correct the way the following words are divided by crossing through inappropriate hyphens and inserting slash marks where the words could more appropriately be divided.

a. cal-lable   d. controll-ing
b. a-gainst   e. hasti-ly
c. self-anal-ysis

21. Frequently Confused Words
Review Section 4.1. Then underline the correct word in each sentence.

a. To be successful, one must (accept, except) a certain amount of stress.

b. Our plans were (all ready, already) when the news came in.

c. The (incidence, incidents) of breakdowns has decreased.

d. No manager can afford to (loose, lose) his or her self-control.

e. Good lines of communication maintain company (moral, morale).

f. I've worked with both Tom and Rita, and I prefer the (later, latter).

g. Civilized people can (defer, differ) in their opinions without getting angry.

h. The (principal, principle) was sound, but the details were misleading.

i. In the future, sales representatives will be assigned (routes, routs) by the Chicago office.

j. See whether this regulation can be (waived, waved).

k. I would (advice, advise) you to hedge your investments.

l. The color of that hat (complements, compliments) the colors in the dress.

m. Because employment matters are so sensitive, you will have to make some (discreet, discrete) inquiries if you want to find out about his previous performance.

n. I have received no greater compliment (than, then) the one she gave me yesterday.

o. That chair is (stationary, stationery), but the other one can be moved.

22. Frequently Misused Words
Review Section 4.2. Then underline the correct or preferable word in each sentence.

a. Each carton contained (fewer, less) packages than were indicated on the outside.

b. His letter (inferred, implied) that there was no charge for the damaged items.

c. We encountered no problems when we (laid, lay) the tiles.

d. We will have (a lot, allot) of openings in six months.

e. The usual mediator was formerly employed by one of the parties to the dispute, so a more (disinterested, uninterested) mediator was assigned to the case.

f. All seated passengers must be able to see the sign, just (as, like) they can on a 747.

g. Our popular poplin dress shirt is (as, like) our executive Essence shirt in many ways.

h. (Many, Much) of our sales effort would be enhanced by a computer.

i. Our Trade Division (corresponds to, corresponds with) their International Division; both have the same function.

j. Apparently I only (implied, inferred) that opinion from her report.

23. Frequently Misspelled Words
Review Section 4.3. Then underline the correct spelling of each word.

a. indispensible	indispensable	indespensable
b. permenent	perminent	permanent
c. consensus	concensus	consencus
d. harrassment	harasment	harassment
e. changable	changeable	changible
f. noticeable	noticable	notisable
g. medeocre	mediocer	mediocre
h. catigory	category	cattegory
i. alignment	alinement	alinment
j. prefered	preferd	preferred

24. Transitional Words and Phrases
Review Section 4.4. Then, of the transitions listed below, choose the most appropriate for each sentence and write your choice in the space provided.

for example	meanwhile
on the contrary	still
in other words	furthermore
on the other hand	therefore
in the second place	in that case

a. Ms. Siegel worked for you in a similar capacity

during the past two years; _____ we are interested in getting your candid comments on her professional abilities.

b. We have experienced difficulties with your ship-

ments of candy before; _____ just last December, 5 of the 22 boxes you shipped arrived empty.

c. The enclosed information sheet contains names and telephone numbers of prospective clients;

_____ it includes mailing addresses and ZIP codes.

d. Because you are a valued customer of Carrillo Images, we are rechecking the figures we used to

prepare your invoice; _____ we are discounting the new price.

e. Your acceptance of these conditions, signaled by your signing the enclosed check, will begin the

process; _____ your signature on this check will release you to begin construction.

25. Grammar and Usage
Edit the following memo so that it conforms to all the rules presented in this chapter as well as the principles of good writing presented in Chapter 7.

MEMO

TO: All department heads
FROM: Alan Kitchener, vice president of human
           relations
DATE: June 22 1997
SUBJECT: In-house training program

Several new training programs have been developed in response to the training needs assessment conducted in February, 1997. (27 highly-informative replies were received; I personally appreciated your comments). Our goal in developing these new programs was to give each employee the skills to do his job better, and to improve employee's moral.

These are the new programs, which will be available beginning July 1.

1. Making the Most of Microcomputers. Reviews microcomputer operations and provides hands-on experience in using the four main software packages owned by us: word processing, spreadsheet; database management and graphics.
2. Keeping Customers Happy. Covers methods for answering the telephone and correspondence—policies for handling complaints and requests for adjustment—as well as general marketing goals as they relate to customer service.
3. Writing Better for Business. Deals with the organization of messages, analyzing purpose and audience, and style and tone.

Each course will be offered once a month beginning at the first week and continuing for 4 sessions. Making the Most of Microcomputers on Tuesdays, Keeping Customers Happy on Wednesdays, and Writing Better for Business on Thursdays. They will be held in the second floor conference room from three to five p.m.

In general these courses have been designed for clerical and supervisory employees; although everybody on your staff who could benefit are welcome to attend. To register an employee must bring a signed authorization form, a packet are included with this memo, to the human relations office, Room 117, at least a week in advance of the start of the course.

Try and send all appropriate staff so that our organization can better meet it's goals!

APPENDIX 2

CORRECTION SYMBOLS

Instructors often use these short, easy-to-remember correction symbols and abbreviations when evaluating students' writing. You can use them too, to understand your instructor's suggestions and to revise and proofread your own letters, memos, and reports. Refer to Appendix I for additional information on grammar and usage.

CONTENT AND STYLE

Acc	Accuracy. Check to be sure information is correct.
ACE	Avoid copying examples.
ACP	Avoid copying problems.
Adp	Adapt. Tailor message to reader.
Assign	Assignment. Review instructions for assignment.
AV	Active verb. Substitute active for passive.
Awk	Awkward phrasing. Rewrite.
BC	Be consistent.
BMS	Be more sincere.
Chop	Choppy sentences. Use longer sentences and more transitional phrases.
Con	Condense. Use fewer words.
CT	Conversational tone. Avoid using overly formal language.
Depers	Depersonalize. Avoid attributing credit or blame to any individual or group.
Dev	Develop. Provide greater detail.
Dir	Direct. Use direct approach; get to the point.
Emph	Emphasize. Develop this point more fully.
EW	Explanation weak. Check logic; provide more proof.
Fl	Flattery. Avoid flattery that is insincere.
FS	Figure of speech. Find a more accurate expression.
GNF	Good news first. Use direct order.
GRF	Give reasons first. Use indirect order.
GW	Goodwill. Put more emphasis on expressions of goodwill.
H/E	Honesty/ethics. Revise statement to reflect good business practices.

Imp	Imply. Avoid being direct.
Inc	Incomplete. Develop further.
Jar	Jargon. Use less specialized language.
Log	Logic. Check development of argument.
Neg	Negative. Use more positive approach or expression.
Obv	Obvious. Do not state point in such detail.
OC	Overconfident. Adopt more humble language.
OM	Omission.
Org	Organization. Strengthen outline.
OS	Off the subject. Close with point on main subject.
Par	Parallel. Use same structure.
Plan	Follow proper organizational plan. (Refer to Chapter 4.)
Pom	Pompous. Rephrase in down-to-earth terms.
PV	Point of view. Make statement from reader's perspective rather than your own.
RB	Reader benefit. Explain what reader stands to gain.
Red	Redundant. Reduce number of times this point is made.
Ref	Reference. Cite source of information.
Rep	Repetitive. Provide different expression.
RS	Resale. Reassure reader that he or she has made a good choice.
SA	Service attitude. Put more emphasis on helping reader.
Sin	Sincerity. Avoid sounding glib or uncaring.
SL	Stereotyped language. Focus on individual's characteristics instead of on false generalizations.
Spec	Specific. Provide more specific statement.
SPM	Sales promotion material. Tell reader about related goods or services.
Stet	Let stand in original form.
Sub	Subordinate. Make this point less important.
SX	Sexist. Avoid language that contributes to gender stereotypes.
Tone	Tone needs improvement.

Trans	Transition. Show connection between points.
UAE	Use action ending. Close by stating what reader should do next.
UAS	Use appropriate salutation.
UAV	Use active voice.
Unc	Unclear. Rewrite to clarify meaning.
UPV	Use passive voice.
USS	Use shorter sentences.
V	Variety. Use different expression or sentence pattern.
W	Wordy. Eliminate unnecessary words.
WC	Word choice. Find a more appropriate word.
YA	"You" attitude. Rewrite to emphasize reader's needs.

GRAMMAR, USAGE, AND MECHANICS

Ab	Abbreviation. Avoid abbreviations in most cases; use correct abbreviation.
Adj	Adjective. Use adjective instead.
Adv	Adverb. Use adverb instead.
Agr	Agreement. Make subject and verb or noun and pronoun agree.
Ap	Appearance. Improve appearance.
Apos	Apostrophe. Check use of apostrophe.
Art	Article. Use correct article.
BC	Be consistent.
Cap	Capitalize.
Case	Use cases correctly.
CoAdj	Coordinate adjective. Insert comma between coordinate adjectives; delete comma between adjective and compound noun.
CS	Comma splice. Use period or semicolon to separate clauses.

DM	Dangling modifier. Rewrite so that modifier clearly relates to subject of sentence.
Exp	Expletive. Avoid expletive beginnings, such as *it is, there are,* and *there is.*
F	Format. Improve layout of document.
Frag	Fragment. Rewrite as complete sentence.
Gram	Grammar. Correct grammatical error.
HCA	Hyphenate compound adjective.
lc	Lowercase. Do not use capital letter.
M	Margins. Improve frame around document.
MM	Misplaced modifier. Place modifier close to word it modifies.
NRC	Nonrestrictive clause. Separate from rest of sentence with commas.
P	Punctuation. Use correct punctuation.
Par	Parallel. Use same structure.
PH	Place higher. Move document up on page.
PL	Place lower. Move document down on page.
Prep	Preposition. Use correct preposition.
RC	Restrictive clause. Remove commas that separate clause from rest of sentence.
RO	Run-on sentence. Separate two sentences with comma or semicolon.
SC	Series comma. Add comma before *and.*
SI	Split infinitive. Do not separate *to* from rest of verb.
Sp	Spelling error. Consult dictionary.
Stet	Let stand in original form.
S-V	Subject-verb pair. Do not separate with comma.
Syl	Syllabification. Divide word between syllables.
WD	Word division. Check dictionary for proper end-of-line hyphenation.
WW	Wrong word. Replace with another word.

PROOFREADING MARKS

Symbol	Meaning	Symbol Used in Context	Corrected Copy
═	Align horizontally	meaningful result	meaningful result
‖	Align vertically	1. Power cable 2. Keyboard	1. Power cable 2. Keyboard
ⓤⓒ	Capitalize	Do not immerse.	DO NOT IMMERSE.
≡	Capitalize	Pepsico, Inc.	PepsiCo, Inc.
⌢	Close up	self-confidence	self-confidence
ℓ	Delete	harrassment and abuse	harassment
ⓢⓣⓔⓣ....	Restore to original	none of the	none of the
∧	Insert	tirquoise shirts	turquoise and white shirts
⋀	Insert comma	a, b and c	a, b, and c
⊙	Insert period	Harrigan et al	Harrigan et al.
/	Lowercase	TULSA, South of here	Tulsa, south of here
⊏	Move left	Attention: Security	Attention: Security
⊐	Move right	February 2, 1995	February 2, 1995
⊔	Move down	Sincerely,	Sincerely,
⊓	Move up	THIRD-QUARTER SALES	THIRD-QUARTER SALES
⊐ ⊏	Center	Awards Banquet	Awards Banquet
⌐	Start new line	Marla Fenton, Manager, Distri-bution	Marla Fenton Manager, Distribution
⊋	Run lines together	Manager, Distribution	Manager, Distribution
⁋	Start paragraph	The solution is easy to determine but difficult to implement in a competitive environment like the one we now face.	The solution is easy to determine but difficult to implement in a competitive environment like the one we now face.
#	Insert space	real-estate testcase	real estate test case
◯	Spell out	COD	cash on delivery
ⓢⓟ	Spell out	Assn. of Biochem. Engrs.	Association of Biochemical Engineers
∿	Transpose	airy, light, casaul tone	light, airy, casual tone

REFERENCES

Chapter 1

1. Scott Kraft, "Disney Magic Is Finally Starting to Work at French Theme Park," *Los Angeles Times,* 4 February 1996, D1, D3, D13; Betsy Streisand, "The Two Michaels Shake Up Hollywood," *U.S. News & World Report,* 28 August–4 September 1995, 42; Ronald Grover and Michael Oneal, "Disney: Room for Two Lion Kings?" *Business Week,* 28 August 1995, 28–29; John Koenig, "Disney Theme-Park President, Judson Green, Takes Fun Seriously," *America West Airlines Magazine,* January 1995, 56–59; *Hoover's Handbook of American Business, 1994* (Austin, Tx.: Reference Press, 1993), 1106; *The Economist,* 1 May 1993, 74; Charlene Marmer Solomon, "How Does Disney Do It?" *Personnel Journal,* December 1989, 50–57; Christopher Knowlton, "How Disney Keeps the Magic Going," *Fortune,* 4 December 1989, 111–132; Douglas C. McGill, "A 'Mickey Mouse' Class—For Real," *New York Times,* 27 August 1989, sec. 3, 4; Richard Turner, "Disney Chairman's 1989 Pay Totals Under $10 Million," *Wall Street Journal,* 16 January 1990, B8; Eric Arndt, "Nobody Does It Better," *IABC Communication World,* May 1988, 26–29; Paul L. Blocklyn, "Making Magic: The Disney Approach to People Management," *Personnel,* December 1988, 28–35; Brian Dumaine, "Creating a New Company Culture," *Fortune,* 15 January 1990, 127–131; Eric J. Wieffering, "Trouble in Camelot," *Business Ethics,* January–February 1991, 19.
2. John D. Ong, "Meeting Communication Challenges at BFGoodrich," *The Bulletin of the Association for Business Communication* 56, no. 4 (1993): 5–9.
3. Carol M. Lehman and G. Stephen Taylor, "A Role-Playing Exercise for Analyzing Intercultural Communication," *The Bulletin of the Association for Business Communication* 57, no. 2 (1994): 23–32.
4. Gary F. Grates, "Communication in the Second Half of the Nineties," *IABC Communication World,* April 1995, 17–19.
5. Joseph N. Scudder and Patricia J. Guinan, "Communication Competencies as Discriminators of Superiors' Ratings of Employee Performance," *Journal of Business Communication* 26, no. 3 (summer 1989): 217–229; Joseph F. Coates, "Today's Events Produce Tomorrow's Communication Issues," *IABC Communication World,* June–July 1991, 20–25.
6. Vanessa Dean Arnold, "The Communication Competencies Listed in Job Descriptions," *The Bulletin of the Association for Business Communication* LV, no. 2 (June 1992): 15–17.
7. "An Ounce of Prevention," *American Management Association,* April 1995, 6; "AT&T Revamps Employee Communications to Emphasize 'New Direction' for '90s," *Public Relations Journal,* November 1990, 41; Thomas J. Peters, "In Search of Communication Excellence," *Communication World,* February 1984, 12–15; Thomas J. Peters and Robert H. Waterman, Jr., *In Search of Excellence* (New York: Warner Books, 1984), 220.
8. J. Michael Sproule, *Communication Today* (Glenview, Ill.: Scott Foresman, 1981), 329.
9. Jaesub Lee and Fredric Jablan, "A Cross-Cultural Investigation of Exit, Voice, Loyalty and Neglect as Responses to Dissatisfying Job Conditions," *Journal of Business Communication* 23, no. 3 (1992): 203–228; Barron Wells and Nelda Spinks, "What Do You Mean People Communicate with Audiences?" *The Bulletin of the Association for Business Communication* LIV, no. 3 (September 1991): 100–102.
10. J. David Pincus, Robert E. Rayfield, and J. Nicholas DeBonis, "Transforming CEOs into Chief Communications Officers," *Public Relations Journal,* November 1991, 22–27.
11. Jim Braham, "A Rewarding Place to Work," *Industry Week,* 18 September 1989, 18.
12. Donald O. Wilson, "Diagonal Communication Links with Organizations," *Journal of Business Communication* 29, no. 2 (spring 1992): 129–143.
13. Valorie A. McClelland and Richard E. Wilmot, "Communication: Improve Lateral Communication," *Personnel Journal,* August 1990, 32–38; Valorie A. McClelland and Dick Wilmot, "Lateral Communication: As Seen Through the Eyes of Employees," *IABC Communication World,* December 1990, 32–35.
14. Carol Hymowitz, "Spread the Word: Gossip Is Good," *Wall Street Journal,* 4 November 1988, B1; Donald B. Simmons, "The Nature of the Organizational Grapevine," *Supervisory Management,* November 1985, 40.
15. J. David Johnson, William A. Donohoe, Charles K. Atkin, and Sally Johnson, "Differences between Formal and Informal Communication Channels," *Journal of Business Communication,* 31, no. 2 (1994): 111–122.
16. Maureen Weiss, "Manager's Tool Kit: Tapping the Grapevine," *Across the Board,* April 1992, 62–63.
17. "Walk More, Talk More," *Across the Board,* December 1992, 57; Jonathan H. Amsbary and Patricia J. Staples, "Improving Administrator/Nurse Communication: A Case Study of 'Management by Wandering Around,'" *Journal of Business Communication* 28, no. 2 (spring 1991): 101–112; Knowlton, "How Disney Keeps the Magic Going," 112.
18. Polly LaBarre, "The Other Network," *Industry Week,* 19 September 1994, 33–36.
19. Gilbert Fuchsberg, "Disaster Plans Gain New Urgency," *Wall Street Journal,* 20 October 1989, B1.
20. "2 Major PR Problems, 2 Approaches," *San Diego Union-Tribune,* 21 January 1990, I1.
21. "Foodmaker, Inc.," *Hoover's MasterList Database* (Austin, Tx.: The Reference Press, 1996), online reference; "Foodmaker Sees Loss for Fiscal 2nd Period Related to Illnesses," *Wall Street Journal,* 25 March 1993, B4; Benjamin A. Holden, "Foodmaker Delays Expansion Plans in Wake of Food-Poisoning Outbreak," *Wall Street Journal,* 16 February 1993, B7; Denise A. Barabet, "Jack in the Box on Spot: How Well Did Chain Respond to Crisis?" *San Diego Union-Tribune,* 12 February 1993, C1, C2; Sarah Lubman, "Foodmaker Says Tainted Burgers Hurt Its Sales," *Wall Street Journal,* 9 February 1993, B6; "Foodmaker Crisis Ads," *Wall Street Journal,* 28 January 1993, B8; Benjamin A. Holden, "State Says Chain Involved in Outbreak Didn't Comply with New Cooking Rule," *Wall Street Journal,* 25 January 1993, A5.
22. See note 21.
23. See note 21.
24. See note 21; Rod Riggs, "Foodmaker in Deal to Sell 236 Chi-Chi's," *San Diego Union-Tribune,* 21 May 1993, C1, C2.
25. Annetta Miller, Vern E. Smith, and Marcus Mabry, "Shooting the Messenger? How Food Lion Handled a Damaging TV Exposé," *Newsweek,* 23 November 1992, 51.
26. "Presumed Guilty: Managing When Your Company's Name Is Mud," *Working Woman,* November 1991, 31.
27. John Huey, "Wal-Mart: Will It Take Over the World?" *Fortune,* 30 January 1989, 56; Patricia Sellers, "Getting Customers to Love You," *Fortune,* 13 March 1989, 39; Stephen Phillips and Amy Dunkin, "King Customer," *Business Week,* 12 March 1990, 91; Charles Leerhsen, "How Disney Does It," *Newsweek,* 3 April 1989, 52.
28. Arndt, "Nobody Does It Better," 27; Knowlton, "How Disney Keeps the Magic Going," 113, 114.
29. Phillip G. Clampitt and Cal W. Downs, "Employee Perceptions of the Relationship Between Communication and Productivity: A Field Study," *Journal of Business Communication* 30, no. 1 (1993): 5–28.
30. Douglas McGregor, *The Human Side of Enterprise* (New York: McGraw-Hill, 1960), 33–34, 47–48.
31. William G. Ouchi, *Theory Z: How American Business Can Meet the Japanese Challenge* (Reading, Mass.: Addison-Wesley, 1981), 17.

32. Shlomo Maital, "Zen and the Art of Total Quality," *Across the Board,* March 1992, 50–51; James C. Shaffer, "Seven Emerging Trends in Organizational Communication," *IABC Communication World,* February 1986, 18.

33. A. Thomas Young, "Ethics in Business: Business of Ethics," *Vital Speeches,* 15 September 1992, 725–730.

34. Bruce W. Speck, "Writing Professional Codes of Ethics to Introduce Ethics in Business Writing," *The Bulletin of the Association for Business Communication* LIII, no. 3 (September 1990): 21–26; H. W. Love, "Communication, Accountability and Professional Discourse: The Interaction of Language Values and Ethical Values," *Journal of Business Ethics* 11 (1992): 883–892; Kathryn C. Rentz and Mary Beth Debs, "Language and Corporate Values: Teaching Ethics in Business Writing Courses," *Journal of Business Communication* 24, no. 3 (summer 1987): 37–48.

35. David Grier, "Confronting Ethical Dilemmas: The View from Inside—A Practitioner's Perspective," *Vital Speeches,* 1 December 1989, 100–104.

36. Joseph L. Badaracco, Jr., "Business Ethics: Four Spheres of Executive Responsibility," *California Management Review,* spring 1992, 64–79; Kenneth Blanchard and Norman Vincent Peale, *The Power of Ethical Management* (Reprint, 1989; New York: Fawcett Crest, 1991), 7–17.

37. John D. Pettit, Bobby Vaught, and Kathy J. Pulley, "The Role of Communication in Organizations," *Journal of Business Communication* 27, no. 3 (summer 1990): 233–249; Kenneth Labich, "The New Crisis in Business Ethics," *Fortune,* 20 April 1992, 167, 168, 172, 176; Kenneth R. Andrews, "Ethics in Practice," *Harvard Business Review,* September–October 1989, 99–104; Priscilla S. Rogers and John M. Swales, "We the People? An Analysis of the Dana Corporation Policies Document," *Journal of Business Communication* 27, no. 3 (summer 1990): 293–313; Larry Reynolds, "The Ethics Audit," *Business Ethics,* July–August 1991, 120–122.

38. Jules Harcourt, "Developing Ethical Messages: A Unit of Instruction for the Basic Business Communication Course," *The Bulletin of the Association for Business Communication* LIII, no. 3 (September 1990): 17–20.

39. Susan L. Fry, "How to Succeed in the New Europe," *Public Relations Journal,* January 1991, 17–21.

40. U.S. Bureau of Labor Statistics, *Occupational Outlook Quarterly,* 1994.

41. Christine Begole, "How to Get the Productivity Edge," *Working Woman,* May 1991, 47, 52, 54, 56, 58, 60.

42. Rick Tetzeli, "Surviving Information Overload," *Fortune,* July 1994, 60–65.

43. "1995 Cost of a Business Letter," *Dartnell Study* (Chicago: The Dartnell Corporation, 1995).

44. Selwyn Feinstein, "Remedial Training," *Wall Street Journal,* 20 February 1990, A1.

45. "When Rumors Disrupt Your Staff," *Working Woman,* October 1992, 36.

46. Keith Denton, "Improving Community Relations," *Small Business Reports,* August 1990, 33–34, 36–41.

Chapter 2

1. Clarence Wooten Jr. and Andre Forde, founders of Metamorphosis Studios, personal communication, 17 July 1996.

2. David Givens, "You Animal! How to Win Friends and Influence Homo Sapiens," *The Toastmaster,* August 1986, 9.

3. Mark L. Hickson III and Don W. Stacks, *Nonverbal Communication: Studies and Applications* (Dubuque, Iowa: Brown, 1985), 4.

4. Gerald H. Graham, Jeanne Unrue, and Paul Jennings, "The Impact of Nonverbal Communication in Organizations: A Survey of Perceptions," *Journal of Business Communication* 28, no. 1 (winter 1991): 45–62.

5. David Lewis, *The Secret Language of Success* (New York: Carroll & Graf, 1989), 67, 170.

6. Nido Qubein, *Communicate Like a Pro* (New York: Berkley Books, 1986), 97.

7. Dale G. Leathers, *Successful Nonverbal Communication: Principles and Applications* (New York: Macmillan, 1986), 19.

8. Graham, Unrue, and Jennings, "The Impact of Nonverbal Communication in Organizations," 45–62.

9. Jill Neimark, "Reach Out and . . ." *Savvy,* February 1985, 42.

10. Margaret Ann Baker, "Reciprocal Accommodation: A Model for Reducing Gender Bias in Managerial Communication," *Journal of Business Communication* 28, no. 2 (spring 1991): 113–127; Graham, Unrue, and Jennings, "The Impact of Nonverbal Communication in Organizations," 45–62.

11. Graham, Unrue, and Jennings, "The Impact of Nonverbal Communication in Organizations," 45–62.

12. Stuart Berg Flexner, "From 'Gadzooks' to 'Nice,' the Language Keeps Changing," *U.S. News & World Report,* 18 February 1985, 59.

13. Erik Larson, "Forever Young," *Inc.,* July 1988, 56.

14. Sandra Blakeslee, "Brain May Sift Writing and Speech Separately," *New York Times,* 28 February 1991, A18.

15. Claudia H. Deutsch, "The Multimedia Benefits Kit," *New York Times,* 14 October 1990, sec. 3, 25.

16. Phillip Morgan and H. Kent Baker, "Building a Professional Image: Improving Listening Behavior," *Supervisory Management,* November 1985, 35, 36.

17. Augusta M. Simon, "Effective Listening: Barriers to Listening in a Diverse Business Environment," *The Bulletin of the Association for Business Communication* LIV, no. 3 (September 1991): 73–74.

18. Irwin Ross, "Corporations Take Aim at Illiteracy," *Fortune,* 29 September 1986, 49.

19. Ross, "Corporations Take Aim at Illiteracy," 52.

20. Judith Valente and Bridget O'Brian, "Airline Cockpits Are No Place to Solo," *Wall Street Journal,* 8 February 1989, B1.

21. Some material adapted from Courtland L. Bovée, John V. Thill, Marian Burk Wood, and George P. Dovel, *Management* (New York: McGraw-Hill, 1993), 537–538.

22. Much of the material contained in the entire section on communication barriers has been adapted from Bovée, Thill, Wood, and Dovel, *Management,* 549–557.

23. Adapted from C. Glenn Pearce, Ross Figgins, and Steve F. Golen, *Principles of Business Communication: Theory, Application, and Technology* (New York: Wiley, 1984), 520–538.

24. Linlin Ku, "Social and Nonsocial Uses of Electronic Messaging Systems in Organizations," *Journal of Business Communication* 33, no. 3 (July 1996): 297–325.

25. Bovée, Thill, Wood, and Dovel, *Management,* 555.

26. See note 1.

27. Thomas C. Hayes, "Medical Care America Hit by New Stock Drop," *New York Times,* 2 October 1992, C3.

Chapter 3

1. Hoover's Company Profile Database (Austin, Tex.: The Reference Press, 1996), online access; P&G Career Center (Cincinnati, Oh.: Procter & Gamble, 1996), online access; Michael Copeland, specialist, international training, personal communication, 24 January 1990; Gabriella Stern, "P&G Will Cut 13,000 Jobs, Shut 30 Plants," *Wall Street Journal,* 16 July 1993, A3; Annetta Miller, "No Cheer for Procter & Gamble," *Newsweek,* 26 July 1993, 38; Brian Dumaine, "P&G Rewrites the Marketing Rules," *Fortune,* 6 November 1989, 34–48; Procter & Gamble Company 1992 Annual Report, 24.

2. Richard A. Melcher, "The Best-Laid Plans of Multinationals . . ." *Business Week,* 5 October 1992, 37–38; Michael J. Mandel, "How to Get America Growing Again," *Business Week Reinventing America 1992,* 22–23, 26, 30, 34–35, 38, 40, 44; Paul Magnusson, "Grabbing New World Orders," *Business Week Reinventing America 1992,* 110–112, 114, 116.

3. Magnusson, "Grabbing New World Orders," 110–112, 114, 116; Jeffrey Hawkins, "Canada: Appetite Remains Strong for U.S. Goods and Services Despite Sluggish Domestic Demand; Recovery Under Way," *Business America,* 19 April 1993, 6–7.

4. Elizabeth Howard, "Going Global: What It Really Means to Communicators," *IABC Communication World,* April 1995, 12–15.

5. Paul Magnusson, "Free Trade? They Can Hardly Wait," *Business Week,* 14 September 1992, 24–25; Bill Javetski, "Continental Drift," *Business Week,* 5 October 1992, 34–36.

6. Bernard Wysocki, Jr., "U.S. Firms Increase Overseas Investments," *Wall Street Journal,* 9 April 1990, A1; "U.S. Affiliates of Foreign Companies: Operations in 1988," *Survey of Current Business* 70 (July 1990): 127–143; Blayne Cutler, "Foreign Staff," *American Demographics,* August 1989, 16; Gene Koretz, "What Happened to the Tidal Wave of Foreign Investment?" *Business Week,* 24 May 1993, 22.

7. John S. McClenahen, "Thinking Globally," *Industry Week,* 21 August 1989, 13.

8. John P. Fernandez, *Managing a Diverse Work Force* (Lexington, Mass.: Lexington Books, 1991), 5; David A. Victor, *International Business*

Communication (New York: HarperCollins, 1992), 7–8; Michael Mandel and Christopher Farrell, "The Immigrants," *Business Week,* 13 July 1992, 114–120, 122; David Jamieson and Julie O'Mara, *Managing Workforce 2000: Gaining the Diversity Advantage* (San Francisco: Jossey-Bass, 1991), 21.

9. "Less Yiddish, More Tagalog," *U.S. News & World Report,* 10 May 1993, 16; Gary Levin, "Marketers Learning New Languages for Ads," *Advertising Age,* 10 May 1993, 33.

10. Marilyn Kern-Foxworth, "Colorizing Advertising: What Ad Clubs Can Do to Make the Business More Inclusive," *American Advertising,* Winter 1991–1992, 26–28; Margaret Ambry and Cheryl Russell, *The Official Guide to the American Marketplace* (Ithaca, N.Y.: New Strategist Publications, 1992), 271.

11. Gus Tyler, "Tokyo Signs the Paychecks," *New York Times Book Review,* 12 August 1990, 7.

12. Carley H. Dodd, *Dynamics of Intercultural Communication,* 3d ed. (Dubuque, Iowa: Brown, 1991), 50; Philip R. Harris and Robert T. Moran, *Managing Cultural Differences,* 3d ed. (Houston: Gulf, 1991), 140.

13. Harris and Moran, *Managing Cultural Differences,* 394–397, 429–430.

14. Tzöl Zae Chung, "Culture: A Key to Management Communication Between the Asian-Pacific Area and Europe," *European Management Journal* 9, no. 4 (December 1991): 419–424.

15. James S. O'Rourke IV, "International Business Communication: Building a Course from the Ground Up," *Bulletin of the Association for Business Communication* 56, no. 4 (1993): 22–27.

16. Larry A. Samovar and Richard E. Porter, "Basic Principles of Intercultural Communication," in *Intercultural Communication: A Reader,* 6th ed., edited by Larry A. Samovar and Richard E. Porter (Belmont, Calif.: Wadsworth, 1991), 12.

17. Kathleen K. Reardon, "It's the Thought that Counts," *Harvard Business Review,* September–October 1984, 141.

18. Otto Kreisher, "Annapolis Has a New Attitude Toward Sexual Harassment," *San Diego Union-Tribune,* 30 July 1990, A6.

19. James Calvert Scott, "Using an International Business-Meal Function to Develop Sociocultural Skills," *Business Communication Quarterly* 58, no. 3 (1995): 55–57.

20. Mary A. DeVries, *Internationally Yours* (New York: Houghton Mifflin, 1994) 194.

21. Robert O. Joy, "Cultural and Procedural Differences that Influence Business Strategies and Operations in the People's Republic of China," *SAM Advanced Management Journal,* Summer 1989, 29–33.

22. "Pakistan: A Congenial Business Climate," *Nation's Business,* July 1986, 50.

23. Victor, *International Business Communication,* 234–239; Mohan R. Limaye and David A. Victor, "Cross Cultural Business Communication Research: State of the Art and Hypotheses for the 1990s," *Journal of Business Communication* 28, no. 3 (Summer 1991): 277–299.

24. Dodd, *Dynamics of Intercultural Communication,* 215.

25. Edward T. Hall, "Context and Meaning," in *Intercultural Communication: A Reader,* 6th ed., edited by Larry A. Samovar and Richard E. Porter (Belmont, Calif.: Wadsworth, 1991), 46–55.

26. Dodd, *Dynamics of Intercultural Communication,* 69–70.

27. Richard E. Porter and Larry A. Samovar, "Basic Principles of Intercultural Communication," in *Intercultural Communication: A Reader,* 6th ed., edited by Larry A. Samovar and Richard E. Porter (Belmont, Calif.: Wadsworth, 1991), 5–22; David A. Victor, personal communication, 1993.

28. Laray M. Barna, "Stumbling Blocks in Intercultural Communication," in *Intercultural Communication: A Reader,* 6th ed., edited by Larry A. Samovar and Richard E. Porter (Belmont, Calif.: Wadsworth, 1991), 345–352.

29. Jean A. Mausehund, Susan A. Timm, and Albert S. King, "Diversity Training: Effects of an Intervention Treatment on Nonverbal Awareness," *Business Communication Quarterly* 38, no. 1 (1995): 27–30.

30. Sharon Ruhly, *Intercultural Communication,* 2d ed., MODCOM (Modules in Speech Communication) (Chicago: Science Research Associates, 1982), 14.

31. Karen P. H. Lane, "Greasing the Bureaucratic Wheel," *North American International Business,* August 1990, 35–37; Arthur Aronoff, "Complying with the Foreign Corrupt Practices Act," *Business America,* 11 February 1991, 10–11; Bill Shaw, "Foreign Corrupt Practices Act: A Legal and Moral Analysis," *Journal of Business Ethics* 7 (1988): 789–795.

32. Harris and Moran, *Managing Cultural Differences,* 260.

33. David J. McIntyre, "When Your National Language Is Just *Another* Language," *IABC Communication World,* May 1991, 18–21.

34. Linda Beamer, "Teaching English Business Writing to Chinese-Speaking Business Students," *Bulletin of the Association for Business Communication* 57, no. 1 (1994): 12–18.

35. David A. Ricks, "International Business Blunders: An Update," *B&E Review,* January–March 1988, 12.

36. Vern Terpstra, *The Cultural Environment of International Business* (Cincinnati: South-Western, 1979), 19.

37. Victor, *International Business Communication,* 36.

38. Doreen Mangan, "What's New in Language Translation: A Tool for Examining Foreign Patents and Research," *New York Times,* 19 November 1989, sec. 3, 15.

39. Victor, *International Business Communication,* 39; Harris and Moran, *Managing Cultural Differences,* 64.

40. Mona Casady and Lynn Wasson, "Written Communication Skills of International Business Persons," *The Bulletin of the Association for Business Communication* 57, no. 4 (1994): 36–40.

41. Geert Hofstede, *Cultures and Organizations* (London: McGraw-Hill, 1991), 211.

42. Richard W. Brislin, "Prejudice in Intercultural Communication," in *Intercultural Communication: A Reader,* 6th ed., edited by Larry A. Samovar and Richard E. Porter (Belmont, Calif.: Wadsworth, 1991), 366–370.

43. Jensen J. Zhao and Calvin Parks, "Self-Assessment of Communication Behavior: An Experiential Learning Exercise for Intercultural Business Success," *Business Communication Quarterly* 58, no. 1 (1995): 20–26; Dodd, *Dynamics of Intercultural Communication,* 142–143, 297–299.

44. Marita van Oldenborgh, "Court with Care," *International Business,* April 1995, 20–22.

45. Susan A. Hellweg, Larry A. Samovar, and Lisa Skow, "Cultural Variations in Negotiation Styles," in *Intercultural Communication: A Reader,* 6th ed., edited by Larry A. Samovar and Richard E. Porter (Belmont, Calif.: Wadsworth, 1991), 185–192.

46. Dumaine, "P&G Rewrites the Marketing Rules," 38.

47. Victor, personal communication, 1993.

48. Copeland, personal communication, 24 January 1990; Dumaine, "P&G Rewrites the Marketing Rules," 34–48; Procter & Gamble Company 1992 Annual Report, 24.

Chapter 4

1. Mike Stevens, systems technology specialist, Hewlett-Packard, personal communication, April 1996.

2. Eric J. Adams, "A Real Global Office," *World Trade,* October 1992, 97–98.

3. *Dialog Database Catalog 1993,* 62–63, 130.

4. Microsoft Corporation, *Encarta,* CD-ROM, 1992–1994.

5. Inspiration demonstration, Disk (Inspiration Software, Inc., 1994).

6. Jack Nimersheim, "Grammar Checker Face-Off," *Home-Office Computing,* July 1992, 49–53.

7. Eric J. Adams, "The Fax of Global Business," *World Trade,* August–September 1991, 34–39.

8. Bill Eager, *Using the Internet* (Indianapolis: Que Corporation, 1994), 13.

9. *The Internet Unleashed,* 2d ed. (Indianapolis: Sams.net Publishing, 1995), 4; Eager, *Using the Internet,* 18.

10. Don Clark and Joan E. Rigdon, "Stripped Down PCs Will Be Talk of Comdex," *Wall Street Journal,* 10 November, 1995, B1.

11. *The Internet Unleashed,* 71.

12. Rosalind Resnick and Dave Taylor, *Internet Business Guide,* 2d ed. (Indianapolis: Sams.net Publishing, 1995), 9.

13. *The Internet Unleashed,* 695.

14. Helen Roper, "Letters from Cyberhell," *Inc. Technology,* 12 September 1995, 67–71.

15. "All About E-mail: Use E-mail to Communicate with Anyone, Anywhere," *Microsoft Magazine,* April–May 1996, 14–26.

16. Eager, *Using the Internet,* 82.

17. William Eager, Larry Donahue, David Forsyth, Kenneth Mitton, and Martin Waterhouse, *Net.search* (Indianapolis: Que Corporation, 1995), 226.

18. Sheri Rosen, "Who Says E-mail Is Mundane?" *IABC Communication World,* September 1995, 42.

19. Jolie Solomon, "As Electronic Mail Loosens Inhibitions, Impetuous Senders Feel Anything Goes," *Wall Street Journal,* 10 December 1990, B1–B2.

20. Michael Rothschild, "When You're Gagging on E-mail," *Forbes ASAP Supplement,* 6 June 1994, 25–26.

21. Rothschild, "When You're Gagging on E-mail," 25–26.
22. Mike Snyder, "E-mail Isn't as Private as You May Think," *USA Today,* 10 October 1995, 6D.
23. Karen Kaplan, "Your Voicemail Box May Have Ears," *Los Angeles Times,* 15 July 1996, D8.
24. Wayne Rash, Jr., "Before You Press That Send Button, Keep in Mind That E-mail Is Forever," *Communications Week,* 16 October 1995, 72.
25. Samuel Greengard, "User Friendly," *Personnel Journal,* September 1995, 165.
26. Michael Mathiesen, *Marketing on the Internet* (Gulf Breeze, Fl.: Maximum Press, 1995), 11–12.
27. Mathiesen, *Marketing on the Internet,* 12–14.
28. Amy Cortese, "Here Comes the Intranet," *BusinessWeek,* 26 February 1996, *BusinessWeek Online,* Online, 15 May 1996 <www.business-week.com/1996/09/b34641.htm>.
29. Cortese, "Here Comes the Intranet."
30. "HP and Netscape Outline Strategic Alliance to Deliver Enterprise Intranet Solutions Across UNIX and NT System Platforms," press release, *Netscape,* Online, 14 May 1996.
31. Don L. Boroughs, "Paperless Profits," *U.S. News & World Report,* 17 July 1995, 40.
32. Boroughs, "Paperless Profits," 40.
33. Cortese, "Here Comes the Intranet."
34. Cortese, "Here Comes the Intranet."
35. Cortese, "Here Comes the Intranet."
36. "Internal Webs as Corporate Information Systems," White paper, *Netscape Communications,* Online, 25 April 1996.
37. Mike Bransby, "Voice Mail Makes a Difference," *Journal of Business Strategy,* January–February 1990, 7–10.
38. Harris Collingswood, "Voice Mail Hangups," *Business Week,* 17 February 1992, 46.
39. Andrew Kupfer, "Prime Time for Videoconferences," *Fortune,* 28 December 1992, 90–95.
40. Michael Finley, "The New Meaning of Meetings," *IABC Communication World,* March 1991, 25–27.
41. Mark Mabrito, "Computer-Mediated Communication and High-Apprehensive Writers: Rethinking the Collaborative Process," *The Bulletin of the Association for Business Communication,* December 1992, 26–29; Susan M. Gelfond, "It's a Fax, Fax, Fax, Fax World," *Business Week,* 21 March 1988, 138.
42. Chris Campbell, "Outerstreaming: The Fourth Communication Paradigm," *IABC Communication World,* December 1990, 18–22.

Chapter 5

1. Jeff Hagen, Director, Consumer Services, General Mills, Personal Communication, 2 July 1997.
2. Mary K. Kirtz and Diana C. Reep, "A Survey of the Frequency, Types, and Importance of Writing Tasks in Four Career Areas," *The Bulletin of the Association for Business Communication* LIII, no. 4 (December 1990): 3–4.
3. Mary Cullinan and Ce Ce Iandoli, "What Activities Help to Improve Your Writing? Some Unsettling Student Responses," *The Bulletin of the Association for Business Communication* LIV, no. 4 (December 1991): 8–10; Ruth Yontz, "Providing a Rationale for the Process Approach," *Journal of Business Communication* 24, no. 1 (winter 1987): 17–19; Annette Shelby, "Note on Process," *Journal of Business Communication* 24, no. 1 (winter 1987): 21.
4. Peter Bracher, "Process, Pedagogy, and Business Writing," *Journal of Business Communication* 24, no. 1 (winter 1987): 43–50.
5. John J. Stallard, Sandra F. Price, and E. Ray Smith, "A Strategy for Teaching Critical-Thinking Skills in Business Communication," *The Bulletin of the Association for Business Communication* LV, no. 3 (September 1992): 20–22.
6. William P. Galle, Jr., Beverly H. Nelson, Donna W. Luse, and Maurice F. Villere, *Business Communication: A Technology-Based Approach* (Chicago: Irwin, 1996), 255; Annette C. Easton, Nancy S. Eickelmann, and Marie E. Flatley, "Effects of an Electronic Meeting System Group Writing Tool on the Quality of Written Documents," *Journal of Business Communication* 31, no. 1 (1994): 27–40; Janis Forman, "Collaborative Business Writing: A Burkean Perspective for Future Research," *Journal of Business Communication* 29, no. 3 (summer 1991): 4–8; Ruth G. Newman, "Communication: Collaborative Writing with Purpose and Style," *Personnel Journal,* April 1988, 37–38.
7. Charles R. Stratton, "Collaborative Writing in the Workplace," *IEEE Transactions on Professional Communication* 32, no. 3 (1989): 178–182.
8. David K. Farkas, "Collaborative Writing, Software Development, and the Universe of Collaborative Activity," in *Collaborative Writing in Industry: Investigations in Theory and Practice,* edited by Mary M. Lay and William M. Karis (Amityville, N.Y.: Baywood Publishing, 1991), 17.
9. Rodney P. Rice and John T. Huguley, Jr., "Describing Collaborative Forms: A Profile of the Team-Writing Process," *IEEE Transactions on Professional Communication* 37, no. 3 (1994), 163–170; Mary Beth Debs, "Recent Research on Collaborative Writing in Industry," *Technical Communication* (November 1991): 476–484.
10. Galle, Nelson, Luse, and Villere, *Business Communication: A Technology-Based Approach,* 255; Cynthia L. Selfe, "Computer-Based Conversations and the Changing Nature of Collaboration," in *New Visions of Collaborative Writing,* edited by Janis Forman (Portsmouth, N.H.: Boynton/Cook, 1992), 147.
11. Galle, Nelson, Luse, and Villere, *Business Communication: A Technology-Based Approach,* 256.
12. Galle, Nelson, Luse, and Villere, *Business Communication: A Technology-Based Approach,* 260.
13. Janet K. Winter and Joan C. Neal, "Group Writing: Student Perceptions of the Dynamics and Efficiency of Groups," *Business Communication Quarterly* 58, no. 2 (1995): 21–25; Rice and Huguley, "Describing Collaborative Forms," 163–170; Debs, "Recent Research on Collaborative Writing in Industry," 476–484.
14. Jack E. Hulbert, "Developing Collaborative Insights and Skills," *The Bulletin of the Association for Business Communication* 57, no. 2 (1994): 53–56; Meg Morgan and Mary Murray, "Insight and Collaborative Writing," in *Collaborative Writing in Industry: Investigations in Theory and Practice,* edited by Mary M. Lay and William M. Karis (Amityville, N.Y.: Baywood Publishing, 1991), 64.
15. Stratton, "Collaborative Writing in the Workplace," 178–182.
16. Debs, "Recent Research on Collaborative Writing in Industry," 476–484.
17. Newman, "Communication: Collaborative Writing with Purpose and Style," 37–38.
18. Galle, Nelson, Luse, and Villere, *Business Communication: A Technology-Based Approach,* 256.
19. Sanford Kaye, "Writing Under Pressure," *Soundview Executive Book Summaries* 10, no. 12, part 2 (December 1988): 1–8.
20. Al Schlachtmeyer and Max Caldwell, "Communicating Creatively," *IABC Communication World,* June–July 1991, 28.
21. Iris I. Varner, "Internationalizing Business Communication Courses," *The Bulletin of the Association for Business Communication* L, no. 4 (December 1987): 7–11.
22. Mary Munter, *Guide to Managerial Communication* (Englewood Cliffs, N.J.: Prentice Hall, 1982), 9.
23. Morgan W. McCall, Jr., and Robert L. Hannon, *Studies of Managerial Work: Results and Methods,* Technical Report no. 9 (Greensboro, N.C.: Center for Creative Leadership, 1978), 6–10.
24. Ernest Thompson, "Some Effects of Message Structure on Listener's Comprehension," *Speech Monographs* 34 (March 1967): 51–57.
25. Laurey Berk and Phillip G. Clampitt, "Finding the Right Path in the Communication Maze," *IABC Communication World,* October 1991, 28–32.
26. Schlachtmeyer and Caldwell, "Communicating Creatively," 26–29.
27. Adapted from Berk and Clampitt, "Finding the Right Path in the Communication Maze," 28–32.
28. Mohan R. Limaye and David A. Victor, "Cross-Cultural Business Communication Research: State of the Art and Hypotheses for the 1990s," *Journal of Business Communication* 28, no. 3 (summer 1991): 277–299.
29. Berk and Clampitt, "Finding the Right Path in the Communication Maze," 28–32.
30. Berk and Clampitt, "Finding the Right Path in the Communication Maze," 28–32.
31. Conover, "Keeping Up with How We Cook," 15; Cameron, *Personal Communication,* 1989.

Chapter 6

1. Julian Santoyo, chief financial officer, Community Health Group, personal communication, March 1996.
2. Carol S. Mull, "Orchestrate Your Ideas," *The Toastmaster,* February 1987, 19.
3. Susan Hall and Theresa Tiggeman, "Getting the Big Picture: Writing to Learn in a Finance Class," *Business Communication Quarterly* 58, no. 1 (1995): 12–15.

4. Bruce B. MacMillan, "How to Write to Top Management," *Business Marketing,* March 1985, 138.

5. MacMillan, "How to Write to Top Management," 138.

6. Based on the Pyramid Model developed by Barbara Minto of McKinsey & Company, management consultants.

7. Philip Subanks, "Messages, Models, and the Messy World of Memos," *The Bulletin of the Association for Business Communication* 57, no. 1 (1994): 33–34.

8. Iris I. Varner, "Internationalizing Business Communication Courses," *The Bulletin of the Association for Business Communication* 50, no. 4 (December 1987): 7–11.

9. Mary A. DeVries, *Internationally Yours* (New York: Houghton Mifflin, 1994), 61.

10. Elizabeth Blackburn and Kelly Belanger, "You-Attitude and Positive Emphasis: Testing Received Wisdom in Business Communication," *The Bulletin of the Association for Business Communication* 56, no. 2 (June 1993): 1–9.

11. Brockman and Belanger, "You-Attitude and Positive Emphasis," 1–9.

12. DeVries, *Internationally Yours,* 61.

13. See note 1.

14. Annette N. Shelby and N. Lamar Reinsch, Jr., "Positive Emphasis and You Attitude: An Empirical Study," *Journal of Business Communication* 32, no. 4 (1995): 303–322.

15. Roger P. Wilcox, *Communication at Work: Writing and Speaking* (Boston: Houghton Mifflin, 1977), 30.

16. John S. Fielden, Jean D. Fielden, and Ronald E. Dulek, *The Business Writing Style Book* (Englewood Cliffs, N.J.: Prentice Hall, 1984), 7.

17. Renee B. Horowitz and Marian G. Barchilon, "Stylistic Guidelines for E-mail," *IEEE Transactions on Professional Communications* 37, no. 4 (December 1994): 207–212.

18. David Angell and Brent Heslop, *The Elements of E-mail Style* (Reading, Mass.: Addison-Wesley, 1994), 10.

19. Jill H. Ellsworth and Matthew V. Ellsworth, *The Internet Business Book* (New York: Wiley, 1994), 91.

20. Lance Cohen, "How to Improve Your E-mail Messages," <http://galaxy.einet/galaxy/Business-and-Commerce/Management/Communications/How_to_Improve_Your_E_Mail.html>.

21. Angell and Heslop, *The Elements of E-mail Style,* 10.

22. Angell and Heslop, *The Elements of E-mail Style,* 20.

23. Angell and Heslop, *The Elements of E-mail Style,* 24.

24. Angell and Heslop, *The Elements of E-mail Style,* 22.

25. Cohen, "How to Improve Your E-mail Messages."

26. Angell and Heslop, *The Elements of E-mail Style,* 20.

27. Horowitz and Barchilon, "Stylistic Guidelines for E-mail," 207–212.

28. Angell and Heslop, *The Elements of E-mail Style,* 28.

29. Cohen, "How to Improve Your E-mail Messages."

30. Angell and Heslop, *The Elements of E-mail Style,* 26–27.

31. Angell and Heslop, *The Elements of E-mail Style,* 18–19.

32. Horowitz and Barchilon, "Stylistic Guidelines for E-mail," 207–212.

33. Cohen, "How to Improve Your E-mail Messages."

34. Angell and Heslop, *The Elements of E-mail Style,* 21.

35. Angell and Heslop, *The Elements of E-mail Style,* 20; Cohen, "How to Improve Your E-mail Messages"; Ellsworth and Ellsworth, *The Internet Business Book,* 101.

36. Cohen, "How to Improve Your E-mail Messages"; Bill Eager, *Using the Internet* (Indianapolis: Que Corporation, 1994), 99.

37. Angell and Heslop, *The Elements of E-mail Style,* 30.

38. Angell and Heslop, *The Elements of E-mail Style,* 117; Ellsworth and Ellsworth, *The Internet Business Book,* 99; Eager, *Using the Internet,* 99.

39. Cohen, "How to Improve Your E-mail Messages."

40. Eager, *Using the Internet,* 99.

41. William Eager, Larry Donahue, David Forsyth, Kenneth Mitton, and Martin Waterhouse, *Net.Search* (Indianapolis: Que Corporation, 1995), 225.

42. Julian Santoyo, personal communication, March 1996.

Chapter 7

1. Adrianne Proeller, corporate communications manager, Turner Broadcasting System, personal communication, March 1993.

2. Robert Half International, "Message Lost in Some Memos," *USA Today,* 25 March 1987, 1A.

3. Iris I. Varner, "Internationalizing Business Communication Courses," *The Bulletin of the Association for Business Communication* 50, no. 4 (December 1987): 7–11.

4. Kevin T. Stevens, Kathleen C. Stevens, and William P. Stevens, "Measuring the Readability of Business Writing: The Cloze Procedure versus Readability Formulas," *Journal of Business Communication* 29, no. 4 (1992): 367–382; Alinda Drury, "Evaluating Readability," *IEEE Transactions on Professional Communication* PC-28 (December 1985): 11.

5. Portions of this section are adapted from Courtland L. Bovée, *Techniques of Writing Business Letters, Memos, and Reports* (Sherman Oaks, Calif.: Banner Books International, 1978), 13–90.

6. Randolph H. Hudson, Gertrude M. McGuire, and Bernard J. Selzler, *Business Writing: Concepts and Applications* (Los Angeles: Roxbury, 1983), 79–82.

7. Hudson, McGuire, and Selzler, *Business Writing,* 79–82; Alan Siegel, "The Plain English Revolution," *Across the Board,* February 1981, 22.

8. James Bredin, "Say It Simply," *Industry Week,* 15 July 1991, 19–20.

9. Kathy M. Kristof, "Mutual Funds Try Something New: Plain English," *Los Angeles Times,* 1 November 1992, D4.

10. William M. Bulkeley, "Software Writers Try to Speak a Language Users Understand," *Wall Street Journal,* 30 June 1992, B6.

11. Peter Crow, "Plain English: What Counts Besides Readability?" *Journal of Business Communication* 25, no. 1 (winter 1988): 87–95.

12. Mary A. DeVries, *Internationally Yours* (Boston: Houghton Mifflin, 1994), 51.

13. DeVries, *Internationally Yours,* 160.

14. Judy E. Pickens, "Terms of Equality: A Guide to Bias-Free Language," *Personnel Journal,* August 1985, 24.

15. Rose Knotts and Mary S. Thibodeaux, "Verbal Skills in Cross-Culture Managerial Communication," *European Business Review* 92, no. 2 (1992): 5–7.

16. Lawrence W. Hugenberg, Renée M. LaCivita, and Andra M. Lubanovic, "International Business and Training: Preparing for the Global Economy," *Journal of Business Communication* 33, no. 2 (1996): 105–222.

17. Lisa Taylor, "Communicating About People with Disabilities: Does the Language We Use Make a Difference?" *The Bulletin of the Association for Business Communication* 53, no. 3 (September 1990): 65–67.

18. Taylor, "Communicating About People with Disabilities," 65–67.

19. Charles E. Risch, "Critiquing Written Material," *Manage* 35, no. 4 (1983): 4–6.

20. Joel Haness, "How to Critique a Document," *IEEE Transactions on Professional Communication* PC-26, no. 1 (March 1983): 15–17.

21. Risch, "Critiquing Written Material," 4–6.

22. Risch, "Critiquing Written Material," 4–6.

23. Varner, "Internationalizing Business Communication Courses," 7–11.

24. DeVries, *Internationally Yours,* 168.

25. Drury, "Evaluating Readability," 12.

26. Portions of the following sections are adapted from Roger C. Parker, *Looking Good in Print,* 2d ed. (Chapel Hill, N.C.: Ventana Press, 1990).

27. Raymond W. Beswick, "Designing Documents for Legibility," *The Bulletin of the Association for Business Communication* 50, no. 4 (December 1987): 34–35.

28. Patsy Nichols, "Desktop Packaging," *The Bulletin of the Association for Business Communication* 54, no. 1 (March 1991): 43–45; Beswick, "Designing Documents for Legibility," 34–35.

29. Beswick, "Designing Documents for Legibility," 34–35.

30. "The Process Model of Document Design," *IEEE Transactions on Professional Communication* PC-24, no. 4 (December 1981): 176–178.

31. "A Misspelling Proves Costly," *New York Times,* 23 November 1991, 29.

32. William Wresch, Donald Pattow, and James Gifford, *Writing for the Twenty-First Century: Computers and Research Writing* (New York: McGraw-Hill, 1988), 192–211; Melissa E. Barth, *Strategies for Writing with the Computer* (New York: McGraw-Hill, 1988), 108–109, 140, 172–177.

33. Proeller, personal communication, March 1993.

34. Milton Moskowitz, Michael Katz, and Robert Levering, eds., *Everybody's Business: An Almanac* (San Francisco: Harper & Row, 1980), 131.

35. Hudson, McGuire, and Selzler, *Business Writing: Concepts and Applications,* 27.

Chapter 8

1. Silva Raker, vice president of merchandise, The Nature Company, personal communication, February 1993; Nature Company home page <www.natureco.com> 13 June 1996.

2. Lennie Copeland and Lewis Griggs, *Going International: How to Make Friends and Deal Effectively in the Global Marketplace,* 2d ed. (New York: Random House, 1985), 24–27.

3. Linda Beamer, "Learning Intercultural Communication Competence," *Journal of Business Communication* 29, no. 3 (1992): 285–303.

4. Owen Edwards, "Send Me a Memo or Better Yet, Don't," *Across the Board,* November 1992, 12–13.

5. Frances A. McMorris, "Ex-Bosses Face Less Peril Giving Honest Job References," *Wall Street Journal,* 8 July 1996, B1, B8.

6. Raker, personal communication, February 1993.

7. Adapted from Reliable Office Supplies Private Customer Sale Catalog, August 1996.

8. Adapted from Kendall Hamilton, "Getting Up, Getting Air," *Newsweek,* 13 May 1996, 68.

9. Trinidad & Tobago advertisement, *Saveur* magazine, March–April 1996, 79.

10. Adapted from "The Pizza Must Go Through: It's the Law in San Francisco," *New York Times,* 14 July 1996, 10Y; "The Politics of Pizza Delivery," *Time,* 22 July 1996, 38.

11. Adapted from Shelley Cryan, "Multimedia Presentations," *Byte,* April 1994, 40, 42.

12. Adapted from *Trek USA 1992 Bicycles, Specialized Bicycles and Accessories,* and *Schwinn 92* catalogs; Champion International Corporation Advertisement, *Wall Street Journal,* 13 September 1991, A2.

13. Adapted from Joanne Cleaver, "Back from the Brink," *Home Office Computing,* April 1995, 58, 60; Webs Are Us classified advertisement, *Computer Edge,* 26 July 1996, 81.

14. Adapted from Bruce V. Bigelow, "Magnificent Magnetics," *San Diego Union-Tribune,* 24 November 1993, E1, E5.

15. Adapted from Associated Press, "Flood of Imports into Argentina Delights Shoppers, Riles Local Industry," *Los Angeles Times,* 6 January 1992, D4.

16. Adapted from Michael M. Phillips, "Carving Out an Export Industry, and Hope, in Africa," *Wall Street Journal,* 18 July 1996, A8.

17. Adapted from Alexandra Peers, "Ruling Britannia, or a Little Portion of It," *Wall Street Journal,* 19 July 1996, B6.

18. Adapted from Sue Shellenbarger, "As More Pregnant Women Work, Bias Complaints Rise," *Wall Street Journal,* 6 December 1993, B1, B2.

19. Adapted from "Periscope: Beanie Mania," *Newsweek,* 3 June 1996, 8.

20. Adapted from Market Watch, "Bookstore Landscape Changing in Burlington, VT," *Bookselling This Week,* 25 April 1994, 4–5; advertising flyers, Andrea Jeffery, Calgary, Alberta, Canada, spring 1994.

21. Adapted from Mary Williams Walsh, "Canadian Firm to Print Ukraine's Money," *Los Angeles Times,* 1 January 1992, D3.

Chapter 9

1. Peter Goodrich, vice president, worldwide concert and artist department, Steinway & Sons, personal communication, April 1993.

2. Daniel P. Finkelman and Anthony R. Goland, "Customers Once Can Be Customers for Life," *Information Strategy: The Executive's Journal,* Summer 1990, 5–9.

3. Cathy Goodwin and Ivan Ross, "Consumer Evaluations of Responses to Complaints: What's Fair and Why," *Journal of Consumer Marketing* 7, no. 2 (spring 1990): 39–46.

4. Maura Dolan and Stuart Silverstein, "Court Broadens Liability for Job References," *Los Angeles Times,* 28 January 1997, A1, A11.

5. Susan Stobaugh, "Watch Your Language," *Inc.,* May 1985, 156.

6. Claudia Mon Pere McIsaac, "Improving Student Summaries Through Sequencing," *The Bulletin of the Association for Business Communication,* September 1987, 17–20.

7. David A. Hayes, "Helping Students GRASP the Knack of Writing Summaries," *Journal of Reading,* November 1989, 96–101.

8. *Techniques for Communicators* (Chicago: Lawrence Ragan Communication, 1995), 34, 36.

9. Claudia H. Deutsch, "Relighting the Fires at Avon Products," *New York Times,* 3 April 1994.

10. Adapted from Donna Larcen, "Authors Share the Words of Condolence," *Los Angeles Times,* December 20, 1991, E11.

11. Goodrich, personal communication, April 1993.

12. Adapted from Timothy Aeppel, "Chlorine-Free Paper Is Clean but Unpopular," *Wall Street Journal,* 4 April 1994, B1, B6.

13. Adapted from "Two Major Piano Makers to Shun Ivory," *San Diego Union-Tribune,* 24 August 1989, A27.

14. Adapted from Eben Shapiro, "The Sincerest Form of Rivalry," *New York Times,* 19 October 1991, C17, C29; Martha T. Moore, "Body Shop: Profits with Principles," *USA Today,* 10 October 1991, B8; The Body Shop by Mail catalogs, brochures, and leaflets, 1991–1992.

15. Adapted from Joanne Lipman, "Do Toll Phone Services Play Fair by Advertising Directly to Kids?" *Wall Street Journal,* 7 July 1989, B1.

16. Adapted from Michele Manges, "Hotel Ads Criticized as Short-Sighted," *Wall Street Journal,* 10 August 1989, B1.

17. Adapted from *L. L. Bean Catalog, Christmas 1986,* 20–21.

18. Adapted from Barbara Carton, "Farmers Begin Harvesting Satellite Data to Boost Yields," *Wall Street Journal,* 11 July 1996, B4.

19. Adapted from "Technology: Sound Chamber," *Newsweek,* 13 May 1996, 10.

20. Adapted from 1993 Campbell Soup Annual Report; Joseph Weber, "Campbell: Now It's M-M-Global," *Business Week,* 15 March 1993, 52–54; Pete Engardio, "Hmm. Could Use a Little More Snake," *Business Week,* 15 March 1993, 53; Joseph Weber, "Campbell Is Bubbling, but for How Long?" *Business Week,* 17 June 1991, 56–57; Joseph Weber, "From Soup to Nuts and Back to Soup," *Business Week,* 5 November 1990, 114, 116; "Here Are the Women to Watch in Corporate America," *Business Month,* April 1989, 40; Alix Freedman and Frank Allen, "John Dorrance's Death Leaves Campbell Soup with Cloudy Future," *Wall Street Journal,* 19 April 1989, A1, A14; Claudia H. Deutsch, "Stirring Up Profits at Campbell," *New York Times,* 20 November 1988, sec. 3, 1, 11; Bill Saporito, "The Fly in Campbell's Soup," *Fortune,* 9 May 1988, 67–70; biography of Zoe Coulson from *Marquis Who's Who,* accessed online, 24 May 1992.

21. Adapted from Yumiko Ono, "Warning: Kool-Aid Seems to Go Straight to Some Kids' Heads," *Wall Street Journal,* 17 July 1996, A1, A7.

22. Adapted from Calvin Sims, "Reporter Disciplined for Reading His Co-workers' Electronic Mail," *New York Times,* 6 December 1993, A8.

23. Adapted from "Olympic Snafus Vault IBM into Limelight of an Unflattering Hue," *Los Angeles Times,* 25 July 1996, D1, D13; Thomas E. Weber and Emory Thomas, Jr., "IBM Olympic Embarrassments Drag On as Computers Produce Late, Bad Data," *Wall Street Journal,* 25 July 1996, B11; Jennifer Oldham, "IBM's Performance at Olympics Not Quite a 10," *Los Angeles Times,* 30 July 1996, D1, D7; Associated Press, "Atlanta Is Stumbling Out of the Blocks," *Los Angeles Times,* 22 July 1996, S1, S5.

24. Adapted from Roger Ricklefs, "Marketers Seek Out Cool Kids for Tomorrow's Mall Trends," *Wall Street Journal,* 11 July 1996, B1, B2.

25. Adapted from Sal D. Rinalla and Robert J. Kopecky, "Recruitment: Burger King Hooks Employees with Educational Incentives," *Personnel Journal,* October 1989, 90–99.

26. Adapted from William Dunn, "Sabbaticals Aim to Cool Job Burnout," *USA Today,* 25 July 1986, 1B, 2B.

27. Adapted from Norihiko Shirouzu, "Japan's Staid Coffee Bars Wake Up and Smell Starbucks," *Wall Street Journal,* 25 July 1996, B1, B13.

28. Adapted from Sewell Chan, "In Frenzy to Recruit, High-Tech Concerns Try Gimmicks, Songs," *Wall Street Journal,* 9 August 1996, B1, B5.

29. Adapted from Leon E. Wynter, "Group Finds Right Recipe for Milk Ads in Spanish," *Wall Street Journal,* 6 March 1996, B1.

30. Adapted from Larcen, "Authors Share the Words of Condolence," E11.

Chapter 10

1. Yia Eason, founder, Olmec Toys, personal communication, September 1996.

2. James Calvert Scott and Diana J. Green, "British Perspectives on Organizing Bad-News Letters: Organizational Patterns Used by Major U.K. Companies," *The Bulletin of the Association for Business Communication* 55, no. 1 (March 1992): 17–19.

3. Iris I. Varner, "Internationalizing Business Communication Courses," *The Bulletin of the Association for Business Communication* 50, no. 4 (December 1987): 7–11.

4. Ram Subramanian, Robert G. Insley, and Rodney D. Blackwell, "Performance and Readability: A Comparison of Annual Reports of Profitable and Unprofitable Corporations," *Journal of Business Communication* 30, no. 2 (1993): 49–61.

5. *Techniques for Communicators* (Chicago: Lawrence Ragan Communication, 1995), 18.

6. Maura Dolan and Stuart Silverstein, "Court Broadens Liability for Job References," *Los Angeles Times,* 28 January 1997, A1, A11; Frances A. McMorris, "Ex-Bosses Face Less Peril Giving Honest Job References," *Wall Street Journal,* 8 July 1996, B1, B8.

7. Thomas S. Brice and Marie Waung, "Applicant Rejection Letters: Are Businesses Sending the Wrong Message?" *Business Horizons,* March–April 1995, 59–62.

8. Gwendolyn N. Smith, Rebecca F. Nolan, and Yong Dai, "Job-Refusal Letters: Readers' Affective Responses to Direct and Indirect Organizational Plans," *Business Communication Quarterly* 59, no. 1 (1996): 67–73; Brice and Waung, "Applicant Rejection Letters," 59–62.

9. Judi Brownell, "The Performance Appraisal Interviews: A Multipurpose Communication Assignment," *Bulletin of the Association for Business Communication* 57, no. 2 (1994): 11–21.

10. Brownell, "The Performance Appraisal Interviews," 11–21.

11. Judith A. Kolb, "Leader Behaviors Affecting Team Performance: Similarities and Differences Between Leader/Member Assessments," *Journal of Business Communication* 32, no. 3 (1995): 233–248.

12. Howard M. Bloom, "Performance Evaluations," *New England Business,* December 1991, 14.

13. David I. Rosen, "Appraisals Can Make—or Break—Your Court Case," *Personnel Journal,* November 1992, 113.

14. Patricia A. McLagan, "Advice for Bad-News Bearers: How to Tell Employees They're Not Hacking It and Get Results," *Industry Week,* 15 February 1993, 42; Michael Lee Smith, "Give Feedback, Not Criticism," *Supervisory Management,* December 1993, 4; "A Checklist for Conducting Problem Performer Appraisals," *Supervisory Management,* December 1993, 7–9.

15. Jane R. Goodson, Gail W. McGee, and Anson Seers, "Giving Appropriate Performance Feedback to Managers: An Empirical Test of Content and Outcomes," *Journal of Business Communication* 29, no. 4 (1992): 329–342.

16. Craig Cox, "On the Firing Line," *Business Ethics,* May–June 1992, 33–34.

17. Cox, "On the Firing Line," 33–34.

18. Eason, personal communication, September 1996.

19. Adapted from Sewell Chan, "A Seattle Blend Is Praised as Rich, Smooth, and Better than Worms," *Wall Street Journal,* 16 July 1996, B1.

20. Adapted from Mark Maremont, "They're All Screaming for Häagen-Dazs," *Business Week,* 14 October 1991, 121; Carla Rapoport, "No Sexy Sales Ads, Please—We're Brits and Swedes," *Fortune,* 21 October 1991, 13.

21. Adapted from Joseph Hanania, "Feeling Sheepish?" *Los Angeles Times,* 30 July 1996, E3.

22. Adapted from Patti Bond, "Hispanics Display Growing Muscle in Entrepreneurship," *The Atlanta Journal-Constitution,* 11 July 1996, B1.

23. Adapted from John M. Glionna, "Owner of Julian Surfing Store Makes Waves with 14-Foot Sign," *Los Angeles Times,* 6 January 1992, B1, B3; Bob Rowland, "Surfing Sign Makes Big Waves in Julian," *San Diego Union-Tribune,* 10 January 1992, B1, B4.

24. Adapted from Michael A. Champ and Michael D. Willinsky, "Farming the Oceans," *The World & I,* April 1994, 200–207.

25. Adapted from International Tesla Society Museum Bookstore Catalog, Fall 1993.

26. Adapted from Pascal Zachary, "Sun Microsystems Apologizes in Letter for Late Payments," *Wall Street Journal,* 11 October 1989, B4.

27. Adapted from Peter Fritsch, "It's Lighter than Glass and Hurts Less When Thrown, but Can Plastic Stack Up?" *Wall Street Journal,* 24 July 1996, B1.

28. Adapted from Robert Johnson, "Your Little Monkey Is So Cuddly. Here, Let Me—OUCH!" *Wall Street Journal,* 2 December 1991, A1, A14.

29. Adapted from Nancy Ann Jeffrey, "Insurers Curb Some Benefits for Disability," *Wall Street Journal,* 25 July 1996, A3, A5.

30. Adapted from Barbara Foley, "Stepping into Something, Um, Ugly," *Los Angeles Times,* 18 December 1991, E1, E8.

31. Adapted from Fleming Meeks, "Shakespeare, Dickens & Hillegass," *Forbes,* 30 October 1989, 206, 208, 209.

32. Adapted from David Colker, "Rest in Space," *Los Angeles Times,* 25 July 1996, B2.

33. Adapted from "I.R.S. Error of $40 Million," *New York Times,* 7 February 1992, C4.

34. Adapted from Laura Shapiro, "Fake Fat: Miracle or Menace?" *Newsweek,* 8 January 1996, 60–61; Raju Narisetti, "P&G Says Fake-Fat Olestra Gets Fewer Complaints than Expected," *Wall Street Journal,* 25 July 1996, B3.

35. Adapted from "Periscope: Color Me . . . Grossed Out," *Newsweek,* 20 November 1995, 8.

36. Adapted from "GTE Headquarters in Connecticut Is Hit by Hepatitis," *Wall Street Journal,* 20 October 1989, A9.

37. Adapted from Gautam Naik, "These Guys Are Junk, and to Mark Tilden That's Just the Point," *Wall Street Journal,* 16 August 1996, A1.

Chapter 11

1. Jeanne Anderson, sales director, Language Line Services, AT&T, personal communication, December 1992.

2. Jeanette W. Gilsdorf, "Write Me Your Best Case for . . ." *The Bulletin of the Association for Business Communication* 54, no. 1 (March 1991): 7–12.

3. Gilsdorf, "Write Me Your Best Case for . . ." 7–12.

4. Mary Cross, "Aristotle and Business Writing: Why We Need to Teach Persuasion," *The Bulletin of the Association for Business Communication* 54, no. 1 (March 1991): 3–6.

5. Abraham H. Maslow, *Motivation and Personality* (New York: Harper & Row, 1954), 12, 19.

6. Robert T. Moran, "Tips on Making Speeches to International Audiences," *International Management,* April 1980, 57–59.

7. Tamra B. Orr, "Persuasion Without Pressure," *The Toastmaster,* January 1994, 19–22; William Friend, "Winning Techniques of Great Persuaders," *Association Management,* February 1985, 82–86; Patricia Buhler, "How to Ask For—and Get—What You Want!" *Supervision,* February 1990, 11–13.

8. Gilsdorf, "Write Me Your Best Case for…" 7–12.

9. John D. Ramage, and John C. Bean, *Writing Arguments: A Rhetoric with Readings,* 3d ed. (Boston: Allyn and Bacon, 1995), 430–442.

10. Ramage and Bean, *Writing Arguments: A Rhetoric with Readings,* 102–117.

11. James Suchan and Ron Dulek, "Toward a Better Understanding of Reader Analysis," *Journal of Business Communication* 25, no. 2 (1988): 29–45.

12. Jeanette W. Gilsdorf, "Executives' and Academics' Perceptions on the Need for Instruction in Written Persuasion," *Journal of Business Communication* 23 (Fall 1986): 67.

13. Robert L. Hemmings, "Think Before You Write," *Fund Raising Management,* February 1990, 23–24.

14. Teri Lammers, "The Elements of Perfect Pitch," *Inc.,* March 1992, 53–55.

15. William North Jayme, quoted in Albert Haas, Jr., "How to Sell Almost Anything by Direct Mail," *Across the Board,* November 1986, 50.

16. Hemmings, "Think Before You Write," 23–24.

17. Hemmings, "Think Before You Write," 23–24.

18. Conrad Squires, "How to Write a Strong Letter, Part Two: Choosing a Theme," *Fund Raising Management,* November 1991, 65–66.

19. Conrad Squires, "Getting the Compassion Out of the Box," *Fund Raising Management,* September 1992, 55, 60.

20. Squires, "How to Write a Strong Letter, Part Two," 65–66.

21. Constance L. Clark, "25 Steps to Better Direct Mail Fundraising," *Nonprofit World,* July–August 1989, 11–13; Squires, "How to Write a Strong Letter, Part Two," 65–66.

22. Squires, "How to Write a Strong Letter, Part Two," 65–66.

23. Clark, "25 Steps to Better Direct Mail Fundraising," 11–13.

24. Conrad Squires, "Why Some Letters Outpull Others," *Fund Raising Management,* January 1991, 67, 72.

25. Squires, "Why Some Letters Outpull Others," 67, 72; Clark, "25 Steps to Better Direct Mail Fundraising," 11–13; Jerry Huntsinger, "My First 29½ Years in Direct-Mail Fund Raising: What I've Learned," *Fund Raising Management,* January 1992, 40–43.

26. "The Ideal Collection Letter," *Inc.,* February 1991, 59–61.

27. Anderson, personal communication, December 1992.

28. Adapted from Norimitsu Onishi, "Making Liberty His Business: Ex-Political Prisoner Turns Freedom's Icon into a Career," *New York Times,* 18 April 1996, B1.

29. Adapted from David Disheneau, "From Hippie to Catnip King—the Long and Strange Trip of Leon Seidman," *Los Angeles Times,* 15 April 1996, D9.

30. Adapted from "Oracle Chief Foresees Internet Appliances from Phone Concerns," *Wall Street Journal,* 10 September 1996, A7.

31. Adapted from Jane Bryant Quinn, "A Primer on Downsizing," *Newsweek,* 13 May 1996, 50; Marshall Loeb, "What to Do if You Get Fired," *Fortune,* 15 January 1996, 77–78; and "Urohealth Sets Sights on Eighth Acquisition," *Los Angeles Times,* 5 May 1996, B1.

32. Adapted from Kevin M. Savetz, "Preventive Medicine for the Computer User," *Multimedia Online* 2, no. 2 (June 1996): 58–60.

33. Adapted from John Case and Jerry Useem, "Six Characters in Search of a Strategy," *Inc.,* March 1996, 46–49.
34. Adapted from Andrew Ferguson, "Supermarket of the Vanities," *Fortune,* 10 June 1996, 30, 32.
35. Adapted from Peter Coy, "Peddling Better Bike Designs," *Business Week,* 1 July 1996, 103.
36. Adapted from Howard Rudnitsky, "Another Agricultural Revolution," *Forbes,* 29 May 1996, 159.
37. Adapted from Greg Johnson, "Taco Bell's Ad Was a Burrito Short of a Combination Plate," *Los Angeles Times,* 2 April 1996, D2.
38. Adapted from Justin Martin, "Confusion Is Killing CD-ROM Sales," *Fortune,* 15 January 1996, 14–15.
39. Adapted from Steve Bass, "ISDN Not; The Agony, the Ecstasy, the Migraines," *Computer Currents,* 7 May 1996, 9.
40. Adapted from "Down These Aisles Is Matrimonial Bliss," *Los Angeles Times,* 22 March 1996, D3.
41. Adapted from Bill Dean, "Viking Pillages Office Superstores," *DM News,* 26 February 1996, 19–26.
42. Adapted from Leslie Earnest, "The Signs of Success," *Los Angeles Times Business Section,* 10 May 1996, D1, D7.
43. Adapted from Ronaleen R. Roha, "Talk Is Cheaper," *Kiplinger Personal Finance Magazine,* May 1996, 105–107.
44. Adapted from Chris Pasles, "Long Beach Opera Cancels Rest of Season as Deal Nears," *Los Angeles Times,* 16 May 1996, F4, F9.
45. Adapted from William G. Flanagan, "Infrequent Flier Blues," *Forbes,* 20 May 1996, 318.
46. Adapted from Marc Levinson, "Riding the Data Highway," *Newsweek,* 21 March 1994, 54–55.
47. Adapted from Rod Riggs, "Mother of Invention," *San Diego Union-Tribune,* 29 March 1994, C1, C2.
48. Tom Morganthau and Seema Nayyar, "Those Scary College Costs," *Newsweek,* 29 April 1996, 52–56; Jane Bryant Quinn, "Save First, then Borrow," *Newsweek,* 29 April 1996, 67–68.
49. Adapted from Edmund Sanders, "Subcontractors Still Waiting for Payoff from Giant Irvine Theater," *The Orange County Register,* 9 May 1996, 2.

Chapter 12

1. Henry Halaiko, manager, recruiting operations, Mobil Corporation, personal communication, 11 January 1990.
2. Nella Barkley, "How to Make Your Career Dreams Come True," *The Bottom Line,* 15 July 1990, 1.
3. Sewell Whitney, "On-Line Résumés Put Job Candidates in Line," *Advertising Age,* 7 March 1985, 48.
4. Joseph E. McKendrick, "Managers Talk About Careers," *Management World,* September–October 1986, 18–19.
5. Robert J. Gerberg, *Robert Gerberg's Job Changing System,* summarized by Macmillan Book Clubs, Inc., in the "Macmillan Executive Summary Program," April 1987, 4.
6. Carol M. Barnum, "Writing Résumés That Sell," *MW,* September–October 1987, 11.
7. Amanda Bennett, "GE Redesigns Rungs of Career Ladder," *Wall Street Journal,* 15 March 1993, B1, B3.
8. Robin White Goode, "International and Foreign Language Skills Have an Edge," *Black Enterprise,* May 1995, 53.
9. Nancy M. Somerick, "Managing a Communication Internship Program," *The Bulletin of the Association for Business Communication* 56, no. 3 (1993): 10–20.
10. Karen W. Arenson, "Placement Offices Leave Old Niches to Become Computerized Job Bazaars," *New York Times,* 17 July 1996, B12.
11. Cheryl L. Noll, "Collaborating with the Career Planning and Placement Center in the Job-Search Project," *Business Communication Quarterly* 58, no. 3 (1995): 53–55.
12. Lee Smith, "Landing that First Real Job," *Fortune,* 16 May 1994, 58–60; Louis S. Richman, "How to Get Ahead," *Fortune,* 16 May 1994, 46–51; Joe Russell, "Finding Solid Ground," *Hispanic Business,* February 1992, 42–46.
13. Pam Stanley-Weigand, "Organizing the Writing of Your Resume," *The Bulletin of the Association for Business Communication* 54, no. 3 (1991): 11–12.
14. Beverly Culwell-Block and Jean Anna Sellers, "Résumé Content and Format—Do the Authorities Agree?" *The Bulletin of the Association for Business Communication* 57, no. 4 (1994): 27–30.
15. Janice Tovey, "Using Visual Theory in the Creation of Resumes: A Bibliography," *The Bulletin of the Association for Business Communication* 54, no. 3 (1991): 97–99.
16. Myra Fournier, "Looking Good on Paper," *Managing Your Career,* Spring 1990, 34–35.
17. Adapted from Burdette E. Bostwick, *How to Find the Job You've Always Wanted* (New York: Wiley, 1982), 69–70.
18. Jennifer J. Laabs, "For Your Information," *Personnel Journal,* August 1993, 16.
19. Pam Dixon and Sylvia Tiersten, *Be Your Own Headhunter Online* (New York: Random House, 1995), 75.
20. Bronwyn Fryer, "Job Hunting the Electronic Way," *Working Woman,* March 1995, 59–60, 78; Joyce Lane Kennedy and Thomas J. Morrow, *Electronic Resume Revolution,* 2d ed. (New York: Wiley, 1995), 30–33; Mary Goodwin, Deborah Cohn, and Donna Spivey, *Netjobs: Use the Internet to Land Your Dream Job* (New York: Michael Wolff, 1996), 149–150; Zane K. Quible, "Electronic Résumés: Their Time Is Coming," *Business Communication Quarterly* 58, no. 3 (1995): 5–9; Alfred and Emily Glossbrenner, *Finding a Job on the Internet* (New York: McGraw-Hill, 1995), 194–197; Dixon and Tiersten, *Be Your Own Headhunter Online,* 80–83.
21. Quible, "Electronic Résumés," 5–9; Goodwin, Cohn, and Spivey, *Netjobs,* 149–150.
22. Richman, "How to Get Ahead," 46–51; Bruce Nussbaum, "I'm Worried About My Job," *Business Week,* 7 October 1991, 94–97.
23. William J. Banis, "The Art of Writing Job-Search Letters," *CPC Annual,* 36th Edition 2 (1992): 42–50.
24. Halaiko, personal communication, 11 January 1990.

Chapter 13

1. Microsoft Web page <http://www.microsoft.com>; Jodi DeLeon, college recruiting manager, Microsoft Corporation, personal communication, May 1993.
2. Paul Plawin, "Job-Hunting Blunders You Don't Have to Make," *Changing Times,* December 1988, 69.
3. Sylvia Porter, "Your Money: How to Prepare for Job Interviews," *San Francisco Chronicle,* 3 November 1981, 54.
4. Albert R. Karr, "Creative Interviewing Takes Firmer Hold as the Job Pinch Worsens," *Wall Street Journal,* 8 April 1990, A1; "The Interviewing Process," *Small Business Reports,* December 1987, 63; James M. Jenks and Brian L. P. Zevnik, "ABCs of Job Interviewing," *Harvard Business Review,* July–August 1989, 39.
5. Charlene Marmer Solomon, "How Does Disney Do It?" *Personnel Journal,* December 1989, 53.
6. Peter Rea, Julie Rea, and Charles Moonmaw, "Training: Use Assessment Centers in Skill Development," *Personnel Journal,* April 1990, 126–131.
7. Barron Wells and Nelda Spinks, "Interviewing: What Small Companies Say," *The Bulletin of the Association for Business Communication* 55, no. 2 (1992): 18–22; Clive Fletcher, "Ethics and the Job Interview," *Personnel Management,* March 1992, 36–39.
8. Eric R. Chabrow, "High-Tech Hiring: CD-ROM and Video Aid Recruiters' Efforts," *Informationweek,* 23 January 1995, 44.
9. Joyce Lain Kennedy and Thomas J. Morrow, *Electronic Resume Revolution* (New York: Wiley, 1995), 208–210.
10. Holly Rawlinson, "Pre-Employment Testing," *Small Business Reports,* April 1989, 20.
11. David Nye, "Son of the Polygraph," *Across the Board,* June 1989, 22.
12. David M. Buckley, "Turning the Tables," *Security Management,* April 1988, 103.
13. Joseph P. Buckley, "Nobody's Perfect," *Security Management,* May 1987, 77.
14. Deborah Veady, "Drug Screening and Your Career," *1992–93 CPC Annual,* 36th ed., 61–62; Heidi Jacobs, "The Handwriting's on the Wall," *Small Business Reports,* February 1992, 11–15; Nye, "Son of the Polygraph," 21; Rawlinson, "Pre-Employment Testing," 24, 26.
15. Michael P. Cronin, "This Is a Test," *Inc.,* August 1993, 64–68.
16. "Read Between the Lines," *Inc.,* June 1995, 90.
17. Joel Russell, "Finding Solid Ground," *Hispanic Business,* February 1992, 42–44, 46.
18. Microsoft 1996 Annual Report, accessed online, 1 July 1997.
19. "Quick Click," *U.S. News & World Report,* 29 April 1996, 70.

20. Robert Gifford, Cheuk Fan Ng, and Margaret Wilkinson, "Nonverbal Cues in the Employment Interview: Links Between Applicant Qualities and Interviewer Judgments," *Journal of Applied Psychology* 70, no. 4 (1985): 729.
21. Dale G. Leathers, *Successful Nonverbal Communication* (New York: Macmillan, 1986), 225.
22. Mary Goodwin, Deborah Cohn, and Donna Spivey, *Netjobs: Use the Internet to Land Your Dream Job* (New York: Michael Wolff, 1996), 170.
23. Shirley J. Shepherd, "How to Get That Job in 60 Minutes or Less," *Working Woman,* March 1986, 119.
24. Shepherd, "How to Get That Job," 118.
25. H. Anthony Medley, *Sweaty Palms: The Neglected Art of Being Interviewed* (Berkeley, Calif.: Ten Speed Press, 1993), 179.
26. Gerald L. Wilson, "Preparing Students for Responding to Illegal Selection Interview Questions," *The Bulletin of the Association for Business Communication* 54, no. 2 (1991): 44–49.
27. Jeff Springston and Joann Keyton, "Interview Response Training," *The Bulletin of the Association for Business Communication* 54, no. 3 (1991): 28–30; Gerald L. Wilson, "An Analysis of Instructional Strategies for Responding to Illegal Selection Interview Questions," *The Bulletin of the Association for Business Communication* 54, no. 3 (1991): 31–35.
28. Stephen J. Pullum, "Illegal Questions in the Selection Process: Going Beyond Contemporary Business and Professional Communication Textbooks," *The Bulletin of the Association for Business Communication* 54, no. 3 (1991): 36–43; Alicia Kitsuse, " 'Have You Ever Been Arrested?' " *Across the Board,* November 1992, 46–49; Christina L. Greathouse, "10 Common Hiring Mistakes," *Industry Week,* 20 January 1992, 22–23, 26.
29. Marilyn Moats Kennedy, "Are You Getting Paid What You're Worth?" *New Woman,* November 1984, 110.
30. Harold H. Hellwig, "Job Interviewing: Process and Practice," *The Bulletin of the Association for Business Communication* 55, no. 2 (1992): 8–14.
31. DeLeon, personal communication, May 1993.

Chapter 14

1. Wesley Van Linda, president, Narada Productions, personal communication, June 1993.
2. Dan Steinhoff and John F. Burgess, *Small Business Management Fundamentals,* 5th ed. (New York: McGraw-Hill, 1989), 37.
3. Joan F. Vesper and Karl H. Vesper, "Writing a Business Plan: The Total Term Assignment," *The Bulletin of the Association for Business Communication* 56, no. 2 (June 1993): 29–32.
4. Elizabeth Conlin, "The Daily Sales Report," *Inc.,* January 1991, 73–75.
5. Tom Peters, "Don't Send Memos!" *The Washington Monthly,* November 1987, 13.
6. Eric D. Randall, "Firms Serve Annual Reports with a Twist," *USA Today,* 17 May 1994, 6B; Patrick Flanagan, "Make Your Annual Report Work Harder," *Management Review,* October 1993, 52–58.
7. Tom Sant, *Persuasive Business Proposals* (New York: American Management Association, 1992), as summarized in *Soundview Executive Book Summaries* 14, no. 10, pt. 2 (October 1992): 3.
8. Iris I. Varner, *Contemporary Business Report Writing,* 2d ed. (Chicago: Dryden Press, 1991), 170.
9. Varner, *Contemporary Business Report Writing,* 178.
10. Susan L. Leach, "SEC Takes Next Leap into Computer Age," *Christian Science Monitor,* 7 June 1994, 8.
11. John Taschek, "New Report Writers Provide Improved Access to Data," *PC Week,* 6 February 1995, 81–85.
12. Stephan Manes, "E-Mail Troubles? You Have No Idea!" *PC World,* July 1996, 39.
13. Van Linda, personal communication, June 1993.

Chapter 15

1. Charley Shin, founder Charley's Steakery, personal communication, June 1996.
2. Bruce McComiskey, "Defining Institutional Problems: A Heuristic Procedure," *Business Communication Quarterly* 58, no. 4 (1995): 21–24.
3. Iris I. Varner, *Contemporary Business Report Writing,* 2d ed. (Chicago: Dryden Press, 1991), 135.
4. F. Stanford Wayne and Jolene D. Scriven, "Problem and Purpose Statements: Are They Synonymous Terms in Writing Reports for Business?" *The Bulletin of the Association for Business Communication,* 54, no. 1 (1991): 30–37.
5. Maridell Fryar and David A. Thomas, *Successful Problem Solving* (Lincolnwood, Ill.: NTC, 1989), 20.
6. David A. Aaker and George S. Day, *Marketing Research,* 2d ed. (New York: Wiley, 1983), 79, 111.
7. Aaker and Day, *Marketing Research,* 88–89.
8. Lisa Gubernick, "Making History Pay," *Forbes,* 13 May 1991, 132.
9. Aaker and Day, *Marketing Research,* 124.
10. Paul L. Riedesel, "Understanding Validity Is Easy; Doing Right Research Is Hard," *Marketing News,* 12 September 1986, 24.
11. "How to Design and Conduct a Study," *Credit Union Magazine,* October 1983, 36–46.
12. TK Associates International, Internet Web site @ <http://www.diyer.com>, accessed 29 July 1996.
13. Charles L. Olson and Mario J. Picconi, *Statistics for Business Decision Making* (Glenview, Ill.: Scott, Foresman, 1983), 105.
14. Olson and Picconi, *Statistics for Business Decision Making,* 105.
15. Shin, personal communication, June 1996.

Chapter 16

1. Michael Fernandez, director of management communications, Eastman Kodak Company, personal communication, March 1996.
2. Alexander Petofi, "The Graphic Revolution in Computers," *The Futurist,* June 1985, 30.
3. Stephanie McKinnon, "Pictures, Signs and Symbols Prove to Be Powerful Tools," *Gannett Suburban Newspapers,* 27 September 1992, 12.
4. Maureen Jones, "Getting Good Graphs," *PC Magazine,* 23 July 1985, 217.
5. Edward R. Tufte, *The Visual Display of Quantitative Information* (Cheshire, Conn.: Graphic Press, 1983), 113.
6. Courtland L. Bovée, Michael J. Houston, and John V. Thill, *Marketing,* 2d ed. (New York: McGraw-Hill, 1995), 250.
7. Sheri Rosen, "What Is Truth?" *IABC Communication World,* March 1995, 40.
8. Fernandez, personal communication, March 1996.

Chapter 17

1. Dierdre Ballou, Education Manager, The San Diego Wild Animal Park, personal communication, 9 July 1997.
2. Milton Wilkins, vice president, plant sciences division, Monsanto Agricultural Company, personal communication, 23 February 1990.
3. Eleanor Rizzo, "Document Design Basics," *Technical Communication,* fourth quarter 1992, 645.
4. A. S. C. Ehrenberg, "Report Writing—Six Simple Rules for Better Business Documents," *Admap,* June 1992, 39–42.
5. Ballou, Personal Communication, October 1992.
6. Adapted from J. Roberto Whitaker-Penteado, "Oil Cos. Pump Up Advertising in Brazil," *Adweek,* 6 September 1993, 14.
7. Adapted from Nancy Jeffrey, "Preparing for the Worst: Firms Set Up Plans to Help Deal with Corporate Crises," *Wall Street Journal,* 7 December 1987, 23.
8. Adapted from Bob Smith, "The Evolution of Pinkerton," *Management Review,* September 1993, 54–58.

Chapter 18

1. Hunter Lovins, co-founder, Rocky Mountain Institute, personal communication, May 1992.
2. Oswald M. T. Ratteray, "Hit the Mark with Better Summaries," *Supervisory Management,* September 1989, 43–45.
3. National Association of Recording Manufacturers, *Annual Survey Results '93* (Marlton, N.J.: NARM, 1994).
4. Lyman W. Porter and Lawrence E. McKibbin, *Management Education and Development: Drift or Thrust into the 21st Century?* (New York: McGraw-Hill, 1988), 1–44.

5. Lovins, personal communication, May 1992.
6. Adapted from American Hotel & Motel Association, "Lodging Guest Research Summary of Major Results," presented to International Hotel, Motel, and Restaurant Association Annual Convention, 14 November 1989.
7. Adapted from Arthur Andersen & Co., "Survey Results of Small and Middle Market Businesses," *Attitudes, Issues and Outlook: Baseline Study* (Arthur Andersen's Enterprise Group and National Small Business United, July 1992).
8. Adapted from Nicholas E. Lefferts, "What's New in the Pet Business," *New York Times,* 3 August 1985, sec. 3, 15.
9. Adapted from Suzanne Alexander, "College 'Parties' Get High Marks as Sales Events," *Wall Street Journal,* 23 October 1992, B1.
10. Adapted from N. R. Kleinfield, "The Ever-Fatter Business of Thinness," *New York Times,* 7 September 1986, sec. 3, 12.
11. Adapted from David J. Jefferson and Thomas R. King, " 'Infomercials' Fill Up Prime Time on Cable, Aim for Prime Time," *Wall Street Journal,* 22 October 1992, A1.

Chapter 19

1. Virginia Johnson, director of human relations, 3M, personal communication, August 1993.
2. Edward F. Walsh, "Telephone Tyranny," *Industry Week,* 1 April 1991, 24–26.
3. Madeline Bodin, "Making the Most of Your Telephone," *Nation's Business,* April 1992, 62.
4. Beverly Davenport Sypher, Robert N. Bastrom, and Joy Hart Seibert, "Listening, Communication Abilities, and Success at Work," *Journal of Business Communication* 26, no. 4 (fall 1989): 293–301.
5. Augusta M. Simon, "Effective Listening: Barriers to Listening in a Diverse Business Environment," *The Bulletin of the Association for Business Communication* 54, no. 3 (September 1991): 73–74.
6. Sypher, Bastrom, and Siebert, "Listening, Communication Abilities, and Success at Work," 293–301.
7. Thomas L. Means, "A Unit to Develop Listening Skill," *The Bulletin of the Association for Business Communication* 54, no. 3 (September 1991): 70–72.
8. Jennifer Lawson, "How I Did It: Persuading Staffers to Get with the Program," *Working Woman,* April 1991, 57–58, 60.
9. Phillip Morgan and H. Kent Baker, "Building a Professional Image: Improving Listening Behavior," *Supervisory Management,* November 1985, 35–36.
10. Andrew D. Wolvin and Carolyn Gwynn Coakley, *Listening* (Dubuque, Iowa: Brown, 1985), 6.
11. Lyman K. Steil, Larry L. Barker, and Kittie W. Watson, *Effective Listening: Key to Your Success* (Reading, Mass.: Addison-Wesley, 1983), 21–22.
12. J. Michael Sproule, *Communication Today* (Glenview, Ill.: Scott, Foresman, 1981), 69.
13. Sproule, *Communication Today,* 69.
14. Sproule, *Communication Today,* 69.
15. Robert A. Luke, Jr., "Improving Your Listening Ability," *Supervisory Management,* June 1992, 7; Madelyn Burley-Allen, "Listening for Excellence in Communication," *The Dynamics of Behavior Newsletter* 2, no. 2 (summer 1992): 1.
16. Jesse S. Nirenberg, *Getting Through to People* (Englewood Cliffs, N.J.: Prentice-Hall, 1973), 134–142.
17. Nirenberg, *Getting Through to People,* 134–142.
18. Nirenberg, *Getting Through to People,* 134–142.
19. Philip R. Harris and Robert T. Moran, *Managing Cultural Differences,* 3d ed. (Houston, Tx.: Gulf, 1991), 56–57.
20. Kevin J. Walsh, "How to Negotiate European Style," *The Journal of European Business,* July–August 1993, 48.
21. Janis Graham, "Sharpen Your Negotiating Skills," *Sylvia Porter's Personal Finance,* December 1985, 54–58.
22. Graham, "Sharpen Your Negotiating Skills," 54–58.
23. Graham, "Sharpen Your Negotiating Skills," 54–58.
24. Thomas L. Brown, "The Art of the Interview," *Industry Week,* 1 March 1993, 19.
25. Claudia H. Deutsch, "Teamwork or Tug of War?" *New York Times,* 26 August 1990, sec. 3, 27.

26. B. Aubrey Fisher, *Small Group Decision Making: Communication and the Group Process,* 2d ed. (New York: McGraw-Hill, 1980), 145–149.
27. Ken Blanchard, "Meetings Can Be Effective," *Supervisory Management,* October 1992, 5.
28. William C. Waddell and Thomas A. Rosko, "Conducting an Effective Off-Site Meeting," *Management Review,* February 1993, 40–44.
29. Kathy E. Gill, "Board Primer: Parliamentary Procedure," *Association Management,* 1993, L-39.
30. Johnson, personal communication, August 1993.

Chapter 20

1. Shirley Crouch, executive vice president and director of operations, Phoenix Management, personal communication, April 1996.
2. Deirdre Fanning, "The Public Equivalent of a Root Canal," *New York Times,* 2 December 1990, sec. 3, 25.
3. Sherron B. Kenton, "Speaker Credibility in Persuasive Business Communication: A Model Which Explains Gender Differences," *Journal of Business Communication* 26, no. 2 (spring 1989): 143–157.
4. Walter Kiechel III, "How to Give a Speech," *Fortune,* 8 June 1987, 180.
5. *Communication and Leadership Program* (Santa Ana, Calif.: Toastmasters International, 1980), 44, 45.
6. The staff of *Presentation Products Magazine,* "Better Presentations for a Better Bottom Line," *Fortune,* 9 October 1989, 24–25.
7. *How to Prepare and Use Effective Visual Aids,* Info-Line series, Elizabeth Lean, managing ed. (Washington, D.C.: American Society for Training and Development, October 1984), 2.
8. Kathleen K. Weigner, "Visual Persuasion," *Forbes,* 16 September 1991, 176; Kathleen K. Weigner, "Showtime!" *Forbes,* 13 May 1991, 118.
9. Eric Arndt, "Nobody Does It Better," *IABC Communication World,* May 1988, 28.
10. Daniel Goleman, "For Victims of Stage Fright, Rehearsal Is the Therapy," *New York Times,* 12 June 1991, B1.
11. Judy Linscott, "Getting On and Off the Podium," *Savvy,* October 1985, 44.
12. Iris R. Johnson, "Before You Approach the Podium," *MW,* January–February 1989, 7.
13. Sandra Moyer, "Braving No Woman's Land," *The Toastmaster,* August 1986, 13.
14. Teresa Brady, "Fielding Abrasive Questions During Presentations," *Supervisory Management,* February 1993, 6.
15. Robert L. Montgomery, "Listening on Your Feet," *The Toastmaster,* July 1987, 14–15.
16. Adapted from Ronald L. Applebaum and Karl W. E. Anatol, *Effective Oral Communication: For Business and the Professions* (Chicago: Science Research Associates, 1982), 240–244.
17. Crouch, personal communication, April 1996.

Component Chapter A

1. Mary A. DeVries, *Internationally Yours* (Boston: Houghton Mifflin, 1994), 9.
2. Patricia A. Dreyfus, "Paper That's Letter Perfect," *Money,* May 1985, 184.
3. "When Image Counts, Letterhead Says It All," *The Advocate and Greenwich Time,* 10 January 1993, F4.
4. Mel Mandell, "Electronic Forms Are Cheap and Speedy," *D&B Reports,* July–August 1993, 44–45.
5. Linda Driskill, *Business & Managerial Communication: New Perspectives* (Orlando, Fla.: Harcourt Brace Jovanovich, 1992), 470.
6. Driskill, *Business & Managerial Communication,* 470.
7. Lennie Copeland and Lewis Griggs, *Going International: How to Make Friends and Deal Effectively in the Global Marketplace,* 2d ed. (New York: Random House, 1985), 24–27.
8. DeVries, *Internationally Yours,* 8.
9. Copeland and Griggs, *Going International,* 24–27.
10. U.S. Postal Service, *Postal Addressing Standards* (Washington, D.C.: GPO, 1992).
11. Copeland and Griggs, *Going International,* 24–27.
12. Renee B. Horowitz and Marian G. Barchilon, "Stylistic Guidelines for E-mail," *IEEE Transactions on Professional Communications* 37, no. 4 (1994): 207–212.

13. Jill H. Ellsworth and Matthew V. Ellsworth, *The Internet Business Book* (New York: Wiley, 1994), 93.
14. Bill Eager, *Using the Internet* (Indianapolis: Que Corporation, 1994), 11.
15. Eager, *Using the Internet,* 10.
16. William Eager, Larry Donahue, David Forsyth, Kenneth Mitton, and Martin Waterhouse, *Net.Search* (Indianapolis: Que Corporation, 1995), 221.
17. Rosalind Resnick and Dave Taylor, *Internet Business Guide* (Indianapolis: Sams.net Publishing, 1995), 117.
18. James L. Clark and Lyn R. Clark, *How 7: A Handbook for Office Workers,* 7th ed. (Cincinnati, Oh.: South-Western, 1995), 431–432.

Component Chapter B

1. Sherwyn Morreale and Courtland Bovée, *Excellence in Public Speaking* (Fort Worth, Tex.: Harcourt Brace, 1997), 173–174.
2. Morreale and Bovée, *Excellence in Public Speaking,* 174–175.
3. Morreale and Bovée, *Excellence in Public Speaking,* 174–175.
4. Dorothy Geisler, "How to Avoid Copyright Lawsuits," *IABC Communication World,* June 1984, 34–37.
5. Robert W. Goddard, "The Crime of Copying," *Management World,* July–August 1986, 20–22.

ACKNOWLEDGEMENTS

Text, Figures, and Tables

4–5 (Communication Skills—Eight Great Ways They Help Advance Your Career): Adapted from Henry H. Bean, "Good Writing: An Underrated Executive Skill," *Human Resource Management,* Spring 1981, 2–7. **8** (F1-2): Adapted from David J. Rachman and Michael H. Mescon, *Business Today,* 5th ed. (Copyright © 1987 by McGraw-Hill, Inc.) 127. **11** (F1-4) Adapted from David J. Rachman and Michael H. Mescon, *Business Today,* 5th ed. (Copyright © 1987 by McGraw-Hill, Inc., 127. **19** (Ethical Boundaries: Where Would You Draw the Line): Adapted from Ben Stein, "An Employer's Bill of Rights," *Business Month,* April 1990, 55; Thomas A. Young, "Ethics in Business: Business of Ethics," *Vital Speeches,* 15 September 1992, 725–730; "Business Ethics: What Are Your Personal Standards?" *Working Woman,* February 1990, 61–62; Kyle Herger, "One Communicator's Gold Star Is Another's Scarlet Letter," *IABC Communication World,* September 1989, 34–36; Barbara D. Langham, "Ethics: Where Do You Stand?" *IABC Communication World,* May 1989, 21–22, 24–25; Frank Yanacek, "A Question of Ethics," *Transportation and Distribution,* December 1988, 48–50. **34** (Actions Speak Louder than Words All Around the World): Adapted from David A. Victor, *International Business Communication* (New York: HarperCollins, 1992); David Wallace, "Mind Your Manners," *World Trade,* October 1992, 52, 54–55; Hannele Duvfa, "Innocents Abroad: The Politics of Cross-Cultural Communication," *Communication and Discourse Across Cultures and Languages,* 1991, 73–89; M. Katherine Glover, "Do's & Taboos: Cultural Aspects of International Business," *Business America* 13 (August 1990): 2–6; C. Barnum and N. Woniansky, "Taking Cues from Body Language," *Management Review,* June 1989, 59–60. **35** (F2-1): Adapted from Phillip Morgan and H. Kent Baker, "Building a Professional Image: Improving Listening Behavior." Reprinted by permission of the publisher, from *Supervisory Management,* November 1985, 34, © 1985 American Management Association, New York. All rights reserved. **39** (F2-3): Adapted from David Lewis, *The Secret Language of Success* (New York: Carroll & Graf Publishers, Inc., 1989), 213. Reprinted by permission. **42** (F2-4): Adapted from Allan D. Frank, *Communicating on the Job* (Glenview, IL: Scott Foresman and Co., 1982), 20. Used with permission of Allan D. Frank. **46–47** (Eight Keys to Achieving Total Quality and Customer Satisfaction): Based on information from Louis C. Williams, Jr., "Hottest Communication Topics Are . . . Improving Quality & Customer Satisfaction," *IABC Communication World,* August 1990, 35–37; Jim Shaffer, "Communication in a World-Class World," *IABC Communication World,* February 1992, 36–38. **60–61** (Test Your Intercultural Knowledge): Adapted from David A. Ricks, "International Business Blunders: An Update," *Business & Economic Review,* January–March 1988, 11–14. Reprinted by permission. **68–69** (Does an 'English Only' Policy Violate Employees' Rights?): Based on information from Arthur F. Silbergeld and Mark B. Tuvim, "English-Only Rules Should Be Narrowly Drawn and Justified by Business Necessity," *Employment Relations Today,* Autumn 1994, 355–364; William E. Lissy, "Workplace Language Rules," *Supervision,* April 1993, 20–21; Norman Sklarewitz, "English-Only on the Job," *Across the Board,* January–February 1992, 18–22; Joseph D'O'Brian, "Only English Speakers Need Apply," *Management Review,* January 1991, 41–45; Jolie Solomon, "Firms Grapple with Language Barriers," *The Wall Street Journal,* 7 November 1989, B1, B12. **88** (F4-1): Netscape Composer © Netscape **89** (F4-2): ACT! © Symantec. Reproduced courtesy Symantec. **90** (F4-3): Courtesy Gateway 2000, Inc. Photo used with permission from © Microsoft Corporation. **104** (F4-6): Courtesy Hewlett Packard. **122** (Understand Intercultural Audiences, and You'll Be Understood): Adapted from Mahalingam Subbiah, "Adding a New Dimension to the Teaching of Audience Analysis: Cultural Awareness," *IEEE Transactions on Professional Communication* 35, no. 1 (March 1992): 14–19; Ronald E. Dulek, John S. Fielden, and John S. Hill, "International Communication: An Executive Primer," *Business Horizons,* January–February 1991, 20–25; Dwight W. Stevenson, "Audience Analysis Across Cultures," *Journal of Technical Writing and Communication* 13, no. 4 (1983): 319–330. **131–132** (F5-3 and 5-4): Courtesy of General Mills, Inc. **134** (F5-5): Octel Unified Messenger/Octel Communications Corporation, Milpitas, CA. **148** (The Tangled Web of Internet Copyrights): *The Internet Unleashed,* 2d ed. (Indianapolis: Sams.net Publishing, 1995), 1056; Alice Bredin, "The Hard Drive: Analog Laws Can't Keep Up with Digital Technology," *Newsday,* 30 April 1995, 2; Ron Coleman, "Copycats on the Superhighway," *ABA Journal* 81 (1 July l995): 68. **168–169** (E-mail Etiquette: Minding Your Manners Online): Adapted from Pamela Sebastian, "E-mail Etiquette Starts to Take Shape for Business Messaging," *The Wall Street Journal,* 12 October 1995, A1; Rosalind Resnick and Dave Taylor, *Internet Business Guide* (Indianapolis: Sams.net Publishing, 1995), 126; Karen S. Nantz and Cynthia Drexel, "Incorporating Electronic Mail into the Business Communication Course," *Business Communication Quarterly* 58, no. 3 (1995): 45–49; David Angell and Brent Heslop, *The Elements of E-mail Style* (Reading, Mass.: Addison-Wesley, 1994), 1–31, 66–69, 113–127; Ed Tittel and Margaret Robbins, *E-mail Essentials* (Cambridge, Mass.: AP Professional, 1994), 21–31, 159–164, 171–187; Bill Eager, *Using the Internet* (Indianapolis: Que Corporation, 1994) 80–101; Renee B. Horowitz and Marian G. Barchilon, "Stylistic Guidelines for E-mail," *IEEE Transactions on Professional Communications* 37, no. 4 (1994): 207–212; Lance Cohen, "How to Improve Your E-mail Messages," <http://galaxy.einet/galaxy/Business-and-Commerce/Management/Communications/How_to_Improve_Your_E_mail.html>. **184–185** (More Than Word for Word—The Importance of Accurate Translation): Adapted from David A. Victor, *International Business Communication* (New York: HarperCollins, 1992), 44; "Heinz Targets Britain's Asians," *Asian Advertising & Marketing,* June 1992, 50; George P. Rimalower, "How Do You Spell Safety?" *Small Business Reports,* September 1992, 11–14; Sandor Albert, "The Traps of Formal Correspondence," paper presented at the Language International Conference, Elsinore, Denmark, 31 May–12 June 1991; Edward Sapir, as quoted in Susan Bassnett-McGuire, "Translation Studies," in *Intercultural Communication: A Reader,* 6th ed., edited by Larry A. Samovar and Richard E. Porter (Belmont, Calif.: Wadsworth, 1991), 251–264; Sue Kapp, "Selling Through a Babel of Tongues," *Business Marketing,* May 1991, 24–28; Richard N. Weltz, "How Do You Say, 'Oops!'" *Business Marketing,* October 1990, 52–54; Martha Dupecher, "Wait a Minute . . . Do These People Speak English?" *IABC Communication World,* August 1990, 24–27; Lynn Tyler, *Intercultural Interacting* (Provo, Utah: David M. Kennedy Center for International Studies, Brigham Young University, 1987), 67–69. **205** (How to Proofread Like a Pro: Tips for Creating the Perfect Document): Adapted from Philip C. Kolin, *Successful Writing at Work,* 2d ed., 102. Used with permission of D. C. Heath and Company; Dennis Hensley, "A Way with Words: Proofreading Can Save Cash and Careers," *Dallas Magazine,* May 1986, 57–58. Reprinted with permission. **206** (F7-6): Grammatik 5, © 1986–93 Reference Software International, a wholly owned subsidiary of WordPerfect Corporation. All rights reserved. Used with permission. **217** (How Direct Is Too Direct?): Adapted from Mary A. DeVries, *Internationally Yours* (Boston: Houghton Mifflin, 1994), 195; Myron W. Lustig and Jolene Koester, *Intercultural Competence* (New York: HarperCollins, 1993), 66–72; Mary Munter, "Cross-Cultural Communication for Managers," *Business Horizons,* May–June 1993, 69–78; David A. Victor, *International Business Communication* (New York: HarperCollins, 1992), 137–168; Larry A. Samovar and Richard E. Porter, *Intercultural Communication: A Reader,* 6th ed. (Belmont, Calif.: Wadsworth, 1991), 109–110; Larry A. Samovar and Richard E. Porter, *Communication Between Cultures* (Belmont, Calif.: Wadsworth, 1991), 235–244; Carley H. Dodd, *Dynamics of Intercultural Communication,* 3d ed. (Dubuque, Iowa: Wm. C. Brown, 1989), 69–73. **250–251** (The

Possibilities and Perils of E-mail): Based on information from Michael R. Overly, "Is Your E-mail Being Tapped?" *Business News,* Spring 1997, 51–52; Alex Markels, "Managers Aren't Always Able to Get the Right Message Across with E-mail," *The Wall Street Journal,* 6 August 1996, B1; William Eager, Larry Donahue, David Forsyth, Kenneth Mitton, and Martin Waterhouse, Net.Search (Indianapolis: Que Corporation, 1995), 221–223; Wayne Rash, Jr., "Before You Press That Send Button, Keep in Mind That E-mail Is Forever," *Communications Week,* 16 October 1995, 72; Michael A. Verespej, "The E-mail Monster," *Industry Week,* 19 June 1995, 52–53; Marc Hequet, "Life's Little E-mail Problems," *Training,* August 1995, 56; Renée B. Horowitz and Marian G. Barchilon, "Stylistic Guidelines for E-mail," *IEEE Transactions on Professional Communication* 37, no. 4 (1994): 207–212; Michael Rothschild, "When You're Gagging on E-mail," *Forbes,* 6 June 1994, 25–26; Jayne A. Pearl, "The E-mail Quandary," *Management Review,* July 1993, 48–51; Barbara Kantrowitz et al., "Love Wires," *Newsweek,* 6 September 1993, 42–49; Jolie Solomon, "As Electronic Mail Loosens Inhibitions, Impetuous Senders Feel Anything Goes," *The Wall Street Journal,* 12 October 1990, B1. **266–267** (Recommendation Letters: What's Right to Right?): Based on information from Maura Dolan and Stuart Silverstein, "Court Broadens Liability for Job References," *The Los Angeles Times,* 28 January 1997, A1, A11; Frances A. McMorris, "Ex-Bosses Face Less Peril Giving Honest Job References," *The Wall Street Journal,* 8 July 1996, B1, B8; Dawn Gunsch, "Gray Matters: Centralize Control of Giving References," *Personnel Journal,* September 1992, 114, 116–117; Betty Southard Murphy, Wayne E. Barlow, and D. Diane Hatch, "Manager's Newsfront: Job Reference Liability of Employees," *Personnel Journal,* September 1991, 22, 26; Ross H. Fishman, "When Silence Is Golden," *Nation's Business,* July 1991, 48–49. **270** (F9-6): News Release provided by Blockbuster Corporate Relations Department, Dallas, Texas. **296** (Good Ways to Send Bad News Around the World): James Calvert Scott and Diana J. Green, "British Perspectives on Organizing Bad-News Letters: Organizational Patterns Used by Major U.K. Companies," *The Bulletin of the Association for Business Communication* 55, no. 1 (March 1992): 17–19; Iris I. Varner, "A Comparison of American and French Business Correspondence," *Journal of Business Communication* 24, no. 4 (Fall 1988): 55–65; Susan Jenkins and John Hinds, "Business Letter Writing: English, French, and Japanese," *TESOL Quarterly* 21, no. 2 (June 1987): 327–349; Saburo Haneda and Hiosuke Shima, "Japanese Communication Behavior as Reflected in Letter Writing," *Journal of Business Communication* 19, no. 1 (1982): 19–32. **312** (How to Take the Sting Out of Criticism and Foster Goodwill): Adapted from Les Giblin, *How to Have Confidence and Power in Dealing with People* (New York: Prentice-Hall, 1956), 132–133. **331** (F11-1): Adapted from Abraham H. Maslow, *Motivation and Personality* (New York: Harper & Row, 1954), 12, 19. Copyright © 1970 by Abraham H. Maslow. Reprinted by permission of HarperCollins Publishers. **350** (Does Some Direct Mail Contain Deliberately Deceptive Copy?): Based on information from Galen Stilson, "Big Sales by Mail: Get the Order Now," *In Business,* October 1992, 44; Herschell Gordon Lewis, "The Future of 'Force-Communication': Power Communication," *Direct Marketing,* April 1991, 51–52; Annetta Miller, "My Postman Has a Hernia!" *Newsweek,* 10 June 1991, 41; Michael R. Hyman and Richard Tansey, "The Ethics of Psychoactive Ads," *Journal of Business Ethics,* February 1990, 105–114; Jill Smolowe, "Read This!!!!!!!!" *Time,* 26 November 1990, 62–67; Laurie P. Cohen, "Direct-Mail Legal Pitches Get Big Boost," *The Wall Street Journal,* 5 July 1988, B21; Milt Pierce, "The Morality of Direct Marketing," *Direct Marketing,* October 1987, 188, 120, 122. **354** (UF11-1): Courtesy MTV. **384–385** (High-Tech Job Hunting: The Secrets of Finding Employment on the World Wide Web): Adapted from Richard Nelson Bolles, *The 1997 What Color Is Your Parachute?* (Berkeley, Calif.: Ten Speed Press, 1996), 129–166; Karen W. Arenson, "Placement Offices Leave Old Niches to Become Computerized Job Bazaars," *The New York Times,* 17 July 1996, B12; Lawrence J. Magid, "Job Hunters Cast Wide Net Online," *Los Angeles Times,* 26 February 1996, 20; Richard Van Doren, "On-Line Career Advice Speeds Search for Jobs," *Network World,* 4 March 1996, 54; Alex Markels, "Job Hunting Takes Off in Cyberspace," *The Wall Street Journal,* 20 September 1996, B1, B2; Michael Chorost, "Jobs on the Web," *Hispanic,* October 1995, 50–53; Zane K. Quible, "Electronic Résumés: Their Time Is Coming," *Business Communication Quarterly* 58, no. 3 (1995): 5–9; Margaret Mannix, "The Home-Page Help Wanteds," *U.S. News & World Report,* 30 October 1995, 88, 90; Pam Dixon and Silvia Tiersten, *Be Your Own Headhunter Online* (New York: Random House, 1995), 53–69. **392–393** (Warning: Deceptive Résumés Can Backfire): Adapted from Joan E. Rigdon, "Deceptive Résumés Can Be Door-Openers but Can Become an Employee's Undoing," *The Wall Street Journal,* 17 June 1992, B1; Diane

Cole, "Ethics: Companies Crack Down on Dishonesty," *Managing Your Career,* Spring 1991, 8–11; Nancy Marx Better, "Résumé Liars," *Savvy,* December 1990–January 1991, 26–29. **421** Handwriting Analysis: Should It Be Used to Determine Your Employment Potential): Daryl Koehn, "Handwriting Analysis in Pre-Employment Screening," *The Online Journal of Ethics* <http://condor.depaul.edu/ethics/hand/html> accessed 11/20/96; Sharon McDonnell, "Your Teacher Was Right About Penmanship: Writing Analysts Help Companies Screen Out Undesirable Applicants," *Newsday,* 17 September 1995; PACE Graphology Web site <http://www.photo-style.co.uk/pace/pacepage/pacewho.htm>; Ron Plotnik, *Introduction to Psychology,* 3d ed. (Pacific Grove, Calif.: Brooks/Cole, 1993), 279, 476. **426–427** (Sixteen Tough Interview Questions: What to Say When You're Stopped in Your Tracks): Adapted from "Career Strategies," *Black Enterprise,* February 1986, 122. Copyright © 1986 Black Enterprise Magazine, The Earl Graves Publishing Co., Inc., New York, NY. All rights reserved. **428** (F13-2): Adapted from *The Northwestern Endicott Report* (Evanston, IL: Northwestern University Placement Center). **429** (F13-3): Adapted from H. Lee Rust, *Job Search: The Completion Manual for Jobseekers* (New York: American Management Association, 1979), 56. **429** (F13-4): Adapted from *The Northwestern Endicott Report* (Evanston, IL: Northwestern University Placement Center). **450–451** (Do You Make These Costly Mistakes When Writing Business Reports): Adapted from Joan Minninger, *The Perfect Memo* (New York: Doubleday, 1990), 169–170. Copyright © 1990 by Joan Minninger. Used by permission of Doubleday, a division of Bantam Doubleday Dell Publishing Group, Inc. **471** (Keeping Pace with Technology): Adapted from Federal Express home page <http://www.fedex.com/svcs_online.html> accessed 14 June 1996; Jack Schember, "Mrs. Fields' Secret Weapon," *Personnel Journal,* September 1991, 56–58; Paul Kondstadt, "Ship 54—Where Are You?" *CIO,* May 1990, 80–81, 84, 86; Bruce G. Posner and Bo Burlingham, "The Hottest Entrepreneur in America," *Inc.,* January 1988, 44–48. **481** (Seven Errors in Logic That Can Undermine Your Reports): Adapted from Christopher Power, "Flops," *Business Week,* 16 August 1993, 79; Mary Munter, *Guide to Managerial Communication,* 2d ed. © 1982, 31. Adapted by permission of Prentice-Hall, Inc., Englewood Cliffs, N.J. **488–490** (F15-4): Gus Venditto, "Search Engine Showdown: IW Lab Tests Seven Internet Search Tools," *Internet World,* May 1996, 79–92; Sandra Stewart, "How to Quickly Locate What You Need to Know on the Internet: Stop Searching and Start Finding," *The Net,* not dated, 35–40; Mitch Wagner, "http: Search engines," *Computerworld,* 23 September 1996, 71; Krista Ostertag, "Rev Up Your Business—Search Engines Are an Integral Part of the Menu for Total Web Solutions," *VarBusiness,* 1 February 1997, 63; Dylan Tweney Yael Li-Ron, "Features: Searching Is My Business: A Gumshoe's Guide to the Web," *PC World Online,* 1 December 1996; Bill Eager, "Web Searcher Shoot-Out," *Websight,* January–February 1996; Infoseek Corporation, Infoseek Home Page, <www.search.yahoo.com>, 1994–97; Excite, Inc., Excite Home Page, <www.excite.com>, 1996; Digital Equipment Corporation, Alta Vista Home Page, <www.altavista.com>, 1996; Cyber Networks, Inc., Cyber411 Home Page, <www.cyber411.com>, 1997; Open Text Corporation, Open Text Home Page, <www.opentext.com>, 1996. **492–493** (How to Avoid Plagiarism): Based on information from Daphne A. Jameson, "The Ethics of Plagiarism: How Genre Affects Writers' Use of Source Materials," *The Bulletin of the Association for Business Communication* 56, no. 2 (June 1993): 18–28; Deni Elliott, "Plagiarism: It's Not a Black and White Issue," *The Quill,* November–December 1991, 15–16; Amy Gamerman, "Unfair Use: Copyright Decision Cramps Writers' Style," *The Wall Street Journal,* 10 April 1990, A16; Pamela S. Zurer, "NIH Panel Strips Researcher of Funding After Plagiarism Review," *Chemical & Engineering News,* 7 August 1989, 24–25; Mark Fitzgerald, "Denver Post Art Critic Fired for Plagiarism," *Editor & Publisher,* 11 March 1989, 22; Edith Skom, "Plagiarism: Quite a Rather Bad Little Crime," *American Association for Higher Education Bulletin,* October 1986, 3–7; Christopher S. Hawley, "The Thieves of Academe: Plagiarism in the University System," *Improving College and University Teaching* 32, no. 1 (winter 1984): 35–39. **496** (15-6): Copyright/trademark of Adaptive Technologies Group/Sawtooth Technologies. **498** (F15-7): From David J. Rachman and Michael H. Mescon, *Business Today,* 5th ed., 587. Copyright © 1987 by McGraw-Hill, Inc. **507** (T16-1): Adapted from Robert Lefferts, *Elements of Graphics,* 18–35. Copyright © 1981 by Robert Lefferts. Reprinted by permission of Harper & Row, Publishers, Inc. **513** (F16-4): Data from U.S. Department of Commerce. **513** (F16-5): Cynthia Kramer, "Production Statistics Raise Intriguing Questions," *Industrial Outlook,* 12 April 1988, 24. **514** (F16-6): Adapted from Gene Zelanzny, *Say It with Charts,* 112. Richard D. Irwin, Inc., © 1985. **515** (F16-8):

Adapted from David J. Rachman and Michael H. Mescon, "Careers in Business" in *Business Today,* 6th ed. (New York: McGraw-Hill, 1990), 592–594.   **516** (F16-10): Reprinted by permission of *The Wall Street Journal,* © 1989 Dow Jones & Company, Inc. All Rights Reserved Worldwide.   **517** (F16-11): Adapted from Robert Lefferts, *How to Prepare Charts and Graphs for Effective Reports* (New York: Harper & Row, Publishers, Inc., 1981).   **518** (F16-12): Adapted from John M. Lannon, *Technical Writing,* 3d ed. Copyright © 1985 by John M. Lannon. Reprinted by permission of HarperCollins College Publishers.   **519** (F16-13): Copyright 1993, *USA Today.* Reprinted with permission.   **522** (UF16-1): © 1997 Picture Perfect.   **522–523** (Creating Colorful Visual Aids with Computers for Maximum Clarity and Impact): Adapted from Peter H. Selby, *Using Graphs and Tables: A Self-Teaching Guide* (New York: Wiley, 1979), 8.   **527** (Visual Aids That Lie: The Use and Abuse of Charts and Graphs): Based on information from A. S. C. Ehrenberg, "The Problem of Numeracy," *Admap,* February 1992, 37–40; Mary S. Auvil and Kenneth W. Auvil, *Introduction to Business Graphics: Concepts and Applications* (Cincinnati, OH.: South-Western, 1992), 40, 192–193; Peter H. Selby, *Using Graphs and Tables: A Self-Teaching Guide* (New York: Wiley, 1979), 8–9.   **536** (UF17-1): © New York Stock Exchange, Inc.   **613–614** (T18-8, 18-9, 18-10): National Restaurant Association.   **615** (T18-11, 18-12, 18-13): Adapted from Thomas D. Dupont, "Consumer Travel: The New Breed of Travel Consumers," *Madison Avenue,* July 1983, 32, 34.   **F18-3, 18-4, 18-5, 18-6, 18-7** Survey of Small and Mid-Sized Businesses conducted by Arthur Andersen's Enterprise Group and National Small Business United.   **631** (Crossing Cultures without Crossing Signals: Your Listening Skills Can Bridge the Gap): Heinz-Dieter Meyer, "The Cultural Gap in Long-Term International Work Groups: A German-American Case Study," *European Management Journal,* March 1993, 99; Kevin J. Walsh, "How to Negotiate European Style," *The Journal of European Business,* July–August 1993, 47.   **633** (F19-1): Copyright, Dr. Lyman K. Steil, President, Communication Development, Inc., St. Paul, MN. Prepared for the Sperry Corporation. Reprinted with permission of Dr. Steil and Unisys Corporation.   **643** (F19-4): Adapted from J. Michael Sproule, *Communication Today,* 1981, by permission of J. Michael Sproule, Copyright, J. Michael Sproule.   **TA-1** Adapted from Doris H. Whalen, *The Secretary's Handbook,* 3d ed., copyright © 1978 by Harcourt Brace & Company, Inc., reprinted by permission of the publisher. **646–647** (Electric Meetings: Work Together—Wherever You Are—to Get the Results You Want): Patrick Flanagan, "Videoconferencing Changes the Corporate Meeting," *Management Review,* February 1994, 7; Intel Web site, <http://www.intel.com>; Pittsburgh Videotech Center Web site, <http:/www.pgh-videotech.com>; Joseph G. Donelan, "Using Electronic Tools to Improve Meetings," *Management Accounting,* March 1993, 42–45; Norman Weizer, "Videoconferencing Comes of Age," *The Journal of European Business,* November–December 1992, 26–28; Brent Gallupe and George Fox, "Facilitated Electronic Meetings: Higher Quality, Less Time," *CMA Magazine,* April 1992, 29–32; Rosemary Hamilton, "Electronic Meetings: No More ZZZZ's," *Computerworld,* 14 September 1992, 109, 113; Michael Finley, "The Best of All Possible Meetings?" *Across the Board,* September 1991, 40–45; Michael Finley, "The New Meaning of Meetings," *IABC Communication World,* March 1991, 25–27; Joanie M. Wexler, "Electronic Meetings Increase," *Computerworld,* 18 February 1991, 55, 58; Gregg Lieberman, "A User's Guide to Videoconferencing," *Meetings & Conventions,* September 1991, 80–84, 88–89; Stephen F. Friedman, "The Electronic Alternative," *Small Business Reports,* July 1991, 68–72; Robert Moskowitz, "Electronic Meetings Raise Effectiveness," *Office Systems,* August 1991, 30–36; Jay Levin, "Video Conferencing Finally in Focus," *Meetings & Conventions,* September 1988, 26–29; Shawn Hartley Hancock, "Electronic Meetings: Ready for Prime Time," *Successful Meetings,* October 1988, 32–37; Ellen Muraskin, "Electronic Meetings," *Meetings & Conventions,* November 1988, 138; Sam Dickey, "Electronic Meetings: Substitutes with Substance?" *Today's Office,* July 1986, 40–46.   **662** (F20-4): Used with permission from © Microsoft Corporation.   **669** (Tired of Being Ignored? Five Ways Guaranteed to Get Attention and Keep It): Eric J. Adams, "Management Focus: User-Friendly Presentation Software," *World Trade,* March 1995, 92.   **688–689** (TA-2): Adapted from James L. Clark and Lyn R. Clark, *How 7: A Handbook for Office Workers,* 7th ed. (Cincinnati, OH.: South-Western, 1995), 257–264.

Photos

1 FPG International   **2** Courtesy of The Walt Disney Company. **3** Fujifotos/The Image Works.   **13** AP/Wide World Photos.   **28** Jim Caldwell/Metamorphosis Studios.   **29** Metamorphosis Studios. **32** The Image Works.   **41** Michael Newman/PhotoEdit.   **49** Seth Resnick/Stock Boston.   **54** Courtesy of Michael Copeland, Proctor & Campbell.   **55** Greg Pease/Tony Stone Images.   **59** Mark Richards, Contact Press Images.   **63** Jeff Greenberg/PhotoEdit and Charles Thatcher/Tony Stone Images.   **84** Courtesy of Michael L. Stevens, Hewlett-Packard Company.   **85** John Coletti/Stock Boston. **93** Courtesy of ..Electric Library® is a service of Infonautics Corporation; ©1998 Infonautics Corporation.   **111** Donal Philby, FPG International. **112** Courtesy of Jeff Hagen.   **113** Courtesy of General Mills. **121** Tom Wagner/SABA Press Photos, Inc.   **138** Courtesy of Julian Santoyo.   **139** Art Montes De Oca, FPG International.   **156** Susan Holtz Image & Film Research.   **174** Courtesy of Adrianne Proeller, CNN Cable News Network, Inc.   **175** Courtesy of CNN Cable News Network, Inc.   **187** Daemmrich/The Image Works.   **192** Rick Kopstein/Monkmeyer.   **213** Frank Siteman/Tony Stone Images. **214** Courtesy of Silva Raker, The Nature Company.   **215** Courtesy of The Nature Company.   **232** Dana White/PhotoEdit.   **239** Eberhard Otto, FPG International.   **243** Leslye Bordon/PhotoEdit.   **246** Peter Dazeley/Tony Stone Images.   **248** Courtesy of Peter Goodrich, Steinway & Sons.   **249** Courtesy of Steinway & Sons.   **253** Michael Newman/PhotoEdit.   **279** Munshi Ahmed Photography.   **280** Courtesy of L.L. Bean.   **284** AP/Wide World Photos.   **288** Courtesy of Yla Eason.   **289** Courtesy of Yla Eason.   **297** The Image Works. **317** Michael Newman/PhotoEdit.   **323** Courtesy of Celestis.   **326** D. Young-Wolff/PhotoEdit.   **328** Courtesy of Jeanne Anderson, AT&T Photo Center.   **329** Courtesy of AT&T Photo Center.   **352** Tony Stone Images.   **354** Courtesy of MTV Networks.   **365** Scott McKiernan/Zurna Press.   **369** Susan Holtz Image & Film Research.   **375** D. Young-Wolff/PhotoEdit.   **377** Robert E. Daemmrich/Tony Stone Images.   **378** Courtesy of Henry Halaiko, Mobil Corporation. **379** David R. Frazier/Tony Stone Worldwide.   **386** The Image Works. **414** Courtesy of Jodi DeLeon, Microsoft Corporation.   **415** Courtesy of Microsoft Corporation.   **430** Bob Daemmrich/The Image Works. **445** Roger Tully/Tony Stone Images.   **446** Courtesy of Wesley Van Linda, Narada Productions.   **447** Courtesy of Narada Productions. **461** Courtesy of Raymond Guardiano and Bruce Rogow.   **474** Courtesy of Charley Shin.   **475** Courtesy of Charley Shin.   **494** Susan Holtz Image & Film Research.   **504** Courtesy of Michael Fernandez, Eastman Kodak Co.   **505** Courtesy of Eastman Kodak Co.   **522** Picture Perfect USA, Inc.   **532, 533, 541** Rob Crandall/Stock Boston.   **569** Kaluzny Thatcher/Tony Stone Images.   **574** Courtesy of L. Hunter Lovins, Rocky Mountain Institute.   **575** Courtesy of Rocky Mountain Institute. **616** Richard Pasley/Stock Boston.   **622** Michael Newman/PhotoEdit. **625** Don Bosler/Tony Stone Images.   **626** Courtesy of 3M Corporation. **627** Courtesy of 3M Corporation.   **638** Michelle Bridwell/PhotoEdit. **643** Peter Menzel/Stock Boston.   **652** Phoenix Management, Inc. **653** Phoenix Management, Inc.   **674** James Shaffer/PhotoEdit. **681** Jim Pickerell/Stock Boston.

ORGANIZATION/COMPANY/BRAND INDEX

SUBJECT INDEX